CJKV Information Processing

CJKV Information Processing

Ken Lunde

O'REILLY®

Beijing · Cambridge · Köln · Paris · Sebastopol · Taipei · Tokyo

CJKV Information Processing
by Ken Lunde

Published by O'Reilly & Associates, Inc., 101 Morris Street, Sebastopol, CA 95472.

Editors: Tim O'Reilly, Peter Mui, and Gigi Estabrook

Production Editors: Ken Lunde and Jane Ellin

Printing History:

January 1999: First Edition.

This book is printed on acid-free paper with 85% recycled content, 15% post-consumer waste. O'Reilly & Associates is committed to using paper with the highest recycled content available consistent with high quality.

ISBN: 1-56592-224-7

This book is dedicated to Ninik Kunti-Utami Lunde,
my friend, life-long companion, lover, and beloved wife.
Without her strong emotional support, encouragement, companionship,
blessing, and love, this book would not have been possible.
I shall love her forever…

Table of Contents

Foreword

In September 1993, an important event in the history of Japanese computing took place: the publication of Ken Lunde's *Understanding Japanese Information Processing*. Even today, no other book brings together such a wealth of information on Japanese data processing. I and my colleague Takeo Suzuki had the unique honor to work on the Japanese translation of this book, a work that made worldwide impact.

Today, an event of even greater importance—a major milestone in the history of East Asian computing—is unfolding: the publication of Ken Lunde's new book: *CJKV Information Processing*. No other book even pretends to approach it in either content or quality. Though the range of issues covered is broad, the treatment of each topic is comprehensive and in-depth.

With the recent spread of Unicode as an international character set and the growing importance of East Asia in the world economy, new CJK applications are appearing at an increasingly rapid pace. Many software publishers are "jumping on the CJK wagon," with the hopes of tapping the potentially huge East Asian market, which has mostly remained closed to non-Asian software developers.

An important reason for the poor market penetration of these products is their low quality. Many of these applications are simply too primitive to adequately meet the practical needs of users.

This state of affairs can be explained by three interrelated factors. First, this is a young market, and developers have not yet acquired sufficient skills and experience. For example, some developers of Japanese software, who have little or no knowledge of the language, hire outside help such as students, often with disastrous results.

Second, developers often do not have access to high-quality data, especially dictionary data, required for the all-important input method (also known as "front-end processor" or FEP) development. It is easy enough to find such data by surfing the Web, but it requires much skill to eliminate the countless errors and adapt it to specific needs.

Third is the lack of good information on CJKV processing. The issues are complex. The developer must contend with multiple, mostly incompatible encoding systems, different character sets, a bewildering variety of locale-dependent input methods, code conversion between incompatible character sets, and support for Unicode, to mention but a few.

How does one acquire reliable and detailed information on these issues? Until the appearance of the present work, this was well-nigh impossible. For the first time, Ken Lunde's pioneering work provides nothing less than an inexhaustible source of accurate and complete information on every aspect of CJKV data processing.

Let me illustrate how useful this information was to the dictionary projects of the Kanji Dictionary Publishing Society (KDPS). We have recently completed *The Kodansha Kanji Learner's Dictionary* (Kodansha International, 1998), based on the *New Japanese-English Character Dictionary* (Kenkyusha, 1990; NTC, 1993) of which I am the chief editor. At the same time, we have been developing DESK, a comprehensive CJK database from which dozens of dictionaries, CJK FEP data, and learning aids are being developed.

Though we are dedicated CJK specialists, the information in Ken Lunde's book was invaluable every step of the way. For example, when we created outline fonts for some 1,350 user-defined characters, it helped us decide on encoding ranges and methods. When we switched to a new platform, it helped us write code conversion routines and build function libraries. When we developed our dictionary page composition system, it guided us in the purchase of software and taught us in depth about typography and font technology. And so on and so on.

As can be seen from our example, the aim of this book is *highly practical*. The author has a very full grasp of the real needs of such diverse users as software developers, lexicographers, and language learners, and provides detailed information for each need with great clarity and precision. I am fully confident that this book shall become an invaluable source of information to everyone interested in CJKV information processing.

Jack Halpern (春遍雀來)
Editor in Chief, CJK Dictionary Publishing Society (CDPS)
http://www.cjk.org/

Preface

Close to six years have passed since *Understanding Japanese Information Processing* was published, and a lot has changed since then. One reason for the delay in getting this new book published was that I decided not only to revise the Japanese portions, but also to include significantly more information about Chinese and Korean, plus add information about Vietnamese—the title was changed accordingly. I was inspired to undertake this significant "CJKV" expansion sometime in 1996, during a lengthy conversation I had at a Togo's near the UC Berkeley campus with Peter Mui, my editor for *Understanding Japanese Information Processing*.

Join me in reading this thick tome of a book, and you shall find that "CJKV" (Chinese, Japanese, Korean, and Vietnamese) will become a standard term in your arsenal of knowledge. But, before we dive in, allow me to use some terms with which you are no doubt familiar. Otherwise, you probably would have no need to continue reading.

Known to more and more people, "internationalization" and "localization" seem to have become household or "buzz" words in the field of computing, and have also become very hot topics among high-tech firms and researchers due to the expansion of software markets to include virtually all parts of the globe. This book is specifically about CJKV-enabling, which is the adaptation of software for one or more CJKV markets. It is my intention that readers will find relevant and useful CJKV-enabling information within these pages.

Virtually every book on internationalization or localization includes information on character sets and encodings, but this book provides much more. In summary, this book provides a brief description of the writing systems, a thorough background of the history and current state of character sets, detailed information on encoding methods, code conversion techniques, input methods, keyboard arrays, font formats, typography, output methods, algorithms with sample source code, tools that perform useful information processing tasks, and how to handle CJKV text with email and in the context of the Web. Expect to find plenty of platform-independent information and discussions about character sets, how CJKV text is encoded and handled on a number of computer systems, and basic guidelines and tips for developing software targeted for CJKV markets.

Now, let me tell you what this book is *not* about. Don't expect to find out how to design your own word processor, how to design your own fonts for use on your computer (I give sources for tools, though), or how to properly handle formats for CJKV numerals, currency, dates, or times. This book is not by any stretch of the imagination a complete reference manual for internationalization or localization, but should serve well as a companion to such reference works (which are, fortunately, slowly becoming more abundant).

It is my intention for this book to become the definitive source for information relating to CJKV information processing issues (*Understanding Japanese Information Processing*, which concentrated on Japanese issues, apparently became the definitive source for that field). Thus, this book focuses heavily on how CJKV text is handled on computer systems in a very platform-independent way. Everything presented in this book can be programmed, categorized, or easily referenced.

This book was written to fill the gap in information relating to CJKV information processing. I first attempted to do this over the course of several years by maintaining an online document that I named *JAPAN.INF* (*Electronic Handling of Japanese Text*). This document had been made publicly available through a number of FTP sites worldwide, and had gained international recognition as *the* source for information relating to Japanese text handling on computer systems. *Understanding Japanese Information Processing* excerpted and further developed key information contained in *JAPAN.INF*. However, since the publication of *Understanding Japanese Information Processing* in 1993, *JAPAN.INF*, well, uh, sort of died. Not a horrible death, mind you, but rather to prepare for its reincarnation as a totally new online document that I have entitled *CJK.INF* (the CJK analog to *JAPAN.INF*). The work I did on *CJK.INF* helped to prepare me to write this new book, which provides updated material plus *significantly* more information about Chinese, Korean, and Vietnamese (to the point that granting the book a new title was deemed appropriate and necessary). I hope that this book becomes as widely accepted as the original.

While I have expended great efforts to provide sufficient amounts of information for Chinese, Japanese, Korean, and Vietnamese computing, you will notice that there is still some bias toward Japanese in many parts of this book. But, almost everything discussed in this book can apply equally to all of these languages.

However, the details of Vietnamese computing in the context of using Chinese characters are still emerging, so its coverage is somewhat limited.

Audience

Anyone interested in how CJKV text is processed on a computer will find this book useful, including those who wish to enter the field of CJKV information processing, and those who are already in the field, but need additional reference material. This book will also be useful for people using any kind of computer and any type of computer operating system: MacOS, MS-DOS, Unix, and Windows.

Although this book is specifically about CJKV information processing, anyone with an interest in creating multilingual software or a general interest in I18N (internationalization) or L10N (localization) will learn a great deal about the issues involved in handling complex writing systems on computers. This is particularly true for people interested in working with CJKV text. Information relating to CJKV-enabling is still, unfortunately, relatively scarce.

I assume that readers have little or no knowledge of a CJKV language (Chinese, Japanese, Korean, or Vietnamese) and its writing system. In Chapter 2, *Writing Systems*, I include material that should provide a good introduction to CJKV languages and their writing systems. If you only know one CJKV language, Chapter 2 should prove to be quite useful.

Conventions Used in this Book

Kanji, *hanzi*, *hanja*, *hangul*, *kana*, *hiragana*, *katakana*, and other terms come up time and time again throughout this book. You will also encounter abbreviations and acronyms, such as ANSI, ASCII, CNS, EUC, GB, ISO, JIS, KS, and TCVN. Terms, abbreviations, and acronyms—along with many others—are usually explained in the text and again in the glossary (Appendix X, *Glossary*, which I encourage you to study).

Hexadecimal values, when used in text, are prefixed with 0x, such as 0x8080. Every two hexadecimal digits beyond 0x represent a single byte. For example, 0x20 represents a one-byte value, but 0x0020 represents a two-byte value. Decimal values appear as themselves. You can use Appendix B, *Notation Conversion Table*, to convert between notations.

Throughout this book I generically use short suffixes such as "J," "K," "S," "T," "V," and "CJKV" to denote locale-specific or CJKV-capable versions of software products. I use these suffixes for the sake of consistency, and because software manufacturers often change the way in which they denote CJKV versions of their products. In practice, you may instead encounter the suffix 日本語版 (*nihon-*

goban, meaning "Japanese version"), the prefix "Kanji," or the prefix 日本語 (*nihongo*, meaning "Japanese") in Japanese product names. For Chinese software, 中文 (*zhōngwén*, meaning "Chinese") is a common prefix. I also refrain from using version numbers for software described in this book (as you know, this sort of information becomes outdated very quickly). I use version numbers only when they represent a significant advancement or development stage in a product.

References to "China" in this book refer to the *People's Republic of China* (PRC; 中华人民共和国 *zhōnghuá rénmín gònghé guó*), also commonly known as Mainland China. References to "Taiwan" in this book refer to the *Republic of China* (ROC; 中華民國 *zhōnghuá mínguó*). Quite often this distinction is necessary.

Name ordering in this book, when transliterated in Latin characters, follows the convention that is used in the West—the given name appears first, followed by the surname. When the name is written using CJKV characters—in parentheses following the transliterated version—the surname appears first, followed by the given name.

"ISO 10646-1:1993" and "Unicode" are used interchangeably throughout this book. Only in some specific contexts are they different.

Italic is used for pathnames, filenames, program names, new terms where they are defined, newsgroup names, and Internet addresses, such as domain names, URLs, and email addresses.

`Constant width` is used in examples to illustrate output from commands, the contents of files, or the text of email messages.

`Constant bold` is used in examples to indicate commands or other text that should be typed literally by the user; occasionally, it is also used to distinguish parts of an example.

`Constant oblique` is used in code fragments and examples to show variables for which a context-specific substitution should be made. The variable *`email address`*, for example, would be replaced by an actual email address.

The `%` (percent) character is used to represent the Unix shell prompt in Unix command lines.

Footnotes are used for parenthetical remarks. Lies are sometimes spoken to simplify or shorten the discussion (especially in Chapter 2 where I introduce the many CJKV writing systems), and the footnotes—usually, but not always—restore the truth.

Organization

Let's now preview the contents of each chapter in this book. Don't feel compelled to read this book linearly, but feel free to jump around from section to section and into the appendixes. Also, the index is there for you to use.

Chapter 1, *CJKV Information Processing Overview*, contains an overview of the issues that are addressed by this book, and will give you an idea of what you can expect to learn. This establishes the context in which this book will become useful in your work or research.

Chapter 2, *Writing Systems*, contains information directly relating to CJKV writing systems. Here you will learn about the various types of characters that compose CJKV texts. This chapter is intended for readers who are not familiar with the Chinese, Japanese, Korean, or Vietnamese languages (or who are familiar with only one or two of those languages). Everyone is bound to learn something new here.

Chapter 3, *Character Set Standards*, describes the two classes of CJKV character set standards: *coded* and *non-coded*. Coded character set standards are further divided into two classes: *national* and *international*. Comparisons are also drawn between CJKV character set standards.

Chapter 4, *Encoding Methods*, contains information on how the character set standards described in Chapter 3 are encoded on computer systems. Encoding is a complex but important step in representing and manipulating human-language text in a computer. Other topics include software for converting from one CJKV encoding to another, and instructions on how to repair damaged CJKV text files.

Chapter 5, *Input Methods*, contains information on how CJKV text is input. First I discuss CJKV input in general terms, then describe several specific methods for inputting CJKV characters on computer systems. Next, we move on to the hardware necessary for CJKV input, specifically keyboard arrays. These range from common keyboard arrays, such as the QWERTY array, to Chinese character tablets containing thousands of individual keys.

Chapter 6, *Font Formats*, contains information about bitmapped and outline font formats as they relate to CJKV. The information presented in this chapter represents my daily work at Adobe Systems, so some sections may suffer from excruciating detail.

Chapter 7, *Typography*, contains information about how CJKV text is properly laid out on a printed page. Having CJKV fonts is not enough—there are rules that govern where characters can and cannot be used, and how different character classes are handled when in proximity. The chapter ends with a description of software programs that provide advanced line layout functionality.

Chapter 8, *Output Methods*, contains information about how to display, print, or otherwise output CJKV text. Here you will find information relating to the latest printing and display technologies.

Chapter 9, *Information Processing Techniques*, contains information and algorithms relating to CJKV code conversion and text handling techniques. The actual mechanics are described in detail, and, where appropriate, include algorithms written in C, Java, and other programming languages. The chapter ends with a brief description of three Japanese code processing tools that I have written and maintained over a period of several years. These tools show how the algorithms can be applied in the context of Japanese.

Chapter 10, *Operating Systems, Text Editors, and Word Processors*, contains information about operating systems, text editors, and word processors that are CJKV-capable, meaning that they support one or more CJKV locale.

Chapter 11, *Dictionaries and Dictionary Software*, contains information about dictionaries, both printed and electronic, that are useful when dealing with CJKV text. Also included are tips on how to more efficiently make use of the various indexes used to locate Chinese characters in dictionaries.

Chapter 12, *The Internet*, contains information on how CJKV text is best handled electronically over networks such as email systems and news readers. Included are tips on how to ensure that what you send is received intact as well as information about the Internet domains that cover the CJKV locales.

Chapter 13, *The World Wide Web*, contains information on displaying CJKV text using various web browsers, and provides instructions for creating your own HTML (HyperText Markup Language) and XML (Extensible Markup Language) documents containing CJKV text. The role of Adobe Acrobat, PDF (Portable Document Format), and CGI (Common Gateway Interface) programming is also discussed in detail.

Appendix A, *Code Conversion Tables*, provides a code conversion table between decimal Row-Cell, hexadecimal ISO-2022, hexadecimal EUC, and hexadecimal Shift-JIS (Japanese-specific) codes. Also included is an extension that handles the Shift-JIS user-defined range.

Appendix B, *Notation Conversion Table*, lists all 256 eight-bit byte values in four common notations: binary, octal, decimal, and hexadecimal.

Appendix C, *Vendor Character Set Standards*, is reference material for those interested in vendor-specific extensions to CJKV character set standards.

Appendix D, *Vendor Encoding Methods*, is reference material for those interested in how the vendor character sets in Appendix C are encoded.

Appendix E, *GB 2312-80 Table*, is a code table for the characters defined in GB 2312-80 (along with the additions and corrections stipulated by GB 6345.1-86), indexed by decimal Row-Cell codes.

Appendix F, *GB/T 12345-90 Table*, is a code table for the characters defined in GB/T 12345-90, indexed by decimal Row-Cell codes.

Appendix G, *CNS 11643-1992 Table*, is a code table for the characters defined in all seven planes of CNS 11643-1992, indexed by decimal Row-Cell codes. Also included are tables that are specific to CNS 11643-1986, such as Plane 15. This is a long appendix, listing well over 50,000 unique hanzi!

Appendix H, *Big Five Table*, is a code table for the characters defined in Big Five, indexed by hexadecimal Big Five codes.

Appendix I, *Hong Kong GCCS Table*, contains a table for the complete set of 3,049 hanzi promulgated by the Hong Kong government, indexed by hexadecimal Big Five codes. Also included is an additional set of 145 hanzi defined by Hong Kong's Department of Judiciary.

Appendix J, *JIS X 0208:1997 Table*, is a code table for the characters defined in JIS X 0208:1997, indexed by decimal Row-Cell codes.

Appendix K, *JIS X 0212-1990 Table*, is a code table for the characters defined in JIS X 0212-1990, indexed by decimal Row-Cell codes. Also included are four additional katakana characters that *may* be added to this standard in the future (but this seems unlikely).

Appendix L, *KS X 1001:1992 Table*, is a code table for the characters defined in KS X 1001:1992, indexed by decimal Row-Cell codes.

Appendix M, *KS X 1002:1991 Hanja Table*, is a code table for *only* the 2,856 hanja defined in KS X 1002:1991, indexed by decimal Row-Cell codes.

Appendix N, *Hangul Reading Table*, contains a complete reading index for all 2,350 modern hangul defined in the KS X 1001:1992 character set standard.

Appendix O, *TCVN 6056:1995 Table*, is a code table for the characters defined in TCVN 6056:1995, indexed by decimal Row-Cell codes.

Appendix P, *Code Table Indexes*, provides various Chinese character indexes—reading, radical, and stroke-count—to be used in conjunction with various appendixes in this book.

Appendix Q, *Character Lists and Mapping Tables*, contains lists of characters and mapping tables referred to throughout this book.

Appendix R, *Chinese Character Lists*, provides a printout of various Chinese character lists—based on non-coded character set standards—as described in Chapter 3, *Character Set Standards*.

Appendix S, *Single-Byte Code Tables*, provides complete ASCII, EBCDIC, EBCDIK, ISO 8859-1:1998, CJKV-Roman, half-width katakana, and half-width jamo code tables, indexed by hexadecimal codes.

Appendix T, *Software and Document Sources*, provides addresses and contact information for software and documents mentioned throughout the book.

Appendix U, *Mailing Lists*, provides information on various (email-based) mailing lists that may be of interest to readers.

Appendix V, *Professional Organizations*, includes information on organizations that deal with CJKV information processing issues.

Appendix W, *Perl Code Examples*, provides Perl equivalents of algorithms found in Chapter 9—along with other goodies.

Appendix X, *Glossary*, defines many of the concepts and terms used throughout this book (and other books).

Finally, the *Bibliography* lists many useful references, some of which I used to write this book.

Acknowledgments

To write a reference work this thick requires interaction with people from around the globe. It is quite impossible for me to list all the people who have helped me over the years—there are literally hundreds.

In some cases, people simply come to me for help on a particular subject (that's what happens, I guess, when people are aware of your email address—to ensure that I will receive a ton of email, in various parts of this book you will find that my email address is *lunde@oreilly.com*). Sometimes I may not know the answer to a particular question, but the question usually inspires me to seek out the truth. The truth *is* out there.

1998 marks seven wonderful years at Adobe Systems, a company that provides me with daily CJKV-related challenges. Its advanced font technology and commitment to customers is what initially attracted me, and this is what keeps me there. Besides, they let me keep a limited-edition three-foot bright-orange super meltdown Godzilla in my office (because my wife won't let it in the house) as a memorial and tribute to *The King* (who quite sadly passed away in the 1995 film

Godzilla versus Destroyah[*]). Speaking of tributes, all aspects of the production of this book are a tribute to Adobe Systems' publishing technology.

To all the people who have read my previous writings, put up with my sometimes dull or otherwise annoying personality at work, pointed out errors in my work, exchanged email with me for whatever reason, or otherwise helped me to become a better person: *thank you!* You should know who you are.

Special thanks go to Tim O'Reilly (the president and founder of O'Reilly & Associates) and Peter Mui for believing in my first book, *Understanding Japanese Information Processing*. It was Peter who encouraged me to expand it to cover the complete CJKV framework. (I am sorry that it took so long to get done—it was a long and painful experience.) Thanks go to Edie Freedman for sticking with my idea of a blowfish for the cover.[†] Mike Sierra graciously helped me through the layout of the book, and nurtured my desire to learn Adobe FrameMaker's particular paradigm. Chris Reilley also deserves a lot of credit for turning my poorly designed figures into works of fine art—for a second time. Gigi Estabrook, the editor, continually pushed me to get this book done. Ellie Fountain Maden performed the copyedit, discovering various errors and oddities.

The following were responsible for reviewing various parts of this book, during the various stages of its prolonged development: Joe Becker, Jim Breen, Robert Bringhurst, Woohyong Choi (최 우형), James Davis, L. Peter Deutsch, James Đỗ (杜伯福), Terry Dowling, Martin Dürst, Gus Fernandez, Jeffrey Friedl, David Gourley, Jerry Hall, Jack Halpern (春遍雀來), Ken'ichi Handa (半田剣一), Dennis Hanks, Ted Harrison, Patty Hay (許珮婷), Carl Hoffman, Chiaki Ishikawa (石川千秋), Matt Jacobs, David Kelly, Hoon Kim (김 훈), Kyongsok Kim (김 경석), Kazuo Koike (小池和夫), Norbert Lindenberg, Toshiaki Maeda (前田年昭), Dirk Meyer, Charles Muller, Terry O'Donnell, Glen Perkins, Etsuko Obata Reiman (エツコ・オバタ・ライマン), Craig Rublee, Limin Shi (施利民), Kohji Shibano (芝野耕司), Jungshik Shin (신 정식), Frank (Yung-Fong) Tang (譚永鋒), Ngô Trung Việt (吳中越), Taro Yamamoto (山本太郎), Koichi Yasuoka (安岡孝一), and Haifeng Zhu (朱海峰). I am grateful to all of them for providing me with useful insights and inspiring ideas. I am, however, responsible for any errors, omissions, or oddities that you may encounter.

* ゴジラ対デストロイア (*gojira tai desutoroia*) in Japanese. As a side-note to this footnote, the creator of Godzilla, Tomoyuki Tanaka, passed away in April of 1997 at the age of 86. The first American-made Godzilla film was released in 1998. Like this book, size *does* matter.

† Michael Slinn made the astute observation that the Babel Fish would have been more appropriate as a cover creature for this book—according to Douglas Adams' *The Hitch Hiker's Guide to the Galaxy*, you simply stick a Babel Fish in your ear, it connects with your brain, and you can suddenly understand all languages. Perhaps the blowfish is still used for this book's cover because there were no nineteenth-century Babel Fish engravings in the Dover Pictorial Archive…

Finally, I wish to thank my beloved wife, Ninik Kunti-Utami Lunde, for her incredible patience with me while I am pursuing my computing interests and a career at Adobe Systems. I apologize to her for all the mornings and nights (and weekends and vacations) I spent working on this book instead of spending more time with her. She's endured two books thus far. Bless her heart for (constantly) reminding me that there is much more to life. To her goes *all* my love. I also thank my parents, Vernon Delano Lunde and Jeanne Mae Lunde, for all of their support throughout the years.

Errors, Omissions, and Updates

A book containing this much highly technical information is bound to contain some errors. No doubt, these errors will be corrected in future printings or editions of this book. In the meantime, any errors will be maintained at the following URL:

ftp://ftp.oreilly.com/pub/examples/nutshell/cjkv/errata/

If you happen to find any errors or notice any omissions, please send them to the following address:

O'Reilly & Associates, Incorporated
101 Morris Street
Sebastopol, CA 95472 USA
800-998-9938 (in the USA or Canada)
+1-707-829-0515 (international or local)
+1-707-829-0104 (facsimile)

You can also send messages electronically. To be put on O'Reilly's mailing list or to request a catalog, send email to:

info@oreilly.com

To ask technical questions or comment on this book, send email to:

bookquestions@oreilly.com

Because this book is filled with hundreds of URLs, I am providing the following web page, which arranges them all by chapter/appendix then by page number, for easier, clickable access (and as a way for me to keep them all up-to-date):

http://www.oreilly.com/~lunde/cjkv-urls.html

In this chapter:
- *Multiple Writing Systems*
- *Character Set Standards*
- *Encoding Methods*
- *Input Methods*
- *Typography*
- *Basic Concepts and Terminology*

1

CJKV Information Processing Overview

A lot of mystique and intrigue surrounds how CJKV—Chinese, Japanese, Korean, and Vietnamese—text is handled on computer systems. Although I agree with there being intrigue, there is far too much mystique, in my opinion. Much of this mystery is due to a lack of information, or simply a lack of information written in a language other than Chinese, Japanese, Korean, or Vietnamese. Nevertheless, many fine folks, like you, would like to know how this all works. To confirm some of your worst fears and speculations, CJKV text *does* require special handling on computer systems. However, it should not be very mysterious after having read this book. You need only break the so-called *one-byte-equals-one-character* barrier—most CJKV characters are represented by more than a single byte (or, to put it in another way, more than eight bits).*

English information processing was a reality soon after the introduction of early computer systems, which were first developed in England and the United States. Adapting software to handle more complex writing systems such as those used to represent CJKV text is a more recent phenomenon. This adaptation developed in various stages, and continues today.

There are several key issues that make CJKV text a challenge to process on computer systems:

- CJKV writing systems use a mixture of different, but sometimes related, writing systems
- CJKV character set standards enumerate thousands or tens of thousands of characters, which is orders of magnitude more than used in the West

* For a greater awareness of (and appreciation for) some of the complexities of dealing with multiple-byte text, you might consider glancing now at the section entitled "Byte Versus Character Handling" in Chapter 9, *Information Processing Techniques*, beginning on page 433.

- There is no universally recognized or accepted CJKV character set standard such as ASCII for writing English—although Unicode can be considered a good first attempt
- There is no universally recognized or accepted CJKV encoding system such as ASCII encoding—again, the various Unicode encodings can be considered an attempt at accomplishing this
- There is no universally recognized or accepted input device such as the QWERTY keyboard array—although this same keyboard array, through a method of transliteration, can be used to input most CJKV text through reading or other means
- CJKV text can be written horizontally or vertically, and requires special typographic rules not found in Western typography, such as spanning tabs and unique line-breaking rules

You will learn that the ASCII character set standard is not as universal as most people think—different flavors of ASCII exist, as do different ASCII encoding methods. You will begin to wonder why so many developers assume that everyone uses ASCII.

This chapter also includes several sections that explain and illustrate some very basic yet important computing concepts, such as notation and byte order, that relate to material in the remainder of this book. If you consider yourself a seasoned software engineer or expert programmer, you may still find value in those sections because they carry much more importance in the context of CJKV information processing. That is, how these concepts relate to CJKV information processing may be slightly different than what you previously learned.

Multiple Writing Systems

CJKV text is typically composed of a mixture of different writing systems. Japanese, as an example, is unique in that it uses four different writing systems. Others, such as Chinese and Korean, use less than four writing systems. Japanese is one of the few, if not the only, languages that exhibit this characteristic of so many writing systems being used together, even in the same sentence (as you will see very soon). This makes Japanese quite complex, orthographically speaking, and poses several problems.* The four Japanese writing systems are Latin characters, hiragana, katakana, and kanji (collectively referred to as "Chinese characters" regardless of the language). You are already familiar with Latin characters because the English language is written with these—this writing system consists of the

* Orthography is a linguistic term that refers to the writing system of a language.

upper- and lowercase Latin alphabet, which are the characters often found on typewriter keys. Hiragana and katakana are native Japanese syllabaries (see Appendix X, *Glossary*, for a definition of "syllabary"). Both hiragana and katakana represent the same set of 108 syllables, and are collectively known as *kana*. Kanji are characters that the Japanese borrowed from China over 1,600 years ago—Chinese characters number in the thousands, and encompass meaning, reading, and shape.

Now let's look at an example sentence composed of these four writing systems. This should serve to illustrate how the different Japanese writing systems can be effectively mixed.

> EUC 等のエンコーディング方法は日本語と英語が混交しているテキストをサポートします。

In case you are curious, this sentence means "Encoding methods such as EUC can support texts that mix Japanese and English." Let's look at this sentence again, but with the Latin characters underlined.

> <u>EUC</u> 等のエンコーディング方法は日本語と英語が混交しているテキストをサポートします。

In this case there is a single abbreviation, EUC (short for *Extended Unix Code*, which refers to a locale-independent encoding method, a topic to be covered in Chapter 4, *Encoding Methods*, of this book). It is quite common to find Latin characters used for abbreviations in CJKV texts. Latin characters used to transliterate Japanese text are called ローマ字 (*rōmaji*) in Japanese.

Now let's underline the katakana characters.

> EUC 等の<u>エンコーディング</u>方法は日本語と英語が混交している<u>テキスト</u>を<u>サポート</u>します。

Each katakana character represents one syllable, typically a lone vowel or a consonant-plus-vowel combination. Katakana characters are commonly used for writing words borrowed from other languages, such as English, French, or German. Table 1-1 lists these three underlined katakana words, along with their meanings and readings.

Table 1-1: Sample Katakana

Katakana	Meaning	Reading[a]
エンコーディング	*encoding*	enkōdingu
テキスト	*text*	tekisuto
サポート	*support*	sapōto

[a] The macron is used to denote long vowel sounds.

Note how their readings closely match that of their English counterparts, from which they were derived. This is no coincidence: it is common for the Japanese readings to be spelled out with katakana characters to closely match the borrowed words.

Next we underline the hiragana characters.

> EUC 等<u>の</u>エンコーディング方法<u>は</u>日本語<u>と</u>英語<u>が</u>混交<u>している</u>テキスト<u>を</u>サポート<u>します</u>。

Hiragana characters, like katakana described above, represent syllables. Hiragana characters are mostly used for writing grammatical words and inflectional endings. Table 1-2 illustrates the usage or meaning of the hiragana in the above sentence.

Table 1-2: Sample Hiragana

Hiragana	Meaning or Usage	Reading
の	possessive marker	no
は	topic marker	wa[a]
と	*and* (conjunction)	to
が	subject marker	ga
している	*doing*... (verb)	shite-iru
を	object marker	o
します	*do*... (verb)	shimasu

[a] This hiragana character is normally read *ha*, but when used as a topic marker, it becomes *wa*.

That's a lot of grammatical stuff! Japanese is a postpositional language, meaning that grammatical markers, such as prepositions as used in English, come after the nouns that they modify. These grammatical markers are called *particles* (助詞 *joshi*) in Japanese.

Finally, we underline the Chinese characters (called *hànzì* in Chinese, *kanji* in Japanese, *hanja* in Korean, and *chữ Hán* in Vietnamese):

> EUC <u>等</u>のエンコーディング<u>方法</u>は<u>日本語</u>と<u>英語</u>が<u>混交</u>しているテキストをサポートします。

At first glance, Chinese characters appear to be more complex than the other characters in the sentence. This happens to be true most of the time. Chinese characters represent meanings, and are often called *ideographs*, *pictographs*, or *logographs*.* Chinese characters are also assigned one or more readings (pronunci-

* Being a widespread convention, this is beyond critique. However, linguists use these terms for different classes of Chinese characters, depending on their etymology.

ations), each of which is determined by context. While their readings differ depending on the language (Chinese, Japanese, Korean, or Vietnamese), Chinese characters often have the same meaning. This makes it possible for Japanese to understand (but not necessarily to pronounce) some very basic Chinese, Korean, and Vietnamese texts. Table 1-3 provides a listing of the underlined Chinese characters and compounds (words composed of two or more Chinese characters) thereof, along with their meanings and readings.

Table 1-3: Sample Chinese Characters and Chinese Character Compounds

Chinese Characters	Meaning	Reading
等	*such as …*	nado
方法	*method*	hōhō
日本語	*Japanese (language)*	nihongo
英語	*English (language)*	eigo
混交	*(to) mix*	konkō

Of course, this example includes only those types of characters that are used in Japanese—other locales use different types of characters. Table 1-4 lists the four CJKV locales, along with what writing systems they use.

Table 1-4: CJKV Locales and Their Writing Systems

Locale	Writing Systems
China	Latin, zhuyin, and hanzi (simplified)
Taiwan	Latin, zhuyin, and hanzi (traditional)
Japan	Latin, hiragana, katakana, and kanji
Korea[a]	Latin, jamo, hangul, and hanja
Vietnam	Latin (Quốc ngữ), chữ Nôm, and chữ Hán

[a] Jamo are the alphabet-like components that make up hangul.

Table 1-5 lists some sample characters from each of the writing systems used in CJKV locales. We discuss these writing systems in greater detail in Chapter 2, *Writing Systems*.

Table 1-5: Sample CJKV Characters

Character Class	Sample Characters
Latin Characters	A B C D E F G H I J … q r s t u v w x y z
Zhuyin	ㄅ ㄆ ㄇ ㄈ ㄉ ㄊ ㄋ ㄌ ㄍ ㄎ … ㄠ ㄡ ㄢ ㄣ ㄤ ㄥ ㄦ ㄧ ㄨ ㄩ
Hiragana	ぁあぃいぅうぇえぉお … りるれろゎわゐゑをん
Katakana	ァアィイゥウェエォオ … ロヮワヰヱヲンヴヵヶ

Table 1-5: Sample CJKV Characters (continued)

Character Class	Sample Characters
Jamo	ㄱㄲㄳㄴㄵㄶㄷㄸㄹㄺ … ㆅㆆᆄᆅᆈᆑᆒᆔㆍㆎ
Hangul	가각간갇갈갉갊감갑값 … 휩휭히힉힌힐힘힙힛힝
Hanzi (simplified)	啊阿埃挨哎唉哀皑癌蔼 … 黪黯鼢鼬鼯鼹鼷鼽鼾齄
Hanzi (traditional)	一乙丁七乃九了二人儿 … 驫鱺鸝灩灪爩麤齾齉龘
Kanji	亜唖娃阿哀愛挨姶逢葵 … 齶龕龜龠堯槇遙瑤凜熙
Hanja	伽佳假價加可呵哥嘉嫁 … 晞曦熙熹熺犧禧稀羲詰

But, how frequently used are each of these character classes? Given an average sampling of Japanese writing, one normally finds 30 percent kanji, 60 percent hiragana, and 10 percent katakana. Actual percentages depend on the nature of the text. For example, you may find a higher percentage of kanji in technical literature, and a higher percentage of katakana in fields such as fashion and cosmetics, which make extensive use of loan words written in katakana. Most Korean texts consist of nothing but hangul, and most Chinese texts are composed of only hanzi.* Latin characters are used the least, except in Vietnam.

So, how many characters do you need to learn in order to read and write CJKV languages effectively? Here are some *very* basic guidelines:

- You must learn hiragana and katakana if you plan to deal with Japanese—this constitutes approximately 200 characters
- Learning hangul is absolutely necessary for Korean, but you can get away with not learning hanja
- You need to have general knowledge of about 1,000 kanji to read over 90 percent of the kanji in typical Japanese texts—more are required for reading Chinese texts because only hanzi are used

If you have not already learned Chinese, Japanese, Korean, or Vietnamese, I encourage you to learn one of them so that you can better appreciate the complexity of their writing systems. Although I discuss character dictionaries (and learning aids to a lesser extent) in Chapter 11, *Dictionaries and Dictionary Software*, they are no substitute for a human teacher.

Character Set Standards

A character set simply provides a common *bucket* of characters. You may have never thought of it this way, but the English alphabet is an example of a character

* Well, you will also find symbol-like characters, such as punctuation marks.

set standard. It specifies 52 upper- and lowercase letters. Character set standards are used to ensure that we learn a minimum number of characters in order to communicate with others in society. In effect, they limit the number of characters we need to learn. There are only a handful of characters in the English alphabet, so nothing is really being limited, and as such, there really is no character set standard *per se*. In the case of languages that use Chinese characters, however, character set standards play an especially vital role. They specify which Chinese characters—out of the tens of thousands in existence—are the most important to learn. The current Japanese set, called Jōyō Kanji (常用漢字 *jōyō kanji*), although advisory, limits the number of Chinese characters to 1,945.* There are similar character sets in China, Taiwan, and Korea. These character set standards were designed with education in mind, and are referred to as *non-coded* character sets.

Character set standards designed for use on computer systems are almost always larger than those used for the purpose of education, and are referred to as *coded* character sets. Establishing coded character set standards for use with computer systems is a way to ensure that everyone is able to view documents created by someone else. ASCII is a Western character set standard, and ensures that their computer systems can communicate with each other. But, as you will soon learn, ASCII is not sufficient for the purpose of professional publishing (neither is its most common extension, ISO 8859-1:1998).

Coded character set standards typically contain characters above and beyond those found in non-coded ones. For example, the ASCII character set standard contains 94 printable characters—42 more than the upper- and lowercase alphabet. In the case of Japanese, there are thousands of characters in the coded character sets in addition to the 1,945 in the basic non-coded character set. The basic coded Japanese character set standard, in its most current form, enumerates 6,879 characters, and is designated JIS X 0208:1997. There are four versions of this character set, each designated by the year in which it was established: 1978, 1983, 1990, and 1997. There are two typical compatibility problems that you may encounter when dealing with different versions of the same character set standard:

- Some of these versions contain different numbers of characters—later versions generally add characters
- Some of these versions are not 100 percent compatible with each other due to changes

In addition, there may be an extended character set standard, such as Japan's JIS X 0212-1990, that defines 6,067 additional characters (most of which are kanji).

* The predecessor of this character set, Tōyō Kanji (当用漢字 *tōyō kanji*), was prescriptive.

Additional incompatibility occurs because operating system developers take these coded character set standards one step further by defining their own extensions. These vendor character set standards are largely, but not completely, compatible, and almost always use one of the national standards as their base. When you factor in vendor character set standards, things appear to be a big mess. This book documents these character sets, making it easier to grapple with such confusion.

Encoding Methods

Encoding is the process of mapping a character to a numeric value. By doing this, you create the ability to uniquely identify a character through its associated numeric value. Ultimately, the computer needs to manipulate the character as a numeric value. Independent of any CJKV language or computerized implementations thereof, indexing encoded values allows a numerically enforced ordering to be mapped onto what might otherwise be a randomly ordered natural language. While there is no universally recognized encoding method, many are commonly used. For example, ISO-2022-KR, EUC-KR, Johab, and Unified Hangul Code (UHC) for Korean.

First, before describing these encoding methods, here's a short explanation of how memory is allocated on computer systems. Computer systems process data called bits. These are the most basic units of information, and can hold one of two possible values: on or off. These are usually mapped to the values 1 or 0, respectively. Bits are strung together into units called bytes. Bytes are usually composed of seven or eight bits. Seven bits in an array allow for up to 128 unique combinations, or values; eight bits allow for up to 256. While these numbers are sufficient for representing most characters in Western writing systems, it does not even come close to accommodating large character sets whose characters number in the thousands, such as those required by the CJKV locales.

The first attempt to encode Chinese characters on computer systems involved the use of Japanese half-width katakana characters. This is a limited set of 63 characters that constitutes a minimal set for representing Japanese text. But there was no support for kanji. The solution to this problem, at least for Japanese, was formalized in 1978, and employed the notion of using two bytes to represent a single character. This did not eliminate the need for one-byte characters, though. The Japanese solution was to extend the notion of one-byte character encoding to include two-byte characters. This allows for text with mixed one- and two-byte characters. How one- and two-byte characters are distinguished depends on the encoding method. Two bytes equal 16 bits, and thus can provide up to 65,536 unique values. This is best visualized as a 256×256 matrix. See Figure 1-1 for an illustration of such a matrix.

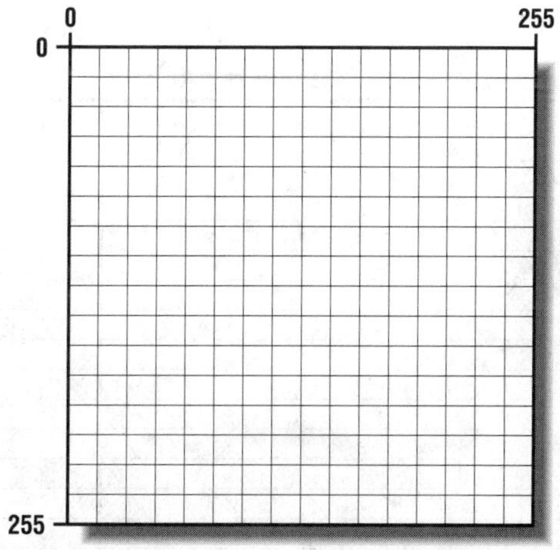

Figure 1-1: 256×256 encoding matrix

However, not all of these 65,536 cells can be used for representing displayable characters. To enable the mixture of one- and two-byte characters within a single text stream, some characters needed to be reserved as control characters, some of which then serve as the characters that signify when a text stream shifts between one- and two-byte modes. In the case of ISO-2022-JP encoding, the upper limit of displayable characters was set at 8,836, which is the size of the code space made from a 94×94 matrix.*

But why do you need to mix one- and two-byte characters anyway? It is to support existing one-byte encoding standards, such as ASCII, within a two-byte encoding system. One-byte encoding methods are here to stay, and it is still a rather efficient means to encode the characters necessary to write English and many other languages. However, languages with large character sets—those spoken in the CJKV locales—require two bytes to encode characters. A mixed one- and two-byte character stream efficiently represents a mixture of English and Chinese text.

Along with discussions about character sets and encodings, you will encounter the terms "row" and "cell" again and again in this book. These refer to the axes of a matrix used to hold and encode characters. A matrix is composed of rows, and a row is made up of cells. The first byte of the character specifies the row, and the second byte specifies the cell within the row. Figure 1-2 illustrates a matrix and how characters' positions correspond to row and cell values.

* *Code space* refers to the area within the (usual) 256×256 encoding matrix that can be used for encoding characters. Most of the figures in Chapter 4 and Appendix D, *Vendor Encoding Methods*, illustrate code spaces that fall within this 256×256 matrix.

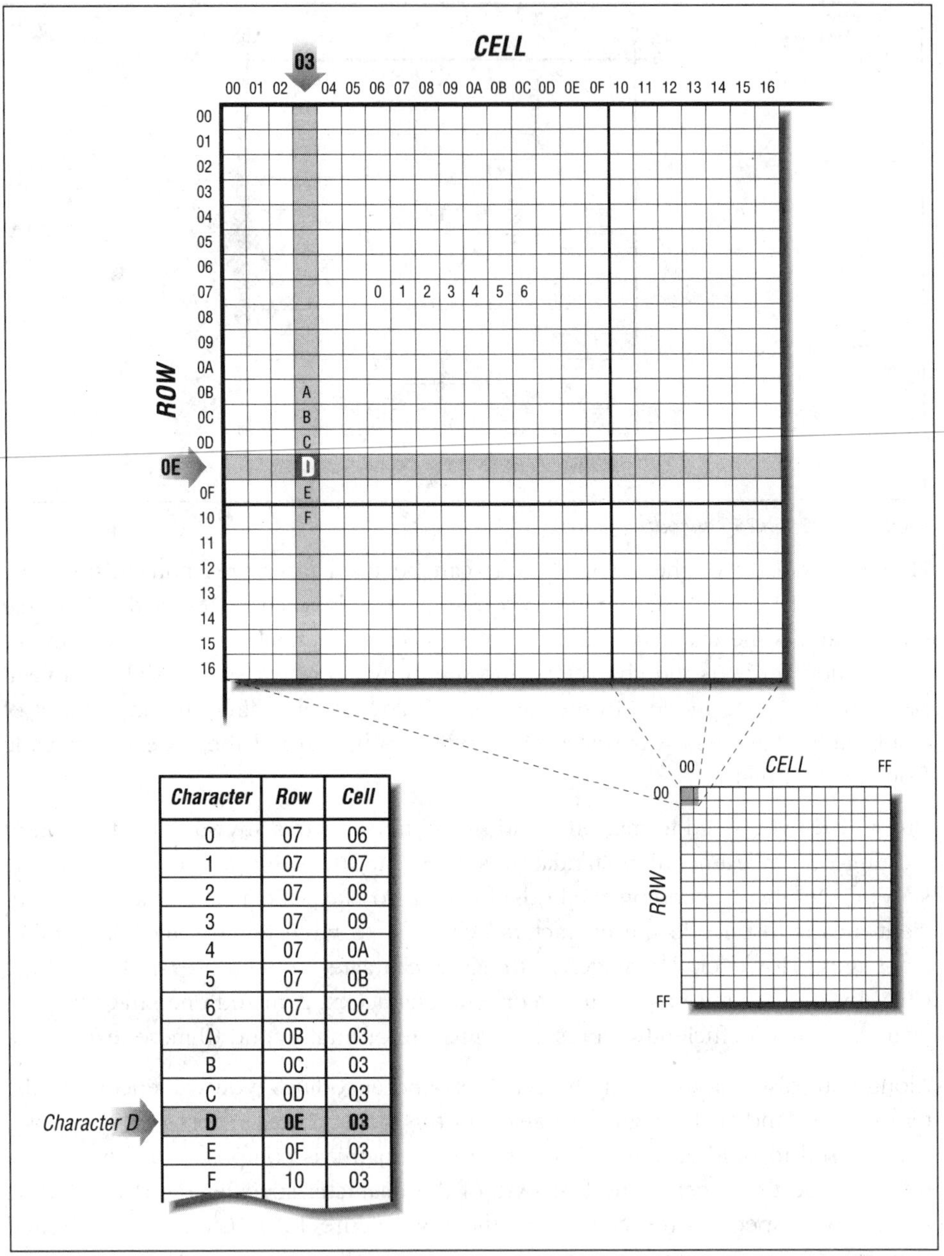

Figure 1-2: Indexing an encoding matrix by row and cell

In an attempt to allow for a mixture of one- and two-byte characters, several CJKV encoding methods have been developed. As you will learn in Chapter 4, these encoding methods are largely, but not completely, compatible. You will also see that there are encoding methods that use three or even four bytes to represent a single character!

The most common Japanese encoding methods are ISO-2022-JP, Shift-JIS, and EUC-JP. ISO-2022-JP, the most basic, uses seven-bit bytes (or, seven bits of a byte) to represent characters, and requires special characters or sequences of characters (called *shifting characters* or *escape sequences*) to shift between one- and two-byte modes. Shift-JIS and EUC-JP encodings make generous use of eight-bit characters, and use the value of the first byte as the way to distinguish one- and multiple-byte characters.

Input Methods

Those who type English text have the luxury of using keyboards that can hold all the keys to represent a sufficient number of characters. CJKV characters number in the thousands, though, so how does one type CJKV text? Large keyboards that hold thousands of individual keys exist, but they require special training and are difficult to use. This has led to software solutions: *input methods* and *conversion dictionaries.*

Most CJKV text is typically input in two stages:

1. The user types raw keyboard input, which the computer interprets using the input method and the conversion dictionary to display a list of *candidate* characters (*candidate* here refers to the character or characters that are mapped to the input string in the conversion dictionary).
2. The user selects one choice from the list of candidate characters, or requests more choices.

How well each stage is handled on your computer depends greatly on the quality (and vintage) of the input software you are using.

Software called an *input method* handles both of these input stages: it is so named because it grabs the user's keyboard input before any other software can use it (specifically, it is the first software to process keyboard input).

The first stage of input requires keyboard input, and can take one of two usual forms:

- Transliteration using Latin characters (type "k" plus "a" to get か, and so on)
- Native-script input (zhuyin for Chinese, hiragana for Japanese, hangul for Korean, and so on)

The form used depends on user preference and the type of keyboard in use. For Japanese, the input method converts transliterated Japanese into hiragana on the fly, so it doesn't really matter which keyboard you are using. In fact, studies show that over 70 percent of Japanese computer users prefer transliterated Japanese input.

Once the input string is complete, it is then parsed in one of two ways: either by the user during input, or by a parser built into the input method. Finally, each segment is run through a conversion process that consists of a lookup into a conversion dictionary. This is very much like a *key-value* lookup. Typical conversion dictionaries have tens of thousands of entries. It seems that the more entries, the better the conversion quality. However, if the conversion dictionary is too large, users are shown a far too lengthy list of candidates. This reduces input efficiency.

Can Chinese characters be input one at a time? While single Chinese-character input is possible, there are three basic units that can be used. These units allow you to limit the number of candidates from which you must choose. Typically, the larger the input unit, the fewer candidates. The units are as follows:

- Single Chinese character
- Chinese character compound
- Chinese character phrase

Early input programs required that each Chinese character be input individually (single Chinese character). Nowadays it is much more efficient to input Chinese characters as they appear in compounds or even phrases. This means that you may input two or more Chinese characters at once by virtue of inputting their combined reading. For example, the Chinese character compound 漢字 (the two Chinese characters for writing the word meaning "Chinese character") can be input as two separate characters, 漢 (read *kan* in Japanese) and 字 (read *ji* in Japanese). Table 1-6 shows the two target Chinese characters, along with other Chinese characters with the same reading.

Table 1-6: Single Chinese Character Input—Japanese

Character	Reading	Chinese Characters with Identical Readings
漢	K A N	乾侃冠寒刊勘勧巻喚堪姦完官寛干幹患感慣憾換敢柑桓棺款歓汗漢澗潅環甘監看竿管簡緩缶翰肝艦莞観諌貫鑑鑑間閑関陥韓館舘
字	J I	事似侍児字寺慈持時次滋治爾璽痔磁示而耳自蒔辞

You can see that there are many other Chinese characters with those readings, so you may have to wade through a long list of candidate Chinese characters before you find the correct one. A more efficient way is to input them as one unit, called a Chinese character compound. This produces a much shorter list of candidates from which to choose. Table 1-7 illustrates the two Chinese characters input as a compound, along with candidate compounds with the same reading.

Table 1-7: Chinese Character Compound Input—Japanese

Compound	Reading	Compounds with Identical Readings
漢字	ＫＡＮＪＩ	漢字 感じ 幹事 監事 完司

Note how the list of Chinese character compounds is much shorter in this case. There is an even higher-level input unit called a Chinese character phrase. This is similar to inputting two or more Chinese characters as a single compound, but adds another element, similar to a preposition in English, that makes the whole string into a phrase. An example of a Chinese character phrase is 漢字は, which means "the Chinese character" in Japanese. Because Chinese-language text is composed solely of hanzi, Chinese character phrase applies only to Japanese, and possibly Korean.

Some of you may know of input software that claims to let you convert whole sentences at once. This is not really true. Such software allows you to input whole sentences, but the sentence is then parsed into smaller units, usually Chinese character phrases, then converted. Inputting whole sentences before any conversion is merely a convenience for the user.

Korean input has some special characteristics that are related to how their most widely used writing system, hangul, is composed. Whether input is by a QWERTY or a Korean keyboard array, Korean input involves the entering of hangul elements called *jamo*. As the jamo are input, the operating system or input software attempts to compose hangul using an automaton. Because of how hangul are composed of jamo, the user may have up to three alternatives for deleting characters:

- Delete entire hangul
- Delete by jamo
- Delete by word

This particular option is specific to Korean, and depends on the input method.

Typography

CJKV text can usually be written or set in one of two orientations: left to right, top to bottom (horizontal setting, as in this book); and top to bottom, right to left (vertical setting). Chapter 7, *Typography*, provides plenty of examples of horizontal versus vertical writing. Vertical writing orientation, more often than not, causes problems with Western-language software. Luckily, it is generally acceptable to set CJKV text in the same horizontal orientation as most Western languages. Traditional novels and short stories are often set vertically, but technical materials, such as science textbooks and the like, are set horizontally.

Vertically set CJKV text is not a simple matter of changing writing direction. Some characters require special handling, such as a different orientation (90-degree clockwise rotation) or a different position within the *em-square*.* Chapter 7 provides some sample text set both horizontally and vertically, and illustrates some characters that require special treatment.

In addition to the two writing directions for CJKV text, there are other special text formatting considerations, such as special rules for wrapping characters at the ends of lines, special justification, metrics adjustment, and a way to annotate characters.

Basic Concepts and Terminology

Now I'll define some basic concepts which will help carry you through this entire book. These concepts are posed as questions. After all, these are questions you might raise as you read this book. If at any time you encounter a new term, please glance at the glossary toward the back of the book: new terms are included and explained there.

What Are All Those Abbreviations and Acronyms?

Most technical fields are flooded with abbreviations and acronyms, and CJKV information processing is no exception. Some of the more important (and confusing) ones are explained in the following section, but when in doubt, consult Appendix X.

What is the difference between GB and GB/T?

Most references to "GB" mean the GB 2312-80 character set standard, which represents the most widely implemented character set for Chinese.

GB stands for "Guo Biao" (国标 *guóbiāo*), which is short for "Guojia Biaozhun" (国家标准 *guójiā biāozhǔn*), and means "National Standard."

Because GB/T character set standards are traditional analogs of existing GB character set standards, some naturally think that the "T" stands for "Traditional." Yet another myth to blow out of the water. The "T" in "GB/T" actually stands for "Tui" (推 *tuī*), which is short for "Tuijian" (推荐 *tuījiàn*), and means "recommended." It

* The term *em-square* refers to a square-shaped space whose height and width roughly correspond to the width of the letter "M." The term *design space* is actually a more accurate way to represent this typographic concept.

means "recommended" in the sense that it is the opposite of "forced" or "mandatory."

The "K" in GBK (an extension to GB 2312-80) comes from the Chinese word 扩展 (*kuòzhǎn*), which means "extension."

What are JIS, JISC, and JSA? How are they related?

In much of the literature in the field of Japanese information processing, you will quite often see references to JISC, JIS, and JSA. The most common of these is JIS, the least JISC. What these refer to can sometimes be confusing, and is often contradicted in reference works.

JIS stands for *Japanese Industrial Standard* (日本工業規格 *nihon kōgyō kikaku*), the name given to the standards used in Japanese industry.* The character 〄 is the symbol for JIS. JIS can refer to several things: the character set standards established by JISC, the encoding method specified in these character set standards, and even the keyboard arrays described in JIS manuals. Context should usually make its meaning clear. The term JIS appears frequently in this book.

JISC stands for *Japanese Industrial Standards Committee* (日本工業標準調査会 *nihon kōgyō hyōjun chōsakai*). This is the name of the governing body that establishes JIS standards and publishes manuals through JSA. The committee that develops and writes each JIS manual is composed of people from Japanese industry who have a deep technical background in the topic to be covered by the JIS manual. Committee members are listed at the end of each JIS manual.

JSA stands for *Japanese Standards Association* (日本規格協会 *nihon kikaku kyōkai*). This organization publishes the manuals for the JIS standards established by JISC, and generally oversees the whole process.

JIS is often used as a blanket term covering JIS, JISC, and JSA, but now you know what they *really* mean.

Several JIS "C" series standards changed designation to "X" series standards on March 1, 1987. Table 1-8 lists the JIS standards—mentioned in this book—that changed designation from "C" to "X" series.

Table 1-8: JIS Standard Designation Changes

JIS "C" Series	JIS "X" Series
JIS C 6220	JIS X 0201
JIS C 6228	JIS X 0202
JIS C 6225	JIS X 0207

* There are even JIS standards for manufacturing toilet paper!

Table 1-8: JIS Standard Designation Changes (continued)

JIS "C" Series	JIS "X" Series
JIS C 6226	JIS X 0208
JIS C 6233	JIS X 6002
JIS C 6235	JIS X 6003
JIS C 6236	JIS X 6004
JIS C 6232	JIS X 9051
JIS C 6234	JIS X 9052

Because these changes took place well over a decade ago, they have long been reflected in software and other documentation.

What is KS?

KS simply stands for "Korean Standard" (한국 공업 규격/韓國工業規格 *hangug gongeob gyugyeog*). All Korean character set standard designations begin with "KS." The character ㉿ is the symbol for KS.

All KS standards also include another letter in their designation. Those that are discussed in this book all include the letter "X," which now indicates electric or electronic standards.*

Several KS "C" series standards changed designation to "X" series standards on August 20, 1997. Table 1-9 lists the KS standards—mentioned in this book—that changed designation from the "C" to "X" series.

Table 1-9: KS Standard Designation Changes

KS "C" Series	KS "X" Series
KS C 5601	KS X 1001
KS C 5657	KS X 1002
KS C 5636	KS X 1003
KS C 5620	KS X 1004
KS C 5700	KS X 1005-1
KS C 5861	KS X 2901
KS C 5715	KS X 5002

Because these changes are very recent, it may take years until they are reflected in software and documentation.

* Other letter designations for KS standards include "B" (mechanical), "D" (metallurgy), and "A" (general guidelines).

Are VISCII and VSCII identical? What about TCVN?

While both VISCII and VSCII are short for *Vietnamese Standard Code for Information Interchange*, they represent completely different character sets and encodings. VISCII is defined in RFC 1456, and VSCII is derived from TCVN 5712:1993 (specifically, VN2), which is a Vietnamese national standard. VSCII is also known as ISO IR 180. The differences among VISCII and VSCII are described in Chapter 3, *Character Set Standards*, beginning on page 78. Appendix S, *Single-Byte Code Tables*, provides complete encoding tables for VISCII and VSCII, which better illustrate their differences.

TCVN stands for *Tiêu Chuẩn Việt Nam*, which means "Vietnamese Standard" in Vietnamese. Like GB, JIS, and KS, it represents the first portion of Vietnamese standard designations.

What Are Internationalization and Localization?

Internationalization (often abbreviated as I18N—the initial letter "I" followed by the middle 18 letters followed by the final letter "N") is a blanket term referring to the process of preparing software so that it can be used by more than one culture, region, or locale.* Localization (often abbreviated as L10N) is the process of adapting software to one specific culture, region, or locale. Japanization (often abbreviated as J10N) is a specific instance of L10N. While this book does not necessarily address all of these issues, you will find information pertinent to internationalization and localization.

Either way, I18N or L10N are often desired by users because they provide menus and documentation written in the language of the target locale. They often require special character set handling because so many non-Latin character sets require more than one byte to represent all their characters.

What Are the Multilingual and Locale Models?

There are two basic models for internationalization: the *locale model* and the *multilingual model*. The locale model implements a set of attributes for specific locales. The user must explicitly switch from one locale to another. The character sets implemented by the locale model are specific to a given culture, region, or locale.

The multilingual model goes one step further by not requiring you to flip between locales—multilingual systems use a character set that contains all the characters

* Quiz time. Guess what CJKV6N, C10N, G11N, K11N, M17N, S32S, and V12N stand for?

necessary for several cultures or regions. But still, there are cases when it is impossible to correctly render characters without knowing the target locale.

What Is Row-Cell?

Row-Cell is the translated form of the Japanese word 区点 (*kuten*), which literally means "ward [and] point" (or, more intuitively, "row [and] cell").* This idea serves as an encoding-independent method for referring to characters in CJKV character set standards. A Row-Cell code usually consists of four decimal digits—the "Row" portion consists of a two-digit number with a range from 1 to 94; likewise, the "Cell" portion also consists of a two-digit number with a range from 1 to 94. For example, the first character in most CJKV character set standards is 01-01 in Row-Cell notation, and is more often than not a "space" character.

When I provide lists of characters throughout this book, I usually include Row-Cell codes. These are useful for future reference of these data (so that you don't have to hunt for the codes yourself!).

Characters and Glyphs—What Is the Difference?

Now here's a topic that is usually beaten to death! The term "character" is an abstract notion indicating a class of shapes declared to have the same meaning or form. The term "glyph" is a specific instance of a character. Sometimes, more than one character can constitute a single glyph, such as the two characters f and i, which can be fused together as the single entity "fi." This glyph "fi" is called a *ligature*. The dollar sign is a good example of a character with several glyphs. There are at least four glyphs for the dollar sign, listed as follows:

- An "S" shape with a single vertical bar: $
- An "S" shape with a single broken vertical bar: $
- An "S" shape with two vertical bars: $
- An "S" shape with two broken vertical bars: $

The differences among these four glyphs are minor, but you cannot deny that they still represent the same character, specifically the "dollar sign." Quite often you see a difference in glyph as a difference in typeface. However, there are some characters that have a dozen or more variant forms. Consider the kanji 辺 (*hen*, used in the Japanese family name 渡辺 *watanabe*), which has only two variant forms that are generally available in Japanese fonts (including Unicode-based fonts): 邊 and

* In Chinese, Row-Cell is expressed as 区位 (*qūwèi*); in Korean as 행렬/行列 (*haengryeol*). Note that if the "Cell" portion of "Row-Cell" is in isolation in Korean that it is expressed instead with the hangul 열 (*yeol*), not 렬 (*ryeol*).

邉. DTP center Biblos, a developer of "Gaiji" fonts, offers fonts that provide the following eight additional variant forms of this kanji:

邊邊邊邉邉邉邉邉

Enfour Media, another developer of "Gaiji" fonts, offers fonts that provide the following 18 variant forms of this kanji:

邊邊邊邊邊邊邊邊邊邉邉邉邉邉邉邉邉邉

Clearly, these variant forms all appear to represent that same character, but are simply different glyphs.

You will find that CJKV character set standards do not define the glyph for the characters contained within their pages. Unfortunately (or, fortunately, as the case may be), many think that the glyphs that appear in these manuals are the official ones. Note, however, that the official Jōyō Kanji Table *does* define the glyph shape, at least for the 1,945 kanji contained within. JSA published two manuals that do, in fact, define glyph shapes: JIS X 9051-1984[*] and JIS X 9052-1983.[†] They were designed for the JIS X 0208-1983 standard. However, these glyphs have not been widely accepted in industry. It seems as though JSA has no intention of ever revising these documents—this may be their way of not enforcing glyphs.

The one Japanese organization that had a chance in establishing a definitive Japanese glyph standard in Japan is called FDPC, which is short for Font Development and Promotion Center (文字フォント開発・普及センター *moji fonto kaihatsu fukyū sentā*). FDPC was a MITI- (Ministry of International Trade and Industry—通商産業省 *tsūshō sangyō shō*) funded organization, and has since been folded in with JSA. This government organization, with the help of developing members, developed a series of Japanese outline fonts called "Heisei" (平成 *heisei*) typefaces. The first two Heisei typefaces that were released are Heisei Mincho W3 (平成明朝W3 *heisei minchō W3*) and Heisei Kaku (squared) Gothic W5 (平成角ゴシックW5 *heisei kaku goshikku W5*). In fact, the standard Japanese typeface used in the production of this book is Heisei Mincho W3. A total of seven weights of both designs have been produced, weights 3 (W3) through 9 (W9). Two weights of Heisei Maru (rounded) Gothic (平成丸ゴシック *heisei maru goshikku*), 4 and 8, have also been developed. The Heisei typefaces have become somewhat commonplace in the Japanese market.

China takes glyph issues *very* seriously, and expended the effort to develop a series of standards, published in a single manual entitled *32×32 Dot Matrix Font Set and Data Set of Chinese Ideograms for Information Interchange* (信息交换用汉字32×32点阵字模集及数据集 *xìnxī jiāohuàn yòng hànzì 32×32 diǎnzhèn zìmújí*

* Previously designated JIS C 6232-1984.

† Previously designated JIS C 6234-1983.

jí shújùjí), that explicitly define glyphs for the GB 2312-80 character set standard in various typeface styles. These standards are listed in Table 1-10.

Table 1-10: Chinese Glyph Standards

Standard	Page Numbers in Manual	Title (in English)
GB 6345.1-86	1–27	*32×32 Dot Matrix Font Set of Chinese Ideograms for Information Interchange*
GB 6345.2-86	28–31	*32×32 Dot Matrix Font Data Set of Chinese Ideograms for Information Interchange*
GB 12034-89	32–55	*32×32 Dot Matrix Fangsongti Font Set and Data Set of Chinese Ideograms for Information Interchange*
GB 12035-89	56–79	*32×32 Dot Matrix Kaiti Font Set and Data Set of Chinese Ideograms for Information Interchange*
GB 12036-89	80–103	*32×32 Dot Matrix Heiti Font Set and Data Set of Chinese Ideograms for Information Interchange*

Songti (specified in GB 6345.1-86), Fangsongti, Kaiti, and Heiti are the most common typeface styles used in Chinese. When the number of available pixels is reduced, it is impossible to completely represent all of a Chinese character's strokes. These standards are useful because they establish bitmapped patterns that offer a compromise between accuracy and legibility. The recent GB 16794.1-1997 standard (信息技术—通用多八位编码字符集48点阵字形 *xìnxì jìshù—tōngyòng duōbāwèi biānmǎ zìfújí 48 diǎnzhèn zìxíng*) is similar to the GB standards listed in Table 1-10, but covers the complete GBK character set and provides 48×48 bitmapped patterns. An older set of GB standards, GB 5007.1-85 (信息交换用汉字24×24点阵字模集 *xìnxī jiāohuàn yòng hànzì 24×24 diǎnzhèn zìmújí*) and GB 5007.2-85 (信息交换用汉字24×24点阵字模数据集 *xìnxī jiāohuàn yòng hànzì 24×24 diǎnzhèn zìmú shújùjí*), provided 24×24 bitmapped patterns for a single design.

Exactly how character and glyph are defined can differ depending on the source. Table 1-11 provides the ISO (International Organization for Standardization) and The Unicode Consortium definitions for the terms character, glyph, and glyph image.

What Is the Difference Between Typeface and Font?

The term *typeface* refers to the printed style of a glyph or character set. A *font*, on the other hand, refers to a single instance of a typeface, such as a specific point size. This is why the commonly used term *outline font* is a misnomer—the outlines are scalable, which means that they are not specific to any one point size. A better term is *outline font instance*.

Table 1-11: Character, Glyph, and Glyph Image Definitions—ISO and Unicode

Terminology	ISO	Unicode[a]
Character	A member of a set of elements used for the organisation, control, or representation of data.[b] An atom of information with an individual meaning, defined by a character repertoire.[c]	(1) The smallest component of written language that has semantic value; refers to the meaning and/or shape, rather than a specific shape, (see also *glyph*) though in code tables some form of visual representation is essential for the reader's understanding.
Glyph	A recognizable abstract graphical symbol which is independent of any specific design.[c]	(1) An abstract form that represents one or more glyph images. (2) A synonym for *glyph image*.
Glyph image	An image of a glyph, as obtained from a glyph representation displayed on a presentation surface.[c]	The actual, concrete image of a glyph representation having been rasterized or otherwise imaged onto some display surface.

[a] *The Unicode Standard, Version 2.0* (Addison-Wesley, 1996).
[b] ISO 10646-1:1993.
[c] ISO 9541-1:1991.

Western typography commonly uses serif, sans serif, and script typeface styles. Table 1-12 lists the common CJKV typeface styles, along with correspondences across locales.

Table 1-12: CJKV Typeface Styles

Western	Chinese[a]	Japanese	Korean
Serif	Song (宋体 *sòngtǐ*)	Mincho (明朝体 *minchōtai*)	Myeongjo (명조체/明朝體 *myeongjoce*)
Sans serif	Hei (黑体 *hēitǐ*)	Gothic (ゴシック体 *goshikkutai*)	Gothic (고딕체/고딕體 *godigce*)
Script	Kai (楷体 *kǎitǐ*)	Kaisho (楷書体 *kaishotai*) Gyosho (行書体 *gyōshotai*) Sosho (草書体 *sōshotai*)	Haeseo (해서체/楷書體 *haeseoce*) Haengseo (행서체/行書體 *haengseoce*) Choseo (초서체/草書體 *coseoce*)
Other	Fangsong (仿宋体 *fǎngsòngtǐ*)	Kyokasho (教科書体 *kyōkashotai*)	

[a] Replace 体 with 體 in these typeface style names for Traditional Chinese.

Table 1-12 by no means constitutes a complete list of CJKV typeface styles—there are numerous typeface styles for hangul, for example.

What Are Half- and Full-Width Characters?

The terms half- and full-width refer to the relative glyph size of characters. These terms are referred to as *hankaku* (半角 *hankaku*) and *zenkaku* (全角 *zenkaku*), respectively, in Japanese.* Half-width is relative to full-width. Full-width refers to the glyph size of standard CJKV characters, such as zhuyin, kana, hangul, and Chinese characters. Latin characters, which appear to take up approximately half the display width of CJKV characters, are considered to be half-width by this standard. The very first Japanese characters to be processed on computer systems were half-width katakana. They have the same approximate display width as Latin characters. There are now full-width Latin and katakana characters. Table 1-13 shows the difference in display width between half- and full-width characters (the katakana character used as the example is read *ka*).

Table 1-13: Half- and Full-Width Characters

	Katakana	Latin
Half-width	ｶｶｶｶｶ	12345
Full-width	カカカカカ	１２３４５

As you can see, full-width characters occupy twice the display width as their half-width versions. At one point in time there was a clear-cut relationship between display width of a glyph and number of bytes used to encode it (the encoding length)—the number of bytes simply determined the display width. Half-width katakana characters were originally encoded with one byte. Full-width ones were encoded with two bytes. Now that there is a much richer choice of encoding methods available, this relationship no longer holds true. Table 1-14 lists several popular encoding methods, along with the number of bytes required to represent half- and full-width characters.

Table 1-14: Half- and Full-Width Character Representations

	ASCII	ISO-2022-JP	Shift-JIS	EUC-JP	ISO 10646-1:1993
Full-width					
Katakana	...	2 bytes	2 bytes	2 bytes	2 or 4 bytes
Latin	...	2 bytes	2 bytes	2 bytes	2 or 4 bytes
Half-width					
Katakana	...	1 byte	1 byte	2 bytes	2 or 4 bytes
Latin	1 byte	1 byte	1 byte	1 byte	2 or 4 bytes

* In Chinese, these terms are 半形 (*bànxíng*) and 全形 (*quánxíng*), respectively. In Korean, perhaps 반각/半角 (*bangag*) and 전각/全角 (*jeongag*), respectively.

Latin Versus Roman Characters

Many people debate whether the 26 letters of the English alphabet should be referred to as *Roman* or *Latin* characters. While some standards, such as those published by ISO, prefer the term Latin, others prefer the term Roman. This book will prefer the term Latin over Roman. Readers of this book should treat both terms synonymously.

When speaking of typeface designs, the use of the term Roman is used in contrast with the term italic.

What Is Notation?

The term notation refers to a method of representing units. A given distance, whether expressed in miles or kilometers, is, after all, the same distance. In computer science, common notations for representing the value of bytes are listed in Table 1-15, and all correspond to a different numeric base.

Table 1-15: Decimal 100 in Common Notations

Notation	Base	Range	Example
Binary	2	0 and 1	`01100100`
Octal	8	0–7	`144`
Decimal	10	0–9	`100`
Hexadecimal	16	0–9 and A–F	`64`

While the numbers in the "Example" column all have the same underlying value, they have been expressed using different notations, and thus take on a different form. Most people (that is, non-nerds) think in decimal notation; however, computers (and some nerds) process information using binary notation (as discussed above, computers process bits, which have two possible values). Below you will find that hexadecimal notation does, however, have distinct advantages when dealing with computers.

What Is an Octet?

We have already discussed the terms bits and bytes. But what about the term octet? At a glance, you can tell it has something to do with the number eight. An octet represents eight bits, and is an eight-bit byte. This becomes confusing when dealing with 16-bit encodings. 16 bits can be broken down into two eight-bit bytes, or two octets. 32 bits, likewise, can be broken down into four eight-bit bytes, or four octets.

Given 16 bits in a row:

```
0110010001011111
```

This string of bits can be broken down into two eight-bit units, specifically octets (bytes):

```
01100100
01011111
```

The first eight bits represent 100 (0x64), and the second 95 (0x5F). All 16 bits together as one unit are usually equal to 25695 in decimal or 0x645F in hexadecimal—it may be different depending on a computer's specific architecture. Divide 25695 by 256 to get the first byte's value as a decimal octet, which results in 100 in this case—the remainder from this division is the value of the second byte, which, in this case, is 95. Table 1-16 lists representations of two octets (bytes) and their 16-bit unit equivalent. This is done for you in different notations.

Table 1-16: Octets and 16-Bit Units in Various Notations

Notation	First Octet	Second Octet	16-Bit Unit
Binary	01100100	01011111	0110010001011111
Octal	144	137	62137
Decimal	100	95	25695
Hexadecimal	64	5F	645F

Note how going from two octets to a 16-bit unit is a simple matter of concatenation in the case of binary and hexadecimal notation. Not so with decimal notation, which requires multiplication of the first octet by 256, then addition of the second octet. The ease of going between different representations (octets versus 16-bit units) depends on the notation that you are using. Of course, string concatenation is easier than two mathematical processes. This is why hexadecimal is used so frequently in computers.

In some cases, the order in which byte concatenation takes place matters, such as when the byte order (endianness) differs depending on the underlying computing architecture. Guess what the next section is about?

What Are Little and Big Endian?

There are two basic computer architectures when it comes to the issue of byte order: little endian and big endian. That is, the order in which the bytes of multiple-byte storage units (such as integers, floats, doubles, and so on) appear.* One-byte storage units, such as char, do not need this special treatment (that is,

* A derivation of little and big endian came from *Gulliver's Travels*, in which there were civil wars fought over which end of a boiled egg to crack.

unless your particular machine or implementation represents them with more than one byte).

- Little endian machines use computing architectures supported by Vax and Intel processors. This typically means that MS-DOS and Windows machines are little endian.
- Big endian machines use computing architectures supported by Motorola and Sun processors. This typically means MacOS and most Unix workstations. Big endian is also known as "network byte order."

Table 1-17 provides an example two-byte value as encoded on little and big endian machines.

Table 1-17: Little and Big Endian Representation

Notation	High Byte	Low Byte	Little Endian	Big Endian
Binary	01100100	01011111	0101111101100100	0110010001011111
Hexadecimal	64	5F	5F64	645F

A four-byte example, such as 0x64, 0x5F, 0x7E, and 0xA1, becomes 0xA17E5F64 on little endian machines, and 0x645F7EA1 on big endian machines. Note how the bytes themselves (not the underlying bits of each byte) are reversed depending on endianness. This is precisely why endianness is also referred to as byte order. The term endian is used to describe what impact the byte at the end has on the overall value. The Unicode value for a "space" character is 0x0020 for big-endian, and 0x2000 for little-endian.

Now that you understand the concept of endianness, the real question that needs answering is when endianness matters. Keep reading…

What Are Multiple-Byte and Wide Characters?

If you have ever read comprehensive books and materials about ANSI C, you more than likely came across the terms multiple-byte and wide characters. Those documents don't do those terms justice. Here you'll get a definitive answer.

When dealing with encodings that are processed on a per-byte basis, endianness is irrelevant. These encodings support what are known as *multiple-byte* characters. So, what encodings are these? Table 1-18 provides an incomplete yet informative list of these encodings.

There are some encodings that require special endian treatment, and cannot be treated on a per-byte basis. These encodings include what are known as *wide* characters, and almost always provide a facility for indicating the byte order. Table 1-19 lists some encodings that use wide characters.

Table 1-18: Multiple-Byte Character Encodings

Encoding	Encoding Length	Locale
ASCII	one-byte	*not applicable*
ISO-2022	one- and two-byte	CJKV
EUC	one- through four-byte, depending on locale	CJKV
GBK	one- and two-byte	China
Big Five	one- and two-byte	Taiwan
Big Five Plus	one- and two-byte	Taiwan
Shift-JIS	one- and two-byte	Japan
Johab	one- and two-byte	Korea
UHC	one- and two-byte	Korea
UTF-8	one- through six-byte	*not applicable*

Table 1-19: Wide Character Encodings

Encoding	Encoding Length
UCS-2	16-bit fixed
UCS-4	32-bit fixed
UTF-16	16-bit variable-length
Unicode Version 2.0	*Same as UTF-16*

It is with endianness that we can more easily distinguish multiple-byte from wide characters. Multiple-byte characters have the same byte order regardless of the underlying processor architecture; the byte order of wide characters is determined by the underlying processor architecture.

In this chapter:
- *Latin Characters and Transliteration*
- *Zhuyin*
- *Kana*
- *Hangul*
- *Chinese Characters*
- *Non-Chinese Chinese Characters*

2
Writing Systems

Now that you have had a taste of what to expect to learn about CJKV information processing, let's begin with a thorough description of the various CJKV writing systems. We've already touched briefly upon this subject in the introductory material, but you need to learn a bit more. After reading this chapter you should have an understanding of the types of characters used to write CJKV text, specifically the following:

- Latin characters
- Zhuyin
- Kana (*hiragana* and *katakana*)
- Hangul (and jamo)
- Chinese characters
- Non-Chinese Chinese characters (Japanese *kokuji*, Korean *gugja*, and Vietnamese *chữ Nôm*)

Each of these types of characters exhibits its own special characteristics, and often has locale-specific usages. This information is absolutely crucial for understanding discussions elsewhere in this book.

Latin Characters and Transliteration

Latin characters (拉丁字母 *lādīng zìmǔ* in Chinese, ラテン文字 *raten moji* or ローマ字 *rōmaji* in Japanese, 로마자 *romaja* in Korean, and Quốc ngữ/國語 in Vietnamese) used in CJKV texts are the same as those used in Western texts, specifically the 52 upper- and lowercase letters of the Latin alphabet, sometimes decorated with accents to indicate length or tone. Also included are the ten numerals 0 through 9. Accented characters, usually vowels, are often required for transliteration purposes. Table 2-1 lists the basic set of Latin characters.

Table 2-1: Latin Characters

Lowercase	abcdefghijklmnopqrstuvwxyz
Uppercase	ABCDEFGHIJKLMNOPQRSTUVWXYZ
Numerals	0123456789

There is really nothing special about these characters. Latin characters are most often used in tables (numerals), in abbreviations (alphabet), or for transcription or transliteration purposes (sometimes with accented characters).

Commonly used transliteration systems for CJKV text that use characters beyond the standard set of Latin characters illustrated above include Pinyin (Chinese), Hepburn (Japanese), Kunrei (Japanese), and Ministry of Education (Korean). These and other CJKV transliteration systems are covered in the following sections.

Chinese Transliteration Methods

Chinese uses two primary transliteration methods: Pinyin (拼音 *pīnyīn*) and Wade-Giles (韋氏 *wéishì*). There is also the Yale method, which is not covered in this book. While there are many similarities between these two transliteration methods, they mainly differ in where they are used. Pinyin is used in China, while Wade-Giles is popular in Taiwan. Historically speaking, Wade-Giles was the originally recognized Chinese transliteration system during the nineteenth century.

Table 2-2 lists the consonant sounds as transliterated by Pinyin and Wade-Giles—zhuyin symbols (described later in this chapter) are included for the purpose of cross-reference.

Table 2-2: Chinese Transliteration—Consonants

Zhuyin	Pinyin	Wade-Giles
ㄅ	B	P
ㄆ	P	P'
ㄇ	M	M
ㄈ	F	F
ㄉ	D	T
ㄊ	T	T'
ㄋ	N	N
ㄌ	L	L
ㄍ	G	K
ㄎ	K	K'

Table 2-2: Chinese Transliteration—Consonants (continued)

Zhuyin	Pinyin	Wade-Giles
ㄏ	H	H
ㄐ	J	CH[a]
ㄑ	Q	CH'[a]
ㄒ	X	HS[a]
ㄓ	ZH	CH
ㄔ	CH	CH'
ㄕ	SH	SH
ㄖ	R	J
ㄗ	Z	TS
ㄘ	C	TS'
ㄙ	S	S

[a] Only before i or ü.

Table 2-3 lists the vowel sounds as transliterated by Pinyin—zhuyin are again included for reference. Note that this table is constructed as a matrix that indicates what zhuyin vowel combinations are possible and how they are transliterated—the two axes themselves serve to indicate the transliterations for single zhuyin vowels.

Table 2-3: Chinese Transliteration—Vowels

	ㄧ I	ㄨ U	ㄩ Ü
ㄚ A	ㄧㄚ IA	ㄨㄚ UA	
ㄛ O		ㄨㄛ UO	
ㄜ E	ㄧㄝ IE		ㄩㄝ ÜE
ㄞ AI		ㄨㄞ UAI	
ㄟ EI		ㄨㄟ UEI	
ㄠ AO	ㄧㄠ IAO		
ㄡ OU	ㄧㄡ IOU		
ㄢ AN	ㄧㄢ IAN	ㄨㄢ UAN	ㄩㄢ ÜAN
ㄣ EN	ㄧㄣ IN	ㄨㄣ UEN	ㄩㄣ ÜN
ㄤ ANG	ㄧㄤ IANG	ㄨㄤ UANG	
ㄥ ENG	ㄧㄥ ING	ㄨㄥ UENG or ONG	ㄩㄥ IONG

The zhuyin character ㄦ, which deserves separate treatment, is usually transliterated *er*.

It is sometimes necessary to use an apostrophe to separate the Pinyin readings of individual hanzi when the result can be ambiguous. Consider the transliterations for the words 先 and 西安, which are *xiān* and *xī'ān*, respectively. Note the use of the apostrophe.

More details about the zhuyin characters themselves appear later in this chapter, starting on page 40. Po-Han Lin (林伯翰 *lín bóhàn*) has developed a Java applet that can convert between the Pinyin, Wade-Giles, and Yale transliteration systems.* He also provides additional details about Chinese transliteration.†

Chinese tone marks

Also of interest is how tone marks are rendered when transliterating Chinese text. Basically, there are two systems for indicating tone. One system, which requires the use of special fonts, employs diacritic marks that serve to indicate tone. The other system uses the numerals 1 through 4 immediately after each hanzi transliteration—no special fonts are required. Pinyin transliteration generally uses diacritic marks, but Wade-Giles uses numerals.

Table 2-4 lists the names of the Chinese tone marks, along with an example hanzi for each. Note that there are cases in which there is no tone required.

Table 2-4: Chinese Tone Mark Examples

Tone	Tone Name	Number	Example	Meaning
None	轻声/輕聲 (*qīngshēng*)	*none*	ma (吗)	question particle
Flat	阴平/陰平 (*yīnpíng*)	1	ma1 or mā (妈)	*mother*
Rising	阳平/陽平 (*yángpíng*)	2	ma2 or má (麻)	*hemp, flax*
Falling-Rising	上声/上聲 (*shǎngshēng*)	3	ma3 or mǎ (马)	*horse*
Falling	去声/去聲 (*qùshēng*)	4	ma4 or mà (骂)	*cursing, swearing*

It is also common to find reference works in which Pinyin readings have no tone marks at all, That is, no numerals and no diacritic marks. I have observed that tone marks can be effectively omitted when the corresponding hanzi are in proximity, such as on the same page—the hanzi themselves can be used to remove any ambiguity that arises from no indication of tones. Pinyin readings provided throughout this book use diacritic marks to indicate tone.

Japanese Transliteration Methods

There are four Japanese transliteration systems worth exploring in the context of this book:

* *http://www.edepot.com/java.html*

† *http://www.edepot.com/taoroman.html*

- The Hepburn system (ヘボン式 *hebon shiki*), developed by James Curtis Hepburn, an American missionary, in 1886—this is considered the most widely used system
- The Kunrei system (訓令式 *kunrei shiki*), developed in 1937, is considered the official transliteration system by the Japanese government
- The Nippon system (日本式 *nippon shiki*), developed in 1881 by Aikitsu Tanakadate (田中館愛橘 *tanakadate aikitsu*)—nearly identical to the Kunrei system, but the least used
- The word processor system (ワープロ式 *wāpuro shiki*) has been developed in a somewhat *ad hoc* fashion over recent years by Japanese word processor and input method manufacturers

The Japanese transliterations in this book adhere to the Hepburn system. Because the word processor system allows for a wide variety of transliteration possibilities (that is the nature of input systems), it is a topic of discussion in Chapter 5, *Input Methods.*

Table 2-5 lists the basic kana syllables (shown here and in other tables of this section using hiragana), transliterated according to the three transliteration systems. Those that are transliterated differently in the three systems have been highlighted for easy differentiation. Table 2-18 on page 43 provides similar information, but presented in a different manner.

Table 2-5: Single Syllable Japanese Transliteration

Kana	Hepburn	Kunrei	Nippon
あ	A	A	A
い	I	I	I
う	U	U	U
え	E	E	E
お	O	O	O
か	KA	KA	KA
が	GA	GA	GA
き	KI	KI	KI
ぎ	GI	GI	GI
く	KU	KU	KU
ぐ	GU	GU	GU
け	KE	KE	KE
げ	GE	GE	GE
こ	KO	KO	KO
ご	GO	GO	GO

Table 2-5: Single Syllable Japanese Transliteration (continued)

Kana	Hepburn	Kunrei	Nippon
さ	SA	SA	SA
ざ	ZA	ZA	ZA
し	SHI	SI	SI
じ	JI	ZI	ZI
す	SU	SU	SU
ず	ZU	ZU	ZU
せ	SE	SE	SE
ぜ	ZE	ZE	ZE
そ	SO	SO	SO
ぞ	ZO	ZO	ZO
た	TA	TA	TA
だ	DA	DA	DA
ち	CHI	TI	TI
ぢ	JI	ZI	DI
つ	TSU	TU	TU
づ	ZU	ZU	DU
て	TE	TE	TE
で	DE	DE	DE
と	TO	TO	TO
ど	DO	DO	DO
な	NA	NA	NA
に	NI	NI	NI
ぬ	NU	NU	NU
ね	NE	NE	NE
の	NO	NO	NO
は	HA	HA	HA
ば	BA	BA	BA
ぱ	PA	PA	PA
ひ	HI	HI	HI
び	BI	BI	BI
ぴ	PI	PI	PI
ふ	FU	HU	HU
ぶ	BU	BU	BU
ぷ	PU	PU	PU
へ	HE	HE	HE
べ	BE	BE	BE

Table 2-5: Single Syllable Japanese Transliteration (continued)

Kana	Hepburn	Kunrei	Nippon
ぺ	PE	PE	PE
ほ	HO	HO	HO
ぼ	BO	BO	BO
ぽ	PO	PO	PO
ま	MA	MA	MA
み	MI	MI	MI
む	MU	MU	MU
め	ME	ME	ME
も	MO	MO	MO
や	YA	YA	YA
ゆ	YU	YU	YU
よ	YO	YO	YO
ら	RA	RA	RA
り	RI	RI	RI
る	RU	RU	RU
れ	RE	RE	RE
ろ	RO	RO	RO
わ	WA	WA	WA
ゐ	WI	WI	WI
ゑ	WE	WE	WE
を	O	O	WO
ん	N or M[a]	N	N

[a] An *m* was once used before the consonants *b*, *p*, or *m*—an *n* is now used in all contexts.

Table 2-6 lists what are considered to be the palatalized syllables—although they represent a single syllable, they are represented with two kana characters. Those that are different in the three transliteration systems are highlighted.

Table 2-6: Japanese Transliteration—Palatalized Syllables

Kana	Hepburn	Kunrei	Nippon
きゃ	KYA	KYA	KYA
ぎゃ	GYA	GYA	GYA
きゅ	KYU	KYU	KYU
ぎゅ	GYU	GYU	GYU
きょ	KYO	KYO	KYO
ぎょ	GYO	GYO	GYO

Table 2-6: Japanese Transliteration—Palatalized Syllables (continued)

Kana	Hepburn	Kunrei	Nippon
しゃ	SHA	SYA	SYA
じゃ	JA	ZYA	ZYA
しゅ	SHU	SYU	SYU
じゅ	JU	ZYU	ZYU
しょ	SHO	SYO	SYO
じょ	JO	ZYO	ZYO
ちゃ	CHA	TYA	TYA
ぢゃ	JA	ZYA	DYA
ちゅ	CHU	TYU	TYU
ぢゅ	JU	ZYU	DYU
ちょ	CHO	TYO	TYO
ぢょ	JO	ZYO	DYO
にゃ	NYA	NYA	NYA
にゅ	NYU	NYU	NYU
にょ	NYO	NYO	NYO
みゃ	MYA	MYA	MYA
みゅ	MYU	MYU	MYU
みょ	MYO	MYO	MYO
ひゃ	HYA	HYA	HYA
びゃ	BYA	BYA	BYA
ぴゃ	PYA	PYA	PYA
ひゅ	HYU	HYU	HYU
びゅ	BYU	BYU	BYU
ぴゅ	PYU	PYU	PYU
ひょ	HYO	HYO	HYO
びょ	BYO	BYO	BYO
ぴょ	PYO	PYO	PYO
りゃ	RYA	RYA	RYA
りゅ	RYU	RYU	RYU
りょ	RYO	RYO	RYO

Table 2-7 lists what are considered to be long (or doubled) vowels—the first five rows are hiragana, and the last five are katakana. Note that only the long hiragana *i* (いい, expressed as *ii*) is common to all three systems, and that the Kunrei and Nippon systems are identical in this regard.

The only difference among these systems' long vowel transliterations is the use of a macron (Hepburn) versus a circumflex (Kunrei and Nippon). Almost all Latin

Table 2-7: Japanese Transliteration—Long Vowels

Kana	Hepburn	Kunrei	Nippon
ああ	Ā	Â	Â
いい	II	II	II
うう	Ū	Û	Û
ええ	Ē	Ê	Ê
えい	EI	EI	EI
おう	Ō	Ô	Ô
アー	Ā	Â	Â
イー	Ī	Î	Î
ウー	Ū	Û	Û
エー	Ē	Ê	Ê
オー	Ō	Ô	Ô

fonts include circumflexed vowels, but those with macroned vowels are still extremely rare.

Finally, Table 2-8 shows some examples of how to transliterate Japanese double consonants, all of which use a small つ or ツ (*tsu*).

Table 2-8: Japanese Transliteration—Double Consonants

Example	Transliteration
かっこ	*kakko*
いっしょ	*issho*
ふっそ	*fusso*
ねっちゅう	*netchū*
しって	*shitte*
ビット	*bitto*
ベッド	*beddo*
バッハ	*bahha*

Korean Transliteration Methods

There are three generally accepted transliteration methods for Korean text: Ministry of Education (문교부/文教部 *mungyobu*; derived from McCune-Reischauer), established on January 13, 1984; Korean Language Society (한글학회/한글學會 *hangeul hakhoe*), established on February 21, 1984;* and ISO/TR 11941:1996 (*Information Documentation—Transliteration of Korean Script into Latin Characters*), estab-

* *http://www.hangeul.or.kr/*

lished in 1996. The Korean text in this book adheres to the ISO/TR 11941:1996 transliteration method, specifically Method 2.* Other transliteration methods, not covered in this book, include the Yale, Lukoff, and Horne methods.

Table 2-9 lists the jamo that represent consonants, along with their representation in these three transliteration methods. Also included are the ISO/TR 11941:1996 transliterations when these jamo serve as the final consonant of a syllable. ISO/TR 11941:1996 Method 1 is used for North Korea (DPRK), and Method 2 is used for South Korea (ROK). Uppercase is used solely for clarity.

Table 2-9: Korean Transliteration—Consonants

Jamo	MOE	KLS	ISO (DPRK)	Final	ISO (ROK)	Final
ㄱ	K/G	G	K	K	G	G
ㄴ	N	N	N	N	N	N
ㄷ	T/D	D	T	T	D	D
ㄹ	R/L	L	R	L	R	L
ㅁ	M	M	M	M	M	M
ㅂ	P/B	B	P	P	B	B
ㅅ	S/SH	S	S	S	S	S
ㅇ	*none*/NG	*none*/NG	*none*	NG	*none*	NG
ㅈ	CH/J	J	C	C	J	J
ㅊ	CH'	CH	CH	CH	C	C
ㅋ	K'	K	KH	KH	K	K
ㅌ	T'	T	TH	TH	T	T
ㅍ	P'	P	PH	PH	P	P
ㅎ	H	H	H	H	H	H
ㄲ	KK	GG	KK	KK	GG	GG
ㄸ	TT	DD	TT	*n/a*	DD	*n/a*
ㅃ	PP	BB	PP	*n/a*	BB	*n/a*
ㅆ	SS	SS	SS	SS	SS	SS
ㅉ	TCH	JJ	CC	*n/a*	JJ	*n/a*

Note that some of the double jamo do not occur at the end of syllables. Also, some of these transliteration methods, most notably the Ministry of Education system, have a number of rules that dictate how to transliterate certain jamo depending on their context. The ㄱ jamo, for example, is transliterated as *k* in most contexts, and *g* when between vowels.

* Notable exceptions include words such as *hangul*, which should really be transliterated as *hangeul*.

ISO/TR 11941:1996 also defines transliterations for compound consonant jamo that appear only at the end of hangul syllables, all of which are listed in Table 2-10.

Table 2-10: ISO/TR 11941:1996 Compound Jamo Transliteration

Jamo	DPRK	ROK
ㄳ	KS	GS
ㄵ	NJ	NJ
ㄶ	NH	NH
ㄺ	LK	LG
ㄻ	LM	LM
ㄼ	LP	LB
ㄽ	LS	LS
ㄾ	LTH	LT
ㄿ	LPH	LP
ㅀ	LH	LH
ㅄ	PS	BS

Table 2-11 lists the jamo that represent vowels and diphthongs, along with their representations in the three transliteration methods. Again, uppercase is used for clarity, and differences have been highlighted.

Table 2-11: Korean Transliteration—Vowels

Jamo	MOE	KLS	ISO (DPRK and ROK)
ㅏ	A	A	A
ㅑ	YA	YA	YA
ㅓ	Ŏ	EO	EO
ㅕ	YŎ	YEO	YEO
ㅗ	O	O	O
ㅛ	YO	YO	YO
ㅜ	U	U	U
ㅠ	YU	YU	YU
ㅡ	Ŭ	EU	EU
ㅣ	I	I	I
ㅐ	AE	AE	AE
ㅒ	YAE	YAE	YAE
ㅔ	E	E	E
ㅖ	YE	YE	YE
ㅘ	WA	WA	WA
ㅙ	WAE	WAE	WAE

Table 2-11: Korean Transliteration—Vowels (continued)

Jamo	MOE	KLS	ISO (DPRK and ROK)
ㅚ	OE	OE	OE
ㅝ	WŎ	WEO	WEO
ㅞ	WE	WE	WE
ㅟ	WI	WI	WI
ㅢ	ŬI	EUI	YI

Note that the ISO/TR 11941:1996 transliteration method is identical for both North and South Korea (DPRK and ROK, respectively).

As with most transliteration methods, there are countless exceptions and special cases. Tables 2-9 and 2-11 provide only the basic transliterations for jamo. It is when you start combining consonants and vowels that exceptions and special cases become an issue. In fact, a common exception is the transliteration of the hangul used for the Korean surname "Lee." More detailed information about Korean transliteration systems can be found on the Web.*

Vietnamese Romanization Methods

Writing Vietnamese using Latin characters—called *Quốc ngữ* (國語)—is considered the most acceptable method for expressing Vietnamese today. In fact, Quốc ngữ is not considered a transliteration method as with Chinese, Japanese, and Korean—it is the currently acceptable means to express Vietnamese in writing. This writing system is based on Latin script, but is decorated with additional characters and many diacritic marks. This complexity serves to account for the very rich Vietnamese sound system, complete with tones.

In addition to the English alphabet, Quốc ngữ requires two additional consonants and twelve additional base characters (that is, characters that do not indicate tone), as shown in Table 2-12.

Table 2-12: Additional Quốc Ngữ Consonants and Base Characters

Lowercase	đ	ăâêôơư
Uppercase	Đ	ĂÂÊÔƠƯ

The modifiers that are used for the base vowels, in the order shown in Table 2-12, are called *breve* or *short* (*trăng* or *mũ ngược* in Vietnamese), *circumflex* (*mũ* in Vietnamese), and *horn* (*móc* or *râu* in Vietnamese).

* *http://www.basistech.com/hpkim/koreanroman.html*

While these additional base characters include diacritic marks and other attachments, they do not indicate tone. There are six tones in Vietnamese, five of which are written with a tone mark. Every Vietnamese word must have a tone. These six tones are shown in Table 2-13, along with their names.

Table 2-13: The Six Vietnamese Tones

Tone Mark	Name (in Vietnamese)	Name (in English)
none	Không dấu	*none*
◌̀	Huyền	Grave
◌̉	Hỏi	Hook above, curl, or *hoi*
◌̃	Ngã	Tilde
◌́	Sắc	Acute
◌̣	Nặng	Dot below, underdot, or *nang*

All of the diacritic-annotated characters that are required for the Quốc ngữ writing system, which are combinations of base characters plus tones, are provided in Table 2-14.

Table 2-14: Quốc Ngữ Base Characters with Tone Marks

	Base Characters											
Tone Marks	a A	ă Ă	â Â	e E	ê Ê	i I	o O	ô Ô	ơ Ơ	u U	ư Ư	y Y
◌̀	à À	ằ Ằ	ầ Ầ	è È	ề Ề	ì Ì	ò Ò	ồ Ồ	ờ Ờ	ù Ù	ừ Ừ	ỳ Ỳ
◌̉	ả Ả	ẳ Ẳ	ẩ Ẩ	ẻ Ẻ	ể Ể	ỉ Ỉ	ỏ Ỏ	ổ Ổ	ở Ở	ủ Ủ	ử Ử	ỷ Ỷ
◌̃	ã Ã	ẵ Ẵ	ẫ Ẫ	ẽ Ẽ	ễ Ễ	ĩ Ĩ	õ Õ	ỗ Ỗ	ỡ Ỡ	ũ Ũ	ữ Ữ	ỹ Ỹ
◌́	á Á	ắ Ắ	ấ Ấ	é É	ế Ế	í Í	ó Ó	ố Ố	ớ Ớ	ú Ú	ứ Ứ	ý Ý
◌̣	ạ Ạ	ặ Ặ	ậ Ậ	ẹ Ẹ	ệ Ệ	ị Ị	ọ Ọ	ộ Ộ	ợ Ợ	ụ Ụ	ự Ự	ỵ Ỵ

In summary, Quốc ngữ requires 134 additional characters beyond the English alphabet. 14 are additional base characters (see Table 2-12), and the remaining 120 include diacritic marks that indicate tone (see Table 2-14).

ASCII-based Vietnamese transliteration methods

When only the ASCII character set is available, it is still possible to represent Vietnamese text using well-established systems. The two most common ASCII-based transliteration methods are called VIQR (Vietnamese Quoted-Readable) and VSCII-MNEM (VSCII Mnemonic). The VIQR system is documented in RFC 1456. Table 2-15 illustrates how Quốc ngữ base characters and tones are represented in these two systems.

Table 2-15: VIQR and VSCII-MNEM Transliteration Methods

	Quốc Ngữ	VIQR	VSCII-MNEM
Base Characters	ă Ă	a(A(	a< A<
	â Â	a^ A^	a> A>
	ê Ê	e^ E^	e> E>
	ô Ô	o^ O^	o> O>
	ơ Ơ	o+ O+	o* O*
	ư Ư	u+ U+	u* U*
	đ Đ	dd DD	dd DD
Tones	à À	a` A`	a! A!
	ả Ả	a? A?	a? A?
	ã Ã	a~ A~	a" A"
	á Á	a' A'	a' A'
	ạ Ạ	a. A.	a. A.

Table 2-16 illustrates how base characters and tones are combined in each system. Note how the base character's ASCII-based annotation comes before the ASCII-based tone mark.

Table 2-16: Base Character Plus Tones Using VIQR and VSCII-MNEM Methods

Quốc Ngữ	VIQR	VSCII-MNEM
ờ Ờ	o+` O+`	o*! O*!
ở Ở	o+? O+?	o*? O*?
ỡ Ỡ	o+~ O+~	o*" O*"
ớ Ớ	o+' O+'	o*' O*'
ợ Ợ	o+. O+.	o*. O*.

Zhuyin

Zhuyin, developed in the early 1900s, is a method for transcribing Chinese text using Chinese character elements for their reading value. It is also known as the *National Phonetic System* (注音符号 *zhùyīn fúhào*) or *bopomofo*. The name bopomofo is derived from the readings of the first four characters in the character set: *b*, *p*, *m*, and *f*. There are a total of 37 characters (representing 21 consonants and 16 vowels), along with five symbols to indicate tone (one of which has no glyph) in the zhuyin character set.

Table 2-17 illustrates each of the zhuyin characters, along with their readings—vowels are at the end of the table.

Table 2-17: Zhuyin Characters

Zhuyin	Reading (Pinyin)
ㄅ	B
ㄆ	P
ㄇ	M
ㄈ	F
ㄉ	D
ㄊ	T
ㄋ	N
ㄌ	L
ㄍ	G
ㄎ	K
ㄏ	H
ㄐ	J
ㄑ	Q
ㄒ	X
ㄓ	ZH
ㄔ	CH
ㄕ	SH
ㄖ	R
ㄗ	Z
ㄘ	C
ㄙ	S
ㄚ	A
ㄛ	O
ㄜ	E
ㄝ	EI
ㄞ	AI
ㄟ	EI
ㄠ	AO
ㄡ	OU
ㄢ	AN
ㄣ	EN
ㄤ	ANG
ㄥ	ENG
ㄦ	ER
ㄧ or 一	I

Table 2-17: Zhuyin Characters (continued)

Zhuyin	Reading (Pinyin)
ㄨ	U
ㄩ	IU

The zhuyin character set is included in character sets developed in China (GB 2312-80 and GB/T 12345-90, Row 8) and Taiwan (CNS 11643-1992, Plane 1, Row 5). This set of characters is identical across these two Chinese locales, with one exception, which is indicated in Table 2-17 with two different characters: "丨" is used in China, and "一" is used in Taiwan.

Kana

The most frequently-used writing system in Japanese text is kana. Kana is made up of two closely related writing systems:

- Hiragana
- Katakana

Although one would expect to find kana characters only in Japanese character sets, they are, in fact, part of some Chinese and Korean character sets, in particular GB 2312-80 and KS X 1001:1992. In fact, kana are encoded at the same code points in the case of GB 2312-80! Why in the world would Chinese and Korean character sets include kana? Most likely for the purposes of creating Japanese-looking text using a Chinese or Korean character set.*

The following sections provide detailed information about kana, along with how they were derived from Chinese characters.

Hiragana

Hiragana (平仮名 *hiragana*) are characters that represent sounds, specifically syllables. A syllable is generally composed of a consonant plus a vowel—sometimes a single vowel will do. In Japanese, there are five vowels: *a*, *i*, *u*, *e*, and *o*; and fourteen basic consonants: *k*, *s*, *t*, *n*, *h*, *m*, *y*, *r*, *w*, *g*, *z*, *d*, *b*, and *p*. It is important to understand that hiragana is a syllabary, not an alphabet—you cannot decompose a hiragana character into a part that represents the vowel and a part that represents the consonant. Hiragana (and katakana, covered in the next section) is one of the

* There is, however, one fatal flaw in the Chinese and Korean implementations of kana. They forgot to include five symbols used with kana, all available in row 1 of JIS X 0208:1997: ヽ (01-19), ヾ (01-20), ゝ (01-21), ゞ (01-22), and ー (01-28).

only true syllabaries still in common use today. Table 2-18 illustrates a matrix containing the basic and extended hiragana syllabary.

Table 2-18: The Hiragana Syllabary

		K	S	T	N	H	M	Y	R	W	G	Z	D	B	P
A	あ	か	さ	た	な	は	ま	や	ら	わ	が	ざ	だ	ば	ぱ
I	い	き	し	ち	に	ひ	み		り	ゐ	ぎ	じ	ぢ	び	ぴ
U	う	く	す	つ	ぬ	ふ	む	ゆ	る		ぐ	ず	づ	ぶ	ぷ
E	え	け	せ	て	ね	へ	め		れ	ゑ	げ	ぜ	で	べ	ぺ
O	お	こ	そ	と	の	ほ	も	よ	ろ	を	ご	ぞ	ど	ぼ	ぽ
N	ん														

The following are some notes to accompany Table 2-18:

- Several hiragana have smaller versions, and are as follows (in parentheses you will find the standard version): ぁ (あ), ぃ (い), ぅ (う), ぇ (え), ぉ (お), っ (つ), ゃ (や), ゅ (ゆ), ょ (よ), and ゎ (わ)
- Two hiragana, ゐ and ゑ, are no longer commonly used
- The hiragana を is read as *o*, not *wo*
- The hiragana ん is considered an independent syllable, and is pronounced approximately *ng*

Notice that some cells do not contain any characters. These sounds are no longer used in Japanese, and thus no longer need a character to represent them. Also, the first block of characters is set in a 5×10 matrix. This is sometimes referred to as the *50 Sounds Table* (50音表 *gojūon hyō*), so named because it has a capacity of 50 cells. The other blocks of characters are the same as those in the first block, but with diacritic marks.

Diacritic marks serve to annotate characters with additional information—usually a variant reading. In the West you commonly see accented characters such as *á*, *à*, *â*, *ä*, *ã*, and *å*. The accents are called diacritic marks.

In Japanese there are two diacritic marks: *dakuten* (also called *nigori*) and *handakuten* (also called *maru*). The dakuten (濁点 *dakuten*) appears as two short strokes (゛) in the upper-right corner of some kana characters. The dakuten serves to voice the consonant portion of the kana character to which it is attached.* Examples of voiceless consonants include *k*, *s*, and *t*. Their voiced counterparts are *g*, *z*, and *d*, respectively. Hiragana *ka* (か) becomes *ga* (が) with the addition of the dakuten. The *b* sound is a special voiced version of a voiced *h* in Japanese.

* Voicing is a linguistic term referring to the vibration of the vocal bands while articulating a sound.

The handakuten (半濁点 *handakuten*) appears as a small open circle (°) in the upper-right corner of kana characters that begin with the *h* consonant. It transforms this *h* sound into a *p* sound.

Hiragana were derived by cursively writing kanji, but no longer carry the meaning of the kanji from which they were derived. Table 2-20 on page 45 lists the kanji from which the basic hiragana characters were derived.

In modern Japanese, hiragana are used to write grammatical words, inflectional endings for verbs and adjectives, and some nouns. They can also be used as a fallback (read "crutch") in case you forget how to write a kanji—the hiragana that represent the reading of a kanji are used in this case. In summary, hiragana are used to write some native Japanese words.

The following characters represent the standard hiragana character set as enumerated in the basic Japanese character set standard, JIS X 0208:1997:

ぁあぃいぅうぇえぉおかがきぎくぐけげこごさざしじすずせぜそぞただちぢっつ
づてでとどなにぬねのはばぱひびぴふぶぷへべぺほぼぽまみむめもゃやゅゆょよ
らりるれろゎわゐゑをん

Note how these characters have a cursive or calligraphic look to them (cursive and calligraphic refer to a smoother, handwritten style of characters). Keep these shapes in mind while we move on to katakana.

Katakana

Katakana (片仮名 *katakana*), like hiragana, is a syllabary, and with minor exceptions, they represent the same set of sounds as hiragana. Their usage, however, differs from hiragana. Where hiragana are used to write native Japanese words, katakana are primarily used to write words of foreign origin, called *gairaigo* (外来語 *gairaigo*), to write onomatopoeic words,* and for emphasis—similar to the use of italics to represent foreign words and to express emphasis in English. For example, the Japanese word for bread is written パン and read *pan*. It was borrowed from the Portuguese word *pão*, which is read sort of like *pown*. Katakana are also used to write foreign names. Table 2-19 illustrates the basic and extended katakana syllabary.

The following are some notes to accompany Table 2-19:

- Several katakana have smaller versions, and are as follows (in parentheses you will find the standard version): ァ (ア), ィ (イ), ゥ (ウ), ェ (エ), ォ (オ), ヵ (カ), ヶ (ケ), ッ (ツ), ャ (ヤ), ュ (ユ), ョ (ヨ), and ヮ (ワ)
- Two katakana, ヰ and ヱ, are no longer commonly used

* Words that serve to describe a sound, such as *buzz* or *hiss* in English. In Japanese, for example, ブクブク (*bukubuku*) represents the sound of a balloon expanding.

- The katakana ヲ is read as *o*, not *wo*
- The katakana ン is considered an independent syllable, and is pronounced approximately *ng*

Table 2-19: The Katakana Syllabary

		K	S	T	N	H	M	Y	R	W	G	Z	D	B	P
A	ア	カ	サ	タ	ナ	ハ	マ	ヤ	ラ	ワ	ガ	ザ	ダ	バ	パ
I	イ	キ	シ	チ	ニ	ヒ	ミ		リ	ヰ	ギ	ジ	ヂ	ビ	ピ
U	ウ	ク	ス	ツ	ヌ	フ	ム	ユ	ル		グ	ズ	ヅ	ブ	プ
E	エ	ケ	セ	テ	ネ	ヘ	メ		レ	ヱ	ゲ	ゼ	デ	ベ	ペ
O	オ	コ	ソ	ト	ノ	ホ	モ	ヨ	ロ	ヲ	ゴ	ゾ	ド	ボ	ポ
N	ン														

Katakana were derived by extracting a single portion of a whole kanji, and, like hiragana, no longer carry the meaning of the kanji from which they were derived. If you compare several of these characters to some kanji, you may recognize common shapes. Table 2-20 lists the basic katakana characters, along with the kanji from which they were derived.

The following characters represent the standard katakana character set as enumerated in the basic Japanese character set standard, JIS X 0208:1997:

ァアィイゥウェエォオカガキギクグケゲコゴサザシジスズセゼソゾタダチヂッツ
ヅテデトドナニヌネノハバパヒビピフブプヘベペホボポマミムメモャヤュユョヨ
ラリルレロヮワヰヱヲンヴヵヶ

Katakana, unlike hiragana, have a squared, more rigid feel to them. Structurally speaking, they are quite similar in appearance to kanji, which we discuss later.

The Development of Kana

You already know that kana were derived from kanji, and Table 2-20 provides a complete listing of kana characters, along with the kanji from which they were derived.

Table 2-20: The Kanji from Which Kana Were Derived

Katakana	Kanji		Hiragana
ア	阿	安	あ
イ	伊	以	い
ウ	宇		う
エ	江	衣	え
オ	於		お

Table 2-20: The Kanji from Which Kana Were Derived (continued)

Katakana	Kanji			Hiragana
カ		加		か
キ		幾		き
ク		久		く
ケ	介		計	け
コ		己		こ
サ	散		左	さ
シ		之		し
ス	須		寸	す
セ		世		せ
ソ		曽		そ
タ	多		太	た
チ	千		知	ち
ツ		川		つ
テ		天		て
ト		止		と
ナ		奈		な
ニ	二		仁	に
ヌ		奴		ぬ
ネ		祢		ね
ノ		乃		の
ハ	八		波	は
ヒ		比		ひ
フ		不		ふ
ヘ		部		へ
ホ		保		ほ
マ	万		末	ま
ミ	三		美	み
ム	牟		武	む
メ		女		め
モ		毛		も
ヤ		也		や
ユ		由		ゆ
ヨ	與		与	よ
ラ		良		ら
リ		利		り
ル	流		留	る

Table 2-20: The Kanji from Which Kana Were Derived (continued)

Katakana	Kanji		Hiragana
レ	礼	禮	れ
ロ	呂		ろ
ワ	和		わ
ヰ	井	為	ゐ
ヱ	恵		ゑ
ヲ	乎	遠	を
ン	尓	无	ん

Note how many of the kanji from which katakana and hiragana characters were derived are the same, and how the shapes of several hiragana/katakana pairs are similar. In fact, many katakana are nearly identical to kanji, and can usually be distinguished by their smaller size. Katakana can usually be distinguished from kanji in that they are usually found in strings containing other katakana. Table 2-21 shows some examples of this phenomenon.

Table 2-21: Katakana and Kanji with Similar Shapes

Katakana	Kanji
エ	工
カ	力
タ	夕
ト	卜
ニ	二
ネ	礻
ハ	八
ヒ	匕
ム	厶
メ	乂
ロ	口

Hangul

Hangul (한글 *hangeul*) are the characters that are used to express contemporary Korean texts in writing.* Unlike Japanese kana, hangul is not a syllabic writing system, but rather a writing system that is composed of elements that represent a pure alphabet. How does one make the distinction between an alphabet and syllabary? Each hangul character can be *easily* decomposed into hangul elements,

* The word "hangul" was coined sometime around 1910, and means "Korean script."

which in turn represent individual sounds (that is, consonants and vowels), not syllables. Hangul elements, which do not carry any meaning, are commonly referred to as *jamo* (자모/字母 *jamo*), literally meaning "alphabet."*

King Sejong (世宗 *sejong*) of the Yi Dynasty initiated the development of what is now referred to as hangul back in the year 1440, and the work was completed in 1446.† Hangul is considered to be one of the most scientific (or well-designed) writing systems due to its extremely regular and predictable structure.‡

Jamo are typically combined with one or two additional jamo to form hangul, which represent syllabic units. Table 2-22 lists a handful of hangul, along with the jamo used to build them.

Table 2-22: Decomposition of Hangul into Jamo

Hangul	Reading	Jamo	Transliterated
가	GA	ㄱ plus ㅏ	*g* plus *a*
갈	GAL	ㄱ plus ㅏ plus ㄹ	*g* plus *a* plus *l*
갉	GALG	ㄱ plus ㅏ plus ㄹ plus ㄱ	*g* plus *a* plus *l* plus *g*

There are exactly six ways to combine simple jamo into modern hangul, as illustrated in Figure 2-1, along with examples ("C" stands for consonant, "V" stands for vowel, and the order in which consonants and vowels are read is indicated with numerals).

Korean has special terms for the jamo that are used to construct hangul, depending on where in the syllable they appear:

- *Coseong* (초성/初聲 *coseong*) for the initial sound, usually a consonant
- *Jungseong* (중성/中聲 *jungseong*) for the middle sound, usually a vowel
- *Jongseong* (종성/終聲 *jongseong*) for the final sound, usually a consonant

The following characters represent the 93 jamo as enumerated in row 4 of the basic Korean character set standard, KS X 1001:1992:

ㄱㄲㄳㄴㄵㄶㄷㄸㄹㄺㄻㄼㄽㄾㄿㅀㅁㅂㅃㅄㅅㅆㅇㅈㅉㅊㅋㅌㅍㅎㅏㅐㅑㅒㅓㅔ
ㅕㅖㅗㅘㅙㅚㅛㅜㅝㅞㅟㅠㅡㅢㅣㅥㅦㅧㅨㅩㅪㅫㅬㅭㅮㅯㅰㅱㅲㅳㅴㅵㅶㅷㅸㅹ
ㅺㅻㅼㅽㅾㅿㆀㆁㆂㆃㆄㆅㆆㆇㆈㆉㆊㆋㆌㆍㆎ

* Sometimes referred to as *jaso* (자소/字素 *jaso*).

† The result of this work was a book entitled 訓民正音 (훈민정음 *hunmin jeongeum*).

‡ Unfortunately, its Latin transliteration methods that we explored earlier in this chapter aren't nearly as regular or predictable.

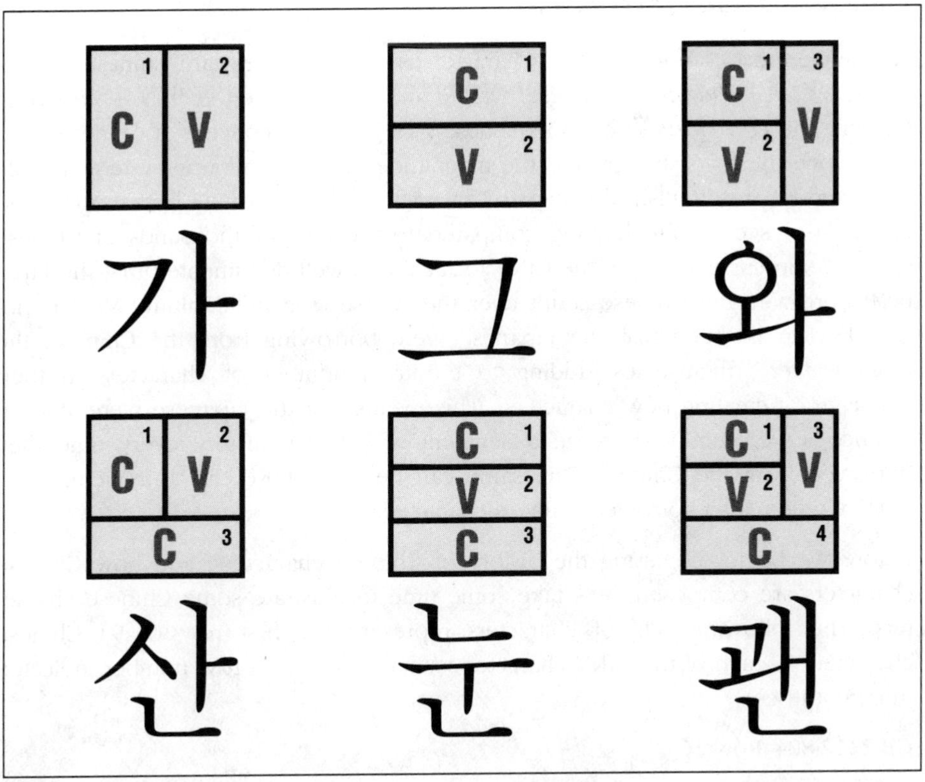

Figure 2-1: Six ways to compose jamo into modern hangul

The first 51 of these jamo are considered modern, and are used in combination to form modern hangul. The remaining 42 jamo are considered ancient.

The following characters represent the first 94 hangul as enumerated in row 16 of the basic Korean character set standard, KS X 1001:1992:

가각간갇갈갉갊감갑값갓갔강갖갗같갚갛개객갠갤갬갭갯갰갱갸갹갼걀걋걍걔걘걜
거걱건걷걸걺검겁것겄겅겆겉겊겋게겐겔겜겝겟겠겡겨격겪견겯결겸겹겻겼경곁계
곈곌곕곗고곡곤곧골곪곬곯곰곱곳공곶과곽관괄괆

Appendix N, *Hangul Reading Table*, provides a complete code table, annotated with readings, for all 2,350 hangul in the KS X 1001:1992 character set standard. This volume is potentially useful for those who do not yet have a good command of hangul, or who do not have access to a Korean-capable operating system. There are also details about hangul on the Web.*

* *http://www.hangul.org/*

Chinese Characters

The single most complex type of character used in CJKV text are Chinese characters (汉字/漢字 *hànzì* in Chinese; 漢字 *kanji* in Japanese; 한자/漢字 *hanja* in Korean; and *chữ Hán*/𡨸漢 in Vietnamese). To grasp the concept of Chinese characters, one must first understand the magnitude of such a writing system. The 26 characters of the English alphabet (52 characters, if one counts both upper- and lower case) seem quite limiting compared to the tens of thousands of Chinese characters in current use by the CJKV locales. It is well documented that the Japanese borrowed the Chinese script over the course of a millennium. What is not well known is that while the Japanese were borrowing from the Chinese, the Chinese were, themselves, adding to the total number of characters in their language by creating new characters.* This means that the Japanese were able, in essence, to capture and freeze a segment of Chinese history every time they borrowed from the Chinese. The same can be said of Korean and Vietnamese, both of whom also borrowed Chinese characters.

Before we begin discussing the history of Chinese characters, and how Chinese characters are composed, let's take some time to illustrate some Chinese characters. The following sets of characters represent the first row of 94 Chinese characters in each of the CJKV character set standards (with row number indicated in parentheses):

GB 2312-80—Row 16

啊阿埃挨哎唉哀皑癌蔼矮艾碍爱隘鞍氨安俺按暗岸胺案肮昂盎凹敖熬翱袄傲奥懊澳
芭捌扒叭吧笆八疤巴拔跋靶把耙坝霸罢爸白柏百摆佰败拜稗斑班搬扳般颁板版扮拌
伴瓣半办绊邦帮梆榜膀绑棒磅蚌镑傍谤苞胞包褒剥

GB/T 12345-90—Row 16

啊阿埃挨哎唉哀皚癌藹矮艾礙愛隘鞍氨安俺按暗岸胺案骯昂盎凹敖熬翱襖傲奥懊澳
芭捌扒叭吧笆八疤巴拔跋靶把耙壩霸罷爸白柏百擺佰敗拜稗斑班搬扳般頒板版扮拌
伴瓣半辦絆邦幫梆榜膀綁棒磅蚌鎊傍謗苞胞包褒剥

CNS 11643-1992 Plane 1—Row 36

一乙丁七乃九了二人儿入八几刀刁力匕十卜又三下丈上丫丸凡久么也乞于亡兀刃勺
千叉口土士夕大女子孑孓寸小尢尸山川工己已巳巾干廾弋弓才丑丐不中丰丹之尹予
云井互五亢仁什仃仆仇仍今介仄元允內六兮公冗凶

* The Chinese are still creating new characters in some locales, especially Hong Kong.

CNS 11643-1992 Plane 2—Row 1

乂乜凵匚厂万丌乇亍囗屮彳丏冇与丮亓仂仉仈冘勼卬厹圠夃夬尐巿旡殳毌气爿丱丼
仨仜仩仡仝仚刌刉匜卌圢圣夗夯宁宄尒尻屴屳帄庀庂忉戉扐氕氶汃氿氻犮犰玊禸肊
阞伎优伬仵伔仱伀价伈伝伂伅伢伓伄仴伒冱刓刐劦

CNS 11643-1992 Plane 3—Row 1

丨丶丿亅丅丄冂冖匸卩厶个亇义凢乆亏亼亾兦凣刄劜卄夂夊宀巛幺广廴彐彑彡阝丈
乣乢亣内仅仏从仌冄円冗汀凤刅办劝勽匀区协卆卝历厷会双叏収圡屮币弌户戸攴攵
无乊生岂仟伕伌夫伉伙伃伖参仝冋同冊写凥切刋刎

CNS 11643-1992 Plane 4—Row 1

𠂆乀乁乚𡿨丂丩乃几刂㔾巜冃日勺卂卪子孑尢屮忄扌犭丒丯亖仐兂冃仌刕刕𠂉叩产
厸叱百壬矢允允币开不氾灬𠆭冈艹辶世丫乍圹仁仢任尢冉亽瓜凷刌刏劲劧医厈尾攴
攴叽㕣另囚囚回先圧尘尔层户产帆羊祀扎扏甲朩禾

CNS 11643-1992 Plane 5—Row 1

㇉𠃋乙乚丘ナ丩乚凵马世𠃛冃去干屯心少𠂢孔仐从仈欠凼刁切叻匆卯厄叒叉艮吃丑
屹岂马朩歹毛爪王亥韦乳尸𡗚冋夙由刎庞𠚥朸勉本夅厍产剋闶叱另妣孙穴尣召叫亓
纡弘礻忆户乎扒此卣毋汴汉年夹犸犱而聿𠂉邶阦阦

CNS 11643-1992 Plane 6—Row 1

乁𠂆㐅丩𠃎乚二三二七巴卜工丂丑牛丸凡乃天个亼六刃勹力可云飞尸兂匕亐且丘历
玉凧禾丬𠀆区仃仓元穴同内丹亢出凶瓜刂刃加亡廾卬丙丙戏丞变及收乜囗囙囗史太
凬寸不出糸王五𢀖乇乑刉廾井式弓弓弓弓弓弓孔忄

CNS 11643-1992 Plane 7—Row 1

壼寚奞奭僊僟僆僪僸僤僶僽僚僔傀僓僕僦兢嬴凫凚凘劃劇劁劏劌劗劖劉戟寫厴厫愿
嗞壼嗝嗶嗇嘀嘊嗟嘩嘰嗞嘁嗹嘖嘿嘰嘻嘸嘈嘍嘎嘍毀賈嘂嘌嗜嗷嘷嘽厤壘圓團團畺墻
壿墻墻墕墕墧墳墤墆墎墪墶墋墍墐墩壽臺堝墨塲翍

CNS 11643-1986 Plane 15—Row 1

乙手乣仅生么㕈尣仈𠒆凧允㞗尤刈匁区匝厄邓𠮛叫囙夲尔龙弓开幺屯虫乔企乍仵佀
夙有丹冗安次充卣厄叨叽叺𡉕𡉚夲夸尥奶孝孖龙尣层叮屶岙旨芊羊纣处彤杢汉水叒
肌辷夲肙底衄亦宋仪伉矣佰佈佊仳伙低侹尔罕汾汻

JIS X 0208:1997—Row 16

亜唖娃阿哀愛挨姶逢葵茜穐悪握渥旭葦芦鯵梓圧斡扱宛姐虻飴絢綾鮎或粟袷安庵按
暗案闇鞍杏以伊位依偉囲夷委威尉惟意慰易椅為畏異移維緯胃萎衣謂違遺医井亥域
育郁磯一壱溢逸稲茨芋鰯允印咽員因姻引飲淫胤蔭

JIS X 0212-1990—Row 16

丂丄丅丌丒丟丣两丨丫丮丯丰丵乀乁乄乇乑乚乜乣乨乩乴乵乹乿亍亖亗亝亯亹仃仐
仚仛仠仡仢仨仯仱仳仵份仾仿伀伂伃伈伋伌伒伕伖众伙伮伱你伳伵伷伹伻伾佀佂佈
佉佋佌佒佔佖佘佟佣佪佬佮佱佷佸佹佺佽佾侁侂侄

KS X 1001:1992—Row 42

伽佳假價加可呵哥嘉嫁家暇架枷柯歌珂痂稼苛茄街袈訶賈跏軻迦駕刻却各恪慤殼珏
脚覺角閣侃刊墾奸姦干幹懇揀杆柬桿澗癎看磵稈竿簡肝艮艱諫間乫喝曷渴碣竭葛褐
蝎鞨勘坎堪嵌感憾戡敢柑橄減甘疳監瞰紺邯鑑鑒龕

KS X 1002:1991—Row 55

仮傢咖哿坷宊斝榎檟珈笳耞舸葭謌卻咯埆搉擱桷偘慳栞榦玕秆茛衎赶迂齦噶楬秸羯
蠍鶡坩埳嵁弇憨撼欿歛泔淦澉矙轗酣鹻韐傋僵壃忼扛杠橿殭矼穅繈罡羌羫茳豇韁剴
匃揩槩玠磕闓硜賡鏗呿昛秬筥籧胠腒苣莒蕖蘧祛裾

TCVN 6056:1995—Row 42

一丁七万丈三上下不与丐丑且丕世丘丙丞丢丫中丰串丸丹主丿乂乃久之乍乎乏乖乘
乙九乞也乱乳乾亂了予事二亍于云互五井亙些亟亡亢交亥亨享京亭人什仁仃仄仆仇
今介仍仔仕他仗付仙仝代令仰件价任份仿企伊伍伎

As you can clearly see, there is quite a variety of character sets available that include Chinese characters. Chapter 3, *Character Set Standards*, will make sense of all these character set standards.

A noteworthy characteristic of Chinese characters is that they can be quite complex (believe it or not, they can get much more complex than the sets of 94 characters illustrated above!). Chinese characters are composed of radicals and radical-like elements, which can be thought of as building-blocks of sorts. Radicals are discussed later in this chapter starting on page 54, in the section entitled "The Structure of Chinese Characters."

Chinese Character Readings

In Japanese, the typical Chinese character has at least two readings—some have more. For example, the Chinese character 生, whose meaning relates to "life," has over 200 readings in Japanese—most of which are used for Japanese given names, which are known for their unusual readings.

Chinese character readings come from two sources:

- Language-specific reading
- Borrowed (and usually approximated) reading

The native Japanese reading was how the Japanese read a word before the Chinese influenced their language and writing system. The native Japanese reading is called the Kun reading (訓読み *kun yomi*).

The borrowed Chinese reading is the Japanese-language approximation of the original Chinese reading of a kanji. These borrowed approximate readings are called On readings (音読み *on yomi*), On being the word for "sound." If a particular kanji was borrowed more than once, multiple readings can result. Table 2-23 lists several kanji, along with their respective readings.

Table 2-23: Chinese Characters and Their Readings—Japanese

Kanji	Meaning	On Readings	Kun Readings
剣	*sword*	ken	akira, haya, tsurugi, tsutomu
窓	*window*	sō	mado
車	*car*	sha	kuruma
万	*ten-thousand*	ban, man	katsu, kazu, susumu, taka, tsumoru, tsumu, yorozu
生	*life, birth*	sei, shō	ari, bu, fu, fuyu, haeru, hayasu, i, ikasu, ikeru, ikiru, iku, ki, mi, nama, nari, nori, o, oki, ou, susumu, taka, ubu, umareru, umu, yo, *and so on*
店	*store, shop*	ten	mise

So, how does one go about deciding which reading to use? Good question! As you learned earlier, the Japanese borrowed kanji as compounds of two or more kanji, and often use the On reading for such compounds. Conversely, when these same kanji appear in isolation, the Kun reading is often used. Table 2-24 provides some examples of individual kanji and kanji compounds.

Table 2-24: Kanji and Kanji Compounds—Japanese

Kanji Compound	Meaning	Readings
自動車	*automobile*	jidōsha (On readings)
車	*car*	kuruma (Kun reading)
剣道	*Kendo*	kendō (On readings)
剣	*sword*	tsurugi (Kun reading)

As with all languages, there are always exceptions to rules! Sometimes you find kanji compounds that use Kun readings for one or all kanji. You may also find kanji in isolation that use On readings. Table 2-25 lists some examples.

Table 2-25: Irregular Uses of Kanji Readings—Japanese

Kanji Compound	Meaning	Reading
重箱	*nest of boxes*	jūbako (On plus Kun reading)
湯桶	*bath ladle*	yutō (Kun plus On reading)

Table 2-25: Irregular Uses of Kanji Readings—Japanese (continued)

Kanji Compound	Meaning	Reading
窓口	*ticket window*	madoguchi (Kun plus Kun reading)
単	*simple, single*	tan (On reading)

Japanese personal names tend to use the Kun readings even though they are in compounds. For instance, 藤本 is read *fujimoto* rather than *tōhon*.

The Structure of Chinese Characters

Chinese characters are composed of smaller, primitive units called radicals, and other non-radical elements, which are used as building blocks. These elements serve as the most basic units for building Chinese characters. 214 radicals are used for indexing Chinese characters. Several radicals stand alone as single, meaningful Chinese characters. Table 2-26 provides some examples of radicals, along with several Chinese characters that can be written with them (examples are taken from Japanese).

Table 2-26: Radicals and Chinese Characters Made from Them

Radical	Variant	Stand-Alone?	Meaning	Examples
木		yes	*tree*	本札朴朶李材条杲林枦栞棚森椳
火	灬	yes	*fire*	灯灰灸災炎点無然熊熟熱燃燭爛
水	氵	yes	*water*	氷永汁江汲沢泉温測港源溢澡濯
辵	辶	no	*running*	辷込辻辺辿迄迅迎近返迚連週還

Note how each radical is placed within Chinese characters—they are stretched or squeezed so that all of the radicals that constitute a Chinese character fit into the general shape of a square. Also note how radicals are positioned within Chinese characters, specifically on the left, right, top, or bottom.

Radicals and radical-like elements, in turn, are composed of smaller units called *strokes*. A radical can consist of one or more strokes. Sometimes a single stroke is considered a radical. There exists one stroke that is considered a single Chinese character: 一, the Chinese character that represents the number one. Figure 2-2 shows how a typical Chinese character is composed of radicals and strokes.

There are many classifications of Chinese characters, but four are the most common: pictographs, simple ideographs, compound ideographs, and phonetic ideographs. Pictographs, the most basic of the Chinese characters, are little pictures, and usually look much like the object they represent.* Table 2-27 lists examples of pictographs.

* Written 象形文字 (*xiàngxíng wénzì*) in Chinese, 象形文字 (*shōkei moji*) in Japanese, and 상형문자/象形文字 (*sanghyeong munja*) in Korean.

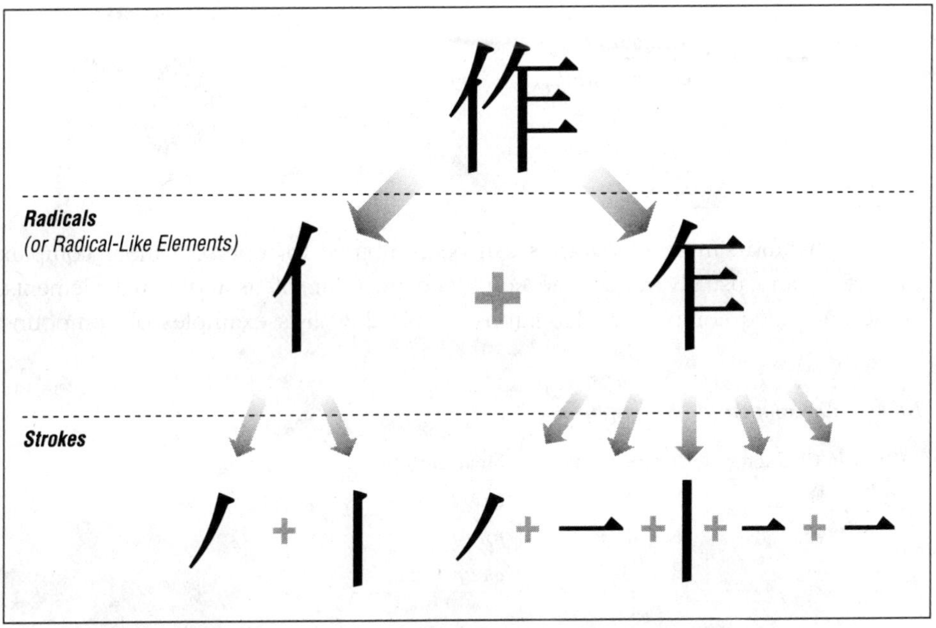

Figure 2-2: Decomposition of Chinese characters into radicals and strokes

Table 2-27: Pictographs

Chinese Character	Meaning
日	*sun*
月	*moon*
山	*mountain*
火	*fire*
木	*tree*
車	*car, cart*
口	*mouth, opening*

Whereas pictographs represent concrete objects, simple ideographs represent abstract concepts or ideas (as the name suggests), such as numbers and directions.* Table 2-28 lists examples of simple ideographs.

Table 2-28: Simple Ideographs

Chinese Character	Meaning
上	*up*
下	*down*

* Written 指事文字 (*zhǐshì wénzì*) in Chinese, 指事文字 (*shiji moji*) in Japanese, and 지사문자/指事文字 (*jisa munja*) in Korean.

Table 2-28: Simple Ideographs (continued)

Chinese Character	Meaning
中	*center, middle*
一	*one*
二	*two*
三	*three*

Pictographs and simple ideographs can be combined to represent more complex characters, and usually reflect the combined meaning of its individual elements. These are called compound ideographs.* Table 2-29 lists examples of compound ideographs.

Table 2-29: Compound Ideographs

Chinese Character	Components	Meaning
林	木 + 木	*woods*
森	木 + 木 + 木	*forest*
明	日 + 月	*clear, bright*

Phonetic ideographs account for more than 90 percent of all Chinese characters.† They usually have at least two components: one to indicate reading, and the other to denote etymological meaning. Table 2-30 provides examples that all use the same base reading component.

Table 2-30: Phonetic Ideographs with Common Reading Component—Japanese

Chinese Character	Meaning	Reading	Meaning Part	Reading Part
銅	*copper*	dō	金 (*metal*)	同 (dō)
洞	*cave*	dō	氵 (*water*)	同 (dō)
胴	*torso*	dō	肉 (*organ*)	同 (dō)
恫	*threat*	dō	忄 (*heart*)	同 (dō)

Note that each uses the 同 radical (*dō*) for its reading component. Table 2-31 lists several Chinese characters that use the same base meaning component.

Table 2-31: Phonetic Ideographs with Common Meaning Component—Japanese

Chinese Character	Meaning	Reading	Meaning Part	Reading Part
雰	*fog*	fun	雨 (*rain*)	分 (fun)
雲	*cloud*	un	雨 (*rain*)	云 (un)

* Written 会意文字/會意文字 (*huìyì wénzì*) in Chinese, 会意文字 (*kaii moji*) in Japanese, and 회의문자/會意文字 (*hoeyi munja*) in Korean.

† Written 形声文字/形聲文字 (*xíngshēng wénzì*) in Chinese, 形声文字 (*keisei moji*) in Japanese, and 형성문자/形聲文字 (*hyeongseong munja*) in Korean.

Table 2-31: Phonetic Ideographs with Common Meaning Component—Japanese (continued)

Chinese Character	Meaning	Reading	Meaning Part	Reading Part
震	*shake*	shin	雨 (*rain*)	辰 (shin)
霜	*frost*	sō	雨 (*rain*)	相 (sō)

Note that each uses the 雨 ("rain") radical for its meaning component. The 雨 radical is another example of a radical that can stand alone as a single Chinese character.

Chinese characters are subsequently combined with other Chinese characters as words to form more complex ideas or concepts. These are called *compounds* (熟語 *jukugo* in Japanese) or *Chinese character compounds* (漢語 *kango* in Japanese). Table 2-32 lists a few examples. Note that you can decompose words into pieces, each piece being a single Chinese character with its own meaning.

Table 2-32: Chinese Character Compounds

Compound	Meaning	Component Chinese Characters and Their Meanings
日本	*Japan*	日 means *sun*, and 本 means *origin*
短刀	*short sword*	短 means *short*, and 刀 means *sword*
酸素	*oxygen*	酸 means *acid*, and 素 means *element* (the acid element)
曲線	*curve*	曲 means *curved*, and 線 means *line* (curved line)
剣道	*Kendo*	剣 means *sword*, and 道 means *path* (the way of the sword)
自動車	*automobile*	自 means *self*, 動 means *moving*, and 車 means *car*
火山	*volcano*	火 means *fire*, and 山 means *mountain* (fire mountain)

There, that should have given you a sense of how Chinese characters are constructed and how they are combined with other Chinese characters to form compounds. But how did they come to be used in Korea and Japan? These and other questions are answered next.

The History of Chinese Characters

This section provides some brief historical context to explain the development of Chinese characters, and how they came to be used in other cultures, such as Korea, Japan, and Vietnam.

The development of Chinese characters

Chinese characters, believe it or not, share a history similar to that of the Latin alphabet. Both writing systems began thousands of years ago as pictures that encompassed meanings. While the Latin alphabet eventually gave up any semantic association with the characters' shapes, Chinese characters retained (and further exploited) this feature. Table 2-33 lists several Chinese reference works whose year of publishing span a period of approximately 2,000 years.

Table 2-33: The Number of Chinese Characters During Different Periods

Year (AD)	Number of Chinese Characters	Reference Work
100	9,353	說文解字
227–239	11,520	聲類
480	18,150	廣雅
543	22,726	玉編
751	26,194	唐韻
1066	31,319	類編
1615	33,179	字彙
1716	47,021	康熙字典
1919	44,908	中華大字典
1969	49,888	中文大辭典
1986	56,000	汉语大字典
1994	85,000	中华字海

Note the nearly five-fold increase in the number of hanzi over this 2,000 year period. The majority of the Chinese characters that sprang into existence during this time were phonetic ideographs (see Tables 2-30 and 2-31 on page 56).

Chinese characters in Korea—hanja

One of the earliest cultures to adapt Chinese characters for their own language was Korea. Although Chinese characters—called *hanja*—were extensively used in years past, most Korean writing today is completely in hangul.

While there appears to be an attempt by the Korean Ministry of Education to restore the use of hanja into its society—by requiring that students learn a basic set of 1,800 hanja—it does not appear to be having much of an effect. This set of 1,800 hanja was introduced in 1972, so there may still be time necessary for it to effectively restore the use of hanja in Korea.

The definitive Korean hanja reference is a dictionary entitled 大字源 (대자원 *daejaweon*), first published in 1972.

Chinese characters in Japan—kanji

There is no evidence to suggest that there was *any* writing system in place in Japan prior to the introduction of Chinese script. In fact, it is quite common for writing systems to develop relatively late in the history of languages. A writing system as complex as that used in Chinese is not really an ideal choice for borrowing, but perhaps this was the only writing system from which the Japanese could choose at the time.

The Japanese borrowed Chinese characters between 222 AD and 1279 AD. During this millennium of borrowing, the Chinese increased their inventory of characters nearly three-fold. Table 2-33 illustrated the number of Chinese characters that were documented in Chinese at different periods. That table clearly indicated that the Chinese, over a period of about 2,000 years, increased their inventory of characters by roughly a factor of five (from 9,353 to 49,888). As you can see, the Japanese were borrowing from the Chinese even while the Chinese were still creating new characters.

The Japanese began borrowing the Chinese script over 1,600 years ago. This massive borrowing took place in three different waves. Several kanji were borrowed repeatedly at different periods, and the reading of each kanji was also borrowed again. This led to different readings for a given kanji depending on which word or words it appeared in, due to dialectal and diachronic differences in China.

The first wave of borrowing took place sometime between 222 and 589 AD by way of Korea, during the Six Dynasties Period in China. Characters borrowed during this period were those used primarily in Buddhist terminology. During this period, the Chinese had between 11,520 and 22,726 hanzi.

The second wave took place between 618 and 907 AD, during the Tang Dynasty in China. Characters borrowed during this period were those used primarily for government and in Confucianism terminology. During this period, the Chinese had between 22,726 and 26,194 hanzi.

The third wave occurred somewhere between 960 and 1279 AD, during the Song Dynasty in China. Characters borrowed during this period were those used in Zen terminology. The Chinese had between 31,319 and 33,179 hanzi by this period.

During all three waves of borrowing, most Chinese characters were borrowed as compounds of two or more kanji, rather than as isolated characters. It is in this context that you find differences in reading of a particular kanji depending on what word it appears in. For example, the kanji 万, meaning "ten thousand," can be found in kanji compounds with either the reading *man* or *ban*, such as 万一 (*man* + *ichi*) and 万歳 (*ban* + *zai*—yes, the actual kanji compound for *banzai*!). This *(m)an/(b)an* alternation would indicate to a trained linguist that these two words were probably borrowed at different periods.

The first two waves of borrowing had the most significant impact on the Japanese lexicon, which accounts for dual On readings for many kanji (lexicon simply refers to the individual words that constitute a language). The third wave of borrowing had very little effect on the Japanese lexicon.

I suggest the front matter of Jack Halpern's *New Japanese-English Character Dictionary* as additional reference material on the history and development of the Japanese writing system. More specifically, pp 50a through 60a of that reference. The definitive Japanese kanji reference is a 13-volume dictionary entitled 大漢和辭典 (*dai kanwa jiten*), first published in 1955.

Chinese characters in Vietnam—chữ Hán

Vietnam also adopted Chinese characters for their language, but in a unique way. There are two ways to represent Vietnamese using Chinese characters. One way is equivalent to Chinese itself (but with approximated readings when pronounced in Vietnamese), and uses characters called *chữ Hán* (genuine Chinese characters). The other way involves characters that look and feel like Chinese characters, but were created by the Vietnamese. These are called *chữ Nôm* (𡨸喃). These methods of writing Vietnamese are unique in that they are never used together in the same text—you write using either chữ Hán (Chinese) or chữ Nôm (Vietnamese). More details about chữ Nôm are provided at the end of this chapter.

Both chữ Hán and chữ Nôm were replaced by *Quốc ngữ* in 1920. Today, chữ Hán and chữ Nôm are still being used—not for the purpose of common communication, but rather for specialized, religious, or historical purposes.

Chinese Character Simplification

Over time, frequently used and complex Chinese characters tend to simplify. Such simplifications have been different depending on the locale using them. For example, Chinese characters in their traditional form are still being used in Taiwan. The same holds true for Korea. Also, Chinese characters in an even more simplified form than found in Japanese are being used in China and Singapore, although there are some exceptions to this rule. A large number of Chinese characters are used in an almost identical form in all CJKV locales. Table 2-34 illustrates several Chinese characters in both traditional and simplified form.

Table 2-34: Traditional and Simplified Chinese Characters

Traditional	Simplified (Japan)	Simplified (China)
廣	広	广
兒	児	儿
兩	両	两
氣	気	气

Table 2-34: Traditional and Simplified Chinese Characters (continued)

Traditional	Simplified (Japan)	Simplified (China)
豐	豊	丰
邊	辺	边
國	国	国
學	学	学
點	点	点
黑	黒	黑
佛	仏	佛
骨	骨	骨

Both the simplified and traditional forms of Chinese characters sometimes coexist within the same character set standard, and some of the pairs from Table 2-34 are such examples—most of them are part of the basic Japanese character set standard, specifically JIS X 0208:1997. You can also see that some simplifications are more extreme than others.

Such simplifications in Japan have led to variants of many characters, and in some character sets both the simplified and traditional forms are included (the examples given above are such cases). As an extreme example, let's examine the JIS X 0208:1997 kanji 剣 (Row-Cell 23-85), whose five variant kanji are also encoded within the same character set standard. These variants are listed in Table 2-35 (Row-Cell values are given).

Table 2-35: Chinese Character Variants in the Same Character Set

Chinese Character	Character Code
劍	49-88
劔	49-89
劒	49-90
剱	49-91
釼	78-63

Non-Chinese Chinese Characters

What is a non-Chinese Chinese character? Simple. Characters that look, feel, and behave like Chinese characters, but were not borrowed from China. The following sections describe this interesting and remarkable phenomenon as it has manifested in Japan, Korea, and Vietnam. Examples are also provided.

Japanese-Made Chinese Characters—Kokuji

The Japanese have created their own Chinese characters known as *kokuji* (国字 *kokuji*), literally meaning "national characters," or, more descriptively, "Japanese-made Chinese characters." Kokuji behave like true Chinese characters, following the same rules of structure, specifically that they are composed of radicals, radical-like elements, and strokes, and can be combined with one or more Chinese characters to form compounds or words. These Chinese characters were created out of a need for characters not borrowed from China.* Most kokuji are used to represent the names of indigenous Japanese plants and fish. They are also used quite frequently in Japanese place and personal names.

Approximately 200 kokuji have been identified in the basic Japanese character set standard, specifically JIS X 0208:1997. There are even more in the supplemental set, specifically JIS X 0212-1990. Table 2-36 provides a few examples of kokuji (JIS X 0208:1997 Row-Cell values are provided).

Table 2-36: Examples of Kokuji

Kokuji		Readings	Meanings
鰯	16-83	iwashi	*sardine*
粂	23-09	kume	Used in personal names
込	25-94	komu	*(to) move inward*
榊	26-71	sakaki	A species of tree called *sakaki*
働	38-15	hataraku, dō[a]	*(to) work*
峠	38-29	tōge	*mountain pass*
畑	40-10	hata, hatake	*dry field*
枠	47-40	waku	*frame*
凩	49-62	kogarashi	*cold, wintry wind*

[a] Considered an On reading.

Additional kokuji were created when the Japanese isolated themselves from the rest of the world for approximately 250 years: from the mid-1600s to the late 1800s. Without direct influence from China, the Japanese resorted to creating their own Chinese characters as necessary. There is at least one kokuji that was subsequently borrowed by China, specifically 腺 (33-03; read *sen*, meaning "gland"). In Chinese it is read *xiàn* (GB 2312-80 47-57).

* In fact, some kokuji were even borrowed back by the Chinese as genuine Chinese characters, as you will soon learn about.

Seven kokuji have made their way into the standard set of 1,945 kanji called Jōyō Kanji, and four are in Jinmei-yō Kanji (Chapter 3 provides a full treatment of these and other related character sets). Those in Jōyō Kanji are 込 (25-94), 働 (38-15), 峠 (38-29), 畑 (40-10), 塀 (42-29), 匁 (44-72), and 枠 (47-40). Those in Jinmei-yō Kanji are 笹 (26-91), 凪 (38-68), 柾 (43-79), and 麿 (43-91). Nozumu Ohara (大原望 *ōhara nozomu*) has compiled a list of kokuji, which includes those that are included in the JIS X 0208:1997 and JIS X 0212-1990 character set standards, plus links to other kokuji-related web sites.*

Korean-Made Chinese Characters—Gugja

Like the Japanese, the Koreans have had the opportunity to create their own Chinese characters. These are known as *gugja* (국자/國字 *gugja*) in Korean. While you'd expect to find gugja only in Korean character set standards, there are approximately 100 gugja included in a Chinese character set standard designated GB 12052-89 (you'll understand why after reading about this character set standard in Chapter 3 starting on page 117).

Gugja—unlike kokuji in Japanese—have many tell-tale signs of their status as non-Chinese Chinese characters. Table 2-37 lists elements of gugja that are used to indicate a final consonant.

Table 2-37: Reading Elements of Gugja

Gugja Element	Reading
乙	L
ㄱ	G
叱	D
ㅇ	NG

Many other gugja look and feel like genuine Chinese characters. It is only after you explore their etymology that you may discover their true Korean origins.

The basic Korean character set standard for use on computers, KS X 1001:1992, includes many gugja. The supplemental Korean character set standard, KS X 1002:1991, includes even more gugja. Table 2-38 provides some examples of gugja, along with their readings and meanings (KS X 1001:1992 Row-Cell values are provided).

* *http://member.nifty.ne.jp/TAB01645/ohara/index.htm*

Table 2-38: Examples of Gugja

Gugja		Reading	Meaning
乫	42-65	갈 gal	Used in personal names
畓	51-44	답 dab	*paddy, wet field*
乭	52-44	돌 dol	Used in personal and place names
唜	56-37	말 mal	Used in place names
鐥	64-54	선 seon	Used in place names
筽	72-04	오 o	Used in place names
岾	79-32	점 jeom	*mountain pass*[a]

[a] Compare with the (Japanese) kokuji 峠 in Table 2-36 on page 62—I find it fascinating that both Japan and Korea created their own Chinese character meaning "mountain pass."

Only one gugja, 畓 (답 *dab*), is known to be included in Korea's standard set of 1,800 hanja called Sangyong Hanja—this gugja is not in the middle school subset of 900 hanja, though.

Vietnamese-Made Chinese Characters—Chữ Nôm

Unlike Japanese and Korean, in which non-Chinese Chinese characters are used together with genuine Chinese characters—a sort of mixing of scripts—Vietnamese has three distinct ways to express its language through writing:

- Latin script (called *Quốc ngữ*)
- Chinese characters (called *chữ Hán*)
- Vietnamese-made Chinese characters (called *chữ Nôm*)

Writing Vietnamese using chữ Hán is considered equivalent to writing in Chinese, not Vietnamese. Using Quốc ngữ or chữ Nôm is considered writing in Vietnamese, not Chinese. For some chữ Nôm characters, there is a corresponding chữ Hán character with the same meaning. Table 2-39 provides a handful of chữ Nôm characters, along with their chữ Hán equivalents (TCVN 5773:1993 and TCVN 6056:1995 Row-Cell codes are provided for chữ Nôm and chữ Hán, respectively).

Table 2-39: Chữ Nôm and Chữ Hán Examples

Chữ Nôm		Reading	Chữ Hán		Reading	Meaning
𠀧	21-47	ba	三	42-06	tam	*three*
𠁑	29-55	giữa	中	42-21	trung	*center, middle*
𡨸	34-02	chữ	字	50-30	tự	*character*
𤾓	35-77	trăm	百	64-02	bá	*hundred*

Because there are far fewer chữ Nôm characters than chữ Hán characters, there are times when chữ Hán characters are used in chữ Nôm context (that is, with chữ Nôm characters). Table 2-40 lists two types of chữ Hán characters: those that have different readings depending on context (chữ Nôm versus chữ Hán), and those that have identical readings regardless of context. TCVN 6056:1995 Row-Cell codes are provided for reference purposes.

Table 2-40: Chữ Hán Characters Used in Chữ Nôm Context

	Character		Chữ Nôm Reading	Chữ Hán Reading	Meaning
Unique	主	42-26	chúa	chủ	*main, primary*
	印	45-85	in	ấn	*printing*
	急	53-14	cấp	kíp	*fast, rapid*
	所	54-35	thửa	sở	*place, location*
Identical	文	56-16	văn	văn	*sentence*
	武	59-22	vũ	vũ	*weapon*
	爭	62-44	tranh	tranh	*war*
	香	76-23	hương	hương	*fragrant*

Chữ Nôm was the accepted method for writing Vietnamese since the 10th century AD. It was not until the 1920s when chữ Nôm was replaced by Quốc ngữ (see a description starting on page 38 of this chapter).

3

Character Set Standards

In this chapter:

- *Non-Coded Character Set Standards*
- *Coded Character Set Standards*
- *International Character Set Standards*
- *Character Set Standard Oddities*
- *Non-Coded Versus Coded Character Sets*
- *Information Interchange Versus Professional Publishing*
- *Advice to Developers*

A rock-solid understanding of and a deep appreciation for CJKV character set standards—what character classes they contain, how many characters they enumerate, how they evolved, and so on—form the foundation on which the remainder of this book is based. Without such a basic understanding, it would be pointless to discuss issues such as encoding methods, input methods, and font formats. This chapter represents what I consider to be the core of this book.

CJKV character sets can be classified into two basic types, depending on their intended purpose and reason for establishment:

- Non-coded (also known as "non-electronic") Character Sets—NCSs
- Coded (also known as "electronic") Character Sets—CCSs

"Non-coded" refers to a character set established without regard to how it would be processed on computer systems, if at all. "Coded" refers to being electronically encoded, that is, such character sets were specifically designed for processing on computer systems. You will soon realize that the characters enumerated in non-coded character sets generally constitute a subset of the characters contained in coded character sets, and sometimes affect their development.

After reading this chapter, you will have a firm understanding about which character classes constitute a particular character set, and information fundamental to dealing with CJKV-related issues.

If you are especially interested in a particular CJKV character set covered in this chapter, I encourage you to obtain the corresponding character set standard document. While this chapter provides some insights not found in the original documents, it does not (and, quite frankly, could not) duplicate all the information that those documents contain.

NOTE Some character sets discussed in this chapter are not yet established—they are in draft form, which means that their designations *may* change. Such character sets are indicated by a trailing "X" in the portion of their designation used to specify the year of establishment. Affected standards include Japan's JIS X 0213:199X and China's GB/T 13131-9X and GB/T 13132-9X.

Non-Coded Character Set Standards

Long before there were any coded character set standards in the CJKV locales (or even before the concept of a coded character set standard existed!), several non-coded standards were defined for pedagogical purposes. These are considered to be the first attempts to limit the number of Chinese characters in common use.

The non-coded character sets described in this book include only Chinese characters. Everyone is expected to learn hiragana and katakana (in Japan) or hangul (in Korea). Only for Chinese characters, which number in the tens of thousands, is there a need to define a set (and thus, limit the number) of characters that are taught in school.

Chapter 2, *Writing Systems*, provided a brief description of Chinese characters. If you skipped that chapter and are unfamiliar with Chinese characters, I suggest going back to read it.

Hanzi in China

The educational system in China requires that students master 3,500 hanzi during their first years of instruction. These hanzi form a subset from a standardized list of 7,000 hanzi defined in 现代汉语通用字表 (*xiàndài hànyǔ tōngyòngzì biǎo*), published on March 25, 1988. We can call this large list Tōngyòng Hànzì. Two other hanzi lists further define this 3,500-hanzi subset. The first list, 现代汉语常用字表 (*xiàndài hànyǔ chángyòngzì biǎo*), defines the 2,500 hanzi that are taught during primary school. The second list, 现代汉语次常用字表 (*xiàndài hànyǔ cìchángyòngzì biǎo*), defines an additional 1,000 hanzi that are taught during middle school. We can call these character sets Chángyòng Hànzì and Cìchángyòng Hànzì. These hanzi lists are commonly abbreviated as 常用字 (*chángyòngzì*) and 次常用字 (*cìchángyòngzì*), respectively, and were published on January 26, 1988. Appendix R provides a complete listing of the 3,500 hanzi defined in 现代汉语常用字表 and 现代汉语次常用字表. The dictionary entitled 汉字写法规范字典 (*hànzì xiěfǎ guīfàn zìdiǎn*) is useful in that it includes both sets of hanzi, and differentiates them through the use of annotations.

In addition, the Chinese government published a document, entitled *Simplified Character Table* (简化字总表 *jiǎnhuàzì zǒngbiǎo*), that enumerates 2,249 simplified hanzi (and illustrates the traditional forms from which they were derived—some simplified hanzi were derived from more than one traditional hanzi). This document is divided into three tables, the contents of which are listed in Table 3-1.

Table 3-1: Simplified Character Table Contents

Table	Characters	Description
1	350	Independently simplified hanzi
2	146	Simplified components used in other hanzi[a]
3	1,753	Hanzi simplified by using simplified components from "Table 2" of the *Simplified Character Table*

[a] Among these, 132 are also used as hanzi themselves.

There has been more than one version of this document, the most recent being published in 1986. It is important to note that its development has not been static—some minor corrections and adjustments have been made over the years, one of which is known to have caused an error in a coded character set, specifically in GB/T 12345-90 (described later in this chapter, starting on page 83). The propagation of errors from one character to another—whether coded, non-coded, or both—is something that *can* occur.

Note that there are many hanzi used in China that do not require further simplification—only those that were deemed frequently used *and* complex were simplified.

Hanzi in Taiwan

The basic set of hanzi in Taiwan is listed in a table called 常用國字標準字體表 (*chángyòng guózì biāozhǔn zìtǐ biǎo*), which enumerates 4,808 hanzi. An additional set of 6,341 hanzi is defined in 次常用國字標準字體表 (*cìchángyòng guózì biāozhǔn zìtǐ biǎo*), 18,480 rare hanzi are defined in 罕用字體表 (*hǎnyòng zìtǐ biǎo*), and 18,609 hanzi variants are defined in 異體國字字表 (*yìtǐ guózì zìbiǎo*). All of these hanzi lists were established by Taiwan's Ministry of Education (教育部 *jiàoyùbù*).

Table 3-2 lists these standards, along with their dates of establishment. These lists, when added together, create a set of 48,238 hanzi.

Table 3-2: Hanzi Lists in Taiwan

Standard	Nickname	Date of Establishment	Number of Hanzi
常用國字標準字體表	甲表 (*jiǎbiǎo*)	September 2, 1982	4,808
次常用國字標準字體表	乙表 (*yǐbiǎo*)	December 20, 1982	6,341
罕用字體表	丙表 (*bǐngbiǎo*)	October 10, 1983	18,480
異體國字字表	*none*	March 29, 1984	18,609

These hanzi lists will become useful when discussing the CNS 11643-1992 and CCCII coded character set standards from Taiwan later in this chapter, starting on pages 93 and 98, respectively. Appendix R provides a complete listing of the hanzi that make up the first two lists, 常用國字標準字體表 and 次常用國字標準字體表.

Compared to other CJKV locales, Taiwan has established non-coded character sets with the most characters.

Kanji in Japan

Non-coded Japanese character sets include Gakushū Kanji (preceded by Kyōiku Kanji)—the 1,006 kanji formally taught during the first six grades in Japanese schools; Jōyō Kanji (preceded by Tōyō Kanji)—the 1,945 kanji designated by the Japanese government as the ones to be used in public documents such as newspapers; and Jinmei-yō Kanji—the 285 kanji sanctioned by the Japanese government for use in writing personal names.* The growth and development of these character sets are listed in Table 3-3 (note that some were renamed).

Table 3-3: Evolving Kanji Lists in Japan

Year	Kyōiku Kanji	Tōyō Kanji	Jinmei-yō Kanji
1946		1,850[a]	
1948	881		
1951			92
1976			120
1977	996 (Gakushū Kanji)		
1981		1,945 (Jōyō Kanji)	166
1990			284
1992	1,006[b]		
1997			285

[a] The corresponding glyph table (当用漢字字体表 *tōyō kanji jitai hyō*) was published in 1949, and likewise, the corresponding reading table (当用漢字音訓表 *tōyō kanji onkun hyō*) was published in 1948.
[b] Established in 1989, but not fully implemented until 1992.

* The 285th kanji added to this list is 琉 (JIS X 0208:1997 46-16).

There is some overlap among these character sets. Gakushū Kanji is a subset of Jōyō Kanji (likewise, Kyōiku Kanji was a subset of Tōyō Kanji).

Table 3-4 shows how you write the names of these character sets in native Japanese orthography, and indicates their meaning.

Table 3-4: The Meanings of Non-Coded Japanese Character Set Standards

Character Set	In Japanese	Meaning	Content
Kyōiku Kanji	教育漢字	*Instructional kanji*	881
Gakushū Kanji	学習漢字	*Educational kanji*	1,006
Tōyō Kanji	当用漢字	*Common use kanji*	1,850
Jōyō Kanji	常用漢字	*Everyday use kanji*	1,945
Jinmei-yō Kanji	人名用漢字	*Personal name use kanji*	285

While this table appears to show that the Gakushū Kanji list gained only ten kanji between 1977 and 1992, the list also experienced some internal shifts. Gakushū Kanji and Kyōiku Kanji can be decomposed into six sets, each corresponding to the grade of school during which they are formally taught. Table 3-5 indicates the six grade levels on the left, along with the number of kanji taught during each one—this is done for Kyōiku Kanji and both versions of Gakushū Kanji.

Table 3-5: The Development of Gakushū Kanji

Grade	1958 (881 Kanji)[a]	1977 (996 Kanji)	1992 (1,006 Kanji)
1	46	76	80
2	105	145	160
3	187	195	200
4	205	195	200
5	194	195	185
6	144	190	181

[a] Kyōiku Kanji was not divided into the six grade levels until 1958.

The general trend shown by Table 3-5 is that more kanji (although not significantly more) are now taught in the earlier grades.

Appendix R provides complete listings of the Jōyō Kanji, Gakushū Kanji, and Jinmei-yō Kanji character sets.

Hanja in Korea

Korea has defined a list of hanja called *Sangyong Hanja* (상용 한자/常用漢字 *sangyong hanja*), and enumerates the 1,800 hanja that students are expected to learn during their school years. The first 900 of these hanja are expected to be learned by students during middle school—the remaining 900 are expected to be learned through high school. These hanja lists were established on August 16, 1972.

When coding these 1,800 hanja electronically, the list expands to 1,953 hanja due to the duplicate hanja in the KS X 1001:1992 character set (covered later in this chapter). Likewise, the list of 900 middle-school hanja expands to 978 hanja for the same reason. Appendix R provides a complete printout of the 1,800 Sangyong Hanja and the 900 hanja taught during middle school (expanded to 1,953 and 978 hanja, respectively, to accommodate the KS X 1001:1992 character set standard—later in this chapter, starting on page 111, you'll know and appreciate why this expansion is necessary).

The Korean Supreme Court (대법원/大法院 *daebeobweon*) also defined, at various periods, lists of hanja that are considered acceptable for use in writing Korean names—these lists are called Inmyeong-yong Hanja (인명용 한자/人名用漢字 *inmyeongyong hanja*). The latest list enumerates 2,964 hanja, and was established in July of 1994. Previous versions of this list were established in January and March of 1991.

Coded Character Set Standards

Proliferation of computer systems necessitated the creation of coded character set standards. Initially, each vendor (such as IBM, Fujitsu, Hitachi, and so on) established their own corporate standard for their products alone. However, the first multiple-byte national coded character set standard among the CJKV locales was established by the Japanese Standards Association (JSA) on January 1, 1978, and was designated JIS C 6226-1978. Without a doubt, the birth of this character set standard sent waves throughout the CJKV locales.

Other CJKV locales, such as Korea and China, being inspired by the success of JIS C 6226-1978, followed soon after by imitating the Japanese solution, and in some cases copied more than merely the encoding method or arrangement of characters. For example, in the case of Taiwan's Big Five character set, it has been claimed that the Taiwanese borrowed many Chinese character forms from Japan's JIS C 6226-1978.

Character Set Standards Overview

The character set standards described in this section constitute those maintained by a government or a government-sanctioned organization within a given country, and are considered the standard character sets for the locale. In addition, some character set standards form the foundation from which other character set standards are derived, such as international or vendor character set standards. (Vendor character set standards are covered in Appendix C, *Vendor Character Set Standards*.)

Tables 3-6 through 3-11 summarize the national character sets described in this chapter, along with the number and classes of characters enumerated by each. I have decided to use separate tables for each locale because one large table would have been far too overwhelming.

Table 3-6: Chinese Character Set Standards—China

Character Set	Level 1	Level 2	Extra Hanzi	Symbols	Control Codes
GB 1988-89[a]				94	34
GB 2312-80	3,755	3,008		682	
GB 6345.1-86	3,755	3,008		814	
GB 8565.2-88	3,755	3,008	636	751	
ISO-IR-165:1992	3,755	3,008	775	905	
GB/T 12345-90	3,755	3,008	103	843	
GB 7589-87	7,237				
GB/T 13131-9X	7,237				
GB 7590-87	7,039				
GB/T 13132-9X	7,039				
GBK	3,755	3,008	14,240	883	

[a] Also known as GB-Roman.

Table 3-7: Chinese Character Set Standards—Taiwan

Character Set	Level 1	Level 2	Extra Hanzi	Symbols	Control Codes
Big Five	5,401	7,652		441	
Big Five Plus	5,401	7,652	7,619	913	
CNS 5205-1989[a]				94	34
CNS 11643-1986	5,401	7,650	13,488[b]	684	
CNS 11643-1992	5,401	7,650	34,976	684	
CCCII[c]	75,684				

[a] Also known as CNS-Roman.
[b] Planes 14 and 15.
[c] The "Level 1" figure represents the total number of characters

Table 3-8: Japanese Character Set Standards

Character Set	Level 1	Level 2	Extra Kanji	Symbols	Control Codes
JIS X 0201-1997[a]				157[b]	34
JIS C 6226-1978	2,965	3,384		453	

Table 3-8: Japanese Character Set Standards (continued)

Character Set	Level 1	Level 2	Extra Kanji	Symbols	Control Codes
JIS X 0208-1983	2,965	3,384	4	524	
JIS X 0208-1990	2,965	3,384	6	524	
JIS X 0208:1997	2,965	3,384	6	524	
JIS X 0212-1990	5,801			266	
JIS X 0213:199X	≈2,000[c]	≈3,000[d]			

[a] Part of this standard includes JIS-Roman.
[b] This figure includes 94 JIS-Roman characters plus 63 half-width katakana characters.
[c] JIS Level 3.
[d] JIS Level 4.

Table 3-9: Korean Character Set Standards

Character Set	Country	Hangul	Hanja	Symbols	Control Codes
KS X 1003:1993[a]	South Korea			94	34
KS X 1001:1992	South Korea	2,350	4,888	986	
KS X 1002:1991	South Korea	3,605[b]	2,856	1,188	
KPS 9566-97	North Korea	2,679	4,653	927	
GB 12052-89	China	5,203[c]	94	682	

[a] Also known as KS-Roman.
[b] These 3,605 hangul are split into two levels, enumerating 1,930 and 1,675 characters, respectively. The second set of hangul (1,675 characters) are considered to be ancient hangul.
[c] These 5,203 hangul are split into three levels, enumerating 2,068, 1,356, and 1,779 characters each.

Table 3-10: Vietnamese Character Set Standards

Character Set	Chinese Characters	Symbols	Control Codes
TCVN 5712:1993[a]		233[b]	34
TCVN 5773:1993	2,357		
TCVN 6056:1995	3,311		

[a] Also known as TCVN-Roman.
[b] This figure includes 94 ASCII characters plus 139 additional (mostly accented) characters, 5 of which are combining marks.

Table 3-11: Other National Character Set Standards

Character Set	Country	Total Characters	Control Codes
ASCII	USA	94	34
ANSI Z39.64-1989	USA	15,686	
Hong Kong GCCS	Hong Kong	3,049	

What a list of standards, eh? If you read this chapter carefully, Tables 3-6 through 3-11 will no longer seem overwhelming. They are also useful for general reference, so be sure to dog-ear these pages.

The national standards that are based on ISO 10646-1:1993, specifically GB 13000.1-93, JIS X 0221-1995, and KS X 1005-1:1995, are covered in the section entitled "International Character Set Standards," beginning on page 120.

The terms Level 1 and Level 2 have not yet been described. They simply refer to the two such groups of Chinese characters usually defined within each CJKV character set standard. Level 1 typically contains frequently-used Chinese characters, whereas Level 2 contains less–frequently-used Chinese characters. Some character sets, such as JIS X 0212-1990 and CNS 11643-1992, contain only a single block of Chinese characters, or else consist of multiple planes.

ASCII

Most readers of this book are familiar with the ASCII encoding, so it is a good place to begin our discussion of coded character set standards, and will serve as a common point of reference.

The ASCII character set is covered in this book because it is quite often mixed with CJKV characters within text. Note, however, that the ASCII character set standard is not specific to any CJKV locale.

ASCII stands for *American Standard Code for Information Interchange*. The ASCII character set standard is described in the standard designated ANSI X3.4-1986;[*] it is the US version and at the same time the International Reference Version (IRV) of ISO 646:1991,[†] which defines the framework for similar national standards.

The ASCII character set is composed of 128 characters, 94 of which are considered printable. There are also 34 other characters, which include a space character and many control characters (such as tab, escape, shift-in, and so on), which are defined in ISO 6429:1992, *Information Technology—Control Functions for Coded Character Sets*. The control codes are technically not part of ASCII or ISO 646:1991. Table 3-12 lists the 94 printable ASCII characters.

Table 3-12: The ASCII Character Set

<table>
<tr><td>Lowercase Latin</td><td>abcdefghijklmnopqrstuvwxyz</td></tr>
<tr><td>Uppercase Latin</td><td>ABCDEFGHIJKLMNOPQRSTUVWXYZ</td></tr>
<tr><td>Numerals</td><td>0123456789</td></tr>
<tr><td>Symbols</td><td>!"#$%&'()*+,-./:;<=>?@[\]^_`{|}~</td></tr>
</table>

* ANSI is short for *American National Standards Institute*; an earlier version of this standard was designated ANSI X3.4-1977.

† ISO is short for *International Organization for Standardization*; an earlier version of this standard was designated ISO 646:1983.

Most of these printable characters are also used in EBCDIC, an encoding method covered in the next chapter. The binary nature of computers allows these 128 characters to be represented using seven bits, but because computers evolved through processing information in eight-bit segments (a typical *byte*), these 128 ASCII characters are usually represented by eight-bit units in which the eighth bit (also known as the highest-order bit) is usually set to zero. Other character sets often incorporate the characters of ASCII.

ASCII Variations

There are, as of this writing, ten variations of the ASCII character sets, all approved by and published through ISO. These character sets contain the ASCII character set as their common base, plus additional characters. Extended ASCII character sets are used to represent other writing systems, such as Arabic, Hebrew, and Cyrillic. There is also an extensive collection of additional Latin characters. These characters are usually additional symbols and accented versions of Latin characters.

Eight-bit representations can theoretically handle 128 more characters than seven-bit representations—the reality is that they handle only up to 94 or 96 additional characters. The documents ISO 8859 Parts 1 through 10 (*Information Processing—8-Bit Single-Byte Coded Graphic Character Sets*) describe character sets that can be encoded in the additional 128 positions when an eight-bit representation is used.* Table 3-13 lists the contents of each of the ten parts of ISO 8859, indicating what languages are supported by each.

Table 3-13: The Ten Parts of ISO 8859

Part	Year	Contents	Languages
1	1998	Latin alphabet No. 1	Danish, Dutch, English, Faeroese, Finnish, French, German, Icelandic, Irish, Italian, Norwegian, Portuguese, Spanish, Swedish
2	1987	Latin alphabet No. 2	Albanian, Czech, English, German, Hungarian, Polish, Rumanian, Serbo-Croatian, Slovak, Slovene
3	1988	Latin alphabet No. 3	Afrikaans, Catalan, Dutch, English, Esperanto, German, Italian, Maltese, Spanish, Turkish
4	1998	Latin alphabet No. 4	Danish, English, Estonian, Finnish, German, Greenlandic, Lappish, Latvian, Lithuanian, Swedish, Norwegian
5	1988	Latin/Cyrillic alphabet	Bulgarian, Byelorussian, English, Macedonian, Russian, Serbo-Croatian, Ukrainian

* *http://czyborra.com/charsets/iso8859.html*

Table 3-13: The Ten Parts of ISO 8859 (continued)

Part	Year	Contents	Languages
6	1987	Latin/Arabic alphabet	Arabic
7	1987	Latin/Greek alphabet	Greek
8	1988	Latin/Hebrew alphabet	Hebrew
9	1989	Latin alphabet No. 5	Danish, Dutch, English, Finnish, French, German, Irish, Italian, Norwegian, Portuguese, Spanish, Swedish, Turkish
10	1998	Latin alphabet No. 6	Danish, English, Estonian, Finnish, German, Greenlandic, Lappish, Latvian, Lithuanian, Swedish, Norwegian

Table 3-14 lists the 95 additional non-ASCII characters from ISO 8859-1:1998 (also known as ISO Latin-1 or ISO-8859-1). Appendix S, *Single-Byte Code Tables*, provides a complete ISO 8859-1:1998 code table.

Table 3-14: ISO 8859-1:1998 Character Samples

Lowercase Latin	àáâãäåæçèéêëìíîïðñòóôõöøùúûüýþÿ
Uppercase Latin	ÀÁÂÃÄÅÆÇÈÉÊËÌÍÎÏÐÑÒÓÔÕÖØÙÚÛÜÝÞß
Symbols	¡¢£¤¥§¨©ª«¬-®¯°±²³´µ¶•¸¹º»¼½¾¿×÷

These characters, as you can probably guess, are not that useful when working with CJKV text. This table simply illustrates the types of characters available in the ISO 8859 series. Note again that these additional ASCII character sets require a full eight bits per character for encoding because they contain far more than 128 characters.

CJKV-Roman

The Chinese, Japanese, Koreans, and Vietnamese have developed their own variants of the ASCII character set, known as GB-Roman (from GB 1988-89), CNS-Roman (from CNS 5205-1989), JIS-Roman (from JIS X 0201-1997), KS-Roman (from KS X 1003:1993), and TCVN-Roman (from TCVN 5712:1993), respectively. Or, CJKV-Roman, collectively. These character sets, like ASCII, consist of 94 printable characters, but there are some minor differences.* The characters that differ are indicated in Table 3-15 (full-width forms are used for illustrative purposes).

Because the difference between ASCII and the CJKV-Roman character sets is minor, they are usually treated as the same throughout this book. You will also find that most terminal software supports only one of these character sets. This

* But one, specifically TCVN 5712:1993, contains more than these 94 characters.

Table 3-15: Special CJKV-Roman Characters

Code	ASCII[a]	GB-Roman	CNS-Roman[b]	JIS-Roman	KS-Roman
0x24	$ (dollar)	¥ (yuan)	$	$	$
0x5C	\ (backslash)	\	\	¥ (yen)	₩ (won)
0x7E	~ (tilde)[c]	‾ (overline)	‾ (overline)	‾ (overline)	‾ (overline)

[a] TCVN-Roman is identical to ASCII as far as these three characters are concerned
[b] CNS-Roman is ambiguous with regard to glyphs. The glyphs shown in this column were made consistent with the other CJKV-Roman character sets.
[c] The vertical positioning of the tilde may vary depending on the implementation.

means that terminals which support only JIS-Roman display the ASCII backslash as the JIS-Roman yen symbol. For systems that require the backslash, such as MS-DOS for indicating directory hierarchy, the yen symbol is used instead. Stranger yet, Perl programs displayed on a terminal that supports GB-Roman would have variables prefixed with yuan symbols (instead of the customary dollar sign). You will also find that most CJKV software supports CJKV-Roman instead of ASCII. It is possible that the computer supports both ASCII and CJKV-Roman. Changing the display from CJKV-Roman to ASCII (and vice versa), though, may be as simple as changing the display font. You will learn in the next chapter that this is because ASCII and CJKV-Roman almost always occupy the same encoding space, which can actually lead to code conversion problems when dealing with Unicode.

It is important to realize that character set standards do *not* prescribe the widths of characters—it is simply customary to associate characters with specific widths, usually half- and full-width.

The document designated GB 1988-89, *Information Processing—7-Bit Coded Character Set for Information Interchange* (信息处理—信息交换用七位编码字符集 *xìnxī chǔlǐ xìnxī jiāohuàn yòng qīwèi biānmǎ zìfújí*), established on July 1, 1990, contains the definition of the GB-Roman character set.* This manual is virtually identical to ISO 646:1991 except that it is written in Chinese.

The document designated CNS 5205-1989, *Information Processing—7-Bit Coded Character Set for Information Interchange* (資訊處理及交換用七數元碼字元集 *zīxùn chǔlǐ jí jiāohuàn yòng qīshùyuán mǎzìyuánjí*), contains the definition of the CNS-Roman character set.† This manual is virtually identical to ISO 646:1991 except that it is written in Chinese.

The document designated JIS X 0201-1997, *7-Bit and 8-Bit Coded Character Sets for Information Interchange* (7ビット及び8ビットの情報交換用符号化文字集合 *nana-bitto oyobi hachi-bitto no jōhō kōkan yō fugōka moji shūgō*), established on January 20, 1997, provides the definition for the JIS-Roman character set.‡ Like GB

* The original version of this standard was designated GB 1988-80.

† Earlier versions of this standard were dated 1980, 1981, and 1983.

‡ JIS X 0201-1997 was formerly designated JIS X 0201-1976 (which itself was reaffirmed in 1984 and in 1989).

1988-89, this manual is virtually identical to ISO 646:1991 except that it is written in Japanese, and defines the extensions for half-width katakana.

The document designated KS X 1003:1993, *Code for Information Interchange* (정보 교환용 부호 (로마 문자) *jeongbo gyohwanyong buho (roma munja)*), established on January 6, 1993, contains the definition of the KS-Roman character set.* Like GB 1988-89, this manual is identical to ISO 646:1991 except that it is written in Korean.

The document designated TCVN 5712:1993, *Công Nghệ Thông Tin—Bộ Mã Chuẩn 8-Bit Kí Tự Việt Dùng Trong Trao Đổi Thông Tin* (*Information Technology—Vietnamese 8-Bit Standard Coded Character Set for Information Interchange*), established on May 12, 1993, contains the definition of the TCVN-Roman character set. TCVN-Roman contains the basic 94 ASCII characters plus up to 139 additional characters, most of which are adorned with diacritic marks (and represent all possible Quốc ngữ characters). Five of these 139 additional characters are combining marks that indicate tone.

Chinese Character Set Standards—China

As you learned earlier, Japan was first to develop and implement a multiple-byte national character set. The other major CJKV locales—China, Taiwan, and Korea—soon followed by developing their own. This section describes the character set standards established by China, or more specifically, the People's Republic of China or PRC (中华人民共和国 *zhōnghuá rénmín gònghé guó*).

All Chinese character set standards begin with the designator GB, which stands for "Guo Biao" (国标 *guóbiāo*), which is short for "Guojia Biaozhun" (国家标准 *guójiā biāozhǔn*), and means "National Standard." Some GB standards have a "/T" tacked onto the "GB" to form "GB/T." The "T" here stands for "Tui" (推 *tuī*), which is short for "Tuijian" (推荐 *tuījiàn*), and means "recommended" (as opposed to "forced" or "mandatory"). The "T" does *not* stand for "traditional" (as in "traditional hanzi").

GB 2312-80

This character set standard, established on May 1, 1981 by the People's Republic of China (PRC), enumerates 7,445 characters. Its official name is *Code of Chinese Graphic Character Set for Information Interchange Primary Set* (信息交换用汉字编

* This standard was previously designated KS C 5636-1993. The original version, KS C 5636-1989, was established on April 22, 1989.

码字符集—基本集 *xìnxī jiāohuàn yòng hànzì qīwèi biānmǎ zìfújí—jīběnjí*). Table 3-16 lists how characters are allocated to each row.

Table 3-16: The GB 2312-80 Character Set

Row	Characters	Content
1	94	Miscellaneous symbols
2	72	Numerals 1–20 with period, parenthesized numerals 1–20, encircled numerals 1–10, parenthesized hanzi numerals 1–20, uppercase Roman numerals 1–12
3	94	Full-width GB 1988-89 (GB-Roman; equivalent to ASCII)
4	83	Hiragana
5	86	Katakana
6	48	Upper- and lowercase Greek alphabet
7	66	Upper- and lowercase Cyrillic alphabet
8	63	26 full-width pinyin characters, 37 zhuyin (bopomofo) characters
9	76	Line-drawing elements
10–15	0	Unassigned
16–55	3,755	Level 1 hanzi (last is 55-89)
56–87	3,008	Level 2 hanzi (last is 87-94)
88–94	0	Unassigned

Level 1 hanzi (第一级汉字 *dìyījí hànzì*) are arranged by reading. Level 2 hanzi (第二级汉字 *dì'èrjí hànzì*) are arranged by radical, then total number of strokes. To give you a feel for the GB 2312-80 character set, Table 3-17 briefly illustrates the types of characters in GB 2312-80.

Table 3-17: GB 2312-90 Character Samples

Character Class	Sample Characters
Miscellaneous symbols	、 。 · ˉ ˇ ¨ 〃 々 — … □ ■ △ ▲ ※ → ← ↑ ↓ 〓
Annotated numerals	1. 2. 3. 4. 5. 6. 7. 8. 9. 10. … Ⅲ Ⅳ Ⅴ Ⅵ Ⅶ Ⅷ Ⅸ Ⅹ Ⅺ Ⅻ
Full-width GB-Roman	！ ＂ ＃ ￥ ％ ＆ ＇ （ ） ＊ … ｕ ｖ ｗ ｘ ｙ ｚ ｛ ｜ ｝ ￣
Hiragana	ぁ あ ぃ い ぅ う ぇ え ぉ お … り る れ ろ ゎ わ ゐ ゑ を ん
Katakana	ァ ア ィ イ ゥ ウ ェ エ ォ オ … ロ ヮ ワ ヰ ヱ ヲ ン ヴ ヵ ヶ
Greek characters	Α Β Γ Δ Ε Ζ Η Θ Ι Κ … ο π ρ σ τ υ φ χ ψ ω
Cyrillic	А Б В Г Д Е Ё Ж З И … ц ч ш щ ъ ы ь э ю я
Full-width pinyin	ā á ǎ à ē é ě è ī í … ǔ ù ü ê ɑ ḿ ń ň ǹ ɡ
Zhuyin (bopomofo)	ㄅ ㄆ ㄇ ㄈ ㄉ ㄊ ㄋ ㄌ ㄍ ㄎ … ㄠ ㄡ ㄢ ㄣ ㄤ ㄥ ㄦ ㄧ ㄨ ㄩ
Line-drawing elements	─ ━ │ ┃ ┄ ┅ ┆ ┇ ┈ ┉ … ┴ ┴ ┴ ┴ ┼ ┼ ┼ ┼ ┼ ┼
Level 1 hanzi	啊阿埃挨哎唉哀皑癌蔼 … 尊遵昨左佐柞做作坐座
Level 2 hanzi	亍丌兀丐廿卅丕亘丞鬲 … 黪黯鼢鼬鼯鼹鼷鼽鼾齄

Encoding methods for GB 2312-80 (and its extensions, described shortly) include ISO-2022-CN, ISO-2022-CN-EXT, EUC-CN, and GBK.

CJKV font developers should be aware that early printings of the GB 2312-80 manual had the code points of two uppercase Cyrillic characters (in row 7) swapped. Table 3-18 illustrates the incorrect and correct order of these characters in GB 2312-80. Note the different ordering of the two uppercase Cyrillic characters Ф (Row-Cell 07-22) and Х (Row-Cell 07-23), both of which have been underlined.

Table 3-18: Uppercase Cyrillic Character Ordering in GB 2312-80

Incorrect	А Б В Г Д Е Ё Ж З И Й К Л М Н О П Р С Т У Х Ф Ц Ч Ш Щ Ъ Ы Ь Э Ю Я
Correct	А Б В Г Д Е Ё Ж З И Й К Л М Н О П Р С Т У Ф Х Ц Ч Ш Щ Ъ Ы Ь Э Ю Я

I have encountered at least one Chinese type foundry whose font data propagates the character-ordering error illustrated in Table 3-18.

There are three common extensions to GB 2312-80, one of which was used to issue two corrections. Table 3-19 illustrates the number of characters in GB 2312-80 and its three extensions.

Table 3-19: GB 2312-80 and Its Three Extensions

Character Set	Characters	Characters Added	Number of Corrections
GB 2312-80	7,445		
GB 6345.1-86	7,577	132	2
GB 8565.2-88	8,150	705	
ISO-IR-165:1992	8,443	998	

These extensions to the GB 2312-80 character set standard are described in the following sections.

GB 6345.1-86—corrections and extensions to GB 2312-80

Corrections for and additions to GB 2312-80 have been issued through a separate character set standard designated GB 6345.1-86, established on December 1, 1986. This standard is entitled *32×32 Dot Matrix Font Set of Chinese Ideograms for Information Interchange* (信息交换用汉字32×32点阵字模集 *xìnxī jiāohuàn yòng hànzì 32×32 diǎnzhèn zìmújí*), and resulted in 132 additional characters for a new total of 7,577 characters (6,763 hanzi plus 814 non-hanzi). Table 3-20 highlights the additional characters for GB 2312-80 specified by GB 6345.1-86.

While Table 3-20 clearly shows what characters were added to GB 2312-80, it does not list the corrections. Table 3-21 shows the two corrections to GB 2312-80 mandated by GB 6345.1-86.

Table 3-20: The GB 6345.1-86 Character Set

Row	Characters	Content
1	94	Miscellaneous symbols
2	72	Numerals 1–20 with period, parenthesized numerals 1–20, encircled numerals 1–10, parenthesized hanzi numerals 1–20, uppercase Roman numerals 1–12
3	94	Full-width GB 1988-89 (GB-Roman; equivalent to ASCII)
4	83	Hiragana
5	86	Katakana
6	48	Upper- and lowercase Greek alphabet
7	66	Upper- and lowercase Cyrillic alphabet
8	69	32 full-width pinyin characters, 37 zhuyin (bopomofo) characters
9	76	Line-drawing elements
10	94	Half-width GB 1988-89 (GB-Roman; equivalent to ASCII)
11	32	Half-width pinyin characters
12–15	0	Unassigned
16–55	3,755	Level 1 hanzi (last is 55-89)
56–87	3,008	Level 2 hanzi (last is 87-94)
88–94	0	Unassigned

Table 3-21: GB 6345.1-86 Corrections

Row-Cell	GB 2312-80	GB 6345.1-86
03-71	g	g
79-81	鍾	锺

The GB 2312-80 character form for Row-Cell 79-81 happens to be the same as in GB/T 12345-90, that is, the traditional form, and at the same code point. GB/T 12345-90 is described shortly. This error is still found in recent publications that list all GB 2312-80 hanzi, so evidently information about this correction is not yet widely known.

GB 8565.2-88—another extension to GB 2312-80

The GB 8565.2-88 standard, established on July 1, 1988, defines additions to the GB 2312-80 character set. This standard is entitled *Information Processing—Coded Character Sets for Text Communication—Part 2: Graphic Characters* (信息处理—文本通信用编码字符集—第二部分—图形字符集 *xìnxī chǔlǐ—wénběn tōngxìn yòng biānmǎ zìfújí—dì'èr bùfen—túxíng zìfújí*). These additions, however, are independent from those specified by GB 6345.1-86. The number of additional characters totals 705, bringing the total number of characters to 8,150 (7,399 hanzi plus 751 non-hanzi).

Table 3-22 provides a listing of characters in GB 8565.2-88, and those above and beyond GB 2312-80 are highlighted.

Table 3-22: The GB 8565.2-88 Character Set

Row	Characters	Content
1	94	Miscellaneous symbols
2	72	Numerals 1–20 with period, parenthesized numerals 1–20, encircled numerals 1–10, parenthesized hanzi numerals 1–20, uppercase Roman numerals 1–12
3	94	Full-width GB 1988-89 (GB-Roman; equivalent to ASCII)
4	83	Hiragana
5	86	Katakana
6	48	Upper- and lowercase Greek alphabet
7	66	Upper- and lowercase Cyrillic alphabet
8	63	26 full-width pinyin characters, 37 zhuyin (bopomofo) characters
9	76	Line-drawing elements
10–12	0	Unassigned
13	50	Hanzi from GB 7589-87 (last is 13-50)
14	92	Hanzi from GB 7590-87 (last is 14-92)
15	93	69 non-hanzi plus 24 hanzi (last is 15-93)
16–55	3,755	Level 1 hanzi (last is 55-89)
56–87	3,008	Level 2 hanzi (last is 87-94)
88–89	0	Unassigned
90–94	470	Hanzi from GB 7589-87 (last is 94-94)

Note how GB 8565.2-88 does not include the additions specified by GB 6345.1-86. But, it does include its corrections as shown in Table 3-21 on page 81.

ISO-IR-165:1992—yet another extension to GB 2312-80

ISO-IR-165:1992, also known as the CCITT (Consultative Committee on International Telephone and Telegraph) Chinese Set, enumerates 8,443 characters.* It is based on the GB 2312-80 character set, and includes all modifications and additions specified in GB 6345.1-86 and GB 8565.2-88. That is, 7,445 characters from GB 2312-80, 132 added due to GB 6345.1-86, 705 added due to GB 8565.2-88, plus 161 added by ISO-IR-165:1992.

Table 3-23 provides a listing of characters in ISO-IR-165:1992, and those rows that have content above and beyond GB 2312-80 are highlighted.

* ISO-IR-165:1992 is short for *ISO International Registry #165*, established on July 13, 1992.

Table 3-23: The ISO-IR-165:1992 Character Set

Row	Characters	Content
1	94	Miscellaneous symbols
2	72	Numerals 1–20 with period, parenthesized numerals 1–20, encircled numerals 1–10, parenthesized hanzi numerals 1–20, uppercase Roman numerals 1–12
3	94	Full-width GB 1988-89 (GB-Roman; equivalent to ASCII)
4	83	Hiragana
5	86	Katakana
6	70	48 upper- and lowercase Greek alphabet, 22 background (shading) characters
7	66	Upper- and lowercase Cyrillic alphabet
8	69	32 full-width pinyin characters, 37 zhuyin (bopomofo) characters
9	76	Line-drawing elements
10	94	Half-width GB 1988-89 (GB-Roman; equivalent to ASCII)
11	32	Half-width pinyin characters
12	94	94 hanzi (last is 12-94)
13	94	50 hanzi from GB 7589-87 plus 44 hanzi (last is 13-94)
14	92	Hanzi from GB 7590-87 (last is 14-92)
15	94	69 non-hanzi plus 25 hanzi (last is 15-94)
16–55	3,755	Level 1 hanzi (last is 55-89)
56–87	3,008	Level 2 hanzi (last is 87-94)
88–89	0	Unassigned
90–94	470	Hanzi from GB 7589-87 (last is 94-94)

ISO-IR-165:1992 is, as you can see, a superset of GB 2312-80 and all previous extensions thereof.

GB/T 12345-90—the traditional analog of GB 2312-80

This character set standard, established on December 1, 1990 by the People's Republic of China, enumerates 7,709 characters (6,866 hanzi plus 843 non-hanzi). Its official name is *Code of Chinese Ideogram Set for Information Interchange Supplementary Set* (信息交换用汉字编码字符集—辅助集 *xìnxī jiāohuàn yòng hànzì biānmǎ zìfújí—fǔzhùjí*). Table 3-24 lists how characters are allocated to each row. Note the similarities to GB 2312-80, and that the GB 6345.1-86 additions are included.

As was the case with GB 2312-80, Level 1 hanzi are arranged by reading, and Level 2 hanzi are arranged by radical and total number of strokes. The 103 additional hanzi are arranged by the order in which their counterparts from Level 1

Table 3-24: The GB/T 12345-90 Character Set

Row	Characters	Content
1	94	Miscellaneous symbols
2	72	Numerals 1–20 with period, parenthesized numerals 1–20, encircled numerals 1–10, parenthesized hanzi numerals 1–20, uppercase Roman numerals 1–12
3	94	Full-width GB 1988-89 (GB-Roman; equivalent to ASCII)
4	83	Hiragana
5	86	Katakana
6	77	48 upper- and lowercase Greek alphabet, 29 vertical-use characters
7	66	Upper- and lowercase Cyrillic alphabet
8	69	32 full-width pinyin characters, 37 zhuyin (bopomofo) characters
9	76	Line-drawing elements
10	94	Half-width GB 1988-89 (GB-Roman; equivalent to ASCII)
11	32	Half-width pinyin characters
12–15	0	Unassigned
16–55	3,755	Level 1 hanzi (last is 55-89)
56–87	3,008	Level 2 hanzi (last is 87-94)
88–89	103	Additional hanzi (last is 89-09)
90–94	0	Unassigned

and 2 hanzi appear. Table 3-25 briefly illustrates the types of characters in GB/T 12345-90.

Table 3-25: GB/T 12345-90 Character Samples

Character Class	Sample Characters		
Miscellaneous symbols	、。・ˉˇ¨〃々—	…	□■△▲※→←↑↓〓
Annotated numerals	1. 2. 3. 4. 5. 6. 7. 8. 9. 10.	…	Ⅲ Ⅳ Ⅴ Ⅵ Ⅶ Ⅷ Ⅸ Ⅹ Ⅺ Ⅻ
Full-width GB-Roman	！＂＃￥％＆＇（）＊	…	ｕｖｗｘｙｚ｛｜｝￣
Hiragana	ぁあぃいぅうぇえぉお	…	りるれろゎわゐゑをん
Katakana	ァアィイゥウェエォオ	…	ロヮワヰヱヲンヴヵヶ
Greek characters	Α Β Γ Δ Ε Ζ Η Θ Ι Κ	…	ο π ρ σ τ υ φ χ ψ ω
Vertical-use characters	，。、：；！？︵︶︹	…	︺︿﹀︽︾﹁﹂﹃﹄︱︙︳︴
Cyrillic characters	А Б В Г Д Е Ё Ж З И	…	ц ч ш щ ъ ы ь э ю я
Full-width pinyin	ā á ǎ à ē é ě è ī í	…	ǚ ǜ ü ê ɑ ḿ ń ň ǹ ɡ
Zhuyin (bopomofo)	ㄅㄆㄇㄈㄉㄊㄋㄌㄍㄎ	…	ㄠㄡㄢㄣㄤㄥㄦㄧㄨㄩ
Line-drawing elements	─━│┃┄┅┆┇┈┉	…	┴┵┶┷┸┹┺┻┼┽┾┿
Half-width GB-Roman	! " # ¥ % & ' ( ) *	…	u v w x y z { | } ‾
Half-width pinyin	ā á ǎ à ē é ě è ī í	…	ǚ ǜ ü ê ɑ ḿ ń ň ǹ ɡ

Table 3-25: GB/T 12345-90 Character Samples (continued)

Character Class	Sample Characters
Level 1 hanzi	啊阿埃挨哎唉哀皚癌藹 … 尊遵昨左佐柞做作坐座
Level 2 hanzi	亍丌兀丐廿卅丕亘丞鬲 … 黲黯鼢鼬鼯鼴鼷鼽鼾齄
Additional hanzi	襬閤錶彆蔔纔厂冲丑齣 … 髒症隻只緻製种硃筑准

Compare Level 1 and 2 hanzi from Table 3-25 with that for GB 2312-80 in Table 3-17 on page 79, and note how the same hanzi are used, but that a handful are in the traditional form. In fact, there are 2,180 traditional hanzi forms in GB/T 12345-90 when compared to GB 2312-80, most of which are replacements for simplified hanzi.

The 2,180 hanzi that are used to transform GB 2312-80 into GB/T 12345-90 can be classified into the two classes, as indicated in Table 3-26.

Table 3-26: GB/T 12345-90 Characters Not in GB 2312-80

Characters	Class
2,118	Traditional hanzi replacements—rows 16 through 87
62	Additional hanzi—scattered throughout rows 88 and 89

In addition to the above replacements and additions, 41 hanzi from GB 2312-80 rows 16 through 87 are scattered throughout GB/T 12345-90 rows 88 and 89, and four pairs of hanzi between Level 1 and Level 2 hanzi were swapped. Appendix Q, *Character Lists and Mapping Tables*, provides more details about the four pairs of swapped hanzi and the mappings for hanzi in rows 88 and 89—it also includes a long and complete listing of the 2,118 traditional hanzi replacements, which is something that even the GB/T 12345-90 does not provide.

Like other character set standards, GB/T 12345-90 is not without errors. Chinese type foundries should take note that the GB/T 12345-90 manual has at least two (but, unfortunately, generally not known) printing errors, as indicated in Table 3-27.

Table 3-27: GB/T 12345-90 Corrections

Original	Corrected	Row-Cell	Original in Unicode	Original in GBK
隷	隸	33-05	`96B7`	`EB5F`
鳧	鳬	57-76	`9CE7`	`F844`

In addition, there is often some misunderstanding of the scope and content of the GB/T 12345-90 character set standard. Some printouts of the GB/T 12345-90 character set use slightly different glyphs from the official standard. One specific instance of GB/T 12345-90 provided to The Unicode Consortium used 22 different glyphs, each of which has a *different* Unicode code point. This causes lots of confusion. Table 3-28 lists these characters, along with their (incorrect) Unicode mappings and GBK cross-references. For all 22 of these characters, their glyphs in GB/T 12345-90 are intended to be identical to those in GB 2312-80.

Table 3-28: Incorrect Mappings Between GB/T 12345-90 and Unicode

Correct	GB 2312-80 and GB/T 12345-90	Incorrect	Unicode	GBK
叠	21-94	疊	758A	AF42
换	27-27	換	63DB	9351
唤	27-29	喚	559A	86BE
痪	27-30	瘓	7613	AF88
焕	27-32	煥	7165	9FA8
涣	27-33	渙	6E19	9C6F
晋	29-90	晉	6649	9578
静	30-18	靜	975C	EC6F
净	30-27	淨	51C8	83F4
栖	38-60	棲	68F2	97AB
弃	38-90	棄	68C4	9789
潜	39-17	潛	6F5B	9D93
挣	53-85	掙	6399	92EA
睁	53-86	睜	775C	B1A0
狰	53-88	猙	7319	AA62
争	53-89	爭	722D	A08E
伫	56-89	佇	4F47	81D0
陧	58-77	隉	9689	EA9F
奂	59-28	奐	5950	8A4A
峥	65-31	崢	5D22	8D98
戬	74-15	戩	6229	91EC
筝	83-61	箏	7B8F	B97E

In summary, GB/T 12345-90 is the traditional analog of GB 2312-80. Because of this relationship, we can say that the scope of GB/T 12345-90 is to include *all* traditional forms of hanzi in GB 2312-80. This brings us to one last error that is in GB/T 12345-90. There is one hanzi in GB/T 12345-90, 囉 (88-51), which actually should not be included because its corresponding simplified form, 啰, is not in GB 2312-80! This hanzi is in both GB 7589-87 (22-51) and GB 8565.2-88 (15-93). The reason why the hanzi 囉 was included in GB/T 12345-90 is due to an error in the 1956 draft version of 简化字总表 (*jiǎnhuàzì zǒngbiǎo*; later corrected in the 1964 version) whereby the two hanzi 羅 and 囉 were mistakenly labeled as traditional forms of the simplified hanzi 罗 (34-62 in GB2312-80)—see Table 3-1 on page 68. Only the hanzi 羅 is the true traditional form of the simplified hanzi 罗.

In the next section, you learn that there are two more Chinese character set standards, GB 7589-87 and GB 7590-87, and that both of them, like GB 2312-80, have traditional analogs. Their traditional analogs, GB/T 13131-9X and GB/T 13132-9X, have not yet been published.

Related Chinese character set standards

There are many other character set standards developed by China, each of which is commonly referred to as a GB standard. All of these GB standards share several common characteristics:

- For every GB standard that includes simplified hanzi, there is a corresponding GB standard that replaces simplified forms by their government-sanctioned traditional forms—GB 2312-80 and GB/T 12345-90, which you read about earlier, represent one such pair of character set standards
- Every GB standard is also referred to by a numeric designation, with the most basic character set being zero (that is, "GB0" for GB 2312-80)

Table 3-29 lists the relevant GB character set standards in a way that indicates their relationship with one another, along with their assigned numeric designation. Note how simplified character sets are indicated by even-numbered designations, and traditional character sets by odd.

Table 3-29: GB Character Set Standards—Simplified and Traditional

Simplified Character Set	Hanzi	Traditional Character Set	Additional Hanzi
GB 2312-80 (GB0)	6,763	GB/T 12345-90 (GB1)	103[a]
GB 7589-87 (GB2)	7,237	GB/T 13131-9X (GB3)	
GB 7590-87 (GB4)	7,039	GB/T 13132-9X (GB5)	

[a] These 103 additional hanzi occupy all of row 88 (94 hanzi) and the first part of row 89 (9 hanzi).

An oddball character set standard in this regard is GB 8565.2-88—it is sometimes referred to as GB8.

The hanzi in GB 7589-87 and 7590-87 (this also applies, of course, to their traditional analogs, specifically GB/T 13131-9X and GB/T 13132-9X) are ordered by radical, then total number of strokes, and begin allocating characters at row 16. GB 7589-87 was established on December 1, 1987, and is entitled *Code of Chinese Ideograms Set for Information Interchange—the Second Supplementary Set* (信息交换用汉字编码字符集—第二辅助集 *xìnxī jiāohuàn yòng hànzì biānmǎ zìfújí—dì'èr fǔzhùjí*). GB 7590-87 was established on the same date, and is entitled *Code of Chinese Ideograms Set for Information Interchange—the Fourth Supplementary*

Set (信息交换用汉字编码字符集—第四辅助集 *xìnxī jiāohuàn yòng hànzì biānmǎ zìfújí—dìsì fǔzhùjí*). Tables 3-30 and 3-31 list the character allocation for GB 7589-87 and GB 7590-87, respectively.

Table 3-30: The GB 7589-87 Character Set

Row	Characters	Content
0–15	0	Unassigned
16–92	7,237	Hanzi (last is 92-93)

Table 3-31: The GB 7590-87 Character Set

Row	Characters	Content
0–15	0	Unassigned
16–90	7,039	Hanzi (last is 90-83)

It is interesting to note that all the hanzi specified in GB 7589-87 and GB 7590-87 are handwritten. Needless to say, fonts that support these character set standards are scarce.

Note that not all hanzi in the simplified character set standards are replaced by a corresponding traditional hanzi. In the case of the GB 2312-80 and GB/T 12345-90 pair, 2,180 additional hanzi are needed to transform GB 2312-80 into GB/T 12345-90. The majority are simple one-to-one replacements, but some are hanzi that swap code points or split into two or more separate hanzi (some simplified hanzi were derived from two or more traditional hanzi).

Appendixes E, *GB 2312-80 Table*, and F, *GB/T 12345-90 Table*, provide complete GB 2312-80 and GB/T 12345-90 code tables, respectively. An inadequate supply of fonts precluded the inclusion of code tables for the other GB character set standards. This volume also includes a reading index for Level 1 hanzi and a radical index for Level 2 hanzi. But note that the GB 2312-80 standard itself, as a printed manual, includes many useful indexes.

GBK—extended GB 2312-80

Another well-known GB character set is aligned to ISO 10646-1:1993 (Unicode Version 1.1), and is designated GB 13000.1-93. It is, for all practical purposes, the Chinese translation of ISO 10646-1:1993. What is interesting about GB 13000.1-93 is the Chinese-specific subset known as GBK.

GBK, known as the *Chinese Internal Code Specification* (汉字内码扩展规范 *hànzì nèimǎ kuòzhǎn guīfàn*), is simply an extension to GB 2312-80 that accommodates the remaining Chinese characters in ISO 10646-1:1993 (GB 13000.1-93). From a character-allocation point of view, GBK is composed as follows:

- GB 2312-80 base (with corrections and additions specified in GB 6345.1-86)
- Non-hanzi from GB/T 12345-90
- 14,240 additional hanzi
- 166 additional symbols

Ten of the 29 non-hanzi specific to GB/T 12345-90, mostly vertical variants, are not included in GBK. But, lowercase Roman numerals 1 through 10 have been added. GBK is logically defined into five parts, as indicated in Table 3-32.

Table 3-32: The Five Parts of GBK

Part	Characters	Content
GBK/1	717	GB 2312-80 and GB/T 12345-90 non-hanzi
GBK/2	6,763	GB 2312-80 hanzi
GBK/3	6,080	Hanzi from ISO 10646-1:1993
GBK/4	8,160	8,059 hanzi from ISO 10646-1:1993 plus 101 additional hanzi
GBK/5	166	Non-hanzi from Big Five and other characters

The number of hanzi in GBK/2 through GBK/4 is 21,003, which is 101 more than are found in the Chinese character block of ISO 10646-1:1993. The 101 additional hanzi in GBK/4 account for this difference.

From a compatibility point of view, there is comfort in knowing that every character in GB 2312-80 is at the *same* code point in GBK. Chapter 4, *Encoding Methods*, provides more details about GBK, to include its encoding specifications.

The Simplified Chinese version of Microsoft Windows 95 and later uses GBK, and this character set is also known as Microsoft Code Page 936.

Chinese Character Set Standards—Taiwan

Taiwan (臺灣 *táiwān*), or more officially Republic of China or ROC (中華民國 *zhōnghuá mínguó*), represents the other standards-producing Chinese locale. Taiwan does not use simplified Chinese characters, and typically uses a larger number of characters than all other CJKV locales—combined.

Big Five

Big Five (大五 *dàwŭ*) is the most widely implemented character set standard used in Taiwan, and was established on May 1st, 1984 by the Institute for Information Industry of Taiwan through the publishing of *Computer Chinese Glyph and Character Code Mapping Table* (電腦用中文字型與字碼對照表 *diànnǎoyòng zhōngwén zìxíngyù zìmǎ duìzhào biǎo*), Technical Report (技術通報 *jìshù tōngbào*) C-26. Its name refers to the five companies that collaborated in its development.

Unlike the other CJKV character set standards, Big Five's character space is set in a disjoint 94×157 matrix, for a maximum capacity of 14,758 cells. The Big Five character set standard specifies 13,494 standard characters (13,053 hanzi plus 441 non-hanzi), but some vendor-specific implementations often have a larger repertoire.

I feel compelled to warn you that Big Five is not a national standard, but is used much more widely than the national character set standard for Taiwan, specifically CNS 11643-1992, described next. In other words, Big Five has become a *de facto* standard for Taiwan. Table 3-33 lists the character allocation of the Big Five character set.

Table 3-33: The Big Five Character Set

Row	Characters	Content
1	157	2 abbreviations, 155 miscellaneous symbols
2	157	9 hanzi for measurements, 9 abbreviations, 21 line-drawing elements, numerals 0–9, uppercase Roman numerals 1–10, Chinese numerals 1–12, upper- and lowercase Latin characters (except for w–z), 38 miscellaneous symbols
3	127	Lowercase Latin characters w–z, 48 upper- and lowercase Greek characters, 37 zhuyin (bopomofo) characters, 5 tone marks, 33 abbreviations for control characters
4–38	5,401	Level 1 hanzi (last is 38-63)
39–40	0	Unassigned
41–89	7,652	Level 2 hanzi (last is 89-116)[a]
90–94	0	Unassigned

[a] CNS 11643-1992, discussed shortly, has only 7,650 characters in Level 2 hanzi—Big Five has two duplicate hanzi which the designers of CNS 11643-1992 decided not to include.

The hanzi in each of the two levels are arranged by increasing total number of strokes, and then by radical (the inverse of the ordering criteria used for Level 2 of both GB 2312-80 and JIS X 0208:1997—their Chinese characters are ordered by radical *then* by increasing total number of strokes).

Table 3-34 illustrates examples for each of the character classes that compose the Big Five character set.

Table 3-34: Big Five Character Samples

Character Class	Sample Characters
Miscellaneous symbols	，、。．‧；：？！ … ㏕㎜㎝㎞㏎㎡㎎㎏㏄°
Hanzi for measurements	兙兛兞兝兡兣嗧瓩糎
Line-drawing elements	▁▂▃▄▅▆▇█▏ ▎ … ├┼┤◢◣◥◤╱╲╳
Numerals	０１２３４５６７８９
Roman numerals	ⅠⅡⅢⅣⅤⅥⅦⅧⅨ … ⅰⅱⅲⅳⅴⅵⅶⅷⅸⅹ

Table 3-34: Big Five Character Samples (continued)

Character Class	Sample Characters		
Short forms for numerals	〡〢〣〤〥〦〧〨〩十	...	卄卅
Latin	A B C D E F G H I J	...	q r s t u v w x y z
Greek	Α Β Γ Δ Ε Ζ Η Θ Ι Κ	...	ο π ρ σ τ υ φ χ ψ ω
Zhuyin (bopomofo)	ㄅㄆㄇㄈㄉㄊㄋㄌㄍㄎ	...	ㄠㄡㄢㄣㄤㄥㄦㄧㄨㄩ
Tone marks[a]	˙ ˊ ˇ ˋ		
Control characters	NULL TC1 (SOH) TC2 (STX) TC3 (ETX) TC4 (EOT) TC5 (ENQ) TC6 (ACK) BELL FE0 (BS) FE1 (HT)	...	TC10 (ETB) CAN EM SUB ESC IS4 (FS) IS3 (GS) IS2 (RS) IS1 (US) DEL
Level 1 hanzi	一乙丁七乃九了二人儿	...	黷豔鑿鸚爨驪鬱鸛鸞籲
Level 2 hanzi	乂乜凵匚厂万丌乇亍囗	...	癵驫鱺鸝灩灪麤齾齉龘

[a] Note that the second tone mark has no form—it is blank.

Table 3-35 illustrates the two hanzi that are duplicately encoded in Big Five. This duplication is a result of an error in design.

Table 3-35: Repeated Hanzi in Big Five

Hanzi	Code Points
兀	`A461,C94A`
嗀	`DCD1,DDFC`

CNS 11643-1992, discussed starting on page 93, corrects this error by eliminating the second instance of each of these two hanzi, specifically 0xC94A and 0xDDFC. Big Five 0xA461 and 0xC94A are the same as CNS 11643-1992 Plane 1's 0x4442, and Big Five 0xDCD1 and 0xDDFC are the same as CNS 11643-1992 Plane 2's 0x4176.

The authors of *An Introduction to Chinese, Japanese and Korean Computing* (World Scientific Publishing, 1989), Jack Huang (黃克東 *huáng kèdōng*) and Timothy Huang (黃大一 *huáng dàyī*), claim that the designers of the Big Five character set actually copied many Chinese characters from JIS C 6226-1978. Many of the same Chinese characters are used in Chinese, Japanese, and Korean, but there are often subtle character-form differences between them. The Big Five character set contains many non-Chinese forms of hanzi (one could go so far as to say that they are actually *kanji*, not *hanzi*!), and no attempt was ever made to remedy this problem (although CNS 11643-1992, described starting on page 93, can be considered a cure).

Big Five Plus

A recent extension to Big Five is known as Big Five Plus (or "Big5+" as a shortened form), and was developed by a number of companies in close collaboration and cooperation, and although the specification for Big Five Plus is finalized, it has yet to be fully implemented in any operating system.* It has, however, been implemented in TwinBridge Chinese Partner, beginning with Version 4.98.†

Big Five Plus includes a total of 21,585 characters (and 2,355 user-defined characters), which come from three distinct sources, indicated as follows:

- 13,463 total characters, consisting of the Big Five character set
- 4,670 total characters, consisting of CNS 11643-1992 Plane 3 hanzi in Unicode (3,875), CNS 11643-1992 Plane 1 characters (88), the 214th radical (missing from CNS 11643-1992), Japanese kana (177), ETen line-drawing characters (34), hanzi "zero" (〇), Unicode "shape" characters (5), and CNS 11643-1992 Plane 4 hanzi in Unicode (489)
- 3,452 total characters, consisting of additional CNS 11643-1992 Plane 4 hanzi in Unicode (402), CNS 11643-1992 Plane 5 hanzi in Unicode (61), CNS 11643-1992 Plane 6 hanzi in Unicode (29), CNS 11643-1992 Plane 7 hanzi in Unicode (16), CNS 11643-1986 Plane 15 hanzi in Unicode (152), additional hanzi in Unicode (247), PRC simplified hanzi (2,105), and Japanese kanji and Korean kanji (440)

The end result of Big Five Plus is a character set comparable to GBK (see page 88) in terms of including all of Unicode's 20,902 Chinese characters. In fact, their encoding definitions, at a high level, are the same. Appendix H, *Big Five Table*, provides a Big Five code table. Table 3-36 shows how these 21,585 Big Five Plus characters, along with user-defined characters, are grouped in terms of encoding.

Table 3-36: The Big Five Plus Character Set

Encoding	Characters	Content
A440–C67E	5,401	Big Five Level 1
C940–F9FE	7,693	Big Five Level 2 and 41 ETen characters from row 0xF9
A140–A3FE	471	Big Five non-hanzi
C6A1–C8FE	408	ETen characters from rows 0xC6 through 0xC8
8180–FEA0	4,158	Hanzi
8140–83FE	471	Hanzi and hanzi variants
8E40–A0FE	2,983	Hanzi, simplified hanzi, kanji, and hanja
FA40–FEFE	785	User-defined characters
8440–8DFE	1,570	User-defined characters

For the sake of compatibility with Big Five, Big Five Plus still includes the two duplicately encoded hanzi that are listed in Table 3-35 on page 91.

* *http://www.cmex.org.tw/service/cmex/project.htm*

† *http://www.twinbridge.com/*

Comparing Big Five and CNS 11643-1992

Although the Big Five and CNS 11643-1992 character sets share many qualities, they are, in fact, different character sets. Here are some facts to consider:

- CNS 11643-1992 Plane 1 enumerates 5,401 hanzi, as does Big Five
- CNS 11643-1992 Plane 2 enumerates 7,650 hanzi, but Big Five has two additional hanzi—both duplicately encoded
- CNS 11643-1992 includes six additional planes of hanzi—Big Five has only two levels
- Big Five does not enumerate the 213 classical radicals of CNS 11643-1992—remember that 187 of these 213 classical radicals are identical to hanzi found in CNS 11643-1992 Planes 1 and 2, which correspond to Big Five Levels 1 and 2
- A handful of character forms are different, such as CNS 11643-1992 Plane 1's 0x213A–0x213D compared to Big Five's 0xA159–0xA15C
- A handful of characters are in a slightly different order, due to corrected stroke counts in CNS 11643-1992—two non-hanzi and six hanzi instances between Big Five Level 1 hanzi and CNS 11643-1992 Plane 1, and 17 hanzi instances between Big Five Level 2 hanzi and CNS 11643-1992 Plane 2
- Big Five has become a *de facto* standard due to its long-standing use on MacOS and Windows

Consider these facts well when comparing and contrasting these two character sets from Taiwan. The mere fact that Big Five has become a *de facto* standard is a often the best reason to adopt its use.

Table 3-50 lists the two non-hanzi and six hanzi that are in a different order between Big Five Level 1 and CNS 11643-1992 Plane 1.

Table 3-50: Different Ordering—Big Five Level 1 and CNS 11643-1992 Plane 1

Hanzi	Big Five Level 1	CNS 11643-1992 Plane 1
←	A1F6	02-56
→	A1F7	02-55
耄	ACFE	55-51
銬	BE52	75-48
薦	C2CB	85-21
羅	C3B9	88-69
繳	C3BA	88-68
嚨	C456	88-13

Table 3-51 lists the 17 hanzi that are in a different order between Big Five Level 2 and CNS 11643-1992 Plane 2.

Table 3-51: Different Ordering—Big Five Level 2 and CNS 11643-1992 Plane 2

Hanzi	Big Five Level 1	CNS 11643-1992 Plane 2
刉	C9BE	01-44
玫	CAF7	02-45
筇	D6CC	30-67
莚	D77A	31-74
笻	DADF	23-79
錡	EBF1	53-43
儈	ECDE	55-02
鏐	EEEB	68-15
曆	F056	61-84
鉠	F0CB	58-08
餮	F16B	71-65
繁	F268	73-20
曡	F4B5	70-45
鐀	F663	74-43
鬮	F9C4	81-70
鸙	F9C5	82-20
爩	F9C6	82-32

I urge you to compare these the code points in Tables 3-50 and 3-51 with the complete Big Five and CNS 11643-1992 code tables in Appendixes G and H to verify that their ordering is indeed different.

CCCII

One of the most well thought-out character set standards from Taiwan is known as CCCII (*Chinese Character Code for Information Interchange*; 中文資訊交換碼 *zhōngwén zīxùn jiāohuànmǎ*), which was developed by the Chinese Character Analysis Group (CCAG; 國字整理小組 *guózì zhěnglǐ xiǎozǔ*) in Taiwan. Its first version was published in 1980, followed by substantial revisions in 1982 and 1987.

CCCII is structured as 16 layers, each of which is composed of up to six consecutive 94×94 planes (there are a total of 94 planes). This results in a 94×94×94 space for encoding characters. Each layer is allocated for a particular class of character. Table 3-52 lists what character classes are allocated to what layers.

Table 3-52: The Structure of CCCII

Layer	Planes	Content
1	1–6	Non-hanzi and hanzi
2	7–12	Simplified hanzi (as used in China)
3–12	13–72	Variant forms of hanzi in Layer 1
13	73–78	Japanese kana and kanji
14	79–84	Korean jamo, hangul, and hanja
15	85–90	Reserved
16	91–94	Other characters

The hanzi in CCCII are arranged according to radical, then by total number of strokes (in ascending order, of course). Table 3-53 illustrates the contents of CCCII Layer 1.

Table 3-53: The Structure of CCCII Layer 1

Plane	Row	Characters	Content
1	1	0	Reserved for control codes
1	2–3		
1	4–10	0	Unassigned
1	11	35	Chinese punctuation
1	12–14	214	Classical radicals
1	15	78	Chinese numerals and phonetic symbols (zhuyin)
1	16–67	4,808	Most frequently-used hanzi
1–3	68–64[a]	17,032	Next most frequently-used hanzi
3–6	65–5[b]	20,583	Other hanzi
6	6–94	0	Unassigned

[a] This range spans Plane 1, row 68 through Plane 3, row 64.
[b] This range spans Plane 3, row 65 through Plane 6, row 5.

CCCII Layer 1 thus provides the basic (but very large) set of hanzi. The remaining layers are used for variant forms of characters found in Layer 1. The relationship between the layers is very important to understand. Table 3-54 illustrates the relationship between variant forms in CCCII—CNS 11643-1992 references are provided for the sake of comparison.

Table 3-54: The Relationship Between CCCII Layers

Hanzi	Layer	Plane	Row-Cell	Status	CNS 11643-1992
來	1	1	17-44	Standard form	Plane 1 43-84
来	2	7	17-44	Simplified form	Plane 4 04-38

Table 3-54: The Relationship Between CCCII Layers (continued)

Hanzi	Layer	Plane	Row-Cell	Status	CNS 11643-1992
倈	3	13	17-44	Variant form	Plane 3 15-47
徠	4	19	17-44	Variant form	Plane 1 58-26

Note how the four hanzi in Table 3-54 all share the same Row-Cell value, but differ only in which layer they exist (while the plane numbers appear to differ, they are all the first plane within each layer). This mechanism provides a very convenient and logical method to access simplified or otherwise variant forms of hanzi. The same cannot be said of CNS 11643-1992.

The latest non-draft version of CCCII, dated February of 1987, defines a total of 53,940 characters. A subsequent revision may have 75,684 characters (44,167 orthographics plus 31,517 variants). Professor Chang, one of the primary CCCII contributors, sadly passed away in 1997, and he left behind some unfinished work, including the finalizing of these 75,684 characters. Professor Ching-Chun Hsieh (謝清俊 *xiè qīngjùn*) and other researchers are working to complete the next CCCII revision. Table 3-55 details the history of CCCII.

Table 3-55: The History of CCCII

Year	Characters	Description
1980	4,808	4,808 most frequently-used hanzi
1982	17,032	17,032 next most frequently-used hanzi—first revision
1985	33,357	Combined 1980 and 1982 sets plus revision
1985	11,517	11,517 additional variants
1987	53,940	Volume III—combined and revision
1989	75,684	First variant revision draft

ANSI Z39.64-1989 (*East Asian Character Code For Bibliographic Use* or EACC) is a derivative work of CCCII that contains a total of 15,686 characters. Some consider EACC to be a "snapshot" of CCCII, but it is actually a fairly important precursor to the development of Unicode, and used extensively for bibliographic applications.

While the structure of CCCII is something to be truly admired in that it establishes relationships between characters, such as simplified and other variants, contemporary font technologies—such as QuickDraw GX, TrueType Open and OpenType described in Chapter 6, *Font Formats*—provide the same level of glyph-substitution functionality at a level beyond encoding.

Chinese Character Set Standards—Hong Kong

Hong Kong (香港 *xiānggǎng*), now a part of China as of 1997, uses many hanzi that are specific to its locale. Of the two most common Chinese character set standards in use today, China's GB 2312-80 and Taiwan's Big Five, Hong Kong has standardized on Big Five. But, Big Five was not sufficient for their needs. Several companies, such as DynaLab and Monotype, have defined their own—conflicting—Hong Kong extensions for Big Five. These vendor-specific Hong Kong extensions are covered in Appendix C.

In 1994, Hong Kong's Special Administrative Region (SAR) Government published a set of 3,049 hanzi that are above and beyond those available in Big Five.* This character set is called Hong Kong GCCS (Government Chinese Character Set). Tze-loi Yeung's dictionary entitled 標準中文輸入碼大字典 (*biāozhǔn zhōngwén shūrùmǎ dà zìdiǎn*, meaning "Big Dictionary of Standard Chinese Input Codes"; Juxian Guan, 1996) provides full coverage of both Big Five (13,053 hanzi) plus this set of 3,049 hanzi published by the Hong Kong government.

Interestingly, this set of 3,049 Hong Kong hanzi includes six characters that are also in the Big Five character set (and thus in CNS 11643-1992), though not in either of its two hanzi levels, but rather in its symbol (non-hanzi) region. Table 3-56 lists these six duplicate hanzi, along with their character codes in both Big Five and in its Hong Kong extension—CNS 11643-1992 Plane 1 Row-Cell codes are also provided for reference.

Table 3-56: Duplicate Hanzi in Big Five and Hong Kong GCCS

Hanzi	"Standard" Big Five	Hong Kong GCCS	CNS 11643-1992
兙	A259	92AF	Plane 1 02-89
兛	A25A	92B0	Plane 1 02-90
兞	A25B	92B2	Plane 1 02-91
兝	A25C	92B1	Plane 1 02-92
瓩	A260	FEAA	Plane 1 03-02
糎	A261	8E7E	Plane 1 03-03
撐	BCB5	FCB9	Plane 1 76-93
釔	D0C0	9BDE	Plane 2 13-65
[illegible]	D8F4	FC4F	Plane 2 27-56
輋	E07C	9D57	Plane 2 40-04
鷰	F86D	9C6B	Plane 2 79-91

* *http://www.info.gov.hk/gccs/*

There is one more hanzi that can also be considered as duplicately encoded if you consider ETen's commonly-used Big Five extension that adds seven hanzi. The hanzi 銹 is available at 0xF9D7 in Big Five and 0x907A in the Hong Kong extension. This hanzi is also in CNS 11643-1992 Plane 3 at 47-48.

Some implementations of this character set also include an additional set of 145 hanzi specified by Hong Kong's Department of Judiciary—they are encoded in rows 0x8A (132 hanzi) and 0x8B (13 hanzi) of Big Five encoding.

Appendix I, *Hong Kong GCCS Table*, provides a complete code table for these 3,049 Hong Kong hanzi plus the 145 hanzi specified by Hong Kong's Department of Judiciary.

Chinese Character Set Standards—Singapore

Singapore (新加坡 *xīnjiāpō*), like Hong Kong as described in the previous section, does not have its own character set standard. But unlike Hong Kong, Singapore uses GB 2312-80 as its character set.

Japanese Character Set Standards

Five coded character sets are widely used in Japan. These character sets are ASCII, JIS-Roman, half-width katakana, JIS X 0208:1997 (and its predecessors), and JIS X 0212-1990. ASCII and JIS-Roman were already discussed. JIS-Roman and half-width katakana* are described in JIS X 0201-1997. These will soon be followed by a sixth standard that defines JIS Levels 3 and 4.

This section includes a description of the latest character set standards established by Japan. JIS X 0221-1995, which is directly aligned with and equivalent to ISO 10646-1:1993, is described in the section about international character set standards, later in this chapter.

Half-width katakana

The Japanese first attempted to adapt their writing system to computer systems through the creation of half-width katakana. This formed a limited set of characters that could be easily encoded on early computer systems because they could be displayed in the same space as ASCII/JIS-Roman characters.† This collection of 63 half-width katakana characters is defined in the document JIS X 0201-1997, and consists of the basic katakana characters, along with enough punctuation marks

* *http://www.ryukyu.ad.jp/~shin/jdoc/hankaku-kana.html*

† Also known as *hankaku* (半角 *hankaku*) katakana. Furthermore, some folks refer to these as half-*wit* katakana, either as a result of a typo or for humorous purposes.

and symbols to write Japanese text—but the result is not very readable.* Table 3-57 illustrates all the characters of this character set.

Table 3-57: The Half-Width Katakana Character Set

Katakana	ｦｧｨｩｪｫｬｭｮｯｱｲｳｴｵｶｷｸｹｺｻｼｽｾｿﾀﾁﾂﾃﾄﾅﾆﾇﾈﾉﾊﾋﾌﾍﾎﾏﾐﾑﾒﾓﾔﾕﾖﾗﾘﾙﾚﾛﾜﾝ
Symbols	｡｢｣､･ﾞﾟｰ

Sometimes a half-width space character is part of this character set, which brings the total to 64 characters.

Half-width katakana occupy half the display width of the equivalent full-width katakana found in JIS X 0208:1997 (described in the following section). The katakana characters enumerated in JIS X 0208:1997 are known as full-width characters.† Full-width, in this case, translates to roughly a square space, meaning that the width and the height of the character are the same. Half-width characters have the same height as full-width characters, but occupy half their width.

The dakuten- and handakuten-annotated counterparts of katakana are not included in the half-width katakana character set. The dakuten (ﾞ) and the handakuten (ﾟ) are used to create additional katakana characters. The dakuten and handakuten are treated as separate characters in the half-width katakana character set. Table 3-58 illustrates the relationship between half- and full-width katakana characters, and how dakuten and handakuten marks are treated as separate characters.

Table 3-58: Dakuten Versus Handakuten and Full- Versus Half-Width

	ka	**ga (dakuten)**	**ha**	**pa (handakuten)**
Full-width	カカカカカ	ガガガガガ	ハハハハハ	パパパパパ
Half-width	ｶｶｶｶｶ	ｶﾞｶﾞｶﾞｶﾞｶﾞ	ﾊﾊﾊﾊﾊ	ﾊﾟﾊﾟﾊﾟﾊﾟﾊﾟ

When the ASCII/JIS-Roman and half-width katakana character set standards are combined into a single collection of characters, this newly-formed character set is often referred to as ANK, short for *Alphabet, Numerals, and Katakana.*

JIS X 0208:1997—formerly JIS X 0208-1990

The first attempt by the Japanese to create a coded character set standard that better represented their written language bore fruit in 1978 by establishing JIS C 6226-1978. The work that eventually became JIS C 6226-1978 actually began as early as 1969. JIS C 6226-1978 represented the very first *national* coded character

* One could therefore argue that katakana is somewhat of a *write-only* writing system when used to completely express Japanese.

† Also known as *zenkaku* (全角 *zenkaku*).

set standard to include Chinese characters, and is also significant in that it broke the *one-byte-equals-one-character* barrier. JIS C 6226-1978 went through three revisions to eventually become JIS X 0208:1997 on January 20, 1997.

The official title of the JIS X 0208:1997 standard is *7-Bit and 8-Bit Double Byte Coded Kanji Sets for Information Interchange* (7ビット及び8ビットの2バイト情報交換用符号化漢字集合 *nana bitto oyobi hachi bitto no ni baito jōhō kōkan yō fugōka kanji shūgō*). The current version of this standard, JIS X 0208:1997, is considered the most basic Japanese coded character set. This character set standard enumerates 6,879 characters, most of which are kanji. The character space is arranged in a 94×94 matrix. Rows 1 through 8 are reserved for non-kanji, rows 9 through 15 are unassigned, rows 16 through 84 are reserved for kanji, and rows 85 through 94 are unassigned. Table 3-59 provides a much more detailed description of the characters allocated to each row (note that character allocation is identical to that of JIS X 0208-1990, but older versions are slightly different).

Table 3-59: The JIS X 0208:1997 Character Set

Row	Characters	Content
1	94	Miscellaneous symbols
2	53	Miscellaneous symbols
3	62	Numerals 0–9, upper- and lowercase Latin alphabet[a]
4	83	Hiragana
5	86	Katakana
6	48	Upper- and lowercase Greek alphabet
7	66	Upper- and lowercase Cyrillic alphabet
8	32	Line-drawing elements
9–15	0	Unassigned
16–47	2,965	JIS Level 1 kanji (last is 47-51)
48–83	3,384	JIS Level 2 kanji (last is 83-94)
84	6	Additional kanji (last is 84-06)[b]
85–94	0	Unassigned

[a] Usually implemented as full-width characters.
[b] The six kanji in row 84 are usually considered part of JIS Level 2 kanji, so the total number of kanji that one would see for JIS Level 2 is 3,390, which includes row 84.

There are 6,355 kanji in this character set. The kanji are broken into two distinct sections. The first section is called *JIS Level 1 kanji* (JIS第一水準漢字 *JIS daiichi suijun kanji*), and the kanji within it are arranged by On (old Chinese) reading.*

* Some kanji do not have an On reading. In these cases, they are arranged by their Kun (Japanese) reading. Also, there is one instance of an incorrectly-ordered kanji in JIS X 0208:1997 Level 1 kanji. The kanji 馨 (*kaori*; 19-30) falls between 浬 (*kairi*; 19-29) and 蛙 (*kaeru*; 19-31), but this reading should come after that of 蛙 (19-31). This means that the sequence 浬馨蛙 should have been 浬蛙馨.

The second section of kanji, called *JIS Level 2 kanji* (JIS第二水準漢字 *JIS daini suijun kanji*), are arranged by radical, then total number of strokes.* The six additional kanji in row 84 are arranged by radical, then number of strokes, like JIS Level 2 kanji. JIS Levels 1 and 2 kanji are mutually exclusive—each level contains no kanji found in the other—together they constitute a set of 6,355 unique kanji.†

A complete code table for the characters that constitute JIS X 0208:1997 can be found in Appendix J, *JIS X 0208:1997 Table*, and Appendix P includes a reading index for JIS Level 1 kanji, and a radical index for JIS Level 2 kanji.

Table 3-60 provides a graphic representation for the first and last characters from each of the character classes (note that the complete set for numerals and additional kanji is provided).

Table 3-60: JIS X 0208:1997 Character Samples

Character Class	Sample Characters
Miscellaneous symbols	、。，．・：；？！ … ∬Å‰♯♭♪†‡¶◯
Numerals	０１２３４５６７８９
Latin	ＡＢＣＤＥＦＧＨＩＪ … ｑｒｓｔｕｖｗｘｙｚ
Hiragana	ぁあぃいぅうぇえぉお … りるれろゎわゐゑをん
Katakana	ァアィイゥウェエォオ … ロヮワヰヱヲンヴヵヶ
Greek	ΑΒΓΔΕΖΗΘΙΚ … οπρστυφχψω
Cyrillic	АБВГДЕЁЖЗИ … цчшщъыьэюя
Line-drawing elements	─│┌┐┘└├┬┤┴ … ┠┯┨┷┿┝┰┥┸╂
JIS Level 1 kanji	亜唖娃阿哀愛挨姶逢葵 … 亙亘鰐詫藁蕨椀湾碗腕
JIS Level 2 kanji	弌丐丕个丱丶丼丿乂乖 … 齦齧齬齪齷齲齶龕龜龠
Additional kanji	堯槇遙瑤凜熙

Symbols include punctuation marks, mathematical symbols, and various types of parentheses. Numerals and Latin characters are what one would normally find in the ASCII character set (less the ASCII/JIS-Roman symbols, which are scattered throughout row 1)—these are full-width, not half-width. The hiragana and katakana characters, too, are full-width, not half-width. Cyrillic and Greek characters are included, perhaps because Japanese technical works include occasional Russian or Greek words. The line-drawing elements are used for building charts on a per-character basis—not terribly useful in this day and age of applications with built-in support for graphics and tables.

* Actually, the ordering is based on the order of entries in the kanji dictionary entitled 新字源 (*shinjigen*). Compare 闊 (79-72) and 濶 (79-73), whose indexing radicals are 門 and 氵(水), respectively. Their 新字源 (1994 edition) index numbers are 8831 and 8832, respectively.

† This is only true if you count character variants as separate entities.

This character set standard was first established on January 1, 1978 as JIS C 6226-1978, modified for the first time on September 1, 1983 as JIS X 0208-1983, modified again on September 1, 1990 as JIS X 0208-1990, and finally became JIS X 0208:1997 on January 20, 1997.* It is widely implemented on a variety of platforms. Encoding methods for JIS X 0208:1997 include ISO-2022-JP, EUC-JP, and Shift-JIS. These three encoding methods are covered in Chapter 4.

JIS X 0208:1997, although it did not add any characters to the character set, does offer some significant improvements to the standard itself, described as follows:

- Explicitly describes ISO-2022-JP and Shift-JIS encodings—previous installments of this standard, specifically the JIS C 6226 and JIS X 0208 series, included no such specifications
- More clearly defines the kanji unification rules and principles, and applies them to the standard
- Provides an extremely thorough treatment of kanji variant forms using these well-established unification principles

You may sometimes encounter systems and documentation that are based on earlier versions of JIS X 0208:1997, the most likely of which is JIS X 0208-1983. That standard was originally known as JIS C 6226-1983. On March 1, 1987, JSA decided to rename many JIS standards from a "C" to an "X" designation (don't ask me why). JIS C 6226-1983, with no substantive changes, was renamed to JIS X 0208-1983. Table 3-61 illustrates this evolution of the JIS X 0208 series.

Table 3-61: The Evolution of JIS X 0208

Year	Designation	Status
1978	JIS C 6226-1978	Establishment
1983	JIS C 6226-1983	Update
1987	JIS X 0208-1983	Designation change
1990	JIS X 0208-1990	Update
1997	JIS X 0208:1997	Update, but no changes in number of characters

Since its conception in 1978, this character set standard has experienced a slight increase in the total number of characters. Table 3-62 lists how characters are allocated to each row in the 1978, 1983, and 1990 (same as 1997) versions.

Table 3-62: Comparing Different Versions of JIS X 0208

Row	1978	1983	1990	Content
1	94	94	94	Miscellaneous symbols
2	14	53	53	Miscellaneous symbols

* It is common practice to review standards every five years or so.

Table 3-62: Comparing Different Versions of JIS X 0208 (continued)

Row	1978	1983	1990	Content
3	62	62	62	Numerals 0–9, upper- and lowercase Latin alphabet
4	83	83	83	Hiragana
5	86	86	86	Katakana
6	48	48	48	Upper- and lowercase Greek alphabet
7	66	66	66	Upper- and lowercase Cyrillic alphabet
8	0	32	32	Line-drawing elements
9–15	0	0	0	Unassigned
16–47	2,965	2,965	2,965	JIS Level 1 kanji (last is 47-51)
48–83	3,384	3,384	3,384	JIS Level 2 kanji (last is 83-94)
84	0	4	6	Additional kanji
85–94	0	0	0	Unassigned

More detailed information about the differences between JIS C 6226-1978, JIS X 0208-1983, JIS X 0208-1990, and JIS X 0208:1997 can be found in Appendix Q.

Some of the similarities between JIS X 0208:1997 and GB 2312-80 (Chinese) are quite close. First, note how the allocation of rows 4 through 7 (hiragana, katakana, Greek, and Cyrillic characters) is identical in both character sets. Also, rows 1 through 15 are reserved for non-Chinese characters. And finally, Chinese characters are divided into two levels, with the first level being the most frequently used and arranged by reading, and the second level being more rarely used and arranged by radical, then total number of strokes.

JIS X 0212-1990—a supplemental character set

A supplemental Japanese character set standard, JIS X 0212-1990, was established by JISC on October 1, 1990, and specified 6,067 characters (5,801 kanji plus 266 non-kanji). These characters are in addition to those found in JIS X 0208:1997, but like that character set standard, JIS X 0212-1990 is also composed of a 94×94 character space. Also like JIS X 0208:1997, rows 1 through 15 are reserved for non-kanji, rows 9 through 15 are unassigned, rows 16 through 84 are reserved for kanji, and rows 85 through 94 are unassigned.

The official title of JIS X 0212-1990 is *Code of the Supplementary Japanese Graphic Character Set for Information Interchange* (情報交換用漢字符号—補助漢字 *jōhō kōkan yō kanji fugō—hojo kanji*). Table 3-63 lists how characters are allocated to each of its 94 rows.

Table 3-63: The JIS X 0212-1990 Character Set

Row	Characters	Content
1	0	Unassigned
2	21	Diacritics and miscellaneous symbols

Table 3-63: The JIS X 0212-1990 Character Set (continued)

Row	Characters	Content
3–5	0	Unassigned
6	21	Greek characters with diacritics
7	26	Eastern European characters
8	0	Unassigned
9–11	198	Miscellaneous alphabetic characters
12–15	0	Unassigned
16–77	5,801	Supplemental kanji (last is 77-67)
78–94	0	Unassigned

The 5,801 kanji are arranged by radical, then total number of strokes (like JIS Level 2 kanji of JIS X 0208:1997). When these data are merged with JIS X 0208:1997, you see that there are now 12,156 unique standard kanji, and 12,946 total characters. However, very few software systems can use these 6,067 supplemental characters. The latest version of GNU Emacs, now a powerful multilingual text editor, is an example of a program that supports the encoding of the JIS X 0212-1990 character set standard. Much of the difficulty in supporting JIS X 0212-1990 is the poor availability of fonts that include its characters.

Table 3-64 illustrates the first and last ten characters in each class of characters listed above.

Table 3-64: JIS X 0212-1990 Character Samples

Character Class	Sample Characters
Miscellaneous symbols	˘ ˇ ¸ ˙ ˝ ¯ ˛ ˚ ~ ΄ … ¡ ¦ ¿ º ª © ® ™ ¤ №
Greek	Ά Έ Ή Ί Ϊ Ό Ύ Ϋ Ώ ά … ή ί ϊ ΐ ό ς ύ ϋ ΰ ώ
Eastern European	Ђ Ѓ Є Ѕ І Ї Ј Љ Њ Ћ … ѕ і ї ј љ њ ћ ќ ў џ
Alphabetic	Æ Đ Ħ Ĳ Ł Ŀ Ŋ Ø Œ Ŧ … ǜ ǘ ǖ ŵ ý ÿ ŷ ź ž ż
Supplemental kanji	丂丄丅丌丒丟乹两丨丫 … 龏龑龔龖龗龞龡龢龣龥

A complete code table for the characters that make up JIS X 0212-1990 can be found in Appendix K, *JIS X 0212-1990 Table*. Also, a radical index for the 5,801 kanji of JIS X 0212-1990 can be found in Appendix P.

JISC may eventually add four katakana characters to JIS X 0212-1990, listed in Table 3-65.

These four characters, although rarely employed, are used for writing foreign words, and can already be found in at least one vendor character set standard (Apple Computer's MacOS-J, covered in Appendix C). Space for these four characters has already been allocated in JIS X 0212-1990—if accepted for inclusion into

Table 3-65: Four Characters that May Be Added to JIS X 0212-1990

Katakana	Reading
ヷ	va
ヸ	vi
ヹ	ve
ヺ	vo

this character set standard, they will be placed in row 5 beginning at cell 87 (that is, 05-87 through 05-90).* Table 3-66 illustrates these proposed changes.

Table 3-66: Proposed Change to the JIS X 0212-1990 Character Set

Row	Characters	Content
1	0	Unassigned
2	21	Diacritics and miscellaneous symbols
3–4	0	Unassigned
5	4	Katakana
6	21	Greek characters with diacritics
7	26	Eastern European characters
8	0	Unassigned
9–11	198	Miscellaneous alphabetic characters
12–15	0	Unassigned
16–77	5,801	Supplemental kanji (last is 77-67)
78–94	0	Unassigned

Incorporating the 6,067 characters of JIS X 0212-1990 into ISO-2022-JP encoding was trivial: a new two-byte character escape sequence (explained in Chapter 4) for this new character set was registered. ISO-2022-JP-2 encoding was subsequently born. It is not possible to encode JIS X 0212-1990 in Shift-JIS encoding because there is not enough space left. EUC-JP encoding does not suffer from this problem of limited encoding space, and in Chapter 4 you will learn how JIS X 0212-1990 is supported by EUC-JP encoding.

JIS X 0213:199X

JSA is currently developing a new character set standard, whose designation is most likely to be JIS X 0213, that will define JIS Levels 3 and 4.† JIS Level 3 will

* There is significance to this starting point. If one were to overlay the non-kanji portions of JIS X 0208:1997 and JIS X 0212-1990 (that is, rows 1 through 16), there would be zero instances of characters in one character set occupying the code point of characters in the other. The katakana in JIS X 0208:1997 end at 05-86, so using 05-87 as the starting code point for these four additional katakana seems like a logical thing to do.

† Some people (mistakenly) refer to JIS X 0212-1990 as *JIS Level 3 kanji*, but the establishment of JIS X 0213:199X will set the record straight once and for all.

contain approximately 2,000 characters, and JIS Level 4 will contain approximately 3,000—for a grand total of approximately 5,000 characters. Of course, this is subject to change.

Because this character set standard is still under development, very few details are known at this time, but its public review commenced at about the same time this book went to press.* This standard is expected to be released in final form sometime in 1999. Early information indicates that many JIS X 0212-1990 non-kanji and kanji will be included, which effectively means that JIS X 0212-1990 may no longer be maintained by JSA.

Relationships among Japanese character set standards

You already read about the slight difference between the ASCII and JIS-Roman character sets. With only one exception, the character set standards JIS X 0208:1997 and JIS X 0212-1990 contain no characters found in the other—together they are designed to form a larger collection of characters (12,156 kanji plus 790 non-kanji). These two characters are illustrated in Table 3-67.

Table 3-67: Duplicate Characters in JIS X 0208:1997 and JIS X 0212-1990

Standard	Kanji	Row-Cell
JIS X 0208:1997	〆	01-26
JIS X 0212-1990	乄	16-17

The characters are the same, with identical meanings, and are used in the same contexts—it is really only a character-classification difference. In JIS X 0208:1997, this character is treated as a non-kanji (in a row of symbols), but in JIS X 0212-1990, it is treated as a full-fledged kanji. This character, in both instances, is read *shime*, and means "deadline," "(to) sum up," or "seal," depending on context.

The internal structures of JIS X 0208:1997 and JIS X 0212-1990 share several unique qualities, the most notable being that they are both composed of a 94×94 character space for a maximum number of 8,836 characters. Thus, they both occupy the same character *space*. Furthermore, the non-kanji characters of both standards are allocated to rows 1 through 15, and the kanji characters are allocated to rows 16 through 84 (that is not to say that all those rows are currently filled, but rather that they have been allocated for those character classes). Chapter 4 discusses how computer systems can distinguish between these two character sets using different encoding methods.

Another interesting aspect of these character set standards is how the non-kanji are arranged so that if one superimposed one set onto the other, there would be absolutely no overlap of assigned character positions. This would make it possible to

* *http://jcs.aa.tufs.ac.jp/*

merge rows 1 through 15 of both standards with no assigned character positions overlapping. In fact, the four katakana characters that may eventually be added to JIS X 0212-1990 are positioned in such a way that they would appear immediately after the katakana assigned to JIS X 0208:1997.*

There is one last tidbit of information to mention about the relationship between these two character set standards. There are 28 kanji in JIS X 0212-1990 that were in JIS C 6226-1978, but were replaced with different glyphs in JIS X 0208-1983. In essence, 28 kanji that were lost during the transition from JIS C 6226-1978 to JIS X 0208-1983 were restored in JIS X 0212-1990. Appendix Q explicitly lists these 28 kanji pairs.

Korean Character Set Standards

Korean character set standards have been developed by South Korea, North Korea, and China, and some of them demonstrate some very unique attributes, such as the following:

- Contain thousands of hangul (alphabetic syllables)
- Hanja (Chinese characters) with multiple readings are encoded more than once

In essence, hangul are treated as though they were Chinese characters as far as character-allocation is concerned. This is quite natural because hangul play an important role in the Korean writing system.

KS X 1001:1992

The most commonly-used Korean character set standard, specified in the document KS X 1001:1992, *Code for Information Interchange (Hangul and Hanja)* (정보 교환용 부호 (한글 및 한자) *jeongbo gyohwanyong buho (hangeul mic hanja)*), enumerates 8,224 characters.† This standard was established on October 15, 1992 by the Korean Industrial Standards Association (also known as the Korean Bureau of Standards) of South Korea (Republic of Korea or ROK; 대한민국/大韓民國 *daehan mingug*).

KS X 1001:1992 contains 4,888 hanja arranged by reading, 2,350 hangul arranged by reading, and 986 symbols. Table 3-68 lists the characters that constitute KS X 1001:1992.

Due to multiple readings of hanja, 268 of the 4,888 hanja in KS X 1001:1992 are duplicates—most of these are single repeats, but a handful of hanja are repeated

* This would be difficult to implement because numerous vendors have effectively filled these open rows of JIS X 0208:1997.

† Formerly KS C 5601-1992.

Table 3-68: The KS X 1001:1992 Character Set

Row	Characters	Content
1	94	Miscellaneous symbols
2	69	6 abbreviations, 63 miscellaneous symbols
3	94	Full-width KS X 1003:1993 (KS-Roman; equivalent to ASCII)
4	94	Jamo (hangul elements)
5	68	Upper- and lowercase Roman numerals 1–10, 48 upper- and lowercase Greek alphabet
6	68	Line-drawing elements
7	79	Abbreviations
8	91	13 alphabetic characters, 28 encircled jamo and hangul, encircled lowercase Latin characters, encircled numerals 1–15, 9 fractions
9	94	16 alphabetic characters, 28 parenthesized jamo and hangul, parenthesized lowercase Latin characters, parenthesized numerals 1–15, 5 superscripts, 4 subscripts
10	83	Hiragana
11	86	Katakana
12	66	Upper- and lowercase Cyrillic alphabet
13–15	0	Unassigned
16–40	2,350	Hangul (last is 40-94)
41	0	Unassigned
42–93	4,888	Hanja (last is 93-94)
94	0	Unassigned

more than once! This effectively means that there are 4,620 unique hanja in KS X 1001:1992, not 4,888. Table 3-69 provides three example hanja from KS X 1001:1992, each repeated a different number of times.

Table 3-69: Repeated Hanja in KS X 1001:1992—Samples

Hanja	Row-Cell
賈	42-25, 45-47
龜	47-47, 48-02, 48-24
樂	49-66, 53-05, 68-37, 72-89

KS X 1001:1992 is the only CJKV character set that multiply encodes Chinese characters due to multiple readings. Big Five includes two duplicate hanzi, but that was due to an error *in* design, not *by* design.

Appendix L, *KS X 1001:1992 Table*, provides a complete KS X 1001:1992 code table, and Appendix Q provides a complete listing of its 268 duplicate hanja. It also provides reading indexes for the hangul and hanja in KS X 1001:1992. Table 3-70 illustrates the many character classes in KS X 1001:1992.

Table 3-70: KS X 1001:1992 Character Samples

Character Class	Sample Characters
Miscellaneous symbols	、 。 · ‥ … ¨ 〃 ― ∥ … ♪ ♬ ㉿ ㈜ № ㏇ ™ ㏂ ㏘ ℡
Full-width KS-Roman	！ ＂ ＃ ＄ ％ ＆ ＇ （ ） ＊ … ｕ ｖ ｗ ｘ ｙ ｚ ｛ ｜ ｝ ￣
Jamo	ㄱ ㄲ ㄳ ㄴ ㄵ ㄶ ㄷ ㄸ ㄹ ㄺ … ㆅ ㆆ ㆇ ㆈ ㆉ ㆊ ㆋ ㆌ ㆍ ㆎ
Roman numerals	ⅰ ⅱ ⅲ ⅳ ⅴ ⅵ ⅶ ⅷ ⅸ ⅹ … Ⅰ Ⅱ Ⅲ Ⅳ Ⅴ Ⅵ Ⅶ Ⅷ Ⅸ Ⅹ
Greek	Α Β Γ Δ Ε Ζ Η Θ Ι Κ … ο π ρ σ τ υ φ χ ψ ω
Line-drawing elements	─ │ ┌ ┐ ┘ └ ├ ┬ ┤ ┴ … ╀ ╁ ╂ ╃ ╄ ╅ ╆ ╇ ╈ ╉
Latin ligatures	㎕ ㎖ ㎗ ℓ ㎘ ㏄ ㎣ ㎤ ㎥ ㎦ … ㎪ ㎫ ㎬ ㏝ ㏐ ㏓ ㏃ ㏉ ㏜ ㏆
Alphabetic characters	Æ Ð ª Ħ Ĳ Ŀ Ł Ø Œ º … ĸ ŀ ł ø œ ß þ ŧ ŋ ŉ
Encircled jamo/hangul	㉠ ㉡ ㉢ ㉣ ㉤ ㉥ ㉦ ㉧ ㉨ ㉩ … ㉲ ㉳ ㉴ ㉵ ㉶ ㉷ ㉸ ㉹ ㉺ ㉻
Encircled Latin/numerals	ⓐ ⓑ ⓒ ⓓ ⓔ ⓕ ⓖ ⓗ ⓘ ⓙ … ⑥ ⑦ ⑧ ⑨ ⑩ ⑪ ⑫ ⑬ ⑭ ⑮
Fractions	½ ⅓ ⅔ ¼ ¾ ⅛ ⅜ ⅝ ⅞
Parenthesized jamo/hangul	㈀ ㈁ ㈂ ㈃ ㈄ ㈅ ㈆ ㈇ ㈈ ㈉ … ㈒ ㈓ ㈔ ㈕ ㈖ ㈗ ㈘ ㈙ ㈚ ㈛
Parenthesized Latin/numerals	⒜ ⒝ ⒞ ⒟ ⒠ ⒡ ⒢ ⒣ ⒤ ⒥ … ⑹ ⑺ ⑻ ⑼ ⑽ ⑾ ⑿ ⒀ ⒁ ⒂
Superscripts and subscripts	^{1} ^{2} ^{3} ^{4} ^{n} $_{1}$ $_{2}$ $_{3}$ $_{4}$
Hiragana	ぁ あ ぃ い ぅ う ぇ え ぉ お … り る れ ろ ゎ わ ゐ ゑ を ん
Katakana	ァ ア ィ イ ゥ ウ ェ エ ォ オ … ロ ヮ ワ ヰ ヱ ヲ ン ヴ ヵ ヶ
Cyrillic	А Б В Г Д Е Ё Ж З И … ц ч ш щ ъ ы ь э ю я
Hangul	가 각 간 갇 갈 갉 갊 감 갑 값 … 흽 힁 히 힉 힌 힐 힘 힙 힛 힝
Hanja	伽 佳 假 價 加 可 呵 哥 嘉 嫁 … 晞 曦 熙 熹 熺 犧 禧 稀 羲 詰

The hanja specified in KS X 1001:1992 are considered to be in the traditional form. Some examples of simplified versus traditional Chinese characters are listed in Chapter 2.

Encoding methods that support the KS X 1001:1992 character set include ISO-2022-KR, EUC-KR, Johab, and Unified Hangul Code (UHC).

This Korean character set standard is similar to JIS X 0208:1997 and GB 2312-80 in that it contains the same set of hiragana, katakana, Greek, and Cyrillic characters (but in different rows). And, although hangul are not considered the same as hanja, they do begin at row 16, like the Chinese characters in JIS X 0208:1997 and friends.

Earlier versions of this standard were designated KS C 5601-1987 and KS C 5601-1989 (the latter was established on April 22, 1989)—their character set being identical. What has changed between versions were the annexes and their contents.

Historically speaking, there was a standard designated KS C 5601-1982, but it enumerated only the 51 basic jamo in a one-byte, seven- and eight-bit encoding. This information is still part of the KS X 1001 series in the form of an annex (Annex 4 of KS X 1001:1992).

In the very early days of Korean information processing, there were character set standards known as KS C 5619-1982 and KIPS (Korean Information Processing System). KS C 5619-1982 enumerated only 51 jamo (modern jamo), 1,316 hangul, and 1,672 hanja. KIPS enumerated 2,058 hangul and 2,392 hanja. Both of these standards were rendered obsolete by KS C 5601-1987 (currently KS X 1001:1992).

KS X 1001:1992—an alternate plane

Annex 3 of the KS X 1001:1992 manual describes an extension whereby all possible modern hangul syllables, 11,172 of them built up using the basic set of 51 jamo, are encoded.* This alternate plane of KS X 1001:1992, which also enumerates the same set of symbols and hanja (but at different code points), is known as *Johab* (조합/組合 *johab*), which means "combining." The standard plane of KS X 1001:1992—the one that enumerates only 2,350 hangul—is known as *Wansung* (완성/完成 *wanseong*), which means "precomposing."

Hangul can be composed of two or three jamo (some jamo are considered compound). Johab uses 19 initial jamo (consonants), 21 medial jamo (vowels), and 27 final jamo (consonants; 28 when you include the "fill" character for hangul containing only two jamo). Multiplying these numbers (19×21×28) results in 11,172.

Johab is best explained in the context of encoding methods, so further discussion is deferred until Chapter 4.

KS X 1002:1991

South Korea (Republic of Korea) developed an extended character set designated KS X 1002:1991, *Code for Information Interchange Supplementary Set* (정보 교환용 부호 확장 세트 *jeongbo gyohwanyong buho hwagjang seteu*).† This character set, established on December 31, 1991, provides an additional 3,605 hangul (all of which, by the way, are covered by Johab, Unified Hangul Code, and Unicode Version 2.0—you will learn about these later in the book), 2,856 hanja (ordered by reading), and 1,188 other characters, for a total of 7,649 characters. These 2,856

* Encoding all 11,172 possible modern hangul is almost like encoding all possible three-letter words in English—while all combinations are possible, only a fraction represent *real* words.

† Formerly KS C 5657-1991.

hanja a listed in Appendix M, *KS X 1002:1991 Hanja Table*. Table 3-71 lists the characters in KS X 1002:1991.

Table 3-71: The KS X 1002:1991 Character Set

Row	Characters	Content
1–7	613	Lowercase and uppercase Latin characters with diacritics
8–10	273	Lowercase and uppercase Greek characters with diacritics
11–13	275	Miscellaneous symbols
14	27	Compound jamo
15	0	Unassigned
16–36	1,930	Hangul (last is 36-50)
37–54	1,675	Yesgeulja[a] (last is 54-77)
55–85	2,856	Hanja (last is 85-36)
86–94	0	Unassigned

[a] Written 옛글자 (*yesgeulja*), meaning "old hangul."

It is interesting to note that the 2,856 hanja enumerated by this standard are handwritten in the official KS X 1002:1991 manual (as was the case in China's GB 7589-87 and GB 7590-87).

I have encountered the following errors and inconsistencies during my perusal of the KS X 1002:1991 manual:

- Page 2 of the manual states that rows 1 through 7 enumerate 615 characters, but I counted only 613—page 19 of the standard seems to include two duplicate characters at Row-Cell values 01-23 (0x2137) and 01-90 (0x217A): "X" and "TM"
- Page 2 of the manual also states that rows 37 through 54 contain 1,677 hangul, but I counted only 1,675

I have not heard of a revised version of KS X 1002:1991, so I assume that these errors and inconsistencies are still present in the standard.

KPS 9566-97

North Korea (officially, Democratic People's Republic of Korea or DPRK; 조선 민주주의 인민 공화국/朝鮮民主主義人民共和國 *coseon mincucuyi inmin konghwakuk*) developed their own character set standard that enumerates hangul and hanja in April of 1997, called KPS 9566-97, *DPRK Standard Korean Graphic Character Set for Information Interchange*. It is similar to South Korea's KS X 1001:1992 in many respects, but also different in many ways. This standard enumerates a total of 8,259 characters.

Table 3-72 lists the characters that make up KPS 9566-97.

Table 3-72: The KPS 9566-97 Character Set

Row	Characters	Content
1	83	55 punctuation symbols plus 28 vertical variants
2	94	Miscellaneous symbols
3	62	Numerals 0–9, upper- and lowercase Latin alphabet
4	71	65 jamo (hangul elements), 6 hangul
5	66	Upper- and lowercase Cyrillic alphabet
6	68	48 upper- and lowercase Greek alphabet, upper- and lowercase Roman numerals 1–10
7	88	Encircled numerals 1–30, 28 encircled jamo and hangul, 10 superscripts 0–9, 10 subscripts 0–9, 10 fractions
8	94	Unit symbols and Latin ligatures
9	68	Line-drawing elements
10	83	Hiragana
11	86	Katakana
12	64	Miscellaneous symbols
13–15	0	Unassigned
16–44	2,679	Hangul (last is 44-47)
45–94	4,653	Hanja (last is 94-47)

The designers of KPS 9566-97 appear to have been inspired by KS X 1001:1992, but chose not to multiply encode hanja with multiple readings. They also decided to directly encode vertical variants in row 1—a total of 28 vertical characters.

Interestingly, row 4 includes six multiple-encoded hangul (not jamo). 04-72 through 04-74 are the three hangul 김일성 (*kim il seong*), which represent the name of the former leader of DPRK, Kim Il Sung. 04-75 through 04-77 are the three hangul 김정일 (*kim ceong il*), which represent the name of the current leader of DPRK, Kim Jong Il (Kim Il Sung's son).

The user-defined region of KPS 9566-97 includes a total of 188 code points, and is comprised of all of row 15 (94 code points), the last half of row 44 (47 code points), and the last half of row 94 (47 code points).

There is one particular hangul in KPS 9566-97 that is not in KS X 1001:1992, and is used to render the name of a famous Korean literary work. The hangul 똠 (*ddom*) as used in the book title 똠방각하 (*ddom bang gag ha*) is available as KPS 9566-97 38-02, Johab 0x99B1, and Unicode 0xB620. This represents a classic example that illustrates why KS X 1001:1992's 2,350 hangul are not sufficient.

GB 12052-89

What is a GB standard doing in a section about Korean character sets? Consider this. There is a rather large Korean population in China (there have been border disputes with China for thousands of years; and many Koreans escaped Japanese colonization, during the period 1910–1945, by moving to the southern parts of China), and they need a character set standard for communicating with each other using hangul.

This character set standard, designated GB 12052-89, *Korean Character Coded Character Set for Information Interchange* (信息交换用朝鲜文字编码字符集 *xìnxī jiāohuàn yòng cháoxiān wénzì biānmǎ zìfújí*), is a Korean character set standard established by China on July 1, 1990, and enumerates a total of 5,979 characters. GB 12052-89 has no relationship nor compatibility with Korea's KS X 1001:1992. Table 3-73 lists the characters in GB 12052-89.

Table 3-73: The GB 12052-89 Character Set

Row	Characters	Content
1	94	Miscellaneous symbols
2	72	Numerals 1–20 with period, parenthesized numerals 1–20, encircled numerals 1–10, parenthesized hanzi numerals 1–20, uppercase Roman numerals 1–12
3	94	Full-width GB 1988-89 (GB-Roman; equivalent to ASCII)[a]
4	83	Hiragana
5	86	Katakana
6	48	Upper- and lowercase Greek alphabet
7	66	Upper- and lowercase Cyrillic alphabet
8	63	26 full-width pinyin characters, 37 zhuyin (bopomofo) characters
9	76	Line-drawing elements
10–15	0	Unassigned
16–37	2,068	Level 1 hangul, Part 1 (last is 37-94)
38–52	1,356	Level 1 hangul, Part 2 (last is 52-40)
53–72	1,873	Level 2 hangul (71-88 is unassigned; last is 72-88)[b]
73–94	0	Unassigned

[a] The yuan symbol that is normally at Row-Cell 03-04 is a dollar sign instead in this character set standard.
[b] The first 1,779 of these characters are hangul (53-01 through 71-87), and the remainder are 94 hanja (71-89 through 72-88).

Rows 1 through 9 look a lot like GB 2312-80, eh? Well, they're identical, except for 03-04, which is a dollar sign (＄) instead of GB 2312-80's yuan symbol (￥).

I have noted the following errors and inconsistencies during my ventures into the GB 12052-89 manual:

- Page 1 of the manual correctly states that a total of 5,979 characters are enumerated (682 symbols plus 5,297 hangul and hanja)
- But, page 3 of the manual states that rows 53 through 72 enumerate 1,876 characters, but I counted only 1,873—rows 53 through 71 enumerate 1,779 hangul, and rows 71 and 72 enumerate 94 hanja

I have not heard of a revised version of GB 12052-89, so I can only assume that these errors and inconsistencies are still present in the standard.

Vietnamese Character Set Standards

Vietnam (Việt Nam) has recently joined the small band of renegade locales that have developed character set standards enumerating thousands of Chinese and Chinese-like characters. They have thus far established two character set standards that enumerate Chinese characters. All Vietnamese standards begin with a TCVN designation, which stands for *Tiêu Chuẩn Việt Nam* (meaning "Vietnamese Standard").

Both standards covered in this section enumerate only Chinese or Chinese-like characters (chữ Hán or chữ Nôm), and are encoded in a single 94×94 matrix as two separate levels. Table 3-74 illustrates the allocation of characters by row.

Table 3-74: The TCVN 5773:1993 and TCVN 6056:1995 Character Sets

Row	Characters	Content
1–15	0	Unassigned; reserved for symbols
16–41	2,357	TCVN 5773:1993 (last is 41-07)
42–77	3,311	TCVN 6056:1995 (last is 77-21)
78–94	0	Unassigned

Note how both character sets are included in one superset—they are more or less treated as separate levels.

TCVN 5773:1993

Vietnam's very first character set that enumerates Chinese characters is designated TCVN 5773:1993, *Công Nghệ Thông Tin—Bộ Mã Chuẩn 16-Bit Chữ Nôm Dùng Trong Trao Đổi Thông Tin (Information Technology—Nom 16-Bit Standard Code Set for Information Interchange)*, and was established on December 31, 1993.

TCVN 5773:1993 enumerates 2,357 Chinese characters, most of which are considered to be "Nom proper" (chữ Nôm) characters. That is, characters that appear to be of Chinese origin, but are in fact of Vietnamese origin. Think of them as Vietnamese-made Chinese characters.* The ordering of the characters is by radical, then total number of strokes. Approximately 600 are considered to be of genuine Chinese origin (chữ Hán).

TCVN 5773:1993 provides mappings to ISO 10646-1:1993 (equivalent for these purposes to Unicode) for every character, as follows:

- 587 characters are included in the standard set of 20,902 Chinese characters in Unicode)
- 1,770 characters map to the user-defined region of ISO 10646-1:1993, beginning at 0xA000 and ending at 0xA6E9

TCVN 5773:1993 distinguishes these two types of mappings *implicitly* by the reference ISO 10646-1:1993 code points. This standard also *explicitly* distinguishes these two types of mappings by using one of two encoding prefixes:

- U+ (for example, U+4EC9) refers to mappings into ISO 10646-1:1993's standard set of 20,902 Chinese characters (the 587 characters from above)
- V+ (for example, V+A000) refers to mappings into ISO 10646-1:1993's user-defined region (the 1,770 characters from above)

TCVN 6056:1995

A second Vietnamese character set standard, designated TCVN 6056:1995, *Công nghệ thông tin—Bộ Mã Chuẩn 16-Bit Chữ Nôm Dùng Trong Trao Đổi Thông Tin—Chữ Nôm Hán* (*Information Technology—Nom 16-Bit Standard Code for Information Interchange—Han Nom Character*), enumerates an additional 3,311 Chinese characters. The original TCVN 6056:1995 enumerated 3,349 characters, but it has since been revised. 38 duplicate characters—duplicates of characters in both TCVN 5773:1993 and TCVN 6056:1995 itself—have been removed from the character set.

While TCVN 5773:1993 included both Chinese (chữ Hán) and "Nom proper" (chữ Nôm) characters, this standard includes only chữ Hán (characters of true Chinese origin). Appendix O, *TCVN 6056:1995 Table*, provides a complete TCVN 6056:1995 code table.

As was the case with TCVN 5773:1993, these characters are ordered by radical, then total number of strokes, and references to ISO 10646-1:1993 code points are provided for reference. All 3,311 of these characters map to ISO 10646-1:1993 BMP

* *Chữ Nôm* are different from Japanese *kokuji* in that they are never used in texts that are written using characters strictly of Chinese origin. See page 64 in Chapter 2 for more details.

code points. Remember that TCVN 5773:1993 mapped most of its characters into ISO 10646-1:1993's user-defined region.

International Character Set Standards

Many organizations, corporations, and researchers have been actively involved in the development of international character set standards in an attempt to provide most of the world's written languages in a single repertoire of characters. One early attempt was Xerox's XCCS (Xerox Character Code Standard). CCCII can also be considered such an attempt. These character sets should be of interest to you because they include tens of thousands of Chinese characters, and thousands of hangul.

Table 3-75 lists the international character set standards covered in this section, all of which are based on different versions of Unicode.

Table 3-75: International Character Set Standards

Standard	Chinese Characters	Hangul	Other	User-defined
Unicode Version 1.0	20,902	2,350	5,049	5,632
Unicode Version 1.1	20,902	6,656[a]	6,610	6,400
Unicode Version 2.0	20,902	11,172	6,811	6,400
Unicode Version 2.1	20,902	11,172	6,813	6,400
ISO 10646-1:1993[b]	*Same as Unicode Version 1.1*			
GB 13000.1-93	*Same as Unicode Version 1.1*			
JIS X 0221-1995	*Same as Unicode Version 1.1*			
KS X 1005-1:1995	*Same as Unicode Version 2.0*			

[a] This figure is composed of 2,350 basic hangul (from KS X 1001:1992), 1,930 Supplemental Hangul A (from KS X 1002:1991), and 2,376 Supplemental Hangul B (source unknown to this author).
[b] ISO 10646-1:1993 with amendments 1 through 7 is identical to Unicode Version 2.0. Amendment 8 makes it identical to Unicode Version 2.1.

Note that Unicode Version 1.0 never became a national or international standard—it is obsolete.

Unicode and ISO 10646-1:1993

The International Organization for Standardization (ISO) and The Unicode Consortium have jointly developed a multilingual character set designed to combine the majority of the world's writing systems and character set standards into a larger repertoire of characters.

ISO designated this standard ISO 10646-1:1993, and the characters have two- and four-byte representations.

The Unicode Consortium calls their standard Unicode, and uses a variable-length 16-bit representation called UTF-16 (for all practical purposes, 16 bits are equivalent to two bytes). Unicode is a subset of ISO 10646-1:1993, from a pure encoding point of view, and is equivalent to what is called the *Basic Multilingual Plane* (BMP) of ISO 10646-1:1993.* It is called the BMP because ISO 10646-1:1993 is composed of groups of planes. The only characters currently defined in either standard are those in the BMP.

Unicode was constructed in an attempt to unify all Chinese characters from the many CJKV national character set standards into a single set of Chinese characters. This effort became incorrectly known as *Han Unification*. "Han" comes from the Chinese reading of the Chinese character 漢—in Chinese, Korean, and Vietnamese it is read *han*, and in Japanese it is read *kan*. Note that this effort does not represent *true* unification of Chinese characters due to the source separation rule (to be explained shortly) and other factors. So, why is Han Unification not an appropriate way to describe the process that took place to create this character set?

If we consider the evolutionary processes that have affected Chinese characters over the course of history, we see that they have diversified into a number of locale-specific variations. That is, they were adapted by several non-Chinese cultures, such as Japan, Korea, and Vietnam. With any borrowing, whether it is from the lexicon (that is, words) or the orthography (writing system), there is a certain amount of change that is almost always guaranteed to take place over time. As Joe Becker so succinctly put it, diversification and variation are the real historical processes that actually took place, but the so-called Han Unification is *not* a real process. Rather, it has been called diversification and variation as seen through a mirror.

The real goal of those who compiled the Chinese characters in Unicode was to simply provide coverage for the major CJKV character set standards existing at the time, so that *every* Chinese character in these standards would have an equivalent code point in Unicode. This provides users and developers with two very important things:

- A much larger repertoire of characters than found in other CJKV character set standards
- Compatibility with the characters in existing CJKV character set standards—this is perhaps more important than you think

Unicode, when encoded according to UCS-2, provides 65,536 16-bit code points. As of this writing, 38,887 of these code points have been assigned characters (that is, for Unicode Version 2.1—38,885 for Version 2.0, 28,301 for Version 1.0, and

* This distinction is somewhat meaningless now that UTF-16 is part of both standards.

34,168 for Version 1.1). The character space for Unicode is set in a 256×256 matrix. Table 3-76 details, by row, how many characters are currently assigned to Unicode (Version 2.1).

Table 3-76: The Unicode Version 2.1 Character Set

Row	Characters	Content
0–16	2,499	Alphabets
17	240	Jamo
18–29	0	Unassigned
30–31	479	Latin and Greek precombined forms
32–39	1,378	Symbols
40–47	0	Unassigned
48–51	842	CJK phonetics and symbols
52–77	0	Unassigned
78–159	20,902	CJK unified ideographs
160–171	0	Unassigned
172–215	11,172	Hangul
216–223	0	Surrogates Area[a]
224–248	0	Private Use Area
249–250	302	CJK compatibility ideographs
251–255	1,073	Compatibility forms and specials

[a] This newly established Surrogates Area provides a mechanism for extending Unicode to support 1,048,576 additional code points. More details about this later in this chapter and in Chapter 4.

The characters from Table 3-76 that are of special interest to this book are the 20,902 Chinese characters and the 11,172 hangul (there are also relevant characters in other blocks, such as those containing CJK phonetics, symbols, and compatibility ideographs). The remaining characters, for the most part, are beyond the scope and interest of this book.

As mentioned above, these 20,902 Chinese characters are the result of merging many character set standards into one larger repertoire. According to *The Unicode Standard, Version 2.0*, most of the Chinese characters contained in the character set standards listed in Table 3-77 have been included.

Table 3-77: Character Sets Included in Unicode Chinese Character Subset

Character Set Standard	Country	Chinese Characters
ANSI Z39.64-1989 (EACC)	USA	13,481
Xerox Chinese	USA	9,776
GB 2312-80	China	6,763

Table 3-77: Character Sets Included in Unicode Chinese Character Subset (continued)

Character Set Standard	Country	Chinese Characters
GB/T 12345-90	China	2,180
GB 7589-87	China	4,835
GB 7590-87	China	2,842
General Use Characters for Modern Chinese[a]	China	41
GB 8565.2-88	China	290
GB 12052-89	China	94
PRC Telegraph Code	China	≈8,000
Big Five[b]	Taiwan	13,053
CCCII, Level 1	Taiwan	4,808
CNS 11643-1986 Planes 1	Taiwan	5,401
CNS 11643-1986 Planes 2	Taiwan	7,650
CNS 11643-1986 Plane 14[c]	Taiwan	4,198
Taiwan Telegraph Code	Taiwan	9,040
JIS X 0208-1990 (and JIS X 0208:1997)[d]	Japan	6,356
JIS X 0212-1990	Japan	5,801
KS X 1001:1992	Korea	4,620
KS X 1002:1991	Korea	2,856
TCVN 6056:1995	Vietnam	3,323

[a] Better known as 现代汉语通用字表 (*xiàndài hànyǔ tōngyòngzì biǎo*).
[b] Two of these hanzi are duplicately encoded, and are mapped into Unicode's compatibility zone.
[c] CNS 11643-1986 Plane 14 contains 6,319 hanzi.
[d] There are normally considered to be 6,355 kanji in JIS X 0208:1997—the extra character, 仝 (01-24), is in its non-kanji region.

Table 3-77 lists approximately 121,000 Chinese characters in total, but when they were merged according to a set of strict and accurate rules, they became 20,902 unique characters. These Chinese characters are subsequently arranged by radical, then of additional strokes excluding the radical (similar to the ordering of GB 2312-80 Level 2 and JIS X 0208:1997 Level 2). Redundant characters among the approximately 121,000 Chinese characters that are represented in Table 3-77 were removed to form the final set of 20,902 characters.

The two Chinese characters in Table 3-78 have similar structure, similar enough, in fact, to unify them. However, they have completely unrelated etymologies and meanings, so merging did not take place.

Table 3-78: Example of Ununified Chinese Characters

Chinese Character	Meaning
土	*earth*
士	*scholar, knight*

As illustrated in Table 3-78, the relative lengths of strokes in Chinese characters *can* change their meaning. However, Chinese characters such as those in Table 3-79 have been unified because their difference lies in their glyphs, which can be thought of as a simple typeface style issue.

Table 3-79: Example of an Unified Chinese Character

Chinese Character	Meaning	Source Set	Row-Cell
父	*father*	JIS X 0208-1983	41-67
父	*father*	JIS X 0208-1990	41-67

Note how these are microscopic variations of the same structure, and that they have the same meaning. They also share the same encoding, but come from different versions of the JIS X 0208 character set standard. The earlier versions of JIS X 0208-1990 are not considered part of the Japanese sources for Unicode—only JIS X 0208-1990 (now JIS X 0208:1997) and JIS X 0212-1990 were used.

Chinese character glyphs can be compared using a three-dimensional model. The X axis (semantic) separates characters by their meaning. The Y axis (abstract shape) separates a character on the X axis into its abstract shapes. Traditional and simplified forms of a particular Chinese character fall into the same X axis position, but have different positions along the Y axis. The Z axis (typeface) separates a character into glyph differences. Only Z-axis differences were merged in Unicode. Table 3-79 provided an example of a Z-axis difference. Glyph differences are usually found when using different typefaces to produce the same character. The same character in different languages may also appear differently because of locale differences that have resulted from diversification. Figure 3-1 illustrates the three-axis model used for comparing Chinese character glyphs.

Unfortunately, early standards were inconsistent in their encoding models for Chinese character glyphs, resulting in separately encoded Y-axis variants. There are four sets of standards from which the Unicode Chinese character subset was derived: Chinese, Taiwanese, Japanese, and Korean character sets. For example, there are two Japanese character sets in the Japanese source set: JIS X 0208-1990 (now JIS X 0208:1997) and JIS X 0212-1990. Unification of two characters cannot take place if they have unique encoded positions within a single source set. Table 3-80 lists the kanji 剣 and its five variants—all of these characters have unique code positions in JIS X 0208:1997, and are thus not unified.* This effectively ensures that round-trip conversion is successful. This is also why the two duplicately encoded hanzi of Big Five and the 268 multiply encoded hanja of KS X 1001:1992 are in Unicode's CJK Compatibility Zone (rows 249 and 250 in Table

* Another variant of 剣 is 剑 (*jiàn*), but that is outside the context of this Japanese-specific discussion.

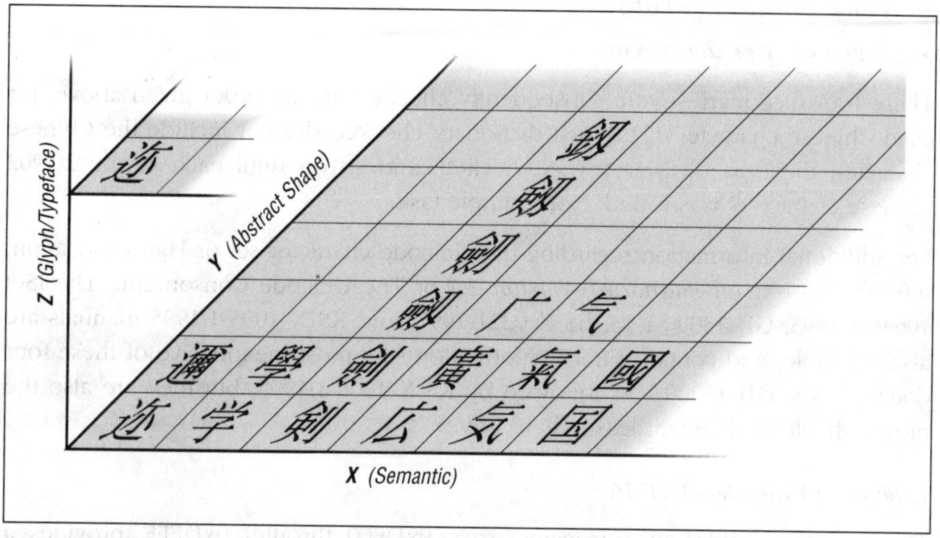

Figure 3-1: Three-axis model for comparing Chinese character glyphs

3-76 on page 122). JIS X 0208:1997 and JIS X 0212-1990 contain many kanji that could potentially be unified: the kanji in Table 3-80 represent but a single example.

Table 3-80: Six Kanji from JIS X 0208:1997 That Are Not Unified

	JIS X 0208:1997	Unicode
剣	23-85	5263
劍	49-88	528D
劔	49-89	5294
劒	49-90	5292
剱	49-91	5271
釼	78-63	91FC

Note how each of these six Chinese characters has unique code points, both in the source character set (JIS X 0208:1997) and in Unicode. This is by design.

The result of all this effort was a collection of Chinese characters whose ordering can be considered culturally neutral. How Chinese characters are ordered by radical is often locale-specific, and devising an ordering that would please all locales that use Chinese characters was a very difficult task. We could call this pan-cultural. The CJK Joint Research Group (CJK-JRG), an ad-hoc committee of ISO/IEC JTC1/SC2/WG2 (Joint Technical Committee 1, Subcommittee 2, Working Group 2), selected four Chinese character dictionaries, reflecting Chinese character usage in CJKV locales:

- Common traditional (康熙字典 *kāngxī zìdiǎn*)
- Japan (大漢和辭典 *dai kanwa jiten*)

- China (汉语大字典 *hànyǔ dà zìdiǎn*)
- Korea (大字源 *daejaweon*)

These four dictionaries were subsequently checked, in the order given above, for each Chinese character. If the first dictionary checked did not include the Chinese character, the next dictionary was checked, and so on until each of the 20,902 Chinese characters was found. Not a simple task.

For additional information regarding the Unicode character set or Han Unification, refer to *The Unicode Standard, Version 2.0* or The Unicode Consortium.* The ISO 10646-1:1993, GB 13000.1-93, JIS X 0221-1995, and KS X 1005-1:1995 manuals are also available, and contain similar information (the most inexpensive of these four documents is GB 13000.1-93 followed by KS X 1005-1:1995, but they are also the most difficult to obtain, at least where I live).

Extending Unicode—UTF-16

The recently established Surrogates Area, 0xD800 through 0xDFFF, provides a method for extending Unicode to accommodate 1,048,576 additional code points. This is better known as UTF-16, which is described in Chapter 4 starting on page 194. Here is how the Surrogates Area works:

- The High Surrogates, 0xD800 through 0xDBFF, represent the first element in a surrogate character
- The Low Surrogates, 0xDC00 through 0xDFFF, represent the second element in a surrogate character

For example, 0xD800DC00 and 0xDBFFDFFF represent the first and last characters in the Surrogates area (big endian), respectively.

In essence, characters encoded in the Surrogates Area are represented by four bytes (or, two 16-bit values). 2,048 code points within the BMP are sacrificed to create an additional 1,048,576 code points. Not a bad trade-off!

One benefit of this technique may not be that obvious: one always knows whether a particular 16-bit unit (or two bytes) represents the first or second element of a surrogate character, by virtue of each element using a different encoding range. This scheme allows software processing to be simpler than if the two ranges overlapped.

131,072 of the code points in the Surrogates Area are reserved for user-defined characters (Private Use). This effectively means that Unicode now provides 137,472 user-defined code points (6,400 plus 131,072).

---

* *http://www.unicode.org/*

Additional Chinese characters for Unicode

The IRG (Ideographic Rapporteur Group*) has compiled an additional set of Chinese characters, 6,582 total, that will eventually become part of Unicode, called "CJK Unified Ideographs Extension A."† It is not yet known exactly where these additional 6,582 characters will be encoded within Unicode, but possibly they will occupy the region left vacant from the 6,656 hangul in Unicode Version 1.1 (this effectively means the range 0x3400 through 0x4DB5).

However, some preliminary mapping data was made available for this set of 6,582 characters, and Table 3-81 lists CJKV character set standards, along with the number of mappings (the number of mappings are according to material dated from February 25, 1997, when there were 6,584 characters in this set—consider the numbers to be approximate figures).

Table 3-81: Mappings for Unicode's CJK Unified Ideographs Extension A

Character Set Standard	Mappings
GB/T 13131-9X	2,391
GB/T 13132-9X	1,226
General Use Characters for Modern Chinese[a]	120
Singapore characters	227
CNS 11643-1992 Plane 3	2,178
CNS 11643-1992 Plane 4	2,912
CNS 11643-1992 Plane 5	392
CNS 11643-1992 Plane 6	194
CNS 11643-1992 Plane 7	133
CNS 11643-1986 Plane 15	71
Unified Japanese IT Vendors Contemporary Ideographs, 1993	660
PKS C 5700-2 1994[b]	1,834
TCVN 5773:1993	128

[a] Better known as 现代汉语通用字表 (*xiàndài hànyǔ tōngyòngzì biǎo*).
[b] This could be a draft of Part 2 of KS X 1005-1:1995.

This set of 6,582 Chinese characters may become the last repertoire of Chinese characters to be added to ISO 10646-1:1993's BMP. Any further additions will be assigned to code points outside of the BMP, hopefully through the newly established Surrogates Area.

* *http://www.cs.cuhk.edu.hk/~irg/*

† The original proposal included 6,585 Chinese characters, but three were found to be duplicates of characters in the CJK compatibility ideographs region and were subsequently excised.

Other characters that are being added to Unicode include a separate listing of the 214 classical radicals (0x2F00 through 0x2FDF), along with 31 radical variants (0x2FE0 through 0x2FFF). Unicode Version 3.0, which is slated to follow Version 2.1, will most likely include all of these additional characters plus more.

CJKV character form differences

The result of the processes that took place when developing Unicode, from a practical point of view, is a set of 20,902 partially unified Chinese characters. This has certain implications for those who feel that they can build a single typeface that will satisfy the character-form criteria for all CJKV locales.

Table 3-82 illustrates several Chinese characters contained in Unicode, along with example representations in four of the CJKV locales.

Table 3-82: CJKV Character Form Differences

Unicode	China	Taiwan	Japan	Korea
4E00	一	一	一	一
4E0E	与	与	与	
5224	判	判	判	判
5668	器	器	器	器
5B57	字	字	字	字
6D77	海	海	海	海
9038	逸	逸	逸	逸
9AA8	骨	骨	骨	骨

Note how 0x4E00 can use the same character form (glyph) across all four CJKV locales, but that the others are slightly different across locales. This is not a criticism of Unicode, but rather the reality one must deal with when building products based on Unicode that are designed to cover more than one CJKV locale.

I must admit that the glyphs illustrated in Table 3-82 can be misleading if not interpreted correctly. In some cases, the differences can be attributed to simple differences in typeface design, but there are clear cases of locale-specific differences that would still exist regardless of typeface design, such as 骨 versus 骨 (specifically, pay attention to the top portion).

GB 13000.1-93

The Chinese translation of ISO 10646-1:1993 is designated GB 13000.1-93 (信息技术—通用多八位编码字符集 (UCS)—第一部分: 体系结构与基本多文种平面 *xīnxì jìshù—tōngyòng duōbāwèi biānmǎ zìfújí (UCS)—dìyī bùfen: tǐxì jiégòu yǔ jīběn duōwénzhǒng píngmiàn*), established on August 1, 1994. GB 13000.1-93 appears to be a straight translation. As indicated in Table 3-75 on page 120, GB 13000.1-93 is aligned with Unicode Version 1.1.

JIS X 0221-1995

The Japanese translation of ISO 10646-1:1993 is designated JIS X 0221-1995 (国際符号化文字集合 (UCS)—第 1 部：体系及び基本多言語面 *kokusai fugōka moji shūgō (UCS)—daiichibu: taikei oyobi kihon tagengomen*), and was established on January 1, 1995. JIS X 0221-1995 contains additional sections (pp 799–1027) that list Japanese-specific information, the most interest of which are the following:

- A table that provides the Chinese 康熙字典 (*kāngxī zìdiǎn*) and Japanese 大漢和辭典 (*dai kanwa jiten*) index numbers for all 20,902 Chinese characters
- A section that describes the Japanese subsets

The Japanese subsets as described in JIS X 0221-1995 are listed in Table 3-83. The subsets are described in terms of seven parts.

Table 3-83: JIS X 0221-1995's Japanese Subrepertoires

Subrepertoire	Characters	Description
Basic Japanese	6,884	JIS X 0208:1997, JIS X 0201-1997
Japanese Non-ideographic Supplement	1,913	JIS X 0212-1990 non-kanji plus other non-kanji
Japanese Ideographic Supplement 1	918	JIS X 0212-1990 kanji
Japanese Ideographic Supplement 2	4,883	Remainder of JIS X 0212-1990
Japanese Ideographic Supplement 3	8,745	Remainder of Chinese characters
Full-width Alphanumeric	94	For compatibility
Half-width Katakana	63	For compatibility

As indicated in Table 3-75 on page 120, JIS X 0221-1995 is aligned with Unicode Version 1.1.

KS X 1005-1:1995

The Korean translation of ISO 10646-1:1993, designated KS X 1005-1:1995 (국제 문자 부호계 (UCS) 제 1 부 : 구조 및 기본 다국어 평면 *gugje munja buhogye (UCS) je 1 bu: gujo mic gibon dagugeo pyeongmyeon*), was established on December 7,

1995.* While the front matter is translated into Korean, the annexes are left untranslated. And, as indicated in Table 3-75 on page 120, KS X 1005-1:1995 is aligned with Unicode Version 2.0.

Character Set Standard Oddities

While the contents of the character set standards are, for the most part, accepted by software developers and users, many of them do exhibit some interesting characteristics. For example, some character set standards contain characters that do not (or, should not) exist (although one could argue that such characters now exist by virtue of being in a character set standard), some do not contain some characters that should have been included (because they are needed to complete character pairs), and some became endowed with fictitious extensions.

Phantom Chinese Characters

While the Chinese characters that are included in non-coded character set standards have been carefully accounted for during the development process, there are documented cases of coded character sets that include Chinese characters whose origins cannot be determined. These are called "phantom" Chinese characters, written 幽霊漢字 (*yūrei kanji*) in Japanese.

During the development of JIS X 0208:1997, a team of researchers lead by Kohji Shibano (芝野耕司 *shibano kōji*) attempted to account for every kanji included in the standard. While some marginal cases were discovered during this lengthy process that involved sifting through countless name records, at least one phantom character was identified. It is 彁, which is JIS X 0208:1997 Row-Cell 55-27. The description of their findings starts on page 291 of the standard document.

Interestingly, any character set standard that is in any way based on JIS X 0208:1997 (such as vendor extensions thereof, and even ISO 10646-1:1993) will inherit this phantom character. The same can be said about other coded character set standard that happen to include phantom characters.

Incomplete Chinese Character Pairs

Several studies of the GB 2312-80 character set standard have been conducted since its establishment, and some of them point out the fact that for several two-hanzi words (or Chinese character pairs), only one of the component hanzi is in GB 2312-80. The most remarkable aspect of this phenomenon is that these hanzi almost always only appear together—almost never with other hanzi or in isola-

* Formerly KS C 5700-1995.

tion. These pairs of hanzi are called 连绵字 or 联绵字 (both transliterated *liánmiánzì*) in Chinese.

One such study, conducted by Dejin Wang (王德进 *wáng déjìn*) and Sheying Zhang (张社英 *zhāng shèyīng*) in 1989, identified six such cases in which one of the component hanzi is in GB 7589-87 (four cases), GB 7590-87 (one case), or GB 13000.1-93 (one case).* The following are two examples of two-hanzi compounds that contain one hanzi not in GB 2312-80:

> 鸺鹠 *xiūliú* (GB 2312-80 80-28, GB 7589-87 62-11), meaning "owlet"
> 欷歔 *xīxū* (GB 2312-80 76-04, GB 7590-87 48-24), meaning "to sob, sigh"

GB 7589-87 62-11 corresponds to ISO 10646-1:1993 0x9DB9 and GBK 0xFA56. GB 7590-87 48-24 corresponds to ISO 10646-1:1993 0x6B54 and GBK 0x9A5B.

Fictitious Character Set Extensions

When the 20,902 Chinese characters in ISO 10646-1:1993 (Unicode) were compiled from numerous national standards, the respective national-standard–developing organizations submitted character set materials to the CJK-JRG (CJK Joint Research Group, now the IRG, Ideographic Rapporteur Group) for inclusion. However, in order to ensure that certain Chinese characters became part of the final set of 20,902 characters, at least two national standards included fictitious extensions. That is, Chinese characters that are not part of the standard, and never likely to be, were added. Affected character sets include China's GB/T 12345-90 and Taiwan's CNS 11643-1986 Plane 14 (keep in mind that CNS 11643-1992 was not yet published at that time).

For GB/T 12345-90, any code point beyond Row-Cell 89-09 should be questioned, and is likely to fall into this area. For CNS 11643-1986 Plane 14, any code point beyond Row-Cell 68-21 should be in doubt. When dealing with CNS 11643-1992 Plane 3 (identical to the first 6,148 hanzi in CNS 11643-1986 Plane 14—the remaining 171 hanzi became scattered throughout CNS 11643-1992 Plane 4), any code point beyond Row-Cell 66-38 may be problematic.

An alternative set of Unicode mapping tables have been developed by Koichi Yasuoka (安岡孝一 *yasuoka kōichi*), ones that do not include these fictitious character set extensions.†

* The study appeared in a paper entitled "Amendments on the GB 2312-80" (关于修改GB 2312-80的几点意见 *guānyú xiūgǎi GB 2312-80 de jǐdiǎn yìjian*), published in *Proceedings Papers of International Symposium on Standardization for Chinese Information Processing* (中文信息处理标准化国际研讨会论文集 *zhōngwén xìnxī chǔlǐ biāozhǔnhuà guójì yántǎohuì lùnwénjí*), 1989, also known as SCIP 89.

† *http://www.kudpc.kyoto-u.ac.jp/~yasuoka/CJK.html*

Non-Coded Versus Coded Character Sets

Non-coded character sets relate to coded ones in a variety of ways, depending on the locale. This section illustrates how coded character set standards attempt to follow and keep pace with non-coded character set standards, using the situations in China, Taiwan, Japan, and Korea as examples.

China

All 2,500 Chángyòng Hànzì are included in GB 2312-80. All but five are in Level 1 hanzi. For the 1,000 Cìchángyòng Hànzì, 998 are in GB 2312-80. 880 are in Level 1 hanzi, 118 in Level 2 hanzi, then finally 2 are in GB 7589-87. Table 3-84 indicates how these two hanzi can be mapped.

Table 3-84: Two Cìchángyòng Hànzì Not in GB 2312-80

Hanzi	GB 7589-87	GB 8565.2-88	GB/T 12345-90	GBK
啰	22-51	15-93	not applicable[a]	86AA
瞭	58-43	93-47	88-49	B274

[a] Oddly enough, its traditional form, 囉, is at 88-51. Neither GB 2312-80 nor GB/T 12345-90 contain the simplified form.

The remaining 3,500 hanzi in the Tōngyòng Hànzì list are distributed as follows. 3,095 are in GB 2312-80 (380 in Level 1 hanzi, and the remaining 2,715 in Level 2 hanzi), 404 are in GB 7589-87, and one is in GB 7590-87.

Appendix R, *Chinese Character Lists*, includes the Chángyòng Hànzì and Cìchángyòng Hànzì hanzi lists broken down into the character sets and the hanzi levels that support them.

Taiwan

The list of 4,808 hanzi, which can be called Taiwan's Chángyòng Hànzì, was used as the basis for Big Five Level 1, CNS 11643-1992 (and -1986) Plane 1, and CCCII. The additional hanzi lists, such as their Cìchángyòng Hànzì, were used to define the remainder of the above coded character sets.

Japan

All of Tōyō Kanji were included in JIS Level 1 kanji of JIS C 6226-1978. When Jōyō Kanji was introduced in 1981, the additional 95 kanji and subsequent glyph changes forced the creation of JIS X 0208-1983 (first called JIS C 6226-1983, then changed to the new designation in 1987)—those extra 95 characters had to be made part of JIS Level 1 kanji (22 simplified and traditional kanji pairs exchanged code points between JIS Level 1 kanji and JIS Level 2 kanji). Appendix Q lists the 95 kanji that were added to Tōyō Kanji in 1981 in order to become Jōyō Kanji.

The kanji specified in Jinmei-yō Kanji, on the other hand, could appear in either JIS Levels 1 or 2 kanji, so that is why four kanji were appended to JIS X 0208-1983, and two to JIS X 0208-1990. Table 3-85 lists the four kanji appended to JIS Level 2 kanji in 1983 to create JIS X 0208-1983.

Table 3-85: Four Kanji Appended to JIS X 0208-1983

	JIS X 0208-1983
堯	84-01
槇	84-02
遙	84-03
瑤	84-04

And, Table 3-86 lists the two kanji that were appended to JIS Level 2 kanji in 1990 to create JIS X 0208-1990.

Table 3-86: Two Kanji Appended to JIS X 0208-1990

	JIS X 0208-1990
凜	84-05
熙	84-06

There is no direct relationship between Gakushū Kanji and coded character sets except for the fact that Gakushū Kanji is a subset of Jōyō Kanji.*

Figure 3-2 illustrates how the current versions of the non-coded Japanese character sets relate to each other, and to JIS Levels 1 and 2 kanji of JIS X 0208:1997.

Korea

The 1,800 hanja enumerated in Sangyong Hanja form a subset of the 4,888 hanja in KS X 1001:1992. But, because 268 of the hanja in KS X 1001:1992 are the result of duplicate encoding due to multiple readings, these 1,800 Sangyong Hanja need to be represented by 1,953 hanja in KS X 1001:1992. Likewise, the middle school subset containing 900 hanja become 978 KS X 1001:1992 code points.

* This means that Gakushū Kanji is a subset of JIS Level 1 kanji.

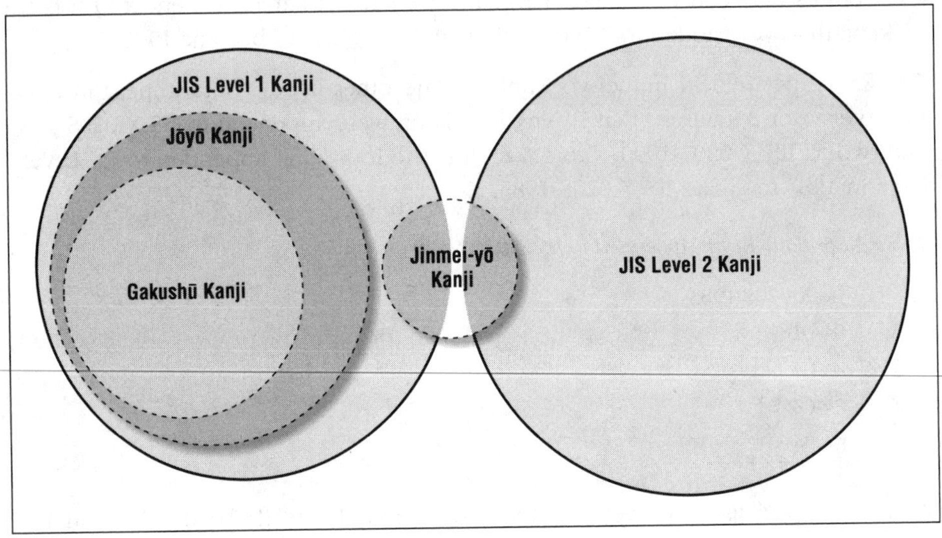

Figure 3-2: Coded versus non-coded Japanese character set standards

Information Interchange Versus Professional Publishing

Ignoring the distinction between non-coded and coded character set standards, there are two types of character sets in use today: those for information interchange, and those for professional publishing. So, what's the big deal? You'll soon find out...

Character Sets for Information Interchange

The majority of character set standards in use today were originally designed for information interchange. Well, after all, look at some of their titles. The title of JIS X 0208:1997 is *7-bit and 8-bit Double Byte Coded Kanji Sets for Information Interchange*, and the title of ASCII (officially called ANSI X3.4-1986) is *Coded Character Set—7-bit American National Standard Code for Information Interchange.* Information interchange can be defined as the process of moving data from one hardware or software configuration to another with no loss of information.

Unicode, although it provides a vast number of characters, was still designed for information interchange—building a superset based on national standards, which were designed for information interchange, still results in a character set for information interchange.

Most of today's CJKV fonts include characters from character set standards designed for information interchange. While the characters that these fonts provide are sufficient for most users' needs, they are far from ideal for professional publishing.

Character Sets for Professional Publishing

The ASCII character set, as you learned earlier, consists of 94 printable characters. ISO 8859-1:1998, the most common extension to ASCII, adds another 95 printable characters. But, these two character sets are still missing characters critical for professional publishing, such as smart (or "curly") quotes, the various dashes (such as the en-dash and em-dash), and so on. Even the most basic English-language publication requires characters outside of ISO 8859-1:1998. Most of today's non-CJKV fonts, such as Type 1 and TrueType, include characters for professional publishing. Their character set specifications evolved out of the needs of the professional publisher, and, at the same time, still provide the basic set of characters (that is, ASCII) for non-professional users.

The same is true for the CJKV locales. JIS X 0208:1997, for example, is missing characters that are necessary for professional publishing. In Japan, the following character classes and features are necessary in character sets for professional publishing:

- Proportional Latin and corresponding italic design—for Latin text
- Macroned vowels, such as ā, ī, ū, ē, and ō—for transliterated Japanese text
- Kanji variants (simplified, traditional, and other forms)
- Additional kanji
- Additional symbols
- Alternate metrics—half-width symbols/punctuation, proportional kana, and so on

More information regarding these character classes and typographic features will be presented in Chapter 7, *Typography*.

Vendors that provide professional publishing systems commonly build or supply fonts based on character sets for information interchange, but heavily supplement such fonts with the character classes listed above, usually at unique code points. Why do these character sets include characters for information interchange? Most documents that are eventually published originate on systems that process character sets for information interchange, so that is why character sets for professional publishing must use those characters as their base.

Examples of character sets for professional publishing include Fujitsu's JEF, Morisawa's MOR-CODE II, and Shaken's SK78. The major disadvantage of these and other character sets for professional publishing is that they are usually restricted to proprietary hardware or software, and thus require a major investment.

Advice to Developers

A difficult question often posed by developers is "What character sets should my product support"? The answer really depends on at least two factors:

- The number of locales that need to be supported by the product
- If the product is an application, the platforms it runs on

If your product is designed for a single CJKV locale (which really assumes two locales: the CJKV locale plus non-CJKV support, such as ASCII), you need to decide which character set to support. If at all possible, you should consider supporting the supplemental character sets (such as GB/T 12345-90 for China, additional Planes of CNS 11643-1992 for Taiwan, JIS X 0212-1990 for Japan, or KS X 1002:1991 for Korea) if resources permit. But, at a bare minimum, the basic character sets should be implemented for each CJKV locale. Table 3-87 lists the four major CJKV locales, along with their most commonly-used character set.

Table 3-87: The Most Common CJKV Character Sets

Locale	Character Set
China and Singapore	GB 2312-80
Taiwan	Big Five or CNS 11643-1992 Planes 1 and 2[a]
Hong Kong	Big Five[b]
Japan	JIS X 0208:1997
South Korea	KS X 1001:1992
North Korea	KPS 9566-97
Vietnam	TCVN 5773:1993 and TCVN 6056:1995

[a] Which one you choose depends on the underlying operating system.
[b] With Hong Kong extensions totalling to 3,049 characters, all hanzi.

Note that supporting Chinese character sets can sometimes cause confusion. Some products try to support both the Chinese locales—China and Taiwan—in a single product (such was the case with Apple Computer's Chinese Language Kit), but that is not an absolute requirement. In fact, it is sometimes beneficial to build separate products for each of the two Chinese locales, for political or other reasons.

But what about Unicode (and the international and national character set standards based on it, specifically ISO 10646-1:1993, GB 13000.1-93, JIS X 0221-1995, and KS X 1005-1:1995)? Unicode *is* here, and is being used to implement *real* software products.

Plan 9 (experimental) by AT&T Bell Laboratories, Solaris by Sun Microsystems, and Microsoft Windows (95, 98, and NT) by Microsoft are operating systems that are based on Unicode today. The Java programming language supports Unicode as its primitive `char` type and for its `String` objects. Although the above environments support Unicode in a more or less native way, developers can still take full advantage of Unicode's benefits by processing Unicode internally using virtually any programming language that supports vectors of 16-bit unsigned integers (or equivalent).

It is safe to say that unless you have a good reason not to support Unicode in your product, you should. Several Unicode-processing applications that have been shipping for years are excellent examples of Unicode's success (and success by using Unicode). JUSTSYSTEM's Ichitaro (一太郎 *ichitarō*) Japanese word processor, for example, processes Unicode internally, yet works as though it is still processing Shift-JIS internally. The following is a small sampling of software developed using Unicode in one way or another (a complete list of such software is *very* large):

- Internet Explorer
- Netscape Communicator
- Microsoft Excel
- Microsoft Word
- Oracle
- Sybase SQL Server

Those developers who need some assistance in supporting Unicode (or are developing on a platform that does not yet support Unicode) should consider the many Unicode-enabling programming environments that are now available. See the section entitled "Other Programming Environments" in Chapter 9, *Information Processing Techniques*, starting on page 413 for more details.

Here is a bit of history that may be of interest. When JIS C 6226-1978 was first introduced in Japan in 1978, it was not met with general acceptance from industry. The problem was that it did not include all the characters found in the major Japanese vendor character set standards already in place at the time. In time, JIS C 6226-1978 did become the standard in Japanese industry, and is now generally accepted. The Unicode Consortium, on the other hand, made sure that all of the characters from the major national standards were included as part of Unicode.* Unicode, like most other character sets, is constantly evolving.

* This also means that Unicode has inherited any and all errors that are in the national standards from which it was designed—with this comes compatibility with such standards.

4

Encoding Methods

In this chapter:

- *Locale-Independent Encoding Methods*
- *Locale-Specific Encoding Methods*
- *Comparing CJKV Encoding Methods*
- *International Encoding Methods*
- *Charset Designations*
- *Code Pages*
- *Code Conversion*
- *Repairing Unreadable CJKV Text*
- *Beware of Little and Big Endian Issues*
- *Advice to Developers*

In this chapter you learn how the coded character set standards presented in Chapter 3, *Character Set Standards*, are encoded for use on computer systems. To recap what you learned earlier, encoding is simply the mapping of a numeric value to a character. While there is no universally recognized CJKV encoding method, you will learn that ISO-2022, EUC, Big Five, and Shift-JIS are the most commonly used—the encodings for ISO 10646-1:1993 and related standards are now becoming more widely used and accepted. Note that the discussions in this chapter apply only to the coded character set standards (that is, they do not apply to Japan's Jōyō Kanji, Gakushū Kanji, Jinmei-yō Kanji, their predecessors, nor equivalent character sets used in other CJKV locales).

There are two encoding methods that are common to virtually every CJKV character set (with the exception of Big Five and ISO 10646-1:1993):

- ISO-2022
- EUC (Extended Unix Code)*

The exact definitions of these two encodings depend greatly on the locale. In other words, there are locale-specific instances of these encodings. There are also

* You will soon realize that although the "U" in EUC stands for "Unix," this encoding is commonly used on other platforms, such as MacOS and Windows.

a number of locale-specific encodings that are currently in use today, such as the following (locale indicated in parentheses):

- GBK (China)
- Big Five and Big Five Plus (Taiwan)
- Shift-JIS (Japan)
- Johab (Korea)

If, after reading this chapter, you have acquired a full understanding of these encoding methods and how they relate to each other, then one important goal of this book will have been achieved. If you happen to absorb the other information in this chapter, well, great! Otherwise, please treat the rest as reference material, and consult it on an as-needed basis.

The encoding methods described in this chapter fall into one of three possible categories:

- Modal
- Non-modal
- Fixed-length

Modal encoding methods require escape sequences or other special characters for the purpose of switching between character sets or different versions of the same character set—this is somewhat related to switching between one- and two-byte modes. Modal encoding methods further use what I would call a two-stage encoding process. The first stage is the mode switching initiated by the escape sequence or mode-switching characters. The second stage is the handling of the actual bytes that represent the characters. Modal encoding methods typically use seven-bit bytes. One example of modal encoding is ISO-2022 encoding, which is by far the most commonly used today. UTF-7 is also considered a modal encoding.

Non-modal encoding methods, on the other hand, make use of the numeric values of bytes in order to decide when to switch between one- and two-byte modes. These encoding methods usually make liberal use of eight-bit bytes (that is, the eighth bit of a byte is turned on or enabled), and are typically variable-length. Examples include Big Five, Big Five Plus, the various locale-specific instances of EUC, GBK, Johab, Shift-JIS, UTF-8, and UTF-16. Non-modal encodings typically use less space, in terms of number of bytes required, than modal and fixed-length encoding methods to represent the same characters. Efficiency and ease-of-use are reasons why fixed-length encodings are often used for the purpose of internal processing.

Fixed-length encoding methods use the same number of bytes to represent *all* the characters in a character set. There is no switching between one- and two-byte modes. This type of encoding method simplifies text-intensive operations, such as searching, indexing, and sorting of text, but can waste a lot of space. Examples of fixed-length encodings include ASCII, UCS-2, and UCS-4.

Note that not all of the encodings described in this chapter have been fully implemented—they have been defined by appropriate agencies, corporations, or committees so that their implementation, once it begins, is simplified.

Table 4-1 lists the common CJKV national character sets, along with the encoding methods that can support them. Most of the "Other" encoding methods are discussed in the next section where we cover locale-specific encodings.

Table 4-1: CJKV Encoding Methods and Supported Character Set Standards

Encoding	Supported Character Sets
ASCII	ASCII, GB-Roman, CNS-Roman, JIS-Roman, half-width katakana, KS-Roman, TCVN-Roman
EBCDIC/EBCDIK	ASCII, GB-Roman, CNS-Roman, JIS-Roman, half-width katakana, KS-Roman, TCVN-Roman
ISO-2022	ASCII, GB-Roman, CNS-Roman, JIS-Roman, half-width katakana, KS-Roman, TCVN-Roman,[a] GB 2312-80, GB/T 12345-90,[a] CNS 11643-1992, JIS X 0208:1997, JIS X 0212-1990, KS X 1001:1992, KS X 1002:1991,[a] TCVN 5773:1993,[a] TCVN 6056:1995[a]
EUC	ASCII, GB-Roman, CNS-Roman, JIS-Roman, half-width katakana, KS-Roman, TCVN-Roman, GB 2312-80, GB/T 12345-90, CNS 11643-1992, JIS X 0208:1997, JIS X 0212-1990, KS X 1001:1992, KS X 1002:1991, TCVN 5773:1993, TCVN 6056:1995
GBK	ASCII, GB-Roman, GB 2312-80, GB/T 12345-90[b]
Big Five	ASCII, CNS-Roman, Big Five
Big Five Plus	ASCII, CNS-Roman, Big Five Plus
Shift-JIS	ASCII, JIS-Roman, half-width katakana, JIS X 0208:1997
Johab	ASCII, KS-Roman, KS X 1001:1992

[a] No escape sequence has been registered for GB/T 12345-90 (and several other GB standards), but its design fits nicely into the ISO-2022 model.
[b] All the characters specific to GB/T 12345-90, the 2,180 traditional hanzi, are included in GBK encoding, but at different code points than in EUC-CN encoding.

Locale-Independent Encoding Methods

This is probably one of the most important sections of this book, and lays the foundation for your complete understanding of the various CJKV encoding methods, so be sure to take some extra time to read and study this material well. Some of the encoding methods described here, specifically ISO-2022 and EUC, will serve as a basis for drawing comparisons between other encodings, and for discussions that appear later in this book.

ASCII/CJKV-Roman Encodings

ASCII and CJKV-Roman (GB-Roman, CNS-Roman, JIS-Roman, KS-Roman, and TCVN-Roman) are considered different character set standards, but they share the same encoding.* The definition of the encoding method for the ASCII character set is found in the document called ISO 646:1991. The encoding method for CJKV-Roman encoding is found in GB 1988-89 (GB-Roman), JIS X 0201-1997 (JIS-Roman), KS X 1003:1993 (KS-Roman), and TCVN 5712:1993 (TCVN-Roman). The ASCII/CJKV-Roman encoding method specifies that seven bits be used, which in turn allows for 128 uniquely encoded characters. Of these 128 encoded characters, 94 comprise the ASCII/CJKV-Roman character set, and are considered printable, meaning that they are displayed on the screen with something other than only whitespace. The remaining 34 characters are non-printing, meaning that they are either control characters or whitespace. Whitespace refers to characters such as tabs and spaces. Table 4-2 lists the encoding ranges for the characters, printable and non-printable, in ASCII/CJKV-Roman encoding.

Table 4-2: ASCII and CJKV-Roman Encoding Specifications

	Decimal	Hexadecimal
Control characters	0–31	00–1F
Space character	32	20
Graphic characters	33–126	21–7E
Delete character	127	7F

Note that these values can be represented with only seven bits (the importance of this is explained later in this chapter). For Japanese, this allows the mixture of the ASCII and half-width katakana character sets when using eight-bit bytes. A more graphic representation of the ASCII/CJKV-Roman encoding method can be found in Figure 4-1.

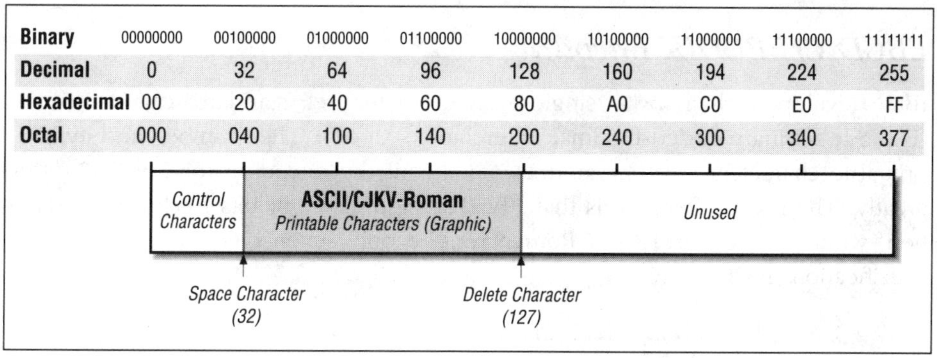

Figure 4-1: ASCII/CJKV-Roman encoding table

* With the possible exception of TCVN-Roman.

The extended ASCII character set encoding defined by ISO 8859 makes use of all eight bits, so more of the 256 possible characters available with eight bits can be encoded with graphic characters. The first 128 character positions are reserved for the ASCII character set and control characters, but the additional 128 character positions made possible with the eighth bit can vary. Exactly which characters are encoded in this extended ASCII character set depends on the implementation. The extended ASCII characters specified in each of these ten parts fall into the range 0xA1–0xFF. However, not all encoded positions in this range are used by every part of ISO 8859.

Figure 4-2 illustrates the encoding range for ASCII and extended ASCII as defined in the ten parts of ISO 8859.

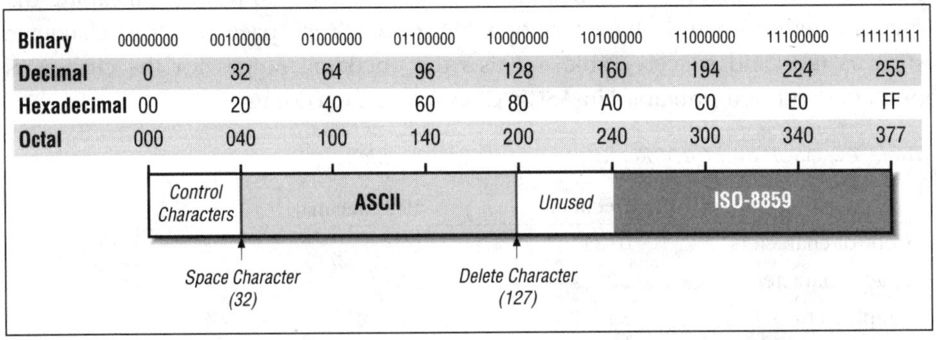

Figure 4-2: ISO 8859 encoding table

Most of the CJKV encoding methods, especially those used as internal codes for computer systems, make generous use of eight-bit characters. This makes it very difficult to mix characters from ISO 8859's ten parts with CJKV text since they all fall into the same encoded range. Some computer platforms deal with this much better than others. Apple Computer's MacOS handles this problem quite well simply by changing the font, which in turn changes the underlying script.

EBCDIC/EBCDIK Encoding

IBM developed their own single-byte character set standard called EBCDIC (Extended Binary-Coded-Decimal Interchange Code). The number and type of printable characters are the same as ASCII, but the encoding for EBCDIC differs greatly. The main difference is that EBCDIC requires eight bits for full representation, whereas ASCII and CJKV-Roman require only seven bits. Table 4-3 lists the specifications for EBCDIC.

Table 4-3: EBCDIC Encoding Specifications

	Decimal	Hexadecimal
Control characters	0–63	00–3F
Space character	64	40

Table 4-3: EBCDIC Encoding Specifications (continued)

	Decimal	Hexadecimal
Graphic characters	65–239	41–EF
Numerals	240–249	F0–F9
Undefined	250–254	FA–FE
Control character	255	FF

The EBCDIC encoding method is not used as often as the encoding for ASCII/CJKV-Roman, and appears to be slowly becoming obsolete. EBCDIC is included in these pages for the sake of completeness, and because three of the encoding methods to follow include EBCDIC as a subset (they are IBM's DBCS-Host, Fujitsu's JEF, and Hitachi's KEIS encoding methods—all of these are vendor-specific encoding methods). Figure 4-3 illustrates the encoding space for EBCDIC encoding.

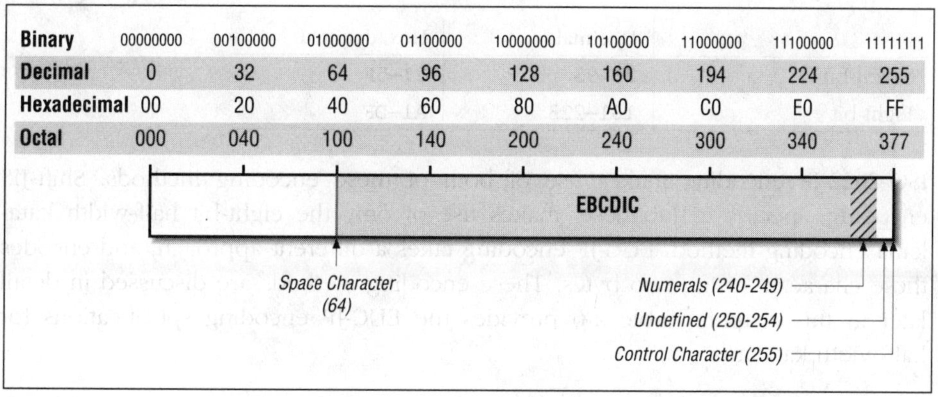

Figure 4-3: EBCDIC encoding table

There is also an encoding called EBCDIK, which stands for *Extended Binary-Coded-Decimal Interchange Kana*. It is an EBCDIC encoding that contains uppercase Latin characters, numerals, symbols, half-width katakana, and control characters (note that there are no lowercase Latin characters). Table 4-4 details the encoding ranges for the characters in EBCDIK.

Table 4-4: EBCDIK Encoding Specifications

	Decimal	Hexadecimal
Control characters	0–63	00–3F
Space character	64	40
Graphic characters	65–239	41–EF
Numerals	240–249	F0–F9
Undefined	250–254	FA–FE
Control character	255	FF

Note how the encoding space is identical to that of EBCDIC (see Figure 4-3 on page 143). Characters appear to be randomly scattered throughout the encoding space, and not all encoding positions have characters assigned to them. For a complete listing of EBCDIC and EBCDIK characters and their code positions, please refer to Appendix S, *Single-Byte Code Tables.*

Half-Width Katakana Encodings

Half-width katakana characters, specific to Japanese, have been encoded in a variety of ways. These characters were chosen to be the first Japanese characters encoded on computers because they are used for Japanese telegrams. As single-byte characters, they are encoded using one of two methods. These two methods are described in the standard designated JIS X 0201-1997. Table 4-5 illustrates the one-byte encoding methods for this small collection of characters.

Table 4-5: Half-Width Katakana Encoding Specifications

	Decimal	Hexadecimal
Seven-bit	33–95	21–5F
Eight-bit	161–223	A1–DF

ISO-2022-JP encoding makes use of both of these encoding methods. Shift-JIS encoding, specific to Japanese, makes use of only the eight-bit half-width katakana encoding method. EUC-JP encoding takes a different approach, and encodes these characters using two bytes. These encoding methods are discussed in detail later in this chapter. Table 4-6 provides the EUC-JP encoding specifications for half-width katakana.

Table 4-6: Half-Width Katakana Encoding Specifications—EUC-JP

	Decimal	Hexadecimal
Packed format		
First byte	142	8E
Second byte range	161–223	A1–DF
Complete two-byte format		
First byte	0	00
Second byte range	161–223	A1–DF

Note how the second byte range is identical to the eight-bit half-width katakana range in the previous table—EUC-JP encoding simply prefixes the byte with the value 0x8E, also known as EUC encoding's SS2 (Single Shift 2) character.

Figure 4-4 illustrates the encoding space for the half-width katakana character set in the various encodings.

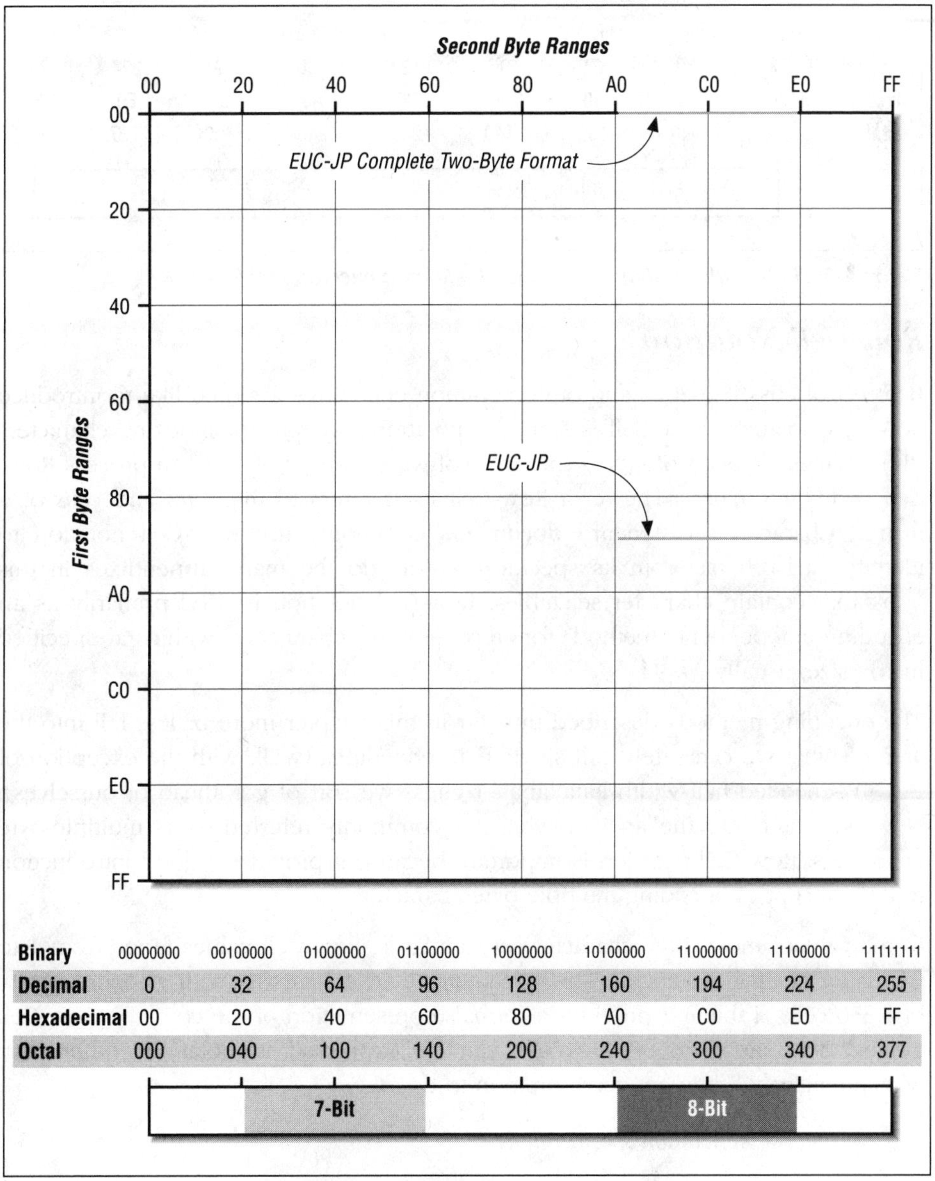

Figure 4-4: Half-width katakana encoding tables

Now note how eight-bit half-width katakana and seven-bit ASCII/JIS-Roman can coexist within the same eight-bit one-byte encoding space. When these two character sets are mixed, the newly formed character set is called ANK (short for Alphabet, Numerals, and Katakana), as illustrated in Figure 4-5.

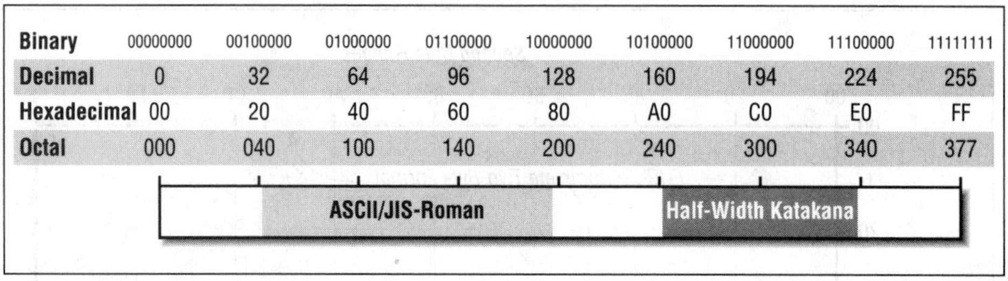

Figure 4-5: Half-width katakana plus ASCII/JIS-Roman encoding table—ANK

Row-Cell Notation

Before I discuss ISO-2022 and other common encodings, I would like to introduce Row-Cell notation. Row-Cell is simply a notational system for indexing characters (the Japanese version of TEX is the only software I know of that can process Row-Cell codes internally). The term Row-Cell itself refers to the *rows* and *cells* of a matrix. Character set standard documents commonly use Row-Cell notation to identify each character in its specification—as do the many appendixes in this book that contain character set tables. Row-Cell notation is used primarily as an encoding-independent method for representing characters within a specified matrix size, usually 94×94.

The encoding methods described thus far in this chapter more or less fall into the area of what we can safely call single-byte encodings (well, with the exception of EUC-JP–encoded half-width katakana—I guess we sort of got ahead of ourselves). Now we enter into the area of what are commonly referred to as multiple-byte encodings. Row-Cell notation is important because it provides a good introduction to the concept of encoding multiple-byte characters.

In the case of most CJKV character set standards, Row-Cell values range from 1 to 94 (using decimal notation). This constitutes a 94×94 matrix, with a total capacity of 8,836 cells. Table 4-7 provides a formal representation of the common Row-Cell ranges. Note how Row-Cell values can be expressed in notations other than decimal, although it is not very common to do so.

Table 4-7: Row-Cell Notation Specifications

	Decimal	Hexadecimal
First byte range	1–94	01–5E
Second byte range	1–94	01–5E

Figure 4-6 illustrates the 94×94 matrix as used by Row-Cell notation. You will quite often see this 94×94 matrix as the same dimensions of other encoding methods.

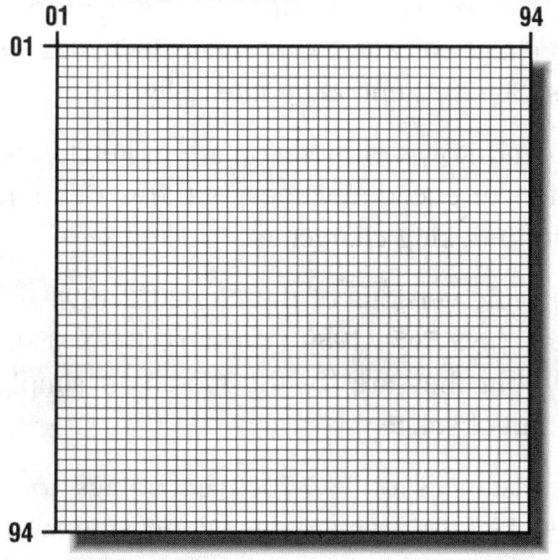

Figure 4-6: Row-Cell table

The section entitled "What Is Row-Cell?," beginning on page 18 of Chapter 1, *CJKV Information Processing Overview*, provides more details about Row-Cell notation, including how it is referred to in Chinese, Japanese, and Korean.

ISO-2022 Encoding

The ISO-2022 encoding method, documented in ISO 2022:1994, *Information technology—Character code structure and extension techniques*, is considered one of the most basic encoding methods used for CJKV text. It is a *modal* encoding, that is, escape sequences or other special characters are used to switch between different modes. Switching "modes" here can refer to either switching between one- and two-byte mode, or among character sets. Some character sets are one-byte, and some are two-byte. To which character set you are switching determines whether you switch into one- or two-byte mode.

The use of "ISO-2022 encoding" in this book is as a generic reference to ISO-2022-CN, ISO-2022-CN-EXT, ISO-2022-JP, ISO-2022-KR, and similar encodings. The full ISO 2022:1994 standard defines a lot of machinery that is rarely used. The encodings described in this section, as a practical matter, implement only a subset of the ISO 2022:1994 standard. In fact, some ISO-2022 encodings are, in fact, incompatible with ISO 2022:1994.

ISO-2022 encoding is not very efficient for internal storage or processing on computer systems. It is used primarily as an information interchange code for moving text between computer systems, such as ever-popular email. This is often called an external code. ISO-2022 encoding is also often referred to as a seven-bit encoding method because all the bytes used to represent characters do not have their eight-bit enabled.

There are some software environments that can process ISO-2022 encoding internally, the most notable of which is GNU Emacs Version 20 and later. Many other programs, such as email software, can create ISO-2022–encoded text, but do not necessarily process ISO-2022 encoding internally.

ISO-2022 encoding and Row-Cell notation are more closely related than you would think. ISO-2022 refers to encoded values, but Row-Cell refers to an encoding-independent notation for indexing characters.

There are locale-specific versions of the ISO 2022:1994 standard available, such as GB 2311-80 (China), CNS 7654-1989 (Taiwan), JIS X 0202:1998 (Japan) and KS X 1004:1995 (Korea),* but they are for the most part simply translations, and some are now outdated and obsolete.

There are several instances of ISO-2022 encodings for representing CJKV text. Table 4-8 lists these ISO-2022 encodings, along with what character sets they are known to support, plus a reference to the RFC (Request For Comments) in which they are officially defined and described (I tell you how to obtain RFCs in the section entitled "Useful URLs" in Appendix T, *Software and Document Sources*, which starts on page 976).

Table 4-8: Character Sets Supported in ISO-2022 Encodings

Encoding	Character Sets	RFC
ISO-2022-CN	ASCII, GB 2312-80, CNS 11643-1992 Planes 1 and 2	1922
ISO-2022-CN-EXT	ISO-2022-CN *plus* CNS 11643-1992 Planes 3–7	1922
ISO-2022-JP[a]	ASCII, JIS-Roman, JIS C 6226-1978, JIS X 0208-1983	1468
ISO-2022-JP-1	ISO-2022-JP *plus* JIS X 0212-1990	2237
ISO-2022-JP-2[b]	ISO-2022-JP *plus* JIS X 0212-1990	1554
ISO-2022-KR	ASCII, KS X 1001:1992	1557

[a] Also includes implied support for JIS X 0208-1990 and JIS X 0208:1997.
[b] ISO-2022-JP-2 encoding, according to the RFC in which it is defined, also supports ISO 8859-1:1998, GB 2312-80, and KS X 1001:1991. But, from a practical point of view, ISO-2022-JP-2 encoding adds support for only JIS X 0212-1990, which makes it equivalent to ISO-2022-JP-1 encoding.

All of these encodings share two common attributes: the encoding ranges for one- and two-byte characters are identical. Table 4-9 provides these encoding ranges.

Table 4-9: One- and Two-Byte Encoding Ranges of ISO-2022 Encoding

	Decimal	Hexadecimal
First byte range[a]	33–126	21–7E
Second byte range	33–126	21–7E

[a] This also corresponds to the one-byte encoding range.

* Formerly KS C 5620-1995.

In other words, the values for all bytes used to encode characters are equivalent to the printable ASCII range. These characters range from the exclamation point (!) at 0x21 to the tilde (~) at 0x7E. Figure 4-7 illustrates the ISO-2022 encoding space.

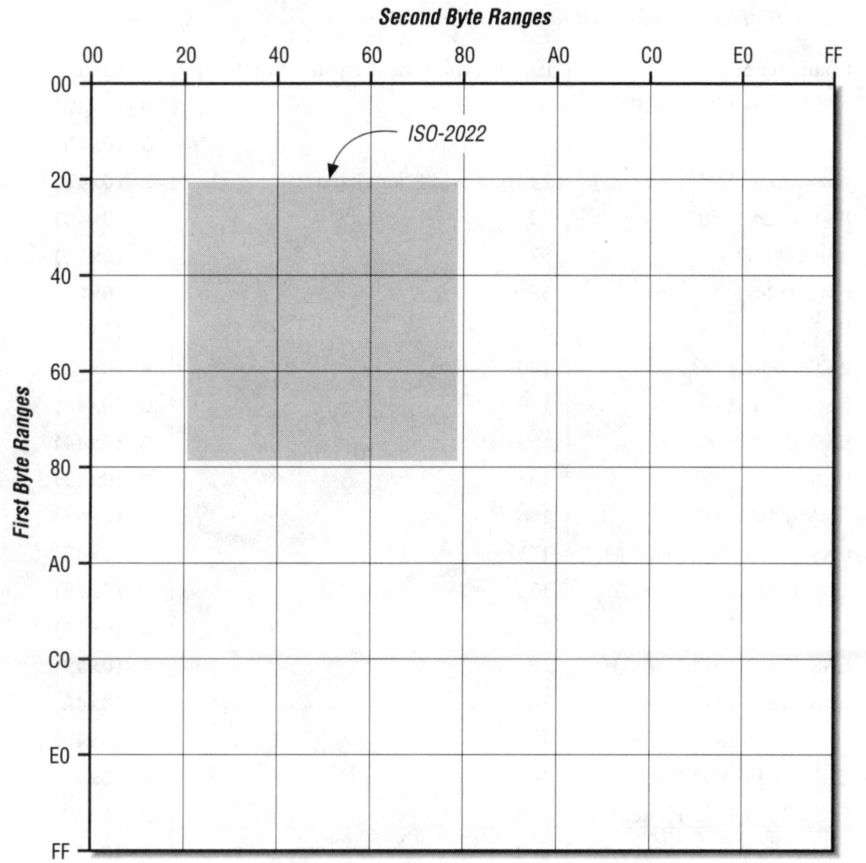

Binary	00000000	00100000	01000000	01100000	10000000	10100000	11000000	11100000	11111111
Decimal	0	32	64	96	128	160	194	224	255
Hexadecimal	00	20	40	60	80	A0	C0	E0	FF
Octal	000	040	100	140	200	240	300	340	377

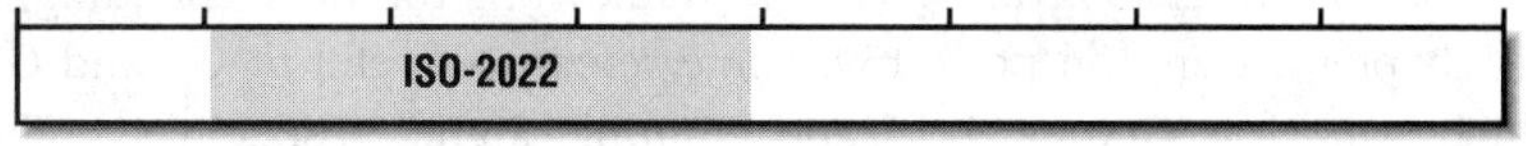

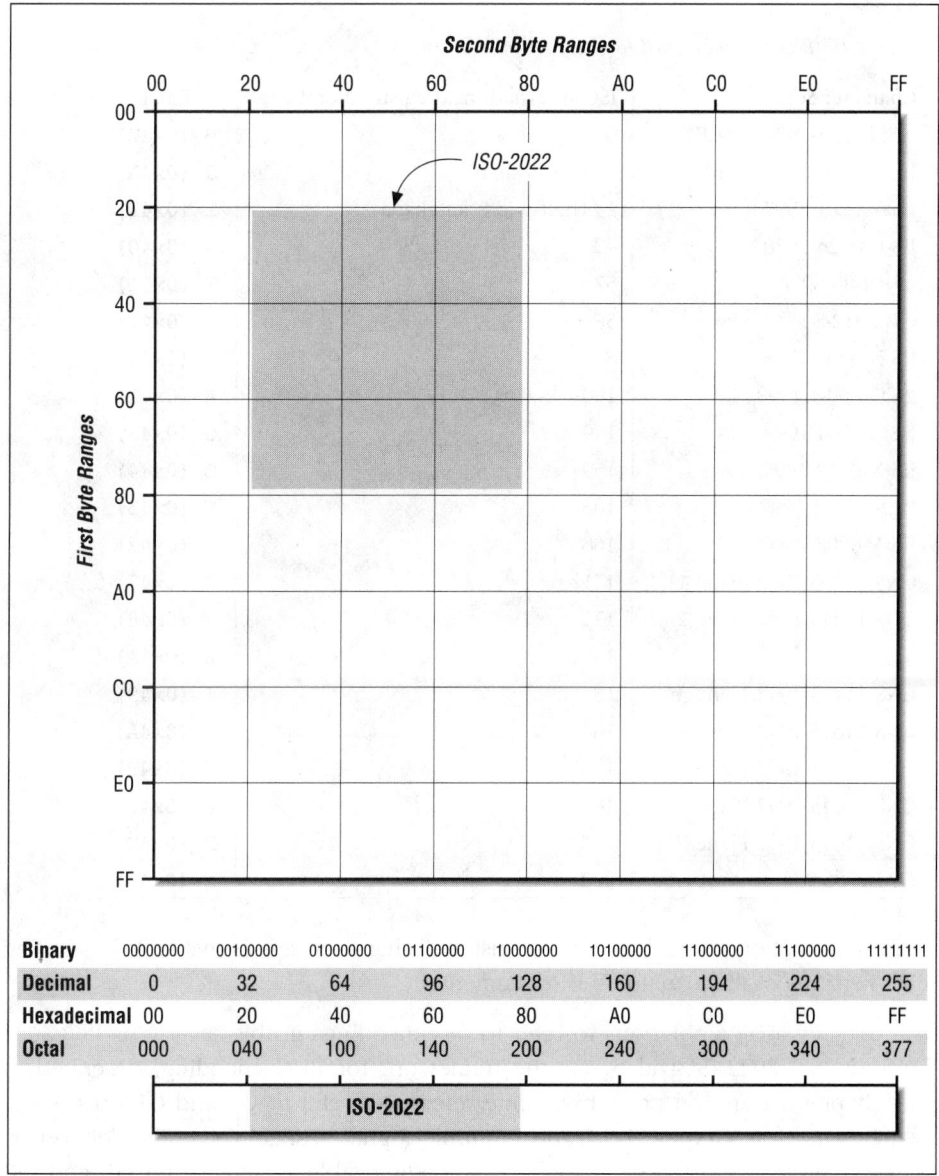

Figure 4-7: ISO-2022 encoding tables

All instances of ISO-2022 encoding support one or more character sets that have been registered with ISO's International Registry for escape sequences. Table 4-10 lists CJKV character sets, along with their ISO International Registry number plus final character (and hexadecimal equivalent) for use in an escape or designator sequence—ordered by ascending ISO International Registry number, which more or less indicates the order in which these character sets were registered with ISO.

Table 4-10: ISO International Registry Numbers

Character Set	ISO International Registry Number	Final
ANSI X3.4-1986 (ASCII)	6	`B (0x42)`
JIS X 0201-1997	13 (JIS-Roman)	`J (0x4A)`
JIS X 0201-1997	14 (half-width katakana)	`I (0x49)`
JIS C 6226-1978	42	`@ (0x40)`
GB 1988-89	57	`T (0x54)`
GB 2312-80	58	`A (0x41)`
JIS X 0208-1983	87	`B (0x42)`
ISO 8859-1:1998	100	`A (0x41)`
KS X 1001:1992	149	`C (0x43)`
JIS X 0212-1990	159	`D (0x44)`
ISO-IR-165:1992	165	`E (0x45)`
JIS X 0208-1990	168	`B (0x42)`
CNS 11643-1992 Plane 1	171	`G (0x47)`
CNS 11643-1992 Plane 2	172	`H (0x48)`
VSCII	180	`Z (0x5A)`
CNS 11643-1992 Plane 3	183	`I (0x49)`
CNS 11643-1992 Plane 4	184	`J (0x4A)`
CNS 11643-1992 Plane 5	185	`K (0x4B)`
CNS 11643-1992 Plane 6	186	`L (0x4C)`
CNS 11643-1992 Plane 7	187	`M (0x4D)`
KPS 9566-97	202	`N (0x4E)`

More information about these ISO-registered character sets is available, including PDF versions of the actual ISO IR documents.*

It is actually a bit ambiguous to refer to the encodings in this section as ISO-2022 because ISO 2022:1994 also sets the framework for EUC encoding, described in this chapter starting on page 159. Some references refer to GL and GR encodings, which stand for "Graphic Left" and "Graphic Right," respectively. Why left versus right? Figure 4-8 illustrates an eight-bit encoding table in which the GL and GR portions are shaded. Note how the GL region is on the left, and the GR region is on the right. This is where GL and GR come from.

* *http://www.itscj.ipsj.or.jp/ISO-IR/*

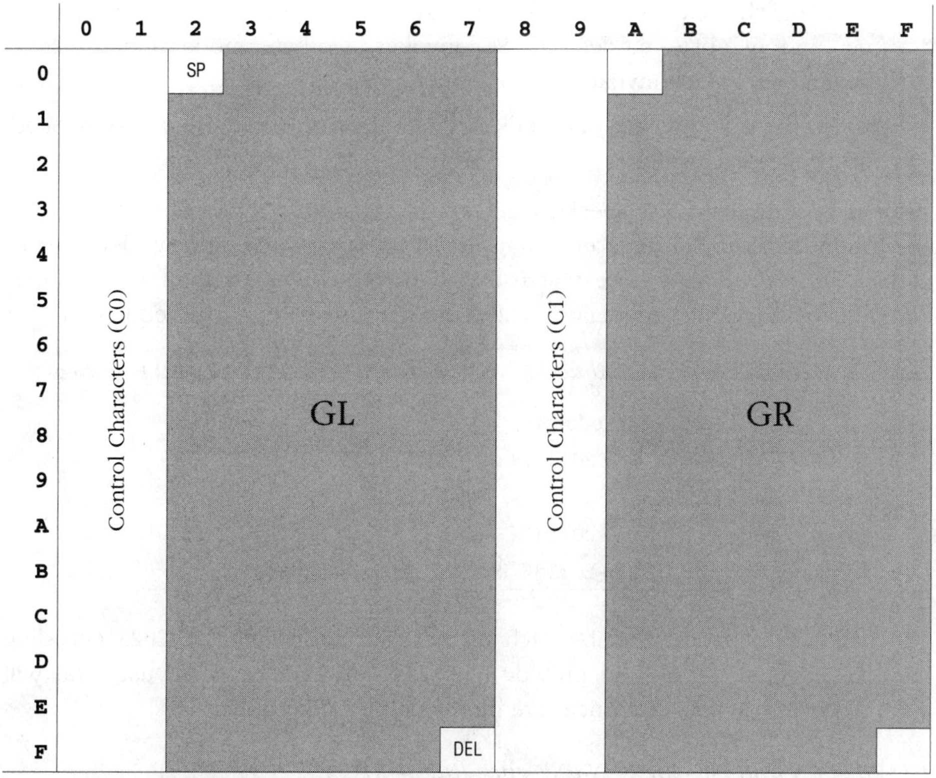

Figure 4-8: GL and GR encodings

The GL range is 0x21 through 0x7E, which is used by ISO-2022 encodings to encode all graphic characters, and by EUC encodings to encode the single-byte ASCII or CJKV-Roman character sets. The GR block is 0xA1 through 0xFE, which is used by EUC encodings to encode all two-byte graphic characters.

My convention is to use "ISO-2022" or locale-specific instances thereof to indicate GL for two-byte encodings, and "EUC" or locale-specific instances thereof to indicate GR for two- or more-byte portions of the encoding.

ISO-2022 encodings use special characters or sequences of characters called *designator sequences*, *single shift sequences*, *shifting characters*, and *escape sequences*. The following are descriptions of each:

- A designator sequence indicates what character set should be invoked when in two-byte mode—it does *not* invoke two-byte mode
- A single shift sequence, indicated by SS2 (0x1B 0x4E) or SS3 (0x1B 0x4F), invokes two-byte mode only for the following two bytes—typically employed for rarely-used character sets

- A shifting character, indicated by SO (0x0E) or SI (0x0F), switches between one- and two-byte modes—an SO invokes two-byte mode until an SI is encountered, which invokes one-byte mode
- An escape sequence not only indicates what character set should be invoked, but invokes it as well

Table 4-11 indicates what special characters or character sequences each locale-specific instance of ISO-2022 encoding uses. Note how there are two basic types of ISO-2022 encodings: those that use designator sequences, shifting characters, and perhaps single shift sequences; and those that use only escape sequences.

Table 4-11: The Use of Special Characters or Character Sequences in ISO-2022 Encodings

Type	Encodings
Designator sequences	ISO-2022-CN, ISO-2022-CN-EXT, ISO-2022-KR
Single shift sequences	ISO-2022-CN, ISO-2022-CN-EXT
Shifting characters	ISO-2022-CN, ISO-2022-CN-EXT, ISO-2022-KR
Escape sequences	ISO-2022-JP, ISO-2022-JP-1, ISO-2022-JP-2

The following sections describe each of these locale-specific ISO-2022 encoding instances in more detail, and provide illustrative examples of their use. You will soon discover that some instances are more complex than others.

ISO-2022-CN and ISO-2022-CN-EXT encodings—RFC 1922

ISO-2022-CN and ISO-2022-CN-EXT encodings, defined in RFC 1922, *Chinese Character Encoding for Internet Messages*, are somewhat complex in that they involve designator sequences, single shift sequences, and shifting characters. This is because these encodings support a rather large number of character sets, from both China and Taiwan.

ISO-2022-CN is distinguished from ISO-2022-CN-EXT in that it supports only ASCII, GB 2312-80, and CNS 11643-1992 Planes 1 and 2. ISO-2022-CN-EXT is equivalent to ISO-2022-CN plus support for many more character sets.

Table 4-12 provides the specifications for the designator sequences used in ISO-2022-CN and ISO-2022-CN-EXT encodings. Note how the designator sequences indicate a character set or subset thereof (such as each plane of CNS 11643-1992).

Table 4-12: ISO-2022-CN and ISO-2022-CN-EXT Specifications—Part 1

Character Set	Decimal	Hexadecimal	Graphical (ASCII)
GB 2312-80	27 36 41 65	1B 24 29 41	<ESC> $) A
CNS 11643-1992 Plane 1	27 36 41 71	1B 24 29 47	<ESC> $) G
CNS 11643-1992 Plane 2	27 36 42 72	1B 24 2A 48	<ESC> $ * H
ISO-IR-165	27 36 41 69	1B 24 29 45	<ESC> $) E
CNS 11643-1992 Plane 3	27 36 43 73	1B 24 2B 49	<ESC> $ + I

Table 4-12: ISO-2022-CN and ISO-2022-CN-EXT Specifications—Part 1 (continued)

Character Set	Decimal	Hexadecimal	Graphical (ASCII)
CNS 11643-1992 Plane 4	`27 36 43 74`	`1B 24 2B 4A`	`<ESC> $ + J`
CNS 11643-1992 Plane 5	`27 36 43 75`	`1B 24 2B 4B`	`<ESC> $ + K`
CNS 11643-1992 Plane 6	`27 36 43 76`	`1B 24 2B 4C`	`<ESC> $ + L`
CNS 11643-1992 Plane 7	`27 36 43 77`	`1B 24 2B 4D`	`<ESC> $ + M`

ISO-2022-CN-EXT actually provides support for additional character sets, including GB/T 12345-90, GB 7589-87, GB 7590-87, and others, but these character sets are not listed above because they are not yet ISO-registered.

Table 4-13 provides the specifications for the single shift sequences and shifting characters used in ISO-2022-CN and ISO-2022-CN-EXT encodings.

Table 4-13: ISO-2022-CN and ISO-2022-CN-EXT Specifications—Part 2

	Decimal	Hexadecimal	Graphical (ASCII)
SS2	`27 78`	`1B 4E`	`<ESC> N`
SS3	`27 79`	`1B 4F`	`<ESC> O`
One-byte shift	`15`	`0F`	`<SI>`
Two-byte shift	`14`	`0E`	`<SO>`

Once you know the designator sequence, you then must find out what kind of shifting is required. Table 4-14 lists the three shifting types, SO, SS2, and SS3, along with what characters are used for each method.

Table 4-14: ISO-2022-CN and ISO-2022-CN-EXT Specifications—Part 3

Shifting Types	Character Sets
SO	GB 2312-80, CNS 11643-1992 Plane 1, ISO-IR-165:1992
SS2	CNS 11643-1992 Plane 2
SS3	CNS 11643-1992 Planes 3–7

The designator sequence must appear once on a line before any instance of the character set it designates. If two lines contain characters from the same character set, both lines must include the designator sequence (this is so that the text can be displayed correctly when scrolled back in a window). This is different behavior from ISO-2022-KR (described later in this chapter), where the designator sequence appears only once in the entire file (this is because ISO-2022-KR supports only one two-byte character set—shifting to two-byte mode is unambiguous).

Sample encoded text, along with ISO-2022-CN-capable software, can now be easily obtained.* CERNET (China Education and Research Network) is promoting the

* *ftp://etlport.etl.go.jp/pub/mule/iso-cn.tgz*

ISO-2022-CN and ISO-2022-CN-EXT encodings, and CITS (China Information Technology Standardization Committee) will promote it in its ninth Five Year Plan.

The predecessor of ISO-2022-CN encoding—HZ encoding

HZ encoding is a simplistic yet powerful system for encoding GB 2312-80 text, which was developed by Fung Fung Lee (李枫峰 *lǐ fēng fēng*)* for exchanging email and posting news in Chinese. HZ encoding is commonly used when exchanging email or posting messages to Usenet News (specifically, to *alt.chinese.text*).

The actual encoding ranges used for one- and two-byte characters are identical to ISO-2022-CN and ISO-2022-CN-EXT encodings, but, instead of using designator sequences and shift characters to shift between character sets, a simple string of two printable characters is used. Table 4-15 lists the two most important shift sequences used in HZ encoding.

Table 4-15: HZ Encoding Shift Sequences

Character Set	Shift Sequence	Decimal	Hexadecimal
ASCII or GB-Roman	`~}`	`126 125`	`7E 7D`
GB 2312-80	`~{`	`126 123`	`7E 7B`

As you can see, the overline or tilde character (0x7E) is interpreted as though it were an escape character in HZ encoding, so it has special meaning. If an overline character is to appear in one-byte mode, it must be doubled (so "~~" would appear as "~"). There is also a fourth escape sequence, specifically "~" followed by a newline character. It is used for maintaining two-byte mode while breaking lines. This effectively means that there are four shift sequences used in HZ encoding, as shown in Table 4-16.

Table 4-16: Meanings of HZ Escape Sequences

Escape Sequence	Meaning
~~	"~" in one-byte mode
~}	Shift into one-byte mode, ASCII or GB-Roman
~{	Shift into two-byte mode, GB 2312-80
~<NL>	Maintain two-byte across lines

HZ encoding typically works without problems because the shift sequences, while being valid two-byte code points, represent empty positions in the very last row of the GB 2312-80 character set's 94×94 matrix (actually, the second- and third-from-last code points). This effectively makes 93 of the 94 rows accessible.

* *lee@umunhum.stanford.edu*

The complete HZ specification is part of the HZ package,* described in RFC 1843, and available in HTML format.†

In addition, RFC 1842 establishes "HZ-GB-2312" as the charset designation for MIME-encoded email headers. Its properties are identical to HZ encoding as described here and in RFC 1843.

ISO-2022-JP encodings—RFCs 1468, 1554, and 2237

ISO-2022-JP encoding, defined in RFC 1468, *Japanese Character Encoding for Internet Messages*, provides support for the ASCII, JIS-Roman, JIS C 6226-1978, and JIS X 0208-1983 character sets. ISO-2022-JP-2 encoding, defined in RFC 1554, *ISO-2022-JP-2: Multilingual Extension of ISO-2022-JP*, is an extension to ISO-2022-JP that adds support for the GB 2312-80, JIS X 0212-1990, and KS X 1001:1992 character sets in addition to two parts of ISO 8859 (Parts 1 and 7). ISO-2022-JP-1, defined in RFC 2237, *Japanese Character Encoding for Internet Messages*, is a modest extension to ISO-2022-JP that simply adds support for JIS X 0212-1990.

All three ISO-2022-JP encodings are incompatible with ISO 2022:1994 because they use escape sequences that do not follow the standard (for JIS C 6226-1978 and JIS X 0208-1983), and because the JIS X 0208-1983 escape sequence is used for introducing JIS X 0208-1990 (see Table 4-20 on page 157).

From a practical point of view, ISO-2022-JP-2 adds support for only JIS X 0212-1990—there are other ISO-2022 encodings better suited to support the GB 2312-80 and KS X 1001:1992 character sets, specifically ISO-2022-CN and ISO-2022-KR, respectively.

Table 4-17 lists the escape sequences supported by ISO-2022-JP encoding.

Table 4-17: ISO-2022-JP Encoding Specifications

Character Set	Decimal	Hexadecimal	Graphical (ASCII)
ASCII	`27 40 66`	`1B 28 42`	<ESC> `( B`
JIS-Roman	`27 40 74`	`1B 28 4A`	<ESC> `( J`
JIS C 6226-1978	`27 36 64`	`1B 24 40`	<ESC> `$ @`
JIS X 0208-1983	`27 36 66`	`1B 24 42`	<ESC> `$ B`

Escape sequences must be fully contained within a line—they should not span newlines or carriage returns. If the last character on a line is represented by two bytes, an ASCII or JIS-Roman character escape sequence should follow before the line terminates. If the first character on a line is represented by two bytes, a two-byte character escape sequence should precede it. Not all these procedures are necessary, but they are useful because they ensure that small communication

* *ftp://ftp.ifcss.org/pub/software/unix/convert/HZ-2.0.tar.gz*

† *http://umunhum.stanford.edu/~lee/chicomp/HZ_spec.html*

errors do not render an entire Japanese document unreadable—each line becomes self-contained. These escape sequences are also known as *kanji-in* and *kanji-out*. Kanji-in corresponds to a two-byte character escape sequence, and kanji-out corresponds to a one-byte character escape sequence.

ISO-2022-JP-1 is identical to ISO-2022-JP encoding except that it adds support for the JIS X 0212-1990 character set. Table 4-18 provides the JIS X 0212-1990 escape sequence as described for ISO-2022-JP-1 encoding.

Table 4-18: ISO-2022-JP-1 Encoding Specifications

Character Set	Decimal	Hexadecimal	Graphical (ASCII)
JIS X 0212-1990	27 36 40 68	1B 24 28 44	<ESC> $ (D

ISO-2022-JP-2, on the other hand, adds support for five additional character sets. These character sets, along with their escape sequences, are listed in Table 4-19.

Table 4-19: ISO-2022-JP-2 Encoding Specifications

Character Set	Decimal	Hexadecimal	Graphical (ASCII)
GB 2312-80	27 36 65	1B 24 41	<ESC> $ A
JIS X 0212-1990	27 36 40 68	1B 24 28 44	<ESC> $ (D
KS X 1001:1992	27 36 40 67	1B 24 28 43	<ESC> $ (C
ISO 8859-1:1998	27 46 65	1B 2E 41	<ESC> . A
ISO 8859-7:1998	27 46 70	1B 2E 46	<ESC> . F

Let's take a look at some ISO-2022-JP–encoded material to see exactly how this encoding method works. The example string is かな漢字, which means "kana [and] kanji." The encoded values are in hexadecimal notation.

Character string				か	な	漢	字			
Escape sequences	<ESC>	$	B					<ESC>	(	J
ISO-2022-JP encoding	1B	24	42	24 2B	24 4A	34 41	3B 7A	1B	28	4A
Graphical (ASCII)				$ +	$ J	4 A	; z			

In this example, the first escape sequence signals a switch in mode to the JIS X 0208-1983 character set (two-byte mode); this is followed by the data for the four characters to be displayed. To terminate the string, a one-byte character escape sequence is used (in this case it is the one for switching to the JIS-Roman character set).

You have already learned that ISO-2022-JP encoding makes use of seven bits for representing two-byte characters. The actual encoded range corresponds to that used for representing the ASCII character set. Thus, the encoded values for the kanji in the above example can be represented with ASCII characters, as shown in the last line of the example.

The predecessor of ISO-2022-JP encoding—JIS encoding

Before RFC 1468 was introduced (June of 1993), which effectively defined ISO-2022-JP encoding, ISO-2022–encoded Japanese text was commonly known as "JIS encoding" (and is still often referred to as such in some contexts). But, what most people do not realize is that what is now known as ISO-2022-JP encoding is actually a subset of what is still known as JIS encoding. Confused? You won't be after reading this section.

JIS encoding can be thought of as a much richer variant of ISO-2022-JP encoding—richer in the sense that it supports more character sets. Table 4-20 provides the specifications for JIS encoding.

Table 4-20: JIS Encoding Specifications

	Decimal	Hexadecimal	Graphical (ASCII)
One-byte characters			
Byte range	33–126	21–7E	
Two-byte characters			
First byte range	33–126	21–7E	
Second byte range	33–126	21–7E	
Escape sequences			
JIS-Roman	27 40 74	1B 28 4A	<ESC> (J
JIS-Roman[a]	27 40 72	1B 28 48	<ESC> (H
ASCII	27 40 66	1B 28 42	<ESC> (B
Half-width katakana	27 40 73	1B 28 49	<ESC> (I
JIS C 6226-1978	27 36 64	1B 24 40	<ESC> $ @
JIS X 0208-1983	27 36 66	1B 24 42	<ESC> $ B
JIS X 0208-1990	27 38 64 27 36 66	1B 26 40 1B 24 42	<ESC> & @ <ESC> $ B
JIS X 0208:1997	27 38 64 27 36 66	1B 26 40 1B 24 42	<ESC> & @ <ESC> $ B
JIS X 0212-1990	27 36 40 68	1B 24 28 44	<ESC> $ (D
JIS7 half-width katakana			
Shift-out	14	0E	<SO>
Byte range	33–95	21–5F	
Shift-in	15	0F	<SI>
JIS8 half-width katakana			
Byte range	161–223	A1–DF	

[a] This is improperly used on some implementations as the one-byte character escape sequence for JIS-Roman. According to the standard designated JIS X 0202:1998, it is actually the one-byte character escape sequence for the Swedish character set. It is a good idea for software to recognize, but not to generate, this one-byte character escape sequence. The correct sequence to use is <ESC> (J.

JIS encoding also supports half-width katakana, and has two different methods called JIS7 and JIS8. JIS7 encoding has all eighth bits cleared, JIS8 does not. JIS7 and JIS8 half-width katakana encodings are not widely used in products, so it is questionable whether all software should necessarily generate such codes. It is, however, important that software recognize and deal with them appropriately.

JIS7 encoding is identical to JIS encoding, but with the addition of another escape sequence for shifting into half-width katakana mode. This method is defined in the document JIS X 0202:1998. This means that a document containing two-byte Japanese, one-byte ASCII, and half-width katakana characters may make use of at least three escape sequences, one for shifting into each of the three modes or character sets. An alternate method for encoding half-width katakana under JIS7 uses the ASCII shift-out (SO) and shift-in (SI) characters instead of an escape sequence. Half-width katakana sequences begin with a shift-out character, and are terminated with a shift-in character. This encoding method is described in the standard designated JIS X 0201-1997.

The encoding range for JIS8 includes eight-bit bytes (its range is 161–233, and is identical to the half-width katakana range in Shift-JIS encoding). The text stream must be in one-byte mode. This encoding is also described in JIS X 0201-1997.

ISO-2022-KR encoding—RFC 1557

ISO-2022-KR encoding, defined in RFC 1557, *Korean Character Encoding for Internet Messages*, specifies how Korean text is to be encoded for email messages or other electronic transmission.

The ISO-2022-KR designator sequence must appear only once in a file, at the beginning of a line, before any KS X 1001:1992 characters. This usually means that it appears by itself on the first line of the file. ISO-2022-KR uses only two shifting sequences (for switching between one- and two-byte modes), and involves neither the escape character nor an escape sequence. Table 4-21 provides a listing of the ISO-2022-KR designator sequence and the two shifting sequences.

Table 4-21: ISO-2022-KR Encoding Specifications

	Decimal	Hexadecimal	Graphical (ASCII)
Designator sequence	27 36 41 67	1B 24 29 43	<ESC> $) C
One-byte shift	15	0F	<SI>
Two-byte shift	14	0E	<SO>

The following is an example of ISO-2022-KR–encoded text, using 김치 (*gimci*) as the example:

Character string						김	치	
Designator sequence	<ESC>	$	)	C				
Shifts					<SO>			<SI>
ISO-2022-KR encoding	1B	24	29	43	0E	31 68	44 21	0F
Graphical (ASCII)						1 h	D !	

Note the similarities with ISO-2022-CN and ISO-2022-CN-EXT encodings, in particular that designator sequences and shifting characters are used.

Other possible ISO-2022 encodings

Although not even officially in existence, one could conceive of ISO-2022–style encodings for North Korea's KPS 9566-97 or Vietnam's TCVN 5773:1993 and TCVN 6056:1995 standards. In fact, the final escape-sequence character for KPS 9566-97 has been registered with ISO, and is set to "N" (0x4E). The stage is now set for ISO-2022-KP encoding. If an ISO-2022-KP encoding is to spring into existence, it is likely to be similar to ISO-2022-KR, except that the designator sequence for KPS 9566-97 would be "`<ESC> $ ) N`" (0x1B 0x24 0x29 0x4E). A likely encoding name for TCVN 5773:1993 and TCVN 6056:1995 is ISO-2022-VN.

EUC Encoding

EUC (Extended Unix Code) encoding is implemented as the internal code for most Unix software configured to support Japanese. EUC is also known in Japan as UJIS (short for Unixized JIS) and AT&T JIS. The definition of EUC, like that of ISO-2022, comes from the standard designated ISO 2022:1994.

EUC was developed as a method for handling multiple character sets, Japanese and otherwise, within a single text stream. The full definition of EUC encoding is quite rich and supports various multiple-byte encodings, but the specific implementations used for CJKV systems usually fall into two specific types: *packed format* and *complete two-byte format*. The Japanese definition (or instance) of EUC, called EUC-JP, was standardized in 1991 by three organizations: OSF (Open Software Foundation), UI (Unix International), and USLP (Unix System Laboratories Pacific). This standardization has subsequently made it easier for other developers to implement Japanese systems, and at the same time reinforced the use of EUC-JP encoding. The definitions of EUC for other CJKV locales have also been defined.

The current trend in software development is to produce systems that process EUC-JP—it is much more extensible than Shift-JIS. Most Unix operating systems process EUC-JP encoding internally.

CJKV implementations of EUC encoding use one specific instance of multiple-length and one specific instance of fixed-length encoding.

The full definition of EUC encoding consists of four code sets. Code set 0 is always set to the ASCII character set or a country's own version thereof (such as, KS-Roman for Korea). The remaining code sets are defined as a set of variants from which each country can select. You will learn how each CJKV locale has implemented EUC later in this chapter.

There are several reserved code positions in EUC that cannot be used to encode printable characters. These code positions and ranges consist of the space character, the delete character, and two independent ranges of control characters. Table 4-22 shows these code ranges in more detail.

Table 4-22: EUC Reserved Code Ranges and Positions

	Decimal	Hexadecimal
Control set 0	0–31	00–1F
Space character	32	20
Delete character	127	7F
Control set 1	128–159	80–9F

This limitation permits two ranges for encoding graphic characters, specifically 0x21–0x7E (94 characters) and 0xA0–0xFF (96 characters). The second range, at least for CJKV implementations, is limited to the range 0xA1–0xFE as a way to stay compatible with encodings that support ranges of only 94 characters, such as ISO-2022. Table 4-23 lists these two encoding ranges in other notations.

Table 4-23: EUC Graphic Character Encoding Ranges

	Decimal	Hexadecimal
First code range	33–126	21–7E
Second code range	160–255	A0–FF

There are also two special characters: SS2 and SS3. SS2 stands for *Single Shift 2*, and serves as a prefix for every character in code set 2. Likewise, SS3 stands for *Single Shift 3*, and serves as a prefix for every character in code set 3. Table 4-24 lists these characters in two notations. Contrast with the SS2 and SS3 characters used in ISO-2022-CN and ISO-2022-CN-EXT encodings in Table 4-13 on page 153. These will become important later when we discuss code sets 2 and 3.

Table 4-24: EUC Encoding's SS2 and SS3 Characters

	Decimal	Hexadecimal
SS2	142	8E
SS3	143	8F

Table 4-25 illustrates the variable-length representation of the four EUC code sets, along with some of their possible permutations (hexadecimal notation is used here for the sake of space), as they may appear in locale-specific instances of EUC encoding.

This representation is often referred to as *EUC packed format*, and represents the most commonly-used instance of EUC encoding. Also, there can be as many variants of this representation as needed to represent a given locale's character sets.

Table 4-25: EUC Variable-Width Representations

	Variant 1	Variant 2	Variant 3
Code set 0	21–7E		
Code set 1	A0–FF	A0–FF + A0–FF	A0–FF + A0–FF + A0–FF
Code set 2	8E + A0–FF	8E + A0–FF + A0–FF	8E + A0–FF + A0–FF + A0–FF
Code set 3	8F + A0–FF	8F + A0–FF + A0–FF	8F + A0–FF + A0–FF + A0–FF

This effectively means that the definition of EUC encoding is locale-specific—each locale implements its own instance of EUC encoding. This is also why specifying EUC encoding itself is somewhat ambiguous. The locale-specific instances of EUC encoding are known as EUC-CN (China), EUC-TW (Taiwan), EUC-JP (Japan), and EUC-KR (Korea). These are each described in the following sections.

There are two fixed-length EUC representations: 16- and 32-bit.* The significance of these fixed-length representations is that all characters are represented by the same number of bits or bytes. While this may waste space, it does make internal processing more efficient. Table 4-26 describes the 16-bit fixed-length representations of EUC encoding.

Table 4-26: EUC 16-Bit Fixed-Length Representations

	Variant 1	Variant 2
Code set 0	00 + 21–7E	
Code set 1	80 + A0–FF	A0–FF + A0–FF
Code set 2	00 + A0–FF	21–7E + A0–FF
Code set 3	80 + 21–7E	A0–FF + 21–7E

This 16-bit fixed-length representation is often referred to as *EUC complete two-byte format*, and is primarily used for internally processing (as opposed to external representation). Note that the SS2 and SS3 characters are not used in this representation—they are not necessary under a fixed-length encoding model. The 32-bit representation gets very long, and since it is not implemented for most locales, there is no need to illustrate its code ranges here.

The following sections describe the locale-specific instances of EUC encoding. Be sure to note the similarities and differences. You will find numerous similarities in code sets 0 and 1, but differences in code sets 2 and 3 (sometimes code sets 2 and 3 are unused).

EUC-CN encoding—China

The instance of EUC encoding used for the China locale is known as EUC-CN (sometimes referred to as eight-bit GB or simply GB encoding outside the context

* Of course, these can also be thought of as two- and four-byte representations.

of EUC encoding). Table 4-27 lists what character set is assigned to what EUC code set. The "Display Width" column in this and similar tables in this chapter corresponds to the number of columns occupied by each character in a code set. A display width value of 1 corresponds to half-width (or proportional, depending on the font), and a display width value of 2 corresponds to full-width.

Table 4-27: EUC-CN Code Set Allocation

	Character Set	Display Width	Number of Bytes
Code set 0	ASCII or GB-Roman	1	1
Code set 1	GB 2312-80	2	2
Code set 2	*unused*		
Code set 3	*unused*		

Note that EUC code sets 2 and 3 are unused in EUC-CN encoding. Table 4-28 lists the EUC-CN encoding specifications.

Table 4-28: EUC-CN Encoding Specifications

	Decimal	Hexadecimal
Code set 0		
Byte range	`33–126`	`21–7E`
Code set 1		
First byte range	`161–254`	`A1–FE`
Second byte range	`161–254`	`A1–FE`
Code set 2	*unused*	*unused*
Code set 3	*unused*	*unused*

EUC-CN encoding is virtually identical to EUC-KR encoding—except for what character sets are allocated to each EUC code set. Figure 4-9 illustrates the encoding regions for EUC-CN and EUC-KR encodings.

EUC-TW encoding—Taiwan

The instance of EUC encoding used for the Taiwan locale is known as EUC-TW. It is by far the most complex instance of EUC encoding in terms of how many characters it encodes—approximately 50,000 characters! Table 4-29 lists what character set is assigned to what code set.

Note that EUC code set 2 is quite overloaded (nearly 50,000 characters are referenced using a four-byte encoding), but EUC code set 3 is completely unused. Table 4-30 lists EUC-TW's encoding specifications.

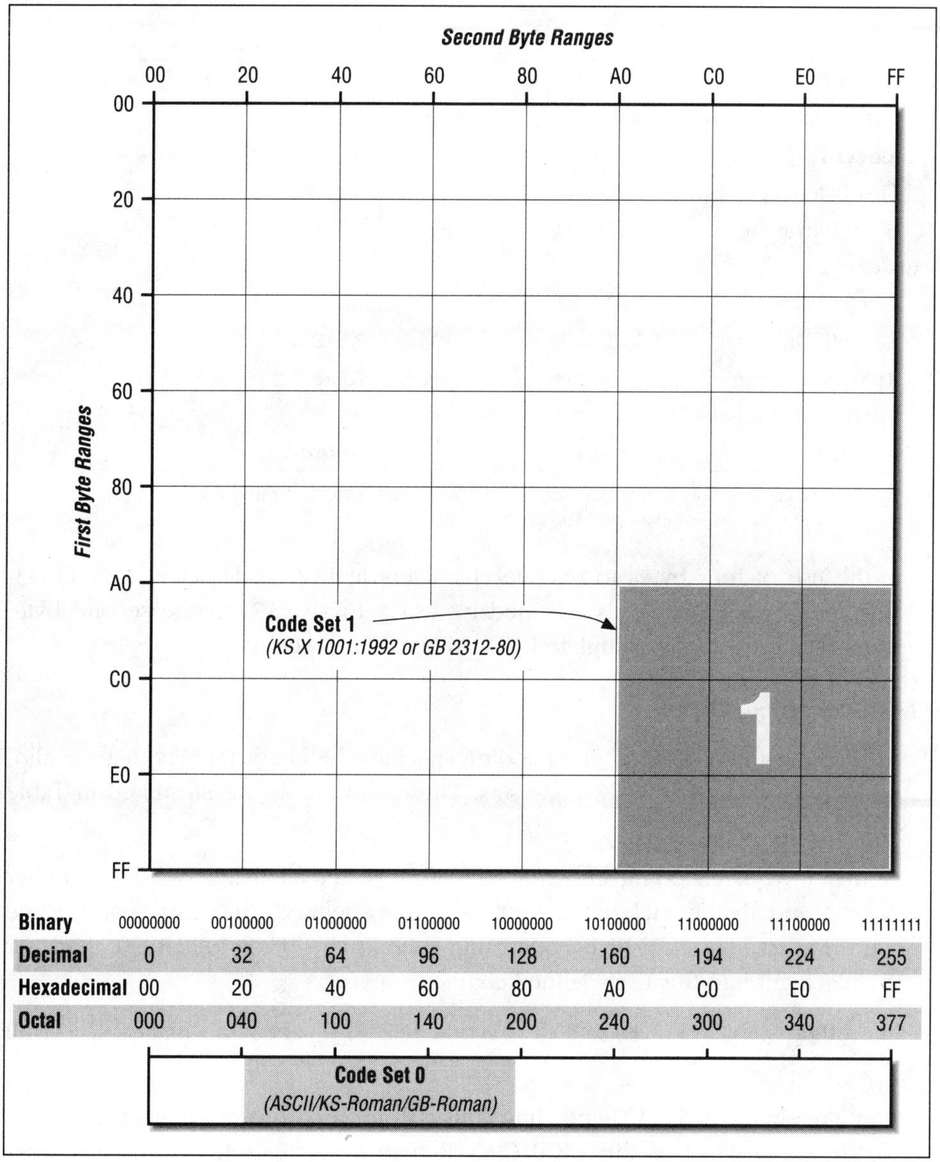

Figure 4-9: EUC-CN and EUC-KR encoding tables

Table 4-29: EUC-TW Code Set Allocation

	Character Set	Display Width	Number of Bytes
Code set 0	ASCII or CNS-Roman	1	1
Code set 1	CNS 11643-1992 Plane 1	2	2
Code set 2[a]	CNS 11643-1992 Planes 1–7	2	4
Code set 3	*unused*		

[a] Note how CNS 11643-1992 Plane 1 is encoded in both EUC code set 1 and 2—this is by design.

Table 4-30: EUC-TW Encoding Specifications

	Decimal	Hexadecimal
Code set 0		
Byte range	33–126	21–7E
Code set 1		
First byte range	161–254	A1–FE
Second byte range	161–254	A1–FE
Code set 2		
First byte (SS2)	142	8E
Second byte range[a]	161–176	A1–B0
Third byte range	161–254	A1–FE
Fourth byte range	161–254	A1–FE
Code set 3	*unused*	*unused*

[a] This value indicates the plane number. Subtract decimal 160 (or 0xA0) from the value to calculate the plane number. For example, 161 means Plane 1.

Note the use of four bytes to encode characters in EUC code set 2. CNS 11643-1992 Plane 7, for example, is encoded by using 167 (0xA7) as the second byte. Figure 4-10 illustrates the complete EUC-TW encoding regions.

EUC-JP encoding—Japan

The official definition of EUC-JP encoding specifies the character sets that are allocated to each of the four EUC code sets. These allocations are illustrated in Table 4-31.

Note that EUC-JP encoding encodes half-width katakana using two bytes rather than one, and that it includes a very large user-defined character space. Large enough, in fact, that EUC-JP encoding implements the JIS X 0212-1990 character set by placing it into this user-defined character space.

Unlike other CJKV instances of EUC encoding, EUC-JP encoding makes use of all four code sets.

As you already learned, EUC encoding consists of four code sets: the primary code set (code set 0) which is the ASCII/CJKV-Roman character set, and three supplemental code sets (code sets 1, 2, and 3) which can be specified by the user, and are usually used for non-Latin characters. Table 4-32 lists the code specifications for all the code sets of EUC-JP encoding.

See Figure 4-11 for an illustration of the EUC-JP encoding space. Note how it requires a three-dimensional encoding space.

You may have noticed that, for each byte of some of the code sets, EUC permits up to 96 characters (that is, the range of 0xA0–0xFF). So why are the above code listings set in a smaller encoding space (specifically 0xA1–0xFE, or 94 characters instead of 96)? As stated earlier, this is done for the sake of compatibility with char-

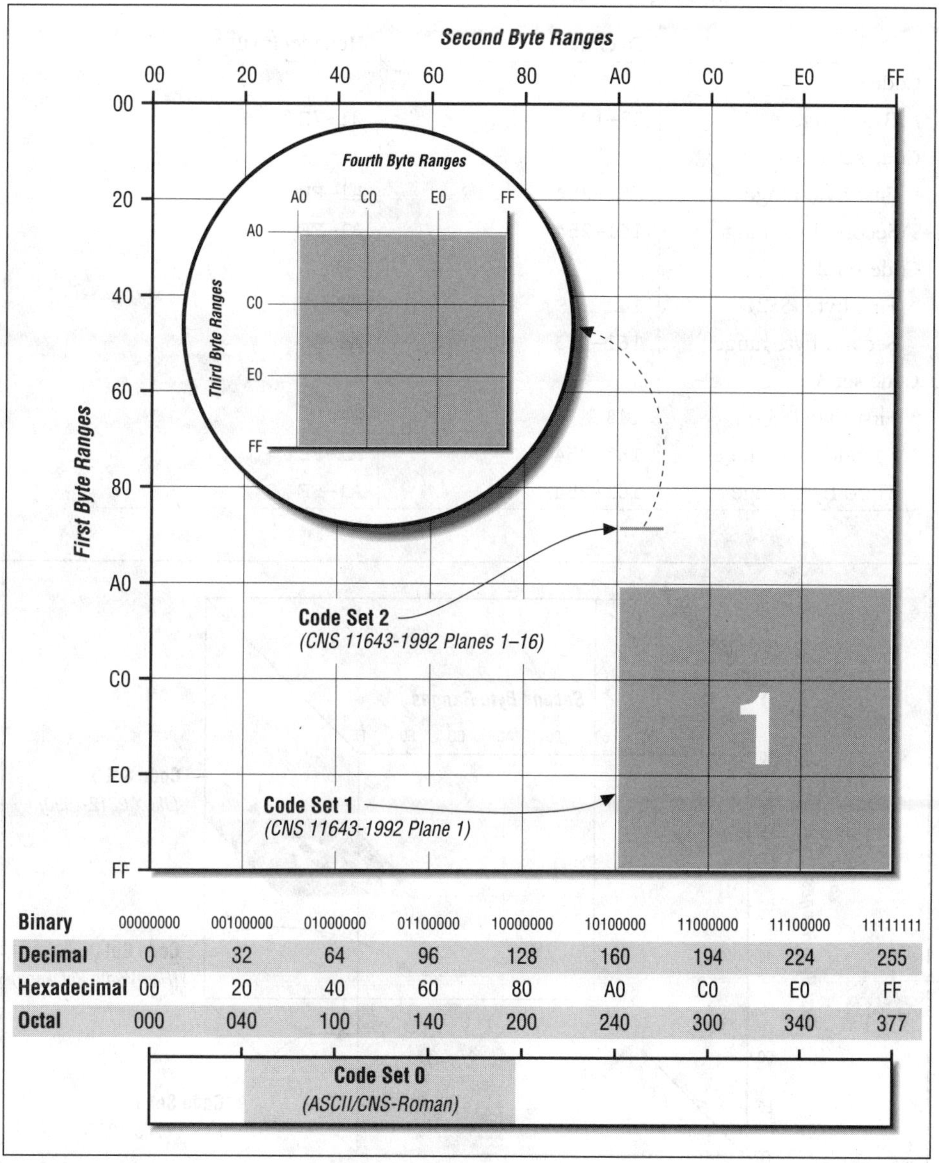

Figure 4-10: EUC-TW encoding tables

Table 4-31: EUC-JP Code Set Allocation

	Character Set	Display Width	Number of Bytes
Code set 0	ASCII or JIS-Roman	1	1
Code set 1	JIS X 0208:1997	2	2
Code set 2	Half-width katakana	1	2
Code set 3	JIS X 0212-1990	2	3

Table 4-32: EUC-JP Encoding Specifications

	Decimal	Hexadecimal
Code set 0		
Byte range	33–126	21–7E
Code set 1		
First byte range	161–254	A1–FE
Second byte range	161–254	A1–FE
Code set 2		
First byte (SS2)	142	8E
Second byte range	161–223	A1–DF
Code set 3		
First byte (SS3)	143	8F
Second byte range	161–254	A1–FE
Third byte range	161–254	A1–FE

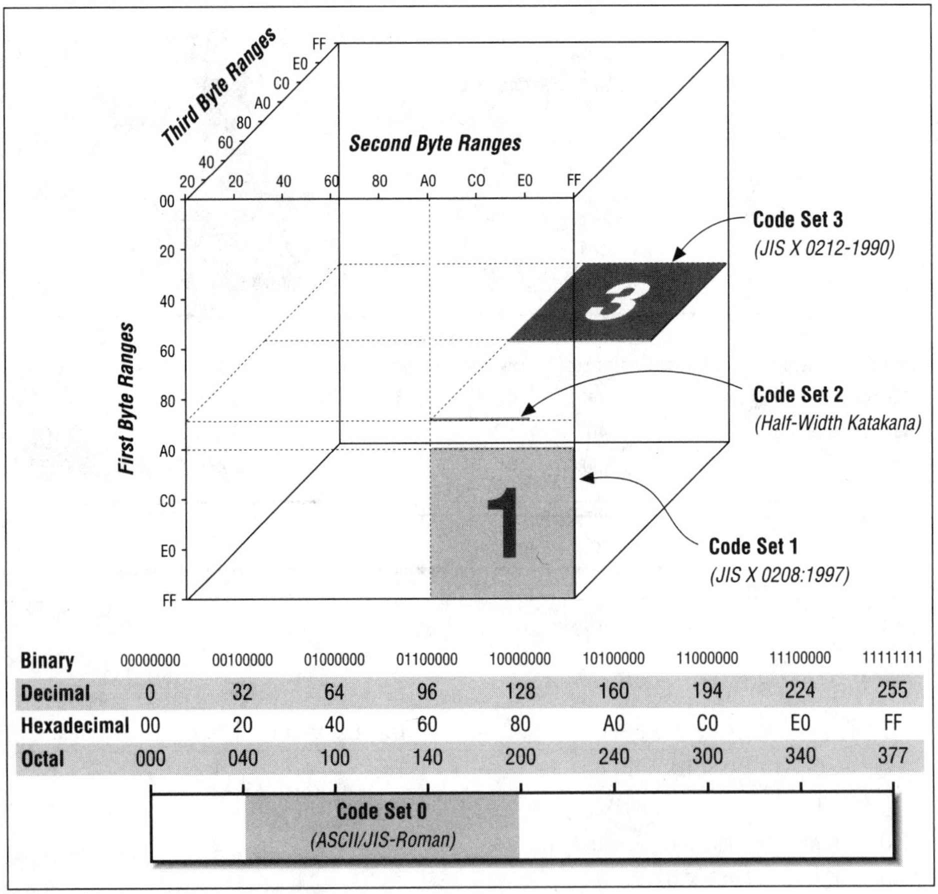

Figure 4-11: EUC-JP encoding tables

acter sets and encodings (most notably, ISO-2022-JP) that are based on a 94×94 matrix. This is not to say that code positions 0xA0 or 0xFF are invalid, but that there are most likely no characters encoded at those rows.

Let's now take a peek at some EUC-JP–encoded material to see how this encoding method works. The example string is かな漢字, which was used in the ISO-2022-JP section (begins on page 155). Like before, the encoded values are in hexadecimal notation, and correspond to characters in the JIS X 0208:1997 character set encoded in EUC-JP code set 1.

Character string	か	な	漢	字
EUC-JP encoding	A4AB	A4CA	B4C1	BBFA

As shown above, there are absolutely no escape sequences or shifting sequences used in EUC-JP encoding.

EUC-KR encoding

The instance of EUC encoding used for the Korean locale is known as EUC-KR (sometimes referred to as "KS_C_5601-1987" or "eight-bit KS" encoding—these are incorrect and dangerous designations, in my opinion), and is defined in the standard designated KS X 2901:1992.* Table 4-33 lists what character sets are assigned to what EUC-KR code sets.

Table 4-33: EUC-KR Code Set Allocation

	Character Set	**Display Width**	**Number of Bytes**
Code set 0	ASCII or KS-Roman	1	1
Code set 1	KS X 1001:1992	2	2
Code set 2	*unused*		
Code set 3	*unused*		

EUC-KR encoding, like EUC-CN encoding covered earlier, does not make use of code sets 2 and 3. This makes it virtually impossible to distinguish EUC-CN encoding from EUC-KR encoding without any sort of language or locale attribute. Table 4-34 details the specifications for EUC-CN encoding.

Table 4-34: EUC-KR Encoding Specifications

	Decimal	**Hexadecimal**
Code set 0		
Byte range	33–126	21–7E

* Formerly KS C 5861-1992.

Table 4-34: EUC-KR Encoding Specifications (continued)

	Decimal	Hexadecimal
Code set 1		
First byte range	161–254	A1–FE
Second byte range	161–254	A1–FE
Code set 2	*unused*	*unused*
Code set 3	*unused*	*unused*

Note the similarities with EUC-CN encoding in Table 4-28 on page 162—apart from character set allocation, the encoding ranges are identical. The EUC-KR encoding is expressed visually in Figure 4-9 on page 163.

Let's now take a peek at some EUC-KR–encoded material, using the same example string for the ISO-2022-KR section (see page 158): 김치. Like before, the encoded values are in hexadecimal notation.

Character string	김	치
EUC-KR encoding	B1E8	C4A1

Other possible EUC encodings

Although not even officially in existence, one could conceive of EUC-style encodings for North Korea's KPS 9566-97 or Vietnam's TCVN 5773:1993 and TCVN 6056:1995 standards. If an EUC-KP encoding is to spring into existence, it is likely to be similar to EUC-KR. A likely encoding name for TCVN 5773:1993 and TCVN 6056:1995 is EUC-VN, but it is unclear how the entire TCVN-Roman character sets, specifically the many characters adorned with diacritic marks, would be handled.

EUC and ISO-2022 encodings

EUC encoding is closely related to ISO-2022 encoding. In fact, every character that can be encoded by ISO-2022 can be converted to an EUC-encoded equivalent. This leads to better information interchange. Figure 4-12 draws a comparison between ISO-2022 and EUC encodings. It is critical to understand that the relationship between the encoding ranges is nothing more than that of seven- versus eight-bit.

In most cases, EUC encoding is simply ISO-2022 encoding with the high bits set, and without escape or shift sequences of any kind.* Algorithms for code conversion are discussed in Chapter 9, *Information Processing Techniques*.

* Some may claim that EUC encoding's SS2 and SS3 characters are shift characters of sorts—it is "officially okay" to think so.

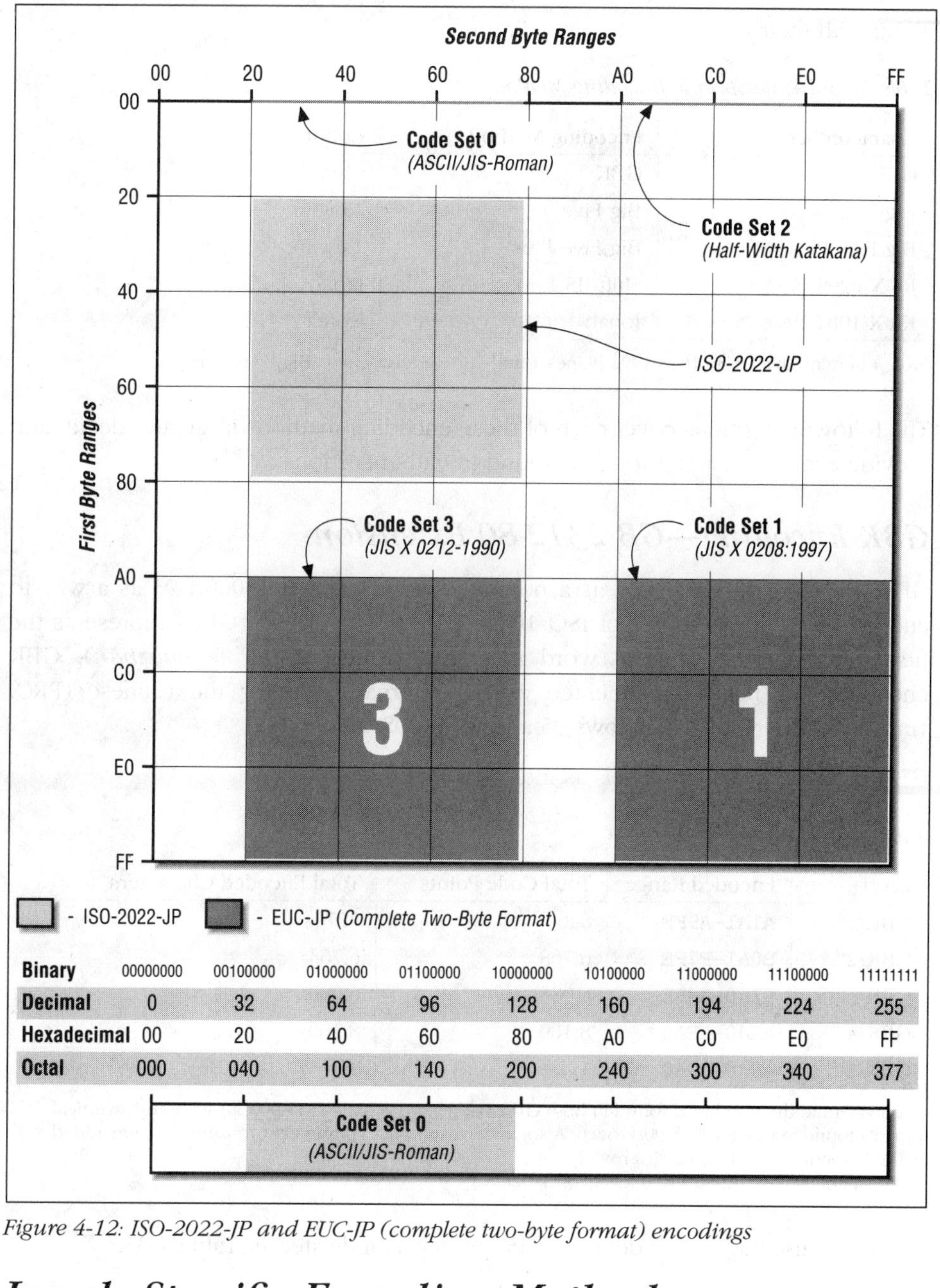

Figure 4-12: ISO-2022-JP and EUC-JP (complete two-byte format) encodings

Locale-Specific Encoding Methods

Included here are descriptions of encoding methods used for specific locales. I find it intriguing that all four of these CJKV locales each have at least one locale-specific encoding method. Table 4-35 lists some CJKV character set standards, along with their locale-specific encoding methods.

Table 4-35: Locale-Specific Encoding Methods

Character Set	Encoding Method	Country
GBK	GBK	China
Big Five[a]	Big Five	Taiwan
Big Five Plus	Big Five Plus	Taiwan
JIS X 0208:1997	Shift-JIS	Japan
KS X 1001:1992	Johab	Korea

[a] Keep in mind that CNS 11643-1992 Planes 1 and 2 are equivalent to Big Five.

The following sections cover each of these encoding methods in greater detail, and provide examples similar to those found in earlier sections.

GBK Encoding—GB 2312-80 Extension

GBK encoding was planned as a normative annex of GB 13000.1-93 as a way to encode the Chinese subset of ISO 10646-1:1993. The "K" in "GBK" represents the first sound in the Chinese word meaning "extension" (扩展 *kuòzhǎn*). GBK encoding has been implemented as the internal code for the Chinese (PRC) versions of Microsoft's Windows 95 and IBM's OS/2.

GBK is divided into five levels as indicated in Table 4-36.

Table 4-36: GBK Levels

Level	Encoded Range	Total Code Points	Total Encoded Characters
GBK/1[a]	`A1A1–A9FE`	846	717
GBK/2[b]	`B0A1–F7FE`	6,768	6,763
GBK/3	`8140–A0FE`	6,080	6,080
GBK/4	`AA40–FEA0`	8,160	8,160
GBK/5	`A840–A9A0`	192	166

[a] Equivalent to the non-hanzi found in both GB 2312-80 and GB/T 12345-90, but without 10 vertical variants found in GB/T 12345-90's row 6. Also, lowercase Roman numerals 1 through 10 were added to the beginning of GB 2312-80's row 2.
[b] Equivalent to GB2312-80's two levels of hanzi.

There are also 1,894 user-defined code points, as indicated in Table 4-37.

Table 4-37: GBK User-Defined Regions

Encoded Range	Total Code Points
`AAA1–AFFE`	564
`F8A1–FEFE`	658
`A140–A7A0`	672

GBK thus provides a total of 23,940 code points, 21,886 of which are assigned characters. Table 4-38 lists the complete encoding specification for GBK encoding.

Table 4-38: GBK Encoding Specifications

	Decimal	Hexadecimal
ASCII or GB-Roman		
Byte range	`33–126`	`21–7E`
GBK		
First byte range	`129–254`	`81–FE`
Second byte ranges	`64–126, 128–254`	`40–7E, 80–FE`

GBK and EUC-CN encodings

Note that the EUC-CN code set 1 encoding range, 0xA1A1 through 0xFEFE, forms a subset of GBK encoding. This is by design, and has the benefit of providing backward compatibility with EUC-CN encoding. Figure 4-13 illustrates the relationship between EUC-CN and GBK encodings.

Big Five Encoding

Big Five encoding has a lot in common with EUC-TW code sets 0 and 1, the main difference being that there is an additional encoding block. This is required because the Big Five character set contains over 13,000 characters—EUC-TW code set 1 simply cannot encode that many characters. Table 4-39 illustrates its encoding specifications.

Figure 4-14 illustrates the Big Five encoding structure, which clearly illustrates the two separate encoding blocks.

Big Five and EUC-TW encodings

It seems a bit silly to compare Big Five and EUC-TW encodings because they are so different from one another. Big Five encoding, on the one hand, is a mixed one- and two-byte encoding whose second-byte values extend into the seven-bit region. EUC-TW, on the other hand, is a mixed one-, two-, and four-byte encoding that is fundamentally made up of planes. They are compatible only in that some parts are equivalent: Big Five Levels 1 and 2 are equivalent to CNS 11643-1992 Planes 1 and 2.

Big Five Encoding—Hong Kong Extension

The Hong Kong extension, consisting of 3,049 hanzi, described in Chapter 3, is encoded in two regions within Big Five, one of which is considered a non-standard region. The portion of this extension that is encoded in the *standard* Big Five

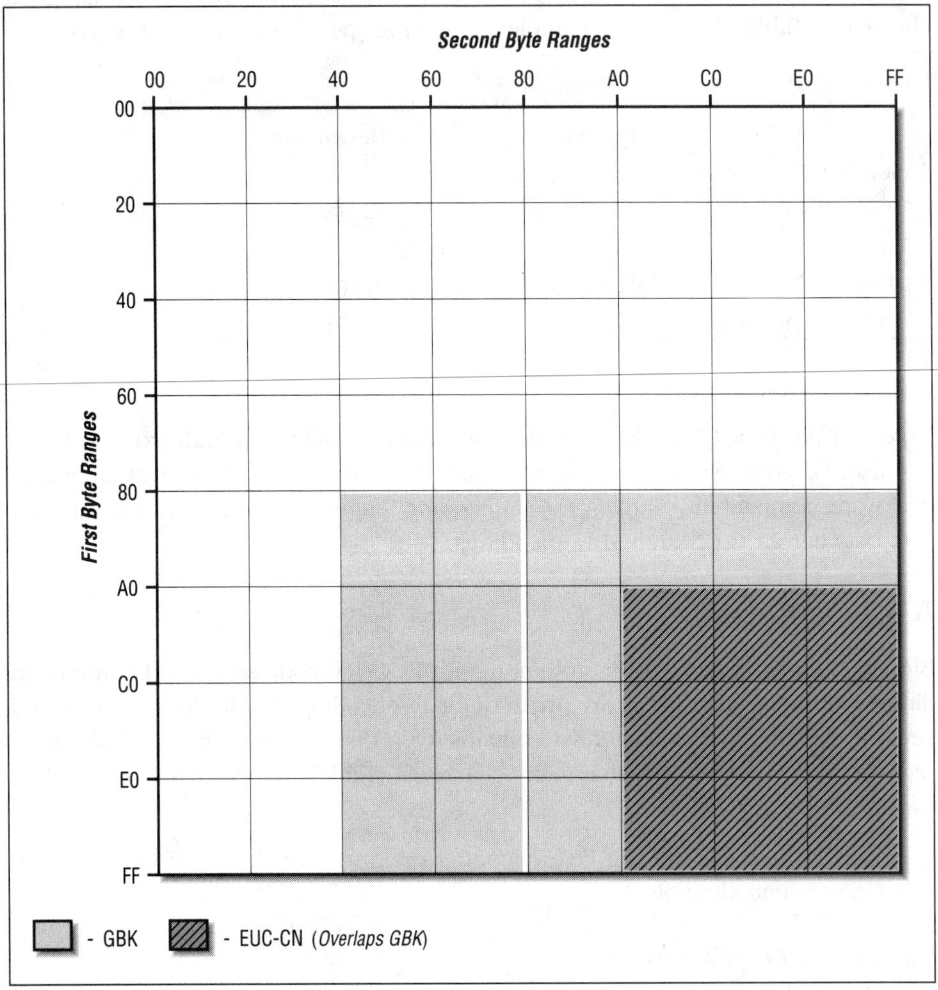

Figure 4-13: EUC-CN and GBK encodings—two-byte regions

Table 4-39: Big Five Encoding Specifications

	Decimal	Hexadecimal
ASCII or CNS-Roman		
Byte range	33–126	21–7E
Big Five		
First byte range	161–254	A1–FE
Second byte ranges	64–126, 161–254	40–7E, A1–FE

encoding region spans rows 0xFA through 0xFE. Because of the non-standard portion of this encoding extension, very few operating systems currently support this Big Five extension.

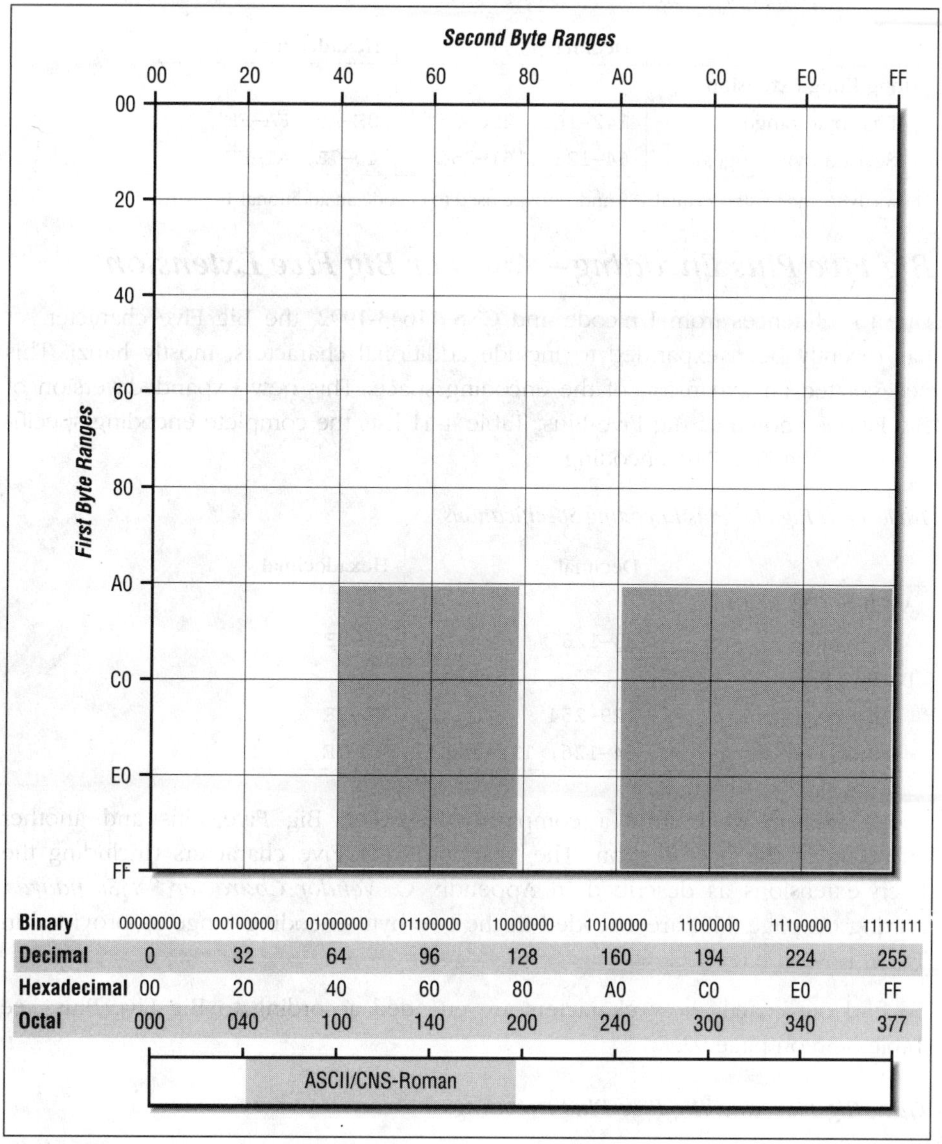

Figure 4-14: Big Five encoding tables

Table 4-40 provides the specification for Hong Kong's extension to Big Five encoding—this should be added to Table 4-39 on page 172 to come up with a complete encoding definition.

Hong Kong's Big Five encoding specification conflicts with the recently established Big Five Plus encoding (described next), and some vendor-specific instances of Big Five encoding, in particular, that used by Apple Computer's MacOS-T.

Table 4-40: Hong Kong's Big Five Encoding Extension

	Decimal	Hexadecimal
Hong Kong Extension		
First byte range	142–160, 250–254	8E–A0, FA–FE[a]
Second byte ranges	64–126, 161–254	40–7E, A1–FE

[a] Rows 0x8A and 0x8B (decimal 138 and 139) are used to encode an additional 145 hanzi.

Big Five Plus Encoding—Another Big Five Extension

Due to influences from Unicode and CNS 11643-1992, the Big Five character set has recently been expanded to include additional characters, mostly hanzi. This necessitated an expansion of the encoding space. This new expanded version of Big Five is known as Big Five Plus. Table 4-41 lists the complete encoding specification for Big Five Plus encoding.

Table 4-41: Big Five Plus Encoding Specifications

	Decimal	Hexadecimal
ASCII or CNS-Roman		
Byte range	33–126	21–7E
Big Five Plus		
First byte range	129–254	81–FE
Second byte ranges	64–126, 128–254	40–7E, 80–FE

Look familiar? We'll draw a comparison between Big Five Plus and another encoding in the next section. The "standard" Big Five characters (including the ETen extensions as described in Appendix C, *Vendor Character Set Standards*, starting on page 559) are encoded in the two-byte encoding range as provided in Table 4-39 on page 172.

To find out exactly how characters are encoded according to Big Five Plus, see Table 3-36 on page 92.

GBK, Big Five, and Big Five Plus encodings

While I have normally preferred to compare encodings within a single locale in this chapter, this is a perfect time to draw comparisons between GBK and Big Five Plus encodings. They share many of the same attributes, but how they were designed pinpoints their differences. GBK began with EUC-CN code set 1 as its base, but Big Five Plus began with Big Five as its base.

Although GBK and Big Five Plus share the same overall encoding structure, their character allocation in the two-byte region is completely different. Figure 4-15 illustrates how Big Five encoding is a subset of Big Five Plus encoding. Compare this with Figure 4-13 on page 172.

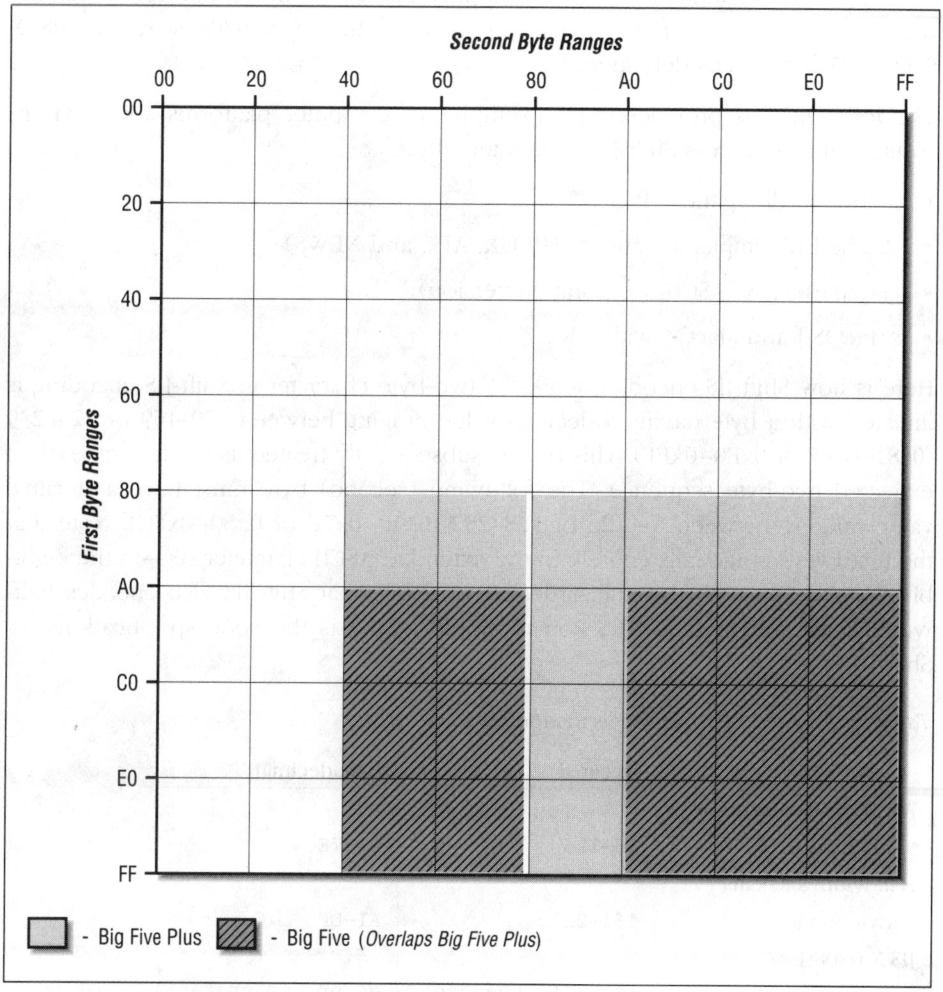

Figure 4-15: Big Five and Big Five Plus encodings—two-byte regions

Shift-JIS Encoding—JIS X 0208:1997

Shift-JIS encoding, originally developed by Microsoft Corporation, is widely implemented as the internal code for a variety of platforms, including Japanese PCs and MacOS-J (including Japanese Language Kit). Shift-JIS is sometimes referred to as MS (for Microsoft) Kanji, MS Code, or SJIS (abbreviated form of Shift-JIS).* Historically, Shift-JIS was so named because of the way the code positions for two-byte characters *shifted* around the code positions for half-width katakana—Japanese PC users were originally restricted to only half-width katakana, so Shift-JIS was devel-

* There are also less flattering permutations of this encoding's name, but they are not suitable for printing in this book.

oped in order to maintain backward compatibility. It was not until recently that the definition of Shift-JIS encoding became part of the JIS X 0208 standard. JIS X 0208:1997 contains its definition.

The following list provides more examples of computer platforms and environments that can process Shift-JIS code internally:

- Virtually all Japanese PCs
- Some Unix implementations (HP-UX, AIX, and NEWS)
- Japanese TEX (ASCII* Corporation version)
- MacOS-J and MacOS with JLK

Here is how Shift-JIS encoding works. A two-byte character in Shift-JIS encoding is initiated with a byte having a decimal value ranging between 129–159 or 224–239 (0x81–0x9F or 0xE0–0xEF). This byte is subsequently treated as the first byte of an expected two-byte sequence. The following (second) byte must have a decimal value ranging between 64–126 or 128–252 (0x40–0x7E or 0x80–0xFC). Note that the first byte's range falls entirely in the extended ASCII character set—in the eight-bit character set with the high-order bit on. Note that Shift-JIS also encodes half-width katakana and ASCII/JIS-Roman. Table 4-42 lists the code specifications for Shift-JIS.

Table 4-42: Shift-JIS Encoding Specifications

	Decimal	Hexadecimal
ASCII or JIS-Roman		
Byte range	33–126	21–7E
Half-width katakana		
Byte range	161–223	A1–DF
JIS X 0208:1997		
First byte ranges	129–159, 224–239	81–9F, E0–EF
Second byte ranges	64–126, 128–252	40–7E, 80–FC

Now let's take a look at some Shift-JIS–encoded material to illustrate exactly how this encoding method works. The example string is かな漢字, which was used in the previous section on ISO-2022-JP encoding. The encoded values are in hexadecimal notation.

Character string	か	な	漢	字
Shift-JIS encoding	82A9	82C8	8ABF	8E9A

* ASCII here refers to the Japan-based company (*http://www.ascii.co.jp/*), not the character set.

Note that no escape sequences are used—this is typical of non-modal encodings, and produces a much tighter encoding. There is, however, no ASCII representation for the two bytes that constitute these characters.

Shift-JIS encoding does not support the characters defined in JIS X 0212-1990. There is simply not enough encoding space left to include these characters, and there is currently no plan to extend Shift-JIS in a manner such that JIS X 0212-1990 can be included. See Figure 4-16 for an illustration of the Shift-JIS encoding space.

Some definitions (in particular, corporate definitions) of Shift-JIS also contain encoding blocks for user-defined characters, or even an encoded position for a half-width katakana space character. Such encoding blocks and encoded positions are not useful if true information interchange is desired because they are encoded in such a way that they do not convert to encoded positions in other Japanese encoding methods (that is, ISO-2022-JP and EUC-JP). Table 4-43 lists these non-standard Shift-JIS encoding blocks and encoded positions.

Note how the second byte range is unchanged from the standard definition of Shift-JIS—only the first byte range differs for the user-defined range.

Figure 4-17 illustrates the standard Shift-JIS encoding space, along with the user-defined character region.

Shift-JIS, ISO-2022-JP, and EUC-JP encodings

The relationship between Shift-JIS and EUC-JP is not very apparent, and requires the use of a somewhat complex code conversion algorithm, examined in detail in Chapter 9, starting on page 414. Figure 4-18 illustrates the two-byte Shift-JIS encoding space and how it relates to EUC-JP and ISO-2022-JP encodings.

Johab Encoding—KS X 1001:1992

The Korean character standard, KS X 1001:1992, is encoded very similarly to JIS X 0208:1997. It is supported by ISO-2022-KR and EUC-KR encodings, which are the Korean analogs to ISO-2022-JP and EUC-JP encodings. KS X 1001:1992 departs from JIS X 0208:1997 only in that we have not yet discussed an encoding method comparable to Shift-JIS. There is a comparable encoding, and it is known as Johab (조합/組合 *johab*). Johab encoding is described in the KS X 1001:1992 standard as an alternate encoding that includes all possible modern hangul—11,172, which is 8,822 more than can be encoded according to ISO-2022-KR or EUC-KR encodings.

The UHC (Unified Hangul Code) character set and encoding—fully described in Appendixes C and D, *Vendor Encoding Methods*, respectively—is character-for-character identical to Johab encoding in terms of its character set, but its encoding is radically different. It is considered to be backward compatible with EUC-KR encoding, and forward compatible with Unicode—two good qualities. Johab is

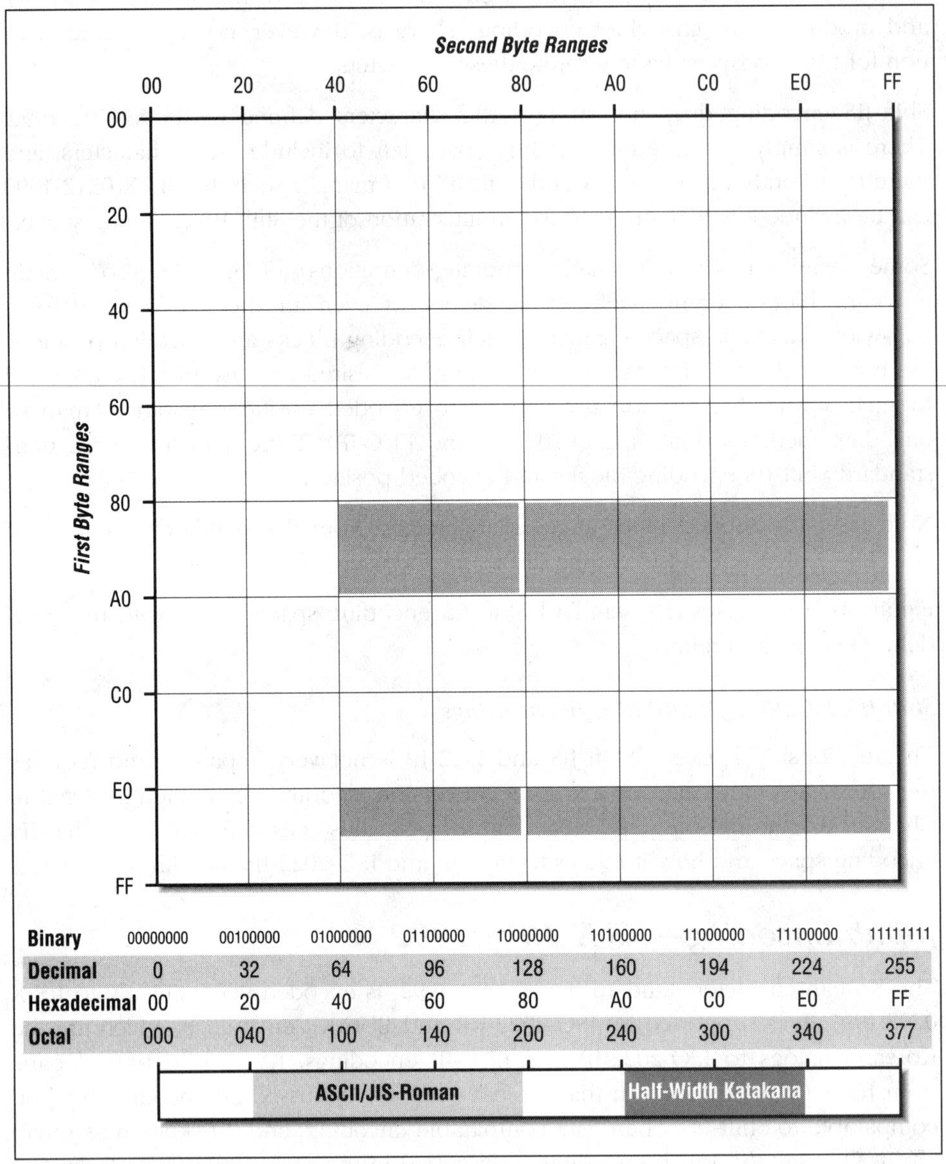

Figure 4-16: Shift-JIS encoding tables

Table 4-43: Shift-JIS User-Defined Character Encoding Specifications

	Decimal	Hexadecimal
Half-width katakana		
Half-width "space" character	160	A0

Table 4-43: Shift-JIS User-Defined Character Encoding Specifications (continued)

	Decimal	Hexadecimal
User-defined characters		
First byte range[a]	240–252	F0–FC
Second byte ranges	64–126, 128–252	40–7E, 80–FC

[a] Some implementations of Shift-JIS encoding implement a smaller user-defined character range, such as rows 0xF0–0xF9 or 0xF0–0xFB.

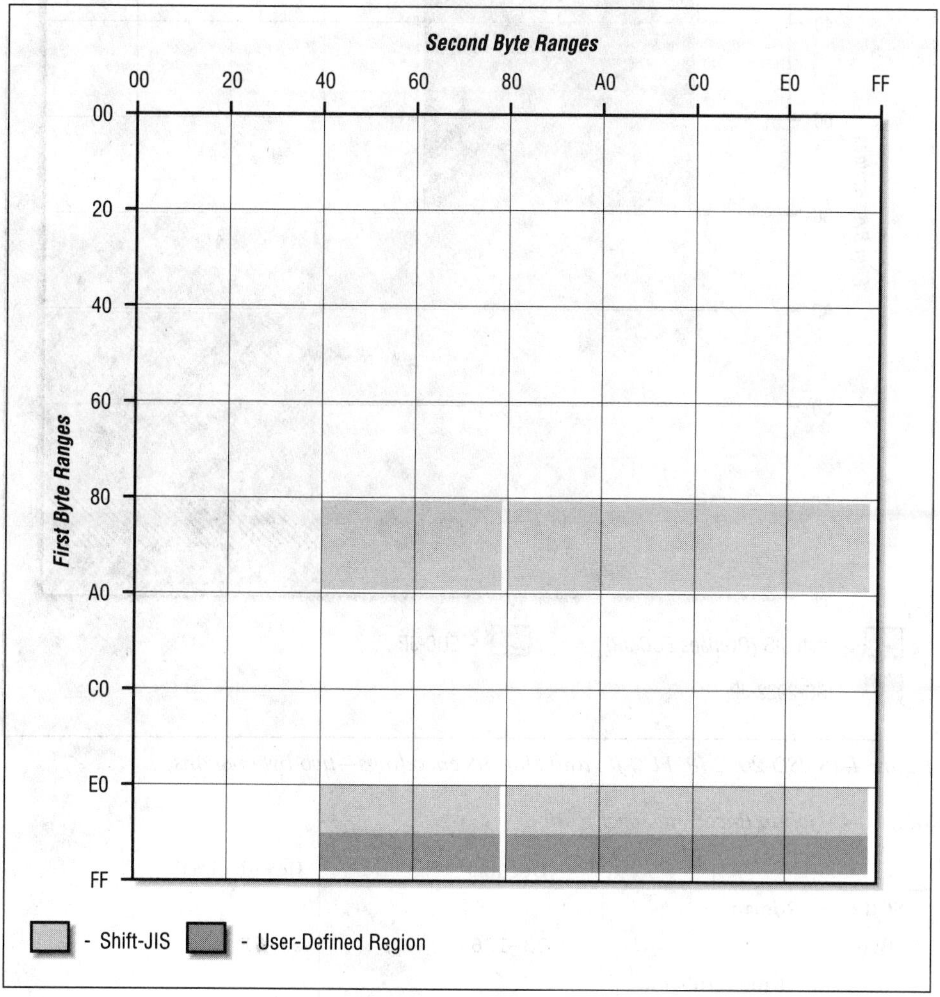

Figure 4-17: Shift-JIS user-defined encoding table—two-byte region

only forward compatible with Unicode. Table 4-44 provides the Johab encoding specifications as described in the KS X 1001:1992 standard.

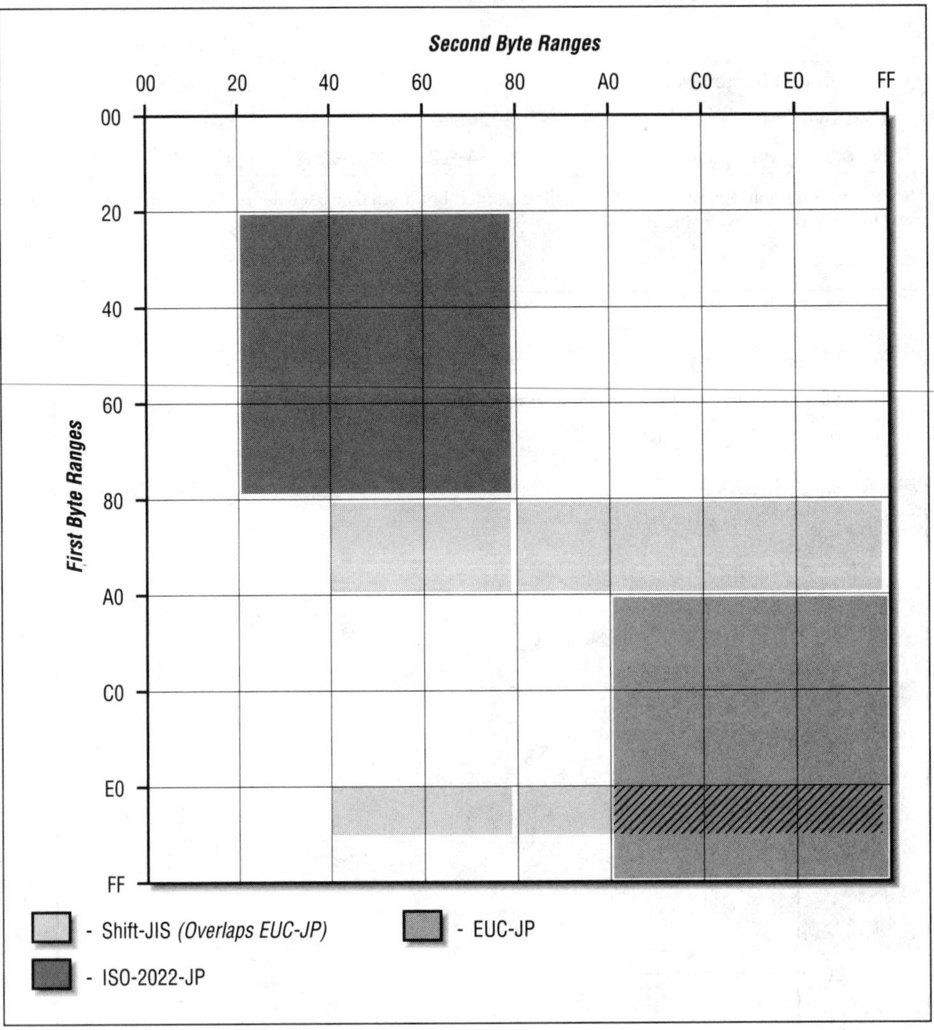

Figure 4-18: ISO-2022-JP, EUC-JP, and Shift-JIS encodings—two-byte regions

Table 4-44: Johab Encoding Specifications

	Decimal	Hexadecimal
ASCII or KS-Roman		
Byte range	33–126	21–7E
Hangul and 51 modern jamo[a]		
First byte range	132–211	84–D3
Second byte ranges	65–126, 129–254	41–7E, 81–FE

Table 4-44: Johab Encoding Specifications (continued)

	Decimal	Hexadecimal
Symbols, hanja, 42 ancient jamo[b]		
First byte ranges	`216–222, 224–249`	`D8–DE, E0–F9`
Second byte ranges	`49–126, 145–254`	`31–7E, 91–FE`

[a] These 51 modern jamo are KS X 1001:1992 04-01 through 04-51.
[b] These 42 ancient jamo are KS X 1001:1992 04-53 through 04-94.

Note how the hangul encoding range is quite different from the symbol and hanja encoding range. They both encode up to 188 characters per row, but the exact encoding range that defines these 188 code points is quite different. Figure 4-19 illustrates the two different two-byte encoding ranges of Johab encoding.

Also note how the hangul encoding range defines 15,040 code points (80 rows of 188 code points), which means that the encoding of the 11,172 hangul is not contiguous.

The hangul portion of Johab encoding is fundamentally based upon three five-bit segments. Five bits are used to represent the three basic positions of jamo within hangul. Five bits can encode up to 32 unique entities. Knowing that there are 19 initial jamo (consonants), 21 medial jamo (vowels), and 27 final jamo (consonants; 28 to cover the "empty" case for two-jamo hangul), we can see that five bits can easily represent the number of unique jamo for each of the three positions. But, three five-bit units become 15 bits. The sixteenth bit, which is the most significant bit (actually, the first bit, not the sixteenth), is always set.

Table 4-45 lists the 32 different binary patterns, along with the jamo they represent in the three positions for composing hangul.

Table 4-46 provides some examples of hangul encoded according to Johab, and illustrates how the binary patterns of the jamo from which they are composed are used to derive the final encoded value. Those five-bit segments that are used to encode a "fill" element are shaded. Note how individual modern jamo are encoded using this scheme using two "fill" elements—hangul use only one "fill" element.

It is critical to understand that KS X 1001:1992 row 4 (the jamo) has special treatment for Johab encoding. The first 51 characters, 04-01 through 04-51, are encoded according to the standard Johab hangul encoding scheme, as illustrated in Table 4-46. The remaining 43 characters, 04-52 through 04-94, are encoded according to the mapping as described in the KS X 1001:1992 manual.

Johab and EUC-KR encodings

The relationship among Johab and EUC-KR encodings is an interesting one. First, their hangul portions are incompatible in that EUC-KR can encode only 2,350.

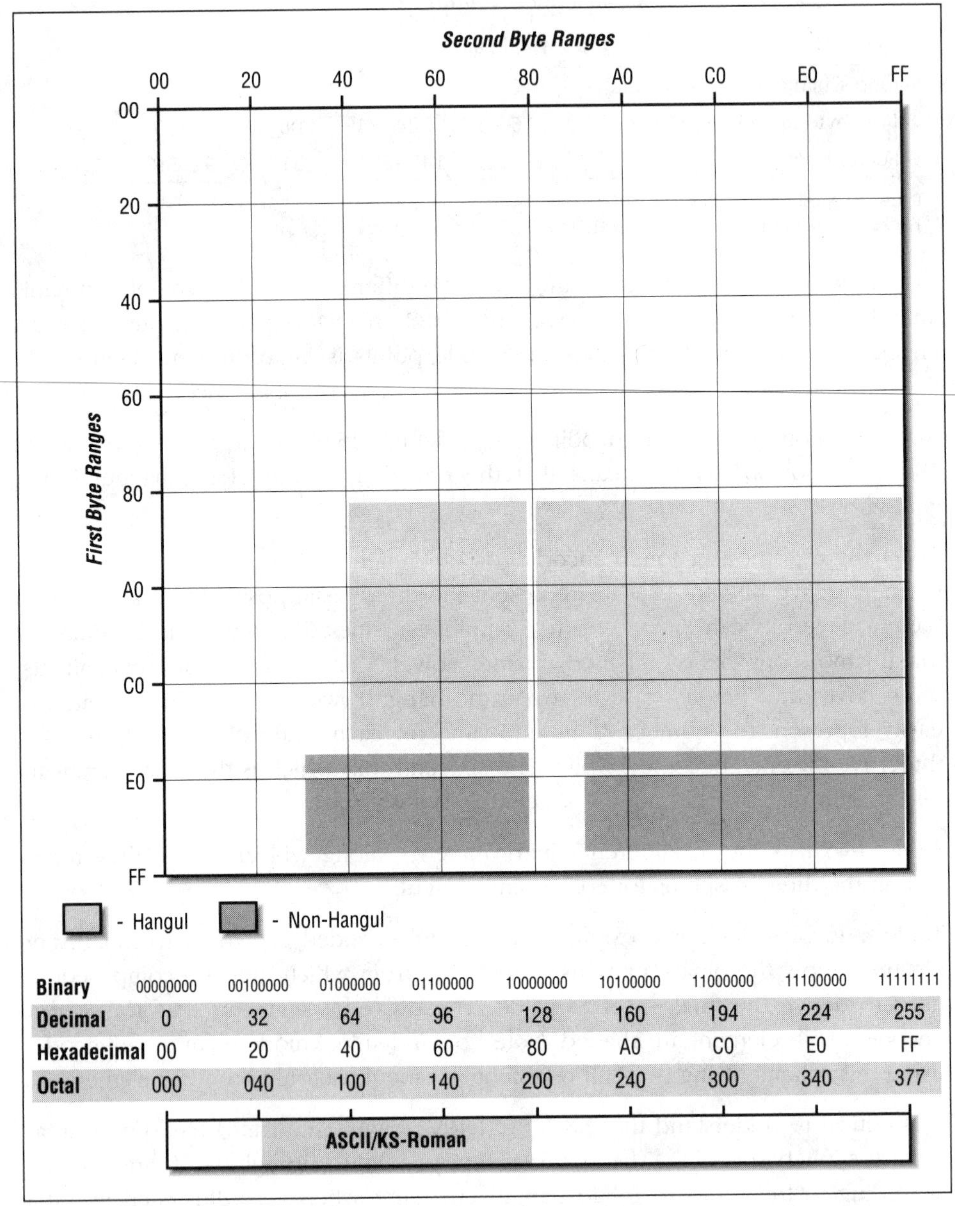

Figure 4-19: Johab encoding tables

Table 4-45: Johab Encoding's Five-Bit Binary Patterns

Binary Pattern	Initial	Medial	Final
00000	*unused*	*unused*	*unused*
00001	"fill"	*unused*	"fill"

Table 4-45: Johab Encoding's Five-Bit Binary Patterns (continued)

Binary Pattern	Initial	Medial	Final
00010	ㄱ	"fill"	ㄱ
00011	ㄲ	ㅏ	ㄲ
00100	ㄴ	ㅐ	ㄳ
00101	ㄷ	ㅑ	ㄴ
00110	ㄸ	ㅒ	ㄵ
00111	ㄹ	ㅓ	ㄶ
01000	ㅁ	*unused*	ㄷ
01001	ㅂ	*unused*	ㄹ
01010	ㅃ	ㅔ	ㄺ
01011	ㅅ	ㅕ	ㄻ
01100	ㅆ	ㅖ	ㄼ
01101	ㅇ	ㅗ	ㄽ
01110	ㅈ	ㅘ	ㄾ
01111	ㅉ	ㅙ	ㄿ
10000	ㅊ	*unused*	ㅀ
10001	ㅋ	*unused*	ㅁ
10010	ㅌ	ㅚ	*unused*
10011	ㅍ	ㅛ	ㅂ
10100	ㅎ	ㅜ	ㅄ
10101	*unused*	ㅝ	ㅅ
10110	*unused*	ㅞ	ㅆ
10111	*unused*	ㅟ	ㅇ
11000	*unused*	*unused*	ㅈ
11001	*unused*	*unused*	ㅊ
11010	*unused*	ㅠ	ㅋ
11011	*unused*	ㅡ	ㅌ
11100	*unused*	ㅢ	ㅍ
11101	*unused*	ㅣ	ㅎ
11110	*unused*	*unused*	*unused*
11111	*unused*	*unused*	*unused*

Table 4-46: Composing Hangul from Jamo According to Johab Encoding

Hangul	Bit 1	Bits 2–6	Bits 7–11	Bits 12–16	Johab Encoding
가	1	00010	00011	00001	8861
김	1	00010	11101	10001	8BB1
치	1	10000	11101	00001	C3A1

Table 4-46: Composing Hangul from Jamo According to Johab Encoding (continued)

Hangul	Bit 1	Bits 2–6	Bits 7–11	Bits 12–16	Johab Encoding
ㄱ	1	00010	00010	00001	8841
ㅏ	1	00001	00011	00001	8461
ㄺ	1	00001	00010	01010	844A

Johab can encode all 11,172 (an additional 8,822). Their symbol and hanja portions, however, are compatible, and there is a proven and convenient code conversion algorithm for converting between them. Figure 4-20 illustrates how the encoding structure of Johab and EUC-KR encodings differ.

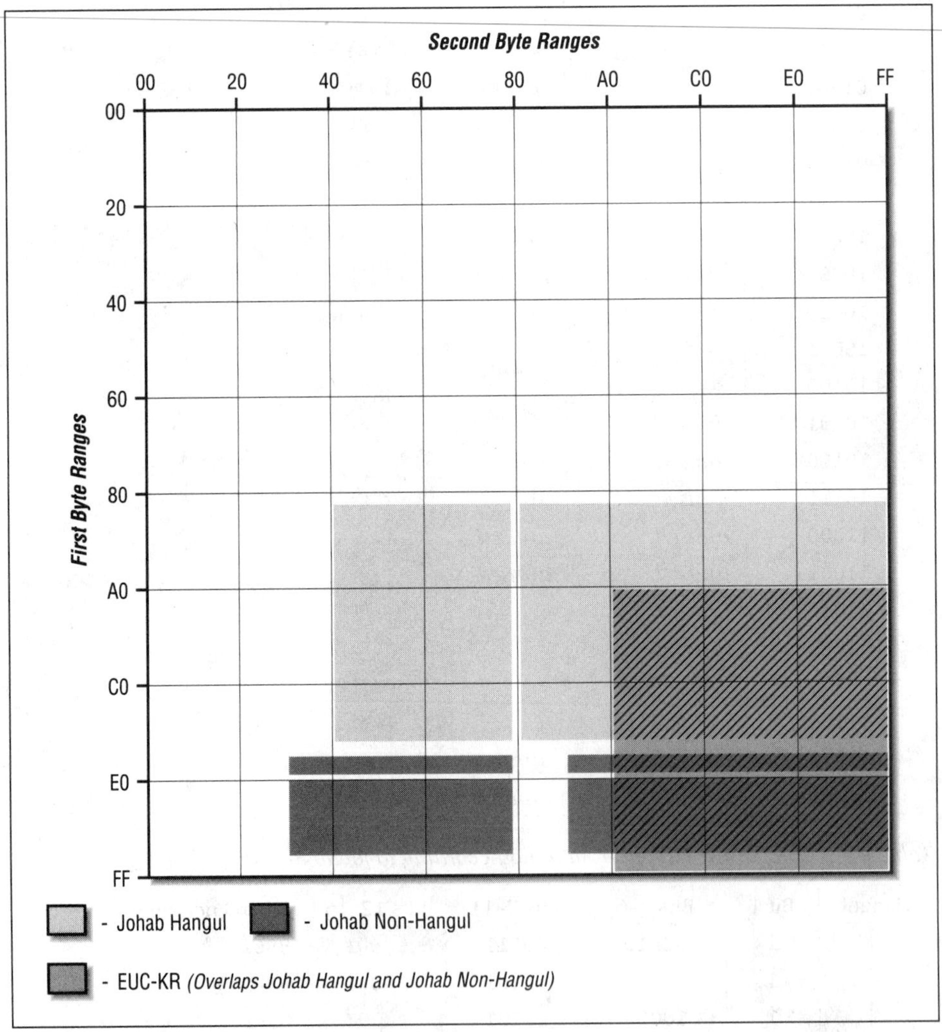

Figure 4-20: Johab and EUC-KR encodings—two-byte regions

A complete machine-readable mapping table that provides correspondences between Johab encoding and Unicode is available.* Other mapping tables provide correspondences among other encodings for the hangul† and non-hangul‡ portions of the Korean character set.

Comparing CJKV Encoding Methods

The repertoire of characters, especially those of Chinese origin, in the CJKV character set standards overlap considerably, although the ordering of the characters is markedly different. This means that any attempt at conversion among them must be done with mapping tables, and there may be cases—sometimes hundreds or thousands—when characters in one standard do not exist in another.

Table 4-47 lists the encoded values for the two Chinese characters 漢 and 字. I am listing them under the most common encoding methods for each locale. Note how there is no correspondence among the encodings of these two characters across the different character sets.

Table 4-47: Chinese Characters Encoded in Different CJKV Character Sets

Locale (Character Set)	ISO-2022 Encoding	Eight-Bit Encodings
China (GB 2312-80)		
汉	`3A3A`	`BABA`
字	`5756`	`D7D6`
Taiwan (CNS 11643-1992)[a]		
漢	`6947`	`E9C7, 8EA1E9C7, BA7E`
字	`4773`	`C7F3, 8EA1C7F3, A672`
Japan (JIS X 0208:1997)[b]		
漢	`3441`	`B4C1, 8ABF`
字	`3B7A`	`BBFA, 8E9A`
South Korea (KS X 1001:1992)[c]		
漢	`7953`	`F9D3, F7D3`
字	`6D2E`	`EDAE, F1AE`
North Korea (KPS 9566-97)		
漢	`7253`	`F2D3`
字	`662F`	`E6AF`

* *http://pantheon.yale.edu/~jshin/faq/JOHAB.TXT.gz*

† *ftp://ftp.oreilly.com/pub/examples/nutshell/cjkv/map/hangul-codes.txt*

‡ *ftp://ftp.oreilly.com/pub/examples/nutshell/cjkv/map/non-hangul-codes.txt*

Table 4-47: Chinese Characters Encoded in Different CJKV Character Sets (continued)

Locale (Character Set)	ISO-2022 Encoding	Eight-Bit Encodings
Vietnam (TCVN 6056:1995)		
漢	5D3E	DDBE
字	523E	D2BE

[a] The eight-bit encodings shown are EUC-TW code set 1, EUC-TW code set 2, and Big Five, respectively.
[b] The eight-bit encodings shown are EUC-JP (code set 1) and Shift-JIS, respectively.
[c] The eight-bit encodings shown are EUC-KR (code set 1) and Johab, respectively.

Although these characters look nearly identical across locales (except for 汉, which is the simplified form of 漢), their character codes (that is, encodings) are quite different.

International Encoding Methods

Thus far the discussions have centered around locale-independent and locale-specific encoding methods: ISO-2022, EUC, Big Five, Shift-JIS, and Johab. Some of these encoding methods are used to form the basis for vendor-specific encoding methods because the character sets they support are nearly identical. In this section you will see radically different encoding methods, ones for encoding a much larger repertoire of characters, such as Unicode. Table 4-48 lists the international character set standards, along with the encoding methods that support them.

Table 4-48: International Character Set Standards and Their Encoding Methods

Character Set	Encoding Methods
Unicode	UCS-2, UTF-7, UTF-8, and UTF-16
ISO 10646-1:1993[a]	UCS-2, UCS-4, UTF-7, UTF-8, and UTF-16

[a] GB 13000.1-93, JIS X 0221-1995, and KS X 1005-1:1995 are identical to ISO 10646-1:1993, encoding-wise.

Two of these encoding methods, UCS-2 and UCS-4, are fixed-length: all characters are represented by the same number of bytes (or 16-bit units). UTF-7 encoding is modal. UTF-8 and UTF-16 encodings are variable-length.

UCS-2 and UCS-4 Encodings

ISO 10646-1:1993 defines two basic encoding methods. The first method is the 32-bit form (actually, a 31-bit form), referred to as UCS-4 (*Universal Character Set containing four bytes*). The second is the 16-bit form, referred to as UCS-2 (*Universal Character Set containing two bytes*). Note that the second method is identical to the encoding used for Unicode. A 16-bit representation can encode up to 65,536 unique code points. A 32-bit representation, on the other hand, can encode up to 4,294,967,296 unique characters.*

These encodings are not modal, and use the same number of bytes to represent each character. All 16 or 32 bits (31 bits) are used for representing characters. ASCII control codes (0x00 through 0x1B and 0x7F), which are usually forbidden in other encodings, are valid for encoding printable characters.† Table 4-49 shows the encoding space for both UCS-2 and UCS-4.

Table 4-49: ISO 10646-1:1993 Encoding Specifications

	Decimal	Hexadecimal
UCS-2		
High byte range	0–255	00–FF
Low byte range	0–255	00–FF
UCS-4		
First byte range	0–127	00–7F
Second byte range	0–255	00–FF
Third byte range	0–255	00–FF
Fourth byte range	0–255	00–FF

Because Unicode and ISO 10646-1:1993 allocate the entire encoding space for characters, it makes no sense to include a diagram showing either the encoding space nor how it compares to other encodings. You will see in the following section that this encoding space is divided into four zones, each one containing one of four different classes of characters.

The following is an example of five characters, "My 河豚," encoded in UCS-2 (in big endian byte order). The same representation holds true for Unicode encoding—UCS-2 and Unicode encodings are identical.

Character string	M	y		河	豚
UCS-2 encoding	004D	0079	0020	6CB3	8C5A

* Considering that UCS-4 is really a 31-bit encoding, there are only 2,147,483,648 available code points. Let's hope that this is enough code points…

† Some control characters, such as 0x09 (tab), 0x0A (newline), and 0x0D (carriage return), are commonly used in almost every textfile.

Next, you see the same characters, but this time encoded according to UCS-4 (in big endian byte order). Note how every character has four bytes, each with the value 0x0000 prefixed.*

Character string	M	y		河	豚
UCS-4 encoding	0000 004D	0000 0079	0000 0020	0000 6CB3	0000 8C5A

It is important to note that *all* characters have the same encoding length. From a computer's point of view, they are treated the same for certain processing operations, such as searching. Variable-length encodings pose difficulties for searching and other processing operations.

Special characters

There are four special characters available in Unicode encodings that are worth mentioning: an "undefined" Chinese character mark (also known as "Geta mark"), the Ideographic Variation Mark, the "Byte Order Mark" (BOM), and a generic "undefined" character.† Table 4-50 lists these four characters' representations in UCS-2 and UCS-4 encodings (taking little and big endian byte order into account).

Table 4-50: Special Unicode Characters

Character	UCS-2	Little Endian	UCS-4	Little Endian
Geta mark	3013	1330	0000 3013	1330 0000
Ideographic Variation Mark	303E	3E30	0000 303E	3E30 0000
Byte Order Mark	FEFF	FFFE	0000 FEFF	FFFE 0000
Undefined	FFFD	FDFF	0000 FFFD	FDFF 0000

The Geta (下駄 *geta*) mark is used to indicate a Chinese character that is in Unicode, but is not available in the font for proper rendering. "Geta" is a Japanese word that refers to a type of wooden shoe whose sole appears as two heavy horizontal bars: 〓 (JIS X 0208:1997 02-14).

The Ideographic Variation Mark, which is not yet officially part of Unicode, is proposed to be used to indicate that the Chinese character that immediately precedes it is not quite the character that was intended, but is the closest that the document author could find. A sort of flag to indicate that what was really intended is not available in Unicode.

The Byte Order Mark has multiple semantics. When it occurs as the first character in a file, its purpose is to explicitly indicate the byte order (thus, it is called a "Byte Order Mark"). When it occurs in other contexts (that is, buried within a file), it is used as a zero-width non-breaking space.

* Or suffixed, if you're dealing with little endian machines.

† They are also available in some of the UTFs, described shortly.

The generic "undefined" character is used for characters that cannot be represented in UCS-2 or UCS-4.

UTF Encodings

UTF refers to a series of encoding methods developed for Unicode and ISO 10646-1:1993. UTF stands for *UCS* (Universal Character Set) *Transformation Format*, and these encodings serve to either transform 16- or 32-bit (31-bit) representations (that is, UCS-2 or UCS-4) so that the data can be passed more reliably through specific environments (UTF-7 and UTF-8), or to provide extensibility (UTF-16).

UTF-7 encoding

UTF-7 encoding, which is designed as a human-unreadable but mail-safe transformation of Unicode, is remarkably similar to Base64 transformation (described starting on page 210), and in fact uses the same set of Base64 characters except for the "pad" character (0x3D, "="). The pad character is not necessary because UTF-7 encoding does not require padding for complete three-byte segments. UTF-7 is also different in that the Base64-like transformation is not applied to an entire file, but only to specific characters.

UTF-7 encoding is described in David Goldsmith and Mark Davis' RFC 2152 (formerly RFC 1642), *UTF-7: A Mail-Safe Transformation Format of Unicode.*

Table 4-51 lists the sixty-four Base64 characters, along with the six-bit values to which they correspond.

The actual binary representation for the values in Table 4-51 are those that correspond to bit arrays of the same values. That is, 0 is 000000 (0x00), and 63 is 111111 (0x3F).

Because UTF-7 does not blindly apply Base64 transformation to an entire file, there are some characters, a subset of ASCII, that represent themselves according to ASCII encoding. Table 4-52 lists the characters that can be directly encoded according to ASCII.

Table 4-53 lists the optional directly encoded characters of UTF-7 encoding. They are optional because these characters, in some contexts, may not be reliably transmitted.

Note that the four characters + (0x2B), = (0x3B), \ (0x5C), and ~ (0x7E) are explicitly excluded from these sets of directly encoded characters.

Those characters that require Base64 transformation according to UTF-7 encoding begin with a "plus" character (+, 0x2B) that functions as an "escape" or "shift" to signify the start of a Base64 sequence. What follows are the Base64 characters

Table 4-51: The Base64 Character Set

Value	Base64	Value	Base64	Value	Base64	Value	Base64
0	A	16	Q	32	g	48	w
1	B	17	R	33	h	49	x
2	C	18	S	34	i	50	y
3	D	19	T	35	j	51	z
4	E	20	U	36	k	52	0
5	F	21	V	37	l	53	1
6	G	22	W	38	m	54	2
7	H	23	X	39	n	55	3
8	I	24	Y	40	o	56	4
9	J	25	Z	41	p	57	5
10	K	26	a	42	q	58	6
11	L	27	b	43	r	59	7
12	M	28	c	44	s	60	8
13	N	29	d	45	t	61	9
14	O	30	e	46	u	62	+
15	P	31	f	47	v	63	/

Table 4-52: UTF-7 Directly-Encoded Characters

Characters	UCS-2/UTF-16 Encoding	UTF-7
'	0027	27
(	0028	28
)	0029	29
,	002C	2C
-	002D	2D
.	002E	2E
/	002F	2F
0 through 9	0030–0039	30–39
:	003A	3A
?	003F	3F
A through Z	0041–005A	41–5A
a through z	0061–007A	61–7A

Table 4-53: UTF-7 Optional Directly-Encoded Characters

Character	UCS-2/UTF-16 Encoding	UTF-7
!	0021	21
"	0022	22

Table 4-53: UTF-7 Optional Directly-Encoded Characters (continued)

Character	UCS-2/UTF-16 Encoding	UTF-7
#	0023	23
$	0024	24
%	0025	25
&	0026	26
*	002A	2A
;	003B	3B
<	003C	3C
=	003D	3D
>	003E	3E
@	0040	40
[	005B	5B
]	005D	5D
^	005E	5E
_	005F	5F
`	0060	60
{	007B	7B
|	007C	7C
}	007D	7D

themselves, and continues until a character not in the Base64 character set is encountered (including line-termination characters), but a hyphen (-, 0x2D) can be used to explicitly terminate a Base64 sequence. The following is an example of UTF-7–encoded text, with UCS-2 encoding (in big endian byte order) provided for reference:

Character string	M	y		河	豚
UCS-2 encoding	004D	0079	0020	6CB3	8C5A
UTF-7 encoding	4D	79	20	+bLOMwg-	

Because UTF-7 is a seven-bit encoding, there is no need to indicate byte order. This means that file-initial instances of the byte order mark (0xFEFF in big endian byte order) can be effectively eliminated when converting to UTF-7 encoding. Of course, the byte order mark should be reinserted when converting back to UCS-2 or UTF-16 encodings.

UTF-7 encoding, by definition, can encode only UCS-2 and UTF-16 encodings, and is applied in big endian byte order. The UTF-16 surrogates are treated as though they were UCS-2 (that is, no special treatment). Note how the escaped portion of this example must span character boundaries. This is because Base64 transformation spans byte boundaries due to the splitting of multiple bytes into six-bit segments.

UTF-8 encoding

UTF-8 encoding was developed as a way to represent Unicode text as a stream of one or more eight-bit bytes (also known as octets) rather than as true 16-bit units.* It is therefore an eight-bit variable-length encoding. UTF-8 encoding converts UCS-2, UCS-4, or UTF-16 encoding into a mixed one- through six-byte encoding, although the BMP (UCS-2 encoding) can be represented using a mixed one-through three-byte encoding. UTF-16, which represents UCS-2 plus a small portion of UCS-4 encoding, can be represented with a mixed one- through four-byte encoding. UTF-8 encoding is fully described in François Yergeau's RFC 2279, *UTF-8, a transformation format of ISO 10646.*

Table 4-54 lists the six different UTF-8 representations as per-octet bit arrays, along with the corresponding UCS-2 and UCS-4 encoding ranges (in big endian byte order).

Table 4-54: UCS-2/UCS-4 Encoding Ranges and UTF-8 Bit Arrays

	Encoding Range	UTF-8 Bit Arrays
UCS-2	0000–007F	0xxxxxxx
	0080–07FF	110xxxxx 10xxxxxx
	0800–FFFF	1110xxxx 10xxxxxx 10xxxxxx
UCS-4	0001 0000–001F FFFF	11110xxx 10xxxxxx 10xxxxxx 10xxxxxx
	0020 0000–03FF FFFF	111110xx 10xxxxxx 10xxxxxx 10xxxxxx 10xxxxxx
	0400 0000–7FFF FFFF	1111110x 10xxxxxx 10xxxxxx 10xxxxxx 10xxxxxx 10xxxxxx

For all but the ASCII-compatible range (0x0000 through 0x007F), the number of first-byte high-order bits set to "1" indicates the byte length. This sequence of two or more bits set to "1" are followed by exactly one bit set to "0." For example, "11110xxx" indicates that the byte length must be four because there are four initial 1s. Bytes 2 through *n* have "10" as the high-order bits.

In order to make the encoding ranges a bit clearer to grasp, Table 4-55 lists the specific encoding ranges that correspond to the bit arrays listed in Table 4-54. All 2,147,483,648 UCS-4 code points can be represented, and note how each encoding range excludes a range that can encode all encoding ranges with less number of bytes—table footnotes explicitly indicate the excluded encoding ranges. Note how all bytes 2 through *n* share the same encoding range, specifically 0x80 through 0xBF.

* UTF-8 was once known as UTF-2 and FSS-UTF (File System Safe UTF).

Table 4-55: UTF-8 Encoding Ranges

	Decimal	Hexadecimal
0000–007F (128 code points)		
Byte range	0–127	00–7F
0080–07FF (1,920 code points)[a]		
First byte range	192–223	C0–DF
Second byte range	128–191	80–BF
0800–FFFF (63,488 code points)[b]		
First byte range	224–239	E0–EF
Second and third byte range	128–191	80–BF
0001 0000–001F FFFF (2,031,616 code points)[c]		
First byte range	240–247	F0–F7
Second through fourth byte range	128–191	80–BF
0020 0000–03FF FFFF (65,011,712 code points)[d]		
First byte range	248–251	F8–FB
Second through fifth byte range	128–191	80–BF
0400 0000–7FFF FFFF (2,080,374,784 code points)[e]		
First byte range	252–253	FC–FD
Second through sixth byte range	128–191	80–BF

[a] 0xC080 through 0xC1BF (128 code points) are not available.
[b] 0xE08080 through 0xE09FBF (2,048 code points) are not available.
[c] 0xF0808080 through 0xF08FBFBF (65,536 code points) are not available.
[d] 0xF880808080 through 0xF887808080 (2,097,152 code points) are not available.
[e] 0xFC8080808080 through 0xFC8380808080 (67,108,864 code points) are not available.

When applying UTF-8 encoding to UTF-16–encoded text, special care must be taken when dealing with the 2,048 surrogate code points. When blindly converting this range (0xD800 through 0xDFFF) to UTF-8 encoding, it becomes 0xEDA080 through 0xEDBFBF. The correct method for dealing with UTF-16 surrogates in UTF-8 encoding is to first convert them into their UCS-4 equivalents, then to apply UTF-8 encoding, which results in four-byte sequences.

There are many attractive and beneficial characteristics of UTF-8 encoding, such as:

- Any valid ASCII string is a valid UTF-8 string—now there's backward compatibility!
- It is possible to probe anywhere within a UTF-8 file and still be able to determine the location of character boundaries.
- UTF-8 encoding, by definition, can have absolutely no instances of 0xFE or 0xFF, which function as components of the byte order mark in UCS-2, UCS-4, and UTF-16 encodings.

Because UTF-8 is an eight-bit encoding, there is no need to indicate byte order. This means that file-initial instances of the byte order mark (0xFEFF in big endian byte order) can be effectively eliminated when converting to UTF-8 encoding. Of course, the byte order mark should be reinserted when converting back to UCS-2, UCS-4, or UTF-16 encodings.

The following is an example of UTF-8–encoded text—the UCS-2 values (in big endian byte order) for each character are provided for the sake of comparison:

Character string	M	y		河	豚
UCS-2 encoding	004D	0079	0020	6CB3	8C5A
UTF-8 encoding	4D	79	20	E6B2B3	E8B19A

Although the Java programming language uses Unicode internally through the use of type `char`, it also provides support for UTF-8 for data import and export purposes. Plan 9, which is briefly described in Chapter 10, *Operating Systems, Text Editors, and Word Processors*, is an experimental operating system that uses UTF-8 to encode Unicode text.

UTF-16 encoding—Unicode Version 2.0 (or greater) encoding

The most pure representation of Unicode Version 2.0 and greater text is referred to as UTF-16 encoding.* UTF-16 is defined in Appendix C.3 of *The Unicode Standard, Version 2.0* (Addison-Wesley, 1996), and in Amendment 1 of ISO 10646-1:1993. Unicode Version 2.0 added the surrogates area that allows for expansion beyond the 16-bit code space. In essence, UTF-16 encodes the BMP according to UCS-2 encoding, but also allows the next 16 planes, which are normally only accessible through UCS-4 encoding, to be encoded—you get the compactness of UCS-2 encoding for the most widely used characters, but also have access to the most useful subset of UCS-4 encoding. More detailed information on UTF-16 encoding can be found in Appendix C.3 of *The Unicode Standard, Version 2.0.*

UTF-16 encoding, which is fundamentally quite simple in design and implementation, works as follows:

- Two blocks of 1,024 code points, called *high surrogates* and *low surrogates* (this is Unicode terminology; ISO terminology is different) are set aside in the BMP (that is, Unicode)
- Combinations of a single high surrogate followed by a single low surrogate are used to address 2^{20} (1024×1024, somewhat more than a million) code points, which correspond to the code points for Planes 1 (0x01) through 16 (0x10) of ISO 10646-1:1993's Group 0 (Plane 0 is the BMP)

* Originally referred to as UCS-2E or Extended UCS-2 encoding.

Currently, Plane 1 (0x01) is planned to consist of historic, synthetic, and miscellaneous scripts, and Plane 2 (0x02) is slated for Chinese characters. Planes 15 and 16 (0x0F and 0x10) are for private use. This effectively allows up to 917,504 additional code points, along with 131,072 private-use codes.

UTF-16 encoding is therefore a variable-length encoding that employs a mixed 16- and 32-bit code space. This effectively means that software that processes UTF-16 encoding internally must deal with issues similar to those in legacy systems that use variable-length encodings. Table 4-56 lists the four levels of support for UTF-16 encoding.

Table 4-56: Four Levels of UTF-16 Support

UTF-16 Support Level	Meaning
UCS-2 only	No interpretation of pairs, and no pair integrity
Weak	Interpretation of pairs, but no pair integrity
Aware	No interpretation of pairs, but pair integrity
Strong	Interpretation of pairs, and pair integrity

Preserving pair integrity simply means that surrogate pairs are treated as a single unit when it comes to processing operations, such as character deleting and inserting. Interpreting pairs simply means that surrogate pairs are treated as UCS-4 characters.

Table 4-57 lists the corresponding code ranges among the first 16 planes of UCS-4 beyond the BMP and the UTF-16 surrogates area. The values are listed in big endian byte order.

Table 4-57: Mapping Sixteen UCS-4 Planes to UTF-16

UCS-4 Plane	UCS-4 Encoding Range	UTF-16 Equivalent
1	`0001 0000–0001 FFFF`	`D800 DC00–D83F DFFF`
2	`0002 0000–0002 FFFF`	`D840 DC00–D87F DFFF`
3	`0003 0000–0003 FFFF`	`D880 DC00–D8BF DFFF`
4	`0004 0000–0004 FFFF`	`D8C0 DC00–D8FF DFFF`
5	`0005 0000–0005 FFFF`	`D900 DC00–D93F DFFF`
6	`0006 0000–0006 FFFF`	`D940 DC00–D97F DFFF`
7	`0007 0000–0007 FFFF`	`D980 DC00–D9BF DFFF`
8	`0008 0000–0008 FFFF`	`D9C0 DC00–D9FF DFFF`
9	`0009 0000–0009 FFFF`	`DA00 DC00–DA3F DFFF`
10	`000A 0000–000A FFFF`	`DA40 DC00–DA7F DFFF`
11	`000B 0000–000B FFFF`	`DA80 DC00–DABF DFFF`
12	`000C 0000–000C FFFF`	`DAC0 DC00–DAFF DFFF`
13	`000D 0000–000D FFFF`	`DB00 DC00–DB3F DFFF`

Table 4-57: Mapping Sixteen UCS-4 Planes to UTF-16 (continued)

UCS-4 Plane	UCS-4 Encoding Range	UTF-16 Equivalent
14	000E 0000–000E FFFF	DB40 DC00–DB7F DFFF
15	000F 0000–000F FFFF	DB80 DC00–DBBF DFFF
16	0010 0000–0010 FFFF	DBC0 DC00–DBFF DFFF

Comparing UCSs and UTFs to Other Encodings

There is no clean conversion algorithm between Unicode and legacy CJKV encodings (that is, those used to encode GB 2312-80, CNS 11643-1992, JIS X 0208:1997, KS X 1001:1992, TCVN 6056:1995, and so on). The basic requirement for converting to and from Unicode is simply a set of mapping tables, and luckily, there is a reliable source for these tables. The Unicode Consortium has developed a tab-delimited database-like file that provides cross-listings among the 20,902 characters in the Unicode Chinese character set (plus the compatibility zone) and the major CJKV character set standards.*

Because the UTFs are simply algorithmic transformations of UCS-2 and UCS-4 encodings, conversion from the UTFs to either UCS-2 or UCS-4 is performed before conversion to non-Unicode encodings is performed. This is simply common sense.

Charset Designations

In this section you will learn about the difference between a character set and an encoding. You will also learn why this distinction is critically important in several important contexts, one of which is information interchange, whether in the form of email or other electronic media. You see, in order to explicitly indicate the content of a document, such as an email message or an HTML file, there is the notion of "charset" (character set), which is used as an identifier.

Character Sets Versus Encodings

The fundamental ways in which character sets are different from encodings—which are especially clear when in the context of CJKV—are as follows:

- Character sets, especially CJKV ones, can usually be encoded in more than one way—consider ISO-2022 and EUC encodings, *both* of which are commonly used to encode most CJKV character sets
- Most CJKV encodings simultaneously support more than one character set—consider EUC-JP for Japan, which supports JIS X 0201-1997, JIS X 0208:1997, and JIS X 0212-1990 in a mixed one-, two-, and three-byte encoding

* *ftp://ftp.unicode.org/Public/MAPPINGS/EASTASIA/*

Table 4-58 lists several CJKV encodings, along with the characters sets that they support. Table 4-1 on page 140 provided similar information.

Table 4-58: CJKV Encodings and the Character Sets They Support

Encoding	Character Sets
EUC-CN	GB 1988-89[a] and GB 2312-80
EUC-TW	CNS 5205-1989[a] and CNS 11643-1992
EUC-JP	JIS X 0201-1997,[b] JIS X 0208:1997, and JIS X 0212-1990
EUC-KR	KS X 1003:1993[a] and KS X 1001:1992
HZ	GB 1988-89[a] and GB 2312-80
GBK	ASCII and GBK
Big Five	ASCII and Big Five
Big Five Plus	ASCII and Big Five Plus
Shift-JIS	JIS X 0201-1997[b] and JIS X 0208:1997
Johab	KS X 1003:1993,[a] KS X 1001:1992, and additional hangul

[a] Or ASCII.
[b] Or ASCII instead of the JIS-Roman portion.

Note that there are some character sets that are supported only by a single encoding, such as GBK and Big Five. Their designations are unique in that they can refer to either their character set or their encoding.

Some charset designations can withstand the test of time, while others cannot. For Korean, there are two camps when it comes to charset designations. One camp prefers to use a designation `KS_C_5601-1978` for EUC-KR encoding. The other camp simply prefers to use for `EUC-KR` encoding. In case it is not obvious, I belong to the latter camp. In 1998, all KS character set standards changed designation. For example, KS C 5601-1992 became KS X 1001:1992. As you can clearly see, the use of `KS_C_5601-1978` as a charset designator did not withstand the test of time. However, the use of `EUC-KR` is still completely valid, and clearly has withstood the test of time.

Charset Registries

Now that the distinction between a character set and an encoding has been made clear, the question now becomes what designation is appropriate for the purpose of relaying content information for documents, such as email and HTML? In my opinion, encoding names make the best charset designators because there is little or no ambiguity or confusion as to what character sets they can support.

There are two primary registries for charset designators, both of which are listed below:

- The ECMA (European Computer Manufacturers Association) Registry*
- The IANA (Internet Assigned Numbers Authority) Registry†

Registering a new charset designation, or changing one, requires that a discussion takes place on the IETF Charset Mailing List (see Appendix U, *Mailing Lists*, for information on how to join). Ned Freed and Jon Postel's RFC 2278, *IANA Charset Registration Procedures*, describes the charset registration process in detail. The latest charset registry is available online.‡

Consider the case when a character set name is used as the charset designator, as is *actually* done in some environments. When a charset designator is set to something like `GB_2312-80` or `KS_C_5601-1987`, it is ambiguous as to what encoding it specifies. This is because these character sets, GB 2312-80 and KS X 1001:1992, can be encoded in at least three ways (see Table 4-58 again if you need a refresher).

Table 4-59 lists charset designators for some of the encodings covered in this book.

Table 4-59: Preferred Charset Designators

Encoding	Charset Designator
ASCII	`US_ASCII`
ISO-2022-CN	`ISO-2022-CN`
ISO-2022-CN-EXT	`ISO-2022-CN-EXT`
HZ	`HZ-GB-2312`
ISO-2022-JP	`ISO-2022-JP`
ISO-2022-JP-2	`ISO-2022-JP-2`
ISO-2022-KR	`ISO-2022-KR`
EUC-CN	`EUC-CN`
EUC-TW	`EUC-TW`
EUC-JP	`EUC-JP`
EUC-KR	`EUC-KR`
GBK	`GBK`
Big Five	`Big_Five`
Shift-JIS	`Shift_JIS`

* *http://www.ecma.ch/*

† *http://www.iana.org/*

‡ *ftp://ftp.isi.edu/in-notes/iana/assignments/character-sets*

Table 4-59: Preferred Charset Designators (continued)

Encoding	Charset Designator
Johab	`Johab`
UTF-7	`UTF-7`
UTF-8	`UTF-8`
UTF-16	`UTF-16`
UCS-2	`ISO-10646-UCS-2`
UCS-4	`ISO-10646-UCS-4`

In order to be compatible with older or poorly written software, it is important to maintain an aliasing mechanism that effectively maps several charset designations to the preferred one.

Code Pages

In the context of IBM and Microsoft documentation there is often mention of a "Code Page." A Code Page is somewhat analogous to charset designations in that it indicates an encoding that supports one or more character sets.

While some of the IBM and Microsoft Code Pages appear to be similar, they should be treated independently of one another because they have several important differences. Specifically, Microsoft's Code Pages define multiple-byte encodings. IBM's define fixed-length encodings that support a single character set, but can combine into multiple-byte entities. For example, IBM's CCSID 00932 differs from Microsoft's Code Page 932 in that it does not include NEC Row 13 nor IBM Selected characters encoded in Rows 89 through 92 (that is, IBM Selected characters encoded according to NEC).

IBM Code Pages

The best way to describe IBM Code Page designations is by first listing the individual SBCS (Single-Byte Character Set), DBCS (Double-Byte Character Set), and TBCS (Triple-Byte Character Set) Code Page designations (those designated by "Host" use EBCDIC-based encodings). The IBM terminology for "Code Page" is Code Page Global Identifier (CPGID), which refers to a number between 00001 and 65534 (decimal) that identifies a code page. Table 4-60 lists several IBM SBCS Code Pages, which are for the most part equivalent to CJKV-Roman as described in Chapter 3.

Table 4-60: IBM SBCS Code Pages

Code Page	Language	Encoding	Additional Details
00367	English	SBCS-PC	ASCII
00836	Simplified Chinese	SBCS-Host	

Table 4-60: IBM SBCS Code Pages (continued)

Code Page	Language	Encoding	Additional Details
00903	Simplified Chinese	SBCS-PC	
01115	Simplified Chinese	SBCS-PC	
00037	Traditional Chinese	SBCS-Host	
00904	Traditional Chinese	SBCS-PC	
01043	Traditional Chinese	SBCS-PC	
00037	Japanese	SBCS-Host	
00290	Japanese	SBCS-Host	EBCDIC
01027	Japanese	SBCS-Host	EBCDIK
00897	Japanese	SBCS-PC	
01041	Japanese	SBCS-PC	
00895	Japanese	SBCS-EUC	EUC-JP JIS-Roman
00896	Japanese	SBCS-EUC	EUC-JP half-width katakana
00833	Korean	SBCS-Host	
00891	Korean	SBCS-PC	
01088	Korean	SBCS-PC	
01129	Vietnamese	SBCS-PC	

Table 4-61 lists some IBM DBCS Code Pages, grouped by language. Some revealing information is provided in the "Additional Details" column.

Table 4-61: IBM DBCS Code Pages

Code Page	Language	Encoding	Additional Details
00837	Simplified Chinese	DBCS-Host	
00928	Simplified Chinese	DBCS-PC	
01380	Simplified Chinese	DBCS-PC	IBM GB
01385	Simplified Chinese	DBCS-PC	GBK encoding
01382	Simplified Chinese	DBCS-EUC	EUC-CN encoding
00835	Traditional Chinese	DBCS-Host	
00927	Traditional Chinese	DBCS-PC	
00947	Traditional Chinese	DBCS-PC	IBM BIG-5
00960	Traditional Chinese	DBCS-EUC	EUC-TW (CNS 11643-1992 Plane 1)
00300	Japanese	DBCS-Host	
00301	Japanese	DBCS-PC	
00941	Japanese	DBCS-PC	Windows-J character set
00952	Japanese	DBCS-EUC	EUC-JP code set 1 (JIS X 0208:1997)
00953	Japanese	DBCS-EUC	EUC-JP code set 3 (JIS X 0212-1990)
00834	Korean	DBCS-Host	
00926	Korean	DBCS-PC	

Table 4-61: IBM DBCS Code Pages (continued)

Code Page	Language	Encoding	Additional Details
00951	Korean	DBCS-PC	IBM KS Code
01362	Korean	DBCS-PC	UHC encoding
00971	Korean	DBCS-EUC	EUC-KR encoding

Table 4-62 lists the only IBM TBCS Code Page that I am aware of.

Table 4-62: IBM TBCS Code Pages

Code Page	Language	Encoding	Additional Details
00961	Traditional Chinese	TBCS-EUC	EUC-TW (CNS 11643-1992 Plane 2)

When we combine the above SBCS, DBCS, and TBCS Code Pages into MBCS (Multiple-Byte Character Set) entities that are assigned unique Coded Character Set Identifiers (CCSIDs), things may become a bit more revealing for those familiar with Microsoft Code Page designations, as shown in Table 4-63.

Table 4-63: IBM MBCS Entities

CCSID	Language	Encoding	Code Page Composition
05031	Simplified Chinese	MBCS-Host	00836 and 00837
00936	Simplified Chinese	MBCS-PC	00903 and 00928
00946	Simplified Chinese	MBCS-PC	01042 and 00928
01383	Simplified Chinese	MBCS-EUC	00367 and 01382
05033	Traditional Chinese	MBCS-Host	00037 and 00835
00938	Traditional Chinese	MBCS-PC	00904 and 00927
00950	Traditional Chinese	MBCS-PC	01114 and 00947
25524	Traditional Chinese	MBCS-PC	01043 and 00927
00964	Traditional Chinese	MBCS-EUC	00367, 00960, and 00961
00930	Japanese	MBCS-Host	00290 and 00300
00939	Japanese	MBCS-Host	01027 and 00300
00932	Japanese	MBCS-PC	00897 and 00301
00943	Japanese	MBCS-PC	01041 and 00941
00954	Japanese	MBCS-EUC	00895, 00952, 00896, and 00953
00933	Korean	MBCS-Host	00833 and 00834
00934	Korean	MBCS-PC	00891 and 00926
00944	Korean	MBCS-PC	01040 and 00926
25525	Korean	MBCS-PC	01088 and 00951
00970	Korean	MBCS-EUC	00367 and 00971

You will see in the next section that many of Microsoft's Code Pages are similar, in both content and designation, to some of these CCSIDs specified by IBM.

More detailed information about IBM Code Pages can be found in IBM's *Character Data Representation Architecture Reference and Registry*.

Microsoft Code Pages

Table 4-64 lists Microsoft's Code Pages, along with a brief description of their composition. Note how many of them have Code Page designations that are the same as IBM CCSIDs listed in Table 4-63 (when the leading zeros are ignored).*

Table 4-64: Microsoft Code Pages

Code Page	Characteristics
932	JIS X 0208:1997 character set, Shift-JIS encoding, Microsoft extensions (NEC Row 13 and IBM Selected Characters duplicately encoded in Rows 89 through 92 and Rows 115 through 119)
936	GBK character set, GBK encoding
949	KS X 1001:1992 character set, Unified Hangul Code encoding, remaining 8,822 hangul as extension
950	Big Five character set, Big Five encoding, Microsoft extensions (actually, only the ETen extensions of Row 0xF9)
1258	TCVN-Roman character set
1361	Johab character set, Johab encoding

While the Code Page designations of Microsoft Code Pages have stayed the same over the years, their contents have been expanded to cover additional characters and new encodings that are true supersets of the previous version. Code Page 936, for example, was once the GB 2312-80 character set encoded according to EUC-CN. Also, Code Page 949 was once the KS X 1001:1992 character set encoded according to EUC-KR.

Code Conversion

Conversion of CJKV text from one encoding to another requires that you alter the numeric values of the bytes used to represent each character. There is a wide variety of CJKV-capable code conversion programs available. Some are portable across platforms, but some are not. Software developers who intend to introduce products into these markets must make their software as flexible as possible—meaning that software should be able to handle more than one CJKV encoding

* Although a hunch, this may have resulted from the fact that Microsoft Code Pages began their life as IBM Code Pages, but then developed on their own.

method. This is not to say that such software should be able to process all possible encodings internally, but that it should at least have the ability to import and export as many encodings as possible, which will result in better information interchange among various platforms. Adobe FrameMaker Version 5.5, for example, allows users to import EUC-JP– and ISO-2022-JP–encoded Japanese text, although it processes Shift-JIS internally.*

Earlier in this chapter you should have taken note how ISO-2022-JP encoding can support the designation of the 1978, 1983, 1990, and 1997 versions of JIS X 0208 by using different escape sequences (although the escape sequences for the 1990 and 1997 versions are identical). In Appendix Q, *Character Lists and Mapping Tables*, you will find material illustrating the differences among these versions of JIS X 0208. Should Japanese code conversion programs account for these differences? I don't recommend it unless you specifically need to refer to a particular vintage of JIS X 0208. Keep in mind that Shift-JIS and EUC-JP encodings support JIS X 0208 without any method for designating its vintage. Any conversion from ISO-2022-JP encoding to Shift-JIS or EUC-JP encoding effectively loses the information that indicates which vintage of JIS X 0208 was used to encode the original text. Likewise, converting Shift-JIS or EUC-JP encoding to ISO-2022-JP encoding requires that an arbitrary version of JIS X 0208 be selected because a two-byte–character escape sequence *must* be used for properly encoding ISO-2022-JP–encoded text.

I have written a tool called JConv which can convert the Japanese encoding within text files.† JConv supports ISO-2022-JP, EUC-JP, and Shift-JIS encodings. JConv is available in a variety of platform-specific executables:

- JConv (MacOS, minimal interface)
- JCONV-DD (MacOS)
- *jconv.exe* (MS-DOS/Windows)
- WinJConv (Windows)

I also distribute this tool as ANSI C source code so that other programmers may benefit from the algorithms used to convert among Japanese encodings, and so that it can be compiled on a variety of platforms. This tool has many useful features: error checking, the ability to automatically detect an input file's encoding, the ability to manually specify the input file's encoding, selective conversion of half-width katakana to their full-width equivalents, a help page, automatic ISO-2022-JP encoding repair, and command-line argument support. A more complete

* You will hear about Adobe FrameMaker in other parts of this book—it is what I used to write and typeset what you are reading right now.

† *http://www.oreilly.com/~lunde/j_tools.html*

description of this tool, including its help page, can be found at the end of Chapter 9, starting on page 448.

Other CJKV code conversion tools are available. They all perform roughly the same tasks, but in different ways, and some are more portable than others. Available tools are listed in Table 4-65.

Table 4-65: CJKV Code Conversion Tools

Tool Name	Language	URL
NCF[a]	Chinese[b]	*http://www.edu.cn/c_resource/software.html* or *ftp://ftp.net.tsinghua.edu.cn/pub/Chinese/ncf/*
ConvChar	Japanese	*http://www.asahi-net.or.jp/~VX1H-KNOY/*
nkf[c]	Japanese	*ftp://ftp.chem.sci.osaka-u.ac.jp/pub/unix/tools/nkf/*
pkf[d]	Japanese	*ftp://ftp.iij.ad.jp/pub/IIJ/dist/utashiro/perl/*
hcode	Korean	*ftp://ftp.kaist.ac.kr/hangul/code/hcode/*

[a] Stands for "Network Chinese Filter."
[b] Many additional Chinese code conversion tools are available at *http://cnapps.ifcss.org/*.
[c] Stands for "Network Kanji Filter."
[d] Perl version of nkf.

Contemporary Unix implementations often include a built-in code conversion utility called *iconv* (it is based on a library that can be used in other programs).

The actual need for stand-alone CJKV code conversion tools is decreasing due to the introduction of built-in code conversion facilities in most CJKV-capable text editors, word processors, and other text-intensive applications.

Chinese Code Conversion

The only frustrating problems that arise when dealing with Chinese code conversion are when it is between the GB 2312-80 and Big Five (or CNS 11643-1992) character sets. There are three basic reasons for this:

- GB 2312-80 contains only 6,763 hanzi, but Big Five contains 13,053—a two-fold difference in character complement
- Approximately one-third of the 6,763 hanzi in GB 2312-80 are considered simplified forms—not available in Big Five
- Many of the simplified hanzi in GB 2312-80 were derived by two or more traditional forms—context tells you which traditional form is appropriate

The use of GB/T 12345-90 conversion tables can sometimes aid in this process, but it doesn't solve the simple fact that Big Five has approximately two times the number of hanzi than GB 2312-80. Even ignoring the simplified/traditional issue, there are characters in GB 2312-80 that do not exist in Big Five.

NCF (Network Hanzi Filter), a Chinese code conversion tool, written in C and includes APIs, represents the core technology of several projects currently underway in China (this is considered a "National Ninth Five-Year Plan Key Project"), such as:

- WinNCF, a Windows version of NCF
- NCFTTY, a pseudo terminal emulator that uses NCF to handle different encodings
- NCF Proxy, a proxy for use with web browsers for automatically handling Chinese code conversion
- NCFDT, a tool for detecting Chinese encodings, written in C and includes APIs

CERNET's Network Compass (a Chinese search engine), developed by Tsinghua University, makes use of NCF and NCFDT.* The URL for NCF and related technologies can be found in Table 4-65 on page 204.

Japanese Code Conversion

Japanese code conversion is not problematic if you are dealing with only the JIS X 0208:1997 character set. The JIS X 0212-1990 character set, for example, cannot be encoded using Shift-JIS. Likewise, there is no single method for encoding half-width katakana in an ISO-2022–like encoding, which causes some confusion (to the point, in my opinion, that half-width katakana are explicitly excluded from the ISO-2022-JP encodings as described starting on page 155). Shift-JIS, as you've learned, is the most commonly used Japanese encoding still today.

One issue that comes up again and again in the context of Japanese code conversion is how to deal with the Shift-JIS user-defined region, specifically the 1,880 code points in the range 0xF040 through 0xF9FC. While ISO-2022-JP and EUC-JP encodings cannot handle these Shift-JIS code points well, Unicode can. In fact, a mapping between this Shift-JIS range and Unicode has already been defined, along with one for EUC-JP encoding.† The corresponding Unicode range is 0xE000 through 0xE757. For EUC-JP encoding, the last 10 rows of JIS X 0208:1997 and JIS X 0212-1990 (rows 85 through 94) are used for this purpose.‡

Table 4-66 provides this mapping on a per-row basis according to Shift-JIS encoding.

* *http://compass.net.edu.cn/* or *http://compass.net.edu.cn:8010/*

† *http://www.opengroup.or.jp/jvc/cde/cde.html*

‡ It seems strange to me that 940 Shift-JIS user-defined code points, 0xF040 through 0xF4FC, map back onto JIS X 0208:1997.

Table 4-66: Shift-JIS to Unicode and EUC-JP for User-Defined Region

Shift-JIS	Unicode	EUC-JP
F040–F0FC	E000–E0BB	F5A1–F5FE, F6A1–F6FE
F140–F1FC	E0BC–E177	F7A1–F7FE, F8A1–F8FE
F240–F2FC	E178–E233	F9A1–F9FE, FAA1–FAFE
F340–F3FC	E234–E2EF	FBA1–FBFE, FCA1–FCFE
F440–F4FC	E2F0–E3AB	FDA1–FDFE, FEA1–FEFE
F540–F5FC	E3AC–E467	8FF5A1–8FF5FE, 8FF6A1–8FF6FE
F640–F6FC	E468–E523	8FF7A1–8FF7FE, 8FF8A1–8FF8FE
F740–F7FC	E524–E5DF	8FF9A1–8FF9FE, 8FFAA1–8FFAFE
F840–F8FC	E5E0–E69B	8FFBA1–8FFBFE, 8FFCA1–8FFCFE
F940–F9FC	E69C–E757	8FFDA1–8FFDFE, 8FFEA1–8FFEFE

Another issue that can affect Japanese developers is the Microsoft Windows Japanese character set when in the context of Unicode. As described in Appendix C, starting on page 591, this character set is an amalgamation of NEC and IBM character sets with a JIS X 0208:1997 base. This results in several duplicate characters at different code points. The code conversion problem can be separated into two categories:

- Code conversion of the 360 IBM Selected Kanji—in NEC and IBM code points
- Code conversion of the non-kanji—affects JIS X 0208:1997 row 2, NEC Row 13, and IBM Selected Non-kanji

Code conversion of the 360 IBM Selected Kanji is easy to describe. When converting from Unicode back into Shift-JIS, the IBM code points are preferred (this follows the third rule provided below). Code conversion of the duplicate non-kanji is not so trivial, and involves a bit of history (keep in mind that the NEC Kanji character set was originally based on JIS C 6226-1978, which didn't have a lot of the characters that are currently in JIS X 0208:1997 row 2). In general, the following rules apply when deciding preference during round-trip conversion:

- If the character is in both JIS X 0208-1983 (and beyond) row 2 and NEC Row 13, the JIS X 0208-1983 row 2 code point is preferred
- If the character is in both NEC Row 13 and IBM Selected Non-kanji, the NEC Row 13 code point is preferred
- If the character is IBM Selected at both NEC and IBM code points, the IBM code point is preferred

Table 4-67 provides the non-kanji mappings for round-trip conversion of the Microsoft Windows-J character set.

Table 4-67: Round-Trip Mapping for Microsoft Windows-J Character Set

Character	Shift-JIS Code Points	To Unicode	Back to Shift-JIS
∪	81BE, 879C	222A	81BE
∩	81BF, 879B	2229	81BF
¬	81CA, EEF9, FA54	FFE2	81CA
∠	81DA, 8797	2220	81DA
⊥	81DB, 8796	22A5	81DB
≡	81DF, 8791	2261	81DF
≒	81E0, 8790	2252	81E0
√	81E3, 8795	221A	81E3
∵	81E6, 879A, FA5B	2235	81E6
∫	81E7, 8792	222B	81E7
Ⅰ	8754, FA4A	2160	8754
Ⅱ	8755, FA4B	2161	8755
Ⅲ	8756, FA4C	2162	8756
Ⅳ	8757, FA4D	2163	8757
Ⅴ	8758, FA4E	2164	8758
Ⅵ	8759, FA4F	2165	8759
Ⅶ	875A, FA50	2166	875A
Ⅷ	875B, FA51	2167	875B
Ⅸ	875C, FA52	2168	875C
Ⅹ	875D, FA53	2169	875D
№	8782, FA59	2116	8782
℡	8784, FA5A	2121	8784
㈱	878A, FA58	3231	878A
ⅰ	EEEF, FA40	2170	FA40
ⅱ	EEF0, FA41	2171	FA41
ⅲ	EEF1, FA42	2172	FA42
ⅳ	EEF2, FA43	2173	FA43
ⅴ	EEF3, FA44	2174	FA44
ⅵ	EEF4, FA45	2175	FA45
ⅶ	EEF5, FA46	2176	FA46
ⅷ	EEF6, FA47	2177	FA47
ⅸ	EEF7, FA48	2178	FA48
ⅹ	EEF8, FA49	2179	FA49
￤	EEFA, FA55	FFE4	FA55
＇	EEFB, FA56	FF07	FA56
＂	EEFC, FA57	FF02	FA57

Korean Code Conversion

Korean code conversion, when dealing with only EUC-KR and ISO-2022-KR encodings, is trivial. However, when Johab encoding is added to the mix, things become less trivial. Converting EUC-KR and ISO-2022-KR to Johab results in no loss of data because all of their characters can be represented in Johab encoding. However, the 8,822 additional hangul made available in Johab encoding cannot convert to EUC-KR and ISO-2022-KR encoding, except as strings of jamo (all of which are encoded in EUC-KR and ISO-2022-KR encodings). A very popular Korean code conversion program, which supports a wide variety of encodings is hcode. Its URL can be found in Table 4-65 on page 204.

Perl subroutines that illustrate algorithmic conversion to and from Johab encoding—they apply to all KS X 1001:1992 characters except for the 51 modern jamo and hangul—are provided in Appendix W, *Perl Code Examples*, starting on page 1013.

Code Conversion Across CJKV Locales

All of the difficult (but interesting) code conversion problems arise when attempting to convert text from one CJKV locale to another. For example, consider times when someone sends me some Chinese text, say the title for a particular book, but may write it in Japanese. If I wanted to render the title in its original Chinese, I'd need to deal with at least one complex issue: *Japanese does not use Chinese characters simplified to the extreme they were in China.* This poses a problem only if you are using an intermediate representation, such as Unicode. This is because Unicode often encodes two versions of the same character: simplified and traditional. But, chances are that all the characters will convert because the author of the text was able to input them.

In order to effectively handle cases of characters that do not have a direct mapping to another character set according to Unicode, making use of information such as simplified/traditional pairs and Chinese character variants can dramatically help. But, there will always be cases of unmappable characters. It is unavoidable.

Basis Technology's Uniconv* (available for Unix and Windows), *tcs*† ("Translate Character Set," available for Unix and Windows), and my own home-grown CJKV-Conv.pl‡ (written in Perl) are examples of tools that can perform code conversion among CJKV locales. Uniconv provides a plethora of options and features. My own

* *http://www.basistech.com/unicode/*

† *ftp://plan9.bell-labs.com/plan9/unixsrc/tcs.shar.Z*, *ftp://ftp.cc.monash.edu.au/pub/nihongo/tcs.zip*, or *ftp://ftp.cc.monash.edu.au/pub/nihongo/tcs_w95.zip*

‡ *ftp://ftp.oreilly.com/pub/examples/nutshell/cjkv/perl/cjkvconv.pl*

CJKVConv.pl uses multiple Chinese character variant database-like tables to assist in resolving unmappable characters.

Code Conversion Tips and Tricks

Understanding the relationships among the many CJKV encoding methods can work to your advantage when it comes time to perform code conversion. Luckily, though, a great many people, because of the environments that they use, are well insulated from having to know details about code conversion.

The first determination you must make with regard to code conversion is whether the text you are attempting to use actually requires code conversion or is simply damaged. If you are using a Korean operating system, and received an ISO-2022-KR–encoded file, it may be difficult to determine whether code conversion is actually what you need.

Consider the following scenario: you are using a Japanese-capable operating system, such as MacOS-J. You receive two files. One file is EUC-JP–encoded, and the other is ISO-2022-JP–encoded, but damaged because its "escape" characters have been stripped. Both files display equally *un*-well when opened in a typical text editor or other text processing application.

The subject of repairing damaged CJKV files, which is closely related to code conversion, is covered next.

Repairing Unreadable CJKV Text

CJKV text files can be damaged in different ways depending on which encoding was used in the file. ISO-2022–encoded text is usually damaged by unfriendly mailers (and news readers) that remove control characters (including the all-important escape and shift characters). You will see that this type of damage is relatively easy to repair for some ISO-2022 encodings because the remaining characters that constitute a valid escape or designator sequence can serve as the context for properly restoring them. However, Big Five, EUC, GBK, Johab, and Shift-JIS encodings make generous use of eight-bit characters, and many mailers (and news readers) are not what many would call *eight-bit clean*, meaning that they effectively turn off the eighth bit of every byte. This has the nasty effect of scrambling the encoding, and renders the text unreadable.

Some data are not damaged *per se*, but rather encoded over again in a way that is intended to preserve the original file's contents. This includes *Quoted-Printable* and *Base64* transformations. Files that contain some binary or eight-bit data are usually converted to Quoted-Printable, and those that contain mostly binary are converted to Base64.

Quoted-Printable Transformation

Quoted-Printable transformation simply converts non-alphanumeric characters into a three-character form: an equals sign (=, 0x3D) followed by the two hexadecimal digits that represent the original character's encoded value. Instances of an equals sign are converted to "=3D" according to Quoted-Printable transformation rules. Quoted-Printable transformation is defined in Ned Freed and Nathaniel Borenstein's RFC 2045, *Multipurpose Internet Mail Extensions (MIME) Part One: Format of Internet Message Bodies.* While most Quoted-Printable–transformed data is in email bodies, it can sometimes be found in email headers, such as in the following I received (the emboldened portions represent the actual data—the rest is part of the transformation process that is explained in Table 4-69 on page 211):

```
Subject: =?Big5?Q?=A6=5E=C2=D0_=3A_Reply_=3A_Tze=2Dloi_Input_Method?=
```

The following short Perl program converts Quoted-Printable data back into its original form:

```
while (defined($line = <STDIN>)) {
  $line =~ s/=([0-9A-Fa-f][0-9A-Fa-f])/chr hex $1/ge;
  $line =~ s/=[\n\r]+$//;
  print STDOUT $line;
}
```

This plus many more Perl programs are provided in Appendix W.

Base64 Transformation

Base64 transformation is more complex than Quoted-Printable in that it involves manipulation of data at the bit level, and is applied to an entire file, not only those bytes that may represent binary data. Base64 transformation, put simply, is a method for transforming arbitrary bytes into the safest 64-character ASCII subset, and like Quoted-Printable is defined in RFC 2045.

Base64 transformation is easy to describe. Every three bytes are transformed into a four-byte sequence. That is, the 24 bits that constitute three bytes are split into four six-bit segments (six bits can encode up to 64 unique characters). Each six-bit segment is then converted into a character in the Base64 character set. A 65th character, = (0x3D), functions as a "pad" character if a full three-byte sequence is not achieved. Zero bits added to the right are used to pad instances of incomplete six-bit segments. The Base64 character set and mappings can be found in Table 4-51 on page 190.

My name, written in Japanese and EUC-JP–encoded, can serve as an example to illustrate the Base64 transformation. The three characters are 小林剣 (0xBEAE, 0xCED3, and 0xB7F5). When the Base64 transformation is applied, the result becomes the following eight Base64 characters:

```
vq7007f1
```

When the three original characters are represented as binary strings, the result is as follows:

```
1011111010101110 (0xBEAE)
1100111011010011 (0xCED3)
1011011111110101 (0xB7F5)
```

Splitting these three binary strings into six-bit segments results in the binary strings and the corresponding Base64 characters as illustrated in Table 4-68.

Table 4-68: An Example of Base64 Transformation

Binary String	Decimal Equivalent	Base64 Character
101111	47 (0x2F)	v
101010	42 (0x2A)	q
111011	59 (0x3B)	7
001110	14 (0x0E)	O
110100	52 (0x34)	0
111011	59 (0x3B)	7
011111	31 (0x1F)	f
110101	53 (0x35)	1

Compare this with the contents of Table 4-51 on page 190. The following short Perl program decodes Base64 data (it requires the "MIME" module):

```
use MIME::Decoder;
my $enc = 'base64';
my $decoder = new MIME::Decoder $enc or die "$enc unsupported";
$decoder->decode(\*STDIN, \*STDOUT);
```

Base64 data is typically delivered in two forms, either embedded within an SMTP header field, or else as an attachment whereby the entire attachment has been Base64-transformed. The following is a Base64-encoded SMTP header field:

```
From: lunde@adobe.com (=?ISO-2022-JP?B?GyRCMk9GWhsoQg==?=)
```

The emboldened portion represents the actual Base64-encoded segment—the rest is syntactic sugar for enabling parsers to more easily identify the Base64-encoded segment. Table 4-69 lists each component of the data within the parentheses (the parentheses themselves are real).

Table 4-69: Base64 in SMTP Header Fields

Component	Explanation
=?	Signals the start of encoded string
ISO-2022-JP	Charset designation ("ISO-2022-JP" is for Japanese)
?	Delimiter
B	Transformation type ("B" for Base64; "Q" for Quoted-Printable)

Table 4-69: Base64 in SMTP Header Fields (continued)

Component	Explanation
?	Delimiter
GyRCMk9GWhsoQg==	Base64-encoded data
?=	Signals the end of encoded string

The following is an example of an attached file that had Base64 transformation applied:


```
SSBhbSB3b25kZXJpbmcgaG93IG1hbnkgcGVvcGxlIHdpbGwgYWN0dWFsbHkgdHlwZSB0aGlzIGlu
IHRvIGZpbmQgb3V0CndoYXQgaXQgc2F5cy4gV2VsbCwgaXQgZG91c24ndCBzYXkgbXVjaC4K
```


I have never encountered a need to Base64-encode data because email client software applies Base64 transformation automatically when required.* If you *really* have a strong desire to Base64-encode some data, you can use the following Perl program (which, again, requires the "MIME" module):

```
use MIME::Base64;
undef $/;
my ($data, $encoded);
$data = <STDIN>;
$encoded = encode_base64($data);
print STDOUT $encoded;
```

Other Types of Encoding Repair

Let's discuss the repair procedure for ISO-2022-JP–encoded files as an example of how encodings may become damaged then repaired. One might receive Japanese email messages or attempt to display Japanese articles from Usenet News which have had their escape characters stripped out by unfriendly email or news reading software. Sometimes the escape characters are simply mangled—converted into a single space (0x20) or into quoted-printable (discussed above). This is a very annoying problem because one usually must throw out such email message or article, or else suffer through the grueling task of manually restoring the escape characters. For example, look at the following strings. The first is an ISO-2022-JP–encoded text string as it should appear when displayed properly, and second is how it could appear if it were damaged. Lots of dollar signs, but these ones won't make you rich, especially if your software is supposed to correctly handle such situations—but doesn't.

```
これは和文の文章の例で、それはEnglishの文章の例です。
$B$3$1$OOBJ8$NJ8>O$NNc$G! $=$1$O(JEnglish$B$NJ8>O$NNc$G$9!#(J
```

I have written a tool that repairs damaged ISO-2022-JP–encoded files by simply scanning for the printable-character portions of the escape sequences that were left

* But frankly, I did need to apply Base64 encoding in order to create the examples for this section.

intact, keeping track of the state of the data stream (that is, whether it is in one- or two-byte mode), and then using this as the context for restoring escape characters. This tool is called JConv, which was briefly described in the previous section—its full description is at the end of Chapter 9 starting on page 448.

Because ISO-2022-CN, ISO-2022-CN-EXT, and ISO-2022-KR encodings use single characters—ASCII's shift-in and shift-out control characters—for switching between one- and two-byte modes, there is not sufficient context for restoring them, so unfortunately, there is no elegant way of repairing eight-bit encodings which have had their eighth bits stripped. Manual repair of EUC encoding is not terribly painful: you simply turn on the eighth bit of character sequences that look like garbage. The only problem is detecting which bytes are used to compose two-byte characters—this is when human intervention and interaction is required. The following is the same Japanese string used in the above ISO-2022-JP–encoded sample, but this time you see how it would appear if the eighth bits were stripped from an EUC-JP–encoded version. Compare it with the corrupt ISO-2022-JP string above—the crucial context-forming strings, specifically `$B` and `(J`, are missing.

Original これは和文の文章の例で、それは `English` の文章の例です。

Corrupt EUC-JP `$3$1$OOBJ8$NJ8>O$NNc$G! $=$1$OEnglish$NJ8>O$NNc$G$9!#`

Providing the same type of example for Shift-JIS is possible, but the results are bit different. See the example strings below.

Original これは和文の文章の例で、それは `English` の文章の例です。

Corrupt Shift-JIS `1 j M a 6 L 6 M L a E A ; j MEnglish L 6 M L a E 7 B`

Depending on the capabilities of your terminal emulation software, this corrupt Shift-JIS string could also appear as the following:

Corrupt Shift-JIS `1jMa6L6MLaEA;jMEnglishL6MLaE7B`

The above example is different from the first example of corrupt Shift-JIS encoding in that it does not contain spaces as place holders for the control characters.

The bottom line is that any encoding repair solution that deals with eight-bit encodings with mixed single- and multiple-byte representations requires interaction with a user. There is simply too much judgement involved, and a (literate) human is needed to guide the repair process. Colin Bootle* has developed such a tool called *Encoding Repair Kit* (ERK), which is available for Windows 95.†

---

* *colin@bootle.dircon.co.uk*

† *http://www.bootle.dircon.co.uk/*

Beware of Little and Big Endian Issues

There are two classes of computers when it comes to the order in which data is interpreted beyond the single-byte level: little endian (such as DOS, Windows, and VMS Vax) and big endian (MacOS and Unix). I suggest that you refer to the section entitled "What Are Little and Big Endian?" in Chapter 1, starting on page 24.

As long as you are dealing with encodings that are byte-driven, such as Shift-JIS for Japanese, byte order makes no difference. For encodings that make use of values that go beyond the single byte (eight bits), such as Unicode (UTF-16), it is absolutely critical.

Unicode encodings that can be represented in both little and big endian byte order can make use of the convenient Byte Order Mark (big endian 0xFEFF or little endian 0xFFFE) to explicitly indicate the byte order of a file. Reverse interpretation of byte order can result in some fairly amusing results. For example, big endian 0x4E00 (the first Chinese character of Unicode: 一) being interpreted as 0x004E would become the Latin character "N" (ASCII 0x4E). Not desired, I think…

Advice to Developers

The information presented in this chapter may have given you the impression that CJKV encoding is a real mess—well, frankly, it can be. However, you should have found that there are two basic CJKV encoding methods (ISO-2022 and EUC) and a host of locale-dependent ones. Furthermore, there are usually convenient algorithms for converting among these encodings—at least, within a single locale. CJKV code conversion algorithms are discussed in Chapter 9.

Now, you may be wondering which CJKV encoding should you choose for your products? In my opinion, that is not the correct question. Better put, what CJKV *encodings* should you support in your product? Note the use of a plural.

My recommendation to software developers is that they should support as many CJKV encodings as possible. At a bare minimum, there should be support for ISO-2022 encoding (for information interchange, such as email). What encoding you select for internal processing really depends on the platform for which your software is designed. But, recognizing other encodings for the purposes of data import and export can go a long way to making your product stand out from others.

Here are some important points to consider when selecting an appropriate internal encoding:

- What CJKV encoding or encodings, if any, are supported by the underlying operating system?

- Does the encoding support all your required (or desired) character sets? For example, Shift-JIS encoding for Japanese does not support the JIS X 0212-1990 character set.
- Does the encoding include regions that cannot be converted to other encodings? For example, the Shift-JIS user-defined region cannot be readily converted to ISO-2022-JP or EUC-JP encodings.

Companies that are interested in a more global market for their products are seriously considering Unicode. In fact, there are several Unicode-based systems currently available or under development, such as Plan 9 (experimental) and Microsoft Windows NT. The process of converting between Unicode and legacy CJKV encodings requires the use of mapping tables—there are no convenient algorithms for this task, and never can be. These extremely useful and necessary mapping tables are provided by the Unicode Consortium.*

* *ftp://ftp.unicode.org/Public/MAPPINGS/EASTASIA/*

5

Input Methods

In this chapter:
- *Transliteration Techniques*
- *Input Techniques*
- *User Interface Concerns*
- *Keyboard Arrays*
- *Other Input Hardware*
- *Input Method Software*

In earlier chapters you learned most of what you need to know about CJKV writing systems, character set standards, and encoding methods. Now it is time for you to learn something about how a user can input the several thousand characters contained in these character set standards.

Because of the vast number of characters defined in CJKV character set standards, there is no simple solution like direct keyboard input such as you would find in the West. Instead, you will find that CJKV input methods fall into two general categories:

- *Direct* methods that employ a unique value for the target character, usually one of its encoded values
- *Indirect* (and usually more convenient) methods that obtain the encoded value of the target character or characters, usually by typing out the reading or shape on a standard or specialized keyboard

You will soon realize that the indirect input methods are the most commonly used, and rightly so, because they usually involve the reading or structure of a character, which is more intuitive. After all, native speakers of CJKV languages learn Chinese characters by their readings. There are Chinese characters, however, that are not commonly known, and these are typically input by means other than their reading. Direct and indirect input methods are covered in this chapter.

To facilitate the explanations to come, at least two examples will be provided per input method. In most cases, the two examples will be the two Chinese characters 漢 and 字 (the two Chinese characters for writing "Chinese character" in most CJKV locales). Other characters will be substituted when appropriate.

There is an easy explanation for why so many different input methods are required for handling CJKV text. First, it is nearly impossible to fit thousands of characters on a keyboard. Mind you, such keyboards do exist, but they are not designed for the casual operator, and do not contain all the character set standards covered in Chapter 3, *Character Set Standards* (an example of this type of keyboard is described below). This forced the CJKV locales to develop more efficient means of input. Second, CJKV text, as you learned in Chapter 4, *Encoding Methods*, is encoded in a variety of ways. This makes using the encoded value of a character in each encoding method a viable method for input.

Other references that either describe input methods or else list input codes for Chinese characters include the following books and dictionaries:

- A Chinese book entitled 常用汉字输入法操作速成 (*chángyòng hànzì shūrùfǎ cāozuò sùchéng*, meaning "Quick Input Method Operations for Frequently Used Chinese Characters") describes many contemporary Chinese input methods
- A Chinese book entitled 计算机汉字输入与编辑实用手册 (*jìsuànjī hànzì shūrù yù biānjí shíyòng shǒucè*) also describes contemporary Chinese input methods, but also includes a large appendix that includes readings and input codes for all GB 2312-80 hanzi
- A Chinese dictionary entitled 常用汉字编码字典 (*chángyòng hànzì biānmǎ zìdiǎn*, meaning "Dictionary of Codes for Frequently Used Chinese Characters") lists nearly two dozen (some obscure) input codes for all 6,763 hanzi in GB 2312-80
- The manuals for a Chinese word processor called NJStar (南极星/南極星 *nánjíxīng*) provide useful descriptions, including examples, for nearly two dozen different input methods
- A Japanese book entitled 中国入力方法の話 (*chūgoku nyūryoku hōhō no hanashi*, meaning "Discussions of Chinese Input Methods") describes the principles behind various Chinese input methods

If you need more information on input methods than is provided in this chapter, I encourage you to explore the above references.

Transliteration Techniques

Before we can even discuss the basics of CJKV input, it is necessary to discuss the issue of transliterated input. This is because the most popular input methods provide a facility to use the world-reknowned QWERTY keyboard array. All CJKV writing systems can be expressed using Latin characters.

Zhuyin Versus Pinyin Input

Zhuyin (also known as *bopomofo*) and Pinyin are related in that there is always a way to represent the same set of sounds using either writing system. Both systems are phonetic, but Pinyin is based on Latin characters.

There are three types of Pinyin input: *Half Pinyin* (简拼/簡拼 *jiǎnpīn*), *Full Pinyin* (全拼 *quánpīn*), and *Double Pinyin* (双拼 *shuāngpīn*). Fortunately, these three methods are easily accommodated using the standard QWERTY keyboard array.

Full Pinyin works by simply typing the Pinyin equivalent of hanzi. Note that any Pinyin-based input methods result in a (sometimes long) list of candidate hanzi from which the user must choose.

Double Pinyin works by first dividing the Pinyin reading into two parts. Certain letter combinations are replaced with single characters according to a set of standardized rules. The resulting characters are used for input. The primary advantage of Double Pinyin is that all hanzi are input using two keystrokes.

Table 5-1 illustrates zhuyin and Pinyin input using both Full Pinyin and Double Pinyin methods of transliteration. Those transliterations that are different from Full Pinyin have been shaded.

Table 5-1: Keystrokes for Zhuyin and Pinyin Characters

Zhuyin	Full Pinyin	Half Pinyin	Double Pinyin
ㄅ	B	B	B
ㄆ	P	P	P
ㄇ	M	M	M
ㄈ	F	F	F
ㄉ	D	D	D
ㄊ	T	T	T
ㄋ	N	N	N
ㄌ	L	L	L
ㄍ	G	G	G
ㄎ	K	K	K
ㄏ	H	H	H
ㄐ	J	J	J
ㄑ	Q	Q	Q
ㄒ	X	X	X
ㄓ	ZH	A	A
ㄔ	CH	I	U
ㄕ	SH	U	I
ㄖ	R	R	R

Table 5-1: Keystrokes for Zhuyin and Pinyin Characters (continued)

Zhuyin	Full Pinyin	Half Pinyin	Double Pinyin
ㄗ	Z	Z	Z
ㄘ	C	C	C
ㄙ	S	S	S
ㄚ	A	A	A
ㄛ	O	O	O
ㄜ	E	E	E
ㄝ	EI	EI	W
ㄞ	AI	L	S
ㄟ	EI	EI	W
ㄠ	AO	K	D
ㄡ	OU	OU	P
ㄢ	AN	J	F
ㄣ	EN	F	R
ㄤ	ANG	H	G
ㄥ	ENG	G	T
ㄦ	ER	ER	Q
ㄧ	I	I	I
ㄧㄚ	IA	IA	B
ㄧㄝ	IE	IE	M
ㄧㄠ	IAO	IK	K
ㄧㄡ	IU	IU	N
ㄧㄢ	IAN	IJ	J
ㄧㄣ	IN	IN	L
ㄧㄤ	IANG	IH	H
ㄧㄥ	ING	Y	;
ㄨ	U	U	U
ㄨㄚ	UA	UA	B
ㄨㄛ	UO	UO	O
ㄨㄞ	UAI	UL	X
ㄨㄟ	UI	UI	V
ㄨㄢ	UAN	UJ	C
ㄨㄣ	UN	UN	Z
ㄨㄤ	UANG	UH	H
ㄨㄥ	ONG	S	Y
ㄩ	V	V	U

Table 5-1: Keystrokes for Zhuyin and Pinyin Characters (continued)

Zhuyin	Full Pinyin	Half Pinyin	Double Pinyin
ㄩㄝ	UE	UE	V
ㄩㄥ	IONG	IS	Y

This means that Full Pinyin requires one to six keystrokes per hanzi, Half Pinyin requires one to three keystrokes per hanzi, and Double Pinyin requires only one or two keystrokes per hanzi. Table 5-2 provides some examples of Pinyin input to better illustrate how these three types of Pinyin work.

Table 5-2: Pinyin Input Examples

Hanzi	Zhuyin	Full Pinyin	Half Pinyin	Double Pinyin
啊	ㄚ	A	A	A
酷	ㄎㄨ	KU	KU	KU
处	ㄔㄨ	CHU	IU	UU
汆	ㄘㄨㄢ	CUAN	CUJ	CC
张	ㄓㄤ	ZHANG	AH	AG
双	ㄕㄨㄤ	SHUANG	UUH	IH

Kana Versus Latin Input

There are two ways to provide reading-based input to Japanese input methods through the keyboard array:

- Transliterated using Latin characters
- Kana

Ultimately, most Japanese input methods require kana input, which means that there must be a mechanism in place for converting, on the fly, transliterated Japanese strings into kana. Almost all (if not all) such software has such a mechanism which permits Western keyboard arrays, such as QWERTY, to be used to input kana, and hence Japanese text.

Table 5-3 lists the basic set of kana characters (hiragana, in this case, but are equally applicable to katakana), along with the most common keystroke or keystrokes necessary to produce them. Some Japanese input software supports alternate keystrokes, and they are separated by slashes.

There are also combinations of two kana characters that require special transliteration. These consist of one of the above kana plus the small versions of や (*ya*), ゆ (*yu*), and よ (*yo*). These are listed in Table 5-4. Like Table 5-3, optional keystrokes are by a slash.

Table 5-3: Keystrokes to Produce Kana Characters

あ	A	い	I	う	U	え	E	お	O
か	KA	き	KI	く	KU	け	KE	こ	KO
が	GA	ぎ	GI	ぐ	GU	げ	GE	ご	GO
さ	SA	し	SI/SHI	す	SU	せ	SE	そ	SO
ざ	ZA	じ	ZI/JI	ず	ZU	ぜ	ZE	ぞ	ZO
た	TA	ち	TI/CHI	つ	TU/TSU	て	TE	と	TO
だ	DA	ぢ	DI	づ	DU/DZU	で	DE	ど	DO
な	NA	に	NI	ぬ	NU	ね	NE	の	NO
は	HA	ひ	HI	ふ	HU/FU	へ	HE	ほ	HO
ば	BA	び	BI	ぶ	BU	べ	BE	ぼ	BO
ぱ	PA	ぴ	PI	ぷ	PU	ぺ	PE	ぽ	PO
ま	MA	み	MI	む	MU	め	ME	も	MO
や	YA			ゆ	YU			よ	YO
ら	RA/LA	り	RI/LI	る	RU/LU	れ	RE/LE	ろ	RO/LO
わ	WA	ゐ	WI			ゑ	WE	を	WO
ん	N/NN/N'								

Table 5-4: Keystrokes to Produce Palatalized Kana Characters

きゃ	KYA	きゅ	KYU	きょ	KYO
ぎゃ	GYA	ぎゅ	GYU	ぎょ	GYO
しゃ	SYA/SHA	しゅ	SYU/SHU	しょ	SYO/SHO
じゃ	ZYA/JA	じゅ	ZYU/JU	じょ	ZYO/JO
ちゃ	TYA/CHA	ちゅ	TYU/CHU	ちょ	TYO/CHO
ぢゃ	DYA	ぢゅ	DYU	ぢょ	DYO
にゃ	NYA	にゅ	NYU	にょ	NYO
ひゃ	HYA	ひゅ	HYU	ひょ	HYO
びゃ	BYA	びゅ	BYU	びょ	BYO
ぴゃ	PYA	ぴゅ	PYU	ぴょ	PYO
みゃ	MYA	みゅ	MYU	みょ	MYO
りゃ	RYA	りゅ	RYU	りょ	RYO

These three small kana characters, ゃ, ゅ, and ょ, can usually be generated by either typing an "x" before their transliterated forms (for example, ゃ can be input with the three-character string "xya") or by pressing the shift key while typing their transliterated forms. Actually, all small kana characters, including ぁ, ぃ, ぅ, ぇ, ぉ, っ, and ゎ, can be handled in this way. Check the documentation of your Japanese input software to find out which method is supported. Also check the documentation for transliteration tables, similar to those above, that specify other special combinations that can be used.

There are additional kana characters that have special methods for input, and these are illustrated in Table 5-5. They are expressed in katakana because they are typically used for transliterating loan words, usually names.

Table 5-5: Keystrokes to Produce Other Special Kana Characters

ファ	FA
フィ	FI
フェ	FE
フォ	FO
ヴ	VU

Japanese long vowels, while transliterated using macroned vowels, are input according to the reading of the kana used to express them. For example, おう (ō) is entered using the two keystrokes "ou," not "oo."

Writing a Latin-to-kana conversion routine is not terribly difficult. Sometimes the authors of Japanese text processing programs encourage others to use their routines, and most Japanese input methods that are freely available come with source code. A Perl version of a Latin-to-kana conversion library called *romkan.pl* is available via FTP (*romkan.pl* requires the Perl library file called *jcode.pl* to function).*

Hangul Versus Transliterated Input

Like bopomofo and kana, each hangul—whether it is composed of multiple or a single jamo—can be represented by equivalent Latin characters. There appears to be several ways to transliterate hangul characters when performing keyboard input. A variety of ways to transliterate jamo are shown in the "Keyboard Input" column of Table 5-6, along with the Ministry of Education, Korean Language Society, and both ISO/TR 11941:1996 systems for comparison (only the syllable-initial transliterations are provided for these systems). The source of these keyboard input transliterations is Apple Computer's Korean Language Kit. Note that case is significant in some instances, in particular an alternate keystroke for the double consonants that involves the use of uppercase.

Table 5-6: Keystrokes to Produce Jamo—Consonants

Jamo	Keyboard Input	MOE	KLS	ISO (ROK)	ISO (DPRK)
ㄱ	g	K/G	G	G	K
ㄴ	n	N	N	N	N

* *ftp://ftp.iij.ad.jp/pub/IIJ/dist/utashiro/perl/*

Table 5-6: Keystrokes to Produce Jamo—Consonants (continued)

Jamo	Keyboard Input	MOE	KLS	ISO (ROK)	ISO (DPRK)
ㄷ	d	T/D	D	D	T
ㄹ	l/r	R/L	R	R	R
ㅁ	m	M	M	M	M
ㅂ	b	P/B	B	B	P
ㅅ	s	S/SH	S	S	S
ㅇ	ng/x	*none*/NG	*none*/NG	*none*/NG	*none*/NG
ㅈ	j	CH/J	J	J	C
ㅊ	c	CH'	CH	C	CH
ㅋ	k	K'	K	K	KH
ㅌ	t	T'	T	T	TH
ㅍ	p/f	P'	P	P	PH
ㅎ	h	H	H	H	H
ㄲ	gg/G	KK	GG	GG	KK
ㄸ	dd/D	TT	DD	DD	TT
ㅃ	bb/Bh	PP	BB	BB	PP
ㅆ	ss/S	SS	SS	SS	SS
ㅉ	jj/J	TCH	JJ	JJ	CC

Table 5-7 illustrates the keystrokes for inputting the jamo that represent vowels. Alternate keystrokes are separated by a slash.

Table 5-7: Keystrokes to Produce Jamo—Vowels

Jamo	Keyboard Input	MOE	KLS	ISO (DPRK and ROK)
ㅏ	a	A	A	A
ㅑ	ya/ia	YA	YA	YA
ㅓ	eo	Ŏ	EO	EO
ㅕ	yeo/ieo/ie	YŎ	YEO	YEO
ㅗ	o	O	O	O
ㅛ	yo/io	YO	YO	YO
ㅜ	u/oo	U	U	U
ㅠ	yu/yw/iu	YU	YU	YU
ㅡ	eu/ew	Ŭ	EU	EU
ㅣ	i/wi	I	I	I
ㅐ	ae/ai	AE	AE	AE
ㅒ	yae/iai	YAE	YAE	YAE
ㅔ	e/ei	E	E	E
ㅖ	ye/ie/iei	YE	YE	YE

Table 5-7: Keystrokes to Produce Jamo—Vowels (continued)

Jamo	Keyboard Input	MOE	KLS	ISO (DPRK and ROK)
ㅘ	wa/ua/oa	WA	WA	WA
ㅙ	wae/uae/oai	WAE	WAE	WAE
ㅚ	oe/oi	OE	OE	OE
ㅝ	weo/ueo/ue	WŎ	WEO	WEO
ㅞ	we/uei	WE	WE	WE
ㅟ	wi/ui	WI	WI	WI
ㅢ	eui/yi/w	ŬI	EUI	YI

Of course, you should always check an input method's documentation to determine exactly what keystrokes are necessary to input each jamo.

Input Techniques

This chapter is intended to describe CJKV input in a platform- and software-independent way. What you learn here can then be applied to a wider variety of CJKV input programs, possibly even ones that have yet to be developed.

Unlike English, which permits direct keyboard entry for the majority of characters, there are two ways to input CJKV characters: direct and indirect. Input by encoded value is a direct means of input, and unambiguously allows you to access CJKV characters.* However, this is not quite intuitive. You can memorize the value 0x4B7C for the hanja 劍 (*geom*), but imagine doing this for thousands of kanji. While input by reading may yield more than one candidate character from which to choose, it is (in a seeming paradox) the most productive and most widely used method yet invented. Figure 5-1 illustrates the four possible stages of input: it shows how the flow of input information travels, and how different input methods and keyboards interface at each stage.

The Input Method

CJKV input software is usually referred to as an *input method* (or FEP, which stands for *front-end processor*). The input method is so named because it grabs the keyboard input, processes the input, then sends it to the application or other software. Typically, the input method runs as a separate process in its own input window, largely independent of the underlying application.

* This is not always true. For example, when an input method can accept ISO-2022 and Row-Cell codes, there are many ambiguous cases, such as the four-digit code 3021. In GB 2312-80, this four-digit code can result in either 啊 (hexadecimal ISO-2022-CN) or 镜 (decimal Row-Cell).

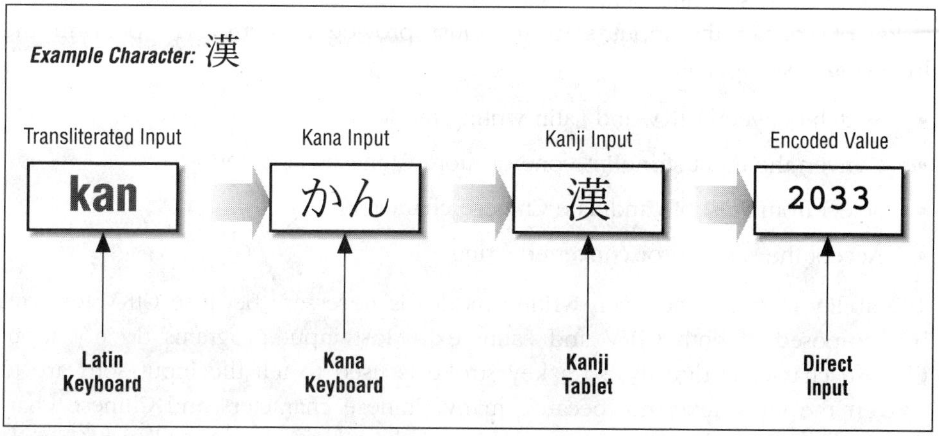

Figure 5-1: Input stages and input method interaction—Japanese

Microsoft Windows systems, at least the Japanese-enabled versions thereof, have several input methods from which to choose. These include ATOK, EGBridge, Katana (刀 *katana*), VJE, and Wnn. Some industrious people have even adapted Unix-based Japanese input software so that they can run under non-Japanese MS-DOS systems. One such example is the adaptation of a program called SKK for use with MOKE, a Japanese text editor. MacOS-based systems (that is, those running MacOS-J) offer several Japanese input software systems such as ATOK, EGBridge, Katana, MacVJE, Wnn, and ことえり (*kotoeri*). Unix offers input methods such as SKK, Wnn, Canna, and kinput2—these are available from a variety of online sources or bundled with other programs. Some of these Japanese input programs are described in more detail at the end of this chapter.

Most input methods run as separate processes from the programs that ultimately use the input, such as text editors and word processors. This allows you to use a single input method with many programs. It can also allow the use of more than one input method (not simultaneously, though, but by switching between them with a special key stroke, menu item, or control panel).

Many of these Japanese input systems allow you to emulate others. For example, MacVJE for MacOS allows you to emulate EGBridge, ATOK, Wnn, and TurboJIP keyboard commands. Some others offer the same flexibility. This may prove to be useful, especially when using multiple platforms where the Japanese input software you prefer to use is not available on the current platform. However, the emulation may not be complete. For example, EGBridge for MacOS can emulate MacVJE, but its emulation does not have the same set of functions. Expect to find slight differences—after all, EGBridge is only *emulating* the other input software.

All CJKV input software shares many similar qualities. Although there are other tasks, of course, the input software must provide a method to perform the following basic operations:

- Switch between CJKV and Latin writing modes
- Convert the input string into one or more Chinese characters
- Select from a list of candidate Chinese characters
- Accept the selected or converted string

The ability to switch between writing modes is necessary because CJKV text can be composed of both CJKV and Latin text. Most input programs do not input Chinese characters directly, so a key stroke is used to tell the input software to convert the input text and, because many Chinese characters and Chinese character compounds share the same reading, it is necessary to list all the Chinese characters or Chinese character compounds with the same reading. The user then selects the Chinese character or Chinese character compound that they intended to input. Finally, the converted input string is sent to the application (this is called accepting the input string). Table 5-8 lists several popular Japanese input programs and the keystrokes used to perform the above input tasks. The "Xfer" and "Nfer" keystrokes in Table 5-8 refer to special keys sometimes found on keyboards.

Table 5-8: Keystrokes for Common Japanese Input Tasks—Japanese

Operations	MacVJE	Wnn	Canna	SKK
Japanese ⇒ English	Cmd-space	F3	Xfer or C-o	l
English ⇒ Japanese	Cmd-space	F3	Xfer or C-o	C-j
Conversion	space or C-c	C-w or C-z	Xfer or space	*uppercase*
Candidate Selection	arrows	up/down arrows	arrows	space
Accepting	return or F10	C-l	Nfer or return	C-j

As you can see, the basic input tasks are common among these various input methods, but the keystrokes used to invoke them are different. For Korean input, the keystroke "shift-space" is usually used to toggle between English and Korean modes. These and other input methods are described at the end of this chapter.

Our discussion will proceed from the most widely used input method to the least widely used. Since most symbols and kana can be input directly, these discussions focus primarily on the input of Chinese characters, and the problems inherent in that process. Chinese characters are problematic because they number in the thousands, and thus require an indirect input method.

The Conversion Dictionary

While the input method provides the mechanical and algorithmic power behind CJKV input, it is the conversion dictionary that allows input strings to be converted into Chinese characters.

Conversion dictionaries come in a variety of formats, and define more than simply readings for Chinese characters. It is also possible to specify additional information to help the input method decide how to use the entry, such as grammatical information (part of speech, type of verb or adjective, and so on).

JSA, in cooperation with several Japanese input method developers, has published the standard designated JIS X 4062:1998, *Format for Information Interchange for Dictionaries of Japanese Input Method* (仮名漢字変換辞書交換形式 *kana kanji henkan jisho kōkan keishiki*). This standard sets a precedent for establishing a common interchange format for representing the contents of input methods' conversion dictionaries.

Input by Reading

The most frequently used CJKV input method is by reading (that is, pronunciation)—it is by far the most intuitive way to input CJKV text. There are three basic units by which input readings can be converted into Chinese characters:

- Single Chinese character
- Chinese character compound (a string of two or more Chinese characters)
- Chinese character phrase (a string of one or more Chinese characters followed by a postposition)—not applicable to all CJKV locales

You may have heard of input software that claims to be able to convert whole sentences at once. In fact, what they are actually describing is the ability to input whole sentences, but these sentences are parsed into smaller units, usually Chinese character phrases, and then converted. This often introduces parsing errors, and it is up to the user to adjust each phrase.

For example, if you want to input the phrase 漢字は (meaning "the Chinese character"), you have three choices: you can input each character, you can input a phrase as a compound, or you can input a phrase as a string of characters. Table 5-9 shows how you can input each character one at a time, and how this results in candidates from which you may choose for each character.

Table 5-9: Input by Reading—Single Chinese Character

Target	Latin Input	Kana Input	Candidates
漢	`K A N (N)`[a]	かん	乾侃冠寒刊勘勧巻喚堪姦完官寛干幹患感慣憾換敢柑桓棺款歓汗漢澗潅環甘監看竿管簡緩缶翰肝艦莞観諌貫還鑑間閑関陥韓館舘

Table 5-9: Input by Reading—Single Chinese Character (continued)

Target	Latin Input	Kana Input	Candidates
字	J I	じ	事似侍児字寺慈持時次滋治爾璽痔磁示而耳自蒔辞
は	H A	は	...[b]

[a] Whether you need to type one or two *n*'s depends on the input method.
[b] The character は resolves as itself—no conversion is necessary.

Table 5-10 illustrates how you can input this phrase as a Chinese character compound plus the following hiragana, and how a shorter list of candidates results.

Table 5-10: Input by Reading—Chinese Character Compound

Target	Latin Input	Kana Input	Candidates
漢字	K A N J I	かんじ	漢字 感じ 幹事 監事 完司
は	H A	は	...[a]

[a] As in Table 5-9, the character は resolves as itself—no conversion is necessary.

Note how the candidate list became shorter, making selection among them much easier. Table 5-11 shows the effect of inputting the entire phrase as a single string of characters. The ability to perform this type of conversion depends on the quality of your input software.

Table 5-11: Input by Reading—Phrase

Target	Latin Input	Kana Input	Candidates
漢字は	K A N J I H A	かんじは	漢字は 感じは 幹事は 監事は 完司は

For Japanese, the kana-to-kanji conversion dictionary (仮名漢字変換辞書 *kana kanji henkan jisho*) makes input by reading possible. Most Japanese input systems are based on a conversion dictionary that takes kana strings as input, and then converts them into strings containing a mixture of kanji and kana. The conversion dictionary uses a key (the reading) to look up possible replacement strings (candidates). Quite often a single search key has multiple replacement strings assigned to it. Conversion dictionaries typically contain tens of thousands of entries.

Most kanji even have multiple readings assigned to them. How many really depends on the conversion dictionary used by your Japanese input software. For example, the kanji 日 can have up to nine unique readings, depending on the context (and the conversion dictionary!). They are び (*bi*), ひ (*hi*), に (*ni*), ぴ (*pi*), か (*ka*), じつ (*jitsu*), にち (*nichi*), につ (*nitsu*), and たち (*tachi*).[*] While this is an extreme example, this phenomenon is not unique.

[*] There are even more readings for this kanji if you consider readings for Japanese names.

As you saw above, the most widely used and most efficient method for inputting kanji by reading is to handle them as kanji compounds or kanji phrases, not as single characters. If you desire a single kanji, it is often more efficient to input it as a compound or phrase, then delete the unwanted character or characters.

Up to this point we have dealt primarily with Chinese characters. What about other characters, such as symbols? Typical CJKV character set standards contain several hundred symbols. As you have seen, Japanese kana and Korean hangul can be input more or less directly. Symbols and other miscellaneous characters may also be input using the symbol's name, reading, or close relative on the keyboard. Table 5-12 provides examples of symbols, along with their candidates.

Table 5-12: Input by Symbol Name for Non-Chinese Characters

Target	Latin Input	Kana Input	Candidates
〒	Y U U B I N (N)	ゆうびん	郵便 〒[a]
】	K A K K O	かっこ	括弧 （ 〔 「 『 【 ） 〕 」 』 】

[a] The character 〒 is not a Chinese character, but rather a postal-code symbol.

Note how Chinese character compounds are also listed as candidates—there are usually perfectly good Chinese character equivalents for these symbol names.

Chinese is unique in that its reading-based input methods provide one additional way to reduce the amount of candidate hanzi: indication of tones. Table 5-13 lists all the hanzi in GB 2312-80 with the reading *han*, followed by how they break down into candidates for each of the four tones. Note how some hanzi have more than one reading—well, same reading, but different tone.

Table 5-13: Reducing the Number of Hanzi Candidates Through Tones

Reading	Number of Hanzi	GB 2312-80 Hanzi
han (no tone)	31	顸 酣 蚶 鼾 憨 邗 邯 韩 晗 含 焓 涵 寒 函 喊 罕 阚 翰 菡 撼 捍 撖 旱 颔 憾 悍 焊 汗 瀚 汉
hān	5	酣 憨 顸 蚶 鼾
hán	10	邯 韩 含 涵 寒 函 汗 邗 晗 焓
hǎn	3	喊 罕 阚
hàn	13	翰 撼 捍 旱 憾 悍 焊 汗 汉 菡 撖 瀚 颔

Nearly all input software uses its own proprietary conversion dictionary or dictionaries. This means that no two input programs behave the same. Luckily, such software allows the user to create a user dictionary in which new search keys can be created and candidate replacement strings assigned. Whether or not there is a logical ordering in a conversion dictionary depends on the dictionary itself. Entries are typically ordered by reading (remember that the key for lookup is usually kana, which implies ordering by reading). The values associated with the keys are typically ordered by their relative frequency of use—more obscure Chinese characters or Chinese character compounds appear further down the list of candidates. It is quite common to find CJKV input method programs that include a learning function (学習機能 *gakushū kinō*). This learning function allows the subtle rearrangement of values associated with keys. The default value for a particular key can change depending on how often the user selects a given candidate. For example, if the default key for the input string けん (*ken*) is 犬 (meaning "dog"), and if I constantly select the candidate 剣 (the Chinese character I use to write my given name), 剣 eventually becomes the default value associated with the key けん. Exactly when the default changes depends on the software—sometimes only one occurrence is necessary.

More advanced input methods implement parsers that use grammatical information for making decisions. This allows users to input whole sentences by reading, then let the software slice the input into units that are manageable for conversion. Like I mentioned earlier, errors in parsing are quite common.

Input by Structure

While input by reading, whether transliterated using Latin characters or not, is by far the most common method for inputting CJKV text; it is also the easiest to learn. But, there are times when input by reading fails to locate the desired Chinese characters, or it is simply not fast enough.

Chinese characters, as described in Chapter 2, *Writing Systems*, are composed of radicals or radical-like elements, which in turn are composed of strokes. Characters with related shapes—which sometimes means that they have somewhat related meanings—can thus be grouped together. All of the following input techniques involve the structure of the character:

- By radical
- By number of strokes
- By stroke shapes
- By corner

In case it is not yet obvious, there exist input techniques that use both structure and reading. Some examples are covered in the section entitled "Input by Multiple Criteria," beginning on page 233.

Input by radical

Some input software allows only certain Chinese characters to be input by radical. This is usually because that is how the characters are arranged in the character set, and it is quite trivial to slice up this collection of characters into sets indexed by the same radical. The Chinese characters in GB 2312-80 Level 2 and JIS X 0208:1997 Level 2, for example, are ordered by radical. The current trend, fortunately, is for input methods to allow users to input all Chinese characters by radical, even those that are ordered differently.

Table 5-14 illustrates examples of input by radical, using two kanji from JIS X 0208:1997 Level 2.

Table 5-14: Input by Radical

Target	Radical	Candidates
漢	氵	水氷永氾汀汁求汎汐汕汗汚汝汞江池汢汨汪汰汲汳決汽 汾沁沂沃沈沌沐漢滝滞滬滲滷滸
字	子	孑孔孕字存孚孛孜孝孟季孥学孩孤孫孰孱孳孵孺

Sophisticated input software programs display a graphic palette of the 214 radicals, or 186 radicals if you are using an input method based on GB 2312-80. These 214 radicals originated in a Chinese dictionary entitled 康熙字典 (*kāngxī zìdiǎn*), which was published in 1716. Each of these 214 radicals has a name or number assigned to it. Some of these radicals even have variants, most of which have unique names. The number represents the relative order within the set of radicals. For example, the last radical is assigned the number 214. You may encounter input software that requires that radicals be input through their names, numbers, or number of strokes. Table 5-15 provides some examples of radicals, along with their names (in Japanese kana), meanings, numbers, and number of strokes.

Table 5-15: Radical Names and Numbers

Radical	Radical Name	Meaning	Number	Strokes
一	一 (*ichi*)	one	1	1
丨	棒 (*bō*)	bar	2	1
女	女 (*onna*)	woman	38	3
子	子 (*ko*)	child	39	3
疒	病垂 (*yamaidare*)	illness enclosure	104	5
石	石 (*ishi*)	stone	112	5
貝	貝 (*kai*)	shell	154	7
鳥	鳥 (*tori*)	bird	196	11
鼻	鼻 (*hana*)	nose	209	14

Appendix P, *Code Table Indexes*, provides a complete listing of the classical 214 radicals, along with their names. China's reduced set of 186 radicals, as used in the GB 2312-80 standard, is also provided in that volume. Other Chinese dictionaries use a different set of radicals, such as 现代汉语词典 (*xiàndài hànyǔ cídiǎn*), which uses a reduced set of 188 radicals.

There are some Chinese characters for which the indexing radical is not obvious. But, it is almost always possible to count the number of strokes. This brings us to the next input technique that involves characters' structure.

Input by number of strokes

Almost all Chinese characters have a unique number of strokes. This paves the way for an input technique whereby the number of strokes is entered by the user, and all the candidates are displayed for selection. However, there are a select few whose actual number of strokes is arguable. This difference is typically a single stroke.* Quality input software accounts for these differences in number of strokes, and allows the user to input characters using multiple stroke counts. Also note that the number of strokes occasionally depends on the glyph shape. For example, an input system based on the JIS C 6226-1978 character set may behave strangely if the JIS X 0208:1997 character set is swapped. Consider Row-Cell 16-02, whose JIS C 6226-1978 glyph is 啞 (11 strokes), and JIS X 0208:1997 glyph is 唖 (10 strokes).

Table 5-16 provides a candidate list for two different numbers of strokes.

Table 5-16: Input by Stroke Count

Target	Stroke Count	Candidates
漢	13	愛葦飴暗意違溢碓園煙猿遠鉛塩嫁暇禍嘩蛾雅解塊慨碍蓋該較隔楽滑褐蒲勧寛幹感漢頑
字	6	旭扱安伊夷衣亥芋印因吋宇羽迂臼曳汚仮会回灰各汗缶企伎危机気吉吃休吸朽汲兇共匡叫仰曲刑圭血件交光向后好江考行合此艮再在旨死糸至字寺次而耳自

Input by stroke shapes

Most users believe that input by radical or by number of strokes is more than sufficient when input by reading fails to turn up the desired character. One of these input methods is known as the Wubi Method (五笔输入法 *wǔbǐ shūrùfǎ*), developed by Yongmin Wang (王永民 *wáng yǒngmín*), which literally means "five strokes." A typical Wubi code consists of the character's overall shape plus its first, second, and final stroke. More details about how the Wubi Method works starts on page 241.

* Some examples of radical or radical-like elements that have an ambiguous number of strokes are provided in Table 11-3 on page 487.

The Shouwei Method (首尾输入法 *shǒuwěi shūrùfǎ*) is a method that specifies the first and final strokes or shapes of a Chinese character.

Input by corner

If we ignore the indexing radical and number of strokes of a Chinese character, it is still possible to input a character by categorizing the shapes that are at each corner. The Four Corner code, which is described in Chapter 11, *Dictionaries and Dictionary Software*, beginning on page 489, is typically used for locating characters in Chinese character dictionaries.

However, the three corner code, invented by Jack Huang (黃克東 *huáng kèdōng*) and others, is designed specifically for character input.

Input by other structure

There are ways to describe the structure of Chinese characters that go beyond indexing radicals, strokes, and corners. Many Chinese input methods take advantage of the fact that Chinese characters can be categorized by shapes.

An input method known as the Cangjie Method (倉頡輸入法 *cāngjié shūrùfǎ*), developed by Bangfu Zhu (朱邦復 *zhū bāngfù*), allows the user to input Chinese characters by radical-like elements. More details about the Cangjie Method starts on page 243. It is commonly used in Taiwan and Hong Kong. In fact, many dictionaries provide Cangjie codes for hanzi.

Also, the Zheng Code Method (郑码输入法 *zhèngmǎ shūrùfǎ*), developed by Yili Zheng (郑易里 *zhèng yìlǐ*) and Long Zheng (郑珑 *zhèng lóng*), also uses radical-like elements for inputting Chinese characters. It is used in all Chinese locales by virtue of being included with Chinese versions of Microsoft Windows.

Input by Multiple Criteria

Some tools were specifically designed to input Chinese or other characters with more than one of the above input methods. This is very useful because a user can significantly narrow a search by giving more than one input criterion.

Like a typical bibliographic search, the more search parameters you provide to the software, the shorter the candidate list becomes. However, don't expect to find very many programs, other than dedicated CJKV character dictionary software, that accept multiple search criteria.

As you will learn in the next section, inputting CJKV characters by their encoded value or dictionary number is a direct method, and always results in a single character match.

Input by structure and reading

The ultimate goal of any indirect input technique should be to reduce the number of candidates from which the user must choose. This is known as reducing the number of collisions. That is, to reduce the number of characters that share the same attributes according to an input technique. It is possible to combine reading and structure attributes to form a new input technique that can effectively reduce the number of collisions.

Examples of input methods that combine reading and structure are the Tze-loi Method (子來輸入法 *zǐlái shūrùfǎ*), developed by Tze-loi Yeung (楊子來 *yáng zǐlái*); and the Renzhi Code Method (认知码输入法 *rènzhī mǎ shūrùfǎ*). A Tze-loi code consists of three keystrokes. The first two are based on the character's structure (the upper-left and lower-right corner), and the third represents the first sound in the character's reading. A Renzhi code, like a Tze-loi code, can consists of three keystrokes. The first keystroke is the first character of its Pinyin reading, and the last two keystrokes are its first and last strokes. Renzhi codes, however, can also consist of other types of elements, and can consist of as little as two keystrokes or as many as four. Table 5-17 lists a handful of hanzi, along with their Tze-loi input codes.

Table 5-17: Examples of "Structure Plus Reading" Input Methods—Tze-Loi Method

Hanzi	Tze-Loi Code	Tze-Loi (QWERTY)
晶	日 + 日 + J	JJJ
品	口 + 口 + B	HHB
法	丶 + 厶 + F	6ZF

Input by Encoding

This CJKV input method is based on fixed values for each character, specifically their encoded values. This is a direct means for input, and is typically used as a last resort for inputting characters. This means that one can unambiguously (that is, without candidates) input a single character. Note that it is most common to use hexadecimal values when inputting characters, with the exception of Row-Cell, which usually requires four decimal digits.

Input by encoding makes use of the encoded values of the target characters. As most systems process only a single code internally, yet accept different encoded values, some sort of conversion between codes is still being performed. For example, many Japanese systems can accept both hexadecimal ISO-2022-JP and Shift-JIS codes since they can be easily distinguished from one another—they occupy separate encoding regions.

Most input software includes character tables indexed by one or more of these encoding methods. Some programs even have these character-indexing tables built in as on-screen palettes so that you need not ever consult the printed documentation.

Many input programs allow the user to select which encoding to use when inputting by code, and those which are really good automatically detect which code the user has selected. This is simple for ISO-2022-JP and Shift-JIS encodings because they occupy different encoding regions, but Row-Cell notation and EUC encoding pose special problems. Some implementations require that a period or other delimiter separate the Row from the Cell of a Row-Cell code. Input by EUC code is quite rare for Japanese, but not for Chinese (GB 2312-80) and Korean (KS X 1001:1992).

Table 5-18 lists two hanja, along with their encoded values according to a variety of Korean encodings (including Unicode), listed from left to right in decreasing frequency/popularity of usage.

Table 5-18: Input by Encoded Value—Korean

Hanja	Row-Cell	EUC-KR	Unicode	ISO-2022-KR	Johab
字	77-14	EDAE	5B57	6D2E	F1AE
漢	89-51	F9D3	6F22	7953	F7D3

Most input systems provide at least two of these input methods, usually Row-Cell and hexadecimal ISO-2022. Sometimes the encoding method supported by the software you are running is another option. For example, Japanese operating systems that process Shift-JIS internally, such as MacOS-J, Windows 3.1J, and Windows 95J, provide input methods that give the user the ability to perform code input by Row-Cell, hexadecimal ISO-2022-JP, and hexadecimal Shift-JIS.

If you need to convert lots of these "codes" into actual characters, you are better off writing a quick tool for this purpose (perhaps using Perl), or else finding software that provides this functionality. JCode, described starting on page 451 of Chapter 9, *Information Processing Techniques*, provides this level of functionality, at least for Japanese.

Input by Other Codes

China's telex code (电报码/電報碼* *diànbàomă*), developed in 1911 for the purpose of hanzi interchange, is yet another code that can be used to unambiguously input Chinese characters—sort of. A telex code is composed of four decimal

* Sometimes referred to as 电报明码/電報明碼 (*diànbàomíngmă*).

digits, and ranges from 0001 to 9999. The ordering of characters in telex code is by radical, then number of strokes.

It is important that you know that a telex code does not distinguish between simplified and traditional Chinese characters—they have been effectively merged into a single telex code. So, for example, the two related hanzi, 剑 and 劍, share the same telex code, specifically 0494.

Other possible codes may include numbers used to index Chinese characters in specific dictionaries. The Four Corner code is also used, but is usually restricted to indexes in Chinese character dictionaries. See Chapter 11's section entitled "Four Corner code," starting on page 489, for a brief description.

Input by Postal Code

Japanese postal codes (郵便番号 *yūbin bangō*) consist of three or seven digits.* Some conversion dictionaries include keys that correspond to these postal codes, and the values associated with those keys are strings that represent the place or places for which the postal codes are used. Table 5-19 includes some examples of three-digit postal code input.

Table 5-19: Input by Postal Code—Three-Digit

Postal Code	Candidate Locations
001	北海道札幌市北区
500	岐阜県岐阜市
999	山形県酒田市, 山形県最上郡, 山形県上山市, 山形県飽海郡, 山形県北村山郡, 山形県尾花沢市, 山形県長井市, 山形県西置賜郡, *and so on*

Japanese place names, especially for the non-native speaker of Japanese, can be difficult to learn. Japanese addresses usually contain postal codes, and for those who use Japanese input software that supports this type of input, much digging in dictionaries to find out how to pronounce (and thus easily enter) each kanji can be avoided.

Input by Association

Input by association (連想入力 *rensō nyūryoku*) is an older Japanese input method, and is often referred to as the two stroke input method (2ストローク入力方式 *ni sutorōku nyūryoku*). It is unlike input by reading in that there is only one kanji associated with each pair of keystrokes—no candidate selection is required.

* Seven-digit Japanese postal codes were introduced in early 1998.

Input by association works by associating two characters, usually kana, to a single kanji. These two kana are usually associated with the kanji by reading or meaning. For example, the two katakana ハハ (read *haha*) are associated with the kanji 母, whose reading happens to be *haha*.

Needless to say, this input method has a long learning curve, but skilled word processor operators can use this input method quite effectively.

There are many in Japan who feel that input by unassociation (無連想入力 *murensō nyūryoku*) is better. This means that the relationship between a kanji and its two keystrokes is arbitrary. In fact, such an input method has been developed, and has quite a following. It is called T-Code, and is available for a variety of operating systems, such as MacOS, MS-DOS, Unix, and Windows. There is even a T-Code mailing list—see Appendix U, *Mailing Lists*, for more information on joining. More information on T-Code itself starts on page 266 of this chapter.

User Interface Concerns

The ability to input CJKV text using a variety of input techniques is not enough to satisfy most users.

Inline Conversion

CJKV input programs typically provide their own input window, because they run as a separate process from the application in which the text will be inserted. CJKV input takes place in the dedicated window, is then sent to the current application, and finally is pasted into the current cursor position. As you can expect, this is far from ideal since you must look at both the current cursor position and the FEP input window. The solution to this problem is called *inline conversion* (インライン変換 *inrain henkan*). There are standard protocols developed by input method manufacturers which can be used in applications such that CJKV input and conversion can take place at the cursor position, not in a dedicated window in an inconvenient location on the screen.

Many CJKV-capable word processors come bundled with an input method, and this usually means inline conversion support, at least for the bundled input method. Read the product literature to find out whether there is inline conversion support for a particular input method. Inline conversion support is, fortunately, very common these days. Windows NT, for example, allows any input method to have inline conversion with any application.

Keyboard Arrays

Our discussion continues with a description of several keyboard arrays in use in CJKV locales, with figures so that comparisons can be drawn among them. Keyboard arrays covered in this chapter are divided into seven categories:

- Two Western keyboard arrays (QWERTY and Dvorak)
- One Chinese character keyboard array (kanji tablet)
- Two Chinese input method keyboard arrays (Wubi and Cangjie)
- Three zhuyin keyboard arrays
- Six kana keyboard arrays (JIS, New-JIS, Thumb-shift, 50 Sounds, and two variations of TRON)
- Two hangul keyboard arrays (KS and Kong)
- Two Latin keyboard arrays (M-style and High-speed Roman)

The market for dedicated Japanese word processors experiences enormous flux in keyboard designs and usage. It seems that for every new computer model a hardware manufacturer introduces to the market, the same manufacturer may introduce two or three dedicated Japanese word processor models. These word processors are much like computers, but the basic software for word processing is usually fixed (that is, cannot be upgraded).

Real computer systems are designed for more general usage, so there is less variety in keyboard arrays. In fact, some dedicated Japanese word processor keyboards may have more than one keyboard array imprinted on their keys. This is done by imprinting more than one character on a key. I once owned and used two dedicated Japanese word processors: the NEC 文豪ミニ5G and the NEC 文豪ミニ7H.* On the tops of their keys were imprints for the QWERTY array and the JIS array; on the sides of the keys were imprints for the 50 Sounds array.

The intent of this chapter is not to teach you how to use these keyboard arrays effectively, but rather to tell you a little bit about them and their characteristics. When it comes to practical usage, the QWERTY keyboard is still the most popular today.

Western Keyboard Arrays

Western keyboard arrays are used quite commonly for CJKV input because typical CJKV input methods allow the user to input text phonemically through the use of Latin characters (the input software subsequently converts this transliterated input

* 文豪ミニ is read *bungō mini*, and means "literary master."

into CJKV characters). In fact, one study claimed that over 70 percent of Japanese computer users input Japanese with Latin characters. This is not to say that keyboard arrays designed specifically for Japanese do not exist, but as you will see in the following sections, there are many to choose from.

QWERTY array

The most widely-used keyboard in the world is known as the QWERTY keyboard array, so named because its first six alphabetic keys are for the characters *q*, *w*, *e*, *r*, *t*, and *y*. It was originally developed so that frequently-used keys were spaced far from each other. In the days of mechanical typewriters, having such keys in close proximity to each other would often result in a jam. However, most keyboards today are not mechanical, but electrical, so the original need for spacing out frequently-used keys is no longer valid.

The QWERTY keyboard array is so well entrenched that it is doubtful that it will ever be replaced. Figure 5-2 illustrates the basic QWERTY keyboard array.

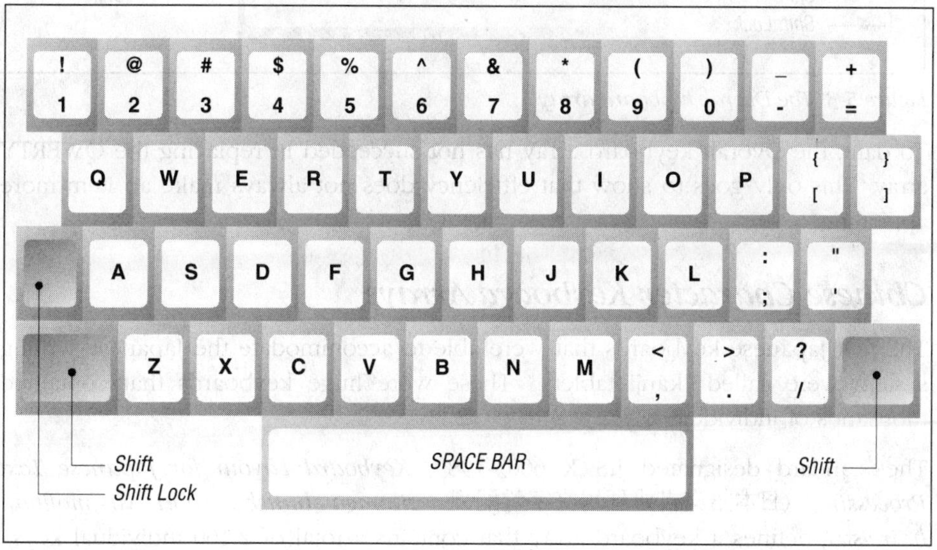

Figure 5-2: The QWERTY keyboard array

Dvorak array

There have been attempts at replacing the QWERTY keyboard array by providing an improved layout of keys, but none of them have succeeded to date. One such attempt was called the Dvorak keyboard array, developed in the 1930s by August Dvorak and William Dealey. Keys on the Dvorak keyboard array are positioned such that approximately 70 percent of English words can be typed with the fingers in the home position. Compare this with only 32 percent in the case of the

QWERTY keyboard array. See Figure 5-3 for an illustration of the Dvorak keyboard array.

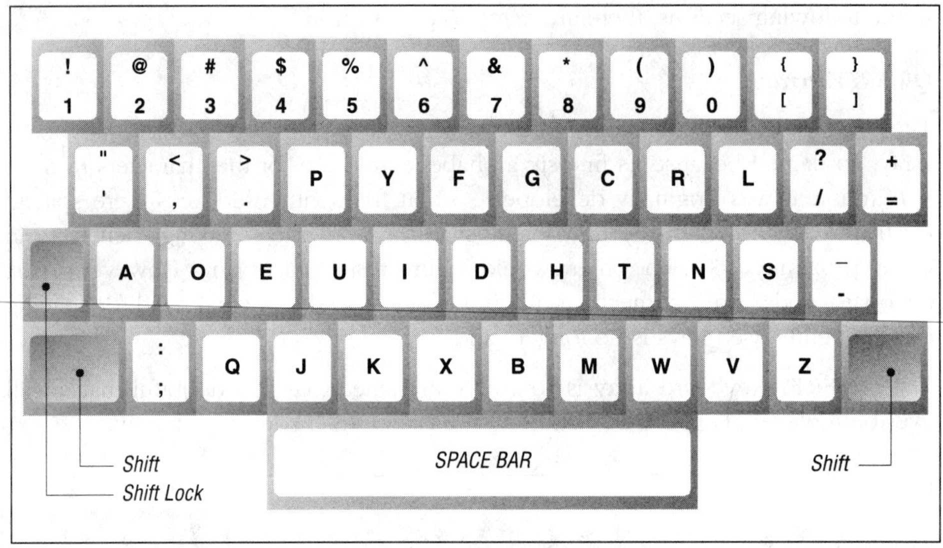

Figure 5-3: The Dvorak keyboard array

To date, the Dvorak keyboard array has not succeeded in replacing the QWERTY array. This only goes to show that efficiency does not always make an item more appealing.

Chinese Character Keyboard Arrays

The first Japanese keyboards that were able to accommodate the Japanese writing system were called "kanji tablets." These were huge keyboards that contained thousands of individual keys.

The standard designated JIS X 6003-1989, *Keyboard Layout for Japanese Text Processing* (日本語文書処理用文字盤配列 *nihongo bunsho shori yō mojiban hairetsu*), defines a keyboard array that contains a total of 2,160 individual keys.*
The kanji tablet shown in Figure 5-4 is 60 keys wide by 36 keys deep (it is also available in another orientation with fewer keys). The 780 most frequently-used kanji are in Level 1, 1,080 additional kanji are in Level 2, and 300 non-kanji are in the remaining keys.

Some Japanese corporations have even defined their own kanji tablet layouts, but this type of Japanese input device is quickly becoming obsolete. Japanese input

* Formerly JIS C 6235-1984.

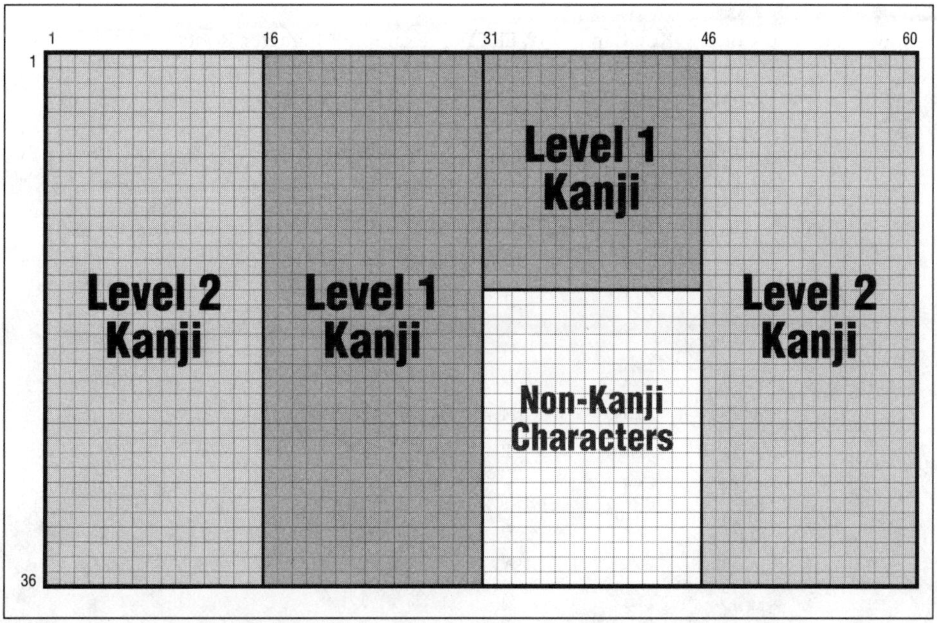

Figure 5-4: The kanji tablet array

software has developed to the point where much smaller keyboard arrays, such as those already discussed, are more efficient and easier to learn.

Chinese Input Method Keyboard Arrays

There have been dozens of keyboard arrays designed for use with specific Chinese input methods. The keys of such keyboard arrays have imprinted on them Chinese characters or Chinese character elements (such as radicals). The two keyboard arrays that are discussed in this section are the Wubi and Cangjie arrays, which appear to be the most popular.

Wubi array

The Wubi array is designed to be used with the Wubi Method, introduced in the section entitled "Input by stroke shapes," starting on page 232. A Wubi code consists of three or four elements, but four elements is the most common. The Wubi Method specifies five basic categories of character roots, according to the first stroke's shape, as shown in Table 5-20. Also provided are the key cap hanzi and their location on the QWERTY keyboard array.

Figure 5-5 illustrates the Wubi array, which demonstrates how the 25 hanzi used as key caps are assigned to the keys of the QWERTY array—all Latin character keys except for "Z."

Table 5-20: Wubi Method Character Roots

Row	Cell	Code	Key Cap	QWERTY	Example Character Roots
Horizontal 1	1	11	王	G	王主一五戋
	2	12	土	F	土士二十干寸雨
	3	13	大	D	大犬三古石厂
	4	14	木	S	木丁西
	5	15	工	A	工匚七弋戈廾廿艹
Vertical 2	1	21	目	H	目丨卜上止
	2	22	日	J	日曰刂早虫
	3	23	口	K	口川
	4	24	田	L	田甲囗四皿车力
	5	25	山	M	山由冂贝几
Curve[a] 3	1	31	禾	T	禾丿竹彳夂攵
	2	32	白	R	白手扌斤
	3	33	月	E	月舟彡衣乃用豕
	4	34	人	W	人亻八
	5	35	金	Q	金钅勹儿夕
Curve[b] 4	1	41	言	Y	言讠亠丶广文方圭
	2	42	立	U	立冫丬六辛疒门
	3	43	水	I	水氵小
	4	44	火	O	火灬米
	5	45	之	P	之辶廴冖宀
Corner 5	1	51	已	N	已己巳乙尸心忄羽
	2	52	子	B	子孑也凵了阝耳卩
	3	53	女	V	巛女刀九彐臼
	4	54	又	C	又厶巴马
	5	55	纟	X	纟幺弓匕

[a] Curves that extend from upper-right to lower-left.
[b] Curves that extend from upper-left to lower-right.

Four of the principles of the Wubi Method can be summarized, in simple terms, as follows:

- If the hanzi is one that is used as a key cap (a limited set of 25 hanzi), then its Wubi code is four instances of that key stroke—for example, the Wubi code for the hanzi 言 is "YYYY"

- If the hanzi is one of the character roots, as shown in the "Example Character Roots" column of Table 5-20, its wubi code consists of that key stroke plus the first, second, and final strokes of the character—for example, the Wubi code

Figure 5-5: The Wubi keyboard array

for the hanzi 西 is "SGHG" ("S" for the 木 key cap, "G" for the first stroke 一, "H" for the second stroke 丨, and "G" for the final stroke 一)

- If the character is not a character root, but whose structure contains four character roots, the Wubi code is the key caps for the character roots—for example, the Wubi code for the hanzi 照 is "JVKO" ("J" for the first element 日, "V" for the second element 刀, "K" for the third element 口, and "O" for the fourth and final element 灬)
- If the character is not a character root, but whose structure contains more than four character roots, the Wubi code is the key caps for the character roots—for example, the Wubi code for the hanzi 照 is "JVKO" ("J" for the first element 日, "V" for the second element 刀, "K" for the third element 口, and "O" for the fourth and final element 灬)

Of course, there are other rules and principles, but to describe them all is well beyond the scope of this book. For example, the "Row" and "Cell" values that make up the "Code" column of Table 5-20 are used for other Wubi principles.

The dictionary entitled 標準中文輸入碼大字典 (*biāozhǔn zhōngwén shūrùmǎ dà zìdiǎn*) provides Wubi codes for most GB 2312-80 hanzi.

Cangjie array

There is a special keyboard array designed for the Cangjie input method, which is one of the most popular input methods for entering Chinese text through the structure of hanzi.* A Cangjie code can consist of as few as one keystroke, or as many as five, depending on the complexity of the hanzi. In many cases, the Cangjie code perfectly reflects the complete structure of hanzi, as illustrated in Table 5-21.

Table 5-21: Intuitive Cangjie Codes

Hanzi	Cangjie Code (QWERTY)	Cangjie Code (Graphic)
一	M	一
二	MM	一 + 一
三	MMM	一 + 一 + 一
日	A	日
昌	AA	日 + 日
晶	AAA	日 + 日 + 日
𣊫	AAAA	日 + 日 + 日 + 日
𣊭	AAAA	日 + 日 + 日 + 日
品	RRR	口 + 口 + 口
堛	GMRW	土 + 一 + 口 + 田
畺	MWMWM	一 + 田 + 一 + 田 + 一

Table 5-22 illustrates less intuitive Cangjie codes, which result from the fact that some graphic Cangjie codes can also represent simple strokes.

Table 5-22: Less Intuitive Cangjie Codes

Hanzi	Cangjie Code (QWERTY)	Cangjie Code (Graphic)
酷	MWHGR	一 + 田 + 竹 + 土 + 口
劍	OOLN	人 + 人 + 中 + 弓

Once you understand that 竹 can represent a downward curved stroke, 中 can represent a vertical stroke, and 弓 can represent a stroke with an angle at the end, these examples become more intuitive. The dictionary entitled 標準中文輸入碼大字典 (*biāozhǔn zhōngwén shūrùmǎ dà zìdiǎn*) provides Cangjie codes for all Big Five hanzi plus the 3,049 hanzi added by the Hong Kong government.

Figure 5-6 illustrates the Cangjie keyboard array, which illustrates the correspondence between QWERTY Cangjie codes and their graphic counterparts.

* Yes indeed, this is the very same keyboard array that effectively stumped British Secret Agent James Bond (007) who always portrays himself as a know-it-all or all-around expert. Chinese Secret Agent Colonel Wai Lin, in the 1997 *Tomorrow Never Dies*, had a hideout somewhere in Vietnam where 007 was confronted with the possibility of using this keyboard array. He threw up his hands and gave up. Too bad this book wasn't available in 1997—imagine 007 whipping out this blowfish-clad tome which he then uses to learn the ins and outs of this keyboard array within moments, just in time to save all of mankind…

Curiously, this keyboard array is not used in China, but rather Taiwan. So what was a Chinese Secret Agent doing with a keyboard array developed in Taiwan?

Figure 5-6: The Cangjie keyboard array

Zhuyin Keyboard Arrays

In order to ease the input of Chinese by reading, several keyboard arrays that include zhuyin characters have been developed over the years. Luckily, only one of these keyboard arrays seems to have taken on the status of being the *de facto* standard.

Figure 5-7 illustrates the most popular instance of a zhuyin keyboard array, the one that is considered the *de facto* standard, which is used on MacOS and Windows.

Figure 5-8 illustrates yet another zhuyin keyboard array, specifically one that expresses the keyboard mappings used by TwinBridge. Note how this particular zhuyin keyboard array does not include keyboard mappings for tones.

Figure 5-9 illustrates a zhuyin keyboard array that was designed for use with the Dai-E input method (大一輸入法 *dàyī shūrùfǎ*), developed by Timothy Huang (黃大一 *huáng dàyī*).

More detailed information about Dai-E can be found in a book co-authored by Timothy Huang, entitled *An Introduction to Chinese, Japanese and Korean Computing* (World Scientific Publishing, 1989).

Kana Keyboard Arrays

The keyboard arrays discussed in this section have kana imprinted on their keys. One word of caution, though: simply because such keyboard arrays are consid-

Figure 5-7: The most popular zhuyin keyboard array

Figure 5-8: The TwinBridge zhuyin keyboard array

ered standard doesn't mean that they have been widely accepted in the Japanese marketplace. Like the QWERTY array in the West, the Japanese have a similar keyboard array called the JIS array—one that is not very efficient, yet is the most commonly used and learned.

JIS array

The standard designated JIS X 6002-1985, *Keyboard Layout for Information Processing Using the JIS 7 Bit Coded Character Set* (情報処理系けん盤配列 *jōhō*

Figure 5-9: The Dai-E zhuyin keyboard array

shori kei kenban hairetsu), specifies what is known as the JIS keyboard array (JIS配列 *JIS hairetsu*).* This keyboard array is the most widely used in Japan (after the QWERTY array, that is), and can be found with almost every computer system sold there. This standard also defines that the QWERTY array be superimposed on the keys of the keyboard. Incidentally, this is how one accesses numerals.

The JIS array is not terribly efficient for Japanese input. Keys are arranged such that all four banks are required for Japanese input. This means that users must move their fingers a lot during typing, and to shift mode in order to access numerals, which are imprinted on the fourth bank of keys, along with kana. In addition, the keys are not logically arranged, so it is difficult to memorize the positions. Figure 5-10 provides an illustration of the JIS array.

Note that the dakuten (゛) and handakuten (゜) have their own keys. This means that characters such as が (hiragana *ga*) must be input as the two keystrokes か (hiragana *ka*) and "゛" (dakuten). The same character が can be input as the two keystrokes *g* and *a* in the case of the QWERTY and other Latin keyboard arrays.

New-JIS array

The standard designated JIS X 6004-1986, *Basic Keyboard Layout for Japanese Text Processing Using Kana-Kanji Translation Method* (仮名漢字変換形日本文入力装置用けん盤配列 *kana kanji henkan kei nihonbun nyŭryoku sōchi yō kenban hairetsu*), specifies what is known as the New-JIS keyboard array (新JIS配列 *shin*

* Formerly JIS C 6233-1980.

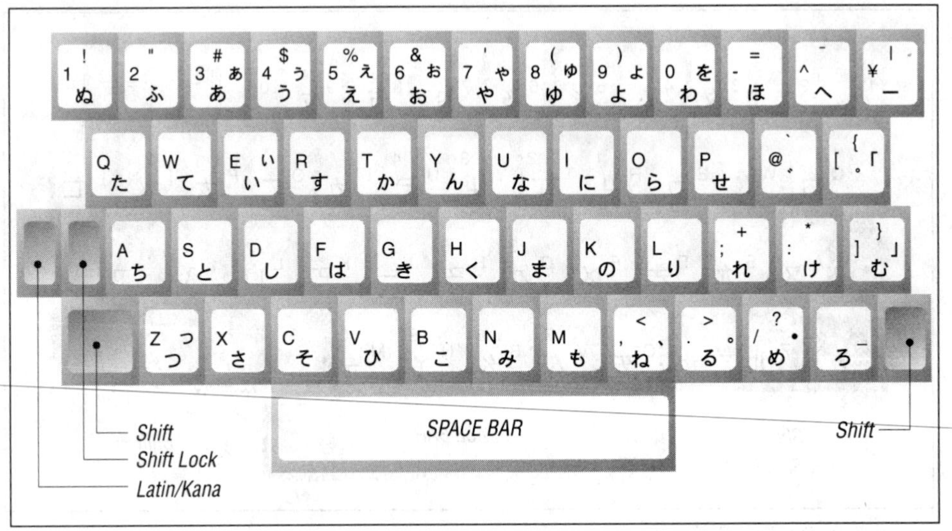

Figure 5-10: The JIS keyboard array

JIS hairetsu).* This keyboard array, too, specifies that the QWERTY array be superimposed on the keyboard keys.

The kana on the keyboard are arranged on the first three banks of keys, and each key holds up to two kana (a shift key is required to access all the kana). This allows the input of numerals without the use of a mode change. Figure 5-11 illustrates the New-JIS keyboard array.

Although this keyboard array seems to be an improvement over the JIS array, it has not been widely accepted in industry. To put it mildly, it failed to replace the standard JIS array (covered above). You will see that its design is similar in some ways to Fujitsu's Thumb-shift array, described next.

Thumb-shift array

In an attempt to improve the input of Japanese text on computers, Fujitsu developed a keyboard known as the Thumb-shift array (親指シフト配列 *oyayubi shifuto hairetsu*). It is very similar in design and concept to the New-JIS array, but has a slightly different keyboard arrangement, and places two special modifier keys in the vicinity of the user's thumbs (these act to shift the keyboard to access more characters).

Like the New-JIS array, the Thumb-shift array assigns two kana characters per key for the first three banks of keys (the fourth bank of keys is reserved for numerals

* Formerly JIS C 6236-1986.

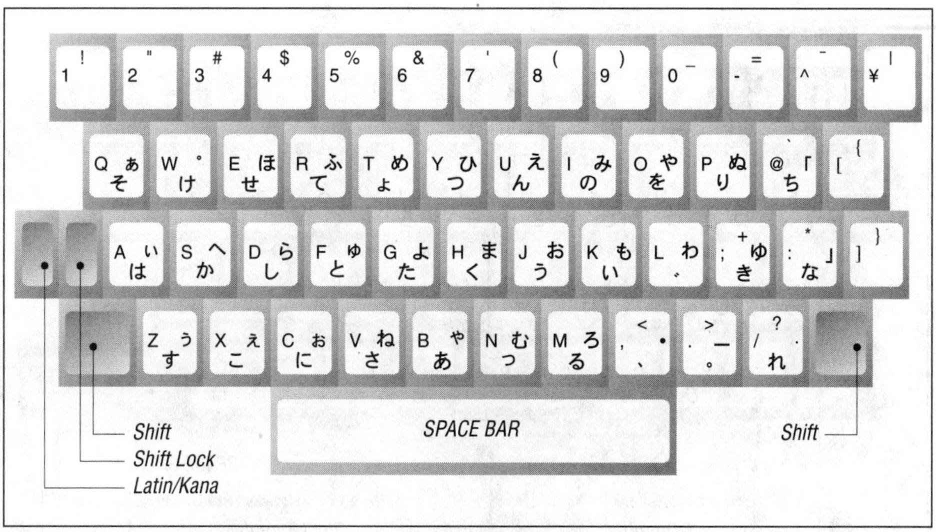

Figure 5-11: The New-JIS keyboard array

and symbols), but diverges in how the dakuten (゛) and handakuten (゜) are applied to kana characters. This is where the thumb-shift keys play a vital role.

The two thumb-shift keys each serve different functions. The left thumb-shift key converts the default character into the version that includes the dakuten. The right thumb-shift key simply shifts the keyboard so that the second character on the key is input. Table 5-23 illustrates some keys, and shows how to derive all possible characters from them (secondary characters for each are in parentheses).

Table 5-23: The Effect of the Thumb-Shift Keys

Key	No Thumb-Shift	Left Thumb-Shift	Right Thumb-Shift
は (み)	は	ば	み
と (お)	と	ど	お
せ (も)	せ	ぜ	も
け (ゆ)	け	げ	ゆ

The trickery used by this keyboard array is that all the characters that can be modified by the dakuten are placed in the no thumb-shift location of each key (that is, the default character). There is a special key used for modifying a character with a handakuten. Figure 5-12 illustrates the entire Thumb-shift keyboard array.

The Thumb-shift keyboard array is probably one of the most widely used in Japan (behind the QWERTY and JIS arrays, that is). In fact, other manufacturers have licensed it for use with their own computer systems.

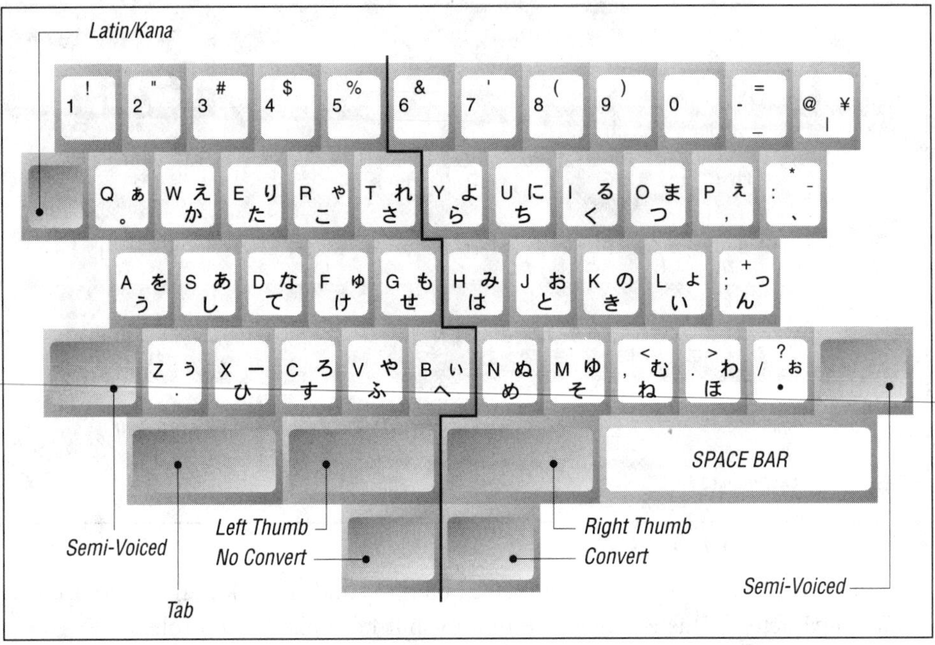

Figure 5-12: The Thumb-shift keyboard array

50 Sounds array

As you may recall from discussions in Chapter 2, the term "50 Sounds" (50音 *gojūon*) refers to the 5×10 matrix that holds the basic kana character set. The 50 Sounds array (50音配列 *gojūon hairetsu*) is based on this same matrix. On one side of the matrix are five vowels: *a*, *i*, *u*, *e*, and *o*. On the other side are nine consonants: *k*, *s*, *t*, *n*, *h*, *m*, *y*, *r*, and *w*. On the same side as the consonants is also a place that represents no consonant, where the vowels can stand alone. This arrangement of kana characters was then used as the basis for a Japanese keyboard array. This array is illustrated in Figure 5-13.

This arrangement of keys is not very efficient: it is almost like having a keyboard array in which the 26 letters of the alphabet are arranged in order—most of the time is spent searching for keys. In fact, there are Western keyboard arrays on which the keys are arranged in alphabetical order! This problem is multiplied for Japanese, which requires nearly 50 separate keys! This keyboard array also suffers from the same problems of the JIS array, specifically that all four banks of keys are required for kana, and that the dakuten (゛) and handakuten (゜) require separate keys. This keyboard array never gained widespread acceptance, and is thus not very widely used in Japan.

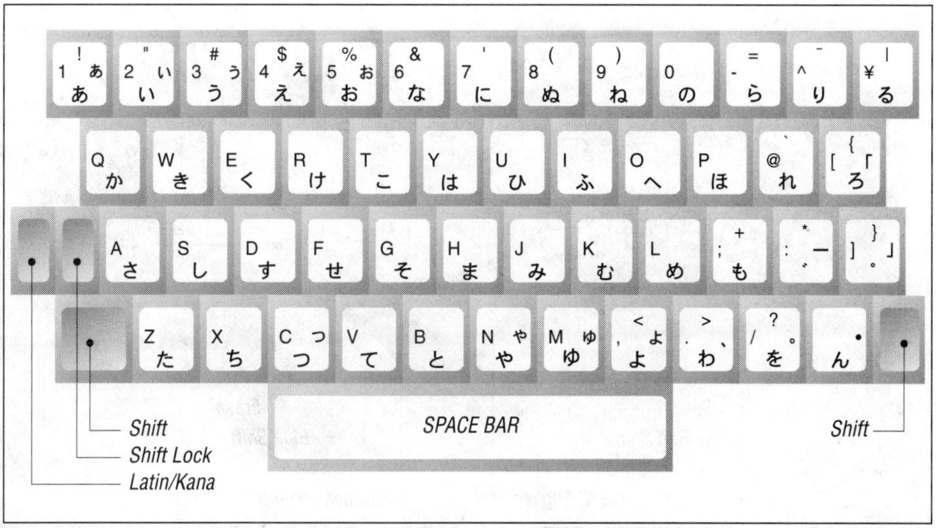

Figure 5-13: The 50 Sounds keyboard array

TRON arrays

Developed by Ken Sakamura (坂村健 *sakamura ken*), the TRON keyboard array is similar in concept to other Japanese keyboard arrays in that several ergonomic and other optimizations were made in its design. TRON stands for *The Real-time Operating system Nucleus*. More information about the TRON Project is available in Appendix C, *Vendor Character Set Standards*, starting on page 595.

There are two common instances of the TRON array: TK1 and μTRON (Micro TRON). Both instances of the TRON keyboard include the Dvorak array for accessing Latin characters (although the figures in this chapter do not show them). The TK1 design is laid out in an ergonomic fashion, as illustrated in Figure 5-14.

The μTRON design is more conventional in arrangement so that it can be used for notebook computers. It is illustrated in Figure 5-15.

Like the thumb-shift keys of Fujitsu's Thumb-shift array, the TRON keyboard arrays include two shift keys that allow the typist to gain access to additional characters. The left shift key is colored red, and the right shift key is colored blue. Table 5-24 lists the standard characters of the TRON keyboard arrays, along with the characters that are made accessible by pressing each of the two shift keys. Keys whose imprinted characters could be confused due to their positioning, such as some punctuation and small kana, are enclosed in boxes with corner reference marks to ease identification.

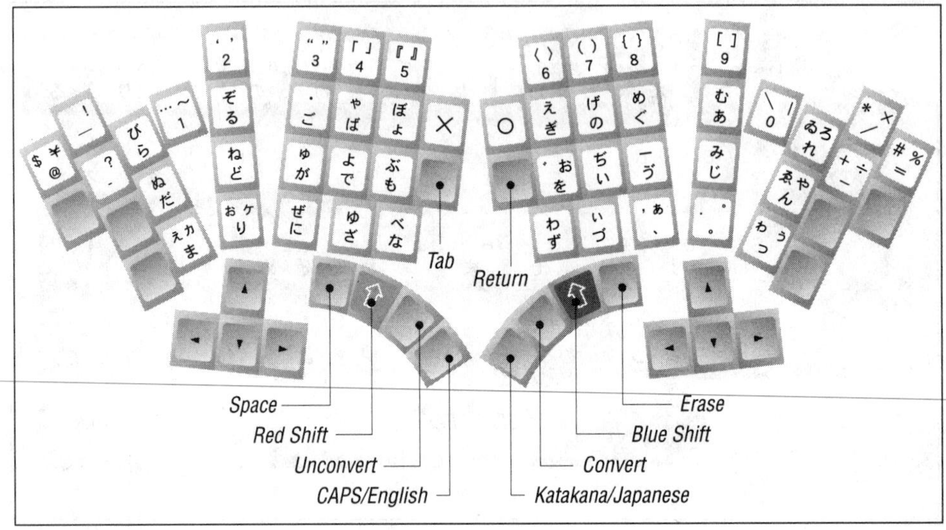

Figure 5-14: The TRON TK1 array

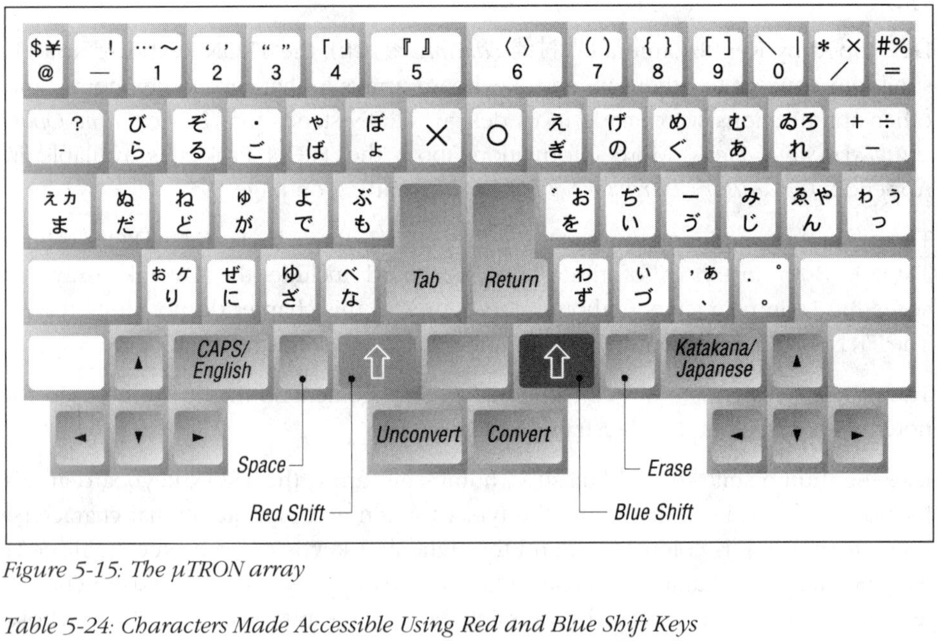

Figure 5-15: The μTRON array

Table 5-24: Characters Made Accessible Using Red and Blue Shift Keys

Unshifted Key	Red Shift Key	Blue Shift Key
@	$	¥
—		!
1	…	～

Table 5-24: Characters Made Accessible Using Red and Blue Shift Keys (continued)

Unshifted Key	Red Shift Key	Blue Shift Key
2	‘	’
3	“	”
4	「	」
5	『	』
6	〈	〉
7	（	）
8	｛	｝
9	［	］
0	＼	｜
／	＊	×
＝	＃	％
‐		？
ら	ひ	び
る	そ	ぞ
こ	・	ご
は	ゃ	ば
ょ	ほ	ぼ
き	ぎ	え
の	げ	け
く	ぐ	め
あ		む
れ	ゐ	ろ
ー	＋	÷
ま	ぇ	ヵ
た	ぬ	だ
と	ね	ど
か	ゅ	が
て	よ	で
も	ふ	ぶ
を	゛	お
い	ぢ	ち
う	づ	ー
し	じ	み
ん	ゑ	や
っ	ゎ	ぅ
り	ぉ	ヶ

Table 5-24: Characters Made Accessible Using Red and Blue Shift Keys (continued)

Unshifted Key	Red Shift Key	Blue Shift Key
に	せ	ぜ
さ	ゆ	ざ
な	へ	べ
す	ず	わ
つ	づ	い
、	，	あ
。	・	。

Hangul Keyboard Arrays

Hangul (and hanja) characters are input through the basic hangul elements, jamo. Up to four jamo comprise a complete hangul character (also referred to as pre-combined hangul). A complete hangul character can also correspond to a single hanja, in which case a hangul-to-hanja conversion dictionary is necessary. There are several hangul keyboard arrays available, most of which are described and illustrated below. The most commonly used Korean keyboard is the KS array.

KS array

The most common hangul keyboard array, known as the KS array, is documented in the standard designated KS X 5002:1992, *Keyboard Layout for Information Processing* (정보 처리용 건반 배열 *jeongbo ceoriyong geonban baeyeol*).* A total of 27 hangul elements are accessed using the three lowest banks of keys (leaving the fourth bank open for numeral access), and an additional seven hangul elements are accessed by shifting the third bank of keys.

Figure 5-16 illustrates the KS keyboard array. Note the additional key, beside the right-side "shift" key, for switching between Korean and Latin mode (labeled "한/영," transliterated *han/yeong*, meaning "Korean/English").

Although this is the most commonly used hangul keyboard array, its biggest drawback is that there is no method for distinguishing initial and final consonants. This is also why the KS array is known as a two-set keyboard array. The two sets are initial and final consonants, and medial vowels. The Kong array, described next, remedies this situation, but at the expense of additional complexity.

* Formerly KS C 5715-1992.

Figure 5-16: The KS keyboard array

Kong array

The Kong array is known as the Dvorak of hangul keyboard arrays, and is considered a three-set keyboard array. This means that all three hangul element positions—initial, medial, and final—are easily distinguished by the keyboard itself. The KS array required distinguishing to be done by software at the operating system level.

The unshifted state provides access to 39 hangul elements using all four banks of keys, and the shifted state provides access to 19 additional hangul elements, again using all four banks of keys.

Figure 5-17 illustrates the Kong keyboard array. Note the position of the numerals, specifically in the shift state of the second and third banks. Also note that some hangul elements are repeated. This is because they are to distinguish between initial and final instances.

Latin Keyboard Arrays for CJKV Input

Keyboard arrays appearing in this section make use of Latin characters rather than kana—there are a smaller number of Latin characters than kana, and these keyboard designs take advantage of that fact. These are unlike the QWERTY and Dvorak keyboard arrays described above in that they are optimized for Japanese input.

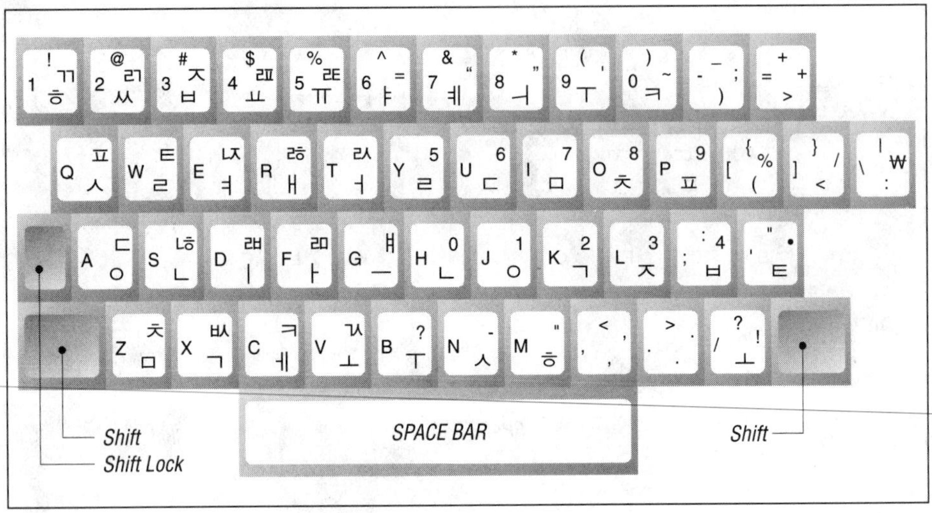

Figure 5-17: The Kong keyboard array

M-style array

Developed by NEC in the early 1980s, the M-style array (M式配列 *emu shiki hairetsu*) defines not only a keyboard, but also a new Japanese input method. The "M" in the name of this keyboard array comes from the last name of its designer, Masasuke Morita (森田正典 *morita masasuke*), a senior engineer at NEC. He has even written two books about this keyboard array and input method. I had a chance to try out the M-style keyboard array connected to two different machines in 1988 while in Japan. I was impressed with the feel of the keyboard, and the efficiency of input.

This keyboard array makes use of only nineteen keys for inputting Japanese text. Five are vowels, specifically *a*, *i*, *u*, *e*, and *o*. The remaining fourteen are consonants, specifically *k*, *s*, *t*, *n*, *h*, *g*, *z*, *d*, *b*, *m*, *y*, *r*, *w*, and *p*. There are, of course, additional keys for the remaining seven characters necessary to input English text (*q*, *l*, *j*, *f*, *c*, *x*, and *v*). Memorizing the locations for nineteen keys is easier than 26 for English, and considerably easier than the nearly 50 required for kana keyboard arrays. See Figure 5-18 for an example of the M-style keyboard array.

At first glance you should notice that the keyboard has a unique design—this is to make it more comfortable to use (less strain on the hands). Next, you should have noticed that the vowels are on the left set of keys, and the consonants are on the right set of keys. Japanese is a syllable-based language, so this vowel and consonant key arrangement provides a right-to-left typing rhythm.

The most important feature of this keyboard array and input system is that the user decides which parts of the input string are to be converted to kanji, which to

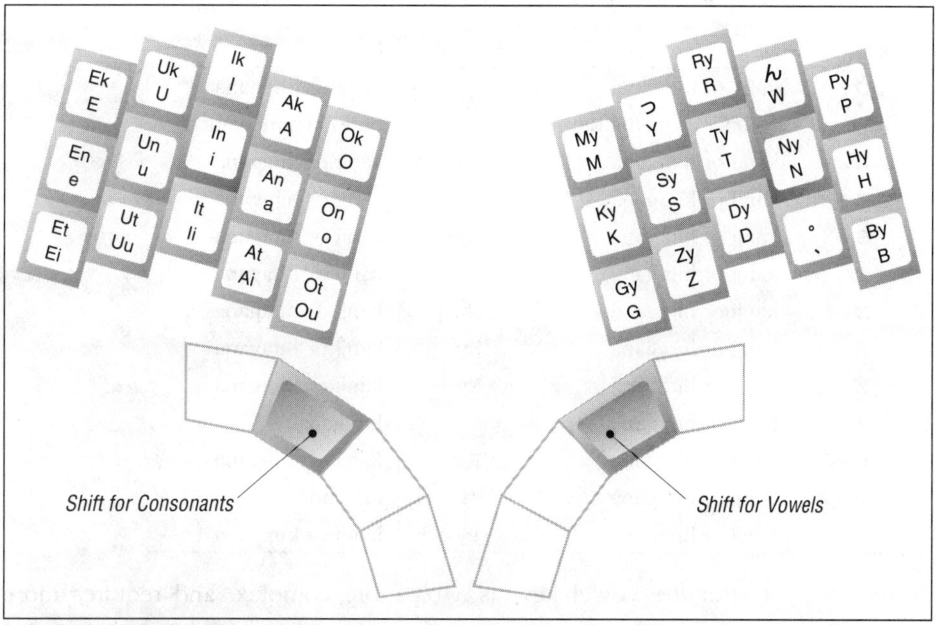

Figure 5-18: The M-style keyboard array

hiragana, and which to katakana. There are three banks of vowel keys, and each bank can also shift to provide even more variations. These different banks specify the target character type for the input segments. With conventional input software the user simply inputs a string of characters, then lets the software decide which parts convert to kanji, and which parts remain as hiragana—this can lead to misconversions.

There are three banks of vowel keys. Each bank contains five keys, one for each of the five Japanese vowels. In addition, a vowel-shift key is located near the user's right thumb. This, in effect, gives you six banks of vowel keys with each bank having a unique purpose. The consonant keys permit only two states, shifted by the consonant-shift key located near the user's left thumb.

The shifted state for the consonant keys in general adds a *y* or palatalized element. This is used to make combinations such as ぎょ (*gyo*) or しゅ (*shu*). Table 5-25 illustrates how the consonant keys shift, and their purpose. Note that some of the shifted versions are not used for kanji input, such as つ and ん.

Table 5-25: The M-Style Keyboard Array's Consonant Keys

Unshifted	Use	Shifted	Use
G	kanji or hiragana	Gy	kanji or hiragana
Z	kanji or hiragana	Zy	kanji or hiragana

Table 5-25: The M-Style Keyboard Array's Consonant Keys (continued)

Unshifted	Use	Shifted	Use
D	kanji or hiragana	Dy	kanji or hiragana
、	comma (punctuation)	。	period (punctuation)
B	kanji or hiragana	By	kanji or hiragana
K	kanji or hiragana	Ky	kanji or hiragana
S	kanji or hiragana	Sy	kanji or hiragana
T	kanji or hiragana	Ty	kanji or hiragana
N	kanji or hiragana	Ny	kanji or hiragana
H	kanji or hiragana	Hy	kanji or hiragana
M	kanji or hiragana	My	kanji or hiragana
Y	kanji or hiragana	っ	hiragana
R	kanji or hiragana	Ry	kanji or hiragana
W	kanji or hiragana	ん	hiragana
P	kanji or hiragana	Py	kanji or hiragana

The shifted state for the vowel keys is a bit more complex, and requires more detailed tables. Some banks of vowel keys are designed to generate hiragana, not kanji. See Tables 5-26 and 5-27 to find out how this works.

Table 5-26: The M-Style Keyboard Array's Vowel Keys—Unshifted

1st Bank	Use	2nd Bank	Use	3rd Bank	Use
Ei	kanji (long vowel)	e	hiragana	E	kanji (single vowel)
Uu	kanji (long vowel)	u	hiragana	U	kanji (single vowel)
Ii	kanji (long vowel)	i	hiragana	I	kanji (single vowel)
Ai	kanji (long vowel)	a	hiragana	A	kanji (single vowel)
Ou	kanji (long vowel)	o	hiragana	O	kanji (single vowel)

Table 5-27: The M-style Keyboard Array's Vowel Keys—Shifted

1st Bank	Use	2nd Bank	Use	3rd Bank	Use
Et	kanji (+ち/つ/っ)	En	kanji (+ん)	Ek	kanji (+き/く/っ)
Ut	kanji (+ち/つ/っ)	Un	kanji (+ん)	Uk	kanji (+き/く/っ)
It	kanji (+ち/つ/っ)	In	kanji (+ん)	Ik	kanji (+き/く/っ)
At	kanji (+ち/つ/っ)	An	kanji (+ん)	Ak	kanji (+き/く/っ)
Ot	kanji (+ち/つ/っ)	On	kanji (+ん)	Ok	kanji (+き/く/っ)

Okay, but what happened to katakana? The M-style keyboard must be shifted into a special state for katakana input to be in effect. Katakana input is quite similar to kanji input in that you can use different vowel keys as shortcuts. Some of the vowel keys change in ways that speed katakana input.

Table 5-28 shows how the M-style keyboard array can be used to specify which characters convert to kanji, and how many kanji to select during conversion. The examples all share the same reading: *daku*.

Table 5-28: Comparisons Among M-Style, Latin, and Kana Input

Word	M-Style Input	Conventional Latin Input[a]	Conventional Kana Input
駄句	D A K U	D A K U	た゛く
諾	D Ak	D A K U	た゛く
抱く	D A K u	D A K U	た゛く
だく	D a K u	D A K U	た゛く

[a] Case makes no difference.

A lot (but not all) of the ambiguity that you will see in conventional Japanese input methods is remedied by the M-style input method.

The M-style keyboard is standard equipment on many of NEC's dedicated Japanese word processing systems.

High-speed Roman array

NEC also developed a keyboard array, partly based on the M-style array, called the High-speed Roman array (快速ローマ字配列 *kaisoku rōmaji hairetsu*). It is set into a conventional keyboard shape, though. The keys are basically set into the same arrangement as with the M-style array, but without the extra vowel keys and the special vowel and consonant modifier keys for distinguishing kanji from kana during input. Figure 5-19 provides an illustration of the High-speed Roman array.

For those who use MacOS, I have experimented with rearranging the keyboard resources within the System file (using ResEdit, the standard resource editor for MacOS) such that this keyboard array can be used for Japanese input (it gave me a chance to experiment with this keyboard array without purchasing special hardware). Modifying keyboard arrays in software is something that almost every platform allows, and this keyboard array can be easily implemented. In fact, you can purchase software kits that allow you to accomplish this more easily. One such kit is called MacQWERTY, distributed by Nisus Software. These kits usually come with stickers to apply to your keys that represent the new keyboard layout. ResEdit can also be used to modify the keyboard layout in software.

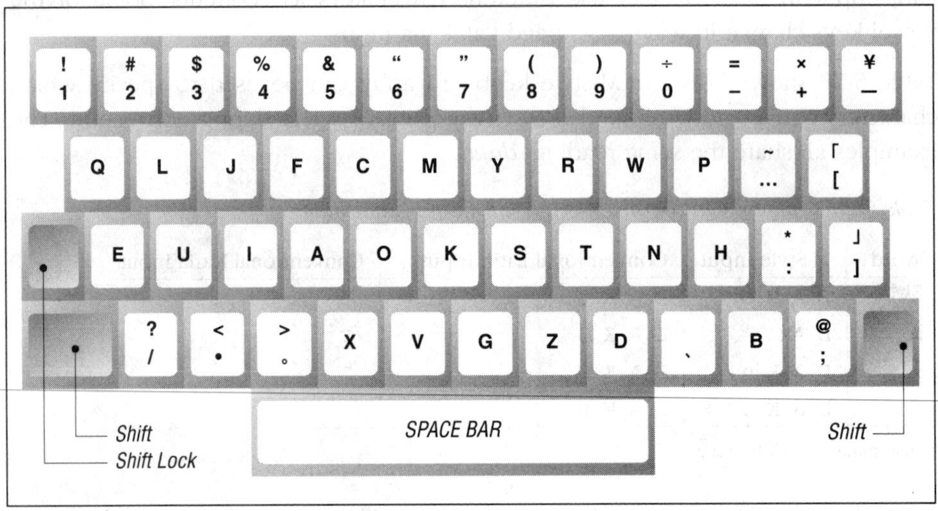

Figure 5-19: The High-speed Roman keyboard array

Other Input Hardware

What has been described so far falls into the category of keyboard arrays. That is, keys are used to input kana and Latin characters. Other more recent hardware methods such as pen input do not require use of conventional keys. Optical character recognition (OCR) is another input system which deals with the problem of transcribing already-printed information. Finally, there are voice input systems.

This area is rapidly changing. Any mention of specifics may make this section obsolete. I do, however, list some systems that use these input systems merely to give you a taste for what has been developed.

Pen Input

GO Corporation, which has since gone out of business after being acquired by AT&T, developed a pen-based operating system and programming environment called PenPoint.* PenPoint did not require the use of conventional keys, but instead used a tablet on which the user physically wrote what was intended. Pen input depends on another technology, specifically optical character recognition (to be covered next). GO Corporation had enhanced their pen-based operating system to handle Japanese through the use of Unicode.

* For an interesting account of GO Corporation's rise and fall, I suggest Jerry Kaplan's *Startup: A Silicon Valley Adventure* (Penguin Books, 1994).

Microsoft's MS-IME, which is the standard input method provided with Windows 95J and Windows NT-J, provides the ability for the user to input characters by writing them on a special on-screen tablet.

Optical Character Recognition

Several OCR systems currently accept CJKV character input, although there are, of course, limitations. The clearer and larger the typefaces, the more reliable such a system is. Some systems do not recognize all the characters in a character set (in the case of GB 2312-80, for example, some recognize only Level 1 hanzi), and some are restricted to certain typeface styles.

You encounter OCR systems more frequently in the West where recognition of a much smaller collection of characters is done. The recognition of thousands of individual characters becomes much more difficult, particularly when each one is fairly complex in structure.

NeocorTech's KanjiScan OCR, available only for Windows, can convert printed material that contains Japanese and English text into a form that can be manipulated as normal text.* For those characters that it cannot recognize, there is a "Kanji Search System" for looking up unrecognized kanji, which automatically suggests alternatives from which to choose.

MacReader/WinReader PRO and e.Typist Bilingual 97 by Media Drive Corporation are examples of OCR software that handles Japanese and English text. They are available for MacOS and Windows.

Voice Input

Voice input systems require users to register their voice patterns so that the voice recognition software can more predictably match the user's voice input with correct character strings. Of course, a voice input system is customized for a specific user, so no others can effectively use voice input unless the system is trained to recognize the new voice. Examples of voice input systems include IBM's ViaVoice (also called VoiceType),† available for Chinese and Japanese, and Apple Computer's Chinese Dictation Kit.‡

Voice-driven software is now becoming more widespread, so expect more sophisticated systems to enter the market. If you think your office environment is

* *http://www.neocor.com/*

† *http://www.software.ibm.com/is/voicetype/*

‡ *http://speech.apple.com/speech/cdk/cdk.html*

distracting now, you can look forward to the joys of entire buildings full of people in cubicles yelling at their computers! Aren't sound-proof walls and doors nice?

Input Method Software

Input methods are the software programs that perform the actual CJKV input. These days it is common practice to refer to these programs as "input methods" rather than FEPs. They make use of one or more conversion dictionaries, and often use special rules to more effectively convert input strings into Chinese characters, or into a mixture of kana and kanji (Japanese) or hangul and hanja (Korean). The actual mechanics of CJKV input were described in detail earlier in this chapter.

Here you will learn a little bit about a select few input methods. Under most environments these programs are separate modules from the text editing or word processing software with which they are used. This allows them to be used with a variety of applications. Some of these programs are dedicated for use within a specific application. For example, Quail is the dedicated input method for Japanese-capable versions of Emacs, such as GNU Emacs Version 20 and greater.

Virtually all input methods have a facility that allows the user to add entries to the conversion dictionary (either to the main conversion dictionary or to a separate user conversion dictionary). This allows users to create entries for hard-to-convert Chinese characters or Chinese character compounds. This also allows adventurous users create specialized or field-specific conversion dictionaries. Adding entries to a conversion dictionary is sometimes a simple task of providing a key in the form of a reading string (using Latin characters, kana, or hangul) followed by one or more names that will act as candidates when the key is encountered during the conversion process. More complex input methods require additional grammatical information, such as part of speech (noun, verb, and so on) or other information to assist in the conversion process.

CJKV Input Method Software

Microsoft is now offering their CJKV-capable "Global IME" for Windows 95, 98, and NT users.* This software can be used with Internet Explorer (Version 4.0 or later), Outlook Express (Version 4.0 or later), Outlook 98, and Netscape Communicator (Version 4.0 or later).

This is a significant development because it means that it is now easier than ever to send CJKV email, browse CJKV web pages, or fill out web-based CJKV forms—

* *http://www.microsoft.com/windows/ie/ie40/ime.htm*

all one needs are Internet Explorer,* Global IME, and one or more Language Packs.† These are all available at no charge from Microsoft's web site.

Chinese Input Method Software

The number of input methods available for Chinese far outnumber those available for Japanese and Korean—combined! One source claims that well over 500 different Chinese input methods have been developed over the years.‡

Jinput

Jinput is a sentence-based Pinyin input system.** Its "Copy to clipboard" feature allows the user to specify Java's \uXXXX format.

NJStar

NJStar? You must be wondering why a Chinese word processor is listed as a Chinese input method. This is because it provides the user with nearly 20 Chinese input methods, each of which can be easily invoked through its menus.

More information about NJStar as a word processor can be found in Chapter 10, *Operating Systems, Text Editors, and Word Processors*, starting on page 481.

Japanese Input Method Software

Some input methods, such as ATOK, VJE, and Wnn, have been ported to multiple platforms, which often means you can exchange their conversion dictionaries among platforms.

The following are some of the available commercial Japanese input methods—some are bundled with operating systems, and others are added on:

- ATOK (JUSTSYSTEM)
- EGBridge (ErgoSoft)
- Katana (SomethingGood)
- Kotoeri (Apple Computer)
- MS-IME97 (Microsoft)
- OAK (Fujitsu)

* *http://www.microsoft.com/windows/ie/*

† *http://www.microsoft.com/msdownload/ieplatform/lang/lang.htm*

‡ Yucheng Liu's MS thesis entitled *Chinese Information Processing* (University of Nevada, Las Vegas, 1995).

** *http://homemade.hypermart.net/jinput/*

- VJE (VACS)
- Wnn (Wnn Consortium)

Some of the above input methods, such as Kotoeri, MS-IME97, and Wnn, are bundled as part of operating systems. After all, a Japanese-capable operating system is meaningless without an input method. The other input methods were developed because some users find the input methods bundled with their operating system inadequate. Finally, some of these input methods have been ported to multiple platforms, such as ATOK, VJE, and Wnn.

Non-commercial input methods include Canna, Quail, SKK, T-Code, Wnn (earlier than Version 6), and so on. Quail and SKK are more or less closely related to GNU Emacs—Quail is actually part of GNU Emacs Version 20 and greater, and SKK is an add-on input method for GNU Emacs. The latest version of Quail uses SKK's conversion dictionary.

ATOK

ATOK (エイトック *ētokku*), developed by JUSTSYSTEM (the developers of the popular Ichitaro Japanese word processing program), is one of the most powerful and popular Japanese input methods available.* ATOK stands for *Advanced Technology of Kana-Kanji transfer*. It is available for both MacOS and Windows.

Canna

Canna (かんな *kanna*) is the name of a Japanese input system originally developed by Akira Kon (今昭 *kon akira*) and several others at NEC, which offers features and a set of conversion dictionaries similar to Wnn, described later in this section.† It is easily customized by the user, and comes with additional utilities for performing tasks such as conversion dictionary maintenance. Much of the customizing is done with LISP-like commands. Canna was one of the first freely-available Japanese input systems for Unix that used automatic conversion and that provided a unified user interface. Canna is now available for Windows 95J and Java.

Kotoeri

Kotoeri (ことえり *kotoeri*) is the name of the input method bundled with MacOS-J Version 7.1 and later (and MacOS with the Japanese Language Kit). Its name during initial development was Akiko (standing for "Apple's kana in kanji out"). Kotoeri literally means "word selector" (こと means "word," and えり means "select"). It is much improved over the input method bundled with earlier versions

---

* *http://www.justsystem.co.jp/atok/*

† *http://www.nec.co.jp/canna/*

of MacOS-J, specifically 2.1変換. The latest version of Kotoeri, Version 2.0, which is bundled with MacOS Version 8.0J, adds improvements that rival third-party input methods, such as the ability to input kanji by using a special Unicode palette. It does, however, remove the ability to input characters by ISO-2022-JP and Shift-JIS codes, but ISO-2022-JP– and Shift-JIS–based palettes are still included. Input by code is now effectively restricted to four-digit Row-Cell codes.

User-defined conversion dictionary entries are entered into a special user conversion dictionary. The main conversion dictionary is considered fixed and thus read-only.

MS-IME

The input method that is bundled with Japanese versions of Windows, whether it is 95, 98, or NT, is called MS-IME (standing for "Microsoft Input Method Editor"). MS-IME provides the user with a full range of input facilities, along with the ability to input characters by writing them on a special on-screen tablet. It is also possible to search for difficult-to-input kanji through the use of built-in radical and stroke count indexes.

MS-IME, when installed on non-Japanese Windows NT (Version 4.0 or later), can be used in the context of some applications, such as Internet Explorer (Version 4.0 or later), to enable Japanese input.*

Because of its status as the bundled input method for Windows, don't expect to see a MacOS version of MS-IME anytime soon!

SKK

SKK, which stands for *Simple Kana Kanji Converter*, is a freely-available Japanese input system intended for use with Japanese-capable versions of text editors based upon GNU Emacs (such as Demacs, GNU Emacs itself, Mule, and NEmacs, which are described in Chapter 10).† This means that Japanese input under SKK is restricted to using Japanese Emacs. Many people use Emacs as their working environment—various tasks, such as sending and receiving email, reading Usenet News, writing and compiling programs, and so on can be done from within Emacs.

SKK comes with three conversion dictionaries. There is no need to install all three since they are inclusive of each other (that is, the large conversion dictionary contains all the entries of the medium one). There is also an interactive tutorial,

---

* *http://www.microsoft.com/windows/ie/ie40/ime.htm*

† *http://skk.kuis.kyoto-u.ac.jp/skk/*

invoked from within GNU Emacs, that is useful for learning the SKK Japanese input method.

SKK and its associated files have been adapted for use with non-Unix systems. For example, MOKE, a commercial Japanese text editor for MS-DOS systems, makes use of the SKK conversion dictionary format for its own Japanese text entry system.

The development of SKK is being managed by Masahiko Sato* (佐藤雅彦 *satō masahiko*). You can even have the entire SKK source sent to you by sending email.†

T-Code

T-Code is a freely-available Japanese input method developed at Yamada Laboratory at Tokyo University.‡ T-Code has been adapted to run under a variety of platforms (MacOS, Unix, and Windows), and uses a two-stroke input method. Each kanji is input by two *arbitrary* key strokes (this is effectively the opposite of input by association, which was an input technique whose description started on page 236).

VJE

VJE is a commercial Japanese input method that has been adapted for a variety of operating systems. VJE is available for Japanese PCs, and MacVJE is available for MacOS. VJE is developed by VACS,** and MacVJE is developed by Dynaware.††

All versions of VJE come with utilities for exchanging conversion dictionaries among operating systems. This is useful if you have more than one version of VJE, or want to send someone your conversion dictionary.

MacVJE comes with two conversion dictionaries. The main conversion dictionary contains well over 100,000 entries. The other dictionary contains Japanese postal codes, along with candidate place names associated with those postal codes. Only one dictionary can be used at a time, but utilities are included for merging dictionaries. The main conversion dictionary can also be decompiled (that is, converted into a large text file for viewing individual entries) with the same utility—this is a feature that many other Japanese input programs do not have. User-specific entries are added directly to the main conversion dictionary.

---

* *masahiko@i.kyoto-u.ac.jp*

† *skk-source@kuis.kyoto-u.ac.jp*

‡ *ftp://ftp.s.u-tokyo.ac.jp/tcode/*

** *http://www.vacs.co.jp/*

†† *http://www.dynaware.co.jp/*

Wnn

Wnn, which is an abbreviation of the transliterated form of the Japanese sentence 私の名前は中野です (*watashi no namae wa nakano desu*, which means "my name is Nakano"), is a freely available Japanese input program for Unix systems developed by the Wnn Consortium. One of the early goals of the Wnn project was to properly parse the above Japanese sentence. Wnn supports a multilingual environment, not only for Japanese, but also for Chinese, Korean, and many European scripts.

Wnn is actually the name of the conversion program that provides a consistent interface between *jserver* (a Japanese multi-client server) and actual Japanese input methods. Wnn also provides a set of conversion dictionaries. The Japanese input method that is provided with Wnn is called *uum*—this represents the word "wnn" rotated 180 degrees so that it is upside down. Uum is the client program that is invoked by the user for Japanese input, and defines the keystroke combinations necessary for Japanese input. Wnn, on the other hand, refers to the entire collection of software included in the distribution.

The conversion dictionaries included with Wnn consist of a main dictionary (about 55,000 entries), single kanji dictionary, personal name dictionary, place name dictionary, grammatical dictionaries, and several field-specific conversion dictionaries (for computer science and biological terms, for example). All these dictionaries are used in the conversion process.

The Ministry of Software (a company, not a government body in Japan) was the first to adapt Wnn for use with MacOS. Yinu System has also adapted Wnn for use with MacOS. Contact the Wnn Consortium for more information on Wnn. Some information on Wnn is available online in English[*] and Japanese,[†] and there is also a useful glossary of Wnn terminology.[‡]

Korean Input Method Software

Because of the hangul-only nature of most Korean text, the fundamental requirements for Korean input are simpler compared to Chinese and Japanese. The input methods bundled with Korean-capable operating systems, such as MacOS and Windows, are the most popular with users. Apple Computer's Korean Language Kit, as well as the Korean versions of Microsoft Windows 95, 98, and NT, come bundled with an input method that supports the input of hanja through the process of hangul-hanja conversion.

---

* *http://web.kyoto-inet.or.jp/people/tomoko-y/biwa/root/wnn_e.html*

† *http://web.kyoto-inet.or.jp/people/tomoko-y/biwa/root/wnn.html*

‡ *http://web.kyoto-inet.or.jp/people/tomoko-y/wnn-yogo.html*

Although not specifically a feature of the input method, Korean input does have one feature not shared by Chinese and Korean. This is the ability to delete hangul as whole characters (hangul) or by element (jamo) while still in "input mode." Once the character string is inserted into the application, the character must be deleted on a per-character (not per-jamo) basis. In any case, good input methods make both delete options available to the user.

Unix input methods, for the X Window System, include Byeroo, KIMS (Korean Input Method Server),* and hanIM.

* *http://www.iworld.net/~bumchul/kims.html*

In this chapter:

- *Typeface Design Issues*
- *Bitmapped Fonts*
- *Outline Fonts*
- *Ruby Fonts*
- *Host-Based Versus Printer-Resident Fonts*
- *Creating Your Own Fonts*
- *External Character Handling*
- *Advice to Developers*

6 Font Formats

One of the most critical aspects of displaying or printing CJKV text is the availability of fonts. Fonts form the very basis of document writing—no matter which writing system is involved—and are available in a wide variety of formats. A fully functional CJKV-capable application is completely worthless (and meaningless) without adequate font support.* Although the internal representation of characters in these formats, which can range from bitmapped to outline, differs considerably, the final result, whether printed, displayed, or otherwise output, is simply a whole bunch of bits or pixels. This is a very important point, so let me reiterate. No matter what format a font happens to be in, the final result consists of nothing but *bits* or *pixels*.

A typical CJKV font consists of the characters from the most common character set standard for a single locale. Only a few years ago, for example, Japanese fonts that provided support for JIS X 0208:1997 Level 2 kanji were somewhat uncommon—now you can start expecting to find font products that support the complete set of 20,902 Chinese characters that form a subset of Unicode—it may take a year or two until there will be font products that support the recent extension to Unicode, specifically 6,582 additional Chinese characters.†

Selecting the point size of a particular font is probably one of the most common tasks one performs within an application.‡ The size of a font is usually described in units called *points*. The point is a term used in typography that represents a measurement that is approximately $\frac{1}{72}$ of an inch (or $\frac{1}{72.28915663}$ of an inch in exact measurements). This means that a 72-point Chinese character is roughly one

* Now you know why I like my job at Adobe Systems so much!

† Well, frankly, as of this writing, these sorts of fonts are still rather uncommon.

‡ But, typing in characters themselves is a much more common task.

inch wide and one inch tall. 10- and 12-point fonts are the most common sizes used in text. The text of this book, for example, is set in 10-point ITC Garamond Light. The subject of typographic units of measurement, including other types of points, is a topic covered in Chapter 7, *Typography*.

This chapter covers what I consider to be the most popular font formats, either because they are widely used, have easily obtainable specifications for developers, or both. There are a myriad of font formats out there—bitmapped, vector, and outline—and it would be impossible (and impractical) to describe them all in this book.

Only the major CJKV type foundries have the appropriate level of design expertise and human resources necessary to create CJKV typefaces that contain thousands of high-quality characters. These CJKV type foundries include Adobe Systems (USA and Japan), Arphic Technology (Taiwan), Bitstream (USA), Dainippon Screen (Japan), DynaLab (Taiwan and Japan), Enfour Media Laboratory (Japan), Fontworks (Hong Kong and Japan), Founder Group (China), Hanyang Systems (Korea), Human Computers (Korea), Monotype (Hong Kong), Morisawa & Company (Japan), Nippon Information Science (Japan), Ryobi (Japan), Seoul Systems (Korea), Shaken (Japan), SinoType (China), SoftMagic (Korea), Tae System & Typefaces (Korea), URW++ (Germany), Yoon Design Institute (Korea), Zhong Yi Electronics (China), and many others. CJKV type was originally cast in metal or wood (or hand-written!), but the current trend, of course, is toward digital type. Those of you who are interested in type may find the newsgroup *comp.fonts* useful.*

Typeface Design Issues

When dealing with multiple typeface designs and different weights, there are many differences that can become apparent. Whether or not these differences are apparent depends on whether you use multiple weights in a single document, the size at which the characters are rendered (of course, differences become more apparent as the size increases).

Figure 6-1 illustrates differences in typeface design that may take place when going from light to heavy weights, using Adobe Systems' 小塚明朝EL and 小塚明朝H (KozMin-ExtraLight and KozMin-Heavy) for the example.† You should take note of two types of differences, one of which is somewhat subtle:

* This newsgroup also has a very useful home page: *http://www.nwalsh.com/comp.fonts/FAQ/*.

† KozMin is short for "Kozuka Mincho." It is named after its designer, Masahiko Kozuka (小塚昌彦 *kozuka masahiko*).

- As the weight increases, some vertical strokes become thinner as they pass through box-like shapes—these are circle-shaded in Figure 6-1
- For serif designs, the horizontal strokes sometimes decrease in weight as the overall weight increases

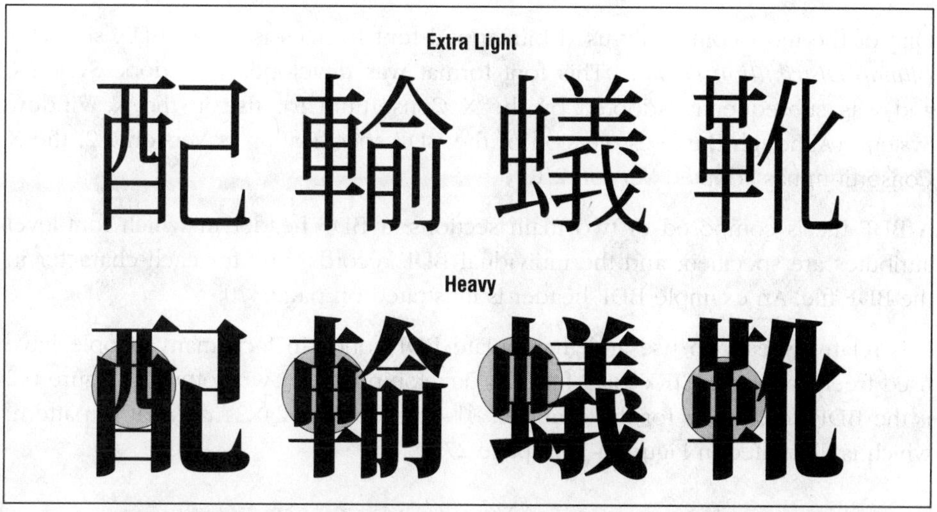

Figure 6-1: Differences in typeface design depending on weight

Bitmapped Fonts

The first CJKV fonts for use on computer systems were bitmapped. This means that each character is constructed from a matrix of dots, each of which could be turned on or off—this is referred to as a dot-matrix. The limitation of this font format is that the resulting bitmapped patterns are restricted to a single point (or pixel) size. Any scaling applied to a bitmapped font almost always produces irregular-looking results (the "jaggies" or the "Lego effect," as many call them). See Figure 8-1 on page 395, which provides an example of a scaled 12-pixel bitmapped character.

Obviously, the larger the dot-matrix pattern, the more memory such a bitmapped font requires, especially when designing a bitmapped CJKV font that contains several thousand characters (or tens of thousands of characters, as the case may be). There is also the problem of having to design a complete set of characters for every pixel size that is required.

It must be stated, however, that bitmapped fonts do have their merits. More advanced font technologies, which you will learn about later in this chapter, may produce poor-quality results at small point sizes and on low-resolution output devices such as computer displays. With bitmapped fonts, the user can have hand-tuned fonts for commonly used point sizes.

There are a myriad of bitmapped font formats available, but there are two common formats that can be used for representing CJKV characters: BDF and HBF. The following sections briefly describe each of these formats.

BDF Fonts

One of the most commonly used bitmapped font formats is called BDF, short for *Bitmap Distribution Format*. This font format was developed by Adobe Systems, and was subsequently adopted by the X Consortium for use in the X Window System. (Although the latest version of the BDF specification is Version 2.2, the X Consortium has adopted Version 2.1.)

A BDF file is composed of two main sections: a BDF header in which font-level attributes are specified; and the individual BDF records, one for each character in the BDF file. An example BDF header is illustrated on page 320.

It is relatively easy to use and manipulate BDF fonts. In fact, many people have used freely available CJKV BDF fonts in developing their own software. Figure 6-2 is the BDF description for the character 剣—this is for a 24×24 dot-matrix pattern, which is illustrated in Figure 6-3 on page 275.

```
STARTCHAR 3775
ENCODING 14197
SWIDTH 1000 0
DWIDTH 24 0
BBX 24 24 0 -2
BITMAP
018007
018006
0360E6
0318C6
060CC6
0C06C6
1866C6
37F0C6
C180C6
218CC6
3FFEC6
318CC6
318CC6
318CC6
318CC6
3FFCC6
318CC6
0340C6
033006
061806
0C1C06
180C06
300C3E
C0000C
ENDCHAR
```

Figure 6-2: A BDF record example

You must be wondering how to interpret this eye-catching BDF bitmap record data. Table 6-1 lists this format's keywords, along with a brief description.

The bitmapped data in each bitmap record of a BDF file that describes 24×24 dot-matrix patterns consists of 24 lines of six characters each. Each line represents 24 pixels, thus each character represents four pixels. Each of these six characters can have a value in the range 0x00–0x0F (that is, 0x00–0x09 or 0x0A–0x0F). This

Table 6-1: BDF Bitmap Record Keyword Descriptions

Keyword	Example	Description
STARTCHAR *name*	STARTCHAR 3775	Character name—can be *anything* (3775 is hexadecimal ISO-2022-JP)
ENCODING *n*	ENCODING 14197	Decimal encoding of character (14197 is decimal ISO-2022-JP)
SWIDTH *x y*	SWIDTH 1000 0	Scalable width expressed as a vector
DWIDTH *x y*	DWIDTH 24 0	Device width expressed as a vector
BBX *w h x y*	BBX 24 24 0 -2	The bounding box for the character in device units
BITMAP	BITMAP	Beginning of bitmapped pattern
ENDCHAR	ENDCHAR	End of character description

allows for up to sixteen unique values, which is the total number of unique patterns that can be generated using four pixels. Table 6-2 illustrates these sixteen values as binary patterns.

Table 6-2: The Sixteen Unique Binary Patterns in BDF Data

Value	Binary Pattern
0	0000
1	0001
2	0010
3	0011
4	0100
5	0101
6	0110
7	0111
8	1000
9	1001
A	1010
B	1011
C	1100
D	1101
E	1110
F	1111

Let's take a closer look at the first line of the BDF bitmap record as shown in Figure 6-2 on page 272:

```
018007
```

The binary pattern that is represented by these data corresponds to a pixel pattern—zeros correspond to white pixels, and ones correspond to black pixels. Table 6-3 illustrates how these binary patterns correspond to their equivalent pixel patterns.

Table 6-3: Binary and Pixel Patterns in BDF Data

BDF Data	0	1	8	0	0	7
Binary Pattern	0000	0001	1000	0000	0000	0111
Pixel Pattern	□□□□	□□□■	■□□□	□□□□	□□□□	□■■■

Note how there are 24 pixels across (and 24 such lines). Compare this pixel pattern with what you see in the first row of pixels in Figure 6-3 on page 275. In fact, it is more efficient to read these binary patterns two characters at a time, into a single byte. A byte can store a binary pattern eight digits long. For example, the first two characters, 01, are stored into a single byte, and its binary pattern is 00000001 (or, more graphically, □□□□□□□■).

BDF files can be reduced in size by converting into binary representations, such as SNF (Server Natural Format) and PCF (Portable Compiled Format). The standard X Window System utilities *bdftosnf* and *bdftopcf*, respectively, are used for this purpose. The X Window System (X11R5 and later) prefers PCF. SNF is older, preferred by X11R4 and earlier, and skips unencoded BDF records.* PCF is newer, and is considered to be superior to SNF in many respects because it uses a more efficient representation.

For a more complete and authoritative description of BDF, fetch the *Glyph Bitmap Distribution Format (BDF) Specification* document (Adobe Systems Tech Note #5005).†

Figure 6-3 is an example of 24×24 and 16×16 dot-matrix patterns for the character 剣. These dot-matrix patterns were taken directly from the JIS manuals JIS X 9052-1983 and JIS X 9051-1984, respectively. These manuals may become useful if your system does not support all the characters in JIS X 0208:1997 (doubtful, unless you're using an ancient operating system).‡ I once put these two manuals to practical use when I was working with EGWord Version 2.2 by Ergosoft on MacOS back in the late 1980s—that word processing software supported only JIS Level 1

* An unencoded BDF record is one whose `ENCODING` field has its value set to -1.

† All of Adobe Systems' Tech Notes that are referenced in this chapter are available as PDF (Adobe Acrobat) files at *http://www.adobe.com/supportservice/devrelations/technotes.html*.

‡ Note that these manuals are based on JIS X 0208-1983—they were never updated by JSA to conform to JIS X 0208-1990 or JIS X 0208:1997.

kanji (versions of EGWord beyond Version 2.2 included support for JIS Level 2 kanji by virtue of running under MacOS-J).

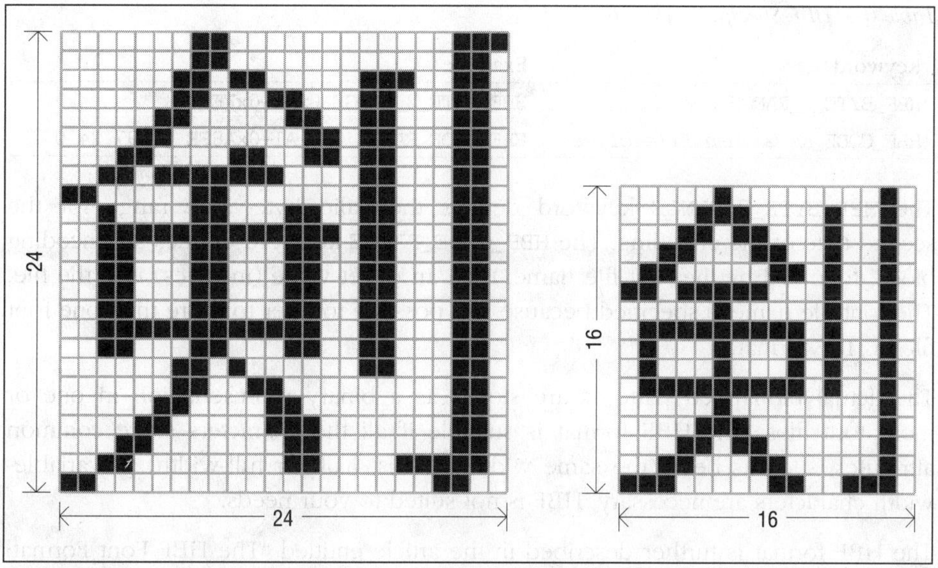

Figure 6-3: Japanese bitmapped characters

You can find bitmapped CJKV fonts at FTP sites, usually in the form of BDF files.* There are easily obtainable tools that allow BDF files to be converted into other formats—some of these tools, such as *bdftosnf* or *bdftopcf*, may be already installed if you are running the X Window System. You can also use Mark Leisher's XmBDFEditor to create and edit BDF files—this X Window System tool is described later in the chapter. The FreeType Project has developed a TrueType to BDF converter called *ttf2bdf*, which is useful for creating CJKV BDF fonts when a suitable BDF font cannot be found.†

HBF Fonts

The HBF (Hanzi Bitmap Font) format is similar to BDF in how it describes the actual character bitmap patterns, but creates a space-saving advantage by assuming that all the characters have certain attributes in common, such as a common display and pixel width.

The HBF format stores the font attributes and common per-bitmap attributes in a human-readable text file, which is based on BDF. This is called the "HBF specifica-

* I suggest that you try *ftp://etlport.etl.go.jp/pub/mule/fonts/*, *ftp://ftp.ifcss.org/pub/software/fonts/*, or even *ftp://ftp.oreilly.com/pub/examples/nutshell/cjkv/fonts/*.

† *http://www.freetype.org/*

tion file." This HBF-specific file introduces several new keywords not found in BDF. Table 6-4 lists these new keywords, along with an example of their use.

Table 6-4: HBF-Specific Keywords

Keyword	Example
`HBF_BYTE_2_RANGE` *`n-n`*	`HBF_BYTE_2_RANGE 0xA1–0xFE`
`HBF_CODE_RANGE` *`n-n file offset`*	`HBF_CODE_RANGE 0xA1A1–0xA8FE jis97.24 0`

The `HBF_BYTE_2_RANGE` keyword defines the valid byte-value range for the second byte of the encoding. The `HBF_CODE_RANGE` keyword defines an encoding block, followed by the font file name, then an offset value (in bytes) into the file. The font file name is specified because it is possible to refer to more than one font file in HBF format.

The actual bitmapped patterns are stored as a binary representation in one or more font files. The HBF format is suitable if all the characters share common attributes, such as being the same width (that is, half- or full-width). If variable-width characters are necessary, HBF is not suited to your needs.

The HBF format is further described in the article entitled "The HBF Font Format: Optimizing Fixed-pitch Font Support" (pp 113–123 of *The X Resource*, Issue 10) and in online resources.* HBF fonts are also available.†

Outline Fonts

During the early 1980s there was a revolution in the publishing industry made possible by the advent of PostScript, the page-description language developed by Adobe Systems. PostScript provides a seamless mixture of text and graphics, and, with the development of laser printers, brought high-quality publishing capability to many more people than ever before. Now, for well under $10,000 (US), anyone can purchase the necessary hardware and software to produce high-quality CJKV text by themselves. As far as CJKV fonts are concerned, the PostScript language supports a number of font formats that represent characters as scalable outlines.

In the late 1980s, Microsoft and Apple Computer collaborated to develop a scalable font format known as TrueType. The two companies went their separate ways, and independently enhanced the TrueType format to the point that the two versions are now incompatible with one another. TrueType, too, is capable of representing CJKV fonts.

* *ftp://ftp.ifcss.org/pub/software/fonts/hbf-discussion/*

† *ftp://ftp.ifcss.org/pub/software/fonts/\{big5,cns,gb,misc,unicode\}/hbf/* (choose one of either *big5*, *cns*, *gb*, *misc*, or *unicode* within the braces)

We will discuss both PostScript and TrueType font formats in greater detail later in this chapter. However, the principles and concepts behind each of these formats have much in common. In both cases, characters are constructed from outlines. This effectively means that each character is described mathematically as a sequence of line segments, arcs, and curves. This outline is scaled to the selected point size, filled, then rendered as bits or pixels to the output device.* A character from an outline font can be used at any conceivable size and resolution.† The design process is also simplified in that the designer need not worry about the point size of the font, and thus does not need to design more than a single point size.‡

Figure 6-4 is an example character from an outline font. The outline is constructed from line segments and curves. The anchor points that describe the outline are marked with small black squares along the actual outline of the character. The offline control points that define the Bézier curves are represented by small black circles with lines drawn to their respective anchor points. In this example, the character **剣** from FDPC's 平成角ゴシックW5 (HeiseiKakuGo-W5) typeface is used.

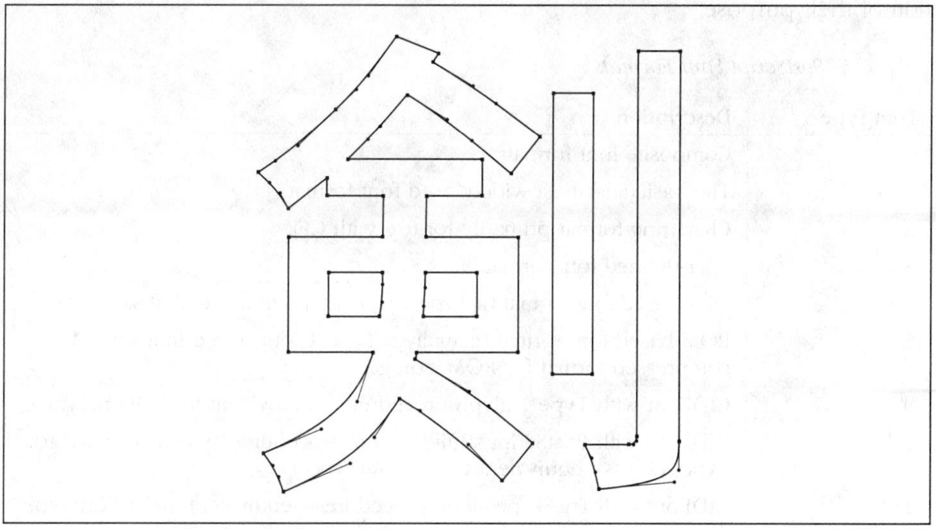

Figure 6-4: Japanese outline character

* In case you're wondering, *rendering* (or scan converting or rasterizing) is the process of converting a scaled outline into a bitmapped image—the outline format is only for more efficient internal representation and storage.

† Unless, of course, the font is resolution-restricted. This means that whether you have a low- or high-resolution device will decide what version of a font you must purchase. Needless to say, the high-resolution version costs more. This is, of course, an artificial restriction.

‡ That is, unless the designer intends to support optical size, in which case Adobe Systems' multiple master font technology, described later in this chapter, comes to the rescue.

Currently, the two most commonly used outline font technologies are PostScript and TrueType. Their primary difference lies in that PostScript uses Bézier curves (also known as cubic splines), and TrueType uses quadratic splines. Exactly what this means is well beyond the scope of this book, but Bézier curves require fewer control points for representation—this leads to fonts that require less disk storage space. Most users do not care on what underlying font technology their fonts are based, so long as they achieve the desired results (that is, that they work).

PostScript Fonts

PostScript is a powerful page-description language backed by a complete programming language. As a programming language, PostScript is syntactically similar to FORTH—both are stack-based languages. As a page-description language, PostScript supports both graphics and text, and, to render text effectively, provides built-in support for fonts.*

PostScript supports several font formats. The most widely used format is called Type 1. Table 6-5 summarizes these PostScript font formats with a brief description of their purpose.

Table 6-5: PostScript Font Formats

Font Type	Description
0	Composite font format
1	The basic and most widely used font format
2	Charstring format primarily for use with CFF
3	User-defined font format
4	Disk-based font format (a Type 1 font stored in a way that saves RAM[a])
5	ROM-based font format (actually a Type 1 font stored in a special compressed format for ROM storage)
9[b]	CIDFont with Type 1 glyph procedures—equivalent to CIDFontType 0
10[b]	CIDFont with PostScript "BuildGlyph" procedures, which is similar to Type 3 fonts—equivalent to CIDFontType 1
11[b]	CIDFont with TrueType glyph procedures—equivalent to CIDFontType 2
42	A TrueType font inside a PostScript wrapper—requires that a TrueType rasterizer be present
CFF	Compact representation for fonts that use Type 1 charstrings (these charstrings can be Type 1)

[a] PostScript junkies usually refer to RAM as VM (virtual memory).
[b] Font Types 9 through 11 represent native-mode implementations of a CIDFont usable as a font resource instance, and only the "glyphshow" operator can be used as their "show" operator.

* But I don't recommend that you go out and use PostScript for your general programming needs. For one thing, most PostScript interpreters are available only in PostScript printers (although Ghostscript and DPS are widely available).

The following is a detailed look at each of these PostScript font formats:

- Type 0 fonts are composite fonts, which are made up of two or more descendant fonts. A *composite* font constitutes a hierarchical structure in which large character sets can be supported. A *descendant* font can be a Type 1, Type 3, or even Type 0 font.* PostScript CJKV fonts are Type 0 fonts. CID-keyed fonts are also Type 0 fonts (with an FMapType value of 9—FMapType is described later in this chapter).
- Type 1 fonts are the most commonly used PostScript fonts. Type 1 fonts use a special, restricted subset of PostScript (along with additional operators), which allows for a more compact (and faster-rendering) font. The Type 1 font format is typically used for all Latin (that is, non-CJKV) fonts issued by Adobe Systems. It is also the format specified by the international standard designated ISO 9541:1991 (*Information Technology—Font Information Interchange*), parts 1, 2, and 3. The Japanese equivalent of this standard has been published as a series of four manuals. Detailed information on the Type 1 font format can be found in Adobe Systems' *Adobe Type 1 Font Format*, Version 1.1 (Addison-Wesley, 1990). Extensions to the Type 1 format are described in *The Type 1 Font Format Supplement* (Adobe Systems Tech Note #5015).
- Type 2 is not a font format, but rather a *charstring* format used within a CFF (Compact Font Format) structure. The word *charstring* (character string) here means the code that forms the description of the outline—think of it as a mini program that describes how to draw a character—as opposed to the entire wrapping mechanism used to contain all the character descriptions for a single font. Type 2 operators form a superset of the Type 1 operators, and provides smaller size and the opportunity for better rendering quality than Type 1. More information on Type 2 can be found in *The Type 2 Charstring Format* (Adobe Systems Tech Note #5177).
- Type 3 is sometimes called a user-defined font format. Type 3 fonts are much like Type 1 fonts, but allow for more complex outlines, such as logos and designs, and permit the use of the full range of PostScript operators. Type 3 fonts are not that common, and do not work with Adobe Type Manager (ATM) software, discussed in Chapter 8, *Output Methods*. They also cannot be hinted (this is true for all practical purposes, but it is possible to hint Type 3 charstrings if and only if you write your own hint procedures—but this still means they will not work with ATM).
- Type 4 fonts are Type 1 fonts, but are disk-based rather than printer-resident. Type 1 fonts now have all the benefits of Type 4, such as being able to be read from disk on an as-needed basis.

---

* A Type 0 font composed of Type 0 descendent fonts is said to be a *nested* composite font.

- Type 5 fonts are Type 1 fonts packaged in a special way for storage within printer ROM.
- Type 9 fonts are CIDFonts (discussed starting on page 288) that use Type 1 character descriptions. All CIDFonts built by Adobe Systems are Type 9. Type 9 is also referred to as CIDFontType 0.
- Type 10 fonts are CIDFonts that use Type 3 character descriptions. That is, they implement the PostScript "BuildGlyph" procedure. Type 10 is also referred to as CIDFontType 1.
- Type 11 fonts are CIDFonts that use TrueType character descriptions. A TrueType rasterizer *must* be present on the PostScript device in order to use Type 11 fonts. Type 11 is also referred to as CIDFontType 2. More information on this TrueType CIDFont format is available in *PostScript Language Extensions for CID-Keyed Fonts* (Adobe Systems Tech Note #5213).
- Type 42 fonts are actually TrueType fonts with a PostScript *wrapper* so that they can reside within PostScript printers, and act much like PostScript fonts. A TrueType rasterizer must be present on the PostScript device in order to use Type 42 fonts. But, why the number 42?*
- CFF (Compact Font Format) is a method that represents Type 1 and CIDFonts much more compactly than ever before. It is a font wrapper or container

* It has been rumored that 42 was chosen by an unidentified (Apple Computer) employee who was being humorous. In the *The Hitch Hiker's Guide to the Galaxy* and its sequels (written by Douglas Adams, published by Pocket Books), a god-like computer named *Deep Thought* is asked to calculate the answer to the *Ultimate Question of Life, the Universe, and Everything*. After computing for thousands of years, Deep Thought returns the value 42.

Reality sets in. In a September 27, 1995 post to *comp.fonts*, Kevin Andresen revealed to the world that he was the person who chose the number 42. I quote:

> I named it, and for you conspiracy theorists out there, it did *not* mean TrueType was the *answer* to Type 1! Maybe the real story later...

In a private email communication, Kevin conveyed the story to me:

> My group back at Xerox had changed their workstation/server/printer naming theme from *Mad Max* to *Hitch Hiker's Guide* just before I left—our main development printer was named "Forty-Two." I picked 42 because I *knew* that Adobe couldn't accidentally go there next, and as a wink and a nudge to my friends back in Rochester. It was only after Adobe and Apple resumed their business relationship that I heard the "conspiracy theory" about the answer to Type 1. By then, we had already released the spec to TrueType developers, so the name stuck.

Kevin also told me that he wrote an unimplemented specification for the disk-resident form of Type 42—similar to Type 4 fonts—called Type 44. He chose 44 because he had a cold at the time, and was guzzling Vicks Formula 44D. Kevin no longer works for Apple Computer.

As a footnote to this footnote, Douglas Adams had a few words to say about the significance of 42, from an email originally sent to Kevin:

> Everybody tries to find significances for 42. In fact, it's the other way around—many more significances have been *created* than previously existed. (Of course, the number that previously existed was zero—it was just a joke.)

designed to be used primarily with Type 1 charstrings (CFF can contain either Type 1 or Type 2 charstrings—Type 2 charstrings are the default). Proper tools can convert Type 1 and CIDFonts to CFF and back again (with no loss of data), so CFF is more like a transformation of existing font formats. CFF is natively supported in PostScript 3 and higher. Information about CFF is found in *The Compact Font Format Specification* (Adobe Systems Tech Note #5176).

Henry McGilton and Mary Campione's *PostScript by Example* (Addison-Wesley, 1992) is an excellent tutorial, and has a chapter on fonts, including a superb tutorial on composite fonts. Adobe Systems' *PostScript Language Reference Manual*, Second Edition (Addison-Wesley, 1990), provides a complete description of the PostScript language, including information on Type 0 and Type 3 fonts. The many Tech Notes authored by Adobe Systems provide additional information about PostScript and related technologies—these Tech Notes are also freely available.*

Type 0 fonts' FMapType

All Type 0 (composite) fonts must specify an FMapType. An FMapType is a PostScript language key (integer) that indicates which mapping algorithm to use when interpreting the sequence of bytes in a string. There are currently eight FMapTypes that have been defined (seven of which are described in the *PostScript Language Reference Manual*, Second Edition). Table 6-6 lists the FMapTypes, along with explanations as provided in the *PostScript Language Reference Manual*, Second Edition.

Table 6-6: FMapTypes for Type 0 Fonts

FMapType	Algorithm	Explanation
2	8/8 mapping	Two bytes are extracted from the "show" string. The first byte is the font number, and the second byte is the character code.
3	Escape mapping	One byte is extracted from the "show" string. If it is equal to the value of the "EscChar" entry, the next byte is the font number, and subsequent bytes (until the next escape code) are character codes for that font. At the beginning of a "show" string, font 0 is selected.
4	1/7 mapping	One byte is extracted from the "show" string. The most significant bit is the font number, and the remaining seven bits are the character code.
5	9/7 mapping	Two bytes are extracted from the "show" string and combined to form a 16-bit number, high-order byte first. The most significant nine bits are the font number, and the remaining seven bits are the character code.

* *http://www.adobe.com/supportservice/devrelations/technotes.html*

Table 6-6: FMapTypes for Type 0 Fonts (continued)

FMapType	Algorithm	Explanation
6	SubsVector mapping	One or more bytes are extracted from the "show" string and decoded according to information in the "SubsVector" entry of the font.
7	Double escape mapping	Similar to FMapType 3. When an escape code is immediately followed by a second escape code, a third byte is extracted from the "show" string. The font number is the value of this byte plus 256.
8	Shift mapping	This mapping provides exactly two descendant fonts. A byte is extracted from the "show" string. If it is the "ShiftIn" code, subsequent bytes are character codes for font 0. If it is the "ShiftOut" code, subsequent bytes are character codes for font 1. At the beginning of the "show" string, font 0 is selected.
9	CMap mapping	One or more bytes are extracted from the "show" string according to information in the "CMap" dictionary. A built-in decoder produces a font number and either a character code, glyph name, or CID.

FMapTypes 7 and 8 are available only in PostScript Level 2 implementations. FMapType 9 is available only on CID-capable PostScript devices.

FMapTypes 3, 7, and 8 support modal encodings (that is, some bytes, such as escape or shifting characters, are used to indicate information other than characters themselves). FMapTypes 2, 4, 5, 6, and 9 support non-modal encodings—all the bytes are used to encode characters themselves.

The composite fonts that are supported in Adobe Systems' Japanese OCF fonts use either FMapType 2 (for strictly two-byte encodings, such as ISO-2022-JP and EUC-JP*) or FMapType 6 (for mixed one- and two-byte encodings, such a Shift-JIS). CID-keyed fonts, of course, use FMapType 9.

Composite fonts

The very first composite fonts offered by Adobe Systems are now referred to as OCF (Original Composite Format) fonts. Adobe Systems produced OCF fonts only for Japanese—Chinese and Korean fonts offered by Adobe Systems will be available only in the newer CID-keyed font file specification.† The actual character

* As you'll soon discover, Adobe Systems' Japanese OCF fonts support only EUC code set 1 (JIS X 0208:1997)—CID-keyed fonts add support for code sets 0 and 1 (ASCII/JIS-Roman and half-width katakana, respectively).

† All of Adobe Systems' Japanese OCF fonts have been upgraded to become CID-keyed fonts, most of which conform to the Adobe-Japan1-2 character collection, described shortly.

descriptions (that is, outlines) in OCF fonts and CID-keyed fonts are identical. The CID-keyed font file specification uses a much more compact and efficient packaging mechanism and file structure, and is highly extensible when it comes to supporting additional or complex encodings.

PostScript CJKV fonts are implemented as collections of composite fonts that support various character sets and encoding methods. They also have special naming conventions not found in other fonts offered by Adobe Systems. A CJKV font name consists of several parts: family name, face name (usually indicating the weight), character set, encoding, and writing direction. The combination of family name and face name represents the base font name. Table 6-7 shows possible values for each of these parts (using examples from OCF fonts).

Table 6-7: PostScript CJKV Font Naming Conventions

Base Font Name	Character Set[a]	Encoding[b]	Writing Direction
Ryumin-Light	83pv[c]	RKSJ[d]	H (horizontal)
GothicBBB-Medium	Add[e]	EUC[f]	V (vertical)
FutoMinA101-Bold	Ext[g]	*and so on*	
MidashiGo-MB31	NWP[h]		
HeiseiMin-W3	*and so on*		
and so on			

[a] When the character set is not specified, the default is the standard JIS character set (meaning JIS X 0208-1983 or JIS X 0208:1997, depending on the vintage of the font).
[b] When the encoding is not specified, the default is ISO-2022-JP encoding.
[c] 83pv stands for "JIS X 0208-1983 plus verticals" (or perhaps "JIS X 0208-1983 plus proportional and verticals"—no one at Adobe Systems really knows for sure), and represents the KanjiTalk Version 6 character set, which also contains the vertically set characters. The writing direction is always specified as -H because most of the characters are horizontal.
[d] RKSJ stands for Roman, (half-width) Kana, and Shift-JIS.
[e] The Add character set represents a version of Fujitsu's FMR Japanese character set.
[f] EUC, as you might have expected, stands for Extended Unix Code. The only recognized EUC-JP code set for OCF fonts is code set 1, for JIS X 0208:1997. CID-keyed fonts, described shortly, support EUC-JP code sets 0, 1, and 2.
[g] The Ext character set represents the NEC Japanese character set.
[h] The NWP character set, short for NEC Word Processor, represents the NEC Japanese character set as implemented on NEC dedicated Japanese word processors.

Note that not all combinations of Character Set and Encoding specified in Table 6-7 are supported. The following are the fully qualified PostScript font names for the typeface called HeiseiMin-W3 (using the OCF version for the example):

```
HeiseiMin-W3-H
HeiseiMin-W3-V
HeiseiMin-W3-Add-H
HeiseiMin-W3-Add-V
HeiseiMin-W3-Ext-H
HeiseiMin-W3-Ext-V
HeiseiMin-W3-NWP-H
```

```
HeiseiMin-W3-NWP-V
HeiseiMin-W3-EUC-H
HeiseiMin-W3-EUC-V
HeiseiMin-W3-RKSJ-H
HeiseiMin-W3-RKSJ-V
HeiseiMin-W3-Add-RKSJ-H
HeiseiMin-W3-Add-RKSJ-V
HeiseiMin-W3-Ext-RKSJ-H
HeiseiMin-W3-Ext-RKSJ-V
HeiseiMin-W3-83pv-RKSJ-H
```

Compare this with Table 6-7 on page 283 to find out what character sets and encoding methods each font instance supports. There are also some special one-byte–encoded fonts that make up Adobe Systems' PostScript Japanese fonts, indicated as follows (again, using the OCF version of HeiseiMin-W3 for the example):

```
HeiseiMin-W3.Hankaku
HeiseiMin-W3.Hiragana
HeiseiMin-W3.Katakana
HeiseiMin-W3.Roman
HeiseiMin-W3.WP-Symbol
```

As of this writing, the Adobe Type Library contains 120 Japanese typefaces (designed by Adobe Systems, and licensed from FDPC,* Kamono Design Laboratory, Morisawa, and TypeBank), 4 simplified Chinese typefaces (licensed from Changzhou SinoType Technology), 4 traditional Chinese typefaces (licensed from Monotype Typography), and 14 Korean typefaces (licensed from Hanyang Systems and SoftMagic). A small sampling of Adobe Systems' PostScript CJKV typefaces is shown in Table 6-8. These typefaces are licensed from the original foundry, then produced by Adobe Systems or their font tools licensees to strictly conform to PostScript font specifications.

Table 6-8: Sample PostScript CJKV Typefaces

Typeface Name[a]	PostScript Name	Foundry	Sample Text
华文宋体	STSong-Light	SinoType	中文简体字范本实例
华文仿宋	STFangsong-Light	SinoType	中文简体字范本实例
华文黑体	STHeiti-Regular	SinoType	**中文简体字范本实例**
华文楷体	STKaiti-Regular	SinoType	中文简体字范本实例
宋體	MSung-Light	Monotype	中文繁體字範本實例
中宋體	MSung-Medium	Monotype	**中文繁體字範本實例**
中黑體	MHei-Medium	Monotype	**中文繁體字範本實例**
楷書	MKai-Medium	Monotype	中文繁體字範本實例
小塚明朝 EL	KozMin-ExtraLight	Adobe	日本語文字のサンプル

* FDPC, if you recall from earlier material, stands for Font Development and Promotion Center (文字フォント開発・普及センター *moji fonto kaihatsu fukyū sentā*).

Table 6-8: Sample PostScript CJKV Typefaces (continued)

Typeface Name[a]	PostScript Name	Foundry	Sample Text
小塚明朝 R	KozMin-Regular	Adobe	日本語文字のサンプル
小塚明朝 M	KozMin-Medium	Adobe	日本語文字のサンプル
小塚明朝 H	KozMin-Heavy	Adobe	日本語文字のサンプル
平成明朝 W3	HeiseiMin-W3	FDPC	日本語文字のサンプル
平成明朝 W9	HeiseiMin-W9	FDPC	日本語文字のサンプル
平成角ゴシック W5	HeiseiKakuGo-W5	FDPC	日本語文字のサンプル
平成丸ゴシック W4	HeiseiMaruGo-W4	FDPC	日本語文字のサンプル
ロゴアール-L	LogoArl-Light	Kamono	わぶんもじのサンプル
ロゴカット-M	LogoCut-Medium	Kamono	わぶんもじのサンプル
ロゴライン-B	LogoLine-Bold	Kamono	わぶんもじのサンプル
ロゴライン-U	LogoLine-Ultra	Kamono	わぶんもじのサンプル
L リュウミン L-KL	Ryumin-Light	Morisawa	日本語文字のサンプル
M 中ゴシック BBB	GothicBBB-Medium	Morisawa	日本語文字のサンプル
新ゴU	ShinGo-Ultra	Morisawa	日本語文字のサンプル
教科書ICA L	KyokaICA-Light	Morisawa	日本語文字のサンプル
タイプバンク明朝M	TypeBankM-m	TypeBank	日本語文字のサンプル
タイプバンク明朝H	TypeBankM-hv	TypeBank	日本語文字のサンプル
TB良寛MM	TBRyokanM-M	TypeBank	わぶんもじのサンプル
TB弘道軒MH	TBKoudoukenM-hv	TypeBank	わぶんもじのサンプル
HY신명조	HYSMyeongJo-Medium	Hanyang	한글과 漢字 샘플
HY중고딕	HYGoThic-Medium	Hanyang	한글과 漢字 샘플
HY둥근고딕M	HYRGoThic-Medium	Hanyang	한글과 漢字 샘플
HY궁서B	HYGungSo-Bold	Hanyang	한글과 漢字 샘플
SM세명조	SMMyungjo-Light	SoftMagic	한글과 漢字 샘플
SM견출명조	SMMyungjo-Bold	SoftMagic	한글과 漢字 샘플
SM중고딕	SMGothic-Medium	SoftMagic	한글과 漢字 샘플
SM태고딕	SMGothic-DemiBold	SoftMagic	한글과 漢字 샘플

[a] These are actually the font names that appear in applications' font menus. While the majority of Adobe Systems' PostScript CJKV fonts share the same menu name across operating systems, there are a handful that do not. They are listed in Table 6-45 on page 321.

Some of those typefaces might look the same, especially the ones called Ryumin-Light and HeiseiMin-W3. Let me assure you, though, that they are not: when set at a much larger point size, they look quite different. The main difference is in the shapes of the serifs (that is, the terminals of the strokes). You may also notice a slight difference in stem weights. Let's take a closer look at a character set at 150-point using two typefaces, Ryumin-Light and HeiseiMin-W3, in Table 6-9.

Table 6-9: Ryumin-Light and HeiseiMin-W3 at 150-point

Ryumin-Light	HeiseiMin-W3
語	語

Do they still look the same? I didn't think so. Ryumin-Light has flared strokes, whereas HeiseiMin-W3 has squared ones. While many typefaces may look the same at text sizes, they are almost always different when printed at larger sizes, such as I have done in Table 6-9.

Companies that develop PostScript CJKV fonts, either by licensing font data or designing font data themselves, are far too numerous to list here.

There are projects that resulted in freely available PostScript CJKV fonts. One of these projects, at WadaLab in Tokyo University (東京大学 *tōkyō daigaku*), resulted in several JIS X 0208:1997 and JIS X 0212-1990 fonts.[*] Another such project, sponsored by Korea's Ministry of Culture and Tourism (문화관광부/文化觀光部 *munhwa gwangwang bu*), resulted in a series of Korean fonts named "Munhwa" (문화/文化 *munhwa*, meaning "culture") that support a hangul-only subset of KS X 1001:1992 (only 2,350 characters).[†] I have since added proportional- and half-width Latin characters to these fonts, which makes them slightly more usable. I have also heard of a similar set of free outline fonts from Taiwan. I have built freely-available CIDFonts (and sfnt-wrapped MacOS versions for most of them) from the above freely available PostScript font data.[‡]

Anyway, there has been much talk thus far about two common PostScript font formats suitable for building CJKV fonts: OCF and CID-keyed fonts. Later sections will set the record straight about their origins and differences.

* *ftp://ftp.ipl.t.u-tokyo.ac.jp/Font/*

† *ftp://cair-archive.kaist.ac.kr/pub/hangul/fonts/munhwa-fonts/*

‡ *ftp://ftp.oreilly.com/pub/examples/nutshell/cjkv/adobe/samples/*

How can I accelerate PostScript fonts?

There are two ways to accelerate the speed at which Type 1 fonts (or font formats that use Type 1 charstrings, such as Adobe Systems' CID-keyed fonts) print, both of which are hardware-dependent:*

- Purchase a PostScript printer whose fonts are stored in ROM (as opposed to being resident on a hard disk, internal or external)
- Purchase a PostScript printer that is equipped with the Adobe Type 1 Coprocessor (such printers are typically bundled with fonts in ROM)

Fonts that are stored in printer ROM are considerably faster than those resident on a hard disk—reading from silicon chips is inherently faster than reading from a disk drive.

The Adobe Type 1 Coprocessor (T1C), also known as Typhoon, is an ASIC (Application Specific Integrated Circuit) developed by Adobe Systems for use under license by their PostScript OEMs (Original Equipment Manufacturers). This chip is essentially a hardware version of Adobe Systems' ATM renderer, which significantly accelerates the rasterization of Type 1 fonts. It was developed primarily to improve the performance of PostScript output devices that support CJKV fonts by reducing the time it takes to process their complex character descriptions.

The first commercial products to support the Adobe Type 1 Coprocessor are Oki Electric's series of PostScript Level 2 Japanese printers: the ML800PSII LT, ML801PSII and ML801PSII+F. They were introduced to the market in January 1993. Other printer manufacturers have also shipped products that include the Adobe Type 1 Coprocessor. It is important to note that T1C is no longer being developed, and as a result does not support Type 2 charstrings as used by CFF.†

What are OCF fonts?

As mentioned earlier, OCF fonts represent the original composite fonts offered by Adobe Systems. The OCF specification was never published or otherwise disclosed, so nearly every major CJKV type foundry took it upon themselves to reverse engineer (er, uh, I meant *creatively re-engineer*) its format.

A typical Japanese OCF font offered by Adobe Systems is made up of nearly 100 separate files spread throughout four directories on a PostScript file system. There are three reasons for the large number of files:

- Adobe Systems' OCF fonts support a large number of character sets and encodings

* As far as host-based (that is, using Adobe Type Manager software) rasterization is concerned, simply using a faster computer usually does the trick.

† This is a polite way of stating that TIC is more or less dead.

- The character set and encoding information, although common across all Adobe Systems' OCF fonts, is duplicated for every font
- The file format itself is complex

The more OCF fonts you install onto a PostScript file system, the more of a headache file management can become. There is nothing inherently wrong or bad about OCF fonts, but their format did not prove itself to be suitably extensible. Work then began on a simpler file format specification: CID-keyed fonts.

What are CID-keyed fonts?

CID-keyed fonts represent the basic underlying technology used for building today's (and tomorrow's) PostScript CJKV fonts. CID stands for *Character ID*, and is a new character and glyph access type. Technically speaking, a CID-keyed font is a Type 0 (composite) font with FMapType 9. A CID-keyed font can also be CIDFontType 0, 1, or 2, depending on the type of character descriptions that are included.

There are two components that comprise a valid a CID-keyed font: a CIDFont file that contains the character descriptions (outlines), along with other data necessary to properly render them (such as hinting information), and a set of one or more CMap (character map) files that are used to establish character-code to CID mappings. The CIDs are ultimately used to index into the CIDFont file for retrieving character descriptions.

A valid CID-keyed font instance consists of a CIDFont plus CMap concatenated using one or two hyphens.* Table 6-10 lists some CIDFonts and CMaps, along with the corresponding valid CID-keyed fonts.

Table 6-10: CIDFonts and CMaps Versus CID-Keyed Fonts

CIDFont	CMap	CID-Keyed Font
Munhwa-Regular	KSC-H	Munhwa-Regular--KSC-H
HeiseiMin-W3	H	HeiseiMin-W3-H
MSung-Light	CNS-EUC-V	MSung-Light--CNS-EUC-V

When is it appropriate to use one versus two hyphens as glue? For CIDFonts and CMaps that were once available as OCF fonts, such as HeiseiMin-W3-H (that is, the "`HeiseiMin-W3`" CIDFont plus "`-`" plus the "`H`" CMap), one hyphen is recommended for compatibility (the OCF font machinery does not understand two

* Two hyphens are recommended because it explicitly tells PostScript and other interpreters what portions represent the CIDFont and CMap. For some CID-capable PostScript clone implementations, two hyphens are required.

hyphens, and will fail to execute or "find" the font); otherwise, two hyphens are recommended.

The best way to learn how to use CID-keyed fonts in a conforming manner is to read *CID Font Tutorial* (Adobe Systems Tech Note #5643).

The CIDFont file

The CIDFont file, which is a container for the character descriptions, assigns a unique character ID (CID) for every glyph. This CID is independent of any normal encoding, and is simply an enumeration beginning at zero. Table 6-11 provides an example of a few CIDs, along with a graphic representation of the characters that are associated with them (examples taken from the Adobe-Japan1-3 character collection).

Table 6-11: Adobe-Japan1-3 CIDs and Their Graphic Representations—Samples

CID	Glyph
0	(.notdef)
1	(proportional-width space)
...	(thousands of CIDs omitted)
7474	堯
7475	槇
7476	遙
7477	瑤
...	(hundreds of CIDs omitted)
8284	凜
8285	熙
...	(hundreds of CIDs omitted)

The CIDFont is constructed from two basic parts, each of which is outlined below, along with a brief description:

- A header that provides global font attributes, such as the font name, number of CIDs, private dictionaries, and so on
- A binary portion that contains offsets to subroutines, the subroutines themselves, offsets to charstrings, and the charstrings themselves

While the header of a CIDFont file is simply PostScript-like ASCII text, the remainder is binary data.

The CMap files

The information that associates encoded values with CIDs is defined in the CMap files. In most cases (or, in a perfect world), an encoding range is associated with a

CID range. The following are example lines taken from the standard Adobe-Japan1-3 CMap file, "H," which specifies ISO-2022-JP encoding:

```
18 begincidrange
... (16 CID ranges omitted)
<7421> <7424> 7474
<7425> <7426> 8284
endcidrange
```

The convention is to use hexadecimal values (enclosed in arrow brackets) for character codes, and decimal values (not enclosed) for CIDs. Carefully note how the encoding ranges are associated with a range of CIDs. The following is how it works: the encoding range is specified by two encoded values, one for each end of the encoding range—sometimes, non-contiguous encoding or CID ranges make one-to-one mappings necessary. In the case above, the two ranges are 0x7421–0x7424 and 0x7425–0x7426. The CID associated with each range indicates the starting point from which encoded positions are associated with CIDs. For example, the two ranges listed above will make the associations between encoded values and CIDs, as listed in Table 6-12.

Table 6-12: Encoded Values Versus CIDs

Encoded Value	CID
<7421>	7474
<7422>	7475
<7423>	7476
<7424>	7477
<7425>	8284
<7426>	8285

Note how two lines of a CMap file can be used to associate many characters with their CIDs. In the case of a complete row of characters, such as the range 0x3021–0x307E (94 characters), the following single line can be used:

```
<3021> <307e> 1125
```

That is, the encoding range 0x3021 through 0x307E is mapped to CIDs 1125 through 1218.

The following is an example CMap file, called UniCNS-UCS2-H, that maps a single character (CID 595) to a Unicode (UCS-2) code point (0x4E00):

```
%!PS-Adobe-3.0 Resource-CMap
%%DocumentNeededResources: ProcSet (CIDInit)
%%IncludeResource: ProcSet (CIDInit)
%%BeginResource: CMap (UniCNS-UCS2-H)
%%Title: (UniCNS-UCS2-H Adobe CNS1 0)
%%Version: 1.000
%%EndComments
```

```
/CIDInit /ProcSet findresource begin

12 dict begin

begincmap

/CIDSystemInfo 3 dict dup begin
  /Registry (Adobe) def
  /Ordering (CNS1) def
  /Supplement 0 def
end def

/CMapName /UniCNS-UCS2-H def
/CMapVersion 1.000 def
/CMapType 1 def

/XUID [1 10 25392] def

/WMode 0 def

2 begincodespacerange
  <0000> <D7FF>
  <E000> <FFFF>
endcodespacerange

1 beginnotdefrange
<0000> <001f> 1
endnotdefrange

1 begincidrange
<4e00> <4e00> 595
endcidrange
endcmap
CMapName currentdict /CMap defineresource pop
end
end

%%EndResource
%%EOF
```

I have emboldened the sections that define the encoding space and the character-code to CID mappings themselves. More detailed information about how to build your own CMap files is available in *Building CMap Files for CID-Keyed Fonts* (Adobe Systems Tech Note #5099).

This is merely a taste of what the CID-keyed fonts offer. This technology will allow developers to make CJKV fonts much more easily, smaller, and more efficiently than ever before. CID-keyed fonts are also portable across platforms. For MacOS, ATM Version 3.5J or later supports CID-keyed fonts as does ATM Version 3.8 (non-Japanese) or later. For Windows (but not Windows NT), ATM Version 3.2J (but not Version 4.0!) supports CID-keyed fonts.

The document entitled *Adobe CMap and CIDFont Files Specification* (Adobe Systems Tech Note #5014) describes CID-keyed fonts in more detail, and is considered to be the engineering specification needed by font developers. A gentler introduction is available in *CID-Keyed Font Technology Overview* (Adobe Systems Tech Note #5092). Adobe Systems Tech Note #5213 (a PostScript Version 2016 supplement) should also be of interest to developers because it describes the various CIDFontTypes. If you are a font developer, I *strongly* encourage you to request a copy of the CID SDK (CID-keyed Font Technology Software Developer's Kit) from the Adobe Developers Association, which is delivered on a single CD-ROM. The CID SDK includes all the documentation and software necessary to implement CID-keyed font technology, including sample CIDFonts.

What is a character collection?

A character collection represents a standardized set of CIDs and characters, meaning that two CIDFont files that conform to the same character collection specification assign the *same* characters to the *same* CIDs. It also means that both CIDFont files can be used with the same set of CMap files.

There are three `/CIDSystemInfo` dictionary entries that are present in every CIDFont and CMap file, indicated by the following code:

```
/CIDSystemInfo 3 dict dup begin
  /Registry (Adobe) def
  /Ordering (CNS1) def
  /Supplement 0 def
end def
```

Yes, this *same* code is present in the header of *both* CIDFont and CMap files! In order for a CIDFont and CMap file to be used together as a valid CID-keyed font, their `/Registry` and `/Ordering` strings *must* be identical. This checking mechanism prevents the mixing of CIDFonts and CMaps from different character collections.

Adobe Systems' CJKV character collections

Adobe Systems' CID-keyed font file specification makes it an almost trivial matter to define new or extend existing CJKV fonts. As part of my enjoyable work at Adobe Systems, I have developed the CJKV character collections specifications listed in Table 6-13.

Table 6-13: Adobe Systems' CJKV Character Collections for CID-Keyed Fonts

Character Collection	CIDs	Previous Supplements	Adobe Systems Tech Note
Adobe-GB1-3	22,353	0, 1, and 2	5079
Adobe-CNS1-2[a]	17,601	0 and 1	5080
Adobe-Japan1-3[b]	9,354	0, 1, and 2	5078

Table 6-13: Adobe Systems' CJKV Character Collections for CID-Keyed Fonts (continued)

Character Collection	CIDs	Previous Supplements	Adobe Systems Tech Note
Adobe-Japan2-0	6,068		5097
Adobe-Korea1-2	18,352	0 and 1	5093

[a] I designed Adobe-CNS1-0, but Dirk Meyer designed Adobe-CNS1-1 and Adobe-CNS1-2.
[b] I did not design Adobe-Japan1-0, but I did design its three supplements, specifically Adobe-Japan1-1, Adobe-Japan1-2, and Adobe-Japan1-3.

The latest supplements of all but one of these character collections—specifically Adobe-GB1-3, Adobe-CNS1-2, Adobe-Japan1-3, and Adobe-Korea1-2—were designed to add pre-rotated instances of all proportional- and half-width characters found in earlier supplements. Their purpose is to significantly improve the vertical handling of such characters in the context of OpenType (see page 308).

The Adobe-Vietnam1-0 character collection, which will support the TCVN 5712:1993, TCVN 5773:1993, and TCVN 6056:1995 character set standards, is under development.

Adobe encourages font developers to conform to these character collection specifications when developing their own CJKV font products. The Adobe Systems Tech Note references in Table 6-13 can be used to obtain the corresponding character collection document from Adobe Systems.* Of course, developers are free to define their own character collections (and corresponding CMap files).

The following sections describe each of these five CJKV character collections in some detail, but please refer to *Adobe CJKV Character Collections and CMaps for CID-Keyed Fonts* (Adobe Systems Tech Note #5094), which is the official documentation that describes the character sets and encodings supported by each of these CJKV character collections.

The Adobe-GB1-3 character collection

The Adobe-GB1-3 character collection, which enumerates 22,353 CIDs, supports the GB 2312-80, GB 1988-89, GB/T 12345-90, and GBK character sets. It also includes the corrections and additions to GB 2312-80 as specified in GB 6345.1-86. Supported encodings include ISO-2022-CN, EUC-CN, and GBK. Table 6-14 lists the CMap files that are included in the Adobe-GB1-3 character collection specification.

Table 6-14: Adobe-GB1-3 CMap Files

CMap Name	Vertical?	Character Set	Encoding
GB-H	Yes	GB 2312-80	ISO-2022-CN
GB-EUC-H	Yes	GB 2312-80	EUC-CN

* *http://www.adobe.com/supportservice/devrelations/technotes.html*

Table 6-14: Adobe-GB1-3 CMap Files (continued)

CMap Name	Vertical?	Character Set	Encoding
GBpc-EUC-H	Yes	GB 2312-80 for MacOS-S	EUC-CN
GBT-H	Yes	GB/T 12345-90	ISO-2022-CN
GBT-EUC-H	Yes	GB/T 12345-90	EUC-CN
GBTpc-EUC-H	Yes	GB/T 12345-90 for MacOS-S	EUC-CN
GBK-EUC-H	Yes	GBK	GBK
UniGB-UCS2-H	Yes	ISO 10646-1:1993 (Unicode)	UCS-2
UniGB-UTF8-H	Yes	ISO 10646-1:1993 (Unicode)	UTF-8
Adobe-GB1-3[a]	No	All CIDs	0x0000–0x57FF

[a] This CMap file is called the Identity CMap, and encodes all characters at their respective CIDs.

The GB/T 12345-90 character set is supported through an additional 2,180 CIDs (which make up the Supplement 1 portion of Adobe-GB1-3—Supplement 0, Adobe-GB1-0, supported only GB 2312-80 and GB 1988-89 by enumerating 7,717 CIDs) which represent traditional hanzi replacements for GB 2312-80 characters plus additional characters found in rows 88 and 89. The complete set of 20,902 Chinese characters in Unicode is supported starting with Adobe-GB1-2.*

Table 6-15 lists the four supplements to this character collection, along with the number of CIDs.

Table 6-15: Adobe-GB1-3 Character Collection Supplements

Character Collection	Number of CIDs	Number of CIDs Added
Adobe-GB1-0	7,717	7,717
Adobe-GB1-1	9,897	2,180
Adobe-GB1-2	22,127	12,230
Adobe-GB1-3	22,353	226

The Adobe-GB1-4 character collection is currently in development, and is expected to add approximately 1,500 Hong Kong hanzi.

The Adobe-CNS1-2 character collection

The Adobe-CNS1-2 character collection, which enumerates 17,601 CIDs, supports the CNS 11643-1992 (Planes 1 and 2 only), CNS 5205-1989, and Big Five character sets. It also includes the popular ETen extensions for the Big Five character set along with several Hong Kong extensions, such as Hong Kong GCCS plus the

* This does not, however, mean that an Adobe-GB1-2 (or Adobe-GB1-3) CIDFont can be used for multiple locales. In fact, its glyphs are designed with the Chinese locale in mind, making them unsuitable for other locales.

DynaLab and Monotype extensions. Supported encodings include ISO-2022-CN, ISO-2022-CN-EXT, EUC-TW, and Big Five. Table 6-16 lists the CMap files that are included as part of the Adobe-CNS1-2 character collection specification.

Table 6-16: Adobe-CNS1-2 CMap Files

CMap Name	Vertical?	Character Set	Encoding
B5-H	Yes	Big Five	Big Five
B5pc-H	Yes	Big Five for MacOS-T	Big Five
ETen-B5-H	Yes	Big Five with ETen extensions	Big Five
HKgccs-B5-H	Yes	Hong Kong GCCS	Big Five (extended)
HKdla-B5-H	Yes	DynaLab HK A	Big Five
HKdlb-B5-H	Yes	DynaLab HK B (665 hanzi only)	Big Five
HKm471-B5-H	Yes	Monotype Hong Kong (471 set)	Big Five
HKm314-B5-H	Yes	Monotype Hong Kong (314 set)	Big Five
CNS1-H	Yes	CNS 11643-1992 Plane 1	ISO-2022-CN
CNS2-H	Yes	CNS 11643-1992 Plane 2	ISO-2022-CN-EXT
CNS-EUC-H	Yes	CNS 11643-1992 Planes 1 and 2	EUC-TW
UniCNS-UCS2-H	Yes	ISO 10646-1:1993 (Unicode)	UCS-2
UniCNS-UTF8-H	Yes	ISO 10646-1:1993 (Unicode)	UTF-8
Adobe-CNS1-2[a]	No	All CIDs	0x0000–0x44FF

[a] This CMap file is called the Identity CMap, and encodes all characters at their respective CIDs.

The ordering of CIDs in the Adobe-CNS1-2 character collection favors that found in CNS 11643-1992, at least for the Adobe-CNS1-0 portion. In addition, the two duplicately encoded hanzi in Big Five are not assigned duplicate CIDs—the Big Five CMap files duplicately encode them.

Table 6-17 lists the three supplements to this character collection, along with the number of CIDs.

Table 6-17: Adobe-CNS1-2 Character Collection Supplements

Character Collection	Number of CIDs	Number of CIDs Added
Adobe-CNS1-0	14,099	14,099
Adobe-CNS1-1	17,408	3,309
Adobe-CNS1-2	17,601	193

The Adobe-Japan1-3 character collection

The Adobe-Japan1-3 character collection, which enumerates 9,354 CIDs, supports the JIS C 6226-1978 (250 JIS78 kanji variants), JIS X 0208:1997, and JIS X 0201-1997 character sets. It also supports the KanjiTalk6, KanjiTalk7, Windows 3.1J, Windows

95J, Fujitsu's FMR, and NEC vendor extensions. Supported encodings include ISO-2022-JP, Shift-JIS, and EUC-JP (code sets 0 through 2). Table 6-18 lists the CMap files included as part of the Adobe-Japan1-3 character collection specification.

Table 6-18: Adobe-Japan1-3 CMap Files

CMap Name	Vertical?	Character Set	Encoding
H	Yes	JIS X 0208:1997	ISO-2022-JP
RKSJ-H	Yes	JIS X 0208:1997	Shift-JIS
EUC-H	Yes	JIS X 0208:1997	EUC-JP
78-H[a]	Yes	JIS C 6226-1978	ISO-2022-JP
78-RKSJ-H[a]	Yes	JIS C 6226-1978	Shift-JIS
78-EUC-H[a]	Yes	JIS C 6226-1978	EUC-JP
83pv-RKSJ-H	No	KanjiTalk Version 6	Shift-JIS
90pv-RKSJ-H[b]	Yes	KanjiTalk Version 7	Shift-JIS
90ms-RKSJ-H	Yes	Windows 3.1J and Windows 95J	Shift-JIS
90msp-RKSJ-H[c]	Yes	Windows 3.1J and Windows 95J	Shift-JIS
78ms-RKSJ-H	Yes	Windows 3.1J and Windows 95J	Shift-JIS
Add-H	Yes	Fujitsu's FMR Japanese	ISO-2022-JP
Add-RKSJ-H	Yes	Fujitsu's FMR Japanese	Shift-JIS
Ext-H	Yes	NEC Japanese	ISO-2022-JP
Ext-RKSJ-H	Yes	NEC Japanese	Shift-JIS
NWP-H	Yes	NEC Word Processor	ISO-2022-JP
Hankaku	No	Half-width Latin and katakana	One-byte
Hiragana	No	Full-width hiragana	One-byte
Katakana	No	Full-width katakana	One-byte
Roman	No	Half-width Latin	One-byte
WP-Symbol	No	Special symbols	One-byte
UniJIS-UCS2-H	Yes	ISO 10646-1:1993 (Unicode)	UCS-2
UniJIS-UTF8-H	Yes	ISO 10646-1:1993 (Unicode)	UTF-8
Adobe-Japan1-3[d]	No	All CIDs	0x0000–0x24FF

[a] These were once available in OCF fonts, but were dropped starting with many early products—they were "brought back from the dead" under CID-keyed font technology.
[b] I chose to use 90pv-RKSJ-H in the spirit of 83pv-RKSJ-H—still, no one *really* knows what the "pv" stands for.
[c] 90ms-RKSJ-H and 90msp-RKSJ-H differ only in that the former uses half-width Latin characters in the single-byte range (0x20 through 0x7E), and the latter uses proportional.
[d] This CMap file is called the Identity CMap, and encodes all characters at their respective CIDs.

Adobe-Japan1-0, the original character collection, enumerates the same number of characters as found in OCF fonts, specifically 8,284 CIDs. Adobe-Japan1-0 did not support JIS X 0208-1990, JIS X 0208:1997, KanjiTalk7, Windows 3.1J, or Windows 95J character sets.

Adobe-Japan1-1, the first supplement, added 75 characters to support JIS X 0208-1990 (and JIS X 0208:1997) and the KanjiTalk7 character set, bringing the total number of CIDs to 8,359.

Adobe-Japan1-2, the second supplement, added 361 characters to support the Windows 3.1J and 95J character sets, bringing the total number of CIDs to 8,720.

Table 6-19 lists the four supplements to this character collection, along with the number of CIDs.

Table 6-19: Adobe-Japan1-3 Character Collection Supplements

Character Collection	Number of CIDs	Number of CIDs Added
Adobe-Japan1-0	8,284	8,284
Adobe-Japan1-1	8,359	75
Adobe-Japan1-2	8,720	361
Adobe-Japan1-3	9,354	634

The Adobe-Japan1-4 character collection, slated to add over 5,000 CIDs, is currently under development. It is being designed to serve the needs of professional publishing.

The Adobe-Japan2-0 character collection

The Adobe-Japan2-0 character collection, which enumerates 6,068 CIDs, supports the entire JIS X 0212-1990 character set. Supported encodings include ISO-2022-JP-2 (and thus ISO-2022-JP-1) and EUC-JP (code set 3 only). Table 6-20 lists the CMap files that are included in the Adobe-Japan2-0 character collection specification.

Table 6-20: Adobe-Japan2-0 CMap Files

CMap Name	Vertical?	Character Set	Encoding
Hojo-H	Yes	JIS X 0212-1990	ISO-2022-JP-2
Hojo-EUC-H	Yes	JIS X 0212-1990	EUC-JP
UniHojo-UCS2-H	Yes	ISO 10646-1:1993 (Unicode)	UCS-2
UniHojo-UTF8-H	Yes	ISO 10646-1:1993 (Unicode)	UTF-8
Adobe-Japan2-0[a]	No	All CIDs	0x0000–0x17FF

[a] This CMap file is called the Identity CMap, and encodes all characters at their respective CIDs.

Because Adobe-Japan2-0 CIDFonts lack certain key characters, such as the half-width or proportional Latin, they are designed to be used in conjunction with Adobe-Japan1-3 CIDFonts.

The Adobe-Korea1-2 character collection

The Adobe-Korea1-2 character collection, which enumerates 18,352 CIDs, supports the KS X 1001:1992 character set, along with all possible 11,172 hangul. Supported encodings include ISO-2022-KR, EUC-KR, UHC, and Johab. The MacOS extension as used by MacOS-KH and KLK, which totals to 1,137 additional characters, is also supported. Table 6-21 lists the CMap files that are included in the Adobe-Korea1-2 character collection specification.

Table 6-21: Adobe-Korea1-2 CMap Files

CMap Name	Vertical?	Character Set	Encoding
KSC-H	Yes	KS X 1001:1992	ISO-2022-KR
KSC-EUC-H	Yes	KS X 1001:1992	EUC-KR
KSCpc-EUC-H	Yes	KS X 1001:1992 for MacOS[a]	EUC-KR[b]
KSC-Johab-H	Yes	KS X 1001:1992 (Johab)[c]	Johab
KSCms-UHC-H	Yes	KS X 1001:1992 (Johab)[c]	UHC[d]
KSCms-UHC-HW-H	Yes	KS X 1001:1992 (Johab)[c]	UHC[d]
UniKS-UCS2-H	Yes	ISO 10646-1:1993 (Unicode)	UCS-2
UniKS-UTF8-H	Yes	ISO 10646-1:1993 (Unicode)	UTF-8
Adobe-Korea1-2[e]	No	All CIDs	0x0000–0x47FF

[a] The MacOS extension includes approximately 1,137 additional symbols.
[b] Apple Computer's EUC-KR includes an expanded second-byte range: 0x41–0x7D and 0x81–0xFE.
[c] Includes all 11,172 hangul.
[d] Unified Hangul Code. See Appendix C, *Vendor Character Set Standards*, for more details.
[e] This CMap file is called the Identity CMap, and encodes all characters at their respective CIDs.

Table 6-22 lists the three supplements to this character collection, along with the number of CIDs.

Table 6-22: Adobe-Korea1-2 Character Collection Supplements

Character Collection	Number of CIDs	Number of CIDs Added
Adobe-Korea1-0	9,333	9,333
Adobe-Korea1-1	18,155	8,822
Adobe-Korea1-2	18,352	197

The 8,822 CIDs that make up Supplement 1 are all hangul, and represent the difference between all 11,172 possible hangul and the 2,350 defined in KS X 1001:1992.

CJKV character collection supplements

Whenever a CJKV character collection is updated, by defining a new supplement, there is almost always a motivation for doing so. The character sets used in each locale are based on national standards and common vendor extensions. When these national standards or vendor extensions change, an update becomes necessary.

For example, there were two motivations for defining the Adobe-Japan1-1 character collection: the release of JIS X 0208-1990 and Apple Computer's definition of the KanjiTalk7 character set. The result was a supplement containing 75 additional characters.

Sometimes, however, two sets of characters that are useful within a single locale are intentionally divided by placing them into two separate supplements (the more frequently used set becomes Supplement 0, and the other becomes Supplement 1), or are used to define two separate character collections.

The Adobe-GB1-1 character collection is an example of the former scenario. Adobe-GB1-0 defines the characters for supporting GB 2312-80, which represents the most basic character set standard for China. Every Chinese typeface design (that is, for China, not Taiwan) must minimally conform to this character set. However, some typeface designs also provide the characters for GB/T 12345-90, the traditional analog of GB 2312-80. When comparing these two character sets in detail, one finds that there are 2,180 hanzi in GB/T 12345-90 that are not available in GB 2312-80. So, these 2,180 hanzi became Supplement 1 (Adobe-GB1-1).

The Adobe-Japan2-0 character collection is an example of the latter scenario. The JIS X 0212-1990 character set, as described in Chapter 3, *Character Set Standards*, enumerates 6,067 characters (5,801 of which are kanji), but very few typeface designs include these characters—FDPC's HeiseiMin-W3 is the only one readily available. So, these 6,067 characters became a separate and independent character collection.

Whether to divide sets of characters into separate supplements of a single character collection or to define them as independent character collections is decided by considering character availability for most typeface designs. Forcing typeface designers to come up with over 6,000 characters per typeface design is not a very reasonable request.

Supporting Unicode in CID-keyed fonts

Because the CID-keyed font file specification is extremely flexible and extensible—primarily because it effectively divorces all encoding information from the font file itself—a large number of encodings can be supported simply by building an appropriate CMap file. Because Unicode is intended as a single character set that provides access to all alphabets (including CJKV characters), it is a natural candidate for one such encoding.

One typical question that is asked regarding Unicode fonts is whether to include all characters. As far as CJKV fonts are concerned, it is not very practical or realistic to build a single set of 20,902 Chinese characters that will conform to the character-design principles of all CJKV locales. Here are some observations to consider:

- Input methods, which represent the typical means by which users input characters, are already restricted to a subset of the corresponding *national* character set standard—having Unicode as the underlying encoding will not magically extend the scope of an input method
- Many characters that are used in one CJKV locale may be totally useless in another—such as the simplified hanzi in China, which are rather useless in Japan
- Character-design principles vary greatly across CJKV locales. Even given the same typeface design, many characters will need to be constructed differently depending on the locale

Of course, having multiple input methods installed, one for each locale, can be useful for users whose work extends beyond a single locale. And, for these same users, having access to characters not normally available in a given locale has advantages.

The next question that people often ask deals with specifying the most useful subset of Unicode for each CJKV locale. This question is already answered by virtue of their existing *national* character set standards for each CJKV locale, such as GB 2312-80 for China. Simply map these CJKV character set standards to Unicode, and you instantly have a useful font for that CJKV locale. It is really that simple. For CID-keyed fonts, it means issuing a new set of Unicode-encoded CMap files—the CIDFonts themselves, which can be several megabytes in size, need not be reissued.

I have developed Unicode (UCS-2– and UTF-8–encoded) CMap files for all five of Adobe Systems' CJKV character collections, and have made them available for developers or anyone else to use.*

Table 6-23 lists each of Adobe Systems' CJKV character collections, along with the name of each Unicode-encoded CMap file.

Table 6-23: Unicode CMap Files

Character Collection	UCS-2	UTF-8
Adobe-GB1-3	UniGB-UCS2-H	UniGB-UTF8-H
Adobe-CNS1-2	UniCNS-UCS2-H	UniCNS-UTF8-H
Adobe-Japan1-3	UniJIS-UCS2-H	UniJIS-UTF8-H

* *ftp://ftp.oreilly.com/pub/examples/nutshell/cjkv/adobe/*

Table 6-23: Unicode CMap Files (continued)

Character Collection	UCS-2	UTF-8
Adobe-Japan2-0	UniHojo-UCS2-H	UniHojo-UTF8-H
Adobe-Korea1-2	UniKS-UCS2-H	UniKS-UTF8-H

All of these Unicode-encoded CMap files have vertical counterparts (for example, the vertical counterpart of UniKS-UCS2-H is UniKS-UCS2-V).

sfnt-wrapped CIDFonts

The latest twist to CID-keyed font technology is referred to as sfnt-wrapped CIDFonts. Font geeks and nerds alike are aware that TrueType fonts reside within what is known as an "sfnt" (scalable font) resource. But, aren't CID-keyed fonts the best thing since sliced bread? Well, yes, but…

CID-keyed font technology provides an extremely flexible mechanism for supporting large character sets and multiple encodings, but lacks host-based support such as user-selected and context-sensitive glyph substitution, alternate metrics (such as half-width symbols and punctuation, proportional kana, and even proportional Chinese characters), and easy vertical substitution. These sort of advanced typographic features will be covered in greater detail in Chapter 7.

An sfnt-wrapped CIDFont looks and smells like a TrueType (actually, QuickDraw GX) font, but instead of having TrueType character descriptions (in the "glyf" table), there is a CIDFont there instead (in the Adobe-established "CID " table). The CIDFont file itself becomes one of the many tables within the "sfnt" resource. Table 6-24 lists the additional "sfnt" tables found in an sfnt-wrapped CIDFont.

Table 6-24: Additional "sfnt" Tables in sfnt-wrapped CIDFonts

Table Tag[a]	Description
`ALMX`	Alternate metrics
`BBOX`	Font bounding box
`CID ` [b]	The CIDFont file
`COFN`	QuickDraw font name for each component in a rearranged font
`COSP`	Code space for a rearranged font
`FNAM`	For QuickDraw compatibility
`HFMX`	Horizontal font metrics
`PNAM`	Fully qualified PostScript font name
`ROTA`	Character rotation
`SUBS`	Subset definition
`VFMX`	Vertical font metrics
`WDTH`	Set widths

[a] Note that all of these table tags are uppercase—this was intentional.
[b] Note that this tag, like the others, consists of four characters: the three letters "CID" followed by a single space.

Note that all lowercase tags are reserved by Apple Computer, so those in Table 6-24 are all uppercase. (The only exception to this policy is the "gasp" table that was defined by Microsoft, which should have included at least one uppercase letter. Gasp!)

In addition, sfnt-wrapped CIDFonts typically include the "bdat," "bloc," "cmap," "feat," "mort," "name," "post," and "subs" tables (these are described later in this chapter in the section entitled "QuickDraw GX," starting on page 306). The TrueType "cmap" table functions as the CMap file for sfnt-wrapped CIDFonts.

The first applications to recognize their typographic features in sfnt-wrapped CIDFonts were Adobe Illustrator Version 5.5J and Adobe PageMaker Version 6.0J—both for MacOS. Macromedia FreeHand 8.0J also recognizes these fonts' typographic features. QuickDraw GX applications can recognize and use these fonts as well, so long as ATM Version 3.9 or later is installed and enabled. More information on sfnt-wrapped CIDFonts can be found in *CID-Keyed sfnt Font File Format for the Macintosh* (Adobe Systems Tech Note #5180).

Multiple Master—a Type 1 Font Format extension

Multiple master technology is an extension to the Type 1 Font Format described earlier in this chapter. This technology allows for the dynamic interpolation of a typeface's attributes, such as width, weight, optical size, and style. Multiple master fonts are a big design effort, and require that many master outlines be made for each character. Exactly how many master outlines there are generally depends on the number of design axes. Table 6-25 illustrates the relationship between design axes and master outlines. Although it may appear that the number of design axes determines the number of master outlines, that is not the case. The number of master outlines must be greater than or equal to the number of axes plus one. For example, Adobe Jenson and Kepler are multiple master fonts that do not follow the "power of two" model. CFF, described earlier in this chapter, allows up to 16 master outlines and 15 design axes.

Table 6-25: Multiple Master Design Axes and Number of Corresponding Master Outlines

Number of Design Axes	Number of Master Outlines
1	2
2	4
3	8
4	16

These master outlines are interpolated to produce a particular font instance. Think of a single axis where one end contains a light version of a character, and the other end contains a bold version of the same character. Now traverse along the axis. The closer you get to the end containing the bold version, the bolder the character becomes. Now imagine doing this with four axes! Let's take a look at a two-axis multiple master character. Table 6-26 illustrates the four master designs of the letter "A." The two axes are for weight and width.

Table 6-26: Sample Character for a Two-Axis Multiple Master Font

Weight	Condensed	Extended
Light	A	A
Bold	**A**	**A**

The number of axes relates to the number of dimensions. For example, a typeface with a single design axis is represented by a straight line, and a line needs two points to be defined. Extend this all the way up to four design axes, at which time you get a hypercube (four dimensions). Needless to say, designing a multiple master font is a great task, but is possible. For those of you who are so inclined, the latest versions of Fontographer for MacOS by Macromedia and FontLab by Pyrus North America for Windows allow designers to create multiple master fonts. Fontographer is currently limited to two-axis designs, while FontLab supports up to four-axis designs.

These techniques can also be applied to a CJKV font. Table 6-27 illustrates several intermediate instances of a Chinese character from an imaginary single-axis multiple master font—the axis is for weight. The two master designs are located at each extreme.

Table 6-27: Sample Kanji for a One-Axis Multiple Master Font with Interpolation

Light					⇔					Bold
京	京	京	京	京	京	京	京	京	京	京

Unfortunately, there are no multiple master CJKV fonts available as of this writing. The design of a CJKV font is itself a large project—designing a multiple master CJKV font is much more work!

TrueType Fonts

TrueType fonts, like PostScript fonts, are described mathematically as outlines, and because of this are fully scalable. TrueType curves are represented as quadratic splines. TrueType fonts are able to reside on PostScript printer hard disks (or in printer RAM or ROM) because the Type 42 font format provides a PostScript wrapper for TrueType fonts.

Many TrueType fonts are also available in Type 1 format—many type vendors market their fonts in both formats to appeal to those dedicated to a particular format.

TrueType CJKV fonts are a more recent addition to TrueType font technology, and are currently usable on MacOS and Windows. In fact, MacOS-J is bundled with seven TrueType Japanese fonts. Apple Computer's Language Kits (CLK, JLK, and KLK) also come bundled with TrueType CJKV fonts—but not nearly as many as are bundled with the fully localized versions of the operating system. These fonts require approximately 20–40 percent more disk space than the equivalent PostScript CJKV fonts.

A TrueType font is contained within a file resource known as "sfnt" (an abbreviation for "Scalable Font"), and consists of many tables. The required and optional tables are listed and described in Table 6-28.

Table 6-28: Standard TrueType Tables

Table Tag	Description	Required?
`cmap`[a]	Character to glyph mapping	Yes
`glyf`	Glyph data	Yes
`head`	Font header	Yes
`hhea`	Horizontal header	Yes
`hmtx`	Horizontal metrics	Yes
`loca`	Index to location	Yes
`maxp`	Maximum profile	Yes
`name`	Naming table	Yes
`post`	PostScript information	Yes
`OS/2`	OS/2- and Windows-specific metrics	Yes
`cvt`	Control Value Table	No
`EBDT`	Embedded bitmap data	No
`EBLC`	Embedded bitmap location data	No
`EBSC`	Embedded bitmap scaling data	No
`fpgm`	Font program	No
`gasp`	Grid-fitting and scan conversion procedure (grayscale)—*read the footnote on page 302*	No
`hdmx`	Horizontal device metrics	No
`kern`	Kerning data	No
`LTSH`	Linear threshold table	No
`prep`	CVT program	No

Table 6-28: Standard TrueType Tables (continued)

Table Tag	Description	Required?
`PCLT`	PCL5	No
`VDMX`	Vertical device metrics table	No
`vhea`	Vertical metrics header	No
`vmtx`	Vertical metrics	No

[a] This is different from Adobe Systems' CMap, which is used in CID-keyed font technology.

It is important to realize that many TrueType developments took place at Apple Computer and Microsoft independently, leading to incompatibilities between the two formats.

More detailed information about the TrueType font format can be found in Microsoft's *TrueType 1.0 Font Files* document.*

TrueType Collections

A recent addition to the TrueType font format is the concept of TrueType Collections (TTCs), a Windows-only font. This allows TrueType fonts to efficiently share data across similar fonts. In short, TTCs embed multiple TrueType fonts within a single file.

Here are some ways in which TTCs can be (and, more importantly, have been) used in the context of CJKV fonts:

- A complete Japanese font, along with its matching kana designs (for example, all of TypeBank's Japanese designs come with five matching kana designs)
- Two or more Korean fonts sharing a single hanja design (not all Korean fonts come with hangul—they are treated somewhat generically)

Of course, there are many other possibilities and uses for TTCs.

TTCs are implemented by including all characters (glyphs) in the "glyf" table. But, there need to be multiple "cmap" tables, one for each font that will appear in applications' font menus. These multiple "cmap" tables *point* to a different subset of the characters found in the "glyf" table. This process of creating a TTC is non-trivial, and requires very precise mapping in the "cmap" tables—each "cmap" table must point to the correct subset of characters in the "glyf" table.

Virtually all TrueType fonts bundled with the various localized versions of Windows 95 are TrueType Collection fonts.

* *http://www.microsoft.com/truetype/*

TTC files can be identified by their filename suffix "TTC" (as opposed to "TTF" for standard TrueType fonts). TrueType Collections are described in Microsoft's *TrueType 1.0 Font Files.*

QuickDraw GX

Apple Computer was the first company to raise the proverbial "bar" with respect to providing advanced typographic features as part of the fonts themselves—their solution is called QuickDraw GX (also referred to as TrueType GX in some circles). However, QuickDraw GX functionality is now called Apple Advanced Typography (AAT), which is used in conjunction with Apple Type Services for Unicode Imaging (ATSUI).*

Table 6-29 lists some of the TrueType tables that Apple Computer has developed on its own for developing QuickDraw GX fonts—meaning that you will not find these tables in TrueType fonts that run under Windows. Some of these tables are specific to QuickDraw GX, and some are not, as noted below.

Table 6-29: QuickDraw GX Tables

Table Tag	Description	GX-specific?
`bdat`[a]	Bitmapped data	No
`bloc`[b]	Bitmapped data locations (offsets)	No
`bsln`	Baseline adjustment information	Yes
`fdsc`	Font descriptor	No
`feat`	QuickDraw GX feature list	Yes
`mort`	QuickDraw GX features	Yes
`trak`	Tracking information	No

[a] Microsoft's TrueType fonts include an "EBDT" table for the same purpose—see Table 6-28 on page 304.
[b] Microsoft's TrueType fonts include an "EBLC" table for the same purpose—see Table 6-28 on page 304.

More information on QuickDraw GX is still available in publications from Apple Computer, such as *QuickDraw GX Font Formats: The TrueType Font Format Specification*, *Inside Macintosh—QuickDraw GX Typography*, and *Inside Macintosh—Text*. The latest developments are available at Apple Computer's web site.†

TrueType Open

TrueType Open is Microsoft's answer to Apple Computer's QuickDraw GX. While QuickDraw GX and TrueType Open attempt to solve the same typographic problems, their approaches are a bit different. TrueType Open fonts are still considered

* When considered a Japanese transliteration, ATSUI means "hot" (熱い *atsui*) or "thick" (厚い *atsui*).

† *http://fonts.apple.com/*

valid TrueType fonts, and are fully compatible with existing applications (but, some applications may not be able to access the tables specific to TrueType Open).

TrueType Open defines five additional tables, each of which is indicated and briefly described in Table 6-30.

Table 6-30: TrueType Open Tables

Table	Table Name	Description
GSUB[a]	Glyph substitution	Substitute glyphs: one to one, one to many, or many to one
GPOS	Glyph positioning	Specific position of glyphs
BASE	Baseline	Baseline adjustment information—useful when mixing different scripts, such as Chinese and Latin characters
JSTF	Justification	Provides additional control over glyph substitution and positioning in justified text—affects spacing
GDEF	Glyph definition	Classifies the font's glyphs, identifies attachment points, and provides positioning data for ligature carets

[a] Apple Computer's QuickDraw GX fonts include a "mort" table for the same basic purpose—see Table 6-29 on page 306.

The "GPOS" table benefits scripts such as romanized Vietnamese in which the exact positioning of accents is crucial. One of the most powerful tables of True-Type Open is "GSUB," which is functionally similar to QuickDraw GX's "mort" table. Table 6-31 lists some of the types of glyph substitution that can be performed by using the "GSUB" table, along with some examples.

Table 6-31: TrueType Open Glyph Substitution

Substitution Type	Example
Single substitution	Vertical substitution: ～ ➡ ⌇
Multiple substitution	Ligature decomposition: ㌕ ➡ キログラム
Alternate substitution	Character variants: 辺 ➡ 邊, 邉, 邊, 邊, 邉, 邉, 邉, 邉, 邉, 邉
Ligature substitution	Ligature construction: キログラム ➡ ㌕

As you can see, building a fully functional TrueType Open font provides a very powerful mechanism for delivering advanced typographic features to applications. Microsoft has published the TrueType Open specification in the *TrueType Open Font Specification* document.* It is designed to be an *open* specification (hence its name), meaning that developers can create their own typographic features.

* *http://www.microsoft.com/truetype/*

OpenType—Merging PostScript and TrueType

Finally. PostScript and TrueType have merged into a single standard called OpenType, sometimes abbreviated OTF.* This effectively means that it will make absolutely no difference whether the underlying character descriptions (*charstrings*) are PostScript (Type 1 or Type 2) or TrueType. Adobe Systems and Microsoft jointly announced this new font format in 1996, and its full specification is available online.†

OpenType fonts are considered *native* under Windows NT Version 5.0 and later, but are supported in Windows 95, Windows 98, Windows NT (Version 4.0), and MacOS through ATM.‡ Because of their native status under Windows NT Version 5.0 and later, OpenType fonts are encoded according to Unicode. That is, they include a Unicode-encoded "cmap" table.

OpenType is an extension to TrueType Open (see page 306), which means that all of its functionality, such as the ability to define advanced typographic features (metrics and glyph substitutions), is available to OpenType fonts.

Up until now, all legacy font formats such as MacOS's FOND resource and Windows' PFM file, did not include information that specified values exclusively for handling vertical writing. Font developers and applications were forced to overload the semantics of available fields, such as those that represent font-level ascent and descent. OpenType provides an elegant solution by including dedicated fields that give applications correct and unambiguous information for vertical writing. The top and bottom of the design space, which are critical for establishing reference points for proper vertical writing, are stored in the "OS/2" table's "sTypoAscender" and "sTypoDescender" fields.

Ruby Fonts

Ruby characters, commonly referred to as *furigana* outside of publishing circles, are specific to Japanese typography, and serve to annotate kanji with readings. How ruby characters are used in line-layout is deferred until Chapter 7, but here we examine the details of a ruby font itself, such as its special design considerations.

A ruby font typically consists of hiragana, katakana, and a handful of symbols. When one compares the kana in a ruby font with those of standard Japanese fonts, there are two important differences to note, indicated as follows:

* The three-character filename extension for OpenType fonts is "otf."

† *http://www.microsoft.com/opentype/otspec/*

‡ More specifically, ATM Version 4.1 or later for Windows, and ATM Version 4.5 or later for MacOS.

- Small kana, such as ぁ, ぃ, ぅ, ぇ, ぉ, っ, ゃ, ゅ, ょ, and ゎ for hiragana, are the same size as their standard-sized equivalents
- Small kana, because they are the same size as their standard-sized equivalents, do not have special vertical-use forms

Ruby Fonts Have Families, Too

Ruby fonts can come in several varieties, depending on the typeface and typeface foundry: generic, generic to a font family, and specific to a typeface:

- Generic ruby fonts are designed to be used with a variety of fonts and font families
- Ruby fonts that are generic to a particular font family are intended for use with all weights of that font family—due to the small size at which ruby characters are set, they do not always benefit from differing weights
- Ruby fonts that are specific to a particular typeface design, although not very common, do serve special purposes—Morisawa's Ryumin font family, for example, includes several ruby fonts, one for nearly every weight

Which type of ruby font you use depends on what is available for the font you are using. Chapter 7 will explore more practical aspects of ruby characters, such as how they are used, and how they differ from their cousins, pseudo-ruby characters.

Table 6-32 illustrates the standard kana and ruby kana from Morisawa's リュウミンL-KL (Ryumin-Light) design.

Table 6-32: Standard Versus Ruby Kana

Character Type	Sample Text
Standard	へのへのもへじのぶんしょう
Ruby	へのへのもへじのぶんしよう

Note how their designs are quite different, although they are included in the same typeface design. In order for ruby characters to be legible at small sizes, they are often slightly heavier than their standard counterparts.

Host-Based Versus Printer-Resident Fonts

An important user and developer concern is how to map host-based fonts to printer-resident fonts. The host-based font either needs to include embedded information that explicitly specifies which printer-resident font it corresponds to, or else a system-level database must exist that maps host-based fonts to printer-resident fonts. The sections below describe how this font mapping occurs on MacOS, Windows (Versions 3.1, 95, and 98), and to a limited extent, the X Window System.

The PostScript File System

PostScript devices use a hierarchical file system composed of several directories (and some subdirectories). Exactly where font components are installed depends on the vintage of the font format. Table 6-33 illustrates how a PostScript Japanese OCF font (note that the base font name, such as "HeiseiMin-W3," has been replaced by an "X" for brevity) is distributed across a PostScript file system.

Table 6-33: OCF Font File Structure

Directory	Contents
fonts	*X-83pv-RKSJ-H, X-83pv-SuppA-H, X-83pv-SuppB-H, X-Add-H, X-Add-RKSJ-H, X-Add-RKSJ-V, X-Add-SuppA-H, X-Add-SuppA-V, X-Add-SuppB-HV, X-Add-V, X-EUC-H, X-EUC-V, X-Ext-H, X-Ext-RKSJ-H, X-Ext-RKSJ-V, X-Ext-SuppA-H, X-Ext-SuppA-V, X-Ext-SuppB-HV, X-Ext-V, X-H, X-JIS.zm_23, X-JIS.zm_29, X-JIS.zm_2E, X-NWP-H, X-NWP-V, X-PropRoman, X-RKSJ-H, X-RKSJ-UserGaiji, X-RKSJ-V, X-SJ.zm_82, X-SJ.zm_82v, X-SJ.zm_85, X-SuppA-H, X-SuppA-V, X-SuppB-HV, X-V, X.Hankaku, X.Hiragana, X.Katakana, X.Oubun, X.Oubun-Add, X.Roman, X.Roman83pv, X.SuppK, X.WP-Symbol*
fsupp	*X-83pv-SuppA_BDY, X-83pv-SuppB_BDY, X-Add-SuppA_BDY, X-Add-SuppB_BDY, X-Add_BDY, X-EUC_BDY, X-Ext-SuppA_BDY, X-Ext-SuppB_BDY, X-Ext_BDY, X-NWP_BDY, X-SuppA_BDY, X-SuppB_BDY, X_BDY*
pgfonts	*X::AlphaNum, X::Alphabetic, X::Dingbats, X::HKana, X::HRoman, X::JIS83-1Kanji, X::JIS83-2, X::Kana, X::KanjiSupp*
pgfsupp	*X::AlphaNum_COD, X::AlphaNum_CSA, X::Alphabetic_COD, X::Alphabetic_CSA, X::Dingbats_COD, X::Dingbats_CSA, X::HKana_COD, X::HKana_CSA, X::HRoman_COD, X::HRoman_CSA, X::JIS83-1Kanji_COD, X::JIS83-1Kanji_CSA, X::JIS83-2_COD, X::JIS83-2_CSA, X::Kana_COD, X::Kana_CSA, X::KanjiSupp_COD, X::KanjiSupp_CSA*

That's a lot of files! 85 to be exact. Keep in mind that *all* of these files are present for *every* PostScript Japanese OCF font. Furthermore, the file structure of an OCF font differs depending on its vintage—the OCF font file structure illustrated in Table 6-33 represents that found in the very last Japanese OCF fonts produced by Adobe Systems. Japanese OCF fonts produced by Adobe Systems are also dependent on a handful of *generic* font files (these font files contain, among other things, the half- and full-width line-drawing elements as found in row 8 of JIS X 0208:1997). The file structure for these files is provided in Table 6-34.

Table 6-34: OCF Font File Structure—Generic Components

Directory	Contents
pgfonts	*Generic::FullWidth, Generic::HalfWidth*
pgfsupp	*Generic::FullWidth_COD, Generic::FullWidth_CSA, Generic::HalfWidth_COD, Generic::HalfWidth_CSA*

In contrast, Table 6-35 illustrates the PostScript file structure for a CIDFont and its associated CMap files. Note the simplicity.

Table 6-35: CID-Keyed Font File Structure

Directory	Contents
Resource/CIDFont	*HeiseiMin-W3*
Resource/CMap	*78-EUC-H, 78-EUC-V, 78-H, 78-RKSJ-H, 78-RKSJ-V, 78-V, 78ms-RKSJ-H, 78ms-RKSJ-V, 83pv-RKSJ-H, 90ms-RKSJ-H, 90ms-RKSJ-V, 90msp-RKSJ-H, 90msp-RKSJ-H, 90pv-RKSJ-H, 90pv-RKSJ-V, Add-H, Add-RKSJ-H, Add-RKSJ-V, Add-V, Adobe-Japan1-0, Adobe-Japan1-1, Adobe-Japan1-2, Adobe-Japan1-3, EUC-H, EUC-V, Ext-H, Ext-RKSJ-H, Ext-RKSJ-V, Ext-V, H, Hankaku, Hiragana, Katakana, NWP-H, NWP-V, RKSJ-H, RKSJ-V, Roman, UniJIS-UCS2-H, UniJIS-UCS2-V, UniJIS-UCS2-HW-H, UniJIS-UCS2-HW-V, UniJIS-UTF8-H, UniJIS-UTF8-V, V, WP-Symbol*

Once you install a set of CMap files for a given CJKV character collection, they need not be installed for subsequent fonts that share the same character collection—they are common across all CIDFonts of the same character collection.

For details on how to install CID-keyed fonts to a PostScript file system, I suggest reading the document *CID-Keyed Font Installation for PostScript File Systems* (Adobe Systems Tech Note #5174).

MacOS

MacOS utilizes the style map of a resource type called "FOND," which is part of each font suitcase, to provide the mapping to a printer-resident font. If a font suitcase includes more than one font, there are multiple instances of the FOND resource. The style map of a FOND resource includes two important pieces of information, which are extremely dependent on one another:

- A string that is a fully qualified PostScript font name, such as "STSong-Light-GBpc-EUC-H." This string then becomes the argument to PostScript's `findfont` procedure when this font is used.
- A byte that indicates the length of this PostScript font name string—this byte appears immediately before the string itself. This byte, for example, has a value of 0x17 (decimal 23) for the string "STSong-Light-GBpc-EUC-H."

The FOND resource also includes other crucial font-related information, such as:

- Menu name, such as "华文宋体" for STSong-Light—this is actually the name of the FOND resource instance, not part of the FOND resource. This is the string that displays in applications' font menus
- FOND ID, which is an internal identifier that serves to indicate the script (locale) of the font
- Widths table, which explicitly lists the widths, expressed in $\frac{1}{4096}$ units, for characters in the range 0x00 through 0xFF (256 characters total)

The FOND ID ranges listed in Table 6-36 are important for CJKV font developers because they indicate to the system how to treat the font in terms of locale and encoding. Note that each of these four CJKV locales is restricted to ranges containing 512 FOND IDs each.

Table 6-36: FOND ID Ranges

FOND ID Range	Script	Character Set	Encoding
16384–16895	Japanese	JIS X 0208:1997	Shift-JIS
16896–17407	Traditional Chinese	Big Five	Big Five
17408–17919	Korean	KS X 1001:1992	EUC-KR
28672–29183	Simplified Chinese	GB 2312-80	EUC-CN

The FOND resource, although typically small, provides the system with the necessary information to put the font in applications' font menus, the font's locale, and the mapping to a printer-resident font.

The contents of the FOND resource are also used by ATM (described in Chapter 8) to decide which host-based outline font to access. It is also possible for two independent FOND resources to reference the same PostScript font name. Table 6-37 illustrates this phenomenon.

Table 6-37: Multiple FOND Resources with Identical PostScript Font Names

Menu Name	Source	PostScript Font Name
細明朝体	MacOS-J	Ryumin-Light-83pv-RKSJ-H
L リュウミン L-KL	Adobe Systems	Ryumin-Light-83pv-RKSJ-H
中ゴシック体	MacOS-J	GothicBBB-Medium-83pv-RKSJ-H
M 中ゴシック BBB	Adobe Systems	GothicBBB-Medium-83pv-RKSJ-H

Although outline font data can be shared by more than one FOND resource, quite often there are differing global metrics information (specified in the "NFNT" resource) that alter the exact placement of characters. One cannot, however, install two FOND resources that share the same menu name.

Also of potential interest is the fact that many of the commonly-used MacOS-J fonts are based on the same designs, but are either in a different format (PostScript versus TrueType) or use a different design space. Table 6-38 lists such MacOS-J fonts.

Table 6-38: Identical Designs in Different MacOS Font Formats

Menu Name	Format	Design Space	Source
L リュウミン L-KL	PostScript	1000×1000	Morisawa's Ryumin Light
リュウミンライト-KL	TrueType	2048×2048	Morisawa's Ryumin Light
M 中ゴシック BBB	PostScript	1000×1000	Morisawa's Gothic BBB Medium
中ゴシックBBB	TrueType	2048×2048	Morisawa's Gothic BBB Medium
平成明朝 W3	PostScript	1000×1000	FDPC's Heisei Mincho W3
平成明朝	TrueType	2048×2048	FDPC's Heisei Mincho W3
平成角ゴシック W5	PostScript	1000×1000	FDPC's Heisei Kaku Gothic W5
平成角ゴシック	TrueType	2048×2048	FDPC's Heisei Kaku Gothic W5
Osaka	TrueType	256×256	FDPC's Heisei Kaku Gothic W5

However, these identical designs in different font formats are not compatible due to metrics differences in the proportional Latin characters of their one-byte range.

Where are the bitmaps?

Latin bitmapped fonts for MacOS are encapsulated in a font suitcase (so named because the icon looks like a suitcase). CJKV bitmapped fonts for MacOS are separated into two basic components:

- Font suitcase
- "fbit" files (so named because its file type is "fbit")*

Legacy fonts (that is, older fonts) typically consist of a rather small (in terms of byte-size) font suitcase plus one or two large "fbit" files. Contemporary fonts consist of a large font suitcase plus one small "fbit" file. Table 6-39 provides information about legacy and contemporary bitmapped fonts for MacOS.

The real difference between legacy and contemporary MacOS bitmapped fonts is the appearance of the "sfnt" resource. Contemporary fonts can store bitmapped data in the "bdat" table (also known as the "sbit" table) of the "sfnt" resource. The "fbit" file's "fbit" resource contains pointers into the data fork of the "fbit" file (for legacy fonts) or into the "bdat" table of the font suitcase (for contemporary fonts). The "sfnt" resource can also store a complete outline font, either TrueType,

* The "fbit" files are not necessary when running under QuickDraw GX or with MacOS Version 8.5 or greater.

Table 6-39: Legacy and Contemporary MacOS Bitmapped Fonts

Vintage	Font Suitcase Resources[a]	"fbit" Resources[a]	Comments
Legacy	FOND, NFNT	fbit	One-byte bitmaps in NFNT resource; two-byte bitmaps in "fbit" file's data fork
Contemporary	FOND, NFNT, sfnt	fbit, fdef, fdnm	One-byte bitmaps in NFNT resource; *all* bitmaps in "sfnt" resource

[a] This file may also contain other resources, such as "vers" (version).

Type 1, or CIDFont. The "fdef" resource allows MacOS to understand the contemporary format. The "fdnm" resource is described in the following section.

While the font suitcases appear the same regardless of CJKV script, the "fbit" files appear differently because they have a different creator. Table 6-40 lists the four CJKV scripts supported by MacOS, along with the file type and creator for their "fbit" files.

Table 6-40: File Type and Creators for "fbit" Files

Script	File Type	Creator
Simplified Chinese	fbit	CSYS
Traditional Chinese	fbit	TSYS
Japanese	fbit	KSYS
Korean	fbit	hfon

Are 512 FOND IDs enough?

512 FOND IDs may seem like plenty at first glance (and, apparently to the designers of MacOS), but with the recent boom in available CJKV fonts, it is not nearly enough. For example, Adobe Systems—as of this writing—has over 100 different Japanese fonts in its type library, which consumes approximately one-fifth of the Japanese FOND ID range. Many Korean type foundries also have well over 100 individual fonts in their type libraries.

Apple Computer was forced to devise a system to handle this situation of too few FOND IDs for non-Latin scripts, and the result was the birth of the Asian Font Arbitrator and the "fdnm" resource, whose function is to dynamically harmonize FOND IDs of CJKV fonts in situations when a user installs a new font whose FOND ID conflicts with one already installed.

MacOS power users know that FOND ID harmonization is something introduced in System7. However, CJKV fonts do not consist of only a font suitcase; they also use the infamous "fbit" files. While the font suitcase includes one-byte bitmapped data in the NFNT resource (one NFNT resource instance per bitmapped size), the "fbit" files contain two-byte bitmapped data, or, for newer fonts, contain pointers into the font suitcases "bdat" table (inside the "sfnt" resource). The "fbit" files contain backpointers to the font suitcase (actually, to its FOND ID). Thus, when standard System7 FOND ID harmonization kicks in, only the FOND ID in the font suitcase becomes harmonized, and the backpointers in the "fbit" files now point off to a non-existent font suitcase.

The Asian Font Arbitrator requires that an "fdnm" resource exist in the "fbit" files, and that an "fdnm" table exist in the corresponding FOND resource. This "resource plus table" combination is linked by a common attribute, which cannot be broken even if FOND ID harmonization takes place. This common attribute is the font's menu name. All CJKV fonts for use on MacOS should include a well-formed "fdnm" resource and table. Contact Apple Computer for more information on the Asian Font Arbitrator.

Where, oh where have my vertical variants gone?

Of the CJKV locales, only Japanese has adequate vertical support on MacOS. Most other operating systems, such as Windows, use a separate font resource for the vertical version of a font. That is, the vertical version of a font appears as a separate entity in applications' font menus. MacOS-J and JLK encode the vertical variants within the same horizontal character set at standard offsets.

KanjiTalk6 and MacOS-J both support the same set of 51 vertical variants for Japanese, but at different offsets. 31 of these have their horizontal versions in row 1 (punctuation and symbols) of JIS X 0208:1997, 10 in row 4 (small hiragana), and 12 in row 5 (small katakana).

Under KanjiTalk6, these 51 vertical variants are at a 10-row offset from their horizontal code points, that is, in rows 11, 14, and 15. For example, small hiragana "a" (ぁ) is normally encoded at Shift-JIS 0x829F (Row-Cell 04-01), but its vertical version is encoded at Shift-JIS 0x879F (Row-Cell 14-01). As far as Shift-JIS encoding is concerned, the shift value is 0x05 (that is, the difference between the first-byte values, which is 0x87 minus 0x82).

Under MacOS-J or JLK, these same 51 vertical variants are at an 84-row offset, that is, in rows 85, 88, and 89. Using the same example as above, small hiragana "a" (ぁ) is normally encoded at Shift-JIS 0x829F (Row-Cell 04-01), but its vertical version is encoded at Shift-JIS 0xEC9F (Row-Cell 88-01). As far as Shift-JIS encoding is concerned, the shift value is 0x6A (that is, the difference between the first-byte values, which is 0xEC minus 0x82).

PostScript Japanese fonts have always had these 51 vertical variants at the 84-row offset. Under KanjiTalk6, MacOS had to further offset vertical variants (which were already offset by 10 rows) by 74 rows when printing to PostScript devices.

Table 6-41 summarizes the two types of offsets for handling vertical variants under KanjiTalk, MacOS-J, and JLK.

Table 6-41: Vertical Variant Row Offsets

MacOS Version	Vertical Offset	Vertical Rows	Value for "tate" Table
KanjiTalk6	10-row	11, 14, and 15	0x05
MacOS-J and JLK	84-row	85, 88, and 89	0x6A

Japanese FOND resources for use under MacOS-J or JLK should include a "tate" (縦 *tate*, meaning "vertical") table, which explicitly indicates which offset should be used for vertical variants. If no "tate" table exists, MacOS assumes that a 10-row offset is desired. PostScript Japanese fonts, therefore, must explicitly indicate an 84-row offset by using the "tate" table and setting its value to 0x6A.

FONDedit, a utility provided to developers by Apple Computer, can properly create and set a "tate" table in FOND resources.

Microsoft Windows—Versions 3.1, 95, and 98

Microsoft Windows, unlike MacOS, typically provides two instances per font: one is horizontal, and the other is the corresponding vertical version. But, how are these instances differentiated for the user? Ever hear of the "at" (@, 0x40) symbol? It is prefixed to the menu name of the vertical font. Table 6-42 illustrates this (for kicks, I also included the equivalent PostScript font name).

Table 6-42: Windows Horizontal and Vertical Fonts

	Menu Name	PostScript Font Name
Horizontal	HY 중고딕	HYGoThic-Medium--KSCms-UHC-H
Vertical	@HY 중고딕	HYGoThic-Medium--KSCms-UHC-V

The critical Windows file that maps host-based fonts to printer-resident fonts is called the PFM (Printer Font Metrics) file. This file provides similar information to that found in the FOND resource on MacOS. Two PFMs are typically required for each CJKV font: one for horizontal, and the other for vertical.

Instead of using a range of FOND IDs whereby specific ranges are set aside for each locale, the PFM includes a single-integer identifier, known as the lfCharset value, to indicate script (locale). Table 6-43 lists the lfCharset values that pertain to CJKV font development.

Table 6-43: CJKV lfCharset Values

lfCharset	Script	Character Set	Encoding
128	Japanese	JIS X 0208:1997	Shift-JIS
129	Korean	KS X 1001:1992	EUC-KR or UHC
131	Korean	KS X 1001:1992	Johab
134	Simplified Chinese	GB 2312-80	EUC-CN or GBK
136	Traditional Chinese	Big Five	Big Five

Extreme care must be taken when creating PFMs due to byte order (I know this from experience, mainly because I wrote a CJKV PFM generator in Perl—this tool runs on big or little endian machines, and creates little endian output). There are many fields within a PFM file that specify two- and four-byte values, such as metrics and other integer-like values, and must be represented in little endian byte order. Practical information on building PFM files for CJKV fonts, including this Perl utility, can be found in *Building PFM Files for PostScript-Language CJK Fonts* (Adobe Systems Tech Note #5178).

Installing and registering PFMs

Once you have built a well-formed PFM file, it needs to be installed and registered to the OS. Installation of a PFM file can be anywhere on the file system, but is typically in the same location as other PFMs.

Registering the PFM to the OS is a matter of visiting and editing a system-level control file called *WIN.INI*. It is in this file where you must specify the full path to the PFM file (this is why a PFM can be stored anywhere on the file system). Let's assume that we installed two PFM files in the following path (the first is the horizontal PFM file, and the second its vertical counterpart):

```
C:\PSFONTS\STSONGLI\METRICS\GKEUC_H.PFM
C:\PSFONTS\STSONGLI\METRICS\GKEUC_V.PFM
```

The following is an example `[PostScript]` section from a *WIN.INI* file, and includes the lines added for the above two PFM files:

```
[PostScript, \\SJ TW 8\panda]
softfonts=2
softfont1=C:\PSFONTS\STSONGLI\METRICS\GKEUC_H.PFM
softfont2=C:\PSFONTS\STSONGLI\METRICS\GKEUC_V.PFM
```

Note that the keyword `softfonts` indicates the number of `softfont` entries, which, in this case, is 2. Note that when you register the PFMs by editing the *WIN.INI* file, you are informing the PostScript driver that the fonts are resident on the printer hard disk. More detailed information on installing PFM files is in *CID-Keyed Font Compatibility with ATM Software* (Adobe Systems Tech Note #5175).

X Window System

The X Window System uses one of two font formats, both bitmapped, and both derivable from BDF: SNF and PCF. SNF (Server Natural Format) is used on X11R4 and earlier, and PCF (Portable Compiled Format) is used on X11R5 and later. If you are running DPS (Display PostScript), you can also use PostScript CJKV fonts.*

X Window System font names are unique in that they are abnormally long, mainly because the name itself includes almost all of its global information. The following is an example taken from a JIS X 0208:1997 font:

```
-Misc-Fixed-Medium-R-Normal--16-150-75-75-C-160-JISX0208.1997-0
```

Hyphens are used to separate the information specified in the font name. Table 6-44 lists each of these fields.

Table 6-44: X Window System Font Names

Field Name	Sample Value	Description
Foundry	Misc	The font developer
Font family	Fixed	The font's family name
Weight	Medium	The font's relative weight
Slant	R	The font's slant angle
Set width	Normal	The font's proportionate width
Additional style		Additional style information
Pixels	16	The font's size measured in pixels
Points	150	The font's size measured in tenths of a point (thus, 15 points)
Horizontal resolution (dpi)	75	The horizontal resolution at which the bitmapped pattern was designed
Vertical resolution (dpi)	75	The vertical resolution at which the bitmapped pattern was designed
Spacing	C	The font's spacing: P for proportional, M for monospaced, and C for character cell (like a box)
Average width	160	The font's average width measured in tenths of a pixel (thus, 16 pixels)
Character set registry	JISX0208.1997	The character set designation
Character set encoding	0	For CJKV fonts, 0 usually means ISO-2022 encoding, and 1 means EUC encoding; for CNS 11643-1992 it is used to indicate plane number

* Sun and SGI systems are often bundled with DPS.

Luckily, the X Window System also has a convenient method for aliasing these excessively long font names to shorter ones, by using a special file called *fonts.alias* in a font directory. An example line from this file is as follows (using the example font name used above):

```
jis97 -Misc-Fixed-Medium-R-Normal--16-150-75-75-C-160-JISX0208.1997-0
```

For more information on X Window System font formats, I suggest Chapter 6, *Font Specification*, in O'Reilly & Associates' *X Window System User's Guide* by Valerie Quercia and Tim O'Reilly. The article entitled "The X Administrator: Font Formats and Utilities" (*The X Resource*, Issue 2, Spring 1992, pp 14–34) by Dinah McNutt and Miles O'Neal provides detailed information about X Window System font formats, including BDF, SNF, and PCF.

Installing and registering X Window System fonts

There are several (easy) steps that must be followed in order to install and register X Window System fonts. These steps are outlined as follows (strings that will change due to different file names or directories are emboldened):

1. Convert a BDF file to SNF or PCF, depending on what version of X Window System you are running:

   ```
   % bdftopcf jiskan16-1997.bdf > k16-97.pcf
   % bdftosnf jiskan16-1997.bdf > k16-97.snf
   ```

2. Copy the resulting SNF or PCF file to a font directory, then run the `mkfontdir` command as follows (assuming that you are creating a directory called *fonts* in your home directory) in order to create a *fonts.dir* file:

   ```
   % mkfontdir ~/fonts
   ```

3. Add this font directory to your font search path by running `xset` with the `+fp` option.

   ```
   % xset +fp ~/fonts
   ```

4. Create and edit the *fonts.alias* file—in the same location as the corresponding *fonts.dir* file. You must run `xset` with the `fp` option in order to make the X Font Server aware of your newly-created alias:

   ```
   % xset fp rehash
   ```

5. You can now display the font using `xfd` (X Font Displayer) with the `-fn` option, as follows:

   ```
   % xfd -fn k16-97
   ```

You can now use this font in other X Window System applications, such as Emacs. It is really that simple.

PostScript extensions for X Window System fonts

MacOS and Windows supported a mechanism whereby the operating system is made aware of the fully qualified PostScript font name that corresponds to the OS-specific font resources. For MacOS, it is the style map of the font suitcase's FOND resource that provides this information; and for Windows, it is a field in the PFM file. The following is the BDF header that corresponds to a PostScript font—the PostScript extensions are emboldened:

```
STARTFONT 2.1
FONT -Adobe-HeiseiMin-W3-R-Normal--12-120-72-72-P-115-Adobe.Japan1-3
SIZE 12 72 72
FONTBOUNDINGBOX 13 12 -2 -3
STARTPROPERTIES 23
FONTNAME_REGISTRY "Adobe"
FOUNDRY "Adobe"
FAMILY_NAME "HeiseiMin"
WEIGHT_NAME "W3"
SLANT "R"
SETWIDTH_NAME "Normal"
ADD_STYLE_NAME ""
PIXEL_SIZE 12
POINT_SIZE 120
RESOLUTION_X 72
RESOLUTION_Y 72
SPACING "P"
AVERAGE_WIDTH 115
CHARSET_REGISTRY "Adobe.Japan1"
CHARSET_ENCODING "3"
CHARSET_COLLECTIONS "Adobe-Japan1"
FONT_ASCENT 9
DEFAULT_CHAR 0
_ADOBE_PSFONT "HeiseiMin-W3-EUC-H"
_ADOBE_XFONT "-Adobe-HeiseiMin-W3-R-Normal--12-120-72-72-P-115-Adobe.Japan1-2"
_DEC_DEVICE_FONTNAMES "PS=HeiseiMin-W3-EUC-H"
COPYRIGHT "Copyright (c) 1996 Adobe Systems Incorporated. All Rights Reserved."
ENDPROPERTIES
CHARS 8720
```

The fully qualified PostScript font name, "HeiseiMin-W3-EUC-H," is provided in two places. PostScript drivers can extract the fully qualified PostScript font name from the arguments of the two fields `_ADOBE_PSFONT` or `_DEC_DEVICE_FONTNAMES`. But, in the case of the `_DEC_DEVICE_FONTNAMES` field, its argument must be split so that the initial `PS=` does not become part of the fully qualified PostScript font name.

Cross-Platform Issues

For purely historical reasons, seven of Adobe Systems' PostScript Japanese fonts have different menu names (that is, the localized font name that appears in applications' font menus) between MacOS and Windows, as far as OCF fonts are concerned. Table 6-45 illustrates these differences (note that the presence or absence of a "space" is sometimes the only difference).

Developers who plan to support PostScript Japanese fonts and are developing cross-platform applications need to be aware of such issues.

Table 6-45: MacOS and Windows Font Menu Names

Base PostScript Font Name	MacOS	Windows
Ryumin-Light	L リュウミン L-KL	リュウミンL-KL
GothicBBB-Medium	M 中ゴシック BBB	中ゴシックBBB
FutoMinA101-Bold	B 太ミン A101	太ミンA101
FutoGoB101-Bold	B 太ゴ B101	太ゴB101
Jun101-Light	L じゅん 101	じゅん101
HeiseiMin-W3	平成明朝 W3	平成明朝W3
HeiseiKakuGo-W5	平成角ゴシック W5	平成角ゴシックW5

Creating Your Own Fonts

If you are interested in creating your own typefaces (that is, rolling your own), by all means endeavor to do so. Be aware, however, that designing typefaces requires special skills, and lots of time, especially for a CJKV typeface that contains thousands (if not tens of thousands) of characters. Designing a CJKV typeface in outline format is never an individual task, but the result of a dedicated group effort. It would literally take several years for an individual to design a complete CJKV typeface of adequate quality. This should not stop you from trying, though. Sometimes you may simply need to add a few characters to an existing typeface. It is also not enough to be able to design individual characters: all the characters you design for a typeface must also match each other in both style and weight.

In addition to the font tools that I describe in the sections that follow, Apple also makes many of its font tools available.*

Bitmapped Font Editors

While nearly all outline font editors (described below) include the ability to create (by generating from outlines) and edit bitmapped fonts, there are also dedicated bitmapped font editors. Because outline fonts are now very common on MacOS and Windows, the need for dedicated bitmapped font editors is not great. However, bitmapped fonts are still a big part of Unix. Mark Leisher's XmBDFEditor is a very good bitmapped font editor for Unix.†

Standard Outline Font Editors

Several high-quality font editors are commercially available, and are quite useful for font development, whether it is at the personal or business level.

* *http://fonts.apple.com/Tools/*

† *ftp://crl.nmsu.edu/CLR/multiling/General/*

One of the most prominent has been Fontographer, developed by Macromedia (Altsys, who originally developed Fontographer, was acquired by Macromedia), available for MacOS and Microsoft Windows.* Fontographer allows users to create fonts for virtually any platform (MacOS, Microsoft Windows, Unix, and so on)—even if the version of Fontographer that is running is not designed for that platform.† Fontographer also supports TrueType fonts, and is available in a Japanese version (Japanese-language interface only). Fontographer allows users to build Type 1 or TrueType fonts from the same source data.

Another font editor that I highly recommend is FontLab by Pyrus North America, available for Windows, and soon to be available for MacOS.‡ The Windows version surpasses Fontographer in some respects, such as offering four-axis multiple master support, native TrueType editing (that is, using TrueType hints and quadratic splines). FontLab also includes a macro language, and provides the ability to define a subroutine library for commonly used "parts" of characters.

CJKV Outline Font Editors

The font editors described in the previous section are limited in that they can create only single-byte–encoded fonts. As design tools, they are of commercial quality. In fact, I have been a devoted Fontographer user for many years. Do not, however, underestimate the usefulness of these one-byte font editors: character design is completely independent from a utility's ability to create multiple-byte–encoded fonts. Luckily, at least one such font editor is finally available: FontLab Composer. TTEdit is a comparable shareware TrueType editor for Windows.**

Pyrus North America has developed an application called FontLab Composer that allows users to create CID-keyed fonts.†† That is, typefaces that contain thousands of characters—genuine multiple-byte–encoded CJKV fonts! FontLab Composer represents the first reasonably priced commercially available software that allows end users and developers alike to build CID-keyed fonts. It is currently available for Windows and MacOS. The Windows version outputs the following files when building a CIDFont:

- CIDFont file
- CID-keyed AFM file‡‡
- Two PFMs: one horizontal and one vertical

* *http://www.macromedia.com/software/fontographer/*

† The sole exception being multiple master font support—only the MacOS version allows users to create these complex Type 1 fonts, and is limited to two axes (four master designs per character).

‡ *http://www.pyrus.com/flfrm.htm*

** *http://www.interq.or.jp/www1/anzawa/ttedit.htm*

†† *http://www.pyrus.com/cpfrm.htm*

‡‡ Built according to the latest AFM (Adobe Font Metrics) specification (Adobe Tech Note #5004).

FontLab Composer is a digital typeface editor designed specifically for creating and manipulating multiple-byte fonts. It provides most of the capabilities found in single-byte font editors, but adds the ability to organize and arrange huge character sets, such as those required for building CJKV fonts.

As a font editor, FontLab Composer provides all the usual tools for working with character outlines. The glyph edit window provides layers for illustrating grids, nodes, control points, guides, hints, bitmapped templates, and character previews. In addition, FontLab Composer includes a special palette of vector paint tools that give the user the ability to create and edit glyphs with standard bitmap-manipulation tools that result in vector forms.

FontLab Composer eases the pain of manipulating fonts with thousands of characters by subdividing them into many *subfonts*, each of which can be viewed independently, and its characters can be freely moved and rearranged. FontLab Composer also provides the user with *the big picture* (the CMap view) that displays the entire font in a single table.

To assist in the process of building CID-keyed fonts that conform to known character collections, FontLab Composer is bundled with several bitmapped templates that correspond to each of the five CJKV character collections that Adobe has developed for building CID-keyed fonts (see Table 6-13 on page 292). Adobe's *public* CMap files, as listed in Tables 6-14 (page 293), 6-16 (page 295), 6-18 (page 296), 6-20 (page 297), and 6-21 (page 298), can be used with such fonts. Users can create their own character collections if desired.

Font Format Conversion

There are utilities, such as Metamorphosis Professional by Macromedia (no longer being sold) and TypeTool,* that allow users to convert fonts from one format to another (for example, from TrueType to Type 1 format and vice versa). TrueKeys, by Xiaolin Allen Zhao (赵小麟 *zhào xiǎolín*), is a shareware program for changing the encoding of TrueType fonts (for example, to change a Shift-JIS–encoded TrueType Japanese font to EUC-JP encoding).† FontLab Composer is also such a tool.

There are two important issues to bear in mind before performing any sort of font-format conversion:

- The license agreement included with most commercial font software may state that the data must not be converted to other formats—this is a *legal* issue
- The font format conversion process always strips out (or renders ineffective) the hinting information that allows the font data to rasterize better at smaller point sizes and at low resolutions—this is a *quality* issue

* *http://www.pyrus.com/ttfrm.htm*

† *http://www.unidocsys.com/TrueKeys.shtml*

These issues may be reasons for not modifying font data. Outline (as opposed to bitmapped) fonts are software (that is, programs—for example, the PostScript language, or a subset thereof, constitutes a complete programming language), and are copyrightable. So why do these tools exist? Well, not all fonts fall under restrictions for conversion to other formats, and many fonts are in the public domain.

Installing and Downloading Fonts

While there are plenty of tools for installing non-CJKV fonts, whether to the host (MacOS or Windows, for example) or to the printer, those designed for handling CJKV fonts are still rare due to the added complexity. Most font manufacturers end up developing their own installation software.

Now that CID-keyed fonts are becoming increasingly popular as the font format of choice for type foundries, the need for installing or downloading such fonts is also increasing. Adobe Systems' and Morisawa's CID-keyed fonts come with their own installer that performs host installation and printer download. InfoLogic's IW PS Font Installer is a tool that can be used to download CIDFont and CMap files, such as those built with FontLab Composer, to a PostScript printer.*

Developers who are serious about developing their own installation and downloading software should read Adobe Systems Tech Notes #5174 (*CID-Keyed Font Installation for PostScript File Systems*) and #5175 (*CID-Keyed Font Installation for ATM Software*), which provide the necessary technical details for performing these tasks.

How Big Can a Font Be?

When building fonts that contain CJKV characters, an obvious concern is file size. Are there limitations on file size or the number of characters? Any limitations could be exposed by using the tools that build fonts (such as FontLab Composer) or by using the fonts on the clients that use them (that is, operating systems, ATM, or PostScript).

Being a professional CJKV font builder, the largest CIDFont that I have ever built contains 55,880 CIDs (that is, characters) and is approximately 40MB in size. It contains all the characters for CNS 11643-1992 and CNS 11643-1986 Plane 15, and was developed specifically for this book.

There is currently a project underway in Japan to build a font that contains approximately 64,000 kanji.† It is called the GT明朝 (*GT minchō*) or 東大明朝

* *http://www.infologic.net/*

† *http://www.um.u-tokyo.ac.jp/DM_CD/DM_TECH/KAN_PRJ/HOME.HTM*

(*tōdai minchō*) font. The "G" stands for 学術振興会 (*gakujutsu shinkokai*), which means "Society for the Promotion of Science." The "T" stands for 東大 (*tōdai*), short for 東京大学 (*tōkyō daigaku*), which means "Tokyo University." It is likely that the first operating system to act as a client for this font is TRON, probably the BTRON instantiation.* Additional details about this project and its progress can be found at its web site (provided above), and at LineLabo's web site.†

External Character Handling

In Appendix C we cover vendor-defined characters within vendor character sets. I state there that these characters, called *gaiji* (外字‡ *gaiji*) in Japanese, do not convert very well between different character set standards. These are referred to here as *external characters*, meaning that they fall outside the range of standard characters, called system-defined characters (SDCs).** External characters are typically used in proper names and for historical or technical purposes, and can be separated into two distinct categories:

- User-defined characters (UDCs)
- System-specific characters (SSCs)

External characters are not used that often, but when they are needed, their support becomes crucial.

User-defined characters are those that a single user creates for personal use. System-specific characters are those characters that are considered standard on a specific operating system—but not across multiple operating systems. In a closed system, there is no difference between SDCs and SSCs, but the moment one bridges multiple operating systems, they can become quite different. For example, the traditional-form kanji 黑 (meaning "black") is considered an SDC under Windows 3.1J and Windows 95J, but because it is also an SSC (that is, specific to Windows), it is not available under other operating systems, such as KanjiTalk or JLK (MacOS). This particular kanji is an external character (that is, a UDC) as far as MacOS is concerned. External characters are not limited to Chinese characters—many are symbols.

Both types of external characters pose problems when information interchange is necessary. The target encoding or character set may not support certain characters that are used in a file. This is especially true for user-defined characters, which are

* *http://tron.um.u-tokyo.ac.jp/* or *http://www.tokyoweb.or.jp/tron/*

† *http://www.linelabo.com/*

‡ 外 means "external," and 字 means "character."

** What's the opposite of *external* characters? You guessed it, *internal* characters! We can call these critters *naiji* (内字 *naiji*) in Japanese.

usually specific to a single person's environment. Even JIS X 0212-1990 characters can be considered external characters if the target system does not support their use.* Some might imagine that Unicode is a solution to this problem. While this appears to be true at first glance (after all, there are nearly 21,000 Chinese characters to pick and choose from!), there are tens of thousands of CNS 11643-1992 hanzi that are not part of Unicode's Chinese character subset.

The success of printing or displaying external characters depends on the fonts you are using. If the font that you have chosen includes the proper external character, you should get proper output. If you need to use a vendor character set on that vendor's operating system, you most likely have access to fonts that correspond to it.

A problem arises when printing user-defined characters. In the case of bitmapped fonts, it is usually possible to create a new bitmapped character, then add it to the repertoire of characters in the font. However, creating a new outline character is a bit more tedious as it requires much more design skill (you may even have to create a corresponding bitmapped character!). Character design software such as Macromedia's Fontographer or Pyrus North America's FontLab (both described earlier in this chapter) are excellent tools for creating your own bitmapped and outline fonts.

The "External Character Problem"

Solving the age-old problem of external characters is not so easy, mainly because it involves so many issues, such as the following:

- How to create external characters
- How to encode external characters
- How to input external characters
- How to display or print external characters
- How to exchange documents containing external characters
- How to search for external characters

So, what can you do about these problems? Unfortunately, there is no elegant solution. A solution would need to somehow allow for the successful transmission of user- and system-specific characters to systems that do not support such characters. Even large character sets do not have all system-specific characters, and that doesn't even touch upon the problem of user-defined characters. A necessary step

* For example, in Shift-JIS encoding, which does not support the JIS X 0212-1990 character set, they are considered external characters. Adobe Systems has released a MacOS font called 平成明朝W3外字 (*heisei minchō W3 gaiji*) that includes all of the JIS X 0212-1990 as a series of one-byte–encoded Type 1 fonts.

in finding a solution might be to embed character data, both bitmapped and outline, into files when they are transmitted. This includes a mechanism for detecting which characters are user-defined. The first person or company to offer a platform-independent solution will be rewarded well by the CJKV computer industry. In my opinion, the CJKV-capable version of Adobe Acrobat—based on PDF Version 1.3 and later—is a step in this direction. More information about Adobe Acrobat and PDF is available in Chapter 13, *The World Wide Web*.

External Character Handling Techniques and Tricks

When one needs to gain access to characters outside the supported character set, there are several proven techniques (none of which provide a high degree of information interchange, but which do result in a correctly printed page). Here are the techniques that I have used to produce this book:

- Accessing special characters not found in common character sets
- Accessing multiple character sets on a single character set system

The first technique, *accessing special characters*, involves producing one or more standard one-byte–encoded Type 1 (or TrueType, if that's your thing) fonts containing all the special characters you require. This can include hacking existing fonts (such as my hacking the ITC Garamond family to make macroned vowels available). Once you have built such fonts, you then need to decide how to access their characters. There are two choices available to you:

- Use the Type 1 (or TrueType) fonts stand-alone
- Add the Type 1 (or TrueType) fonts to the user-defined region of an existing CJKV font

The second choice requires a tool for adding these special characters to existing fonts. Adobe Type Composer is such a tool designed to interact with PostScript fonts, but is currently limited to Japanese and MacOS. It is discussed in the next section.

The second technique, *accessing multiple character sets*, offers some degree of information interchange. Suppose that you prefer to work in a single CJKV environment, such as MacOS-J or MacOS with JLK, but you need to produce a (rather large, say book-length) document that includes characters from Chinese, Korean, and Vietnamese character sets.* You could obtain and install the appropriate system resources, but for some character sets, such as JIS X 0212-1990, none exist for MacOS (or for Windows, for that matter). What to do? It turns out that almost all CJKV character sets are based on a 94×94 matrix. My solution for producing this book was to first take existing CIDFont files for the necessary CJKV character sets.

* Uh huh, like this book.

I then created Shift-JIS–encoded CMap files for each character set, sometimes separating character sets into separate planes when necessary to be compatible with Shift-JIS encoding. Table 6-46 details the character sets I needed to support, along with the CIDFont files and CMap files used.

Table 6-46: Shift-JIS–Encoded CJKV Fonts

Character Set	CIDFont File	CMap File
GB 2312-80	STSong-Light	GB-RKSJ-H
GB/T 12345-90	STSong-Light	GBT-RKSJ-H
CNS 11643-1992 Plane 1	MingTiEG-Medium	CNS01-RKSJ-H
CNS 11643-1992 Plane 2	MingTiEG-Medium	CNS02-RKSJ-H
CNS 11643-1992 Plane 3	MingTiEG-Medium	CNS03-RKSJ-H
CNS 11643-1992 Plane 4	MingTiEG-Medium	CNS04-RKSJ-H
CNS 11643-1992 Plane 5	MingTiEG-Medium	CNS05-RKSJ-H
CNS 11643-1992 Plane 6	MingTiEG-Medium	CNS06-RKSJ-H
CNS 11643-1992 Plane 7	MingTiEG-Medium	CNS07-RKSJ-H
CNS 11643-1986 Plane 15	MingTiEG-Medium	CNS15-RKSJ-H
Hong Kong GCCS	HKSong-Regular	HK-RKSJ-H
JIS X 0212-1990	HeiseiMin-W3H	Hojo-RKSJ-H
KS X 1001:1992	HYSMyeongJo-Medium	KS-RKSJ-H
KS X 1002:1991	HYSMyeongJo-SMedium	KS2-RKSJ-H
TCVN 6056:1995	MingTiEGV-Medium	TCVN-RKSJ-H

Although this technique does not allow easy input of characters because the KanjiTalk input methods are geared toward the JIS X 0208:1997 character set, it does simplify and trivialize in the building of character set tables, and provides for the occasional use of CJKV characters. Perfect for my needs. If you feel that this technique would be useful for your own publishing needs, I have made these special Shift-JIS–encoded CMap files available for public use (but, note that these special CMap files are not officially supported by Adobe Systems).*

No matter what technique you choose to use, you must consider how to input the additional or non-standard characters. The dictionaries for conventional CJKV input methods either need to be extended, or else code input is mandated. But, for some special purposes, code input is completely adequate.

* *ftp://ftp.oreilly.com/pub/examples/nutshell/cjkv/adobe/rksj-cmaps.tar.Z*

XKP—an External Character Handling Initiative

XKP, short for *Extended Kanji Processing*, is a specification developed by a Microsoft-sponsored consortium for extending operating systems so that developers can access, define, create, display, and print user-defined characters in a standardized way. Moving from a Shift-JIS to Unicode architecture effectively increases the total number of available UDCs from 1,800 to 6,400.*

While XKP is currently Japanese-specific, its techniques can be easily adapted for use with other CJKV locales. XKP doesn't simply provide a method to encode user-defined characters, but provides other information to aid input and searches. Table 6-47 lists the sort of information that can be associated with each UDC.†

Table 6-47: XKP's User-Defined Character Information

Field Name	Example	Description
Yomi	Yomi= ケン つるぎ	Readings
Busyu	Busyu=18	Radical
Kakusu	Kakusu=9	Number of strokes
URP	URP=0x5263	Unified Representative Point[a]
FontPath	FontPath=*STKAIREG.TTF*	The file name of the UDC font
FontName	FontName= 华文楷体	The name of the UDC font
FontCodePoint	FontCodePoint=0xBDA3	The code point in the UDC font

[a] A code point reference that represents the "parent" or standard version of the UDC. It effectively means that the UDC will be treated as a variant of the parent character for purposes such as searching.

Once you have properly registered your UDCs, you can then start making use of them in your documents. There are two ways in which UDCs can be referenced:

- As a user-defined code point (in UCS-2's PUA‡), such as the value 0xE000
- As an ampersand-prefixed eight-digit hexadecimal string, such as "&00000001"

XKP also defines three character sets (Basic, Extended, and Compatibility) and three implementation levels (1, 2, and 3) for Japanese. These are referred to as SDCs in XKP. Two of the character sets refer to Japanese subrepertoires specified in JIS X 0221-1995. Table 6-48 lists these implementation levels, along with references to the Japanese subrepertoires specified in JIS X 0221-1995.

* If the newly-established Surrogates Area is taken into account, this 6,400 figure could well become 137,472 (6,400 plus 131,072). See Chapter 3 for more details.

† Bonus points (or extra credit) will be awarded to those who can figure out what the glyph is for the character described in Table 6-47.

‡ Private Use Area—a fancy way to write "user-defined region."

Table 6-48: XKP's JIS X 0221-1995 Implementation Levels

Implementation Level	Character Set	JIS X 0221-1995 Reference
1	Basic	1, 6, and 7
2	Basic, Compatibility	1, 6, 7, and Windows 95J-specific characters
3	Basic, Compatibility, Extended	1, 2, 3, 4, 6, and 7

The only Japanese subrepertoire that is not covered by XKP is number 5, which represents the 8,745 remaining Chinese characters in Unicode.

More information about XKP is available in the form of documentation and an SDK (Software Developer's Kit).*

Adobe Type Composer: External Character Front-End

Adobe Type Composer (ATC) is software that allows you to rearrange the characters of Japanese typefaces, and also lets you add new characters to the same—PostScript Japanese typefaces, that is. Adobe Type Composer has three basic functions:

- Add new characters to an existing Japanese typeface in the user-defined character range (0xF041 through 0xFBFC)
- Substitute characters from one Japanese typeface for another Japanese typeface, such as kana and symbols
- Change the baseline for the built-in proportional Latin font

The result can be considered a "virtual" font that is installed at the system level, meaning that it is available to all applications. It is virtual in the sense that it contains no character outlines, but is simply a recipe for combining parts of other fonts into a new font resource.

Anyway, here is what each of ATC's functions can do for you. First, you can add new characters, up to a maximum of 2,256 (this is composed of 12 rows of 188 characters each), to existing PostScript Japanese fonts. You can either create or purchase additional characters, and add them to encoded positions of a font. Second, you can substitute the kana characters or some select symbols with others of a different style. Since kana characters constitute over 70 percent of typical Japanese text, you can dramatically change the look and feel of a document simply by using different kana characters. This is an inexpensive way to add more functionality to a smaller Japanese type library. Look at the Japanese text in Table 6-49. The block on the left is set in a single Japanese typeface, whereas the block on the right uses a different typeface for the kana and punctuation.

* *http://www.xkp.or.jp/*

Table 6-49: The Effect of Changing the Kana Design

HeiseiMin-W3	HeiseiMin-W3 and TBRyokanM-M
普通の和文フォントは明朝体とゴシック体ですが、スペシャルなフォントもあります。例えば、丸ゴシック体、楷書体、毛筆体、および教科書体というフォントに人気があります。	普通の和文フォントは明朝体とゴシック体ですが、スペシャルなフォントもあります。例えば、丸ゴシック体、楷書体、毛筆体、および教科書体というフォントに人気があります。

See what I mean? The abundance of kana clearly allows you to change the "look and feel" of Japanese text. Of course, this mixing of typefaces can be performed by most word processing software simply by selecting the kana and changing them to another font—this can be a tedious task for long documents. But what about software, such as simple text editors, that allows only a single font selection per document? That is one of those circumstances when this functionality becomes crucial.

Adobe Type Composer makes it more feasible for type foundries (and individual designers) to design kana-only fonts for mixing with kanji from a different Japanese typeface.

Adobe Type Composer software currently rearranges only 90pv-RKSJ-H– and 83pv-RKSJ-H–based fonts, both of which are accessible only on MacOS. This means that the user-defined character area pertains only to Shift-JIS–encoded ("RKSJ") fonts.

Note that Adobe Type Composer is simply a front-end to a very powerful font rearrangement technology available on all PostScript devices capable of supporting CID-keyed fonts. A resource instance called "AdobeTypeComposer" is made available on such PostScript devices.

Some applications provide functionality similar to Adobe Type Composer, but the resulting fonts are accessible only within the application. Adobe FrameMaker, Adobe PageMaker, and QuarkXPress provide users with the ability to create virtual fonts that can substitute character classes, such as the Latin characters. SMI EDICOLOR, as an exception, also allows the user to specify fonts for two types of external characters: system and user. See the description of SMI EDICOLOR in Chapter 7, starting on page 381, for more details.

Creating Your Own Rearranged Fonts

If the Adobe Type Composer application's functionality does not suit your specific needs (or if you cannot make use of it due to its operating environment or other limitations), you can build your own rearranged fonts. In order to use this newly defined font, you need to ensure that the rearranged font file itself, along with all font components to which it refers are installed onto the PostScript device. This effectively means that the following scenarios are possible, and will result in proper execution of a rearranged font:

- Explicitly download all referenced font components to the PostScript device, either to its hard disk (permanently) or to RAM (temporarily)
- Download the referenced fonts followed by the rearranged font within the PostScript stream—the referenced fonts and the rearranged font are available only for the duration of the job, and vanish from memory once it is over

Anything else will result in failure.

The following is a completely valid rearranged font file. It depends on the presence of a PostScript ProcSet (Procedure Set—a fancy name for a program) called *AdobeTypeComposer*. All CID-capable PostScript devices include this ProcSet.

In a nutshell, this rearranged font file defines a new PostScript font name called `HeiseiMin-W3-Fugu-RKSJ-H`, which uses `HeiseiMin-W3-90ms-RKSJ-H` as its template font, then adds the contents of the fonts `MyUDC1` and `MyUDC2`, each containing 94 characters in the range 0x21 through 0x7E, to the first row of the Shift-JIS user-defined range, specifically 0xF040 through 0xF0FC.* I have emboldened non-boilerplate information.

```
%%BeginResource: Font (HeiseiMin-W3-Fugu-RKSJ-H)
%%DocumentNeededResources: ProcSet (AdobeTypeComposer)
%%+ Font (HeiseiMin-W3-90ms-RKSJ-H)
%%+ Font (MyUDC1)
%%+ Font (MyUDC2)
%%IncludeResource: ProcSet (AdobeTypeComposer)
%%IncludeResource: Font (HeiseiMin-W3-90ms-RKSJ-H)
%%IncludeResource: Font (MyUDC1)
%%IncludeResource: Font (MyUDC2)
%%Version: 1.000

1 dict begin /FontName /HeiseiMin-W3-Fugu-RKSJ-H def end

/languagelevel where { pop languagelevel 2 ge } { false } ifelse

{ /CIDInit /ProcSet resourcestatus
  { pop pop /CIDInit /ProcSet findresource }
  { /AdobeTypeComposer /ProcSet findresource }
  ifelse
}
{ AdobeTypeComposer }
```

* PostScript fonts, such as Type 1, typically have three names associated with them: *FontName*, *FullName*, and *FamilyName*. The only one that matters to PostScript (and thus to rearranged font files) is FontName. While FullName and FamilyName are used only for informational purposes, and contain strings as their values (PostScript strings are delimited by parentheses), FontName contains a font object as its value (PostScript objects are prefixed with a slash). See the following examples taken from a valid Type 1 font:

```
/FullName (Jeffrey Special) readonly def
/FamilyName (Jeffrey) readonly def
/FontName /JeffreySpecial def
```

```
ifelse
begin
%ADOStartRearrangedFont
/HeiseiMin-W3-Fugu-RKSJ-H [ /HeiseiMin-W3-90ms-RKSJ-H
                            /MyUDC1 /MyUDC2 ]
beginrearrangedfont
  1 usefont
    2 beginbfrange
    <f040> <f07e> <21>
    <f080> <f09e> <60>
    endbfrange
  2 usefont
    1 beginbfrange
    <f09f> <f0fc> <21>
    endbfrange
endrearrangedfont
end
%%EndResource
%%EOF
```

Note that this file's syntax is quite simple, and basically defines the following information:

- The new PostScript font name: *HeiseiMin-W3-Fugu-RKSJ-H*
- The template font: *HeiseiMin-W3-90ms-RKSJ-H*
- Additional fonts: *MyUDC1* and *MyUDC2**
- The code points in the template font where the additional fonts are to be encoded, also specifying at what code point in the additional fonts to begin referencing characters

The template and additional fonts must be valid font instances, such as a Type 1 (or Type 42, if a TrueType rasterizer is available), OCF, or CID-keyed font. Note that a CIDFont by itself (that is, without a CMap to impose an encoding) is not a valid component within a rearranged font file.

If Type 1 fonts are to be used as the additional fonts, there are some special considerations. Typical Type 1 fonts use what is known as *StandardEncoding*. The presence of the following line in a Type 1 font confirms the presence of StandardEncoding:

```
/Encoding StandardEncoding def
```

* These are typically Type 1 fonts, but can be another composite font, such as a CID-keyed font (that is, a CIDFont plus CMap combination that forms a valid font instance). You can even use the same font that was specified as the template font in order to perform cute tricks such as *really* rearranging the characters within the font.

Type 1 fonts that specify StandardEncoding can be affected by what is known as *font re-encoding*. Font re-encoding usually affects characters in the extended ASCII range (0x7F and above), which exists to accommodate the slight difference in encoding for some accented characters and symbols on different operating systems. But, font re-encoding can effectively mangle Type 1 fonts that were not intended to be used as typical Type 1 fonts.

To avoid font re-encoding, most font editing software allows fonts to be built using custom encodings. But, some operating systems try to be smart, and ignore the fact that a font specifies a custom encoding.* This can be easily circumvented by using non-standard character names. A convention that I use is to name each character according to its encoding. I do this with the character "`c`" (meaning "character") followed by a two-digit hexadecimal code (such as "`20`" for 0x20). This results in character names that can range from "`c00`" (for 0x00) to "`cFF`" (for 0xFF).

Let's rip apart some of these sections for further analysis and explanation. First, the section that specifies the name of the rearranged font, its template, and additional fonts:

```
/HeiseiMin-W3-Fugu-RKSJ-H [ /HeiseiMin-W3-90ms-RKSJ-H
                            /MyUDC1 /MyUDC2 ]
```

The string `HeiseiMin-W3-Fugu-RKSJ-H`, which is the name of the rearranged font, is followed by an array containing three elements (delimited by brackets). The first element, `HeiseiMin-W3-90ms-RKSJ-H`, represents the template font. The rearranged font, thus, becomes a copy of this font, and inherits all of its attributes, such as character complement, writing direction, and so on. The remaining elements, `MyUDC1` and `MyUDC2`, represent the additional fonts used for rearrangement.

Between the two keywords `beginrearrangedfont` and `endrearrangedfont` is the code that performs the actual rearrangement. There is one section for each of the additional fonts specified in the above array—the first element of the array, which represents the template font, is considered the 0th element. Thus, the following rearrangement code refers to the `MyUDC1` font:

```
1 usefont
  2 beginbfrange
  <f040> <f07e> <21>
  <f080> <f09e> <60>
  endbfrange
```

* Such operating systems often peek at the names of the characters within the font to determine whether or not to re-encode.

The numeral that appears before the keyword `usefont` refers to an element of the font array, which means `MyUDC1` in the case of the value 1. The section that follows describes the rearrangement in terms of an encoding range within the template font (that is, what encoding range to modify in the template font) followed by a beginning code point from which to begin referencing characters from the additional font. In other words, the encoding range 0xF040–0xF07E in `HeiseiMin-W3-90ms-RKSJ-H` is replaced by characters from `MyUDC1` encoded in the range 0x21–0x5F. The integer value that appears before the `beginbfrange` keyword specifies the number of lines of rearrangement code, and must agree with the actual number of lines of rearrangement code.

As you can see, once you understand the simple syntax of a rearranged font file, it becomes a trivial task to create rearranged fonts of your own. Or, if you are a developer, to build your own front-end to this powerful PostScript-based technology.

Obtaining External Characters

While it is possible to create your own external characters, it is perhaps easier for most users to simply purchase them as commercial products.* Nearly all type foundries sell external character packages, but some type foundries specialize in external character products. DTP center Biblos† and Enfour Media‡ are companies that market Japanese external character (also known as "Gaiji") products. Appendix C of this book lists their standard Gaiji character sets starting on pages 570 and 575, respectively.

Advice to Developers

Many users will discover that a suitable set of CJKV fonts may be right in front of their very eyes in the form of the fonts (usually outline fonts these days) that were bundled with their operating system. Users that require designs beyond the basic fonts provided by the operating system will look to font developers for additional offerings.

Developers need to be aware of the pros and cons of each font format so that they can decide when it is appropriate to implement one format over another. Incorporating an outline font into a product, for example, will require that an appropriate rasterizer be present in order to render bitmaps from outlines.

---

* After all, most users, even power users, are not professional type designers.

† *http://www.biblosfont.co.jp/*

‡ *http://www.enfour.com/*

7

Typography

In this chapter:

- *Rules, Rules, Rules...*
- *Typographic Units and Measurements*
- *Horizontal and Vertical Layout*
- *Line Breaking and Word Wrapping*
- *Character Spanning*
- *Alternate Metrics*
- *Kerning*
- *Line Length Issues*
- *Multilingual Text*
- *Glyph Substitution*
- *Annotations*
- *Typographic Software*

The foundation for producing printed works in *any* language—no matter how basic—involves typography. It is in this chapter where we are finally able to apply what we have learned in earlier chapters: Chapter 3, *Character Set Standards*, illustrated the thousands of characters at our disposal; Chapter 4, *Encoding Methods*, showed how these characters can be encoded; Chapter 5, *Input Methods*, provided information about the input of these characters through software (*input methods*); and Chapter 6, *Font Formats*, provided details about fonts and font formats. It all comes together here. After all, the ultimate goal of processing CJKV text is to produce documents, whether printed or in electronic form.

Most people have a basic understanding that CJKV text can be set horizontally and vertically, but there is much more to CJKV typography than these two simple writing modes. There are also many formatting considerations, such as line breaking, justification, spacing, alternate metrics, kerning, alternate glyphs, and so on. You will soon realize that CJKV text does not follow all Western-language–style composition rules, and for good reasons.

An excellent reference on typography is Robert Bringhurst's *The Elements of Typographic Style*, Second Edition (Hartley & Marks, 1996). Seybold Publications' *Seybold Report on Publishing Systems* and *Seybold Report on Internet Publishing* sometimes contain information of a CJKV nature. More detailed information on Japanese line-layout can be found in the standard designated JIS X 4051-1995 (whose contents are described throughout this chapter, and a discussion about compliance with this standard is in the next section), and in Mitsuo Fukawa's (府川充男 *fukawa mitsuo*) book entitled 組版原論—タイポグラフィと活字・写植・DTP (*kumihan genron—taipogurafi to katsuji, shashoku, DTP*) (太田出版, 1996). Other books about typography, some of them written in languages other than English, can be found in this book's bibliography.

Note that while most of the examples provided in this chapter are Japanese, the principles are applicable to all text of CJKV locales. Also, most of the typographic examples provided in this chapter are created directly in Adobe FrameMaker, but some—in particular examples that involve vertical writing—were created with a variety of applications, such as Adobe Illustrator, Macromedia FreeHand-J, QuarkXPress-J, and SMI EDICOLOR.

Rules, Rules, Rules...

When one reads information about CJKV line-layout, sets of rules are often presented (such as those rules outlined in the standard designated JIS X 4051-1995). And, many line-layout programs allow the user to adhere to these rules. While line-layout rules are often based on sound and proven typographic principles, they do not always need to be followed to the letter—they can be broken when the situation or context permits.

The most important aspect of line-layout is *consistency*. The formation and obeying of line-layout rules results in consistency. Whatever rules you choose to apply, they need to be applied in a consistent manner. If a set of pre-defined rules happen to work well with the document that you are typesetting, by all means follow them. This book, for example, follows the book-design rules set forth by the book designers of O'Reilly & Associates.

Keep in mind while reading this chapter that typography *is* an art form. Providing an unskilled painter with a set of painting rules will not result in an aesthetically pleasing piece of art. All artists have their own set of rules—usually unwritten—and they obey or break them when the situation demands.

JIS X 4051-1995 Compliance

JIS X 4051-1995, *Line Composition Rules for Japanese Documents* (日本語文書の行組版方法 *nihongo bunshō no gyō kumihan hōhō*), is the standard that provides the rules necessary for setting Japanese documents.* Several publishing-quality applications, such as Adobe FrameMaker, Adobe Illustrator, Adobe PageMaker-J,

* Originally designated JIS X 4051-1993.

Macromedia FreeHand-J, QuarkXPress-J, and SMI EDICOLOR now provide full or partial JIS X 4051-1995 compliance.

The most important aspect of JIS X 4051-1995 is that it is the first national standard that attempts to document line-layout rules for any type of CJKV text. Many of the line-layout rules for Japanese were either inconsistently documented in proprietary documentation or else not documented at all. While I wrote in the beginning of this chapter that consistency is more important than a set of rules, you must realize that consistency arises from adhering to a set of rules. JIS X 4051-1995 provides application developers and typographers with a starting point from which to define their own set of typographic rules.

Many of the typographic rules described in JIS X 4051-1995 are loosely described in this chapter. If your work, research, or interests involve Japanese typography, I encourage you to explore what JIS X 4051-1995 has to offer.

If you are a member of a standards committee in China, Korea, Taiwan, or Vietnam, I *strongly* encourage you to consider publishing a standard that describes a basic set of your locale's line-layout rules, similar to Japan's JIS X 4051-1995.

GB/T 15834-1995 and GB/T 15835-1995

China has published two standards that provide some amount of line-layout guidance: GB/T 15834-1995, *Use of Punctuation Marks* (标点符号用法 *biāodiǎn fúhào yòngfǎ*); and GB/T 15835-1995, *General Rules for Writing Numerals in Publications* (出版物上数字用法的规定 *chūbǎn wùshàng shùzì yòngfǎ de guīdìng*). While these two standards are not nearly as comprehensive as Japan's JIS X 4051-1995, they do provide general principles for composing Chinese text in both horizontal and vertical writing modes.

Typographic Units and Measurements

Before one begins to construct lines of text for a document, there must be a consistent and established set of units and measurements in place for the purpose of specifying the size of text and spacing. If one is to consider only non-proprietary typesetting systems, there is little benefit to discussing typographic units other than points. But, many proprietary typesetting systems are still in use today, and many typographic guides still make use of other typographic units. Knowing how to convert between these typographic units can often be of benefit.

Before the days of easily scaled type, names were given to the various type sizes. Table 7-1 lists some of these names, along with their sizes in (American) points.

Because most typographic units of measurement have long and sometimes misunderstood histories, such discussions are beyond the scope of this book. As written

Table 7-1: Historical Names for Type Sizes

Name	Size in Points
Diamond	4
Pearl	4.5
Ruby	5
Nonpareil	6
Emerald	6.5
Minion	7
Brevier	7.5
Bourgeois	8
Long primer	9
Elite	10
Small pica	11
Pica	12
English	14
Great primer	16
Paragon	18
Two-line small pica	22
Two-line pica	24
Two-line English	28
Two-line great primer	32
Three-line pica	36
Four-line pica	48
Four-line English	56
Five-line pica	60
Six-line pica	72

above, what is important in the context of this book is to know that there are many typographic units, and that you can convert between them.

Two Important Points—Literally

Quite literally, there are two types of *points* used in typography today. The point is a unit of measurement used to specify the size of characters, and also for specifying types of spaces, such as leading and letterspacing. Which point is being used—the American or Didot—is important because they represent different sizes.

It is important to realize that the American point has become the predominant typographic unit of measurement.

The American point

The American point (or simply "point") is the most commonly used typographic unit today, at least for American and British systems. The point is usually considered to be $\frac{1}{72}$ of one inch, which also means 0.3515 millimeters, 0.01383 inches, or $\frac{1}{12}$ of one *pica*.* To be exact, there are 72.28915663 points per inch—the result of the mathematical operation 12 ÷ 0.166 (the number of points per pica divided by the length of one pica in inches).

Some programs allow the user to alter the definition of the point. QuarkXPress, for example, allows the user the change the definition of a point—the default is 72 points per inch according to the PostScript imaging model. This is useful if you have been using a different typographic scale, and want to stick with it.

The Didot point

The Didot point is still widely used in continental Europe, and is approximately seven percent larger than the American point. It represents 0.38 millimeters, 0.01483 inches, or $\frac{1}{12}$ of one *cicero*. The cicero is similar to a pica, but like the American versus Didot point, it is approximately seven percent larger than the pica.

Other Typographic Units

The two types of points are Western typographic units, but surely there must have been typographic units developed in non-Western cultures. Indeed there are, and three other typographic units are still used in some proprietary typesetting systems in CJKV locales, written as follows in CJKV locales:

- 级数/級數 *jíshù* in Chinese, 級数 *kyūsū* in Japanese, and 급수/級數 *geubsu* in Korean
- 齿数/齒數 *chǐshù* in Chinese, 歯数 *hasū* in Japanese, and 치수/齒數 *cisu* in Korean
- 号数/號數 *hàoshù* in Chinese, 号数 *gōsū* in Japanese, and 호수/號數 *hosu* in Korean

I will refer to these three typographic units below as Q,† H, and G, respectively. The use of Q and H as abbreviations for the first two units is actually common practice in Japan. The Q unit is defined in JIS X 0207-1979 (formerly JIS C 6225-1979) and GB 3937-83.

* A pica is traditionally 4.22 millimeters or 0.166 inches, but the convention today is to consider a pica to be the same as $\frac{1}{6}$ of one inch.

† I feel obliged to point out that there is no relation between Q (the unit of typographic measurement), "Q" (an omnipotent being from the contemporary *Star Trek* series), and "Q" (007's personal spy-gadget technician).

Q and H are equivalent to one-fourth of one millimeter (0.25 mm)—although both units represent the same size, they are used for completely different purposes, as follows:

- Q are used solely for specifying type size
- H are used solely for specifying leading, escapement, line length, and spaces—everything but type size

Adobe FrameMaker, FIT, Macromedia FreeHand, QuarkXPress, and SMI EDICOLOR are the few non-proprietary page-layout systems that allow the user to specify Q for units of typographic measurement. Although these applications do not currently support the use of H as a unit of typographic measurement, the use of Q suffices because it represents the same size. These applications may eventually support the use of Q and H as they were originally intended. Providing support for Q and H in non-proprietary page-layout systems makes it easier for users of proprietary equipment to transition to non-proprietary software.

So, you may be wondering why there is a need for both Q and H—time for a little Q and A (*questions and answers*). When one specifies how text is to be laid out into lines, it is common to specify both type size and leading. The text of this book, for example, is laid out as 10/13, which means 10-point type and 13-point leading. The leading here refers to the distance from the baseline of one line of text to another: 10 points for the characters themselves plus 3 points of lead as extra space. There are other conventions that specify *only* the additional space instead of the point size plus the additional space. This could result in 10/3. Needless to say, this can become confusing because it is not always clear which value is the type size and which is the leading (whether the value includes the type size or not). But, the use of Q and H makes this obvious. Text laid out as 10Q/13H uses 10Q (2.5 mm or 7.112-point) type size plus 13H (3.25 mm or 9.246-point) leading.

The other typographic unit, which I am calling G, is unique in that its scale is the reverse of what one finds in the other typographic units. That is, the higher the value of G, the smaller the size. And, like the Q unit, G is used strictly for type size. This typographic unit was developed in Japan by Shozo Motoki (本木昌造 *motoki shōzō*) in 1933, and was supposedly based on a traditional Japanese metric system called Kujira-Jaku (鯨尺 *kujira jaku*).

Various sizes on the G scale relate to one another in terms of being either half or double the size of other sizes in the same scale. The following sizes on the G scale relate to one another in terms of being multiples of one another:

- 1G, 4G, and 7G
- 0G (Initial G), 2G, 5G, and 8G
- 3G and 6G

Table 7-2 provides these same G units together, along with the equivalent sizes in points so that it is clear how they are related.

Table 7-2: The G Typographic Unit

	0G (42 points)	
1G (27.5 points)	2G (21 points)	3G (16 points)
4G (13.75 points)	5G (10.5 points)	6G (8 points)
7G (6.875 points)	8G (5.25 points)	

Needless to say, the G is a typographic unit of measurement whose scale limits the maximum size of a character to 42 points. It is also no longer used.

Some page-layout systems also use the notion of "character" as a typographic unit. FIT and SMI EDICOLOR, for example, allow the user to specify dimensions in terms of number of characters, for both the horizontal and vertical direction. For writing systems whose characters are uniform in size (which means that they can be set on a rigid grid), this has many advantages.

Horizontal and Vertical Layout

CJKV text, from a traditional point of view, is set vertically. Columns begin at the right side of the page, and work their way to the left. Also, books are read beginning from what in the West is considered the back of the book. Fortunately, it is also acceptable to set CJKV text horizontally, and to read books in "Western" direction. There are, however, a few punctuation marks and other characters that require special handling when set vertically, such as their positioning within the design space or 90-degree clockwise rotation.

PostScript's flexible text handling capabilities allow you to set CJKV text vertically, accomplished through the use of a vertical font instance.* Whether or not you can actually typeset CJKV text vertically depends greatly upon the operating systems and software you are using—the underlying PostScript CJKV fonts have inherent vertical support. MacOS, for example, does not have any built-in vertical support, so application developers who wish to provide their users with the ability to set text vertically must implement vertical support themselves.

One critical aspect of vertical layout is the relative position of the vertical origin, typically centered over the top of the design space. As you will see in Figure 7-1 on page 367, the typical design space found in CJKV fonts is negatively offset from the baseline (Y coordinate 0) anywhere from 120 to 200 units. This really means that the relative position from the horizontal baseline—Y coordinate 0—depends

* That is, PostScript fonts whose `/WMode` value is set to 1.

on the design space of the font. However, contemporary font resources, such as the "FOND" resource for MacOS and the PFM file for Windows, do not have any place to encapsulate this information. It is information specific to vertical writing mode, but most host-based font-resource formats were not designed with vertical writing in mind. The fields that contain values for font-level ascent and descent are sometimes (incorrectly and dangerously, in my opinion) overloaded or changed to encapsulate the design space rather than the true font-level ascent and descent values.

Another aspect of vertical layout is *escapement*. That is, the amount of space from one character to the next, also referred to as a character's set width. If a character's set width is 1000 units—a typical CJKV character—then its escapement, whether in horizontal or vertical writing mode, is the same as the point size. That is, a 10-point character will have 10-point escapement. Typical typeface designs that are used to compose newspapers, however, are set in a non-square design space, such as 1000×800 (that is, 1000 units wide, 800 units high). More about non-square designs in the next section.

Table 7-3 provides some examples of Japanese text set horizontally and vertically, including some of the characters that require special vertical handling.

Table 7-3: Horizontal and Vertical Layout—Japanese

Horizontal	Vertical
普通の「DTPシステム」は 縦書きレイアウトをサポー トしていますが、簡単なワ ープロやテキストエディタ ーはサポートしません。縦 書きのサポートの為にはフ ォントも必要です。全ての ポストスクリプト中日韓越 フォントには縦書きフォン トも含まれています。	普通の「DTPシステム」は 縦書きレイアウトをサポー トしていますが、簡単なワ ープロやテキストエディタ ーはサポートしません。縦 書きのサポートの為にはフ ォントも必要です。全ての ポストスクリプト中日韓越 フォントには縦書きフォン トも含まれています。

Programs that provide the capability for vertically set CJKV text often allow you edit text vertically—this is a new experience for those not accustomed to it. The cursor is usually a horizontal bar, and moves top to bottom then right to left. Some simpler software only permits users to enter and edit text horizontally, but may print vertically. Not a particularly fine WYSIWYG situation, eh?

Non-Square Design Space

As mentioned in the previous section, there are some fonts whose design space is not square, in particular those fonts that are used for printing newspapers. It is also possible, using today's page-layout systems, to artificially scale square designs so that they fit in a non-square design space, but the results from such an operation are far from pleasing.

Table 7-4 provides an example of text that was set using a font with a square design space, using Morisawa's リュウミンL-KL (Ryumin-Light) typeface design, and one with a non-square design space, using Morisawa's 毎日新聞明朝L (MNewsM-Light) typeface design.

Table 7-4: Square and Non-Square Design Spaces

Ryumin-Light	MNewsM-Light
ぁあぃいぅうぇえ ぉおかがきぎくぐ 亜唖娃阿哀愛挨姶 逢葵茜穐悪握渥旭 ─│┌┐└├┬ ┴┼━┃┏┓	ぁあぃいぅうぇえ ぉおかがきぎくぐ 亜唖娃阿哀愛挨姶 逢葵茜穐悪握渥旭 ─│┌┐└├┬ ┴┼━┃┏┓

Newspaper publishers prefer to use these "compressed" typeface designs because they can fit more text in the same amount of space. I included the generic line-drawing characters because they illustrate that simple scaling is not used to create these designs—they are designed in a non-square design space. Morisawa's 毎日新聞明朝L (MNewsM-Light) typeface design is ideally set in a 1000×800 design space.

Although a typeface design set in a 1000×800 design space *can* be used for horizontal writing, it is not very common, and the results are not very pleasing (but may be appropriate under some circumstances). Some Korean typeface designs, in particular their hangul, are set in a 800×1000 design space, giving them a compressed effect, but intended for horizontal writing.

The "Character Grid"

An essential element in CJKV typography is the ability for the user to establish a character-based grid, if desired. Some applications, such as SMI EDICOLOR, allow the user to establish a character grid, and also allow the user to use "character" as a unit of measurement for determining line lengths and so on.

Because most CJKV characters, such as zhuyin, kana, hangul, and Chinese characters, are typically set in a uniform design space, usually square, it is natural to set characters in a character-based grid. However, the inclusion of some punctuation or Latin characters can cause this grid to break down.

Table 7-5 provides an example of a character-based grid. Note how punctuation is still allowed to dangle (see the end of the fourth line). Details about dangling punctuation can be found in the section entitled "Line Breaking and Word Wrapping," starting on page 352.

Table 7-5: Character Grid Example

普	通	の	「	D	T	P	シ	ス	テ	ム	」	は	縦	書	き	レ	イ	ア	ウ
ト	は	サ	ポ	ー	ト	し	て	い	ま	す	。	簡	単	な	ワ	ー	プ	ロ	や
テ	キ	ス	ト	エ	デ	ィ	タ	ー	は	サ	ポ	ー	ト	し	ま	せ	ん	。	縦
書	き	の	サ	ポ	ー	ト	の	為	に	は	フ	ォ	ン	ト	も	必	要	で	す。
全	て	の	ポ	ス	ト	ス	ク	リ	プ	ト	中	日	韓	越	フ	ォ	ン	ト	に
は	縦	書	き	フ	ォ	ン	ト	も	含	ま	れ	て	い	ま	す	。			

Morisawa's Fuzzy完全箱組 (*fajī kanzen hakogumi*, meaning "fuzzy perfect-box layout") software, an Adobe Illustrator plug-in, performs various calculations that enable grid-like behavior for Adobe Illustrator, but doesn't actually set up a grid as shown in Table 7-5. Its purpose is to perform the necessary calculations in order to fill the selected text box with the text that is inside (which may need to be stretched or otherwise enlarged in order to fill it).

Vertical Character Variants

While the majority of characters appear the same regardless of writing direction, some characters, due to their orientation or position within the design space, must somehow change to accommodate different writing directions.

Table 7-6 illustrates how some characters change their orientation or positioning within their design space depending on whether they are being set horizontally or vertically (these characters' design spaces have been highlighted for much easier comparison). Additionally, there are some characters that must undergo more than one transformation in order to change from the horizontal form to the vertical form. Consider the characters ～ (a wave or swung dash) and ー (long vowel mark—Japanese-specific) whose corresponding vertical forms are ≀ and ｜, respectively. Note how these two characters are rotated 90 degrees *and* flipped in order to become the vertical variant. Some font vendors often forget to flip these characters when creating their vertical variants—it is a very easy mistake to make, unfortunately.

Table 7-6: Sample Characters that Require Special Vertical Handling—Japanese

Description	Horizontal	Vertical
Ideographic period	。	︒
Ideographic comma	、	︑
Long vowel symbol	ー	｜
Opening bracket	「	﹁
Closing bracket	」	﹂
Small katakana *i*	ィ	ィ
Small katakana *o*	ォ	ォ

Table 7-7 provides a much more complete list of characters that are *known* to have vertical variants in at least one implementation, listed in the order they appear in ISO 10646-1:1993 (Unicode). Included for reference are Row-Cell values from the GB 2312-80, CNS 11643-1992, JIS X 0208:1997, and KS X 1001:1992 character set standards (for China, Taiwan, Japan, and Korea, respectively).

Table 7-7: Characters with Vertical Variants

Unicode	China		Taiwan		Japan		Korea[a]	
00B0	°	01-67	°	22-78	° → °	01-75	°	01-38
2010	‐	03-13			‐ → '	01-30	‐ → |	01-09
2015	― → |	01-10[b]	― → |	01-25	― → |	01-29[c]	― → |	01-10
2016	‖ → ═	01-12	‖ → ═	02-61	‖ → ═	01-34	‖ → ═	01-11
2018	‘	01-14	‘	01-68	‘ → ‘	01-38[c]	‘	01-14
2019	’	01-15	’	01-69	’ → ’	01-39[c]	’	01-15
201C	“	01-16	“	01-70	“ → 〃	01-40[c]	“	01-16
201D	”	01-17	”	01-71	” → 〃	01-41[c]	”	01-17

Table 7-7: Characters with Vertical Variants (continued)

Unicode	China		Taiwan		Japan		Korea[a]	
2025			‥→︰	01-13	‥→︰	01-37[c]	‥→︰	01-05
2026	…→︙	01-13[b]	…→︙	01-12	…→︙	01-36[d]	…→︙	01-06
2032	′	01-68	′	01-75	′→,	01-76	′	01-39
2033	″	01-69	″	01-73	″→„	01-77	″	01-40
3001	、→︑	01-02[b]	、	01-03	、→︑	01-02[d]	、→︑	01-02[e]
3002	。→︒	01-03[b]	。	01-04	。→︒	01-03[d]	。→︒	01-03[e]
3008	〈→︿	01-20[b]	〈→︿	01-50[f]	〈→︿	01-50[d]	〈→︿	01-20
3009	〉→﹀	01-21[b]	〉→﹀	01-51[f]	〉→﹀	01-51[d]	〉→﹀	01-21
300A	《→︽	01-22[b]	《→︽	01-46[f]	《→︽	01-52[d]	《→︽	01-22
300B	》→︾	01-23[b]	》→︾	01-47[f]	》→︾	01-53[d]	》→︾	01-23
300C	「→﹁	01-24[b]	「→﹁	01-54[f]	「→﹁	01-54[d]	「→﹁	01-24
300D	」→﹂	01-25[b]	」→﹂	01-55[f]	」→﹂	01-55[d]	」→﹂	01-25
300E	『→﹃	01-26[b]	『→﹃	01-58[f]	『→﹃	01-56[d]	『→﹃	01-26
300F	』→﹄	01-27[b]	』→﹄	01-59[f]	』→﹄	01-57[d]	』→﹄	01-27
3010	【→︻	01-30[b]	【→︻	01-42[f]	【→︻	01-58[d]	【→︻	01-28
3011	】→︼	01-31[b]	】→︼	01-43[f]	】→︼	01-59[d]	】→︼	01-29
3013	〓→‖	01-94			〓→‖	02-14	〓→‖	01-75
3014	〔→︹	01-18[b]	〔→︹	01-38[f]	〔→︹	01-44[d]	〔→︹	01-18
3015	〕→︺	01-19[b]	〕→︺	01-39[f]	〕→︺	01-45[d]	〕→︺	01-19
3016	〖→︗	01-28[b]						
3017	〗→︘	01-29[b]						
301C	〜→≀	01-11	〜→≀	02-36	〜→≀	01-33[d]	〜→≀	01-13
3041	ぁ	04-01			ぁ→ぁ	04-01[c]	ぁ	10-01
3043	ぃ	04-03			ぃ→ぃ	04-03[c]	ぃ	10-03
3045	ぅ	04-05			ぅ→ぅ	04-05[c]	ぅ	10-05
3047	ぇ	04-07			ぇ→ぇ	04-07[c]	ぇ	10-07
3049	ぉ	04-09			ぉ→ぉ	04-09[c]	ぉ	10-09
3063	っ	04-35			っ→っ	04-35[c]	っ	10-35
3083	ゃ	04-67			ゃ→ゃ	04-67[c]	ゃ	10-67
3085	ゅ	04-69			ゅ→ゅ	04-69[c]	ゅ	10-69
3087	ょ	04-71			ょ→ょ	04-71[c]	ょ	10-71
308E	ゎ	04-78			ゎ→ゎ	04-78[c]	ゎ	10-78
30A1	ァ	05-01			ァ→ァ	05-01[c]	ァ	11-01
30A3	ィ	05-03			ィ→ィ	05-03[c]	ィ	11-03
30A5	ゥ	05-05			ゥ→ゥ	05-05[c]	ゥ	11-05
30A7	ェ	05-07			ェ→ェ	05-07[c]	ェ	11-07

Table 7-7: Characters with Vertical Variants (continued)

Unicode	China		Taiwan		Japan		Korea[a]	
30A9	ォ	05-09			ォ→ォ	05-09[c]	ォ	11-09
30C3	ッ	05-35			ッ→ッ	05-35[c]	ッ	11-35
30E3	ャ	05-67			ャ→ャ	05-67[c]	ャ	11-67
30E5	ュ	05-69			ュ→ュ	05-69[c]	ュ	11-69
30E7	ョ	05-71			ョ→ョ	05-71[c]	ョ	11-71
30EE	ヮ	05-78			ヮ→ヮ	05-78[c]	ヮ	11-78
30F5	ヵ	05-85			ヵ→ヵ	05-85[c]	ヵ	11-85
30F6	ヶ	05-86			ヶ→ヶ	05-86[c]	ヶ	11-86
30FC					ー→｜	01-28[d]		
FF01	！→︕	03-01[b]	！	01-10	！	01-10	！→︕	03-01
FF08	（→︵	03-08[b]	（→︵	01-30[f]	（→︵	01-42[d]	（→︵	03-08
FF09	）→︶	03-09[b]	）→︶	01-31[f]	）→︶	01-43[d]	）→︶	03-09
FF0C	，→︐	03-12[b]	，	01-02	，→︐	01-04	，→︐	03-12
FF0E	．→︒	03-14	．	01-05[g]	．→︒	01-05	．→︒	03-14
FF1A	：→︓	03-26[b]	：	01-08	：→‥	01-07[c]	：→︓	03-26
FF1B	；→︔	03-27[b]	；	01-07	；	01-08	；→︔	03-27
FF1D	＝→‖	03-29	＝→‖	02-24	＝→‖	01-65[d]	＝→‖	03-29
FF1F	？→︖	03-31[b]	？	01-09	？	01-09	？→︖	03-31
FF3B	［→﹇	03-59			［→﹇	01-46[d]	［→﹇	03-59
FF3D	］→﹈	03-61			］→﹈	01-47[d]	］→﹈	03-61
FF3F	＿→︳	03-63[b]	＿	02-05	＿→︳	01-18	＿→︳	03-63
FF5B	｛→︷	03-91[b]	｛→︷	01-34[f]	｛→︷	01-48[d]	｛→︷	03-91
FF5C	｜	03-92	｜→－	01-24	｜→－	01-35	｜→－	03-92
FF5D	｝→︸	03-93[b]	｝→︸	01-35[f]	｝→︸	01-49[d]	｝→︸	03-93
FFE3	￣→｜	03-94	￣	02-03	￣→｜	01-17	￣→｜	03-94

[a] Some implementations of vertically set Korean text use Western-style punctuation that are simply rotated 90 degrees. This affects the vertical variants ‘ (0x2018), ’ (0x2019), “ (0x201C), ” (0x201D), ！ (0xFF01), ， (0xFF0C), ． (0xFF0E), ： (0xFF1A), ； (0xFF1B), and ？ (0xFF1F). Sometimes, the half- or proportional-width forms of these characters are simply rotated 90 degrees clockwise.

[b] Specified in GB/T 12345-90—vertical variants are encoded from 06-57 through 06-85. See Appendix F, *GB/T 12345-90 Table*, for a complete GB/T 12345-90 code table.

[c] Specified beginning in JIS X 0208:1997.

[d] Specified beginning in JIS C 6226-1978.

[e] For some implementations, the vertical form is the standard form.

[f] The vertical variant of this character is encoded exactly two code points forward. For example, the vertical variant of 01-50 is encoded at 01-52.

[g] One must wonder how ． (a period) is differentiated from a centered dot—contrast ． with ・.

Note how some characters' vertical forms, such as Unicode 0xFF1A (full-width colon), are arranged differently among CJKV locales—shifted to the upper-right corner in China and Korea, as-is in Taiwan, and rotated 90 degrees clockwise in Japan. Ligatures that are composed of Chinese characters, katakana, or hangul also have vertical variants. Although none of these ligatures are included in national character set standards, they are commonplace in vendor extensions (see Appendix C, *Vendor Character Set Standards*). Table 7-37 on page 372 provides some examples of these ligatures that require vertical variants.

As illustrated in Table 7-7, some CJKV locales use different conventions for handling vertical characters. Taiwan, for example, uses centered punctuation instead of left- or top-justified ones. Contrast 。 with 。 (an ideographic period) and 、 with 、 (an ideographic comma). This technique permits the same *glyph* to be used for both horizontal and vertical writing.

There are some differences between how vendors have defined vertical variants and how they have been defined in national character sets. Using JIS X 0208:1997 as an example, we find that the way they defined vertical variants are, by and large, the same. Apple Computer's extension to JIS X 0208:1997 (both versions, used on different vintages of MacOS-J) share the same set of 53 vertical variants. JIS X 0208:1997 also defines a set of 53 vertical variants. Yet, they are not the same. Table 7-8 lists the characters that are common and specific to these two vertical variant definitions.

Table 7-8: Common and Implementation-Specific Vertical Variants—Japanese

Common	**26 symbols**	、 。 ー — ～ … ‥ （ ） 〔 〕 ［ ］ ｛ ｝ 〈 〉 《 》 「 」 『 』 【 】 ＝
	10 small hiragana	ぁ ぃ ぅ ぇ ぉ っ ゃ ゅ ょ ゎ
	12 small katakana	ァ ィ ゥ ェ ォ ッ ャ ュ ョ ヮ ヵ ヶ
Specific	**JIS X 0208:1997**	： ‘ ’ “ ”
	MacOS-J	￣ ＿ - ‖ ｜

All versions of MacOS-J actually encode the vertical variants—very early versions of MacOS-J (KanjiTalk Version 6 and earlier) encode them 10 rows after their horizontal versions, and current versions (KanjiTalk Version 7 and later) encode them 74 rows after their horizontal versions. This effectively means that the vertical version of Row-Cell 01-02 (ideographic comma) is encoded at either 11-02 or 85-02, depending on the vintage of MacOS-J.

Other implementations, such as the character set used for the Japanese versions of Microsoft Windows (Versions 3.1J, 95J, 98J, and NT-J), define additional vertical variants, including some of those listed in the Table 7-7 on page 346. In addition to the *identical* set of 53 vertical variants currently specified by MacOS-J, the Japanese versions of Microsoft Windows specify the use of vertical versions of the following characters: comma (01-04), period (01-05), "geta" mark (02-14), and 16 katakana ligatures (not part of JIS X 0208:1997). Furthermore, it specifies that the four arrows and 30 of the 32 line-drawing elements in JIS X 0208:1997 be rearranged as shown in Table 7-9 (ISO 10646-1:1993 codes shown in parentheses).

Table 7-9: Rearranging Horizontal Characters for Vertical Use

	Horizontal	Vertical
02-10 (2192)	→	↓
02-11 (2190)	←	↑
02-12 (2191)	↑	→
02-13 (2193)	↓	←
08-01 (2500)	─	│
08-02 (2502)	│	─
08-03 (250C)	┌	┐
08-04 (2510)	┐	┘
08-05 (2518)	┘	└
08-06 (2514)	└	┌
08-07 (251C)	├	┬
08-08 (252C)	┬	┤
08-09 (2524)	┤	┴
08-10 (2534)	┴	├
08-12 (2501)	━	┃
08-13 (2503)	┃	━
08-14 (250F)	┏	┓
08-15 (2513)	┓	┛
08-16 (251B)	┛	┗
08-17 (2517)	┗	┏
08-18 (2523)	┣	┳
08-19 (2533)	┳	┫
08-20 (252B)	┫	┻
08-21 (253B)	┻	┣
08-23 (2520)	┠	┯
08-24 (252F)	┯	┨
08-25 (2528)	┨	┷
08-26 (2537)	┷	┠
08-27 (253F)	┿	╂
08-28 (251D)	┝	┰
08-29 (2530)	┰	┥

Table 7-9: Rearranging Horizontal Characters for Vertical Use (continued)

	Horizontal	Vertical
08-30 (2525)	┥	┸
08-31 (2538)	┸	┝
08-32 (2542)	╂	┿

Note that all of the vertical forms are a result of 90-degree clockwise rotation. The line-drawing elements 08-11 (┼) and 08-22 (╋) do not require rearranging for vertical use because the same form results from 90-degree clockwise rotation (ISO 10646-1:1993 0x253C and 0x254B, respectively).

Vertically Set Latin Text

While the transformation from horizontal to vertical layout is somewhat straightforward for most CJKV characters, and involves mainly punctuation and symbols (and small kana in the case of Japanese), handling Latin text in vertical writing mode requires special considerations and has more than one option. As they say about Perl: TIMTOWTDI.*

PostScript CJKV fonts, by default, treat Latin characters the same as everything else when it comes to vertical writing mode—their orientation remains the same. The preferred way to vertically set Latin text, however, involves 90-degree clockwise rotation.

The following are the ways in which Latin characters can be set vertically, in order of perceived preference:

- Rotated 90 degrees clockwise
- Converted to full-width forms then set as-is—most Latin characters used in CJKV text are half- or proportional-width
- Set together horizontally in the same *cell* using half- or third-width forms if they consist of only two or three characters, respectively—this is sometimes referred to as *tatechuyoko* (縦中横 *tatechūyoko*) in Japanese, which means "horizontal in vertical"†
- Set *as-is*—this is rarely desirable unless you are writing a document that needs to illustrate the various ways to set Latin text vertically‡

* The classic Perl slogan: *There Is More Than One Way To Do It*.

† Adobe Illustrator (Version 8.0 or greater), Founder FIT, Macromedia FreeHand, and QuarkXPress use this term, but SMI EDICOLOR uses 連文字 (*ren moji*). Adobe Illustrator Version 7.0 used 組み文字 (*kumi moji*).

‡ Like this book, or any book for that matter that includes information about CJKV typography. It is also the default way in which PostScript images such characters.

Table 7-10 illustrates these four methods for setting Latin text vertically using the sample Japanese text “これはJPテキストだ” (meaning “This is JP text”). It is only the two uppercase Latin characters “JP” that change in the four examples.

Table 7-10: Vertically Set Latin Text

Rotated 90 Degrees Clockwise	Full-Width	Horizontal in Vertical	As-Is
これはJPテキストだ	これはＪＰテキストだ	これはJPテキストだ	これはJPテキストだ

As I wrote earlier, you will find that most users will prefer these methods in the order presented in Table 7-10. Exactly which one is preferable may depend on the length of the embedded Latin text. Some applications, by default, rotate these characters 90 degrees clockwise. Any other setting may require explicit direction from the user.

Line Breaking and Word Wrapping

Most CJKV text requires special handling for the beginning and ends of lines, which is commonly called *line breaking*, *word wrapping*, or sometimes *hyphenation*. In Japanese, this is known as 禁則処理 (*kinsoku shori*), which literally means “prohibited [character] processing.” There are some characters, usually punctuation and enclosing characters, that should not begin a new line, and likewise, there are characters that should not terminate a line. There are similar rules in English, but they are much more important for CJKV text because there are no spaces between words—punctuation marks are treated like any other character.*

* Korean and any transliterated CJKV text are considered to be exceptions to this general rule—spaces are used to delimit words.

Table 7-11 lists the characters that should not begin a new line. These include characters such as punctuation marks, closing quotes, closing bracket-like characters, small kana (Japanese-specific), and some symbols. The characters in the first rank have priority in processing, at least in Japanese. Some software handles only some ranks. From a semantic or syntactic point of view, most of these characters act as modifiers for or appear immediately after text.

Table 7-11: Characters Prohibited from Beginning Lines

Rank	Characters
1	、 。 ， ． ： ； ？ ！ ’ ” ） 〕 ］ ｝ 〉 》 」 』 】
2[a]	々ーぁぃぅぇぉっゃゅょゎァィゥェォッャュョヮヵヶ
3	゛ ゜ ヽ ヾ ゝ ゞ — ‐ ° ′ ″ ℃ ℉ ¢ ％ ‰

[a] Of course, most of the characters in this rank—the kana—are Japanese-specific.

Table 7-12 lists the characters that should not terminate a line. These are basically opening quotes, opening bracket-like characters, and some symbols—they are ranked into two groups. From a syntactic point of view, most of these characters appear immediately before text that they modify.

Table 7-12: Characters Prohibited from Terminating Lines

Rank	Characters
1	‘ “ （ 〔 ［ ｛ 〈 《 「 『 【
2	￥ ＄ ￡ ＠ § 〒 ＃

Of course, vertical variants of characters in Tables 7-11 and 7-12 are to be handled accordingly. Also, whether a character is full-width or not should not should not affect its treatment during line breaking—the characters illustrated in Tables 7-11 and 7-12 have been rendered as full-width, but the non–full-width counterparts, whether they are half-width or proportional, require the same treatment.

There are three fundamental methods used to line-break or word-wrap CJKV text. Which one you use often depends upon the program you are using, and most high-end line-layout–capable software allows the user to choose which style to use in any particular situation. Adobe FrameMaker, for example, will automatically use wrap-up or wrap-down line breaking in order to maintain optimal spacing as the user dictated in the paragraph designer.

The first line breaking method is known as *wrap-up* (in Japanese, 追い込み禁則処理 *oikomi kinsoku shori*). Wrap-up line breaking works by moving characters that are prohibited from beginning a new line back up to the end of the previous line.

It can also shift up a character from the following line such that characters that are prohibited from terminating a line do not. Table 7-13 provides two example texts before any line breaking is applied.

Table 7-13: Before Line Breaking

　□□□□□□□□□□□「□□□□□□□」□□□□□□□□□□□□□□□□
□□□□□□□□□□□、□□□□□□□□。

　□□□□□□□□□□□□□□□□□□□□□□□□□「□□□□□□□」、「
□□□□□□□」□□□□□□□□□□□・□□□□□□□□□□□、□□□□□□
□□□□□□□□□□□。

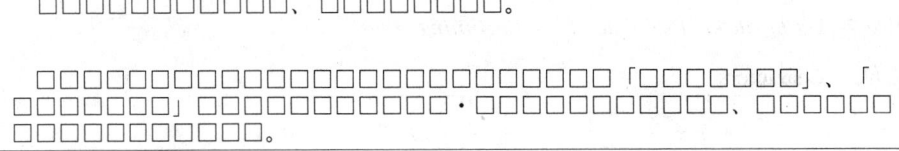

Table 7-14 illustrates what happens after wrap-up line breaking is applied to the two texts in Table 7-13.

Table 7-14: After Wrap-Up Line Breaking

　□□□□□□□□□□□「□□□□□□□」□□□□□□□□□□□□□□□□、
□□□□□□□□□□□、□□□□□□□□。

　□□□□□□□□□□□□□□□□□□□□□□□□□「□□□□□□□」、「□
□□□□□□」□□□□□□□□□□□・□□□□□□□□□□□、□□□□□□□
□□□□□□□□□□。

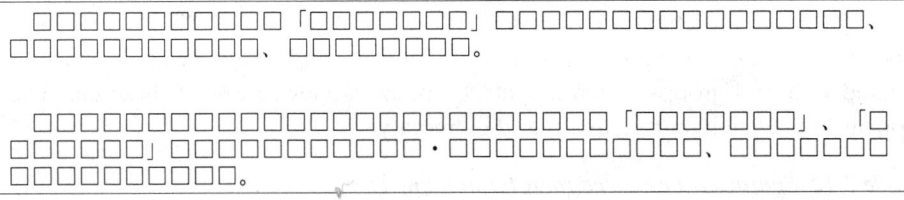

The first text in Table 7-14 involved an ideographic comma shifting up to the end of the previous line, and the second text involved shifting up a non-wrapping character.

A second line breaking method is called *wrap-down* (in Japanese, 追い出し禁則処理 *oidashi kinsoku shori*). Wrap-down line breaking works by forcing characters that are prohibited from terminating a line to shift down to the next line. It is also possible for a character to shift down to the next line so that it precedes a character that is prohibited from beginning a line. Table 7-15 illustrates wrap-down line breaking being applied to the texts from Table 7-13.

Table 7-15: After Wrap-Down Line Breaking

　□□□□□□□□□□□「□□□□□□□」□□□□□□□□□□□□□□□
□、□□□□□□□□□□□、□□□□□□□□。

　□□□□□□□□□□□□□□□□□□□□□□□□□「□□□□□□□」、
「□□□□□□□」□□□□□□□□□□□・□□□□□□□□□□□、□□□□□□
□□□□□□□□□□□。

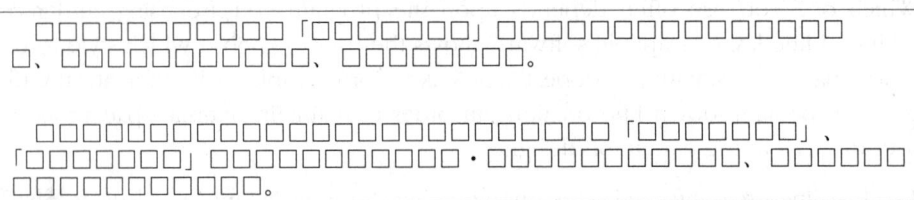

Note how wrap-down line breaking can result in lines that appear to prematurely end. While the characters used in the example text provided in Tables 7-13

through 7-15 are set using equal set widths (full-width), other aspects of typography, specifically spacing and alternate metrics, can help to adjust the result.

A third line breaking technique is called *dangling* or *hanging punctuation* (in Japanese, ぶら下がり禁則処理 *burasagari kinsoku shori*). This method employs a strategy whereby a character—almost always punctuation, such as a period or comma (Western or ideographic)—is left hanging (or dangling) on the right margin.* These characters appear to hang or dangle off the end of the line, hence this method's name. Some implementations of this line breaking method can dangle more than one character. Dangling punctuation is often provided as an option for wrap-up line breaking. Table 7-16 provides text in a state before dangling punctuation is applied. Note how the right side of the text block is flush.

Table 7-16: Before Dangling Punctuation

□□□□□□□□□□「□□□□□□□」、「□□□□□□□」□□□□□□□
、□□□・□□□□□□□□□□□、□□□□□□□□□□□□□□□□□。□□
□□□□□□□□「□□□□□□□」□□□□□□□□□□□□□□□□、□□□
□□□□□□□、□□□□□□□□。□□□□□□□□□□□□□□□□□□□□
□□□□□□□□□□、□□□□□□□□□□□、□□□□□□□□。

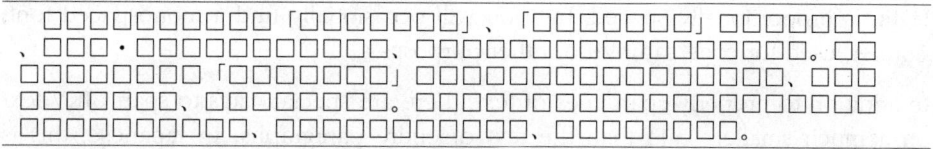

Table 7-17 illustrates the result of applying dangling punctuation to the text in Table 7-16.

Table 7-17: After Dangling Punctuation

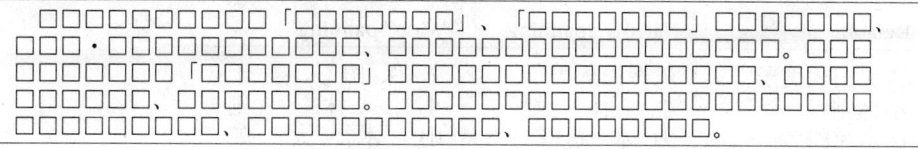

□□□□□□□□□□「□□□□□□□」、「□□□□□□□」□□□□□□□、
□□□・□□□□□□□□□□□、□□□□□□□□□□□□□□□□□。□□□
□□□□□□□「□□□□□□□」□□□□□□□□□□□□□□□□、□□□□
□□□□□□、□□□□□□□□。□□□□□□□□□□□□□□□□□□□□□
□□□□□□□□□、□□□□□□□□□□□、□□□□□□□□。

Proper application of line breaking is absolutely crucial if a program is to succeed in the market. Some developers have implemented all the line breaking methods described above, and permit the user to select which one or ones to use.

After CJKV text has been properly line-broken using one or more of the methods described previously, there still remains the issue of how to right-justify (or bottom-justify if in vertical writing mode) the text in case a ragged edge is not desired. This is the topic of the section entitled "Line Length Issues," starting on page 365.

* Unjustified text is considered to have a *ragged* right side.

Character Spanning

In the West, we usually think of tabs in terms of the white space that serves as an alternate to the use of spaces.* Common tabs include left, right, centered, and decimal. A spanning tab is unique in that it adjusts the spacing between every character that appears before it.

Most CJKV words are strung together with no intervening spaces, so adjusting the inter-character spacing becomes mandatory. Under most implementations, CJKV characters—kana, hangul, and Chinese characters—have equal set widths (that is, they are considered full-width), which effectively means that every character occupies the same amount of typographic space.† Latin characters are typically spaced proportionally, meaning that the widths of characters differ depending on their shape and typeface design. The Latin typeface used in this book, ITC Garamond Light, is proportionally spaced, but you will occasionally find a monospaced font, Courier, used for code samples or other purposes.

In addition to properly span lines of text, there are special ways to span CJKV text on a much smaller scale than the text of entire paragraphs. In Japanese, this is known as 均等割 (*kintō wari*) or 均等割付 (*kintō waritsuke*). This technique is most often used when listing names. Table 7-18 provides an example of a list of Japanese names justified in various ways.

Table 7-18: Examples of Character Spanning

Default	Narrow Spanning	Wide Spanning
久保田久美子	久保田久美子	久 保 田 久 美 子
小林剣	小　林　剣	小　　林　　剣
山本太郎	山 本 太 郎	山　本　太　郎
泉均	泉　　　均	泉　　　　　均
藤本みどり	藤 本 み ど り	藤　本　み　ど　り

Note how the justification takes place within units such as small text blocks, and that all the characters are adjusted such that they line up equally on both sides. You can think of this as text-level justification as opposed to the usual page-level justification. Nisus Writer, a CJKV-capable word processor for MacOS, has provided this type of text-level justification for quite some time through the use of a special type of tab stop.

* The golden rule is that you should use a tab whenever you feel the urge to type more than one space.

† It is true that kana and a handful of Chinese characters benefit from proportional metrics, and typesetting systems are moving in that direction. Proprietary typesetting systems already have this capability.

Alternate Metrics

Most users of CJKV-capable word processors and other text processing applications are all too familiar with the concept of *full-width* characters. You may have experienced a feeling of being trapped in the mindset that CJKV-specific characters—zhuyin, kana, hangul, and Chinese characters—must *always* be set using equal set widths. Not always true. However, bear in mind that some CJKV locales, such as China and Taiwan, still follow the convention of setting *all* characters on a very rigid grid, except perhaps punctuation and bracket-like symbols.

A new twist to desktop CJKV type technology is the ability to supplement CJKV fonts with alternate metrics—alternate in the sense that the default metrics are still preserved as full-width, but that the user can now choose alternate widths. Alternate metrics can encompass character classes such as punctuation, symbols, kana, and even Chinese characters. Some fonts have implemented alternate metrics through additional font instances that appear in applications' font menus—this means that two fonts now appear in applications' font menus where before there was only one. One is typically the fixed-width font, and the other is the one with half-width and proportional metrics. An example of this can be found when exploring Microsoft's Windows 95J (or 98J or NT-J) operating system. It includes two basic fonts, MS明朝 (*MS minchō*) and MSゴシック (*MS goshikku*). The versions of these fonts that include alternate metrics—proportional kana, half-width symbols and punctuation, and condensed katakana—are called MS P明朝 (*MS P minchō*) and MS Pゴシック (*MS P goshikku*), respectively. The "P" presumably stands for "proportional."

The examples that I provide in the following sections will clearly illustrate the use of alternate metrics through contrast with the default (full-width) metrics. And, *all* of these examples use the alternate metrics that are built into the commercially available versions of the fonts—sfnt-wrapped CIDFonts for MacOS. Some MacOS QuickDraw GX fonts and some Microsoft Windows TrueType Open fonts also provide alternate metrics.

Applications, such as Adobe Illustrator and Adobe FrameMaker, refer to alternate or proportional metrics as *tsume* (詰め *tsume*), which is a Japanese word meaning "squeezing" or "stuffing." In almost all cases, alternate metrics result in either proportional or half-width metrics.

Half-Width Symbols and Punctuation

It turns out that most punctuation and enclosing (bracket-like) characters do not completely fill a full-width cell—they almost always occupy less than half of the cell, leaving a lot of unused whitespace on one side, or on all sides.

Table 7-19 lists six classes of traditionally full-width characters that can be set with half-width alternate metrics.

Table 7-19: Half-Width Symbols and Punctuation Classes

Half-Width Classes[a]	Example Characters
50 percent left	（〔［｛〈《「『【‘“
50 percent right	、。，．）〕］｝〉》」』】’”
50 percent top[b]	︵︹﹇︷︿︽﹁﹃︻ ‘ “
50 percent bottom[b]	︑︒，．︶︺﹈︸﹀︾﹂﹄︼ ’ ”
25 percent left and right	：；！
25 percent all sides	・

[a] The percentages listed in this column refer to the amount of empty space that is trimmed from the full-width design space in order to end up with half-width metrics.

[b] These are vertical variants of characters two rows above—note that some do not have vertical variants.

Note how some characters are specific to vertical writing, but that some characters, such as ・ (centered dot), are the same regardless of writing direction.

Table 7-20 provides an example of Japanese text that uses half-width symbols and punctuation in horizontal writing mode. Whether all of these modes are possible depends on the line-layout software you are using.

Table 7-20: Full-Width Versus Half-Width Symbols and Punctuation—Horizontal

Full-Width	あっ。剣、劍、及び「ふぐ・河豚本」だ。
Half-Width	あっ。剣、劍、及び「ふぐ・河豚本」だ。
Combination[a]	あっ。剣、劍、及び「ふぐ・河豚本」だ。

[a] The ideographic periods and commas are half-width, but the brackets are full-width.

As a side note, if the Japanese line-layout rules set forth in JIS X 4051-1995 were to be applied together with half-width metrics for the symbols and punctuation, the example Japanese text in Table 7-20 would look identical to the full-width example.

Table 7-21 provides the same example of Japanese text as found in Table 7-20, but this time in vertical writing mode.

According to the JIS X 4051-1995 standard, all of these characters, by default, should use half-width metrics. But, when they come into contact with other char-

Table 7-21: Full-Width Versus Half-Width Symbols and Punctuation—Vertical

Full-Width	Half-Width
あっ。剣、剣、及び「ふぐ・河豚本」だ。	あっ。剣、剣、及び「ふぐ・河豚本」だ。

acter classes, such as kana or kanji, they should be given additional space (usually a half-width space, which in a way makes them full-width again). These characters themselves are separated into two classes: those that are considered "opening" (see the first line of characters in Table 7-19), and those that are considered "closing" (see the second line of characters in Table 7-19).

If a closing character is immediately followed by an opening character—such as in the text "字典」「新漢"—then a half-width space is inserted after the closing character, effectively making the closing character full-width and the opening character half-width. However, if two closing or opening characters come together—such as in the text "とは秘密）、及び"—there is no additional space inserted. Table 7-22 illustrates these same two texts set horizontally with and without the application of these rules. Morisawa's リュウミンL-KL (Ryumin-Light) typeface is used for the example.

Table 7-22: The Application of Spacing Rules

No Rules	字典」　「新漢
With Rules	字典」「新漢

Table 7-22: The Application of Spacing Rules (continued)

No Rules	とは秘密）　、及び
With Rules	とは秘密）、及び

The JIS X 4051-1995 standard includes much more detailed information about such spacing rules.

Proportional Symbols and Punctuation

Some of the same punctuation and symbols listed in the previous section (see Table 7-19 on page 358) can also be set with proportional widths—as opposed to fixed half-width metrics. In fact, there are some characters that must use proportional widths because their design is too large for half-width metrics. A prime example is the full-width Latin characters that are typical of all CJKV fonts.

Table 7-23 illustrates the word "Typography" set horizontally using the full-width Latin characters of Morisawa's リュウミンL-KL (Ryumin-Light) typeface.

Table 7-23: Full-Width and Proportional Latin Characters—Horizontal

Full-Width	Ｔｙｐｏｇｒａｐｈｙ
Proportional	Typography

Table 7-24 illustrates the same word as Table 7-23 using the same typeface design, but this time set vertically.

There are, of course, other characters that require proportional rather than half-width metrics. Depending on the typeface design, they *may* include full-width versions of the question mark (？) and kana iteration marks (ヽ, ヾ, ゝ, and ゞ).

Proportional Kana

While most Japanese users are accustomed to using full-width kana in their documents, those who have been using proprietary typesetting equipment know that most kana designs are inherently conducive to being set with proportional widths.

Table 7-25 illustrates a short Japanese sentence, using both full-width and alternate (proportional, in this case) metrics for the kana. TypeBank's タイプバンク明朝M (TypeBankM-m) is used in this example.

Table 7-24: Full-Width and Proportional Latin Characters—Vertical

Full-Width	Proportional
Typography	Typography

Table 7-25: Full-Width and Proportional Kana

Full-Width	きょう、本を買った。
Proportional	きょう、本を買った。

Note how the small kana—the characters ょ and っ in this example—have undergone the most drastic reduction in set width, which results in improved readability. While this is typical for standard kana designs, it is by no means a steadfast rule.

Table 7-26 illustrates the same Japanese sentence, but this time using an alternate kana design, TypeBank's TB良寛MM (TBRyokanM-M) combined with TypeBank's タイプバンク明朝M (TypeBankM-m) for the kanji.

Table 7-26: Full-Width and Proportional Kana—Alternate Kana

Full-Width	きょう、本を買った。
Proportional	きょう、本を買った。

Note how the alternate kana design illustrated in Table 7-26 results in a more drastic difference in metrics between full-width and proportional. Even the standard kana (that is, not only the small kana) have undergone a drastic reduction in set width.

Table 7-27 includes the same examples as provided in Tables 7-25 on page 361 and 7-26, but set vertically. This clearly demonstrates that proportional metrics also benefit kana when set vertically.

Table 7-27: Full-Width and Proportional Kana—Vertical

Full-Width	Proportional	Full-Width	Proportional
きょう、本を買った。	きょう、本を買った。	きょう、本を買った。	きょう、本を買った。

Note how the alternate kana design provides less of a contrast than with the horizontally set example.

Proportional Chinese Characters

It is a generally accepted notion that Chinese characters fit within a square design space. While this notion is true most of the time, there are, of course, exceptions.

Table 7-28 illustrates a short string of Chinese characters, 中日韓越 ("CJKV"), set horizontally. Note how the second character, 日 (the "J" of "CJKV"), is no longer full-width when proportional metrics are applied. Morisawa's リュウミンL-KL (Ryumin-Light) is used for the example.

Table 7-28: Full-Width and Proportional Chinese Characters—Horizontal

Full-Width	中日韓越
Proportional	中日韓越

Similarly, there are other Chinese characters whose shapes benefit from proportional metrics when set vertically. Table 7-29 illustrates a short Chinese-character string, 第一勧業 (*daiichi kangyō*, the name of a famous Japanese bank), set vertically. Note how the second character, 一 (*ichi*, meaning "one"), has undergone a drastic reduction in overall set width. Again, Morisawa's リュウミンL-KL (Ryumin-Light) typeface design is used for the example.

Table 7-29: Full-Width and Proportional Chinese Characters—Vertical

Full-Width	Proportional
第	第
一	一
勧	勧
業	業

Believe it or not, there are instances when applying proportional metrics to Chinese characters does more harm than good. That is when kerning comes to the rescue...

Kerning

While alternate metrics provide a way to escape from the trap or mindset of using only full-width characters, it sometimes introduces new problems. Luckily, such problems are solved through the use of *kerning*, which is the process of adjusting inter-character spacing according to context. The context in the case of kerning happens to be the proximity of two characters. These are called *kerning pairs*. In Western typography using Latin characters, the most common kerning pairs are in the uppercase set. "A" and "V" (such as in the pair-kerned instance "JAVA"—"JAVA" is not a pair-kerned instance) represent one kerning pair—when set together they appear to be too far apart, and are thus kerned.

Kerning, like alternate metrics, is a typeface-dependent attribute. This means that the actual kerning values change depending on the typeface design.

Table 7-30 illustrates a short kana phrase, どうして (*dōshite*, meaning "why"), set using full-width and proportional metrics with Morisawa's リュウミンL-KL (Ryumin-Light). When this high-frequency phrase is set using proportional metrics, the inter-character spacing between し (*shi*) and て (*te*) appears to be too great. This problem is addressed through the use of proper kerning.

Table 7-30: Kerning Kana Characters

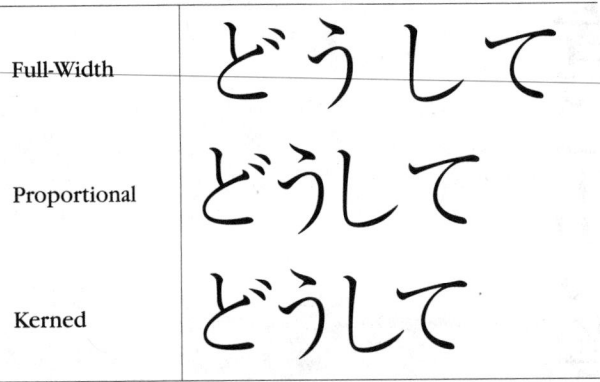

Full-Width	どうして
Proportional	どうして
Kerned	どうして

There are also times when *negative kerning* (increase inter-character spacing) is required for CJKV text. Take, for instance, 一二 ("one" and "two"), when set vertically. Both of these characters are candidates for proportional metrics. However, if these two characters are in proximity, they require negative kerning, otherwise they *may* resemble 三 ("three") or may simply look bad, depending on the typeface design. Table 7-31 illustrates this phenomenon using kanji from Morisawa's リュウミンL-KL (Ryumin-Light).

As you can see, the introduction of alternate metrics, along with proper kerning, can make a world of difference in the overall appearance and quality of CJKV documents.

Morisawa & Company* has developed an Adobe Illustrator plug-in called Fuzzyカーニング (*fajī kāningu*, meaning "Fuzzy Kerning") that provides the ability to kern Japanese text. They have also developed a QuarkXPress XTension (plug-in) called Dr.カーニング ("Dr. Kerning"). Demo versions of both are available from Morisawa's web site.

* *http://www.morisawa.co.jp/*

Table 7-31: Kerning Chinese Characters

Full-Width	Proportional	Kerned
元	元	元
年	年	年
二	二	二
月	月	月

Line Length Issues

Once you begin applying alternate metrics or adjusting other spacing aspects of CJKV text, you are then left with the problem of how to calculate line length to perform common typographic tasks, such as right justification. When dealing with text that is set on a rigid grid, such as Chinese, calculating line length becomes a bit more trivial.

The inclusion of Latin text—even one character—is the typical culprit for causing line-length calculation problems in CJKV text. Another culprit is the application of line-breaking rules—adjusting text so that certain characters do not begin or terminate lines. The following sections provide methods for adjusting spacing so that right justification can be performed.

Manipulating Symbol and Punctuation Metrics

As described earlier in this chapter, many symbols and most punctuation marks have forms that lend themselves to being set with half-width or proportional metrics. One of the first methods for adjusting spacing is to apply alternate metrics to one or more symbols or punctuation marks. The preference is usually to apply such metrics to punctuation marks, then symbols.

Table 7-32 illustrates an example three-line text that requires the use of half-width symbols or punctuation marks due to the application of line breaking.

Table 7-32: Adjusting Symbol and Punctuation Mark Metrics

□□□□□□□□□□□□、□□□□□□□□、□□□□□□□□□□□□□□□□□□ □□□「□□□□□□□□□□□」□□□□□□□□□□□□□□。□□□□□□□□□ 「□□□□□□」□□□□□□□□□□、□□□□□□□□□□□□□□□□□□□□□□。
□□□□□□□□□□□□、□□□□□□□□、□□□□□□□□□□□□□□□□□□□ □□「□□□□□□□□□□□」□□□□□□□□□□□□□□。□□□□□□□□□「□ □□□□□」□□□□□□□□□□、□□□□□□□□□□□□□□□□□□□□□□。

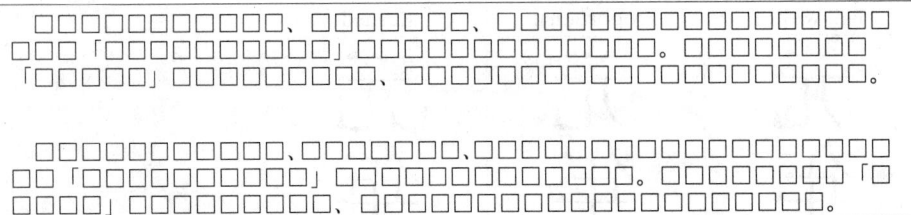

The two ideographic commas in the first line are converted to half-width forms, which has the side-effect of reversing the effect of line breaking by allowing another character to terminate the second line instead of the opening bracket.

Manipulating Inter-Character Spacing

Texts that include only full-width characters with a few punctuation, and symbols thrown in can be set fully justified by manipulating the spacing of punctuation and symbols—as illustrated in the previous section. However, when *any* proportional characters come into play, inter-character spacing often needs to be adjusted in order to achieve right-justification.

Table 7-33 illustrates an example of inter-character spacing being used to help right-justify text that includes characters with proportional widths.

Table 7-33: Adjusting Inter-Character Spacing

Japan、 California、 □□□ Wisconsin □□□□□□□□□□□□□□□□□□□□ □□「□□□□□□□□□□」□□□□□□□□□□□□□。□□□□□□「□□□□□ □□□」□□□□□□□□□□、□□□□□□□□□□□□□□□□□□□□□。
Japan、 California、 □□□ Wisconsin □□□□□□□□□□□□□□□□□□□□ □□「□□□□□□□□□□」□□□□□□□□□□□□□。□□□□□□「□□□□□ □□□」□□□□□□□□□□、□□□□□□□□□□□□□□□□□□□□□。

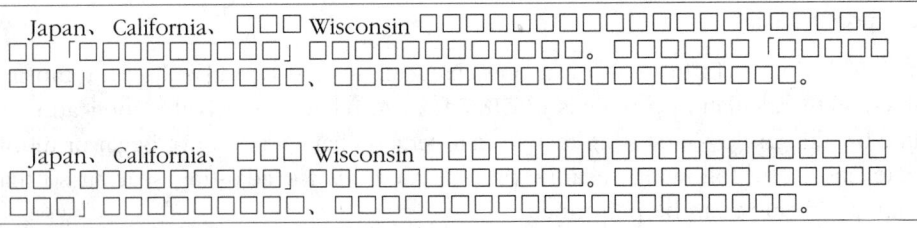

Note how the inter-character spacing of the characters in the first line of the text is adjusted so that it can be properly right-justified.

Multilingual Text

Mixing Latin and CJKV characters together in a single document—multilingual text—requires that you consider several typographic issues, such as the Latin base line, the spacing between Latin and CJKV characters, and selecting appropriate typeface designs. Let us explore each of these issues in the following sections.

Latin Baseline Adjustment

CJKV-specific characters, such as zhuyin, kana, hangul, and Chinese characters, do not rest on a baseline as is the case for Latin characters—they are, instead, optically centered within the character cell.* This creates the first obstacle you will encounter when mixing Latin and CJKV text.

All of Adobe Systems' CJKV fonts include CJKV-specific characters that are set in a 1000-unit design space that extends from the coordinates 0,–120 to 1000,880. That is, a 1000×1000 cell that is lowered 120 units in relation to the baseline at Y coordinate 0. Figure 7-1 illustrates this design space using characters from Changzhou Sinotype's 华文宋体 (STSong-Light) typeface.

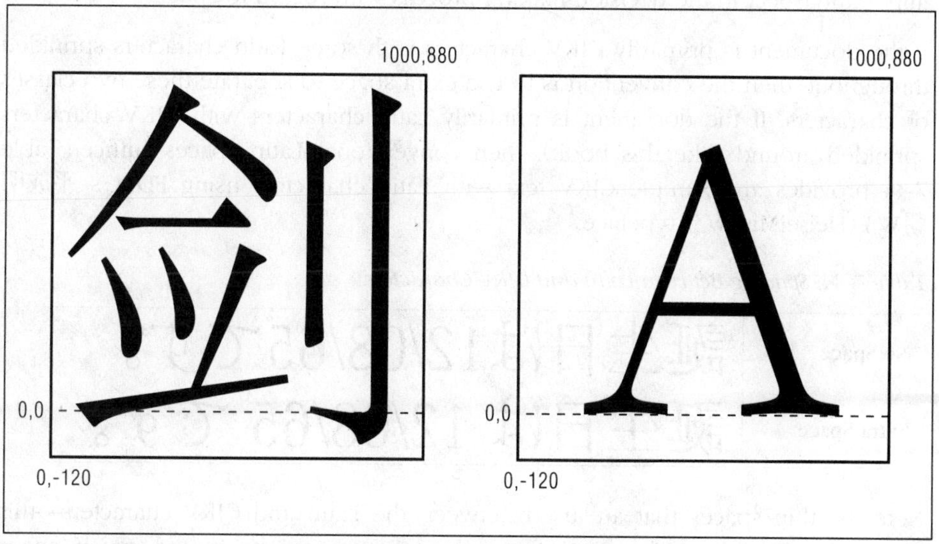

Figure 7-1: 1000×1000 character design space

Note how the full-width Latin character "A" is resting comfortably on the baseline located at Y coordinate 0, but the hanzi 剑 *(jiàn)* is optically centered within the entire 1000×1000 cell without regard to the baseline at Y coordinate 0.

Other type foundries, however, often use a different design space for CJKV-specific characters. 0,–200 to 1000,800 is widely used by many CJKV type foundries, such as Changzhou SinoType, Seoul Systems, SoftMagic, and Yoon Design Institute. I have also encountered font data that use the following design spaces:

- 0,–110 to 1000,890 (Monotype)
- 0,–130 to 1000,870 (EulHae)

* Some CJKV-specific characters, such as the small number of small kana used in Japanese, are exceptions to this general rule.

- 0,–160 to 1000,840 (Fontworks)
- 0,–166 to 1000,834 (Hanyang Systems)

Adobe FrameMaker, among other high-end page-layout applications, allows the user to adjust the baseline and size ratios in order to better adapt Latin fonts for use with CJKV characters.

Spacing Latin and CJKV Characters

Exactly how you space Latin and CJKV characters that are in proximity—that is, adjacent—depends on the nature of the document that you are creating. Different types of documents have different quantities of these characters, and this is an important aspect in the decision-making process with regard to spacing.

If the document is primarily CJKV characters with some Latin characters sprinkled throughout, then the convention is to use extra space to separate these two classes of characters. If the document is primarily Latin characters with CJKV characters sprinkled around (like this book), then conventional Latin spaces suffice. Table 7-34 provides an example CJKV text with Latin characters using FDPC's 平成明朝W3 (HeiseiMin-W3) typeface.

Table 7-34: Spacing Between Latin and CJKV Characters

No Space	誕生日は12/08/65です。
Extra Space	誕生日は 12/08/65 です。

Note the thin spaces that are used between the Latin and CJKV characters—this improves readability. The use of *standard* spaces results in too much space between these two character classes. Most CJKV-capable page-layout applications either provide the ability to use thin spaces (which is not desirable because it becomes a manual operation) or else the ability to automatically insert extra space when appropriate (based on line-layout rules).

According to the JIS X 4051-1995 standard, there should be a quarter-width space between Latin and CJKV characters, but sophisticated line-layout applications allow the user to adjust this value as necessary. The bottom line is that *some* space should be used to separate Latin and CJKV characters. While the JIS X 4051-1995 standard provides guidance in this regard, you are free to use whatever amount of space you see fit.

Mixing Latin and CJKV Typeface Designs

Every CJKV font, perhaps with the exception of Vietnamese, comes with a minimally functional set of Latin characters, usually encoded in the one-byte range. On MacOS, these Latin characters are almost always proportional-width. Although these Latin characters look well with the rest of the font, there are times when a different Latin font needs to be used. This book, for example, uses a variety of CJKV fonts for printing CJKV text, but the Latin portion is consistently the same: ITC Garamond (Light, Light Italic, Book, and Book Italic). I have even developed *edited* (that is, modified or hacked) versions of ITC Garamond to accommodate certain typographic aspects of this book, such as the macroned vowels used for transliterated Japanese text.

Okay, so when do the built-in Latin characters suffice, and when is a separate Latin font required? It depends on the nature of the text. Documents that consist primarily of CJKV characters with a few Latin characters sprinkled throughout typically do not require the "typographically correct" characters that are typically found in Latin fonts. These includes smart (or curly) quotes, the various dashes, and ligatures. CJKV fonts either have these characters available—usually as full-width forms—or else have no need for them. This is why the built-in Latin characters of CJKV fonts usually suffice for these types of documents. Text that is composed primarily of Latin characters requires Latin fonts in order to provide typographically pleasing results.

Another consideration is whether cross-platform compatibility is an issue. Many CJKV-capable applications these days are available for multiple operating systems. Adobe FrameMaker, for example, is available for MacOS, Unix, and Windows. However, the built-in Latin characters of most CJKV fonts sometimes have different metrics depending on the operating system on which they are installed. PostScript Japanese fonts installed onto MacOS typically use proportional-width Latin characters, but the same fonts installed onto Windows typically use half-width Latin characters. Simply selecting an independent Latin font for Latin characters, besides providing access to typographically correct characters (such as the various dashes, smart quotes, and Latin ligatures), will ensure cross-platform compatibility. This book, for example, is set in ITC Garamond Light, an independent Latin font. The CJKV characters come from a variety of CJKV fonts, as listed in this book's colophon.

Vietnamese typeface issues

A complete Vietnamese font, one that includes both Latin and Chinese characters, is an example that brings together the complexities from both worlds of typography. While readers of this book should now be well aware of the issues that surround the use of Chinese characters in typography, Latin characters used in

Vietnamese, called Quốc ngữ, require extensive use of diacritic marks for base characters and tones. Chinese, Japanese, and Korean text, when transliterated, requires diacritic marks to indicate vowel length, tone, or other phonetic attribute. However, these transliteration systems are not considered the primary orthography for these locales, so their fonts do not require these additional characters. Vietnamese fonts, on the other hand, require these additional characters.

It is safe to say that the ideal environment for a complete Vietnamese font is Unicode, where all necessary characters are easily available. Table 7-35 illustrates lowercase simple vowels, including y, along with the required permutations for Vietnamese Quốc ngữ.

Table 7-35: Simple Vowels and Their Quốc Ngữ Permutations—Lowercase

Simple Vowel	Required Quốc Ngữ Permutations
a	à ả ã á ạ ă ằ ẳ ẵ ắ ặ â ầ ẩ ẫ ấ ậ
e	è ẻ ẽ é ẹ ê ề ể ễ ế ệ
i	ì ỉ ĩ í ị
o	ò ỏ õ ó ọ ô ồ ổ ỗ ố ộ ơ ờ ở ỡ ớ ợ
u	ù ủ ũ ú ụ ư ừ ử ữ ứ ự
y	ỳ ỷ ỹ ý ỵ

That's right, there are anywhere from five to seventeen required permutations for a single unadorned vowel.

Glyph Substitution

A very useful typographic trick is called *glyph substitution*, which is the act of substituting one form of a character for another. There are four basic types of glyph substitution that benefit CJKV fonts:

- Vertical substitution
- Variant substitution
- Ligature construction
- Ligature decomposition

Vertical substitution is a form of glyph substitution that takes effect when in vertical writing mode. It is considered something that is invoked automatically when a document is being set in vertical mode. The remaining types of glyph substitution are explicitly invoked by the user.

Character Variants

When considering the various types of characters found in CJKV text, one of the most common types of substitution involves the ability to select different forms of a character, such as traditional, simplified, or variant (异体字/異體字 *yìtǐzì* in Chinese, 異体字 *itaiji* in Japanese, and 이체자/異體字 *iceja* in Korean) forms. Some variants can be defined more specifically, such as JIS78 (JIS C 6226-1978) for Japanese. And, some variants do not involve Chinese characters at all, such as annotated forms.

Table 7-36 lists several classes of character variants, along with appropriate examples for each using a variety of typeface designs.

Table 7-36: Character Variant Examples

Feature	Default	After Substitution
To Traditional	台	臺, 颱, or 檯
To Simplified	國	国
To Variant	辺	邊, 邊, 邊, 邊, 邉, 邉, 邉, 邉, 邉, 邉, and so on
To JIS78	唖	啞
To Hangul	樂	낙, 락, 악, or 요
To Annotated	イ	(イ), ㋑, イ, イ, イ, イ, イ, and so on

Note the numerous cases of one-from-*n* substitutions. You may encounter one-to-one and one-from-*n* substitutions, depending on the class of variant substitution.

A good example of a Japanese phrase that clearly illustrates the benefits of applying glyph substitution is as follows:

学校の桜並木に黒い虫

This phrase was coined by Kazuo Koike (小池和夫 *koike kazuo*) on the Font-G mailing list, and means "black bugs stick on the cherry trees in the schoolyard." When this phrase is rendered using alternate forms made accessible through glyph substitution, the result is as follows (modified forms have been underlined for your convenience):

學校の櫻竝木に黑い蟲

On MacOS, for example, some of these alternate forms are not easily accessible simply because they are not available in the character set. These include the kanji 校 (JIS83 variant of 校) and 黑 (traditional form of 黒).

Ligatures

Ligatures, single characters whose underlying glyphs are those of other characters, are also very common, especially in Japanese.* This is also known as one-to-*n* substitution. The most common types of CJKV ligatures include those composed of kana, hangul, Chinese characters, and Latin characters. Variants of ligatures—but not *all* ligatures—include abbreviated and vertical forms. Table 7-37 illustrates examples of ligatures for CJKV text.

Table 7-37: Ligature Examples

Ligature Type	Original Text	Ligature Form	Vertical Variant
Kana ligature	キログラム[a]	キロ グラム	グキ ラ ムロ
Hangul ligature	주식회사[b]	주식 회사	회주 사식
Chinese character ligature	株式会社[c]	株式 会社	会株 社式
Latin ligature	FAX[d]	FAX	*not applicable*

[a] Read *kiroguramu*, meaning "kilogram."
[b] Read *jusig hoesa*, meaning "incorporated."
[c] Read *kabushiki gaisha*, meaning "incorporated."
[d] Short for "facsimile," in case you didn't know.

Some ligatures have abbreviated forms. That is, not all of the underlying glyphs that serve to compose the ligature need to be in the abbreviated form—they are also enclosed. The abbreviated ligature form of the four characters 株式会社, for example, is ㈱. It is also considered to be a form of the kanji 株 annotated with parentheses.

Annotations

While many of the typographic features described thus far may have seemed Japanese-specific due to the frequent use of Japanese examples, most apply equally to Chinese, Korean, and Vietnamese text as well. And, most of the features make perfect typographic sense, such as rules that forbid certain classes of characters from beginning or terminating lines. But, there are some other aspects of typography that are very much Japanese-specific. This includes compliance with JIS X 4051-1995, the use of ruby characters and other annotations, and inline notes.

* Actually, ligatures are the most common in Korean, whose hangul are ligatures based on jamo. Does this mean that the hangul ligature example in Table 7-37 is actually a nested ligature?

Ruby Characters

Ruby (ルビ *rubi*) characters, put simply, are reduced-size kana characters that appear above (or sometimes below) one or more kanji, and act to annotate characters by indicating their reading—this often helps readers, both native and non-native, to understand the meaning or reading of rarely used words.* When in vertical writing mode, ruby typically appear to the right of kanji. Ruby characters are sometimes referred to as *furigana* (振り仮名 *furigana*) or as *glosses*.

All the *genuine* Japanese ruby characters used in this chapter are from Morisawa's リュウミン L-KL (Ryumin-Light) design, and as explained in Chapter 6, are genuine ruby designs.

Applying ruby

There are two contexts in which ruby characters are used. One context is global in the sense that *all* kanji are annotated with ruby to indicate their readings. Children's books use ruby characters quite extensively—Japanese children learn kana first, then kanji. These small annotations written in reduced-size kana allow Japanese children (and foreigners who are learning to read Japanese) to learn kanji readings.

The other context are typical documents in which there may appear rarely used or non-standard kanji—only words containing these kanji are annotated with ruby. Native Japanese are expected to be able to read the unannotated kanji.

Mono ruby

The simplest type of ruby are called *mono ruby* (モノルビ *mono rubi* in Japanese)—thus named because one or more ruby characters serve to annotate only a single character. Because readings for kanji can require up to as many as five kana, the number of required ruby characters must match. Table 7-38 provides examples of mono ruby that consist of one to five ruby characters.

Table 7-38: Mono Ruby Examples—Japanese

One Ruby	Two Ruby	Three Ruby	Four Ruby	Five Ruby
こ 小	けん 剣	はやし 林	あらかじ 予	こころざし 志

This brings us to another issue with regard to ruby characters, specifically how they are aligned with respect to the characters that they annotate. The examples

* No one can read *all* kanji.

provided in Table 7-38 on page 373 were all center-aligned, but Table 7-39 illustrates examples of left-, center-, and right-alignment.

Table 7-39: Mono Ruby Examples—Alignment Variations—Japanese

	Left	Center	Right
One Ruby	こ 小	こ 小	こ 小
Three Ruby	はやし 林	はやし 林	はやし 林

There is no point in discussing alignment of mono ruby consisting of two ruby characters—they align in only one way.

Of course, all of these alignment principles apply equally well when the text is set vertically—the ruby characters appear on the right side of the characters that they annotate.

Group ruby

One of the most common types of ruby are called *group ruby* (グループルビ *gurūpu rubi* in Japanese). That is, they are ruby characters that serve to annotate two or more characters, usually kanji. Exactly how they are aligned becomes more of an issue than with mono ruby.

Table 7-40 provides some examples of kanji compounds annotated with ruby characters according to group ruby principles.

Table 7-40: Group Ruby Examples—Japanese

か ん じ 漢字	かぶしきがいしや 株式会社	はんちゆう 範 疇
kanji	kabushiki gaisha	hanchū
kanji	*incorporated*	*category*

It is also possible to combine the two ruby principles for strings of kanji that have logical separations, such as personal names in which there is precedent to distinguish family from given names. Table 7-41 provides two examples of applying both types of ruby principles to Japanese names.

Table 7-41: Combining Mono and Group Ruby Principles—Japanese

Group Plus Group	Mono Plus Group
やまもとたろう	はやし と も こ
山本太郎	林とも子
yamamoto tarō	hayashi tomoko

Pseudo ruby

There are also special-purpose ruby characters, which basically can mean one of two things—or both:

- The ruby characters are not part of a specialized ruby font
- The use of characters other than hiragana and katakana (and a few specialized ruby-specific symbols), such as Latin characters or kanji

These are called *pseudo ruby* (擬似ルビ *giji rubi* in Japanese) characters. For example, words written using katakana can be annotated with ruby characters that are actually reduced-size kanji—these are most often used to indicate the Japanese equivalent of loan words. Kanji compounds can also be annotated with ruby characters that are reduced-size Latin characters. Table 7-42 provides some examples of pseudo ruby.

Table 7-42: Pseudo Ruby Examples—Japanese

Kanji	Kanji	Latin Characters
拳　銃	計　算　機	N E C
ピストル	コンピュータ	日本電気
pisutoru	konpyūta	nippon denki
pistol	*computer*	*NEC*

You may find some Japanese word processing software that supports ruby characters, but it is a more common feature of page-layout software. Adobe FrameMaker Version 5.5 and later, for example, includes support for ruby characters.

One can imagine how ruby characters can be applied to Chinese, Korean, and Vietnamese. Chinese text can be annotated with Pinyin or zhuyin, Korean text (that is, hanja) can be annotated with hangul, and Vietnamese text (that is, chữ Hán and chữ Nôm) can be annotated with Quốc ngữ. In fact, Chinese text annotated with zhuyin characters—as readings—is quite common.

Inline Notes—Warichu

Japanese text can be set as inline or inset notes, called *warichu* (割注 *warichū*) in Japanese. The text for inline notes is the same as ruby characters (that is, half-size), but are set within the text using two lines enclosed by a set of parentheses. Table 7-43 provides an example of text with an inline note.

Table 7-43: Inline Note Example

Example	情報処理（この本のテーマは 中日韓越情報処理）です。

While it is theoretically possible to *fake* kana, hangul, and Chinese character ligatures using the principles of inline notes, the results are not typographically pleasing. While the characters used for inline notes are purposely reduced in size, applying the same technique for constructing ligatures will result in characters that do not match the surrounding text, and will look more like inline notes. Table 7-44 provides an example of genuine versus faked katakana ligatures in text set using FDPC's 平成角ゴシックW5 (HeiseiKakuGo-W5) typeface.

Table 7-44: Genuine and Faked Katakana Ligatures

Genuine Ligature	身長は 188㌢です。
Faked Ligature	身長は 188センチです。

Pay close attention to how the vertical spacing and relative weight of the two types of ligatures differ. The ligature form in question is ㌢ (*senchi*, short for and meaning "centimeter"). The genuine ligature blends with the surrounding text while the faked one does not. The faked ligature's vertical spacing is such that it looks like two separate lines of text—this is what inline notes entails.

More information on inline note composition can be found in JIS X 4051-1995. Adobe Illustrator Version 7.0 and later supports inline notes.

Other Annotations

In addition to annotating Chinese or other characters with readings or meanings, it is also possible to add annotations that simply add emphasis, similar to the use of an underline in Western texts. In Japanese, these marks are called *boten* (傍点 *bōten*), and appear above (in horizontal writing) or to the right (in vertical writing) of the characters to which they add emphasis. These marks are sometimes referred to as *kenten* (圏点 *kenten*).

Table 7-45 illustrates the most common type of boten marks in Japanese, along with an alternative type, set using Adobe Systems' 小塚明朝H (KozMin-Heavy) typeface.

Table 7-45: Standard and Alternate Japanese Boten Marks

Standard Boten	このサンプルは重要です。
Alternate Boten	このサンプルは重要です。

Page-layout systems such as QuarkXPress allow these two types of boten marks. SMI EDICOLOR, provides nearly a dozen types of character annotations, and also permits the user to define their own.

Typographic Software

Although typical word processing software allows the user to typeset most documents, there are often circumstances when significantly more typographic control is necessary, such as when composing books or other complex documents.

Today, page-layout and some graphics applications provide the user with a high level of typographic functionality—many also offer CJKV-specific features. What I describe below are what I consider to be the most widely used typographic software.

Page-Layout Systems

Page-layout programs are considered the most complex CJKV text processing tools available because they allow users to typeset text in a variety of ways, and with much greater precision than tools such as text editors and word processors. There are many dedicated CJKV-capable page-layout systems available, but they are proprietary in nature, and are very expensive and not easily upgraded.

Most page-layout systems—with the exception of Adobe FrameMaker and perhaps QuarkXPress—are not very efficient for text entry. It is usually necessary to first enter the text using conventional word processing software (such as Microsoft Word), then import the text into the page-layout software for further manipulation. There are usually filters available that allow you to retain certain attributes of the text during the import process, such as the fonts used (names, point sizes, styles, and so on), tab settings, and line spacing. Some page-layout systems, such as Adobe FrameMaker, have always been effective for text entry—there is absolutely no need to use a word processor.

You can expect to find features such as a vertical writing mode (except for the current version of Adobe FrameMaker), multiple columns, full control over character, word, and line spacing, a table editor, and a graphics interface (although it is usually better to create graphics using a dedicated graphics application, such as Adobe Illustrator or Macromedia FreeHand, then import as an EPS file).

While my personal preference for page layout is Adobe FrameMaker, you will find that most software (not only page-layout software) has extremely loyal followings. As the complexity of a program increases, so does its learning curve. This is especially true of page-layout systems which use a slightly different paradigm for laying out text. While fierce competition in this market has led to competitive upgrades and import filters among these programs, completely transitioning from one page-layout system to another is not so simple, and can literally take months of learning. Sticking with the system that you currently use has the advantage that you are most likely aware of its strengths and weaknesses, and know how to compensate for its weaknesses. Learning the strengths and weaknesses of a new page-layout system can be a time-consuming process.

I must also point out that some word processors, such as the Japanese version of Microsoft Word, have evolved to the point where they provide very sophisticated page-layout facilities, rivaling some of those described in this section.

Adobe FrameMaker

Adobe FrameMaker is an extremely powerful page-layout system that is popular in technical and book-making circles, and has been developed for MacOS, Unix, and Windows (95, 98, and NT).* It is the only page-layout system that allows users to exchange files between today's three major operating systems (let alone be available for all three of these operating systems).

Adobe FrameMaker was designed to handle complex page layout for highly structured documents, such as books and technical reports. But, many have found that it can also serve well as a word processor. This is a feature not shared by other popular page-layout software, such as Adobe PageMaker. For many page-layout systems, one usually composes the text in a word processor, then imports that text for further page layout refinements.

* Adobe FrameMaker was formerly known as simply FrameMaker—Frame Technologies merged with Adobe Systems in late 1995. Try looking at *http://www.adobe.com/prodindex/framemaker/*.

Two of the most outstanding features of Adobe FrameMaker, in my opinion, are its ability to create and edit tables, and to gracefully handle footnotes. Some chapters in this book have more tables than number of pages, so table support was a critical aspect in the production of this book. Footnote support was also important. Other useful features of Adobe FrameMaker not found in other page-layout systems include footnotes and an equation editor.

For those who develop documents based on SGML (Standard Generalized Markup Language), Adobe FrameMaker+SGML provides SGML facilities.

Adobe FrameMaker Version 5.1 and greater for MacOS is WorldScript-II–compatible, which effectively means that it is CJKV-capable. This book was created (that is, text entry *and* page layout) using Adobe FrameMaker Version 5.5, which provides additional CJKV enhancements, such as ruby support, alternate metrics, and JIS X 4051-1995 compliance.

Adobe PageMaker

Adobe has developed a very popular page-layout system called Adobe PageMaker, which has been enhanced to handle CJKV text as fully localized Chinese, Japanese, and Korean versions.* It is available for both MacOS and Windows. One of the main enhancements to the localized versions of this program, besides the obvious handling of multiple-byte characters, is the ability to set CJKV text vertically. A Japanese-specific feature is support for ruby characters.

Adobe PageMaker, in my opinion, is ideally suited for creating complex documents that have different layouts from page to page. The latest version of Adobe PageMaker provides text manipulation tools, such as a search and replace function and spell checker—these functions are made accessible in the context of its "story editor." As a side note, Adobe PageMaker Versions 4.0J and 4.5J were used to typeset *Understanding Japanese Information Processing* (O'Reilly & Associates, 1993).

FIT

FIT, short for "Focus on Integrated Typesetting (飞腾 *fēiténg*; meaning "to soar")," is a page-layout system developed by Peking University Founder Group (北大方正集团公司 *běidà fāngzhèng jítuán gōngsī*), available for MacOS and Windows.† It is worth noting that it is not based on a page-layout system originally developed for English-speaking users.

---

* Adobe PageMaker was formerly known as Aldus PageMaker—Aldus merged with Adobe Systems in 1994. Try looking at *http://www.adobe.com/prodindex/pagemaker/*.

† *http://www.founderpku.com/*

Although the original version of FIT was designed for use in China (Simplified Chinese), it has since been made available for use in Taiwan (Traditional Chinese) and Japan (called "Founder FIT"),* and there are plans for a Korean version.

Some of the more noteworthy features of FIT include the following:

- A ruby feature that supports zhuyin and pinyin—the positioning options are quite rich (top, bottom, left, or right of parent characters)
- Various options for writing direction
- Various options for punctuation marks (full-width, proportional, or even centered)
- Observation of line-breaking rules

Also of interest is that it provides an equation editor and table tool. Like SMI EDICOLOR (described on page 381), it allows the use of "character" as a unit of measurement. Of course, it also supports the Q unit. Some interesting details about FIT are available online.†

QuarkXPress

QuarkXPress, developed by Quark Incorporated, is another very popular and sophisticated page-layout system available for MacOS and Windows.‡ The latest localized versions have the option to use English menus and dialogs.

QuarkXPress allows the user to use a wide variety of typographic units, such as the Q. It also allows users to redefine typographic measurements such as the point (the PostScript imaging model defines there to be 72 points per inch, but that can be easily changed in QuarkXPress). Other significant features of CJKV versions of QuarkXPress include:

- Ruby support
- CJKV support in kerning table editor—horizontal and vertical kerning are supported
- Modification of the line-breaking character set—there are pre-defined weak and strong sets, and the user can change their definitions or create new ones
- Definition of font sets that allow users to select a different font for different types of scripts, such as Chinese characters, kana, Latin characters, numerals, and symbols—the font specified for each script can be baseline shifted or scaled at the time of the definition

---

* *http://www.founder.co.jp/*

† *http://www.jagat.or.jp/asia/report/China3.htm*

‡ *http://www.quark.com/*

Although not CJKV-specific, the QuarkXPress "Text to Box" feature allows the user to convert text into a (editable) text box in the shape of the characters themselves—similar to the text-to-outline feature available in Adobe Illustrator and Macromedia FreeHand, both of which are described shortly. This feature works with both PostScript and TrueType fonts, and ATM (Adobe Type Manager) is required. Of course, this feature does not work for fonts whose outlines are not available or are protected.

As an avid user of Adobe FrameMaker, I would miss features such as tables and footnotes if using QuarkXPress. However, QuarkXPress provides extended functionality through third-party plug-ins called *XTensions*. Quark maintains a list of XTension developers.* Note that some XTensions may not work properly with CJKV versions of QuarkXPress. SOFTWARE Too, a Japanese company, also maintains a list of XTensions that can be used with QuarkXPress-J (and perhaps other CJKV versions as well).† TableWorks, for example, is an XTension that adds table support to QuarkXPress-J. The XTension called fXT adds footnote support.

Demo versions of QuarkXPress, including CJKV-capable versions, are available from Quark.‡ This provides the potential user the ability to test-drive the software before making a purchase. A very useful guide for QuarkXPress is Donnie O'Quinn's *QuarkXPress in a Nutshell* (O'Reilly & Associates, 1998). Although it is written for the English version of QuarkXPress, it is nonetheless useful for those using the CJKV-capable versions.

SMI EDICOLOR

Sumitomo Metal Industries' (住友金属工業株式会社 *sumitomo kinzoku kōgyō kabushiki gaisha*) Publishing Systems Division (パブリッシングシステムズ事業室 *paburisshingu shisutemu jigyōshitsu*) has developed a page-layout system called SMI EDICOLOR (エス エム アイ エディカラー *esu emu ai edikarā*), available for MacOS and Windows.** EDICOLOR stands for *EDItors' COLOR Layout Software*. Fully-functional demo versions of SMI EDICOLOR are available at their web site.

SMI EDICOLOR is unique from other common page-layout systems, such as Adobe PageMaker and QuarkXPress, in two ways:

- It is not based on an English page-layout system—as is the case for Adobe FrameMaker, Adobe PageMaker, and QuarkXPress
- It is unlikely that it will ever support languages other than Japanese, such as Chinese and Korean (although it is within the realm of extreme possibilities)

---

* *http://www.quark.com/xtensions/xt3rdparty2.html*

† *http://www.swtoo.com/topics/quark4j-np/pages/Quark4XTensionInfo.html*

‡ *http://www.quark.com/demo004.htm*

** *http://www.smisoft.ssd.co.jp/ps/*

SMI EDICOLOR provides the user with a wide variety of typographic controls, including many Japanese-specific features (such as ruby support, a character-based layout grid, and the use of the Q typographic unit), in order to create the desired page design. It also includes a special font, called "SMI外字" (*SMI gaiji*), that includes many symbol characters that are typically found in "Gaiji" font products, such as those developed by DTP center Biblos and Enfour Media. A well-integrated table editor is also part of SMI EDICOLOR.

SMI EDICOLOR's かな詰め (*kana tsume*, meaning "proportional kana") feature makes use of character-level bounding box information of AFM (Adobe Font Metrics) files to create proportional metrics for kana and a handful of additional characters. AFM files for a large number of Japanese fonts is included with SMI EDICOLOR, which allows users to compose documents using Japanese fonts that are not actually installed onto their system. Table 7-46 illustrates four types of proportional metrics for a short string of katakana characters set in Adobe Systems' 小塚明朝H (KozMin-Heavy) typeface: the hand-tuned proportional metrics developed by Adobe Systems, along with three levels of proportional metrics made available in SMI EDICOLOR, each mathematically calculated from its AFM file.

Table 7-46: Hand-Tuned and AFM-Derived Proportional Metrics

Full-width	トラッキング&カーニング
Adobe Systems	トラッキング&カーニング
SMI Loose	トラッキング&カーニング
SMI Standard	トラッキング&カーニング
SMI Tight	トラッキング&カーニング

SMI EDICOLOR also allows the user to define font sets. That is, the ability to specify what font to use for what character class. In addition to being able to specify specific fonts for standard characters (kanji, kana, Latin, and numerals), it also allows the user to specify fonts for system- and user-defined characters (the "SMI外字" font is, by default, set to be used for the system-defined characters).*

* It is possible to create fonts so that they are recognized by SMI EDICOLOR as system- or user-gaiji. If a font's menu name begins with "ＳＭＩ外字," "システム外字," or "SmiGaiji," then it is treated as a system-gaiji font. If a font's menu name begins with "ユーザー外字," "ユーザー創作," or "Edigai," then it is treated as a user-gaiji font.

While QuarkXPress allows the user to freely define or redefine the line-breaking character sets, SMI EDICOLOR also permits the user to modify what punctuation marks are allowed to dangle.

Graphics Software

Another class of software that often includes advanced typographic capabilities is more graphics-oriented than page-layout–oriented. These programs are known as graphics software. While most word processors and page-layout programs include a very basic set of built-in graphics tools, they are not nearly as powerful as dedicated software. All figures and some tables in this book required intervention by one or more graphics applications—this is typical for most books.

Adobe Dimensions

Adobe Dimensions provides users with the ability to create three-dimensional objects that can be completely constructed using Adobe Dimensions itself, or can be exported to other applications, such as Adobe Illustrator or Adobe Photoshop for further editing or manipulation.*

While it is possible to emulate three-dimensional objects using standard illustration tools, you cannot rotate or otherwise change the orientation of such objects and still expect them to *look* correct. This is what makes Adobe Dimensions useful. Adobe Dimensions Version 3.0 or later (including the standard or unlocalized version) provides the ability to manipulate CJKV text using three dimensions. Figure 7-2 illustrates Korean text—specifically, the characters 김치 (*gimci*, meaning "kimchi") set using hangul from Hanyang Systems' HY신명조 (HYSMyeongJo-Medium) design—extruded to become three-dimensional. Needless to say, Adobe Dimensions can provide documents with some very interesting effects.

Adobe Illustrator

One of the most well-known illustration programs is Adobe Illustrator.† It allows extremely precise layout of text and graphics objects within the context of a single page. While Adobe Illustrator does not constitute a full-featured page-layout system, it is very useful for short works, such as one-page advertisements and so on. Many of the diagrams and illustrations used in this book, for example, were created with Adobe Illustrator. Adobe Illustrator provides the user with the ability to set text in both horizontal and vertical mode—for both CJKV and Latin text. All of the variations of setting Latin text vertically (as illustrated in Table 7-10 on page 352) constitute a built-in feature of Adobe Illustrator. Also of significance is that as of Version 7.0, the *standard* (that is, the unlocalized or domestic) version of Adobe

* *http://www.adobe.com/prodindex/dimensions/*

† *http://www.adobe.com/prodindex/illustrator/*

Figure 7-2: Three-dimensional Korean text

Illustrator is CJKV-capable. And, believe it or not, you are not even required to have an underlying CJKV-capable operating system!*

Using Adobe Illustrator is very much like having the entire PostScript programming language at your disposal through a convenient graphical interface. Almost every attribute of every object you create can be modified to your heart's content. You can even set text along a curve, and convert text—set using either PostScript or TrueType fonts—into editable outlines.†

Like Adobe PageMaker, Adobe Illustrator provides the user with the ability to adhere to the Japanese line-layout rules set forth in JIS X 4051-1995. Also of importance is the ability to use a font's built-in alternate metrics and certain classes of glyph substitution.

All of the typographic samples provided in this chapter were produced with Adobe Illustrator using the fonts' built-in typographic features.

* Before you get too excited, let me warn you that one critical piece of software provided by CJKV-capable operating systems is one or more input methods. Without an input method, you cannot enter CJKV text—but you can display it. Also, you need to somehow find and install CJKV fonts—these are also included as part of CJKV-capable operating systems.

† You cannot, however, convert text into editable outlines if the selected font has its outlines protected. Morisawa's Japanese fonts, for example, currently impose this restriction (but this may change in the future).

Adobe Photoshop

The most widely used bitmap-graphics–manipulation program is Adobe Photoshop.* Every aspect of a scanned or created image can be modified using Adobe Photoshop. But, you may be wondering why it is being mentioned in this book.

Adobe Photoshop does not currently provide the user with advanced typographic functionality, but the localized versions provide the user with the ability to include CJKV text in their images. This can become especially useful if the client of the images does not have a CJKV-capable operating system, or if the fonts are protected in such a way that prevents access to outlines. A bitmap image of a character, rendered at the final output device's resolution, can be easily printed from any computer running Adobe Photoshop. Adobe Photoshop Version 5.0 and later provides much better text services than previous versions.

A useful reference for Adobe Photoshop is Donnie O'Quinn and Matt LeClair's *Photoshop in a Nutshell* (O'Reilly & Associates, 1997).

Macromedia FreeHand

Macromedia FreeHand, developed by Macromedia, provides features comparable to those provided by Adobe Illustrator, and like Adobe Illustrator is available for MacOS and Windows.† Some of the more salient features of Macromedia FreeHand include:

- Convert characters into editable outlines, along with one-step path simplification
- Access to sfnt-wrapped CIDFonts' glyph substitutions and alternate metrics—MacOS version only
- Support for the Q typographic unit in selecting type size (Japanese version only)
- Localized versions for Chinese, Japanese, and Korean—a localized version is required in order to handle CJKV text (for example, the Korean version is required to handle Korean text)
- Character spanning (see page 356 of this chapter for more details)
- JIS X 4051-1995 compliance for character classes, spacing, and line-layout algorithms

* It is also the most widely pirated program. Try looking at *http://www.adobe.com/prodindex/photoshop/*.

† Macromedia FreeHand was formerly known as Aldus FreeHand—Altsys Corporation originally developed FreeHand, but Aldus marketed it. When Aldus merged with Adobe Systems in 1994, FreeHand was relinquished to Altsys, but soon after Macromedia bought Altsys.

- Incremental font downloading
- Ability to edit characters used in hanging punctuation

Additional information about Macromedia FreeHand is available, including demo versions.*

* *http://www-asia.macromedia.com/jp/* and *ftp://zorba.uafadm.alaska.edu/pub/freehand/*

In this chapter:
- *Where Can Fonts Live?*
- *Printer Output*
- *PostScript CJKV Printers*
- *Computer Monitor Output*
- *Other Printing Methods*
- *The Role of Printer Drivers*
- *Output Tips and Tricks*
- *Advice to Developers*

8
Output Methods

It is now time to discuss how CJKV text is output or displayed using devices such as printers and computer monitors. You learned about font formats in Chapter 6, *Font Formats*, then typography in Chapter 7, *Typography*, but now comes the time when you must finally display, print, or otherwise output the CJKV text that you so carefully prepared. Printers can range from low-resolution dot-matrix printers to high-resolution photo imagesetters costing tens of thousands of dollars.* Most computer monitors and virtually all dot-matrix printers are considered low-resolution devices.

No matter what output device is being used, whether it is a computer monitor, a dot-matrix printer, or even a high-resolution photo imagesetter, the most basic unit of output is either a *pixel* (in the case of computer monitors) or a *dot* (in the case of printers). The resolution of both types of devices is usually expressed in units called *dpi*, short for *dots-per-inch*. The most commonly-used printers today are 600-dpi or greater laser printers, although inexpensive 1200-dpi and greater plain-paper printers have already emerged. The most commonly-used computer monitors have 72-dpi or greater resolution (72-dpi for MacOS, and 96- or 120-dpi for Windows).

Exactly what is considered high- or low-resolution is extremely relative, and depends on your background. To people who use a 1270-dpi photo imagesetter, 600-dpi and below is considered low-resolution, but those who recently upgraded from a dot-matrix printer to a 300-dpi laser printer may think that they are now the proud owner of a high-resolution printer. As you can see, it is all relative…

* Or yuan, yen, or won as the case may be—actual amounts may depend on currency fluctuations.

Where Can Fonts Live?

Before we discuss how to actually print or display CJKV text, let's discuss for a moment where fonts live in relation to the host and the printer.

PostScript fonts, in the beginning, felt at home only when resident on a printer, either in VM (also known as RAM), in ROM, or on a hard disk. With the introduction of ATM, PostScript fonts also feel at home on the host. It is only with the introduction of OpenType that PostScript fonts share many of the same advantages of TrueType fonts in a host environment, such as a single-file format.

TrueType fonts, although they can be downloaded to and rendered on most contemporary PostScript devices, feel most at home on a host. This is because their format was designed with the host environment in mind.

Non-CJKV PostScript fonts, usually in Type 1 format, can be explicitly downloaded to a PostScript device on a permanent basis. This is known as a *static* download. These same fonts can also be automatically downloaded when the PostScript driver senses that the PostScript device does not have one or more fonts available. This is known as a *dynamic* download. It is also possible to download only those characters that are referenced in the document to be printed. This is known as *partial* or *incremental* download. In the absence of incremental downloading capability, it is also possible to send bitmaps of the appropriate resolution to PostScript devices. In fact, sending bitmaps is the only course of action for some classes of printers, such as most ink-jet devices.

Most CJKV fonts, because they are typically several megabytes in size, do not lend themselves to dynamic downloading because of the download time and the amount of printer memory required. They are installed through a static download. However, contemporary PostScript drivers have made it possible to incrementally download CJKV fonts. A typical Japanese document is 70 percent kana, so the number of kanji will be limited for most documents, leading to a font that is considerably smaller than the original when incrementally downloaded.*

Now that computers and the communication channel between host and printer are considerably faster than only a few years ago, the advantage of having fonts resident on the PostScript device is decreasing. Even with the ability to incrementally download fonts, some CJKV fonts may be restricted in such a way that prevents incremental downloading. Static downloading may still be required.

* Of course, if you are printing complete character set tables, most if not all of a CJKV font will be incrementally downloaded.

Printer Output

Several years ago you could print CJKV text using only bitmapped fonts. In fact, some printers required that the bitmapped characters be resident in the printer hardware itself—in its ROM. As discussed in Chapter 6, bitmapped fonts are not ideal (and quite frankly, extremely poor) for printing high-quality CJKV text. Fortunately, there are now many ways you can improve the quality of CJKV text when output to a wide variety of devices.

Printing devices range from low-resolution dot-matrix printers to high-resolution photo imagesetters. Some of these devices, usually printers and photo imagesetters, usually support PostScript, which means that they have a built-in PostScript interpreter—we discuss why this is a "good thing" later in this section.

At the beginning of this chapter, I stated that any printing or displaying eventually results in the rasterization or rendering of a font into dots or pixels. Ultimately, every font, no matter what its format, is ultimately resolved into a bitmap. For outline fonts, printing speed and performance are heavily dependent on where the outlines are scaled and subsequently rendered into bitmapped patterns:

- The characters (as outlines) can be rendered into bitmaps on the computer, then sent to the printer
- The instructions for rendering the outlines into bitmaps can be sent to the printer, which subsequently renders the outlines into bitmaps of the appropriate size and resolution

The latter is usually faster, but both result in the same printed page as long as the software performing the rendering is the same or at least similar. Hardware and software for both methods are described throughout this chapter.

PostScript CJKV Printers

One of the very first solutions available for obtaining high-quality CJKV output was to obtain a PostScript Japanese printer. One of the most common models was the Apple LaserWriter II NTX-J, a PostScript Level 1 printer with built-in composite font support. The Apple LaserWriter II NTX-J came with a 40MB hard disk containing two PostScript Japanese fonts, Morisawa's Ryumin-Light and GothicBBB-Medium. There are now many PostScript Japanese printers that come bundled with five or more PostScript Japanese fonts. These fonts include the two listed above (sometimes baked into ROM rather than stored on an internal or external hard disk—accessing ROM-based fonts is *much* faster) plus Morisawa's FutoMinA101-Bold, FutoGoB101-Bold, and Jun101-Light. Companies such as Apple Computer, Canon, Dainippon Printing, Digital, Electronics for Imaging (EFI), Epson, Fuji-Xerox,

Hewlett-Packard, Linotype-Hell, Oki Electric, Varityper, Xerox, and other companies manufacture PostScript CJKV printers. The products developed by these companies range from laser printers to high-resolution photo imagesetters. Other companies, such as LaserMaster Corporation and Harlequin, manufacture PostScript-compatible CJKV printers, also called PostScript *clones*.

The definitive guide to PostScript (specifically, PostScript Level 2) is Adobe Systems' *PostScript Language Reference Manual*, Second Edition (Addison-Wesley, 1990). This book will eventually be revised to conform to PostScript 3.*

Genuine PostScript

Adobe Systems released PostScript Level 2 to the marketplace during the latter part of 1991. PostScript Level 2 has built-in composite font support (that is, support for Type 0 fonts). Specifically, PostScript Version 2011 and greater includes the complete composite font extensions—a handful of PostScript Version 2010 printers exist, such as Apple's LaserWriter IIf and IIg, which do not have a complete implementation of the composite font extensions.† Contrary to popular belief (or myth), having the composite font extensions does not automatically give you the ability to use Japanese or other CJKV fonts. This is because special system files must be resident in ROM or on the printer hard disk. Having these composite font extensions does, however, make it easier for printer manufacturers to produce PostScript CJKV printers by licensing the necessary system files from Adobe Systems. It also makes it possible for users to CJKV-enable such PostScript devices by downloading a contemporary CJKV font using Adobe Systems' installer.‡

Versions of PostScript prior to PostScript Level 2, now called PostScript Level 1, did not have composite font support (exceptions being PostScript Japanese Level 1 printers, such as Apple's LaserWriter II NTX-J mentioned above).

No matter which version of PostScript you have in your printer, if the font with which you are attempting to print is resident on the printer (resident here refers to being baked into ROM or on the printer's hard disk whether internal or external), the font is rendered on the printer. To give you an example of the size of a Post-

* Note that I did not write "PostScript Level 3" here—Adobe has explicitly stated that the official designation for this post-PostScript Level 2 is "PostScript 3."

† The following two-line PostScript program, when sent to any PostScript device, will echo back the specific version number of the PostScript interpreter that is resident on the device:

```
%!
version ==
```

‡ That is, one very useful side effect of downloading a CID-keyed font from Windows or MacOS to a PostScript device that is not yet CJKV-enabled (and has all the other requirements, such as PostScript Version 2011 or greater, enough RAM, and a hard disk) is the installation of the necessary system files that make the PostScript device CJKV-enabled.

Script file compared to sending bitmapped data to the printer from the computer, see the following code, which represents the PostScript file for printing my Japanese pen-name (小林剣) set vertically at 200-point:

```
%!
/Ryumin-Light-V findfont
200 scalefont
setfont
306 720 moveto
<3e2e 4e53 3775> show
showpage
```

The above PostScript code example provides the necessary rendering instructions to the PostScript interpreter resident on the printer. The printer then renders the characters per the instructions. Compare that with a file that contains bitmapped data for three 200-point characters, which may be a file that is more than 100 times as large. It should be rather obvious which method is faster for sending from the computer (host) to the printer.

Adobe Systems is now in the process of developing and releasing PostScript 3, which the next step beyond PostScript Level 2.

Clone PostScript

Not everyone, especially individual users, has enough money to purchase a CJKV printer equipped with genuine PostScript from Adobe Systems, so this opened the door for the development of PostScript clones.

One of the most prominent (and easily obtainable) clone PostScript implementations is called Ghostscript, developed by Aladdin Systems.* Some of the more interesting features (interesting at least in the context of this book) of Ghostscript include support for PDF Version 1.2, CFF, and CID-keyed fonts. Ghostscript is also likely to provide PostScript 3 support.

Another PostScript clone is Jaws,† developed by 5D Solutions Limited,‡ and is available only as an OEM product. The current implementation of Jaws supports CID-keyed fonts. Jaws is very similar in concept to Adobe Systems' CPSI (Configurable PostScript Interpreter), which means that it runs on a standard computer (MacOS, Unix, and Windows) that is attached to a printing engine, such as an imagesetter.

Keep in mind that some PostScript clone implementations may lack features and functionality that are required to support CJKV fonts, in particular CID-keyed fonts.

---

* *http://www.cs.wisc.edu/~ghost/* or *ftp://ftp.cs.wisc.edu/ghost/aladdin/*

† Stands for "Just Another Window Server."

‡ *http://www.5-d.com/*

Ghostscript and Jaws, as exceptions to this general rule, do not appear to have this problem. Harlequin's latest version of their ScriptWorks RIP also supports CID-keyed fonts.

Using CID-keyed fonts in Ghostscript

It is not always obvious how to use CID-keyed fonts in Ghostscript, so the following is a detailed outline that clearly demonstrates how to properly install and use CID-keyed fonts in Ghostscript. Although the procedures written below are for a Korean CID-keyed font, the procedure itself is generic.

1. Obtain a CIDFont file. For example, you can obtain the Munhwa-Regular CIDFont file from the following URL:

   ftp://ftp.oreilly.com/pub/examples/nutshell/cjkv/adobe/samples/
2. Obtain the CMap files that correspond to the character collection of the CIDFont, which in this case is Adobe-Korea1. For example, the following URL contains the Adobe-Korea1-1 CMap files:

   ftp://ftp.oreilly.com/pub/examples/nutshell/cjkv/adobe/ak11.tar.Z
3. Create a "font-stub" for the CID-keyed font, Munhwa-Regular-KSC-EUC-H, by making a file with the following name:

   Munhwa-Regular-KSC-EUC-H.gsf

   The following represents the complete contents of the newly-created *Munhwa-Regular-KSC-EUC-H.gsf* file:

   ```
   /Munhwa-Regular-KSC-EUC-H
   /Munhwa-Regular (Munhwa-Regular)
   /KSC-EUC-H (KSC-EUC-H)

   1 index /CMap resourcestatus
   {pop pop pop}
   {runlibfile} ifelse
   /CMap findresource

   3 1 roll
   1 index /CIDFont resourcestatus
   {pop pop pop}
   {runlibfile} ifelse
   /CIDFont findresource

   [ exch ] composefont pop
   ```
4. Place the *Munhwa-Regular-KSC-EUC-H.gsf* and *KSC-EUC-H* files in the font path (such as */usr/lib/ghostscript/fonts/*).
5. Add a fontmap entry for Munhwa-Regular to the *Fontmap* file:

   ```
   % CID-Keyed font
   % Korean(Adobe)
   /Munhwa-Regular-KSC-EUC-H (Munhwa-Regular-KSC-EUC-H.gsf);
   ```

6. With all of these steps completed, you can simply use PostScript commands to use the CID-keyed font. What follows demonstrates how this Korean CID-keyed font can be used in Ghostscript (user-entered commands are emboldened):

```
GS>/Munhwa-Regular-KSC-EUC-H findfont 100 scalefont setfont
Loading Munhwa-Regular-KSC-EUC-H font from ./Munhwa-Regular-KSC-EUC-H.gsf...
411 7896 2702441 4104584 2791079 0 done.
GS>100 100 moveto <B0A1 B0A2> show showpage
```

Passing Characters to PostScript

There is more than one method for passing characters to PostScript as an argument to the show operator. The show operator is quite important because it is the only method to display text using fonts. The `findfont` and `selectfont` operators are used to indicate what font to use for the characters passed to the show operator. When handling normal ASCII text, the standard convention is to simply pass characters as-is to the show operator using parentheses, as illustrated by the following PostScript program:

```
%!
/Courier findfont 12 scalefont setfont
100 100 moveto
(This is ASCII text) show
showpage
```

But, when you are dealing with characters whose values go beyond seven-bit ASCII encoding, some care must be taken to do things correctly. Remember that most CJKV encodings make generous use of eight-bit characters. The following PostScript program illustrates two acceptable methods for passing eight-bit characters to the show operator (using EUC-CN encoding for the three-character string 小林剑 *xiǎolín jiàn*):

```
%!
/STFangsong-Light-GB-EUC-H findfont 12 scalefont setfont
100 100 moveto
<d0a1 c1d6 bda3> show
(\320\241\301\326\275\243) show
showpage
```

The first method (the fourth line of code) uses hexadecimal codes in angled brackets—spaces are ignored, and hexadecimal digits "a" through "f" can be upper- or lowercase. The second method (the fifth line of code) uses octal codes delimited by standard parentheses. If we use the same text, but specify an encoding that does not use eight-bit characters, such as ISO-2022-CN, there is a third possibility: pass the characters as-is. See the sixth line of the following code:

```
%!
/STFangsong-Light-GB-H findfont 12 scalefont setfont
100 100 moveto
```

```
<5021 4156 3d23> show
(\120\041\101\126\075\043) show
(P!AV=#) show
showpage
```

While the sixth line of the above PostScript program illustrates how seven-bit CJKV characters codes can be passed to the show operator as-is, there are some characters that need to be escaped with a single slash character (/) when this is done: left parenthesis, right parenthesis, and the slash character itself.

Computer Monitor Output

Being able to output CJKV text onto a computer monitor or other display device is a very basic requirement in order to successfully input or otherwise manipulate text. Without the ability to display text, imagine for a moment how you would go about processing CJKV text. You'd be literally blind.

A computer monitor or display screen image consists of pixels, with each pixel representing the most fundamental unit of display. In the case of monochrome displays, each pixel can be either white or black. These days there are better display technologies that offer grayscale, color, and even anti-aliasing options. Anti-aliasing is a technique that allows complex Chinese characters to be displayed at small sizes and still be legible.

As we will discuss below, ATM (Adobe Type Manager) and TrueType can be used to provide high-quality output for display devices. They are also useful for printing to environments that do not have the fonts resident, such as non-PostScript devices, or PostScript devices that simply do not have the necessary fonts installed.* There is also *Display PostScript* (DPS), which is like ATM but has the entire range of PostScript available. DPS provides what is known as full WYSIWYG (What You See Is What You Get), meaning that what is displayed on the screen is what you will get when printed. Currently, some Digital, IBM, SGI, Sun, and other workstations support DPS.

The X Window System for Unix is a graphical user interface, and as such, handles the display of a variety of fonts. It is usually necessary to use a special window for CJKV output, such as a *kterm* (Japanese-specific), *exterm*, or equivalent. Some X Window System applications, such as GNU Emacs (Version 20 or greater), provide their own CJKV-capable windows.

* There are some printers that include all of their CJKV fonts in ROM, and have no hard disk nor hard disk port. There is no permanent download option for such printers.

Adobe Type Manager—ATM

Adobe Systems developed a font-rendering program called Adobe Type Manager (ATM), which can be thought of as the font-rendering software used in a PostScript interpreter. ATM resides on the computer (often called the host), which allows users to place printer fonts on the computer and use them with ATM for high-quality computer monitor output. As mentioned above, ATM is also used for printing to printers on which the fonts are not resident. ATM works with non-PostScript printers, too. The first versions of ATM could handle only Latin fonts, but late in 1991 Adobe Systems released ATM-J, the Japanese version of ATM. This software package came with two PostScript Japanese fonts (Morisawa's Ryumin-Light and GothicBBB-Medium), which the user installed onto a computer hard disk. The current version of ATM, although not advertised, includes full CJKV font support.

If the typeface is resident on both the computer and printer, ATM does not render the characters, but lets the printer do it instead. In fact, it is the printer driver that must request bitmaps from ATM—ATM itself does not communicate with the printer. And for display purposes, ATM is used to render point sizes for which a bitmapped font is not installed.

Figure 8-1 illustrates the Chinese character 剣 printed at 216-point (scaled) in three ways: using a 12-point bitmapped font (ugh!), on a screen display with ATM turned on (72-dpi), and finally printer output with ATM turned on (300-dpi). Notice the difference ATM makes in the output quality of the character. The same figure applies to TrueType, which is covered very soon.

Figure 8-1: The effect of ATM on a 216-point character

As of this writing, you can purchase over 100 Adobe PostScript Japanese fonts that work with ATM—this number is expected to grow. Third-party developers also offer CJKV fonts that function with ATM. ATM currently runs on MacOS and Microsoft Windows, and a Deluxe version considerably helps with font management issues, such as auto-activation and grouping into sets.

SuperATM

SuperATM is an extension to ATM, and makes use of the multiple master technology described in Chapter 6. Well, to be a bit more clear, SuperATM offers font substitution technology, something that is part of Adobe Acrobat. So, you may ask, what problem does SuperATM attempt to solve? Consider a case in which someone provides you with a document, but you do not have the typefaces which were used to create it. What usually happens is that the computer substitutes Courier, a mono-spaced font (“`this is Courier`”), which totally destroys the layout and line-breaks of the document. SuperATM solves this problem through the use of multiple master font technology. Typefaces with identical metrics are generated, but are otherwise very close in appearance to those used in the document. SuperATM uses two generic multiple master fonts to accomplish this feat: one is a serif font, and the other is sans serif. So how are SuperATM and multiple master different? When you select a different weight, width, optical size, or even style for a multiple master font, the interpolation ratios are applied equally to every character in the typeface. In the case of SuperATM, however, the matching of metrics is done at the character, not typeface, level. This means that every character in a substituted font may have a unique interpolation ratio. SuperATM (and Adobe Acrobat, discussed next) uses a database of font metrics information to accomplish this. ATM Deluxe, in addition to offering superb font management and activation services, includes SuperATM font substitution functionality.

Adobe Acrobat

The primary goal and function of Adobe Acrobat is to achieve true document portability (you may have heard about it under its code name *Carousel* while it was under development—more recent code names are *Amber* and *Stout*). This is more or less the same as information interchange, but carried one step further. This further step is to preserve the look and feel of a document across platforms. This includes the typefaces (font substitution technology, such as that used by SuperATM, is key here), graphics, and even color. No longer will you need the application that created the original document, and no longer will Courier be used to replaced missing fonts. You may have guessed that Adobe Acrobat uses SuperATM technology's font metrics database to accomplish part of its goals.

Adobe Acrobat works by first interpreting a PostScript file—these can come from a variety of sources. Adobe Acrobat then outputs a new file that conforms to PDF specifications (PDF stands for *Portable Document Format*). PDF files *can* contain only seven-bit ASCII characters, so that they are easily transported across different platforms. Adobe Acrobat Distiller is the work-horse program that converts PostScript files to PDF files. Adobe Acrobat Reader, which is freely available for operating systems such as MacOS, MS-DOS, Unix, Windows, and so on, is used to display and print PDF files.* More information on Adobe Acrobat and PDF is provided in Chapter 13, *The World Wide Web*, where they are described in the context of the Web.

The full PDF specification is available in Tim Bienz and Richard Cohen's *Portable Document Format Reference Manual* (Addison-Wesley, 1993).

TrueType

In Chapter 6 we discussed TrueType as a font format, but here we discuss TrueType as font-rendering machinery. TrueType font-rendering technology is fundamentally the same as used by ATM in that it renders character descriptions (outlines) on the computer, then uses the resulting bitmapped fonts for both display and printing (of course, generating bitmaps of different resolutions to accommodate screen display and printing). The TrueType font-rendering machinery has been an integral part of MacOS since System 7, and likewise since Microsoft Windows Version 3.1.

Like ATM, TrueType began as a Latin-only font rendering technology. In mid-1992, Apple Computer released a package called *Kanji TrueType*, which included two TrueType Japanese fonts: Ryobi's 本明朝-M (*hon minchō M*) and FDPC's 平成角ゴシック (*heisei kaku goshikku*).

Late in 1992, Apple Computer subsequently released KanjiTalk Version 7.1, which was bundled with seven TrueType Japanese fonts—the two listed above plus Osaka (actually, this font is identical to 平成角ゴシック, but is set in a 256×256 design space, as opposed to the more usual TrueType 2048×2048 design space), FDPC's 平成明朝 (*heisei minchō*), Ryobi's 丸ゴシック -M (*maru goshikku M*), Morisawa's 中ゴシックBBB (*chū goshikku BBB*), and Morisawa's リュウミンライト-KL (*ryūmin raito KL*).† The Chinese and Korean versions of MacOS also come bundled with TrueType fonts appropriate for the locale.

TrueType fonts do have many merits, such as their use of an excellent font caching mechanism that makes subsequent displaying (well, to be more precise, re-displaying) of characters extremely fast.

Microsoft and Apple Computer have further developed their (incompatible) TrueType formats in order to incorporate what most people refer to as advanced typographic functionality. These new technologies are known as TrueType Open

* *http://www.adobe.com/prodindex/acrobat/*

† As discussed in Chapter 6, the localized menu names for these two Morisawa fonts are not the same as their PostScript counterparts, and the proportional Latin characters are metrically incompatible with these PostScript counterparts (although some contemporary PostScript printers include a solution that allows the TrueType version to effectively alias to the PostScript version resident on the printer, and compensates for the metrics incompatibility).

and QuickDraw GX, respectively. TrueType Open will effectively transition into OpenType, as discussed in Chapter 6.

Other Printing Methods

Many of you may not have access to the above printing methods, probably because you do not use a platform that is supported by the font-rendering software (that is, ATM and TrueType), or do not own or otherwise have access to a PostScript CJKV printer. Fortunately, you will usually find that the CJKV text-processing software you are using comes with at least a bare-bones method for outputting CJKV text to a printer, whether it uses outline or bitmapped fonts.

There are freely available and dedicated CJKV printing kits these days, such as CNPRINT, available for MS-DOS, Unix, and VMS, by Yidao Cai (蔡依道 *cài yīdào*).* These programs accept CJKV text files as input, then format the text for printing. These printing kits often come bundled with at least a minimal set of bitmapped fonts, but you are not always limited to using those. Some word processors that do not require an underlying CJKV-capable OS almost always have similar printing facilities.

A future release of JWP, Stephen Chung's freely-available Japanese word processor for Windows, should work quite nicely with ATM for Windows.

Besides PostScript and these printing kits, there are other typesetting and page-description languages in use today. Examples include *ditroff*, *triroff*, *troff*, TEX, and LATEX. Some of these, such as TEX and LATEX, have had CJKV-capable versions available for some time. In fact, there are many slightly different versions of TEX available, such as NTT and ASCII versions. Japanese TEX, for example, makes use of fonts from Dainippon Printing. There are also quite a few Korean-enabled versions of LATEX available.†

For more information on TEX in general, I suggest Norman Walsh's *Making TEX Work* (O'Reilly & Associates, 1994). Chapter 7 of that book includes some useful information on CJKV-capable versions of TEX.

As sort of a section summary, the material in this chapter concentrates on PostScript because it produces a high-quality printed page on virtually any output device, and because the most commonly-available outline fonts are in PostScript format. Also of importance is that these other typesetting and page-description languages can generate PostScript.

* *ftp://ftp.ifcss.org/pub/software/unix/print/*

† *http://pantheon.yale.edu/~jshin/faq/htex.html*

The Role of Printer Drivers

Whenever a document is to be printed, there is mandatory interaction with software called a printer driver. The printer driver communicates with the printer, and whether the printer driver can query the printer (that is, it asks the printer a question about its configuration, such as available paper sizes or resident fonts, then expects an answer) depends on the operating system on which it is running (and perhaps the vintage of the operating system). For most applications, it is the printer driver that is responsible for generating the PostScript code that is ultimately sent to the printer for imaging. For what are considered high-end applications (graphics or page-layout programs, such as those described at the end of Chapter 7), the printer driver does not usually generate PostScript code, but rather acts as a pass-through agent. In other words, the printer driver simply takes the PostScript code generated by an application, then merely sends it, without modification, to the printer.

Printer drivers can also play other critical roles, such as font subsetting and embedding. Although it is common practice to embed Type 1 fonts in PostScript files (to ensure that the printer will use the correct fonts), doing the same for CJKV fonts is more problematic for a variety of reasons, such as:

- CJKV fonts are typically many megabytes in size, which often exceeds the RAM capacity of most printers and imagesetters—these fonts are usually downloaded to its hard disk*
- CJKV fonts typically require additional resources and infrastructure that may or may not be present on the printer
- Only a fraction of the characters in a CJKV font are used in a typical document, which makes font subsetting *extremely* attractive—consider that 70 percent of typical Japanese text consists of kana (less than 200 characters when totalled)

These are all good reasons why CJKV font embedding has been difficult to implement. It is actually the printer driver that is responsible for performing font subsetting, which consists of three basic steps:

- Determine what characters in a given font are used in the requested document
- Build a new version of the font with only the characters referenced in the document
- Embed the newly-built subsetted font into the PostScript file

* While the average size of the CJKV fonts I used to produce this book is approximately 5MB, the largest is over 40MB!

Font subsetting and embedding is a topic that will be discussed in Chapter 13 in the context of Adobe Acrobat and its file format, PDF.

Microsoft Windows Printer Drivers

The availability of appropriate printer drivers on MS Windows is critical in getting your documents to print correctly. Windows has traditionally been a platform that did not allow the printer driver to query the printer. This is why the infamous PPD (PostScript Printer Description) files are absolutely necessary.

PPDs contain the printer's configuration information in a convenient (and local) form that can be easily understood by printer drivers. PPDs are, in general, read-only documents, but some applications retain their own set of (writable) PPDs in order to manage fonts that are subsequently added to the printer (that is, after-market fonts that are downloaded).

Fortunately, there are three suitable printer drivers available for MS Windows, listed in Table 8-1.

Table 8-1: MS Windows' Printer Drivers

Printer Driver	Developer
AdobePS	Adobe Systems
PS Print	EAST
PScript	Microsoft

Adobe Systems' AdobePS printer driver represents an ongoing development effort to improve the printing architecture for Windows environments.

Although Version 3.0 and earlier were never adapted for CJKV use, its latest version is CJKV-capable, and runs under Windows 95 and 98 (a version for Windows NT is planned).* AdobePS also provides users and developers alike with plug-in functionality.

EAST's PS Print printer driver is available in a variety of versions, depending on what version of Windows you are using, and what resolution of printer you expect to use.† One feature unique to PS Print is its crop-mark editor (crop-marks are called トンボ *tombo* in Japanese). Unfortunately, the PS Print series is currently available only for Japanese.

Finally, PScript is Microsoft's version of a PostScript printer driver for Windows 95 co-developed with Adobe Systems. Adobe enhanced PScript's features, and made

* *http://www.adobe.com/prodindex/printerdrivers/windows.html*

† *http://www4.est.co.jp/psprint/*

it available as AdobePS (described above). PScript does not provide any sort of plug-in functionality. The version of PScript included in Windows NT Version 4.0 and earlier was developed by Microsoft alone, but the version that will be included in Windows NT Version 5.0 is being co-developed with Adobe Systems once again.

MacOS Printer Drivers

MacOS users commonly encounter the following PostScript printer drivers:

- AdobePS
- LaserWriter
- LaserWriter 8
- PSPrinter

How are each different? Who developed them? When should one be chosen over another? Good questions…

Both LaserWriter and LaserWriter 8 are maintained by Apple Computer (LaserWriter 8 was originally developed by Adobe Systems as PSPrinter)—they are different only in that LaserWriter 8 is of more recent vintage than LaserWriter.

PSPrinter, now called AdobePS, is developed by Adobe Systems, and is bundled with virtually all Adobe Systems' products.

Korean printing issues

PostScript printing of Korean text on MacOS, unlike for Chinese and Japanese text, can come in one of two forms:

- One-byte printing
- Two-byte printing

The "one-byte printing" method assumes that the Korean fonts resident on the PostScript printer are a series of one-byte–encoded Type 1 fonts—that is, not a true composite font. The "two-byte printing" method is more along the lines of Chinese and Japanese, in which the Korean fonts that are resident on the PostScript printer are true composite fonts. A Control Panel, included with MacOS-KH, called *Hangul Jojung* (한글 조중 *hangeul jojung*), controls what printing method is to be used. As we discovered at Adobe Systems shortly after Apple Computer's Korean Language Kit was released at the end of 1996, this Control Panel was not included. The result was that only one-byte–encoded Korean fonts on PostScript printers would work. Apple Computer subsequently released this Control Panel for KLK users.*

* *ftp://ftp.info.apple.com/Apple_Support_Area/Apple_Software_Updates/US/Macintosh/System/Language_Kits/*

Output Tips and Tricks

Printing CJKV documents can be problematic for some users, depending on their hardware and software environment. Here I present some tips and tricks that may help some readers to produce CJKV documents in unusual environments.*

Creating CJKV Documents for Non-CJKV Systems

One of the most common questions I get asked is how to create a document that includes CJKV text, but can be exported for use on non-CJKV systems, either for displaying or printing. Fortunately, there are several ways to create these types of documents, such as the following:

- Convert CJKV text into outline graphics
- Convert CJKV text into bitmapped graphics
- Use CJKV-capable Adobe Acrobat

A very brief introduction to Adobe Acrobat was provided in earlier sections of this chapter, and other aspects of Adobe Acrobat are covered in Chapter 13. The following sections detail methods for converting CJKV text into graphic objects, either outline objects or bitmapped graphics.

Converting CJKV text into outline graphics

Converting CJKV text into outline graphics requires an application that can perform this function. The CJKV-capable versions of Adobe Illustrator or Macromedia FreeHand are suitable applications for this task.

This operation is extremely simple. First, you compose and lay out the text as desired. Second, you select the command for converting text to editable outlines (consult the manual to determine exactly where in the user interface this command is available). Finally, you save the file as an EPS (Encapsulated PostScript) file. As you can see, the end result of this operation is an EPS file that can be imported into other applications, such as page-layout programs, as graphics.

For some graphic designers, this feature is necessary whether or not they are using a CJKV-capable operating system or have a CJKV-capable printer—they want access to characters' outlines so that they can make changes. Graphic designers may simply want to "fill" the character's outline with some kind of funky pattern, or else change its shape slightly for some wild advertisement.

* The use of the term "unusual" here usually refers to non-CJKV–capable environments.

Anyway, the following are some time-saving notes and tips that are very much worth mentioning at this time:

- Creating outline graphics has the advantage that the EPS file can be scaled to virtually any size
- Converting text to outline graphics results in a form that no longer contains hinting information that benefits small point sizes at low resolution—when these EPS files are output at high-resolution, you simply cannot tell the difference
- Because text that has been converted into outlines can no longer be edited as text, you will need to save the text for possible future editing; a good way to do this is to include two identical layers in your document whereby one layer contains the actual text (set so that it does not print) and the other contains the text after converting to outlines (this is the layer that should be set to print)—trust me, this tip alone can save you plenty of time!
- Some fonts, such as those from Morisawa, are protected in such a way that their outlines are not accessible through these applications' features

Keep the above points in mind when creating EPS files containing text converted to outline graphics. Fortunately, there are still ways to work with fonts that do not allow access to their outlines, as described in the following section.

Converting CJKV text into bitmapped graphics

A technique that turns text into bitmapped graphics is desirable only under circumstances when a font's outlines are protected in such a way that prevents applications from accessing their outlines. However, if such fonts are required for the final document, there may be no other choice.

Converting text into bitmapped graphics first and foremost requires an application suited for the task—Adobe Photoshop is an appropriate tool. All of the steps outlined above for converting text into editable outlines apply here, except that the conversion to bitmapped graphics is more or less an automatic process as you input text. Also, you need to determine what the final output resolution of the document is so that you can set the resolution of the document workspace.*

* Note, however, that creating a full-page Adobe Photoshop document whose resolution is equivalent to that of a photo imagesetter (1270-dpi or greater) will require many megabytes of disk space. It is not a decision to make lightly.

Advice to Developers

This section presents some of my opinions regarding the acquisition of a CJKV-capable publishing system, including hardware and software. I also provide some practical advice regarding how to think about printing technologies and how they may impact your own work.

Acquiring a CJKV-Capable Publishing System

After reading the material in this and earlier chapters, you should be well convinced that using outline fonts for generating high-quality CJKV output is indeed the best choice all around. Investing in a publishing system is something that should be done with great care in order to ensure the best possible results.

Only a few years ago, you would have needed to spend tens of thousands of dollars to produce high-quality CJKV documents. But, believe it or not, you can now purchase an entire hardware and software system for producing high-quality CJKV documents for well under $10,000 (US). The actual price may fluctuate depending on how many CJKV typefaces you decide to purchase and other factors (for example, you may already own some of the hardware or software).

My personal recommendations for a basic CJKV publishing system, at least when I wrote this book, are listed in Table 8-2.

Table 8-2: CJKV Publishing System Hardware and Software Recommendations

Hardware/Software	Description	Estimated Cost
Printer	600-dpi PostScript Level 2 or higher with SCSI hard disk	$2,000
Typefaces	Serif, sans serif, and script designs in text and display weights	$3,000
CPU	At least 64MB RAM plus 2GB hard disk	$2,000
Operating system	Localized OS (or Language Kit for MacOS)	$150–$500
Page-layout software[a]	Adobe FrameMaker,[b] Adobe PageMaker, FIT, QuarkXPress, or SMI EDICOLOR[c]	$500–$2000
Graphics software	Adobe Photoshop plus Adobe Illustrator[d] or localized Macromedia FreeHand	$1000–$1500

[a] If you choose Adobe PageMaker, FIT, or SMI EDICOLOR, you will also need to acquire a CJKV-capable word processor—Adobe FrameMaker and QuarkXPress are suitable for text entry as well as page layout.
[b] Version 5.1 and later for MacOS is WorldScript II compatible—Version 5.5 or later is recommended.
[c] If you intend to publish Japanese-only documents.
[d] Version 7.0 and later for MacOS is WorldScript II compatible.

If you cannot stretch your budget to afford even the most basic outline font software, there are sources for bitmapped fonts, many of them freely available. Most

CJKV-capable operating systems and operating system extensions that are available today, such as MacOS, Apple Computer's Language Kits, Windows 95, and Windows NT, come bundled with a basic but functional set of outline fonts.

Some Practical Advice

You may be wondering, even after reading this chapter and earlier chapters, which outline font format to use: PostScript or TrueType. Most of what I covered here and in Chapter 6 may have seemed focused on (or biased toward) PostScript fonts.

I suggest working with PostScript fonts, and there are a number of reasons for this. First, Adobe Systems' entire corporate direction lies in the further development of the PostScript language and its supported font formats, so by using PostScript you are likely to be using more advanced font technologies much sooner—companies that develop TrueType fonts often make their livelihood in other ways (such as developing entire operating systems), so they may not be as committed to advancing the technology. Second, most printing bureaus accept only documents formatted using PostScript fonts. High-end users, who generally insist on the highest quality fonts, tend to prefer PostScript over TrueType.

As discussed previously, TrueType fonts are not without their merits. On MacOS, TrueType fonts have always been very easy for the user to install (the same can be said of sfnt-wrapped CIDFonts, but that is a more recent phenomenon). Also, TrueType fonts use an excellent disk caching mechanism.

In *Understanding Japanese Information Processing*, which was written way back in 1993, I speculated that PostScript and TrueType technologies may eventually merge or at least become somewhat indistinguishable.* That is exactly what is now happening in the context of OpenType, discussed in Chapter 6.

* For this sort of technology, 1993 is considered a long time ago (but not in a galaxy far, far away).

9

Information Processing Techniques

In this chapter:

- *Language, Country, and Script Codes*
- *Programming Languages*
- *Code Conversion Algorithms*
- *Java Programming Examples*
- *Miscellaneous Algorithms*
- *Byte Versus Character Handling*
- *Character Sorting*
- *Natural Language Processing*
- *Regular Expressions*
- *Search Engines*
- *Code Processing Tools*

As you have learned in earlier chapters, CJKV character set standards and encoding methods have many qualities that make each unique, but within a given locale, there is comfort in knowing that at least some effort was made to keep various encoding methods somewhat compatible. This becomes increasingly important—even critical—when you are dealing with CJKV information processing on multiple platforms. Not all computer systems use the same encoding method. Using Japanese as an example, Shift-JIS encoding is typically used on Windows- and MacOS-based machines, EUC-JP encoding on Unix-based machines, and ISO-2022-JP encoding for electronic transmission, such as email and news. Faced with the difficulties of converting, manipulating, and generating Japanese text, I developed a suite of tools for performing such tasks. Although I have not yet done so myself, these tools can be extended or enhanced to accommodate other CJKV encoding methods.*

A new aspect of programming and operating systems is the ability to use what is known as the *locale model*. The locale model is a system that predefines many

* Two of these tools *have* been extended, but have taken on different forms: *JChar* is now the *CJKV Character Set Server*, as described at the end of this chapter, starting on page 451; and some of JConv's functionality is available in CJKVConv.pl, as described in the section entitled "Code Conversion Across CJKV Locales," starting on page 208 in Chapter 4, *Encoding Methods*.

attributes that are language- and locale-specific, such as the number of bytes per character, date formats, time formats, currency formats, and so on. The actual attributes are located in a library or locale object file, and are loaded when required. The locale model as defined by X/Open's XPG4 (X/Open Portability Guide 4) and IEEE's POSIX (Portable Operating System Interface) contains several categories of features: code set information, time and date formats, numeric formatting, collation information, and so on.

Language, Country, and Script Codes

A locale name is typically composed of two parts, separated by as underscore. The first part specifies a language identifiers ("en" for English, "ja" for Japanese, "ko" for Korean, "zh" for Chinese, "vi" for Vietnamese, and so on).* The second part specifies a country codes ("US" for USA, "CN" for China, "TW" for Taiwan, "HK" for Hong Kong, "SG" for Singapore, "JP" for Japan, "KR" for South Korean (Republic of Korea), "KP" for North Korea (Democratic People's Republic of Korea), "VN" for Vietnam, and so on).† Note the use of upper- versus lowercase—it is intentional.

There are now three-letter language codes as defined in ISO 639-2, *Codes for the Representation of Names of Languages—Part 2: Alpha-3 Code* (draft).‡ Table 9-1 lists ISO languages codes that are of interest to readers of this book.

Table 9-1: ISO 639 Two- and Three-Letter Language Codes

Language	ISO 639	Terminological (ISO 639-2/T)	Bibliographic (ISO 639-2/B)
English	`en`	`eng`	`eng`
Chinese	`zh`	`zho`	`chi`
Japanese	`ja`	`jpn`	`jpn`
Korean	`ko`	`kor`	`kor`
Vietnamese	`vi`	`vie`	`vie`

Note how the two types of three-letter language codes are identical except for Chinese. Three-letter country codes have also been established recently. Table 9-2 lists some of them, along with their two-letter counterparts.

* ISO 639:1988, *Code for the Representation of Names of Languages*, is the ISO standard that serves to register two-letter language identifiers. Also see RFC 1766, *Tags for the Identification of Languages*, for more information. See *http://www.indigo.ie/egt/standards/iso639/iso639-1-en.html*.

† ISO 3166-1:1997, *Codes for the Representation of Names of Countries and Their Subdivisions—Part 1: Country Codes*, is the standard that serves to register country codes (the two-letter codes found in most email addresses). Also see RFC 1766, *Tags for the Identification of Languages*, for more information. See *http://www.indigo.ie/egt/standards/iso3166-en.html*.

‡ *http://www.indigo.ie/egt/standards/iso639/iso639-2-en.html*

Table 9-2: Two- and Three-Letter Country Codes

Country	Two-Letter	Three-Letter
United States	US	USA
China	CN	CHN
Taiwan	TW	TWN
Hong Kong	HK	HKG
Singapore	SG	SGP
Japan	JP	JPN
South Korea	KR	KOR
North Korea	KP	PRK
Vietnam	VN	VNM

The locale "zh_CN," for example, refers to Chinese as used in China, and would include a Chinese code set (such as GB 2312-80), a yuan (¥) for the currency symbol, and so on. The locale "zh_TW" refers to Chinese as used in Taiwan, and would use locale attributes specific to Taiwan. For more information on the locale model, I suggest that you obtain three X/Open CAE Specifications books (CAE stands for *Common Applications Environment*) and the *X/Open Guide: Internationalisation Guide*. See this book's bibliography for more information.

Another useful technique is to be able to identify the script. A language can use multiple scripts (for example, Korean uses Latin characters, hangul, and hanja), so this technique is useful for identifying blocks of text. Table 9-3 lists scripts, along with their ISO 15924 (*Codes for the Representation of Names of Scripts*—draft) two-letter codes and ISO 10179:1996 (*Information Technology—Processing Languages—Document Style Semantics and Specification Language (DSSSL)*) public identifiers. Note the use of upper- then lowercase for the two-letter ISO 15924 codes.

Table 9-3: Script Codes and Identifiers

Script	ISO 15924	DSSSL
Bopomofo	Bp	Script::Bopomofo
Chữ Nôm	Cu	*none*
Chinese characters	Hn	Script::Han
Hangul	Hg	Script::Hangul
Hiragana	Hr	Script::Hiragana
Katakana	Kk	Script::Katakana
Latin	La	Script::Latin
Undetermined script	Zy	*none*
Unwritten languages	Zx	*none*

When used and applied wisely, country, language, and script codes can be used to enhance the performance and reliability of software when handling multilingual information.

Another programming trend that is catching on are variables and data structures that use multiple-byte or wide characters.* Although C and C++ were enhanced to support these variables and data structures, widespread support has never been achieved. That has since changed with the introduction of the Java programming language, created by James Gosling and Bill Joy of Sun Microsystems.

Most of the algorithms and techniques provided in this chapter make use of the Java Version 1.2 API, which provides programmers with exceptional internationalization support. Providing C or C++ examples that make use of the locale model or multiple-byte and wide character data structures is not very useful because many compilers still do not support them (ensuring non-portability from day one). Programmers who use C or C++ generally resort to writing their own input and output mechanisms for handling issues such as representing two or more bytes as a single character. If you are a programmer, I encourage you to explore the Java programming language.

This chapter first discusses programming languages, followed by algorithms for actual byte value conversion (this is the heart of the CJKV code conversion process). However, that is not all that is required. Next, we move on to text stream handling, which serves as the wrapper for the code conversion routines—as you'll soon realize, the Java Version 1.2 API simplifies this task *immensely*. Programming languages such as Java can perform much of this code conversion using built-in methods, which saves programmers significant time, effort, and energy. There are, however, specialized algorithms that may or may not be available as built-in methods or functions, such as half- to full-width katakana conversion (Japanese-specific) and automatic code detection.† But, even implementing these algorithms in Java provides much simplification due to the use of Unicode (UCS-2 encoding) internally. This chapter continues with information about handling multiple bytes as a single unit for operations such as text insertion, deletion, and searching. CJKV implications for sorting, parsing, and regular expressions are covered last.

In most cases, workable C or Java source code, along with an explanation of the algorithm is provided (Appendix W, *Perl Code Examples*, provides Perl equivalents of some of these algorithms). Feel free to use these code fragments in your own programs—that is why they are included in this book. The code samples that

* The issue of multiple-byte versus wide characters was discussed in Chapter 1, *CJKV Information Processing Overview*, starting on page 25.

† After all, before you can convert from one encoding to another, you need to know what the original encoding is.

I provide here may not be the most efficient code, but *do* work.* Feel free to adapt what you find here to suit your own programming style or taste. The entire source code for these algorithms and examples is available in machine-readable form.†

Programming Languages

A short discussion of several popular programming languages—C/C++, Java, Perl, Python, and Tcl—is necessary before we can meaningfully discuss the information processing techniques presented in the remainder of this chapter. While what I write in the following sections is by no means a complete description or treatment of these programming languages, it does provide information about their salient features and virtues as they relate to CJKV programming.

While it is easy (and, quite frankly, sort of childish) to explore and argue about the strengths and weaknesses of programming languages, it is ultimately the method of deployment that usually determines what programming language is chosen for a specific task.

C/C++

Most CJKV-capable programs today are written in C or C++. The wide availability of C/C++ compilers has made this possible. However, because of the weak or non-existent support for internationalization in such compilers, C/C++ is no longer the best choice.

It is important to understand (or at least appreciate) the programming paradigms and structures offered by C/C++ because they have been instrumental in forming the foundations for more contemporary programming languages, covered next. Many of their programming constructs, such as conditional statements and loops, have been "borrowed" into languages such as Java, Perl, and Python. This makes it a much easier task for C/C++ programmers to learn and master these other languages.

One pitfall of the C programming language is that it has the concept of signed and unsigned characters (type `char`), and the default is signed. For all meaningful string comparisons using multiple-byte encodings, the programmer must set everything to unsigned `char`, which can cause compiler warnings because prototypes do not agree. And, things won't work correctly if unsigned `char` is used. Some compiler developers, bless their hearts, give programmers the ability to change the default to unsigned `char`.

* If they do not work, I want to know about it!

† *ftp://ftp.oreilly.com/pub/examples/nutshell/cjkv/Ch9/*

Java

The first programming language that experts consider to be fully suitable for CJKV programming is Java.* Java was touted as being the first programming language to include support for Unicode, but it was not until the Version 1.1 release of the language that this feature was fully realized.

The standard Java I/O (input/output) package provides built-in support for converting between Unicode (UCS-2 or UTF-8 encodings) and numerous encoding methods (including those covered in Chapter 4 of this book). This can effectively render most of this chapter no longer necessary, but luckily for me there are some tips, tricks, pitfalls, and caveats that developers need to be aware of before diving into Java.

A lot of thought has been put into the design of Java. One problem that is almost always encountered when writing programs is *portability*. This usually results from differing data type sizes for different architectures. Table 9-4 lists data types and their sizes as specified by Java.

Table 9-4: Java Data Types and Sizes

Data Type	Size (in Bits)
Boolean	1
Char[a]	16
Byte	8
Short	16
Int	32
Long	64
Float	32
Double	64

[a] A Unicode-encoded character.

With almost any other programming language, the data type sizes listed in Table 9-4 differ depending on the underlying architecture. Java is like a programmer's dream come true because it uses data sizes that programmers prefer to think in (with the possible exception of type `char`).

An excellent guide to the Java programming language is David Flanagan's *Java in a Nutshell*, Second Edition (O'Reilly & Associates, 1997). The *comp.lang.java* newsgroup also includes articles relating to internationalization from time to time.

* My wife is from Java, but she doesn't write Java programs (well, not yet). Unless, of course, you count participating in a Javanese dance performance a program of sorts…

Perl

Usually described as a scripting language, Perl, developed by Larry Wall, is much, much more than that. Perl's main strengths include rapid development, regular expressions (described later in this chapter),* and hashes (associative arrays). It is not so much these individual features that provide Perl with extraordinary text-manipulation capabilities, but rather how these features are intertwined with one another. Other programming languages offer similar features, but there is often no convenient way for them to function together. In Perl, for example, a regular expression can be used to parse text, and at the same time used to store the resulting items into a hash for subsequent lookup.

Perl is the programming language of choice for those who write CGI programs or do other web-related programming (a topic that is discussed at the end of Chapter 13, *The World Wide Web*), because it is well suited for the task.

Although the current incarnation of Perl has no built-in support for internationalization (to the level that Java currently has), it is something that is being discussed by its developers. There are, however, clever ways to use Perl for handling multiple-byte data, most of which make use of regular expression tricks and techniques. The Perl code examples provided in Appendix W should be studied by any serious Perl programmer. Gisle Aas and Martin Schwartz have been diligently working on some extremely useful Unicode modules† for Perl (such as `Unicode::String`, `Unicode::Map8`, and `Unicode::Map`), so you can expect some useful and interesting things to happen in the future. The `Unicode::Map` module by Martin Schwartz, in particular, already supports code conversion between Unicode and a number of legacy CJKV encodings.

Kazumasa Utashiro (歌代和正 *utashiro kazumasa*)‡ has developed a useful Japanese-enabling Perl library called *jcode.pl*, which includes Japanese code conversion routines.** Some may find the Japanese version of Perl, called JPerl,†† to be useful, although I suggest using programming techniques that avoid JPerl for optimal portability. JPerl adds Japanese support to the following features: regular expressions, formats, some built-in functions (`chop` and `split`), and the `tr///` operator.

* Tom Christiansen and Nathan Torkington, in *Perl Cookbook* (O'Reilly & Associates, 1998), describe Perl's regular expression implementation in the following sentence: "It's more like string searching with mutant wildcards on steroids."

† *http://www.perl.com/CPAN/authors/Gisle_Aas/* and *http://www.perl.com/CPAN/authors/Martin_Schwartz/*

‡ *utashiro@iij.ad.jp*

** *ftp://ftp.iij.ad.jp/pub/IIJ/dist/utashiro/perl/*

†† *http://www.perl.com/CPAN/authors/Hirofumi_Watanabe/*

The definitive guide to Perl is *Programming Perl*, Second Edition, by Larry Wall et al. (O'Reilly & Associates, 1996). Tom Christiansen and Nathan Torkington's *Perl Cookbook* (O'Reilly & Associates, 1998) is also highly recommended as a companion volume to *Programming Perl*. The *comp.lang.perl.misc* newsgroup should also be of interest. The best place to find Perl is at CPAN (Comprehensive Perl Archive Network).*

Python

Like Perl, Python is also sometimes described as a scripting language. Python was developed by Guido van Rossum, and is a high-level programming language that provides valuable programming features such as hashes and regular expressions.

An excellent guide to Python is Mark Lutz's *Programming Python* (O'Reilly & Associates, 1996). The *comp.lang.python* newsgroup should also be of interest if you want to learn about recent Python developments and join discussions. There is also a Python web site from which Python itself is available.†

Tcl

Tcl, which stands for *Tool Command Language*, is a programming language that was originally developed by John Ousterhout while a professor at UC Berkeley.‡ Like Perl and Python, Tcl is considered a high-level scripting language that provides built-in facilities for hashes and regular expressions. John later founded Scriptics Corporation where Tcl is now being advanced.

Some important milestones in Tcl's history include its byte-code compiler introduced for Version 8.0, and support for Unicode (in the form of UTF-8 encoding) that began with Version 8.1. Tcl will also have a regex package comparable to Perl's by the time you read this. The lack of a byte-code compiler has always kept Tcl slower than Perl.

Tcl is rarely used alone, but rather with its GUI (Graphical User Interface) component called TK (standing for Tool Kit).

Other Programming Environments

While it is possible to write multiple-byte–enabled programs using all of the programming languages mentioned above, there are some programming environments that have done all this work for you, meaning that you need not worry

* *http://www.perl.com/CPAN/CPAN.html*

† *http://www.python.org/*

‡ *http://www.scriptics.com/*

about multiple-byte enabling your own source code because you depend on a module to do it for you. This may not sound terribly exciting for companies with sufficient resources and multiple-byte expertise, but may be a savior for smaller companies with limited resources.

One example of such a programming environment is Visix's Galaxy Global, a multilingual product based on their Galaxy product. (Visix Software has since gone out of business.)

Perhaps of greater interest is Basis Technology's "Rosette: C++ Library for Unicode," which is a compact, general-purpose Unicode-based source code library.* Embedded into an application, this library adds Unicode text processing capabilities that are robust and efficient across a variety of platforms (MacOS, Unix, Windows, and so on). Its functions adhere to the latest Unicode specifications. Major functions include code conversion between major legacy encodings and Unicode encodings, character classification (identification of a character), and character property conversion (such as half- to full-width katakana conversion). Basis Technology also offers a general-purpose code conversion utility, called "Uniconv," built using this library. Also of interest is UniScape's Global C and Global Checker packages,† Sybase's Unilib,‡ and Alis Technologies' Batam (their own Tango web browser is an example of this library's usage in a real product).**

Code Conversion Algorithms

It is very important to understand that only the encoding methods for the national character sets are mutually compatible, and work quite well for round-trip conversion.†† The vendor-defined character sets often include characters that do not map to anything meaningful in the national character set standards. When dealing with the Japanese ISO-2022-JP, Shift-JIS, and EUC-JP encodings, for example, algorithms are used to perform code conversion—this involves mathematical operations that are applied equally to every character represented under an encoding method. This is known as *algorithmic* conversion.

However, dealing with encodings such as UCS-2 and UTF-16 (used to encode ISO 10646-1:1993 and Unicode), and when mapping from one locale to another, require mapping tables.‡‡ (Mapping tables are necessary when no code conver-

* *http://www.basistech.com/unicode/*

† *http://www.uni-scape.com/*

‡ *http://www.sybase.com/*

** *http://montreal.alis.com/castil/batam.en.html*

†† The only possible exceptions lie in user-defined regions, which do not exist in all encodings of a given locale; and the JIS X 0212-1990 character set, which is supported by Shift-JIS encoding.

‡‡ The conversion between Unicode and ASCII/ISO 8859-1:1998, as one exception, is algorithmic.

sion algorithm exists, which usually means that character ordering is different.) This is known as *table-driven*, *tabular*, or *hard-coded* conversion. Table-driven conversion deals with every character on a case-by-case basis. Table 9-5 provides examples that illustrate algorithmic versus table-driven conversion, specifically the first four kanji in JIS X 0208:1997 (for brevity, all code points are expressed in hexadecimal notation).

Table 9-5: Algorithmic Versus Table-Driven Conversion

Character	Algorithmic (ISO-2022-JP to EUC-JP)[a]	Table-Driven (UTF-16 to EUC-JP)
亜	0x3021 becomes 0xB0A1	0x4E9C maps to 0xB0A1
唖	0x3022 becomes 0xB0A2	0x5516 maps to 0xB0A2
娃	0x3023 becomes 0xB0A3	0x5A03 maps to 0xB0A3
阿	0x3024 becomes 0xB0A4	0x963F maps to 0xB0A4

[a] The algorithm used here is simply "add 0x80 to each byte."

Figure 9-1 illustrates the difference between algorithmic and table-driven conversion, using the information presented in Table 9-5. Note how algorithmic conversion alters every character in the *same* way—they are in the same relative position in the new encoding. However, table-driven conversion introduces apparent randomness—each character code is treated as a special case.

One advantage of converting between legacy encodings and Unicode is that the redundancy in Unicode, in the form of its various "compatibility zones," allows for round-trip (that is, one-to-one) conversion. In fact, this is a fundamental design feature of Unicode. However, when dealing with conversion between character sets of different locales, such as between GB 2312-80 and Big Five, the relationship is not always one-to-one, thus round-trip conversion is not always possible.

The code conversion techniques in this section cover three CJKV encoding methods: ISO-2022, EUC, and Shift-JIS (Japanese-specific). Information on conversion to and from Row-Cell notation is also covered. These techniques can be easily applied to any CJKV locales.

It is best to treat the vendor encoding methods, as described in Appendix D, *Vendor Encoding Methods*, as exceptional cases. It is also best to avoid using such encoding methods and character sets if your software requires the maximum amount of flexibility and information interchange—this is a portability issue.

The following sections contain more detailed information about dealing with the conversion of these and other encoding methods. Two of the conversion algorithms require the use of functions for maximum efficiency (at least, when writing code in a language other than Java). The other types of conversion make use of these functions, or perform simple assignments.

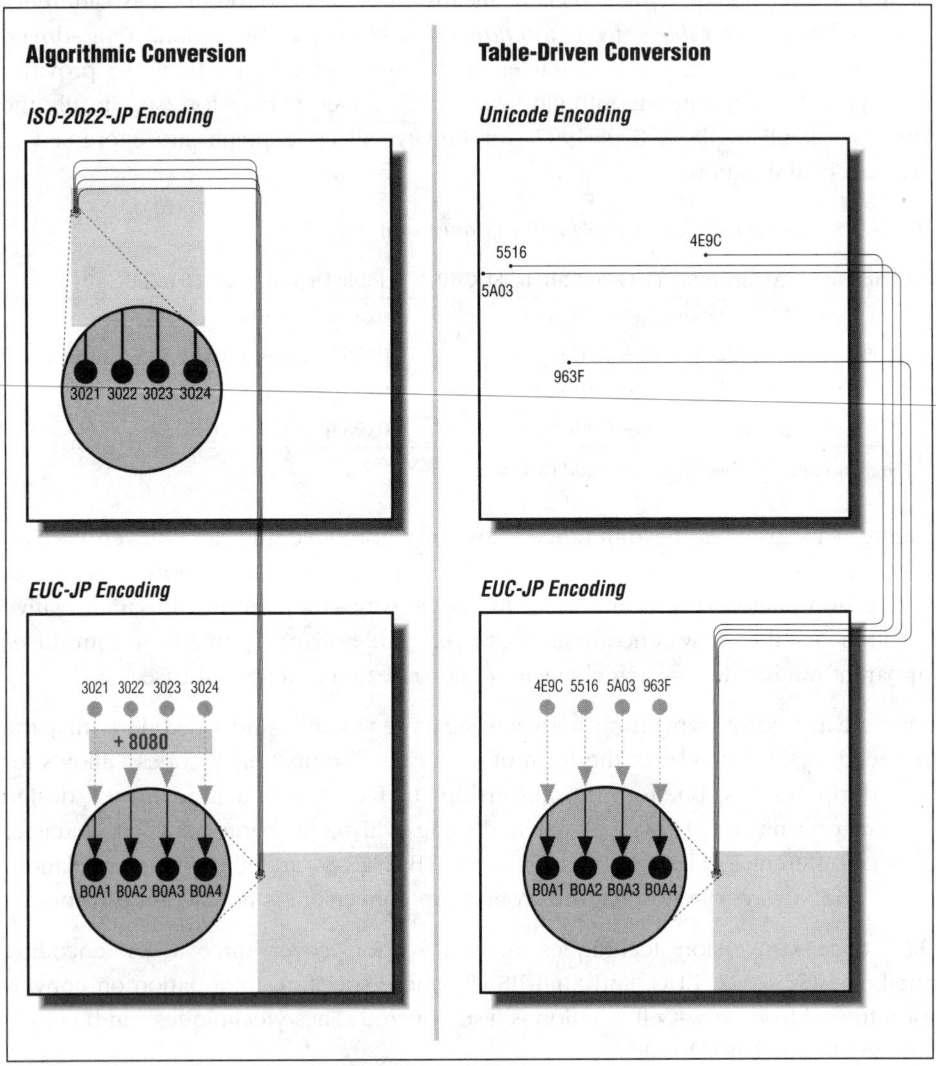

Figure 9-1: Algorithmic versus table-driven conversion—visually

Conversion Between ISO-2022 and EUC

EUC encoding is what I often refer to as escape-sequence– or shift-*less* ISO-2022 encoding with the eighth bit set. Some email transport systems (and news readers) strip the eighth bits from email messages—if one sends an EUC-encoded file through such mailers, the file becomes damaged (and unreadable) because it is transformed into escape-sequence– or shift-less ISO-2022. This should indicate to you that conversion between ISO-2022 and EUC is a simple matter of subtracting or adding 128 (0x80), applied to both bytes—this has the effect of toggling the eighth bit.* Although the conversion of bytes is a simple process, one must properly detect and insert designator sequences, escape sequences, or shift characters for ISO-2022–encoded text.

First, we assume two variables, one for holding each of the two bytes to be converted:

```
int p1,p2;
```

I am not showing how you go about assigning the initial values to these variables—I assume that they already contain appropriate values.

Converting ISO-2022 to EUC is a simple matter of using the following two assignment statements in C:

```
p1 += 128;
p2 += 128;
```

These assignment statements have an effect of adding 128 (0x80) to the current values of the variables `p1` and `p2`. These statements could also have been written as follows:

```
p1 = p1 + 128;
p2 = p1 + 128;
```

Both styles perform the same task. C (and other programming languages) has a shorthand method for doing these sort of variable assignments. There are even shorthand methods for turning the eighth bit on or off.

Next, converting EUC to ISO-2022 requires the following two statements (or their equivalent):

```
p1 -= 128;
p2 -= 128;
```

These assignment statements have an effect of subtracting 128 (0x80) from the current value of the variables `p1` and `p2`. That's really all there is to do.

One difficult issue to contend with is how to handle half-width katakana, which can be represented in EUC-JP encoding using code set 2, but have no official representation in ISO-2022-JP encoding. I suggest that they be converted into their full-width counterparts (see the section entitled "Half- to Full-Width Katakana Conversion—in Java," starting on page 429).

Conversion Between ISO-2022 and Row-Cell

Conversion from ISO-2022 to Row-Cell is a matter of subtracting 32 (0x20) from each of the ISO-2022 bytes.† Similarly, conversion from Row-Cell to ISO-2022 is a

* Or, if you prefer to treat both bytes as a single unit, you subtract or add 32,896 (0x8080).

† Or, if you prefer to treat both bytes as a single unit, use 8,224 (0x2020) instead.

matter of adding 32 (0x20) to each of the Row-Cell bytes (or, more properly, adding 32 (0x20) to the Row and 32 (0x20) to the Cell). This may not be very useful for converting Japanese text since Row-Cell is not typically used internally to represent characters on computer systems—there are exceptions, of course. It may often be useful to determine the Row-Cell value for CJKV characters, such as for indexing into a dictionary whose entries are listed by Row-Cell code.

To convert from ISO-2022 to Row-Cell, use the following assignment statements:

```
p1 -= 32;
p2 -= 32;
```

The reverse conversion (Row-Cell to ISO-2022) uses the following assignment statements:

```
p1 += 32;
p2 += 32;
```

ISO-2022 and Row-Cell are related more closely than you would think. They are different only in the fact that ISO-2022 is the encoded value, which does not happen to begin at value 1, and that Row-Cell represents an encoding-independent way of indexing characters within the 94×94 character matrix. The only software system I know of that processes CJKV characters by Row-Cell values is the Japanese version of TEX, a typesetting language. For other systems it is simply not very efficient or practical to process Row-Cell codes internally.

Conversion Between ISO-2022-JP and Shift-JIS

The ability to convert between ISO-2022-JP and Shift-JIS encodings is fundamental for most software that is designed to support Japanese. Half-width katakana, which can be represented in Shift-JIS encoding, have no official representation in ISO-2022-JP encoding. As with conversion from EUC-JP, I suggest that these characters be converted into their full-width counterparts.

ISO-2022-JP to Shift-JIS conversion

Conversion from ISO-2022-JP to Shift-JIS requires the use of the following conversion algorithm (given in C code), or its equivalent. A call to this function must pass variables for both bytes to be converted, and pointers are used to return the values back to the calling statement. Here is the algorithm:

```
void jis2sjis(int *p1, int *p2)
{
  unsigned char c1 = *p1;
  unsigned char c2 = *p2;
  int rowOffset = c1 < 95 ? 112 : 176;
  int cellOffset = c1 % 2 ? (c2 > 95 ? 32 : 31) : 126;
  *p1 = ((c1 + 1) >> 1) + rowOffset;
  *p2 += cellOffset;
}
```

Assuming that variables have been defined already, a typical call to this function may take the following form:

```
jis2sjis(&p1,&p2);
```

Table 9-6 provides a step-by-step listing of the conversion process used in the above function. The target character is 漢 (*kan*; the "kan" from the Japanese word 漢字 *kanji*). Its ISO-2022-JP code is 52-65, and the Shift-JIS code is 138-191. Changes are highlighted.

Table 9-6: ISO-2022-JP to Shift-JIS Conversion Example

Variable	Line 1	Line 2	Line 3	Line 4	Line 5	Line 6
`c1`	52	52	52	52	52	52
`c2`	…	65	65	65	65	65
`rowOffset`	…	…	112	112	112	112
`cellOffset`	…	…	…	126	126	126
`*p1`	52	52	52	52	138	138
`*p2`	65	65	65	65	65	191

Now for some explanation by line number:

Line 1 The variable `c1` is assigned the value of the object to which `*p1` points. In this case, it is the value of the first byte, specifically 52.

Line 2 The variable `c2` is assigned the value of the object to which `*p2` points. In this case, it is the value of the second byte, specifically 65.

Line 3 The variable `rowOffset` is initialized by testing a condition. This condition is whether the value of the variable `c1` is less than 95. If its value is less than 95, `rowOffset` is initialized to 112. Otherwise, it is initialized to 176. Because `c1` is less than 95 in the example, `rowOffset` is initialized to 112.

Line 4 The variable `cellOffset` is initialized by testing one or more conditions. The first condition is whether the variable `c1` is odd. If this first condition is not met, `cellOffset` is initialized to 126. If this first condition is met, another condition is tested. If the variable `c2` is greater than 95, `cellOffset` will be initialized to 32; 31 otherwise. Because `c1` is not odd in the example, `cellOffset` is initialized to 126.

Line 5 The object to which `*p1` points is assigned the value of adding 1 to `c1` (52 + 1 = 53), performing a right-shift, which is the same as dividing a number by two and throwing away the remainder (53 ÷ 2 = 26), then finally adding `rowOffset` (26 + 112 = 138).

Line 6 The object to which `*p2` points is assigned the value of adding `cellOffset` to itself (126 + 65 = 191).

Besides simple code conversion, it is also very important to be able to detect the escape sequences used in ISO-2022-JP encoding. Escape sequences signal the software when to change modes. Good software should also keep track of the current *n*-byte-per-character mode so that redundant escape sequences can be ignored (and absorbed). Remember that Shift-JIS encoding does not use escape sequences, so you will have to make sure that they are not written to the resulting output file.

Shift-JIS to ISO-2022-JP conversion

Conversion from Shift-JIS to ISO-2022-JP is not as simple as simply reversing the above algorithm, but requires the use of the following dedicated conversion algorithm (given again in C code), or its equivalent. A call to this function must pass variables for both bytes to be converted, and pointers are used to return the values back to the calling statement.

```
        void sjis2jis(int *p1, int *p2)
        {
Line 1    unsigned char c1 = *p1;
Line 2    unsigned char c2 = *p2;
Line 3    int adjust = c2 < 159;
Line 4    int rowOffset = c1 < 160 ? 112 : 176;
Line 5    int cellOffset = adjust ? (c2 > 127 ? 32 : 31) : 126;
Line 6    *p1 = ((c1 - rowOffset) << 1) - adjust;
Line 7    *p2 -= cellOffset;
        }
```

Assuming that variables have been defined already, a typical call to this function may take the following form:

```
sjis2jis(&p1,&p2);
```

Table 9-7 provides a step-by-step table of the conversion process used in the above function. The target character is 漢 again. Its Shift-JIS code is 138-191, and its ISO-2022-JP code is 52-65. Changes are highlighted.

Table 9-7: Shift-JIS to ISO-2022-JP Conversion Example

Variable	Line 1	Line 2	Line 3	Line 4	Line 5	Line 6	Line 7
`c1`	138	138	138	138	138	138	138
`c2`	...	191	191	191	191	191	191
`adjust`	...	...	0	0	0	0	0
`rowOffset`	...	...	...	112	112	112	112
`cellOffset`	...	...	...	...	126	126	126
`*p1`	138	138	138	138	138	52	52
`*p2`	191	191	191	191	191	191	65

Now for some explanation by line number:

Line 1 The variable `c1` is assigned the value of the object to which `*p1` points. In this case, it is the value of the first byte, specifically 138.

Line 2 The variable `c2` is assigned the value of the object to which `*p2` points. In this case, it is the value of the second byte, specifically 191.

Line 3 The variable `adjust` is assigned the value 0 or 1, depending on the result of a test. This test checks whether the value of the variable `c2` is less than 159. If the result of this test results in true, then the variable `adjust` is assigned the value 1, otherwise it is assigned the value 0. In this example, the variable `c2` is 191, which is not less than 159, so `adjust` is assigned the value 0.

Line 4 The variable `rowOffset` is initialized by testing a condition. This condition is whether the value of the variable `c1` is less than 160. If its value is less than 160, `rowOffset` is initialized to 112. Otherwise, it is initialized to 176. Because `c1` is less than 160 in the example, `rowOffset` is initialized to 112.

Line 5 The variable `cellOffset` is initialized by testing one or more conditions. The first condition is whether the variable `adjust` is equal to 1. If this first condition is not met, `cellOffset` is initialized to 126. If this first condition is met, another condition is tested. If the variable `c2` is greater than 127, `cellOffset` will be initialized to 32; 31 otherwise. Because `c1` is not equal to 1 in the example, `cellOffset` is initialized to 126.

Line 6 The object to which `*p1` points is assigned the value of subtracting `rowOffset` from `c1` (138 – 112 = 26), performing a left-shift, which is equivalent to multiplying a number by two (26 × 2 = 52), then finally subtracting `adjust` (52 – 0 = 52).

Line 7 The object to which `*p2` points is assigned the value of subtracting `cellOffset` from itself (191 – 126 = 65).

Again, it is also very important to be able to properly insert escape sequences into ISO-2022-JP–encoded text streams. Be sure that redundant escape sequences are not written.

Conversion Between EUC-JP and Shift-JIS

There is no need to elaborately explain how one goes about converting Shift-JIS to EUC-JP here. What you have already learned is sufficient. You simply need to use ISO-2022-JP encoding as the middle ground for JIS X 0208:1997 characters.* The

* ISO-2022-JP encoding cannot be used as the middle ground for half-width katakana because the official definition of ISO-2022-JP encoding explicitly excludes half-width katakana.

only exceptional handling that is required is for those pesky half-width katakana, which require a one-byte representation in Shift-JIS, but a two-byte representation in EUC-JP. The relationship between them is useful to know—the second byte of EUC-JP–encoded half-width katakana is the same as the Shift-JIS equivalent. Converting Shift-JIS half-width katakana to EUC-JP encoding is a matter of prefixing a byte with the value of 142 (0x8E, also known as SS2) to each half-width katakana byte. Likewise, converting EUC-JP–encoded half-width katakana to Shift-JIS is a simple matter of removing the first byte, specifically 142 (0x8E). Note that escape-sequence handling is not required for either encoding.

Other Code Conversion Types

What you have learned already is enough to guide you through additional code conversion types, so we haven't covered every type of code conversion. Table 9-8 details how to implement other conversions. (The values used in Table 9-8 are in decimal notation.)

Table 9-8: Code Conversion Matrix

From | To	ISO-2022	Shift-JIS	EUC	Row-Cell
ISO-2022	...	jis2sjis	+128	−32
Shift-JIS	sjis2jis	...	sjis2jis then +128	sjis2jis then −32
EUC	−128	−128 then jis2sjis	...	−160
Row-Cell	+32	+32 then jis2sjis	+160	...

The string *jis2sjis* refers to the ISO-2022-JP to Shift-JIS conversion algorithm; likewise, *sjis2jis* refers to the Shift-JIS to ISO-2022-JP conversion algorithm—both were described in detail earlier in this chapter. The numbers prefixed with either + (plus) or – (minus) mean that you must add or subtract those amounts, in decimal, from both bytes. Also note in the table how ISO-2022 is used as the middle ground for code conversion when Shift-JIS encoding is involved—this does not mean such implementation is absolutely necessary, but I find it efficient to do so.

Java Programming Examples

The following sections illustrate, with example code, how trivial CJKV code conversion can be when using the Java programming language. Specifically, code conversion and text stream handling techniques are provided.

Java Code Conversion

The Java programming language, beginning with Version 1.1, provides extremely useful built-in code conversion facilities that allow the programmer to easily convert between legacy (that is, non-Unicode) encodings and Unicode. This is a significant development because the proper handling of multiple encodings has always been a tricky issue for programmers developing software that manipulates CJKV text or data.

The Java code examples in this section demonstrate how to take advantage of Java's built-in code conversion facilities for handling small chunks of data, such as single characters or short strings of characters. You will notice that these examples are short and concise, which clearly illustrates how Java trivializes code conversion.

Non-Unicode to Unicode conversion—import

One of the ways in which non-Unicode data can be converted to Unicode using Java is to simply convert byte arrays into String objects. The following is sample code that first creates a byte array (containing the two-byte value 0xB0EC for the EUC-JP–encoded kanji 一 meaning "one") then converts it into Unicode:

```
byte[] my_eucjp_data = {(byte)0xB0,(byte)0xEC};
String my_unicode_data = new String(my_eucjp_data,"EUC_JP");
```

Simply specifying a "charset" value, such as `EUC_JP` for EUC-JP encoding, as the second argument to the String object creation method is sufficient to invoke code conversion on the byte array `my_eucjp_data`. It is really that simple.

The String object `my_unicode_data` ends up containing the Unicode value 0x4E00 (expressed as `\u4E00` in Java notation).

Unicode to non-Unicode conversion—export

Because the Java programming language processes Unicode internally, it may become necessary to convert an internal Unicode representation into a legacy encoding when dealing with non-Unicode environment.

```
String my_unicode_data = "\u4E00";
byte[] my_eucjp_data = my_unicode_data.getBytes("EUC_JP");
```

It is really amazing to realize how trivial code conversion can become when using Java's built-in facilities, as the above two lines of Java code demonstrate.

Java Text Stream Handling

This section provides example code for handling text streams in Java through the underlying use of the standard (but private) `ByteToCharConverter` and `CharTo-ByteConverter` classes found in the *sun.io* package. These algorithms fall into two basic types:

- Non-Unicode to Unicode (considered a text "import")
- Unicode to non-Unicode (considered a text "export")

None of these text stream conversion types require *any* special handling, such as the proper handling of designator sequences, escape sequences, or shifting characters as used in ISO-2022 encoding.

Before Java, keeping track of the current *n*-byte-per-character mode and current character set was very important when dealing with ISO-2022–encoded data. Java performs the following tasks for you:

- Recognize and remove redundant escape sequences
- Ensure that lines terminate in one-byte mode
- Ensure that the file terminates in one-byte mode

This list may not seem very important to you now, but as you begin to encounter ISO-2022–encoded files with redundant or missing escape sequences, you will soon appreciate it.

Non-Unicode to Unicode conversion—import

Converting a text stream from a non-Unicode encoding to Unicode is greatly simplified in Java through its text stream classes. Non-Unicode encodings are treated as *raw* data by Java. The following three lines of Java open a file called *input* and proceed to convert its contents to Unicode as it is being read:

```
File i = new File("input");
FileInputStream tmpin = new FileInputStream(i);
BufferedReader in = new BufferedReader(new InputStreamReader(tmpin,"SJIS"));
```

Once the BufferedReader `in` is established, as accomplished above, data can be read using the `readLine()` method. The following is an example use of this method:

```
inputStr = in.readLine();
```

Note the use of `SJIS` as the second argument to the `InputStreamReader()` method. This parameter invokes the built-in conversion to Unicode assuming Shift-JIS (`SJIS`) encoding as input.

As you can see, Java takes away all of the pain associated with importing non-Unicode data. This is actually a big win for programmers because what has traditionally been a formidable task in developing CJKV-capable software is now trivialized.

Unicode to non-Unicode conversion—export

Properly handling conversion from a seven-bit code to an eight-bit encoding requires that escape sequences be recognized, handled, then absorbed. The example code provided below handles conversion of an ISO-2022-JP–encoded text stream to Shift-JIS encoding. Another example is ISO-2022-JP to EUC-JP conversion.

Here is the Java code for converting a Unicode–encoded text stream into Shift-JIS encoding. Notice that this function does not return any information to the calling statement—it merely reads in a text stream, and outputs to another text stream.

```
File o = new File("output.sjs");
FileOutputStream tmpout = new FileOutputStream(o);
BufferedWriter out = new BufferedWriter(new OutputStreamWriter(tmpout,"SJIS"));
```

After the BufferedWriter `out` object is established, Unicode data that is subsequently output is automatically converted to Shift-JIS encoding.

```
out.println("\u6CB3\u8C5A");
out.close();
```

The two Unicode characters 0x6CB3 (河) and 0x8C5A (豚) that are fed to the `println()` method become Shift-JIS 0x89CD and 0x93D8 in the output file called *output.sjs*. Creating a UTF-8–encoded output file is accomplished in the same way, but the `UTF8` charset designator should be used instead of `SJIS`.

It is also possible to output directly in Unicode, demonstrated as follows:

```
PrintWriter out = new PrintWriter (
  new BufferedWriter (
    new OutputStreamWriter (
      new FileOutputStream("output.ucs"), "Unicode"
    )
  )
);
```

We can then output the same Unicode characters, without any code conversion applied, as follows:

```
out.println("\u6CB3\u8C5A");
out.close();
```

This time, the output is exactly 0x6CB3 (河) and 0x8C5A (豚).

Java "Charset" Designators

In order to take advantage of Java's built-in code conversion facilities, you need to be aware of the valid "charset" designators in order to properly invoke them. While Java has "preferred" charset designators for each meaningful character set and encoding combination, it also supports an aliasing mechanism to support alternate charset names.

Table 9-9 provides a partial listing of Java's charset designators, along with the encodings and character sets that they support. Alternate charset designators have been explicitly excluded from this table (to discourage their use). These charset designators can be used to invoke the built-in code conversion routines.

Table 9-9: Java's Charset Designators—Examples

Charset Designator	Encoding	Character Sets
`ASCII`	ASCII	ASCII
`ISO8859_1`	ISO 8859-1:1998	ISO 8859-1:1998
`UTF8`	UTF-8	Unicode
`ISO2022CN_CNS`	ISO-2022-CN-EXT	ASCII, CNS 11643-1992
`ISO2022CN_GB`	ISO-2022-CN	ASCII/GB-Roman, GB 2312-80
`ISO2022JP`	ISO-2022-JP	ASCII/JIS-Roman, half-width katakana, JIS X 0208:1997, JIS X 0212-1990
`ISO2022KR`	ISO-2022-KR	ASCII/KS-Roman, KS X 1001:1992
`EUC_CN`	EUC-CN	ASCII/GB-Roman, GB 2312-80
`EUC_JP`	EUC-JP	ASCII/JIS-Roman, half-width katakana, JIS X 0208:1997, JIS X 0212-1990
`EUC_KR`	EUC-KR	ASCII/KS-Roman, KS X 1001:1992
`EUC_TW`	EUC-TW	ASCII, CNS 11643-1992
`GBK`	GBK	ASCII, GBK
`Big5`	Big Five	ASCII, Big Five
`SJIS`	Shift-JIS	ASCII/JIS-Roman, half-width katakana, JIS X 0208:1997

A much more complete and up-to-date listing of Java charset designators is available online—be sure to consult the latest Java programming language specification to ensure that you are using the correct charset designators, which will best guarantee that your program will function in all environments.*

Miscellaneous Algorithms

This section covers three miscellaneous algorithms that are useful, but are not directly associated with either code conversion or text stream handling, as covered in the two previous sections.

The first algorithm is for the automatic detection of the input file's encoding. Some software requires that you specify the encoding method used by the input file: many people who use Japanese code conversion utilities may not be familiar with the various Japanese encoding methods. If you do not know, all you can do is guess. The Japanese code detection algorithm examines the

* *http://java.sun.com/products/jdk/1.1/docs/guide/intl/encoding.doc.html*

input file in order to determine the encoding method. This usually makes it unnecessary to specify the input file's encoding method. However, there are times when the input file's encoding may be ambiguous—the Shift-JIS and EUC-JP encoding ranges overlap considerably, for example.

The second algorithm converts half-width katakana into their full-width counterparts. Some environments do not provide half-width katakana support, so this algorithm converts these characters into their full-width versions, which are more commonly supported. This algorithm is also quite useful as a filter for outgoing email transmissions to ensure that information interchange is maintained on the receiving end.

The third and last algorithm repairs damaged ISO-2022-JP–encoded files; that is, files which had their escape sequences stripped out by unfriendly email or news reading software. I occasionally received email in this damaged format, and spent a lot of time reinserting those lost escape characters. This algorithm is simply a way to automate this repair process.

The C functions described in this section use the following C `#define` statements in addition to those listed in the previous section:

```
#define NEW         1
#define OLD         2
#define NEC         3
#define EUC         4
#define SJIS        5
#define EUCORSJIS   6
#define ASCII       7
#define SS2         142
#define ESC         27
```

Japanese Code Detection

This algorithm is useful for automatically detecting the Japanese encoding used in a Japanese text file. This is useful when you receive Japanese text files with various encodings: it is not always obvious what encoding a given text file uses, so it is easier to let the software decide for you.

This C function requires only an input stream as a parameter, but returns a value to the calling statement indicating what Japanese code, if any, was detected. This value can either specify the Japanese encoding detected or that none was detected (or was ambiguous). If Japanese encoding was detected, possible values include JIS C 6226-1978 (also called Old-JIS), JIS X 0208-1983 (also called New-JIS), NEC Kanji (also called NEC-JIS), EUC-JP (packed format), and Shift-JIS. It also returns special values if no Japanese encoding was detected, or if the Japanese encoding was ambiguous (Shift-JIS and EUC-JP overlap considerably, and it is possible to encounter text streams that may be ambiguous). I use this algorithm in two of the tools described at the end of this chapter, specifically JConv and JCode. A typical call to this function takes the following form:

```
DetectCodeType(in);
```

Below is a C function for detecting the Japanese encoding of an input stream. Most of the statements check encoded value ranges. The results of these checks are then used to determine whether a particular encoding has been detected in the stream. ISO-2022 encodings are easily detected by the occurrence of escape characters, along with other characters that constitute a valid two-byte character escape sequence.

```
int DetectCodeType(FILE *in)
{
  int c = 0;
  int whatcode = ASCII;               /* The detected code, set to ASCII. */
  while ((whatcode == EUCORSJIS || whatcode == ASCII) && c != EOF) {
    if ((c = fgetc(in)) != EOF) {  /* Read one byte until EOF. */
      if (c == ESC) {                 /* Maybe ISO-2022-JP encoding. */
        c = fgetc(in);
        if (c == '$') {               /* Maybe two-byte escape sequence. */
          c = fgetc(in);
          if (c == 'B')
            whatcode = NEW;           /* JIS X 0208-1983 detected. */
          else if (c == '@')
            whatcode = OLD;           /* JIS C 6226-1978 detected. */
        }
        else if (c == 'K')
          whatcode = NEC;             /* NEC Japanese detected. */
      }
      else if ((c >= 129 && c <= 141) || (c >= 143 && c <= 159))
        whatcode = SJIS;
      else if (c == SS2) {            /* Maybe EUC-JP half-width katakana. */
        c = fgetc(in);
        if ((c >= 64 && c <= 126) || (c >= 128 && c <= 160) || (c >= 224 && c <= 252))
          whatcode = SJIS;            /* Shift-JIS detected. */
        else if (c >= 161 && c <= 223)
          whatcode = EUCORSJIS;       /* Ambiguous (Shift-JIS or EUC-JP). */
      }
      else if (c >= 161 && c <= 223) {
        c = fgetc(in);
        if (c >= 240 && c <= 254)
          whatcode = EUC;             /* EUC-JP detected. */
        else if (c >= 161 && c <= 223)
          whatcode = EUCORSJIS;       /* Ambiguous (Shift-JIS or EUC-JP). */
        else if (c >= 224 && c <= 239) {
          whatcode = EUCORSJIS;       /* Ambiguous (Shift-JIS or EUC-JP). */
          while (c >= 64 && c != EOF && whatcode == EUCORSJIS) {
            if (c >= 129) {
              if (c <= 141 || (c >= 143 && c <= 159))
                whatcode = SJIS;      /* Shift-JIS detected. */
              else if (c >= 253 && c <= 254)
                whatcode = EUC;       /* EUC-JP detected. */
            }
            c = fgetc(in);
          }
        }
        else if (c <= 159)
          whatcode = SJIS;            /* Shift-JIS detected. */
      }
      else if (c >= 240 && c <= 254)
        whatcode = EUC;               /* EUC-JP detected. */
      else if (c >= 224 && c <= 239) {
```

```
        c = fgetc(in); /* Read next byte to c. */
        if ((c >= 64 && c <= 126) || (c >= 128 && c <= 160))
          whatcode = SJIS;          /* Shift-JIS detected. */
        else if (c >= 253 && c <= 254)
          whatcode = EUC;           /* EUC-JP detected. */
        else if (c >= 161 && c <= 252)
          whatcode = EUCORSJIS;     /* Ambiguous (Shift-JIS or EUC-JP). */
      }
    }
  }
  return whatcode;                  /* Return the detected code. */
}
```

Appendix W provides Perl code for a much more flexible way to automatically detect the encoding of CJKV text files, not only those for Japanese. That Perl code shows how powerful regular expressions can be when used in specific contexts.

Half- to Full-Width Katakana Conversion—in Java

It sometimes is necessary to convert half-width katakana to their full-width counterparts. This is most useful as a filter to ensure that no half-width katakana characters are included within email messages. It is also useful when you need to move files from one platform to another and the new platform does not support half-width katakana characters. Example usage of this Java method is as follows:

```
String half = "\uFF76\uFF9E";
String full = KatakanaFilter.halfToFullWidthKatakana(half);
```

There is no simple conversion algorithm that you can use to accomplish this task. In fact, such conversion requires a mapping table between half- and full-width katakana (table-driven conversion), as well as special handling to accommodate dakuten and handakuten, the marks that modify kana characters. You see, these marks are encoded as separate characters in the half-width katakana character set, but in the case of full-width katakana, they are integrated with katakana characters within the same encoded character.

The following Java class defines a method called `halfToFullWidthKatakana()` that represents the algorithm for converting half-width katakana to their full-width counterparts, and includes proper handling for dakuten and handakuten marks.

```
public class KatakanaFilter {

  // Zero-base table for mapping half-width katakana to full-width
  private final static char FWKatakana[] = {
    '\u3002','\u300C','\u300D','\u3001','\u30FB', // U+FF61 - U+FF65
    '\u30F2','\u30A1','\u30A3','\u30A5','\u30A7', // U+FF66 - U+FF6A
    '\u30A9','\u30E3','\u30E5','\u30E7','\u30C3', // U+FF6B - U+FF6F
    '\u30FC','\u30A2','\u30A4','\u30A6','\u30A8', // U+FF70 - U+FF74
    '\u30AA','\u30AB','\u30AD','\u30AF','\u30B1', // U+FF75 - U+FF79
    '\u30B3','\u30B5','\u30B7','\u30B9','\u30BB', // U+FF7A - U+FF7E
    '\u30BD','\u30BF','\u30C1','\u30C4','\u30C6', // U+FF7F - U+FF83
    '\u30C8','\u30CA','\u30CB','\u30CC','\u30CD', // U+FF84 - U+FF88
    '\u30CE','\u30CF','\u30D2','\u30D5','\u30D8', // U+FF89 - U+FF8D
```

```
    '\u30DB','\u30DE','\u30DF','\u30E0','\u30E1', // U+FF8E - U+FF92
    '\u30E2','\u30E4','\u30E6','\u30E8','\u30E9', // U+FF93 - U+FF97
    '\u30EA','\u30EB','\u30EC','\u30ED','\u30EF', // U+FF98 - U+FF9C
    '\u30F3','\u309B','\u309C'                    // U+FF9D - U+FF9F
  };

  // Class method for converting half-width katakana to full-width
  public static String halfToFullWidthKatakana (String string_input) {
    int ixIn = 0;
    int ixOut = 0;
    int bufferLength = string_input.length();
    char[] input = string_input.toCharArray();
    char[] output = new char[bufferLength + 1];

    while (ixIn < bufferLength) {
      if (input[ixIn] >= '\uFF61' && input[ixIn] <= '\uFF9F') {
        if (ixIn + 1 >= bufferLength) {
          output[ixOut++] = FWKatakana[input[ixIn++] - '\uFF61'];
        } else {
          if (input[ixIn + 1] == '\uFF9E' || input[ixIn + 1] == '\u3099'
          || input[ixIn + 1] == '\u309B') {
            if (input[ixIn] == '\uFF73') {
              output[ixOut++] = '\u30F4';
              ixIn += 2;
            } else if (input[ixIn] >= '\uFF76' && input[ixIn] <= '\uFF84'
              || input[ixIn] >= '\uFF8A' && input[ixIn] <= '\uFF8E') {
              output[ixOut] = FWKatakana[input[ixIn] - '\uFF61'];
              output[ixOut++]++;
              ixIn += 2;
            } else {
              output[ixOut++] = FWKatakana[input[ixIn++] - '\uFF61'];
            }
          } else if (input[ixIn + 1] == '\uFF9F'
            || input[ixIn + 1] == '\u309A' || input[ixIn + 1] == '\u309C') {
            if (input[ixIn] >= '\uFF8A' && input[ixIn] <= '\uFF8E') {
              output[ixOut] = FWKatakana[input[ixIn] - '\uFF61'];
              output[ixOut++] += 2;
              ixIn += 2;
            } else {
              output[ixOut++] = FWKatakana[input[ixIn++] - '\uFF61'];
            }
          } else {
            output[ixOut++] = FWKatakana[input[ixIn++] - '\uFF61'];
          }
        }
      } else {
        output[ixOut++] = input[ixIn++];
      }
    }
    String output_string = new String(output);
    return output_string.substring(0,ixOut);
  }
}
```

Appendix W provides a half- to full-width katakana conversion program written in Perl. It is different in that it is not based on Unicode, but rather supports EUC-JP and Shift-JIS encodings.

Encoding Repair

ISO-2022-JP–encoded files often become damaged or corrupt from software that strips out escape characters. Some programs have a tendency to filter out control characters from files, and the escape character (0x1B), which is an essential part of ISO-2022-JP encoding, is a control character. Luckily, there are ways to repair corrupted ISO-2022-JP–encoded files.

You can make a few assumptions before you proceed to repair damaged ISO-2022-JP–encoded files. The first assumption is that the text stream begins, and also ends, in one-byte mode. In addition, each line begins and ends in one-byte mode. The next assumption is that the other characters that make up a complete escape sequence are still intact. These may include such strings as `$@`, `$B`, `(J`, and `(B`. Depending on the *n*-byte-per-character mode, you need to scan for different strings.

While in one-byte mode, you need only to scan for the string `$B` or `$@`, which should signify the beginning of two-byte mode. The chances of encountering such strings of characters while in one-byte mode are quite low (but can happen!). You need to repair such string occurrences by inserting an escape character immediately before the string that determined the context for it (in this case, either `$B` or `$@`). The current mode is then shifted to two-byte.

While in two-byte mode, you need to scan for the strings `(J` and `(B`. Also, since you are in two-byte mode, you must scan two characters, then compare them to the search strings. The two bytes that represent the strings `(J` and `(B` are within the ISO-2022-JP encoding space, but have no characters assigned to them. This means that you should never run into those strings other than when they are part of a damaged escape sequence. Like before, you need to insert an escape character right before the string that was found (in this case, either `(J` or `(B`). The current mode is then shifted to one-byte.

Other processing may be necessary if you reach the end of a line, but are still in two-byte mode. You must then insert a whole escape sequence.

The following C function represents an algorithm for automatically inserting escape sequences into a damaged ISO-2022-JP–encoded file. Note that undamaged escape sequences are also recognized by this C function. A modified version of this function is used in one of the Japanese code processing tools (specifically, JConv) described at the end of this chapter, starting on page 448.

```
void repairjis(FILE *in,FILE *out)
{
  int p1;                                    /* First byte. */
  int p2;                                    /* Second byte. */
  int p3;                                    /* Third byte. */
  int shifted_in = FALSE;                    /* The initial one-byte mode. */
  while ((p1 = getc(in)) != EOF) {
    if (shifted_in) {                        /* If in two-byte mode. */
      if (p1 == ESC) {
        p2 = getc(in);
        if (p2 == '(') {
          p3 = getc(in);
          switch (p3) {
            case 'J' :                       /* JIS-Roman. */
            case 'B' :                       /* ASCII. */
            case 'H' :                       /* False JIS-Roman. */
              shifted_in = FALSE;            /* Change to one-byte mode. */
              break;
            default :
              break;
          }
          fprintf(out,"%c%c%c",p1,p2,p3);    /* Print the escape sequence. */
        }
      }
      else if (p1 == '(') {                  /* If p1 is (. */
        p2 = getc(in);
        switch (p2) {
          case 'J' :                         /* JIS-Roman. */
          case 'B' :                         /* ASCII. */
          case 'H' :                         /* False JIS-Roman. */
            shifted_in = FALSE;              /* Change to one-byte mode. */
            fprintf(out,"%c%c%c",ESC,p1,p2); /* Print the escape sequence. */
            break;
          default :
            fprintf(out,"%c%c",p1,p2);       /* Print p1 and p2. */
            break;
        }
      }
      else {
        p2 = getc(in);
        fprintf(out,"%c%c",p1,p2);           /* Print p1 and p2. */
      }
    }
    else {                                   /* If in one-byte mode. */
      if (p1 == ESC) {
        p2 = getc(in);
        if (p2 == '$') {
          p3 = getc(in);
          switch (p3) {
            case 'B' :                       /* JIS X 0208-1983. */
            case '@' :                       /* JIS C 6226-1978. */
              shifted_in = TRUE;             /* Change to two-byte mode. */
              break;
            default :
              break;
          }
          fprintf(out,"%c%c%c",p1,p2,p3);    /* Print the escape sequence. */
        }
      }
      else if (p1 == '$') {
        p2 = getc(in);
        switch (p2) {
          case 'B' :                         /* JIS X 0208-1983. */
          case '@' :                         /* JIS C 6226-1978. */
            shifted_in = TRUE;               /* Change to two-byte mode. */
            fprintf(out,"%c%c%c",ESC,p1,p2); /* Print the escape sequence. */
            break;
          default :
```

```
                fprintf(out,"%c%c",p1,p2);          /* Print p1 and p2. */
                break;
            }
          }
          else
            fprintf(out,"%c",p1);                   /* Print p1. */
        }
      }
    }
```

Yep, you guessed it, Appendix W provides a similar program, but written in Perl. I encourage you to compare and contrast the C and Java examples in this chapter with Perl versions in Appendix W.

Byte Versus Character Handling

Most Western encoding methods have the luxury of assuming that one byte equals one character, so inserting, deleting, and searching text becomes a simple matter of comparing one byte with another. However, this is not the case with encodings that require more than one byte to represent a single character, such as those used for representing CJKV text. Life gets much more complex! A multiple-byte character is still a character. Consider it an "atomic" unit. After all, you would gawk at Western-style software that split characters into four-bit units for some strange design reason. What I discuss below falls into what I would call text processing behavior, because it is what one would expect from programs such as text editors, word processors, and the like.

What you should learn from this section is that a multiple-byte character should never be broken down into its component bytes. This whole discussion points out the best reason for adapting fixed 16- or 32-bit representations inside your software—you can much more safely deal with atomic units. The topics that follow are examples of areas in which many text processing programs fail to handle multiple-byte characters properly. There are many examples of programs that fall into this category—unless a program was specifically designed to handle multiple-byte characters, it is unlikely that multiple-byte characters are handled properly. For example, the *standard* (that is, unlocalized) version of Microsoft Word (for MacOS) is one of the most popular word processing programs ever, but fails to handle two-byte characters properly.

Character Deletion

It is quite likely that you will encounter text processing software that deletes only one byte of a two-byte character. Those that have been properly adapted to CJKV locales are able to detect whether the character in front of the insertion point is represented by two bytes, and subsequently deletes both bytes. This problem can be avoided if you remember to press the delete key twice when dealing with two-byte characters. If you are not careful, loss or corruption of data may result.

Let's take a closer look at this problem. Table 9-10 provides a sample Shift-JIS–encoded Japanese text string. The first process that will be applied is the deletion of the last character. The first example deletes the last *character* (consisting of two bytes), and the second deletes the last *byte* (more precisely, the last *byte* of the last *character*). Finally, we add another character, 典, at the insertion point. Note how the undeleted first byte left over from the second example affects the interpretation of the added character (the encoded value of this added character is highlighted).

Table 9-10: Character Deletion Example—Shift-JIS

	Text Representation	Shift-JIS Representation				
Original string	漢字辞書	漢	字	辞	書	
		8ABF	8E9A	8EAB	8F91	
Delete (correct)	漢字辞	漢	字	辞		
		8ABF	8E9A	8EAB		
Add character	漢字辞典	漢	字	辞	典	
		8ABF	8E9A	8EAB	9354	
Delete (incorrect)	漢字辞	漢	字	辞		
		8ABF	8E9A	8EAB	8F	
Add character	漢字辞諸T	漢	字	辞	諸	T
		8ABF	8E9A	8EAB	**8F93**	**54**

A lack of synch occurs when the first byte of a two-byte character is left behind. Any two-byte characters that follow will be interpreted incorrectly—their first byte will be interpreted as the second byte for the previous character, and their second byte will be interpreted as a first byte.

Table 9-11 illustrates what happens with the same character string, but when EUC-JP–encoded.

Table 9-11: Character Deletion Example—EUC-JP

	Text Representation	EUC-JP Representation			
Original string	漢字辞書	漢	字	辞	書
		B4C1	BBFA	BCAD	BDF1
Delete (correct)	漢字辞	漢	字	辞	
		B4C1	BBFA	BCAD	
Add character	漢字辞典	漢	字	辞	典
		B4C1	BBFA	BCAD	C5B5

Table 9-11: Character Deletion Example—EUC-JP (continued)

	Text Representation	EUC-JP Representation				
Delete (incorrect)	漢字辞	漢	字	辞		
		B4C1	BBFA	BCAD	BD	
Add character	漢字辞重	漢	字	辞	重	
		B4C1	BBFA	BCAD	**BDC5**	**B5**

This problem is fixed by keeping track of the characters at the insertion point—whether they are represented by one or more bytes. If a byte happens to be the second byte of a two-byte character, both bytes must be deleted with a single keystroke. In the case of three-byte characters (for example, characters from EUC-JP code set 3—JIS X 0212-1990 characters), three bytes must be deleted. An extreme example is EUC-TW encoding, which includes a four-byte representation.

Character Insertion

Inserting characters is problematic only when the insertion point (that is, the cursor) is between the two bytes that represent a two-byte character. This then splits the two-byte character, and results in data loss. This section, as you may have expected, relates to cursor movement.

Let's now look at some examples of inserting characters between the two bytes of a two-byte character. The example string is 仮名漢字, and the character と is mistakenly inserted between the two bytes of the character 名—in an ideal world, it should be added between the two *characters* 名 and 漢. Table 9-12 provides an example that is Shift-JIS–encoded, and the byte values for the inserted character are highlighted.

Table 9-12: Character Insertion Example—Shift-JIS

	Text Representation	Shift-JIS Representation					
Original string	仮名漢字	仮	名	漢	字		
		89BC	96BC	8ABF	8E9A		
Correct	仮名と漢字	仮	名	と	漢	字	
		89BC	96BC	82C6	8ABF	8E9A	
Incorrect	仮魔ﾆｼ漢字	仮	魔	ﾆ	ｼ	漢	字
		89BC	96**82**	**C6**	BC	8ABF	8E9A

Notice how the two-byte character 名 is split right down the middle, and that unexpected characters have resulted, two of which are interpreted as half-width katakana. Now you can see why incorrect character insertion must never be allowed to happen—it leads to corruption and data loss. Integrity is retained only with proper handling of two-byte characters.

Table 9-13 provides this same example, but this time EUC-JP–encoded. Notice how different characters result from incorrect insertion—the expected 名と string becomes the unexpected 未半.

Table 9-13: Character Insertion Example—EUC-JP

	Text Representation	EUC-JP Representation				
Original string	仮名漢字	仮	名	漢	字	
		B2BE	CCBE	B4C1	BBFA	
Correct	仮名と漢字	仮	名	と	漢	字
		B2BE	CCBE	A4C8	B4C1	BBFA
Incorrect	仮未半漢字	仮	未	半	漢	字
		B2BE	CC**A4**	**C8**BE	B4C1	BBFA

The solution to this problem is simply to have the cursor move one or more bytes—the number of bytes to move corresponds to the number of bytes used to represent the current character.

Character Searching

The various instances of the *grep* program represent the most commonly-used utilities on Unix and some other platforms—*grep* is short for *Global Regular Expression Print* (jokingly, one source suggests that *grep* represents the first letters of its authors' last names: Gregior, Ritchie, Ebersole, and Pike). The *grep* program performs a search based on regular expressions (covered later in this chapter). The standard Unix version of *grep*, unfortunately, does not treat two or more bytes (that constitute a single character) as a single unit. Some versions of Unix, such as IBM's AIX, include versions of *grep* that recognize multiple-byte characters.

So, you may ask, what problem does this cause? Well, take, for instance, a case when you are searching for the kanji 剣 in a large Japanese file. Assuming Shift-JIS encoding, you may end up with matches in quite unexpected places. In fact, some lines for which a match is reported may not even contain the kanji 剣 because comparison that is performed during searching is done on a per-byte basis. This means that one byte is compared to another without regard to multiple-byte characters. In the case of a search pattern that contains multiple-byte characters, the following conditions *must* be met:

- One or more bytes of the search string must be compared with one or more bytes in the document being searched.
- The current index into the text being searched must advance either one or more bytes depending on whether the character at that index is represented by one or more bytes. This simply means that the index must advance one *character*, which is not always represented by one byte.

- Because CJKV character sets are supported by multiple encodings, the search engine must be completely aware of the encoding used in the search string *and* in the document to be searched. If the encodings are different, they must be made compatible (the easiest approach would be to convert the search string into the same encoding used in the document to be searched).

If these conditions are not met, matches may sometimes be made with the second or subsequent bytes of one multiple-byte character plus the first or subsequent bytes of the next. This, of course, produces completely undesirable results. Table 9-14 provides an example using the character 剣 as the search string in a Shift-JIS–encoded file (the codes of matches are highlighted).

Table 9-14: Character Searching Example—Shift-JIS

	Characters	**Shift-JIS Codes**		
Search string	剣	剣		
		8C95		
Correct	剣道	剣	道	
		8C95	93B9	
Incorrect	白血病	白	血	病
		9492	8C**8C**	**95**61

Note how the example of an incorrect match spans two characters, specifically the second byte of one character and the first byte of the next. The incorrect match was made by treating every byte as a single character—the *one-byte-equals-one-character* barrier must be overcome in order to handle CJKV text properly. This is a crucial issue for those who are writing multiple-byte–capable search engines, a topic covered in the section entitled "Search Engines," starting on page 447.

Line Breaking

Many text processing programs allow users to break long lines into shorter ones, usually by specifying a maximum number of columns per line. As you can expect, breaking a line between the bytes of a two-byte character can result in a loss of information and end up corrupting surrounding characters.

Let's look at what may happen when ISO-2022-JP, Shift-JIS, and EUC-JP strings are broken into two lines. In the example below a line break is inserted between the two bytes that represent the katakana character サ (*sa*). Note how that character is apparently lost, and how some characters after the line break become scrambled. Some Japanese telecommunications programs (such as ASLTelnet) insert their own one-byte character escape sequences at the end of each line to ensure that no errors take place. This means when a line is broken, the software automatically inserts a one-byte character escape sequence. However, when the line is broken in this fashion, the lack of an additional two-byte character escape sequence causes the line following to be interpreted as one-byte mode. Here is the original string and one example of ISO-2022-JP–encoded text:

Original String	カキクケコサシスセソタチツテト
Broken ISO-2022-JP	カキクケコ
	`5%7%9%;%=%?%A%D%F%H`

Here is another example of ISO-2022-JP encoding. This time the software (in this case, NinjaTerm) does not automatically insert one-byte character escape sequences at the ends of lines. The second byte of the split character サ is now treated as the first byte for the following two-byte character, which causes a lack of synch. Also note how the following line does not start on the left margin.

Original String	カキクケコサシスセソタチツテト
Broken ISO-2022-JP	カキクケコ
	汽礬好札愁織船張謄

Here is a Shift-JIS example. This time there is no lack of synch. The only character that is lost is the one that was split. The first byte, since it is in the eight-bit range, is invisible, and since the second byte (at least for this particular character) falls into the seven-bit range, it is not treated as the first byte of a two-byte character.

Original String	カキクケコサシスセソタチツテト
Broken Shift-JIS	カキクケコ
	Tシスセソタチツテト

Finally, here is an EUC-JP example. You should see the lack of synch problem here again. The first byte is invisible, and the second byte is now treated as the first byte of a two-byte character.

Original String	カキクケコサシスセソタチツテト
Broken EUC-JP	カキクケコ
	汽礬好札愁織船張謄

As you can see from these examples, this problem varies in intensity depending on the encoding method, and even on the software you are using (compare the two types of output you get for ISO-2022 encoding, using different software). Some encodings require slightly more overhead than simplistically treating two-byte characters as an inseparable unit. For example, when dealing with ISO-2022 encoding, you must also remember to insert and perhaps even delete escape sequences.

Character Attribute Detection Using C Macros

A useful function often supported in CJKV text processing programs (or for that matter in most text processing systems) is the ability to determine the attributes of characters within a file. For example, it is often convenient to obtain a listing of the numbers of Chinese characters, kana, and other characters in a file. One can even break those categories down further, such as kana into katakana and hiragana, Chinese characters into separate levels, and so on.

The C programming language has a useful macro facility which allows programmers to specify simple commands that can be used often within a program. Macros are similar in concept to functions, but require less work (but more thought).

As an example, several C macro definitions for detecting the attributes of Japanese (JIS X 0208:1997) characters are provided. They all assume Row-Cell values as input. How you implement this depends on the purpose of the program you are writing. You simply need to convert the Japanese code of each character to Row-Cell values right before executing each of these macros. The macros are as follows:

```
#define ISLEVEL1(A) (A >= 16 && A <= 47)
#define ISLEVEL2(A) (A >= 48 && A <= 84)
#define ISKANJI(A) (ISLEVEL1(A) || ISLEVEL2(A))
#define ISHIRAGANA(A) (A == 4)
#define ISKATAKANA(A) (A == 5)
#define ISKANA(A) (ISKATAKANA(A) || ISHIRAGANA(A))
#define ISKANAKANJI(A) (ISKANA(A) || ISKANJI(A))
```

Seasoned C programmers should be able to recognize what each of these macro definitions does.

The first two macros:

```
#define ISLEVEL1(A) (A >= 16 && A <= 47)
#define ISLEVEL2(A) (A >= 48 && A <= 84)
```

use the first byte (row) value to determine if a character is in JIS Level 1 or 2 kanji. You may recall that in JIS X 0208:1997 the kanji are contained in two ranges—rows 16 through 47, and rows 48 through 84—exactly what the macro checks for.

The next macro:

```
#define ISKANJI(A) (ISLEVEL1(A) || ISLEVEL2(A))
```

combines the first two macros. Quite often you won't care whether a kanji is in JIS Level 1 or 2 kanji, but rather if it is a kanji at all. Again, it is sufficient to use only the first byte as input to this macro.

The next three macros:

```
#define ISHIRAGANA(A) (A == 4)
#define ISKATAKANA(A) (A == 5)
#define ISKANA(A) (ISHIRAGANA(A) || ISKATAKANA(A))
```

do the same as the first three macros, but with kana. The first two detect whether a character is a hiragana or katakana, and the last one combines them. Like before, only the first byte is used for this.

The last macro:

```
#define ISKANAKANJI(A) (ISKANA(A) || ISKANJI(A))
```

checks for a larger set of characters, kana and kanji.

Similar macros can be written to accommodate other languages, such as Korean (KS X 1001:1992):

```
#define ISJAMO(A) (A == 4)
#define ISHANGUL(A) (A >= 16 && A <= 40)
#define ISHANJA(A) (A >= 42 && A <= 93)
#define ISHANGULHANJA(A) (ISHANGUL(A) || ISHANJA(A))
```

And Chinese (GB 2312-80):

```
#define ISLEVEL1(A) (A >= 16 && A <= 55)
#define ISLEVEL2(A) (A >= 56 && A <= 87)
#define ISHANZI(A) (ISLEVEL1(A) || ISLEVEL2(A))
```

Writing such macro definitions can be carried to almost any extreme, and represent a very useful tool in the hands of a C or C++ programmer. Of course, these macros could have been implemented as C functions, or written in yet other programming languages.

Character Sorting

You can sort English text in a multitude of ways—low to high, high to low, dictionary, numeric—the possibilities are almost endless. CJKV locales have even more possibilities for sorting text. In English, despite all the possible variations, there are really only two basic ways to sort text. The first is case-insensitive, meaning that upper- and lowercase Latin characters are sorted as though they were the same. The other is an ASCII sort which sorts by increasing value of the byte which represents each character, which has the effect of separating upper- and lowercase Latin characters whereby uppercase is sorted first. This is sometimes referred to as sorting *ASCIIbetically*.

Japanese, for example, has the equivalent of an ASCII sort, that is, characters are ordered by the values of the bytes used to represent them. This is often called a *JIS sort*. In Chapter 3, *Character Set Standards*, you learned that JIS X 0208:1997 Level 1 kanji are arranged by reading, and that JIS X 0208:1997 Level 2 kanji are arranged by radical, then the total number of strokes of the non-radical part. Consequently, a JIS sort produces a list of characters sorted in that way. And although they represent the same set of sounds, hiragana and katakana are separated when performing a JIS sort—the hiragana come first.

The *iroha* order is another collation sequence in addition to the 50 Sounds order. The name of this ordering comes from its first three sounds, specifically *i*, *ro*, and *ha*, the Japanese analogy to *a*, *b*, and *c*. The iroha collation sequence is not commonly used, and is based on the Buddhist poem listed in Table 9-15.

Table 9-15: The Iroha Order as a Poem

Japanese	Transliterated
いろはにほへと	i ro ha ni ho he to
ちりぬるを	chi ri nu ru (w)o
わかよたれそ	wa ka yo ta re so
つねならむ	tsu ne na ra mu
うゐのおくやま	u (w)i no o ku ya ma
けふこえて	ke fu ko e te
あさきゆめみし	a sa ki yu me mi shi
ゑひもせす	(w)e hi mo se su

Other types of sorts include by radical, by total number of strokes, and by pronunciation. Yes, these were listed above in the JIS sort, but I am referring to the coverage of *all* kanji. For example, a sort by radical should include JIS Level 1 kanji, too. The implementation of these various sorting methods is limited to the database of information you have. Hiragana and katakana can also be sorted together like a case-insensitive sort of Latin characters, but some dictionaries sort hiragana separately from katakana.

Due to the unique nature of kana, the examples provided in Table 9-16 consist of four words written solely with kana, and will serve to illustrate some issues that arise when sorting kana.

Table 9-16: Sorting Kana

Unordered	Byte-Value Order	Desired Order
バンドフ	はんとう	ハンド
はんとう	ハントン	はんとう
ハンドン	ハンド	バンドフ
ハント	バンドフ	ハントン

All four words share several characteristics with regard to their first three characters. All begin with the kana whose basic (unannotated) form is read *ha* (バ, は, or ハ), followed by a syllabic *n* (ン or ん), then finally the kana whose basic form is read *to* (ド, と, or ト). Note how the byte-value order—also known as the *JIS order* because it is also the order in which these characters appear in JIS X 0208:1997—produces a significantly different result from the desired order. There are two things going on here to cause these radically different results:

- The distinction between hiragana and katakana is ignored—all hiragana come before any katakana in JIS X 0208:1997; this can be considered a form of case-folding
- The distinction between unannotated and annotated kana is ignored—unannotated forms come before the annotated ones in JIS X 0208:1997

Kana sorting can also be affected by small kana (which always come before the standard forms).

JSA published the standard designated JIS X 4061-1996, *Collation of Japanese Character String* (日本語文字列照合順番 *nihongo mojiretsu shōgō junban*), which provides detailed information and suggestions for sorting characters found in the Japanese character set standards. I suggest that you use this standard for guidance.

Chinese text, written using hanzi, is usually sorted by Pinyin reading. Pinyin transliteration, because it uses Latin characters, is thus sorted according to the English alphabet.

An example that illustrates different sorting requirements for the same writing system is Korean hangul. North and South Korea (DPRK and ROK, respectively), although they use the same set of jamo for constructing hangul, sort them differently. Table 9-17 illustrates the sequence in which jamo are sorted in the two Korean locales, subcategorized by the position in which they appear in hangul: initial (consonants), medial (vowels), and final (consonants).

Table 9-17: Korean Jamo Sorting Sequences

	Locale	Sorting Sequence
Initial	DPRK	ㄱ ㄴ ㄷ ㄹ ㅁ ㅂ ㅅ ㅈ ㅊ ㅋ ㅌ ㅍ ㅎ ㄲ ㄸ ㅃ ㅆ ㅉ ㅇ
	ROK	ㄱ ㄲ ㄴ ㄷ ㄸ ㄹ ㅁ ㅂ ㅃ ㅅ ㅆ ㅇ ㅈ ㅉ ㅊ ㅋ ㅌ ㅍ ㅎ
Medial	DPRK	ㅏ ㅑ ㅓ ㅕ ㅗ ㅛ ㅜ ㅠ ㅡ ㅣ ㅐ ㅒ ㅔ ㅖ ㅚ ㅟ ㅢ ㅘ ㅝ ㅙ ㅞ
	ROK	ㅏ ㅐ ㅑ ㅒ ㅓ ㅔ ㅕ ㅖ ㅗ ㅘ ㅙ ㅚ ㅛ ㅜ ㅝ ㅞ ㅟ ㅠ ㅡ ㅢ ㅣ
Final	DPRK	ㄱ ㄳ ㄴ ㄵ ㄶ ㄷ ㄹ ㄺ ㄻ ㄼ ㄽ ㄾ ㄿ ㅀ ㅁ ㅂ ㅄ ㅅ ㅇ ㅈ ㅊ ㅋ ㅌ ㅍ ㅎ ㄲ ㅆ
	ROK	ㄱ ㄲ ㄳ ㄴ ㄵ ㄶ ㄷ ㄹ ㄺ ㄻ ㄼ ㄽ ㄾ ㄿ ㅀ ㅁ ㅂ ㅄ ㅅ ㅆ ㅇ ㅈ ㅊ ㅋ ㅌ ㅍ ㅎ

In general, North Korea sorts double consonants after all other consonants. The vowels, in medial position, are also sorted quite differently.

Natural Language Processing

Attempting to derive meaning from text requires natural language processing. The most fundamental level of natural language processing is the ability to parse the text into words. Applications for this technology include spelling and grammar checkers. The following sections will explore natural language processing techniques, along with some of its applications.

Word Parsing

Parsing most Western language text into words is a somewhat trivial operation due to the intervening (and necessary) spaces between words. Other than the occasional punctuation and dealing with case issues, there is very little difficulty. Most CJKV text, however, offers significant challenges in this area of information processing. The ultimate goal of parsing text into its component words is for common purposes such as determining the key words of a document. This is useful for categorizing or indexing documents based on their content.

Most CJKV texts, such as Chinese and Japanese, have no intervening spaces between words. Korean, on the other hand, *does* use spaces to separate words. Typical Chinese texts include only hanzi, along with a select few punctuation marks and symbols—how does one decide how to break up the words when there are only hanzi to deal with? Typical Japanese texts include mostly kana plus some kanji, and to make matters worse, some Japanese words are combinations of kana and kanji.

In order to successfully parse any CJKV text, a suitable dictionary is required. This dictionary can be very simple, listing only words of the language. Any parsing that is performed must result in *chunks* that match entries in this dictionary. More complex parsing dictionaries may be necessary to handle language-specific phenomena such as inflectional endings.

Because Japanese text seems to be laced with the most difficulty, let's examine a sample Japanese sentence that includes some typical words that need to be identified: 漢字が含まれているテキストは読み易い。* Table 9-18 lists the words that make up this Japanese sentence.

Table 9-18: A Parsed Japanese Sentence

Word	Reading	Meaning
漢字	kanji	*kanji*
が	ga	subject marker

* This sentence can be translated into English as "Texts that include kanji are easy to read."

Table 9-18: A Parsed Japanese Sentence (continued)

Word	Reading	Meaning
含まれている	fukumarete iru	*included*
テキスト	tekisuto	*text*
は	wa	topic marker
読み	yomi	*read*
易い	yasui	*easy*

Some complex or compound words, such as 日本語情報処理 (*nihongo jōhō shori*, meaning "Japanese information processing"), can cause additional problems, such as determining how to break up the compound word into its component words. It can also be treated as one unit. Anyway, there are several ways in which this compound word can be broken up, usually described as levels of a hierarchy. Table 9-19 illustrates the various levels to which this particular compand Japanese word can be parsed.

Table 9-19: Parsing Compound Words

Compound Word	First Level Parsing	Second Level Parsing
日本語情報処理	日本語 ("Japanese")	日本 ("Japan")
		語 ("language")
	情報処理 ("information processing")	情報 ("information")
		処理 ("processing")

Chinese and Japanese texts are typically laced with compound words (composed of hanzi and kanji, respectively). Korean is too, to some extent, but with hangul instead of hanja.

Fujitsu Laboratories in Japan has developed a Japanese morphological analyzer called *Breakfast* that can parse Japanese text into morphemes, and has a customizable POS (part-of-speech) system.[*] This feature enables Breakfast to use the dictionaries of JUMAN and ChaSen. It currently runs under Japanese versions of Windows. Other Japanese word parsers include JUMAN (寿満 *juman*),[†] which runs on Unix, Sumomo (すもも *sumomo*),[‡] which also runs on Unix, and ChaSen (茶筌 *chasen*),[**] which runs under Windows. A classical Japanese extension to JUMAN has been developed, and requires JPerl (Japanese Perl) and software called 古典対照語い表フロッピー版 (*koten taishō goi hyō furoppī ban*) published by 笠間書院 (*kasama shoin*).[††]

* *http://www.fujitsu.co.jp/hypertext/free/breakfast/*

† *ftp://pine.kuee.kyoto-u.ac.jp/pub/juman/*

‡ *http://www.brl.ntt.co.jp/sumomo/*

** *http://cactus.aist-nara.ac.jp/lab/nlt/chasen.html*

†† *ftp://ftp.oreilly.com/pub/examples/nutshell/cjkv/Ch9/kojuman.tar.gz*

Spelling and Grammar Checking

Spelling and grammar checking software is extremely common for English, especially spelling checking software. In fact, most word processors and page-layout systems include spelling checkers. However, finding such software for languages spoken in CJKV locales can be a daunting task.

SpellViser (日本語文書校正支援ライブラリ *nihongo bunsho kōsei shien raiburari* in Japanese), developed by Sumitomo Metal Industries, is an example of the Japanese equivalent to a spelling and grammar checker that is bundled with some MacOS and Windows applications.* This technology is included in the latest versions of Microsoft Word-J, Corel's Japanese products (such as Word Perfect-J and DRAW-J), Ergosoft's EGWord, and Kuni Research's Eudora Pro-J.

JUSTSYSTEM also developed a similar Japanese grammar-checking technology called 修太 (*shūta*), and is in their Japanese word processor called 一太郎 (*ichitarō*), accessible through its 文書校正 (*bunsho kōsei*) feature.

Regular Expressions

Regular expressions (regexes is a short way to express this; 正規表現 *seiki hyōgen* in Japanese) provide a *very* powerful mechanism to search for, replace, shred, or otherwise manipulate text or data. The most common regex engines, as found in popular Unix tools such as *awk*, GNU Emacs, *grep*, Perl, *sed*, Tcl, and so on, have no inherent CJKV-specific capabilities. However, several CJKV-specific regex implementations have been developed over the years. The most noteworthy of these include JPerl (Japanese Perl) and GNU Emacs (Version 20 or greater).

Adding CJKV or multiple-byte support to regex engines is a matter of being able to use multiple-byte characters in places where one-byte characters are expected. This may sound simple enough at first glance, but there is much complexity to consider. The character-class feature of regexes, for example, is an immediate candidate for this sort of extension. The following is a typical regex character class definition in Perl:

```
/[0-9A-Fa-f]/
```

This character class includes any upper- or lowercase hexadecimal digit, and the entire regex (that is, what appears between the slashes) matches exactly one character in this character class. However, when we deal with CJKV text, the following character class would be *very* useful:

```
/[あ-んア-ケ]/
```

* *http://www.smisoft.ssd.co.jp/product/sv/index.html*

This character class is intended to include all hiragana and katakana characters. JPerl allows you to specify such character classes. Without explicit Japanese (or, multiple-byte) support, the above regex would be meaningless (or, at least, result in an incorrect match).* There are, however, clever ways to fake such character classes, covered later in this section. You may think that the following is equivalent to the above kana character class:

```
/[\xA4-\xA5][\xA1-\xFE]/
```

This regex should match any character in the range 0xA4A1 through 0xA5FE, which means the hiragana and katakana rows in EUC-JP encoding, right? Nope. Because standard (that is, those that are not CJKV-capable) regex engines match on a per-byte basis, a match may be made with the second byte of a two-byte character followed by the first byte of the next two-byte character. See the "Character Searching" section on page 436 for more details on why this is important to avoid at all costs.

The only reliable way to handle multiple-byte encodings using standard regex engines is to use techniques that effectively trap all characters. You may not need to perform any transformations on most of the trapped characters—they can be easily output as-is. This means that there are two types of operations to consider:

- Process all characters or all characters of a particular class—some sort of converter or filter (a side-effect of applying a regex to all characters in a file allows an encoding-integrity check to be performed with little additional effort)
- Selectively process characters—search or search/replace

Other aspects of regexes that need to be extended for supporting multiple-byte characters include the definitions of many metacharacters, such as . (*dot*). This metacharacter matches any (one) *byte*, and to make it useful in the context, CJKV information processing requires that it match any (one) *character*.

JPerl is unique in that its regex engine provides a way to directly use Japanese characters. Other regex engines, such as those found in GNU Emacs, pre-define Japanese-specific character classes as metacharacters. Table 9-20 provides a listing of these pre-defined character classes, according to the latest version of GNU Emacs, along with a definition plus the equivalent JPerl regex.

When running GNU Emacs in other language modes, such as Chinese or Korean, additional multiple-byte metacharacters spring into existence. In particular, `\ch` (matches any KS X 1001:1992 character) and `\cc` (matches any GB 2312-80, CNS 11643-1992, or Big Five character). The `\cA`, `\cG`, `\cH`, `\cK`, and `\cY` multiple-byte

* This regex, if EUC-JP–encoded, would be interpreted as `/[\xA4\xA1-\xA4\xF3\xA5\xA1-\xA5\xF6]/`, and would match a single byte whose values are in the following ranges: 0xA1–0xA5, 0xF3, and 0xF6. Not what you would expect, eh?

Table 9-20: Japanese-Specific Regular Expression Implementations

GNU Emacs	GNU Emacs Definition	JPerl Equivalent
`\cA`	Alphanumeric (row 3)	[０-９Ａ-Ｚａ-ｚ]
`\cH`	Hiragana (01-11, 01-12, 01-21, 01-22, row 4)	[゛゜ゝゞぁ-ん]
`\cK`	Katakana (01-11, 01-12, 01-19, 01-20, 01-28, row 5)	[゛゜ヽヾーァ-ヶ]
`\cG`	Greek (row 6)	[Α-Ωα-ω]
`\cY`	Cyrillic (row 7)	[А-Яа-я]
`\cC`	Kanji (01-24 through 01-27, 05-86, rows 16–84)	[仝-〇ヶ亜-腕弌-熙]

metacharacters also function for Chinese and Korean, but match characters in the appropriate rows.

I encourage you to study the Perl code examples found in Appendix W to learn more about how regexes can be used to manipulate CJKV text.

For more information on regular expressions, I highly suggest Jeffrey Friedl's *Mastering Regular Expressions* (O'Reilly & Associates, 1997).* *X/Open Guide: Internationalisation Guide* also includes a chapter on internationalized regular expressions.

Search Engines

One important function of the Web is the ability to conduct searches for particular items. While most of the popular search engines accept only ASCII characters (or regexes that reflect ASCII text) for this task, there are now a number of CJKV-capable search engines available.

The toughest issues faced by CJKV-capable search-engine developers include the following:

- The proper handling of multiple-byte characters that appear in the search string, including multiple-byte support for regexes
- The proper handling of multiple encodings for both the search string and searched text (for example, a user-entered Korean EUC-KR search string must be able to match in documents encoded according to EUC-KR and ISO-2022-KR encodings), which effectively means that the encodings for the search string and searched text must be regularized (because the searched text may be large, it is much easier to regularize the search string to match the encoding of the searched text)

* *http://enterprise.ic.gc.ca/~jfriedl/regex/*

Japanese-enabled search engines include NTT's Goo[*] and Lycos.[†] Korean-enabled search engines include Lycos.[‡] AltaVista appears to provide Chinese, Japanese, and Korean support in their search engine.[**]

Code Processing Tools

Below you will find brief descriptions of and the printed help pages for three Japanese code processing tools that I have written and maintained until 1993: JConv, JChar, and JCode. Also included is a description of JChar's replacement: the CJKV Character Set Server, available online as a web server. This section also includes some contexts in which these tools may be useful to your work. The latest source code for these tools is available online.[††]

Three of these tools were written in ANSI C, and are portable on compilers that conform to this standard. This means that their source code, without any modifications, should compile on multiple platforms, and this has been confirmed by their many users. Each of these three tools displays its help page by using the `-h` option on the command line. These same help pages are listed below, and are provided n order to illustrate the full potential of the tools' functionality.

JConv—Code Conversion Tool

The most basic Japanese text processing requirement is a tool that converts Japanese text from one encoding to another. This is most important when moving Japanese text from one platform to another, and when receiving email messages or news articles. All in all, such a tool is a general workhorse tool; I use it often.

This tool, called JConv, implements the routines for converting from one Japanese encoding to another. The main features of JConv are that it:

- Supports the JIS X 0208:1997 character set
- Handles ISO-2022-JP, Shift-JIS, and EUC-JP encodings
- Lists code specifications for Japanese encoding methods
- Filters half-width katakana by converting them to their full-width counterparts
- Repairs damaged ISO-2022-JP–encoded files
- Can forcibly damage ISO-2022-JP–encoded files (so they can be restored later with the repair option)

* *http://www.goo.ne.jp/*

† *http://www-jp.lycos.com/*

‡ *http://www-kr.lycos.com/*

** *http://www.altavista.com/*

†† *ftp://ftp.oreilly.com/pub/examples/nutshell/cjkv/src/*

- Lets one check files for their encoding without actually performing any code conversion
- Includes a verbose mode option that displays more information about what the tool is doing

Many of the algorithms and routines listed and explained earlier in this chapter are used in this code processing tool.

Here is this tool's help page:

```
** jconv v3.0 (July 1, 1993) **
Written by Ken R. Lunde, Adobe Systems Incorporated
lunde@adobe.com
Usage: jconv [-options] [infile] [outfile]
Tool description: This tool is a utility for converting the Japanese code of
textfiles, and supports Shift-JIS, EUC, New-JIS, Old-JIS, and NEC-JIS for
both input and output. It can also display a file s input code, repair
damaged Old- or New-JIS files, and display the specifications for any of the
handled codes.
Options include:
  -c        Displays the detected input code, then exits -- the types
            reported include EUC, Shift-JIS, New-JIS, Old-JIS, NEC-JIS, ASCII
            (no Japanese), ambiguous (Shift-JIS or EUC), and unknown (note
            that this option overrides "-iCODE")
  -f        Converts half-width katakana to their full-width equivalents (this
            option is forced when output code is New-, Old-, or NEC-JIS)
  -h        Displays this help page, then exits
  -iCODE    Forces input code to be recognized as CODE
  -o[CODE]  Output code set to CODE (default is Shift-JIS if this option is
            not specified, or if the specified CODE is invalid)
  -r[CODE]  Repairs damaged New- and Old-JIS encoded files by restoring lost
            escape characters, then converts it to the CODE specified (the
            default is to convert the file to New-JIS if CODE is not
            specified -- cannot be used in conjunction with "-s")
  -s[f]     Removes escape characters from valid escape sequences of New- and
            Old-JIS encoded files -- "f" will force all escape characters
            to be removed (default extension is .rem -- cannot be used in
            conjunction with "-r")
  -t[CODE]  Prints a table listing the specifications for the specified CODE,
            then exits (all code tables will be displayed if CODE is not
            specified, or if CODE is invalid)
  -v        Verbose mode -- displays information such as automatically
            generated file names, detected input code, number of escape
            characters restored/removed, etc.
NOTE: CODE has five possible values (and default outfile extensions):
      "e" = EUC (.euc); "s" = Shift-JIS (.sjs); "j" = New-JIS (.new);
      "o" = Old-JIS (.old); and "n" = NEC-JIS (.nec)
```

JConv has been ported to MacOS, MS-DOS, and MS Windows. One of the MacOS ports was done by Natsu Sakimura, and is called JCONV-DD (DD standing for "Drag and Drop").

If you are interested in cross-locale code conversion, consider using CJKVConv.pl, *tcs*, or Uniconv (described in Chapter 4's "Code Conversion Across CJKV Locales," starting on page 208).

JChar—Character Set Generation Tool

Another general Japanese code processing need is the ability to generate a listing of Japanese character sets. Generating a file that contains a complete electronically encoded Japanese character set can be done most effectively with the use of loops found in most programming languages. After all, who wants to manually input several thousand characters? Generating the coded character sets is trivial, as loops do all the work for you. The problem is when you want to generate a list containing only the characters in a non-coded character set, such as Jōyō Kanji. There is no algorithm you can use, since the necessary kanji are scattered throughout JIS X 0208:1997 Level 1 kanji. The only way to handle such a task is to key them in manually, and then to be sure to save your work!

I have written a tool, called JChar, that generates these problematic character sets (and non-problematic ones, too!). Listings of these non-coded Japanese character set standards, as generated by JChar, are in Appendix R, *Chinese Character Lists.*

The JChar tool has many features and options that you will find useful at some time or another—the main ones are that it:

- Supports the JIS X 0208:1997, ASCII/JIS-Roman, half-width katakana, Jōyō Kanji, Gakushū Kanji, and Jinmei-yō Kanji character sets
- Outputs data in ISO-2022-JP, Shift-JIS, or EUC-JP encoding
- Wraps output lines at *n* columns
- Can suppress header information

Algorithms used in this tool are primarily loops (for the coded character sets) and data structures (for the non-coded character sets). Encoding range bounds are used, though, to generate the whole character encoding space, and not only the code positions that contain characters. For example, when choosing to generate the JIS X 0208:1997 list, it does not generate 6,879 code positions, but 8,836 code positions, which is what you get from a complete 94×94 matrix.

Here is this tool's help page:

```
** jchar v3.0 (July 1, 1993) **
Written by Ken R. Lunde, Adobe Systems Incorporated
lunde@adobe.com
Usage: jchar [-options] [outfile]
Tool description: This tool is a utility for generating various Japanese
character sets in any code. This includes all the characters specified in
JIS X 0208-1990, half-width katakana (EUC and Shift-JIS output only), the
94 printable ASCII/JIS-Roman characters, the 1945 Joyo Kanji, the 284
Jinmei-yo Kanji, and the 1006 Gakushu Kanji.
```

```
Options include:
  -a        Builds an ASCII/JIS-Roman list (printable characters only)
  -g        Builds the Gakushu Kanji list
  -h        Displays this help page, then exits
  -j        Builds the Joyo Kanji list
  -k        Builds the JIS X 0208-1990 list
  -o[CODE]  Builds lists in CODE format (default is Shift-JIS if this option
            is not specified, if CODE is not specified, or if CODE is invalid)
  -p        Builds the Jinmei-yo Kanji list
  -s        Suppresses headers and row number information
  -w[NUM]   Wraps output lines at NUM columns (if NUM is not specified, 78
            is used as the default value)
NOTE: CODE has five possible values: "e" = EUC; "s" = Shift-JIS;
      "j" = New-JIS; "o" = Old-JIS; and "n" = NEC-JIS
```

CJKV Character Set Server

Late-breaking news! Well, sort of. JChar has been upgraded—sometime in 1996—to support CJKV character sets and encodings, and instead of being available as C source code that must be compiled then run on specific operating systems (and available as MacOS and MS-DOS executables), it is now a web server (a CGI program is under the hood).* The underlying CGI program is written in Perl.

Like JChar, the CJKV Character Set Server supports both coded and non-coded character sets. And, you can decide whether you'd like a file mailed to you (automatically uuencoded for safety if there are any eight-bit characters used in the selected encoding) or else display the character set directly in your web browser.

JCode—Text File Examination Tool

Every programmer (or even non-programmer types with enough interest) may occasionally like to take a closer peek at Japanese codes and how they relate to each other. The non-Japanese analogy is a hex dump of a file. However, since most Japanese characters consist of two bytes, a normal hex dump may not be very useful. Such a tool designed for use with Japanese text should treat two-byte characters as single entities. It should also make use of all the routines for converting between the various encoding methods, but instead of converting characters, it lists each character, along with its associated value in a variety of encodings.

A tool I wrote, called JCode, fills this gap, and offers two basic functions, indicated as follows:

- Accepts actual encoded Japanese characters in a variety of encodings, then performs the equivalent of a hex dump

* *http://www.oreilly.com/~lunde/cjkv-char.html*

- Accepts four- and five-digit codes, one per line, that represent the encoded value of a character (for instance, JIS X 0208:1997 "3021" or "k1601" for the kanji 亜), then performs the equivalent of a hex dump

Using a hex dump as the non-Japanese analogy to this tool is not entirely correct. The tool JCode also allows you to perform an octal or decimal dump, depending on what notation you want (the default is to use hexadecimal notation).

Now it's time to see some sample output of JCode. First, you will see how this tool can handle actual Japanese text. Note that the file cannot be of a mixed encoding (that is, Shift-JIS plus EUC-JP, and so on). The following four characters serve as the example input to JCode:

かな漢字

They are read *ka na kan ji* (meaning "kana [and] kanji"). The resulting output is shown in Table 9-21.

Table 9-21: JCode Output—First Example

Character	Shift-JIS	EUC	JIS	ASCII	KUTEN
か	82-A9	A4-AB	24-2B	$+	04-11
な	82-C8	A4-CA	24-4A	$J	04-42
漢	8A-BF	B4-C1	34-41	4A	20-33
字	8E-9A	BB-FA	3B-7A	;z	27-90

Next, you will see how this tool can handle four- and five-digit codes. To automatically detect all the main encodings, you must add a prefix before EUC-JP and Row-Cell (called KUTEN in its output) values, and require hexadecimal notation for ISO-2022-JP, Shift-JIS, and EUC-JP encodings. Here is the input I used:

```
82A9
xa4cA
3441
k2790
```

The first line is a hexadecimal Shift-JIS code, the second line is a hexadecimal EUC-JP code (note the "x" prefix), the third line is a hexadecimal ISO-2022-JP code, and the last line is a Row-Cell (KUTEN) code (note the "k" prefix). Table 9-22 provides the output.

Table 9-22: JCode Output—Second Example

Character	Shift-JIS	EUC	JIS	ASCII	KUTEN
か	**82-A9**	A4-AB	24-2B	$+	04-11
な	82-C8	**A4-CA**	24-4A	$J	04-42
漢	8A-BF	B4-C1	**34-41**	4A	20-33
字	8E-9A	BB-FA	3B-7A	;z	**27-90**

As you can see, a different set of input produced the same output. Also note how the handling of the four- and five-digit codes is not case-sensitive, and how each line can use a different encoding.

This tool has other options, most of which allow you to better format the output, as follows:

- Supports octal, decimal, and hexadecimal notations for output (the default is hexadecimal)
- Pads columns with spaces or a tab (the default is padding with spaces)
- Shows control characters
- Includes a verbose mode that provides more information, such as which Japanese encoding was detected

This tool, as you might expect, uses many of the code conversion algorithms and routines described earlier in this chapter. The remainder is simply fancy formatting of the output.

Now for this tool's help page:

```
** jcode v3.0 (July 1, 1993) **
Written by Ken R. Lunde, Adobe Systems Incorporated
lunde@adobe.com
Usage: jcode [-options] [infile] [outfile]
Tool description: This tool is a utility for displaying the electronic values
of Japanese characters within textfiles, and supports Shift-JIS, EUC, New-JIS,
Old-JIS, and NEC-JIS for both input and output.
Options include:
  -c[DATA]      Reads codes, one per line, rather than characters as input --
                if DATA is specified, only that code is treated, then exits
                (KUTEN codes must be prefixed with "k," and EUC codes with
                "x" -- EUC, JIS, and Shift-JIS codes must be hexadecimal)
  -h            Displays this help page, then exits
  -iCODE        Forces input code to be recognized as CODE
  -n[NOTATION]  Output notation set to NOTATION (default is hexadecimal if this
                option is not specified, if NOTATION is not specified, or if
                the specified NOTATION is invalid)
  -o[CODE]      Output code set to CODE (default is Shift-JIS if this option
                is not specified, if CODE is not specified, or if the
                specified CODE is invalid)
  -p[CHOICE]    Pads the columns with CHOICE whereby CHOICE can be either  t
                for tabs or "s" for spaces (default is spaces if this option
                is not specified, if CHOICE is not specified, or if the
                specified CHOICE is invalid)
  -s            Shows control characters (except escape sequences)
  -v            Verbose mode -- displays information such as automatically
                generated file names, detected input code, etc.
NOTE: CODE has five possible values:
      "e" = EUC; "s" = Shift-JIS; "j" = New-JIS; "o" = Old-JIS;
      and "n" = NEC-JIS
NOTE: NOTATION has three possible values:
      "o" = octal; "d" = decimal; and "h" = hexadecimal
```

Other Useful Tools

There are many more tools that perform very useful and time-saving tasks that are in one way or another CJKV-related. Below is a brief listing of some more well-known sources for such utilities or data:

- Mark Leisher's multilingual tools[*]
- Erik Peterson's Chinese tools[†]
- Tsinghua Network Center's Chinese tools[‡]
- Yahoo!'s localization page[**]
- Koichi Yasuoka's CJK mapping tables[††]
- Koichi Yasuoka's "Kanji Bukuro" (漢字袋 *kanji bukuro*)[‡‡]

I encourage you to explore these URLs, along with the many books that are listed in this book's *Bibliography*, to find suitable tools or data for your needs. It is best not to reinvent the wheel.

---

* *ftp://crl.nmsu.edu/CLR/multiling/*

† *http://www.erols.com/eepeter/chtools.html*

‡ *ftp://ftp.net.tsinghua.edu.cn/pub/Chinese/*

** *http://www.yahoo.com/Computers_and_Internet/Software/Localization/*

†† *http://www.kudpc.kyoto-u.ac.jp/~yasuoka/CJK.html*

‡‡ *http://www.kudpc.kyoto-u.ac.jp/~yasuoka/kanjibukuro/*

In this chapter:
- *Viewing CJKV Text on Non-CJKV Systems*
- *Operating Systems*
- *Hybrid Environments*
- *Text Editors*
- *Word Processors*
- *Dedicated Word Processors*

10

Operating Systems, Text Editors, and Word Processors

Some of the code processing tools described at the end of Chapter 9, *Information Processing Techniques*, are relatively specialized programmers' tools that I developed. In this chapter, I discuss software that companies and individuals have developed, which, when properly integrated and configured, provides the ability to create, format, read, print, send, or receive CJKV text electronically. Figure 10-1 illustrates how various text processing tools interact with each other.

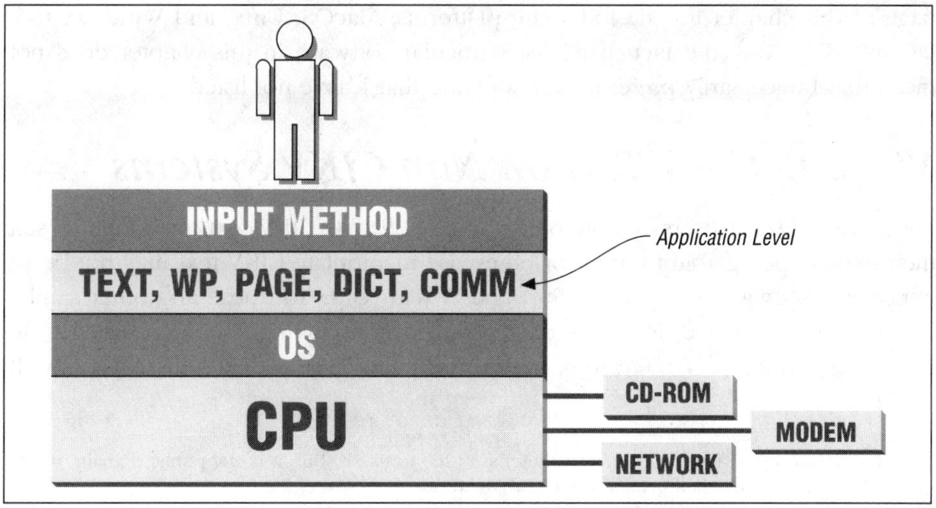

Figure 10-1: The interaction of text processing tools

The goal of this chapter is to give you a basic knowledge of the types of CJKV text processing tools available, and what capabilities to expect from each. Note that certain classes of these tools have already been discussed in earlier and more appropriate chapters: code conversion tools in Chapter 4, *Encoding Methods*; input methods in Chapter 5, *Input Methods*; and page-layout and graphics software in Chapter 7, *Typography*. Others are discussed in later and again more appropriate chapters: dictionary software and learning aids in Chapter 11, *Dictionaries and Dictionary Software*; and communication software in Chapter 12, *The Internet*.

The capabilities of these types of tools range from the most basic to very complex functions. With all of their differences, they share one common feature: they are all multiple-byte–aware. That is, they treat multiple-byte characters as a single unit. Not all software has been localized for all CJKV locales, but some programs provide a generic level of CJKV support, such as multiple-byte awareness. This is especially true of MacOS software that is considered to be WorldScript II compatible—it is multiple-byte–aware when the appropriate script (language) resources are installed into the operating system, either due to the use of a fully-localized operating system or else the installation of one or more of Apple Computer's Language Kits.

The software listed as examples consists of freeware,* shareware,† and commercial software.‡ This chapter will provide you with a basic working knowledge of what functions to expect, but stops short of providing all the information about this software. If you are interested in a particular package, I encourage you to obtain more detailed information on it from its creator, manufacturer, or distributor.

I attempt to describe at least one tool for each of the categories listed on the first page of this chapter for the following platforms: MacOS, Unix, and Windows (95, 98, and NT). And, the fact that I list particular software in this chapter does not mean that I necessarily prefer it over software that I have not listed.

Viewing CJKV Text on Non-CJKV Systems

For a great deal of users, simply being able to *display* CJKV text is enough to suit their needs—being able to input or otherwise manipulate CJKV text may not be so important. Software, such as AsiaSurf and NJWin (URLs for these and other similar software are provided in the section entitled "Displaying Web Documents" in Chapter 13, *The World Wide Web*, starting on page 533), provide this capability. If

* Freeware software is free, meaning that there is no fee to use it. But, it is *not* public domain, which means that the developer still maintains the copyright.

† Shareware software is usually freely available, but there is a minimal fee that you must pay the developer in order to continue using it. This allows you to effectively *try-before-you-buy*. If you end up regularly using shareware programs, I strongly encourage you to pay the license fee in fairness to the software author who spent countless hours developing it.

‡ Some commercial programs are available as demo versions at no charge, which means that you are able to *try-before-you-buy*, but unlike shareware, there are many more restrictions, such as the inability to print or save files. If you're interested in a particular commercial program, I strongly encourage you to seek out a demo version, either at the company's web site or by making a telephone call.

you do not fall into this category of user, I strongly urge you to consider obtaining an operating system or other environment that provides a full range of CJKV support, not simply the ability to display CJKV text.

I encourage you to explore the online information that describes the best ways to enable the display of CJKV text in non-CJKV environments.*

The Microsoft Office 97 (and later) and the latest Microsoft Windows NT CD-ROMs include a variety of what Microsoft calls "Language Packs" in the *LANGPACK* directory. These Language Packs are also available at Microsoft's web site.† If you install the appropriate Language Pack, it will enable the display (but not input) of the corresponding CJKV text in many applications, such as Internet Explorer (Version 3.0 and later) and Netscape Communicator (Version 4.0 and later).‡

MacOS, from Version 8.5, includes the appropriate fonts and scripts for displaying Chinese, Japanese, and Korean text as part of its Multilingual Internet Access.

Operating Systems

Many of the text processing tools listed in the sections that follow (or described in previous chapters) may require that you either have a CJKV-capable operating system, or else that you add CJKV support to your computer's current operating system. This may involve replacing your operating system entirely with a fully-localized version, or else adding extensions to your current operating system.

CJKV-capable operating systems usually provide three main benefits. First, they provide multiple-byte handling at the system level—this often (but not always) makes non-CJKV (or unlocalized) software able to handle multiple-byte characters. Second, they provide menus and dialogs written in the target language (in Chinese, for example, in a Chinese operating system)—this is a *major* convenience for users who happen to be native speakers of the locale targeted by the operating system developer.

This section will specify what hardware or software environments are required for such operating systems or operating system extensions. This material lays the foundation for the discussions that follow this section.

There are far too many operating systems and operating system extensions to describe in this book. What is provided below are brief descriptions of CJKV-capable operating systems and operating system extensions—in essence, how to add CJKV support to computers. What is *not* described below are the computers

* *ftp://rtfm.mit.edu/pub/usenet/news.answers/chinese-text/faq* or *http://www.cathay.net/help/read-chn.shtml*

† *http://www.microsoft.com/msdownload/ieplatform/lang/lang.htm*

‡ Installation instructions can be found at *http://www.basistech.com/articles/browsing.html*.

manufactured specifically for CJKV locales. Older computers required special ROM to support CJKV locales—the fonts to support the locale, for example, were in the ROM. Today's trend—fortunately—is to use *standard* hardware.

MS-DOS

MS-DOS (Microsoft Disk Operating System) represents the classic operating system for personal computers. In the past it was necessary for the computer itself to contain special ROM that contained CJKV fonts and CJKV text handling routines. Well, that day came to an abrupt end with IBM's introduction of DOS J/V, which allowed anyone to install a Japanese-capable operating system onto non-Japanese IBM PC and compatible computers. IBM DOS J/V processes Shift-JIS code internally.

The hardware requirements for IBM DOS J/V, as shown below, are considered extremely minimal by today's standards:

- PS/55, PC/AT compatible, or PS/2 computer
- VGA, XGA, or PS/55 display adaptor
- 80286 CPU or greater
- 1MB of RAM (4MB is recommended)

There was also CCDOS, which was a very popular Chinese version of MS-DOS back in the early 1990s.

More and more software these days runs under Windows 95, 98, or NT (or under all of them), so the number of users of MS-DOS has decreased significantly. In my opinion, the greatest achievement of Microsoft Windows (described next) is the ability to effectively bridge incompatible hardware. For example, there were countless versions of MS-DOS available, each of which was designed to run under a different underlying architecture. When you purchased software that ran under MS-DOS, you had to be sure that it was designed for the particular version of MS-DOS running on your computer. When you buy Windows software, it will run on Windows regardless of the underlying architecture.

Microsoft Windows 95 and 98

Microsoft has developed several localized versions of Windows 95 and 98, including five for CJKV locales: Simplified Chinese, Traditional Chinese, Japanese, Korean, and Vietnamese.* Starting with Windows 95, there is no longer the requirement for an underlying MS-DOS. Windows 95 is in itself an operating system, not

* The Vietnamese capabilities provided in Windows 95V support only Quốc ngữ at this time.

only a windowing environment for MS-DOS, which was the case for Windows Version 3.1 and earlier.

Every version of Windows 95 and 98 is bundled with everything you need to process the language for which it was localized. This includes a localized interface (menus and dialog), a minimal set of TrueType fonts, and one or more input methods.

Although Windows 95 and 98 still processes *native* encodings internally—EUC-CN, GBK, or Big Five for Chinese; Shift-JIS for Japanese; and EUC-KR or UHC for Korean—many aspects of the operating system have already been migrated to Unicode. The most notable of these is the bundled fonts. In Windows 95J and 98J, for example, the bundled fonts, called MS明朝 (*MS minchō*) and MSゴシック (*MS goshikku*), have absolutely no trace of Shift-JIS encoding. They have only Unicode encoding. So, how do Shift-JIS–based applications work with such Unicode-encoded fonts? The operating system converts between native encodings (Shift-JIS, for example) and Unicode on the fly whenever necessary. This is actually quite seamless, and users really have no idea that conversion between Unicode and native encodings is even occurring. Microsoft has effectively insulated users from the issues.

Developers of Windows 95 and 98 software should consult Nadine Kano's *Developing International Software for Windows 95 and Windows NT* (Microsoft Press, 1995). Tim O'Reilly and Troy Mott's *Windows 95 in a Nutshell* (O'Reilly & Associates, 1998) and *Windows 98 in a Nutshell* (O'Reilly & Associates, 1999) are both useful as general Windows 95 or 98 references.

Microsoft Windows NT

Windows NT is a completely Unicode-based operating system, which means that there is no fallback to what I like to refer to as *native* encodings, such as the various locale-specific instances of EUC encoding, Big Five, and Shift-JIS. Its architecture was also designed in such a way that is intended to prevent system crashes and freezes. In short, Windows NT is a very solid and stable operating system, and is often used for servers.*

In addition, a new breed of font will be considered the *native* format for Windows NT Version 5.0 and beyond: OpenType, a font format that effectively bridges the two most common outline font formats, specifically PostScript and TrueType. OpenType was a subject of discussion in Chapter 6, *Font Formats*.

* Needless to say, it is not a good thing when your server crashes.

Developers of Windows NT software should consult Nadine Kano's *Developing International Software for Windows 95 and Windows NT* (Microsoft Press, 1995). I suggest Eric Pearce's *Windows NT in a Nutshell* (O'Reilly & Associates, 1997) for Windows NT users.

The following sections describe various aspects of the localized versions of Windows NT, and list the bundled TrueType fonts. The default system fonts will be shaded in the tables that follow.

Although not fully described here, there is also a Pan Chinese Windows NT that supports the Hong Kong Government extension to Big Five (supported as both Big Five and GBK extensions).*

Chinese Windows NT—for China

The TrueType and TrueType Collection fonts that are included in Windows NT for China are the same as those included in Windows 95 for China, which means full GBK support (this translates to all 21,000 or so Chinese characters found in Unicode). This makes the transition to Unicode much easier. Table 10-1 lists the TrueType and TrueType Collection files, along with their font instances.

Table 10-1: Chinese Windows NT TrueType Files and Font Instances—Simplified

TrueType Font File	Font Instances	Source
Simfang.ttf	FangSong_GB2312	Great Wall Computer
Simhei.ttf	SimHei	Zhong Yi Electronics
Simkai.ttf	KaiTi_GB2312	Great Wall Computer
Simsun.ttc	SimSun (Songti) NsimSun	Zhong Yi Electronics

Chinese Windows NT—for Taiwan

The Chinese version of Windows NT, designed for use in Taiwan and Hong Kong, includes TrueType and TrueType Collection fonts that were developed by DynaLab—these two types of fonts are easily differentiated by their filename extensions. Table 10-2 lists the TrueType and TrueType Collection font files, along with their font instances.

Table 10-2: Chinese Windows NT TrueType Files and Font Instances—Traditional

TrueType Font File	Font Instances
KaiU.ttf	DFKai-SB
MingliU.ttc	MingliU PmingliU

* *http://www.microsoft.com/hk/pcntw/*

Japanese Windows NT

The Japanese version of Windows NT includes TrueType Collection fonts that were developed by Ricoh. In addition, it comes with Microsoft's MS-IME, which is the latest Japanese input method developed by Microsoft. Although this input method was described in some detail in Chapter 5, it is useful to note again that it includes a hand-written recognition system for accessing hard-to-input kanji.

Table 10-3 lists the TrueType Collection font files, along with their font instances (that is, what appears in applications' font menus).

Table 10-3: Japanese Windows NT TrueType Files and Font Instances

TrueType Collection File	Font Instances
Msmincho.ttc	MS明朝 (*MS minchō*) MSP明朝 (*MSP minchō*)
Msgothic.ttc	MSゴシック (*MS goshikku*) MSPゴシック (*MSP goshikku*)

As discussed in Chapter 6, the difference between the two font instances is that the ones that include a "P" in their name use proportional characters (proportional-width Latin characters, kana, punctuation, and some symbols). These same TrueType Collection fonts, including their "P" instances, were also bundled with Windows 95J.

Korean Windows NT

The Korean version of Windows NT includes TrueType Collection fonts that were developed by Hanyang Systems. It is useful to note that the bundled Korean input method is quite powerful. Actually, powerful to the point that there are effectively no popular third-party Korean input methods for Korean Windows NT.

Table 10-4 lists the TrueType Collection font files bundled with Korean Windows NT, along with their font instances. Note how each TrueType Collection font includes two basic font instances—ignoring the "che" versus non-"che" difference for the moment. While the two basic font instances have different hangul designs, they both share the same hanja designs.

Table 10-4: Korean Windows NT TrueType Files and Font Instances

TrueType Font File	Font Instances
Batang.ttc	바탕 (*batang*) 바탕체 (*batangce*) 궁서 (*gungseo*) 궁서체 (*gungseoce*)
Gulim.ttc	굴림 (*gurim*) 굴림체 (*gurimce*) 돋움 (*dodum*) 돋움체 (*dodumce*)

Like with Japanese Windows NT, these same TrueType Collection fonts were included as part of Windows 95K.

There is some interesting history behind these font instance names—the "ce" versus non-"ce" difference. They are somewhat confusing, so this may help users to understand why they are named so. For example, we can see that there are pairs of related font instances, such as Batang and Batangce. In this case, Batang contains proportional Latin characters, but Batangce contains half-width Latin characters. The difference in their name, "ce" (체 *ce*), must apparently mean "proportional." Not true. When writing 체 using hanja, 體, we can clearly see that it is simply a common suffix that means "typeface." Versions of these fonts that included half-width Latin characters were part of Windows 3.1K, and were named with the final "ce." When instances of these fonts with proportional Latin characters were created, whoever was in charge of font naming decided to simply drop the final "ce" (체).

MacOS

The developers of the Apple Macintosh computer have always been committed to making Macintosh a multilingual platform. Development of a localized Japanese version of its operating system, up until recently known as KanjiTalk (漢字Talk *kanji tōku*), began very early on. MacOS-J currently processes Shift-JIS encoding internally.

Beginning with System 7.1, Apple Computer introduced operating system extensions called WorldScript I and WorldScript II. Before System 7, similar functionality came from a system component called ScriptManager. WorldScript I supports non-Latin one-byte–encoded scripts, such as Arabic, Cyrillic, Hebrew, Thai, and so on; and WorldScript II supports non-Latin two-byte–encoded scripts, such as Chinese, Japanese, and Korean. These operating system extensions allow you to add multilingual support to unlocalized versions of MacOS. This effectively makes localized versions of MacOS no longer necessary for those who do not need a localized interface. Apple Computer currently offers *Language Kits* for Chinese, Japanese, and Korean*—they are discussed later in this chapter in the section entitled "Hybrid Environments," starting on page 468.

However, you must be warned that adding CJKV support to your Macintosh by installing a localized version of MacOS or one of the Language Kits does *not* automatically make all of your English-language applications handle CJKV text (that is, multiple-byte functionality). It is best to check with the application vendor before you buy. One of the first applications to be WorldScript-II–compatible is the word

* These happen to be the WorldScript II Language Kits. Apple Computer also offers many WorldScript I Language Kits.

processor called Nisus Writer developed by Nisus Software. Nisus Writer is described later in this chapter on page 481.

MacOS-S—formerly HanziTalk

MacOS-S is the version of MacOS that is for Simplified Chinese based on GB 2312-80. The encoding used by MacOS-S is based on EUC-CN. A variety of input methods and TrueType Simplified Chinese fonts are included.

MacOS-T—formerly ChineseTalk

MacOS-T is the version of MacOS that is for Traditional Chinese based on the Big Five character set. The encoding used by MacOS-T is, of course, based on Big Five. A variety of input methods and TrueType Traditional Chinese fonts are included. Included input methods are Cangjie, Dayi, Parrot, Pinyin, and zhuyin.

MacOS-J—formerly KanjiTalk

The most current release of the localized Japanese operating system for Macintosh is called MacOS-J. MacOS-J provides a complete Japanese environment, and includes seven Japanese outline fonts (TrueType format).* Expect this system to consume approximately 50MB of hard disk space if you install all seven fonts. At least 16MB of RAM is recommended when running the latest version of this operating system. MacOS-J also comes with an excellent Japanese input system called ことえり (*kotoeri*)—discussed in greater detail at the end of Chapter 5, starting on page 264. KanjiTalk Version 6.0.7, which is now several years old, included a Japanese input method called 2.1変換, and even earlier versions of KanjiTalk included one called 2.0変換.

The cost of obtaining this Japanese operating system can range from a couple to several hundred dollars, depending on your MacOS-J registration status. It is, of course, included with newly-purchased Macintosh computers in Japan, and is available on a single CD-ROM. Luckily, obtaining MacOS-J is not the only way to process Japanese on Macintosh computers: JLK (Japanese Language Kit), which is described later in this chapter, is also a viable solution for some people.

MacOS-KH—formerly HangulTalk

MacOS-KH is not developed by Apple Computer, but rather by Elex Computer in Korea. Apple Computer's closest thing to a Korean operating system is its Korean Language Kit, which is described later in this chapter.

---

* Six, if you consider the Osaka system font identical to Heisei Kaku Gothic W5—they share the same design for all two-byte characters, but have different design spaces. Osaka uses a 256×256 design spaces, and the others use the conventional TrueType 2048×2048 design space.

Unix

One of the oldest operating systems still in use today is Unix. Unlike PC-based operating systems such as Windows and MacOS, Unix protects itself from user-inflicted damage through the allocation of a privileged or super-user account called *root*—all other users are never granted the permissions necessary to modify operating-system–level resources. While there are two primary Unix implementations available today, BSD (Berkeley Standard Distribution) and System V, countless derivatives have been developed.

Each Unix workstation manufacturer offers its own proprietary Unix variant with manufacturer-specific enhancements. In addition, there are various "free" and "copylefted" versions of Unix around—some are more robust than others.

One aspect of Unix to be careful of—in the context of this book—is the fact that the behavior of some of its utilities changes depending on what "language" is set by the user. That is, the `LANG` environment variable. The most basic `LANG` setting is "C." Using the C shell, one can set the `LANG` environment variable as follows:

```
% setenv LANG C
```

When you use common Unix tools when `LANG` is set to "C," such as wc for example, it predictably calculates the number of words and characters based on the number of *bytes* in the file.* But, when the `LANG` environment variable is set to a value such as "Japanese," this command instead calculates the number of words and characters based on the number of *characters* (which may be composed of more than one byte) in the file.

I find Jerry Peek, Tim O'Reilly, and Mike Loukides' *UNIX Power Tools*, Second Edition (O'Reilly & Associates, 1997) to be an overall useful Unix reference, with a focus on time-saving tips. *The UNIX CD Bookshelf* (O'Reilly & Associates, 1998) provides the greatest amount of Unix reference material I have ever seen.

AIX—RISC System/6000

AIX (Advanced Interactive Executive) is a fully internationalized Unix operating system developed by IBM. Japanese language support was added beginning with Version 3.2. Support for other CJKV locales, such as Chinese and Korean, was added beginning with Version 3.2.3.

Being fully internationalized means that AIX can handle multiple-byte characters in almost all library functions, kernel routines, commands, utilities, and so on. Tools such as *vi*, *sed*, *awk*, *grep*, *diff*, *sdiff*, *cat*, *more*, and so on function correctly.

* Note that *wc* stands for "word count," not "water closet."

Command-line arguments, filenames, and the like can also use multiple-byte characters.

AIX internationalization is based on the XPG4 locale model (the locale model was briefly described in the beginning of Chapter 9). This means that character classification and case conversion (CTYPE), collation order (COLLATE), date and time formats (TIME), numeric and non-monetary formatting (NUMERIC), monetary formatting (MONETARY), and the language to be used for informative and diagnostic messages and interactive responses (MESSAGES) are all controlled by the user-selected locale. Changing locales is usually as simple as the following command line:

```
% export LANG=Ja_JP
```

This sets the current locale to handle Japanese characters and cultural aspects of Japan. If you list all the locale categories, along with their associated values, you may see the following:

```
% locale
LANG=Ja_JP
LC_COLLATE="Ja_JP"
LC_CTYPE="Ja_JP"
LC_MONETARY="Ja_JP"
LC_NUMERIC="Ja_JP"
LC_TIME="Ja_JP"
LC_MESSAGES="Ja_JP
LC_ALL=
```

The following command line sets the current locale to English and cultural aspects of the US:

```
% export LANG=En_US
```

Displaying Japanese text under AIX still requires that you run the X Window System or some other Unix windowing environment. The following command line opens a Japanese-capable window, using *aixterm*:

```
% aixterm -lang Ja_JP
```

There are actually two Japanese locales supported by AIX: `Ja_JP` and `ja_JP`. Note the case difference. The difference is in the encoding method supported by each. The locale `Ja_JP` supports Shift-JIS encoding, and the locale `ja_JP` supports EUC-JP encoding.

For more information on AIX, contact IBM directly, or else obtain *AIX Version 3.2 for RISC System/6000: Internationalization of AIX Software—A Programmer's Guide.*

IRIX—SGI workstations

IRIX is the name of the operating system for all Silicon Graphics' workstations. International support based on the locale model began with Version 5.0. The locale name for Japanese is `ja_JP.EUC` (EUC-JP encoding), but there is support for ISO-2022-JP encoding for processes such as email and news posting. EUC-JP remains the internally-processed code.

Versions of IRIX in Japan prior to Version 5.0 include JLS (Japanese Language System)—this consisted of adding Japanese language support to the operating system, and included Japanese versions of many of the utilities. IRIX Version 5.0 in Japan comes bundled with JLS Version 3.0. JLS Version 3.0 is available elsewhere as an option. Switching to Japanese under IRIX Version 5.0 is a simple matter of changing the locale to `ja_JP.EUC` (if JLS is installed).

There are also Chinese and Korean versions of IRIX available. There is also built-in support for CID-keyed fonts. Contact Silicon Graphics for more information.[*]

Solaris

The Unix-based operating system developed by Sun Microsystems is called Solaris, and there are localized versions available.[†] Like IRIX, Solaris also supports CID-keyed fonts through the use of DPS. The latest versions are also Unicode-enabled, and include a CJKV-capable email client called DtMail.

Plan 9

Plan 9 is an experimental multilingual Unix-based operating system under seemingly constant development at AT&T Bell Laboratories.[‡] Plan 9's multilingual support is not based on the locale model, but instead uses Unicode as its standard character set. No switching between code sets is necessary because all the characters necessary for many cultures or regions are included within the Unicode character set.

The encoding specified by Unicode is a fixed-length 16-bit representation (now better known as UTF-16). This is unsuitable for Unix systems whose text processing functions come in the form of tools and pipes working in unison. Plan 9 makes use of UTF-8, a method of transforming Unicode text so that it can be handled more reliably through Unix pipes and processes.

---

* *http://www.sgi.com/*

† *http://www.sun.com/solaris/*

‡ *http://plan9.bell-labs.com/plan9/*

BeOS

BeOS, developed by Be, Incorporated, is a fairly new operating system that runs on PowerPC or Intel architectures (the same architectures that are used for running MacOS and Windows).*

BeOS supports Unicode (through UTF-8 encoding) throughout the system, and with appropriate fonts, can display CJKV text.

Japanese appears to be the first CJKV locale that is being fully supported in BeOS, but I expect other locales to be supported soon. The online documentation for BeOS describes how to set up NetPositive, the BeOS web browser, to display Japanese web pages.†

The Be Development Team's *Be Developer's Guide* (O'Reilly & Associates, 1997) and *Be Advanced Topics* (O'Reilly & Associates, 1998) are useful references for those who plan to develop software for BeOS.

FreeBSD

FreeBSD is yet another freeware version of Unix, similar to Linux in that it is designed to run on PC compatibles.‡ FreeBSD is based on advanced BSD Unix. While new versions of the Linux kernel are released frequently, FreeBSD's releases are more infrequent.

Linux

Linux (りぬくす *rinukusu* in Japanese) is a rapidly-developing Unix-compatible operating system that runs on ordinary Intel-processor–powered PCs.** Linux also runs on Alphas, MIPS4000s, and M68000s. Linus Torvalds represents the primary force behind Linux in that he is responsible for the kernel. But, there is a cast of thousands doing actual development on Linux as a whole.

Japanese support in Linux has been available for the longest time, but support for Chinese and Korean seems to be increasing. WZCE (Wei Zhong Chinese Environment), developed by Wei Zhong Gong (龚为众 *gōng wèi zhòng*), is an example of software that adds Chinese processing capability to Linux.††

* *http://www.be.com/*

† *http://www.be.com/documentation/user_docs/05_beos_customize.html*

‡ *http://www.freebsd.org/*

** *http://www.linux.org/*

†† *http://sunsite.unc.edu/pub/Linux/apps/chinese/*

A good introduction to Linux is Matt Welsh and Lar Kaufman's *Running Linux*, Second Edition (O'Reilly & Associates, 1996), and Jessica Hekman's *Linux in a Nutshell* (O'Reilly & Associates, 1997) provides useful reference material.

MkLinux

MkLinux is, simply put, Linux for computers that use the PowerPC chip, such as the Power Macintosh series by Apple Computer.* MkLinux is a joint project of Apple Computer and The Open Group Research Institute,† and stands for *Microkernel Linux for the Power Macintosh*.

OS/2

OS/2 is an operating system developed by IBM for use on personal computers. The Chinese version of OS/2 was one of the first operating systems to support the GBK character set and its encoding. There is now some information about CJKV-enabling OS/2 available, courtesy of Alan Barbour.‡

TRON

Personal Media Corporation in Japan has developed the BTRON operating system, which is an instance of TRON.** TRON is unique in that it supports the JIS X 0212-1990 character set.

The most up-to-date information about TRON can be found online,†† and in *TRON-WARE* magazine, published bi-monthly in Japanese by Personal Media Corporation.

Hybrid Environments

The software described up until now are considered to be fully-functional operating systems, even when localized. They are not add-ons to existing operating systems, but rather wholly replace your current operating system with something new. The software described in this section are considered hybrids of operating systems that add CJKV functionality.

If you are a serious user or developer, I *strongly* suggest that you use a fully-localized operating system. If you do not feel that such an investment is right for you, these hybrid operating systems may provide an acceptable level of CJKV function-

* *http://www.mklinux.org/* or *http://www.mklinux.apple.com/*

† *http://www.opengroup.org/*

‡ *http://userzweb.lightspeed.net/~abarbour/os2cjk.htm*

** *http://www.personal-media.co.jp/*

†† *http://tron.um.u-tokyo.ac.jp/* or *http://www.tokyoweb.or.jp/tron/*

ality for your needs. There are also those who need the ability to process CJKV data, but whose language skills are not sufficiently developed to understand a fully-localized interface (its menus or dialogs). For this class of user, these hybrid environments become more enticing.

MacOS Language Kits

Apple Computer's Language Kits provide all the system extensions necessary for processing CJKV text on Macintosh computers, such as a minimum set of TrueType fonts, input methods, and so on. In a way, these Language Kits can be considered a poor-man's version of fully-localized versions of MacOS. But, they are also ideal for people who need the ability to process CJKV text, but would be unable to easily understand all of the localized menus and dialogs. Apple Computer maintains online information about all Language Kits, including pricing and availability.*

Unlike the fully-localized versions of MacOS, all of the Language Kits can be combined to form a single operating system that can process multiple languages. Note that you should *never*, *ever* install a Language Kit onto a fully-localized version of MacOS. Doing so can damage your operating system beyond repair.† Anyway, there is usually a specific order in which to install Apple Computer's Language Kits if more than one is desired. It is very difficult to describe the order in which to install Language Kits in fashion that will not be obsolete by the time you read this, but, in general, you should install the oldest Language Kits first.

Chinese Language Kit

Apple Computer's Chinese Language Kit (CLK for short) is actually two Language Kits in one. It includes installers for both Simplified (based on GB 2312-80) and Traditional Chinese (based on Big Five), and each comes with many TrueType fonts and a variety of input methods. "*Beijing*" is the System Font for Simplified Chinese, and "*Taipei*" is the System Font for Traditional Chinese.

Japanese Language Kit

The Japanese Language Kit (JLK) was the first CJKV-capable Language Kit developed by Apple Computer—it was also the very first Language Kit of them all. It was and still is extremely popular, even in Japan.

* *http://macos.apple.com/multilingual/* or *http://www.apple.com/macos/multilingual/languagekits.html*

† I know because I have tried it and ended up ruining my installation of MacOS-J—I tried to install CLK onto MacOS-J.

Korean Language Kit

The Korean market was unique for Apple Computer in that it did not directly control the fully-localized Korean version of MacOS (called HangulTalk). Elex Computer performed all of the development. When Apple Computer released the Korean Language Kit (KLK) in late 1996, it was the result of re-engineering many tasks already done by Elex Computer.

The Korean Language Kit comes bundled with five TrueType Korean fonts: AppleGothic, AppleMyungjo, Gungseouche (displays as "#궁서체" *gungseoce*), Pilgiche (displays as "#필기체" *pilgice*), and Seoul (the System Font). Also provided in its input method is the ability to perform hangul-hanja conversion.

An alternative to Apple Computer's KLK is HanSoft's Han Korean Kit (HKK), which adds Korean functionality to MacOS, and provides support for all 11,172 modern hangul (KLK and MacOS-KH support only the basic set of 2,350 hangul).*

MASS—Microsoft Windows and Unix

MASS, which stands for *Multilingual Application Support Service*, is a Unicode-based multilingual environment developed by Star+Globe Technologies, available for Unix and Windows.† The Unix version is called xMASS (for the X Window System), and the Windows version is called WinMASS.

PanALE—MacOS

PanALE (Pan-Asia Language Environment, also called Oriental Express), shareware written by Xiaolin Allen Zhao (赵小麟 *zhào xiǎolín*),‡ provides CJK (Chinese, Japanese, and Korean) support without the need for a localized MacOS or even one or more of Apple Computer's Language Kits.**

RichWin—Microsoft Windows

The RichWin products, available for Windows NT and OS/2, create a Chinese-enabled environment that allows users to manipulate Chinese text using ordinary unlocalized applications.†† RichWin also comes bundled with a Chinese-English dictionary for convenient lookup of words, and Chinese fonts. There is also a

* *http://www.hansoft.com/hkk/hkk.html*

† *http://www.starglobe.com.sg/*

‡ *xlz@kagi.com*

** *http://www.unidocsys.com/PanALE.shtml*

†† *http://www.richwin.com/*

version of RichWin that works in conjunction with web browsers to display Chinese, Japanese, and Korean text.

TwinBridge—Microsoft Windows

TwinBridge provides CJKV functionality on non-CJKV versions of Windows, including input methods and TrueType fonts.*

UnionWay—Microsoft Windows

UnionWay, like TwinBridge, provides CJKV functionality on non-CJKV versions of Windows, including input methods and TrueType fonts.†

X Window System—Unix

The X Window System (also known as X11R6, meaning "X Window System, Version 11, Release 6"), developed by the now disbanded MIT X Consortium, is a graphical user interface (GUI), windowing system, and general multilingual environment that runs on top of a Unix operating system, but has recently become available for MacOS and MS-DOS.

Each flavor of Unix has taken its own path towards localization and internationalization. Many flavors require that the operating system be language-localized: a `LANG` environment variable effectively sets the language used on the machine. Other Unix variants, like OSF/1, are adopting Unicode as their standard for internationalization.

The locales defined in X11R6 are somewhat different from those you learned about in the description of AIX above. For example, Table 10-5 lists the possible locales for Japanese under X11R6.

Table 10-5: Japanese Locales in X11R6

Locale	Japanese Encoding Method
`ja_JP.jis7`	JIS7
`ja_JP.jis8`	JIS8
`ja_JP.mscode`	Shift-JIS
`ja_JP.pjis`	ISO-2022-JP
`ja_JP.ujis`	EUC-JP

* *http://www.twinbridge.com/*

† *http://www.unionway.com/*

Some of the most advanced work in this area is coming from Japan itself. There is an effort at Waseda University (早稲田大学 *waseda daigaku*) to internationalize, rather than localize, both Unix and the X Window System. Supported by NTT and Omron, it is an attempt to create a fully-internationalized workstation environment which will allow for multiple languages to be used simultaneously with a minimum of overhead.

Here's how it works: one additional locale is defined, called `wr_WR.ct`. This locale contains information for over 20 character sets, such as Japanese, Korean, Chinese, and many for Western languages. The encodings are based on the escape sequences defined in ISO 2022:1994 (or JIS X 0202:1998, which is the Japanese equivalent). You learned in Chapter 4 that Chinese, Japanese, and Korean all can be encoded using the ISO-2022 model. While this is usually used for information interchange purposes, the locale `wr_WR.ct` takes advantage of this to provide a multilingual environment. For more information, contact Yutaka Kataoka (片岡裕 *kataoka yutaka*)* or visit his web site.†

For more information on X11R6 in general, I suggest getting one or more volumes from the *X Window System Series*, published by O'Reilly & Associates.

Text Editors

The most basic text processing tool is a text editor. This tool allows you to input and save text. The functions are very basic, but, believe it or not, there are cases when you would choose a text editor over a word processor. One such circumstance is if you are composing CJKV text for transmission by email—special formatting such as you would expect from a word processor does not travel well over email. The characters and formatting that you are limited to with text editors are precisely what usually travels well through email.

The features found in text editors are limited, yet useful. Most of them come with search and replace functions, and some even allow the user to write complex macros. Limitations sometimes include lack of word wrap, font limitations, font size limitations, and font style limitations.

Of the text editors that are currently available, they can be categorized into two basic types:

- Those that require an underlying CJKV-capable operating system to correctly handle CJKV data
- Those that provide their own CJKV support independently of the underlying operating system

* *kataoka@mling.waseda.ac.jp* or *kataoka@otani.ac.jp*

† *http://www.mling.waseda.ac.jp/*

My overall favorite text editor is GNU Emacs because there is no dependency on a mouse for *any* editing command, and its built-in editing commands are *extremely* powerful. I had been using its multilingual version—called Mule—for years. Mule's multilingual functionality has recently been integrated back into GNU Emacs (as of Version 20). I also use a Japanese-capable version of Emacs designed for MacOS called Nitemacs. If you haven't yet explored Emacs and its multilingual variants, I encourage you to do so. If you are a *vi* fan, there are also CJKV-capable versions of *vi* available.

Most contemporary text editors actually eliminate the need for dedicated code conversion tools in some important contexts because they provide import/export functionality for multiple character sets and encodings.

MacOS Text Editors

Nearly all CJKV-capable text editors for MacOS require that you use either a fully-localized version of MacOS or else a Language Kit. And most Japanese ones support ISO-2022-JP and EUC-JP encodings for import or export purposes—they process Shift-JIS encoding internally because that is what MacOS-J processes internally.

While I list only a few MacOS text editors below, there are many available. BBedit is popular, and works well in conjunction with programming tools (because the built-in editors of most MacOS programming environments are either not CJKV-capable or are simply inadequate for most editing needs).

ASLEdit+

The Japanese text editor called ASLEdit+, written by Hiroo Yamada (山田浩大 *hiroo yamada*), is one of the most stable and reliable text editors I have used. This freeware was designed as a MacOS text editor for use with compilers (the programs used to transform source code written in a programming language, such as C, into an executable program). ASLEdit+ was designed to be used as a replacement for compilers' built-in text editor. Underlying Japanese capability is required for ASLEdit+—otherwise it behaves like a standard English-language text editor.

ASLEdit+ does not really have any special Japanese features other than being able to handle two-byte characters correctly. Many times, this is all that is necessary, especially for a text editor. It does have a very powerful search and replace function, including multiple file and regular expression support.

The name ASLEdit+ comes from the author's amateur radio call sign, which is JK1ASL. The author has written other freeware MacOS software such as ASLTelnet, a Japanese-capable telnet client, which is described in Chapter 12.*

---

* *http://www.activeopen.co.jp/ASL/*

Jedit

Jedit is a Japanese text editor for MacOS that provides useful editing facilities, along with import/export abilities for encodings such as ISO-2022-JP and EUC-JP (Shift-JIS is processed by default due to MacOS-J).*

King's Edit

King's Edit is shareware developed by Naoki Hirata (平田直毅 *hirata naoki*) and Akito Fujiwara (藤原彰人 *fujiwara akito*).† It is a very powerful text editor that offers many features not commonly available, such as:

- Rectangular selection, useful for selecting columns of text
- Ability to use *awk* and *sed* filters, useful for applying regex-based operations against the contents of a file
- Extensively customizable character transformations

Also of significance is King's Edit's ability to import and export Japanese encodings other than Shift-JIS, specifically ISO-2022-JP and EUC-JP.

Nitemacs

Nitemacs is a freeware Emacs clone developed by Shigeru Chiba (千葉滋 *chiba shigeru*).‡ While it does not offer all the features found in GNU Emacs (described shortly), such as rectangular selection and regex support, it does provide a convenient and fast Emacs-like environment, along with the ability to import and export files that are encoded according to ISO-2022-JP and EUC-JP.

SaLLY

Makoto Inage (稲毛誠 *inage makoto*) developed SaLLY, which is yet another Emacs clone.** Unlike other Emacs clones, SaLLY supports regex-based search/replace, along with rectangular editing.

Windows Text Editors

There are an incredible number of CJKV-capable text editors for Windows, and unlike those for MacOS, many do not require underlying CJKV support in the operating system.

---

* *http://www.matsumoto.co.jp/*

† *http://www.page.sannet.ne.jp/warajy/*

‡ *http://www.softlab.is.tsukuba.ac.jp/~chiba/nitemacs.html*

** *http://www.bekkoame.or.jp/~m-inage/*

Popular Japanese-capable Windows text editors include Hidemaru (秀丸 *hidemaru*),* MIFES,† and WZ.‡ Some of these text editors offer extremely powerful text-mangling facilities through the use of regular expressions.

Emacs and GNU Emacs Variants

Described in this section are several freely-available variants of Emacs and GNU Emacs. Emacs is a text editor that has been ported to many platforms. If you have more than one working environment, you can use the software described below to have similar text-editing features and functionality.

All of these Emacs and GNU Emacs variants depend on a CJKV-capable environment for displaying CJKV characters on the screen—they handle only the internal manipulation of CJKV character codes.

Most variants of Emacs or GNU Emacs can be extensively customized by the user. In fact, these programs can also constitute a complete working environment (at least on most Unix systems)—email can be processed, source code can be compiled, and so on. Customizing is usually done by adding entries to the configuration file called *.emacs* ("dot" emacs), or by writing Emacs LISP programs. Extensive tutorials are also included in the complete GNU Emacs distribution.

There are a large number of Emacs and GNU Emacs variants available for a number of operating systems. While I describe only the most widely-used versions, there are also variants such as Demacs, Han Emacs, Mg, Ng, Nitemacs, and SaLLY. I have become particularly fond of Nitemacs because it is for MacOS.

For more information on GNU Emacs in general, I suggest that you obtain Debra Cameron and Bill Rosenblatt's *Learning GNU Emacs*, Second Edition (O'Reilly & Associates, 1996) and Richard Stallman's *GNU Emacs Manual*, Thirteenth Edition (Free Software Foundation, 1997). The latter is likely to be most useful because it documents the multilingual features and functionality that have been integrated into GNU emacs since Version 20. More about this below.

GNU Emacs, NEmacs, and Mule

GNU Emacs and its variants are developed by the Free Software Foundation,** and are copylefted software distributed under the terms of the GNU General Public

* *http://hidemaru.xaxon.co.jp/*

† *http://www.megasoft.co.jp/products/*

‡ *http://www.villagecenter.co.jp/WZ30/*

** *http://www.gnu.org/*

License.* The terms of the GNU General Public License protect software from being exploited for commercial use.

There have been two major CJKV-capable GNU Emacs developments over the years: NEmacs and Mule, each of which is installed as a series of patches to the GNU Emacs source code. NEmacs stands for *Nihongo Emacs* ("nihongo," written 日本語, is the Japanese word that means "Japanese [language]"). Mule stands for *MULtilingual enhancement to GNU Emacs.* While it may be obvious by their names, NEmacs was a Japanese-only version of GNU Emacs, and Mule provided support for a large number of languages, including Chinese, Japanese, and Korean.

Both NEmacs and Mule were developed by a core team made up of Ken'ichi Handa† (半田剣一 *handa ken'ichi*), Satoru Tomura (戸村哲 *tomura satoru*), and Mikiko Nishikimi (錦見美貴子 *nishikimi mikiko*). Mule was one of the very first programs to support the characters and encoding methods for the JIS X 0212-1990 character set standard. Both ISO-2022-JP-2 and EUC-JP encodings are supported for the encoding of this character set in Mule.

GNU Emacs Version 20 and greater incorporates all functionality of Mule—the Mule extensions were integrated back into the standard GNU Emacs distribution.‡ The following are some lines that I include in my *.emacs* file to enable a Japanese language environment:

```
(set-language-environment 'Japanese)
(setq-default buffer-file-coding-system 'iso-2022-jp)
```

Although I have specified ISO-2022-JP as the default buffer encoding when using GNU Emacs, it will still recognize (and preserve) files that use Shift-JIS and EUC-JP encodings. There is also an elaborate aliasing mechanism that recognizes a wide variety of encoding names so that there is more than one way to set such variables.

With GNU Emacs, it is possible to use any encodings in any language environment. Changing the language environment only affects the following behavior:

- Which encoding is used as the default
- The priority of encodings while GNU Emacs is automatically detecting a file's encoding

The following are possible language designators for establishing a Chinese environment in GNU Emacs: `Chinese-GB`, `Chinese-BIG5`, and `Chinese-CNS`. As expected, these establish environments that are based on the GB 2312-80, Big

* *http://www.gnu.org/copyleft/gpl.html*

† *handa@etl.go.jp*

‡ *ftp://prep.ai.mit.edu/pub/gnu/*

Five, and CNS 11643-1992 character sets, respectively. For Korean, one simply specifies `Korean`.

Nitemacs and SaLLY, described starting on page 474, are Japanese-capable Emacs clones for MacOS.

vi and vi Variants

The *vi* text editor is another popular editing environment, and there are now several CJKV-capable versions available. Unlike GNU Emacs, which recently had multilingual extensions integrated back into its own source code, the original *vi* editor is still ASCII-only software. This means that there is little point in describing *vi* itself in the context of this book—describing CJKV-capable variants is much more appropriate. For those who wish to learn *vi*, I suggest Linda Lamb and Arnold Robbins' *Learning the vi Editor*, Sixth Edition (O'Reilly & Associates, 1998).

Jstevie

Jstevie, written by Junn Ohta (太田純 *ōta jun*),* supports most *vi* and *ex* commands and Japanese input. ISO-2022-JP, Shift-JIS, and EUC-JP encodings are supported, but the user must choose one encoding at compile time. *Jstevie* is easily ported to different platforms, and is based on STEVIE 3.69 written by Tony Andrews.

Jstevie does not support the input or display of Japanese characters—it simply handles the internal processing of Japanese codes. Other software such as Wnn and *kterm* is required to enter and display Japanese text.

Jim Breen has modified *Jstevie* to handle JIS X 0212-1990.† Apart from GNU Emacs and *nvi-m17n* (described shortly), it is the only other editor capable of handling the JIS X 0212-1990 character set.

jelvis

Another Japanese-capable *vi* clone is called *jelvis*, and is based on *elvis* written by Steve Kirkendall. The Japanese-enabling patches were originally written by Jun-ichiro Itoh (伊藤純一郎 *itō junichirō*),‡ and like *elvis* itself, are freely available. Like *Jstevie*, ISO-2022-JP, Shift-JIS, and EUC-JP encodings are supported, but the user does not need to choose one at compile time—Japanese encodings can be set from the command line or from within *jelvis*.

---

* *ohta@src.ricoh.co.jp*

† *ftp://ftp.cc.monash.edu.au/pub/nihongo/jstevie_212.tar.gz*

‡ *itojun@itojun.org*

The further development of *jelvis*, specifically for Version 2.1 (based on *elvis* Version 2.1) and beyond, is being done by the people who make up the *jelvis* Mailing List.*

Multilingual nvi—nvi-m17n

Perhaps of wider interest is *multilingual nvi* (also known as *nvi-m17n*), available as a multilingual patch for Keith Bostic's *nvi*, and written by Jun-ichiro Itoh (伊藤純一郎 *itō junichirō*) of *jelvis* fame.† What separates *nvi-m17n* from other *vi* clones is that it supports a wide variety of character sets and encodings, and it uses a generic ISO-2022 engine for handling ISO-2022–style encodings.

The following Japanese encodings are supported by *nvi-m17n*:

- EUC-JP (all four code sets)
- ISO-2022-JP
- ISO-2022-JP-1
- ISO-2022-JP-2
- Shift-JIS

The following Chinese encodings are supported:

- EUC-CN
- HZ
- ISO-2022-CN
- ISO-2022-CN-EXT
- Big Five
- EUC-TW

The following Korean encodings are supported:

- EUC-KR
- ISO-2022-KR

The ISO 8859 series is also handled by *nvi-m17n* in a very meaningful way. This seems to be the only *vi* clone with extensive CJKV support.

Hangul Elvis

A Korean-enabled version of *elvis* is called Hangul Elvis. It supports the basic Korean encodings, and requires a Korean-enabled operating system.‡

* *jelvis@itojun.org*

† *ftp://ftp.foretune.co.jp/pub/tools/nvi-m17n/*

‡ *ftp://sunsite.kren.nm.kr/shortcut/hangul/editor/HElvis/*

Word Processors

Word processors (ワードプロセッサ *wādopurosessa* or ワープロ *wāpuro* in Japanese) are the next step up from text editors. Supported features usually include multiple fonts (that is, you can select different fonts at the character level), multiple font styles, multiple point sizes, word wrap, various types of justification, CJKV line breaking, somewhat complex formatting capabilities, multiple tab styles, and sometimes a basic set of graphics-building tools. Some word processors even rival the features of page-layout software.

Of the large number of word processors on the market that provide CJKV functionality, there are those that depend on an underlying CJKV-capable operating system, and there are those that establish their own environment, making them usable on unlocalized operating systems.

Because there are far more word processors available today than can conceivably be described in a book such as this, this section provides a mere sampling of what is currently available on the market.

AppleWorks—MacOS

Apple Computer's AppleWorks (formerly ClarisWorks) is software that consists of a variety of applications, including word processing, spreadsheet, graphics, and so on.* It is widely bundled on Macintosh computers. Note that the standard (that is, unlocalized) version is WorldScript II compatible, which means that you may already have this software available to you.

HWP—Microsoft Windows

The Korean word processor called HWP (Hangul Word Processor), developed by a company called Hangul & Computer, provides full Korean functionality, but does not require an underlying Korean operating system.†

HWP has already been ported to many Unix-like operating systems, and there are plans to do the same for MacOS and OS/2.

Ichitaro—MacOS and Microsoft Windows

JUSTSYSTEM's Ichitaro (一太郎 *ichitarō*) is one of the most widely-used Japanese word processors, and is available for MacOS and Windows.‡ It also one of the first

* *http://www.apple.com/appleworks/*

† *http://www.hnc.co.kr/*

‡ *http://www.justsystem.co.jp/ichitaro/*

Japanese word processors that is now completely Unicode-based internally. Their engineers have effectively insulated the users from ever knowing this.*

JWP—Microsoft Windows

Stephen Chung† developed a freeware Japanese word processor that runs under standard (that is, unlocalized) Microsoft Windows (95, 98, or NT).‡ It is distributed under the terms of the GNU General Public License. JWP requires the following environment:

- Microsoft Windows Version 3.0 or later
- 80286 CPU (80386 or higher is recommended)
- 2MB of RAM (4MB is recommended)

These are, I think you'll agree, very minimal requirements by today's computer-hardware standards.

JWP is very rich in features, and rivals commercial products with its capabilities. Version 2.0 and later will also work with CID-keyed fonts by virtue of its hooks for ATM Version 3.2J.**

The author of JWP is constantly adding new features, and accepts suggestions for changes and improvements. Requested features may or may not get implemented depending on his busy schedule.

KanjiWORD—Microsoft Windows

KanjiWORD, developed by Pacific Software Publishing, is a fully-functional Japanese word processor that runs under Windows.†† Like other word processors that establish their own Japanese environment, it supports the import and export of multiple Japanese encodings, and comes with its own fonts and input methods.

Microsoft Office—Microsoft Windows

An excellent word processing package is the appropriately-localized version of Microsoft Office—excellent in that in addition to a full-featured and powerful word processor, Microsoft Word, it includes other useful programs, including Microsoft Excel (spreadsheet software), Microsoft PowerPoint (presentation software), and

* Well, at least until Ichitaro users read this page.

† *stephen.chung@monsanto.com*

‡ *ftp://ftp.cc.monash.edu.au/pub/nihongo/*

** ATM Version 3.2J does *not* run under Windows NT.

†† *http://www.pspinc.com/LSG/kword.htm*

MS Mail (email software). Quite often, Microsoft Office provides users with a basic set of software to get their job done.

Microsoft Word 97 (and later), Microsoft Excel 97 (and later), and Microsoft PowerPoint 97 (and later) are Unicode-enabled. The "Language Packs" that are included with the Microsoft Office CD-ROM can effectively CJKV-enable these and other Windows applications. See page 456 for more details.

Nisus Writer—MacOS

Nisus Writer (formerly simply Nisus) was one of the very few word processors that could handle CJKV text adequately although it was not designed for CJKV handling *per se*. An effort began to localize Nisus Writer to the Japanese market, and to add extra features specific to Japanese text handling. The resulting software was called SoloWriter. Nisus Software continued to develop this software, and now it is considered one of the top-rated word processors.

Many of Nisus Writer's most notable features are not necessarily specific to handling CJKV text. It is also one of the easiest word processors to obtain outside of the CJKV locales—most MacOS mail order companies carry Nisus Writer.

There is also a light version of Nisus Writer available: Nisus Compact. It has slightly fewer features than Nisus Writer, and thus requires less RAM to run effectively. It was designed with the Apple Macintosh PowerBook series laptop computers in mind—RAM and hard disk space were at a premium on early models.

Nisus Writer was used to produce the manuscript for *Understanding Japanese Information Processing*. A free demo version of Nisus Writer is available.* This demo version is fully functional except that it will not permit you to save documents. Joe Kissell's *The Nisus Way* (MIS:Press, 1996) is an excellent guide for Nisus Writer, and comes with a CD-ROM containing a time-expiring version of Nisus Writer plus a fully-functional Nisus Compact.

NJStar—Microsoft Windows

NJStar (南极星/南極星 *nánjíxīng*), a commercial program written by Hongbo Ni (倪鸿波 *ní hóngbō*), who also went on to found NJStar Software Corporation, was originally designed as a Chinese word processor, but was modified to handle Japanese in a dedicated Japanese version—this means that there are now Chinese and Japanese versions of NJStar available.† Its interface includes pull-down menus and mouse support, and the ability to use English menus. It also has rich editing func-

* *http://www.nisus.com/*

† *http://www.njstar.com/*

tions to include multiple file editing, undo, two-direction fast search, flexible replace, and extensive block manipulations. NJStar does not require a localized operating system because it establishes its own Chinese or Japanese environment, as appropriate.

The lowest price version of NJStar (the "Basic" version) includes only bitmapped fonts, but the "Pro" versions include TrueType fonts that can be used for better-quality printing.

The Chinese version of NJStar supports EUC-CN, Big Five, and HZ encodings for import and export purposes, and provides the user with nearly 20 Chinese input methods (some of which were described in Chapter 5 of this book). In fact, the NJStar manuals are useful for understanding these Chinese input methods. Also provided is instant access for a Chinese-English dictionary.

The Japanese version of NJStar supports ISO-2022-JP, EUC-JP, and Shift-JIS encodings for import and export purposes, includes approximately 10 Japanese input methods, and provides users with instant access to a Japanese-English dictionary.

UniText—MacOS

UniText (formerly Unicorn Editor), written by Xiaolin Allen Zhao (赵小麟 *zhào xiǎolín*), provides CJK (Chinese, Japanese, and Korean) editing capability when using unlocalized MacOS *and* without a Language Kit.* UniText is very useful for users who simply cannot afford to purchase a fully-localized version of MacOS, or who require simultaneous use of Chinese, Japanese, and Korean (but still cannot afford to purchase Apple Computer's Language Kits). UniText is included in his Pan-Asia Language Environment (PanALE), which is a hybrid environment described starting on page 470.

Dedicated Word Processors

The word processors described in the previous section are software that you can purchase, install, and run on various platforms. There are, however, systems that have word processing software built in. These are called *dedicated* word processors (日本語ワープロ専用機 *nihongo wāpuro senyōki* in Japanese). Their word processing software is almost always *fixed* (that is, not upgradable). The very first dedicated Japanese word processor, Toshiba's JW-10 (東芝JW-10 *tōshiba JW-10*), was released in the fall of 1978.

These machines may be ideal for those who do not wish to invest in a fully-functional computer system. The features offered on some of these machines are often

* *http://www.unidocsys.com/UniText.shtml*

quite impressive, and many come with file exchange facilities (for example, they can read and write MS-DOS disks) and telecommunication software (and sometimes even an internal modem!). There are even some with Lotus 1-2-3 (a very popular spreadsheet program) built in. Most of these machines now have built-in outline fonts, and their printers (often built-in ink-jet or thermal) produce reasonably good quality output.

Almost every major computer manufacturer, at least in Japan, produces a series of these machines. There was a Japanese periodical, published quarterly from 1986 until 1993, entitled 最新ワープロ大百科 (*saishin wāpuro daihyakka*, meaning "New Word Processor Encyclopedia"), that did a excellent job at providing a current listing of dedicated Japanese word processors. This periodical usually highlighted some of the latest models. Full specifications of all current models were listed at the end of each issue. It is a shame that this periodical had been discontinued, but I hear that it has since been revived.

A friend of mine from Japan, Yukihiro Furuse* (古瀬幸広 *furuse yukihiro*), once told me why he prefers to use dedicated word processors rather than word processing software for personal computers: he does not experience system crashes or freezes while using the dedicated machines. Indeed, something to think about…

* *http://ir.sr.rikkyo.ac.jp/~furuse/*

11

Dictionaries and Dictionary Software

In this chapter:

- *Chinese Character Dictionary Indexes*
- *Character Dictionaries*
- *Other Useful Dictionaries*
- *Dictionary Hardware*
- *Dictionary Software*
- *Machine Translation Software*
- *Machine Translation Services*
- *Learning Aids*

You may be wondering why there is even mention of—let alone a dedicated chapter on—dictionaries in a book about information processing. The usefulness of dictionaries should be quite obvious once you give it some thought: they provide users and developers the ability to locate information about words (for most CJKV locales, this usually entails meaningful sequences of one of more Chinese characters) and individual Chinese characters. Having the ability to rapidly access information about words and the Chinese characters that are used to compose them—or to be able to access this type of information at all—makes using and developing software a much more pleasant experience.

Software, such as that which performs machine-aided translation or aid a student in studying a language, is related to dictionaries. Some very basic information about these related topics is covered near the end of this chapter.

Chinese Character Dictionary Indexes

In order to begin taking advantage of the wealth of information contained within Chinese character dictionaries, you first need to know how to use them. The typical Chinese character dictionary contains two main parts:

- Main entries, which provide all the useful information in one place
- One or more indexes, which provide ways to find the target main entry

Needless to say, the more indexes a dictionary contains, the greater chance that you can find the target main entry—many Chinese characters are difficult to find in dictionaries for a variety of reasons, such as due to rare readings, difficult-to-find radicals, ambiguous stroke counts, and so on.

The main entries in Chinese character dictionaries are typically ordered in a standard way, such as by radical, number of strokes, or reading. The most common of these is by radical. In fact, there is usually a simple radical index right inside the front (or back) cover of most Chinese character dictionaries to aid in quick lookup.

The following sections describe these indexing methods in greater detail, and provide tips for faster lookup.

Reading Index

One of the most effective ways to locate Chinese characters in a dictionary is by their reading. Once you locate the appropriate reading in the reading index, you will then usually find the Chinese characters ordered by radical or number of strokes.

However, there are some things to bear in mind when making use of reading indexes:

- Many Chinese characters have multiple readings, which means that some reading indexes may include multiple entries for such Chinese characters
- Not all Chinese characters have well-known readings, which means that some reading indexes may not have a single entry for such Chinese characters

The fact that Chinese characters often have multiple reading actually can work to your advantage. In the case of Japanese, for example, kanji with multiple readings often have a reading that is fairly frequent (that is, many other kanji share the same reading: *homophones*) and one that is rather infrequent. In short, searching for a Chinese character using an uncommon reading is typically faster because there are less homophones to consider. Table 11-1 lists several kanji, along with frequent and infrequent readings.

Table 11-1: Kanji Readings of Different Frequency

Kanji	Frequent Reading	Infrequent Reading
剣	ケン (*ken*)	つるぎ (*tsurugi*)
中	チュウ(*chū*)	なか (*naka*)
生	セイ (*sei*), ショウ (*shō*)	なま (*nama*)
犬	ケン (*ken*)	いぬ (*inu*)

Many rare Chinese characters do not have very well-known readings. But, even if you happen to know a reading for a particular Chinese character, that doesn't necessarily mean that all reading indexes will include an entry for it. This is when other indexes come into play.

Radical Index

Chinese characters are most frequently categorized by radical. As discussed in Chapters 2, *Writing Systems*, and 5, *Input Methods*, radicals and radical-like components are the basic building blocks of Chinese characters. Radicals thus serve as a way to organize and categorize Chinese characters. Some character set standards order Chinese characters according to their radical, such as Level 2 of JIS X 0208:1997 and GB 2312-80, JIS X 0212-1990, and ISO 10646-1:1993.

The most commonly-used set of radicals today is the classic 214. This set of radicals, along with its classification system, was established in the classic Chinese character dictionary entitled 康熙字典 (*kāngxī zìdiǎn*), which is nearly 300 years old. This radical-indexing scheme is widely used in Japan, Korea, and Taiwan. China, because of its hanzi simplifications, uses a reduced set of 186 radicals. Both of these common radical systems are listed in Appendix P, *Code Table Indexes*.

Radical indexes require that the user first identify what is considered to be the *indexing* radical. Once the indexing radical has been determined, the next task is to count the remaining strokes in the Chinese character. Table 11-2 lists several hanzi, along with their indexing radical and remaining strokes, using the two common radical systems: the classic 214 system and the simplified 186 system.

Table 11-2: Identifying Hanzi Using Different Radical Systems

Hanzi	214 Radicals	186 Radicals	Remaining Elements and Residual Strokes
剑	刀 (18)	刂 (11)[a]	佥, 7 strokes
汉	水 (85)	氵 (55)[b]	又, 2 strokes
林	木 (75)	木 (72)	木, 4 strokes
边	辵 (162)	辶 (57)[c]	力, 2 strokes
语	言 (149)	讠 (22)[d]	吾, 7 strokes

[a] A variant of 刀.
[b] A variant of 水.
[c] A variant of 辵.
[d] The simplified form of 言.

Appendix P provides radical indexes for Level 2 of JIS X 0208:1997 and GB 2312-80, and JIS X 0212-1990. While the two JIS standards conform to the set of 214 classical radicals, Level 2 of GB 2312-80 uses the reduced set of 186 based on the principles of simplified hanzi.

Some Chinese character dictionaries that use a reduced set radicals include a table that provides a cross-reference to equivalent radicals in the classical set of 214 radicals. And, some dictionaries include special indexes that list Chinese characters whose indexing radical is not very obvious.

Stroke Count Index

This kind of index is the least effective of the three principal ways to locate a Chinese character. The first two methods discussed in this chapter, accessed through reading and radical indexes, are almost always more effective.

A stroke count index first separates Chinese characters into groups whose common characteristic is their number of total strokes. The Chinese characters within each stroke-count group then need to be ordered—otherwise, you'd sometimes need to scan several hundred characters to find the one you're looking for. The most common ordering within each stroke-count group is by radical.*

Many character dictionaries published in China use a very useful and effective method for ordering hanzi within each stroke-count group. The characters are ordered according to the shape of their first strokes. This system employs a total of five such strokes, indicated as follows, along with their names:

- 一 (横 *héng*)
- 丨 (竖/豎 *shù*)
- 丿 (撇 *piě*)
- 丶 (点/點 *diǎn*)
- 乙 (折 *zhé* or 横折 *héngzhé*)

The hanzi 中 can thus be described using the following four strokes: 丨, 乙, 一, and 丨. The convention in dictionaries' stroke-count indexes is to use a single stroke to order characters whose stroke counts are either small or great (because there are not that many characters under such stroke counts), but two strokes for those stroke counts that include a large number of characters. This is done for the sake of searching efficiency.

Note that some Chinese characters are known to have ambiguous stroke counts, typically because there are multiple ways to write their radicals or radical-like components. Table 11-3 lists some radicals that have ambiguous stroke counts, either due to variations of the radical or different ways in which to write the radical.

Table 11-3: Radicals with Ambiguous Stroke Counts

Radical	Stroke Counts	Reason for Discrepancy
臣	6 or 7	Different ways to write radical
食	9 or 10	Different ways to write radical

* This is sort of the reverse of radical lookup whereby you first find the radical, then you count the number of strokes or the number of remaining strokes, depending on how the dictionary was designed.

Table 11-3: Radicals with Ambiguous Stroke Counts (continued)

Radical	Stroke Counts	Reason for Discrepancy
舛	6 or 7	Different ways to write radical
阝	2 or 3	Different ways to write radical
⻌, ⻍	3 or 4	Different number of strokes
礻, 示	4 or 5	Variations

Good dictionaries include Chinese characters with ambiguous stroke counts in all applicable stroke-count groups.

Other Indexes

While reading, radical, and stroke count indexes are the most frequently found in Chinese character dictionaries, they are not necessarily the most efficient in terms of lookup speed. Other indexes include Jack Halpern's SKIP, the four-corner method, and character codes themselves.

SKIP

One particularly efficient Chinese character index method is known as SKIP (System of Kanji Indexing with Patterns), developed and patented by Jack Halpern, implemented in his own dictionary for the ordering of the main entries, and included (by permission) in Jim Breen's KANJIDIC file (described later in this chapter, starting on page 502). In fact, KANJIDIC includes SKIP codes for all JIS X 0208:1997 kanji, not only those that appear in Jack Halpern's *New Japanese-English Character Dictionary* (Kenkyusha, 1990; NTC, 1993).[*] Jack Halpern also maintains a useful web page.[†]

A SKIP code consists of three numbers separated by a hyphen. The first part represents the basic pattern. SKIP identifies four basic patterns, and numbers them accordingly:

1. Left-right
2. Top-bottom
3. Enclosure
4. Solid

For the first three SKIP patterns, the second number in the SKIP code represents the number of strokes in the pattern (Pattern 1: left side; Pattern 2: top; Pattern 3:

* Jim Breen's KANJD212 (see page 504) also includes SKIP codes.

† *http://www.kanji.org/*

the enclosure), and the third and final number in the SKIP code represents the remaining number of strokes. Table 11-4 provides three examples.

Table 11-4: Example SKIP Codes

Kanji	SKIP Code	Description
剣	1-8-2	1st pattern, 8 strokes in pattern, 2 remaining strokes
書	2-6-4	2nd pattern, 6 strokes in pattern, 4 remaining strokes
国	3-3-5	3rd pattern, 3 strokes in pattern, 5 remaining strokes

The fourth pattern, Solid, has four subpatterns, as follows:

1. Top line
2. Bottom line
3. Through line
4. Others

The second SKIP code for the fourth pattern is the total number of strokes. The third SKIP part is the subpattern. An example is 下, whose SKIP code is 4-3-1 (4th pattern, 3 total strokes, 1st subpattern).

Although SKIP has thus far been used only for Japanese, it is applicable to other CJKV locales as well. Werner Lemberg has developed a Quail-based SKIP input method for GNU Emacs.*

Four Corner code

The Four Corner code has been used for many years in China and Japan as a way to identify Chinese characters using exactly four digits. This system is apparently losing popularity in China due to the now widespread use of Pinyin. Japan's thirteen-volume 大漢和辭典 *(dai kanwa jiten)* and China's 辭源 *(cíyuán)*, for example, include a Four Corner code index.

There are a number of rules that effectively describe how this system works and its underlying principles:

- The Four Corner code elements are divided into ten shapes, numbered 0 through 9—these are described in Table 11-5 on page 490
- The four digits that comprise a Four Corner code are derived from the four corners in a Z-shaped sequence—upper-left, upper-right, lower-left, then lower-right

* *ftp://ftp.etl.go.jp/pub/mule/emacs-contrib/skip.tar.gz*

- A shape is only used once—if it fills several corners, it is counted as 0 (zero) in subsequent corners
- When the upper or lower half of a character is comprised of only a single shape, it is, regardless of its position, counted as a left-corner code—the right corner is counted as 0 (zero)
- When there is no additional element to the four sides of the characters 口, 門, 鬥 (and the split form of 行), whatever is inside these characters is taken as the lower two corners

Table 11-5 lists the ten elements that can be used to build Four Corner codes, along with some notes about their use.

Table 11-5: The Ten Four-Corner Code Elements

Code	Name	Example Shapes	Description
0	头/頭 (*tóu*)	亠	Lid
1	横 (*héng*)	一	Horizontal bar
2	垂 (*chuí*)	丨 丿	Vertical bar
3	点/點 (*diǎn*)	丶	Dot
4	叉 (*chā*)	十	Cross
5	插 (*chā*)	扌	Skewer
6	方 (*fāng*)	口	Box
7	角 (*jiǎo*)	乙	Angle
8	八 (*bā*)	八人入	Eight
9	小 (*xiǎo*)	小个忄	Small

Character code

When dealing with Chinese characters across multiple locales, there are often cases when finding a Chinese character in one locale is easier than in another. For example, if you happen to be well-versed in Japanese, it may be relatively easy to input most kanji. But, trying to input that same character in Chinese or Korean may prove to be a difficult or impossible task.* The character code itself can serve as a cross-reference to the Chinese or Korean equivalents.

Consider the contents of Table 11-6, which provide various character codes for the Chinese character 中 (meaning "middle" or "center").

* Especially if you're trying to write a book entitled *CJKV Information Processing* on a Japanese-only operating system with only Japanese input methods and Shift-JIS–encoded Chinese, Korean, and Vietnamese fonts.

Table 11-6: CJKV Character Code Indexes

Character Set	Row-Cell	ISO-2022	EUC	Other
JIS X 0208:1997	35-70	4366	C3E6	9286 (Shift-JIS)
GB 2312-80	54-48	5650	D6D0	
CNS 11643-1992	36-67	4463	C4E3	A4A4 (Big Five)
KS X 1001:1992	81-73	7169	F1E9	F3E9 (Johab)
KPS 9566-97	74-27	6A3B	EABB	
TCVN 6056:1995	42-21	4A35	CAB5	

Note that all of the various code points listed in Table 11-6 refer to the *same* UCS-2 or UTF-16 code point, specifically 0x4E2D. A dictionary that provides cross-references or indexes for character codes, as you can see, can be quite useful at times.

But, in order for this type of index to be useful, it must also account for character form differences between locales. Character form differences, such as the simplifications used in China, can often render simplistic cross-references useless. Consider the case as illustrated in Table 11-7. This table provides the cross-reference information as provided by ISO 10646-1:1993 in the "Traditional" column, but what is considered to be the more correct cross-reference is in the "Simplified" column.

Table 11-7: Chinese Character Cross-Referencing Issues

Locale	Traditional (Unicode 0x6F22)	Simplified (Unicode 0x6C49)
China	漢 GB/T 12345-90 26-26	汉 GB 2312-80 26-26
Taiwan	漢 CNS 11643-1992 Plane 1 73-39	*not applicable*
Japan	漢 JIS X 0208:1997 20-33	*not applicable*
South Korea	漢 KS X 1001:1992 89-51	*not applicable*
North Korea	漢 KPS 9566-97 82-51	*not applicable*
Vietnam	漢 TCVN 6056:1995 61-30	*not applicable*

Note how the character code for the example from China is the same for both traditional and simplified, but the character set designation differs. This is by design. As you learned in Chapter 3, *Character Set Standards*, GB/T 12345-90 is the traditional analog of GB 2312-80.

Character Dictionaries

Dictionaries represent one of the most useful resources for inputting or otherwise accessing CJKV characters. Yep, these are usually good ol' fashioned books!* In

* The nice thing about books is that you can take them virtually anywhere—often to places where computers or other electronic devices dare not venture.

fact, many of this book's appendixes, to some extent, can fill this purpose. What you will find in this book's appendixes are complete listings of characters enumerated in the most common CJKV character sets, followed by reading and radical indexes. The dictionaries discussed in this section go one step further in helping you to more easily access characters from those CJKV character set standards.

Character dictionaries that are CJKV-specific typically fall into one of two categories, described as follows:

- Conventional dictionaries that provide information such as readings, compounds, or words in which the character occurs, and perhaps even a short definition—these dictionaries were not necessarily designed with computer users in mind
- Specialized dictionaries that give you information, such as readings, one or more *encoded values*, and perhaps other information, such as compounds or words in which the character occurs

Needless to say, conventional dictionaries are most useful to the student or scholar of a language, but specialized dictionaries are a valuable resource for the computer user and software developer, and typically contain entries for all the characters in one or more CJKV character set standards, such as GB 2312-80 or GB/T 12345-90 for Chinese. One of the largest conventional CJKV character dictionaries was published in Japan. It is entitled 大漢和辭典 (*dai kanwa jiten*), contains 50,294 kanji, and is published as a thirteen-volume set.

Dictionaries that include the encoded value of characters prove their usefulness when you are trying to input a particular Chinese character, and the input method that you are using simply doesn't seem to know it exists. Mind you, there are Chinese characters that are not included in any CJKV character set standard, but those Chinese characters are not frequently used. There are many Chinese characters, such as those enumerated in JIS X 0208:1997 Level 2 kanji and GB 2312-80 Level 2 hanzi, that typically cannot be input by reading, and the user must finally resort to unintuitive means, such as input by encoded value (also known as code input).

Most input methods provide a mechanism for code input, and come with character tables—printed or available in software—arranged by encoded value. The usefulness of these character tables is very limited. Remember that GB 2312-80 Level 1 hanzi are arranged by reading, so forget about trying to locate a hanzi there by its indexing radical. GB 2312-80 Level 2 hanzi, on the other hand, are arranged by radical, so this makes locating hanzi a bit easier. However, there are always circumstances when you may wish to use other means to locate Chinese characters, such as by reading (or multiple readings), number of strokes, indexing radical, or radical-like parts—for both GB 2312-80 Level 1 and 2 hanzi. This is when a specialized Chinese character dictionary becomes invaluable. These dictionaries go far beyond what CJKV character set tables offer—they offer two or more methods for locating *all* characters in CJKV character set standards. I highly recommend purchasing at least one of these types of dictionaries. I have purchased several such dictionaries over the years.

Character Set Standards as Character Dictionaries

The CJKV character set standards themselves—in the form of a printed manual—can function as a limited-use character dictionary strictly for the purpose of locating characters more effectively than the inherent ordering of characters itself.

Table 11-8 lists the major CJKV character set standards, along with information about what type of indexes they provide.

Table 11-8: Chinese Character Indexes Provided by CJKV Standards

Character Set Standard	Indexes
ISO 10646-1:1993	Cross-references to character codes in CJKV national standards[a]
GB 2312-80[b]	Radical, stroke-count (limited), reading (ordered by Pinyin), and simplified versus traditional
CNS 11643-1992	None[c]
JIS X 0208:1997	Radical and reading, plus cross-references to variants, 大漢和辭典 and 新字源
JIS X 0212-1990	Radical plus cross-references to variants
JIS X 0221-1995	Cross-references to 大漢和辭典 and 康熙字典
KS X 1001:1992	None[d]
KS X 1002:1991	None[d]
TCVN 5773:1993	Reading
TCVN 6056:1995	Cross-references to *Tự Điển Chữ Nôm* and *Bảng Tra Chữ Nôm*

[a] *The Unicode Standard, Version 2.0* (Addison-Wesley, 1996) provides a radical index.
[b] Level 1 hanzi entries are annotated with Pinyin readings, and Level 2 hanzi entries are annotated with radicals (hanzi that represent the first using a particular radical are printed in Hei style—all others are in Song style).
[c] Each hanzi entry includes fields that indicate its total number of strokes, its indexing radical, and the number of strokes that make up the indexing radical.
[d] The hanja themselves are annotated with hangul to indicate reading.

I have personally found the indexes provided in the GB 2312-80 manual to be very useful and complete. These indexes have been repeated verbatim in the appendixes of the Chinese character dictionary entitled 常用汉字编码字典 (described in the very next section). Kohji Shibano's JIS漢字字典 includes the same indexes as in the JIS X 0208:1997 manual, which makes obtaining the actual JIS X 0208:1997 for the purpose of obtaining its indexes somewhat pointless.*

* Besides, computer-oriented Chinese character dictionaries are typically cheaper and easier to find than the character set standards that they cover.

Locale-Specific Character Dictionaries

Every CJKV locale has published a number of Chinese character dictionaries. While most of these dictionaries are not directly applicable to computer users and software developers, a handful have been designed with computers in mind. A handful of these computer-oriented dictionaries are briefly described below.

The specialized character dictionaries that I have used over the years provide access to different sets of characters, offer different methods for locating characters, and provide different information once you locate the target character:

- The Chinese character dictionary entitled 常用汉字编码字典 (*chángyòng hànzì biānmǎ zìdiǎn*, meaning "Character Dictionary of Codes for Frequently Used Chinese Characters") contains the same hanzi indexes found in the GB 2312-80 character set standard, along with nearly two dozen assorted input codes for all 6,763 GB 2312-80 hanzi.
- The Chinese character dictionary entitled 汉字属性字典 (*hànzì shǔxìng zìdiǎn*, meaning "Character Dictionary of Chinese Character Properties") is essentially a giant database of information for all 6,763 hanzi in the GB 2312-80 character set standard. It provides cross-references to other CJKV character set standards, such as Japan's JIS X 0208 series and Taiwan's CCCII.
- A pocket-size Chinese dictionary entitled 汉字输入速查手册 (*hànzì shūrù sùchá shǒucè*, meaning "Handbook of Chinese Character Input and Searching") allows lookup only through Pinyin readings (with no tones), and lists codes for two input methods (Renzhi and Wubi), along with Row-Cell values.
- The Chinese character dictionary entitled 標準中文輸入碼大字典 (*biāozhǔn zhōngwén shūrùmǎ dà zìdiǎn*, meaning "Big Character Dictionary of Standard Chinese Input Codes") provides stroke-count, reading, and radical indexes for the Big Five character set, and provides cross-references to the GB 2312-80 character set standard (using EUC-CN character codes). Also included are approximately 3,000 Hong Kong hanzi that are not part of the standard Big Five definition (it is published in Hong Kong).
- The Japanese character dictionary entitled パソコンワープロ漢字辞典 (*pasokon wāpuro kanji jiten*, meaning "Personal Computer and Word Processor Kanji Dictionary") allows users to locate all of the characters found in JIS X 0208-1983 (not the 1990 or 1997 vintages) by reading, indexing radical, and total number of strokes. It then provides hexadecimal ISO-2022-JP, hexadecimal Shift-JIS, Row-Cell, and the two printable ASCII characters that correspond to the two hexadecimal ISO-2022-JP bytes.
- The Japanese character dictionary entitled 最新JIS漢字辞典 (*saishin JIS kanji jiten*, meaning "New JIS Kanji Dictionary") allows users to locate all the char-

acters in JIS X 0208-1990 and JIS X 0212-1990 by radical and reading. It then provides hexadecimal ISO-2022-JP and Row-Cell values for JIS X 0208-1990 characters, and only the Row-Cell value for JIS X 0212-1990 characters.

- Although the Japanese character dictionary entitled 大漢語林 (*dai kango rin*, meaning "Large Chinese Word Forest") is on the expensive side due to its professional-level quality, it is extremely authoritative, being authored by two students of the author of the thirteen-volume 大漢和辭典 (*dai kanwa jiten*). It includes entries for all the kanji in JIS X 0208-1990 and JIS X 0212-1990, and provides Row-Cell and hexadecimal ISO-2022-JP codes (Row-Cell only for JIS X 0212-1990).
- JSA itself published a Japanese character dictionary entitled JIS漢字字典 (*JIS kanji jiten*, meaning "JIS Kanji Dictionary"), which provides extensive information and cross-references based on the JIS X 0208:1997 character set standard. This dictionary provides Row-Cell, GL (ISO-2022-JP), GR (EUC-JP), Shift-JIS, and CJK (Unicode) code points for each kanji, and includes a staggering amount of readings. Also included for every entry are cross-references to 大漢和辭典 (*dai kanwa jiten*) and 新字源 (*shinjigen*). I consider this dictionary a model for others based on national standards to follow.

There are a number of other computer-oriented character dictionaries available, at least another two dozen such titles in Japan alone, most of which support some flavor of the JIS X 0208 series (a select few cover JIS X 0212-1990 to varying degrees as well).* I have found the ones listed above to be exceptionally useful in my work. Strangely, I have not yet been able to discover a computer-oriented hangul or hanja dictionary from Korea—Appendix N, *Hangul Reading Table*, represents my attempt to provide such a reference for hangul.

大漢語林 (*dai kango rin*) or its smaller sibling 漢語林 (*kango rin*) set a precedent in Japan for conventional kanji dictionaries to include character codes, such as Row-Cell. They were apparently the very first conventional kanji dictionaries to do so. Andrew Nelson and John Haig's *The New Nelson Japanese-English Character Dictionary* (Charles E. Tuttle Company, 1997), a favorite among English-speaking learners of Japanese, has joined this pack. As some dictionaries demonstrate, a Chinese character dictionary does not need to include all the characters in a character set standard (such as JIS X 0208:1997) in order for the inclusion of character codes (such as Row-Cell) to be useful to its readership. In fact, I have categorized conventional Japanese kanji dictionaries in the five ways listed in Table 11-9.

Ever since I began working with Chinese, Korean, and Vietnamese character sets, I have been searching for character dictionaries that span more than a single CJKV locale. There are times when I need to quickly determine the Chinese or Korean

* *http://www.oreilly.com/~lunde/paperdict.html*

Table 11-9: Categories of Conventional Japanese Kanji Dictionaries

Coverage of JIS Standards	Dictionaries
None	新字源
Partial JIS X 0208:1997	*The Kodansha Kanji Learner's Dictionary*
Complete JIS X 0208:1997	*The New Nelson Japanese-English Character Dictionary*, 漢語林
Partial JIS X 0208:1997 and JIS X 0212-1990	角川必携漢和辞典, 福武漢和辞典, 旺文社漢和辞典
JIS X 0208:1997 and JIS X 0212-1990	大漢語林, 五十音引き講談社漢和辞典

character code for a kanji in a Japanese character set standard. The limited indexes provided in *The Unicode Standard, Version 2.0* run out of steam far too quickly, although once you find the Chinese character, there are useful cross-references to various CJKV character set standards.

Vendor Character Dictionaries and Character Tables

A number of vendor character set standards are described in Appendix C, *Vendor Character Set Standards*. Where do they fit into this discussion of character dictionaries? Most companies that develop their own CJKV character set standards, such as operating system and font manufacturers, also publish a character dictionary, or at least a set of code tables, along with some indexes, that allows users to locate all of its special characters. I have a large collection of such references.

It goes without saying that some of these references are more useful than others. For example, a Japanese code table from Hewlett-Packard is identical to a JIS X 0208-1983 code table, except that it lists the Shift-JIS, ISO-2022-JP, and Row-Cell values for each character—this doesn't help you much in finding obscure characters. The set of Japanese character dictionaries published by NEC, on the other hand, are superb, and allow users to search by radical, reading, total number of strokes, and encoding. The moral of the story is that you should look before you buy (or else get a recommendation from someone whose opinion you trust).

CJKV Character Dictionaries

The world's very first CJKV character dictionary—designed for computer users and software developers—is slated to be entitled *Dictionary of Unified CJK Characters—for the Unicode Standard* (日中韓統合漢字字典—ユニコード規格対応 *nitchūkan tōgō kanji jiten—yunikōdo kikaku taiō*), and is being compiled by the *CJK Dictionary Publishing Society* (CDPS or 日中韓字典刊行会 *nitchūkan jiten kankō kai*). It will be the first character dictionary that truly bridges CJK standards.

This character dictionary will be based on the 20,902 Chinese characters that are included in Unicode. It will go well beyond what the ISO 10646-1:1993 manual and *The Unicode Standard, Version 2.0* offer in terms of information, content, and cross-references:

- Reading indexes for Chinese, Japanese, and Korean
- Character code indexes for cross-referencing among CJK character set standards

There will also be an abundance of information at each of the 20,902 main entries, such as a variety of character codes, readings, cross-references to related characters, classification symbols, indexing radical, stroke count, and so on.

Other Useful Dictionaries

Believe it or not, there are *many* non-computer–oriented dictionaries that are in some way useful in the context of this book. Below I categorize several such dictionaries in the hope that you will also find them useful for your own work or research.

Conventional Dictionaries

In my attempts to understand Korean text, I have found a particularly useful dictionary. It is *Dong-A's Prime Korean-English Dictionary*, Second Edition (Doosan Dong-A Company, 1996). This dictionary is useful in that it illustrates the hanja that correspond to the hangul that are conventionally used to express Korean words. Because of my experience in dealing with Chinese characters, once I can see the hanja that correspond to hangul, my comprehension of Korean text increases significantly. Those of you with limited Korean experience but with extensive Chinese or Japanese knowledge may find this and similar dictionaries useful.

I'll provide you with an example of what I mean. Suppose I come across the Korean phrase 정보 교환 (*jeongbo gyohwan*). When I look up this word in the dictionary, as two separate words 정보 (*jeongbo*) and 교환 (*gyohwan*), I am immediately greeted with the hanja 情報 and 交換. Because I am familiar with the equivalent words in Japanese, specifically 情報 (*jōhō*) and 交換 (*kōkan*), I gain an instant understanding of the Korean text. These two words together mean "information processing."

Variant Character Dictionaries

When working with Chinese characters there is always the issue of simplified or variant characters to wrestle with. Some dictionaries, such as 汉字写法规范字典

(*hànzì xiěfǎ guīfàn zìdiǎn*), illustrate the traditional forms of simplified hanzi. Still other dictionaries, such as 漢字簡繁體字對照字典 (*hànzì jiǎnfántǐzì duìzhào zìdiǎn*) and 简化字 繁体字 异体字辨析手册 (*jiǎnhuàzì fántǐzì yìtǐzì biànxī shǒucè*), are specialized in the sense that they only serve to provide information on the relationship between traditional, simplified, and variant hanzi.

For Japanese, Jack Halpern's *New Japanese-English Character Dictionary* (NTC, 1993; Kenkyusha, 1990) is a literal gold mine of kanji variant information and cross-references. 漢字異体字典 (*kanji itai jiten*; Nichigai Associates, 1994) is a specialized kanji variant dictionary. Also of interest is 誤字俗字・正字一覧表 (*goji zokuji seiji ichiranhyō*; Teihan, 1995), which lists kanji variants that were registered for use in Japanese names.

A CD-ROM–based product called 今昔文字鏡 (*konjaku moji kyō*) provides approximately 80,000 Chinese characters and their variants—it runs under Windows 95 or Windows NT.*

The relationships among traditional, simplified, and variant Chinese characters are somewhat locale-specific, especially when dealing with characters that were either created or simplified within a single locale. This is why dedicated reference materials are indispensible if you are serious about fully understanding the relationship among Chinese characters and their variants.

Dictionary Hardware

Non-paper dictionaries can come in the form of dedicated hardware. Well, to be perfectly honest, these devices still use software (to be more precise, dedicated software) for searching and other purposes.

Canon and Seiko, among other companies, manufacture hand-held electronic character dictionaries that support the languages used in CJKV locales. Canon's WordTank series has been exceptionally popular with students studying Japanese. I myself once owned a model ID 7100.

The main disadvantage of dedicated dictionary hardware is that, due to its hardware nature, it cannot be easily upgraded. While many of these devices have optional dictionaries, usually specialized, there is no way to add entries to the main dictionary. WYBIWYG.†

* *http://www.infonia.ne.jp/~nature/kanji/konjaku/*

† What You Buy Is What You Get.

Dictionary Software

Character dictionaries that reside in software are a more recent phenomenon. Some are conventional, some are specialized, and some are even a combination of both. These electronic dictionaries take the form of dictionary software for your computer, and may or may not require that you use a CJKV-capable OS.

Dictionary CD-ROMs

Electronic dictionary software is a very useful resource for computer users. Such software allows you to look up individual characters, words, and even phrases. This software usually comes in two parts: the actual dictionary, which is machine-readable text in a database format, and software that accesses the information and displays it to the screen. Sometimes software packages include both parts.

A recent market trend is to store dictionaries on a single CD-ROM. CD-ROMs can store several hundred megabytes of data, and make an excellent media for large distributions of software (and music!). Most of these have been designed to be interfaced using an electronic book player. These are commonly referred to as electronic books (電子ブック *denshi bukku* in Japanese). Creative people and companies have written software that allows you to read these CD-ROMs on platforms such as MacOS and Windows using standard CD-ROM drives. The following is a short list of currently available Japanese-related electronic books:

広辞苑 by 岩波書店 (YRRS-7 1)
大辞林 by 三省堂 (YRRS-082)
新英和・和英中辞典 by 研究社 (YRRS-9 1)
漢字源 by 学研 (YRRS-050)
辞書パック10 by 三省堂
新漢英字典電子ブック版 by 日外アソシエーツ (YRRS-224)
科学技術用語大辞典 by 日外アソシエーツ
25万語医学用語大辞典 by 日外アソシエーツ
コンピュータ用語辞典 by 日外アソシエーツ

These and other electronic books can usually be ordered through Kinokuniya and other Japanese bookstores in the US and Japan (see Appendix T, *Software and Document Sources*, for more information). They may even have certain titles in stock now that they are becoming more popular. Prices usually begin at about $50 (US). Note that these are always 8cm CD-ROMs—most CD-ROM drives accept 12cm CD-ROMs. Most music stores sell adapters that let you play 8cm CD-ROMs in 12cm CD-ROM drives.

Front-End Software for Dictionary CD-ROMs

There are a number of freeware and commercial software packages that serve as front-ends for dictionary CD-ROMs.

Syokendai (書見台 *shokendai*) is freeware for MacOS that lets you display the contents of and search for text in several electronic books designed for electronic book players.* Syokendai was written by Naritoshi Yoshinaga (吉永成利 *yoshinaga naritoshi*), and the routines for accessing electronic books were borrowed from source code written by Shigeo Suwa (諏訪茂男 *suwa shigeo*) and Nobuhiro Miyatake (宮武伸裕 *miyatake nobuhiro*).

Using Syokendai is the most economical way to interface electronic book dictionaries. The only expenses that you need to worry about are the cost of the actual electronic book dictionaries and the cost of a standard CD-ROM drive (if you do not currently own one) or an electronic book player.

Sentius Software has developed the Sentius Electronic Book Player and Sentius Read! programs, both commercial programs available for MacOS.† If you are using a Unix system, you can try *dserver*.‡

Dictionary Files

Jim Breen has managed and coordinated the development of several useful machine-readable dictionary files for Japanese: COMPDIC, EDICT, ENAMDICT, GEODIC, KANJIDIC, and KANJD212.** These dictionary files—except for COMPDIC and GEODIC—are described below, followed by a listing of programs that act as front-ends to one or more of them. COMPDIC provides computer-related terms, and GEODIC provides geological terms. Paul Denisowski has initiated a similar effort for Chinese. His first work is CEDICT, which is the Chinese analog of Jim Breen's EDICT. I am hopeful that other dictionary files, perhaps a HANZIDIC (the Chinese analog of Jim Breen's KANJIDIC), will result from Paul Denisowski's continuing efforts.

These dictionary projects represent ongoing efforts, and contributions are always welcome. Contact Jim Breen†† or Paul Denisowski‡‡ for more information.

---

* *ftp://ftp.oreilly.com/pub/examples/nutshell/cjkv/mac/*

† *http://www.sentius.com/*

‡ *ftp://ftp.csis.oita-u.ac.jp/pub/misc/CD-ROM/dserver-2.0.tar.Z*

** *ftp://ftp.cc.monash.edu.au/pub/nihongo/*

†† *j.breen@csse.monash.edu.au* or *http://www.csse.monash.edu.au/~jwb/*

‡‡ *paul_denisowski@mindspring.com* or *http://www.mindspring.com/~paul_denisowski/*

CEDICT—Chinese-English dictionary

Started in the fall of 1997, CEDICT is work that was inspired by Jim Breen's suite of Japanese dictionary files.* CEDICT is a Chinese-English dictionary file whose development is being managed by Paul Denisowski. As of this writing, CEDICT has well over 20,000 entries, and is expected to grow significantly over time. The following are some example entries from CEDICT:

笔画 [bi3 hua4] /strokes of a Chinese character/

汉字 [han4 zi4] /Chinese character/

人权 [ren2 quan2] /human rights/

中华人民共和国 [zhong1 hua2 ren2 min2 gong4 he2 guo2] /People's Republic of China/

中日韩越 [zhong1 ri4 han2 yue4] /China, Japan, Korea, and Vietnam/

字集 [zi4 ji2] /character set/

自由 [zi4 you2] /freedom/free/liberty/

The CEDICT file itself is in EUC-CN encoding, and consists of three basic fields:

- One or more hanzi
- Reading in Pinyin
- One or more English glosses

The objective of the CEDICT project is to create an online, downloadable (as opposed to searchable-only) public-domain Chinese-English dictionary. For the most part, the project is modelled on Jim Breen's highly successful EDICT (Japanese-English dictionary) project and is intended to be a collaborative effort, with users providing entries and corrections to the main file. For specific limitations regarding its use, please see the CEDICT license file (*cedict_license*). Also of potential interest is that CEDICT has been adapted for NJStar use.

EDICT—Japanese-English dictionary

EDICT is a freeware Japanese-English dictionary in machine-readable form. It was intended initially for use with Moke (Mark's Own Kanji Editor) and related software such as JDIC. However, this file has the potential to be used in a large number of situations. The copyright on EDICT and its documentation is held by Jim Breen, however it is freely available for non-commercial use. EDICT is in the EDICT format specified by MOKE, and uses EUC-JP encoding for the Japanese portions. It is a text file with one entry per line. Here are a few examples of EDICT entries:

* *http://www.mindspring.com/~paul_denisowski/cedict.html*

教科書 [きょうかしょ] /text book/

字体 [じたい] /type/font/lettering/

字典 [じてん] /character dictionary/

辞書 [じしょ] /dictionary/

辞典 [じてん] /dictionary/

電子計算機 [でんしけいさんき] /computer/

日本 [にっぽん] /Japan/

日本 [にほん] /Japan/

日本語 [にほんご] /Japanese language/

和英辞典 [わえいじてん] /Japanese-English dictionary/

辭典 [じてん] /dictionary/

EDICT now has over 60,000 entries, and is similar in size to a good-quality commercial dictionary. The *edict.doc* file distributed with EDICT describes its history, its lexicographical principles, its usage license statement, and lists its many contributors.

ENAMDICT—Japanese name dictionary

ENAMDICT, which contains over 110,000 Japanese personal and place name entries, was once part of EDICT. Because this portion of EDICT caused it to bloat considerably, Jim decided to split it into two separate entities: EDICT, which now has the personal and place names removed; and ENAMDICT, which contains the personal and place names formerly part of EDICT. The following are some sample entries from the ENAMDICT file:

剣 [けん] /Ken (g)/

小塚 [こづか] /Kozuka (s)/

太郎 [たろう] /Tarou (p,m)/

山本 [やまもと] /Yamamoto (p,s)/

For those who prefer to have both dictionaries in a merged format, the *EDICT_BIG* file is available.

KANJIDIC—JIS X 0208:1997 kanji

KANJIDIC is simply a kanji database file. There are 6,355 entries, one per line, and one for each of the kanji in JIS X 0208:1997. The first two fields of each entry are *always* the kanji itself (EUC-JP–encoded) followed by its hexadecimal ISO-2022-JP code. The remaining fields correspond to additional information. Table 11-10 lists the prefixes and the information their values present (some may not mean much unless you have a particular dictionary handy).

KANJIDIC, like EDICT and ENAMDICT, has a copyright. However, Jim has made it freely available on the same basis as EDICT. The copyright on some fields is held by others. For example, the SKIP field was included with the permission of Jack Halpern and his publishers. Again, the *kanjidic.doc* file explains the copyright details and usage procedures.

Table 11-10: Explanations of KANJIDIC Fields

Field	Meaning
B	Radical number assigned by Nelson's kanji dictionary (from a set of 214)
C	Classical radical number (from the standard set of 214) when assigned differently from Nelson's kanji dictionary
E	Index number from Kenneth Henshall's *A Guide to Remembering Japanese Characters*
F	Frequency-of-use ranking, if present (applies only to 2,135 kanji, based on Jack Halpern's *New Japanese-English Character Dictionary*)
G	*Jōyō Kanji*, *Gakushū Kanji*, and *Jinmei-yō Kanji* field (a value of 1 to 6 indicates the grade level for Gakushū Kanji; a value of 8 indicates Jōyō Kanji; and a value of 9 indicates Jinmei-yō Kanji)
H	Index number from Jack Halpern's *New Japanese-English Character Dictionary*
I	Index number from Mark Spahn and Wolfgang Hadamitzky's *The Kanji Dictionary* and *Kana & Kanji*
K	Gakken dictionary index number
L	Index number from James Heisig's *Remembering the Kanji* series
M	Index number from Morohashi's 大漢和辭典
N	Index number from Andrew Nelson's *The Modern Reader's Japanese-English Character Dictionary*
O	Index number from P.G. O'Neill's *Japanese Names*
P	SKIP pattern code
Q	Four Corner code
S	Total number of strokes (more than one such field is acceptable in the case of kanji with varying stroke counts)
U	Hexadecimal Unicode value (UCS-2 encoding)
V	Index number from Andrew Nelson and John Haig's *The New Nelson Japanese-English Character Dictionary*
W	Korean reading
X	Cross-reference code
Y	Pinyin reading
Z	Mis-classification code

The final fields are one or more pronunciations written in kana and English meanings. English meanings are enclosed in curly braces. The *kanjidic.doc* file included with KANJIDIC explains these fields in greater detail.

The following are some sample lines taken from KANJIDIC. Compare the information to the listing given above.

> 漢 3441 U6f22 N2662 B85 S13 G3 H657 F1393 P1-3-10 L1578 K1394 I3a10.17 O1860 Whan Yhan4 Q3413.4 MN18068P MP7.0189 E442 カン T1 はん {Sino-} {China}

> 剣 3775 U5263 N696 B18 S10 G8 H1672 F1177 P1-8-2 L1671 K1248 I2f8.5 O1151 Wgeom Yjian4 XJ05178 XJ05179 XJ0517A XJ0517B XJ06E5F Q8250.0 MN2076 MP2.0295 E1214 ケン つるぎ {sabre} {sword} {blade} {clock hand}

> 和 4f42 U548c N3268 B115 S8 G3 H1130 F166 P1-5-3 L897 K151 I5d3.1 O638 Whwa Yhe2 Yhe4 Yhuo2 Yhuo4 Yhuo5 Yhai1 Yhe5 XJ16D61 Q2690.0 MN3490 MP2.0969 E416 ワ オ カ やわ.らぐ やわ.らげる なご.む なご.やか T1 あい いず かず かつ かつり かづ たけ ち とも な にぎ まさ やす よし より わだこ わっ {harmony} {Japanese style} {peace} {soften} {Japan}

KANJD212—JIS X 0212-1990 kanji

The KANJD212 dictionary file is the JIS X 0212-1990 analog of the KANJIDIC file, and includes 5,801 entries, one for each of the kanji enumerated in the JIS X 0212-1990 character set standard. Its format is different from that of KANJIDIC in only the following respects:

- EUC-JP encoding, code set 3 (KANJIDIC uses code set 1)
- Includes only the following KANJIDIC fields: U, B, S, M, W, and Y (see Table 11-10 for a description of these fields)

Japanese readings are also included. The following are some sample entries from the KANJD212 file:

> 圕 3729 U5715 B31 S13 MN4829 Ytu2shu1guan3 トショカン ショ トショク

> 辵 6133 U8fb5 B162 S3 H1945 MN38700 Ychuo4 チャク しんにょう しんにゅう

> 辶 6134 U8fb6 B162 S3 H1932 MN38702 Ychuo4 チャク しんにょう しんにゅう

Whether or not this dictionary file can be used in your environment depends on whether your OS supports the JIS X 0212-1990 character set. Read the *kanjd212.doc* for more details.

EDICLSD3—Japanese-English life sciences dictionary

Although its development is not coordinated by Jim Breen, the EDICLSD3 dictionary (coordinated by the *Life Science Dictionary Project* led by Shuji Kaneko*) is nonetheless another useful dictionary file that has been adapted to the same format as the previously described dictionary files.†

* *skaneko@pharm.kyoto-u.ac.jp*

† *http://lsd.pharm.kyoto-u.ac.jp/*

This dictionary file contains over 30,000 entries for terms used in the life sciences—physiology, pharmacology, biophysics, biochemistry, organic chemistry, biology, and so on—along with their corresponding English terms. The following are some example entries—some not very suitable for discussion at the dinner table—from the EDICLSD3 dictionary:

甲状腺機能低下症 [こうじょうせんきのうていかしょう] /hypothyroidism/

ジアスターゼ [じあすたーぜ] /diastase/*

手根管症候群 [しゅこんかんしょうこうぐん] /carpal tunnel syndrome/

虫垂炎 [ちゅうすいえん] /appendicitis/

腸 [ちょう] /intestine/intestinal/bowel/gut/entero/

Needless to say, EDICLSD3 is useful for those who deal with the life sciences and Japanese.

Front-End Software for Dictionary Files

There are a variety of programs, freeware and commercial software, that serve as excellent front-ends to Jim Breen's various dictionary files: EDICT, ENAMDICT, KANJIDIC, and KANJD212. These front-ends also work with the EDICLSD3 file. There is also one, CEL (Chinese-English Lookup), that serves as a front-end to Paul Denisowski's CEDICT. Table 11-11 lists these programs, and includes information about what platform they run on, who authored them, and so on.

Table 11-11: Dictionary Front-End Software

Program	Platform	Availability
CEL	Windows	Freeware by Richard Warmington[a]
edict.el	GNU Emacs	Freeware by Stephen Turnbull[b]
JavaDict	Java	Freeware by Todd Rudick[c]
JDIC	MS-DOS	Freeware by Jim Breen; does not require Japanese-capable OS
JREADER	MS-DOS	Freeware by Jim Breen; does not require a Japanese-capable OS
MacJDic	MacOS	Freeware by Dan Crevier[d]
RJ	Windows	Commercial software by Basis Technology;[e] does not require Japanese-capable OS
tkjdic	Unix	Tcl/Tk front-end to XJDIC
UniDict	MacOS, Newton	Commercial software by Dan Crevier, distributed by Enfour Media[f]

* $2.50.

Table 11-11: Dictionary Front-End Software (continued)

Program	Platform	Availability
WinJDIC	Windows	Freeware by Mark Edwards;[g] does not require Japanese-capable OS
XJDIC	Unix	Freeware by Jim Breen

[a] *http://inside.com.tw/user/richwarm/cel.htm*
[b] *turnbull@sk.tsukuba.ac.jp* or *ftp://ftp.xemacs.org/pub/xemacs/packages/*
[c] *http://www.cs.arizona.edu/japan/JavaDict/*
[d] *dan.crevier@pobox.com* or *http://www.boingo.com/dan/software/MacJDic.html*
[e] *http://rj.basistech.com/*
[f] *http://www.enfour.co.jp/unidict/e/*
[g] *medwards@minn.net* or *http://www1.minn.net/~medwards/winjdic.html*

Some word processors, such as JWP and NJStar, also provide support for these dictionary files as a way for users to input text or look up unknown words.

There are other front-end software packages for dictionary files, but these are in what I consider to be proprietary formats. Such software includes KanjiWorks for MacOS by Jouni Kerman.*

Hirofumi Fujiwara's (藤原博文 *fujiwara hirofumi*) Kanrakugai (漢楽街 *kanrakugai*) deserves a look because it provides access to tens of thousands of kanji.†

Web-Based Dictionaries

There are now many dictionaries and dictionary-like resources that are accessible through the Web. Some of these simply act as a front-end to dictionaries that are easily accessible, and some are accessible only through the Web. The following are some samples of those that are currently available—more and more are coming online everyday:

- Jim Breen's own web front-end to his various dictionary files—a must-visit site‡
- Jeffrey Friedl's front-end to Jim Breen's Japanese dictionary files—that is, EDICT, KANJIDIC, and so on—has been a long mainstay on the Web**
- Rick Harbaugh's *Chinese Character Genealogy* (based on his software called *Zhongwen Zipu*)†† and *Chinese Characters Dictionary Web* (really cool because it links together about a dozen web dictionaries)‡‡

* *http://www.kerman.com/kanji/*

† *http://www.pro.or.jp/~fuji/japanese/kanrakugai.html*

‡ *http://www.csse.monash.edu.au/projects/wwwjdic/* or *http://enterprise.ic.gc.ca/~jbreen/wwwjdic.html*

** *http://enterprise.ic.gc.ca/cgi-bin/j-e/*

†† *http://zhongwen.com/*

‡‡ *http://zhongwen.com/zi.htm*

- Kyodai Jinbunken's (京大人文研 *kyōdai jinbunken*, short for 京都大学人文科学研究所 *kyōto daigaku jinbun kagaku kenkyūjo*, which means "Institute for Humanities Research, Kyoto University") "e漢字" (*e kanji*) dictionary*
- *Muller's CJK-English Character Dictionary* by Charles Muller†
- Erik Peterson's *Chinese-English Dictionary*‡ and *Chinese Character Dictionary***
- Christian Wittern's *KanjiBase*††
- Hongjie Xin's (忻宏杰 *xīn hóngjié*) *English-Chinese Online Dictionary*‡‡

Some of these web dictionaries—in particular, Charles Muller's, Jim Breen's, and Rick Harbaugh's—have been cross-linked at the character level. This represents an exciting development in web-based lexicography.

Expect to find more and more dictionaries accessible through the Web as time goes on.

Machine Translation Software

Machine translation (MT) software is a bit different from electronic dictionaries in that it handles not only single characters, words, and phrases, but whole sentences. Machine translation software is best used to perform the first pass translation, thus reducing the translation burden for humans. The state of machine translation technology is not yet to the point where human intervention is not required.*** These programs are best referred to as machine-*aided* translation software—they merely assist you in translating text faster.

Because these programs do not provide a perfect translation, pre- and post-editing functions are usually available. Pre-editing is a form of *massaging* input text so that the translation software does a better job. Post-editing is the process of correcting errors in translation made by the software.

One of the keys to adequate translation is the availability of specialized dictionaries that contain terms specific to fields of study. Such fields include computer science, medicine, and science. Very few machine translation programs come bundled with specialized dictionaries—they are available for additional cost.

---

* *http://www.zinbun.kyoto-u.ac.jp/~ekanji/*

† *http://www.human.toyogakuen-u.ac.jp/~acmuller/cjkdict.htm*

‡ *http://www.erols.com/eepeter/worddict.html*

** *http://www.erols.com/eepeter/chardict.html*

†† *http://www.kb.oas.hist.uni-goettingen.de/kb/query.htm*

‡‡ *http://www.tigernt.com/dict.shtml*

*** We can all dream about the time when there will be a "universal translator" as used in *Star Trek* and other science fiction series.

One of the highest rated machine translation programs available is Language Engineering Corporation's LogoVista E to J, available for MacOS and Windows.* In fact, a free demo version of LogoVista E to J is available on CD-ROM. Unfortunately, there is no Japanese to English version yet available.

NeocorTech offers Tsunami MT (English to Japanese) and Typhoon MT (Japanese to English) as their machine translation products, both of which can run on non-Japanese versions of Windows, come bundled with TrueType Japanese fonts for ease of viewing and printing, and are highly rated.† Both include a built-in input method for Japanese text entry. When you indicate the subject of the text to be translated, the quality of the resulting translations can be increased.

Others include ATLAS‡ (Japanese to English and English to Japanese versions available) by Fujitsu; and これ和英 (*kore waei*; Japanese to English)** and コリャ英和 (*korya eiwa*; English to Japanese) by Catena Corporation,†† both of which are available for MacOS or Windows.

Machine Translation Services

With the explosive growth of the Web comes the need to translate information on the same medium.

InTransNet,‡‡ Language Engineering Corporation,*** and NeocorTech††† provide commercial online machine translation services. The software behind LEC's is their own LogoVista E to J, and the one behind NeocorTech's is their own Tsunami Server (a server-based version of Tsunami MT).

The procedure is to first sign up with their service, then submit materials to be translated through email. It is also possible to submit materials through HTML forms, but that is not typically convenient for longer or complex items.

Rich Morrow has written a simple web-based translation program, called CAMALT (Clear As Mud Asian Language Translator), that makes use of Jim Breen's dictio-

* *http://www.lec.com/*

† *http://www.neocor.com/*

‡ *http://www.fsc.fujitsu.com/fsc/language/atlas.htm*

** *http://www.catena.co.jp/sp/koremac/koremac.htm* (MacOS) or *http://www.catena.co.jp/sp/korewa/korewa.htm* (Windows).

†† *http://www.catena.co.jp/sp/koryam/koryam.htm* (MacOS) or *http://www.catena.co.jp/sp/korya98/korya98.htm* (Windows).

‡‡ *http://www.intransnet.bc.ca/intrans/intra.htm*

*** *http://www.lec.com/transserv/transserv_overview.html*

††† *http://www.neocor.com/server/*

nary files for Japanese, and Paul Denisowski's CEDICT for Chinese.* It is based on a program originally written by Tuomas Lukka.

Learning Aids

This section provides information on some of the Japanese learning aids that are available—this does not mean that similar software for Chinese, Korean, or Vietnamese does not exist.

The learning of a foreign language can often be supplemented or reinforced through the use of software.† There are many software-based learning aids available, far too many to exhaustively list here. If you plan to study (or have already studied) a language such as Chinese, Japanese, Korean, or Vietnamese, I encourage you to seek out software-based learning aids.

Table 11-12 lists some of the learning aids of which I am aware—there are many, many more available. Note that some of these programs are much more than simply learning aids—some also function as electronic dictionaries or full-featured word processors.

Table 11-12: Learning Aids

Software	Platform	Availability
Chinese Character Tutor	Windows	Commercial software by FlashWare International[a]
Japanese WordMage	MacOS/Windows	Commercial software by Lava Software[b]
KanjiCard	Windows	Commercial software by Eli Charne[c]
Kanji-Flash/BTJ	MS-DOS	Commercial software by Kanji-Flash Softworks[d]
KanjiWorks	MacOS	Commercial software by Jouni Kerman[e]
MacSunrise Script	MacOS	Commercial software distributed by Stone Bridge Press[f]
Mikan	MacOS	Commercial software by Sentius Software[g]
Smart Characters	Windows	Commercial software by Apropos[h]

[a] *http://ourworld.compuserve.com/homepages/fergab/*
[b] *http://www.lavasoft.com/*
[c] *echarne@acm.org* or *http://www.eclecticbits.com/*
[d] *http://ourworld.compuserve.com/homepages/KanjiFlash/*
[e] *jouni@kerman.com* or *http://www.kerman.com/kanji/*
[f] *http://www.stonebridge.com/*
[g] *http://www.sentius.com/*
[h] *http://www.aproposinc.com/*

* *http://livid.vivid.com/~rich/cgi-bin/honyaku/camalt.html*

† But make no mistake, while software-based learning aids are useful in the language-learning process, they are by no means a substitute for genuine human interaction, especially during the early stages of learning.

I suggest that you explore World Language Resources as a source for language-learning products.*

Many readers may also require classroom study of the Japanese language. If local classes are not available, or if there is a group within a company that wants to learn Japanese, there are still options open. Some schools, such as The University of Wisconsin-Madison, offer Technical Japanese programs that cater to the working professional through distance education.†

* *http://www.worldlanguage.com/*

† *http://epdwww.engr.wisc.edu/japan/*

In this chapter:
- *Email*
- *News*
- *FTP and Telnet*
- *Network Domains*
- *Getting Connected*
- *Internet Software*

12

The Internet

This chapter describes methods for handling CJKV text in electronic media such as email, news, and other Internet information services. To some extent, these discussions also apply to accessing CJKV online database services.

The handling of CJKV text within email systems falls into the realm of *information interchange* (信息交换 *xìnxī jiāohuàn* or 資訊交換 *zīxùn jiāohuàn* in Chinese, 情報交換 *jōhō kōkan* in Japanese, and 정보교환/情報交換 *jeongbo gyohwan* in Korean), whereby data are sent from one computer to another without, one hopes, any loss of data. How CJKV text is handled internally by a single computer system is not necessarily the same as the external handling of the same data. Here we can make a distinction between an internal and external code. An internal code is one which is most efficiently processed directly on a computer system. Examples of internal codes include the various locale-specific instances of EUC encoding (EUC-CN, EUC-JP, EUC-KR, and EUC-TW) and Unicode. An external code, however, is used somewhat as a machine-independent code which allows the transfer of data from one encoding to another—an external code is also called an information interchange code. Example of external codes include the various instances of ISO-2022 encoding and UTF-7—they are designed to be transmitted quite reliably through most email networks.

Let's look at an example of information interchange in action. Figure 12-1 illustrates how Japanese data can be moved from a system processing Shift-JIS to one processing EUC-JP, using ISO-2022-JP as the common encoding for electronic transmission.

Note how ISO-2022-JP encoding is used as the information interchange code. The ISO-2022-JP encoding step may be bypassed if the Japanese data are being moved by other means, such as by a direct connection or by exchangeable media (such as a floppy disk).

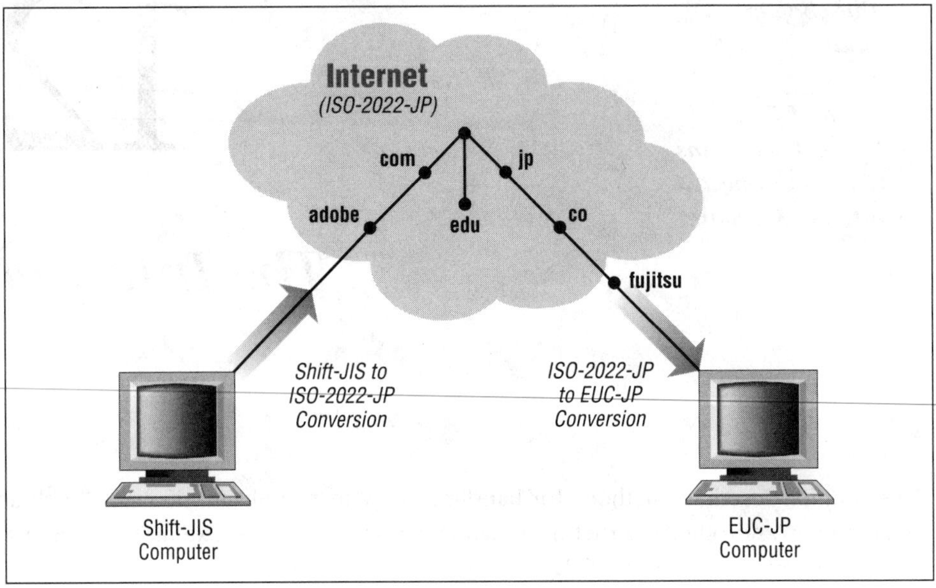

Figure 12-1: Information interchange

True information interchange is achieved when data is moved from one platform to another (and perhaps even from one encoding to another) with no loss of information. Information interchange is usually a simple affair when using the ASCII character set, but in the case of CJKV text there are more problems, such as different encoding methods (for example, ISO-2022-KR, EUC-KR, and Johab for Korean) and multiple character sets. Not all encodings support all the character sets. An example is the lack of support in Shift-JIS encoding for the JIS X 0212-1990 character set standard. These factors must be taken into consideration when deciding how to implement information interchange in your working environment.

Email

One of the most commonly used Internet services is email or electronic mail, and represents the most basic form of electronic communication today. People often wonder how to send and receive email in languages other than English. That is what this section is all about.

Sending Email

There are different environments under which users can send CJKV text from their computer to a mainframe computer for subsequent transmission through email. Many of these environments are specific to particular types of mainframe computers or electronic services. The algorithms for converting between CJKV encodings are covered in Chapter 9, *Information Processing Techniques*; the techniques and tools for doing this are described in Chapter 4, *Encoding Methods*.

You must make a few preparations before a CJKV text file can be reliably transmitted through email networks. I suggest that these guidelines be followed as closely as possible:

- Break long lines to fewer than 80 columns (75 columns or fewer is preferred)
- Compose the document using a monospaced font (most communication software uses monospaced fonts for display purposes)
- Do not include any half-width katakana characters since they are not fully supported in all environments—this applies only to Japanese
- Convert the text file to an ISO-2022 encoding, according to the appropriate RFC

Jun Murai, Erik van der Poel, and Mark Crispin have written RFC (Request For Comments) 1468, *Japanese Character Encoding for Internet Messages*. This RFC describes how Japanese is encoded for use in email systems. Similar RFCs have been published to deal with Chinese and Korean.* Table 12-1 lists these RFCs, along with the encodings they define and the languages they support.

Table 12-1: RFCs that Define ISO-2022 Encodings

RFC	Encoding	Character Sets
1922	ISO-2022-CN, ISO-2022-CN-EXT	ASCII, GB 2312-80, CNS 11643-1992
1468	ISO-2022-JP	ASCII, JIS-Roman, JIS C 6226-1978, JIS X 0208-1983[a]
2237	ISO-2022-JP-1	ISO-2022-JP *plus* JIS X 0212-1990
1554	ISO-2022-JP-2	ISO-2022-JP *plus* JIS X 0212-1990[b]
1557	ISO-2022-KR	ASCII, KS X 1001:1992

[a] Support for JIS X 0208-1990 and JIS X 0208:1997 is also implied.
[b] As you've read in Chapter 4, ISO-2022-JP-2 also supports GB 2312-80, KS X 1001:1992, and two parts of ISO 8859, but the GB 2312-80, KS X 1001:1992 character sets are better handled through RFCs 1922 and 1557, respectively.

If the CJKV text is not composed on the system that is running the email software, you must first transfer the text (as a file) to such a system. The most reliable method is to upload the file with a standard file transfer protocol (for example, X-Modem, Kermit, FTP, and so on), then send it as an included (but not attached) file in an email message (check your email documentation to find out how to perform this task). The "`C-x i`" key command as used in GNU Emacs' *mail* or

* See the section entitled "Useful URLs" in Appendix T, *Software and Document Sources*, starting on page 976 to find out how to obtain RFCs.

mh-e package accomplishes this task, and prompts for a file to include into the message buffer. The file's Japanese code can be converted either before or after transferring to the computer with the email system, depending on where the code conversion software is available.

Some email networks, such as Bitnet, occasionally strip escape characters from email messages. In my experience, Bitnet can handle eight-bit characters much more reliably than escape or shift characters—this may make sending CJKV text files in Shift-JIS, EUC, Big Five, or Johab encoding more reliable! The ISO-2022-JP encoding repair tool and algorithm, discussed in Chapter 9, can help remedy this problem.

As a last resort, if you are using a Unix system, you can uuencode the text file before sending it in an email message. The file can then be uudecoded when it is received. This method, however, assumes that the receiving party has uudecode available. Sending text as a binary file is generally not recommended because there is nothing binary about text files, even if they include eight-bit characters.

Receiving Email

Receiving CJKV text is considerably easier than sending it, as you will soon learn below. Whether or not CJKV text is displayed properly online depends heavily on whether your computer, terminal, or communication software has the ability to display CJKV text. CompuServe and most Unix email software seems to permit escape characters to function properly, so users should be able to view CJKV text online like normal English text. That is, as long as their terminal emulation software allows CJKV to be displayed. A mainframe computer, if acting as a host, simply stores the electronic codes, and your computer, if acting as a Japanese terminal, simply interprets these electronic codes accordingly. The other problem you may encounter is when receiving a file that is in a CJKV encoding not supported by your displaying software. This requires conversion from one Japanese encoding to one that is supported by your software. In Chapter 4 we discussed methods for converting from one CJKV encoding to another.

Some email systems, such as those used under VMS systems, do not allow control characters to function (that is, if they didn't simply strip them out!). This has the effect of rendering CJKV text unreadable within the mail system even if you are using CJKV-capable terminal emulation software. For example, you may sometimes see some text that looks like this:

```
$B$3$1$OOBJ8$NJ8>O$NNc$G!"$=$1$O(JEnglish$B$NJ8>O$NNc$G$9!#(J
```

There sure are a lot of "$" (dollar) characters—those happen to represent the first byte of hiragana characters. This should tell you that something has gone wrong.

You may be able to trick your email software into permitting those characters to perform their proper functions. For example, on VMS systems, you can often use the *extract* command followed by "`tt:`" (two t's followed by a single colon) to accomplish this. Here is an example command line within the VMS email subsystem:

```
Mail> extract tt:
```

If this works, and if the CJKV text has not been damaged, the above text should display properly as a mixture of CJKV and English text, such as the following sample Japanese text:

これは和文の文章の例で、それは English の文章の例です。

If there is no method with which you can coerce your email software into displaying CJKV text, you are then forced to save the message to a file, exit the email system, and then attempt to view the message by other means. The most likely method involves saving the email message as a file outside your email program, then, if necessary, downloading the file to your computer. Unix newsreaders often have a similar problem—to display an article, save the article to a text file, then view it.

For those who must view CJKV text offline due to hardware or software limitations, some type of file transfer protocol (for example, X-Modem, Kermit, FTP, and so on) must be used to move the file to a place where it can be viewed. If your viewer requires the file to be in Big Five, Shift-JIS, or some other CJKV encoding, you may need to convert the file to the appropriate encoding for viewing (if the file originated from an email system, it is most likely in one of the locale-specific instances of ISO-2022 encoding).

Email Addressing Templates

Although this section does not relate to CJKV information processing *per se*, it is useful in case a correspondent happens to use an email service other than your own. Because the Internet is probably the most widely-used network, addressing templates revolve around how to send email to and from the Internet. For detailed information on email networks and email addressing techniques in general, I suggest obtaining one or both of the following books:

- Kiersten Conner and Ed Krol's *The Whole Internet: The Next Generation* (O'Reilly & Associates, 1999)
- Donnalyn Frey and Rick Adams' *!%@:: A Directory of Electronic Mail Addressing & Networks* (O'Reilly & Associates, 1994)

Email Troubles and Tricks

Most of the problems you will encounter when sending Japanese text through email will most likely relate to encodings becoming damaged, or else to using the wrong encoding method (for instance, sending Japanese text in Shift-JIS encoding—eight-bit encodings do not survive through most network paths). These problems have already been addressed earlier in this chapter, but there is a bit more to cover.

There are times when the escape sequences become scrambled in Japanese text for one reason or another. This might be due to poorly-written telecommunication software, or simply a problem with the integrity of the Japanese text, such as it ending in two-byte mode. This can leave you stuck in two-byte mode—text, such as your system prompt, will be interpreted as two bytes per character, and will make no sense at all. A solution to this is to create a short script with an embedded *one-byte–character* escape sequence. The following two lines can be added to your *.cshrc* file (if you are using the C shell on a Unix system):

```
set e = "`echo x | /bin/tr x \\033`"
alias ko 'echo "${e}(J"; echo "*** FORCED KANJI-OUT ***"'
```

The first line sets the value of the variable `e` to be the same as the escape character. This variable is then used in the second line to complete the one-byte–character escape sequence. It is not wise to directly use an escape character in this sort of settings file—it may be detected as a redundant escape sequence by certain CJKV-capable text editors, and subsequently (and appropriately) deleted. When invoked, this newly-established alias "`ko`" outputs two lines to the terminal: the first is a valid one-byte–character escape sequence, and the second is simply a line that informs you that you have successfully returned to one-byte mode.

Mail delivery problems can also be quite common. These can happen whether or not the email message contains CJKV text. The two types of mail delivery problems that you may encounter are outlined below:

- Your mail software does not recognize the email address
- Other mail software, such as a gateway, does not permit your email to pass

You may also experience a combination of both problems.

When your mail software does not recognize the email address, the solution is to use a relay. In the early days of the CJKV networks, the use of relays was required so that email could be sent from the US to those countries. Fortunately, this is no longer the case for the majority of CJKV.

What do you do when your email is refused passage? Almost all information services have the ability to exchange email with Internet users. However, some gateways may limit usage with those sites that are physically located within the country. Such restrictions are usually due to the lack of an international communication license required by the laws of some countries.

There have been reports of users having problems sending non-ASCII email (such as ISO-2022-JP) using some email clients that are particularly strict about the "Charset" header. These email clients may refuse to accept any non-ASCII text if the header is set to "`us-ascii`."

News

Besides spending (or wasting) phenomenal amounts of time sending and receiving email, Internet users can also avoid work (and family) by reading Usenet News. As with email, it is possible to both read (receive) and post (send) news articles in languages other than English.

Posting News

Many of the same techniques recommended for sending CJKV text through email are also applicable when posting news articles containing such text. Refer to the bulleted items in the previous section. Most of the problems that you will encounter will relate to *displaying* news—this topic is covered later in this chapter.

The transmission of news from one site to another usually follows the same paths as email messages. Some of these paths are not friendly to eight-bit data, which is why ISO-2022 encodings are also recommended for CJKV news articles.

Displaying News

If you are on a system that allows you to read news off the network, you most likely have access to Usenet News and Japanese newsgroups. The Usenet News newsgroup *sci.lang.japan* often has articles with Japanese text. In the case of Japanese newsgroups—whose names all begin with the two letters *fj* (meaning "from Japan")—most articles are in nothing but Japanese text. Japanese text that is included within these news articles is typically ISO-2022-JP–encoded. As you learned in Chapter 4, ISO-2022-JP encoding makes use of the escape character. Most news reading programs do not allow these control characters to pass, thus making Japanese text display improperly.

Displaying Japanese text using news reading software, such as *rn*, can often be problematic. There are ways around these problems, usually in the form of programs or patches.

There are newer news reading programs that do allow escape characters to pass. These include C News and INN. If your system administrator has been keeping up with the latest news reading programs, you may be able to use these programs right now to read Japanese news.

Programs such as *rn* and Bnews require a patch to pass escape characters—these patches are available through FTP. One of the best Japanese patches is called *krn*, which is the Japanese patch for *rn*. It not only patches *rn* to pass escape characters, but also has all menus, error messages, and prompts written in Japanese. Other such programs include *knn*, *ktin*, and *ktrn*.

If you do not wish to replace or patch your news reading programs, there are still ways to display Japanese news. A simple trick is to pipe the article through the standard Unix commands *cat*, *page*, or *more*. The following is an example of a prompt you may see at the end of a news article, along with a piped command:

```
End of article 1 (of 1)--what next? [npq] | more
```

Another more severe problem you may encounter is lost escape characters. Some news posting programs actually strip out control characters in a particular range. Neither patching your news reading program nor Unix pipes can help you here. You must save the article to a file, then use a tool to reinsert the lost escape characters. A tool for performing this type of repair is described at the end of Chapter 9.

FTP and Telnet

FTP (File Transfer Protocol) and telnet are perhaps the most widely-used Internet services—besides email and news, that is. FTP allows users to transfer files between local or remote sites. Telnet allows users to establish interactive sessions between local or remote hosts (although connections with local hosts are normally done using *rlogin*).

FTP Concerns

While it is not the purpose of this book to show you how to establish an FTP connection nor how to transfer files using FTP, there are some valid concerns that relate to the transfer of CJKV data. So that you know, there are two ways to use FTP:

- Using the *ftp* program itself (if you happen to be using a Unix operating system)
- Using a web browser—you provide a URL that specifies "ftp" as the Internet protocol

The first thing that you should learn is that nearly all native CJKV encoding methods, such as Big Five, EUC, ISO-2022, Shift-JIS, and so on, do *not* represent binary data. Sure, some of these encoding methods use generous amounts of eight-bit data and even some control characters thrown in. But, data that use these encoding methods are still considered to be text data. In most cases, though, transferring CJKV text through a binary FTP connection is not harmful—it will result in the preservation of line-termination. In case you are not aware, different operating systems use different characters or different combinations of characters to terminate lines. Table 12-2 lists the three most common line termination methods, along with the operating systems that make use of them.

Table 12-2: Line Termination Conventions

Line Termination	Encoding	Operating Systems
Carriage Return[a]	13 (0x0D)	MacOS
Carriage Return + Line Feed[b]	13 (0x0D) + 10 (0x0A)	MS-DOS and Windows
Line Feed[c]	10 (0x0A)	Unix

[a] Also expressed as CR.
[b] Also expressed as CR + LF or CR + NL (*newline*).
[c] Also expressed as LF or NL.

A non-binary file transfer session will convert the line-termination characters appropriately. My work, for example, deals with MacOS, Windows, and Unix operating systems, so the automatic translation of line termination characters using the (default) ASCII file transfer mode of FTP serves an important role in my productivity.

Files that contain *real* binary data *must* be transferred in binary transfer mode, otherwise their data *will* become corrupt. Compressed files are the most commonly encountered binary files. Binary data, for example, may contain embedded carriage return or line feed characters, and when these characters are converted the entire file becomes damaged.

Some encodings must be treated as binary data, such as those for ISO 10646-1:1993 or Unicode: UCS-2, UCS-4, and UTF-16. My recommendation is to effect FTP transfers in binary mode when in doubt—*any* doubt.

Telnet Concerns

Establishing a CJKV-capable telnet session requires that you initiated that session from a CJKV-capable terminal. If the telnet session still does not behave properly in a CJKV context, the Unix-side terminal may not be set to handle eight-bit characters properly.

Network Domains

The Internet, as it is used today, began as a defense-funded network known as ARPANET. The identity of each node on the network was first categorized into different *domains*. This tells users, for example, that *adobe.com* represents a commercial node and that *nasa.gov* is a government node. The "classic" Internet domains are listed in Table 12-3.

Table 12-3: Classic Internet Domains

Domain	Example	Description
com	*adobe.com*	Commercial entities
edu	*wisc.edu*	Educational institutions
gov	*nasa.gov*	Government
mil	*army.mil*	Military
net	*flash.net*	Network providers
org	*gsj.org*	Non-profit organizations

In 1997, however, additional Internet domains were established to provide a more meaningful set for today's commercial Internet. Table 12-4 lists these newly-established Internet domains.

Table 12-4: New Internet Domains

Domain	Description
firm	General businesses
store	Online shopping services
web	Web-related activities
arts	Artistic and cultural institutions
rec	Recreation and entertainment
info	Information services
nom	Individuals

The United States is also divided into regional domains, all with a trailing *us* (short for "United States"). The state of Wisconsin, for example, would be *wi.us* according to this scheme. The use of the classic Internet domains has traditionally been restricted to sites in the United States (due to the initial US-centricity of the Internet), but that trend has changed. Now, it is almost impossible to determine the location of Internet sites that use the domains specified in Tables 12-3 or 12-4.

Keep in mind that the networking environment throughout the world is ever changing and improving. URLs are included for each NIC (Network Information Center) so that more up-to-date information on each domain can be obtained.

The CN Domain

The CN domain, which covers China, is managed by CNNIC (China Network Information Center).* This domain includes four subdomains, as indicated in Table 12-5.

Table 12-5: CN Subdomains

Subdomain	Example	Description
ac	*ios.ac.cn*	Managed by Chinese Academy of Sciences
co	*intercom.co.cn*	Corporations
edu	*tsinghua.edu.cn*	Covers all schools and universities, and is managed by CERNET (China Education and Research Network)
net	*bta.net.cn*	Networks

Note that no private Internet Service Providers (ISPs) are permitted in the CN domain.

The JP Domain

The Internet domain that specifies sites in Japan is the two-letter country code JP. So, how can you send email to someone whose address is in the JP domain? First, each JP subdomain must be specified within the email address. Some entities, such as NTT, originally belonged to the JP domain itself as *ntt.jp*—it did not belong to a subdomain, but rather formed its own subdomain of sorts. NTT is now *ntt.co.jp*, under the expected *co* subdomain. KEK (High Energy Accelerator Research Organization) is still in JP domain, as *kek.jp*. Table 12-6 lists the JP subdomains.

Table 12-6: JP Subdomains

Subdomain	Example	Description
ac	*keio.ac.jp*	Academic institutions
ad	*nic.ad.jp*	Administration
co	*morisawa.co.jp*	Commercial entities (corporations)
go	*etl.go.jp*	Government
gr	*almighty.gr.jp*	Individual entities
ne	*nifty.ne.jp*	Commercial networks
or	*aegis.or.jp*	Organizations

Other new subdomains that have been planned include *shop* and *web*. The most current listing of subdomain entities of the JP domain can be easily obtained.†

* *http://www.cnc.ac.cn/*

† *http://www.nic.ad.jp/jpnic/domain/domain-list-e.txt*

The KR Domain

The KR domain is managed by KRNIC (Korea Network Information Center).* Table 12-7 lists the KR subdomains.

Table 12-7: KR Subdomains

Subdomain	Example	Description
ac	*kaist.ac.kr*	Academic institutions
co	*hanyang.co.kr*	Companies
go	*scourt.go.kr*	Government
ne[a]	*kornet.ne.kr*	Networks
or	*nic.or.kr*	Organizations
re	*sdi.re.kr*	Research institutes

[a] Originally, this subdomain was "nm," but has been transitioning to "ne."

Note that geographical domains, such as *seoul.kr* and *pusan.kr*, are also being planned.

The TW Domain

The TW domain is managed by TWNIC (Taiwan Network Information Center).† Table 12-8 lists the TW subdomains.

Table 12-8: TW Subdomains

Subdomain	Example	Description
com	*dynalab.com.tw*	Companies
edu	*nsysu.edu.tw*	Educational institutions
gov	*npm.gov.tw*	Government
net	*seeder.net.tw*	Networks

Getting Connected

This chapter ends with a few suggestions on how to get connected to an email service. I hope most of you are already connected to some such service, but for those who are not, please read on. Being connected will bring to you a wide variety of information and software, most of which is free. If you are an employee at a corporation or if you are a student or faculty member at an educational institution, there is probably an email service you can obtain access to. Contact the

* *http://www.krnic.net/* or *http://www.nic.or.kr/*

† *http://www.twnic.net/*

computing services department to see what is available; in many cases access may be free.

You most likely have heard of (or, perhaps more appropriately, been bombarded with information from) many different Internet Service Providers (or ISPs for short), such as America Online, CompuServe, FlashNet, GEnie, MCIMail, Prodigy, and so on. Some ISPs offer access only through web browsers (which makes *telnet* sessions impossible). For those in Japan, TWICS or Aegis may turn out to be inexpensive alternatives to NIFTY-Serve, PC-VAN, or CompuServe. Contact information for some ISPs is provided in Appendix T.

But, before you go knocking down an ISP's door, I suggest that you pick up a copy of Kiersten Conner and Ed Krol's *The Whole Internet: The Next Generation* (O'Reilly & Associates, 1999) and Valerie Quercia's *Internet in a Nutshell* (O'Reilly & Associates, 1997). The first book lists a number of ISPs that offer worldwide connectivity. You may find an ISP nearby with local dialups and PPP access. Unless you want to incur long-distance telephone charges, select one that is close to where you live.

If you plan to use the many free web-based email services, such as those provided by a wide variety of companies for a wide variety of languages,* you still need an ISP to which to connect in order to gain web access in the first place.

Internet Software

Internet software allows you to communicate with a host computer for accessing higher-level functions, such as reading Usenet News or sending and receiving email. These are usually more complex than other telecommunications software you may have used in that they must be able to handle multiple CJKV encodings on the fly. There are some, however, that can handle only a single CJKV encoding, such as Shift-JIS for Japanese.

With MacOS and Windows, it is often necessary to connect to a mainframe computer, by modem or network, in order to access an email facility. This is when Internet software is required.

Email Clients

The availability of email clients is always on the rise because it is by far the most widely used (and abused) Internet service. However, obtaining an appropriate CJKV-capable email client can be a bit more difficult.

* *http://www.emailaddresses.com/email_language.htm*

Although I only list Becky!, Eudora, and *mh-e* as email clients in this section, most contemporary web browsers, such as Microsoft's Internet Explorer and Netscape Communications' Netscape Communicator, provide an email facility that is usually as good or better than most dedicated clients. In addition, these browsers also provide adequate CJKV support. Solaris Version 2.7 and later includes a CJKV-capable email client called DtMail. CTM Development's PowerMail for MacOS uses the MacOS Text Encoding Converter facility to provide CJKV capability.* Dedicated Korean-capable email clients are also widely available.† Information about Japanese-capable email clients is also available on the Web.‡

Becky!—Windows

RimArts' Becky! is a Windows-based email client whose standard version includes CJKV support.** Becky! supports ISO-2022-JP (Japanese), ISO-2022-KR (Korean), and HZ (Chinese) encodings. Its FAQ provides a lot of useful tips and techniques.††

Eudora

Eudora is one of the most popular email programs for MacOS and Windows. Although localized versions are available, plug-ins that enable CJKV support appear to be popular, especially for those who prefer the standard English-language menus or are on a budget.

Hideki Itoh (伊東秀喜 *itō hideki*) has written a shareware ($8 US) Japanese-enabling plug-in for Eudora (MacOS version) called Japanese Plug-In.‡‡ It works with both the Pro and Light versions. This plug-in adds a couple of useful features beyond simply enabling Japanese support:

- Adds a "`Content-Type: text/plain; charset=iso-2022-jp`" field to all outgoing email messages
- A command that can encode or decode Base64 data in the email header

Tim Burress has written a Japanese code conversion plug-in for Eudora called Kanji Conversion Plug-In that performs, among other things, code conversion among the three major Japanese encodings used today: ISO-2022-JP, EUC-JP, and Shift-JIS.***

* *http://www.ctmdev.com/*

† *http://scorpion.kaist.ac.kr/email.html*

‡ *http://www.forest.impress.co.jp/mail.html*

** *http://www.rimarts.co.jp/becky.htm*

†† *http://www4.est.co.jp/~shimaya/becky/faq.html*

‡‡ *http://www.vcnet.com/hide/*

*** *http://www.twics.com/~kanji/*

The important thing to understand is that the standard versions of Eudora Light and Eudora Pro are not CJKV-capable by default.

GNU Emacs' mh-e

I have always been a fan of GNU Emacs' *mh-e* package, which is based on and depends on the availability of the popular MH mail system. When used with GNU Emacs Version 20 or later, *mh-e* inherits its CJKV support.

Kmail—Windows

Developed by Kureo Technology Limited in Canada, Kmail is a lightweight Japanese-capable email client that runs on English versions of Windows 3.1 and 95.* Kmail supports ISO-2022-JP, Shift-JIS, and EUC-JP encodings, and also can decode Base64, Quoted-Printable, and uuencoded material.

Web Browsers

By far the most popular and utilitarian Internet tool is the category of web browsers. I list only Microsoft's Internet Explorer and Netscape Communications' Netscape Communicator here because they are by far the most widely used, provide an adequate level of CJKV support, and are easily obtained (usually bundled with operating systems).

Internet Explorer

Internet Explorer (IE) is one of the most popular browsers available, and is CJKV-capable without modifications.† Internet Explorer is included with Microsoft Windows, and is also available at no charge from Microsoft's web site. Although the original version was only for Windows, there are now MacOS and Unix versions available.

Outlook Express, which is the email client that is included with Internet Explorer, is also CJKV-capable.‡

Netscape Communicator

Although Netscape Communications' famous Netscape Communicator (formerly known as Netscape Navigator, and sometimes still available as this stand-alone designed strictly for web browsing services)—available for MacOS, Unix, and Windows—was originally designed as a web browser, it has developed into a very

* *http://www.kureo.com/k-mail.htm*

† *http://www.microsoft.com/windows/ie/*

‡ *http://www.microsoft.com/windows/ie/ie40/oe/*

useful email program and news reader.* The most current version allows users to go directly into the email facility when the program first starts up. The email facility is sometimes known as Netscape Messenger, and handles Usenet News in addition to email.

It is possible to use Microsoft's "Language Packs" with Netscape Communicator to facilitate the display of CJKV text when using a non-CJKV version of Windows. One of the biggest needs is CJKV fonts.†

Telnet Clients

My preferred method to access Internet services, such as email, news, FTP, telnet, and so on, is through a Unix shell (running what some people may consider to be "primitive" tools). I also prefer to make connections to a Unix system through a telnet client running on another operating system, such as MacOS or Windows. Telnet clients, described in this section, allow users to establish multiple telnet sessions, which has great advantages over traditional terminal software that establishes only a single interactive session. Telnet clients also permit FTP transfers, which, in my opinion, beat the traditional transfer protocols (X-Modem, Y-Modem, Kermit, and so on) hands down.

The localized versions of Microsoft Windows NT come bundled with a telnet client (called "telnet") that adequately supports the locale. That is, Windows NT-J comes bundled with a telnet client that supports ISO-2022-JP, EUC-JP, and Shift-JIS encodings. It does not, however, support FTP within telnet—a separate FTP client is provided for that purpose.

Japanese telnet clients

ASLTelnet‡ and NCSA Telnet-J appear to be the most popular telnet clients for MacOS-J, and are both freeware. Both of these telnet clients provide the ability to recognize Japanese encodings beyond merely Shift-JIS, such as ISO-2022-JP and EUC-JP.

Korean telnet clients

There are many Korean versions of telnet clients available for MacOS-KH, all of which seem to handle multiple Korean encodings:** Hangul NiftyZTelnet, Hangul NiftyTelnet, Hangul Telnet, and NCSA Telnet-K.††

* *http://www.netscape.com/*

† *http://people.netscape.com/ftang/communicatorfont.html*

‡ *http://www.activeopen.co.jp/ASL/*

** *http://scorpion.kaist.ac.kr/telnet.html*

†† *ftp://salmosa.kaist.ac.kr/pub/mac/internet-sw/*

Anzio—Windows

Rasmussen Software's Anzio, a telnet client that runs on Windows (95, 98, and NT), has been recently upgraded to become CJKV-capable.* Anzio takes advantage of Unicode in order to provide this level of CJKV functionality. Of course, appropriate fonts need to be installed for proper display, but they can be easily obtained through Microsoft's Language Packs.† A less-expensize Anzio Lite is also available.

MacBlueTelnet—MacOS

MacBlueTelnet is a freeware MacOS telnet client that supports Chinese, Japanese, and Korean without the use of a fully-localized MacOS nor a Language Kit.‡ Its only real limitation is that only single encodings are supported for each locale: EUC-CN for Simplified Chinese, Big Five for Traditional Chinese, EUC-JP for Japanese, and EUC-KR for Korean.

For those who plan to use MacBlueTelnet with CJKV-capable editors (such as GNU Emacs) while connected to a Unix host, there is one feature that needs to be disabled. MacBlueTelnet's "Use HanZi Editing" option, selectable through terminal preferences, automatically doubles certain keystrokes in order to simulate double-byte handling. This includes the delete and cursor key. Because GNU Emacs (Version 2.0 or later) has its own multiple-byte support, this MacBlueTelnet feature ends up deleting two multiple-byte characters (when the "delete" key is pressed) or advancing two characters (when the advancing cursor key is pressed).

MacBlueTelnet provides support for Chinese, Japanese, and Korean display through the use of add-on bitmap fonts. You can also add input methods.**

Terminal Software

Although the use of terminal software is decreasing due to the explosive growth of the Web—access to the Web typically requires a special type of network connection, such as SLIP, PPP, or a dedicated network or dialup. However, there are still contexts in which terminal software can be useful, so I cover them here briefly.

NinjaTerm—MacOS-J

If you need to use modems to connect to a mainframe host computer for email purposes, NinjaTerm, written by Michiharu Ariza (有座道春 *ariza michiharu*), is

* *http://www.anzio.com/products/anziowin.htm*

† *http://www.microsoft.com/msdownload/ieplatform/lang/lang.htm*

‡ *ftp://ftp.ifcss.org/pub/software/mac/networking/MacBlueTelnet/*

** *ftp://ftp.ifcss.org/pub/software/mac/input/*

an older, yet still useful, freely-available Japanese telecommunications program. NinjaTerm supports Shift-JIS, ISO-2022-JP, and EUC-JP encodings, but does not support more than one at a time like ASLTelnet can. It has a buffering system that keeps a log of your communications session. This log file is both a text file (that can be opened by text editors for retrieving data) and a settings file for NinjaTerm itself. The only supported file transfer protocol is X-Modem.

NinjaTerm, unfortunately, is no longer being maintained by its author. In fact, the last release was all the way back in 1988 (Version 0.962)! With the introduction of newer operating systems, such as KanjiTalk 7.1, compatibility problems have crept in, the most notable of which is the lack of 32-bit mode compatibility. A patched version that remedies this problem is available.

ActiveTalk—MacOS-J

Hiroo Yamada, the author of ASLTelnet (telnet client) and ASLEdit+ (text editor), has developed an inexpensive commercial terminal program called ActiveTalk. It provides full Japanese functionality (such as the ability to handle multiple encodings), as expected.

Terminal-J—MacOS-J

Terminal-J is another freely-available Japanese telecommunications program.* Terminal-J is based on Terminal, written by Erny Tontlinger. A version that was previously available recognized only Shift-JIS encoded material. This made it useful for tasks such as connecting to a Japanese BBS (most of them run on PCs, and thus use Shift-JIS encoding). However, a more diverse choice of encodings is desirable when dealing with other host computers and email systems. Fortunately, a second flavor of Terminal-J has been released, and can user-selectably change the encoding method. Choices include ISO-2022-JP, Shift-JIS, and EUC-JP.

Terminal-J offers a wide variety of file transfer protocols, such as Y-Modem and Z-Modem. These are more modern protocols, and are much faster than those such as X-Modem.

Terminal-J is developed by a team consisting of Minoru Yoshida (吉田稔 *yoshida minoru*) and Masashi Oka† (岡昌志 *oka masashi*).

YKH—MS-DOS

YKH is a freely-available Japanese DEC VT-320 terminal emulator developed by Bryan McNett for MS-DOS. YKH supports the display and entry of Japanese text in

* *http://www.big.or.jp/~yoshida/techlab/Terminal-J/*

† *oka@anritsu.co.jp*

ISO-2022-JP, Shift-JIS, and EUC-JP encodings, and is able to make a connection through modems on *com1* or *com2* ports, and over some local area networks (for instance, using DECNET LAT and DECNET CTERM network terminal protocols). YKH stands for *Yaki Kemono Hosuto*, and in Japanese is written 焼き獣ホスト (*yaki kemono hosuto*). The original non-Japanese version was called RBH, which stands for *Roastie-Beastie Host*—Yaki Kemono Hosuto is the Japanese equivalent.

One unique feature of YKH is that it is able to fix and display Japanese text that has been mangled by newsreader software (such as *rn*). Without such a feature, those who wish to read Japanese text on Usenet News must either compile a special Japanese-aware version of their newsreading software (usually in the form of a patch), or else save the article to a file then view it later.

YKH requires about 64K of RAM and a VGA graphics adapter. YKH is available through anonymous FTP, and under the terms of the GNU general public license, the full source code for YKH is available free of charge—contact the author at the following email address for a copy of the full source code.

News Readers

As with email clients, the contemporary web browsers described earlier in this chapter also provide a news-reading facility. When used on a CJKV-capable operating system, these web browsers almost always provide the ability to read and post news articles containing CJKV text. Of course, I still use *rn* for reading Usenet News. Information about how to obtain and effectively use Japanese-capable news reading software is available online.*

* *http://www.forest.impress.co.jp/netnews.html*

13

The World Wide Web

In this chapter:
- *Content Versus Presentation*
- *Displaying Web Documents*
- *Authoring HTML Documents*
- *Authoring XML Documents*
- *Authoring PDF Documents*
- *Character References*
- *CGI Programming Examples*
- *Shall We Surf?*

This chapter describes various methods for displaying and otherwise handling CJKV text in the context of the World Wide Web (WWW or W3 for short). As you are no doubt aware, there has been explosive growth of the Web in recent years. Virtually every company has established a "home page" for letting Internet users know of their products and services—television, radio, and billboard advertisements these days often boldly include URLs. But, how do you go about displaying or creating web documents that include CJKV text? Good questions with reasonable and understandable answers. An excellent book whose focus is on viewing and creating multilingual web documents is Yoshihiko Mikami's (三上吉彦 *mikami yoshihiko*) マルチリンガルWEBガイド (*maruchiringaru WEB gaido*, meaning "Multilingual WEB Guide"; O'Reilly Japan, 1997).

People who are already comfortable with using web browsers, such as Netscape Communicator, Internet Explorer (both graphics-based), and Lynx (text-based), will find comfort in knowing that their current browser either has inherent CJKV support, or can be easily patched to do so.

Content Versus Presentation

HTML (HyperText Markup Language), an application of SGML (Standard Generalized Markup Language, described in ISO 8879:1986), provides the author with full control over the *content* of web documents, but it is up to the individual browser to handle *presentation*. When including graphics in your web documents, for example, you must keep in mind that text-based browsers, such as Lynx, exist, and therefore cannot display them directly.

Adobe Acrobat provides the author with full control over both the content *and* presentation of web documents. This means that the "look and feel" of the original document is *fully* preserved. These documents are known as PDF (Portable Document Format) files. Adobe Acrobat Version 3.0, based on PDF Version 1.2, provides complete CJKV support, and can also plug into Netscape Communicator so that PDF files display directly in the browser window (as opposed to running Adobe Acrobat as a separate process or application). Adobe Acrobat Version 4.0, based on PDF Version 1.3, will provide slightly more enhanced CJKV support, such as the ability to embed CJKV fonts.

XML (Extensible Markup Language), which may soon replace HTML, provides much better control over presentation, and also has better overall CJKV support.

HTML, XML, and other advanced web developments are usually coordinated by the World Wide Web Consortium (W3C).*

HTML—HyperText Markup Language

HTML, first documented in RFC 1866, is a language used to describe the content and structure of web documents, and originally specified ISO 8859-1:1998 (also known as ISO Latin 1 or ISO-8859-1) as the default character set. RFC 2070, *Internationalization of the Hypertext Markup Language*, effectively changes the default character set for HTML from ISO 8859-1:1998 to ISO 10646-1:1993 (Unicode), and also extends HTML to be more suitable for multilingual purposes. The latest HTML specification is Version 4.0.†

Many companies, such as Microsoft and Netscape Communications, have defined their own extensions to HTML in the form of additional tags. These tags are not part of the official HTML specification, and are guaranteed to work only in that vendor's browser.

With the large number of HTML books on the market, it can be difficult for the beginner to choose an appropriate title. My favorite is Chuck Musciano and Bill Kennedy's *HTML: The Definitive Guide*, Third Edition (O'Reilly & Associates, 1998).

XML—Extensible Markup Language

XML, put simply, makes SGML available for web use. Unlike HTML, it does not restrict the user to a fixed set of tags. On the contrary, it allows the user to freely define tags. Its default character set is ISO 10646-1:1993.

* *http://www.w3.org/*

† *http://www.w3.org/Markup/*

The XML specification is available online.* An excellent printed source of information for XML is *XML: Principles, Tools, and Techniques*, edited by Dan Connolly (*World Wide Web Journal*, Winter 1997 issue, O'Reilly & Associates, 1997), which is a collection of XML-related papers. Also of interest is Rick Jelliffe's *The XML & SGML Cookbook: Recipes for Structured Information* (Prentice-Hall, 1998).

PDF—Portable Document Format

PDF, short for *Portable Document Format*, is a special PostScript-derived language for describing documents in a platform-independent manner.† But, some of you may have heard that PostScript itself was designed to be platform-independent. PostScript, as a programming language, is typically written (or generated) by other programs, such as high-end publishing applications and PostScript printer drivers. The quality and integrity of the resulting PostScript files varied greatly. There was also the issue of font availability—if the fonts that are referenced in a PostScript file are not available to the PostScript interpreter, the document will not print.‡ These were all motivations for developing a truly portable format for interchanging documents. In the beginning, PDF was a write-only format, meaning that once you created a PDF file (using the Adobe Acrobat Distiller application or the PDFWriter printer driver), you could only view, print, and search its contents. Today, many of Adobe Systems' applications, such as Adobe Illustrator and Adobe FrameMaker, can open and edit PDF files, or can save them in PDF format (as a function of the "Save As…" command).

The initial releases of Adobe Acrobat (and the PDF specifications on which they were based) did not include any CJKV support. While some people have discovered that there were ways to embed CJKV characters as graphics, this method has three serious drawbacks:

- It is not possible to search for text—the text that was converted to graphics is now, well, simply graphics
- Embedding graphics requires specifying an output resolution—the document may display fine at screen resolutions, but may print horribly (or vice versa)
- Embedding higher-resolution graphics takes up a lot of space—the resulting files are larger

PDF Version 1.2, which has been incorporated into Adobe Acrobat Version 3.0, provides a minimal level of CJKV support. PDF Version 1.3 provides a much more

* *http://www.w3.org/XML/*

† *http://www.adobe.com/prodindex/acrobat/adobepdf.html*

‡ Or may print, but using Courier as the substitution font, which results in typographic chaos.

enhanced level of CJKV support, intended for use beginning in Adobe Acrobat Version 4.0.

Displaying Web Documents

There are many more people who are browsing (surfing) the Web than people who are creating web documents. This means that displaying web documents is critical. After all, if no one can display your web document correctly, what is the point in creating it? Things can become a bit tricky when it comes to displaying CJKV text.

There are five common methods for correctly displaying CJKV text in web browsers:

- Obtain a web browser that includes CJKV support, such as Netscape Communicator or Internet Explorer (an underlying CJKV-capable OS *may* be required)
- Patch your web browser to support CJKV text (again, an underlying CJKV-capable OS *may* be required)
- Use a gateway that transforms CJKV text into graphic images, such as Shodouka*—not terribly useful for text-based browsers, such as Lynx†
- Use an application that forces display of CJKV text, such as DynaLab's AsiaSurf,‡ Kureo Technology's Kview,** or NJStar Software's NJWin†† (this technique is also quite useful outside the context of web browsing software—it can be used to view CJKV text in most non-CJKV applications)
- Use Adobe Acrobat Version 3.0 or later—if the URL resolves to a PDF file, and if the Adobe Acrobat Version 3.0 plug-in is installed into your browser, everything displays correctly (a CJKV-capable OS that includes a basic collection of CJKV fonts *may* be required)

Note that the gateway method requires that you use a graphics-based browser, and can be painfully slow. Text-based browsers, such as Lynx, do not (and, obviously, cannot) directly support graphics or images of any kind. It is possible, however, for Lynx to use a "helper application," such as *xv*, for displaying graphics. Worse yet, web documents that make use of Java (such as Java Applets) or JavaScript are not usable in today's text-based browsers. Too bad.

* *http://www.shodouka.com/*

† *http://lynx.browser.org/*

‡ *http://www.dynalab.com/Products/html/AsiaSurf/asiasurf.htm*

** *http://www.kureo.com/k-mail.htm*

†† *http://www.njstar.com/njwin/*

There are currently two widely-used web browsers available: Netscape Communications' Netscape Communicator,* Microsoft's Internet Explorer.† There is also Alis Technologies' Tango.‡ These companies, especially Netscape Communications and Microsoft, are trying to out-perform the others in this fiercely competitive market. This strong competition is resulting in better and better browsing software, and is ultimately a *win* situation for all users, especially for those who need to display CJKV documents.**

Basis Technology has assembled a lot of useful tips and techniques for correctly handling Japanese in web browsers, specifically in Windows.†† There is also information about enabling Chinese in web browsers.‡‡ These tips and techniques can be applied for all CJKV locales.

I currently use Netscape Communicator running under MacOS-J, the X Window System, and Windows NT-J. I sometimes use Lynx from a Japanese-capable Unix terminal. These tools provide me with plenty of net surfin' capability.

Note that while many browsers support the display of CJKV text, some browsers cannot correctly display CJKV text on the page header or on HTML form buttons (such as "Submit" and "Reset").

Authoring HTML Documents

The most widely-used CJKV encodings—EUC, ISO-2022, Big Five, Shift-JIS, and so on—all support a mixed one- and two-byte code space.*** All the special HTML tags fall within the printable ASCII set, which is fully supported by virtually all CJKV encoding methods.

The following example represents a minimal HTML document with no multilingual content:

```
<HTML>
<HEAD>
<META HTTP-EQUIV="Content-Type" CONTENT="text/html; CHARSET=us-ascii">
<TITLE>Ken Lunde's Home Page</TITLE>
</HEAD>
```

* *http://www.netscape.com/*

† *http://www.microsoft.com/windows/ie/*

‡ *http://www.alis.com/internet_products/*

** Such as the sort of person who would read this book.

†† *http://www.basistech.com/articles/browsing.html*

‡‡ *http://chinese.yahoo.com/docs/info/download.html*

*** If you have read Chapter 4, *Encoding Methods*, very carefully, you'd know I'm sort of lying. EUC-JP defines a mixed one-, two-, and three-byte code space; EUC-TW defines a mixed one-, two-, and four-byte code space; and UTF-8 defines a mixed one- through six-byte code space.

```
<BODY>
<H1>Ken Lunde's Home Page</H1>
</BODY>
</HTML>
```

(HTML tags stand out better if they are in uppercase, but they do not need to be—this is more important if you write your own HTML.) The following is the same HTML document, but this time in Japanese (and indicates Shift-JIS encoding):

```
<HTML>
<HEAD>
<META HTTP-EQUIV="Content-Type" CONTENT="text/html; CHARSET=euc-jp">
<TITLE>小林劍のホームページ</TITLE>
</HEAD>
<BODY>
<H1>小林劍のホームページ</H1>
</BODY>
</HTML>
```

As you can see, creating multilingual HTML documents is actually quite simple. The real question is how to go about creating the raw HTML. Do you prefer to use a front-end tool, your favorite word processor, or do you want to write your own HTML?

Special HTML Attributes and Tags

The current HTML specification defines several attributes and tags that allow the document author to define multilingual aspects of a document. More information about these and other attributes and tags can be found in *HTML: The Definitive Guide*, Third Edition (O'Reilly & Associates, 1998).

The LANG attribute

HTML's `LANG` attribute provides the ability to tag smaller portions of text with language-related attributes. While it is typically necessary to indicate the character set and encoding of the entire document (covered next), this special tag allows a similar type of specification on a much smaller scale.

Examples of this tag in use can be illustrated when dealing with Unicode data. A Unicode code point by itself does not carry with it sufficient information to properly render most CJKV texts, particularly Chinese characters. While such a document may be flagged as Unicode, the `LANG` attribute allows the HTML author the ability to indicate the language of the text, thus allowing the characters to be correctly displayed.

The <META> tag

Did you notice the `<META>` tag in the previous HTML sample? It is now possible to explicitly specify character set and encoding information between the balancing

<HEAD> and </HEAD> tags. This sequence uses the <META> tag extension (as described in a proposal for internationalizing HTML), and looks like the following, which indicates EUC-KR encoding:

```
<HEAD>
<META HTTP-EQUIV="Content-Type" CONTENT="text/html; CHARSET=euc-kr">
</HEAD>
```

Some of the values for CHARSET (MIME Charsets) recognized by Netscape Communicator Version 4.0 and later include `us-ascii`, `iso-8859-1`, `x-mac-roman`, `iso-8859-2`, `x-mac-ce`, `iso-2022-jp`, `x-sjis`, `x-euc-jp`, `euc-kr`, `iso-2022-kr`, `gb2312`, `gb_2312-80`, `x-euc-tw`, `x-cns11643-1`, `x-cns11643-2`, and `big5`.

Embedding this tag is not only useful for HTML documents that include CJKV text, but also for non-CJKV ones. In case an HTML document includes accented Latin characters, such as those found in ISO 8859-1:1998, specifying `iso-8859-1` will ensure that the accented Latin characters are not accidentally interpreted as though they were encoded according to a CJKV encoding.

The CHARSET value is subsequently passed to the from server to client as part of the HTTP negotiation. There are many other uses for the <META> tag beyond simply providing character set and encoding information to browsers.*

Providing charset information—where and how?

There is a big debate about which method for indicating character and encoding information is best. There are two methods available:

- Embed the character set and encoding information using the LANG attribute or the <META> tag, as described in the previous section
- Require that the server send the character set and encoding information separately from the document itself to the client in the HTTP header—the LANG attribute may still be necessary, depending on the character set and encoding

Instead of arguing which method is best, why not simply support both methods whenever possible? Consider a situation where you receive a CD-ROM packed full of HTML files. There is no server present to send the character set and encoding information to the client for the documents because the client must open the documents as local files. You must then rely on embedded information.

Automatic encoding detection issues

Most contemporary browsers provide a feature that automatically detects what encoding is being used. EUC-JP and Shift-JIS encodings used for Japanese text can

* *http://people.netscape.com/ftang/meta.html* or *http://vancouver-webpages.com/META/*

often be difficult to differentiate. There is a useful trick that can help browsers more reliably detect the encoding by including an HTML comment near the top of the HTML file. This comment includes a single character whose encoding is unambiguously either EUC-JP or Shift-JIS encoding. I suggest the following two meaningful characters for this purpose: 東京 (*tōkyō*, meaning "Tokyo"). The character codes for these two characters are 0xC5EC 0xB5FE for EUC-JP, and 0x938C 0x8B9E for Shift-JIS. Note how the second kanji is unambiguously either EUC-JP or Shift-JIS. The following is an example HTML comment that includes these two kanji:

```
<!--- 東京 used for correct automatic encoding detection --->
```

This technique provides a reliable backup for the technique of specifying the character set and encoding using the <META> tag.

HTTP language negotiation

Many web sites can serve different versions of HTML document, such as *index.html* and *index-jp.html*, where one provides English-language content, and the other provides Japanese-language content. It is possible, through HTTP negotiation, to serve either version automatically, depending on how the client server is configured.

HTTP negotiation involves a conversation or dialog between a *client* (your browser, for example) and a *server* (the machine specified by the URL). It is during this negotiation when each party tells the other its capabilities and preferences. The client, for example, can inform the server that it prefers Korean-language content. If the server has a file named something like *index-kr.html*, that document can be provided to the client instead of the default *index.html* file.

For more information about HTTP negotiation between clients and servers, I suggest Clinton Wong's *Web Client Programming in Perl* (O'Reilly & Associates, 1997).

HTML Authoring Tools

Some of the many HTML authoring tools available today include Adobe PageMill (a Japanese version is available),* Netscape Composer (part of Netscape Communicator), Dreamweaver, Microsoft FrontPage, and NetObjects Fusion. Many word processors and page-layout programs, such as Nisus Writer and Adobe FrameMaker, include features for saving documents in HTML or XML format—you compose to your heart's delight, then save as an HTML or XML file.

* *http://www.adobe.com/prodindex/pagemill/*

Because I maintain a single URL—my home page—I prefer to craft my own HTML documents and write my own CGI programs, using GNU Emacs and Perl, respectively. Learning the simple HTML syntax is really a no-brainer, and such knowledge is downright useful when special HTML tools are not available when something goes wrong. If I were to maintain many URLs, for example, as a full-time job, I would immediately start looking for tools to ease the pain.

Embedding CJKV Text as Graphics

If you expect that your target audience is not equipped with CJKV-display capability (sort of doubtful these days given the current states of most browsers), you can embed CJKV text as graphics. The most common format to use for this purpose is GIF (Graphics Interchange Format), developed by the folks that bring you CompuServe. Most graphics applications, such as Adobe Photoshop, can create GIF files.*

Authoring XML Documents

Authoring XML document is a lot like authoring HTML documents, but there are well-defined places in XML to encapsulate "character set and encoding" information that tells the browser or other display software how to display the document.

The following is a small XML file that is a lot like the HTML example provided earlier, but includes two additional lines at the beginning that are for XML:

```
<?xml version="1.0" encoding="euc-kr"?>
<!DOCTYPE HTML PUBLIC "-//W3C//DTD HTML 4.0 Transitional//EN"
  "http://www.w3.org/TR/REC-html40/loose.dtd">
<HTML>
<HEAD>
<TITLE>켄 런디의 홈페이지</TITLE>
</HEAD>
<BODY>
<H1>켄 런디의 홈페이지</H1>
</BODY>
</HTML>
```

The first line identifies the document as XML, and also provides encoding information. If no encoding information is provided, UTF-8 is assumed. Because UTF-8 includes seven-bit ASCII, this is an acceptable default for compatibility. The second line indicates the DTD (Document Type Definition), which tells software how to handle the document as far as information structure is concerned.

* "What a waste of ammo!" Using Adobe Photoshop for the purpose of creating CJKV text as graphic images is a lot like driving in a thumb tack with a sledge hammer. But what the heck, it does the trick.

Including these first two lines, with meaningful values, has benefits for the following three reasons:

- The character set and encoding of the document is unambiguous—this is mandatory in XML
- The fact that the document is XML is unambiguous—this is mandatory in XML
- The DTD that the document uses is unambiguous—the "DOCTYPE" declaration is not mandatory in XML; W3C even recommends its use in HTML

Developers should take note that there are already XML parsers available. One is James Clark's Expat (XML Parser Toolkit), written in C.* Masato Yoshida (吉田正人 *yoshida masato*) has written an XML Parser Module for Ruby that uses Expat.† As a side note, Ruby is a relatively new object-oriented programming language whose facilities are similar to those in Perl, Python, and Tcl, and includes modules for handling Japanese encodings and Unicode (UTF-8 and UCS-2), called Kconv and Uconv, respectively.‡ Microsoft has also developed an XML parser for Java.**

Authoring PDF Documents

PDF files can be created in a number of ways, and several options regarding font embedding are made available in Adobe Acrobat Version 4.0 and later. Adobe Systems' Tech Note #5641, *Enabling PDF Font Embedding for CID-Keyed Fonts*, illustrates to developers how they may enable their CID-keyed fonts for embedding in PDF.

PDF files begin their life as documents created using common word processing or publishing applications. My favorite happens to be Adobe FrameMaker. There are three methods for converting such documents into PDF:

- Select PDFWriter instead of a printer, then print the document as usual—the result is a PDF file instead of output to a printer
- Print the document to a PostScript file, then use the Adobe Acrobat Distiller application to convert the PostScript file to PDF—this is by far the most reliable way to create a PDF file
- Save the document as PDF—some applications, such as Adobe Illustrator Version 7.0 or greater and Adobe FrameMaker Version 5.5 or greater, have this *very* useful feature

* *http://www.jclark.com/xml/expat.html*

† *http://www.bekkoame.ne.jp/~yoshidam/xmlparser_en.txt*

‡ *http://www.netlab.co.jp/ruby/*

** *http://www.microsoft.com/xml/default.asp*

If the original document includes embedded EPS (Encapsulated PostScript) graphics, then PDFWriter is useless, and the Adobe Acrobat Distiller application *must* be used.

Don't be alarmed by the size of PostScript files that you plan to push through the Adobe Acrobat Distiller application—the resulting PDF file is usually a fraction of the size of the original PostScript file. Of course, YMMV.*

One of the more difficult decisions that must be made when creating PDF files is whether or not to embed font information.† There are advantages and disadvantages of each approach, as shown in Table 13-1.

Table 13-1: To Embed or Not To Embed, That Is the Question

Font Embedding	Advantages	Disadvantages
No	Reduced file size	Adobe Acrobat viewers require fonts
Yes	Display or print anywhere	Increased file size
Yes (restricted)	Display anywhere	Increased file size, and print to devices of specific resolutions

So, how does one decide whether or not to embed font information in PDF files? First of all, PDF files never include the entire font (that is, unless every character in the font is referenced in the document—sort of doubtful). All the referenced characters are subsetted before embedding. In Japanese, for example, 70 percent of running text is composed of kana, which represents approximately 200 unique characters—the rest are kanji and other symbols, which may or may not take up much space.

Unless you can guarantee that all people who display your PDF file have the same (or equivalent) fonts used to create it, you are better off embedding font information. Embedding usually leads to slightly larger files, but a small and undisplayable document is useless.

PDF Eases Publishing Pains

Most individuals do not own their own typesetting hardware, such as a photo imagesetter, and for good reason: it is a big expense, and requires frequent maintenance. This is where service bureaus live up to the first word in their title: *service*.

* Your Mileage May Vary.

† No embedding of CJKV fonts is available in Adobe Acrobat Version 3.0.

There are many service bureaus that provide CJKV support. Service bureaus today typically accept "jobs" in one of two formats:

- Application files
- PostScript files

Both of these methods of submitting jobs to service bureaus have major disadvantages, indicated as follows:

- Submitting application files requires that the service bureau have the same application (and perhaps the *same* version of the application) installed onto at least one of their computers, along with the same fonts
- Submitting PostScript files does not require the presence of the application or fonts from which they were generated, but they cannot be previewed—it also requires that the service bureau have the same fonts unless they were embedded in the PostScript files

Submitting documents to service bureaus in the form of PDF files suffers from none of these problems. In short, PDF does not require that the original application and fonts be available, and can be previewed before printing using freely-available viewers. But, the service bureau will usually need to have the fonts available on their photo imagesetters due to resolution restrictions when embedding some CJKV fonts.

Some fonts, due to their licensing restrictions, are not allowed to be embedded within a PDF file. Some fonts *can* be embedded, but stipulate a resolution restriction (for example, such documents cannot be printed to output devices whose resolution is 1201-dpi and higher—if the output device has the font resident, the document *will* print). The font's license should indicate any such restrictions. Read or inquire before you buy.

In summary, PDF can act as a reliable "digital master" if the fonts referenced in the document are embedded, which is possible in the context of Adobe Acrobat Version 4.0 and greater (PDF Version 1.3). This means the ability to print directly from PDF to plate. Those in the professional publishing industry will immediately recognize this benefit.

Character References

Besides the obvious method of using characters themselves, it is also possible to use character references in HTML, XML, and SGML. Common character references, known to most HTML authors, include things like `&` for an ampersand. Note that character references, whether they are mnemonic or numeric, are delimited by an ampersand (`&`, 0x26) and a semicolon (`;`, 0x3B).

When using character codes, only decimal notation was possible in traditional SGML and HTML up until Version 3.2. Hexadecimal notation is possible in HTML Version 4.0, XML, and SGML (after a correction). Hexadecimal notation is preferred for Unicode-encoded characters. These are called "Numeric Character References."

The character encoded at hexadecimal 0xFF (decimal 255) can take on the following two forms:

`ÿ` (hexadecimal)
`ÿ` (decimal)

Note that Unicode 0x4E00 should only be represented as `一`. While Internet Explorer and Netscape Communicator Versions 4.0 do not recognize hexadecimal character references, the next major releases of each program should.

CGI Programming Examples

There is much more to the Web than simply static HTML and PDF documents. One can dynamically provide content through what is known as CGI (Common Gateway Interface) programming. The most common programming language that drives CGI programs is Perl. But, virtually *any* programming language will do.

CGI programming involves interaction between HTML *forms* and a program that does something (hopefully) intelligent with data from the forms—a prime example of a client-server relationship. Users fill out HTML forms much like they would fill out conventional forms. Once the form is complete, the user submits the form (to the server) to be processed. This is when the CGI program takes over.

There are two ways in which the data in HTML forms are passed to a CGI program: the GET and POST methods. The GET method provides the form data to the CGI program on the server in a single step by appending the data to the URL. The POST method uses two steps: the server is first contacted, then the form data is supplied in a separate transmission.

Once you have handled some simple HTML-related parsing tasks, such as managing the HTML form data, the rest is simply normal programming. The following are two functions (written in Perl) that I use for parsing HTML form data:

```
sub parse_form_data {
  local(*DATA) = @_;
  local($method,$query_string,@key_value_pairs,$key_value,$key,$value);

  $method = $ENV{REQUEST_METHOD};
  if ($method eq "GET") {
    $query_string = $ENV{QUERY_STRING};
  } elsif ($method eq "POST") {
    read(STDIN,$query_string,$ENV{CONTENT_LENGTH});
  } else {
```

```
      &return_error(500,"Server Error","Server uses unsupported method");
    }
    $query_string =~ tr/+/ /;
    @key_value_pairs = split(/&/,$query_string);
    foreach $key_value (@key_value_pairs) {
      ($key,$value) = split(/=/,$key_value);
      $value =~ s/%([0-9A-Fa-f][0-9A-Fa-f])/chr hex $1/eg;
      if (defined($DATA{$key})) {
        $DATA{$key} = join("\0",$DATA{$key},$value);
      } else {
        $DATA{$key} = $value;
      }
    }
  }
  sub return_error {
    local($status,$keyword,$message) = @_;

    print "Content-type: text/html\n";
    print "Status: $status $keyword\n\n";
    print "<TITLE>CGI Program - Unexpected Error</TITLE>\n";
    print "<H1>$keyword</H1>\n<HR>$message</HR>\n";
    print "Please contact lunde\@oreilly.com for more information.\n";
    exit(1);
  }
```

Now for some explanations. It is not until the following line that we start manipulating the data provided by the HTML form:

```
@key_value_pairs = split(/&/,$query_string);
```

Each key-value pair in the query string returned by the HTML form is separated by an ampersand (&, 0x26) character, so we need to split each pair using an ampersand as the separator. Each pair is stuffed into its own element of an array.

Next we iterate through the array that contains each key-value pair:

```
foreach $key_value (@key_value_pairs) {
  ...
}
```

With each iteration of the loop we copy the next key-value pair into the temporary variable `$key_value`. The body of this loop is as follows:

```
($key,$value) = split(/=/,$key_value);
$value =~ tr/+/ /;
$value =~ s/%([0-9A-Fa-f][0-9A-Fa-f])/chr hex $1/eg;
if (defined($DATA{$key})) {
  $DATA{$key} = join("\0",$DATA{$key},$value);
} else {
  $DATA{$key} = $value;
}
```

While key-value pairs were separated by an ampersand, the keys and values themselves are separated by an equals sign (=, 0x3D). Thus, we must split each key-value pair using an equals sign as the separator. Once we have split a key-value pair into its key and value, we must *decode* the result. Because most non-alphanumeric characters are not permitted to be sent as form data through HTTP (HyperText Transfer Protocol), they have been converted or otherwise encoded to mask their true identity. Most everything that is non-alphanumeric is converted into a three-character string: a percent sign (%, 0x25) followed by two hexadecimal digits (known as "URL transformation"). For example, a hyphen (-, 0x2D) is represented as %2D according to this method. Eight-bit characters that are so commonly used for CJKV encodings, such as 0xA1, can also be passed using this method: %A1. The following single line of Perl decodes this type of encoded data:

```
$value =~ s/%([0-9A-Fa-f][0-9A-Fa-f])/chr hex $1/eg;
```

Spaces have also been converted, either to a plus sign (+, 0x2B) or according to the encoding described above, so we must convert them back:

```
$value =~ tr/+/ /;
```

The above line of code *must* be executed before the general decoding takes place, as follows:

```
$value =~ tr/+/ /;
$value =~ s/%([0-9A-Fa-f][0-9A-Fa-f])/chr hex $1/eg;
```

The resulting keys and values are stored in a hash (associative array) called %DATA for subsequent lookup.

The only other aspect of CGI programming to be aware of is that sending results back to the user requires a valid HTTP header. This effectively means that the very first data sent back must be the text `Content-type: text/html` followed by not one but *two* newline characters. The following single line of Perl code is all you need:

```
print STDOUT "Content-type: text/html\n\n";
```

Of course, if you'd like to avoid dealing with all of these CGI headaches and concentrate on writing some cool CGI program, I highly suggest using Lincoln Stein's excellent CGI.pm module, which is now part of the standard Perl distribution as of Version 5.004. It gracefully handles all tricky aspects of CGI programming—so that you don't have to.

There is *much* more to CGI programming than I provide here. Shishir Gundavaram's *CGI Programming on the World Wide Web* (O'Reilly & Associates, 1996) is an excellent guide for writing CGI programs, as is Lincoln Stein's own *Official Guide to Programming with CGI.pm: The Standard for Building Web Scripts* (John Wiley & Sons, 1998).

There are many URLs that provide content through the magic of CGI programming. Jeffrey Friedl's Japanese-English Dictionary Server[*] and my own CJKV Character Set Server[†] are a couple of examples that serve multilingual content. Check them out! In both cases, the Perl programming language is being used to handle multilingual text.

Shall We Surf?

There are two types of web users: those who author documents and those who view (that is, "surf") them. Many, like me, are both. One of the most addicting aspects of the Web is the ability to follow links to virtually no end. This can be good and bad. It is good in that you may come across some useful information (which means you want to keep the direct URL handy for future reference by creating a bookmark in your favorite browser), but is bad in that you probably have other work you should be doing instead (like what you're probably being paid to do).

An excellent way to find your way around the Web is to search for items using an Internet search engine such as AltaVista, or else through an Internet guide, such as Excite, Infoseek, Lycos, or Yahoo!

Anyway, now that you're done reading this book, or at least its chapters, I encourage you to check out my home page, which will provide late-breaking information relating to this book:

http://www.oreilly.com/~lunde/

My home page should serve as one way to start exploring the numerous CJKV information resources available.

Cheers!

小林劍

* *http://enterprise.ic.gc.ca/cgi-bin/j-e/*

† *http://www.oreilly.com/~lunde/cjkv-char.html*

A

Code Conversion Tables

The first table in this appendix, which spans the following two pages, is useful when dealing with material indexed by the various native CJKV encoding methods. The second table provides the correspondences between Row-Cell rows 95 through 120 and the Shift-JIS user-defined encoding range.

All of these columns are fairly self-explanatory, except perhaps for the two Shift-JIS columns. Confusion may occur when you try to convert the first Shift-JIS byte to another code, or when you try to convert the second byte of another code to Shift-JIS. The following two sets of rules should help:

Row-Cell/ISO-2022/EUC to Shift-JIS

1. The first byte converts using both conversion tables—find the first byte value in Row-Cell/ISO-2022/EUC code, then simply slide over to the "SJIS First Byte" column.
2. The second byte is a bit tricky. If the first byte (yes, the first byte!) of the Row-Cell/ISO-2022/EUC code is odd (the hexadecimal digits B, D, and F are odd), select the left-hand value in the "SJIS Second Byte" column. Otherwise, select the right-hand value.

Shift-JIS to Row-Cell/ISO-2022/EUC

1. If the second Shift-JIS byte is the left-hand entry in the "SJIS Second Byte" column, use the first occurrence of the first Shift-JIS byte to determine the first byte value of another code. Otherwise, use the second occurrence of the first Shift-JIS byte.
2. The second Shift-JIS byte converts unambiguously using the code conversion table.

Row-Cell	ISO-2022	EUC	SJIS First Byte	SJIS Second Byte	
01	21	A1	81	40	9F
02	22	A2	81	41	A0
03	23	A3	82	42	A1
04	24	A4	82	43	A2
05	25	A5	83	44	A3
06	26	A6	83	45	A4
07	27	A7	84	46	A5
08	28	A8	84	47	A6
09	29	A9	85	48	A7
10	2A	AA	85	49	A8
11	2B	AB	86	4A	A9
12	2C	AC	86	4B	AA
13	2D	AD	87	4C	AB
14	2E	AE	87	4D	AC
15	2F	AF	88	4E	AD
16	30	B0	88	4F	AE
17	31	B1	89	50	AF
18	32	B2	89	51	B0
19	33	B3	8A	52	B1
20	34	B4	8A	53	B2
21	35	B5	8B	54	B3
22	36	B6	8B	55	B4
23	37	B7	8C	56	B5
24	38	B8	8C	57	B6
25	39	B9	8D	58	B7
26	3A	BA	8D	59	B8
27	3B	BB	8E	5A	B9
28	3C	BC	8E	5B	BA
29	3D	BD	8F	5C	BB
30	3E	BE	8F	5D	BC
31	3F	BF	90	5E	BD
32	40	C0	90	5F	BE
33	41	C1	91	60	BF
34	42	C2	91	61	C0
35	43	C3	92	62	C1
36	44	C4	92	63	C2
37	45	C5	93	64	C3
38	46	C6	93	65	C4
39	47	C7	94	66	C5
40	48	C8	94	67	C6
41	49	C9	95	68	C7
42	4A	CA	95	69	C8
43	4B	CB	96	6A	C9
44	4C	CC	96	6B	CA
45	4D	CD	97	6C	CB
46	4E	CE	97	6D	CC
47	4F	CF	98	6E	CD

Row-Cell	ISO-2022	EUC	SJIS First Byte	SJIS Second Byte	
48	50	D0	98	6F	CE
49	51	D1	99	70	CF
50	52	D2	99	71	D0
51	53	D3	9A	72	D1
52	54	D4	9A	73	D2
53	55	D5	9B	74	D3
54	56	D6	9B	75	D4
55	57	D7	9C	76	D5
56	58	D8	9C	77	D6
57	59	D9	9D	78	D7
58	5A	DA	9D	79	D8
59	5B	DB	9E	7A	D9
60	5C	DC	9E	7B	DA
61	5D	DD	9F	7C	DB
62	5E	DE	9F	7D	DC
63	5F	DF	E0	7E	DD
64	60	E0	E0	80	DE
65	61	E1	E1	81	DF
66	62	E2	E1	82	E0
67	63	E3	E2	83	E1
68	64	E4	E2	84	E2
69	65	E5	E3	85	E3
70	66	E6	E3	86	E4
71	67	E7	E4	87	E5
72	68	E8	E4	88	E6
73	69	E9	E5	89	E7
74	6A	EA	E5	8A	E8
75	6B	EB	E6	8B	E9
76	6C	EC	E6	8C	EA
77	6D	ED	E7	8D	EB
78	6E	EE	E7	8E	EC
79	6F	EF	E8	8F	ED
80	70	F0	E8	90	EE
81	71	F1	E9	91	EF
82	72	F2	E9	92	F0
83	73	F3	EA	93	F1
84	74	F4	EA	94	F2
85	75	F5	EB	95	F3
86	76	F6	EB	96	F4
87	77	F7	EC	97	F5
88	78	F8	EC	98	F6
89	79	F9	ED	99	F7
90	7A	FA	ED	9A	F8
91	7B	FB	EE	9B	F9
92	7C	FC	EE	9C	FA
93	7D	FD	EF	9D	FB
94	7E	FE	EF	9E	FC

The following table provides the correspondences between Row-Cell and Shift-JIS encodings for the Shift-JIS user-defined region (0xF0 through 0xFC). The principles for the previous code conversion table apply to this table.

Row-Cell	SJIS First Byte
95	F0
96	F0
97	F1
98	F1
99	F2
100	F2
101	F3
102	F3
103	F4
104	F4
105	F5
106	F5
107	F6
108	F6
109	F7
110	F7
111	F8
112	F8
113	F9
114	F9
115	FA
116	FA
117	FB
118	FB
119	FC
120	FC

B

Notation Conversion Table

The following two-page table lists all 256 eight-bit byte values in binary (base 2), octal (base 8), decimal (base 10), and hexadecimal (base 16) notations. While I commonly use decimal and hexadecimal notations throughout this book, there are some readers who are more familiar with other notations, such as octal. It is unlikely that many readers will be converting between binary and other notations, but you never know.

Use this table as your guide for converting data throughout this book between notations. The 94 printable ASCII characters are included, when appropriate, for reference purposes.

Base 2	Base 8	Base 10	Base 16	ASCII
00000000	000	0	00	<NUL>
00000001	001	1	01	<SOH>
00000010	002	2	02	<STX>
00000011	003	3	03	<ETX>
00000100	004	4	04	<EOT>
00000101	005	5	05	<ENQ>
00000110	006	6	06	<ACK>
00000111	007	7	07	<BEL>
00001000	010	8	08	<BS>
00001001	011	9	09	<HT>
00001010	012	10	0A	<LF>
00001011	013	11	0B	<VT>
00001100	014	12	0C	<FF>
00001101	015	13	0D	<CR>
00001110	016	14	0E	<SO>
00001111	017	15	0F	<SI>
00010000	020	16	10	<DLE>
00010001	021	17	11	<DC1>
00010010	022	18	12	<DC2>
00010011	023	19	13	<DC3>
00010100	024	20	14	<DC4>
00010101	025	21	15	<NAK>
00010110	026	22	16	<SYN>
00010111	027	23	17	<ETB>
00011000	030	24	18	<CAN>
00011001	031	25	19	<EM>
00011010	032	26	1A	<SUB>
00011011	033	27	1B	<ESC>
00011100	034	28	1C	<FS>
00011101	035	29	1D	<GS>
00011110	036	30	1E	<RS>
00011111	037	31	1F	<US>
00100000	040	32	20	<SP>
00100001	041	33	21	!
00100010	042	34	22	"
00100011	043	35	23	#
00100100	044	36	24	$
00100101	045	37	25	%
00100110	046	38	26	&
00100111	047	39	27	'
00101000	050	40	28	(
00101001	051	41	29	)
00101010	052	42	2A	*
00101011	053	43	2B	+
00101100	054	44	2C	,
00101101	055	45	2D	-
00101110	056	46	2E	.
00101111	057	47	2F	/
00110000	060	48	30	0
00110001	061	49	31	1
00110010	062	50	32	2
00110011	063	51	33	3
00110100	064	52	34	4
00110101	065	53	35	5
00110110	066	54	36	6
00110111	067	55	37	7
00111000	070	56	38	8
00111001	071	57	39	9
00111010	072	58	3A	:
00111011	073	59	3B	;
00111100	074	60	3C	<
00111101	075	61	3D	=
00111110	076	62	3E	>
00111111	077	63	3F	?

Base 2	Base 8	Base 10	Base 16	ASCII
01000000	100	64	40	@
01000001	101	65	41	A
01000010	102	66	42	B
01000011	103	67	43	C
01000100	104	68	44	D
01000101	105	69	45	E
01000110	106	70	46	F
01000111	107	71	47	G
01001000	110	72	48	H
01001001	111	73	49	I
01001010	112	74	4A	J
01001011	113	75	4B	K
01001100	114	76	4C	L
01001101	115	77	4D	M
01001110	116	78	4E	N
01001111	117	79	4F	O
01010000	120	80	50	P
01010001	121	81	51	Q
01010010	122	82	52	R
01010011	123	83	53	S
01010100	124	84	54	T
01010101	125	85	55	U
01010110	126	86	56	V
01010111	127	87	57	W
01011000	130	88	58	X
01011001	131	89	59	Y
01011010	132	90	5A	Z
01011011	133	91	5B	[
01011100	134	92	5C	\
01011101	135	93	5D	]
01011110	136	94	5E	^
01011111	137	95	5F	_
01100000	140	96	60	`
01100001	141	97	61	a
01100010	142	98	62	b
01100011	143	99	63	c
01100100	144	100	64	d
01100101	145	101	65	e
01100110	146	102	66	f
01100111	147	103	67	g
01101000	150	104	68	h
01101001	151	105	69	i
01101010	152	106	6A	j
01101011	153	107	6B	k
01101100	154	108	6C	l
01101101	155	109	6D	m
01101110	156	110	6E	n
01101111	157	111	6F	o
01110000	160	112	70	p
01110001	161	113	71	q
01110010	162	114	72	r
01110011	163	115	73	s
01110100	164	116	74	t
01110101	165	117	75	u
01110110	166	118	76	v
01110111	167	119	77	w
01111000	170	120	78	x
01111001	171	121	79	y
01111010	172	122	7A	z
01111011	173	123	7B	{
01111100	174	124	7C	|
01111101	175	125	7D	}
01111110	176	126	7E	~
01111111	177	127	7F	<DEL>

Base 2	Base 8	Base 10	Base 16	ASCII
10000000	200	128	80	
10000001	201	129	81	
10000010	202	130	82	
10000011	203	131	83	
10000100	204	132	84	
10000101	205	133	85	
10000110	206	134	86	
10000111	207	135	87	
10001000	210	136	88	
10001001	211	137	89	
10001010	212	138	8A	
10001011	213	139	8B	
10001100	214	140	8C	
10001101	215	141	8D	
10001110	216	142	8E	
10001111	217	143	8F	
10010000	220	144	90	
10010001	221	145	91	
10010010	222	146	92	
10010011	223	147	93	
10010100	224	148	94	
10010101	225	149	95	
10010110	226	150	96	
10010111	227	151	97	
10011000	230	152	98	
10011001	231	153	99	
10011010	232	154	9A	
10011011	233	155	9B	
10011100	234	156	9C	
10011101	235	157	9D	
10011110	236	158	9E	
10011111	237	159	9F	
10100000	240	160	A0	
10100001	241	161	A1	
10100010	242	162	A2	
10100011	243	163	A3	
10100100	244	164	A4	
10100101	245	165	A5	
10100110	246	166	A6	
10100111	247	167	A7	
10101000	250	168	A8	
10101001	251	169	A9	
10101010	252	170	AA	
10101011	253	171	AB	
10101100	254	172	AC	
10101101	255	173	AD	
10101110	256	174	AE	
10101111	257	175	AF	
10110000	260	176	B0	
10110001	261	177	B1	
10110010	262	178	B2	
10110011	263	179	B3	
10110100	264	180	B4	
10110101	265	181	B5	
10110110	266	182	B6	
10110111	267	183	B7	
10111000	270	184	B8	
10111001	271	185	B9	
10111010	272	186	BA	
10111011	273	187	BB	
10111100	274	188	BC	
10111101	275	189	BD	
10111110	276	190	BE	
10111111	277	191	BF	

Base 2	Base 8	Base 10	Base 16	ASCII
11000000	300	192	C0	
11000001	301	193	C1	
11000010	302	194	C2	
11000011	303	195	C3	
11000100	304	196	C4	
11000101	305	197	C5	
11000110	306	198	C6	
11000111	307	199	C7	
11001000	310	200	C8	
11001001	311	201	C9	
11001010	312	202	CA	
11001011	313	203	CB	
11001100	314	204	CC	
11001101	315	205	CD	
11001110	316	206	CE	
11001111	317	207	CF	
11010000	320	208	D0	
11010001	321	209	D1	
11010010	322	210	D2	
11010011	323	211	D3	
11010100	324	212	D4	
11010101	325	213	D5	
11010110	326	214	D6	
11010111	327	215	D7	
11011000	330	216	D8	
11011001	331	217	D9	
11011010	332	218	DA	
11011011	333	219	DB	
11011100	334	220	DC	
11011101	335	221	DD	
11011110	336	222	DE	
11011111	337	223	DF	
11100000	340	224	E0	
11100001	341	225	E1	
11100010	342	226	E2	
11100011	343	227	E3	
11100100	344	228	E4	
11100101	345	229	E5	
11100110	346	230	E6	
11100111	347	231	E7	
11101000	350	232	E8	
11101001	351	233	E9	
11101010	352	234	EA	
11101011	353	235	EB	
11101100	354	236	EC	
11101101	355	237	ED	
11101110	356	238	EE	
11101111	357	239	EF	
11110000	360	240	F0	
11110001	361	241	F1	
11110010	362	242	F2	
11110011	363	243	F3	
11110100	364	244	F4	
11110101	365	245	F5	
11110110	366	246	F6	
11110111	367	247	F7	
11111000	370	248	F8	
11111001	371	249	F9	
11111010	372	250	FA	
11111011	373	251	FB	
11111100	374	252	FC	
11111101	375	253	FD	
11111110	376	254	FE	
11111111	377	255	FF	

C

Vendor Character Set Standards

The material presented in this appendix supplements Chapter 3, *Character Set Standards*, by including detailed information on vendor CJKV character set standards. This appendix is primarily intended as reference material in the event that you need to deal with one of the included character set standards. The character set tables that are included supplement those that appear later in this book. This book's *Bibliography* has information on the documentation for some of the character set standards covered in this appendix.

Nearly all of the vendor character sets described in this appendix are based on one or more national standards, and usually provide additional symbols and Chinese characters. In addition, you will learn that many vendor-defined Chinese characters can be found in supplemental national character set standards, such as in Japan's JIS X 0212-1990 for Japanese vendor character sets.

The vendor character set standards covered in this appendix do not represent an exhaustive list—nearly every major computer manufacturer that does business in one or more CJKV locales has developed its own character set standard. This material shows you not only how diverse character sets can be, but also how they are not fully compatible with one another nor with the national character set standards covered in Chapter 3.

The Ideographic Rapporteur Group* (IRG; formerly CJK-JRG) has diligently worked on adding 6,582 more Chinese characters to Unicode. These additional characters have been approved and have mappings. Some of the characters you find in this appendix may soon become part of the Unicode character set (if they are not included already).

* *http://www.cs.cuhk.edu.hk/~irg/*

Many pages of this chapter are dedicated to IBM's Chinese, Japanese, and Korean character sets. For more detailed information on IBM's character sets, to include machine-readable mapping tables on CD-ROM, I strongly suggest that you buy IBM's *Character Data Representation Architecture Reference and Registry* (1995, IBM part number SC09-2190-00). Page 982 in Appendix T, *Software and Document Sources*, provides phone numbers and a URL for ordering this IBM publication.

Chinese Vendor Character Sets—China

Besides the GBK character set, which is an extended version of GB 2312-80, there are vendor character sets developed by Apple for MacOS-S and by IBM for its operating systems. All of these vendor character sets are based on GB 2312-80, as shown in Table C-1.

Table C-1: Vendor Character Set Standards—China

Character Set	Other	User-Defined
DEC Hanzi		8,178
IBM Simplified Chinese	31	1,900[a]
MacOS-S	4	

[a] IBM Simplified Chinese DBCS-Host encoding permits up to 1,900 user-defined characters, but IBM Simplified Chinese DBCS-PC encoding permits only up to 1,880.

DEC Hanzi

The DEC Hanzi character set is the GB 2312-80 character set in the standard 94×94 matrix plus an additional 94×94 matrix set aside for user-defined characters. Specifically, rows 1 through 87 of this additional matrix are for user-defined characters.

IBM Simplified Chinese

The Simplified Chinese character set as used by IBM is based on GB 2312-80, and adds 31 additional characters that are considered to be IBM Simplified Chinese Selected Characters. Depending on the encoding, 1,900 (DBCS-Host) or 1,880 (DBCS-PC) user-defined characters are available.

The 6,763 hanzi in the IBM Simplified Chinese character set are in the same order as in GB 2312-80. The same is true for the GB 2312-80 non-hanzi, but only for DBCS-PC encoding—DBCS-Host encoding uses a completely different ordering for these characters.

The IBM Simplified Chinese DBCS-Host character set, also known as IBM Code Page 00837, is arranged as shown in Table C-2.

Table C-2: IBM Simplified Chinese DBCS-Host Character Set

Character Type	Number of Characters
Full-width space	1
Non-hanzi[a]	712
GB 2312-80 Level 1 hanzi	3,755
GB 2312-80 Level 2 hanzi	3,008
User-defined characters	1,900

[a] Includes the 31 IBM Selected Characters.

Table C-3 illustrates the IBM Simplified Chinese DBCS-PC character set, also known as IBM Code Page 00928. Note how the 31 IBM Selected Characters are separate from the GB 2312-80 non-hanzi, but are combined in the IBM DBCS-Host character set.

Table C-3: IBM Simplified Chinese DBCS-PC Character Set

Character Type	Number of Characters
GB 2312-80 non-hanzi	682
GB 2312-80 Level 1 hanzi	3,755
GB 2312-80 Level 2 hanzi	3,008
User-defined characters	1,880
IBM Selected Characters	31

According to older IBM documentation (from 1985), GB 2312-80 79-81 has the form 鍾, but according to more recent IBM documentation (from 1993), the correct form, 锺, is used. The IBM Simplified Chinese DBCS-Host and DBCS-PC encodings for this character are 0x6892 and 0xA891, respectively.

The single-byte portion of IBM's equivalent to GB 1988-89 (GB-Roman) is different from both ASCII and GB-Roman. Table C-4 illustrates the differences among these character sets for two code points.

Table C-4: IBM Variation of GB 1988-89

Code Point	ASCII	GB 1988-89	IBM
24	$ (dollar)	¥ (yuan)	$ (dollar)
5C	\ (backslash)	\ (backslash)	¥ (yuan)

The 31 IBM Selected Characters that are included in the IBM Simplified Chinese character set are listed below in a DBCS-PC encoding table.

Row FA	0	1	2	3	4	5	6	7	8	9	A	B	C	D	E	F
4		ⅰ	ⅱ	ⅲ	ⅳ	ⅴ	ⅵ	ⅶ	ⅷ	ⅸ	ⅹ					
5	￢	￤	＇													
6	ー	￥	゛	゜	ヽ	ヾ										
7	-	仝	〆	〇	〒	㈱	℡	‥	ゝ	ゞ	▽	▼				
8																
9																
A																
B																
C																
D																
E																
F																

Table C-5 lists the correspondences among these 31 IBM Selected Characters in DBCS-PC and DBCS-Host encodings.

Table C-5: DBCS-PC and DBCS-Host Encoding for 31 IBM Selected Characters

Character	DBCS-PC	DBCS-Host
ⅰ	FA41	41B1
ⅱ	FA42	41B2
ⅲ	FA43	41B3
ⅳ	FA44	41B4
ⅴ	FA45	41B5
ⅵ	FA46	41B6
ⅶ	FA47	41B7
ⅷ	FA48	41B8
ⅸ	FA49	41B9
ⅹ	FA4A	41BA
￢	FA50	425F
￤	FA51	426A
＇	FA52	427D
ー	FA60	4358
￥	FA61	435B
゛	FA62	43BE
゜	FA63	43BF

Table C-5: DBCS-PC and DBCS-Host Encoding for 31 IBM Selected Characters (continued)

Character	DBCS-PC	DBCS-Host
ヽ	FA64	43DC
ヾ	FA65	43DD
-	FA70	445A
仝	FA71	445C
〆	FA72	445E
○	FA73	445F
〒	FA74	446C
㈱	FA75	446D
℡	FA76	446F
‥	FA77	447E
ゝ	FA78	44DC
ゞ	FA79	44DD
▽	FA7A	44EB
▼	FA7B	44EC

MacOS-S Character Set

The MacOS-S character set, put simply, is based on the GB 2312-80 character set, encoded according to EUC-CN encoding, with some minor differences in the single-byte range.

The single-byte range, used for encoding ASCII or GB-Roman, uses four additional code points, as illustrated in Table C-6.

Table C-6: Additional MacOS-S Single-Byte Characters

Code Point	Character
80	ü ("u" with diaeresis)
FD	© (copyright)
FE	™ (trademark)
FF	… (ellipsis)

Two of these additional single-byte code points, specifically 0xFD and 0xFE, affect EUC-CN encoding by making rows 0xFD and 0xFE unavailable for encoding two-byte characters (there are no characters in those rows, so there are no adverse effects).

Chinese Vendor Character Sets—Taiwan

Nearly all vendors in Taiwan have standardized on Big Five for their character set, and use it as their base. Thus, most of the vendor character sets described in this section are based on Big Five, as shown in Table C-7.

Table C-7: Vendor Character Set Standards—Taiwan

Character Set	Additional Hanzi	Other	User-defined
DEC Hanyu	13,446[a]		3,587
ETen	7	399	
IBM Traditional Chinese	3	563	6,204
MacOS-T		34	
Microsoft Traditional Chinese	7	34	

[a] CNS 11643-1992 Planes 3 and 4.

DEC Hanyu

The DEC Hanyu ("Hanyu" is the transliterated form of the Chinese word 漢語 *hànyŭ* that means "Chinese") character set is CNS 11643-1992 Planes 1 through 4 set in four standard 94×94 matrixes. Empty code points in Planes 1 and 2 are used for providing up to 3,587 user-defined characters, specifically the ranges that are provided in Table C-8.

Table C-8: DEC Hanyu User-Defined Regions

Plane	Range	Number of Code Points
1	FDCC–FEFE	145
1	AAA1–C1FE	2,256
2	F245–FE7E	1,186

The most common implementation of DEC Hanyu includes only CNS 11643-1992 Planes 1 and 2 (more or less compatible with Big Five), but Planes 3 and 4 are also available as an extension called DTSCS (Digital Taiwan Supplementary Character Set).

ETen Character Set

ETen (倚天資訊股份有限公司 *yĭtiān zīxùn gŭfèn yŏuxiàn gōngsī*) has developed what appears to be the most widely-used Big Five extension. Microsoft's Traditional Chinese character set includes the second block of the ETen character set, (that is, the 7 hanzi and 34 non-hanzi at the end of row 0xF9).

The ETen character set's extension to Big Five includes two blocks of characters, as follows:

- The first block that contains 365 characters begins at 0xC6A1 and extends, without gaps, to 0xC8D3. This block includes encircled numerals 1–10, parenthesized numerals 1–10, lowercase Roman numerals 1–10, radicals and radical-like elements, Japanese characters (including kana), the upper- and lowercase Cyrillic alphabet, and ETen input codes (used for ETen's "Row Column" input method*).
- The second block, consisting of seven hanzi (碁銹裏墻恒粧嫺; 0xF9D6 through 0xF9DC) and 34 line-drawing characters, begins at 0xF9D6 and extends, without gaps, to 0xF9FE. Note that 0xF9D5 is the last Big Five hanzi.

The following tables illustrate all 406 ETen-specific characters, as encoded according to Big Five:

Row C6	0	1	2	3	4	5	6	7	8	9	A	B	C	D	E	F
4																
5																
6																
7																
A		①	②	③	④	⑤	⑥	⑦	⑧	⑨	⑩	⑴	⑵	⑶	⑷	⑸
B	⑹	⑺	⑻	⑼	⑽	ⅰ	ⅱ	ⅲ	ⅳ	ⅴ	ⅵ	ⅶ	ⅷ	ⅸ	ⅹ	⼂
C	⼃	⼅	⼇	⼌	⼍	⼎	⼓	⼕	⼙	⼛	⼢	⼧	⼮	⼳	⼴	⼵
D	⼹	⼺	⽀	⽆	⽧	⽨	⾌	⾪	¨	ˆ	ヽ	ヾ	ゝ	ゞ	〃	仝
E	々	〆	〇	ー	［	］	✽	ぁ	あ	ぃ	い	ぅ	う	ぇ	え	ぉ
F	お	か	が	き	ぎ	く	ぐ	け	げ	こ	ご	さ	ざ	し	じ	

Row C7	0	1	2	3	4	5	6	7	8	9	A	B	C	D	E	F
4	す	ず	せ	ぜ	そ	ぞ	た	だ	ち	ぢ	っ	つ	づ	て	で	と
5	ど	な	に	ぬ	ね	の	は	ば	ぱ	ひ	び	ぴ	ふ	ぶ	ぷ	へ
6	べ	ぺ	ほ	ぼ	ぽ	ま	み	む	め	も	ゃ	や	ゅ	ゆ	ょ	よ
7	ら	り	る	れ	ろ	ゎ	わ	ゐ	ゑ	を	ん	ァ	ア	ィ	イ	
A		ゥ	ウ	ェ	エ	ォ	オ	カ	ガ	キ	ギ	ク	グ	ケ	ゲ	コ
B	ゴ	サ	ザ	シ	ジ	ス	ズ	セ	ゼ	ソ	ゾ	タ	ダ	チ	ヂ	ッ
C	ツ	ヅ	テ	デ	ト	ド	ナ	ニ	ヌ	ネ	ノ	ハ	バ	パ	ヒ	ビ
D	ピ	フ	ブ	プ	ヘ	ベ	ペ	ホ	ボ	ポ	マ	ミ	ム	メ	モ	ャ
E	ヤ	ュ	ユ	ョ	ヨ	ラ	リ	ル	レ	ロ	ヮ	ワ	ヰ	ヱ	ヲ	ン
F	ヴ	ヵ	ヶ	А	Б	В	Г	Д	Е	Ё	Ж	З	И	Й	К	

* Written 行列輸入法 (*hánglìè shūrùfǎ*) in Chinese.

Row C8	0	1	2	3	4	5	6	7	8	9	A	B	C	D	E	F
4	Л	М	Н	О	П	Р	С	Т	У	Ф	Х	Ц	Ч	Ш	Щ	Ъ
5	Ы	Ь	Э	Ю	Я	а	б	в	г	д	е	ё	ж	з	и	й
6	к	л	м	н	о	п	р	с	т	у	ф	х	ц	ч	ш	щ
7	ъ	ы	ь	э	ю	я	⇧	↸	⇆	㇏	㇆	㇗	㇇	刂	䒑	
A		⻍	冈	⊠	㐆	1-	58	3⁹₈	3-	3²₁	4-	5-	6-	81	7-	8-
B	9-	7⁰₈	6⁰₇	9²₁	01	1²₁	41	2-	5²₁	71	4⁹₈	2²₁	2⁹₈	6²₁	1⁰₈	1⁶₃
C	2⁵₃	3⁶₃	4⁶₃	5⁶₃	6⁶₃	7⁶₃	86	9⁶₅	0⁶₃	88	9⁹₈	08	0-	¬	¦	'
D	"	㈱	No.	Tel												
E																
F																

Row F9	0	1	2	3	4	5	6	7	8	9	A	B	C	D	E	F
4																
5																
6																
7																
A																
B																
C																
D							碁	銹	裏	墻	恒	粧	嫺	┌	┬	┐
E	├	┼	┤	└	┴	┘	┌	┬	┐	├	┼	┤	└	┴	┘	┌
F	┬	┐	├	┼	┤	└	┴	┘	│	─	╭	╮	╰	╯	■	

It is interesting to note that all seven ETen-specific hanzi map to CNS 11643-1992 Plane 3, as detailed in Table C-9.

Table C-9: Mapping Seven ETen Hanzi to CNS 11643-1992 Plane 3

Hanzi	ETen Code	CNS 11643-1992 Plane 3
碁	F9D6	35-23
銹	F9D7	47-48
裏	F9D8	36-46
墻	F9D9	48-42
恒	F9DA	12-61
粧	F9DB	29-94
嫺	F9DC	43-60

IBM Traditional Chinese

Table C-10 illustrates the IBM Traditional Chinese DBCS-Host character set, also known as IBM Code Page 00835.

Table C-10: IBM Traditional Chinese DBCS-Host Character Set

Character Type	Number of Characters
Full-width space	1
Non-hanzi	1,003
Big Five Level 1 hanzi	5,402[a]
Big Five Level 2 hanzi	7,654[b]
User-defined characters	6,204

[a] Includes 1 IBM Traditional Chinese Selected Hanzi appended at the end.
[b] Includes 2 IBM Traditional Chinese Selected Hanzi appended at the end.

Table C-11 illustrates the IBM Traditional Chinese DBCS-PC character set, also known as IBM Code Page 00927.

Table C-11: IBM Traditional Chinese DBCS-PC Character Set

Character Type	Number of Characters
Non-hanzi	1,004
Big Five Level 1 hanzi	5,402[a]
Big Five Level 2 hanzi	7,654[b]
User-defined characters	6,204

[a] Includes 1 IBM Traditional Chinese Selected Hanzi appended at the end.
[b] Includes 2 IBM Traditional Chinese Selected Hanzi appended at the end.

The only difference between IBM Traditional Chinese DBCS-Host and DBCS-PC is that the full-width space character is treated specially in DBCS-Host, but included with the other non-hanzi in DBCS-PC. The 1,004 non-hanzi consist of the 441 non-hanzi in Big Five, another 243 that are specific to CNS 11643-1992 (introduced in CNS 11643-1986), and another 320 that are in neither Big Five nor CNS 11643-1992.

As alluded to in the table notes of Tables C-10 and C-11, there are a total of three IBM Traditional Chinese Selected Hanzi. These three hanzi are listed in Table C-12, which also shows how they relate to CNS 11643-1992.

Table C-12: Three IBM Traditional Chinese Selected Hanzi

Hanzi	DBCS-PC	DBCS-Host	CNS 11643-1992
撐	A8CA	68CB	Plane 1 76-93
糹	D1C5	91C6	Plane 2 22-24
溹	D1C6	91C7	Plane 2 36-19

These three IBM Traditional Chinese Selected Hanzi, curiously, are in CNS 11643-1992 Planes 1 or 2. You might be wondering about this, knowing that CNS 11643-1992 Planes 1 and 2 are equivalent to Big Five. Put simply, these three hanzi are considered IBM Selected Hanzi in DBCS-PC and DBCS-Host, and represent the hanzi forms that are now in use by Big Five and CNS 11643-1992. The Level 1 and 2 hanzi in IBM Traditional Chinese are based on hanzi forms found in the original Big Five definition published in 1984. Table C-13 illustrates how these three hanzi and their variant forms are included in IBM Traditional Chinese, and how they map to Big Five and CNS 11643-1992 (those that are considered IBM Traditional Chinese Selected Hanzi—that is, appended at the end of Level 1 and Level 2—are emboldened).

Table C-13: Three IBM Traditional Chinese Selected Hanzi and Their Variants

Hanzi	DBCS-PC	DBCS-Host	CNS 11643-1992	Big Five	Big Five (1984)
撐	**A8CA**	**68CB**	Plane 1 76-93	BCB5	
撑	A09C	609D	Plane 3 44-27	**F286**[a]	BCB5
柒	**D1C5**	**91C6**	Plane 2 22-24	D5D4	
桼	B3B7	73B8	Plane 3 28-19	**F287**[a]	D5D4
溱	**D1C6**	**91C7**	Plane 2 36-19	DE4D	
溱	BAB3	7AB4	Plane 3 34-13	**F288**[a]	DE4D

[a] IBM Selected Hanzi code points.

It is interesting that what is considered IBM Selected Hanzi depends on what encoding is used. The older IBM encodings, DBCS-Host and DBCS-PC, share the same definition of what is considered IBM Selected Hanzi, but more contemporary IBM encodings consider the other forms to be IBM Selected Hanzi.

MacOS-T Character Set

The MacOS-T character set is based on the Big Five character set with the addition of 30 annotated numerals (the same 30 that constitute CNS 11643-1992 Plane 1's row 6, specifically encircled, parenthesized, and lowercase Roman numeral forms of 1 through 10).

In addition, the single-byte range, used for encoding ASCII or CNS-Roman, uses four additional code points, as illustrated in Table C-14.

Table C-14: Additional MacOS-T Single-Byte Characters

Code Point	Character
80	ü ("u" with diaeresis)
FD	© (copyright)

Table C-14: Additional MacOS-T Single-Byte Characters (continued)

Code Point	Character
FE	™ (trademark)
FF	… (ellipsis)

Like with the MacOS-S character set, 0xFD and 0xFE are used as single-byte characters, so they are not available for encoding two-byte characters. This affects any vendor extension that encodes characters in either of these two rows. DynaLab's Hong Kong extension, for example, normally encodes characters in rows 0xFD and 0xFE.

Microsoft Traditional Chinese

The Microsoft Traditional Chinese character set, known as Microsoft Code Page 950, is based on Big Five, and includes only the second block of ETen characters, specifically those hanzi and non-hanzi from row 0xF9 (0xF9D6 through 0xF9FE).

Chinese Vendor Character Sets—Hong Kong

While the largest Hong Kong character set is clearly that designed by the Hong Kong government, two major Big Five extensions for Hong Kong have been developed independently of and conflicting with one another. Table C-15 lists three Hong Kong extensions.

Table C-15: Vendor Character Set Standards—Hong Kong

Character Set	Base Set	Hanzi	Other
DynaLab HK A	Big Five	784	
DynaLab HK B	Big Five	665	746
Monotype Hong Kong	Big Five	471	

For more detailed information on these and other Hong Kong extensions, I highly recommend reading Dirk Meyer's informative article entitled "Dealing With Hong Kong Specific Characters" (*MultiLingual Communications & Technology*, Number 19, Volume 9, Issue 3, April 1998, pp 35–38).

DynaLab Hong Kong Extensions

DynaLab (華康科技開發股份有限公司 *huákāng kējì kāifā gǔfèn yǒuxiàn gōngsī*), headquartered in Taiwan, developed two of its own Hong Kong extensions for Big Five. One extension contains 784 hanzi (Dirk Meyer calls this "DynaLab HK A") spread over five rows: 0xFA through 0xFE; and the other contains 1,411 characters (665 hanzi plus 746 symbols, which Dirk calls "DynaLab HK B"). However,

DynaLab's font products for Hong Kong appear to be shifting toward Hong Kong GCCS, which was described in Chapter 3.

The DynaLab HK A set includes several duplicate hanzi. Both groups of duplicate hanzi, listed in Table C-16, consists of 30 hanzi each. The first group, on the left, are those that are duplicately encoded within the DynaLab HK A set itself, and the second group, on the right, are those that are duplicates of standard Big Five hanzi.

Table C-16: Duplicate Hanzi in DynaLab HK A

Hanzi	DynaLab HK A	Hanzi	DynaLab HK A	Big Five
礆	FB52,FD5A	靚	FAC8	E8B0
祇	FB53,FD5E	祇	FB53	ACE9
褸	FB54,FD60	蟄	FB5C	EE68
秄	FB55,FD62	呶	FBD1	A94C
瘻	FB56,FD6E	唉	FBD3	ADFC
癎	FB57,FD70	姒	FBF4	A971
絝	FB59,FDB0	姘	FBF7	ABB9
鑘	FB5A,FDB7	帙	FC4A	CC6F
膀	FB5B,FDC5	徽	FC5D	E975
蟄	FB5C,FDD0	悛	FC61	D1AA
蟮	FB5D,FDD3	惚	FC63	B1AB
衩	FB5E,FDDC	憩	FC6F	BECD
袜	FB5F,FDDE	撐	FCA3	BCB5
罸	FB60,FDE5	攢	FCA5	F6E3
葬	FB61,FDEF	朵	FCAC	A6B7
蘯	FB62,FDFA	杲	FCB0	AA58
覞	FB63,FE40	涅	FCD1	AF49
卹	FB64,FE5C	煆	FCE5	B7DA
鉢	FB65,FE70	焊	FCE8	E667
鋉	FB66,FE71	斑	FCFA	D670
颸	FB67,FEB9	祇	FD5E	ACE9
舘	FB68,FEBC	祕	FD5F	AFA6
餡	FB69,FEC0	筋	FD77	B5AC
饍	FB6A,FEC2	籙	FDA2	F6FC
騌	FB6B,FEC6	腓	FDC2	B5CC
髗	FB6C,FECA	蟄	FDD0	EE68
髴	FB6D,FECF	祛	FDDF	D7B6
鷄	FB6E,FEEB	讞	FE4A	F9A9

Table C-16: Duplicate Hanzi in DynaLab HK A (continued)

Hanzi	DynaLab HK A	Hanzi	DynaLab HK A	Big Five
馨	FB6F,FEF1	鋨	FE72	E872
鼦	FB70,FEF7	隃	FEA1	DCA2

If you examine the contents of Table C-16 carefully, you'll discover that two hanzi include three instances each, one in Big Five, and two in DynaLab HK A: 衹 (0xACE9, 0xFB53, and 0xFD5E) and 蟄 (0xEE68, 0xFB5C, 0xFDD0).

The following five encoding tables illustrate the complete DynaLab HK A extension for Big Five, which contains 784 hanzi. Note that 0xFA40 is intentionally left empty.

Row FA	0	1	2	3	4	5	6	7	8	9	A	B	C	D	E	F
4		弌	丏	甲	由	氹	叶	亘	両	吖	吔	坳	邨	呍	汹	剅
5	担	効	宝	叁	[illegible]	[illegible]	拃	攜	揑	怱	咗	[illegible]	哝	[illegible]	[illegible]	哋
6	枱	[illegible]	啱	[illegible]	肶	笋	迹	响	珏	烟	疱	峯	冧	[illegible]	啫	𠝹
7	[illegible]	埗	啤	舦	呃	咔	猪	[illegible]	嗞	掹	梘	咭	[illegible]	吓	啩	
A		欖	啲	脷	葱	琼	着	靭	揸	鈎	疴	[illegible]	廸	掾	廻	廼
B	搵	喺	疊	㗎	嘅	鈪	𨋢	韮	滙	菓	賍	嘷	嗰	[illegible]	䘏	悞
C	綉	嘢	嗺	煅	嫲	蔴	糍	諗	靚	剷	噏	噃	瞓	螆	踭	膶
D	湴	[illegible]	衞	燶	湼	[illegible]	餸	刦	蠄	嚀	嚓	鎅	坂	鐣	[illegible]	鰂
E	[illegible]	画	鉄	[illegible]	鑛	鱲	攞	[illegible]	拎	攣	醃	祢	决	[illegible]	矾	碍
F	浜	[illegible]	却	羣	踪	栢	煊	躭	綫	軚	虬	[illegible]	沢	羗	粮	

Row FB	0	1	2	3	4	5	6	7	8	9	A	B	C	D	E	F
4	窰	牀	壳	毡	塲	隣	麫	學	胆	膺	拗	芪	肽	[illegible]	杧	洚
5	塱	葛	礆	衹	褸	秄	瘦	癎	筋	絝	鑪	勝	蟄	蜡	衸	袜
6	罸	莽	藴	覸	邮	鉢	録	颸	舘	餡	饍	騌	髗	髴	鷄	馨
7	鼦	个	丞	从	仮	仔	休	伹	伲	俤	俥	侫	偖	㑳	倮	
A		倣	偬	偦	働	僙	儎	僭	儁	凭	凴	㓮	剢	刻	剳	劚
B	勅	勑	勠	勳	双	叙	冲	况	冴	凉	凑	凓	凟	匁	畆	凾
C	匲	匬	匳	厫	厠	厨	厦	厪	厮	厐	咏	呩	吡	咜	呪	吲
D	咤	[illegible]	叚	唉	啳	喆	嗯	喰	㖎	嗽	啗	嗪	[illegible]	嘑	噍	嗥
E	[illegible]	噔	嗒	[illegible]	哚	噟	嘎	坟	坆	坺	坧	堺	埦	埝	塀	壻
F	塩	堦	壜	妋	姒	妬	姙	姘	姹	媏	娟	尅	尠	届	屬	

Row FC	0	1	2	3	4	5	6	7	8	9	A	B	C	D	E	F
4	炭	峑	峩	嵗	嵆	嶎	𡻕	巵	帋	帒	帙	帮	幞	弌	彍	宂
5	灾	穽	寃	窻	廊	廹	园	国	彺	徫	徤	徧	徺	徼	㲎	您
6	恩	悛	惧	惚	悳	惩	惣	悧	惛	悓	慂	憔	惰	慙	慯	憇
7	憾	慤	慜	憙	懢	戚	戹	扨	扚	抂	抦	拕	掘	拼	捬	
A		捿	携	撐	擥	攢	晈	晧	暎	晋	朞	条	朶	栃	枠	栅
B	呆	柹	栂	梶	椬	椚	楟	椀	棊	楕	楳	榀	楡	樋	榲	槀
C	榊	槼	槺	槩	欄	樫	橺	橒	檝	櫊	欝	歒	毹	泪	洫	泎
D	洤	涅	湏	涹	漱	潜	濟	澅	瀞	濼	濶	炉	畑	炁	炑	点
E	焇	煹	煶	煱	熒	煆	㷆	熵	熚	燹	牐	牕	犇	猬	犲	狢
F	猂	献	猛	猨	獏	獱	斅	縠	氳	珉	珽	瑝	瑠	瑨	瑭	

Row FD	0	1	2	3	4	5	6	7	8	9	A	B	C	D	E	F
4	瓧	瓱	瓲	瓰	甅	甎	瓸	甞	畚	畊	畠	畺	疎	皞	皁	盌
5	盖	眤	眫	眦	䁥	瞹	砣	磓	碱	磘	礆	磁	礐	礉	祇	祕
6	禝	禩	秄	秔	𥞊	稭	稾	稺	竓	竝	竚	竪	痃	瘇	瘦	瘂
7	痼	癧	癯	癮	䇆	笔	笹	筋	笊	箒	箣	篏	篍	篼	篩	
A		籑	籙	籯	籰	籾	粆	粃	粬	糇	糂	糏	糀	糕	紝	絚
B	絝	綳	緜	緵	縧	繮	罇	罎	耝	聢	聣	聰	聛	脉	脇	肦
C	脃	脂	腓	脈	腈	勝	臈	皐	臯	臸	舚	舜	艢	蝨	蟓	盤
D	蟄	䗥	蟎	蟮	蟳	蟖	蠋	蠏	蠘	蠭	衂	衅	衹	衮	袜	袪
E	袵	袠	䘯	褁	褋	罫	罱	罸	芦	苷	苽	苦	苐	莅	荼	莽
F	萠	䖃	蓚	蒽	蒭	蔲	蔬	薛	藥	蘐	蘯	覇	覉	覊	覔	

Row FE	0	1	2	3	4	5	6	7	8	9	A	B	C	D	E	F
4	覗	覩	覼	訩	諔	謌	讃	譃	讁	譌	讞	貭	賫	賣	贌	贖
5	趂	趦	跔	踨	踁	䟘	蹷	蹵	躧	軀	轃	轜	邮	郄	酐	酖
6	酜	酙	酞	酧	醯	醎	醻	辷	辻	込	迋	迚	適	遡	遻	釾
7	鉢	録	鋨	鍈	鍪	鉣	鍮	鎺	鐗	閅	閧	阫	阸	陁	陡	
A		隃	隖	隁	隽	霂	霦	靍	靆	靟	鞟	鞴	韠	鞺	鞾	韈
B	韵	頟	頪	顩	頳	顋	顚	顥	颭	颷	飜	飦	舘	饂	餹	餻
C	餡	饊	饍	馱	駄	駚	騌	騐	骺	骽	髗	鬪	鬮	鬭	髦	髴
D	鬂	鬖	鬠	鬘	鬛	魰	鮏	鮎	鮝	鮗	鮰	鰌	鰕	鰊	鯿	鰯
E	鰐	鰮	鱅	鱉	鰺	嶋	鳰	鵞	鵇	鶍	鶇	鶏	鸜	麁	麄	麐
F	麢	麘	麞	麨	麯	麿	黈	鼦	鼂	竈	齅	齓	齚	齩	齸	

When DynaLab HK A is implemented on MacOS-T, rows 0xFD and 0xFE are not accessible because those two code points are reserved for single-byte characters, as indicated in Table C-14 on page 563.

Monotype Hong Kong Extension

Monotype's Hong Kong extension to Big Five contains exactly 471 hanzi spread over three rows: 0xFA through 0xFC. Knowing that each Big Five row contains exactly 157 characters, encoded in the ranges 0x40–0x7E and 0xA1–0xFE, tells us that all three of these rows are completely full (in terms of Big Five encoding principles).

The following tables constitute Monotype's Hong Kong extension:

Row FA	0	1	2	3	4	5	6	7	8	9	A	B	C	D	E	F
4	両	亘	画	畺	氹	宄	衮	裏	仔	伲	佪	侫	倮	偬	傈	働
5	傻	儎	健	円	冚	冧	冪	决	冲	冸	凉	凓	凭	凴	凾	刅
6	刧	刼	刽	刱	劉	劏	劵	効	勅	勠	勺	卬	却	鄂	厓	雁
7	壓	叁	参	叚	叠	叶	卟	吓	吖	吔	呍	吡	呋	咗	咔	
A		咝	咏	呪	响	哋	哝	哌	哐	咟	咤	唂	唞	唓	啫	啱
B	啲	啩	咀	唿	㖼	咕	喺	喼	嘅	喋	嗞	喹	啍	嗰	嗘	㗎
C	嗎	嗪	㗉	嗙	噉	嘢	嗺	嘞	嘡	嗬	嘑	啓	噃	噍	嘭	噏
D	噔	嗒	噝	嗥	噻	噼	嚡	噟	嘮	嚒	嚟	嚤	嚿	嚩	圩	坂
E	坳	坆	壳	埗	型	塱	堺	堦	塲	墻	壜	壠	囪	妬	姙	媖
F	嬎	嫏	媁	嫲	嫺	孭	宝	寗	屘	屌	尅	岢	岪	峯	峩	

Row FB	0	1	2	3	4	5	6	7	8	9	A	B	C	D	E	F
4	崐	崕	嵆	嵖	嵛	嵴	帋	帙	幞	乾	幺	庽	庛	廊	廸	廹
5	廼	廻	弍	彍	徧	怤	怱	恒	悞	惧	憜	憋	慙	憹	懢	抅
6	拗	抐	担	抦	拃	捞	拪	挵	掹	捬	揸	揘	掾	掿	搸	携
7	摚	撐	搔	擧	攜	擡	攞	攣	敍	甴	曱	肶	胆	脉	脇	
A		脷	脈	腊	腭	膄	膶	腸	曝	杧	枱	栀	栢	梘	椁	楳
B	榘	榻	榲	樋	樫	橈	欝	欸	毡	毑	汹	沢	浜	涖	湼	滙
C	滘	澗	潤	澟	灩	点	畑	烟	烱	煱	燜	煶	煊	煅	煲	燶
D	燓	燨	牀	犂	犏	狍	猂	猄	猵	猹	猬	猨	献	珐	珏	珉
E	琼	畋	疎	疴	疱	痨	瘇	瘢	痐	瘻	瘩	癦	癪	癧	癵	皀
F	眜	盌	眫	着	睸	睺	瞓	瞹	矾	䂙	砵	碍	碁	碱	䃈	

Row FC	0	1	2	3	4	5	6	7	8	9	A	B	C	D	E	F
4	磘	礮	祢	袂	禝	秆	稭	穅	穉	穷	窑	窰	竚	竪	笋	箒
5	筅	簕	粧	粮	粦	糍	糉	紮	絝	綫	綉	綳	縧	繮	縛	罇
6	罎	羗	羓	羣	羮	卧	耻	舦	芭	芪	茉	菓	葛	萘	莖	韮
7	葱	蒓	蔴	虬	蚲	蚺	螆	螋	蟎	蟮	蠄	蟖	衅	衞	𧘹	
A		袜	袴	袵	䘏	褡	裯	覉	覊	靚	覥	訩	誺	譌	謟	謭
B	賍	跖	踪	踭	蹱	蹚	躭	躰	軚	䡈	轅	轉	込	迹	逈	逾
C	邨	酞	酰	酧	酶	醌	鈎	鈪	銽	鉄	鉢	銃	銹	鍥	錭	鑛
D	鐪	閚	闃	隣	靭	韜	韹	韵	顥	颴	餎	餜	餸	饈	饍	饟
E	駡	騐	驫	骶	髗	鬃	鬪	鬭	鮎	鮍	鯏	鰂	鰐	鯿	鰺	鰛
F	鰺	鱅	鱉	鱲	鴳	鶓	鶇	鷄	麖	麪	麬	麯	鼦	齇	教	

The ordering of Monotype's Hong Kong extension follows indexing radical, then total number of strokes. The only exception appears to be the very last hanzi, encoded at 0xFCFE (教).

This Big Five extension is not limited to Monotype's own font products. Arphic Technology, for example, has standardized on Monotype's Hong Kong Big Five extension for their Chinese fonts intended to be used in the Hong Kong market.

Japanese Vendor Character Sets

A large number of Japanese developers have established their own extensions to JIS X 0208:1997 (or earlier versions), usually to accommodate non-JIS characters that are important for their users. The following sections describe many vendor-defined Japanese character sets, all of which are based on JIS X 0208:1997 or earlier. Table C-17 summarizes these character sets.

Table C-17: Vendor Character Set Standards—Japan

Character Set	Base Set	Additional Kanji	Other	User-Defined
Biblos Gaiji Set	*not applicable*	365	1,406	
DEC Kanji	JIS X 0208:1997			2,914
Enfour Gaiji Set	*not applicable*	348	1,156	
FMR Kanji	JIS X 0208-1983		3	2,444
Fontworks Japanese	JIS X 0208-1990	530	207	
HP Kanji	JIS X 0208-1983			5,366
IBM Japanese	JIS X 0208-1990	360	28	4,370[a]
IKIS	JIS X 0208-1983[b]		63	376
JEF	JIS C 6226-1978	4,039	1,010	3,102[c]
KanjiTalk6	JIS X 0208-1983		135	2,444
KanjiTalk7	JIS X 0208-1990		313	2,444

Table C-17: Vendor Character Set Standards—Japan (continued)

Character Set	Base Set	Additional Kanji	Other	User-Defined
KEIS78	JIS C 6226-1978	2,042	1,021	3,008
KEIS83	JIS X 0208-1983	2,200	966	3,008
NEC Kanji	JIS C 6226-1978	3,382	1,090	2,256[d]
NTT Kanji	JIS C 6226-1978	5,238	261	2,820
Super DEC Kanji	JIS X 0208:1997	5,801[e]	266[f]	11,374
TRON Code[g]	JIS X 0208-1990	5,801[e]	266[f]	27,720
Windows Japanese	JIS X 0208-1990	720[h]	42	1,880

[a] IBM Japanese DBCS-Host encoding permits up to 4,370 user-defined characters, but IBM Japanese DBCS-PC encoding permits only up to 1,880, and IBM Japanese DBCS-EUC encoding permits up to 2,538.
[b] That is, JIS X 0208-1983 less 32 line-drawing elements.
[c] 457 of these have been pre-assigned under some implementations.
[d] There are 2,256 user-defined characters in the Shift-JIS–encoded version of this character set. The ISO-2022-JP–encoded version is usually limited to 188 user-defined characters.
[e] JIS X 0212-1990 kanji.
[f] JIS X 0212-1990 non-kanji.
[g] Can also include GB 2312-80 and KS X 1001:1992.
[h] The 360 IBM Selected Kanji appear twice, which is where this figure comes from.

Information about additional Japanese vendor character set standards is available online.*

Biblos Gaiji Character Set

In addition to there being various vendor-specific extensions to JIS X 0208:1997, a company called DTP center Biblos has developed a series of "Gaiji" fonts that have become extremely popular in Japan.† One reason for their popularity, especially in professional publishing, is that they match most of Morisawa's typeface designs. As of this writing, there are Biblos Gaiji sets that match 23 Morisawa typeface designs.

The following tables represent the standard Biblos Gaiji character set, which extends from Shift-JIS row 0xF0 to 0xF9. Rows 0xF0 through 0xF7 contain 1,395 symbols, and rows 0xF8 and 0xF9 contain 365 kanji plus 11 parenthesized kanji numerals. The range 0xF790 through 0xF7FC (109 code points) is left open for user-defined characters.

* *http://www.opengroup.or.jp/jvc/cde/sjis-e.html*
† *http://www.biblosfont.co.jp/*

Row F0	0	1	2	3	4	5	6	7	8	9	A	B	C	D	E	F
4	0⃝	1⃝	2⃝	3⃝	4⃝	5⃝	6⃝	7⃝	8⃝	9⃝	10⃝	11⃝	12⃝	13⃝	14⃝	15⃝
5	16⃝	17⃝	18⃝	19⃝	20⃝	21⃝	22⃝	23⃝	24⃝	25⃝	26⃝	27⃝	28⃝	29⃝	30⃝	31⃝
6	32⃝	33⃝	34⃝	35⃝	36⃝	37⃝	38⃝	39⃝	40⃝	41⃝	42⃝	43⃝	44⃝	45⃝	46⃝	47⃝
7	48⃝	49⃝	50⃝	51⃝	52⃝	53⃝	54⃝	55⃝	56⃝	57⃝	58⃝	59⃝	60⃝	61⃝	62⃝	
8	63⃝	64⃝	65⃝	66⃝	67⃝	68⃝	69⃝	70⃝	71⃝	72⃝	73⃝	74⃝	75⃝	76⃝	77⃝	78⃝
9	79⃝	80⃝	81⃝	82⃝	83⃝	84⃝	85⃝	86⃝	87⃝	88⃝	89⃝	90⃝	91⃝	92⃝	93⃝	94⃝
A	95⃝	96⃝	97⃝	98⃝	99⃝	100⃝	a⃝	b⃝	c⃝	d⃝	e⃝	f⃝	g⃝	h⃝	i⃝	j⃝
B	k⃝	l⃝	m⃝	n⃝	o⃝	p⃝	q⃝	r⃝	s⃝	t⃝	u⃝	v⃝	w⃝	x⃝	y⃝	z⃝
C	A⃝	B⃝	C⃝	D⃝	E⃝	F⃝	G⃝	H⃝	I⃝	J⃝	K⃝	L⃝	M⃝	N⃝	O⃝	P⃝
D	Q⃝	R⃝	S⃝	T⃝	U⃝	V⃝	W⃝	X⃝	Y⃝	Z⃝	0⃞	1⃞	2⃞	3⃞	4⃞	5⃞
E	6⃞	7⃞	8⃞	9⃞	10⃞	11⃞	12⃞	13⃞	14⃞	15⃞	16⃞	17⃞	18⃞	19⃞	20⃞	21⃞
F	22⃞	23⃞	24⃞	25⃞	26⃞	27⃞	28⃞	29⃞	30⃞	31⃞	32⃞	33⃞	34⃞			

Row F1	0	1	2	3	4	5	6	7	8	9	A	B	C	D	E	F
4	35⃞	36⃞	37⃞	38⃞	39⃞	40⃞	41⃞	42⃞	43⃞	44⃞	45⃞	46⃞	47⃞	48⃞	49⃞	50⃞
5	51⃞	52⃞	53⃞	54⃞	55⃞	56⃞	57⃞	58⃞	59⃞	60⃞	61⃞	62⃞	63⃞	64⃞	65⃞	66⃞
6	67⃞	68⃞	69⃞	70⃞	71⃞	72⃞	73⃞	74⃞	75⃞	76⃞	77⃞	78⃞	79⃞	80⃞	81⃞	82⃞
7	83⃞	84⃞	85⃞	86⃞	87⃞	88⃞	89⃞	90⃞	91⃞	92⃞	93⃞	94⃞	95⃞	96⃞	97⃞	
8	98⃞	99⃞	100⃞	a⃞	b⃞	c⃞	d⃞	e⃞	f⃞	g⃞	h⃞	i⃞	j⃞	k⃞	l⃞	m⃞
9	n⃞	o⃞	p⃞	q⃞	r⃞	s⃞	t⃞	u⃞	v⃞	w⃞	x⃞	y⃞	z⃞	A⃞	B⃞	C⃞
A	D⃞	E⃞	F⃞	G⃞	H⃞	I⃞	J⃞	K⃞	L⃞	M⃞	N⃞	O⃞	P⃞	Q⃞	R⃞	S⃞
B	T⃞	U⃞	V⃞	W⃞	X⃞	Y⃞	Z⃞	(0)	(1)	(2)	(3)	(4)	(5)	(6)	(7)	(8)
C	(9)	(10)	(11)	(12)	(13)	(14)	(15)	(16)	(17)	(18)	(19)	(20)	(21)	(22)	(23)	(24)
D	(25)	(26)	(27)	(28)	(29)	(30)	(31)	(32)	(33)	(34)	(35)	(36)	(37)	(38)	(39)	(40)
E	(41)	(42)	(43)	(44)	(45)	(46)	(47)	(48)	(49)	(50)	(51)	(52)	(53)	(54)	(55)	(56)
F	(57)	(58)	(59)	(60)	(61)	(62)	(63)	(64)	(65)	(66)	(67)	(68)	(69)			

Row F2	0	1	2	3	4	5	6	7	8	9	A	B	C	D	E	F
4	(70)	(71)	(72)	(73)	(74)	(75)	(76)	(77)	(78)	(79)	(80)	(81)	(82)	(83)	(84)	(85)
5	(86)	(87)	(88)	(89)	(90)	(91)	(92)	(93)	(94)	(95)	(96)	(97)	(98)	(99)	(100)	(a)
6	(b)	(c)	(d)	(e)	(f)	(g)	(h)	(i)	(j)	(k)	(l)	(m)	(n)	(o)	(p)	(q)
7	(r)	(s)	(t)	(u)	(v)	(w)	(x)	(y)	(z)	(A)	(B)	(C)	(D)	(E)	(F)	
8	(G)	(H)	(I)	(J)	(K)	(L)	(M)	(N)	(O)	(P)	(Q)	(R)	(S)	(T)	(U)	(V)
9	(W)	(X)	(Y)	(Z)	●0	●1	●2	●3	●4	●5	●6	●7	●8	●9	●10	●11
A	●12	●13	●14	●15	●16	●17	●18	●19	●20	●21	●22	●23	●24	●25	●26	●27
B	●28	●29	●30	●31	●32	●33	●34	●35	●36	●37	●38	●39	●40	●41	●42	●43
C	●44	●45	●46	●47	●48	●49	●50	●51	●52	●53	●54	●55	●56	●57	●58	●59
D	●60	●61	●62	●63	●64	●65	●66	●67	●68	●69	●70	●71	●72	●73	●74	●75
E	●76	●77	●78	●79	●80	●81	●82	●83	●84	●85	●86	●87	●88	●89	●90	●91
F	●92	●93	●94	●95	●96	●97	●98	●99	●100	●a	●b	●c	●d			

Row F3	0	1	2	3	4	5	6	7	8	9	A	B	C	D	E	F
4	e	f	g	h	i	j	k	l	m	n	o	p	q	r	s	t
5	u	v	w	x	y	z	A	B	C	D	E	F	G	H	I	J
6	K	L	M	N	O	P	Q	R	S	T	U	V	W	X	Y	Z
7	0	1	2	3	4	5	6	7	8	9	10	11	12	13	14	
8	15	16	17	18	19	20	21	22	23	24	25	26	27	28	29	30
9	31	32	33	34	35	36	37	38	39	40	41	42	43	44	45	46
A	47	48	49	50	51	52	53	54	55	56	57	58	59	60	61	62
B	63	64	65	66	67	68	69	70	71	72	73	74	75	76	77	78
C	79	80	81	82	83	84	85	86	87	88	89	90	91	92	93	94
D	95	96	97	98	99	100	a	b	c	d	e	f	g	h	i	j
E	k	l	m	n	o	p	q	r	s	t	u	v	w	x	y	z
F	A	B	C	D	E	F	G	H	I	J	K	L	M			

Row F4	0	1	2	3	4	5	6	7	8	9	A	B	C	D	E	F
4	N	O	P	Q	R	S	T	U	V	W	X	Y	Z	0	1	2
5	3	4	5	6	7	8	9	10	11	12	13	14	15	16	17	18
6	19	20	21	22	23	24	25	26	27	28	29	30	31	32	33	34
7	35	36	37	38	39	40	41	42	43	44	45	46	47	48	49	
8	50	51	52	53	54	55	56	57	58	59	60	61	62	63	64	65
9	66	67	68	69	70	71	72	73	74	75	76	77	78	79	80	81
A	82	83	84	85	86	87	88	89	90	91	92	93	94	95	96	97
B	98	99	100	a	b	c	d	e	f	g	h	i	j	k	l	m
C	n	o	p	q	r	s	t	u	v	w	x	y	z	A	B	C
D	D	E	F	G	H	I	J	K	L	M	N	O	P	Q	R	S
E	T	U	V	W	X	Y	Z	0.	1.	2.	3.	4.	5.	6.	7.	8.
F	9.	0	1	2	3	4	5	6	7	8	9	○	□			

Row F5	0	1	2	3	4	5	6	7	8	9	A	B	C	D	E	F
4	☎	✆	☎	☎	☎	▥	📠	TEL	TEL	FAX	FAX	oo	0120	0120 FreeDial	(Q)	🚗
5	〠	〶	🔥	JAS	Ⓖ	S	ST	♳	アルミ	スチール	♲	♻	❂	❂	©	◉
6	⭘	◦	•	◯	❏	◍	▨	⟐	◈	❖	⧈	▣	◘	⧈	▣	⊞
7	■	⇨	⇦	⇧	⇩	⇐	═	⇒	⇑	‖	⇓	➡	⬅	⬆	⬇	
8	⬅	▬	➡	⬆	▮	⬇	⮊	⮈	⮉	⮋	⍈	⍇	⍐	⍗	▷	◁
9	▶	◀	←	─	→	↑	│	↓	⇠	┄	⇢	⇡	┆	⇣	↖	↙
A	↘	↗	♤	♡	♧	♢	♠	♥	♣	◆	♩	♪	♬	═	━	┿
B	〜	‖	┃	‡	≀	❀	✲	✕	▩	✵	⧉	╪	⫽	▢	❏	Ⅰ
C	Ⅱ	Ⅲ	Ⅳ	Ⅴ	Ⅵ	Ⅶ	Ⅷ	Ⅸ	Ⅹ	Ⅺ	Ⅻ	ⅰ	ⅱ	ⅲ	ⅳ	ⅴ
D	ⅵ	ⅶ	ⅷ	ⅸ	ⅹ	ⅺ	ⅻ	㎚	㎛	㎜	㎝	m	㎞	㎟	㎠	㎡
E	㎢	㎣	㎤	㎥	㎦	㎍	㎎	g	㎏	㎖	㎗	ℓ	㎘	㎱	㎲	㎳
F	sec	min	㎈	㎉	㏄	℃	℉	°K	㏈	㎐	㌰	㌨	㍃			

Row F6	0	1	2	3	4	5	6	7	8	9	A	B	C	D	E	F
4	ミリ	センチ	キロ	メガ	ギガ	テラ	メートル	ミクロン	グラム	トン	リットル	カロリー	デシベル	ヘルツ	ボルト	アンペア
5	ワット	ビット	バイト	ボー	アール	ヘクタール	インチ	フィート	マイル	ヤード	エーカー	オンス	ポンド	ガロン	バーレル	ドル
6	セント	シリング	フラン	マルク	リラ	ペソ	ペセタ	パーセント	ページ	ピコ	ナノ	マイクロ	ミリ	センチ	キロ	メガ
7	ギガ	テラ	メートル	ミクロン	グラム	トン	リットル	カロリー	デシベル	ヘルツ	ボルト	アンペア	ワット	ビット	バイト	
8	ボー	アール	ヘクタール	インチ	フィート	マイル	ヤード	エーカー	オンス	ポンド	ガロン	バーレル	ドル	セント	シリング	フラン
9	マルク	リラ	ペソ	ペセタ	パーセント	ページ	(株)	(有)	(資)	(名)	(相)	(社)	(財)	(学)	(宗)	(医)
A	(協)	(共)	(特)	(監)	(労)	(企)	(機)	(本)	(支)	(営)	(事)	(販)	(研)	(自)	(至)	(普)
B	(当)	(代)	(呼)	(休)	(祝)	(祭)	(日)	(月)	(火)	(水)	(木)	(金)	(土)	( )	株式会社	株式会社
C	有限会社	有限会社	社団法人	社団法人	財団法人	財団法人	学校法人	学校法人	宗教法人	宗教法人	印⃞	印⃝	秘⃝	営⃝	問⃝	円⃝
D	控⃝	当⃝	メ⃝	休⃝	祝⃝	祭⃝	日⃝	月⃝	火⃝	水⃝	木⃝	金⃝	土⃝	日⃞	月⃞	火⃞
E	水⃞	木⃞	金⃞	土⃞	●印	●秘	●営	●問	●円	●控	●当	●メ	●休	●祝	●祭	●日
F	●月	●火	●水	●木	●金	●土	■日	■月	■火	■水	■木	■金	■土			

Row F7	0	1	2	3	4	5	6	7	8	9	A	B	C	D	E	F
4	「	」	「	」	﹁	﹂	﹁	﹂	」、	」。	」,	」.	﹂、	﹂。	『	』
5	『	』	﹃	﹄	﹃	﹄	』、	』。	』,	』.	﹄、	﹄。	〝	〟	〝	〟
6	„	″	″	″	“	”	“	”	„	”	“	⸨	⸩	⸨	⸩	
7	︽	︾	︽	︾	〚	〛	〚	〛	﹇	﹈	﹇	﹈	〘	〙	〘	
8	〙	︹	︺	︹	︺	〈	〉	〈	〉	︿	﹀	︿	﹀	‥	‼	⁉
9																
A																
B																
C																
D																
E																
F																

Row F8	0	1	2	3	4	5	6	7	8	9	A	B	C	D	E	F
4	啞	逢	芦	飴	溢	茨	鰯	淫	迂	噓	鬱	廐	廐	噂	餌	益
5	焰	襖	鷗	迦	牙	恢	拐	晦	慨	概	喝	葛	鞄	嚙	澗	翰
6	舘	翫	徽	祇	吉	汲	笈	俠	卿	教	橋	橋	槗	鄕	饗	僅
7	謹	軀	喰	櫛	屑	靴	莱	莱	薫	祁	恵	慧	稽	繋	荊	
8	隙	倦	嫌	拳	捲	鹼	諺	巷	廣	昂	溝	高	麴	鵠	黑	甑
9	采	冴	榊	崎	寄	栅	薩	鯖	捌	錆	珊	飼	屢	社	遮	杓
A	灼	爵	繡	酋	遵	曙	渚	緒	薯	藷	諸	哨	廠	昇	松	梢
B	祥	蔣	醬	鞘	埴	蝕	侵	浸	真	神	靱	靱	靭	靭	逗	翠
C	摺	瀨	逝	靑	靜	静	蟬	撰	栓	煎	煽	煽	穿	箭	詮	噌
D	遡	創	掻	曺	巢	瘦	揃	遜	驒	腿	黛	臺	才	啄	濯	琢
E	蛸	巽	辿	棚	鱈	樽	簞	註	瀦	猪	凋	捗	槌	鎚	塚	摑
F	辻	鄭	擢	溺	塡	顚	堵	屠	菟	賭	土	塘	禱			

Row F9	0	1	2	3	4	5	6	7	8	9	A	B	C	D	E	F
4	鴇	德	瀆	瀞	噸	遁	頓	那	謎	灘	檜	迩	禰	祢	囊	牌
5	這	秤	剝	箸	潑	醱	抜	叛	挽	扉	樋	柊	稗	逼	媛	謬
6	廟	濱	瀕	頻	福	蔽	瞥	篇	邊	邉	邉	邊	邊	邉	邉	邉
7	娩	庖	泡	蓬	頬	鱒	迄	麵	儲	餅	戻	籾	栁	栟	鑓	
8	愉	愈	癒	猶	猷	猷	祐	熔	耀	莱	頼	隆	龍	遼	漣	煉
9	簾	蓮	朗	榔	蠟	郎	兎	冉	冕	冤	凜	辧	吩	唳	嘲	嚥
A	堋	媾	兖	屏	悗	捩	搆	攢	艷	枦	枴	梛	梍	榆	榉	湮
B	渣	熙	爨	珎	甄	甍	甕	皓	硼	稱	穐	箙	粐	粮	綛	綮
C	緥	翔	舮	芎	苒	蒖	葱	蔗	蛛	螂	蟒	褊	覯	諞	諱	跚
D	踉	輓	迪	遘	釁	霤	靠	頤	鬮	鮗	鮄	麪	龜	唖	鰺	飴
E	溢	鰯	淫	柑	噦	漚	煇	琪	杦	炫	侊	姤	你	暲	鮭	鄧
F	侔	埇	(〇)	㈠	㈡	㈢	㈣	㈤	㈥	㈦	㈧	㈨	㈩			

There are additional Biblos gaiji products that serve specific purposes, such as characters specifically designed for cloth handling, as illustrated below.

DEC Kanji

Digital Equipment Corporation (ディジタルイクイップメント株式会社 *dijitaru ikuippumento kabushikigaisha*) developed two Japanese character set standards: DEC Kanji and Super DEC Kanji.

DEC Kanji consists of a 94×94 matrix identical to that used for JIS X 0208:1997, plus another 94×94 matrix for additional characters. Rows 1 through 31 (2,914 code points) of this additional character space are reserved for user-defined characters, and rows 32 through 94 (5,922 code points) are reserved for private Digital use (but are unused). Rows 9 through 15 and rows 85 through 94 of the JIS X 0208:1997 table are also reserved for Digital use (and are currently unused). Table C-18 shows how characters are allocated to the additional 94×94 matrix.

Table C-18: The DEC Extended Character Set

Rows	Characters	Content
1–31	0	Unassigned (free)
32–94	0	Unassigned (maintained by Digital)

Super DEC Kanji was designed to be a superset of what is available in DEC Kanji and in the full definition of EUC-JP encoding (meaning JIS X 0201-1997, JIS X 0208:1997, and JIS X 0212-1990). It also provides a total of 11,374 user-defined code points, from the encoding regions as illustrated in Table C-19.

Table C-19: Super DEC Kanji User-Defined Regions

Character Set	Rows	Encoding Ranges	Number of Code Points
JIS X 0208:1997	85–94	F5A1–FEFE	940
JIS X 0212-1990	78–94	8FEEA1–8FFEFE	1,598
User-defined	1–94	A121–FE7E	8,836

Enfour Gaiji Character Set

Enfour Media (エヌフォー), like DTP center Biblos, is in the business of developing "Gaiji" products that serve professional publishing needs in Japan. In addition to the standard Enfour Gaiji Set described in this section, Enfour Media also develops Gaiji sets for medical and dental use, and also those that include the IBM and KanjiTalk7 characters (see pages 583 and 588, respectively).

Unlike the Biblos fonts, which match 23 of Morisawa's typeface designs, Enfour Media's fonts are considered more generic in design, but do match five of Morisawa's typeface designs (Mincho Light, Mincho Bold, Gothic Medium, Gothic Bold, and Rounded Gothic Light—try to guess what Morisawa typeface designs these five style and weight combinations correspond to).

The standard Enfour Gaiji Set includes 1156 non-kanji (most of which are annotated numbers) and 348 kanji (including many JIS78 variants and IBM Selected Kanji), encoded in rows 0xF0 through 0xF7.

The character set tables that span pages 576 through 578 represent the standard Enfour Gaiji character set.

Fontworks Japanese Character Set

Fontworks, a Hong Kong–based Japanese type foundry, provides additional characters beyond JIS X 0208:1997 in their "Pro" series of PostScript font products. This character set includes KanjiTalk7 characters, some JIS78 kanji, some IBM Selected Kanji, and other kanji variants. There are a total of 207 non-kanji and 530 kanji in Fontworks' extension to JIS X 0208:1997.

The character set tables that span pages 579 and 580 illustrate the characters in Fontworks' extension to JIS X 0208:1997.

Row F0	0	1	2	3	4	5	6	7	8	9	A	B	C	D	E	F
4	◯~	Ⓐ	Ⓑ	Ⓒ	Ⓓ	Ⓔ	Ⓕ	Ⓖ	Ⓗ	Ⓘ	Ⓙ	Ⓚ	Ⓛ	Ⓜ	Ⓝ	Ⓞ
5	Ⓟ	Ⓠ	Ⓡ	Ⓢ	Ⓣ	Ⓤ	Ⓥ	Ⓦ	Ⓧ	Ⓨ	Ⓩ	⊕	⊖	⊗	⨸	⊜
6	™	ⓐ	ⓑ	ⓒ	ⓓ	ⓔ	ⓕ	ⓖ	ⓗ	ⓘ	ⓙ	ⓚ	ⓛ	ⓜ	ⓝ	ⓞ
7	ⓟ	ⓠ	ⓡ	ⓢ	ⓣ	ⓤ	ⓥ	ⓦ	ⓧ	ⓨ	ⓩ	∓	≃	≲	≳	
8	©	(A)	(B)	(C)	(D)	(E)	(F)	(G)	(H)	(I)	(J)	(K)	(L)	(M)	(N)	(O)
9	(P)	(Q)	(R)	(S)	(T)	(U)	(V)	(W)	(X)	(Y)	(Z)	Ā	Ē	Ī	Ō	Ū
A	®	[A]	[B]	[C]	[D]	[E]	[F]	[G]	[H]	[I]	[J]	[K]	[L]	[M]	[N]	[O]
B	[P]	[Q]	[R]	[S]	[T]	[U]	[V]	[W]	[X]	[Y]	[Z]	ā	ē	ī	ō	ū
C	⓪	㉑	㉒	㉓	㉔	㉕	㉖	㉗	㉘	㉙	㉚	㉛	㉜	㉝	㉞	㉟
D	㊱	㊲	㊳	㊴	㊵	㊶	㊷	㊸	㊹	㊺	㊻	㊼	㊽	㊾	㊿	◯51
E	◯52	◯53	◯54	◯55	◯56	◯57	◯58	◯59	◯60	◯61	◯62	◯63	◯64	◯65	◯66	◯67
F	◯68	◯69	◯70	◯71	◯72	◯73	◯74	◯75	◯76	◯77	◯78	◯79	◯80			

Row F1	0	1	2	3	4	5	6	7	8	9	A	B	C	D	E	F
4	◯81	◯82	◯83	◯84	◯85	◯86	◯87	◯88	◯89	◯90	◯91	◯92	◯93	◯94	◯95	◯96
5	◯97	◯98	◯99	◯100	(0)	(21)	(22)	(23)	(24)	(25)	(26)	(27)	(28)	(29)	(30)	(31)
6	(32)	(33)	(34)	(35)	(36)	(37)	(38)	(39)	(40)	(41)	(42)	(43)	(44)	(45)	(46)	(47)
7	(48)	(49)	(50)	(51)	(52)	(53)	(54)	(55)	(56)	(57)	(58)	(59)	(60)	(61)	(62)	
8	(63)	(64)	(65)	(66)	(67)	(68)	(69)	(70)	(71)	(72)	(73)	(74)	(75)	(76)	(77)	(78)
9	(79)	(80)	(81)	(82)	(83)	(84)	(85)	(86)	(87)	(88)	(89)	(90)	(91)	(92)	(93)	(94)
A	(95)	(96)	(97)	(98)	(99)	(100)	[0]	[1]	[2]	[3]	[4]	[5]	[6]	[7]	[8]	[9]
B	[10]	[11]	[12]	[13]	[14]	[15]	[16]	[17]	[18]	[19]	[20]	[21]	[22]	[23]	[24]	[25]
C	[26]	[27]	[28]	[29]	[30]	[31]	[32]	[33]	[34]	[35]	[36]	[37]	[38]	[39]	[40]	[41]
D	[42]	[43]	[44]	[45]	[46]	[47]	[48]	[49]	[50]	[51]	[52]	[53]	[54]	[55]	[56]	[57]
E	[58]	[59]	[60]	[61]	[62]	[63]	[64]	[65]	[66]	[67]	[68]	[69]	[70]	[71]	[72]	[73]
F	[74]	[75]	[76]	[77]	[78]	[79]	[80]	[81]	[82]	[83]	[84]	[85]	[86]			

Row F2	0	1	2	3	4	5	6	7	8	9	A	B	C	D	E	F
4	[87]	[88]	[89]	[90]	[91]	[92]	[93]	[94]	[95]	[96]	[97]	[98]	[99]	[100]	⓿	❿
5	⓫	⓬	⓭	⓮	⓯	⓰	⓱	⓲	⓳	⓴	●21	●22	●23	●24	●25	●26
6	●27	●28	●29	●30	●31	●32	●33	●34	●35	●36	●37	●38	●39	●40	●41	●42
7	●43	●44	●45	●46	●47	●48	●49	●50	●51	●52	●53	●54	●55	●56	●57	
8	●58	●59	●60	●61	●62	●63	●64	●65	●66	●67	●68	●69	●70	●71	●72	●73
9	●74	●75	●76	●77	●78	●79	●80	●81	●82	●83	●84	●85	●86	●87	●88	●89
A	●90	●91	●92	●93	●94	●95	●96	●97	●98	●99	●100	●+	●−	●×	●÷	●=
B	10.	11.	12.	13.	14.	15.	16.	17.	18.	19.	20.	∮	⊿	MB	GB	TB
C	cm	mm²	mm³	km³	ℓ	kℓ	sec	min	hr	cal	kcal	dB	∭	ħ	vs.	⌘
D	␣	[F1]	[F2]	[F3]	[F4]	[F5]	[F6]	[F7]	[F8]	[F9]	[F10]	[F11]	[F12]	[F13]	[F14]	[F15]
E	[caps]	[control]	[delete]	[enter]	[esc]	[option]	[return]	[space]	[tab]	[.]	[◁]	[⌘]	[⌘]	[↩]	◯↩	[↩]
F	apple	apple (filled)	↔	↗	↙	↖	↘	⤡	⤢	▶	◀	▷	◁			

Row F3	0	1	2	3	4	5	6	7	8	9	A	B	C	D	E	F
4	☼	☁	⛅	☂	☃	○	⦶	◎	●	●キ	●ニ	●ツ	⊛	⊛ニ	◒	△⃝
5	▲⃝	◒	⦿	∞⃝	S⃝	⊕	⊗	台⃝	◉	♨	⊠	⊗	Y⃞	文⃝	✚	⌂
6	⛩	卍	†	☼	☼	⚓	⚑	⛵	✈	🚃	🚌	🚗	Ⓟ	⛽	☕	🍴
7	AND	OR	XOR	NOT	ON	OFF	½	⅓	⅔	¼	¾	⅕	⅖	⅗	⅘	
8	•	○	■	□	☚	☛	☜	☞	✂	✂	✂	✂	✂	✂	✂	✂
9	い⃝	ろ⃝	は⃝	に⃝	ほ⃝	へ⃝	と⃝	ち⃝	り⃝	ぬ⃝	る⃝	を⃝	わ⃝	か⃝	よ⃝	た⃝
A	れ⃝	そ⃝	つ⃝	ね⃝	な⃝	ら⃝	む⃝	う⃝	ゐ⃝	の⃝	お⃝	く⃝	や⃝	ま⃝	け⃝	ふ⃝
B	こ⃝	え⃝	て⃝	あ⃝	さ⃝	き⃝	ゆ⃝	め⃝	み⃝	し⃝	ゑ⃝	ひ⃝	も⃝	せ⃝	す⃝	ん⃝
C	㋑	㋺	㋩	㋥	㋭	㋬	㋣	㋠	㋷	㋦	㋸	㋾	㋻	㋕	㋵	㋟
D	㋹	㋞	㋡	㋧	㋤	㋶	㋰	㋒	㋼	㋨	㋔	㋗	㋳	㋮	㋘	㋫
E	㋙	㋓	㋢	㋐	㋚	㋖	㋴	㋱	㋯	㋛	㋽	㋪	㋲	㋝	㋜	ン⃝
F	(い)	(ろ)	(は)	(に)	(ほ)	(へ)	(と)	(ち)	(り)	(ぬ)	(る)	(を)	(わ)			

Row F4	0	1	2	3	4	5	6	7	8	9	A	B	C	D	E	F
4	(か)	(よ)	(た)	(れ)	(そ)	(つ)	(ね)	(な)	(ら)	(む)	(う)	(ゐ)	(の)	(お)	(く)	(や)
5	(ま)	(け)	(ふ)	(こ)	(え)	(て)	(あ)	(さ)	(き)	(ゆ)	(め)	(み)	(し)	(ゑ)	(ひ)	(も)
6	(せ)	(す)	(ん)	(イ)	(ロ)	(ハ)	(ニ)	(ホ)	(ヘ)	(ト)	(チ)	(リ)	(ヌ)	(ル)	(ヲ)	(ワ)
7	(カ)	(ヨ)	(タ)	(レ)	(ソ)	(ツ)	(ネ)	(ナ)	(ラ)	(ム)	(ウ)	(ヰ)	(ノ)	(オ)	(ク)	
8	(ヤ)	(マ)	(ケ)	(フ)	(コ)	(エ)	(テ)	(ア)	(サ)	(キ)	(ユ)	(メ)	(ミ)	(シ)	(ヱ)	(ヒ)
9	(モ)	(セ)	(ス)	(ン)	ミリグラム	ミリ	メートル	キロメートル	フィート	アール	マイル	エーカー	ガロン	バーレル	ダース	カートン
A	ケース	ノット	ビット	バイト	メガ	ギガ	サイクル	ボルト	アンペア	ガウス	ポンド	マルク	フラン	ペセタ	ペソ	リラ
B	ウォン	ルーブル	パーツ	マンション	明治	社団法人	学校法人	医療法人	宗教法人	キロメートル	インチ	フィート	ミリグラム	キログラム	ヘルツ	サイクル
C	ボルト	アンペア	日⃝	月⃝	火⃝	水⃝	木⃝	金⃝	土⃝	祝⃝	休⃝	祭⃝	呼⃝	内⃝	自⃝	至⃝
D	企⃝	協⃝	資⃝	社⃝	名⃝	特⃝	注⃝	障⃝	株⃝	有⃝	支⃝	販⃝	営⃝	事⃝	学⃝	普⃝
E	高⃝	昼⃝	夜⃝	前⃝	後⃝	〒⃝	(休)	(内)	(注)	(大)	(中)	(小)	(上)	(下)	(左)	(右)
F	(支)	(販)	(営)	(事)	(普)	(研)	(昼)	(夜)	(前)	(後)	(株)	印⃞	溢			

Row F5	0	1	2	3	4	5	6	7	8	9	A	B	C	D	E	F
4	溢	迂	噂	餌	焰	鷗	迦	恢	晦	喝	葛	噛	潤	諫	徽	祇
5	旣	廐	俠	卿	軀	櫛	屑	祁	倦	嫌	捲	巷	麴	鵠	甑	釆
6	榊	薩	鯖	錆	珊	屢	社	繡	酋	曙	渚	薯	藷	梢	蔣	醬
7	鞘	蝕	逝	蟬	撰	噌	遡	搔	遜	驒	腿	黛	啄	琢	辿	
8	樽	簞	偸	瀦	槌	鎚	塚	摑	壺	鄭	迪	塡	堵	屠	賭	禱
9	瀆	德	瀞	遁	謎	楢	禰	囊	蠅	剝	箸	潑	醱	樋	逼	蓬
A	頰	鱒	麵	儲	餠	籾	鑓	愈	癒	猷	萊	遼	漣	煉	蓮	榔
B	蠟	乚	𠃌	乁	八	丷	刂	𠂇	㔾	𠂉	⺈	𠆢	⺌	⺍	龷	⺿
C	⺕	⺆	䒑	忄	扌	氵	犭	阝	辶	⻌	丬	⺳	⺮	⺣	⺌	夂
D	⺹	罒	禸	氺	疒	衤	覀	⺷	羽	臼	走	食	飠	青	麻	黑
E	D♭	E♭	G♭	A♭	B♭	C♯	D♯	F♯	G♯	A♯	C♮	D♮	E♮	F♮	G♮	A♮
F	B♮	m7	M7	△7	+7	(♭5)	(♯5)	(♭9)	(♯9)	(♭11)	(♯11)	(♭13)	(♯13)			

Row F6	0	1	2	3	4	5	6	7	8	9	A	B	C	D	E	F
4	[shift]	[clear]	[help]	[home]	[up]	[down]	[end]	[F16]	[F17]	[F18]	[F19]	[F20]	[F21]	[F22]	[F23]	[F24]
5	[⌦]	[←]	[→]	[↓]	[↑]	「	」	『	』	┐	└	┐	└	／	／゛	＼
6	⌇	〜	‼	⁉	⁇	!	‼	⁉	⁇	¡	¿	○	□	□	( )	⌒
7	↷	↶	//	▱	$\overline{x}$	$\overline{X}$	T/C	L/C	a/c	c/o	c/s	m/h	m/s	kΩ	MΩ	
8	μm	μA	μN	μW	μF	μl	ø	ポイント	ヘクト	パスカル	[問]	[答]	[例]	◯円	◯男	◯女
9	◯本	◯正	◯副	◯写	◯原	◯国	◯公	◯私	◯衆	◯参	◯相	◯連	◯宗	◯幼	◯問	◯答
A	◯泊	◯往	◯復	◯歩	◯電	◯飛	◯適	◯項	◯専	◯新	◯旧	◯再	◯変	◯禁	◯暴	◯共
B	◯済	◯当	◯非	◯税	◯申	◯低	◯朝	(本)	(正)	(副)	(写)	(原)	(国)	(公)	(私)	(衆)
C	(参)	(相)	(連)	(宗)	(幼)	(泊)	(往)	(復)	(歩)	(電)	(飛)	(専)	(新)	(旧)	(共)	(当)
D	(税)	(控)	(高)	(低)	(朝)	(医)	(一)	(二)	(三)	(四)	(五)	(六)	(七)	(八)	(九)	(十)
E	マイル	エーカー	ガロン	バーレル	ダース	カートン	ケース	ノット	ビット	バイト	メガ	ギガ	ガウス	ポンド	マルク	フラン
F	ペセタ	ペソ	リラ	ウォン	ルーブル	バーツ	ポイント	ヘクト	パスカル	社団法人	学校法人	医療法人	宗教法人			

Row F7	0	1	2	3	4	5	6	7	8	9	A	B	C	D	E	F
4	啞	飴	或	迤	迤	瑋	昱	今	鰯	淫	英	叚	會	會	海	角
5	嵩	神	舘	監	寬	熙	熙	澌	㐂	起	祺	祈	軌	吉	櫸	祛
6	教	髙	槗	尭	仰	嶔	栞	栞	慧	恵	惠	稽	絜	崄	鹼	黃
7	廣	廣	昻	昜	髙	槗	叻	皓	皥	暐	顥	沆	壷	齊	齋	
8	﨑	碕	寄	璨	視	你	您	姝	琇	蘒	祝	葰	緒	翔	祥	祥
9	将	崧	暲	傷	情	穠	丈	聎	埴	真	眞	愼	愼	瀨	淸	靖
A	精	静	靜	靜	鮏	箭	操	揃	尊	泰	才	瀧	巽	棚	猪	辻
B	鉄	都	土	唐	鋕	鄧	黨	藤	那	灘	灘	栖	袨	覇	菈	博
C	鐗	扉	彥	濵	敏	榑	福	邉	邉	邉	邉	邉	邉	邉	邉	邉
D	邊	邊	邊	邊	邊	邊	邊	邊	邊	穗	邦	邦	芳	昴	昪	每
E	侔	栁	槐	栜	喻	庾	裕	祐	祐	雄	仔	旺	鍚	賴	龍	龍
F	龍	隆	淩	蓼	梁	簗	礼	禮	璐	郎	朗	脇	篗			

Fujitsu Character Sets

Fujitsu (富士通 *fujitsū*) has developed two Japanese character set standards, JEF and FMR Kanji. They are used for entirely different environments, specifically Fujitsu's mainframe and personal computers, respectively.

JEF

JEF, short for *Japanese processing Extended Feature*, is the Fujitsu character set primarily used on their mainframe computers called FACOM and some of their OASYS series personal word processors. JEF includes the JIS C 6226-1978 char-

Row F0	0	1	2	3	4	5	6	7	8	9	A	B	C	D	E	F
4	(1)	(2)	(3)	(4)	(5)	(6)	(7)	(8)	(9)	(10)	(11)	(12)	(13)	(14)	(15)	(16)
5	(17)	(18)	(19)	(20)	❶	❷	❸	❹	❺	❻	❼	❽	❾	0.	1.	2.
6	3.	4.	5.	6.	7.	8.	9.	XI	XII	XIII	XIV	XV	i	ii	iii	iv
7	v	vi	vii	viii	ix	x	xi	xii	xiii	xiv	xv	(a)	(b)	(c)	(d)
8	(e)	(f)	(g)	(h)	(i)	(j)	(k)	(l)	(m)	(n)	(o)	(p)	(q)	(r)	(s)	(t)
9	(u)	(v)	(w)	(x)	(y)	(z)	㎟	㎠	㎤	㎥	㎢	mℓ	dℓ	ℓ	kℓ	ms
A	μs	ns	ps	℉	mb	HP	Hz	KB	MB	GB	TB	FAX	♤	♧	♡	♢
B	♠	♣	♥	♦	〠	☎	[illegible]	☞	☜	☝	☟	⇆	⇄	⇅	⇵	⇨
C	⇦	⇧	⇩	➡	⬅	⬆	⬇	(日)	(月)	(火)	(水)	(木)	(金)	(土)	(祭)	(祝)
D	(自)	(至)	(呼)	(資)	(名)	(学)	(財)	(社)	(特)	(監)	(企)	(協)	(労)	大⃝	小⃝	医⃝
E	財⃝	優⃝	労⃝	印⃝	控⃝	秘⃝	キロメートル	インチ	フィート	ヤード	キログラム	ヘルツ	ホーン	アパート	コーポ	ハイツ
F	ビル	マンション	平成	株式会社	有限会社	財団法人	ヾ	ゞ	ゔ	ヷ	ヸ	ヹ	ヺ			

Row F1	0	1	2	3	4	5	6	7	8	9	A	B	C	D	E	F
4	乇	丯	丬	仐	仿	你	侊	侔	俠	侵	侮	倦	僅	僧	儲	兎
5	兔	冉	冤	冴	凋	凴	凞	剝	創	勉	勤	卌	卋	卑	即	卿
6	厓	厩	厩	厲	叛	吉	呈	咜	咩	哨	嗤	啞	啄	唹	唳	喰
7	喝	噓	嘆	噌	噂	嘲	噦	器	噸	囓	嚥	囊	圡	圣	圳	
8	埇	埴	堋	堵	塚	塡	塘	增	壔	奭	妥	姉	娄	娜	娩	媛
9	嫌	媾	宵	寃	寃	寬	屑	屛	層	屨	層	嵜	嵓	崎	巠	巣
A	巷	巽	庖	廊	廠	廣	廟	徵	德	徽	恢	悔	悗	悗	恖	恵
B	愉	愈	慨	慧	憎	懲	戾	扁	扈	扉	拐	拔	拳	挽	掤	掺
C	捲	捩	揭	揄	揑	搆	搔	摑	摺	撰	擊	擢	攢	教	敏	斃
D	昱	昻	曺	晦	晚	晸	晛	晃	冕	暑	暲	曆	曙	朗	腿	縢
E	杓	杦	枦	枻	枴	柵	柊	柗	栁	桒	栓	栟	梢	梅	梛	椛
F	椛	棚	楡	楢	榉	榊	槌	樃	槪	槁	樋	橋	槁			

Row F2	0	1	2	3	4	5	6	7	8	9	A	B	C	D	E	F
4	橫	樽	櫛	櫛	欄	欤	歎	步	歷	穀	每	毬	氏	汲	泔	泡
5	海	涉	浸	淫	淚	湮	渴	渣	渚	溢	溫	溝	溺	漢	滬	漣
6	澗	潑	濯	濵	澑	瀆	瀞	瀦	瀕	瀨	瀧	灘	灼	炫	焰	煇
7	煎	煮	煉	熥	煽	熔	熙	熙	燗	燜	爨	爵	狀	牌	牙	
8	猪	猶	猷	玆	珊	珎	琪	琢	璣	甄	豊	甑	甕	痤	瘍	瘦
9	瘙	瘭	癒	皓	眞	睪	瞽	砺	碑	硼	祁	社	祈	祇	祉	祢
A	祝	神	祐	祖	祥	福	禍	禎	禱	禰	秤	稗	稱	稽	穐	穿
B	突	笈	箒	箙	節	箭	箸	篇	簞	簾	籔	籐	籾	粐	粮	綛
C	緊	綟	緣	緖	練	縕	繁	繫	繡	罡	署	羽	翅	翆	翔	翠
D	翫	翩	翩	翰	耀	者	耾	臭	臺	舮	船	艏	芍	芦	苒	茨
E	葱	荊	菀	莫	菟	萊	萠	葛	著	蔰	蔣	蓬	蓮	蔗	蔽	薩
F	薰	藷	藷	蘒	虛	虜	蛛	蜓	蛸	蜷	蝕	蝙	螂			

Row F3	0	1	2	3	4	5	6	7	8	9	A	B	C	D	E	F
4	蟒	蟬	蠅	蠟	褊	襃	襖	視	覯	角	註	詮	謁	諺	諸	諞
5	謎	譁	謹	謦	謬	賓	賭	贈	趙	跚	跟	踩	軀	輓	辦	辻
6	迂	迄	辿	迦	迹	迪	逌	這	逝	逗	逢	逸	遁	逼	遘	遡
7	遜	遮	邉	遵	邉	邉	遼	邉	邊	邊	邉	邊	那	郎	都	
8	鄕	鄭	鄧	邦	酉	醬	醱	釁	釆	釚	鉄	鋏	錆	錄	鍊	鎚
9	鑓	镸	隆	隙	雞	難	霂	霤	靑	靜	静	靠	靭	靭	靱	靴
A	靤	鞘	響	頚	頓	頣	頤	頬	頻	頼	顛	類	顥	颪	飫	飴
B	飼	餃	餌	餌	餉	餅	舘	餡	饅	饗	饜	騙	騸	驒	髙	鬭
C	鬮	欝	鮗	鮏	鯁	鯖	鯵	鰊	鰯	鱈	鱒	鴇	鴿	鷗	靏	靍
D	麪	麴	麵	麻	黃	黑	墨	黛	鹼	龍	龜	’	·	゛	°	‘
E	,	‘	“	”	„	“	°	′	″	‖	か	け	か	け		
F																

acter set as a subset, along with thousands of other characters. Table C-20 lists the characters included in JEF.

Table C-20: The JEF Character Set—Overview

Character Type	Number of Characters
JIS C 6226-1978	6,802
JEF Extended kanji	4,039
JEF Extended non-kanji	1,010
User-defined characters	3,102[a]

[a] Some implementations of JEF have 457 of these 3,102 code points allocated for kanji specified by Japan's Ministry of Labor (労働省 *rōdōshō*).

As you would expect, the JEF Extended characters are arranged into rows of 94 characters. They are assigned Row-Cell values beginning from 101. Table C-21 shows how JEF Extended characters are allocated to rows 101 through 163.

Table C-21: The JEF Extended Character Set

Rows	Characters	Contents
101–148	4,039	JEF Extended kanji
149–161	917	JEF Extended non-kanji
162	0	Unused
163	93	JEF Extended non-kanji

For the most part, the 4,039 extended kanji are ordered by indexing radical. However, there is what appears to be a compatibility zone containing 71 kanji at the end of the JEF Extended kanji set, which are also ordered by indexing radical.

The JEF Extended kanji area is not fully used—the block of JEF Extended kanji has many empty character positions scattered throughout. JEF actually predates JIS C 6226-1978, and has undergone modifications so that conversion from the JIS X 0208 series is possible.

Most implementations of JEF also include ASCII/JIS-Roman and half-width katakana characters made accessible through the use of shifting characters in an EBCDIC-based encoding.

FMR Kanji

The Fujitsu FM-R series of personal computers make use of a Japanese character set different from JEF both in terms of character set and encoding. This character set is called FMR Kanji. FMR Kanji contains the JIS X 0208 series as its base, yet still makes use of many JIS C 6226-1978 glyphs. It also has three additional hiragana characters not found in JIS X 0208:1997, as illustrated in Table C-22.

Table C-22: Three Non-JIS Hiragana in FMR Kanji

Hiragana	Row-Cell	Transliteration
ゔ	04-84	vu
ゕ	04-85	ka (small version of か)
ゖ	04-86	ke (small version of け)

You may recall from Chapter 3 that there are 83 hiragana and 86 katakana. The difference among these numbers happens to be three characters. The three hiragana characters listed above bring the hiragana set up to 86 characters, like katakana (that is, these three hiragana characters have katakana analogs in JIS X 0208:1997).

Also included in the FMR Kanji character set are the ASCII/JIS-Roman and half-width katakana character set standards, and a user-defined character area that can hold up to 2,444 characters.

Hitachi Character Sets

Hitachi (日立 *hitachi*) developed a character set standard known as KEIS, short for *Kanji processing Extended Information System*. This character set standard comes in two forms: KEIS78 and KEIS83. The former is based heavily on JIS C 6226-1978, and includes 36 additional characters used for print formatting. The latter is based on JIS X 0208-1983. I have a hunch that there is a KEIS90 or KEIS97 in the works or already exists, based on JIS X 0208-1990 or JIS X 0208:1997.

KEIS78

KEIS78 is based on JIS C 6226-1978, and represents Hitachi's original Japanese character set. It also includes 71 non-kanji that were introduced in JIS X 0208-1983. More importantly, its glyphs conform to JIS C 6226-1978, which is important for some classes of users.

KEIS83

After JIS X 0208-1983 was established, Hitachi followed with a version of KEIS that conformed to it. Some shifting of characters took place to accommodate changes that were introduced in JIS X 0208-1983.

Under both KEIS78 and KEIS83, JIS Level 1 kanji and JIS non-kanji are in what Hitachi calls the KEIS Basic Character Set. JIS Level 2 kanji in its entirety makes up KEIS Extended Character Set 1. Corporate-defined kanji and non-kanji are in KEIS Extended Character Set 3 (the kanji are arranged by radical then stroke count, identical to JIS Level 2 kanji). Oddly enough, there is no mention of a KEIS Extended Character Set 2. Table C-23 lists the number of characters in KEIS78 and KEIS83, arranged by its three character sets.

Table C-23: The KEIS78 and KEIS83 Character Sets

	Basic Character Set	Extended Character Set 1	Extended Character Set 3
KEIS78	3,454[a]	3,384	3,027[b]
KEIS83	3,489	3,388	3,166[c]

[a] This is the same as JIS C 6226-1978 Level 1 kanji and non-kanji plus 36 formatted printing characters.
[b] This includes 71 JIS X 0208-1983 non-kanji, 914 Hitachi non-kanji, and 2,042 kanji.
[c] This includes 966 Hitachi non-kanji and 2,200 kanji.

KEIS78 and KEIS83 also includes a user-defined character range. This area can hold up to 3,008 characters (equivalent to 32 rows of 94 characters).

HP Kanji

The Japanese character set implemented by Hewlett-Packard (HP) consists of the 94 printable ASCII/JIS-Roman characters, the 63 half-width katakana characters, and JIS X 0208-1983. Nothing out of the ordinary here. However, in Appendix D, *Vendor Encoding Methods*, which discusses HP Kanji's encoding methods, you will see a departure from this apparent lack of ordinariness in that there is a large user-defined character area that can hold up to 5,366 characters.

IBM Japanese

IBM (アイ・ビー・エム *ai bī emu*) was one of the first companies to develop a Japanese vendor character set standard, called "IBM Japanese" in the scope of this book. This vendor character set standard includes those characters from JIS X 0208:1997 plus an additional 360 kanji and 28 non-kanji known as IBM Selected Kanji and IBM Selected Non-kanji, respectively. IBM Japanese has followed the JIS X 0208 standard very closely. For example, when JIS X 0208-1990 superseded JIS X 0208-1983 in late 1990, IBM quickly moved to standardize to JIS X 0208-1990 by including the two kanji 凜 (84-05) and 熙 (84-06).

IBM Japanese does have a peculiar twist, though. There are three encodings for this character set, and although these encoding methods handle the same set of characters, their characters are arranged differently. Table C-24 shows how the characters are defined under one encoding method, IBM Japanese DBCS-Host, also known as IBM Code Page 00300.

Table C-24: IBM Japanese DBCS-Host Character Set

Character Type	Number of Characters
Full-width space	1
Non-kanji	551
Basic kanji	3,226
Extended kanji	3,489
User-defined characters	4,370

Under the other two encoding methods, IBM DBCS-PC and IBM DBCS-EUC, you clearly see that the break-down of IBM Japanese is quite different. IBM Japanese DBCS-PC is also known as IBM Code Page 00301. Table C-25 illustrates this, and note that the first three entries of Table C-25 comprise the JIS X 0208:1997 character set.

Table C-25: IBM Japanese DBCS-PC and DBCS-EUC Character Set

Character Type	Number of Characters
Non-kanji	524
JIS X 0208 Level 1 kanji	2,965
JIS X 0208 Level 2 kanji	3,390
IBM Selected Non-kanji	28
IBM Selected Kanji	360
User-defined characters	1,880[a]

[a] IBM DBCS-EUC encoding permits up to 2,538 user-defined characters.

With the exception of the number of user-defined characters, the total number of characters is identical, specifically 7,267. The current number of IBM Selected Non-kanji happens to be 26. The difference between that number and the number in the above table, 28, consists of two characters that were not included in JIS C 6226-1978, but became part of JIS X 0208-1983. After IBM standardized to JIS X 0208-1983, these two characters were dropped, thus reducing IBM Selected Non-kanji to 26 characters. I refer to 28 IBM Selected Non-kanji for backward compatibility, and because some implementations include all 28 of these characters, such as Microsoft's Japanese character set (see page 591). These two characters are shown in Table C-26.

Table C-26: Special Mappings for Two IBM DBCS-PC Characters

Character	IBM DBCS-PC Code	JIS X 0208:1997
¬	`FA54`	02-44
∵	`FA5B`	02-72

I once conducted a short study in which I tried to match the 360 IBM Selected Kanji with kanji from JIS X 0212-1990. The outcome of this study was that 279 kanji in JIS X 0212-1990 matched those in IBM Selected Kanji. There was even one that matched a kanji in JIS X 0208:1997. The remaining 80 kanji map to the JIS X 0212-1990 user-defined region, and in fact there are two such mappings as listed in Appendix Q, *Character Lists and Mapping Tables*. Approximately 70 of these remaining 80 kanji are common to the JEF character set standard, covered earlier in this chapter starting on page 578.

IBM Japanese also includes the ASCII/JIS-Roman and half-width katakana character sets. These fall into what is called SBCS (Single-Byte Character Set). A DBCS (Double-Byte Character Set) and an SBCS (Single-Byte Character Set) together are referred to as an MBCS (Multiple-Byte Character Set).

Other vendors have included IBM Selected Kanji and Non-kanji into their products or even into their own character set standards. As an example, some of NEC's PC-9800 computer systems include all 360 IBM Selected Kanji in rows 89 through 92 of JIS X 0208, and 14 of the 28 IBM Selected Non-kanji in the remainder of row 92 (see page 592 for more details). Microsoft has also included the IBM Selected Kanji and Non-kanji in two regions, specifically in regions defined by *both* IBM and NEC. The character set tables on page 585 illustrate the characters specific to IBM Japanese, specifically IBM Selected Kanji and Non-kanji.

IKIS

Nippon (Japan) Data General (日本データゼネラル *nippon dēta zeneraru*) developed a character set standard very similar to JIS X 0208-1983, except that it

Row FA	0	1	2	3	4	5	6	7	8	9	A	B	C	D	E	F
4	ⅰ	ⅱ	ⅲ	ⅳ	ⅴ	ⅵ	ⅶ	ⅷ	ⅸ	ⅹ	Ⅰ	Ⅱ	Ⅲ	Ⅳ	Ⅴ	Ⅵ
5	Ⅶ	Ⅷ	Ⅸ	Ⅹ	￢	￤	＇	＂	㈱	№	℡	∵	纊	褜	鍈	銈
6	蓜	俉	炻	昱	棈	鋹	曻	彅	丨	仡	仼	伀	伃	伹	佖	侒
7	侊	侚	侔	俍	偀	倢	俿	倞	偆	偰	偂	傔	僴	僘	兊	
8	兤	冝	冾	凬	刕	劜	劦	勀	勛	匀	匇	匤	卲	厓	厲	叝
9	﨎	咜	咊	咩	哿	喆	坙	坥	垬	埈	埇	﨏	塚	增	墲	夋
A	奓	奛	奝	奣	妤	妺	孖	寀	甯	寘	寬	尞	岦	岺	峵	崧
B	嵓	﨑	嵂	嵭	嶸	嶹	巐	弡	弴	彧	德	忞	恝	悅	悊	惞
C	惕	愠	惲	愑	愷	愰	憘	戓	抦	揵	摠	撝	擎	敎	昀	昕
D	昻	昉	昮	昞	昤	晥	晗	晙	晴	晳	暙	暠	暲	暿	曺	朎
E	朗	杦	枻	桒	柀	栁	桄	棏	﨓	楨	﨔	榘	槢	樰	橫	橆
F	橳	橾	櫢	櫤	毖	氿	汜	沆	汯	泚	洄	涇	浯			

Row FB	0	1	2	3	4	5	6	7	8	9	A	B	C	D	E	F
4	涖	涬	淏	淸	淲	淼	渹	湜	渧	渼	溿	澈	澵	濵	瀅	瀇
5	瀨	炅	炫	焏	焄	煜	煆	煇	凞	燁	燾	犱	犾	猤	猪	獷
6	玽	珉	珖	珣	珒	琇	珵	琦	琪	琩	琮	瑢	璉	璟	甁	畯
7	皂	皜	皞	皛	皦	益	睆	劯	砡	硎	硤	硺	礰	礼	神	
8	祥	禔	福	禛	竑	竧	靖	竫	箞	精	絈	絜	綷	綠	緖	繒
9	罇	羡	羽	茁	荢	荿	菇	菶	葈	蒴	蕓	蕙	蕫	﨟	薰	蘒
A	﨡	蠇	裵	訒	訷	詹	誧	誾	諟	諸	諶	譓	譿	賰	賴	贒
B	赶	﨣	軏	﨤	逸	遧	郞	都	鄕	鄧	釚	釗	釞	釭	釮	釤
C	釥	鈆	鈐	鈊	鈺	鉀	鈼	鉎	鉙	鉑	鈹	鉧	銧	鉷	鉸	鋧
D	鋗	鋙	鋐	﨧	鋕	鋠	鋓	錥	錡	鋻	﨨	錞	鋿	錝	錂	鍰
E	鍗	鎤	鏆	鏞	鏸	鐱	鑅	鑈	閒	隆	﨩	隝	隯	霳	霻	靃
F	靍	靏	靑	靕	顗	顥	飯	飼	餧	館	馞	驎	髙			

Row FC	0	1	2	3	4	5	6	7	8	9	A	B	C	D	E	F
4	髜	魵	魲	鮏	鮱	鮻	鰀	鵰	鵫	鶴	鸙	黑				
5																
6																
7																
8																
9																
A																
B																
C																
D																
E																
F																

contains the half-width katakana character set within the 94×94 character space—these characters are placed in row 8. In addition, only rows 9 through 12 are assigned as a user-defined character space. This character set standard is referred to as IKIS, which stands for *Interactive Kanji Information System*. Table C-27 illustrates the differences between IKIS and JIS X 0208-1983.

Table C-27: Comparing JIS X 0208-1983 and IKIS

Rows	Characters	Content
8	63	Half-width katakana
9–12	0	Unassigned (free)
13–15	0	Unassigned (reserved)

K-JIS

Developed by 共同通信社 (*kyōdō tsūshinsha*) and 配信先新聞社 (*haishinsen shinbunsha*) for writing newspaper articles. The book entitled 記者ハンドブック (*kisha handobukku*) includes a complete listing of K-JIS–specific kanji and non-kanji. Also of interest is that many K-JIS–specific kanji are part of JIS X 0212-1990.

MacOS-J Character Sets

Apple Computer (アップルコンピュータ *appuru konpyūta*) developed their own Japanese character set with the introduction of KanjiTalk (漢字Talk *kanji tōku*), the Japanese operating system for the Macintosh computer, which is now called MacOS-J. This character set is based on JIS X 0208-1983, but has 82 additional characters in row 13, and 53 vertically-set variants. I call this character set the KanjiTalk6 character set. This character set is implemented in MacOS-J prior to Version 7.1.

The KanjiTalk6 and KanjiTalk7 character sets share the same set of characters for the one-byte range, which is ASCII/JIS-Roman plus four additional characters. These four additional characters are illustrated in Table C-28.

Table C-28: Additional KanjiTalk6 and KanjiTalk7 Single-Byte Characters

Code Point	Character
80	\ (backslash)
FD	© (copyright)
FE	™ (trademark)
FF	… (ellipsis)

0x5C is normally used to encode a backslash in ASCII, but JIS-Roman replaces it with a yen symbol. The KanjiTalk6 and KanjiTalk7 character sets encode the ASCII backslash at 0x80.

The KanjiTalk6 character set

The KanjiTalk6 character was originally developed out of a collaborative effort involving Adobe Systems and Apple Computer. The very first PostScript Japanese fonts, Morisawa's Ryumin-Light and GothicBBB-Medium, were first made accessible on MacOS-J in the late 1980s on the Apple LaserWriter II NTX-J printer. Table C-29 illustrates the differences between JIS X 0208-1983 and the KanjiTalk6 character set.

Table C-29: Comparing JIS X 0208-1983 and KanjiTalk6 Character Sets

Row	Characters	Content
11	31	Vertical variants of row 1 (miscellaneous symbols)
13	82	Encircled numerals 1–20, uppercase Roman numerals 1–10, 16 katakana ligatures, 10 abbreviations, 3 two-kanji ligatures, 5 encircled kanji, 3 parenthesized kanji, 15 miscellaneous symbols
14	10	Vertical variants of row 4 (hiragana)
15	12	Vertical variants of row 5 (katakana)

One note is that row 13 was actually copied from NEC Kanji. NEC Kanji now defines 83 characters in this row, though. So why the difference? The KanjiTalk6 character set does not include the two-kanji Japanese era name ligature ㍻ (*heisei*), which is a relatively recent addition to NEC Kanji.

The following tables illustrate the characters that are included in the KanjiTalk6 character set.

Row 11		01	02	03	04	05	06	07	08	09	10	11	12	13	14	15	16	17	18	19
00			︑	︒														￤	￤	
20									丨	︱	╵			≀	＝	—	︙	︰		
40			︵	︶	︹	︺	﹇	﹈	︷	︸	︿	﹀	︽	︾	﹁	﹂	﹃	﹄	︻	︼
60						‖														
80																				

Row 13		01	02	03	04	05	06	07	08	09	10	11	12	13	14	15	16	17	18	19
00		①	②	③	④	⑤	⑥	⑦	⑧	⑨	⑩	⑪	⑫	⑬	⑭	⑮	⑯	⑰	⑱	⑲
20	⑳	Ⅰ	Ⅱ	Ⅲ	Ⅳ	Ⅴ	Ⅵ	Ⅶ	Ⅷ	Ⅸ	Ⅹ		㍉	㌔	㌢	㍍	㌘	㌧	㌃	㌶
40	㍑	㍗	㌍	㌦	㌣	㌫	㍊	㌻	㎜	㎝	㎞	㎎	㎏	㏄	㎡					
60					〝	〟	№	㏍	℡	㊤	㊥	㊦	㊧	㊨	㈱	㈲	㈹	㍾	㍽	㍼
80	≒	≡	∫	∮	∑	√	⊥	∠	∟	⊿	∵	∩	∪							

Row 14	01	02	03	04	05	06	07	08	09	10	11	12	13	14	15	16	17	18	19
00	ぁ		ぃ		ぅ		ぇ		ぉ										
20															っ				
40																			
60							ゃ		ゅ		ょ							ゎ	
80																			

Row 15	01	02	03	04	05	06	07	08	09	10	11	12	13	14	15	16	17	18	19
00	ァ		ィ		ゥ		ェ		ォ										
20															ッ				
40																			
60							ャ		ュ		ョ							ヮ	
80					ヵ	ヶ													

Although KanjiTalk6 (the operating system) is now years old and no longer used, the KanjiTalk6 character set is still being used by many Japanese fonts for MacOS-J, including those developed by Adobe Systems and Morisawa.

The KanjiTalk7 character set

Apple Computer developed a new Japanese character set with the introduction of KanjiTalk 7.1 in late 1992. This character set is based on JIS X 0208-1990. I call this Japanese character set the KanjiTalk7 character set. This character set contains ASCII/JIS-Roman, half-width katakana, and JIS X 0208-1990. Rows 9 through 15 of this character set standard contain 260 characters above and beyond JIS X 0208-1990, plus the same 53 vertical variants that are included in the KanjiTalk6 character set. Table C-30 illustrates the differences between JIS X 0208-1990 and the KanjiTalk7 character set.

Table C-30: Comparing JIS X 0208:1997 and KanjiTalk7 Character Sets

Rows	Characters	Content
9	59	Encircled numerals 1–20, parenthesized numerals 1–20, black-encircled numerals 1–9, numerals 0–9 with period
10	56	Upper- and lowercase Roman numerals 1–15, parenthesized lowercase Latin characters
11	34	Abbreviations
12	27	Miscellaneous symbols
13	39	25 parenthesized kanji, 14 encircled kanji
14	35	28 katakana ligatures, 4 two-kanji ligatures, 3 four-kanji ligatures
15	10	5 miscellaneous symbols, 1 hiragana, 4 katakana
85	31	Vertical variants of row 1 (miscellaneous symbols)

Table C-30: Comparing JIS X 0208:1997 and KanjiTalk7 Character Sets (continued)

Rows	Characters	Content
88	10	Vertical variants of row 4 (hiragana)
89	12	Vertical variants of row 5 (katakana)

As you learned in Chapter 7, *Typography*, a four-kanji ligature is a single character that contains four reduced-size kanji characters within its design space. One is ㍿, which is a single character that represents the kanji compound 株式会社 (*kabushikigaisha*), and means "stock company" or "Incorporated." Another is ㈲, which represents the kanji compound 有限会社 (*yūgengaisha*), and means "limited liability company" or "Limited." The third one is 財団法人 (as a single ligature character), which represents the kanji compound 財団法人 (*zaidanhōjin*), and means "juridical foundation" or "foundation." The following tables illustrate the rows specific to the KanjiTalk7 character set:

Row 9		01	02	03	04	05	06	07	08	09	10	11	12	13	14	15	16	17	18	19
00		①	②	③	④	⑤	⑥	⑦	⑧	⑨	⑩	⑪	⑫	⑬	⑭	⑮	⑯	⑰	⑱	⑲
20	⑳											(1)	(2)	(3)	(4)	(5)	(6)	(7)	(8)	(9)
40	(10)	(11)	(12)	(13)	(14)	(15)	(16)	(17)	(18)	(19)	(20)									
60		❶	❷	❸	❹	❺	❻	❼	❽	❾										
80		0.	1.	2.	3.	4.	5.	6.	7.	8.	9.									

Row 10		01	02	03	04	05	06	07	08	09	10	11	12	13	14	15	16	17	18	19
00		I	II	III	IV	V	VI	VII	VIII	IX	X	XI	XII	XIII	XIV	XV				
20		i	ii	iii	iv	v	vi	vii	viii	ix	x	xi	xii	xiii	xiv	xv				
40																				
60		(a)	(b)	(c)	(d)	(e)	(f)	(g)	(h)	(i)	(j)	(k)	(l)	(m)	(n)	(o)	(p)	(q)	(r)	(s)
80	(t)	(u)	(v)	(w)	(x)	(y)	(z)													

Row 11		01	02	03	04	05	06	07	08	09	10	11	12	13	14	15	16	17	18	19
00		mm	mm²	cm	cm²	cm³	m	m²	m³	km	km²	mg	g	kg	cc	mℓ	dℓ	ℓ	kℓ	ms
20	μs	ns	ps	°F	mb	HP	Hz	KB	MB	GB	TB									
40																				
60																				
80												No.	K.K.	TEL	FAX					

Row 12		01	02	03	04	05	06	07	08	09	10	11	12	13	14	15	16	17	18	19
00		♤	♧	♡	◇	♠	♣	♥	♦											
20		〠	☎	[illegible]																
40		☞	☜	☝	☟	⇆	⇄	⇅	⇵	⇨	⇦	⇧	⇩	➡	⬅	⬆	⬇			
60																				
80																				

Row 13		01	02	03	04	05	06	07	08	09	10	11	12	13	14	15	16	17	18	19
00		(日)	(月)	(火)	(水)	(木)	(金)	(土)	(祭)	(祝)	(自)	(至)	(代)	(呼)	(株)	(資)	(名)	(有)	(学)	(財)
20	(社)	(特)	(監)	(企)	(協)	(労)														
40																				
60																				
80		㊤大	小	上	中	下	左	右	医	財	優	労	印	控	秘					

Row 14		01	02	03	04	05	06	07	08	09	10	11	12	13	14	15	16	17	18	19
00		ミリ	センチ	メートル	キロ	キロメートル	インチ	フィート	ヤード	アール	ヘクタール	グラム	キログラム	トン	リットル	ミリバール	ヘルツ	ワット	カロリー	ホーン
20	セント	ドル	ページ	パーセント								アパート	コーポ	ハイツ	ビル	マンション				
40																				
60												明治	大正	昭和	平成					
80													株式会社	有限会社	財団法人					

Row 15		01	02	03	04	05	06	07	08	09	10	11	12	13	14	15	16	17	18	19
00		§	∟	⊿																
20		゛	゛																	
40		ゔ		ヴ	ヸ	ヹ	ヺ													
60																				
80																				

Row 85		01	02	03	04	05	06	07	08	09	10	11	12	13	14	15	16	17	18	19
00			︑	︒														｜	｜	
20									︱	︲	'			︴	＝	—	︙	︰		
40			︵	︶	︹	︺	﹇	﹈	︷	︸	︿	﹀	︽	︾	﹁	﹂	﹃	﹄	︻	︼
60						‖														
80																				

Row 88		01	02	03	04	05	06	07	08	09	10	11	12	13	14	15	16	17	18	19
00		あ		い		う		え		お										
20																つ				
40																				
60								や		ゆ		よ							わ	
80																				

Row 89		01	02	03	04	05	06	07	08	09	10	11	12	13	14	15	16	17	18	19
00		ア		イ		ウ		エ		オ										
20																ツ				
40																				
60								ヤ		ユ		ヨ							ワ	
80						カ	ケ													

There are some characters used in Japanese, mainly punctuation marks, parentheses, and small versions of kana, that need to be positioned differently within their em-square when set vertically. Vertical Japanese text is described in Chapter 7. These characters are found in rows 1, 3, and 4. Rows 85, 88, and 89 in the KanjiTalk7 character set contain the vertical variants of rows 1, 4, and 5, respectively. Likewise, rows 11, 14, and 15 in the KanjiTalk6 character set contain the vertical variants of rows 1, 4, and 5, respectively. This difference between the KanjiTalk6 and KanjiTalk7 character sets is not found in the characters contained in these rows, but rather in the offsets used. Table C-31 details this difference between the KanjiTalk6 and KanjiTalk7 character sets.

Table C-31: Vertical Character Positions in the KanjiTalk6 and KanjiTalk7 Character Sets

	Row Offset	Row 1	Row 4	Row 5
KanjiTalk6	10	11	14	15
KanjiTalk7	84	85	88	89

You can imagine what a headache this row offset value change caused developers who produced software that relied on a value of 10 to access the vertically-set variants of those rows. Apple Computer has plans to eventually phase out these vertically-set variants altogether. I don't mean that you will no longer be able to set Japanese vertically on a Macintosh, but that they will be removed from the character set. This may mean that they are stored internally at the same code positions as their horizontally-set counterparts.

The KanjiTalk6 and KanjiTalk7 character sets both provide 2,444 user-defined character positions. This amounts to 13 rows of 188 characters, which is equivalent to 26 rows of 94 characters.

The PostScript equivalent of the KanjiTalk6 character set is *fontname*-83pv-RKSJ-H, and the PostScript equivalent of the KanjiTalk7 character set is *fontname*-90pv-RKSJ-H. See Chapter 6, *Font Formats*, for more details.

Microsoft Japanese

The character sets in Windows 3.1J and Win95J are identical, and can be described as JIS X 0208-1990 with NEC Row 13 plus the IBM Selected Kanji and Non-kanji sets (in both IBM and NEC positions). See the IBM Japanese and NEC Kanji sections for more information on these character sets, on pages 583 and 592 of this chapter, respectively. For details about Shift-JIS encoding, see page 175 in Chapter 4, *Encoding Methods*. This character set is also known as Microsoft Code Page 932.

The Japanese fonts bundled with Microsoft Windows and some of Microsoft's Japanese applications, such as Microsoft Word-J, were recently expanded to include all of JIS X 0212-1990, along with hundreds of additional characters found in Unicode.

The PostScript equivalent of the Windows 95J character set is *fontname*-90ms-RKSJ-H (horizontal) and *fontname*-90ms-RKSJ-V (vertical). See Chapter 6 for more details.

NEC Kanji

Nippon (Japan) Electronics Corporation (NEC; 日本電気株式会社 *nippon denki kabushikigaisha*) developed its own character set for use on its personal computers and dedicated Japanese word processors. This character set is based on JIS C 6226-1978, and also includes JIS-Roman and half-width katakana. The basic NEC Kanji character set also includes the 360 IBM Selected Kanji and 14 of the 28 IBM Selected Non-kanji set into rows 89 through 92. There are three ways in which the NEC implementation of the IBM Selected Kanji and Non-kanji differ from IBM's own implementation:

- They are encoded in a different region, specifically within the 94×94 matrix
- The 360 kanji come first followed by the non-kanji
- Only 14 of the 28 IBM Selected Non-kanji are included because the remaining 14 characters are already included in NEC Row 13

Table C-32 lists the differences between NEC Kanji and JIS X 0208:1997 (note that row numbers 2, 8, and 84 are identical to JIS C 6226-1978—compare with Table 3-62 on page 106).

Table C-32: The Differences Between JIS X 0208:1997 and NEC Kanji

Rows	Characters	Content
2	14	Miscellaneous symbols
8	0	Unassigned (reserved)
9	94	Half-width JIS-Roman characters
10	94	63 standard half-width katakana, 31 additional half-width katakana
11	93	76 half-width line-drawing elements, 17 half-width miscellaneous symbols
12	76	Full-width line-drawing elements
13[a]	83	Circled numerals 1–20, uppercase Roman numerals 1–10, 16 katakana ligatures, 10 abbreviations, 4 two-kanji ligatures, 5 encircled kanji, 3 parenthesized kanji, 15 miscellaneous symbols
84	0	Unassigned (reserved)
89–92	374	360 IBM Selected Kanji and 14 IBM Selected Non-kanji

[a] This row initially contained only 82 characters. Sometime after 1989 the two-kanji ligature for the Japanese era name ㍻ was added to this row to bring the total up to 83. This character is a ligature form of the kanji compound 平成 (*heisei*), which stands for the Heisei Era (1989–present).

Note the inclusion of half-width characters here, specifically the JIS-Roman and half-width katakana character sets. Some implementations include one-fourth size characters in rows 14 and 15.

NEC Kanji can also include an extended character set. Let's call this NEC Extended Kanji. These characters are arranged into a separate 94×94 matrix, and include 682 non-kanji and 3,382 kanji. Table C-33 lists the contents of this extended character set.

Table C-33: The NEC Extended Kanji Character Set

Rows	Characters	Content
1	94	Miscellaneous symbols
2	93	Miscellaneous symbols
3	92	Miscellaneous symbols
4	94	Miscellaneous symbols
5	94	Miscellaneous symbols
6	63	41 katakana ligatures, 20 parenthesized kanji, 2 encircled kanji
7–15	0	Unassigned (free)
16–17	152	Cursive kana characters
18–53	3,382	Kanji arranged by radical then stroke count
54–94	0	Unassigned (free)

Many of these 3,382 kanji are common to JIS X 0212-1990. NEC Extended Kanji was developed nearly 10 years before JIS X 0212-1990, and doesn't appear to be in very common use.

There seems to be a shift at NEC whereby its character set is becoming compatible with JIS X 0208:1997. Two NEC products released in late 1991 (both dedicated Japanese word processors) boasted support for the JIS X 0208-1990 character set.

The following tables illustrate how NEC Row 13, IBM Selected Kanji, and IBM Selected Non-kanji are encoded according to the NEC Kanji character set:

Row 13		01	02	03	04	05	06	07	08	09	10	11	12	13	14	15	16	17	18	19
00		①	②	③	④	⑤	⑥	⑦	⑧	⑨	⑩	⑪	⑫	⑬	⑭	⑮	⑯	⑰	⑱	⑲
20	⑳	Ⅰ	Ⅱ	Ⅲ	Ⅳ	Ⅴ	Ⅵ	Ⅶ	Ⅷ	Ⅸ	Ⅹ		㍉	㌔	㌢	㍍	㌘	㌧	㌃	㌶
40	㍑	㍗	㌍	㌦	㌣	㌫	㍊	㌻	㎜	㎝	㎞	㎎	㎏	㏄	㎡					
60				㍻	〝	〟	№	㏍	℡	㊤	㊥	㊦	㊧	㊨	㈱	㈲	㈹	㍾	㍽	㍼
80	≒	≡	∫	§	∑	√	⊥	∠	∟	⊿	∵	∩	∪							

Row 89		01	02	03	04	05	06	07	08	09	10	11	12	13	14	15	16	17	18	19
00		纊	褜	鍈	銈	蓜	俉	炻	昱	棈	鋹	曻	彅	丨	仡	仼	伀	伃	伹	佖
20	侒	侊	侚	侔	俍	偀	倢	俿	倞	偆	偰	偂	傔	僴	僘	兊	兤	冝	冾	凬
40	刕	劜	劦	勀	勛	匀	匇	匤	卲	厓	厲	叝	﨎	咜	咊	咩	哿	喆	坙	坥
60	垬	埈	埇	﨏	塚	增	墲	夋	奓	奛	奝	奣	妤	妺	孖	寀	甯	寘	寬	尞
80	岦	岺	峵	崧	嵓	﨑	嵂	嵭	嶸	嶹	巐	弡	弴	彧	德					

Row 90		01	02	03	04	05	06	07	08	09	10	11	12	13	14	15	16	17	18	19
00		忞	恝	悅	悊	惞	惕	愠	惲	愑	愷	愰	憘	戓	抦	揵	摠	撝	擎	敎
20	昀	昕	昻	昉	昮	昞	昤	晥	晗	晙	晴	晳	暙	暠	暲	暿	曺	朎	朗	杦
40	枻	桒	柀	栁	桄	棏	﨓	楨	﨔	榘	槢	樰	橫	橆	橳	橾	櫢	櫤	毖	氿
60	汜	沆	汯	泚	洄	涇	浯	涖	涬	淏	淸	淲	淼	渹	湜	渧	渼	溿	澈	澵
80	濵	瀅	瀇	瀨	炅	炫	焏	焄	煜	煆	煇	凞	燁	燾	犱					

Row 91		01	02	03	04	05	06	07	08	09	10	11	12	13	14	15	16	17	18	19
00		犾	猤	猪	獷	玽	珉	珖	珣	珒	琇	珵	琦	琪	琩	琮	瑢	璉	璟	甁
20	畯	皂	皜	皞	皛	皦	益	睆	劯	砡	硎	硤	硺	礰	礼	神	祥	禔	福	禛
40	竑	竧	靖	竫	箞	精	絈	絜	綷	綠	緖	繒	罇	羡	羽	茁	荢	荿	菇	菶
60	葈	蒴	蕓	蕙	蕫	﨟	薰	蘒	﨡	蠇	裵	訒	訷	詹	誧	誾	諟	諸	諶	譓
80	譿	賰	賴	贒	赶	﨣	軏	﨤	逸	遧	郞	都	鄕	鄧	釚					

Row 92		01	02	03	04	05	06	07	08	09	10	11	12	13	14	15	16	17	18	19
00		釗	釞	釭	釮	釤	釥	鈆	鈐	鈊	鈺	鉀	鈼	鉎	鉙	鉑	鈹	鉧	銧	鉷
20	鉸	鋧	鋗	鋙	鋐	﨧	鋕	鋠	鋓	錥	錡	鋻	﨨	錞	鋿	錝	錂	鍰	鍗	鎤
40	鏆	鏞	鏸	鐱	鑅	鑈	閒	隆	﨩	隝	隯	霳	霻	靃	靍	靏	靑	靕	顗	顥
60	飯	飼	餧	館	馞	驎	髙	髜	魵	魲	鮏	鮱	鮻	鰀	鵰	鵫	鶴	鸙	黑	
80		ⅰ	ⅱ	ⅲ	ⅳ	ⅴ	ⅵ	ⅶ	ⅷ	ⅸ	ⅹ	￢	￤	＇	＂					

Some of the characters in NEC Row 13 come in slightly different forms depending on the implementation. Table C-34 lists some of these characters, along with a known variation.

Table C-34: Alternate Forms for NEC Row 13 Characters

NEC Form	Alternate Form
㌢	㌢
㌘	㌘
㌃	㌃
㍗	㍗
㌣	㌣
㌻	㌻

Table C-34: Alternate Forms for NEC Row 13 Characters (continued)

NEC Form	Alternate Form
K.K.	K.K.
TEL	TEL

NTT Kanji

Nippon (Japan) Telegraph and Telephone (NTT; 日本電信電話 *nippon denshin denwa*) developed a character set that includes a non-kanji portion identical to JIS X 0208-1983, and a kanji portion identical to JIS C 6226-1978. There are also 261 NTT-specific symbols in the non-kanji region. These include lowercase and uppercase Roman numerals, additional mathematical symbols, symbols for units of measurement, additional line-drawing characters, and graphic representations for ASCII control characters.

NTT Kanji includes an additional 94×94 character space for kanji above and beyond those specified in JIS C 6226-1978. The first 60 rows of this additional character space (5,640 code points) have 5,238 kanji allocated to them, 4,048 of which are kanji found in the dictionary entitled 新字源 (*shinjigen*, meaning "new character origins"), but not in JIS C 6226-1978; the remaining 1,190 kanji are for use in writing person and place names. Within the first 60 rows of this character space, rows 1 through 44 are called Level 1 (4,048 kanji), and rows 45 through 57 are called Level 2 (1,190 kanji). Rows 61 through 64 (376 total code points) are allocated for extended non-kanji, but have yet to be assigned characters. Rows 65 through 94 (2,820 total code points) are reserved for user-defined characters. Table C-35 shows how characters are allocated to the additional 94×94 matrix.

Table C-35: The NTT Kanji Character Set

Rows	Characters	Content
1–44	4,048	Level 1 kanji
44–60	1,190	Level 2 kanji
61–64	0	Unassigned (reserved for extended non-kanji)
65–94	0	Unassigned (free)

TRON Character Set

The TRON character set, which is used on various instances of TRON, such as BTRON, is composed of four zones, labelled A through D, and supports the JIS X 0208:1997 and JIS X 0212-1990 character sets.* JIS X 0208:1997 and JIS X 0212-1990 are allocated to zones A and B, respectively.

* *http://tron.um.u-tokyo.ac.jp/* or *http://www.tokyoweb.or.jp/tron/*

Zone A is used for the most commonly-used character set. For Japanese, this is obviously JIS X 0208:1997. Zone B, as expected, is used for the next most commonly-used character set, which is JIS X 0212-1990. A recent development in TRON is that China's GB 2312-80 and Korea's KS X 1001:1992 are allocated to Zones C and D, respectively.

Korean Vendor Character Sets

There are two important Korean vendor character sets, specifically those for the Korean versions of MacOS and Microsoft Windows, along with IBM's Korean implementations. All are based on KS X 1001:1992, as shown in Table C-36.

Table C-36: Vendor Character Set Standards—Korea

Character Set	Additional Hangul	Additional Hanja	Other	User-Defined
DEC Korean				
HangulTalk			1,137	188
IBM Korean	270	377	6	1,880[a]
Unified Hangul Code	8,822			

[a] IBM Korean DBCS-Host encoding permits up to 1,880 user-defined characters, but IBM Korean DBCS-PC encoding permits only up to 1,227.

DEC Korean

The DEC Korean character set is identical to KS X 1001:1992, and appears to provide no support for user-defined characters.

HangulTalk Character Set

The HangulTalk character set, which is used on MacOS-KH, was originally developed by Elex Computer. It is based on the KS X 1001:1992 character set, but adds 1,137 additional characters, many of which are typeface-independent. Elex Computer designed this character set, and includes many symbols that are normally available in proprietary typesetting systems.

The single-byte range, used for encoding ASCII or KS-Roman, uses five additional code points, as illustrated in Table C-37.

Table C-37: Additional HangulTalk Single-Byte Characters

Code Point	Character
81	₩ ("won" symbol)
82	– (minus)
83	© (copyright)

Table C-37: Additional HangulTalk Single-Byte Characters (continued)

Code Point	Character
FE	™ (trademark)
FF	... (ellipsis)

The following tables illustrate the 1,137 characters that make up the KS X 1001:1992 extension of the HangulTalk character set, arranged according to their encoding:

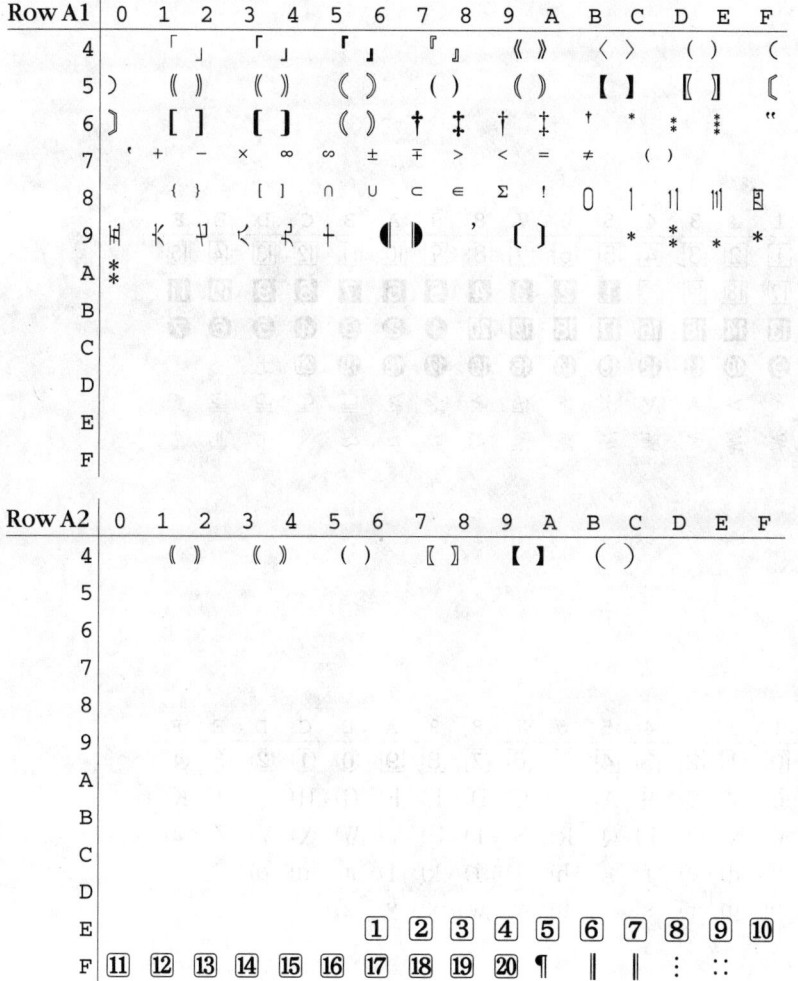

Row A1	0	1	2	3	4	5	6	7	8	9	A	B	C	D	E	F
4		「	」	「	」	「	」	『	』	《	》	〈	〉	(	)	(
5	)	⦅	⦆	⦅	⦆	(	)	(	)	(	)	【	】	〖	〗	〘
6	〙	[	]	[	]	(	)	†	‡	†	‡	†	*	⁑	⁂	"
7	'	+	−	×	∞	∽	±	∓	>	<	=	≠	(	)		
8		{	}	[	]	∩	∪	⊂	∈	Σ	!	0	1	11	111	目
9	[illegible]	[illegible]	[illegible]	[illegible]	[illegible]	+	◖	◗	'	[	]		*	⁑	*	*
A	⁑															
B																
C																
D																
E																
F																

Row A2	0	1	2	3	4	5	6	7	8	9	A	B	C	D	E	F
4		《	》	《	》	(	)	〖	〗	【	】	(	)			
5																
6																
7																
8																
9																
A																
B																
C																
D																
E							①	②	③	④	⑤	⑥	⑦	⑧	⑨	⑩
F	⑪	⑫	⑬	⑭	⑮	⑯	⑰	⑱	⑲	⑳	¶	‖	‖	⋮	∷	

Row A3	0	1	2	3	4	5	6	7	8	9	A	B	C	D	E	F
4		[1]	[2]	[3]	[4]	[5]	[6]	[7]	[8]	[9]	[10]	[11]	[12]	[13]	[14]	[15]
5	[16]	[17]	[18]	[19]	[20]	❶	❷	❸	❹	❺	❻	❼	❽	❾	❿	⓫
6	⓬	⓭	⓮	⓯	⓰	⓱	⓲	⓳	⓴	(A)	(B)	(C)	(D)	(E)	(F)	(G)
7	(H)	(I)	(J)	(K)	(L)	(M)	(N)	(O)	(P)	(Q)	(R)	(S)	(T)	(U)		
8		(V)	(W)	(X)	(Y)	(Z)	Ⓐ	Ⓑ	Ⓒ	Ⓓ	Ⓔ	Ⓕ	Ⓖ	Ⓗ	Ⓘ	Ⓙ
9	Ⓚ	Ⓛ	Ⓜ	Ⓝ	Ⓞ	Ⓟ	Ⓠ	Ⓡ	Ⓢ	Ⓣ	Ⓤ	Ⓥ	Ⓦ	Ⓧ	Ⓨ	Ⓩ
A																
B																
C																
D																
E																
F																

Row A4	0	1	2	3	4	5	6	7	8	9	A	B	C	D	E	F
4		[1]	[2]	[3]	[4]	[5]	[6]	[7]	[8]	[9]	[10]	[11]	[12]	[13]	[14]	[15]
5	[16]	[17]	[18]	[19]	[20]	■1	■2	■3	■4	■5	■6	■7	■8	■9	■10	■11
6	■12	■13	■14	■15	■16	■17	■18	■19	■20	➊	➋	➌	➍	➎	➏	➐
7	➑	➒	➓	⓫	⓬	⓭	⓮	⓯	⓰	⓱	⓲	⓳	⓴	⨦		
8		<	>	∧	∨	≮	≯	≰	≱	≲	≳	⫅	⫋	⫆	⫌	≶
9	≷	≹	⋚	⋛	⪋	⪌	⪑	⪒	∢	≅	≃	≈	⦣	⊤	⫫	⫽
A																
B																
C																
D																
E																
F																

Row A5	0	1	2	3	4	5	6	7	8	9	A	B	C	D	E	F
4		[0]	[1]	[2]	[3]	[4]	[5]	[6]	[7]	[8]	[9]	⓪	①	②	③	④
5	⑤	⑥	⑦	⑧	⑨	A)	B)	C)	D)	E)	F)	G)	H)	I)	J)	K)
6	L)	M)	N)	O)	P)	Q)	R)	S)	T)	U)	V)	W)	X)	Y)	Z)	a)
7	b)	c)	d)	e)	f)	g)	h)	i)	j)	k)	l)	m)	n)	o)		
8		p)	q)	r)	s)	t)	u)	v)	w)	x)	y)	z)				
9																
A																
B																
C																
D											!	∘	′	″	‴	
E																
F										●27	●28	●29	●30			

Row A6	0	1	2	3	4	5	6	7	8	9	A	B	C	D	E	F
4		⚜	⚜	†	††	‡‡	‡	§	♯	*	*	⁑	**	⁂	*	⁑
5	**	⁂	✻	⚹	✱	•	◈	◈	◆	◇	〈	〉	《	》	☜	☞
6	◈	◈	⊠	◘	▣	◆	◙	▣	◎	◎	◬	▲	✚	✖	◉	○
7	○	□	✣	❖	⊠	◌	⬚	□	□	❖	❖	✲	✱	═		
8		⛬	◎	◒	●	✧	✖	✲	✠	◈	▨			❀	❖	IIIII
9	₩	⚘	卍	☯			✗	◓	☯	❀	❀	❋			☺	❁
A																
B																
C																
D																
E						❶	❷	❸	❹	❺	❻	❼	❽	❾	❿	⓫
F	⓬	⓭	⓮	⓯	⓰	⓱	⓲	⓳	⓴	㉑	㉒	㉓	㉔	㉕	㉖	

Row A7	0	1	2	3	4	5	6	7	8	9	A	B	C	D	E	F
4		♂	〒	〶	○	△	□	⬠	⬡	□	▭	⏢	⏢	⏢	◇	⊔
5	⊓	Δ	⊿	∟	∪	//	✗	∩	≓	∻	≦	≧	∓	⊕	⊖	⊗
6	⨸	▽	≠	≢	≠	≠	▱	∺	∢	≐	∅	⊥	⊣	⊥	≢	∢
7	⋫	⊅	⊄	∉	∌	⊻	⊼	⊻	⊼	∞	▽	±	補	주식 회사		
8		회주 사식	㊞	印	‼	!?	‼	⁇	◇	◇	◇	◆	▫	□	□	■
9	∘	○	○	●	▽	△	▷	◁	♦	●	■	◭	◇	㈱	㈹	TP
A																
B																
C																
D																
E																
F	⑯	⑰	⑱	⑲	⑳	㉑	㉒	㉓	㉔	㉕	㉖	㉗	㉘	㉙	㉚	

Row A8	0	1	2	3	4	5	6	7	8	9	A	B	C	D	E	F
4		→	←	↑	↓	↖	↗	↘	↙	⇐	⇏	⇍	⇔	→	←	↑
5	↓	↔	↕	⬅	➡	⬆	⬇	⍇	⍈	⍐	⍗	⯇	⯈	⯅	⯆	⬅
6	➡	⬆	⬇	⇦	⇨	⇧	⇩	◀((·	·))▶	◄	►	⬅	➡	⬆	⬇	⇚
7	⇛	⇈	⇊	⬅	➡	⬆	⬇	←	→	↑	↓	↲	↱	↰		
8		⬎	⬐	↳	⬏	⬑	⤶	↷	↶	⤵	↶	⤷	⤶	⤴	⇦	⇨
9	⇧	⇩	←	→	✥	⬄	⇨	⇦	⇀	↽	⇾	⇽	⇨	⇦	⇄	⇅
A																
B																
C																
D																
E																
F																

Row A9	0	1	2	3	4	5	6	7	8	9	A	B	C	D	E	F
4		A.	B.	C.	D.	E.	F.	G.	H.	I.	J.	K.	L.	M.	N.	O.
5	P.	Q.	R.	S.	T.	U.	V.	W.	X.	Y.	Z.	a.	b.	c.	d.	e.
6	f.	g.	h.	i.	j.	k.	l.	m.	n.	o.	p.	q.	r.	s.	t.	u.
7	v.	w.	x.	y.	z.											
8																
9																
A																
B																
C																
D																
E																
F																

Row AA	0	1	2	3	4	5	6	7	8	9	A	B	C	D	E	F
4		문	답	주	명	대	형	부	전	접	수	동	비	반	자	타
5	감	약	인	뜻	印	註	예	感	冠	答	代	頭	動	名	目	反
6	補	本	副	序	連	影	例	源	子	前	節	接	助	指	他	派
7	形	조	문	답	주	뜻	註	교	역	음	정	해	예	존		
8		라	마	바	사	아	자	차	카	타	파	높	낮	명	대	형
9	부	전	접	수	동	비	게	반	속	인	본	약	숙	유	관	冠
A																
B																
C																
D																
E																
F						(16)	(17)	(18)	(19)	(20)	(21)	(22)	(23)	(24)	(25)	(26)

Row AB	0	1	2	3	4	5	6	7	8	9	A	B	C	D	E	F
4		조	국	감	印	衣	末	거	답	변	상	센	신	여	예	원
5	작	준	큰	외	활	간	같	실	感	慣	代	動	名	反	副	自
6	前	電	接	助	注	參	本	新	現	形	間	國	中	他	빠	시
7	입	으	음	직	표	가	나	다	하	마	바	사	아	자		
8		차	카	타	파	하	비	답	빠	본	단	센	시	여	예	으
9	음	입	제	존	준	표	해	느	높	낮	반	가	나	다	라	외
A																
B																
C																
D																
E																
F									(27)	(28)	(29)	(30)				

Row AC	0	1	2	3	4	5	6	7	8	9	A	B	C	D	E	F
4		⇨	⇦	➳	→	←	➡	⬌	➤	◀	↣	↢	⇀	↼	➡	⬅
5	↰	↱	⤸	⤹	⤷	⇦	⇨	⇧	⇩	⇦	⇨	⇧	⇩	←	→	↞
6	↑	↓	←	→	↑	↓	⇦	⇨	⇧	⇩	⇠	⇢	⇡	⇣	⬅	➡
7	⬆	⬇	⇦	⇨	⇧	⇩	⤶	⤴	⤹	⤵	⤺	⤷	⤶	⤴		
8		⤶	⤴	⤹	⤵	⤺	⤷	⤶	⤴	⇦	⇨	⇧	⇩	☝	☟	☝
9	☞	(단)	(참)	(소)	(종)	(일)	(이)	(휴)								
A																
B																
C			❶	❷	❸	❹	❺	❻	❼	❽	❾	❿	⓫	⓬	⓭	⓮
D	⓯															
E																
F			⓰	⓱	⓲	⓳	⓴									

Row AD	0	1	2	3	4	5	6	7	8	9	A	B	C	D	E	F
4		一	二	三	四	五	六	七	八	九	十	十一	十二	十三	十四	十五
5	十六	十七	十八	十九	二十	一	二	三	四	五	六	七	八	九	十	十一
6	十二	十三	十四	十五	十六	十七	十八	十九	二十	日	月	火	水	木	金	土
7	㊐	㊊	㊋	㊌	㊍	㊎	㊏	日	月	火	水	木	金	土		
8																
9																
A		「	」	『	』	⇨	⇦	⇧	⇩	〃	〃	⸗	⸗	ˋ	ˎ	⬆
B	!															
C																
D																
E																
F																

I have noticed that some Korean type foundries have the Yin-Yang (음양/陰陽 *eumyang*, meaning "negative [and] positive") symbols reversed when implementing this character set. This symbol is called 태극/太極 (*taegeug*) in Korean. Row 0xA6 includes three instances of this character: ◒ (0xA693), ◓ (0xA697), and ◐ (0xA698). Notice how they appear to be rotating in the counter-clockwise direction, which is considered to be correct.

Many of the gaps in the HangulTalk character set are actually by design, specifically so that it can be overlaid on the KS X 1001:1992 character set encoded according to EUC-KR with no overlapping of characters. You can compare these tables with the KS X 1001:1992 code table in Appendix L, *KS X 1001:1992 Table*, to see how they overlay.

IBM Korean

The IBM Korean character set is based on KS X 1001:1992, and adds 377 hanja, 270 hangul, and 6 symbols. As with other IBM character sets, their Korean character set has been implemented using two different encodings: DBCS-Host and DBCS-PC.

The IBM Korean DBCS-Host character set, also known as IBM Code Page 00834, is arranged as shown in Table C-38.

Table C-38: IBM Korean DBCS-Host Character Set

Character Type	Number of Characters
Full-width space	1
Symbols[a]	991
Hanja[b]	5,265
Hangul[c]	2,620
User-defined characters	1,880

[a] Includes the 6 IBM Selected Characters.
[b] Includes the 377 IBM Selected Hanja
[c] Includes the 270 IBM Selected Hangul

Interestingly, the 2,620 hangul that are included in IBM Korean DBCS-Host are encoded according to Johab encoding, as described in Chapter 4 starting on page 177.

Table C-39 illustrates the IBM Korean DBCS-PC character set, also known as IBM Code Pages 00926 or 00951. Note how the three sets of IBM Selected Characters are separate from the KS X 1001:1992 characters, but are combined with them in the IBM DBCS-Host character set. Also note how the 1,227 user-defined characters are separated into three regions. The last two user-defined regions, with 94 available code points each, are from KS X 1001:1992 itself.

Table C-39: IBM Korean DBCS-PC Character Set

Character Type	Number of Characters
User-defined characters	1,039
IBM Selected Characters	6
IBM Selected Hanja	377
IBM Selected Hangul	270
KS X 1001:1992 symbols	986
KS X 1001:1992 hangul	2,350
User-defined characters	94

Table C-39: IBM Korean DBCS-PC Character Set (continued)

Character Type	Number of Characters
KS X 1001:1992 hanja	4,888
User-defined characters	94

The following tables illustrate the IBM Korean Selected Characters, encoded according to IBM Korean DBCS-PC encoding (where these IBM-specific characters are consolidated to seven rows):

Row 9A	0	1	2	3	4	5	6	7	8	9	A	B	C	D	E	F
A							≠	≦	≧	°K	¦	＂	喀	擱	羯	酣
B	醲	骼	蒹	哽	扃	檠	頴	畊	稧	雞	杲	瞽	詁	栱	槓	箜
C	蝌	霍	盥	鸛	鉸	佝	傴	媾	嫗	晷	甌	覯	颶	掬	跪	巹
D	漌	岌	笈	覊	鰭	炁	糯	喃	囊	迺	佞	獰	孥	閙	靻	怛
E	闥	韃	党	蟷	碓	菟	咄	垌	肚	蚪	滕	灯	鐙	犖	幱	埒
F	榔	涼	魎	癘	膂	蠡	鑢	櫟	鬣	呤	泠	苓	蛉	潦	艫	

Row 9B	0	1	2	3	4	5	6	7	8	9	A	B	C	D	E	F
A		轤	漉	淥	轆	籟	蕾	誄	寥	僂	髏	窿	凜	廩	提	漓
B	离	螭	魑	痳	岦	媽	蟇	謾	鏝	鬘	魍	昧	莓	脉	俛	耄
C	鉡	濛	朦	瀰	糜	閩	婆	欂	膊	胖	髣	魴	潘	翻	辟	汴
D	辮	遍	駢	鷩	迸	鴇	黼	蝠	丰	葑	仆	罘	苻	蜉	頫	鮒
E	吩	蕡	巿	鬅	黻	妣	沙	沘	睥	篦	腓	轡	髀	擯	蘋	贇
F	鼙	鬢	姒	麝	楂	槎	笥	槊	鑠	畝	鍤	霎	殤	鰓	噬	

Row 9C	0	1	2	3	4	5	6	7	8	9	A	B	C	D	E	F
A		婿	齟	射	單	尠	愃	洗	燹	霰	偰	契	挈	艘	霄	蟀
B	瑣	叟	宿	晬	溲	祟	睢	鶉	虱	啻	寺	緦	矧	瑟	蓴	贗
C	鴈	戞	遏	嵒	諳	黯	鞅	欸	皚	礙	靉	阨	射	篛	籥	牂
D	敔	恚	射	羨	臙	蠕	讌	塩	饜	嬰	睨	翳	蕋	邀	媼	蘊
E	鰛	蕘	舂	蛹	吁	熨	蜿	暐	衞	囿	帷	蕤	黝	鬻	櫽	垠
F	齦	挹	栮	頤	仞	眥	粢	耔	觜	赭	柞	涔	蚕	嶂	瘴	

Row 9D	0	1	2	3	4	5	6	7	8	9	A	B	C	D	E	F
A		裝	纔	柢	蛆	豬	糴	囀	巔	磚	翦	窃	椄	梃	晢	瑅
B	踶	吊	噪	皁	竈	笊	糶	絛	鯛	樅	蹤	蔟	肘	隼	則	証
C	痣	滄	慚	搠	悵	鼈	簀	蜴	躑	濺	簷	蜻	砌	隷	峭	綃
D	鈔	鞘	數	躅	髑	怱	葱	摧	槌	甃	箒	鞦	麁	麤	杻	舳
E	沖	橇	贅	巵	徵	鴟	忱	拆	橐	駄	幀	蝙	庖	炮	舖	鉋
F	鞄	分	蓖	蹕	瘧	邯	鬨	炕	廨	慊	篋	陜	皥	醐	鶻	

Row 9E	0	1	2	3	4	5	6	7	8	9	A	B	C	D	E	F
A		鑊	圜	懽	鬟	媓	怳	囂	猴	篌	忻	迄	頡	갂	갊	겱
B	겆	겐	곪	곺	괙	괨	괫	귓	귕	귭	긂	긏	긑	긧	긺	깄
C	깉	깢	꺠	꼄	꼳	꽌	꽘	꽛	꽨	꾓	꿎	꾿	뀐	뀟	꿕	꿩
D	끠	낐	낸	내	넏	넞	녇	녓	녙	녯	뉵	놧	놰	뉫	늦	닁
E	닑	닉	당	대	덨	덪	뎜	돐	됀	됏	됐	둔	뒷	뒴	듁	듊
F	딮	뚝	딷	뜷	따	때	뗴	뚀	뛰	뜌	래	렌	뢔	름	뤳	

Row 9F	0	1	2	3	4	5	6	7	8	9	A	B	C	D	E	F
A		릐	맟	맻	매	멫	멭	몀	몯	뫃	뫠	믁	뭉	믜	뮌	밎
B	밨	밴	뱜	배	벘	벅	벹	볌	볏	볒	볔	봣	붖	뷐	븘	븡
C	븨	빈	빤	뺴	뻭	뼨	뼬	뼷	뼤	뽜	뾔	뿀	뿕	뿝	쀡	쀠
D	쀡	쁙	삐	샤	샵	샳	샺	샹	샌	섥	섿	셑	셨	숀	숏	슌
E	슳	싀	싦	쌂	썃	썟	쌰	썃	쌔	썻	쎅	쎙	쎠	쎼	쏼	쒯
F	쑷	쒓	쒷	쓔	씄	씿	얇	앙	얐	앳	워	엱	연	옝	옫	

Row A0	0	1	2	3	4	5	6	7	8	9	A	B	C	D	E	F
A		옺	욷	웏	윋	윳	잂	잦	잪	젇	젔	죻	젹	졋	좐	좜
B	좠	좬	좰	좸	죨	죰	죱	줫	쥭	즤	짔	쨰	쩖	쪨	쪗	쪠
C	쫒	쬬	쮀	쯥	찌	찟	찦	찬	찾	찮	챱	채	쳣	청	쵀	췃
D	츼	칸	캔	캘	캐	컬	켈	퀙	퀜	퀫	큔	킹	킈	태	텠	텩
E	퇫	튓	퉁	틧	팊	팦	퍙	패	펠	펵	폇	퐤	풰	퓩	픅	픐
F	픙	픠	핀	한	핡	핬	핱	해	헌	헴	혹	흠	훕	휌	흭	

DBCS-PC 0x9AA6 has a glyph identical to most implementations of KS X 1001:1992 01-33 (specifically, ≠) because the actual KS X 1001:1992 standard uses the glyph ≠ for 01-33. This symbol's meaning is "not equal."

Unified Hangul Code

Microsoft introduced an expanded Korean character set, called Unified Hangul Code (UHC), beginning with Microsoft Windows 95K. Unified Hangul Code is also known as Microsoft Code Page 949.* UHC's encoding is identical to EUC-KR encoding in terms of how KS X 1001:1992 characters are encoded, but includes the additional 8,822 hangul necessary to complete the set of 11,172 hangul in the Johab set.

* Unified Hangul Code was originally called Extended Wansung.

D

Vendor Encoding Methods

The material covered in this appendix supplements Chapter 4, *Encoding Methods*, and Appendix C, *Vendor Character Set Standards*. Like Appendix C, it is intended as reference material in the event that you need to work with a particular vendor character set. The material here should provide enough information.

Most of the vendor encoding methods share similar encodings with the national character set encodings. This is appropriate since, as you have already learned, most vendor character set standards share many of the same characters with only slight variations. Table D-1 lists these vendor character sets, along with the encodings that support them. Some of the character sets described in Appendix C are not described in this appendix simply because they share the same encoding as described in Chapter 4 (or I couldn't find any encoding information for them).

Table D-1: CJKV Vendor Encoding Method Overview

Encoding	Supported Character Sets
ISO-2022	NEC Kanji, NTT Kanji
EUC	MacOS-S, DEC Korean, IKIS, NEC Kanji
EUC extension	DEC Hanyu, DEC Hanzi, DEC Kanji, HP-16 (Japanese), HangulTalk, Super DEC Kanji, Unified Hangul Code
Big Five	ETen, MacOS-T, DynaLab Hong Kong, Monotype Hong Kong
Shift-JIS	Enfour Gaiji, FMR Kanji, MacOS-J, Microsoft Japanese, NEC Kanji
Shift-JIS extension	HP-15 (Japanese)
IBM DBCS-PC	All IBM
IBM DBCS-Host	All IBM
IBM DBCS-EUC	All IBM
IBM TBCS-EUC	IBM Traditional Chinese
Other	JEF, KEIS78, KEIS83, TRON

At appropriate times in this appendix, comparisons are drawn between vendor encoding methods and those covered in Chapter 4.

Brief Overview of IBM Encodings

IBM has defined four basic multiple-byte language-independent encoding methods: DBCS-PC, DBCS-EUC, TBCS-EUC, and DBCS-Host (the abbreviation DBCS stands for Double-Byte Character Set; likewise, the abbreviation TBCS stands for Triple-Byte Character Set). TBCS-EUC is not used to encode Japanese. IBM manufactures and supports a wide variety of computing environments, such as host computers, PCs, and Unix workstations, and thus requires many encoding methods. While each locale has its own variation for each of these encodings, the tables in this section define these encodings in a generic way.

IBM DBCS-PC Encoding

Table D-2 provides the generic definition for IBM DBCS-PC encoding, which basically uses ASCII or equivalent in the one-byte range and a large and disjoint two-byte range.

Table D-2: IBM DBCS-PC Encoding Specifications—Generic

	Decimal	Hexadecimal
ASCII/CJKV-Roman		
Byte range	33–126	21–7E
Two-byte characters		
First byte range	129–254	81–FE
Second byte ranges	64–126, 128–254	40–7E, 80–FE

Note how the second-byte range is identical to the second-byte range of Shift-JIS encoding.

IBM DBCS-EUC and TBCS-EUC Encodings

IBM has developed EUC encodings that have been implemented identically to EUC encoding as described in Chapter 4. Note that there are two types of IBM EUC encodings, specifically DBCS-EUC and TBCS-EUC. TBCS-EUC refers to characters encoded using three bytes. In IBM terminology, the use of SS2 and SS3 does not count when totalling the number of bytes per character (they are treated as shift characters). So, TBCS-EUC is used only to refer to EUC-TW code set 2 (CNS 11643-1992 Planes 1 through 16).

IBM DBCS-Host Encoding

Table D-3 provides the generic definition for IBM DBCS-Host encoding, which is EBCDIC-based.

Table D-3: IBM DBCS-Host Encoding Specifications—Generic

	Decimal	Hexadecimal
One-byte characters		
Byte range	65–249	41–F9
Full-width space		
First byte	64	40
Second byte	64	40
Two-byte characters		
First byte range	65–254	41–FE
Second byte range	65–254	41–FE
Shifting characters		
One-byte character	15	0F
Two-byte character	14	0E

Note the use of shifting characters, which clearly shows that this encoding is modal. Also, the one-byte range is EBCDIC-based, not ASCII. All multiple-byte encodings that use EBCDIC for the one-byte range turn out to be modal.

Chinese Vendor Encodings—China

While most Chinese vendor character sets follow the GB 2312-80 character set standard and its most widely used encoding (EUC-CN), IBM has developed several other encodings that encapsulate the same character set, along with some IBM extensions.

DEC Hanzi Encoding

DEC Hanzi encoding is identical to EUC-CN encoding except that there is an additional 94×94 region for encoding user-defined characters. Table D-4 illustrates DEC Hanzi encoding.

Table D-4: DEC Hanzi Encoding Specifications

	Decimal	Hexadecimal
ASCII/GB-Roman		
Byte range	33–126	21–7E

Table D-4: DEC Hanzi Encoding Specifications (continued)

	Decimal	Hexadecimal
GB 2312-80		
First byte range	161–254	A1–FE
Second byte range	161–254	A1–FE
User-defined characters		
First byte range	161–254	A1–FE
Second byte range	33–126	21–7E

IBM Simplified Chinese Encodings

IBM has developed a number of encodings for handling Simplified Chinese, specifically for those character sets that are based on GB 2312-80. The following sections describe the Simplified Chinese encodings originally developed by IBM, specifically DBCS-PC and DBCS-Host encodings. IBM has recently adopted GBK (as DBCS-PC), and has their own version of EUC-CN encoding (called DBCS-EUC). Please refer to IBM documentation for details about their EUC-CN and GBK implementations.

IBM Simplified Chinese DBCS-PC encoding

Table D-5 provides the encoding specifications for IBM Simplified Chinese DBCS-PC encoding.

Table D-5: IBM Simplified Chinese DBCS-PC Encoding Specifications

	Decimal	Hexadecimal
ASCII/GB-Roman		
Byte range	33–126	21–7E
GB 2312-80[a]		
First byte range	129–172	81–AC
Second byte ranges	64–126, 128–252	40–7E, 80–FC
User-defined characters		
First byte range	240–249	F0–F9
Second byte ranges	64–126, 128–252	40–7E, 80–FC
IBM Selected Characters		
First byte range	250–251	FA–FB
Second byte ranges	64–126, 128–252	40–7E, 80–FC
Reserved		
First byte ranges	176–239, 252	B0–EF, FC
Second byte ranges	64–126, 128–252	40–7E, 80–FC

[a] The last defined character in this region is 0xAC9E.

IBM Simplified Chinese DBCS-Host encoding

Table D-6 provides the encoding specifications for IBM Simplified Chinese DBCS-Host encoding.

Table D-6: IBM Simplified Chinese DBCS-Host Encoding Specifications

	Decimal	Hexadecimal
One-byte characters		
Byte range	65–249	41–F9
Full-width space		
First byte	64	40
Second byte	64	40
Two-byte characters[a]		
First byte range	65–111	41–6F
Second byte ranges	65–127, 129–253	41–7F, 81–FD
User-defined characters		
First byte range	118–127	76–7F
Second byte ranges	65–127, 129–253	41–7F, 81–FD
Shifting characters		
One-byte character	15	0F
Two-byte character	14	0E
Reserved		
First byte ranges	112–117, 128–254	70–75, 80–FE
Second byte ranges	65–127, 129–253	41–7F, 81–FD

[a] The last defined character in this region is 0x6C9F.

MacOS-S Encoding

The encoding used on MacOS-S is identical to EUC-CN except that it accommodates additional one-byte characters (see Table C-6 on page 558). In fact, the existence of two of these additional one-byte characters, at code points 0xFD and 0xFE, effectively reduces the size of the two-byte encoding region by 188 code points.

Table D-7 illustrates the MacOS-S encoding specifications, which show the reduced two-byte encoding region: 0xA1A1 through 0xFCFE.

Table D-7: MacOS-S Encoding Specifications

	Decimal	Hexadecimal
ASCII/GB-Roman		
Byte ranges	33–126, 128, 253–255	21–7E, 80, FD–FF

Table D-7: MacOS-S Encoding Specifications (continued)

	Decimal	Hexadecimal
GB 2312-80		
First byte range	161–252	A1–FC
Second byte range	161–254	A1–FE

Chinese Vendor Encodings—Taiwan

There are many vendor extensions to Big Five. This is because Big Five is much more widely implemented than CNS 11643-1992. See Table 4-39 on page 172 for a complete description of Big Five encoding. DEC Hanyu seems to be the only vendor implementation that is based on CNS 11643-1992.

DEC Hanyu Encoding

DEC Hanyu encoding consists of a mixed one-, two-, and four-byte encoding. It differs from EUC-TW encoding in two major ways:

- CNS 11643-1992 Planes 1 and 2 are encoded using two bytes
- CNS 11643-1992 Planes 3 and 4 are encoded using four bytes, but the first two bytes are always 0xC2 and 0xCB

Table D-8 provides the DEC Hanyu encoding specifications, illustrating the complete one- through four-byte encoding region.

Table D-8: DEC Hanyu Encoding Specifications

	Decimal	Hexadecimal
ASCII/CNS-Roman		
Byte ranges	33–126	21–7E
CNS 11643-1992 Plane 1		
First byte range	161–254	A1–FE
Second byte range	161–254	A1–FE
CNS 11643-1992 Plane 2		
First byte range	161–254	A1–FE
Second byte range	33–126	21–7E
CNS 11643-1992 Plane 3		
First byte	194	C2
Second byte	203	CB
Third byte range	161–254	A1–FE
Fourth byte range	161–254	A1–FE

Table D-8: DEC Hanyu Encoding Specifications (continued)

	Decimal	Hexadecimal
CNS 11643-1992 Plane 4		
First byte	194	C2
Second byte	203	CB
Third byte range	161–254	A1–FE
Fourth byte range	33–126	21–7E

ETen Encoding

The encoding used by the ETen character set is simply Big Five. The ETen-specific characters are encoded in rows 0xC6 through 0xC8 and 0xF9, which are within the Big Five encoding definition.

IBM Traditional Chinese Encodings

While the most widely used IBM Traditional Chinese encoding is IBM DBCS-Big5, there are a number of encodings for IBM Traditional Chinese, some of which are covered in this section. IBM Traditional Chinese DBCS-EUC and TBCS-EUC encodings support the CNS 11643-1992 character set, at least Planes 1 through 3, and is identical to EUC-TW encoding.

IBM Traditional Chinese DBCS-PC encoding

Table D-9 provides the encoding specifications for IBM Traditional Chinese DBCS-PC encoding.

Table D-9: IBM Traditional Chinese DBCS-PC Encoding Specifications

	Decimal	Hexadecimal
ASCII/CNS-Roman		
Byte range	33–126	21–7E
Two-byte characters[a]		
First byte range	129–209	81–D1
Second byte ranges	64–126, 128–252	40–7E, 80–FC
User-defined characters		
First byte range	219–251	DB–FB
Second byte ranges	64–126, 128–252	40–7E, 80–FC
Reserved		
First byte ranges	210–218, 252	D2–DA, FC
Second byte ranges	64–126, 128–252	40–7E, 80–FC

[a] The last defined character in this region is 0xD1C6.

IBM Traditional Chinese DBCS-Host encoding

Table D-10 provides the encoding specifications for IBM Traditional Chinese DBCS-Host encoding.

Table D-10: IBM Traditional Chinese DBCS-Host Encoding Specifications

	Decimal	Hexadecimal
One-byte characters		
Byte range	65–249	41–F9
Full-width space		
First byte	64	40
Second byte	64	40
Two-byte characters[a]		
First byte range	65–145	41–91
Second byte ranges	65–127, 129–253	41–7F, 81–FD
User-defined characters		
First byte range	194–226	C2–E2
Second byte ranges	65–127, 129–253	41–7F, 81–FD
Shifting characters		
One-byte character	15	0F
Two-byte character	14	0E
Reserved		
First byte ranges	74–75, 146–193, 227–254	4A–4B, 92–C1, E3–FE
Second byte ranges	65–127, 129–253	41–7F, 81–FD

[a] The last defined character in this region is 0x91C7.

MacOS-T Encoding

The encoding used by the MacOS-T character set is slightly reduced Big Five encoding (to accommodate two of its four additional one-byte characters, as illustrated in Table C-14 on page 563). Table D-11 provides a complete description of the Big Five encoding used on MacOS-T.

Table D-11: MacOS-T Encoding Specifications

	Decimal	Hexadecimal
ASCII/CNS-Roman		
Byte ranges	33–126, 128, 253–255	21–7E, 80, FD–FF
Big Five		
First byte range	161–252	A1–FC
Second byte ranges	64–126, 161–254	40–7E, A1–FE

Microsoft Traditional Chinese Encoding

The encoding used by the Microsoft Traditional Chinese character set is simply Big Five. Characters from the ETen character set are encoded in row 0xF9, which is within the Big Five encoding definition (the ETen characters encoded in rows 0xC6 through 0xC8 are not included).

Chinese Vendor Encodings—Hong Kong

All of the encodings that support Hong Kong extensions are based on Big Five encoding. In fact, Big Five is still considered the *de facto* character set and encoding for the Hong Kong locale. While the Hong Kong government has developed its own Hong Kong extension to Big Five (which itself required an extension to Big Five encoding), those Hong Kong extensions developed by vendors keep its characters encoded within the standard Big Five definition. This is important for compatibility with existing operating systems that are based on Big Five.

DynaLab Hong Kong Encoding

The encoding used by DynaLab's Hong Kong extension is simply Big Five. However, when implemented on MacOS-T, 0xFD and 0xFE are unavailable as the first byte or a two-byte character because they are reserved for single-byte characters. Table D-11 on page 612 showed how the MacOS-T implementation of Big Five encoding treats rows 0xFD and 0xFE as part of the single-byte range, not as the first byte of a two-byte character. Under these circumstances, the DynaLab Hong Kong hanzi encoded in rows 0xFD and 0xFE are simply not available.

Monotype Hong Kong Encoding

The encoding used by the Monotype Hong Kong character set is simply Big Five. The Hong Kong characters are encoded in rows 0xFA through 0xFC. This makes it possible to implement this character set on MacOS-T because row 0xFC is still considered to be part of the two-byte encoding region. Table D-11 on page 612 showed how the MacOS-T implementation of Big Five encoding treats rows 0xFD and 0xFE as part of the single-byte range, not as the first byte of a two-byte character.

Japanese Vendor Encodings

All of the major Japanese encodings—ISO-2022-JP, EUC-JP, and Shift-JIS—have been adopted by at least one Japanese vendor for use in their products. There have also been other encodings developed, some of them pre-dating ISO-2022-JP, EUC-JP, and Shift-JIS encodings.

DEC Kanji Encoding

DEC Kanji encoding is very similar to EUC-JP complete two-byte format. The equivalent of EUC-JP code sets 0, 1, and 3 are supported. Note that the ASCII/JIS-Roman portion of DEC Kanji encoding is identical to EUC-JP packed format (that is, one-byte). Also note that the equivalent of EUC-JP code set 2, specifically half-width katakana, is not supported. Table D-12 shows the encoding.

Table D-12: DEC Kanji Encoding Specifications

	Decimal	Hexadecimal
ASCII/JIS-Roman		
Byte range	33–126	21–7E
JIS X 0208:1997		
First byte range	161–254	A1–FE
Second byte range	161–254	A1–FE
User-defined characters		
First byte range	161–254	A1–FE
Second byte range	33–126	21–7E

Super DEC Kanji encoding expands upon the encoding regions provided by DEC Kanji encoding. Put simply, Super DEC Kanji encoding is DEC Kanji encoding with the rest of EUC-JP encoding thrown in. Table D-13 provides the complete encoding specifications for Super DEC Kanji encoding.

Table D-13: Super DEC Kanji Encoding Specifications

	Decimal	Hexadecimal
ASCII/JIS-Roman		
Byte range	33–126	21–7E
JIS X 0208:1997		
First byte range	161–254	A1–FE
Second byte range	161–254	A1–FE
Half-width katakana		
First byte	142	8E
Second byte range	161–223	A1–DF
JIS X 0212-1990		
First byte	143	8F
Second byte range	161–254	A1–FE
Third byte range	161–254	A1–FE

Table D-13: Super DEC Kanji Encoding Specifications (continued)

	Decimal	Hexadecimal
User-defined characters		
First byte range	161–254	A1–FE
Second byte range	33–126	21–7E

DEC Kanji, Super DEC Kanji, and EUC-JP encodings

DEC Kanji encoding is identical to EUC-JP complete two-byte format without code set 2 (half-width katakana). Also note that the equivalent of EUC-JP code set 3 is not specified to be used for the JIS X 0212-1990 character set.

Super DEC Kanji encoding, however, is a superset of DEC Kanji and EUC-JP encodings.

Fujitsu Japanese Encodings

Fujitsu has developed both mainframe and personal computers, and the character sets and encodings used on each are different. The JEF character set and encoding are used on their FACOM mainframe computers, and the FMR Kanji character set and encoding are used on their personal computers.

JEF encoding

JEF encoding is quite unusual. First, it does not use the ASCII/JIS-Roman character set or encoding—it uses EBCDIC/EBCDIK instead. This allows for a quite different encoding structure, yet you will see some similarities with EUC-JP encoding. The first byte's value spans the seven- and eight-bit range. This does not allow such an encoding to make use of the byte's value to determine whether it represents itself, or is part of an expected two-byte sequence. JEF, instead, uses special characters for performing such shifts of state. The code specifications for JEF are listed in Table D-14.

Table D-14: JEF Encoding Specifications

	Decimal	Hexadecimal
One-byte characters		
Byte range	65–249	41–F9
Full-width space		
First byte	64	40
Second byte	64	40
JIS C 6226-1978[a]		
First byte range	161–254	A1–FE
Second byte range	161–254	A1–FE

Table D-14: JEF Encoding Specifications (continued)

	Decimal	Hexadecimal
JEF Extended characters		
First byte ranges	65–125, 127	41–7D, 7F
Second byte range	161–254	A1–FE
User-defined characters		
First byte range	128–160	80–A0
Second byte range	161–254	A1–FE
Shifting characters		
One-byte character	41	29
Two-byte character	40	28

[a] 0xA1A1 is not a valid code position.

First, the encoding for the JIS C 6226-1978 character set is identical to EUC-JP code set 1. The remainder is unique to JEF, except for the special encoding for the full-width space, which is shared by IBM Japanese DBCS-Host encoding (see page 623).

Figure D-1 illustrates the JEF encoding space. Note that it is similar to EUC-JP encoding (the JIS C 6226-1978 portion shares the same encoding with EUC-JP code set 1), and that the full-width space character is off by itself within the encoding space.

JEF and EUC-JP encodings

The JIS C 6226-1978 portion of JEF encoding is identical to that of EUC-JP code set 1. The rest of JEF encoding, as you saw, is quite different.

FMR Kanji encoding

The FMR Kanji encoding is identical to Shift-JIS encoding. There is not much more to say about it here. See Figure 4-16 on page 178 for an illustration of Shift-JIS encoding, and Table 4-42 on page 176 for a listing of its specifications. Also see Table 4-43 on page 178 for a listing of the user-defined character area. The first byte range for these characters is from 0xF0 to 0xFC.

HP Kanji Encodings

Hewlett-Packard developed two Japanese encoding methods called HP-15 and HP-16. Both encode the same set of characters, but in a different way. HP-15 is a superset of Shift-JIS encoding, and HP-16 is similar to EUC-JP encoding. These encoding methods are fully compatible with one another, and Hewlett-Packard

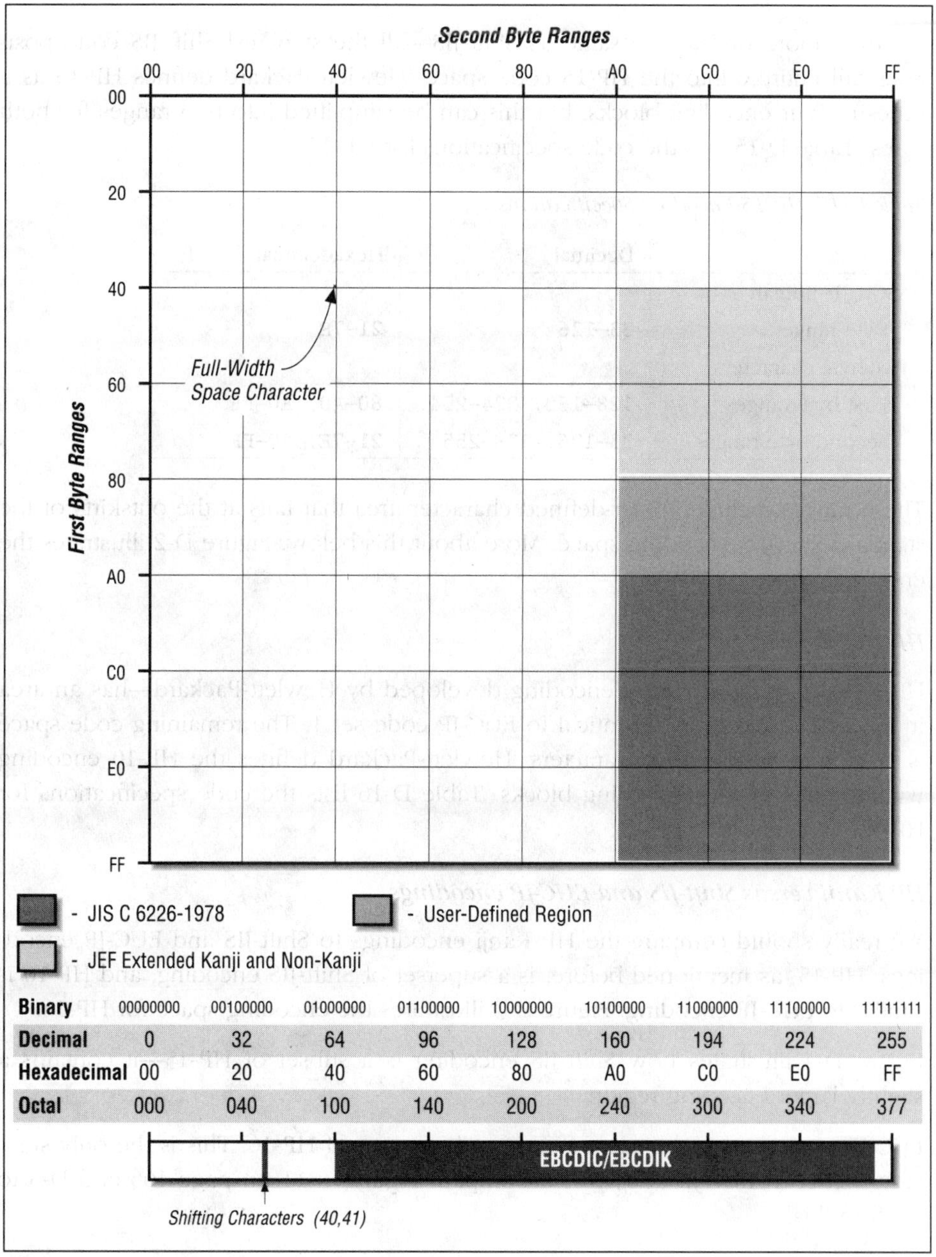

Figure D-1: JEF encoding tables

software is able to convert between them. I have seen the mapping tables, and they are not in a form that can be readily digested.

HP-15 encoding

HP-15 is more or less the same as Shift-JIS—all the standard Shift-JIS code positions fall entirely into the HP-15 code space. Hewlett-Packard defines HP-15 as a series of four encoding blocks, but this can be simplified into two ranges for both bytes. Table D-15 lists the code specifications for HP-15.

Table D-15: HP-15 Encoding Specifications

	Decimal	Hexadecimal
ASCII/JIS-Roman		
Byte range	33–126	21–7E
Two-byte characters		
First byte ranges	128–160, 224–254	80–A0, E0–FE
Second byte ranges	33–126, 128–255	21–7E, 80–FF

These ranges include a user-defined character area that falls at the outskirts of the standard Shift-JIS encoding space. More about this below. Figure D-2 illustrates the encoding space for HP-15.

HP-16 encoding

HP-16—the other Japanese encoding developed by Hewlett-Packard—has an area in its code space that is identical to EUC-JP code set 1. The remaining code space is used for user-defined characters. Hewlett-Packard defines the HP-16 encoding with a series of four encoding blocks. Table D-16 lists the code specifications for HP-16.

HP Kanji versus Shift-JIS and EUC-JP encodings

We really should compare the HP Kanji encodings to Shift-JIS and EUC-JP encodings. HP-15, as mentioned before, is a superset of Shift-JIS encoding, and HP-16 is similar to EUC-JP encoding. Figure D-3 illustrates the encoding space for HP-16.

Figure D-4 illustrates how Shift-JIS encoding is a subset of HP-15—it contains a slightly larger encoding region.

EUC-JP code set 1 is the same as the main portion of HP-16. This is the only similarity between EUC-JP and HP-16. Compare Figures 4-11 on page 166 and D-3 to confirm this.

IBM Japanese Encodings

In this section you will learn about Japanese-specific implementations of IBM's encoding methods.

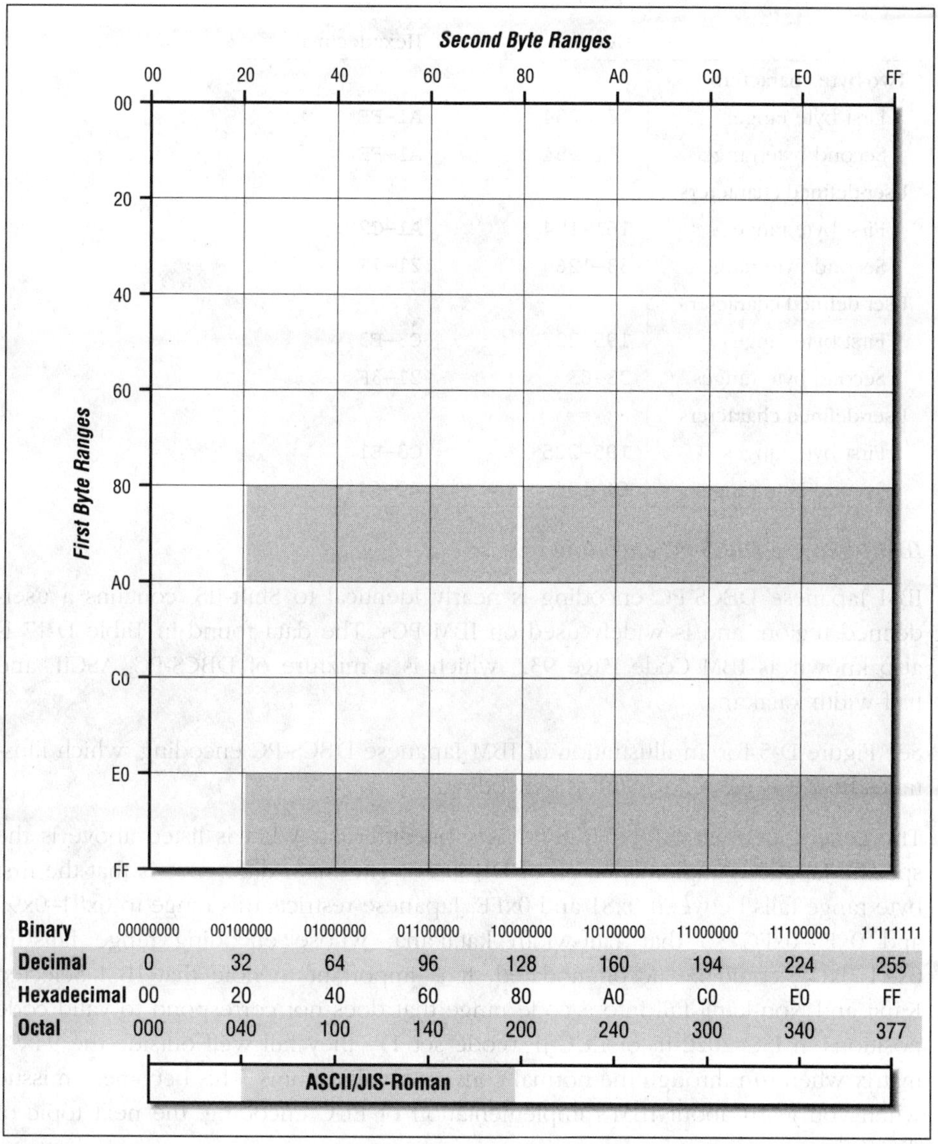

Figure D-2: HP-15 encoding tables

Table D-16: HP-16 Encoding Specifications

	Decimal	Hexadecimal
ASCII/JIS-Roman		
Byte range	33–126	21–7E

Table D-16: HP-16 Encoding Specifications (continued)

	Decimal	Hexadecimal
Two-byte characters		
First byte range	161–254	A1–FE
Second byte range	161–254	A1–FE
User-defined characters		
First byte range	161–194	A1–C2
Second byte range	33–126	21–7E
User-defined characters		
First byte ranges	195–227	C3–E3
Second byte ranges	33–63	21–3F
User-defined characters		
First byte ranges	195–225	C3–E1
Second byte ranges	64–100	40–64

IBM Japanese DBCS-PC encoding

IBM Japanese DBCS-PC encoding is nearly identical to Shift-JIS, contains a user-defined region, and is widely used on IBM PCs. The data found in Table D-17 is also known as IBM Code Page 932, which is a mixture of DBCS-PC, ASCII, and half-width katakana.

See Figure D-5 for an illustration of IBM Japanese DBCS-PC encoding, which illustrates how it is related to Shift-JIS encoding.

The generic definition for DBCS-PC is a bit different. What is listed above is the specific Japanese implementation of DBCS-PC. The main difference is that the first byte range falls between 0x81 and 0xFE. Japanese restricts this range to 0x81–0x9F and 0xE0–0xFC so that half-width katakana, whose encoding range falls in 0xA1–0xDF, could be accommodated. It is important to note that IBM Selected Kanji and Non-kanji fall into a code range that does not correspond to valid code positions in ISO-2022-JP or EUC-JP (code set 1)—they fall well outside the 94×94 matrix when run through the normal conversion algorithms. This becomes an issue when you learn about IBM's implementation of EUC encoding, the next topic of discussion.

IBM Japanese DBCS-EUC encoding

DBCS-EUC encoding is essentially identical to EUC, which was covered in detail in a previous section. All four code sets are implemented. This encoding is primarily found on the AIX environment, and the Japanese implementation is commonly known as IBM-eucJP. TBCS-EUC is defined by IBM for future standardization, and is currently not specified for handling Japanese.

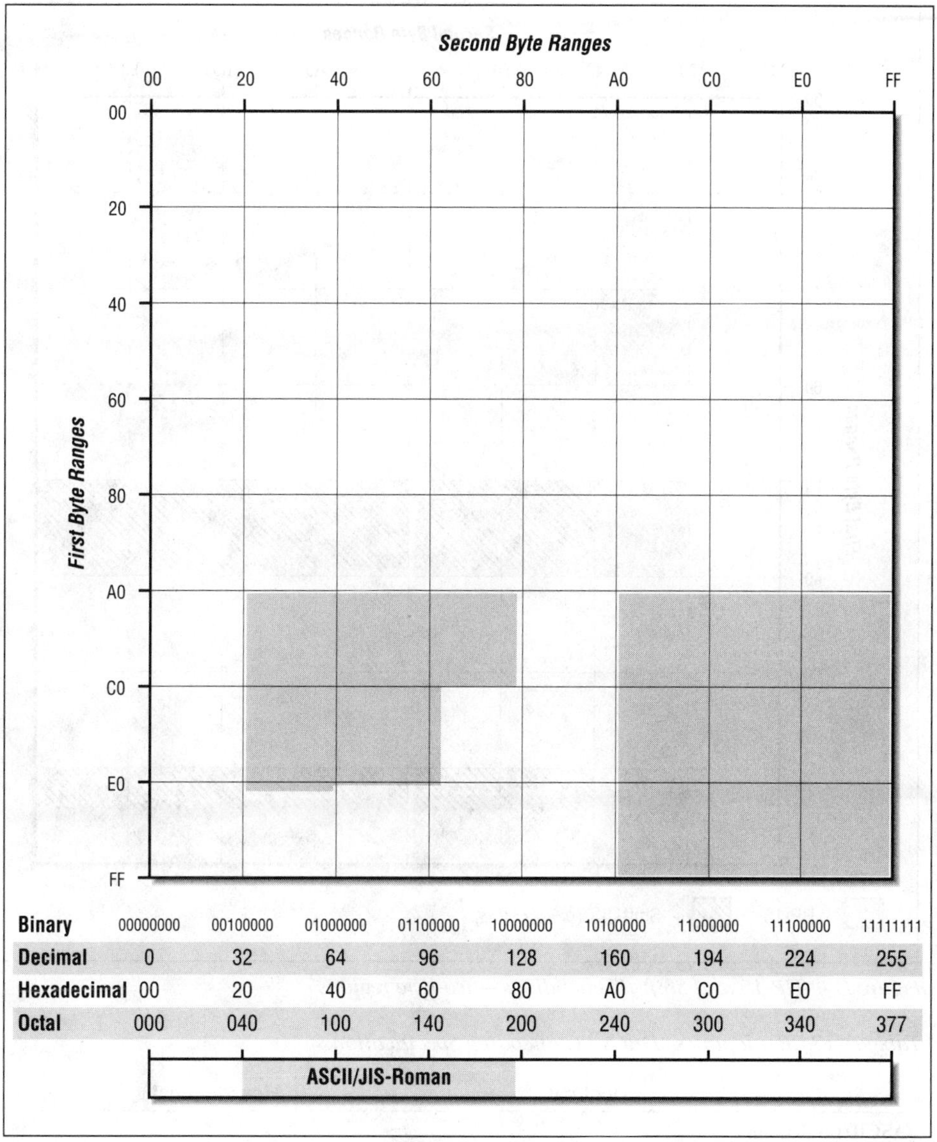

Figure D-3: HP-16 encoding tables

You may be asking how DBCS-EUC handles IBM Selected Kanji and Non-kanji. The answer is that these characters are mapped to JIS X 0208:1997 and JIS X 0212-1990 code positions. Table D-18 summarizes how these characters are mapped.

25 of the 28 IBM Selected Non-kanji are mapped to row 83 of JIS X 0212-1990, and 80 of the 360 IBM Selected Kanji are mapped to row 84 of JIS X 0212-1990. Appendix Q, *Character Lists and Mapping Tables*, shows how the 388 IBM

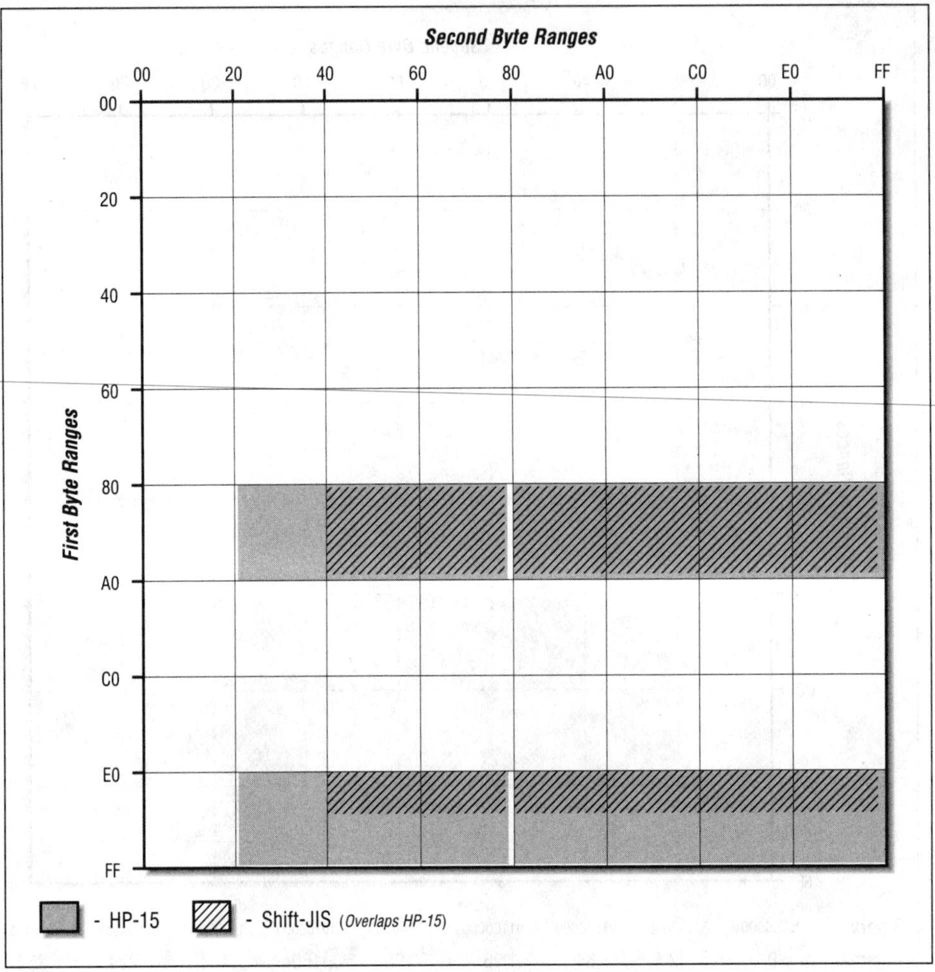

Figure D-4: HP-15 and Shift-JIS encodings—two-byte regions

Table D-17: IBM Japanese DBCS-PC Encoding Specifications

	Decimal	Hexadecimal
ASCII/JIS-Roman		
Byte range	33–126	21–7E
Half-width katakana[a]		
Byte range	161–223	A1–DF
JIS X 0208:1997[b]		
First byte ranges	129–132, 136–159, 224–234	81–84, 88–9F, E0–EA
Second byte ranges	64–126, 128–252	40–7E, 80–FC

Table D-17: IBM Japanese DBCS-PC Encoding Specifications (continued)

	Decimal	Hexadecimal
User-defined characters		
First byte range	240–249	F0–F9
Second byte ranges	64–126, 128–252	40–7E, 80–FC
IBM Selected Characters		
First byte range	250–252	FA–FC
Second byte ranges	64–126, 128–252	40–7E, 80–FC
Reserved[c]		
First byte ranges	133–135, 235–239	85–87, EB–EF
Second byte ranges	64–126, 128–252	40–7E, 80–FC

[a] Sometimes the code position 0xA0 is used for a half-width katakana space.
[b] The last defined character in this region is 0xEAA4—the same as Shift-JIS encoding.
[c] Note that these ranges correspond to code points within the JIS X 0208:1997 94×94 matrix.

Selected Kanji and Non-kanji are mapped to JIS X 0208:1997 and JIS X 0212-1990 code points. The results of this mapping process, at least for the 360 IBM Selected Kanji, concur with the findings of my own study that compared them with JIS X 0212-1990.

There are three user-defined character areas defined for IBM's Japanese DBCS-EUC implementation. They are listed in Table D-19.

IBM Japanese DBCS-Host encoding

DBCS-Host encoding, usually found on host computer systems, has a much larger character encoding space than DBCS-PC encoding. This two-byte encoding space can hold up to 36,481 unique characters. It is also used in conjunction with EBCDIC. This encoding method also existed long before any similar national standards existed. It is listed in Table D-20.

Figure D-6 illustrates the structure of IBM DBCS-Host encoding, which clearly shows how the full-width space is treated separately from other two-byte characters.

Converting Japanese text between IBM Japanese DBCS-Host and IBM Japanese DBCS-PC/EUC requires the use of mapping tables—no code conversion algorithm exists, which means that every character must be treated as a special case. These mapping tables exist in machine-readable form as part of IBM's *Character Data Representation Architecture Reference and Registry* (1995, IBM part number SC09-2190-00).

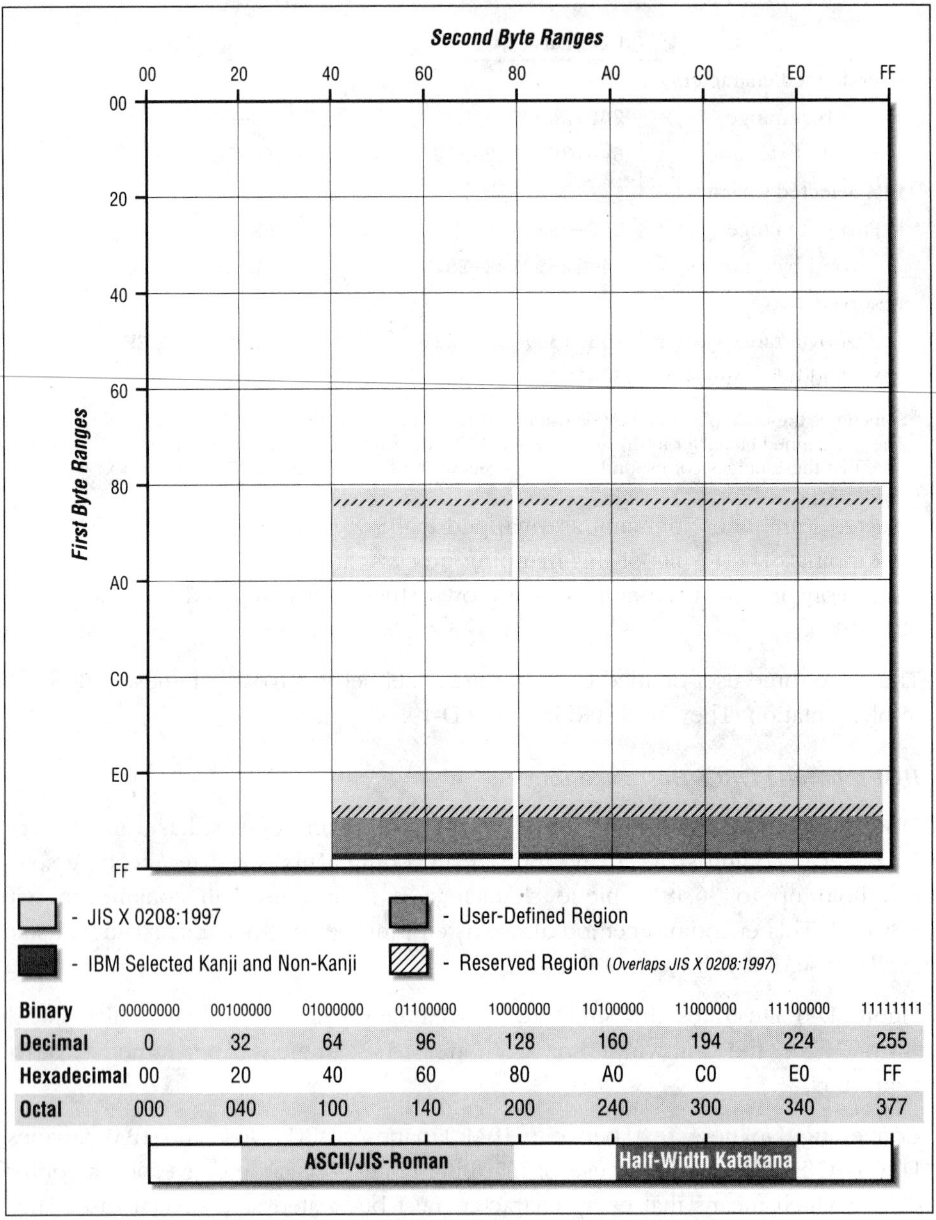

Figure D-5: IBM Japanese DBCS-PC encoding tables

IBM Japanese encodings versus Shift-JIS and EUC-JP encodings

IBM Japanese DBCS-Host encoding does not correspond to ISO-2022-JP, Shift-JIS, or EUC-JP encoding. IBM Japanese DBCS-PC corresponds to Shift-JIS encoding with the addition of a user-defined region (this is where the 386 IBM Selected

Table D-18: IBM Selected Kanji and Non-Kanji Mappings

	Total	JIS X 0208:1997	JIS X 0212-1990	User-Defined
IBM Selected Kanji	360	1	279	80
IBM Selected Non-kanji	28	2	1	25

Table D-19: IBM Japanese DBCS-EUC User-Defined Character Regions

Area	Location	Number of Code Points
Primary	Rows 85–94 of JIS X 0208:1997	940
Secondary	Rows 85–94 of JIS X 0212-1990	940
Tertiary	Rows 78–84 of JIS X 0212-1990	658

Table D-20: IBM Japanese DBCS-Host Encoding Specifications

	Decimal	Hexadecimal
One-byte characters		
Byte range	65–249	41–F9
Full-width space		
First byte	64	40
Second byte	64	40
Two-byte characters[a]		
First byte range	65–104	41–68
Second byte range	65–254	41–FE
User-defined characters[b]		
First byte range	105–114	69–72
Second byte range	65–254	41–FE
Shifting characters		
One-byte character	15	0F
Two-byte character	14	0E
Reserved		
First byte ranges	115–254	73–FE
Second byte range	65–254	41–FE

[a] The last defined character in this region is 0x6885.
[b] The last user-defined character in this region is 0x72EA.

Kanji and Non-kanji are encoded). IBM Japanese DBCS-EUC corresponds to EUC-JP encoding. You learned how the 386 IBM Selected Kanji and Non-kanji are mapped to appropriate positions in IBM Japanese DBCS-EUC encoding.

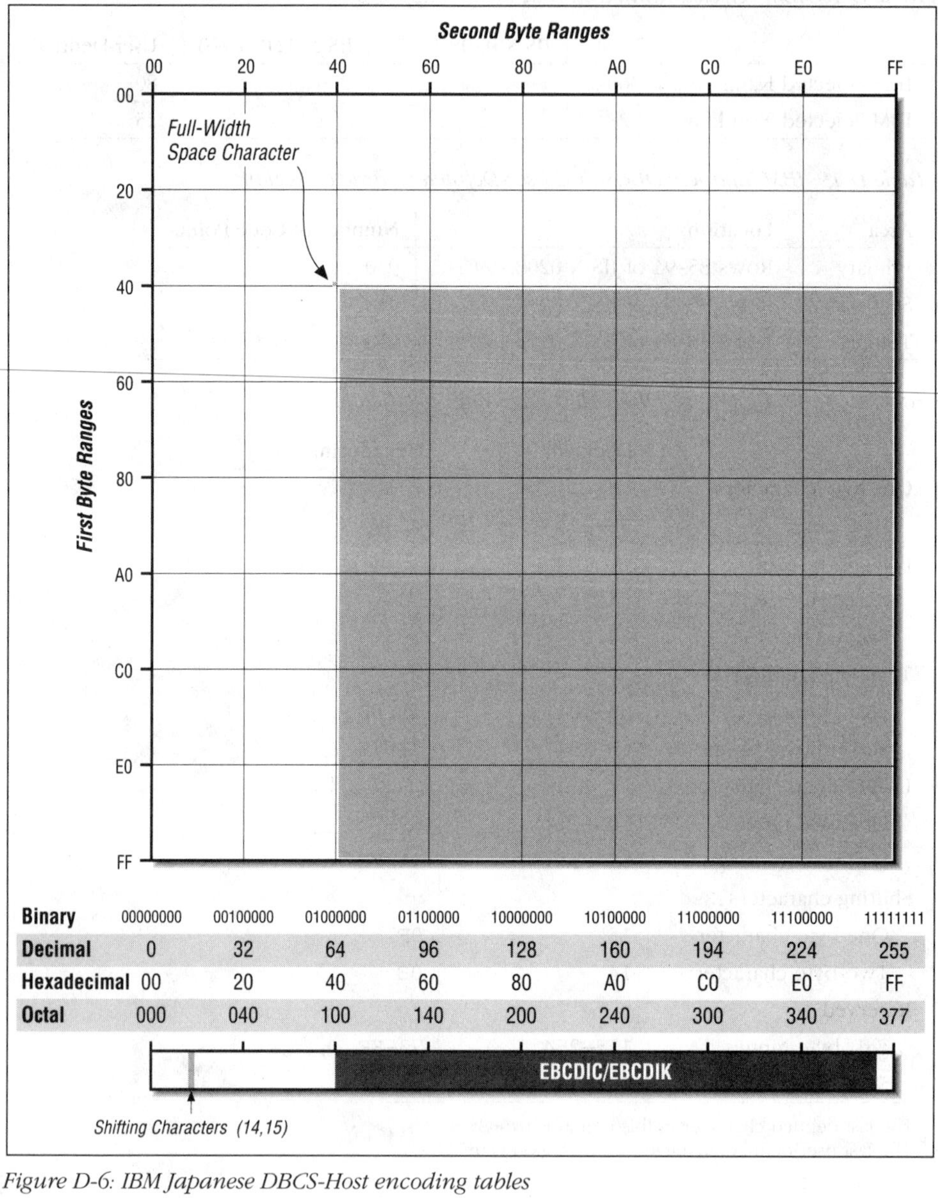

Figure D-6: IBM Japanese DBCS-Host encoding tables

IKIS Encoding

The encoding method for IKIS closely resembles EUC-JP, but lacks two of the code sets (code set 2 for half-width katakana, and code set 3 for JIS X 0212-1990). Remember from our discussion in Appendix C that the half-width katakana character set is included within the JIS X 0208-1983 character space, specifically in row

8 (where the line-drawing characters are normally found). Table D-21 illustrates IKIS' encoding specifications.

Table D-21: IKIS Encoding Specifications

	Decimal	Hexadecimal
ASCII/JIS-Roman		
Byte range	33–126	21–7E
JIS X 0208-1983		
First byte range	161–254	A1–FE
Second byte range	161–254	A1–FE

IKIS and EUC-JP encodings

IKIS encoding is identical to the encoding specified in EUC-JP complete two-byte format. Only the equivalent of EUC-JP code sets 0 and 1 is supported by IKIS.

KEIS Encoding

The encoding method used for KEIS includes encoding ranges found in parts of EUC-JP encoding, specifically EUC-JP code set 1. It also uses shifting sequences to shift between one- and two-byte-per-character modes. KEIS encoding is used in conjunction with EBCDIK. The valid two-byte encoding region for KEIS is actually quite large, but a large chunk of it is reserved and apparently unused. Table D-22 illustrates this large two-byte encoding region.

Table D-22: KEIS Two-Byte Encoding Region

	Decimal	Hexadecimal
Two-byte characters		
First byte range	65–254	41–FE
Second byte range	65–254	41–FE

Note that the KEIS two-byte encoding region is identical to generic instance of IBM DBCS-Host encoding.

You may recall from Appendix C that KEIS Basic Character Set and KEIS Extended Character Set 1 together constitute the JIS X 0208 character set.

Table D-23 provides the full specifications for KEIS encoding.

Table D-23: KEIS Encoding Specifications

	Decimal	Hexadecimal
One-byte characters		
Byte range	65–249	41–F9

Table D-23: KEIS Encoding Specifications (continued)

	Decimal	Hexadecimal
Full-width space[a]		
First byte	64 or 161	40 or A1
Second byte	64 or 161	40 or A1
KEIS Basic set		
First byte range	161–207	A1–CF
Second byte range	161–254	A1–FE
KEIS Extended Set 1		
First byte range	208–254	D0–FE
Second byte range	161–254	A1–FE
KEIS Extended Set 3		
First byte range	89–128	59–80
Second byte range	161–254	A1–FE
User-defined characters		
First byte range	129–160	81–A0
Second byte range	161–254	A1–FE
Shifting sequences		
One-byte character	10 65	A0 42
Two-byte character	10 66	A0 42

[a] A full-width space can be represented by either 0x4040 or 0xA1A1.

KEIS and EUC-JP encodings

The encoding for KEIS Basic Character Set and KEIS Extended Character Set 1 is identical to the encoding used for EUC-JP code set 1. The encoding for KEIS Extended Character Set 3 and KEIS user-defined characters departs from what we find in EUC-JP encoding, and does not correspond to ISO-2022-JP nor Shift-JIS encodings.

The big difference is that KEIS encoding is modal; it uses shifting sequences to switch between one- and two-byte characters.

MacOS-J Encoding

Apple's MacOS-J encoding, used for the KanjiTalk6 and KanjiTalk7 character sets, is Shift-JIS plus an additional encoding range for up to 2,444 user-defined characters equal to 26 extra rows of 94 characters each.* This additional encoding range,

* Or 13 rows of 188 characters each when thinking in terms of Shift-JIS encoding.

however, is not compatible with other encodings such as ISO-2022-JP and EUC-JP—they do not convert to valid code points in those encoding methods.

Table D-24 illustrates the encoding space for MacOS-J.

Table D-24: MacOS-J Encoding Specifications

	Decimal	Hexadecimal
ASCII/JIS-Roman		
Byte ranges	33–126, 128, 253–255	21–7E, 80, FD–FF
Half-width katakana		
Byte range	161–223	A1–DF
Two-byte characters		
First byte ranges	129–159, 224–239	81–9F, E0–EF
Second byte ranges	64–126, 128–252	40–7E, 80–FC
User-defined characters		
First byte range	240–252	F0–FC
Second byte ranges	64–126, 128–252	40–7E, 80–FC

MacOS-J and Shift-JIS encodings

The encoding method used by MacOS-J is more or less identical to Shift-JIS, except that there is an extra user-defined character encoding area and three additional single-byte code points (0x80 and 0xFD–0xFF). Both MacOS-J character sets, KanjiTalk6 and KanjiTalk7, use the same encoding as described above.

Microsoft Japanese Encoding

The encoding used by the Microsoft Japanese character set is simply Shift-JIS. Characters from IBM Japanese and NEC Kanji have been included. The Shift-JIS user-defined region is required because it is used to encoded the IBM Japanese Selected characters.

NEC Kanji Encoding

NEC Kanji can be encoded similarly to ISO-2022-JP, Shift-JIS, and EUC-JP encodings, depending on the environment. The ISO-2022–like implementation is sometimes referred to as NEC-JIS. ASCII/JIS-Roman (half-width) and half-width katakana are also in the same encoding space as kanji, and thus can be encoded using two bytes. This can simplify the handling of text streams (no need to have any state shifting between one- and two-byte modes), but significantly increases the storage requirements for documents not written in Japanese. Table D-25 lists its specifications.

Table D-25: NEC Kanji Encoding Specifications

	Decimal	Hexadecimal	Graphical (ASCII)
JIS-Roman			
Byte range	33–126	21–7E	
JIS C 6226-1978			
First byte range	33–126	21–7E	
Second byte range	33–126	21–7E	
NEC Extended Set			
First byte range	161–254	A1–FE	
Second byte range	161–254	A1–FE	
Escape sequences			
JIS-Roman	27 72	1B 48	<ESC> H
JIS C 6226-1978	27 75	1B 4B	<ESC> K
JIS8 half-width katakana			
Byte range	161–223	A1–DF	

Refer to Tables 4-42 and 4-32 for descriptions of the Shift-JIS and EUC-JP implementations of the NEC Kanji character set on pages 176 and 166, respectively. Note that Shift-JIS does not support the NEC Extended Character Set, but includes the 360 IBM Selected Kanji and 14 of the 28 IBM Selected Non-kanji encoded in rows 89 through 92.

NEC Kanji and ISO-2022-JP encodings

The escape sequences for NEC Kanji encoding are unique in that they are made up of the escape character followed by only a single printable character. While this makes the escape sequences shorter, it does not leave much context with which you may insert lost escape characters (the restoration of lost escape characters and otherwise mangled escape sequences was discussed in Chapter 4 and Chapter 7, *Typography*).

NTT Kanji Encoding

NTT Kanji encoding is much like ISO-2022-JP encoding, except that there is an additional two-byte character escape sequence defined for the extended character set. See Table D-26 for a listing of its encoding specifications.

Table D-26: NTT Kanji Encoding Specifications

	Decimal	Hexadecimal	Graphical (ASCII)
One-byte characters			
Byte range	33–126	21–7E	

Table D-26: NTT Kanji Encoding Specifications (continued)

	Decimal	Hexadecimal	Graphical (ASCII)
Two-byte characters			
First byte range	33–126	21–7E	
Second byte range	33–126	21–7E	
Escape sequences			
JIS-Roman	27 40 74	1B 28 4A	<ESC> (J
JIS C 6226-1978	27 36 64	1B 24 40	<ESC> $ @
NTT Extended	27 36 41 48	1B 24 29 30	<ESC> $) 0

NTT Kanji and ISO-2022-JP encodings

NTT Kanji encoding is like ISO-2022-JP plus an additional two-byte escape sequence for the extended character set. Note that only the JIS C 6226-1978 character set is supported through a single escape sequence.

TRON Encoding

The encoding used by operating systems based on TRON (such as BTRON) is a mixed one- and two-byte modal encoding. The two-byte encoding region includes four zones, designated "A" through "D." Zone A is used for encoding JIS X 0208:1997, Zone B for JIS X 0212-1990, Zone C for GB 2312-80, and Zone D for KS X 1001:1992. Table D-27 provides the complete TRON encoding definition.

Table D-27: TRON Encoding Specifications

	Decimal	Hexadecimal
Single-byte characters		
Byte ranges	33–126, 128–253	21–7E, 80–FD
Two-byte control characters		
First byte	0	00
Second byte range	0–254	00–FE
Zone "A" (8,836 code points)		
First byte range	33–126	21–7E
Second byte range	33–126	21–7E
Zone "B" (11,844 code points)		
First byte range	128–253	80–FD
Second byte range	33–126	21–7E
Zone "C" (11,844 code points)		
First byte range	33–126	21–7E
Second byte range	128–253	80–FD

Table D-27: TRON Encoding Specifications (continued)

	Decimal	Hexadecimal
Zone "D" (15,876 code points)		
First byte range	128–253	80–FD
Second byte range	128–253	80–FD
Two-byte language specifiers (94)		
First byte	254	FE
Second byte range	33–126	21–7E
One-byte language specifiers (127)		
First byte	254	FE
Second byte range	128–254	80–FE
Special codes (94)		
First byte	255	FF
Second byte range	33–126	21–7E
Escapes (127)		
First byte	255	FF
Second byte range	128–254	80–FE
EOF (End-Of-File) mark		
First byte	255	FF
Second byte	255	FF

JIS X 0212-1990 is encoded in Zone B of TRON encoding, which represents a 126×94 matrix. So, how does a 94×94 character set fit into this matrix? The last row of JIS X 0212-1990 is ignored, forming a 93×94 matrix that fits into the highest bounds of zone B (0xA121–0xFD7E).

Perhaps of greater curiosity is how GB 2312-80 and KS X 1001:1992, both 94×94 character sets, fit into a 94×126 and 126×126 matrix, respectively. Zero-based code conversion techniques are used to fit them so that they fill up encoding rows consisting of 126 code points each. Table D-28 lists ISO-2022 and EUC encoding ranges, along with the corresponding TRON encoding range.

Table D-28: GB 2312-80 and KS X 1001:1992 in TRON Encoding

Character Set	ISO-2022	EUC	TRON[a]
GB 2312-80	2121–7E7E	A1A1–FEFE	2180–678F
KS X 1001:1992	2121–7E7E	A1A1–FEFE	B780–FD8F

[a] Although the second-byte values appear to end at 0x8F, it does, in fact, use the range 0x80–0xFD. This is an artifact of zero-based code conversion.

The language specifiers are used for the modal aspect of TRON encoding. There are two language specifiers that are always defined in TRON. 0xFE21 is for "Japanese" (two-byte language), and 0xFE80 is for "English" (one-byte language). There are 93 remaining two-byte language specifiers, and 126 remaining one-byte language specifiers.

There are three types of "space" characters according to TRON encoding, as illustrated in Table D-29.

Table D-29: Three Types of "Space" Characters in TRON Encoding

	Japanese Mode	English Mode
Full-width space	`2121`	*not applicable*
Half-width space	`00A0`	`A0`
Proportional space	`0020`	`20`

Figure D-7 illustrates the four two-byte zones and other encoding regions defined by TRON encoding.

The algorithms for converting between TRON encoding and encodings that support GB 2312-80 (ISO-2022-CN and EUC-CN) and KS X 1001:1992 (ISO-2022-KR and EUC-KR) can be found in the section entitled "TRON Code Conversion," starting on page 1015 in Appendix W, *Perl Code Examples*.

Korean Vendor Encodings

Nearly all Korean vendor encodings are based on EUC-KR encoding. Exceptions to this are some of the IBM encodings. The following sections provide encoding tables for a number of Korean vendor encodings.

DEC Korean Encoding

DEC Korean encoding is identical to EUC-KR encoding, meaning that it is a simple mixed one- and two-byte encoding that encodes the ASCII/KS-Roman plus KS X 1001:1992 character sets.

HangulTalk Encoding

Table D-30 provides the complete specification for HangulTalk encoding, which includes an enlarged two-byte region to accommodate an extension defined by Elex Computer, and adopted by Apple Computer. Also note that the second byte range is shortened to 0xA1 through 0xFD to accommodate one single-byte character at 0xFE.

IBM Korean Encodings

As you observed in previous sections regarding Chinese and Japanese encodings, IBM has developed a number of encodings for use on their various operating systems. The following sections describe some of IBM's Korean encodings.

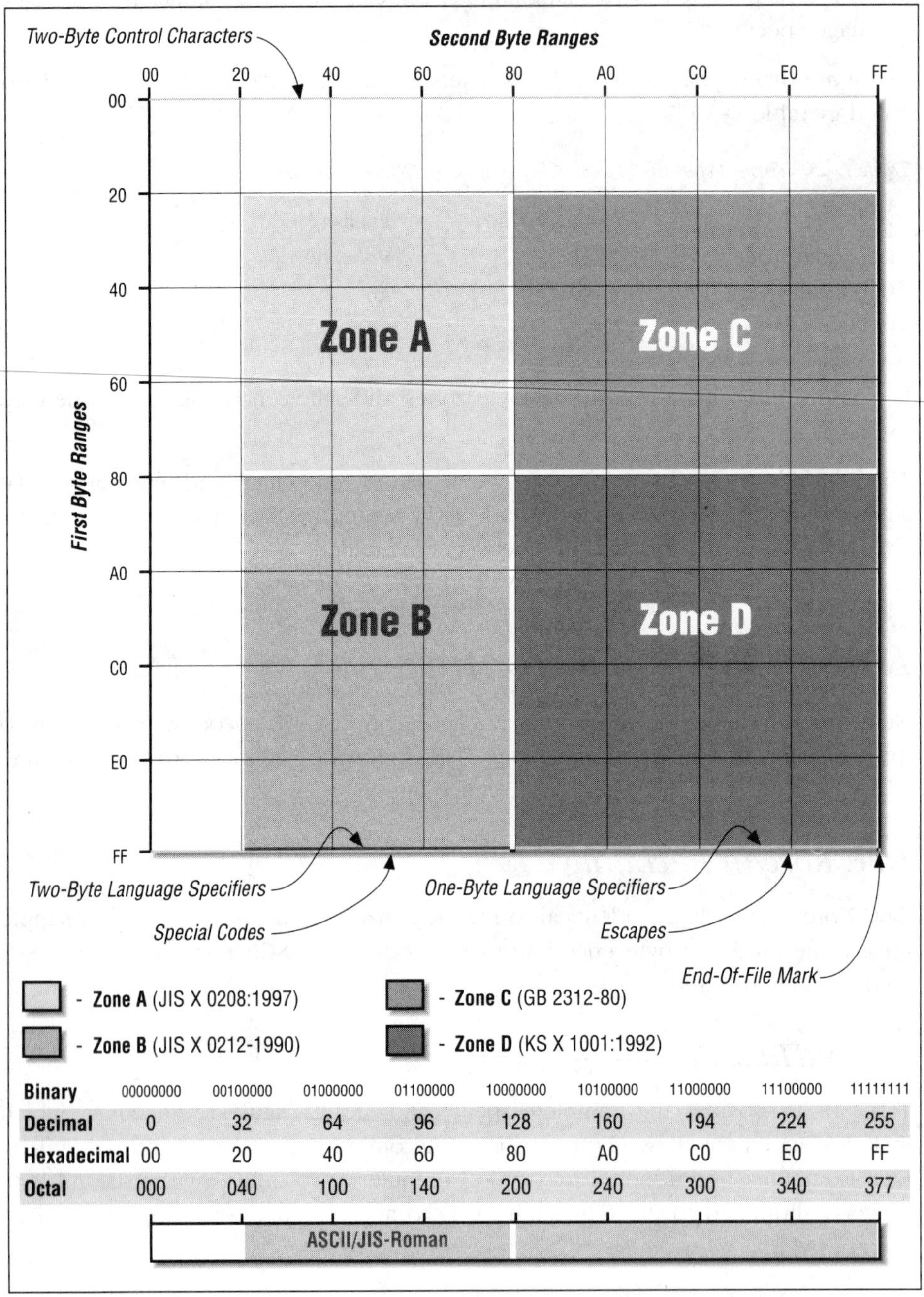

Figure D-7: TRON encoding tables

Table D-30: HangulTalk Encoding Specifications

	Decimal	Hexadecimal
ASCII/KS-Roman		
Byte ranges	33–126, 129–131, 254–255	21–7E, 81–83, FE–FF
Two-byte characters		
First byte range	161–253	A1–FD
Second byte ranges	65–125, 129–254	41–7D, 81–FE

IBM Korean DBCS-PC encoding

Table D-31 provides the encoding specifications for IBM Korean DBCS-PC encoding. It is important to note how the IBM Selected Characters, which are encoded in the range of rows 0x9A through 0xA0, are encoded in a separate block, not mixed in with the rest of the characters. In IBM DBCS-Host encoding, they are mixed in with the rest of the characters.

Table D-31: IBM Korean DBCS-PC Encoding Specifications

	Decimal	Hexadecimal
ASCII/KS-Roman		
Byte range	33–126	21–7E
User-defined characters[a]		
First byte ranges	143–154, 201, 254	8F–9A, C9, FE
Second byte range	161–254	A1–FE
IBM Selected Characters[b]		
First byte range	154–160	9A–A0
Second byte range	161–254	A1–FE
KS X 1001:1992[c]		
First byte ranges	161–172, 176–253	A1–AC, B0–FD
Second byte range	161–254	A1–FE
Reserved		
First byte ranges	129–143, 173–175	81–8E, AD–AF
Second byte range	161–254	A1–FE

[a] The range 0x9AA6 through 0x9AFE is for IBM Selected Characters.
[b] The first IBM Selected Character is at 0x9AA6; 0x9AA1 through 0x9AA5 are user-defined code points.
[c] The last defined character in this region is 0xFDFE—the same as EUC-KR encoding.

IBM Korean DBCS-Host encoding

Table D-32 provides the encoding specifications for IBM Korean DBCS-Host encoding, which clearly shows that characters are allocated slightly differently than in DBCS-PC encoding. Like other instances of IBM DBCS-Host encoding, shifting characters are used for switching between one- and two-byte modes.

Table D-32: IBM Korean DBCS-Host Encoding Specifications

	Decimal	Hexadecimal
One-byte characters		
Byte range	65–249	41–F9
Full-width space		
First byte	64	40
Second byte	64	40
Two-byte characters[a]		
First byte ranges	65–75, 80–108, 132–211	41–4B, 50–6C, 84–D3
Second byte range	65–254	41–FE
User-defined characters		
First byte range	212–221	D4–DD
Second byte ranges	65–127, 129–253	41–7F, 81–FD
Shifting characters		
One-byte character	15	0F
Two-byte character	14	0E
Reserved		
First byte ranges	76–79, 109–131, 222–254	4C–4F, 6D–83, DE–FE
Second byte range	65–254	41–FE

[a] The last defined character in this region is 0xD3B7. Also, the range 0x8441–0xD3FE is not only similar to Johab encoding, but the hangul are encoded according to the Johab encoding principles.

Unified Hangul Code Encoding

The encoding for Unified Hangul Code (UHC) is simply an extension to EUC-KR encoding that is used to encode 8,822 additional hangul. It is supported by the Korean version of Microsoft Windows 95. Table D-33 provides the full specifications for Unified Hangul Code encoding.

Table D-33: Unified Hangul Code Encoding Specifications

	Decimal	Hexadecimal
ASCII/KS-Roman		
Byte range	33–126	21–7E
Two-byte characters		
First byte range	129–254	81–FE
Second byte ranges	65–90, 97–122, 129–254	41–5A, 61–7A, 81–FE

Figure D-8 illustrates three distinct two-byte regions defined by Unified Hangul Code encoding. One region is a superset of EUC-KR encoding (0xA1A1–0xFEFE), and the others' sole purpose is to encode the additional 8,822 hangul.

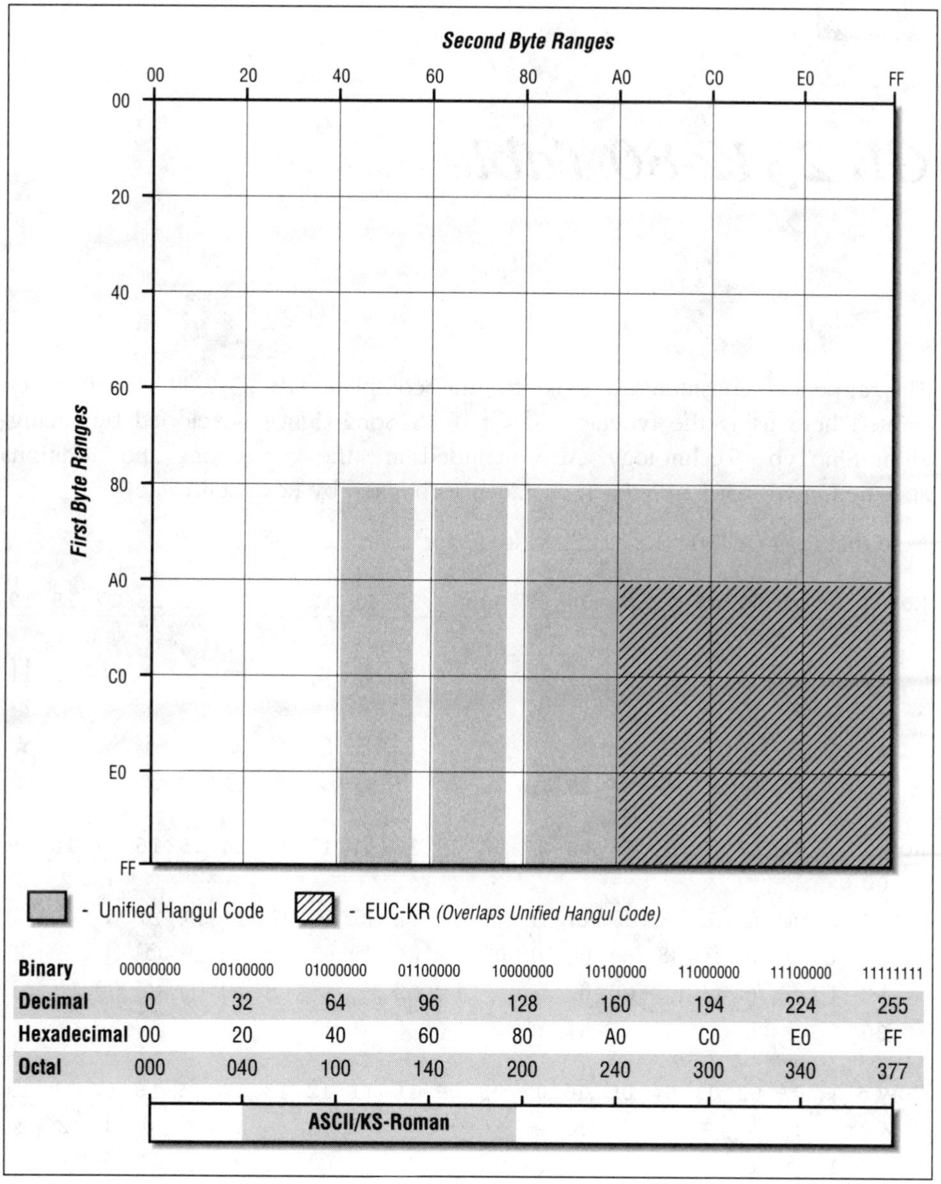

Figure D-8: Unified Hangul Code encoding tables

E

GB 2312-80 Table

This appendix constitutes a table for the complete GB 2312-80 character set, printed here using the typeface 华文宋体 (STSong-Light), developed by Changzhou SinoType Technology. Also included are the corrections and additions specified in GB 6345.1-86. Each character is indexed by Row-Cell value.

Note that Row-Cell 01-01 is a full-width space character.

Row 1		01	02	03	04	05	06	07	08	09	10	11	12	13	14	15	16	17	18	19
00			、	。	·	ˉ	ˇ	¨	〃	々	—	～	‖	…	‘	’	“	”	〔	〕
20	〈	〉	《	》	「	」	『	』	〖	〗	【	】	±	×	÷	∶	∧	∨	∑	∏
40	∪	∩	∈	∷	√	⊥	∥	∠	⌒	⊙	∫	∮	≡	≌	≈	∽	∝	≠	≮	≯
60	≤	≥	∞	∵	∴	♂	♀	°	′	″	℃	＄	¤	￠	￡	‰	§	№	☆	★
80	○	●	◎	◇	◆	□	■	△	▲	※	→	←	↑	↓	〓					

Row 2		01	02	03	04	05	06	07	08	09	10	11	12	13	14	15	16	17	18	19
00																		⒈	⒉	⒊
20	⒋	⒌	⒍	⒎	⒏	⒐	⒑	⒒	⒓	⒔	⒕	⒖	⒗	⒘	⒙	⒚	⒛	⑴	⑵	⑶
40	⑷	⑸	⑹	⑺	⑻	⑼	⑽	⑾	⑿	⒀	⒁	⒂	⒃	⒄	⒅	⒆	⒇	①	②	③
60	④	⑤	⑥	⑦	⑧	⑨	⑩			㈠	㈡	㈢	㈣	㈤	㈥	㈦	㈧	㈨	㈩	
80		Ⅰ	Ⅱ	Ⅲ	Ⅳ	Ⅴ	Ⅵ	Ⅶ	Ⅷ	Ⅸ	Ⅹ	Ⅺ	Ⅻ							

Row 3		01	02	03	04	05	06	07	08	09	10	11	12	13	14	15	16	17	18	19
00		！	＂	＃	￥	％	＆	＇	（	）	＊	＋	，	－	．	／	０	１	２	３
20	４	５	６	７	８	９	：	；	＜	＝	＞	？	＠	Ａ	Ｂ	Ｃ	Ｄ	Ｅ	Ｆ	Ｇ
40	Ｈ	Ｉ	Ｊ	Ｋ	Ｌ	Ｍ	Ｎ	Ｏ	Ｐ	Ｑ	Ｒ	Ｓ	Ｔ	Ｕ	Ｖ	Ｗ	Ｘ	Ｙ	Ｚ	［
60	＼	］	＾	＿	｀	ａ	ｂ	ｃ	ｄ	ｅ	ｆ	ｇ	ｈ	ｉ	ｊ	ｋ	ｌ	ｍ	ｎ	ｏ
80	ｐ	ｑ	ｒ	ｓ	ｔ	ｕ	ｖ	ｗ	ｘ	ｙ	ｚ	｛	｜	｝	￣					

Row 4		01	02	03	04	05	06	07	08	09	10	11	12	13	14	15	16	17	18	19
00		ぁ	あ	ぃ	い	ぅ	う	ぇ	え	ぉ	お	か	が	き	ぎ	く	ぐ	け	げ	こ
20	ご	さ	ざ	し	じ	す	ず	せ	ぜ	そ	ぞ	た	だ	ち	ぢ	っ	つ	づ	て	で
40	と	ど	な	に	ぬ	ね	の	は	ば	ぱ	ひ	び	ぴ	ふ	ぶ	ぷ	へ	べ	ぺ	ほ
60	ぼ	ぽ	ま	み	む	め	も	ゃ	や	ゅ	ゆ	ょ	よ	ら	り	る	れ	ろ	ゎ	わ
80	ゐ	ゑ	を	ん																

Row 5		01	02	03	04	05	06	07	08	09	10	11	12	13	14	15	16	17	18	19
00		ァ	ア	ィ	イ	ゥ	ウ	ェ	エ	ォ	オ	カ	ガ	キ	ギ	ク	グ	ケ	ゲ	コ
20	ゴ	サ	ザ	シ	ジ	ス	ズ	セ	ゼ	ソ	ゾ	タ	ダ	チ	ヂ	ッ	ツ	ヅ	テ	デ
40	ト	ド	ナ	ニ	ヌ	ネ	ノ	ハ	バ	パ	ヒ	ビ	ピ	フ	ブ	プ	ヘ	ベ	ペ	ホ
60	ボ	ポ	マ	ミ	ム	メ	モ	ャ	ヤ	ュ	ユ	ョ	ヨ	ラ	リ	ル	レ	ロ	ヮ	ワ
80	ヰ	ヱ	ヲ	ン	ヴ	ヵ	ヶ													

Row 6		01	02	03	04	05	06	07	08	09	10	11	12	13	14	15	16	17	18	19
00		Α	Β	Γ	Δ	Ε	Ζ	Η	Θ	Ι	Κ	Λ	Μ	Ν	Ξ	Ο	Π	Ρ	Σ	Τ
20	Υ	Φ	Χ	Ψ	Ω									α	β	γ	δ	ε	ζ	η
40	θ	ι	κ	λ	μ	ν	ξ	ο	π	ρ	σ	τ	υ	φ	χ	ψ	ω			
60																				
80																				

Row 7		01	02	03	04	05	06	07	08	09	10	11	12	13	14	15	16	17	18	19
00		А	Б	В	Г	Д	Е	Ё	Ж	З	И	Й	К	Л	М	Н	О	П	Р	С
20	Т	У	Ф	Х	Ц	Ч	Ш	Щ	Ъ	Ы	Ь	Э	Ю	Я						
40										а	б	в	г	д	е	ё	ж	з	и	й
60	к	л	м	н	о	п	р	с	т	у	ф	х	ц	ч	ш	щ	ъ	ы	ь	э
80	ю	я																		

Row 8		01	02	03	04	05	06	07	08	09	10	11	12	13	14	15	16	17	18	19
00		ā	á	ǎ	à	ē	é	ě	è	ī	í	ǐ	ì	ō	ó	ǒ	ò	ū	ú	ǔ
20	ù	ǖ	ǘ	ǚ	ǜ	ü	ê	ɑ	ḿ	ń	ň	ǹ	ɡ					ㄅ	ㄆ	ㄇ
40	ㄈ	ㄉ	ㄊ	ㄋ	ㄌ	ㄍ	ㄎ	ㄏ	ㄐ	ㄑ	ㄒ	ㄓ	ㄔ	ㄕ	ㄖ	ㄗ	ㄘ	ㄙ	ㄚ	ㄛ
60	ㄜ	ㄝ	ㄞ	ㄟ	ㄠ	ㄡ	ㄢ	ㄣ	ㄤ	ㄥ	ㄦ	ㄧ	ㄨ	ㄩ						
80																				

Row 9		01	02	03	04	05	06	07	08	09	10	11	12	13	14	15	16	17	18	19
00					─	━	│	┃	┄	┅	┆	┇	┈	┉	┊	┋	┌	┍	┎	┏
20	┐	┑	┒	┓	└	┕	┖	┗	┘	┙	┚	┛	├	┝	┞	┟	┠	┡	┢	┣
40	┤	┥	┦	┧	┨	┩	┪	┫	┬	┭	┮	┯	┰	┱	┲	┳	┴	┵	┶	┷
60	┸	┹	┺	┻	┼	┽	┾	┿	╀	╁	╂	╃	╄	╅	╆	╇	╈	╉	╊	╋
80																				

Row 10		01	02	03	04	05	06	07	08	09	10	11	12	13	14	15	16	17	18	19
00		!	"	#	¥	%	&	′	(	)	*	+	,	-	.	/	0	1	2	3
20	4	5	6	7	8	9	:	;	<	=	>	?	@	A	B	C	D	E	F	G
40	H	I	J	K	L	M	N	O	P	Q	R	S	T	U	V	W	X	Y	Z	[
60	\	]	^	_	`	a	b	c	d	e	f	g	h	i	j	k	l	m	n	o
80	p	q	r	s	t	u	v	w	x	y	z	{	|	}	‾					

Row 11		01	02	03	04	05	06	07	08	09	10	11	12	13	14	15	16	17	18	19
00		ā	á	ǎ	à	ē	é	ě	è	ī	í	ǐ	ì	ō	ó	ǒ	ò	ū	ú	ǔ
20	ù	ǖ	ǘ	ǚ	ǜ	ü	ê	ɑ	ḿ	ń	ň	ǹ	ɡ							
40																				
60																				
80																				

Row 16		01	02	03	04	05	06	07	08	09	10	11	12	13	14	15	16	17	18	19
00		啊	阿	埃	挨	哎	唉	哀	皑	癌	蔼	矮	艾	碍	爱	隘	鞍	氨	安	俺
20	按	暗	岸	胺	案	肮	昂	盎	凹	敖	熬	翱	袄	傲	奥	懊	澳	芭	捌	扒
40	叭	吧	笆	八	疤	巴	拔	跋	靶	把	耙	坝	霸	罢	爸	白	柏	百	摆	佰
60	败	拜	稗	斑	班	搬	扳	般	颁	板	版	扮	拌	伴	瓣	半	办	绊	邦	帮
80	梆	榜	膀	绑	棒	磅	蚌	镑	傍	谤	苞	胞	包	褒	剥					

Row 17		01	02	03	04	05	06	07	08	09	10	11	12	13	14	15	16	17	18	19
00		薄	雹	保	堡	饱	宝	抱	报	暴	豹	鲍	爆	杯	碑	悲	卑	北	辈	背
20	贝	钡	倍	狈	备	惫	焙	被	奔	苯	本	笨	崩	绷	甭	泵	蹦	迸	逼	鼻
40	比	鄙	笔	彼	碧	蓖	蔽	毕	毙	毖	币	庇	痹	闭	敝	弊	必	辟	壁	臂
60	避	陛	鞭	边	编	贬	扁	便	变	卞	辨	辩	辫	遍	标	彪	膘	表	鳖	憋
80	别	瘪	彬	斌	濒	滨	宾	摈	兵	冰	柄	丙	秉	饼	炳					

Row 18		01	02	03	04	05	06	07	08	09	10	11	12	13	14	15	16	17	18	19
00		病	并	玻	菠	播	拨	钵	波	博	勃	搏	铂	箔	伯	帛	舶	脖	膊	渤
20	泊	驳	捕	卜	哺	补	埠	不	布	步	簿	部	怖	擦	猜	裁	材	才	财	睬
40	踩	采	彩	菜	蔡	餐	参	蚕	残	惭	惨	灿	苍	舱	仓	沧	藏	操	糙	槽
60	曹	草	厕	策	侧	册	测	层	蹭	插	叉	茬	茶	查	碴	搽	察	岔	差	诧
80	拆	柴	豺	搀	掺	蝉	馋	谗	缠	铲	产	阐	颤	昌	猖					

Row 19		01	02	03	04	05	06	07	08	09	10	11	12	13	14	15	16	17	18	19
00		场	尝	常	长	偿	肠	厂	敞	畅	唱	倡	超	抄	钞	朝	嘲	潮	巢	吵
20	炒	车	扯	撤	掣	彻	澈	郴	臣	辰	尘	晨	忱	沉	陈	趁	衬	撑	称	城
40	橙	成	呈	乘	程	惩	澄	诚	承	逞	骋	秤	吃	痴	持	匙	池	迟	弛	驰
60	耻	齿	侈	尺	赤	翅	斥	炽	充	冲	虫	崇	宠	抽	酬	畴	踌	稠	愁	筹
80	仇	绸	瞅	丑	臭	初	出	橱	厨	躇	锄	雏	滁	除	楚					

Row 20		01	02	03	04	05	06	07	08	09	10	11	12	13	14	15	16	17	18	19
00		础	储	矗	搐	触	处	揣	川	穿	椽	传	船	喘	串	疮	窗	幢	床	闯
20	创	吹	炊	捶	锤	垂	春	椿	醇	唇	淳	纯	蠢	戳	绰	疵	茨	磁	雌	辞
40	慈	瓷	词	此	刺	赐	次	聪	葱	囱	匆	从	丛	凑	粗	醋	簇	促	蹿	篡
60	窜	摧	崔	催	脆	瘁	粹	淬	翠	村	存	寸	磋	撮	搓	措	挫	错	搭	达
80	答	瘩	打	大	呆	歹	傣	戴	带	殆	代	贷	袋	待	逮					

Row 21		01	02	03	04	05	06	07	08	09	10	11	12	13	14	15	16	17	18	19
00		怠	耽	担	丹	单	郸	掸	胆	旦	氮	但	惮	淡	诞	弹	蛋	当	挡	党
20	荡	档	刀	捣	蹈	倒	岛	祷	导	到	稻	悼	道	盗	德	得	的	蹬	灯	登
40	等	瞪	凳	邓	堤	低	滴	迪	敌	笛	狄	涤	翟	嫡	抵	底	地	蒂	第	帝
60	弟	递	缔	颠	掂	滇	碘	点	典	靛	垫	电	佃	甸	店	惦	奠	淀	殿	碉
80	叼	雕	凋	刁	掉	吊	钓	调	跌	爹	碟	蝶	迭	谍	叠					

Row 22		01	02	03	04	05	06	07	08	09	10	11	12	13	14	15	16	17	18	19
00		丁	盯	叮	钉	顶	鼎	锭	定	订	丢	东	冬	董	懂	动	栋	侗	恫	冻
20	洞	兜	抖	斗	陡	豆	逗	痘	都	督	毒	犊	独	读	堵	睹	赌	杜	镀	肚
40	度	渡	妒	端	短	锻	段	断	缎	堆	兑	队	对	墩	吨	蹲	敦	顿	囤	钝
60	盾	遁	掇	哆	多	夺	垛	躲	朵	跺	舵	剁	惰	堕	蛾	峨	鹅	俄	额	讹
80	娥	恶	厄	扼	遏	鄂	饿	恩	而	儿	耳	尔	饵	洱	二					

Row 23		01	02	03	04	05	06	07	08	09	10	11	12	13	14	15	16	17	18	19
00		贰	发	罚	筏	伐	乏	阀	法	珐	藩	帆	番	翻	樊	矾	钒	繁	凡	烦
20	反	返	范	贩	犯	饭	泛	坊	芳	方	肪	房	防	妨	仿	访	纺	放	菲	非
40	啡	飞	肥	匪	诽	吠	肺	废	沸	费	芬	酚	吩	氛	分	纷	坟	焚	汾	粉
60	奋	份	忿	愤	粪	丰	封	枫	蜂	峰	锋	风	疯	烽	逢	冯	缝	讽	奉	凤
80	佛	否	夫	敷	肤	孵	扶	拂	辐	幅	氟	符	伏	俘	服					

Row 24		01	02	03	04	05	06	07	08	09	10	11	12	13	14	15	16	17	18	19
00		浮	涪	福	袱	弗	甫	抚	辅	俯	釜	斧	脯	腑	府	腐	赴	副	覆	赋
20	复	傅	付	阜	父	腹	负	富	讣	附	妇	缚	咐	噶	嘎	该	改	概	钙	盖
40	溉	干	甘	杆	柑	竿	肝	赶	感	秆	敢	赣	冈	刚	钢	缸	肛	纲	岗	港
60	杠	篙	皋	高	膏	羔	糕	搞	镐	稿	告	哥	歌	搁	戈	鸽	胳	疙	割	革
80	葛	格	蛤	阁	隔	铬	个	各	给	根	跟	耕	更	庚	羹					

Row 25		01	02	03	04	05	06	07	08	09	10	11	12	13	14	15	16	17	18	19
00		埂	耿	梗	工	攻	功	恭	龚	供	躬	公	宫	弓	巩	汞	拱	贡	共	钩
20	勾	沟	苟	狗	垢	构	购	够	辜	菇	咕	箍	估	沽	孤	姑	鼓	古	蛊	骨
40	谷	股	故	顾	固	雇	刮	瓜	剐	寡	挂	褂	乖	拐	怪	棺	关	官	冠	观
60	管	馆	罐	惯	灌	贯	光	广	逛	瑰	规	圭	硅	归	龟	闺	轨	鬼	诡	癸
80	桂	柜	跪	贵	刽	辊	滚	棍	锅	郭	国	果	裹	过	哈					

Row 26		01	02	03	04	05	06	07	08	09	10	11	12	13	14	15	16	17	18	19
00		骸	孩	海	氦	亥	害	骇	酣	憨	邯	韩	含	涵	寒	函	喊	罕	翰	撼
20	捍	旱	憾	悍	焊	汗	汉	夯	杭	航	壕	嚎	豪	毫	郝	好	耗	号	浩	呵
40	喝	荷	菏	核	禾	和	何	合	盒	貉	阂	河	涸	赫	褐	鹤	贺	嘿	黑	痕
60	很	狠	恨	哼	亨	横	衡	恒	轰	哄	烘	虹	鸿	洪	宏	弘	红	喉	侯	猴
80	吼	厚	候	后	呼	乎	忽	瑚	壶	葫	胡	蝴	狐	糊	湖					

Row 27		01	02	03	04	05	06	07	08	09	10	11	12	13	14	15	16	17	18	19
00		弧	虎	唬	护	互	沪	户	花	哗	华	猾	滑	画	划	化	话	槐	徊	怀
20	淮	坏	欢	环	桓	还	缓	换	患	唤	痪	豢	焕	涣	宦	幻	荒	慌	黄	磺
40	蝗	簧	皇	凰	惶	煌	晃	幌	恍	谎	灰	挥	辉	徽	恢	蛔	回	毁	悔	慧
60	卉	惠	晦	贿	秽	会	烩	汇	讳	诲	绘	荤	昏	婚	魂	浑	混	豁	活	伙
80	火	获	或	惑	霍	货	祸	击	圾	基	机	畸	稽	积	箕					

Row 28		01	02	03	04	05	06	07	08	09	10	11	12	13	14	15	16	17	18	19
00		肌	饥	迹	激	讥	鸡	姬	绩	缉	吉	极	棘	辑	籍	集	及	急	疾	汲
20	即	嫉	级	挤	几	脊	己	蓟	技	冀	季	伎	祭	剂	悸	济	寄	寂	计	记
40	既	忌	际	妓	继	纪	嘉	枷	夹	佳	家	加	荚	颊	贾	甲	钾	假	稼	价
60	架	驾	嫁	歼	监	坚	尖	笺	间	煎	兼	肩	艰	奸	缄	茧	检	柬	碱	硷
80	拣	捡	简	俭	剪	减	荐	槛	鉴	践	贱	见	键	箭	件					

Row 29		01	02	03	04	05	06	07	08	09	10	11	12	13	14	15	16	17	18	19
00		健	舰	剑	饯	渐	溅	涧	建	僵	姜	将	浆	江	疆	蒋	桨	奖	讲	匠
20	酱	降	蕉	椒	礁	焦	胶	交	郊	浇	骄	娇	嚼	搅	铰	矫	侥	脚	狡	角
40	饺	缴	绞	剿	教	酵	轿	较	叫	窖	揭	接	皆	秸	街	阶	截	劫	节	桔
60	杰	捷	睫	竭	洁	结	解	姐	戒	藉	芥	界	借	介	疥	诫	届	巾	筋	斤
80	金	今	津	襟	紧	锦	仅	谨	进	靳	晋	禁	近	烬	浸					

Row 30		01	02	03	04	05	06	07	08	09	10	11	12	13	14	15	16	17	18	19
00		尽	劲	荆	兢	茎	睛	晶	鲸	京	惊	精	粳	经	井	警	景	颈	静	境
20	敬	镜	径	痉	靖	竟	竞	净	炯	窘	揪	究	纠	玖	韭	久	灸	九	酒	厩
40	救	旧	臼	舅	咎	就	疚	鞠	拘	狙	疽	居	驹	菊	局	咀	矩	举	沮	聚
60	拒	据	巨	具	距	踞	锯	俱	句	惧	炬	剧	捐	鹃	娟	倦	眷	卷	绢	撅
80	攫	抉	掘	倔	爵	觉	决	诀	绝	均	菌	钧	军	君	峻					

Row 31		01	02	03	04	05	06	07	08	09	10	11	12	13	14	15	16	17	18	19
00		俊	竣	浚	郡	骏	喀	咖	卡	咯	开	揩	楷	凯	慨	刊	堪	勘	坎	砍
20	看	康	慷	糠	扛	抗	亢	炕	考	拷	烤	靠	坷	苛	柯	棵	磕	颗	科	壳
40	咳	可	渴	克	刻	客	课	肯	啃	垦	恳	坑	吭	空	恐	孔	控	抠	口	扣
60	寇	枯	哭	窟	苦	酷	库	裤	夸	垮	挎	跨	胯	块	筷	侩	快	宽	款	匡
80	筐	狂	框	矿	眶	旷	况	亏	盔	岿	窥	葵	奎	魁	傀					

Row 32		01	02	03	04	05	06	07	08	09	10	11	12	13	14	15	16	17	18	19
00		馈	愧	溃	坤	昆	捆	困	括	扩	廓	阔	垃	拉	喇	蜡	腊	辣	啦	莱
20	来	赖	蓝	婪	栏	拦	篮	阑	兰	澜	谰	揽	览	懒	缆	烂	滥	琅	榔	狼
40	廊	郎	朗	浪	捞	劳	牢	老	佬	姥	酪	烙	涝	勒	乐	雷	镭	蕾	磊	累
60	儡	垒	擂	肋	类	泪	棱	楞	冷	厘	梨	犁	黎	篱	狸	离	漓	理	李	里
80	鲤	礼	莉	荔	吏	栗	丽	厉	励	砾	历	利	傈	例	俐					

Row 33		01	02	03	04	05	06	07	08	09	10	11	12	13	14	15	16	17	18	19
00		痢	立	粒	沥	隶	力	璃	哩	俩	联	莲	连	镰	廉	怜	涟	帘	敛	脸
20	链	恋	炼	练	粮	凉	梁	粱	良	两	辆	量	晾	亮	谅	撩	聊	僚	疗	燎
40	寥	辽	潦	了	撂	镣	廖	料	列	裂	烈	劣	猎	琳	林	磷	霖	临	邻	鳞
60	淋	凛	赁	吝	拎	玲	菱	零	龄	铃	伶	羚	凌	灵	陵	岭	领	另	令	溜
80	琉	榴	硫	馏	留	刘	瘤	流	柳	六	龙	聋	咙	笼	窿					

Row 34		01	02	03	04	05	06	07	08	09	10	11	12	13	14	15	16	17	18	19
00		隆	垄	拢	陇	楼	娄	搂	篓	漏	陋	芦	卢	颅	庐	炉	掳	卤	虏	鲁
20	麓	碌	露	路	赂	鹿	潞	禄	录	陆	戮	驴	吕	铝	侣	旅	履	屡	缕	虑
40	氯	律	率	滤	绿	峦	挛	孪	滦	卵	乱	掠	略	抡	轮	伦	仑	沦	纶	论
60	萝	螺	罗	逻	锣	箩	骡	裸	落	洛	骆	络	妈	麻	玛	码	蚂	马	骂	嘛
80	吗	埋	买	麦	卖	迈	脉	瞒	馒	蛮	满	蔓	曼	慢	漫					

Row 35		01	02	03	04	05	06	07	08	09	10	11	12	13	14	15	16	17	18	19
00		谩	芒	茫	盲	氓	忙	莽	猫	茅	锚	毛	矛	铆	卯	茂	冒	帽	貌	贸
20	么	玫	枚	梅	酶	霉	煤	没	眉	媒	镁	每	美	昧	寐	妹	媚	门	闷	们
40	萌	蒙	檬	盟	锰	猛	梦	孟	眯	醚	靡	糜	迷	谜	弥	米	秘	觅	泌	蜜
60	密	幂	棉	眠	绵	冕	免	勉	娩	缅	面	苗	描	瞄	藐	秒	渺	庙	妙	蔑
80	灭	民	抿	皿	敏	悯	闽	明	螟	鸣	铭	名	命	谬	摸					

Row 36		01	02	03	04	05	06	07	08	09	10	11	12	13	14	15	16	17	18	19
00		摹	蘑	模	膜	磨	摩	魔	抹	末	莫	墨	默	沫	漠	寞	陌	谋	牟	某
20	拇	牡	亩	姆	母	墓	暮	幕	募	慕	木	目	睦	牧	穆	拿	哪	呐	钠	那
40	娜	纳	氖	乃	奶	耐	奈	南	男	难	囊	挠	脑	恼	闹	淖	呢	馁	内	嫩
60	能	妮	霓	倪	泥	尼	拟	你	匿	腻	逆	溺	蔫	拈	年	碾	撵	捻	念	娘
80	酿	鸟	尿	捏	聂	孽	啮	镊	镍	涅	您	柠	狞	凝	宁					

Row 37		01	02	03	04	05	06	07	08	09	10	11	12	13	14	15	16	17	18	19
00		拧	泞	牛	扭	钮	纽	脓	浓	农	弄	奴	努	怒	女	暖	虐	疟	挪	懦
20	糯	诺	哦	欧	鸥	殴	藕	呕	偶	沤	啪	趴	爬	帕	怕	琶	拍	排	牌	徘
40	湃	派	攀	潘	盘	磐	盼	畔	判	叛	乓	庞	旁	耪	胖	抛	咆	刨	炮	袍
60	跑	泡	呸	胚	培	裴	赔	陪	配	佩	沛	喷	盆	砰	抨	烹	澎	彭	蓬	棚
80	硼	篷	膨	朋	鹏	捧	碰	坯	砒	霹	批	披	劈	琵	毗					

Row 38		01	02	03	04	05	06	07	08	09	10	11	12	13	14	15	16	17	18	19
00		啤	脾	疲	皮	匹	痞	僻	屁	譬	篇	偏	片	骗	飘	漂	瓢	票	撇	瞥
20	拼	频	贫	品	聘	乒	坪	苹	萍	平	凭	瓶	评	屏	坡	泼	颇	婆	破	魄
40	迫	粕	剖	扑	铺	仆	莆	葡	菩	蒲	埔	朴	圃	普	浦	谱	曝	瀑	期	欺
60	栖	戚	妻	七	凄	漆	柒	沏	其	棋	奇	歧	畦	崎	脐	齐	旗	祈	祁	骑
80	起	岂	乞	企	启	契	砌	器	气	迄	弃	汽	泣	讫	掐					

Row 39		01	02	03	04	05	06	07	08	09	10	11	12	13	14	15	16	17	18	19
00		恰	洽	牵	扦	钎	铅	千	迁	签	仟	谦	乾	黔	钱	钳	前	潜	遣	浅
20	谴	堑	嵌	欠	歉	枪	呛	腔	羌	墙	蔷	强	抢	橇	锹	敲	悄	桥	瞧	乔
40	侨	巧	鞘	撬	翘	峭	俏	窍	切	茄	且	怯	窃	钦	侵	亲	秦	琴	勤	芹
60	擒	禽	寝	沁	青	轻	氢	倾	卿	清	擎	晴	氰	情	顷	请	庆	琼	穷	秋
80	丘	邱	球	求	囚	酋	泅	趋	区	蛆	曲	躯	屈	驱	渠					

Row 40		01	02	03	04	05	06	07	08	09	10	11	12	13	14	15	16	17	18	19
00		取	娶	龋	趣	去	圈	颧	权	醛	泉	全	痊	拳	犬	券	劝	缺	炔	瘸
20	却	鹊	榷	确	雀	裙	群	然	燃	冉	染	瓤	壤	攘	嚷	让	饶	扰	绕	惹
40	热	壬	仁	人	忍	韧	任	认	刃	妊	纫	扔	仍	日	戎	茸	蓉	荣	融	熔
60	溶	容	绒	冗	揉	柔	肉	茹	蠕	儒	孺	如	辱	乳	汝	入	褥	软	阮	蕊
80	瑞	锐	闰	润	若	弱	撒	洒	萨	腮	鳃	塞	赛	三	叁					

Row 41		01	02	03	04	05	06	07	08	09	10	11	12	13	14	15	16	17	18	19
00		伞	散	桑	嗓	丧	搔	骚	扫	嫂	瑟	色	涩	森	僧	莎	砂	杀	刹	沙
20	纱	傻	啥	煞	筛	晒	珊	苫	杉	山	删	煽	衫	闪	陕	擅	赡	膳	善	汕
40	扇	缮	墒	伤	商	赏	晌	上	尚	裳	梢	捎	稍	烧	芍	勺	韶	少	哨	邵
60	绍	奢	赊	蛇	舌	舍	赦	摄	射	慑	涉	社	设	砷	申	呻	伸	身	深	娠
80	绅	神	沈	审	婶	甚	肾	慎	渗	声	生	甥	牲	升	绳					

Row 42		01	02	03	04	05	06	07	08	09	10	11	12	13	14	15	16	17	18	19
00		省	盛	剩	胜	圣	师	失	狮	施	湿	诗	尸	虱	十	石	拾	时	什	食
20	蚀	实	识	史	矢	使	屎	驶	始	式	示	士	世	柿	事	拭	誓	逝	势	是
40	嗜	噬	适	仕	侍	释	饰	氏	市	恃	室	视	试	收	手	首	守	寿	授	售
60	受	瘦	兽	蔬	枢	梳	殊	抒	输	叔	舒	淑	疏	书	赎	孰	熟	薯	暑	曙
80	署	蜀	黍	鼠	属	术	述	树	束	戍	竖	墅	庶	数	漱					

Row 43		01	02	03	04	05	06	07	08	09	10	11	12	13	14	15	16	17	18	19
00		恕	刷	耍	摔	衰	甩	帅	栓	拴	霜	双	爽	谁	水	睡	税	吮	瞬	顺
20	舜	说	硕	朔	烁	斯	撕	嘶	思	私	司	丝	死	肆	寺	嗣	四	伺	似	饲
40	巳	松	耸	怂	颂	送	宋	讼	诵	搜	艘	擞	嗽	苏	酥	俗	素	速	粟	僳
60	塑	溯	宿	诉	肃	酸	蒜	算	虽	隋	随	绥	髓	碎	岁	穗	遂	隧	祟	孙
80	损	笋	蓑	梭	唆	缩	琐	索	锁	所	塌	他	它	她	塔					

Row 44		01	02	03	04	05	06	07	08	09	10	11	12	13	14	15	16	17	18	19
00		獭	挞	蹋	踏	胎	苔	抬	台	泰	酞	太	态	汰	坍	摊	贪	瘫	滩	坛
20	檀	痰	潭	谭	谈	坦	毯	袒	碳	探	叹	炭	汤	塘	搪	堂	棠	膛	唐	糖
40	倘	躺	淌	趟	烫	掏	涛	滔	绦	萄	桃	逃	淘	陶	讨	套	特	藤	腾	疼
60	誊	梯	剔	踢	锑	提	题	蹄	啼	体	替	嚏	惕	涕	剃	屉	天	添	填	田
80	甜	恬	舔	腆	挑	条	迢	眺	跳	贴	铁	帖	厅	听	烃					

Row 45		01	02	03	04	05	06	07	08	09	10	11	12	13	14	15	16	17	18	19
00		汀	廷	停	亭	庭	挺	艇	通	桐	酮	瞳	同	铜	彤	童	桶	捅	筒	统
20	痛	偷	投	头	透	凸	秃	突	图	徒	途	涂	屠	土	吐	兔	湍	团	推	颓
40	腿	蜕	褪	退	吞	屯	臀	拖	托	脱	鸵	陀	驮	驼	椭	妥	拓	唾	挖	哇
60	蛙	洼	娃	瓦	袜	歪	外	豌	弯	湾	玩	顽	丸	烷	完	碗	挽	晚	皖	惋
80	宛	婉	万	腕	汪	王	亡	枉	网	往	旺	望	忘	妄	威					

Row 46		01	02	03	04	05	06	07	08	09	10	11	12	13	14	15	16	17	18	19
00		巍	微	危	韦	违	桅	围	唯	惟	为	潍	维	苇	萎	委	伟	伪	尾	纬
20	未	蔚	味	畏	胃	喂	魏	位	渭	谓	尉	慰	卫	瘟	温	蚊	文	闻	纹	吻
40	稳	紊	问	嗡	翁	瓮	挝	蜗	涡	窝	我	斡	卧	握	沃	巫	呜	钨	乌	污
60	诬	屋	无	芜	梧	吾	吴	毋	武	五	捂	午	舞	伍	侮	坞	戊	雾	晤	物
80	勿	务	悟	误	昔	熙	析	西	硒	矽	晰	嘻	吸	锡	牺					

Row 47		01	02	03	04	05	06	07	08	09	10	11	12	13	14	15	16	17	18	19
00		稀	息	希	悉	膝	夕	惜	熄	烯	溪	汐	犀	檄	袭	席	习	媳	喜	铣
20	洗	系	隙	戏	细	瞎	虾	匣	霞	辖	暇	峡	侠	狭	下	厦	夏	吓	掀	锨
40	先	仙	鲜	纤	咸	贤	衔	舷	闲	涎	弦	嫌	显	险	现	献	县	腺	馅	羡
60	宪	陷	限	线	相	厢	镶	香	箱	襄	湘	乡	翔	祥	详	想	响	享	项	巷
80	橡	像	向	象	萧	硝	霄	削	哮	嚣	销	消	宵	淆	晓					

Row 48		01	02	03	04	05	06	07	08	09	10	11	12	13	14	15	16	17	18	19
00		小	孝	校	肖	啸	笑	效	楔	些	歇	蝎	鞋	协	挟	携	邪	斜	胁	谐
20	写	械	卸	蟹	懈	泄	泻	谢	屑	薪	芯	锌	欣	辛	新	忻	心	信	衅	星
40	腥	猩	惺	兴	刑	型	形	邢	行	醒	幸	杏	性	姓	兄	凶	胸	匈	汹	雄
60	熊	休	修	羞	朽	嗅	锈	秀	袖	绣	墟	戌	需	虚	嘘	须	徐	许	蓄	酗
80	叙	旭	序	畜	恤	絮	婿	绪	续	轩	喧	宣	悬	旋	玄					

Row 49		01	02	03	04	05	06	07	08	09	10	11	12	13	14	15	16	17	18	19
00		选	癣	眩	绚	靴	薛	学	穴	雪	血	勋	熏	循	旬	询	寻	驯	巡	殉
20	汛	训	讯	逊	迅	压	押	鸦	鸭	呀	丫	芽	牙	蚜	崖	衙	涯	雅	哑	亚
40	讶	焉	咽	阉	烟	淹	盐	严	研	蜒	岩	延	言	颜	阎	炎	沿	奄	掩	眼
60	衍	演	艳	堰	燕	厌	砚	雁	唁	彦	焰	宴	谚	验	殃	央	鸯	秧	杨	扬
80	佯	疡	羊	洋	阳	氧	仰	痒	养	样	漾	邀	腰	妖	瑶					

Row 50		01	02	03	04	05	06	07	08	09	10	11	12	13	14	15	16	17	18	19
00		摇	尧	遥	窑	谣	姚	咬	舀	药	要	耀	椰	噎	耶	爷	野	冶	也	页
20	掖	业	叶	曳	腋	夜	液	一	壹	医	揖	铱	依	伊	衣	颐	夷	遗	移	仪
40	胰	疑	沂	宜	姨	彝	椅	蚁	倚	已	乙	矣	以	艺	抑	易	邑	屹	亿	役
60	臆	逸	肄	疫	亦	裔	意	毅	忆	义	益	溢	诣	议	谊	译	异	翼	翌	绎
80	茵	荫	因	殷	音	阴	姻	吟	银	淫	寅	饮	尹	引	隐					

Row 51		01	02	03	04	05	06	07	08	09	10	11	12	13	14	15	16	17	18	19
00		印	英	樱	婴	鹰	应	缨	莹	萤	营	荧	蝇	迎	赢	盈	影	颖	硬	映
20	哟	拥	佣	臃	痈	庸	雍	踊	蛹	咏	泳	涌	永	恿	勇	用	幽	优	悠	忧
40	尤	由	邮	铀	犹	油	游	酉	有	友	右	佑	釉	诱	又	幼	迂	淤	于	盂
60	榆	虞	愚	舆	余	俞	逾	鱼	愉	渝	渔	隅	予	娱	雨	与	屿	禹	宇	语
80	羽	玉	域	芋	郁	吁	遇	喻	峪	御	愈	欲	狱	育	誉					

Row 52		01	02	03	04	05	06	07	08	09	10	11	12	13	14	15	16	17	18	19
00		浴	寓	裕	预	豫	驭	鸳	渊	冤	元	垣	袁	原	援	辕	园	员	圆	猿
20	源	缘	远	苑	愿	怨	院	曰	约	越	跃	钥	岳	粤	月	悦	阅	耘	云	郧
40	匀	陨	允	运	蕴	酝	晕	韵	孕	匝	砸	杂	栽	哉	灾	宰	载	再	在	咱
60	攒	暂	赞	赃	脏	葬	遭	糟	凿	藻	枣	早	澡	蚤	躁	噪	造	皂	灶	燥
80	责	择	则	泽	贼	怎	增	憎	曾	赠	扎	喳	渣	札	轧					

Row 53		01	02	03	04	05	06	07	08	09	10	11	12	13	14	15	16	17	18	19
00		铡	闸	眨	栅	榨	咋	乍	炸	诈	摘	斋	宅	窄	债	寨	瞻	毡	詹	粘
20	沾	盏	斩	辗	崭	展	蘸	栈	占	战	站	湛	绽	樟	章	彰	漳	张	掌	涨
40	杖	丈	帐	账	仗	胀	瘴	障	招	昭	找	沼	赵	照	罩	兆	肇	召	遮	折
60	哲	蛰	辙	者	锗	蔗	这	浙	珍	斟	真	甄	砧	臻	贞	针	侦	枕	疹	诊
80	震	振	镇	阵	蒸	挣	睁	征	狰	争	怔	整	拯	正	政					

Row 54		01	02	03	04	05	06	07	08	09	10	11	12	13	14	15	16	17	18	19
00		帧	症	郑	证	芝	枝	支	吱	蜘	知	肢	脂	汁	之	织	职	直	植	殖
20	执	值	侄	址	指	止	趾	只	旨	纸	志	挚	掷	至	致	置	帜	峙	制	智
40	秩	稚	质	炙	痔	滞	治	窒	中	盅	忠	钟	衷	终	种	肿	重	仲	众	舟
60	周	州	洲	诌	粥	轴	肘	帚	咒	皱	宙	昼	骤	珠	株	蛛	朱	猪	诸	诛
80	逐	竹	烛	煮	拄	瞩	嘱	主	著	柱	助	蛀	贮	铸	筑					

Row 55		01	02	03	04	05	06	07	08	09	10	11	12	13	14	15	16	17	18	19
00		住	注	祝	驻	抓	爪	拽	专	砖	转	撰	赚	篆	桩	庄	装	妆	撞	壮
20	状	椎	锥	追	赘	坠	缀	谆	准	捉	拙	卓	桌	琢	茁	酌	啄	着	灼	浊
40	兹	咨	资	姿	滋	淄	孜	紫	仔	籽	滓	子	自	渍	字	鬃	棕	踪	宗	综
60	总	纵	邹	走	奏	揍	租	足	卒	族	祖	诅	阻	组	钻	纂	嘴	醉	最	罪
80	尊	遵	昨	左	佐	柞	做	作	坐	座										

Row 56		01	02	03	04	05	06	07	08	09	10	11	12	13	14	15	16	17	18	19
00		亍	丌	兀	丐	廿	卅	丕	亘	丞	鬲	孬	噩	丨	禺	丿	匕	乇	夭	爻
20	卮	氐	囟	胤	馗	毓	睾	鼗	丶	亟	鼐	乜	乩	亓	芈	孛	啬	嘏	仄	厍
40	厝	厣	厥	厮	靥	赝	匚	叵	匦	匮	匾	赜	卦	卣	刂	刈	刎	刭	刳	刿
60	剀	剌	剞	剡	剜	蒯	剽	劂	劁	劐	劓	冂	罔	亻	仃	仉	仂	仨	仡	仫
80	仞	伛	仳	伢	佤	仵	伥	伧	伉	伫	佞	佧	攸	佚	佝					

Row 57		01	02	03	04	05	06	07	08	09	10	11	12	13	14	15	16	17	18	19
00		佟	佗	伲	伽	佶	佴	侑	侉	侃	侏	佾	佻	侪	佼	侬	侔	俦	俨	俪
20	俅	俚	俣	俜	俑	俟	俸	倩	偌	俳	倬	倏	倮	倭	俾	倜	倌	倥	倨	偾
40	偃	偕	偈	偎	偬	偻	傥	傧	傩	傺	僖	儆	僭	僬	僦	僮	儇	儋	仝	氽
60	佘	佥	俎	龠	汆	籴	兮	巽	黉	馘	冁	夔	勹	匍	訇	匐	凫	夙	兕	亠
80	兖	亳	衮	袤	亵	脔	裒	禀	嬴	蠃	羸	冫	冱	冽	冼					

Row 58		01	02	03	04	05	06	07	08	09	10	11	12	13	14	15	16	17	18	19
00		凇	冖	冢	冥	讠	讦	讧	讪	讴	讵	讷	诂	诃	诋	诏	诎	诒	诓	诔
20	诖	诘	诙	诜	诟	诠	诤	诨	诩	诮	诰	诳	诶	诹	诼	诿	谀	谂	谄	谇
40	谌	谏	谑	谒	谔	谕	谖	谙	谛	谘	谝	谟	谠	谡	谥	谧	谪	谫	谮	谯
60	谲	谳	谵	谶	卩	卺	阝	阢	阡	阱	阪	阽	阼	陂	陉	陔	陟	陧	陬	陲
80	陴	隈	隍	隗	隰	邗	邛	邝	邙	邬	邡	邴	邳	邶	邺					

Row 59		01	02	03	04	05	06	07	08	09	10	11	12	13	14	15	16	17	18	19
00		邸	邰	郏	郅	邾	郐	郄	郇	郓	郦	郢	郜	郗	郛	郫	郯	郾	鄄	鄢
20	鄞	鄣	鄱	鄯	鄹	酃	酆	刍	奂	劢	劬	劭	劾	哿	勐	勖	勰	叟	燮	矍
40	廴	凵	凼	鬯	厶	弁	畚	巯	坌	垩	垡	塾	墼	壅	壑	圩	圬	圪	圳	圹
60	圮	圯	坜	圻	坂	坩	垅	坫	垆	坼	坻	坨	坭	坶	坳	垭	垤	垌	垲	埏
80	垧	垴	垓	垠	埕	埘	埚	埙	埒	垸	埴	埯	埸	埤	埝					

Row 60		01	02	03	04	05	06	07	08	09	10	11	12	13	14	15	16	17	18	19
00		堋	堍	埽	埭	堀	堞	堙	塄	堠	塥	塬	墁	墉	墚	墀	馨	鼙	懿	艹
20	艽	艿	芏	芊	芨	芄	芎	芑	芗	芙	芫	芸	芾	芰	苈	苊	苣	芘	芷	芮
40	苋	苌	苁	芩	芴	芡	芪	芟	苄	苎	芤	苡	茉	苷	苤	茏	茇	苜	苴	苒
60	苘	茌	苻	苓	茑	茚	茆	茔	茕	苠	苕	茜	荑	荛	荜	茈	莒	茼	茴	茱
80	莛	荞	茯	荏	荇	荃	荟	荀	茗	荠	茭	茺	茳	荦	荥					

Row 61		01	02	03	04	05	06	07	08	09	10	11	12	13	14	15	16	17	18	19
00		荨	茛	荩	荬	荪	荭	荮	莰	荸	莳	莴	莠	莪	莓	莜	莅	荼	莶	莩
20	荽	莸	荻	莘	莞	莨	莺	莼	菁	萁	菥	菘	堇	萘	萋	菝	菽	菖	萜	萸
40	萑	萆	菔	菟	萏	萃	菸	菹	菪	菅	菀	萦	菰	菡	葜	葑	葚	葙	葳	蒇
60	蒈	葺	蒉	葸	萼	葆	葩	葶	蒌	蒎	萱	葭	蓁	蓍	蓐	蓦	蒽	蓓	蓊	蒿
80	蒺	蓠	蒡	蒹	蒴	蒗	蓥	蓣	蔌	甍	蔸	蓰	蔹	蔟	蔺					

Row 62		01	02	03	04	05	06	07	08	09	10	11	12	13	14	15	16	17	18	19
00		蕖	蔻	蓿	蓼	蕙	蕈	蕨	蕤	蕞	蕺	瞢	蕃	蕲	蕻	薤	薨	薇	薏	蕹
20	薮	薜	薅	薹	薷	薰	藓	藁	藜	藿	蘧	蘅	蘩	蘖	蘼	廾	弈	夼	奁	耷
40	奕	奚	奘	匏	尢	尥	尬	尴	扌	扪	抟	抻	拊	拚	拗	拮	挢	拶	挹	捋
60	捃	掭	揶	捱	捺	掎	掴	捭	掬	掊	捩	掮	掼	揲	揸	揠	揿	揄	揞	揎
80	摒	揆	掾	摅	摁	搋	搛	搠	搌	搦	搡	摞	撄	摭	撖					

Row 63		01	02	03	04	05	06	07	08	09	10	11	12	13	14	15	16	17	18	19
00		摺	撷	撸	撙	撺	擀	擐	擗	擤	擢	攉	攥	攮	弋	忒	甙	弑	卟	叱
20	叽	叩	叨	叻	吒	吖	吆	呋	呒	呓	呔	呖	呃	吡	呗	呙	吣	吲	咂	咔
40	呷	呱	呤	咚	咛	咄	呶	呦	咝	哐	咭	哂	咴	哒	咧	咦	哓	哔	呲	咣
60	哕	咻	咿	哌	哙	哚	哜	咩	咪	咤	哝	哏	哞	唛	哧	唠	哽	唔	哳	唢
80	唣	唏	唑	唧	唪	啧	喏	喵	啉	啭	啁	啕	唿	啐	唼					

Row 64		01	02	03	04	05	06	07	08	09	10	11	12	13	14	15	16	17	18	19
00		唷	啖	啵	啶	啷	唳	唰	啜	喋	嗒	喃	喱	喹	喈	喁	喟	啾	嗖	喑
20	啻	嗟	喽	喾	喔	喙	嗪	嗷	嗉	嘟	嗑	嗫	嗬	嗔	嗦	嗝	嗄	嗯	嗥	嗲
40	嗳	嗌	嗍	嗨	嗵	嗤	辔	嘞	嘈	嘌	嘁	嘤	嘣	嗾	嘀	嘧	嘭	噘	嘹	噗
60	嘬	噍	噢	噙	噜	噌	噔	嚆	噤	噱	噫	噻	噼	嚅	嚓	嚯	囔	囗	囝	囡
80	囵	囫	囹	囿	圄	圊	圉	圜	帏	帙	帔	帑	帱	帻	帼					

Row 65		01	02	03	04	05	06	07	08	09	10	11	12	13	14	15	16	17	18	19
00		帷	幄	幔	幛	幞	幡	岌	屺	岍	岐	岖	岈	岘	岙	岑	岚	岜	岵	岢
20	岽	岬	岫	岱	岣	峁	岷	峄	峒	峤	峋	峥	崂	崃	崧	崦	崮	崤	崞	崆
40	崛	嵘	崾	崴	崽	嵬	嵛	嵯	嵝	嵫	嵋	嵊	嵩	嵴	嶂	嶙	嶝	豳	嶷	巅
60	彳	彷	徂	徇	徉	後	徕	徙	徜	徨	徭	徵	徼	衢	彡	犭	犰	犴	犷	犸
80	狃	狁	狎	狍	狒	狨	狯	狩	狲	狴	狷	猁	狳	猃	狺					

Row 66		01	02	03	04	05	06	07	08	09	10	11	12	13	14	15	16	17	18	19
00		狻	猗	猓	猡	猊	猞	猝	猕	猢	猹	猥	猬	猸	猱	獐	獍	獗	獠	獬
20	獯	獾	舛	夥	飧	夤	夂	饣	饧	饨	饩	饪	饫	饬	饴	饷	饽	馀	馄	馇
40	馊	馍	馐	馑	馓	馔	馕	庀	庑	庋	庖	庥	庠	庹	庵	庾	庳	赓	廒	廑
60	廛	廨	廪	膺	忄	忉	忖	忏	怃	忮	怄	忡	忤	忾	怅	怆	忪	忭	忸	怙
80	怵	怦	怛	怏	怍	怩	怫	怊	怿	怡	恸	恹	恻	恺	恂					

Row 67		01	02	03	04	05	06	07	08	09	10	11	12	13	14	15	16	17	18	19
00		恪	恽	悖	悚	悭	悝	悃	悒	悌	悛	惬	悻	悱	惝	惘	惆	惚	悴	愠
20	愦	愕	愣	惴	愀	愎	愫	慊	慵	憬	憔	憧	憷	懔	懵	忝	隳	闩	闫	闱
40	闳	闵	闶	闼	闾	阃	阄	阆	阈	阊	阋	阌	阍	阏	阒	阕	阖	阗	阙	阚
60	丬	爿	戕	氵	汔	汜	汊	沣	沅	沐	沔	沌	汨	汩	汴	汶	沆	沩	泐	泔
80	沭	泷	泸	泱	泗	沲	泠	泖	泺	泫	泮	沱	泓	泯	泾					

Row 68		01	02	03	04	05	06	07	08	09	10	11	12	13	14	15	16	17	18	19
00		洹	洧	洌	浃	浈	洇	洄	洙	洎	洫	浍	洮	洵	洚	浏	浒	浔	洳	涑
20	浯	涞	涠	浞	涓	涔	浜	浠	浼	浣	渚	淇	淅	淞	渎	涿	淠	渑	淦	淝
40	淙	渖	涫	渌	涮	渫	湮	湎	湫	溲	湟	溆	湓	湔	渲	渥	湄	滟	溱	溘
60	滠	漭	滢	溥	溧	溽	溻	溷	滗	溴	滏	溏	滂	溟	潢	潆	潇	漤	漕	滹
80	漯	漶	潋	潴	漪	漉	漩	澉	澍	澌	潸	潲	潼	潺	濑					

Row 69		01	02	03	04	05	06	07	08	09	10	11	12	13	14	15	16	17	18	19
00		濉	澧	澹	澶	濂	濡	濮	濞	濠	濯	瀚	瀣	瀛	瀹	瀵	灏	灞	宀	宄
20	宕	宓	宥	宸	甯	骞	搴	寤	寮	褰	寰	蹇	謇	辶	迓	迕	迥	迮	迤	迩
40	迦	迳	迨	逅	逄	逋	逦	逑	逍	逖	逡	逵	逶	逭	逯	遄	遑	遒	遐	遨
60	遘	遢	遛	暹	遴	遽	邂	邈	邃	邋	彐	彗	彖	彘	尻	咫	屐	屙	孱	屣
80	屦	羼	弪	弩	弭	艴	弼	鬻	屮	妁	妃	妍	妩	妪	妣					

Row 70		01	02	03	04	05	06	07	08	09	10	11	12	13	14	15	16	17	18	19
00		妗	姊	妫	妞	妤	姒	妲	妯	姗	妾	娅	娆	姝	娈	姣	姘	姹	娌	娉
20	娲	娴	娑	娣	娓	婀	婧	婊	婕	娼	婢	婵	胬	媪	媛	婷	婺	媾	嫫	媲
40	嫒	嫔	媸	嫠	嫣	嫱	嫖	嫦	嫘	嫜	嬉	嬗	嬖	嬲	嬷	孀	尕	尜	孚	孥
60	孳	孑	孓	孢	驵	驷	驸	驺	驿	驽	骀	骁	骅	骈	骊	骐	骒	骓	骖	骘
80	骛	骜	骝	骟	骠	骢	骣	骥	骧	纟	纡	纣	纥	纨	纩					

Row 71		01	02	03	04	05	06	07	08	09	10	11	12	13	14	15	16	17	18	19
00		纭	纰	纾	绀	绁	绂	绉	绋	绌	绐	绔	绗	绛	绠	绡	绨	绫	绮	绯
20	绱	绲	缍	绶	绺	绻	绾	缁	缂	缃	缇	缈	缋	缌	缏	缑	缒	缗	缙	缜
40	缛	缟	缡	缢	缣	缤	缥	缦	缧	缪	缫	缬	缭	缯	缰	缱	缲	缳	缵	幺
60	畿	巛	甾	邕	玎	玑	玮	玢	玟	珏	珂	珑	玷	玳	珀	珉	珈	珥	珙	顼
80	琊	珩	珧	珞	玺	珲	琏	琪	瑛	琦	琥	琨	琰	琮	琬					

Row 72		01	02	03	04	05	06	07	08	09	10	11	12	13	14	15	16	17	18	19
00		琛	琚	瑁	瑜	瑗	瑕	瑙	瑷	瑭	瑾	璜	璎	璀	璁	璇	璋	璞	璨	璩
20	璐	璧	瓒	璺	韪	韫	韬	杌	杓	杞	杈	杩	枥	枇	杪	杳	枘	枧	杵	枨
40	枞	枭	枋	杷	杼	柰	栉	柘	栊	柩	枰	栌	柙	枵	柚	枳	柝	栀	柃	枸
60	柢	栎	柁	柽	栲	栳	桠	桡	桎	桢	桄	桤	梃	栝	桕	桦	桁	桧	桀	栾
80	桊	桉	栩	梵	梏	桴	桷	梓	桫	棂	楮	棼	椟	椠	棹					

Row 73		01	02	03	04	05	06	07	08	09	10	11	12	13	14	15	16	17	18	19
00		椤	棰	椋	椁	楗	棣	椐	楱	椹	楠	楂	楝	榄	楫	榀	榘	楸	椴	槌
20	榇	榈	槎	榉	楦	楣	楹	榛	榧	榻	榫	榭	槔	榱	槁	槊	槟	榕	槠	榍
40	槿	樯	槭	樗	樘	橥	槲	橄	樾	檠	橐	橛	樵	檎	橹	樽	樨	橘	橼	檑
60	檐	檩	檗	檫	猷	獒	殁	殂	殇	殄	殒	殓	殍	殚	殛	殡	殪	轫	轭	轱
80	轲	轳	轵	轶	轸	轷	轹	轺	轼	轾	辁	辂	辄	辇	辋					

Row 74		01	02	03	04	05	06	07	08	09	10	11	12	13	14	15	16	17	18	19
00		辍	辎	辏	辘	辚	軎	戋	戗	戛	戟	戢	戡	戥	戤	戬	臧	瓯	瓴	瓿
20	甏	甑	甓	攴	旮	旯	旰	昊	昙	杲	昃	昕	昀	炅	曷	昝	昴	昱	昶	昵
40	耆	晟	晔	晁	晏	晖	晡	晗	晷	暄	暌	暧	暝	暾	曛	曜	曦	曩	贲	贳
60	贶	贻	贽	赀	赅	赆	赈	赉	赇	赍	赕	赙	觇	觊	觋	觌	觎	觏	觐	觑
80	牮	犟	牝	牦	牯	牾	牿	犄	犋	犍	犏	犒	挈	挲	掰					

Row 75		01	02	03	04	05	06	07	08	09	10	11	12	13	14	15	16	17	18	19
00		搿	擘	耄	毪	毳	毽	毵	毹	氅	氇	氆	氍	氕	氘	氙	氚	氡	氩	氤
20	氪	氲	攵	敕	敫	牍	牒	牖	爰	虢	刖	肟	肜	肓	肼	朊	肽	肱	肫	肭
40	肴	肷	胧	胨	胩	胪	胛	胂	胄	胙	胍	胗	朐	胝	胫	胱	胴	胭	脍	脎
60	胲	胼	朕	脒	豚	脶	脞	脬	脘	脲	腈	腌	腓	腴	腙	腚	腱	腠	腩	腼
80	腽	腭	腧	塍	媵	膈	膂	膑	滕	膣	膪	臌	朦	臊	膻					

Row 76		01	02	03	04	05	06	07	08	09	10	11	12	13	14	15	16	17	18	19
00		臁	膦	欤	欷	欹	歃	歆	歙	飑	飒	飓	飕	飙	飚	殳	彀	毂	觳	斐
20	齑	斓	於	旆	旄	旃	旌	旎	旒	旖	炀	炜	炖	炝	炻	烀	炷	炫	炱	烨
40	烊	焐	焓	焖	焯	焱	煳	煜	煨	煅	煲	煊	煸	煺	熘	熳	熵	熨	熠	燠
60	燔	燧	燹	爝	爨	灬	焘	煦	熹	戾	戽	扃	扈	扉	礻	祀	祆	祉	祛	祜
80	祓	祚	祢	祗	祠	祯	祧	祺	禅	禊	禚	禧	禳	忑	忐					

Row 77		01	02	03	04	05	06	07	08	09	10	11	12	13	14	15	16	17	18	19
00		怼	恝	恚	恧	恁	恙	恣	悫	愆	愍	慝	憩	憝	懋	懑	戆	肀	聿	沓
20	泶	淼	矶	矸	砀	砉	砗	砘	砑	斫	砭	砜	砝	砹	砺	砻	砟	砼	砥	砬
40	砣	砩	硎	硭	硖	硗	砦	硐	硇	硌	硪	碛	碓	碚	碇	碜	碡	碣	碲	碹
60	碥	磔	磙	磉	磬	磲	礅	磴	礓	礤	礞	礴	龛	黹	黻	黼	盱	眄	眍	盹
80	眇	眈	眚	眢	眙	眭	眦	眵	眸	睐	睑	睇	睃	睚	睨					

Row 78		01	02	03	04	05	06	07	08	09	10	11	12	13	14	15	16	17	18	19
00		睢	睥	睿	瞍	睽	瞀	瞌	瞑	瞟	瞠	瞰	瞵	瞽	町	畀	畎	畋	畈	畛
20	畲	畹	疃	罘	罡	罟	詈	罨	罴	罱	罹	羁	罾	盍	盥	蠲	钅	钆	钇	钋
40	钊	钌	钍	钏	钐	钔	钗	钕	钚	钛	钜	钣	钤	钫	钪	钭	钬	钯	钰	钲
60	钴	钶	钷	钸	钹	钺	钼	钽	钿	铄	铈	铉	铊	铋	铌	铍	铎	铐	铑	铒
80	铕	铖	铗	铙	铘	铛	铞	铟	铠	铢	铤	铥	铧	铨	铪					

Row 79		01	02	03	04	05	06	07	08	09	10	11	12	13	14	15	16	17	18	19
00		铩	铫	铮	铯	铳	铴	铵	铷	铹	铼	铽	铿	锃	锂	锆	锇	锉	锊	锍
20	锎	锏	锒	锓	锔	锕	锖	锘	锛	锝	锞	锟	锢	锪	锫	锩	锬	锱	锲	锴
40	锶	锷	锸	锼	锾	锿	镂	锵	镄	镅	镆	镉	镌	镎	镏	镒	镓	镔	镖	镗
60	镘	镙	镛	镞	镟	镝	镡	镢	镤	镥	镦	镧	镨	镩	镪	镫	镬	镯	镱	镲
80	镳	锺	矧	矬	雉	秕	秭	秣	秫	稆	嵇	稃	稂	稞	稔					

Row 80		01	02	03	04	05	06	07	08	09	10	11	12	13	14	15	16	17	18	19
00		稹	稷	穑	黏	馥	穰	皈	皎	皓	皙	皤	瓞	瓠	甬	鸠	鸢	鸨	鸩	鸪
20	鸫	鸬	鸲	鸱	鸶	鸸	鸷	鸹	鸺	鸾	鹁	鹂	鹄	鹆	鹇	鹈	鹉	鹋	鹌	鹎
40	鹑	鹕	鹗	鹚	鹛	鹜	鹞	鹣	鹦	鹧	鹨	鹩	鹪	鹫	鹬	鹱	鹭	鹳	疒	疔
60	疖	疠	疝	疬	疣	疳	疴	疸	痄	疱	疰	痃	痂	痖	痍	痣	痨	痦	痤	痫
80	痧	瘃	痱	痼	痿	瘐	瘀	瘅	瘌	瘗	瘊	瘥	瘘	瘕	瘙					

Row 81		01	02	03	04	05	06	07	08	09	10	11	12	13	14	15	16	17	18	19
00		瘛	瘼	瘢	瘠	癀	瘭	瘰	瘿	瘵	癃	瘾	瘳	癍	癞	癔	癜	癖	癫	癯
20	翊	竦	穸	穹	窀	窆	窈	窕	窦	窠	窬	窨	窭	窳	衤	衩	衲	衽	衿	袂
40	袢	裆	袷	袼	裉	裢	裎	裣	裥	裱	褚	裼	裨	裾	裰	褡	褙	褓	褛	褊
60	褴	褫	褶	襁	襦	襻	疋	胥	皲	皴	矜	耒	耔	耖	耜	耠	耢	耥	耦	耧
80	耩	耨	耱	耋	耵	聃	聆	聍	聒	聩	聱	覃	顸	颀	颃					

Row 82		01	02	03	04	05	06	07	08	09	10	11	12	13	14	15	16	17	18	19
00		颉	颌	颍	颏	颔	颚	颛	颞	颟	颡	颢	颥	颦	虍	虔	虬	虮	虿	虺
20	虼	虻	蚨	蚍	蚋	蚬	蚝	蚧	蚣	蚪	蚓	蚩	蚶	蛄	蚵	蛎	蚰	蚺	蚱	蚯
40	蛉	蛏	蚴	蛩	蛱	蛲	蛭	蛳	蛐	蜓	蛞	蛴	蛟	蛘	蛑	蜃	蜇	蛸	蜈	蜊
60	蜍	蜉	蜣	蜻	蜞	蜥	蜮	蜚	蜾	蝈	蜴	蜱	蜩	蜷	蜿	螂	蜢	蝽	蝾	蝻
80	蝠	蝰	蝌	蝮	螋	蝓	蝣	蝼	蝤	蝙	蝥	螓	螯	螨	蟒					

Row 83		01	02	03	04	05	06	07	08	09	10	11	12	13	14	15	16	17	18	19
00		蟆	螈	螅	螭	螗	螃	螫	蟥	螬	螵	螳	蟋	蟓	螽	蟑	蟀	蟊	蟛	蟪
20	蟠	蟮	蠖	蠓	蟾	蠊	蠛	蠡	蠹	蠼	缶	罂	罄	罅	舐	竺	竽	笈	笃	笄
40	笕	笊	笫	笏	筇	笸	笪	笙	笮	笱	笠	笥	笤	笳	笾	笞	筘	筚	筅	筵
60	筌	筝	筠	筮	筻	筢	筲	筱	箐	箦	箧	箸	箬	箝	箨	箅	箪	箜	箢	箫
80	箴	篑	篁	篌	篝	篚	篥	篦	篪	簌	篾	篼	簏	簖	簋					

Row 84		01	02	03	04	05	06	07	08	09	10	11	12	13	14	15	16	17	18	19
00		簟	簪	簦	簸	籁	籀	臾	舁	舂	舄	臬	衄	舡	舢	舣	舭	舯	舨	舫
20	舸	舻	舳	舴	舾	艄	艉	艋	艏	艚	艟	艨	衾	袅	袈	裘	裟	襞	羝	羟
40	羧	羯	羰	羲	籼	敉	粑	粝	粜	粞	粢	粲	粼	粽	糁	糇	糌	糍	糈	糅
60	糗	糨	艮	暨	羿	翎	翕	翥	翡	翦	翩	翮	翳	糸	絷	綦	綮	繇	纛	麸
80	麴	赳	趄	趔	趑	趱	赧	赭	豇	豉	酊	酐	酎	酏	酤					

Row 85		01	02	03	04	05	06	07	08	09	10	11	12	13	14	15	16	17	18	19
00		酢	酡	酰	酩	酯	酽	酾	酲	酴	酹	醌	醅	醐	醍	醑	醢	醣	醪	醭
20	醮	醯	醵	醴	醺	豕	鹾	趸	跫	踅	蹙	蹩	趵	趿	趼	趺	跄	跖	跗	跚
40	跞	跎	跏	跛	跆	跬	跷	跸	跣	跹	跻	跤	踉	跽	踔	踝	踟	踬	踮	踣
60	踯	踺	蹀	踹	踵	踽	踱	蹉	蹁	蹂	蹑	蹒	蹊	蹰	蹶	蹼	蹯	蹴	躅	躏
80	躔	躐	躜	躞	豸	貂	貊	貅	貘	貔	斛	觖	觞	觚	觜					

Row 86		01	02	03	04	05	06	07	08	09	10	11	12	13	14	15	16	17	18	19
00		觥	觫	觯	訾	謦	靓	雩	雳	雯	霆	霁	霈	霏	霎	霪	霭	霰	霾	龀
20	龃	龅	龆	龇	龈	龉	龊	龌	黾	鼋	鼍	隹	隼	隽	雎	雒	瞿	雠	銎	銮
40	鋈	錾	鍪	鏊	鎏	鐾	鑫	鱿	鲂	鲅	鲆	鲇	鲈	稣	鲋	鲎	鲐	鲑	鲒	鲔
60	鲕	鲚	鲛	鲞	鲟	鲠	鲡	鲢	鲣	鲥	鲦	鲧	鲨	鲩	鲫	鲭	鲮	鲰	鲱	鲲
80	鲳	鲴	鲵	鲶	鲷	鲺	鲻	鲼	鲽	鳄	鳅	鳆	鳇	鳊	鳋					

Row 87		01	02	03	04	05	06	07	08	09	10	11	12	13	14	15	16	17	18	19
00		鳌	鳍	鳎	鳏	鳐	鳓	鳔	鳕	鳗	鳘	鳙	鳜	鳝	鳟	鳢	靼	鞅	鞑	鞒
20	鞔	鞯	鞫	鞣	鞲	鞴	骱	骰	骷	鹘	骶	骺	骼	髁	髀	髅	髂	髋	髌	髑
40	魅	魃	魇	魉	魈	魍	魑	飨	餍	餮	饕	饔	髟	髡	髦	髯	髫	髻	髭	髹
60	鬈	鬏	鬓	鬟	鬣	麽	麾	縻	麂	麇	麈	麋	麒	鏖	麝	麟	黛	黜	黝	黠
80	黟	黢	黩	黧	黥	黪	黯	鼢	鼬	鼯	鼹	鼷	鼽	鼾	齄					

F

GB/T 12345-90 Table

This appendix constitutes a table for the complete GB/T 12345-90 character set, printed here using the typeface 华文宋体 (STSong-Light), developed by Changzhou SinoType Technology. Each character is indexed by Row-Cell value.

Note that Row-Cell 01-01 is a full-width space character.

Row 1	00	01	02	03	04	05	06	07	08	09	10	11	12	13	14	15	16	17	18	19
00			、	。	·	ˉ	ˇ	¨	〃	々	—	～	‖	…	‘	’	“	”	〔	〕
20	〈	〉	《	》	「	」	『	』	〖	〗	【	】	±	×	÷	∶	∧	∨	∑	∏
40	∪	∩	∈	∷	√	⊥	∥	∠	⌒	⊙	∫	∮	≡	≌	≈	∽	∝	≠	≮	≯
60	≤	≥	∞	∵	∴	♂	♀	°	′	″	C	＄	¤	￠	￡	‰	§	№	☆	★
80	○	●	◎	◇	◆	□	■	△	▲	※	→	←	↑	↓	〓					

Row 2	00	01	02	03	04	05	06	07	08	09	10	11	12	13	14	15	16	17	18	19
00																		1.	2.	3.
20	4.	5.	6.	7.	8.	9.	10.	11.	12.	13.	14.	15.	16.	17.	18.	19.	20.	(1)	(2)	(3)
40	(4)	(5)	(6)	(7)	(8)	(9)	(10)	(11)	(12)	(13)	(14)	(15)	(16)	(17)	(18)	(19)	(20)	①	②	③
60	④	⑤	⑥	⑦	⑧	⑨	⑩			㈠	㈡	㈢	㈣	㈤	㈥	㈦	㈧	㈨	㈩	
80		Ⅰ	Ⅱ	Ⅲ	Ⅳ	Ⅴ	Ⅵ	Ⅶ	Ⅷ	Ⅸ	Ⅹ	Ⅺ	Ⅻ							

Row 3	00	01	02	03	04	05	06	07	08	09	10	11	12	13	14	15	16	17	18	19
00		！	＂	＃	￥	％	＆	＇	（	）	＊	＋	，	－	．	／	０	１	２	３
20	４	５	６	７	８	９	：	；	＜	＝	＞	？	＠	Ａ	Ｂ	Ｃ	Ｄ	Ｅ	Ｆ	Ｇ
40	Ｈ	Ｉ	Ｊ	Ｋ	Ｌ	Ｍ	Ｎ	Ｏ	Ｐ	Ｑ	Ｒ	Ｓ	Ｔ	Ｕ	Ｖ	Ｗ	Ｘ	Ｙ	Ｚ	［
60	＼	］	＾	＿	｀	ａ	ｂ	ｃ	ｄ	ｅ	ｆ	ｇ	ｈ	ｉ	ｊ	ｋ	ｌ	ｍ	ｎ	ｏ
80	ｐ	ｑ	ｒ	ｓ	ｔ	ｕ	ｖ	ｗ	ｘ	ｙ	ｚ	｛	｜	｝						

Row 4		01	02	03	04	05	06	07	08	09	10	11	12	13	14	15	16	17	18	19
00		ぁ	あ	ぃ	い	ぅ	う	ぇ	え	ぉ	お	か	が	き	ぎ	く	ぐ	け	げ	こ
20	ご	さ	ざ	し	じ	す	ず	せ	ぜ	そ	ぞ	た	だ	ち	ぢ	っ	つ	づ	て	で
40	と	ど	な	に	ぬ	ね	の	は	ば	ぱ	ひ	び	ぴ	ふ	ぶ	ぷ	へ	べ	ぺ	ほ
60	ぼ	ぽ	ま	み	む	め	も	ゃ	や	ゅ	ゆ	ょ	よ	ら	り	る	れ	ろ	ゎ	わ
80	ゐ	ゑ	を	ん																

Row 5		01	02	03	04	05	06	07	08	09	10	11	12	13	14	15	16	17	18	19
00		ァ	ア	ィ	イ	ゥ	ウ	ェ	エ	ォ	オ	カ	ガ	キ	ギ	ク	グ	ケ	ゲ	コ
20	ゴ	サ	ザ	シ	ジ	ス	ズ	セ	ゼ	ソ	ゾ	タ	ダ	チ	ヂ	ッ	ツ	ヅ	テ	デ
40	ト	ド	ナ	ニ	ヌ	ネ	ノ	ハ	バ	パ	ヒ	ビ	ピ	フ	ブ	プ	ヘ	ベ	ペ	ホ
60	ボ	ポ	マ	ミ	ム	メ	モ	ャ	ヤ	ュ	ユ	ョ	ヨ	ラ	リ	ル	レ	ロ	ヮ	ワ
80	ヰ	ヱ	ヲ	ン	ヴ	ヵ	ヶ													

Row 6		01	02	03	04	05	06	07	08	09	10	11	12	13	14	15	16	17	18	19
00		Α	Β	Γ	Δ	Ε	Ζ	Η	Θ	Ι	Κ	Λ	Μ	Ν	Ξ	Ο	Π	Ρ	Σ	Τ
20	Υ	Φ	Χ	Ψ	Ω									α	β	γ	δ	ε	ζ	η
40	θ	ι	κ	λ	μ	ν	ξ	ο	π	ρ	σ	τ	υ	φ	χ	ψ	ω	︐	︒	︑
60	︓	︔	︕	︖	︵	︶	︹	︺	︿	﹀	︽	︾	﹁	﹂	﹃	﹄	︗	︘	︻	︼
80	︷	︸	︱	︙	︳	︴														

Row 7		01	02	03	04	05	06	07	08	09	10	11	12	13	14	15	16	17	18	19
00		А	Б	В	Г	Д	Е	Ё	Ж	З	И	Й	К	Л	М	Н	О	П	Р	С
20	Т	У	Ф	Х	Ц	Ч	Ш	Щ	Ъ	Ы	Ь	Э	Ю	Я						
40										а	б	в	г	д	е	ё	ж	з	и	й
60	к	л	м	н	о	п	р	с	т	у	ф	х	ц	ч	ш	щ	ъ	ы	ь	э
80	ю	я																		

Row 8		01	02	03	04	05	06	07	08	09	10	11	12	13	14	15	16	17	18	19
00		ā	á	ǎ	à	ē	é	ě	è	ī	í	ǐ	ì	ō	ó	ǒ	ò	ū	ú	ǔ
20	ù	ǖ	ǘ	ǚ	ǜ	ü	ê	ɑ	ḿ	ń	ň	ǹ	ɡ					ㄅ	ㄆ	ㄇ
40	ㄈ	ㄉ	ㄊ	ㄋ	ㄌ	ㄍ	ㄎ	ㄏ	ㄐ	ㄑ	ㄒ	ㄓ	ㄔ	ㄕ	ㄖ	ㄗ	ㄘ	ㄙ	ㄚ	ㄛ
60	ㄜ	ㄝ	ㄞ	ㄟ	ㄠ	ㄡ	ㄢ	ㄣ	ㄤ	ㄥ	ㄦ	ㄧ	ㄨ	ㄩ						
80																				

Row 9		01	02	03	04	05	06	07	08	09	10	11	12	13	14	15	16	17	18	19
00					─	━	│	┃	┄	┅	┆	┇	┈	┉	┊	┋	┌	┍	┎	┏
20	┐	┑	┒	┓	└	┕	┖	┗	┘	┙	┚	┛	├	┝	┞	┟	┠	┡	┢	┣
40	┤	┥	┦	┧	┨	┩	┪	┫	┬	┭	┮	┯	┰	┱	┲	┳	┴	┵	┶	┷
60	┸	┹	┺	┻	┼	┽	┾	┿	╀	╁	╂	╃	╄	╅	╆	╇	╈	╉	╊	╋
80																				

Row 10		01	02	03	04	05	06	07	08	09	10	11	12	13	14	15	16	17	18	19
00		!	"	#	¥	%	&	'	(	)	*	+	,	-	.	/	0	1	2	3
20	4	5	6	7	8	9	:	;	<	=	>	?	@	A	B	C	D	E	F	G
40	H	I	J	K	L	M	N	O	P	Q	R	S	T	U	V	W	X	Y	Z	[
60	\	]	^	_	`	a	b	c	d	e	f	g	h	i	j	k	l	m	n	o
80	p	q	r	s	t	u	v	w	x	y	z	{	|	}	‾					

Row 11		01	02	03	04	05	06	07	08	09	10	11	12	13	14	15	16	17	18	19
00		ā	á	ǎ	à	ē	é	ě	è	ī	í	ǐ	ì	ō	ó	ǒ	ò	ū	ú	ǔ
20	ù	ǖ	ǘ	ǚ	ǜ	ü	ê	ɑ	ḿ	ń	ň	ǹ	ɡ							
40																				
60																				
80																				

Row 16		01	02	03	04	05	06	07	08	09	10	11	12	13	14	15	16	17	18	19
00		啊	阿	埃	挨	哎	唉	哀	皚	癌	藹	矮	艾	礙	愛	隘	鞍	氨	安	俺
20	按	暗	岸	胺	案	骯	昂	盎	凹	敖	熬	翱	襖	傲	奥	懊	澳	芭	捌	扒
40	叭	吧	笆	八	疤	巴	拔	跋	靶	把	耙	壩	霸	罷	爸	白	柏	百	擺	佰
60	敗	拜	稗	斑	班	搬	扳	般	頒	板	版	扮	拌	伴	瓣	半	辦	絆	邦	幫
80	梆	榜	膀	綁	棒	磅	蚌	鎊	傍	謗	苞	胞	包	褒	剥					

Row 17		01	02	03	04	05	06	07	08	09	10	11	12	13	14	15	16	17	18	19
00		薄	雹	保	堡	飽	寶	抱	報	暴	豹	鮑	爆	杯	碑	悲	卑	北	輩	背
20	貝	鋇	倍	狽	備	憊	焙	被	奔	苯	本	笨	崩	繃	甭	泵	蹦	迸	逼	鼻
40	比	鄙	筆	彼	碧	蓖	蔽	畢	斃	毖	幣	庇	痹	閉	敝	弊	必	辟	壁	臂
60	避	陛	鞭	邊	編	貶	扁	便	變	卞	辨	辯	辮	遍	標	彪	膘	表	鱉	憋
80	别	癟	彬	斌	瀕	濱	賓	擯	兵	冰	柄	丙	秉	餅	炳					

Row 18		01	02	03	04	05	06	07	08	09	10	11	12	13	14	15	16	17	18	19
00		病	并	玻	菠	播	撥	鉢	波	博	勃	搏	鉑	箔	伯	帛	舶	脖	膊	渤
20	泊	駁	捕	卜	哺	補	埠	不	布	步	簿	部	怖	擦	猜	裁	材	才	財	睬
40	踩	采	彩	菜	蔡	餐	參	蠶	殘	慚	慘	燦	蒼	艙	倉	滄	藏	操	糙	槽
60	曹	草	厠	策	側	册	測	層	蹭	插	叉	茬	茶	查	碴	搽	察	岔	差	詫
80	拆	柴	豺	攙	摻	蟬	饞	讒	纏	鏟	産	闡	顫	昌	猖					

Row 19		01	02	03	04	05	06	07	08	09	10	11	12	13	14	15	16	17	18	19
00		場	嘗	常	長	償	腸	廠	敞	暢	唱	倡	超	抄	鈔	朝	嘲	潮	巢	吵
20	炒	車	扯	撤	掣	徹	澈	郴	臣	辰	塵	晨	忱	沉	陳	趁	襯	撑	稱	城
40	橙	成	呈	乘	程	懲	澄	誠	承	逞	騁	秤	吃	痴	持	匙	池	遲	弛	馳
60	耻	齒	侈	尺	赤	翅	斥	熾	充	衝	蟲	崇	寵	抽	酬	疇	躊	稠	愁	籌
80	仇	綢	瞅	醜	臭	初	出	橱	厨	躇	鋤	雛	滁	除	楚					

Row 20		01	02	03	04	05	06	07	08	09	10	11	12	13	14	15	16	17	18	19
00		礎	儲	矗	搐	觸	處	揣	川	穿	椽	傳	船	喘	串	瘡	窗	幢	床	闖
20	創	吹	炊	捶	錘	垂	春	椿	醇	唇	淳	純	蠢	戳	綽	疵	茨	磁	雌	辭
40	慈	瓷	詞	此	刺	賜	次	聰	蔥	囪	匆	從	叢	湊	粗	醋	簇	促	躥	篡
60	竄	摧	崔	催	脆	瘁	粹	淬	翠	村	存	寸	磋	撮	搓	措	挫	錯	搭	達
80	答	瘩	打	大	呆	歹	傣	戴	帶	殆	代	貸	袋	待	逮					

Row 21		01	02	03	04	05	06	07	08	09	10	11	12	13	14	15	16	17	18	19
00		怠	耽	擔	丹	單	鄲	撣	膽	旦	氮	但	憚	淡	誕	彈	蛋	當	擋	黨
20	蕩	檔	刀	搗	蹈	倒	島	禱	導	到	稻	悼	道	盜	德	得	的	蹬	燈	登
40	等	瞪	凳	鄧	堤	低	滴	迪	敵	笛	狄	滌	翟	嫡	抵	底	地	蒂	第	帝
60	弟	遞	締	顛	掂	滇	碘	點	典	靛	墊	電	佃	甸	店	惦	奠	澱	殿	碉
80	叼	雕	凋	刁	掉	吊	釣	調	跌	爹	碟	蝶	迭	諜	疊					

Row 22		01	02	03	04	05	06	07	08	09	10	11	12	13	14	15	16	17	18	19
00		丁	盯	叮	釘	頂	鼎	錠	定	訂	丟	東	冬	董	懂	動	棟	侗	恫	凍
20	洞	兜	抖	鬥	陡	豆	逗	痘	都	督	毒	犢	獨	讀	堵	睹	賭	杜	鍍	肚
40	度	渡	妒	端	短	鍛	段	斷	緞	堆	兌	隊	對	墩	噸	蹲	敦	頓	囤	鈍
60	盾	遁	掇	哆	多	奪	垛	躲	朵	跺	舵	剁	惰	墮	蛾	峨	鵝	俄	額	訛
80	娥	惡	厄	扼	遏	鄂	餓	恩	而	兒	耳	爾	餌	洱	二					

Row 23		01	02	03	04	05	06	07	08	09	10	11	12	13	14	15	16	17	18	19
00		貳	發	罰	筏	伐	乏	閥	法	琺	藩	帆	番	翻	樊	礬	釩	繁	凡	煩
20	反	返	範	販	犯	飯	泛	坊	芳	方	肪	房	防	妨	仿	訪	紡	放	菲	非
40	啡	飛	肥	匪	誹	吠	肺	廢	沸	費	芬	酚	吩	氛	分	紛	墳	焚	汾	粉
60	奮	份	忿	憤	糞	豐	封	楓	蜂	峰	鋒	風	瘋	烽	逢	馮	縫	諷	奉	鳳
80	佛	否	夫	敷	膚	孵	扶	拂	輻	幅	氟	符	伏	俘	服					

Row 24		01	02	03	04	05	06	07	08	09	10	11	12	13	14	15	16	17	18	19
00		浮	涪	福	袱	弗	甫	撫	輔	俯	釜	斧	脯	腑	府	腐	赴	副	覆	賦
20	復	傅	付	阜	父	腹	負	富	訃	附	婦	縛	咐	噶	嘎	該	改	概	鈣	蓋
40	溉	幹	甘	杆	柑	竿	肝	趕	感	稈	敢	贛	岡	剛	鋼	缸	肛	綱	崗	港
60	杠	篙	皋	高	膏	羔	糕	搞	鎬	稿	告	哥	歌	擱	戈	鴿	胳	疙	割	革
80	葛	格	蛤	閣	隔	鉻	個	各	給	根	跟	耕	更	庚	羹					

Row 25		01	02	03	04	05	06	07	08	09	10	11	12	13	14	15	16	17	18	19
00		埂	耿	梗	工	攻	功	恭	龔	供	躬	公	宮	弓	鞏	汞	拱	貢	共	鈎
20	勾	溝	苟	狗	垢	構	購	夠	辜	菇	咕	箍	估	沽	孤	姑	鼓	古	蠱	骨
40	谷	股	故	顧	固	雇	刮	瓜	剮	寡	挂	褂	乖	拐	怪	棺	關	官	冠	觀
60	管	館	罐	慣	灌	貫	光	廣	逛	瑰	規	圭	硅	歸	龜	閨	軌	鬼	詭	癸
80	桂	櫃	跪	貴	劊	輥	滾	棍	鍋	郭	國	果	裹	過	哈					

Row 26

		01	02	03	04	05	06	07	08	09	10	11	12	13	14	15	16	17	18	19
00		骸	孩	海	氦	亥	害	駭	酣	憨	邯	韓	含	涵	寒	函	喊	罕	翰	撼
20	捍	旱	憾	悍	焊	汗	漢	夯	杭	航	壕	嚎	豪	毫	郝	好	耗	號	浩	呵
40	喝	荷	菏	核	禾	和	何	合	盒	貉	閡	河	涸	赫	褐	鶴	賀	嘿	黑	痕
60	很	狠	恨	哼	亨	横	衡	恒	轟	哄	烘	虹	鴻	洪	宏	弘	紅	喉	侯	猴
80	吼	厚	候	後	呼	乎	忽	瑚	壺	葫	胡	蝴	狐	糊	湖					

Row 27

		01	02	03	04	05	06	07	08	09	10	11	12	13	14	15	16	17	18	19
00		弧	虎	唬	護	互	滬	户	花	嘩	華	猾	滑	畫	劃	化	話	槐	徊	懷
20	淮	壞	歡	環	桓	還	緩	換	患	喚	瘓	豢	煥	渙	宦	幻	荒	慌	黄	磺
40	蝗	簧	皇	凰	惶	煌	晃	幌	恍	謊	灰	揮	輝	徽	恢	蛔	回	毁	悔	慧
60	卉	惠	晦	賄	穢	會	燴	匯	諱	誨	繪	葷	昏	婚	魂	渾	混	豁	活	伙
80	火	獲	或	惑	霍	貨	禍	擊	圾	基	機	畸	稽	積	箕					

Row 28

		01	02	03	04	05	06	07	08	09	10	11	12	13	14	15	16	17	18	19
00		肌	饑	迹	激	譏	鷄	姬	績	緝	吉	極	棘	輯	籍	集	及	急	疾	汲
20	即	嫉	級	擠	幾	脊	己	薊	技	冀	季	伎	祭	劑	悸	濟	寄	寂	計	記
40	既	忌	際	妓	繼	紀	嘉	枷	夾	佳	家	加	莢	頰	賈	甲	鉀	假	稼	價
60	架	駕	嫁	殲	監	堅	尖	箋	間	煎	兼	肩	艱	奸	緘	繭	檢	柬	碱	鹼
80	揀	撿	簡	儉	剪	減	薦	檻	鑒	踐	賤	見	鍵	箭	件					

Row 29

		01	02	03	04	05	06	07	08	09	10	11	12	13	14	15	16	17	18	19
00		健	艦	劍	餞	漸	濺	澗	建	僵	姜	將	漿	江	疆	蔣	槳	獎	講	匠
20	醬	降	蕉	椒	礁	焦	膠	交	郊	澆	驕	嬌	嚼	攪	鉸	矯	僥	脚	狡	角
40	餃	繳	絞	剿	教	酵	轎	較	叫	窖	揭	接	皆	秸	街	階	截	劫	節	桔
60	杰	捷	睫	竭	潔	結	解	姐	戒	藉	芥	界	借	介	疥	誡	届	巾	筋	斤
80	金	今	津	襟	緊	錦	僅	謹	進	靳	晋	禁	近	燼	浸					

Row 30

		01	02	03	04	05	06	07	08	09	10	11	12	13	14	15	16	17	18	19
00		盡	勁	荆	兢	莖	睛	晶	鯨	京	驚	精	粳	經	井	警	景	頸	静	境
20	敬	鏡	徑	痙	靖	竟	競	净	炯	窘	揪	究	糾	玖	韭	久	灸	九	酒	厩
40	救	舊	臼	舅	咎	就	疚	鞠	拘	狙	疽	居	駒	菊	局	咀	矩	舉	沮	聚
60	拒	據	巨	具	距	踞	鋸	俱	句	懼	炬	劇	捐	鵑	娟	倦	眷	卷	絹	撅
80	攫	抉	掘	倔	爵	覺	决	訣	絶	均	菌	鈞	軍	君	峻					

Row 31

		01	02	03	04	05	06	07	08	09	10	11	12	13	14	15	16	17	18	19
00		俊	竣	浚	郡	駿	喀	咖	卡	咯	開	揩	楷	凱	慨	刊	堪	勘	坎	砍
20	看	康	慷	糠	扛	抗	亢	炕	考	拷	烤	靠	坷	苛	柯	棵	磕	顆	科	殼
40	咳	可	渴	克	刻	客	課	肯	啃	墾	懇	坑	吭	空	恐	孔	控	摳	口	扣
60	寇	枯	哭	窟	苦	酷	庫	褲	誇	垮	挎	跨	胯	塊	筷	儈	快	寬	款	匡
80	筐	狂	框	礦	眶	曠	况	虧	盔	巋	窺	葵	奎	魁	傀					

Row 32		01	02	03	04	05	06	07	08	09	10	11	12	13	14	15	16	17	18	19
00		饋	愧	潰	坤	昆	捆	困	括	擴	廓	闊	垃	拉	喇	蠟	臘	辣	啦	萊
20	來	賴	藍	婪	欄	攔	籃	闌	蘭	瀾	讕	攬	覽	懶	纜	爛	濫	琅	榔	狼
40	廊	郎	朗	浪	撈	勞	牢	老	佬	姥	酪	烙	澇	勒	樂	雷	鐳	蕾	磊	累
60	儡	壘	擂	肋	類	泪	棱	楞	冷	厘	梨	犁	黎	籬	狸	離	灕	理	李	裏
80	鯉	禮	莉	荔	吏	栗	麗	厲	勵	礫	歷	利	傈	例	俐					

Row 33		01	02	03	04	05	06	07	08	09	10	11	12	13	14	15	16	17	18	19
00		痢	立	粒	瀝	隸	力	璃	哩	倆	聯	蓮	連	鐮	廉	憐	漣	簾	斂	臉
20	鏈	戀	煉	練	糧	涼	梁	粱	良	兩	輛	量	晾	亮	諒	撩	聊	僚	療	燎
40	寥	遼	潦	了	撂	鐐	廖	料	列	裂	烈	劣	獵	琳	林	磷	霖	臨	鄰	鱗
60	淋	凜	賃	吝	拎	玲	菱	零	齡	鈴	伶	羚	凌	靈	陵	嶺	領	另	令	溜
80	琉	榴	硫	餾	留	劉	瘤	流	柳	六	龍	聾	嚨	籠	窿					

Row 34		01	02	03	04	05	06	07	08	09	10	11	12	13	14	15	16	17	18	19
00		隆	壟	攏	隴	樓	婁	摟	簍	漏	陋	蘆	盧	顱	廬	爐	擄	滷	虜	魯
20	麓	碌	露	路	賂	鹿	潞	祿	錄	陸	戮	驢	呂	鋁	侶	旅	履	屢	縷	慮
40	氯	律	率	濾	綠	巒	攣	孿	灤	卵	亂	掠	略	掄	輪	倫	侖	淪	綸	論
60	蘿	螺	羅	邏	鑼	籮	騾	裸	落	洛	駱	絡	媽	麻	瑪	碼	螞	馬	罵	嘛
80	嗎	埋	買	麥	賣	邁	脉	瞞	饅	蠻	滿	蔓	曼	慢	漫					

Row 35		01	02	03	04	05	06	07	08	09	10	11	12	13	14	15	16	17	18	19
00		謾	芒	茫	盲	氓	忙	莽	猫	茅	錨	毛	矛	鉚	卯	茂	冒	帽	貌	貿
20	麼	玫	枚	梅	酶	霉	煤	没	眉	媒	鎂	每	美	昧	寐	妹	媚	門	悶	們
40	萌	蒙	檬	盟	錳	猛	夢	孟	眯	醚	靡	糜	迷	謎	彌	米	秘	覓	泌	蜜
60	密	冪	棉	眠	綿	冕	免	勉	娩	緬	面	苗	描	瞄	藐	秒	渺	廟	妙	蔑
80	滅	民	抿	皿	敏	憫	閩	明	螟	鳴	銘	名	命	謬	摸					

Row 36		01	02	03	04	05	06	07	08	09	10	11	12	13	14	15	16	17	18	19
00		摹	蘑	模	膜	磨	摩	魔	抹	末	莫	墨	默	沫	漠	寞	陌	謀	牟	某
20	拇	牡	畝	姆	母	墓	暮	幕	募	慕	木	目	睦	牧	穆	拿	哪	吶	鈉	那
40	娜	納	氖	乃	奶	耐	奈	南	男	難	囊	撓	腦	惱	鬧	淖	呢	餒	內	嫩
60	能	妮	霓	倪	泥	尼	擬	你	匿	膩	逆	溺	蔫	拈	年	碾	攆	捻	念	娘
80	釀	鳥	尿	捏	聶	孽	嚙	鑷	鎳	涅	您	檸	獰	凝	寧					

Row 37		01	02	03	04	05	06	07	08	09	10	11	12	13	14	15	16	17	18	19
00		擰	濘	牛	扭	鈕	紐	膿	濃	農	弄	奴	努	怒	女	暖	虐	瘧	挪	懦
20	糯	諾	哦	歐	鷗	毆	藕	嘔	偶	漚	啪	趴	爬	帕	怕	琶	拍	排	牌	徘
40	湃	派	攀	潘	盤	磐	盼	畔	判	叛	乓	龐	旁	耪	胖	拋	咆	刨	炮	袍
60	跑	泡	呸	胚	培	裴	賠	陪	配	佩	沛	噴	盆	砰	抨	烹	澎	彭	蓬	棚
80	硼	篷	膨	朋	鵬	捧	碰	坯	砒	霹	批	披	劈	琵	毗					

Row 38		01	02	03	04	05	06	07	08	09	10	11	12	13	14	15	16	17	18	19
00		啤	脾	疲	皮	匹	痞	僻	屁	譬	篇	偏	片	騙	飄	漂	瓢	票	撇	瞥
20	拼	頻	貧	品	聘	乒	坪	蘋	萍	平	憑	瓶	評	屏	坡	潑	頗	婆	破	魄
40	迫	粕	剖	撲	鋪	僕	莆	葡	菩	蒲	埔	樸	圃	普	浦	譜	曝	瀑	期	欺
60	棲	戚	妻	七	淒	漆	柒	沏	其	棋	奇	歧	畦	崎	臍	齊	旗	祈	祁	騎
80	起	豈	乞	企	啓	契	砌	器	氣	迄	弃	汽	泣	訖	掐					

Row 39		01	02	03	04	05	06	07	08	09	10	11	12	13	14	15	16	17	18	19
00		恰	洽	牽	扦	釺	鉛	千	遷	簽	仟	謙	乾	黔	錢	鉗	前	潛	遣	淺
20	譴	塹	嵌	欠	歉	槍	嗆	腔	羌	墻	薔	强	搶	橇	鍬	敲	悄	橋	瞧	喬
40	僑	巧	鞘	撬	翹	峭	俏	竅	切	茄	且	怯	竊	欽	侵	親	秦	琴	勤	芹
60	擒	禽	寢	沁	青	輕	氫	傾	卿	清	擎	晴	氰	情	頃	請	慶	瓊	窮	秋
80	丘	邱	球	求	囚	酋	泅	趨	區	蛆	曲	軀	屈	驅	渠					

Row 40		01	02	03	04	05	06	07	08	09	10	11	12	13	14	15	16	17	18	19
00		取	娶	齲	趣	去	圈	顴	權	醛	泉	全	痊	拳	犬	券	勸	缺	炔	瘸
20	却	鵲	榷	確	雀	裙	群	然	燃	冉	染	瓤	壤	攘	嚷	讓	饒	擾	繞	惹
40	熱	壬	仁	人	忍	韌	任	認	刃	妊	紉	扔	仍	日	戎	茸	蓉	榮	融	熔
60	溶	容	絨	冗	揉	柔	肉	茹	蠕	儒	孺	如	辱	乳	汝	入	褥	軟	阮	蕊
80	瑞	鋭	閏	潤	若	弱	撒	灑	薩	腮	鰓	塞	賽	三	叁					

Row 41		01	02	03	04	05	06	07	08	09	10	11	12	13	14	15	16	17	18	19
00		傘	散	桑	嗓	喪	搔	騷	掃	嫂	瑟	色	澀	森	僧	莎	砂	殺	刹	沙
20	紗	傻	啥	煞	篩	曬	珊	苫	杉	山	删	煽	衫	閃	陝	擅	贍	膳	善	汕
40	扇	繕	墒	傷	商	賞	晌	上	尚	裳	梢	捎	稍	燒	芍	勺	韶	少	哨	邵
60	紹	奢	賒	蛇	舌	捨	赦	攝	射	懾	涉	社	設	砷	申	呻	伸	身	深	娠
80	紳	神	沈	審	嬸	甚	腎	慎	滲	聲	生	甥	牲	升	繩					

Row 42		01	02	03	04	05	06	07	08	09	10	11	12	13	14	15	16	17	18	19
00		省	盛	剩	勝	聖	師	失	獅	施	濕	詩	尸	虱	十	石	拾	時	什	食
20	蝕	實	識	史	矢	使	屎	駛	始	式	示	士	世	柿	事	拭	誓	逝	勢	是
40	嗜	噬	適	仕	侍	釋	飾	氏	市	恃	室	視	試	收	手	首	守	壽	授	售
60	受	瘦	獸	蔬	樞	梳	殊	抒	輸	叔	舒	淑	疏	書	贖	孰	熟	薯	暑	曙
80	署	蜀	黍	鼠	屬	術	述	樹	束	戍	竪	墅	庶	數	漱					

Row 43		01	02	03	04	05	06	07	08	09	10	11	12	13	14	15	16	17	18	19
00		恕	刷	耍	摔	衰	甩	帥	栓	拴	霜	雙	爽	誰	水	睡	税	吮	瞬	順
20	舜	説	碩	朔	爍	斯	撕	嘶	思	私	司	絲	死	肆	寺	嗣	四	伺	似	飼
40	巳	鬆	聳	慫	頌	送	宋	訟	誦	搜	艘	擻	嗽	蘇	酥	俗	素	速	粟	僳
60	塑	溯	宿	訴	肅	酸	蒜	算	雖	隋	隨	綏	髓	碎	歲	穗	遂	隧	祟	孫
80	損	笋	蓑	梭	唆	縮	瑣	索	鎖	所	塌	他	它	她	塔					

Row 44		01	02	03	04	05	06	07	08	09	10	11	12	13	14	15	16	17	18	19
00		獺	撻	蹋	踏	胎	苔	抬	臺	泰	酞	太	態	汰	坍	攤	貪	癱	灘	壇
20	檀	痰	潭	譚	談	坦	毯	袒	碳	探	嘆	炭	湯	塘	搪	堂	棠	膛	唐	糖
40	倘	躺	淌	趟	燙	掏	濤	滔	絛	萄	桃	逃	淘	陶	討	套	特	藤	騰	疼
60	謄	梯	剔	踢	銻	提	題	蹄	啼	體	替	嚏	惕	涕	剃	屜	天	添	填	田
80	甜	恬	舔	腆	挑	條	迢	眺	跳	貼	鐵	帖	廳	聽	烴					

Row 45		01	02	03	04	05	06	07	08	09	10	11	12	13	14	15	16	17	18	19
00		汀	廷	停	亭	庭	挺	艇	通	桐	酮	瞳	同	銅	彤	童	桶	捅	筒	統
20	痛	偷	投	頭	透	凸	禿	突	圖	徒	途	塗	屠	土	吐	兔	湍	團	推	頹
40	腿	蛻	褪	退	吞	屯	臀	拖	托	脫	鴕	陀	馱	駝	橢	妥	拓	唾	挖	哇
60	蛙	窪	娃	瓦	襪	歪	外	豌	彎	灣	玩	頑	丸	烷	完	碗	挽	晚	皖	惋
80	宛	婉	萬	腕	汪	王	亡	枉	網	往	旺	望	忘	妄	威					

Row 46		01	02	03	04	05	06	07	08	09	10	11	12	13	14	15	16	17	18	19
00		巍	微	危	韋	違	桅	圍	唯	惟	爲	濰	維	葦	萎	委	偉	僞	尾	緯
20	未	蔚	味	畏	胃	喂	魏	位	渭	謂	尉	慰	衛	瘟	温	蚊	文	聞	紋	吻
40	穩	紊	問	嗡	翁	瓮	撾	蝸	渦	窩	我	斡	卧	握	沃	巫	嗚	鎢	烏	污
60	誣	屋	無	蕪	梧	吾	吳	毋	武	五	捂	午	舞	伍	侮	塢	戊	霧	晤	物
80	勿	務	悟	誤	昔	熙	析	西	硒	矽	晰	嘻	吸	錫	犧					

Row 47		01	02	03	04	05	06	07	08	09	10	11	12	13	14	15	16	17	18	19
00		稀	息	希	悉	膝	夕	惜	熄	烯	溪	汐	犀	檄	襲	席	習	媳	喜	銑
20	洗	系	隙	戲	細	瞎	蝦	匣	霞	轄	暇	峽	俠	狹	下	廈	夏	嚇	掀	鍁
40	先	仙	鮮	纖	咸	賢	銜	舷	閑	涎	弦	嫌	顯	險	現	獻	縣	腺	餡	羨
60	憲	陷	限	綫	相	厢	鑲	香	箱	襄	湘	鄉	翔	祥	詳	想	響	享	項	巷
80	橡	像	向	象	蕭	硝	霄	削	哮	囂	銷	消	宵	淆	曉					

Row 48		01	02	03	04	05	06	07	08	09	10	11	12	13	14	15	16	17	18	19
00		小	孝	校	肖	嘯	笑	效	楔	些	歇	蝎	鞋	協	挾	携	邪	斜	脅	諧
20	寫	械	卸	蟹	懈	泄	瀉	謝	屑	薪	芯	鋅	欣	辛	新	忻	心	信	釁	星
40	腥	猩	惺	興	刑	型	形	邢	行	醒	幸	杏	性	姓	兄	凶	胸	匈	洶	雄
60	熊	休	修	羞	朽	嗅	銹	秀	袖	綉	墟	戌	需	虚	噓	須	徐	許	蓄	酗
80	叙	旭	序	畜	恤	絮	婿	緒	續	軒	喧	宣	懸	旋	玄					

Row 49		01	02	03	04	05	06	07	08	09	10	11	12	13	14	15	16	17	18	19
00		選	癬	眩	絢	靴	薛	學	穴	雪	血	勛	熏	循	旬	詢	尋	馴	巡	殉
20	汛	訓	訊	遜	迅	壓	押	鴉	鴨	呀	丫	芽	牙	蚜	崖	衙	涯	雅	啞	亞
40	訝	焉	咽	閹	烟	淹	鹽	嚴	研	蜒	岩	延	言	顔	閻	炎	沿	奄	掩	眼
60	衍	演	艷	堰	燕	厭	硯	雁	唁	彦	焰	宴	諺	驗	殃	央	鴦	秧	楊	揚
80	佯	瘍	羊	洋	陽	氧	仰	癢	養	樣	漾	邀	腰	妖	瑤					

Row 50		01	02	03	04	05	06	07	08	09	10	11	12	13	14	15	16	17	18	19
00		搖	堯	遙	窑	謠	姚	咬	舀	藥	要	耀	椰	噎	耶	爺	野	冶	也	頁
20	掖	業	葉	曳	腋	夜	液	一	壹	醫	揖	銥	依	伊	衣	頤	夷	遺	移	儀
40	胰	疑	沂	宜	姨	彝	椅	蟻	倚	已	乙	矣	以	藝	抑	易	邑	屹	億	役
60	臆	逸	肄	疫	亦	裔	意	毅	憶	義	益	溢	詣	議	誼	譯	异	翼	翌	繹
80	茵	蔭	因	殷	音	陰	姻	吟	銀	淫	寅	飲	尹	引	隱					

Row 51		01	02	03	04	05	06	07	08	09	10	11	12	13	14	15	16	17	18	19
00		印	英	櫻	嬰	鷹	應	纓	瑩	螢	營	熒	蠅	迎	贏	盈	影	穎	硬	映
20	喲	擁	傭	臃	癰	庸	雍	踴	蛹	咏	泳	涌	永	恿	勇	用	幽	優	悠	憂
40	尤	由	郵	鈾	猶	油	游	酉	有	友	右	佑	釉	誘	又	幼	迂	淤	于	盂
60	榆	虞	愚	輿	餘	俞	逾	魚	愉	渝	漁	隅	予	娱	雨	與	嶼	禹	宇	語
80	羽	玉	域	芋	鬱	吁	遇	喻	峪	御	愈	欲	獄	育	譽					

Row 52		01	02	03	04	05	06	07	08	09	10	11	12	13	14	15	16	17	18	19
00		浴	寓	裕	預	豫	馭	鴛	淵	冤	元	垣	袁	原	援	轅	園	員	圓	猿
20	源	緣	遠	苑	願	怨	院	曰	約	越	躍	鑰	岳	粤	月	悦	閱	耘	雲	鄖
40	匀	隕	允	運	蘊	醖	暈	韵	孕	匝	砸	雜	栽	哉	災	宰	載	再	在	咱
60	攢	暫	贊	贓	臟	葬	遭	糟	鑿	藻	棗	早	澡	蚤	躁	噪	造	皂	竈	燥
80	責	擇	則	澤	賊	怎	增	憎	曾	贈	扎	喳	渣	札	軋					

Row 53		01	02	03	04	05	06	07	08	09	10	11	12	13	14	15	16	17	18	19
00		鍘	閘	眨	栅	榨	咋	乍	炸	詐	摘	齋	宅	窄	債	寨	瞻	氈	詹	粘
20	沾	盞	斬	輾	嶄	展	蘸	棧	占	戰	站	湛	綻	樟	章	彰	漳	張	掌	漲
40	杖	丈	帳	賬	仗	脹	瘴	障	招	昭	找	沼	趙	照	罩	兆	肇	召	遮	折
60	哲	蟄	轍	者	鍺	蔗	這	浙	珍	斟	真	甄	砧	臻	貞	針	偵	枕	疹	診
80	震	振	鎮	陣	蒸	掙	睜	徵	猙	争	怔	整	拯	正	政					

Row 54		01	02	03	04	05	06	07	08	09	10	11	12	13	14	15	16	17	18	19
00		幀	癥	鄭	證	芝	枝	支	吱	蜘	知	肢	脂	汁	之	織	職	直	植	殖
20	執	值	侄	址	指	止	趾	祇	旨	紙	志	摯	擲	至	致	置	幟	峙	制	智
40	秩	稚	質	炙	痔	滯	治	窒	中	盅	忠	鐘	衷	終	種	腫	重	仲	衆	舟
60	周	州	洲	謅	粥	軸	肘	帚	咒	皺	宙	晝	驟	珠	株	蛛	朱	猪	諸	誅
80	逐	竹	燭	煮	拄	矚	囑	主	著	柱	助	蛀	貯	鑄	築					

Row 55		01	02	03	04	05	06	07	08	09	10	11	12	13	14	15	16	17	18	19
00		住	注	祝	駐	抓	爪	拽	專	磚	轉	撰	賺	篆	樁	莊	裝	妝	撞	壯
20	狀	椎	錐	追	贅	墜	綴	諄	準	捉	拙	卓	桌	琢	茁	酌	啄	着	灼	濁
40	兹	咨	資	姿	滋	淄	孜	紫	仔	籽	滓	子	自	漬	字	鬃	棕	踪	宗	綜
60	總	縱	鄒	走	奏	揍	租	足	卒	族	祖	詛	阻	組	鑽	纂	嘴	醉	最	罪
80	尊	遵	昨	左	佐	柞	做	作	坐	座										

Row 56		01	02	03	04	05	06	07	08	09	10	11	12	13	14	15	16	17	18	19
00		亍	丌	兀	丐	廿	卅	丕	亘	丞	鬲	孬	噩	丨	禺	丿	匕	乇	夭	爻
20	卮	氐	囟	胤	馗	毓	睾	鼗	丶	亟	鼐	乜	乩	亓	芈	孛	嗇	嘏	仄	厙
40	厝	厴	厥	厮	靨	贋	匚	叵	匭	匱	匾	賾	卦	卣	刂	刈	刎	剄	刳	劌
60	剴	剌	剞	剡	剜	蒯	剽	劂	劁	劐	劓	冂	罔	亻	仃	仉	仂	仨	仡	仫
80	仞	傴	仳	伢	佤	仵	倀	傖	伉	佇	佞	佧	攸	佚	佝					

Row 57		01	02	03	04	05	06	07	08	09	10	11	12	13	14	15	16	17	18	19
00		佟	佗	伲	伽	佶	佴	侑	侉	侃	侏	佾	佻	儕	佼	儂	侔	儔	儼	儷
20	俅	俚	俁	俜	俑	俟	俸	倩	偌	俳	倬	倏	倮	倭	俾	倜	倌	倥	倨	僨
40	偃	偕	偈	偎	傯	僂	儻	儐	儺	傺	僖	儆	僭	僬	僦	僮	儇	儋	仝	氽
60	佘	僉	俎	龠	汆	糴	兮	巽	黌	馘	囅	夔	勹	匍	訇	匐	鳧	夙	兕	亠
80	兗	亳	衮	袤	褻	臠	裒	稟	嬴	蠃	羸	冫	冱	冽	冼					

Row 58		01	02	03	04	05	06	07	08	09	10	11	12	13	14	15	16	17	18	19
00		凇	冖	冢	冥	訁	訐	訌	訕	謳	詎	訥	詁	訶	詆	詔	詘	詒	誆	誄
20	詿	詰	詼	詵	詬	詮	諍	諢	詡	誚	誥	誑	誒	諏	諑	諉	諛	諗	諂	誶
40	諶	諫	謔	謁	諤	諭	諼	諳	諦	諮	諞	謨	讜	謖	謚	謐	謫	譾	譖	譙
60	譎	讞	譫	讖	卩	巹	阝	阢	阡	阱	阪	阽	阼	陂	陘	陔	陟	隉	陬	陲
80	陴	隈	隍	隗	隰	邗	邛	鄺	邙	鄔	邡	邴	邳	邶	鄴					

Row 59		01	02	03	04	05	06	07	08	09	10	11	12	13	14	15	16	17	18	19
00		邸	邰	郟	郅	邾	鄶	郄	郇	鄆	酈	郢	郜	郗	郛	郫	郯	郾	鄄	鄢
20	鄞	鄣	鄱	鄯	鄹	酃	酆	芻	奐	勱	劬	劭	劾	哿	勐	勖	勰	叟	燮	矍
40	廴	凵	凼	鬯	厶	弁	畚	巰	坌	堊	垡	塾	墼	壅	壑	圩	圬	圪	圳	壙
60	圮	圯	壢	圻	坂	坩	壟	坫	壚	坼	坻	坨	坭	坶	坳	埡	垤	垌	塏	埏
80	垧	堖	垓	垠	埕	塒	堝	塤	埒	垸	埴	埯	埸	埤	埝					

Row 60		01	02	03	04	05	06	07	08	09	10	11	12	13	14	15	16	17	18	19
00		堋	堍	埽	埭	堀	堞	堙	塄	堠	塥	塬	墁	墉	墚	墀	馨	鼙	懿	艹
20	艽	艿	芏	芊	芨	芄	芎	芑	薌	芙	芫	蕓	芾	芰	藶	苊	苣	芘	芷	芮
40	莧	萇	蓯	芩	芴	芡	芪	芟	苄	苧	芤	苡	茉	苷	苤	蘢	茇	苜	苴	苒
60	苘	茌	苻	苓	蔦	茚	茆	塋	煢	苠	苕	茜	荑	蕘	蓽	茈	莒	茼	茴	茱
80	莛	蕎	茯	荏	荇	荃	薈	荀	茗	薺	茭	茺	茳	犖	滎					

Row 61		01	02	03	04	05	06	07	08	09	10	11	12	13	14	15	16	17	18	19
00		蕁	茛	藎	蕒	蓀	葒	葤	莰	荸	蒔	萵	莠	莪	莓	莜	蒞	荼	薟	莩
20	荽	蕕	荻	莘	莞	莨	鶯	蓴	菁	萁	菥	菘	堇	萘	萋	菝	菽	菖	萜	萸
40	萑	萆	菔	菟	萏	萃	菸	菹	菪	菅	菀	縈	菰	菡	葜	葑	葚	葙	葳	蕆
60	蒈	葺	蕢	葸	萼	葆	葩	葶	蔞	蒎	萱	葭	蓁	蓍	蓐	驀	蒽	蓓	蓊	蒿
80	蒺	蘺	蒡	蒹	蒴	蒗	鎣	蕷	蔌	甍	蔸	蓰	蘞	蔟	藺					

Row 62		01	02	03	04	05	06	07	08	09	10	11	12	13	14	15	16	17	18	19
00		蕖	蔻	蓿	蓼	蕙	蕈	蕨	蕤	蕞	蕺	瞢	蕃	蘄	蕻	薤	薨	薇	薏	蕹
20	藪	薜	薅	薹	薷	薰	蘚	藁	藜	藿	蘧	蘅	蘩	蘖	蘼	廾	弈	夼	奩	耷
40	奕	奚	奘	匏	尢	尥	尬	尷	扌	捫	摶	抻	拊	拚	拗	拮	撟	拶	挹	捋
60	捃	掭	揶	捱	捺	掎	摑	捭	掬	掊	捩	掮	摜	揲	揸	揠	撳	揄	揞	揎
80	摒	揆	掾	攄	摁	搋	搛	搠	搌	搦	搡	摞	攖	摭	撖					

Row 63		01	02	03	04	05	06	07	08	09	10	11	12	13	14	15	16	17	18	19
00		摺	擷	擼	撙	攛	擀	擐	擗	擤	擢	攉	攥	攮	弋	忒	甙	弒	卟	叱
20	嘰	叩	叨	叻	吒	吖	吆	呋	嘸	囈	呔	嚦	呃	吡	唄	咼	吣	吲	咂	咔
40	呷	呱	呤	咚	嚀	咄	呶	呦	噝	哐	咭	哂	咴	噠	咧	咦	嘵	嗶	呲	咣
60	噦	咻	咿	哌	噲	哚	嚌	咩	咪	咤	噥	哏	哞	嘜	哧	嘮	哽	唔	哳	嗩
80	唣	唏	唑	唧	唪	嘖	喏	喵	啉	囀	啁	啕	唿	啐	唼					

Row 64		01	02	03	04	05	06	07	08	09	10	11	12	13	14	15	16	17	18	19
00		唷	啖	啵	啶	啷	唳	唰	啜	喋	嗒	喃	喱	喹	喈	喁	喟	啾	嗖	喑
20	啻	嗟	嘍	嚳	喔	喙	嗪	嗷	嗉	嘟	嗑	囁	嗬	嗔	嗦	嗝	嗄	嗯	嗥	嗲
40	噯	嗌	嗍	嗨	嗵	嗤	轡	嘞	嘈	嘌	嘁	嚶	嘣	嗾	嘀	嘧	嘭	噘	嘹	噗
60	嘬	噍	噢	噙	嚕	噌	噔	嚆	噤	噱	噫	噻	噼	嚅	嚓	嚯	囔	囗	囝	囡
80	圇	囫	囹	囿	圄	圊	圉	圜	幃	帙	帔	帑	幬	幘	幗					

Row 65		01	02	03	04	05	06	07	08	09	10	11	12	13	14	15	16	17	18	19
00		帷	幄	幔	幛	幞	幡	岌	屺	岍	岐	嶇	岈	峴	岙	岑	嵐	岜	岵	岢
20	崬	岬	岫	岱	岣	峁	岷	嶧	峒	嶠	峋	崢	嶗	崍	崧	崦	崮	崤	崞	崆
40	崛	嶸	崾	崴	崽	嵬	嵛	嵯	嶁	嵫	嵋	嵊	嵩	嵴	嶂	嶙	嶝	豳	嶷	巔
60	彳	彷	徂	徇	徉	后	徠	徙	徜	徨	徭	征	徼	衢	彡	犭	犰	犴	獷	獁
80	狃	狁	狎	狍	狒	狨	獪	狩	猻	狴	狷	猁	狳	獫	狺					

Row 66		01	02	03	04	05	06	07	08	09	10	11	12	13	14	15	16	17	18	19
00		狻	猗	猓	玀	猊	猞	猝	獼	猢	猹	猥	猬	猸	猱	獐	獍	獗	獠	獬
20	獯	獾	舛	夥	飧	夤	夂	飠	餳	飩	餼	飪	飫	飭	飴	餉	餑	余	餛	餷
40	餿	饃	饈	饉	饊	饌	饢	庀	廡	庋	庖	庥	庠	庹	庵	庾	庳	賡	廒	廑
60	廛	廨	廩	膺	忄	忉	忖	懺	憮	忮	慪	忡	忤	愾	悵	愴	忪	忭	忸	怙
80	怵	怦	怛	怏	怍	怩	怫	怊	懌	怡	慟	懨	惻	愷	恂					

Row 67		01	02	03	04	05	06	07	08	09	10	11	12	13	14	15	16	17	18	19
00		恪	惲	悖	悚	慳	悝	悃	悒	悌	悛	愜	悻	悱	惝	惘	惆	惚	悴	慍
20	憒	愕	愣	惴	愀	愎	愫	慊	慵	憬	憔	憧	憷	懍	懵	忝	隳	閂	閆	闈
40	閎	閔	閌	闥	閭	閫	鬮	閬	閾	閶	鬩	閿	閽	閼	闃	闋	闔	闐	闕	闞
60	丬	爿	戕	氵	汔	汜	汊	灃	沅	沐	沔	沌	汨	汩	汴	汶	沆	溈	泐	泔
80	沭	瀧	瀘	泱	泗	沲	泠	泖	濼	泫	泮	沱	泓	泯	涇					

Row 68		01	02	03	04	05	06	07	08	09	10	11	12	13	14	15	16	17	18	19
00		洹	洧	洌	浹	湞	洇	洄	洙	洎	洫	澮	洮	洵	洚	瀏	滸	潯	洳	涑
20	浯	淶	潿	浞	涓	涔	浜	浠	浼	浣	渚	淇	淅	淞	瀆	涿	淠	澠	淦	淝
40	淙	瀋	涫	淥	涮	渫	湮	湎	湫	溲	湟	漵	湓	湔	渲	渥	湄	灧	溱	溘
60	灄	漭	瀅	溥	溧	溽	溻	溷	潷	溴	滏	溏	滂	溟	潢	瀠	瀟	漤	漕	滹
80	漯	漶	瀲	瀦	漪	漉	漩	澉	澍	澌	潸	潲	潼	潺	瀨					

Row 69		01	02	03	04	05	06	07	08	09	10	11	12	13	14	15	16	17	18	19
00		濉	澧	澹	澶	濂	濡	濮	濞	濠	濯	瀚	瀣	瀛	瀹	瀵	灝	灞	宀	宄
20	宕	宓	宥	宸	甯	騫	搴	寤	寮	褰	寰	蹇	謇	辶	迓	迕	迥	迮	迤	邇
40	迦	逕	迨	逅	逄	逋	邐	逑	逍	逖	逡	逵	逶	逭	逯	遄	遑	遒	遐	遨
60	遘	遢	遛	暹	遴	遽	邂	邈	邃	邋	彐	彗	彖	彘	尻	咫	屐	屙	孱	屣
80	屨	羼	弳	弩	弭	艴	弼	鬻	屮	妁	妃	妍	嫵	嫗	妣					

Row 70		01	02	03	04	05	06	07	08	09	10	11	12	13	14	15	16	17	18	19
00		妗	姊	媯	妞	妤	姒	妲	妯	姍	妾	婭	嬈	姝	孌	姣	姘	姹	娌	娉
20	媧	嫻	娑	娣	娓	婀	婧	婊	婕	娼	婢	嬋	胬	媼	媛	婷	婺	媾	嫫	媲
40	嬡	嬪	媸	嫠	嫣	嬙	嫖	嫦	嫘	嫜	嬉	嬗	嬖	嬲	嬤	孀	尕	尜	孚	孥
60	孳	孑	孓	孢	駔	駟	駙	騶	驛	駑	駘	驍	驊	駢	驪	騏	騍	騅	驂	騭
80	騖	驁	騮	騸	驃	驄	驏	驥	驤	糹	紆	紂	紇	紈	纊					

Row 71		01	02	03	04	05	06	07	08	09	10	11	12	13	14	15	16	17	18	19
00		紜	紕	紓	紺	紲	紱	縐	紼	絀	紿	絝	絎	絳	綆	綃	綈	綾	綺	緋
20	緔	緄	綞	綬	綹	綣	綰	緇	緙	緗	緹	緲	繢	緦	緶	緱	縋	緡	縉	縝
40	縟	縞	縭	縊	縑	繽	縹	縵	縲	繆	繅	纈	繚	繒	繮	繾	繰	繯	纘	幺
60	畿	巛	甾	邕	玎	璣	瑋	玢	玟	玨	珂	瓏	玷	玳	珀	珉	珈	珥	珙	頊
80	琊	珩	珧	珞	璽	琿	璉	琪	瑛	琦	琥	琨	琰	琮	琬					

Row 72		01	02	03	04	05	06	07	08	09	10	11	12	13	14	15	16	17	18	19
00		琛	琚	瑁	瑜	瑗	瑕	瑙	璦	瑭	瑾	璜	瓔	璀	璁	璇	璋	璞	璨	璩
20	璐	璧	瓚	璺	韙	韞	韜	杌	杓	杞	杈	榪	櫪	枇	杪	杳	枘	梘	杵	棖
40	樅	梟	枋	杷	杼	柰	櫛	柘	櫳	柩	枰	櫨	柙	枵	柚	枳	柝	梔	柃	枸
60	柢	櫟	柁	檉	栲	栳	椏	橈	桎	楨	桄	榿	梃	栝	桕	樺	桁	檜	桀	欒
80	桊	桉	栩	梵	梏	桴	桷	梓	桫	櫺	楮	棼	櫝	槧	棹					

Row 73		01	02	03	04	05	06	07	08	09	10	11	12	13	14	15	16	17	18	19
00		欏	棰	椋	椁	楗	棣	椐	楱	椹	楠	楂	楝	欖	楫	榀	榘	楸	椴	槌
20	櫬	櫚	槎	櫸	楦	楣	楹	榛	榧	榻	榫	榭	槔	榱	槁	槊	檳	榕	櫧	榍
40	槿	檣	槭	樗	樘	橥	槲	橄	樾	檠	橐	橛	樵	檎	櫓	樽	樨	橘	櫞	檑
60	檐	檁	檗	檫	猷	獒	歿	殂	殤	殄	殞	殮	殍	殫	殛	殯	殪	軔	軛	軲
80	軻	轤	軹	軼	軫	軤	轢	軺	軾	輊	輇	輅	輒	輦	輞					

Row 74	01	02	03	04	05	06	07	08	09	10	11	12	13	14	15	16	17	18	19
00		輟	輜	輳	轆	轔	軎	戔	戧	戛	戟	戢	戡	戥	戤	戩	臧	甌	瓴	瓿
20	甏	甑	甓	攴	旮	旯	旰	昊	曇	杲	昃	昕	昀	炅	曷	昝	昴	昱	昶	昵
40	耆	晟	曄	晁	晏	暉	晡	晗	晷	暄	暌	曖	暝	暾	曛	曜	曦	曩	賁	貰
60	貺	貽	贄	貲	賅	贐	賑	賚	賕	賫	賧	賻	覘	覬	覡	覿	覦	覯	覲	覷
80	牮	犟	牝	牦	牯	牾	牿	犄	犋	犍	犏	犒	挈	挲	掰					

Row 75	01	02	03	04	05	06	07	08	09	10	11	12	13	14	15	16	17	18	19
00		搿	擘	耄	毪	毳	毽	毿	毹	氅	氌	氆	氍	氕	氘	氙	氚	氡	氬	氤
20	氪	氳	攵	敕	敫	牘	牒	牖	爰	虢	刖	肟	肜	肓	肼	朊	肽	肱	肫	肭
40	肴	肷	朧	腖	胩	臚	胛	胂	胄	胙	胍	胗	朐	胝	脛	胱	胴	胭	膾	脎
60	胲	胼	朕	脒	豚	腡	脞	脬	脘	脲	腈	腌	腓	腴	腙	腚	腱	腠	腩	腼
80	膃	腭	腧	塍	媵	膈	膂	臏	滕	膣	膪	臌	朦	臊	膻					

Row 76	01	02	03	04	05	06	07	08	09	10	11	12	13	14	15	16	17	18	19
00		臁	膦	歟	欷	欹	歃	歆	歙	颮	颯	颶	颼	飆	飈	殳	彀	轂	觳	斐
20	齏	斕	於	旆	旄	旃	旌	旎	旒	旖	煬	煒	炖	熗	炻	烀	炷	炫	炱	燁
40	烊	焐	焓	燜	焯	焱	煳	煜	煨	煆	煲	煊	煸	煺	熘	熳	熵	熨	熠	燠
60	燔	燧	燹	爝	爨	灬	燾	煦	熹	戾	戽	扃	扈	扉	礻	祀	祆	祉	祛	祜
80	祓	祚	禰	祗	祠	禎	祧	祺	禪	禊	禚	禧	禳	忑	忐					

Row 77	01	02	03	04	05	06	07	08	09	10	11	12	13	14	15	16	17	18	19
00		懟	恝	恚	恧	恁	恙	恣	慤	愆	愍	慝	憩	憝	懋	懣	戇	肀	聿	沓
20	澩	淼	磯	矸	碭	砉	硨	砘	砑	斫	砭	碸	砝	砹	礪	礱	砟	砼	砥	砬
40	砣	砩	硎	硭	硤	磽	砦	硐	硇	硌	硪	磧	碓	碚	碇	磣	碡	碣	碲	碹
60	碥	磔	磙	磉	磬	磲	礅	磴	礓	礤	礞	礴	龕	黹	黻	黼	盱	眄	瞘	盹
80	眇	眈	眚	眢	眙	眭	眦	眵	眸	睞	瞼	睇	睃	睚	睨					

Row 78	01	02	03	04	05	06	07	08	09	10	11	12	13	14	15	16	17	18	19
00		睢	睥	睿	瞍	睽	瞀	瞌	瞑	瞟	瞠	瞰	瞵	瞽	町	畀	畎	畋	畈	畛
20	畬	畹	疃	罘	罡	罟	詈	罨	羆	罱	罹	羈	罾	盍	盥	蠲	釒	釓	釔	釙
40	釗	釕	釷	釧	釤	鍆	釵	釹	鈈	鈦	鉅	鈑	鈐	鈁	鈧	鈄	鈥	鈀	鈺	鉦
60	鈷	鈳	鉕	鈽	鈸	鉞	鉬	鉭	鈿	鑠	鈰	鉉	鉈	鉍	鈮	鈹	鐸	銬	銠	鉺
80	銪	鋮	鋏	鐃	鋣	鐺	銱	銦	鎧	銖	鋌	銩	鏵	銓	鉿					

Row 79	01	02	03	04	05	06	07	08	09	10	11	12	13	14	15	16	17	18	19
00		鎩	銚	錚	銫	銃	鐋	銨	銣	鐒	錸	鋱	鏗	鋥	鋰	鋯	鋨	銼	鋝	鋶
20	鐦	鐧	鋃	鋟	鋦	錒	錆	鍩	錛	鍀	錁	錕	錮	鍃	錇	錈	錟	錙	鍥	鍇
40	鍶	鍔	鍤	鎪	鍰	鎄	鏤	鏘	鐨	鎇	鏌	鎘	鐫	鎿	鎦	鎰	鎵	鑌	鏢	鏜
60	鏝	鏍	鏞	鏃	鏇	鏑	鐔	鐝	鏷	鑥	鐓	鑭	鐠	鑹	鏹	鐙	鑊	鐲	鐿	鑔
80	鑣	鍾	矧	矬	雉	秕	秭	秣	秫	稆	嵇	稃	稂	稞	稔					

Row 80		01	02	03	04	05	06	07	08	09	10	11	12	13	14	15	16	17	18	19
00		稹	稷	穡	黏	馥	穰	皈	皎	皓	皙	皤	瓞	瓠	甬	鳩	鳶	鴇	鴆	鴣
20	鶇	鸕	鴝	鴟	鷥	鴯	鷙	鴰	鵂	鸞	鵓	鸝	鵠	鵒	鷴	鵜	鵡	鶓	鵪	鵯
40	鶉	鶘	鶚	鷀	鶥	鶩	鷂	鶼	鸚	鷓	鷚	鷯	鷦	鷲	鷸	鸌	鷺	鸛	疒	疔
60	癤	癘	疝	癧	疣	疳	痾	疸	痄	疱	疰	痃	痂	瘂	痍	痣	癆	痦	痤	癇
80	痧	瘃	痱	痼	痿	瘐	瘀	癉	瘌	瘞	瘊	瘥	瘻	瘕	瘙					

Row 81		01	02	03	04	05	06	07	08	09	10	11	12	13	14	15	16	17	18	19
00		瘛	瘼	瘢	瘠	癀	瘭	瘰	癭	瘵	癃	癮	瘳	癍	癩	癔	癜	癖	癲	癯
20	翊	竦	穸	穹	窀	窆	窈	窕	竇	窠	窬	窨	窶	窳	衤	衩	衲	衽	衿	袂
40	袢	襠	袷	袼	裉	褳	裎	襝	襇	裱	褚	裼	裨	裾	裰	褡	褙	褓	褸	褊
60	襤	褫	褶	襁	襦	襻	疋	胥	皸	皴	矜	耒	耔	耖	耜	耠	耮	耥	耦	耬
80	耩	耨	耱	耋	耵	聃	聆	聹	聒	聵	聱	覃	頇	頎	頏					

Row 82		01	02	03	04	05	06	07	08	09	10	11	12	13	14	15	16	17	18	19
00		頡	頜	潁	頦	頷	顎	顓	顳	顢	顙	顥	顬	顰	虍	虔	虯	蟣	蠆	虺
20	虼	虻	蚨	蚍	蚋	蜆	蚝	蚧	蚣	蚪	蚓	蚩	蚶	蛄	蚵	蠣	蚰	蚺	蚱	蚯
40	蛉	蟶	蚴	蛩	蛺	蟯	蛭	螄	蛐	蜓	蛞	蠐	蛟	蛘	蛑	蜃	蜇	蛸	蜈	蜊
60	蜍	蜉	蜣	蜻	蜞	蜥	蜮	蜚	蜾	蟈	蜴	蜱	蜩	蜷	蜿	螂	蜢	蝽	蠑	蝻
80	蝠	蝰	蝌	蝮	螋	蝓	蝣	螻	蝤	蝙	蝥	螓	螯	蟎	蟒					

Row 83		01	02	03	04	05	06	07	08	09	10	11	12	13	14	15	16	17	18	19
00		蟆	螈	螅	螭	螗	螃	螫	蟥	螬	螵	螳	蟋	蟓	螽	蟑	蟀	蟊	蟛	蟪
20	蟠	蟮	蠖	蠓	蟾	蠊	蠛	蠡	蠹	蠼	缶	罌	罄	罅	舐	竺	竽	笈	篤	笄
40	筧	笊	笫	笏	筇	笸	笪	笙	笮	笱	笠	笥	笤	笳	籩	笞	筘	篳	筅	筵
60	筌	箏	筠	筮	筻	筢	筲	筱	箐	簀	篋	箸	箬	箝	籜	箅	簞	箜	箢	簫
80	箴	簣	篁	篌	篝	篚	篥	篦	篪	簌	篾	篼	簏	籪	簋					

Row 84		01	02	03	04	05	06	07	08	09	10	11	12	13	14	15	16	17	18	19
00		簟	簪	簦	簸	籟	籀	臾	舁	舂	舄	臬	衄	舡	舢	艤	舭	舯	舨	舫
20	舸	艫	舳	舴	舾	艄	艉	艋	艏	艚	艟	艨	衾	裊	袈	裘	裟	襞	羝	羥
40	羧	羯	羰	羲	秈	敉	粑	糲	糶	粞	粢	粲	粼	粽	糝	糇	糌	糍	糈	糅
60	糗	糨	艮	暨	羿	翎	翕	翥	翡	翦	翩	翮	翳	糸	縶	綦	綮	繇	纛	麩
80	麴	赳	趄	趔	趑	趲	赧	赭	豇	豉	酊	酐	酎	酏	酤					

Row 85		01	02	03	04	05	06	07	08	09	10	11	12	13	14	15	16	17	18	19
00		酢	酡	酰	酩	酯	釅	釃	酲	酴	酹	醌	醅	醐	醍	醑	醢	醣	醪	醭
20	醮	醯	醵	醴	醺	豕	鹺	躉	跫	踅	蹙	蹩	趵	趿	趼	趺	蹌	跖	跗	跚
40	躒	跎	跏	跛	跆	跬	蹺	蹕	跣	躚	躋	跤	踉	跽	踔	踝	踟	躓	踮	踣
60	躑	踺	蹀	踹	踵	踽	踱	蹉	蹁	蹂	躡	蹣	蹊	躕	蹶	蹼	蹯	蹴	躅	躪
80	躔	躐	躦	躞	豸	貂	貊	貅	貘	貔	斛	觖	觴	觚	觜					

Row 86		01	02	03	04	05	06	07	08	09	10	11	12	13	14	15	16	17	18	19
00		觥	觫	觶	訾	謦	靚	雩	靂	雯	霆	霽	霈	霏	霎	霪	靄	霰	霾	齔
20	齟	齙	齠	齜	齦	齬	齪	齷	黽	黿	鼉	隹	隼	雋	雎	雒	瞿	讎	銎	鑾
40	鋈	鏨	鍪	鏊	鎏	鐾	鑫	魷	魴	鮁	鮃	鮎	鱸	穌	鮒	鱟	鮐	鮭	鮚	鮪
60	鮞	鱭	鮫	鯗	鱘	鯁	鱺	鰱	鰹	鰣	鰷	鯀	鯊	鯇	鯽	鯖	鯪	鯫	鯡	鯤
80	鯧	鯝	鯢	鯰	鯛	鯴	鯔	鱝	鰈	鰐	鰍	鰒	鰉	鯿	鰠					

Row 87		01	02	03	04	05	06	07	08	09	10	11	12	13	14	15	16	17	18	19
00		鰲	鰭	鰨	鰥	鰩	鰳	鰾	鱈	鰻	鰵	鱅	鱖	鱔	鱒	鱧	靼	鞅	韃	鞽
20	鞔	韉	鞫	鞣	鞲	鞴	骱	骰	骷	鶻	骶	骺	骼	髁	髀	髏	髂	髖	髕	髑
40	魅	魃	魘	魎	魈	魍	魑	饗	饜	餮	饕	饔	髟	髡	髦	髯	髫	髻	髭	髹
60	鬈	鬏	鬢	鬟	鬣	么	麾	縻	麂	麇	麈	麋	麒	鏖	麝	麟	黛	黜	黝	黠
80	黟	黢	黷	黧	黥	黲	黯	鼢	鼬	鼯	鼴	鼷	鼽	鼾	齇					

Row 88		01	02	03	04	05	06	07	08	09	10	11	12	13	14	15	16	17	18	19
00		襬	闆	錶	彆	蔔	纔	厂	冲	丑	齣	噹	党	淀	鼕	斗	噁	髮	范	丰
20	複	干	穀	颳	广	閤	鬍	划	迴	彙	穫	飢	几	傢	价	荐	薑	儘	据	捲
40	剋	夸	睏	蜡	腊	纍	里	曆	帘	瞭	鹵	囉	黴	濛	懞	矇	瀰	麵	衊	鬭
60	苹	凭	扑	仆	朴	韆	籤	縴	鞦	麯	确	舍	术	松	嚥	台	颱	檯	[illegible]	涂
80	糰	万	係	繫	鹹	嚮	鬚	葯	叶	郁	禦	籲	愿	云	髒					

Row 89		01	02	03	04	05	06	07	08	09	10	11	12	13	14	15	16	17	18	19
00		症	隻	只	緻	製	种	硃	筑	准										
20																				
40																				
60																				
80																				

G

CNS 11643-1992 Table

This appendix constitutes a table for the complete CNS 11643-1992 character set, printed here using the typeface 文鼎中明CNS11643 (MingTiEG-Medium), developed by Arphic Technology. Each character is indexed by Row-Cell value, and each plane is in a separate section.

The last 171 hanzi of CNS 11643-1986 Plane 14 (which became scattered throughout CNS 11643-1992 Plane 3) are listed in Appendix Q, *Character Lists and Mapping Tables*, but all of CNS11643-1986 Plane 15 are included in this appendix.

CNS 11643-1992 Plane 1

The following rows constitute CNS 11643-1992 Plane 1. Note that Row-Cell 01-01 of Plane 1 is a full-width space character.

Row 1		01	02	03	04	05	06	07	08	09	10	11	12	13	14	15	16	17	18	19
00			，	、	。	．	‧	；	：	？	！	︰	…	‥	﹐	﹑	﹒	·	﹔	﹕
20	﹖	﹗	｜	–	︱	—	︳	╴	︴	﹏	（	）	︵	︶	｛	｝	︷	︸	〔	〕
40	︹	︺	【	】	︻	︼	《	》	︽	︾	〈	〉	︿	﹀	「	」	﹁	﹂	『	』
60	﹃	﹄	﹙	﹚	﹛	﹜	﹝	﹞	‘	’	“	”	〝	〞	‵	′	＃	＆	＊	※
80	§	〃	○	●	△	▲	◎	☆	★	◇	◆	□	■	▽	▼					

Row 2		01	02	03	04	05	06	07	08	09	10	11	12	13	14	15	16	17	18	19
00		㊣	℅	¯	￣	＿	ˍ	﹉	﹊	﹍	﹎	﹋	﹌	﹟	﹠	﹡	＋	－	×	÷
20	±	√	＜	＞	＝	≦	≧	≠	∞	≒	≡	﹢	﹣	﹤	﹥	﹦	～	∩	∪	⊥
40	∠	∟	⊿	㏒	㏑	∫	∮	∵	∴	♀	♂	⊕	⊙	↑	↓	→	←	↖	↗	↙
60	↘	∥	∣	／	＼	∕	﹨	＄	￥	〒	￠	￡	％	＠	℃	℉	﹩	﹪	﹫	㏕
80	㎜	㎝	㎞	㏎	㎡	㎎	㎏	㏄	°	兙	兛	兞	兝	兡	兣					

Row 3	01	02	03	04	05	06	07	08	09	10	11	12	13	14	15	16	17	18	19
00		嗧	瓩	糎	▁	▂	▃	▄	▅	▆	▇	█	▏	▎	▍	▌	▋	▊	▉	┼
20	┴	┬	┤	├	▔	─	│	▕	┌	┐	└	┘	╭	╮	╰	╯	═	╞	╪	╡
40	◢	◣	◥	◤	╱	╲	╳													
60																				
80																				

Row 4	01	02	03	04	05	06	07	08	09	10	11	12	13	14	15	16	17	18	19
00		0	1	2	3	4	5	6	7	8	9	Ⅰ	Ⅱ	Ⅲ	Ⅳ	Ⅴ	Ⅵ	Ⅶ	Ⅷ	Ⅸ
20	Ⅹ	〡	〢	〣	〤	〥	〦	〧	〨	〩	十	卄	卅	A	B	C	D	E	F	G
40	H	I	J	K	L	M	N	O	P	Q	R	S	T	U	V	W	X	Y	Z	a
60	b	c	d	e	f	g	h	i	j	k	l	m	n	o	p	q	r	s	t	u
80	v	w	x	y	z	Α	Β	Γ	Δ	Ε	Ζ	Η	Θ	Ι	Κ					

Row 5	01	02	03	04	05	06	07	08	09	10	11	12	13	14	15	16	17	18	19
00		Λ	Μ	Ν	Ξ	Ο	Π	Ρ	Σ	Τ	Υ	Φ	Χ	Ψ	Ω	α	β	γ	δ	ε
20	ζ	η	θ	ι	κ	λ	μ	ν	ξ	ο	π	ρ	σ	τ	υ	φ	χ	ψ	ω	ㄅ
40	ㄆ	ㄇ	ㄈ	ㄉ	ㄊ	ㄋ	ㄌ	ㄍ	ㄎ	ㄏ	ㄐ	ㄑ	ㄒ	ㄓ	ㄔ	ㄕ	ㄖ	ㄗ	ㄘ	ㄙ
60	ㄚ	ㄛ	ㄜ	ㄝ	ㄞ	ㄟ	ㄠ	ㄡ	ㄢ	ㄣ	ㄤ	ㄥ	ㄦ	ㄧ	ㄨ	ㄩ	˙		ˊ	ˇ
80	ˋ																			

Row 6	01	02	03	04	05	06	07	08	09	10	11	12	13	14	15	16	17	18	19
00		①	②	③	④	⑤	⑥	⑦	⑧	⑨	⑩	⑴	⑵	⑶	⑷	⑸	⑹	⑺	⑻	⑼
20	⑽	ⅰ	ⅱ	ⅲ	ⅳ	ⅴ	ⅵ	ⅶ	ⅷ	ⅸ	ⅹ									
40																				
60																				
80																				

Row 7	01	02	03	04	05	06	07	08	09	10	11	12	13	14	15	16	17	18	19
00		一	丨	丶	丿	乙	亅	二	亠	人	儿	入	八	冂	冖	冫	几	凵	刀	力
20	勹	匕	匚	匸	十	卜	卩	厂	厶	又	口	囗	土	士	夂	夕	大	女	子	宀
40	寸	小	尢	尸	屮	山	巛	工	己	巾	干	幺	广	廴	廾	弋	弓	彐	彡	彳
60	心	戈	戶	手	支	攴	文	斗	斤	方	无	日	曰	月	木	欠	止	歹	殳	毋
80	比	毛	氏	气	水	火	爪	父	爻	爿	片	牙	牛	犬	玄					

Row 8	01	02	03	04	05	06	07	08	09	10	11	12	13	14	15	16	17	18	19
00		玉	瓜	瓦	甘	生	用	田	疋	疒	癶	白	皮	皿	目	矛	矢	石	示	禸
20	禾	穴	立	竹	米	糸	缶	网	羊	羽	老	而	耒	耳	聿	肉	臣	自	至	臼
40	舌	舛	舟	艮	色	艸	虍	虫	血	行	衣	襾	見	角	言	谷	豆	豕	豸	貝
60	赤	走	足	身	車	辛	辰	辵	邑	酉	釆	里	金	長	門	阜	隶	隹	雨	青
80	非	面	革	韋	韭	音	頁	風	飛	食	首	香	馬	骨	高					

Row 9		01	02	03	04	05	06	07	08	09	10	11	12	13	14	15	16	17	18	19
00		髟	鬥	鬯	鬲	鬼	魚	鳥	鹵	鹿	麥	麻	黃	黍	黑	黹	黽	鼎	鼓	鼠
20	鼻	齊	齒	龍	龜	龠														
40																				
60																				
80																				

Row 34		01	02	03	04	05	06	07	08	09	10	11	12	13	14	15	16	17	18	19
00		NULL	TC_1 (SOH)	TC_2 (STX)	TC_3 (ETX)	TC_4 (EOT)	TC_5 (ENQ)	TC_6 (ACK)	BELL	FE_0 (BS)	FE_1 (HT)	FE_2 (LF)	FE_3 (VT)	FE_4 (FF)	FE_5 (CR)	SO	SI	TC_7 (DLE)	DC_1	DC_2
20	DC_3	DC_4	TC_8 (NAK)	TC_9 (SYN)	TC_{10} (ETB)	CAN	EM	SUB	ESC	IS_4 (FS)	IS_3 (GS)	IS_2 (RS)	IS_1 (US)	DEL						
40																				
60																				
80																				

Row 36		01	02	03	04	05	06	07	08	09	10	11	12	13	14	15	16	17	18	19
00		一	乙	丁	七	乃	九	了	二	人	儿	入	八	几	刀	刁	力	匕	十	卜
20	又	三	下	丈	上	丫	丸	凡	久	么	也	乞	于	亡	兀	刃	勺	千	叉	口
40	土	士	夕	大	女	子	孑	孓	寸	小	尢	尸	山	川	工	己	已	巳	巾	干
60	廾	弋	弓	才	丑	丐	不	中	丰	丹	之	尹	予	云	井	互	五	亢	仁	什
80	仃	仆	仇	仍	今	介	仄	元	允	內	六	兮	公	冗	凶					

Row 37		01	02	03	04	05	06	07	08	09	10	11	12	13	14	15	16	17	18	19
00		分	切	刈	勻	勾	勿	化	匹	午	升	卅	卞	厄	友	及	反	壬	天	夫
20	太	夭	孔	少	尤	尺	屯	巴	幻	廿	弔	引	心	戈	戶	手	扎	支	文	斗
40	斤	方	日	曰	月	木	欠	止	歹	毋	比	毛	氏	水	火	爪	父	爻	片	牙
60	牛	犬	王	丙	世	丕	且	丘	主	乍	乏	乎	以	付	仔	仕	他	仗	代	令
80	仙	仞	充	兄	冉	冊	冬	凹	出	凸	刊	加	功	包	匆					

Row 38		01	02	03	04	05	06	07	08	09	10	11	12	13	14	15	16	17	18	19
00		北	匝	仟	半	卉	卡	占	卯	卮	去	可	古	右	召	叮	叩	叨	叼	司
20	叵	叫	另	只	史	叱	台	句	叭	叻	四	囚	外	央	失	奴	奶	孕	它	尼
40	巨	巧	左	市	布	平	幼	弁	弘	弗	必	戊	打	扔	扒	扑	斥	旦	朮	本
60	未	末	札	正	母	民	氐	永	汁	汀	氾	犯	玄	玉	瓜	瓦	甘	生	用	甩
80	田	由	甲	申	疋	白	皮	皿	目	矛	矢	石	示	禾	穴					

Row 39		01	02	03	04	05	06	07	08	09	10	11	12	13	14	15	16	17	18	19
00		立	丞	丟	乒	乓	乩	亙	交	亦	亥	仿	伉	伙	伊	伕	伍	伐	休	伏
20	仲	件	任	仰	仳	份	企	伋	光	兇	兆	先	全	共	再	冰	列	刑	划	刎
40	刖	劣	匈	匡	匠	印	危	吉	吏	同	吊	吐	吁	吋	各	向	名	合	吃	后
60	吆	吒	因	回	囝	圳	地	在	圭	圬	圯	圩	夙	多	夷	夸	妄	奸	妃	好
80	她	如	妁	字	存	宇	守	宅	安	寺	尖	屹	州	帆	并					

Row 40		01	02	03	04	05	06	07	08	09	10	11	12	13	14	15	16	17	18	19
00		年	式	弛	忙	忖	戎	戌	戍	成	扣	扛	托	收	早	旨	旬	旭	曲	曳
20	有	朽	朴	朱	朵	次	此	死	氖	汝	汗	汙	江	池	汐	汕	污	汛	汍	汎
40	灰	牟	牝	百	竹	米	糸	缶	羊	羽	老	考	而	耒	耳	聿	肉	肋	肌	臣
60	自	至	臼	舌	舛	舟	艮	色	艾	虫	血	行	衣	西	阡	串	亨	位	住	佇
80	佗	佞	伴	佛	何	估	佐	佑	伽	伺	伸	佃	佔	似	但					

Row 41		01	02	03	04	05	06	07	08	09	10	11	12	13	14	15	16	17	18	19
00		佣	作	你	伯	低	伶	余	佝	佈	佚	兌	克	免	兵	冶	冷	別	判	利
20	刪	刨	劫	助	努	劬	匣	即	卵	吝	吭	吞	吾	否	呎	吧	呆	呃	吳	呈
40	呂	君	吩	告	吹	吻	吸	吮	吵	吶	吠	吼	呀	吱	含	吟	听	囪	困	囤
60	囫	坊	坑	址	坍	均	坎	圾	坐	坏	圻	壯	夾	妝	妒	妨	妞	妣	妙	妖
80	妍	妤	妓	妊	妥	孝	孜	孚	孛	完	宋	宏	尬	局	屁					

Row 42		01	02	03	04	05	06	07	08	09	10	11	12	13	14	15	16	17	18	19
00		尿	尾	岐	岑	岔	岌	巫	希	序	庇	床	廷	弄	弟	彤	形	彷	役	忘
20	忌	志	忍	忱	快	忸	忪	戒	我	抄	抗	抖	技	扶	抉	扭	把	扼	找	批
40	扳	抒	扯	折	扮	投	抓	抑	抆	改	攻	攸	旱	更	束	李	杏	材	村	杜
60	杖	杞	杉	杆	杠	杓	杗	步	每	求	汞	沙	沁	沈	沉	沅	沛	汪	決	沐
80	汰	沌	汨	沖	沒	汽	沃	汲	汾	汴	沆	汶	沍	沔	沘					

Row 43		01	02	03	04	05	06	07	08	09	10	11	12	13	14	15	16	17	18	19
00		沂	灶	灼	災	灸	牢	牡	牠	狄	狂	玖	甬	甫	男	甸	皂	盯	矣	私
20	秀	禿	究	系	罕	肖	肓	肝	肘	肛	肚	育	良	芒	芋	芍	見	角	言	谷
40	豆	豕	貝	赤	走	足	身	車	辛	辰	迂	迆	迅	迄	巡	邑	邢	邪	邦	那
60	酉	釆	里	防	阮	阱	阪	阬	並	乖	乳	事	些	亞	享	京	佯	依	侍	佳
80	使	佬	供	例	來	侃	佰	併	侈	佩	佻	侖	佾	侏	侑					

Row 44		01	02	03	04	05	06	07	08	09	10	11	12	13	14	15	16	17	18	19
00		佺	兔	兒	兕	兩	具	其	典	冽	函	刻	券	刷	刺	到	刮	制	剁	劾
20	劻	卒	協	卓	卑	卦	卷	卸	卹	取	叔	受	味	呵	咖	呸	咕	咀	呻	呷
40	咄	咒	咆	呼	咐	呱	呶	和	咚	呢	周	咋	命	咎	固	垃	坷	坪	坩	坡
60	坦	坤	坼	夜	奉	奇	奈	奄	奔	妾	妻	委	妹	妮	姑	姆	姐	姍	始	姓
80	姊	妯	妳	姒	姅	孟	孤	季	宗	定	官	宜	宙	宛	尚					

Row 45		01	02	03	04	05	06	07	08	09	10	11	12	13	14	15	16	17	18	19
00		屈	居	屆	岷	岡	岸	岩	岫	岱	岳	帘	帚	帖	帕	帛	帑	幸	庚	店
20	府	底	庖	延	弦	弧	弩	往	征	彿	彼	忝	忠	忽	念	忿	怏	怔	怯	怵
40	怖	怪	怕	怡	性	怩	怫	怛	或	戕	房	戾	所	承	拉	拌	拄	抿	拂	抹
60	拒	招	披	拓	拔	拋	拈	抨	抽	押	拐	拙	拇	拍	抵	拚	抱	拘	拖	拗
80	拆	抬	拎	放	斧	於	旺	昔	易	昌	昆	昂	明	昀	昏					

Row 46		01	02	03	04	05	06	07	08	09	10	11	12	13	14	15	16	17	18	19
00		昕	昊	昇	服	朋	杭	枋	枕	東	果	杳	杷	枇	枝	林	杯	杰	板	枉
20	松	析	杵	枚	枓	杼	杪	杲	欣	武	歧	歿	氓	氛	泣	注	泳	沱	泌	泥
40	河	沽	沾	沼	波	沫	法	泓	沸	泄	油	況	沮	泗	泅	泱	沿	治	泡	泛
60	泊	沬	泯	泜	泖	泠	炕	炎	炒	炊	炙	爬	爭	爸	版	牧	物	狀	狎	狙
80	狗	狐	玩	玨	玟	玫	玥	甽	疝	疙	疚	的	盂	盲	直					

Row 47		01	02	03	04	05	06	07	08	09	10	11	12	13	14	15	16	17	18	19
00		知	矽	社	祀	祁	秉	秈	空	穹	竺	糾	罔	羌	羋	者	肺	肥	肢	肱
20	股	肫	肩	肴	肪	肯	臥	臾	舍	芳	芝	芙	芭	芽	芟	芹	花	芬	芥	芯
40	芸	芣	芰	芾	芷	虎	虱	初	表	軋	迎	返	近	邵	邸	邱	邶	采	金	長
60	門	阜	陀	阿	阻	附	陂	隹	雨	青	非	亟	亭	亮	信	侵	侯	便	俠	俑
80	俏	保	促	侶	俘	俟	俊	俗	侮	俐	俄	係	俚	俎	俞					

Row 48		01	02	03	04	05	06	07	08	09	10	11	12	13	14	15	16	17	18	19
00		侷	兗	冒	冑	冠	剎	剃	削	前	剌	剋	則	勇	勉	勃	勁	匍	南	卻
20	厚	叛	咬	哀	咨	哎	哉	咸	咦	咳	哇	哂	咽	咪	品	哄	哈	咯	咫	咱
40	咻	咩	咧	咿	囿	垂	型	垠	垣	垢	城	垮	垓	奕	契	奏	奎	奐	姜	姘
60	姿	姣	姨	娃	姥	姪	姚	姦	威	姻	孩	宣	宦	室	客	宥	封	屎	屏	屍
80	屋	峙	峒	巷	帝	帥	帟	幽	庠	度	建	弈	弭	彥	很					

Row 49		01	02	03	04	05	06	07	08	09	10	11	12	13	14	15	16	17	18	19
00		待	徊	律	徇	後	徉	怒	思	怠	急	怎	怨	恍	恰	恨	恢	恆	恃	恬
20	恫	恪	恤	扁	拜	挖	按	拼	拭	持	拮	拽	指	拱	拷	拯	括	拾	拴	挑
40	挂	政	故	斫	施	既	春	昭	映	昧	是	星	昨	昱	昤	曷	柿	染	柱	柔
60	某	柬	架	枯	柵	柩	柯	柄	柑	枴	柚	查	枸	柏	柞	柳	枰	柙	柢	柝
80	柒	歪	殃	殆	段	毒	毗	氟	泉	洋	洲	洪	流	津	洌					

Row 50		01	02	03	04	05	06	07	08	09	10	11	12	13	14	15	16	17	18	19
00		洱	洞	洗	活	洽	派	洶	洛	泵	洹	洧	洸	洩	洮	洵	洎	洫	炫	為
20	炳	炬	炯	炭	炸	炮	炤	爰	牲	牯	牴	狩	狠	狡	玷	珊	玻	玲	珍	珀
40	玳	甚	甭	畏	界	畎	畋	疫	疤	疥	疢	疣	癸	皆	皇	皈	盈	盆	盃	盅
60	省	盹	相	眉	看	盾	盼	眇	矜	砂	研	砌	砍	祆	祉	祈	祇	禹	禺	科
80	秒	秋	穿	突	竿	竽	籽	紂	紅	紀	紉	紇	約	紆	缸					

Row 51		01	02	03	04	05	06	07	08	09	10	11	12	13	14	15	16	17	18	19
00		美	羿	耐	耍	耑	耶	胖	胥	胚	胃	胄	背	胡	胛	胎	胞	胤	胝	致
20	舢	苧	范	茅	苣	苛	苦	茄	若	茂	茉	苒	苗	英	茁	苜	苔	苑	苞	苓
40	苟	苯	茆	虐	虹	虻	虺	衍	衫	要	觔	計	訂	訃	貞	負	赴	赳	趴	軍
60	軌	述	迦	迢	迪	迥	迭	迫	迤	迨	郊	郎	郁	郃	酋	酊	重	閂	限	陋
80	陌	降	面	革	韋	韭	音	頁	風	飛	食	首	香	乘	亳					

Row 52		01	02	03	04	05	06	07	08	09	10	11	12	13	14	15	16	17	18	19
00		倌	倍	倣	俯	倦	倥	俸	倩	倖	倆	值	借	倚	倒	們	俺	倀	倔	倨
20	俱	倡	個	候	倘	俳	修	倭	倪	俾	倫	倉	兼	冤	冥	冢	凍	凌	准	凋
40	剖	剜	剔	剛	剝	匪	卿	原	厝	叟	哨	唐	唁	唷	哼	哥	哲	唆	哺	唔
60	哩	哭	員	唉	哮	哪	哦	唧	唇	哽	唏	圃	圄	埂	埔	埋	埃	堉	夏	套
80	奘	奚	娑	娘	娜	娟	娛	娓	姬	娠	娣	娩	娥	娌	娉					

Row 53		01	02	03	04	05	06	07	08	09	10	11	12	13	14	15	16	17	18	19
00		孫	屘	宰	害	家	宴	宮	宵	容	宸	射	屑	展	屐	峭	峽	峻	峪	峨
20	峰	島	崁	峴	差	席	師	庫	庭	座	弱	徒	徑	徐	恙	恣	恥	恐	恕	恭
40	恩	息	悄	悟	悚	悍	悔	悌	悅	悖	扇	拳	挈	拿	捎	挾	振	捕	捂	捆
60	捏	捉	挺	捐	挽	挪	挫	挨	捍	捌	效	敉	料	旁	旅	時	晉	晏	晃	晒
80	晌	晅	晁	書	朔	朕	朗	校	核	案	框	桓	根	桂	桔					

Row 54		01	02	03	04	05	06	07	08	09	10	11	12	13	14	15	16	17	18	19
00		栩	梳	栗	桌	桑	栽	柴	桐	桀	格	桃	株	桅	栓	栘	桁	殊	殉	殷
20	氣	氧	氨	氦	氤	泰	浪	涕	消	涇	浦	浸	海	浙	涓	浬	涉	浮	浚	浴
40	浩	涌	涊	浹	涅	浥	涔	烊	烘	烤	烙	烈	烏	爹	特	狼	狹	狽	狸	狷
60	玆	班	琉	珮	珠	珪	珞	畔	畝	畜	畚	留	疾	病	症	疲	疳	疽	疼	疹
80	痂	疸	皋	皰	益	盍	盎	眩	真	眠	眨	矩	砰	砧	砸					

Row 55		01	02	03	04	05	06	07	08	09	10	11	12	13	14	15	16	17	18	19
00		砝	破	砷	砥	砭	砠	砟	砲	祕	祐	祠	祟	祖	神	祝	祗	祚	秤	秣
20	秧	租	秦	秩	秘	窄	窈	站	笆	笑	粉	紡	紗	紋	紊	素	索	純	紐	紕
40	級	紜	納	紙	紛	缺	罟	羔	翅	翁	耆	耄	耘	耕	耙	耗	耽	耿	胱	脂
60	胰	脅	胭	胴	脆	胸	胳	脈	能	脊	胼	胯	臭	臬	舀	舐	航	舫	舨	般
80	芻	茫	荒	荔	荊	茸	荐	草	茵	茴	荏	茲	茹	茶	茗					

Row 56		01	02	03	04	05	06	07	08	09	10	11	12	13	14	15	16	17	18	19
00		荀	茱	茨	荃	虔	蚊	蚪	蚓	蚤	蚩	蚌	蚣	蚜	衰	衷	袁	袂	衽	衹
20	記	訐	討	訌	訕	訊	託	訓	訖	訏	訑	豈	豺	豹	財	貢	起	躬	軒	軔
40	軏	辱	送	逆	迷	退	迺	迴	逃	追	逅	迸	邕	郡	郝	郢	酒	配	酌	釘
60	針	釗	釜	釙	閃	院	陣	陡	陛	陝	除	陘	陞	隻	飢	馬	骨	高	鬥	鬲
80	鬼	乾	偺	偽	停	假	偃	偌	做	偉	健	偶	偎	偕	偵					

Row 57		01	02	03	04	05	06	07	08	09	10	11	12	13	14	15	16	17	18	19
00		側	偷	偏	倏	偯	偭	兜	冕	凰	剪	副	勒	務	勘	動	匐	匏	匙	匿
20	區	匾	參	曼	商	啪	啦	啄	啞	啡	啃	啊	唱	啖	問	啕	唯	啤	唸	售
40	啜	唬	啣	唳	啁	啗	圈	國	圉	域	堅	堊	堆	埠	埤	基	堂	堵	執	培
60	夠	奢	娶	婁	婉	婦	婪	婀	娼	婢	婚	婆	婊	孰	寇	寅	寄	寂	宿	密
80	尉	專	將	屠	屜	屝	崇	崆	崎	崛	崖	崢	崑	崩	崔					

Row 58		01	02	03	04	05	06	07	08	09	10	11	12	13	14	15	16	17	18	19
00		崙	崢	崧	崗	巢	常	帶	帳	帷	康	庸	庶	庵	庾	張	強	彗	彬	彩
20	彫	得	徙	從	徘	御	徠	徜	恿	患	悉	悠	您	惋	悴	惦	悽	情	悻	悵
40	惜	悼	惘	惕	惆	惟	悸	惚	惇	戚	戛	扈	掠	控	捲	掖	探	接	捷	捧
60	掘	措	捱	掩	掉	掃	掛	捫	推	掄	授	掙	採	掬	排	掏	掀	捻	捩	捨
80	捺	敝	敖	救	教	敗	啟	敏	敘	敕	敔	斜	斛	斬	族					

Row 59		01	02	03	04	05	06	07	08	09	10	11	12	13	14	15	16	17	18	19
00		旋	旌	旎	晝	晚	晤	晨	晦	晞	曹	勗	望	梁	梯	梢	梓	梵	桿	桶
20	梱	梧	梗	械	梃	棄	梭	梆	梅	梔	條	梨	梟	梡	梂	欲	殺	毫	毬	氫
40	涎	涼	淳	淙	液	淡	淌	淤	添	淺	清	淇	淋	涯	淑	涮	淞	淹	涸	混
60	淵	淅	淒	渚	涵	淚	淫	淘	淪	深	淮	淨	淆	淄	涪	淬	涿	淦	烹	焉
80	焊	烽	烯	爽	牽	犁	猜	猛	猖	猓	猙	率	琅	琊	球					

Row 60		01	02	03	04	05	06	07	08	09	10	11	12	13	14	15	16	17	18	19
00		理	現	琍	瓠	瓶	瓷	甜	產	略	畦	畢	異	疏	痔	痕	疵	痊	痍	皎
20	盔	盒	盛	眷	眾	眼	眶	眸	眺	硫	硃	硎	祥	票	祭	移	窒	窕	笠	笨
40	笛	第	符	笙	笞	笮	粒	粗	粕	絆	絃	統	紮	紹	紼	絀	細	紳	組	累
60	終	紲	紱	缽	羞	羚	翌	翎	習	耜	聊	聆	脯	脖	脣	脫	脩	脰	脤	舂
80	舵	舷	舶	船	莎	莞	莘	荸	莢	莖	莽	莫	莒	莊	莓					

Row 61		01	02	03	04	05	06	07	08	09	10	11	12	13	14	15	16	17	18	19
00		莉	莠	荷	荻	荼	莆	莧	處	彪	蛇	蛀	蚶	蛄	蚵	蛆	蛋	蚱	蚯	蛉
20	術	袞	袈	被	袒	袖	袍	袋	覓	規	訪	訝	訣	訥	許	設	訟	訛	訢	豉
40	豚	販	責	貫	貨	貪	貧	赧	赦	趾	趺	軛	軟	這	逍	通	逗	連	速	逝
60	逐	逕	逞	造	透	逢	逖	逛	途	部	郭	都	酗	野	釵	釦	釣	釧	釭	釩
80	閉	陪	陵	陳	陸	陰	陴	陶	陷	陬	雀	雪	雩	章	竟					

Row 62		01	02	03	04	05	06	07	08	09	10	11	12	13	14	15	16	17	18	19
00		頂	頃	魚	鳥	鹵	鹿	麥	麻	傢	傍	傅	備	傑	傀	傖	傘	傚	最	凱
20	割	剴	創	剩	勞	勝	勛	博	厥	啻	喀	喧	啼	喊	喝	喘	喂	喜	喪	喔
40	喇	喋	喃	喳	單	喟	唾	喲	喚	喻	喬	喱	啾	喉	喫	喙	圍	堯	堪	場
60	堤	堰	報	堡	堝	堠	壹	壺	奠	婷	媚	婿	媒	媛	媧	孳	孱	寒	富	寓
80	寐	尊	尋	就	嵌	嵐	崴	嵇	巽	幅	帽	幀	幃	幾	廊					

Row 63		01	02	03	04	05	06	07	08	09	10	11	12	13	14	15	16	17	18	19
00		廁	廂	廄	弼	彭	復	循	徨	惑	惡	悲	悶	惠	愜	愣	惺	愕	惰	惻
20	惴	慨	惱	愎	惶	愉	愀	愒	戟	扉	掣	掌	描	揀	揩	揉	揆	揍	插	揣
40	提	握	揖	揭	揮	捶	援	揪	換	摒	揚	揹	敞	敦	敢	散	斑	斐	斯	普
60	晰	晴	晶	景	暑	智	晾	晷	曾	替	期	朝	棺	棕	棠	棘	棗	椅	棟	棵
80	森	棧	棹	棒	棲	棣	棋	棍	植	椒	椎	棉	棚	楮	棻					

Row 64		01	02	03	04	05	06	07	08	09	10	11	12	13	14	15	16	17	18	19
00		款	欺	欽	殘	殖	殼	毯	氮	氯	氬	港	游	湔	渡	渲	湧	湊	渠	渥
20	渣	減	湛	湘	渤	湖	湮	渭	渦	湯	渴	湍	渺	測	湃	渝	渾	滋	溉	渙
40	湎	湣	湄	湲	湩	湟	焙	焚	焦	焰	無	然	煮	焜	牌	犄	犀	猶	猥	猴
60	猩	琺	琪	琳	琢	琥	琵	琶	琴	琯	琛	琦	琨	甥	甦	畫	番	痢	痛	痣
80	痙	痘	痞	痠	登	發	皖	皓	皴	盜	睏	短	硝	硬	硯					

Row 65		01	02	03	04	05	06	07	08	09	10	11	12	13	14	15	16	17	18	19
00		稍	稈	程	稅	稀	窘	窗	窖	童	竣	等	策	筆	筐	筒	答	筍	筋	筏
20	筑	粟	粥	絞	結	絨	絕	紫	絮	絲	絡	給	絢	絰	絳	善	翔	翕	耋	聒
40	肅	腕	腔	腋	腑	腎	脹	腆	脾	腌	腓	腴	舒	舜	菩	萃	菸	萍	菠	菅
60	萋	菁	華	菱	菴	著	萊	菰	萌	菌	菽	菲	菊	萸	萎	萄	菜	萇	菔	菟
80	虛	蛟	蛙	蛭	蛔	蛛	蛤	蛐	蛞	街	裁	裂	袱	覃	視					

Row 66		01	02	03	04	05	06	07	08	09	10	11	12	13	14	15	16	17	18	19
00		註	詠	評	詞	証	詁	詔	詛	詐	詆	訴	診	訶	詖	象	貂	貯	貼	貳
20	貽	賁	費	賀	貴	買	貶	貿	貸	越	超	趁	跎	距	跋	跚	跑	跌	跛	跆
40	軻	軸	軼	辜	逮	逵	週	逸	進	逶	鄂	郵	鄉	鄔	酣	酥	量	鈔	鈕	鈣
60	鈉	鈞	鈍	鈐	鈇	鈑	閔	閏	開	閑	間	閒	閎	隊	階	隋	陽	隅	隆	隍
80	陲	隄	雁	雅	雄	集	雇	雯	雲	韌	項	順	須	飧	飪					

Row 67		01	02	03	04	05	06	07	08	09	10	11	12	13	14	15	16	17	18	19
00		飯	飩	飲	飭	馮	馭	黃	黍	黑	亂	傭	債	傲	傳	僅	傾	催	傷	傻
20	傯	僇	剿	剷	剽	募	勦	勤	勢	勣	匯	嗟	嗨	嗓	嗦	嗎	嗜	嗇	嗑	嗣
40	嗤	嗯	嗚	嗡	嗅	嗆	嗥	嗉	園	圓	塞	塑	塘	塗	塚	塔	填	塌	塭	塊
60	塢	塒	塋	奧	嫁	嫉	嫌	媾	媽	媼	媳	嫂	媲	嵩	嵯	幌	幹	廉	廈	弒
80	彙	徬	微	愚	意	慈	感	想	愛	惹	愁	愈	慎	慌	慄					

Row 68		01	02	03	04	05	06	07	08	09	10	11	12	13	14	15	16	17	18	19
00		慍	愾	愴	愧	愍	慆	愷	戡	戢	搓	搾	搞	搪	搭	搽	搬	搏	搜	搔
20	損	搶	搖	搗	搆	敬	斟	新	暗	暉	暇	暈	暖	暄	暘	暍	會	榔	業	楚
40	楷	楠	楔	極	椰	概	楊	楨	楫	楞	楓	楹	榆	楝	楣	楛	歇	歲	毀	殿
60	毓	毽	溢	溯	滓	溶	滂	源	溝	滇	滅	溥	溘	溼	溺	溫	滑	準	溜	滄
80	滔	溪	溧	溴	煎	煙	煩	煤	煉	照	煜	煬	煦	煌	煥					

Row 69		01	02	03	04	05	06	07	08	09	10	11	12	13	14	15	16	17	18	19
00		煞	煆	煨	煖	爺	牒	猷	獅	猿	猾	瑯	瑚	瑕	瑟	瑞	瑁	琿	瑙	瑛
20	瑜	當	畸	瘀	痰	瘁	痲	痱	痺	痿	痴	痳	盞	盟	睛	睫	睦	睞	督	睹
40	睪	睬	睜	睥	睨	睢	矮	碎	碰	碗	碘	碌	碉	硼	碑	碓	硿	祺	祿	禁
60	萬	禽	稜	稚	稠	稔	稟	稞	窟	窠	筷	節	筠	筮	筧	粱	粳	粵	經	絹
80	綑	綁	綏	條	置	罩	罪	署	義	羨	群	聖	聘	肆	肄					

Row 70		01	02	03	04	05	06	07	08	09	10	11	12	13	14	15	16	17	18	19
00		腱	腰	腸	腥	腮	腳	腫	腹	腺	腦	舅	艇	蒂	葷	落	萱	葵	葦	葫
20	葉	葬	葛	萼	萵	葡	董	葩	葭	葆	虞	虜	號	蛹	蜓	蜈	蜇	蜀	蛾	蛻
40	蜂	蜃	蜆	蜊	衙	裟	裔	裙	補	裘	裝	裡	裊	裕	裒	覜	解	詫	該	詳
60	試	詩	詰	誇	詼	詣	誠	話	誅	詭	詢	詮	詬	詹	詻	訾	詨	豢	貊	貉
80	賊	資	賈	賄	貲	賃	賂	賅	跡	跟	跨	路	跳	跺	跪					

Row 71		01	02	03	04	05	06	07	08	09	10	11	12	13	14	15	16	17	18	19
00		跤	跦	躲	較	載	軾	輊	辟	農	運	遊	道	遂	達	逼	違	遐	遇	遏
20	過	遍	遑	逾	遁	鄒	鄗	酬	酪	酩	釉	鈷	鉗	鈸	鈽	鉀	鈾	鉛	鉋	鉤
40	鉑	鈴	鉉	鉍	鉅	鈹	鈿	鉚	閘	隘	隔	隕	雍	雋	雉	雊	雷	電	雹	零
60	靖	靴	靶	預	頑	頓	頊	頒	頌	飼	飴	飽	飾	馳	馱	馴	髡	鳩	麂	鼎
80	鼓	鼠	僧	僮	僥	僖	僭	僚	僕	像	僑	僱	僎	僩	兢					

Row 72		01	02	03	04	05	06	07	08	09	10	11	12	13	14	15	16	17	18	19
00		凳	劃	劂	匱	厭	嗾	嘀	嘛	嘗	嗽	嘔	嘆	嘉	嘍	嘎	嗷	嘖	嘟	嘈
20	嘐	嗶	團	圖	塵	塾	境	墓	墊	塹	墅	塽	壽	夥	夢	夤	奪	奩	嫡	嫦
40	嫩	嫗	嫖	嫘	嫣	孵	寞	寧	寡	寥	實	寨	寢	寤	察	對	屢	嶄	嶇	幛
60	幣	幕	幗	幔	廓	廖	弊	彆	彰	徹	慇	愿	態	慷	慢	慣	慟	慚	慘	慵
80	截	撇	摘	摔	撤	摸	摟	摺	摑	摧	搴	摭	摻	敲	斡					

Row 73		01	02	03	04	05	06	07	08	09	10	11	12	13	14	15	16	17	18	19
00		旗	旖	暢	暨	暝	榜	榨	榕	槁	榮	槓	構	榛	榷	榻	榫	榴	槐	槍
20	榭	槌	榦	槃	榣	歉	歌	氳	漳	演	滾	漓	滴	漩	漾	漠	漬	漏	漂	漢
40	滿	滯	漆	漱	漸	漲	漣	漕	漫	漯	澈	漪	滬	漁	滲	滌	滷	熔	熙	煽
60	熊	熄	熒	爾	犒	犖	獄	獐	瑤	瑣	瑪	瑰	瑭	甄	疑	瘧	瘍	瘋	瘉	瘓
80	盡	監	瞄	睽	睿	睡	磁	碟	碧	碳	碩	碣	禎	福	禍					

Row 74		01	02	03	04	05	06	07	08	09	10	11	12	13	14	15	16	17	18	19
00		種	稱	窪	窩	竭	端	管	箕	箋	筵	算	箝	箔	箏	箸	箇	箄	粹	粽
20	精	綻	綰	綜	綽	綾	綠	緊	綴	網	綱	綺	綢	綿	綵	綸	維	緒	緇	綬
40	罰	翠	翡	翟	聞	聚	肇	腐	膀	膏	膈	膊	腿	膂	臧	臺	與	舔	舞	艋
60	蓉	蒿	蓆	蓄	蒙	蒞	蒲	蒜	蓋	蒸	蓀	蓓	蒐	蒼	蓑	蓊	蜿	蜜	蜻	蜢
80	蜥	蜴	蜘	蝕	蜷	蜩	裳	褂	裴	裹	裸	製	裨	褚	裯					

Row 75		01	02	03	04	05	06	07	08	09	10	11	12	13	14	15	16	17	18	19
00		誦	誌	語	誣	認	誡	誓	誤	說	誥	誨	誘	誑	誚	誧	豪	貍	貌	賓
20	賑	賒	赫	趙	趕	跼	輔	輒	輕	輓	辣	遠	遘	遜	遣	遙	遞	遢	遝	遛
40	鄙	鄘	鄞	酵	酸	酷	酴	鉸	銬	銀	銅	銘	銖	鉻	銓	銜	銨	鉼	銑	閡
60	閨	閩	閣	閥	閤	隙	障	際	雌	雒	需	靼	鞅	韶	頗	領	颯	颱	餃	餅
80	餌	餉	駁	骯	骰	髦	魁	魂	鳴	鳶	鳳	麼	鼻	齊	億					

Row 76		01	02	03	04	05	06	07	08	09	10	11	12	13	14	15	16	17	18	19
00		儀	僻	僵	價	儂	儈	儉	儅	凜	劇	劈	劉	劍	劊	勰	厲	嘮	嘻	嘹
20	嘲	嘿	嘴	嘩	噓	噎	噗	噴	嘶	嘯	嘰	墀	墟	增	墳	墜	墮	墩	墦	奭
40	嬉	嫻	嬋	嫵	嬌	嬈	寮	寬	審	寫	層	履	嶝	嶔	幢	幟	幡	廢	廚	廟
60	廝	廣	廠	彈	影	德	徵	慶	慧	慮	慝	慕	憂	慼	慰	慫	慾	憧	憐	憫
80	憎	憬	憚	憤	憔	憮	戮	摩	摯	摹	撞	撲	撈	撐	撰					

Row 77		01	02	03	04	05	06	07	08	09	10	11	12	13	14	15	16	17	18	19
00		撥	撓	撕	撩	撒	撮	播	撫	撚	撬	撙	撢	撳	敵	敷	數	暮	暫	暴
20	暱	樣	樟	槨	樁	樞	標	槽	模	樓	樊	槳	樂	樅	槭	樑	歐	歎	殤	毅
40	毆	漿	潼	澄	潑	潦	潔	澆	潭	潛	潸	潮	澎	潺	潰	潤	澗	潘	滕	潯
60	潠	潟	熟	熬	熱	熨	牖	犛	獎	獗	瑩	璋	璃	瑾	璀	畿	瘠	瘩	瘟	瘤
80	瘦	瘡	瘢	皚	皺	盤	瞎	瞇	瞌	瞑	瞋	磋	磅	確	磊					

Row 78		01	02	03	04	05	06	07	08	09	10	11	12	13	14	15	16	17	18	19
00		碾	磕	碼	磐	稿	稼	穀	稽	稷	稻	窯	窮	箭	箱	範	箴	篆	篇	篁
20	箠	篌	糊	締	練	緯	緻	緘	緬	緝	編	緣	線	緞	緩	綞	緙	緲	緹	罵
40	罷	羯	翩	耦	膛	膜	膝	膠	膚	膘	蔗	蔽	蔚	蓮	蔬	蔭	蔓	蔑	蔣	蔡
60	蔔	蓬	蔥	蓿	蔆	螂	蝴	蝶	蝠	蝦	蝸	蝨	蝙	蝗	蝌	蝓	衛	衝	褐	複
80	褒	褓	褕	褊	誼	諒	談	諄	誕	請	諸	課	諉	諂	調					

Row 79		01	02	03	04	05	06	07	08	09	10	11	12	13	14	15	16	17	18	19
00		誰	論	諍	誶	誹	諛	豌	豎	豬	賠	賞	賦	賤	賬	賭	賢	賣	賜	質
20	賡	赭	趟	趣	踫	踐	踝	踢	踏	踩	踟	踡	踞	躺	輝	輛	輟	輩	輦	輪
40	輜	輞	輥	適	遮	遨	遭	遷	鄰	鄭	鄧	鄱	醇	醉	醋	醃	鋅	銻	銷	鋪
60	鋤	鋁	銳	銼	鋒	鋇	鋰	銲	閭	閱	霄	霆	震	霉	靠	鞍	鞋	鞏	頡	頫
80	頜	颳	養	餓	餒	餘	駝	駐	駟	駛	駑	駕	駒	駙	骷					

Row 80		01	02	03	04	05	06	07	08	09	10	11	12	13	14	15	16	17	18	19
00		髮	髯	鬧	魅	魄	魷	魯	鴆	鴉	鴃	麩	麾	黎	墨	齒	儒	儘	儔	儐
20	儕	冀	冪	凝	劑	劓	勳	噙	噫	噹	噩	噤	噸	噪	器	噥	噱	噯	噬	噢
40	噶	壁	墾	壇	壅	奮	嬝	嬴	學	寰	導	彊	憲	憑	憩	憊	懍	憶	憾	懊
60	懈	戰	擅	擁	擋	撻	撼	據	擄	擇	擂	操	撿	擒	擔	撾	整	曆	曉	暹
80	曄	曇	暸	樽	樸	樺	橙	橫	橘	樹	橄	橢	橡	橋	橇					

Row 81		01	02	03	04	05	06	07	08	09	10	11	12	13	14	15	16	17	18	19
00		樵	機	橈	歙	歷	氅	濂	澱	澡	濃	澤	濁	澧	澳	激	澹	澶	澦	澠
20	澴	熾	燉	燐	燒	燈	燕	熹	燎	燙	燜	燃	燄	獨	璜	璣	璘	璟	璞	瓢
40	甌	甍	瘴	瘸	瘺	盧	盥	瞠	瞞	瞟	瞥	磨	磚	磬	磧	禦	積	穎	穆	穌
60	穋	窺	篙	簑	築	篤	篛	篡	篩	篦	糕	糖	縊	縑	縈	縛	縣	縞	縝	縉
80	縐	罹	羲	翰	翱	翮	耨	膳	膩	膨	臻	興	艘	艙	蕊					

Row 82	00	01	02	03	04	05	06	07	08	09	10	11	12	13	14	15	16	17	18	19
00		蕙	蕈	蕨	蕩	蕃	蕉	蕭	蕪	蕞	螃	螟	螞	螢	融	衡	褪	褲	褥	褫
20	褡	親	覦	諦	諺	諫	諱	謀	諜	諧	諮	諾	謁	謂	諷	諭	諳	諶	諼	豫
40	豭	貓	賴	蹄	踱	踴	蹂	踹	踵	輻	輯	輸	輳	辨	辦	遵	遴	選	遲	遼
60	遺	鄴	醒	錠	錶	鋸	錳	錯	錢	鋼	錫	錄	錚	錐	錦	錡	錕	錮	錙	閻
80	隧	隨	險	雕	霎	霑	霖	霍	霓	霏	靛	靜	靦	鞘	頰					

Row 83	00	01	02	03	04	05	06	07	08	09	10	11	12	13	14	15	16	17	18	19
00		頸	頻	頷	頭	頹	頤	餐	館	餞	餛	餡	餚	駭	駢	駱	骸	骼	髻	髭
20	鬨	鮑	鴕	鴣	鴦	鴨	鴒	鴛	默	黔	龍	龜	優	償	儡	儲	勵	嚎	嚀	嚐
40	嚅	嚇	嚏	壕	壓	壑	壎	嬰	嬪	嬤	孺	尷	屨	嶼	嶺	嶽	嶸	幫	彌	徽
60	應	懂	懇	懦	懋	戲	戴	擎	擊	擘	擠	擰	擦	擬	擱	擢	擭	斂	斃	曙
80	曖	檀	檔	檄	檢	檜	櫛	檣	橾	檗	檐	檠	歜	殮	毚					

Row 84	00	01	02	03	04	05	06	07	08	09	10	11	12	13	14	15	16	17	18	19
00		氈	濘	濱	濟	濠	濛	濤	濫	濯	澀	濬	濡	濩	濕	濮	濰	燧	營	燮
20	燦	燥	燭	燬	燴	燠	爵	牆	獰	獲	璩	環	璦	璨	癆	療	癌	盪	瞳	瞪
40	瞰	瞬	瞧	瞭	矯	磷	磺	磴	磯	礁	禧	禪	穗	窿	簇	簍	篾	篷	簌	篠
60	糠	糜	糞	糢	糟	糙	糝	縮	績	繆	縷	縲	繃	縫	總	縱	繅	繁	縴	縹
80	繈	縵	縿	縯	罄	翳	翼	聱	聲	聰	聯	聳	臆	臃	膺					

Row 85	00	01	02	03	04	05	06	07	08	09	10	11	12	13	14	15	16	17	18	19
00		臂	臀	膿	膽	臉	膾	臨	舉	艱	薪	薄	蕾	薜	薑	薔	薯	薛	薇	薨
20	薊	薦	虧	蟀	蟑	螳	蟒	蟆	螫	螻	螺	蟈	蟋	褻	褶	襄	褸	褽	覬	謎
40	謗	謙	講	謊	謠	謝	謄	謐	豁	谿	豳	賺	賽	購	賸	賻	趨	蹉	蹋	蹈
60	蹊	轄	輾	轂	轅	輿	避	遽	還	邁	邂	邀	鄹	醣	醞	醜	鍍	鎂	錨	鍵
80	鍊	鍥	鍋	錘	鍾	鍬	鍛	鍰	鍚	鍔	闊	闋	闌	闈	闆					

Row 86	00	01	02	03	04	05	06	07	08	09	10	11	12	13	14	15	16	17	18	19
00		隱	隸	雖	霜	霞	鞠	韓	顆	颶	餵	騁	駿	鮮	鮫	鮪	鮭	鴻	鴿	麋
20	黏	點	黜	黝	黛	鼾	齋	叢	嚕	嚮	壙	壘	嬸	彝	懣	戳	擴	擲	擾	攆
40	擺	擻	擷	斷	曜	朦	檳	檬	櫃	檻	檸	櫂	檮	檯	歟	歸	殯	瀉	瀋	濾
60	瀆	濺	瀑	瀏	燻	燼	燾	燸	獷	獵	璧	璿	甕	癖	癘	癒	瞽	瞿	瞻	瞼
80	礎	禮	穡	穢	穠	竄	竅	簫	簧	簪	簞	簣	簡	糧	織					

Row 87	00	01	02	03	04	05	06	07	08	09	10	11	12	13	14	15	16	17	18	19
00		繕	繞	繚	繡	繒	繙	罈	翹	翻	職	聶	臍	臏	舊	藏	薩	藍	藐	藉
20	薰	薺	薹	蟯	蟬	蟲	蟠	覆	覲	觴	謨	謹	謬	謫	豐	贅	蹙	蹣	蹦	蹤
40	蹟	蹕	軀	轉	轍	邇	邃	邈	醫	醬	釐	鎔	鎊	鎖	鎢	鎳	鎮	鎬	鎰	鎘
60	鎚	鎗	闔	闖	闐	闕	離	雜	雙	雛	雞	霤	鞣	鞦	鞭	韹	額	顏	題	顎
80	顓	颺	餾	餿	餽	餮	馥	騎	髁	鬃	鬆	魏	魎	魍	鯊					

Row 88		01	02	03	04	05	06	07	08	09	10	11	12	13	14	15	16	17	18	19
00		鯉	鯽	鯈	鯀	鵑	鵝	鵠	黠	鼕	鼬	儳	嚥	嚨	壞	壟	壢	寵	龐	廬
20	懲	懷	懶	懵	攀	攏	曠	曝	櫥	櫝	櫚	櫓	瀛	瀟	瀨	瀚	瀝	瀕	瀘	爆
40	爍	牘	犢	獸	獺	璽	瓊	瓣	疇	疆	癟	癡	矇	礙	禱	穫	穩	簾	簿	簸
60	簽	簷	籀	繫	繭	繹	繩	繪	繳	羅	羶	羹	羸	臘	藩	藝	藪	藕	藤	藥
80	藷	蟻	蠅	蠍	蟹	蟾	襠	襟	襖	襞	譁	譜	識	證	譚					

Row 89		01	02	03	04	05	06	07	08	09	10	11	12	13	14	15	16	17	18	19
00		譎	譏	譆	譙	贈	贊	蹼	蹲	躇	蹶	蹬	蹺	蹴	轔	轎	辭	邊	邋	醱
20	醮	鏡	鏑	鏟	鏃	鏈	鏜	鏝	鏖	鏢	鏍	鏘	鏤	鏗	鏨	關	隴	難	霪	霧
40	靡	韜	韻	類	願	顛	颼	饅	饉	騖	騙	鬍	鯨	鯧	鯖	鯛	鶉	鵡	鵲	鵪
60	鵬	麒	麗	麓	麴	勸	嚷	嚶	嚴	嚼	壤	孀	孃	孽	寶	巉	懸	懺	攘	攔
80	攙	曦	朧	櫬	瀾	瀰	瀲	爐	獻	瓏	癢	癥	礦	礪	礬					

Row 90		01	02	03	04	05	06	07	08	09	10	11	12	13	14	15	16	17	18	19
00		礫	竇	競	籌	籃	籍	糯	糰	辮	繽	繼	纂	罌	耀	臚	艦	藻	藹	蘑
20	藺	蘆	蘋	蘇	蘊	蠔	蠕	襤	覺	觸	議	譬	警	譯	譟	譫	贏	贍	躉	躁
40	躅	躂	醴	釋	鐘	鐃	鏽	闡	霰	飄	饒	饑	馨	騫	騰	騷	騵	鰓	鰍	鹹
60	麵	黨	鼯	齟	齣	齡	儷	儸	囁	囀	囂	夔	屬	巍	懼	懾	攝	攜	斕	曩
80	櫻	欄	櫺	殲	灌	爛	犧	瓖	瓔	癩	矓	籐	纏	續	羼					

Row 91		01	02	03	04	05	06	07	08	09	10	11	12	13	14	15	16	17	18	19
00		蘗	蘭	蘚	蠣	蠢	蠡	蠟	襪	襬	覽	譴	護	譽	贓	躊	躍	躋	轟	辯
20	醺	鐮	鐳	鐵	鐺	鐸	鐲	鐫	闢	霸	霹	露	響	顧	顥	饗	驅	驃	驀	騾
40	髏	魔	魑	鰭	鰥	鶯	鶴	鷂	鶸	麝	黯	鼙	齜	齦	齧	儼	儻	囈	囊	囉
60	孿	巔	巒	彎	懿	攤	權	歡	灑	灘	玀	瓤	疊	癮	癬	禳	籠	籟	聾	聽
80	臟	襲	襯	觼	讀	贖	贗	躑	躓	轡	酈	鑄	鑑	鑒	霽					

Row 92		01	02	03	04	05	06	07	08	09	10	11	12	13	14	15	16	17	18	19
00		霾	韃	韁	顫	饕	驕	驍	髒	鬚	鱉	鰱	鰾	鰻	鷓	鷗	鼴	齬	齪	龔
20	囌	巖	戀	攣	攫	攪	曬	欐	瓚	竊	籤	籣	籥	纓	纖	纔	臢	蘸	蘿	蠱
40	變	邐	邏	鑣	鑠	鑤	靨	顯	饜	驚	驛	驗	髓	體	髑	鱔	鱗	鱖	鷥	麟
60	黴	囑	壩	攬	灞	癱	癲	矗	罐	羈	蠶	蠹	衢	讓	讒	讖	艷	贛	釀	鑪
80	靂	靈	靄	韆	顰	驟	鬢	魘	鱟	鷹	鷺	鹼	鹽	鼇	齷					

Row 93		01	02	03	04	05	06	07	08	09	10	11	12	13	14	15	16	17	18	19
00		齲	廳	欖	灣	籬	籮	蠻	觀	躡	釁	鑲	鑰	顱	饞	髖	鬣	黌	灤	矚
20	讚	鑷	韉	驢	驥	纜	讜	躪	釅	鑽	鑾	鑼	鱷	鱸	黷	豔	鑿	鸚	爨	驪
40	鬱	鸛	鸞	籲																
60																				
80																				

CNS 11643-1992 Plane 2

Row 1		01	02	03	04	05	06	07	08	09	10	11	12	13	14	15	16	17	18	19
00		乂	乜	凵	匚	厂	万	丌	乇	亍	囗	屮	彳	丏	冇	与	丮	亓	仂	仉
20	仈	冘	勼	卬	厹	圠	夃	夬	尐	巿	旡	殳	毌	气	爿	丱	丼	仨	仜	仩
40	仡	仝	仚	刌	刉	匜	卌	圢	圣	夗	夯	宁	宄	尒	尻	屴	屳	帄	庀	庂
60	忉	戉	扐	氕	氶	汃	氿	氻	犮	犰	玊	禸	肊	阞	伎	优	伬	仵	伔	仱
80	伀	价	伈	伝	伂	伅	伢	伓	伄	仴	伒	冱	刓	刐	劦					

Row 2		01	02	03	04	05	06	07	08	09	10	11	12	13	14	15	16	17	18	19
00		匢	匟	卍	厊	吇	囡	囟	圮	圪	圴	夼	攺	奼	妅	奻	奾	奷	奿	孖
20	尕	尥	屼	屺	屻	屾	巟	幵	庄	异	弚	彴	忕	忔	忏	扜	扞	扤	扡	扦
40	扢	扙	扠	扚	扥	攷	旯	旮	朾	朹	朸	朻	机	朿	朼	朳	氘	汆	汒	汜
60	汏	汊	汔	汋	汌	灱	牞	犴	犵	玎	甪	癿	穵	网	艸	艼	芀	艽	艿	虍
80	襾	邙	邗	邘	邛	邔	阢	阤	阠	阣	佖	伻	佢	佉	体					

Row 3		01	02	03	04	05	06	07	08	09	10	11	12	13	14	15	16	17	18	19
00		佤	伾	佧	佒	佟	佁	佘	伭	伳	伿	佡	冏	冹	刜	刞	刡	劭	劮	匉
20	卣	卲	厎	厏	吰	吷	吪	呔	呅	吙	吜	吥	吘	吽	呏	呁	吨	吤	呇	囮
40	囧	囥	坁	坅	坌	坉	坋	坒	夆	奀	妦	妘	妠	妗	妎	妢	妐	妏	妧	妡
60	宎	宒	尨	尪	岍	岏	岈	岋	岉	岒	岊	岆	岓	岕	巠	帊	帎	庋	庉	庌
80	庈	庍	弅	弝	彸	彶	忒	忑	忐	忭	忨	忮	忳	忡	忤					

Row 4		01	02	03	04	05	06	07	08	09	10	11	12	13	14	15	16	17	18	19
00		忣	忺	忯	忷	忻	怀	忴	戺	抃	抌	抎	抏	抔	抇	扱	扻	扺	扰	抁
20	抈	扷	扽	扲	扴	旰	旴	旳	旲	旵	杅	杇	杙	杕	杌	杈	杝	杍	杚	杋
40	毐	氙	氚	汸	汧	汫	沄	沋	沏	汱	汯	汩	沚	汭	沇	沕	沜	汦	汳	汥
60	汻	沎	灴	灺	牣	犿	犽	狃	狆	狁	犺	狅	玕	玗	玓	玔	玒	町	甹	疔
80	疕	皁	礽	耴	肕	肙	肐	肒	肜	芐	芏	芅	芎	芑	芓					

Row 5		01	02	03	04	05	06	07	08	09	10	11	12	13	14	15	16	17	18	19
00		芊	芃	芄	豸	迉	辿	邟	邡	邥	邞	邧	邠	阰	阨	阯	阭	丳	侘	佼
20	侅	佽	侀	侇	佶	佴	侉	侄	佷	佌	侗	佪	侚	佹	侁	佸	侐	侜	侔	侞
40	侒	侂	侕	佫	佮	冞	冼	冾	刵	刲	刳	剆	刱	劼	匊	匋	匼	厒	厔	咇
60	呿	咁	咑	咂	咈	呫	呺	呾	呥	呬	呴	呦	咍	呯	呡	呠	咘	呣	呧	呤
80	囷	囹	坯	坲	坭	坫	坱	坰	坶	垀	坵	坻	坳	坴	坢					

Row 6		01	02	03	04	05	06	07	08	09	10	11	12	13	14	15	16	17	18	19
00		坨	坽	夌	奅	妵	妺	姏	姎	姐	姌	姁	妶	妼	姃	姖	妱	妽	妖	姈
20	婜	㚴	孢	孥	宓	宕	屄	屇	岮	岤	岠	岵	岯	岨	岬	岟	岣	岺	岢	岪
40	岩	岸	岥	岶	岰	岦	帗	帔	帙	弨	弢	弣	弤	彔	徂	彾	彽	忞	忥	怭
60	怦	怙	怲	怋	怴	怊	怗	怳	怚	怞	怬	怢	怍	怐	怮	怓	怑	怌	怉	怜
80	戔	屒	抭	抴	拑	抾	抪	抶	拊	抮	抳	抯	抻	抩	抰					

Row 7		01	02	03	04	05	06	07	08	09	10	11	12	13	14	15	16	17	18	19
00		抸	攽	斨	斻	昉	旼	昄	昒	昈	旻	昃	昋	昍	昅	旽	昑	昐	曶	朊
20	枅	杭	枎	枒	杶	杻	枘	枆	构	杴	柃	枌	杺	枟	枑	枙	枃	杽	极	杸
40	枇	枔	欥	殀	歾	毞	氝	沓	泬	泫	泮	泙	沶	泔	沭	泧	沷	泐	洞	沺
60	泃	泆	泭	泲	泒	泝	沴	炏	沝	泘	泞	泂	洰	泍	泇	沰	泹	泏	泩	泑
80	炔	炘	炅	炓	炆	炄	炑	炖	炂	炚	炃	牪	狖	狋	狘					

Row 8		01	02	03	04	05	06	07	08	09	10	11	12	13	14	15	16	17	18	19
00		狉	狜	狒	狔	狚	狌	狑	玤	玡	玭	玦	玢	玠	玬	玝	瓟	瓨	甿	畀
20	甾	疌	疘	皯	盳	盱	盰	盵	矸	矼	矹	矻	矺	矷	祂	礿	秅	穸	穻	竻
40	籵	紅	耵	肏	肮	肣	肸	肵	肭	舠	芠	苀	芫	芚	芘	芛	芵	芧	芮	芼
60	芞	芺	芴	芨	芡	芩	苂	芤	苃	芶	芢	虰	虯	虭	虮	豖	迒	迋	迓	迍
80	迖	迕	迗	邲	邴	邯	邳	邰	阹	阽	阼	阺	陃	俍	俅					

Row 9		01	02	03	04	05	06	07	08	09	10	11	12	13	14	15	16	17	18	19
00		俓	侲	俉	俋	俁	俔	俜	俙	侻	侳	俛	俇	俖	俈	俀	侹	俬	剄	剉
20	勍	勂	匽	卼	厗	厖	厙	厘	咺	咡	咭	咥	哏	哃	茍	咷	咮	哖	咶	哅
40	哆	咠	呰	咼	咢	咾	呲	哞	咰	垵	垞	垟	垤	垌	垗	垝	垛	垔	垘	垏
60	垙	垥	垚	垕	壴	复	奓	姡	姞	姮	娀	姱	姝	姺	姽	姼	姶	姤	姲	姷
80	姛	姩	姳	姵	姠	姾	姴	婺	宨	屌	峐	峘	峌	峗	峋					

Row 10		01	02	03	04	05	06	07	08	09	10	11	12	13	14	15	16	17	18	19
00		峛	峞	峑	峉	峇	峊	峖	峓	峔	峏	峈	峆	峎	峟	峸	巹	帡	帢	帣
20	帠	帤	庰	庤	庢	庛	庣	庥	弇	弮	彖	徆	恋	怹	恔	恲	恞	恅	恓	恇
40	恉	恛	恌	恀	恂	恟	怤	恄	恘	恦	恮	扂	扃	拏	挍	挋	拵	挎	挃	拫
60	拹	挏	挌	拸	拶	挀	挓	挔	拺	挕	挾	拰	敁	敀	斪	斿	昶	昡	昲	昵
80	昜	昦	昢	昳	昫	昺	昝	昴	昹	㫚	胐	胊	柁	柲	柈					

Row 11		01	02	03	04	05	06	07	08	09	10	11	12	13	14	15	16	17	18	19
00		株	柜	柑	柸	柘	柀	枷	柅	柫	柤	柟	枵	柍	枳	柷	柶	柮	柣	柂
20	枹	柎	柧	柰	枲	柼	柆	柭	柌	枮	柦	柛	柺	柉	柊	柃	柪	柋	欨	殂
40	殄	殶	毖	毘	毴	氟	氡	洨	洴	洭	洟	洼	洿	洒	洊	泚	洳	洄	洙	洺
60	洚	洑	洀	洝	浂	洁	洘	洷	洃	洏	浀	洇	洠	沨	洈	洢	洉	洐	炷	炟
80	炾	炱	炰	烅	炴	炵	炩	牁	牉	牊	牬	牰	牳	牮	狊					

Row 12		01	02	03	04	05	06	07	08	09	10	11	12	13	14	15	16	17	18	19
00		狤	狨	狫	狟	狪	狦	狣	玅	珌	珂	珈	珅	玹	玶	玵	玴	珫	玿	珇
20	玾	珃	珆	玸	珋	瓬	瓮	甪	畇	畈	疧	疪	癹	盄	眈	眃	眄	眅	眊	盷
40	盻	盺	矧	矨	砆	砑	砒	砅	砐	砏	砎	砉	砃	砓	祊	祌	祋	祅	祄	秕
60	种	秏	秖	秎	窀	穾	竑	笀	笁	籺	籸	籹	籿	粀	粁	紃	紈	紁	罘	羑
80	羍	羾	耇	耎	耏	耔	耷	胘	胇	胠	胑	胈	胂	胐	胅					

Row 13		01	02	03	04	05	06	07	08	09	10	11	12	13	14	15	16	17	18	19
00		胣	胙	胜	胊	胕	胉	胏	胗	胦	胍	臿	舡	芔	苙	苾	苹	茇	苨	茀
20	苕	茺	苫	苖	苴	苬	苡	苲	苵	茌	苻	苶	苰	苪	苤	苠	苺	苳	苭	虷
40	虴	虼	虳	衁	衎	衧	衪	衩	觓	訄	訇	赲	迣	迡	迮	迠	郱	邽	邿	郕
60	郅	邾	郇	郋	郈	釔	釓	陔	陏	陑	陓	陊	陎	倞	倅	倇	倓	倢	倰	倛
80	俵	俴	倳	倷	倬	俶	俷	倗	倜	倠	倧	倵	倯	倱	倎					

Row 14		01	02	03	04	05	06	07	08	09	10	11	12	13	14	15	16	17	18	19
00		党	冔	冓	凊	凄	凅	凈	凎	剡	剚	剒	剞	剟	剕	剢	勍	匎	厞	唦
20	哢	唗	唒	哧	哳	哤	唚	哿	唄	唈	哫	唑	唅	哱	唊	哻	哷	哸	哠	唎
40	唃	唋	圁	圂	埌	堲	埕	埒	垺	埆	垽	垼	垸	垶	垿	埇	埐	垹	埁	夎
60	奊	娙	娖	娭	娮	娕	娏	娗	娊	娞	娳	孬	宧	宭	宬	尃	屖	屔	峬	峿
80	峮	峱	峷	崀	峹	帩	帨	庨	庮	庪	庬	弳	弰	彧	恝					

Row 15		01	02	03	04	05	06	07	08	09	10	11	12	13	14	15	16	17	18	19
00		恚	恧	恁	悢	悈	悀	悒	悁	悝	悃	悕	悛	悗	悇	悜	悎	戙	扆	拲
20	挐	捖	挬	捄	捅	挶	捃	揤	挹	捋	捊	挼	挩	捁	挴	捘	捔	捙	挭	捇
40	挳	捚	捑	挸	捗	捀	捈	敊	敆	旆	旃	旄	旂	晊	晟	晇	晑	朒	朓	栟
60	栚	桉	栲	栳	栻	桋	桏	栖	栱	栜	栵	栫	栭	栯	桎	桄	栴	栝	栒	栔
80	栦	栨	栮	桍	栺	栥	栠	欬	欯	欭	欱	欴	歭	肂	殈					

Row 16		01	02	03	04	05	06	07	08	09	10	11	12	13	14	15	16	17	18	19
00		毦	毤	毨	毣	毢	毧	氥	浺	浣	浤	浶	洍	浡	涒	浘	浢	浭	浯	涑
20	涍	淯	浿	涆	浞	浧	浠	涗	浰	浼	浟	涂	涘	洯	浨	涋	浾	涀	涄	洖
40	涃	浻	浽	浵	涐	烜	烓	烑	烝	烋	缹	烢	烗	烒	烞	烠	烔	烍	烅	烆
60	烇	烚	烎	烡	牂	牸	牷	牶	猀	狺	狴	狾	狶	狳	狻	猁	珓	珙	珥	珖
80	玼	珧	珣	珩	珜	珒	珛	珔	珝	珚	珗	珘	珨	瓞	瓟					

Row 17		01	02	03	04	05	06	07	08	09	10	11	12	13	14	15	16	17	18	19
00		瓴	瓵	甡	畛	畟	疰	痁	疻	痄	痀	疿	疶	疺	皊	盉	眝	眛	眐	眓
20	眒	眣	眑	眕	眙	眚	眢	眧	砣	砬	砢	砵	砯	砨	砮	砫	砡	砩	砳	砪
40	砱	祔	祛	祏	祜	祓	祒	祑	秫	秬	秠	秮	秭	秪	秜	秞	秝	窆	窉	窅
60	窋	窌	窊	窇	竘	笐	笄	笓	笅	笏	笈	笊	笎	笉	笒	粄	粑	粊	粌	粈
80	粍	粅	紞	紝	紑	紎	紘	紖	紓	紟	紒	紏	紌	罜	罡					

Row 18		01	02	03	04	05	06	07	08	09	10	11	12	13	14	15	16	17	18	19
00		罘	罠	罝	罛	羖	羒	翃	翂	耼	耖	耾	耹	胺	胲	胹	胵	朓	胻	脋
20	舁	舯	舥	茳	茭	荄	茙	茣	茥	荖	茿	荁	茦	茜	荆	荂	荎	茛	茪	茈
40	茼	莜	茖	茤	茠	茷	茯	茩	荐	荅	荌	荓	茞	荏	荋	茧	荈	虓	虒	蚢
60	蚨	蚖	蚍	蚑	蚞	蚇	蚗	蚆	蚋	蚚	蚅	蚥	蚙	蚡	蚧	蚕	蚘	蚎	蚝	蚐
80	蚔	衃	衄	衭	衵	衶	衲	袀	衱	衿	衯	袃	衾	衻	衼					

Row 19		01	02	03	04	05	06	07	08	09	10	11	12	13	14	15	16	17	18	19
00		訒	豇	豗	豻	貤	貣	赶	赸	趵	趷	趼	軑	軓	迾	迵	适	迿	迻	逄
20	迼	迶	邳	郠	郙	郚	郣	郟	郰	郘	郛	郗	郜	郤	酐	酎	酏	釕	釢	釚
40	陜	陟	隼	飣	髟	鬯	乿	偰	偪	偡	偞	偠	偓	偋	偝	偲	偈	偍	偁	偭
60	偶	偢	倕	偅	偟	偩	偫	偣	偤	偆	偀	偮	偳	偗	偑	凐	剫	剭	剬	剮
80	勖	勘	匭	厜	啵	啶	唼	啍	啐	唴	唪	啑	啢	唶	唵					

Row 20		01	02	03	04	05	06	07	08	09	10	11	12	13	14	15	16	17	18	19
00		唰	啒	啅	唌	唲	啥	啎	唹	啈	唭	唻	啀	啋	圊	圇	埻	堔	埢	埶
20	埜	埴	堀	埭	埽	堈	場	堋	埳	埏	堇	埮	埣	埲	埥	埬	埡	堎	埼	堐
40	埧	堁	堌	埱	埩	埰	堍	堄	埾	婠	婘	婕	婧	婞	娸	娵	婭	婐	婟	婥
60	娙	婓	婤	婗	婃	婝	婒	婄	婛	婈	媎	娾	婍	婱	婌	婰	婩	婇	婑	婖
80	婂	婜	孲	孮	寁	寀	屙	崞	崋	崝	崚	崠	崌	崨	崍					

Row 21		01	02	03	04	05	06	07	08	09	10	11	12	13	14	15	16	17	18	19
00		崦	崥	崏	崰	崒	崣	崟	崮	帾	帴	庱	庴	庹	庲	庳	弶	弸	徛	徖
20	徟	悊	悐	悆	悾	悰	悺	惓	惔	惏	惤	惙	惝	惈	悱	惛	悷	惊	悿	惃
40	惍	惀	挲	捥	掊	掂	捽	掽	掞	掭	掝	掗	掫	掎	捯	掇	掐	据	捎	捵
60	捝	捭	掮	捼	掤	挻	掟	捸	掅	掁	掑	掍	捰	敆	旍	晥	晡	晛	晙	晜
80	晢	朘	桹	梇	梐	梜	桭	桮	梮	梫	楖	桯	梣	梬	梩					

Row 22		01	02	03	04	05	06	07	08	09	10	11	12	13	14	15	16	17	18	19
00		桵	桴	梲	梏	梙	梒	桼	桫	桲	梪	梀	桱	梮	梛	梖	梋	梠	梑	梎
20	桸	桻	楸	梌	桀	桬	欶	歒	欷	欽	殑	殏	殍	殎	殌	氪	淀	涫	涴	涳
40	湴	涬	淩	淢	涷	淶	淔	渀	淈	淠	淟	淖	涾	淥	淜	淝	淛	淴	淊	涽
60	淭	淰	涺	淕	淂	淏	淉	淐	淲	淓	淽	淗	淍	淣	涻	烺	焍	烷	焗	烴
80	焌	烰	焄	烳	焐	烼	烿	焆	焓	焀	烸	烶	焈	烾	焎					

Row 23		01	02	03	04	05	06	07	08	09	10	11	12	13	14	15	16	17	18	19
00		牾	牻	牼	牿	猝	猗	猇	猑	猘	猊	猈	狿	猏	猞	玈	珶	珸	珵	琄
20	琔	珽	琇	琀	珺	珼	珿	琌	琋	珴	琈	畤	畣	痎	痒	痏	痋	痌	痑	痐
40	皏	皉	盓	眹	眯	眭	眱	眲	眴	眳	眽	眥	眻	眵	硈	硒	硉	硍	硊	硌
60	砦	硅	硐	祤	祧	祩	祪	祣	祫	祡	离	秺	秸	秶	秷	窏	窔	窐	笵	筇
80	笴	笥	第	笢	笞	笳	笘	笪	笝	笱	笫	笭	筊	笄	筦					

Row 24	01	02	03	04	05	06	07	08	09	10	11	12	13	14	15	16	17	18	19
00		笚	笣	粔	粘	粖	粣	紵	紽	絓	紶	紺	絅	紬	紩	絁	絇	紾	紿	絉
20	缺	[illegible]	罜	羑	羜	羝	羛	翊	翋	翍	翐	翑	翇	翏	[illegible]	耟	耞	耛	聇	聃
40	聈	脘	脥	脙	脛	脭	脟	脬	脞	脡	脕	脧	脝	脢	舑	舸	舳	舺	舴	舲
60	艴	莐	莣	莨	莍	[illegible]	荳	莤	荴	莏	莁	莕	莙	[illegible]	莔	莩	荽	莃	莌	莝
80	莛	莪	莋	菱	莥	莯	莈	莗	莰	荿	莴	莇	莮	荂	虙					

Row 25	01	02	03	04	05	06	07	08	09	10	11	12	13	14	15	16	17	18	19
00		虖	蚿	蚷	蚑	蛁	蛅	蚺	蚰	蛈	蚹	蚳	蚸	蛌	蚴	蚻	蚼	蛃	蚽	蚾
20	衒	袉	袕	袨	袢	袪	袚	袑	袡	袟	袘	袧	袙	袛	袗	袤	衮	袠	袓	袎
40	覂	觖	觓	觕	訰	訧	訬	訞	谹	谻	豣	豝	豽	貥	赽	赻	赹	趼	跂	趹
60	趿	跁	軘	軞	軝	軜	軗	軠	軡	迣	逋	逑	逜	逌	逡	郟	郪	郰	郴	郲
80	郳	郔	郫	郬	郩	酖	酘	酚	酓	酕	釬	釴	釱	釳	釸					

Row 26	01	02	03	04	05	06	07	08	09	10	11	12	13	14	15	16	17	18	19
00		釤	釹	釨	釪	釷	釾	釮	镺	閆	閈	陼	陭	陫	陱	陯	隿	靪	頄	飥
20	馗	傛	傕	傔	傞	傋	傣	傃	傌	傎	傝	偨	傜	傒	傂	傇	兟	凔	匒	匑
40	厤	厧	喑	喨	喥	喭	啷	嗚	喢	喓	喈	喏	喵	喁	喣	喒	喤	啍	喌	喦
60	啿	喕	喡	喎	圌	堩	堷	堙	堞	堧	堣	堨	埵	塈	堥	堜	堛	堳	堿	堉
80	堮	堹	堸	堭	堬	堻	奡	媯	媔	媟	婺	媢	媞	婸	媦					

Row 27	01	02	03	04	05	06	07	08	09	10	11	12	13	14	15	16	17	18	19
00		婼	媥	媬	媕	媮	娷	媄	媊	媗	媃	媋	媩	媂	婽	媌	媜	媏	媓	媝
20	寪	寍	寋	寔	寖	寘	寎	尌	尰	崷	嵃	嵫	嵁	嵋	崿	崵	嵑	嵎	嵕	崳
40	㡘	嵒	崽	嵮	嵙	嵂	崹	嵉	嵿	崼	崲	嵔	嵟	嵗	幄	幀	㡬	徦	徥	徫
60	惉	惪	惌	惢	惎	惄	愔	惲	愊	愖	愌	惵	愓	惸	惼	惾	惁	愃	愘	愝
80	愐	惿	愄	愋	扊	掔	掱	掰	揎	揥	揨	揯	揃	撝	揳					

Row 28	01	02	03	04	05	06	07	08	09	10	11	12	13	14	15	16	17	18	19
00		揊	揠	揶	揕	揲	揵	摡	揟	掾	揝	揜	揄	揘	揓	揂	揇	揌	揋	揈
20	揰	揗	揙	攲	敧	敪	敤	敜	敨	敥	斌	斝	斞	斮	旐	旒	晼	晬	晻	晀
40	晱	晹	晪	晲	晵	椌	棓	棲	棜	椪	棬	棪	棱	椏	棖	棷	棫	棤	棶	椓
60	椐	棳	棡	椇	棌	椈	楰	梴	椑	棯	棆	椔	棸	棐	棽	棼	棨	椋	椊	椗
80	棎	棈	棝	棞	棦	棴	棑	椆	棔	棩	椕	椥	棇	欹	欻					

Row 29	01	02	03	04	05	06	07	08	09	10	11	12	13	14	15	16	17	18	19
00		欿	欼	殔	殗	殙	殕	殽	毰	毲	毳	氰	淼	湆	滳	渟	湉	溈	渼	淢
20	湅	湢	渫	渿	湁	湝	湳	湈	渳	湋	湀	湑	渻	渃	渮	湞	湨	湜	湡	渱
40	渨	湠	渚	湫	渹	渢	渰	湓	湥	渧	湸	湤	湷	湕	湹	湒	湦	渵	渶	湚
60	焠	焞	焯	烻	焮	焱	焣	焥	焢	焲	焟	焆	焩	閔	牋	牚	犈	犉	犆	犅
80	犋	猒	猋	猰	猢	猱	猳	猧	猲	猭	猦	猣	猵	猌	琮					

Row 30		01	02	03	04	05	06	07	08	09	10	11	12	13	14	15	16	17	18	19
00		琬	琰	琫	琖	琚	琡	琭	琱	琤	琣	琝	琩	琠	琲	瓻	甯	畯	畬	痧
20	痵	痡	痦	痝	痼	痤	痗	皕	睋	盔	睆	睇	睄	睍	睅	睊	睎	睋	睌	矞
40	矬	硍	硤	硥	硜	硭	硱	硪	确	硰	硩	硨	硞	硢	祴	祳	祲	祰	稂	稊
60	稃	稌	稄	窣	竦	竤	筊	笻	筄	筈	筌	筎	筀	筘	筅	粢	粞	粨	粡	絘
80	絯	絣	絓	絖	絧	絪	絏	絭	絜	絫	絒	絔	絩	絑	絟					

Row 31		01	02	03	04	05	06	07	08	09	10	11	12	13	14	15	16	17	18	19
00		絎	缾	缿	罥	罦	羢	羠	羡	翑	聑	聏	聐	胾	胔	腃	腊	腒	腏	腇
20	脽	腍	脺	臦	臮	臷	臸	臹	舄	舼	舽	舿	艵	茻	菏	菹	萣	菀	菨	菸
40	菧	菤	菼	菶	葏	菆	菈	菫	菣	莿	萁	菝	菥	菘	菿	菡	菋	菎	菖	菵
60	菉	萉	萏	菞	萑	萆	菂	菳	菕	萺	菇	菑	菪	萓	莚	菃	落	萀	菄	菻
80	菗	萢	萛	萠	菾	蛘	蛢	蛦	蛓	蛣	蛚	蛪	蛝	蛫	蛜					

Row 32		01	02	03	04	05	06	07	08	09	10	11	12	13	14	15	16	17	18	19
00		蛬	蛩	蛗	蛨	蛑	衈	衖	衕	袺	裗	袹	袸	裀	袾	袶	袼	袷	袽	袲
20	褁	裉	峴	覘	覗	觝	觚	觛	詎	詍	訹	詙	詀	詗	詘	詄	詅	詒	詈	詑
40	詊	詌	詏	豟	貁	貀	貺	貾	貰	貹	貵	趄	趀	趉	跘	跓	跍	跇	跖	跜
60	跏	跕	跙	跈	跗	跅	軯	軷	軺	軹	軦	軮	軥	軵	軧	軨	軶	軫	軱	軬
80	軴	軩	逭	逴	逯	鄆	鄬	鄄	郿	郼	郹	郻	鄈	鄁	鄀					

Row 33		01	02	03	04	05	06	07	08	09	10	11	12	13	14	15	16	17	18	19
00		鄉	鄅	鄃	酡	酤	酟	酢	酠	鈁	鈊	鈥	鈃	鈚	鈦	鈏	鈌	鈀	鈒	釿
20	釽	鈆	鈄	鈧	鈂	鈜	鈤	鈘	鈗	鈅	鈖	镻	閅	閌	閜	隇	陾	隁	隉	隃
40	隀	雂	雈	雃	雱	雺	靬	靰	靮	頇	颩	飫	馲	黹	兆	亄	亶	傽	僞	僆
60	傮	僄	僊	傴	僈	僂	傰	傯	傺	傱	僋	僉	傶	傸	凗	務	剸	剻	剹	嗃
80	嗛	嗌	嗐	嗋	嗩	嗝	嗀	嗔	嗄	嗩	喿	嗒	㗅	嗏	嗕					

Row 34		01	02	03	04	05	06	07	08	09	10	11	12	13	14	15	16	17	18	19
00		嗢	嗖	𠹭	嗲	嗍	嗙	嗂	圔	塓	堞	塤	塏	塍	塉	塯	塕	塎	塝	塙
20	塥	塛	堽	塗	塑	壼	嫇	嫄	嫋	嬍	媸	媱	媵	嫐	媿	嫈	嫛	嫆	媷	嫀
40	嫊	嫏	媶	嫍	媹	嫑	寖	寘	寙	尟	尳	嵱	嵣	嵊	嵥	嵲	嵬	嵞	嵨	嵧
60	嵢	巰	幏	幎	幀	幍	幣	廅	廌	廆	廋	廇	彀	徯	徭	惷	慉	慊	愫	慅
80	愶	愲	愮	慆	愯	慏	愼	慀	戠	截	戣	戥	戤	掔	搴					

Row 35		01	02	03	04	05	06	07	08	09	10	11	12	13	14	15	16	17	18	19
00		搫	搐	搒	搉	搠	搤	搳	揁	摲	搕	搘	搞	搷	搢	搣	搌	搦	搰	搨
20	揌	搵	搯	搊	擠	搗	搥	搧	搋	挈	搛	摽	搸	搎	敼	斒	旓	曨	暌	暕
40	暐	暋	暊	暏	暔	最	朠	楦	楟	椸	楎	楢	楱	椿	楅	楪	椹	楂	楗	楙
60	楺	楈	楉	椵	楬	椳	椽	楥	棰	楸	椴	楩	楀	楯	楄	楶	楘	楁	楴	椮
80	椻	楋	楲	楜	楏	楑	椲	楒	椯	楻	椼	歆	歅	歃	歂					

Row 36		01	02	03	04	05	06	07	08	09	10	11	12	13	14	15	16	17	18	19
00		歈	歍	殗	毻	毼	毹	毷	毸	湠	滚	滈	溏	滀	溟	溓	溔	溠	溱	溹
20	滆	滒	溽	滁	溞	滉	溷	溰	滍	溦	滏	溲	溾	滃	滜	滘	溙	溒	溎	溍
40	溤	溡	溿	溳	滐	滊	溗	溮	溣	煇	煔	煒	煣	煠	煁	煝	煢	煲	煸	煪
60	煡	熚	煘	煃	煋	熅	煟	煐	煓	煄	煍	煛	牏	犍	犌	犑	犐	犎	猼	獂
80	猻	猺	獀	獊	獉	瑄	瑊	瑋	瑒	瑑	瑗	瑀	瑏	瑐	瑎					

Row 37		01	02	03	04	05	06	07	08	09	10	11	12	13	14	15	16	17	18	19
00		瑂	瑆	瑍	瑔	瓡	瓿	瓾	瓽	甝	畹	畷	榃	痯	瘏	瘃	痷	痾	痼	痹
20	痸	瘐	痻	痶	痭	痵	痽	皙	皵	盝	睕	睟	睠	睒	睖	睚	睩	睧	睔	睙
40	睭	矠	碇	碚	碔	碏	碄	碕	碅	碆	碡	碃	硹	碙	碀	碖	硻	祼	禂	祽
60	祹	稑	稘	稙	稒	稗	稕	稢	稓	稛	稐	窣	窢	窞	竫	筦	筤	筭	筴	筩
80	筸	筶	筳	筱	筰	筡	箄	箁	粡	粶	粴	粯	綈	綆	綀					

Row 38		01	02	03	04	05	06	07	08	09	10	11	12	13	14	15	16	17	18	19
00		綍	絿	綅	絺	綎	絻	綃	絼	綌	綔	綄	絽	綒	罭	罫	罧	罨	罬	羦
20	羥	羧	翛	翜	耡	腤	腠	腷	腜	腩	腛	腢	腲	朡	腞	腶	腧	腯	腄	腡
40	舝	艉	艄	艀	艂	艅	蓱	萿	葖	葶	葹	蒏	蒍	葥	葑	葀	萋	葧	萰	蒀
60	葽	葚	葙	葳	葴	葝	蔇	葞	葪	萺	萴	葺	葃	葸	萲	葅	萩	菙	葋	蒷
80	葂	萬	葟	葰	萹	葎	葌	葒	葯	蓅	蒎	萻	蒃	萶	萳					

Row 39		01	02	03	04	05	06	07	08	09	10	11	12	13	14	15	16	17	18	19
00		蒖	蒽	葄	蓄	葠	葔	葮	葢	蜋	蜄	蛷	蜌	蛺	蛖	蛵	蝍	蛸	蜎	蜉
20	蜁	蛶	蜍	蜅	裖	裋	裍	裎	裞	裛	裚	裌	裐	覅	覛	觟	觥	觤	觡	觠
40	觢	觜	触	詶	誆	詿	詡	訿	詷	誂	誄	詵	誃	誁	訽	詺	谼	豋	豊	豥
60	豤	豦	貆	貄	貅	賌	赨	赩	趑	趌	趎	趏	趍	趓	趔	趐	趒	跰	跠	跬
80	跱	跮	跐	跩	跣	跢	跧	跲	跫	跴	輆	軿	輁	輀	輅					

Row 40		01	02	03	04	05	06	07	08	09	10	11	12	13	14	15	16	17	18	19
00		輇	輈	輂	輋	遒	逿	遄	遉	逽	鄐	鄍	鄏	鄑	鄖	鄔	鄋	鄎	酮	酯
20	鉈	鉒	鈰	鈺	鉦	鈳	鉥	鉞	銃	鈮	鉊	鉆	鉭	鉬	鉏	鉠	鉧	鉯	鈶	鉡
40	鉰	鈱	鉔	鉣	鉐	鉲	鉎	鉓	鉌	鉖	鈲	閟	閜	閞	閛	隒	隓	隑	隗	雎
60	雺	雽	雸	雵	靳	靷	靸	靲	頏	頍	頎	颬	飶	飹	馯	馲	馰	馵	骭	骫
80	魛	鳩	鳭	鳧	麀	黽	僦	僔	僗	僨	僳	僛	僪	僝	僤					

Row 41		01	02	03	04	05	06	07	08	09	10	11	12	13	14	15	16	17	18	19
00		僓	僬	僰	僯	僣	僠	凘	劀	劁	勩	勫	匰	厬	嘧	嘕	嘌	嘒	嗼	嘏
20	嘜	嘁	嘓	嘂	嗺	嘝	嘄	嘖	嗹	墉	塼	墐	墘	墆	墁	塿	塴	墋	塺	墇
40	墑	墎	塶	墂	墈	塻	墔	墏	壾	奫	嫜	嫮	嫥	嫕	嫪	嫚	嫭	嫫	嫳	嫢
60	嫠	嫛	嫬	嫞	嫝	嫙	嫨	嫟	孷	寠	寣	屣	嶂	嶀	嵽	嶆	嵺	嶁	嵷	嶊
80	嶉	嶈	嵾	嵼	嶍	嵹	嵿	幘	幙	幓	廘	廑	廗	廎	廜					

Row 42		01	02	03	04	05	06	07	08	09	10	11	12	13	14	15	16	17	18	19
00		廕	廙	廒	廔	彄	彃	彯	徶	愬	愨	慁	慞	慱	慳	慒	慓	慲	慬	憀
20	慴	慔	慺	慛	慥	愻	慪	慡	慖	戩	戧	戫	搫	摍	摛	摝	摴	摶	摲	摳
40	摽	摵	摦	撦	摎	撂	摞	摜	摋	摓	摠	摐	摿	搿	摬	摫	摙	摥	摷	敳
60	斠	暡	暠	暟	朅	朄	朢	榱	榶	槉	榠	槎	榖	榰	榬	榼	榑	榙	榎	榧
80	榍	榩	榾	榯	榿	槄	榽	榤	槔	榹	槊	榚	槏	榳	榓					

Row 43		01	02	03	04	05	06	07	08	09	10	11	12	13	14	15	16	17	18	19
00		榪	榡	榞	槙	榗	榐	槂	榵	榥	槆	歊	歍	歋	殞	殟	殠	毃	毄	毾
20	滎	滵	滱	漃	漥	滸	漷	滻	漮	漉	潎	漙	漚	漧	漘	漻	漒	滭	漊	漶
40	潳	滹	滮	漭	潀	漰	漼	漵	滫	漇	漎	潃	漅	滽	滶	漹	瀅	濙	漺	漟
60	漍	漞	漈	漡	熇	熐	熉	熀	熅	熂	熏	煻	熆	熁	熗	牄	牓	犗	犕	犓
80	獃	獍	獑	獌	瑢	瑳	瑱	瑵	瑲	瑧	瑮	甀	甂	甃	畽					

Row 44		01	02	03	04	05	06	07	08	09	10	11	12	13	14	15	16	17	18	19
00		疐	瘖	瘈	瘌	瘕	瘑	瘊	瘔	皸	瞁	睼	瞅	瞂	睮	瞀	瞖	睾	瞃	磃
20	碪	碴	碭	碨	硾	碫	碞	碥	碠	碬	碢	碤	禘	禊	禋	禖	禕	禔	禓	禗
40	禈	禒	禐	稫	穊	稰	稯	稨	稦	窨	窫	窬	竮	箈	箜	箊	箑	箐	箖	箍
60	箌	箛	箎	箅	箘	箚	箙	箤	箂	粻	粿	粼	粺	綧	綷	緂	綣	綪	緁	緀
80	緅	綝	緎	緄	緆	緋	緌	綯	綹	綖	綼	綟	綦	綮	綩					

Row 45		01	02	03	04	05	06	07	08	09	10	11	12	13	14	15	16	17	18	19
00		綡	緉	罳	翢	翣	翥	翞	耤	聝	聜	膉	膆	膃	膇	膍	膌	膋	舕	蒗
20	蒤	蒡	蒟	蒺	蓎	蓂	蒬	蒮	蒫	蒹	蒴	蓁	蓍	蒪	蒚	蒱	蓐	蒝	蒧	蒻
40	蒢	蒔	蓇	蓌	蒛	蒩	蒯	蒨	蓖	蒘	蒶	蓏	蒠	蓗	蓔	蓒	蓛	蒰	蔎	虡
60	蜳	蜣	蜨	蝫	蝀	蜮	蜞	蜡	蜙	蜛	蝃	蜬	蝁	蜾	蝆	蜠	蜲	蜪	蜭	蜼
80	蜒	蜺	蜱	蜵	蝂	蜦	蜧	蜸	蜤	蜚	蜰	蜑	裷	裧	裱					

Row 46		01	02	03	04	05	06	07	08	09	10	11	12	13	14	15	16	17	18	19
00		裲	裺	裾	裮	裼	裶	裻	裰	裬	裫	覝	覡	覟	覞	觩	觫	觨	誫	誙
20	誋	誒	誏	誖	谽	豨	豩	賕	賏	賗	趖	踉	踂	跿	踍	跽	踊	踃	踇	踆
40	踅	踛	踀	踄	輐	輑	輎	輍	鄣	鄜	鄠	鄢	鄟	鄝	鄚	鄤	鄡	鄛	酺	酲
60	酹	酳	銥	銖	鉶	銛	鉺	銠	銔	銪	銍	銦	銚	銫	鉹	銗	鉿	銣	鋮	鋈
80	銂	銕	銢	鉽	銈	銡	銊	銆	銌	銙	銧	鉾	銇	銩	銝					

Row 47		01	02	03	04	05	06	07	08	09	10	11	12	13	14	15	16	17	18	19
00		鋋	鋬	隞	隡	雿	靘	靽	靺	靾	鞃	鞀	鞂	靻	鞄	鞁	靿	韎	韍	頖
20	颭	颮	餂	餀	餇	馝	馜	駃	馹	馻	馺	駂	骫	骳	骱	髣	髡	魃	魆	魠
40	魡	魟	鳱	鳲	鳵	麧	僄	儃	僞	僸	儆	儇	僶	僾	儋	儌	僽	儊	剩	劌
60	勱	勯	噈	噂	噌	嘵	噁	噊	噉	噆	噘	噚	噀	嘳	嘽	嘬	嘾	嘸	嘪	嘺
80	圚	墫	墝	墱	墠	墣	墯	墬	墥	墡	壿	嫿	嫴	嫽	嫷					

Row 48		01	02	03	04	05	06	07	08	09	10	11	12	13	14	15	16	17	18	19
00		嫶	嫢	嬉	嬂	嫹	嬁	嬇	嬅	嬏	屪	嶙	嶗	嶟	嶒	嶢	嶓	嶕	嶠	嶜
20	嶡	嶛	嶞	幩	幝	幠	幜	縻	廛	廞	廡	彉	徲	憨	惷	慹	憱	憍	憢	憉
40	憛	憓	憯	憭	憟	憒	憪	㦗	憰	憗	憳	戭	擎	摯	撖	撠	撅	撗	撜	撏
60	撊	撋	撌	撣	撟	㩘	撱	撘	敶	敺	敹	敻	斲	斳	暵	暰	暩	暲	暷	暪
80	暯	樀	樆	樗	樥	樧	樕	標	樋	樠	槿	㯉	槢	樛	樝					

Row 49		01	02	03	04	05	06	07	08	09	10	11	12	13	14	15	16	17	18	19
00		槾	樧	槲	槮	樸	槷	槧	榼	樈	槦	槻	樍	槼	槫	梜	樄	樘	樥	樏
20	槶	樫	樇	樞	翕	歔	殨	殣	殢	殦	毷	氀	毿	麾	潁	漦	潾	澇	濆	澒
40	澍	澉	澌	潢	潏	澅	潚	澖	潶	潬	澂	潕	潲	潒	潐	潗	澔	澓	潝	漀
60	潡	潫	潽	潧	澐	潓	澋	潩	潿	澕	潣	潷	潪	潻	熲	熯	熛	熰	熠	熚
80	熩	熵	熝	熥	熞	燈	熡	熪	熜	熒	熳	犘	犚	獘	獒					

Row 50		01	02	03	04	05	06	07	08	09	10	11	12	13	14	15	16	17	18	19
00		獞	獟	獠	獢	獛	獡	獚	獥	獝	璇	璉	璊	璆	璁	瑽	璅	璈	瑼	璖
20	甈	甇	畾	瘥	瘞	瘙	瘝	瘜	瘣	瘚	瘨	瘛	皜	皝	皞	皛	瞍	睘	瞉	瞈
40	磍	碻	磏	磌	磑	磎	磔	磈	磃	磄	磀	禚	禡	禠	禜	禢	禛	稾	稹	窫
60	窴	窳	箷	篋	箭	箸	篎	箯	箹	篊	箵	糅	糈	糌	糒	緷	緛	緪	緧	緗
80	緡	縃	緺	緦	緶	緱	緰	緮	緟	罶	羬	羰	羭	翭	翫					

Row 51		01	02	03	04	05	06	07	08	09	10	11	12	13	14	15	16	17	18	19
00		翪	翬	翦	翨	聤	聨	膣	膟	膞	膕	膢	膙	膗	舖	艏	艓	艒	艐	艎
20	艑	蔤	蔻	蔏	蔀	蔩	蔎	蔉	蔍	蔟	蔊	蔧	蔜	蓻	蔫	蓺	蔈	蔌	蓴	蔪
40	蓲	蔕	蓷	蓫	蓳	蓼	蔒	蓪	蓩	蔰	蓾	蔨	蔝	蔮	蔂	蓽	蔓	蓶	蔱	蔦
60	蓧	蓨	蓰	蓯	蓹	蔘	蔠	蔖	蔋	蔙	蔯	虢	蝖	蝣	蝤	蝷	蟡	蝳	蝘	蝔
80	蝛	蝒	蝡	蝚	蝑	蝞	蝭	蝪	蝐	蝎	蝟	蝝	蝯	蝬	蝺					

Row 52		01	02	03	04	05	06	07	08	09	10	11	12	13	14	15	16	17	18	19
00		蝮	蝜	蝥	蝏	蝻	蝵	蝢	蝧	蝩	衚	褅	褌	褔	褋	褗	褘	褙	褆	褖
20	褑	褎	褉	覢	覤	覣	觭	觰	觬	諏	諆	諮	諓	諑	諔	諕	諎	諗	誾	諀
40	諅	諘	諃	諫	説	諙	谾	豍	貏	賥	賟	賙	賨	賚	賝	賧	趠	趜	趡	趛
60	踠	踣	踥	踤	踮	踕	踛	踖	踑	踙	踦	踧	踔	踒	踘	踓	踜	踗	踚	輬
80	輤	輘	輚	輠	輣	輖	輗	遳	遰	遯	遧	遫	鄯	鄫	鄬					

Row 53		01	02	03	04	05	06	07	08	09	10	11	12	13	14	15	16	17	18	19
00		鄭	鄲	鄦	鄮	醅	醆	醊	醁	醂	醄	醀	鋐	鋃	鋄	鋀	鋙	錄	鋏	鉽
20	鋟	鋘	鋩	鋗	鋝	鋌	鋯	鋂	鋨	鋊	鋈	鋎	鋦	鋍	鋕	鋉	鋠	鋞	鋧	鋑
40	鋓	鋔	鋡	鋣	鋆	鋚	𨱏	閴	閳	閺	閜	隤	隢	雓	雺	霈	霂	靚	鞊	鞎
60	鞈	韐	韏	頞	頝	頍	頨	頧	頠	頮	頣	颲	飻	飺	餑	餔	餖	餗	餕	駜
80	駍	駏	駓	駔	駎	駉	駖	駘	駋	駗	駌	骳	髶	髫	髳					

Row 54	01	02	03	04	05	06	07	08	09	10	11	12	13	14	15	16	17	18	19
00		髮	髺	魊	魃	魧	魴	魱	魦	魶	魵	魰	魨	魮	魬	鴂	鴩	鳽	鳿	鴑
20	鴇	鴶	鴏	鴔	鴈	鴅	鴄	麀	黙	鼏	鼒	儜	儓	儗	儚	儑	凞	匴	叡	噰
40	噠	噮	嚧	噦	噣	噭	噌	噞	噉	圜	圛	壈	墽	壉	墿	墺	壂	墼	壆	嬗
60	嬙	嬛	嬡	嫶	嬓	嬐	嬖	嬨	嬚	嬠	嬞	寯	嶬	嶱	嶩	嶧	嶵	嶰	嶮	嶪
80	嶨	嶲	嶭	嶯	嶴	幧	幨	幦	幯	廩	廧	廦	廨	廥	彋					

Row 55	01	02	03	04	05	06	07	08	09	10	11	12	13	14	15	16	17	18	19
00		徼	徻	憝	憨	憖	懅	憴	懆	懁	懌	憺	憿	憸	懇	擗	擖	擐	擻	擉
20	撽	擎	擃	擛	擳	擙	趬	斂	敼	斣	曈	暾	曀	曊	曋	曏	暽	暻	暺	曌
40	朣	樴	橦	橉	橧	樲	橨	樾	橝	橲	橶	橛	橑	樨	橚	樻	樿	橗	橪	橤
60	橐	橏	檄	橯	橩	檨	檽	橞	檏	樘	橌	橎	橆	歑	歔	歖	殧	殪	殫	毈
80	毇	毹	毶	氆	灉	濋	澣	濇	澼	濎	濈	潞	濄	澽	澞					

Row 56	01	02	03	04	05	06	07	08	09	10	11	12	13	14	15	16	17	18	19
00		濊	澨	瀄	澥	澮	澺	澬	澪	濏	澿	澸	澢	濉	澫	澻	澯	澲	澰	燅
20	燂	熿	熸	燖	燀	燁	燋	燔	燊	燇	燏	熽	燗	熼	燆	燚	爂	犝	犞	獩
40	獦	獧	獬	獥	獫	獪	瑿	璚	璠	璔	璒	璕	璡	甋	疀	瘯	瘭	瘱	瘇	瘳
60	瘼	瘵	瘲	瘰	皻	盦	瞚	瞝	瞡	瞜	瞛	瞢	瞦	瞕	瞙	瞗	磝	磩	磥	磪
80	磞	磣	磛	磡	磢	磭	磟	磠	禤	穄	穈	穇	窶	窸	窵					

Row 57	01	02	03	04	05	06	07	08	09	10	11	12	13	14	15	16	17	18	19
00		篨	篩	篁	篣	篧	篝	篕	篥	篚	篠	篹	篔	篪	篢	篜	篫	篘	篟	糒
20	糔	糗	糐	糑	縒	縡	縗	縌	縟	縠	縓	縎	縜	縕	縚	縢	縋	縏	縖	縍
40	縔	縥	縤	罃	罻	罼	罺	羱	翯	耪	耩	聬	膱	膦	膮	膹	膵	膫	膰	膬
60	膴	膲	膷	膧	艆	艕	艖	艗	蕖	蕅	蕫	蕍	蕓	蕡	蕘	蕀	蕆	蕤	蕁	蕢
80	蕄	蕑	蕇	蕣	蔾	蕛	蕱	蕎	蕮	蕵	蕕	蕧	蕠	薌	蕦					

Row 58	01	02	03	04	05	06	07	08	09	10	11	12	13	14	15	16	17	18	19
00		蕝	蕔	蕥	蕬	虣	虥	虤	虦	螛	螏	螗	螓	螒	螈	螁	蟳	螘	蝹	螇
20	螣	螅	螐	螑	螝	螄	螔	螫	螚	螉	褞	褦	褰	褭	褮	褧	褱	褢	褩	褣
40	褫	褬	褟	觱	諠	諢	諲	諴	諵	諝	諕	諤	諟	諰	諈	諞	諡	諨	諿	諯
60	諻	貑	貒	貐	賵	賷	賱	賰	賳	赬	赮	趥	趧	踳	踾	踸	蹀	踣	踶	踼
80	踽	蹁	踰	踿	躽	輶	輮	輵	輲	輹	輷	輴	遶	遹	遻					

Row 59	01	02	03	04	05	06	07	08	09	10	11	12	13	14	15	16	17	18	19
00		遾	鄨	鄹	鄝	鄶	醘	醐	醑	醍	醏	錧	錞	錈	錟	錆	錏	鍺	錸	錼
20	錛	錣	錒	錁	鍆	錭	錎	錍	鋋	錝	鋺	鋧	鋹	鋷	錴	錂	錤	鋿	錩	錥
40	錵	錪	錔	錌	錋	鋾	錉	錀	鋻	鋫	閝	闍	閾	閹	閿	閶	閺	閵	闇	隩
60	雔	霎	霒	霐	鞙	鞗	鞔	鞂	韸	頶	頨	頲	餤	餟	餧	餩	馞	駮	駬	駥
80	駤	駰	駣	駪	駩	駧	骹	骿	骴	骻	髶	髺	髹	髷	鬳					

Row 60		01	02	03	04	05	06	07	08	09	10	11	12	13	14	15	16	17	18	19
00		鮀	鮅	鮇	魼	魾	魻	鮦	鮓	鮒	鮐	魺	鮎	魽	鮈	鴥	鴂	鴡	鴞	鴔
20	鳺	鴅	鴋	鴭	鴐	鴗	鴟	麈	麐	麇	麮	麭	黕	黖	黺	鼒	鼽	儦	儥	儢
40	儤	儹	儩	勴	嚓	嚌	嚧	嚆	嚄	嚃	嚐	嚂	嚃	嚁	壖	壔	壏	壒	嬭	嬥
60	孋	嬣	嬬	嬧	嬦	嬯	嬮	孻	寱	寲	嶷	幬	幪	徾	徻	懃	憵	憾	懧	懠
80	懤	懨	懞	擯	擩	擣	擫	擤	擨	斁	斀	斶	旚	曒	檍					

Row 61		01	02	03	04	05	06	07	08	09	10	11	12	13	14	15	16	17	18	19
00		檖	檁	檥	檉	檟	檛	檡	檞	檇	檓	檎	檕	檃	檨	檤	檑	橿	檦	檚
20	檅	檌	檒	歛	殭	氉	濌	澩	濴	濔	濣	濜	濭	濧	濦	濞	濲	濝	濢	濨
40	燡	燱	燨	燲	燤	燰	燢	獳	獮	獯	璗	璲	璫	璐	璪	璭	璱	璥	璸	甎
60	甗	甂	甏	瞵	癃	癈	癉	癄	皤	盩	瞵	瞫	瞲	瞷	瞶	瞴	瞱	瞨	矰	磳
80	磽	礂	磻	磼	磿	礀	礅	礃	礇	礄	禫	穖	穜	穛	穖					

Row 62		01	02	03	04	05	06	07	08	09	10	11	12	13	14	15	16	17	18	19
00		穘	穔	穚	窾	竀	竁	簅	簏	篲	簀	篿	簻	簎	篴	簋	篳	簂	簉	簃
20	簁	篸	篽	簆	篰	篱	簐	簊	糨	縭	縼	繂	縳	顈	縸	縪	繉	繀	繇	縩
40	繌	縰	縻	縶	繄	縺	罅	罿	罾	罽	翴	翲	耬	膻	臄	臌	臊	臅	臇	膼
60	臩	艛	艚	艜	薃	薀	薏	薧	薕	薠	薋	薣	蕻	薤	薚	薞	蕷	蕼	薉	薡
80	蕺	蕸	蕗	薎	薖	薆	薍	薙	薝	薁	薢	薂	薈	薅	蕹					

Row 63		01	02	03	04	05	06	07	08	09	10	11	12	13	14	15	16	17	18	19
00		蕶	蕯	蕵	蕟	彪	螾	螪	螭	蟅	螰	螬	螹	螵	螼	螮	蟉	蟃	蟂	蟌
20	螷	螯	蟄	蟊	螴	螶	螿	螸	螽	蟞	螲	褵	褳	褼	褾	襁	襒	褷	襂	覭
40	覯	覮	觲	觳	謞	謘	謖	謑	謅	謋	謢	謏	謒	謕	謇	謍	謈	謆	謜	謓
60	謚	豏	豰	豲	豱	豯	貕	貔	賹	赯	蹎	蹍	蹓	蹐	蹌	蹇	轃	轀	邅	遾
80	鄸	醚	醢	醛	醙	醟	醡	醝	醠	鎡	鎃	鎯	鍤	鍖	鍇					

Row 64		01	02	03	04	05	06	07	08	09	10	11	12	13	14	15	16	17	18	19
00		鍼	鍘	鍜	鍶	鍉	鍐	鍑	鍠	鍭	鎏	鍌	鍪	鍹	鍗	鍕	鍒	鍏	鍱	鍷
20	鍻	鍡	鍞	鍣	鍧	鎀	鍎	闇	闉	闉	闃	闅	閷	隮	隰	隬	霠	霟	霘	霝
40	霙	鞚	鞡	鞜	鞞	鞝	韕	韔	韱	顁	顄	顊	顉	顅	顃	餥	餫	餬	餪	餳
60	餲	餯	餭	餱	餰	馘	馣	馡	騂	駺	駴	駷	駹	駸	駶	駻	駽	駾	駼	騃
80	骾	髾	髽	鬁	髼	魈	鮚	鮨	鮞	鮛	鮦	鮡	鮥	鮤	鮆					

Row 65		01	02	03	04	05	06	07	08	09	10	11	12	13	14	15	16	17	18	19
00		鮢	鮠	鮯	鴳	鵁	鵧	鴶	鴮	鴯	鴱	鴸	鴰	鵅	鵂	鵃	鴾	鴷	鵀	鴽
20	翵	鴭	麊	麉	麍	麰	黈	黚	黻	黿	鼤	鼣	鼢	齔	龠	儱	儭	儮	嚘	嚜
40	嚗	嚚	嚝	嚙	嚥	嚮	嚪	嚟	嚬	巇	巁	瀯	懟	懭	懮	懱	懪	懰	懫	懖
60	懩	擿	攄	擽	擸	攁	擃	擼	斔	旛	曚	曛	曘	櫅	檹	檽	櫡	櫆	檺	檶
80	檷	櫇	檴	檭	歈	歝	氋	瀇	瀌	瀍	瀁	瀅	瀔	瀎	瀏					

Row 66		01	02	03	04	05	06	07	08	09	10	11	12	13	14	15	16	17	18	19
00		瀀	瀆	瀦	濼	灕	瀊	爁	燿	燚	爍	燽	獿	璸	瓀	璵	瓁	璾	璶	𤩽
20	瑤	甋	甓	癜	癤	癙	癐	癥	癗	癚	皦	皻	盬	矂	瞺	礝	礓	礔	礉	礐
40	礒	礑	禭	禬	穟	𥨍	篣	簙	簠	簟	簮	簝	簦	簨	簢	簥	簰	縳	繌	繳
60	繣	繘	繢	繟	繑	縈	繗	繓	羵	羳	翾	翽	聵	臑	臒	臐	艟	𦪻	薴	蕐
80	葵	蔎	蔡	薳	薵	薽	藇	藆	薿	藋	藎	藈	藅	薱	蕹					

Row 67		01	02	03	04	05	06	07	08	09	10	11	12	13	14	15	16	17	18	19
00		藁	藡	薸	薷	薾	虢	蟧	蟦	蟢	蟚	蟫	蟪	蟥	蟟	蟳	蟤	螵	蟜	蟓
20	蟭	螑	蟣	蟗	蟙	蠁	螹	蠇	蟂	襓	襋	襏	襌	襆	襐	襑	襇	謪	謧	謣
40	謳	謰	謵	譇	譃	謼	謾	謱	謥	謷	謦	謶	謮	謤	䜈	譼	謺	𧳜	豵	貙
60	貘	貗	賾	贄	賿	賢	蹈	蹢	蹠	蹗	蹃	蹎	蹥	蹧	蹛	蹚	蹡	蹝	蹩	蹔
80	轆	轇	轈	轋	䜬	鄭	鄨	鄮	醨	醥	醧	醶	醪	鎵	鎌					

Row 68		01	02	03	04	05	06	07	08	09	10	11	12	13	14	15	16	17	18	19
00		鎒	鎷	鎛	鎝	鍚	鎧	鎎	鎪	鎞	鎦	鎕	鎈	鎙	鎟	鏒	鎄	鎱	鎑	鋭
20	鎤	鎨	鎴	鎣	闒	闓	闌	隊	雗	雈	嶲	雟	雘	雝	霣	霢	霶	鞬	鞮	鞨
40	鞫	鞼	鞶	鞢	鞥	韗	韙	韖	韘	頢	顛	顊	顒	颸	饁	餼	餺	騏	騋	騉
60	騍	騄	騑	騊	騅	騇	騆	髀	髃	鬈	鬄	鬋	鬩	鬵	魊	魌	魋	鯇	鯆	鯃
80	魟	鯁	鯢	鮸	鯓	鮶	鮇	鮹	鮽	鵝	鵏	鵪	鵴	鵛	鵢					

Row 69		01	02	03	04	05	06	07	08	09	10	11	12	13	14	15	16	17	18	19
00		鵙	鵖	駼	鶐	鶍	鵔	䳽	鶠	鶂	麛	麚	黟	鼃	鼄	鼖	鼥	鼤	鼪	鼩
20	鼶	齌	齕	儴	儵	劖	勷	厴	嚫	嚭	嚦	嚧	嚪	嚬	壚	壝	壛	夒	嬽	嬾
40	嬿	巃	幰	徿	懻	攇	攐	攍	攉	攌	攎	斄	旞	旝	曞	櫧	櫠	櫌	櫑	櫙
60	櫋	櫟	櫜	櫐	櫫	櫏	櫍	櫞	歠	殰	氌	瀙	瀧	瀠	瀖	瀫	瀡	瀢	瀣	瀩
80	瀗	瀤	瀜	瀪	爌	爊	爇	爂	爅	犥	犦	犤	犣	犡	瓋					

Row 70		01	02	03	04	05	06	07	08	09	10	11	12	13	14	15	16	17	18	19
00		瓅	璷	瓃	甖	癠	矉	矊	矄	矱	礝	礛	礡	礜	礗	礞	禰	穧	穨	簳
20	簼	簹	簬	簻	糬	糪	繶	繵	繸	繰	繷	繯	繺	繲	繴	繨	罋	罊	羃	羆
40	羷	翽	翾	聸	臗	臕	艓	艤	艡	艣	藫	藱	藭	藙	藡	藨	藚	藗	藬	藲
60	藸	藘	藟	藣	藜	藑	藰	藦	藯	藞	藢	蠀	蟺	蠃	蟶	蟷	蠉	蠌	蠋	蠆
80	蟼	蠈	蟿	蠊	蠂	襢	襚	襛	襗	襡	襜	襘	襝	襙	覈	覷				

Row 71		01	02	03	04	05	06	07	08	09	10	11	12	13	14	15	16	17	18	19
00		覾	觟	譑	譊	譆	譐	譙	譒	譓	譔	譙	譍	譊	譕	譖	譗	豷	豶	貚
20	贆	贇	贉	趬	趪	趭	趫	蹭	蹸	蹳	蹪	蹯	蹻	軂	轒	轑	轏	轐	轓	辴
40	酀	鄿	醰	醭	鏞	鏇	鏏	鏂	鏚	鏐	鏹	鏬	鏌	鏙	鎩	鏦	鏊	鏔	鏮	鏣
60	鏕	鏄	鏎	鏀	鏒	鏧	鏨	闚	闛	闠	雟	霪	霫	霬	霮	霯	鞳	鞷	鞶	韝
80	韞	韟	顜	顙	顝	顗	颾	颽	颻	颼	饈	饇	饃	馦	馧					

Row 72		01	02	03	04	05	06	07	08	09	10	11	12	13	14	15	16	17	18	19
00		騚	騕	騥	騝	騤	騛	騢	騠	騧	騣	䮾	騜	騔	骼	髺	髼	髳	髻	骰
20	鯪	鰕	鯠	鯞	鯤	鯦	鯢	鯰	鯔	鯗	鯬	鯜	鯙	鯥	鯕	鯡	鯚	鵷	鶈	鵩
40	鵲	鶄	鵽	鶀	鵿	鶆	鶌	鶋	鶏	鶉	鶐	鶂	鶍	鵬	鶔	鶊	鵻	鶇	鶈	鶩
60	鶣	鶫	鶬	麔	麑	麢	黐	鼪	鼫	齁	齍	齖	齗	齘	匷	嚲	嚵	嚳	嚹	孅
80	巆	巇	廮	廯	忀	忁	懹	攗	攖	攕	攓	旟	曨	曣	曤

Row 73		01	02	03	04	05	06	07	08	09	10	11	12	13	14	15	16	17	18	19
00		櫳	櫰	櫪	櫨	櫹	櫱	櫮	櫯	瀼	瀵	瀯	瀷	瀴	瀱	灂	瀸	瀿	瀺	瀹
20	灀	瀻	瀳	灁	爓	爔	犨	獽	獼	璺	皫	皪	皾	盭	矌	矎	矏	矍	矲
40	礥	礣	礧	礨	礤	礩	禲	穮	穬	穭	竷	籉	籈	籊	籇	籅	糮	繻	繾	纁
60	纀	羺	翷	耰	臛	臙	舋	艕	蘢	藿	蘁	藾	蘃	蘐	蘆	蘄	蘉	蘅	蘌	蘏
80	蠙	蠐	蠑	蠗	蠓	蠖	襣	襦	覹	觷	譠	譪	譝	譨	譣

Row 74		01	02	03	04	05	06	07	08	09	10	11	12	13	14	15	16	17	18	19
00		譥	譧	譭	趮	躆	躈	躄	轙	轖	轗	轕	轘	轚	邍	酄	酅	醷	醲	醳
20	醳	鐋	鐓	鏻	鐠	鐏	鐔	鐎	鐟	鐐	鐨	鐙	鐍	鏵	鐀	鏷	鏽	鐎	鐖	鐒
40	鏺	鐉	鏸	鐊	鏿	鏼	鐌	鏶	鐑	鐆	闞	闠	闟	霮	霯	鞹	鞻	韽	韾	顠
60	顢	顣	顐	飄	颾	饐	饎	饙	饌	饋	饓	騲	騴	騱	騬	騪	騶	騩	騮	騸
80	騭	髇	髊	髆	鬐	鬒	鬑	鰋	鰈	鯷	鰅	鰒	鯸	鱀

Row 75		01	02	03	04	05	06	07	08	09	10	11	12	13	14	15	16	17	18	19
00		鯀	鯉	鯺	鰗	鰔	鰉	鶟	鶙	鶤	鶝	鶒	鶘	鶐	鶛	鷗	鶠	鶕	鶚	鶡
20	鶪	鶚	鶠	鶞	鶌	鶮	鶱	鶭	鶵	鷩	鶷	麙	麛	麚	黥	黭	黮	黯	鼰	鼮
40	齞	齠	齙	齝	齙	龑	儺	儹	劘	劗	囃	嚽	嚾	孈	孇	巋	巏	廱	懽	攛
60	欂	櫼	欃	櫸	欀	灃	灄	灊	灈	灉	灅	灆	爝	爚	爙	獾	甗	癪	矐	礭
80	礱	礯	籔	籓	糲	纊	纇	纈	纋	纆	纍	罍	羻	耰	贏

Row 76		01	02	03	04	05	06	07	08	09	10	11	12	13	14	15	16	17	18	19
00		蘘	蘪	蘲	蘟	蘣	蘜	蘙	蘧	蘮	蘡	蘠	蘩	蘞	蘥	蠩	蠝	蠛	蠠	蠤
20	蠜	蠫	衊	襭	襩	襮	襫	觺	譹	譸	譅	譺	譻	贐	贔	趯	躎	躌	轞	轛
40	轝	酆	酇	酈	醹	鐿	鐻	鐶	鐩	鐽	鐼	鐰	鐹	鐪	鐷	鐬	鑀	鐱	闥	闤	闣
60	霵	霺	鞿	韡	顤	飉	飆	飀	饘	饖	騹	騽	驆	驄	驂	驁	騺	騿	髍	鬕
80	鬗	鬘	鬖	鬺	魒	鰫	鰝	鰜	鰬	鰣	鰨	鰩	鰤	鰡	鶷

Row 77		01	02	03	04	05	06	07	08	09	10	11	12	13	14	15	16	17	18	19
00		鶶	鶼	鷁	鷇	鷊	鷏	鶾	鷅	鷃	鶻	鶵	鷎	鶹	鶺	鶬	鷈	鶱	鶭	鷌
20	鶳	鷍	鶲	鹺	麜	黫	黮	黭	鼛	鼘	鼚	鼙	齎	齥	齸	龒	亹	囆	囇	囋
40	奱	孋	孌	巕	巑	廲	攡	攠	攦	攢	欋	欈	欉	氍	灕	灖	灗	灒	爞	爟
60	犩	獿	瓘	瓕	瓙	瓗	癭	皭	礵	禴	穰	穱	籗	籜	籙	籛	籚	糴	糱	纑
80	罏	羇	臞	艫	蘴	虀	蘦	蘬	蘳	蘶	蠬	蠨	蠦	蠪	蠥

Row 78		01	02	03	04	05	06	07	08	09	10	11	12	13	14	15	16	17	18	19
00		襱	覿	觀	𦪇	譾	謳	讂	譽	譒	譓	𨈖	躕	躔	躚	躒	躐	𨇽	𨘼	轠
20	轢	鄭	鑌	鑐	鑊	鑿	鑏	鑇	鑅	鑈	鑑	鑆	霿	韣	顡	顐	飀	饔	饛	驎
40	驓	驔	驌	騳	驕	驊	驉	驒	驐	髐	鬠	鬫	鬻	魖	魕	鱆	鱈	鱝	鱄	鯹
60	鰳	鯅	鰼	鰷	鰴	鰲	鰽	鰶	鷉	鶽	鶇	鷚	鷂	鷐	鷃	鴣	鷟	鷩	鷙	鷔
80	鷖	鵩	鷕	鶾	鷸	黰	黲	鼰	鼶	齂	齫	龕	龢	儽	劙					

Row 79		01	02	03	04	05	06	07	08	09	10	11	12	13	14	15	16	17	18	19
00		壨	壧	𦉪	孍	巘	廬	彏	懟	㦗	懾	攩	攥	曡	曫	欑	欒	欋	𣫥	灛
20	灚	麣	獑	獵	玃	癰	矐	籧	籦	纕	艬	蘺	蘲	蘹	蘼	蘱	蘻	𧟌	蠰	蠲
40	蠮	蠳	襶	襴	襳	𦪓	譕	讎	讐	讈	讋	贙	躘	轤	轣	醼	鑢	鑕	鑝	鑗
60	鑞	韄	韅	護	驖	驙	鬞	鬟	鬡	鱒	鱘	鱐	鱊	鱍	鱋	鱕	鱙	鱌	鱎	鱜
80	鷜	鷀	鷃	鷫	鷸	鷤	鷶	鷡	鷮	鷦	鷩	鷲	鷹	鷶	鷵					

Row 80		01	02	03	04	05	06	07	08	09	10	11	12	13	14	15	16	17	18	19
00		鷳	鷯	鷭	麡	黐	黲	黳	鼆	鼕	鼸	鼷	鼲	齃	齍	齀	齰	齮	齯	囓
20	囍	孎	屭	攇	曭	曮	欓	灟	灡	灝	灚	爣	瓛	癵	矕	礸	禶	襸	籪	纗
40	纚	艭	蘶	蠸	蠷	蠵	蠹	讘	讕	躞	躟	躔	躝	醾	醹	釂	鑫	鑨	鑩	鑴
60	雝	霍	霳	韇	韣	驞	髕	鬤	鱣	鱧	鱦	鱳	鱞	鱠	鸂	鸄	鸇	鸃	鸆	鸈
80	鸉	鼊	鼞	鼜	鼟	鼛	鼲	鼟	齆	齉	齵	齶	囔	攮	斸					

Row 81		01	02	03	04	05	06	07	08	09	10	11	12	13	14	15	16	17	18	19
00		欘	欙	欗	欐	灢	爦	犪	矘	矙	礹	籩	籫	糶	纙	纘	纛	纙	臠	虊
20	虆	虇	虈	襹	襺	襻	襼	觾	讗	讙	躣	躤	躍	鑮	鑭	鑯	鑱	鑳	靉	顪
40	饟	鰽	鱮	鱭	鸋	鸍	鸐	鸏	鸒	鸑	麢	黱	鼉	鼳	齈	齻	齺	囖	圞	灟
60	爧	蠼	趲	躜	醿	鑴	鑸	鑶	鑵	驠	鬮	鱴	鱳	鱱	鱵	鸓	鸔	鸑	鼊	齸
80	灨	爨	爤	爥	蠾	蠽	蠿	讞	貜	躩	軉	靋	顳	顴	飌					

Row 82		01	02	03	04	05	06	07	08	09	10	11	12	13	14	15	16	17	18	19
00		饡	蠢	驤	驨	驧	鬤	鸕	鸗	齇	戇	欞	爟	虌	躨	钂	钀	钁	驩	驨
20	鬮	虋	讟	钃	鑵	麷	癵	驫	鱺	鸝	灩	灪	爩	麤	齾	齉	龘			
40																				
60																				
80																				

CNS 11643-1992 Plane 3

Row 1		01	02	03	04	05	06	07	08	09	10	11	12	13	14	15	16	17	18	19
00		丨	丶	丿	亅	丅	丄	冂	冖	匚	卩	厶	个	亇	乂	九	夂	亐	亼	亾
20	亾	九	刃	尣	廾	夊	攵	宀	巛	幺	广	廴	彐	彑	彡	阝	丈	乣	乢	亣
40	内	仅	仫	从	仌	冄	円	冗	冮	凤	刅	办	劝	勽	匀	区	协	卆	卝	历
60	厷	厺	双	圣	収	圡	屮	币	弍	户	戸	攴	攵	无	乇	生	岂	仠	伕	仈
80	夫	仉	仦	仍	伎	参	全	回	冋	册	写	尻	切	刋	幼					

Row 2		01	02	03	04	05	06	07	08	09	10	11	12	13	14	15	16	17	18	19
00		团	匃	匈	匆	匆	匡	卟	卬	厉	厺	叐	叺	叶	号	叹	叽	台	図	坊
20	圤	処	夘	夲	夰	头	夻	奵	文	宂	对	尔	尽	屼	尖	尖	岁	吕	帆	庁
40	広	式	归	行	忊	忇	戹	扨	执	旧	术	歺	氹	汇	汎	氷	汄	污	玌	疒
60	癶	邓	邛	邔	阞	両	丠	丢	乱	争	亘	伴	仯	俩	併	仸	伆	伃	任	仮
80	伖	伒	伨	佧	伇	会	仓	众	兊	合	关	再	冴	决	冲					

Row 3		01	02	03	04	05	06	07	08	09	10	11	12	13	14	15	16	17	18	19
00		沃	凮	凶	刔	刉	劦	刘	动	卉	吉	协	平	卐	厷	压	序	去	吏	叒
20	吖	叿	叱	吁	吴	吅	吓	吕	吆	囲	团	圵	坴	圱	圩	壮	夅	乔	奔	奺
40	奂	妣	妖	妏	姜	妆	学	安	宇	当	尘	厚	尽	屸	屿	岙	岊	岜	出	巟
60	师	帆	庆	序	庑	廵	式	弔	弜	忞	忏	忚	忉	忛	戋	戏	扝	扟	执	扗
80	齐	㫃	旫	旪	曳	杒	朷	朳	杂	欢	毎	毜	汘	汑	汥					

Row 4		01	02	03	04	05	06	07	08	09	10	11	12	13	14	15	16	17	18	19
00		炏	休	污	汜	汓	灯	灱	灮	灰	风	欠	犰	犲	玜	玏	玌	到	百	礼
20	辛	肌	冐	芌	芳	艽	辶	边	邮	邚	阤	两	乱	况	亜	佅	佊	伹	伷	㑥
40	伲	征	俩	佄	佋	侮	侣	伵	你	兑	兎	児	兔	网	具	冝	沰	况	泮	凮
60	刨	刧	刦	劭	别	删	労	劳	劬	匥	医	却	应	居	厍	叻	咩	呍	味	呔
80	吺	吤	呙	呇	吽	吣	呷	吲	呋	吡	哅	吳	呉	呐	㕣					

Row 5		01	02	03	04	05	06	07	08	09	10	11	12	13	14	15	16	17	18	19
00		告	呑	吆	启	哂	囩	囲	図	国	园	囬	囦	坑	坪	坄	坅	呈	坓	坙
20	抖	坟	坃	坧	块	坒	均	坊	坆	均	圽	坳	坂	坐	坠	壱	壳	声	夋	麦
40	囱	夽	奈	妔	妌	妉	妜	妁	妅	妟	姘	妛	妡	妧	妚	奼	孛	宆	宍	宖
60	对	寿	孚	尪	岬	岄	岎	岂	岦	岐	岅	卮	帉	帕	希	帋	戊	庄	庐	弃
80	弦	弞	彣	忪	忧	忔	忦	応	忑	怓	忼	忟	忬	忶	忕					

Row 6		01	02	03	04	05	06	07	08	09	10	11	12	13	14	15	16	17	18	19
00		忲	忰	忹	忿	戓	或	成	戾	戼	扛	扜	扙	托	拐	扎	扐	択	报	抛
20	抜	抒	抍	拘	拗	扲	孜	牵	吃	时	旯	旵	旱	曳	杇	朴	杔	杒	机	屎
40	杆	杊	条	汁	浮	沑	沛	浅	汮	泮	沟	泠	宋	岽	沢	汹	汷	没	次	沪
60	泒	沿	炖	斧	灾	炒	灵	夷	牤	犴	狮	犽	狇	犹	犾	状	犻	犷	玘	玗
80	玗	巩	叭	疬	皀	皁	皃	盅	盈	盱	矻	矴	矵	秎	肌					

Row 7		01	02	03	04	05	06	07	08	09	10	11	12	13	14	15	16	17	18	19
00		廾	紀	肟	肑	肷	肶	苏	艾	芌	芭	芗	芟	虬	虿	辵	达	过	迂	迋
20	邓	邡	邛	邞	邢	邮	阧	队	阫	阳	阴	阩	丽	矛	叁	律	侊	侏	佩	佫
40	侎	侠	俩	価	侟	侣	侃	佫	伯	佥	兖	兔	具	冐	洪	洞	洤	凭	函	刵
60	刑	刧	剶	刹	効	券	势	单	卣	卻	叠	厓	厎	叁	参	叕	音	啦	咳	呃
80	咉	咲	黾	咏	哧	咄	咢	咔	咒	咊	咱	国	囻	匝	匣					

Row 8		01	02	03	04	05	06	07	08	09	10	11	12	13	14	15	16	17	18	19
00		固	囯	坦	坎	坐	坧	坤	坮	均	坿	垩	坐	壳	奋	奂	姘	妊	姊	妭
20	姛	姃	姗	妃	妚	妩	妳	姫	妥	娑	要	姊	妸	姤	娐	姖	婷	姝	姗	姈
40	孛	孙	弦	实	宝	実	宝	宮	尉	尚	尿	尾	屉	届	岥	岷	峁	岙	岍	岣
60	峄	岞	岴	岺	岊	帓	帒	弁	庢	库	庎	庙	庝	廸	迴	廹	耕	弄	弡	弤
80	弥	录	彭	彤	徂	径	徍	恅	恒	恸	恢	忝	恶	恳	忩					

Row 9		01	02	03	04	05	06	07	08	09	10	11	12	13	14	15	16	17	18	19
00		怽	怈	怵	怙	抹	抲	抗	抷	抻	択	抳	抑	抓	抡	扩	拝	抦	抯	担
20	挄	拟	拶	拓	拒	斉	斛	所	旂	映	昨	昏	冥	易	昳	晋	昨	昐	昳	杜
40	枖	枂	柳	杭	枣	枠	枢	栅	栌	柿	柰	欤	欧	走	步	朔	殁	殴	毑	毡
60	氧	氤	沛	泙	泱	沂	泮	泰	泵	泟	泫	泪	泗	泅	浮	浼	泎	洺	炉	炜
80	炰	炑	炊	炙	炆	炉	炻	炁	炁	炌	畗	烝	烊	欣	朋					

Row 10		01	02	03	04	05	06	07	08	09	10	11	12	13	14	15	16	17	18	19
00		牥	牦	犺	狂	狃	狍	狓	狛	狂	狏	玧	玠	玞	珃	环	玟	玫	玲	珋
20	帪	畋	畄	画	畀	界	疛	疜	疰	秄	秃	秆	秬	秕	秇	杆	秊	突	笆	笄
40	籸	籴	紉	紃	圂	罕	罙	胖	朊	肤	肰	服	肳	朋	肤	肚	肧	肬	胊	肦
60	臥	舍	芓	芽	芜	芾	芽	莎	苹	茚	芪	药	茈	茸	芰	芦	苍	虐	卒	迒
80	迌	这	迊	还	达	邸	郎	郇	邹	陉	阳	陁	阾	隶	青					

Row 11		01	02	03	04	05	06	07	08	09	10	11	12	13	14	15	16	17	18	19
00		面	乘	亁	亲	京	亯	亱	侊	保	侢	侼	侹	俖	侸	侳	侽	侾	俆	俌
20	俥	俣	俞	俞	冢	冟	冦	凍	凋	凂	凃	剄	剆	剅	剈	剏	剄	刾	勅	勀
40	勄	匧	単	卽	庯	叝	叜	叚	叙	咹	咠	咺	咴	咰	咽	咣	哚	哆	哘	咲
60	哘	哶	哛	哦	哧	响	哞	哌	囮	囧	垬	垑	垎	垍	垒	垡	垄	垦	垶	垌
80	垛	垍	垧	垘	垩	垜	垡	垚	夆	变	条	麦	奁	奎	姌					

Row 12		01	02	03	04	05	06	07	08	09	10	11	12	13	14	15	16	17	18	19
00		姟	姩	姫	姚	姰	姕	娍	娄	姹	娂	姸	娟	姙	姧	孛	宎	宴	宫	宯
20	尛	尯	屎	昼	屑	厨	峠	峚	峇	峦	峡	峍	峴	峛	峃	峥	巻	巽	帞	帱
40	庡	庫	庭	廼	廻	弯	弮	弫	彦	形	徆	徍	恜	恭	恈	恑	恩	点	恙	怱
60	恼	恒	恎	恠	恊	恡	恁	战	扁	挆	挆	挄	挓	拘	拍	挟	挗	拪	挡	挠
80	挼	拓	敊	敉	敀	敥	敏	旆	昳	昧	昛	昏	昣	昬	春					

Row 13		01	02	03	04	05	06	07	08	09	10	11	12	13	14	15	16	17	18	19
00		昰	昻	昞	昷	昸	昹	昤	柣	柨	柹	柖	柤	柸	桒	栞	栟	栘	柾	荣
20	查	栬	枱	柳	栅	栀	枀	枲	歂	歫	歭	殈	殂	殀	毡	毤	浓	洣	浪	洔
40	洅	涑	洆	洙	浺	洧	沓	盅	洂	浅	洴	洦	洧	净	洼	洤	炥	炢	炣	炶
60	炦	炻	炠	炪	炯	炭	炨	炶	炲	炧	炶	炏	点	爮	爼	爼	牠	牭	牸	牻
80	狧	狭	狣	独	狥	狢	垩	珄	珣	珐	珉	珁	珐	珌	珎					

Row 14		01	02	03	04	05	06	07	08	09	10	11	12	13	14	15	16	17	18	19
00		瓬	瓮	瓴	瓯	畉	畐	畆	畊	畈	畇	疾	疲	疣	疲	疨	皏	皅	盇	盷
20	㪷	眛	矦	矻	矸	砄	砋	砇	砐	砕	砈	祊	秓	秔	秐	秄	窊	窀	穾	穽
40	窃	窄	竔	竌	竕	竓	竐	竒	笆	笂	粍	籼	类	紆	紀	紂	紆	罗	罘	罘
60	罜	羒	胛	胆	胋	胒	胈	胍	胢	胟	胆	舦	舤	苷	苘	苝	莽	芝	苸	茔
80	芙	茉	苜	苍	茴	茶	苐	茎	苢	苠	茫	兹	虸	虰	虾					

Row 15		01	02	03	04	05	06	07	08	09	10	11	12	13	14	15	16	17	18	19
00		虿	蚇	虵	虽	虾	衂	衶	衶	覌	訅	訙	訓	訑	負	趴	迲	迧	迹	迸
20	郊	郋	郖	郘	郛	郥	郝	郍	邢	郱	郡	酏	閂	陕	皂	倲	偭	軌	俿	倚
40	俐	倃	丧	併	倄	倣	值	倈	俱	倮	傷	倏	倸	倹	倣	偖	倄	冣	冦	冢
60	涬	凄	凇	凉	剅	剈	剙	剥	剧	剡	剣	剮	剺	剻	勀	勑	勎	勐	勅	勈
80	匽	匪	粂	哘	哏	哋	哖	哯	哵	呼	哈	唀	唪	哥	启					

Row 16		01	02	03	04	05	06	07	08	09	10	11	12	13	14	15	16	17	18	19
00		哰	哶	咩	哆	啾	圓	圅	埉	埕	埧	埍	埌	埌	埑	埠	埙	埰	埛	埈
20	埄	堕	埑	埊	埀	婞	娦	婎	娪	娻	婚	娺	娋	娽	娲	婕	娵	娢	娑	娶
40	婓	婂	娖	娱	娓	娯	娚	娒	娏	媁	娭	娾	娩	寇	寋	宷	尅	将	屖	屓
60	峎	峈	峺	峫	峿	峸	崁	峩	峯	峇	帳	帰	帮	帬	带	庯	庲	庳	廼	弰
80	徎	従	徏	恏	悙	悟	悋	悎	悥	恋	悬	恵	悪	患	悤					

Row 17		01	02	03	04	05	06	07	08	09	10	11	12	13	14	15	16	17	18	19
00		悩	悋	悦	悚	悓	悞	悮	悧	悆	挬	挦	挮	挌	挵	捏	招	挩	挙	挐
20	舒	挱	挩	挪	挵	挪	括	捜	挿	敓	敊	敕	斋	斛	斜	晐	晆	晎	晀	晢
40	晋	晈	显	晠	晄	晍	朖	样	栤	栦	械	栛	梱	栳	桅	栙	桖	栔	栾	栞
60	桒	栭	栢	栧	栫	栯	栮	栰	栣	欶	欽	欿	歬	殑	残	殸	毬	毨	毭	浶
80	浵	浕	涽	涑	涖	浣	浰	浮	涏	浛	枭	涚	涛	浿	涁					

Row 18	01	02	03	04	05	06	07	08	09	10	11	12	13	14	15	16	17	18	19
00		淋	浱	淉	淀	浲	浜	渱	烄	烛	焮	烸	焥	烟	裵	裁	裂	威	焦	狠
20	牿	牳	牺	猘	猇	猂	垡	琎	琅	珴	瑲	珹	珮	珦	珸	琠	珋	珽	琏	琹
40	瓿	瓳	瓷	瓽	瓶	瓟	畕	畘	畗	畝	痃	痟	痞	疴	痁	疱	皅	盈	盔	盌
60	眪	眲	睨	眏	眹	眘	眽	眫	睐	眤	貼	眡	眷	矜	砎	砇	砲	砶	袣	袮
80	祩	祑	祢	秤	秙	秅	秡	秥	秨	秛	秬	秢	称	窐	窜					

Row 19	01	02	03	04	05	06	07	08	09	10	11	12	13	14	15	16	17	18	19
00		竒	竏	竚	竝	竓	竛	竜	笉	笁	笍	笋	笔	粎	粆	粃	粇	粊	粋	粡
20	缺	紃	紕	紤	紻	紩	絅	紥	罢	羓	美	羗	翊	翌	羜	翠	耇	耕	耵	耽
40	聃	耻	胶	胿	脝	脉	脃	脇	脆	脴	舀	甜	胡	舭	舲	航	舩	華	茂	荀
60	茉	苦	荐	学	荨	荽	荔	荘	菜	荼	虡	虤	虔	蚄	蚟	蚛	蚕	蚦	蚒	蚓
80	蚉	衎	衸	袠	袞	袡	袄	袦	贠	尋	訍	訋	訙	訖	趾					

Row 20	01	02	03	04	05	06	07	08	09	10	11	12	13	14	15	16	17	18	19
00		軓	軕	迒	迣	迹	迼	迥	郅	郎	酐	酞	酕	釛	釟	釞	釰	釓	閅	陠
20	陙	陓	陖	陷	雄	隽	飳	飋	偂	偙	偵	偄	偦	偒	偔	偱	偐	偻	偼	偘
40	像	偹	偨	偬	偷	冨	凑	减	割	剢	勔	堤	厕	叄	叅	啘	啌	啨	啭	啉
60	啯	啰	啝	啛	喜	啓	啓	啽	啚	啶	啸	嗯	啥	埪	埬	埯	埱	埦	埝	堅
80	型	埞	埦	埧	埨	堎	埅	壷	梦	够	森	奝	奞	奞	套					

Row 21	01	02	03	04	05	06	07	08	09	10	11	12	13	14	15	16	17	18	19
00		娆	娫	娃	婡	婼	婪	婡	婔	婮	婋	婫	婸	媘	婤	婎	婨	婇	婆	婴
20	婯	婵	婍	婳	娬	婙	婓	娩	媏	寊	寐	寈	寘	寃	宿	屛	屡	屦	崡	崊
40	崉	崌	崠	崈	崍	崓	崪	崕	崗	崐	崮	崣	崯	崘	崰	巢	崚	崛	帺	帲
60	幓	庎	庢	庶	庻	庺	弴	弹	彫	徕	徛	徖	匽	悐	惐	悳	惓	惆	惗	悪
80	悆	悡	悤	悠	惮	惘	惧	惧	惨	惞	戫	挈	掐	掋	揀					

Row 22	01	02	03	04	05	06	07	08	09	10	11	12	13	14	15	16	17	18	19
00		掿	掽	掴	掓	掤	掘	掳	掽	掭	掮	捷	掳	揭	掺	掁	掹	掽	掭	敊
20	敚	教	教	敍	竟	斎	断	旍	旋	旒	旙	専	既	既	晗	晷	晰	晧	朚	朙
40	朖	朘	桶	梞	梶	梘	梓	梐	梚	梞	梥	梢	梥	梁	梲	梄	梩	梛	梕	梆
60	棉	梀	梸	梹	梧	欲	欵	殍	殏	殼	毬	毦	氪	沓	淒	淃	淎	淐	淴	浸
80	淝	淳	淩	湉	淤	洴	済	淛	淜	淵	淺	淠	清	渌	淴					

Row 23	01	02	03	04	05	06	07	08	09	10	11	12	13	14	15	16	17	18	19
00		淲	渀	浸	渴	涉	渁	渗	渆	渒	焐	焲	焃	焇	焁	焒	焗	煚	焎	烝
20	羔	埊	犇	牸	犋	猚	猇	猎	琂	琰	琪	琎	琘	琜	琓	爽	甛	産	畡	畨
40	畄	署	痤	痞	痜	皐	皛	盔	盗	盗	盖	睉	睑	眦	眝	着	看	眞	硋	硑
60	硂	硇	硅	硋	硎	研	硂	硆	裀	祮	裎	秲	稀	稒	稇	秳	稚	栖	票	窅
80	窚	窓	窯	竡	筀	筜	筫	笛	筄	筨	笑	筅	粘	粓	粙					

Row 24		01	02	03	04	05	06	07	08	09	10	11	12	13	14	15	16	17	18	19
00		粧	宲	紝	絉	紑	紴	紷	紓	紭	紙	経	組	絇	絔	䑙	䑸	瓵	翎	翓
20	翆	翵	耈	䎱	秌	耝	聅	聉	联	聄	肅	胮	䏹	脪	脮	舦	䏲	脱	脨	脚
40	䏦	䐑	舐	䑴	芍	茝	苨	茰	茛	堇	茞	唠	莎	莑	莅	荅	莭	荓	莏	莫
60	萄	莅	莜	获	虘	虚	處	虐	蚲	蛆	蚔	蚤	蛩	蛛	蚌	袜	袦	袘	袏	袥
80	袩	袖	袊	衺	袐	覎	覐	覔	訃	訦	訷	訨	訥	託	訜					

Row 25		01	02	03	04	05	06	07	08	09	10	11	12	13	14	15	16	17	18	19
00		豞	訬	訠	詌	詾	訮	訨	訙	詅	谺	豇	豵	豘	貀	豰	貥	貮	貭	赦
20	赹	赾	赿	趑	趆	趁	趽	跅	跢	跀	跈	躭	躯	軖	軼	軪	軏	軙	軚	軷
40	軨	退	逓	逎	迴	逥	逓	郿	鄙	郒	郷	酦	酙	醉	釲	釰	釸	鈋	鈍	閂
60	閅	陡	陚	陗	陑	陮	陰	陦	陙	陷	雫	凔	飦	飢	黄	黒	亀	亁	乾	偡
80	偙	傈	傉	傊	傿	傻	兆	冕	冦	冪	凓	凘	凅	凒	凖					

Row 26		01	02	03	04	05	06	07	08	09	10	11	12	13	14	15	16	17	18	19
00		剳	剶	剩	剻	匬	卿	厨	厦	叅	喗	嗞	喗	喞	喖	喊	喛	喓	喂	喛
20	喠	嗌	呰	唇	喆	喥	嗑	嗙	喝	嗂	嗠	嗒	喞	喉	喩	圏	圓	堚	堰	塖
40	堼	堼	埢	堾	堦	堨	堺	堭	堢	壵	塙	奣	奩	臭	媨	媃	媂	媈	媡	媞
60	媘	媙	媙	媠	媉	媁	媖	媀	媩	媷	媑	媲	媙	媎	媼	鄉	媭	媭	媻	媢
80	媃	嫂	媣	嫡	媉	嫑	媍	嫫	媗	媪	媤	媠	媮	孰	寍					

Row 27		01	02	03	04	05	06	07	08	09	10	11	12	13	14	15	16	17	18	19
00		寓	尋	尉	尞	屡	属	嵄	嵝	嵉	嵈	嵊	嵂	嵛	嵍	崋	嵋	嵗	嵝	嵓
20	嵏	嵲	嵴	嵇	嵏	嵘	嵑	幇	幝	幈	廋	廌	廇	廅	弑	彊	弾	弻	弼	强
40	彰	彩	徨	徧	惁	惪	惦	愇	愢	愌	惢	惡	悳	惷	惒	愗	惣	愬	徭	愴
60	慃	慂	愲	愶	愼	愞	愠	惱	戞	戟	揢	揞	揦	揻	揃	揅	揨	揸	揵	揾
80	損	搭	揷	揑	敟	敪	敭	散	斮	旑	朞	晫	晽	晫	晿					

Row 28		01	02	03	04	05	06	07	08	09	10	11	12	13	14	15	16	17	18	19
00		晹	晣	晳	暁	晭	晚	晷	朧	朞	棭	棙	棝	椋	椗	椛	棤	棼	棫	棨
20	椂	楼	棰	棄	棊	椀	棡	椁	椘	椆	棏	椚	椮	棅	棿	棆	検	棃	款	歯
40	歸	歮	殔	殽	毷	毰	氰	毶	湷	湵	湇	湠	湅	湮	湈	湗	湞	湺	湾	湪
60	湰	湶	湽	湬	湭	湬	湆	湾	湙	湥	湗	湋	満	湘	湶	温	湶	湡	湌	焭
80	焱	焵	焬	焯	焝	焸	焹	焽	焞	焿	焫	焳	焧	焢	焚					

Row 29		01	02	03	04	05	06	07	08	09	10	11	12	13	14	15	16	17	18	19
00		焭	爲	犃	犂	犇	犕	猴	猸	猪	猬	猫	猗	猯	猨	琗	琭	琚	琙	琸
20	琈	琟	琔	琼	琙	琜	琿	瑉	琹	瓶	甤	甤	甡	畃	畆	畭	畱	疎	痒	痥
40	痺	痩	痼	痯	皔	皵	盝	盙	睸	睉	睉	睃	睪	睐	矞	矟	硞	碿	碍	硎
60	碰	碤	祦	祱	祹	程	祶	禄	祵	稏	稇	稃	税	稉	稘	稐	窅	窴	窘	竨
80	竩	竢	笭	笪	笙	笛	笹	笩	笓	笄	笔	笛	粉	粱	粧					

Row 30		01	02	03	04	05	06	07	08	09	10	11	12	13	14	15	16	17	18	19
00		粠	莽	粤	絴	絑	絙	緝	絠	絗	絬	絾	絤	䋈	絚	絝	䋚	䋞	䋯	絶
20	紝	絵	綔	翃	翎	毧	翥	聠	脁	腅	脻	𦝁	腈	腂	脫	腀	腐	胼	腊	皐
40	䑕	舄	舩	落	菽	萲	萘	萛	萖	菌	萀	萵	萔	䒴	萗	萠	萏	萈	萶	萂
60	萂	莧	萒	萓	虙	虡	蛸	蛡	蛢	蛋	蛣	蛕	蛮	蜹	衆	裃	裓	裥	裂	袿
80	袴	裑	裖	覎	覚	該	詆	誠	詛	詎	詘	訳	詗	詠	詂					

Row 31		01	02	03	04	05	06	07	08	09	10	11	12	13	14	15	16	17	18	19
00		詉	詝	詇	詾	詟	詈	谾	豉	豠	豞	豿	豾	貊	貹	貾	赹	赺	赻	赼
20	赽	趀	趄	趆	趋	趑	趺	跀	跇	跡	跔	跉	躰	躰	躴	軮	軲	軤	軳	軸
40	軳	輊	軸	辝	逕	逪	逨	逨	逶	逬	逰	逺	逺	遊	逿	逻	鄎	鄉	酙	酟
60	酠	釾	鈠	鉀	鈋	鈧	鈘	鉢	鈗	鉞	鈃	鉒	鉤	鈺	閖	閔	閑	閏	閒	隁
80	陪	陻	陿	隁	隙	陰	雄	集	雩	雉	雌	雹	雺	霓	雭					

Row 32		01	02	03	04	05	06	07	08	09	10	11	12	13	14	15	16	17	18	19
00		韭	靬	靮	靿	訌	韷	韵	飣	飻	飺	飰	飦	馵	骲	骯	高	髮	髡	廉
20	襄	傛	僘	僙	僋	傪	僥	僜	僳	備	働	冀	圖	劉	剬	剷	勦	勠	勧	剿
40	厰	厘	厩	疊	嗪	嘌	嗗	嗂	嗼	嗁	圕	塼	塬	臺	塚	塮	塡	塯	塩	塛
60	塠	堙	墊	夢	奰	奨	嫐	媼	嫎	媹	嫅	嫃	媺	嫆	嫐	嫕	嫇	嫱	嬖	嫫
80	娟	孴	孳	寍	寕	寚	寛	寖	尠	嵭	嵦	嵲	嵱	嵮	嵼					

Row 33		01	02	03	04	05	06	07	08	09	10	11	12	13	14	15	16	17	18	19
00		嵠	嵘	彚	彨	慈	愫	愰	慔	慣	愹	愙	慊	慆	愽	慍	慖	摯	搈	摝
20	搸	搡	握	撊	搙	搃	揖	搵	搉	搩	搷	撇	搇	搛	撑	搱	摆	搖	搊	搜
40	携	搲	搶	敫	敨	数	斅	斞	斲	晢	暃	暎	暻	暋	睹	暴	暝	暒	暠	暵
60	暍	槫	榫	榧	槑	楷	楸	槬	槵	榎	楶	槧	榆	榧	楼	榁	榓	楳	楂	榷
80	榏	楕	榅	榴	楞	榻	榠	櫻	榾	楡	槼	楽	歇	款	歱					

Row 34		01	02	03	04	05	06	07	08	09	10	11	12	13	14	15	16	17	18	19
00		歲	殜	殙	殠	毂	毀	毷	毹	氲	氳	滐	溰	溹	溨	滝	溳	溻	潤	溚
20	滝	滐	滆	滊	滜	溵	滌	滨	溇	滝	滚	滦	滢	滛	漏	溹	滙	滬	滩	滛
40	滵	煯	煝	煰	煈	熒	煊	煫	煍	熅	煐	煴	熆	熜	煌	煅	煑	熈	煭	牑
60	牐	牕	犌	獁	獂	献	獆	琗	琞	瑖	瑹	瑓	瑎	瑣	瑝	瑕	瑆	瑆	瑇	瑃
80	瑘	瑎	瑹	瑌	瑅	瑆	甀	瓶	甞	畽	畷	疊	痕	痖	睭					

Row 35		01	02	03	04	05	06	07	08	09	10	11	12	13	14	15	16	17	18	19
00		睛	習	盔	睖	督	睤	瞋	睘	碂	碐	碊	碄	碅	碖	碟	碋	碑	碒	碉
20	碍	碏	硂	碁	祾	禃	禇	祫	禇	禀	禊	禁	稝	稏	稇	稒	稝	稜	窽	窟
40	竧	竩	竪	筥	筢	筫	筥	筞	筓	筹	箸	筶	筋	筨	粷	粿	粮	粯	糒	粨
60	粰	綒	綐	綪	綊	經	綋	継	綕	綼	綇	綗	綱	綉	綘	綠	罝	罜	羣	翎
80	翑	翐	翗	耿	聋	腣	腪	腬	腏	脾	腜	腝	腵	腵	腔					

Row 36		01	02	03	04	05	06	07	08	09	10	11	12	13	14	15	16	17	18	19
00		脲	腽	腭	臺	辞	艁	蓮	蒄	莿	萺	菖	菓	萪	葳	菒	葤	萮	葜	淇
20	葕	菨	葄	葟	盇	葚	葐	蒃	葱	蒼	葬	荇	菑	虛	蚫	蚲	蜱	蛽	蛻	蛘
40	蛐	蛤	蛪	蛩	蝬	衕	裹	袌	覙	覗	觥	衛	觧	誏	誀	誧	詯	詥	誓	詸
60	訮	誈	詍	詗	詵	詾	詉	詧	豣	貐	貣	賍	貾	賉	趌	跭	跻	跰	踈	踈
80	躬	躲	躹	躱	軗	衛	軏	辤	辠	遂	遆	遈	遲	遉	遝					

Row 37		01	02	03	04	05	06	07	08	09	10	11	12	13	14	15	16	17	18	19
00		鄢	巷	鄘	鄓	鄕	酮	醛	酧	鉝	鉅	鈉	鉀	鉙	鉗	鈼	鉶	鉟	鉪	鉢
20	鉟	鉫	鉮	鋁	鉄	鉁	閚	閜	閙	隝	隚	隔	随	陷	隖	雁	雄	雄	雩	雹
40	雵	靖	靗	鞆	靿	鞊	韲	韮	韵	韺	頋	颫	飳	飲	飶	飷	飿	飵	餉	養
60	飧	餮	飻	馚	馸	髢	髟	魝	鳨	鳶	鳫	鳳	鴩	麁	鼓	僐	僙	僜	僘	僟
80	僡	僫	僤	僷	僩	僢	僞	僚	僋	潔	滭	剩	劕	劈	勣					

Row 38		01	02	03	04	05	06	07	08	09	10	11	12	13	14	15	16	17	18	19
00		勫	勢	匲	厨	厮	厰	叡	嗻	嘯	嗷	嘐	嘇	嘟	嘗	嗨	嘯	嘞	嘣	嘘
20	嘑	嘷	嘅	圖	墒	墩	墟	墚	墟	墈	墶	墣	增	墕	墸	墤	墦	塹	夐	夥
40	奬	嫆	嫧	嫙	嫤	嫦	嫰	嫯	嫚	嫩	嫩	嫩	嫝	嵊	嶄	嶍	嶆	嶋	嶌	嶋
60	嵷	幒	幓	廜	廐	廏	弊	德	徵	寨	慫	慧	慻	慬	慯	慖	慎	慂	慜	慁
80	慈	慠	慩	慽	慳	戳	戩	搖	搓	搌	摗	摼	撓	撗	摕.					

Row 39		01	02	03	04	05	06	07	08	09	10	11	12	13	14	15	16	17	18	19
00		摢	摱	撕	摖	搴	摔	撈	搼	摋	摵	攄	搗	摷	摿	搗	敱	新	暚	暥
20	暚	普	暗	曆	暷	暤	榏	槅	槈	榻	榲	槵	槵	榆	椅	槀	槀	槑	榟	槨
40	榼	槤	槮	樹	樤	槹	檅	槥	盇	槩	歀	歷	殯	滬	滰	滴	漉	漩	滲	漌
60	漝	漴	漨	漗	潡	漱	漋	漄	漑	漎	潊	熑	熎	熄	熋	熔	熥	熌	熜	熇
80	熒	熈	熙	犇	犪	犥	獖	獕	獥	獏	獔	瑬	瑥	瑪	瑚					

Row 40		01	02	03	04	05	06	07	08	09	10	11	12	13	14	15	16	17	18	19
00		瑫	瑨	瑤	瑮	瑠	瑣	瑴	甆	瘃	痳	瘇	瘟	皛	皣	皫	皺	盬	盡	暉
20	睫	睶	睵	瞟	睸	瞎	暖	睺	睘	暄	碦	碮	碸	碖	磇	碿	碱	磁	禋	禉
40	褚	褡	稹	稩	稸	稪	稫	稭	稬	稷	稻	稈	竮	竰	箬	箞	箙	箋	箒	箘
60	箣	箟	箓	箪	箢	粸	粷	粿	糁	粻	粺	綉	綍	綶	絣	緑	綨	綨	綫	縄
80	綳	緍	絟	総	綮	緊	綹	綱	罯	罱	罭	罳	羳	羵	羻					

Row 41		01	02	03	04	05	06	07	08	09	10	11	12	13	14	15	16	17	18	19
00		翗	翰	聛	聬	聡	翻	膁	膉	膌	膄	膓	艊	艗	艙	蒊	蒚	蒜	蒠	蓝
20	蓀	蓆	蓃	蓦	蒷	蓄	蒵	蒳	蓧	蔆	蓘	蓕	蓡	蒷	蓏	蓚	蒓	蜯	蜋	蜳
40	蜗	蜽	蜫	蝇	蛶	蜜	蜑	蜚	裚	裿	裀	裣	裹	裬	褀	褫	褚	褆	裥	褓
60	觧	誁	誃	誎	誏	誔	誜	誕	誐	誩	說	誂	誖	谿	語	誋	豉	豧	貕	賻
80	賧	賒	賔	趧	趚	趛	趝	趞	踑	踋	踈	踁	躴	躳	輀					

Row 42		01	02	03	04	05	06	07	08	09	10	11	12	13	14	15	16	17	18	19
00		辡	辢	遉	遚	遒	遡	遟	郲	鄚	鄎	醇	醅	醂	銥	銉	銃	錦	銭	銒
20	鉤	鉤	鉞	鋈	鋆	鋆	閒	閰	閣	関	閧	閪	隋	隑	隟	隔	隠	隖	隟	雇
40	雒	雜	霌	霓	静	靤	靤	鞁	鞃	頤	頙	頡	頕	頢	頸	颬	餃	餀	餁	餅
60	餐	餦	餫	駍	駐	駭	駰	駮	駾	駿	騂	騁	騄	馱	馶	駘	駟	散	骯	髹
80	髩	髡	髮	髯	髿	鬦	鬫	鬫	魀	魋	魵	鳪	鳮	鴈	鴈					

Row 43		01	02	03	04	05	06	07	08	09	10	11	12	13	14	15	16	17	18	19
00		麪	麽	黖	僱	僆	僷	儎	僪	僷	僅	僼	僾	儁	潹	澤	凛	劆	劒	勴
20	匳	厱	嗷	噇	嘭	噔	嘫	噋	噒	噣	嚗	噚	噐	嘫	噆	噍	嘷	噏	墢	墷
40	墽	墲	墶	墼	墵	墰	墪	墴	墤	墧	墘	嫯	嫾	嫨	嬉	嬆	嫖	嫺	嬀	嫢
60	嫺	嬓	嫣	嫷	嶐	嶗	嶌	嶑	嶡	嶏	嶐	嶘	嶢	嶛	嶕	嶠	巤	幫	幓	幜
80	幞	廡	徸	憖	憗	憥	憕	憈	憚	憣	憏	歷	憝	憝	慙					

Row 44		01	02	03	04	05	06	07	08	09	10	11	12	13	14	15	16	17	18	19
00		懯	懩	懃	憇	憞	憪	憶	憘	憜	懌	戠	戱	擊	撛	撎	撍	撔	撦	撼
20	撨	擊	擎	撹	擎	撴	撯	撐	撳	撿	擀	擆	暶	暳	暯	暫	暬	暽	暭	榴
40	樹	樜	樚	樼	樿	樋	樺	樵	樻	樣	樢	樷	樣	槃	樒	樚	樕	横	樫	樜
60	樇	樫	権	槹	樬	樬	樤	梟	槩	敵	歎	歡	歛	氳	漐	漂	漖	濆	潩	潤
80	潔	潛	潌	潜	潳	澧	潝	潘	瀧	滖	澁	澀	澗	潙	潴					

Row 45		01	02	03	04	05	06	07	08	09	10	11	12	13	14	15	16	17	18	19
00		熥	熮	熯	熼	熭	熧	熢	熫	熣	燧	燙	勲	牗	牕	犙	獐	璢	瓔	璖
20	璒	瑱	璄	璅	瑺	瑻	璓	璤	瓁	瓶	甂	瞇	甾	疐	瘪	皾	瞎	暟	皛	翁
40	磚	磓	磜	磒	磈	磂	禛	禟	禝	禞	穏	穕	穃	稭	稡	穂	穑	穊	稾	窰
60	篔	篺	篰	箾	篿	篙	箹	箴	箹	篼	箱	箴	篛	糒	糒	糗	糢	糌	糍	糂
80	糆	糖	糉	糇	槃	經	緉	綢	緇	緼	緂	緡	緐	総	縁					

Row 46		01	02	03	04	05	06	07	08	09	10	11	12	13	14	15	16	17	18	19
00		緆	緒	緌	緤	緾	緰	緞	緼	緽	緕	緵	総	緧	縂	緳	罰	羮	翧	瞅
20	聥	聡	聦	聨	聫	膔	膌	膒	膖	膓	艐	蕿	蕈	蕡	蔓	蓮	蓵	蔾	蔄	蒶
40	蔗	蔁	蔠	蔛	蔃	蔳	蔴	蔨	蕭	蔬	蔵	蔆	蔄	蕚	蔩	蝁	蝬	蝽	蝶	蝭
60	蝗	螎	衛	衞	褎	褏	褛	褸	覙	覞	觪	諕	諄	諌	諎	諔	諑	諗	諝	諡
80	諃	諂	諛	諁	諿	諣	謍	谿	豼	豬	貌	賝	賀	賨	賛					

Row 47		01	02	03	04	05	06	07	08	09	10	11	12	13	14	15	16	17	18	19
00		賮	賫	趦	趨	趤	趛	趥	踠	踽	踻	踪	踨	踕	楚	踦	躶	躹	躷	輢
20	輫	輧	輙	辤	遫	遳	遧	遱	遪	遨	鄹	醆	醌	銿	鋭	錴	錠	鋥	鈔	錦
40	鋔	鋖	鋈	鋚	鋭	鋳	錍	銙	銹	鋝	鋫	閦	閮	閲	闌	閫	隡	隟	隣	隥
60	雉	雊	雩	霆	霊	霓	鞇	鞉	鞏	韯	頪	頥	頤	頟	餇	餙	餔	駊	駃	駄
80	駢	駒	駞	駔	駠	骬	骶	骵	骭	髯	鬩	魷	魩	魲	魣					

Row 48		01	02	03	04	05	06	07	08	09	10	11	12	13	14	15	16	17	18	19
00		鮁	鳶	鳵	鴂	鴦	鴬	鳫	鳨	鴆	鳾	鳩	麄	麇	麪	麩	傑	儖	儫	像
20	儞	儛	劐	翪	䎗	叡	嗞	噧	噿	噻	觭	曆	噡	嚮	墄	壇	墍	臺	壇	壅
40	壃	壞	墻	壀	壄	壼	嬟	嬘	嬑	嬕	嬩	嬒	嬃	嬁	孃	嬖	嶦	嶶	嶤	嶫
60	廩	廲	彝	彩	徤	憷	懎	憹	憽	懏	懀	懚	懋	懟	懍	懷	懄	戲	擂	擁
80	擀	擿	擨	擩	擛	擨	擮	擈	擕	擕	曃	曇	曾	曦	曄					

Row 49		01	02	03	04	05	06	07	08	09	10	11	12	13	14	15	16	17	18	19
00		曞	暤	曁	朂	朥	朤	檽	檏	檼	檯	櫗	檮	檠	櫅	檞	橺	檊	櫃	櫊
20	輮	棶	槼	檍	檚	櫫	櫥	櫂	櫑	櫒	櫈	櫓	櫔	檁	櫋	隳	櫒	歘	歞	罄
40	磬	毦	氈	毯	漾	滌	濇	濜	澾	澲	濫	濍	澌	濂	澟	濇	澇	濵	熷	熛
60	熻	燹	燑	燌	燨	燀	燉	燌	燬	燓	燓	璛	璹	璠	璪	璢	璝	甗	甎	甑
80	瞜	癑	癓	癜	癭	癱	皞	暶	膊	矔	矉	瞖	矑	磃	磃					

Row 50		01	02	03	04	05	06	07	08	09	10	11	12	13	14	15	16	17	18	19
00		磖	磫	礐	磜	褸	禥	禩	頴	穓	穅	穋	穏	檠	竂	窻	竱	篅	簬	篬
20	篭	篟	糙	瀫	雜	糭	縃	緝	縩	縕	繇	緣	縱	臬	聜	聮	膯	臚	膞	臢
40	齎	膪	舘	舜	藹	蓐	蔲	薩	蕌	蘩	蔎	蔡	蕙	薀	蘐	蔄	蕚	蔬	蔦	蠊
60	蠦	螋	螽	蝙	蟉	螽	蟸	衞	衠	褭	覽	諄	譁	諹	諣	謰	謂	諿	謽	踰
80	踶	豎	貗	賨	賫	賶	贊	趦	趚	踐	踤	踽	踸	踼	蹠					

Row 51		01	02	03	04	05	06	07	08	09	10	11	12	13	14	15	16	17	18	19
00		輱	輰	輴	輭	轀	辦	辥	遞	遯	遹	鄷	醋	醎	醽	醞	醢	鉣	錊	鈹
20	錋	錞	錗	錜	錇	鑫	錄	鍊	鉥	鍫	黎	闕	闍	闞	闉	閷	閵	閱	閹	隨
40	隤	隸	雝	雞	雛	霆	霄	霜	霨	霧	鞜	鞓	鞴	鞘	穎	頪	頡	頿	頼	賴
60	頮	頯	頦	頹	顢	颸	館	餩	餠	餜	餹	韷	韐	騬	騋	駒	駪	駖	騂	騂
80	罵	鴦	髷	髑	鬂	鬍	鬻	魍	鮃	鮔	鮄	鮔	鮋	鮏	鮟					

Row 52		01	02	03	04	05	06	07	08	09	10	11	12	13	14	15	16	17	18	19
00		鮌	鮢	鮉	鮔	鮎	鯆	鮑	鮍	鴤	鴐	鳶	鵊	鵇	鴿	鶕	鵏	鵖	鴻	駉
20	鮑	鴻	鴎	鴅	麧	麠	麬	黕	黔	黗	齓	儀	價	儹	瀆	劉	匱	嚴	嚛	嚊
40	嚭	嚉	壈	壍	壐	壧	嫸	嬳	嬩	孇	嬱	孍	巙	巉	巆	巐	巇	巏	巓	巁
60	懛	懝	懜	懚	懞	懙	懱	攄	攦	攃	攀	擡	擥	攕	攇	斲	曒	曕	曚	壘
80	曑	曎	曗	曒	櫨	櫨	櫛	櫫	櫬	權	櫺	欂	櫰	櫹	欒					

Row 53		01	02	03	04	05	06	07	08	09	10	11	12	13	14	15	16	17	18	19
00		檰	櫲	櫱	櫼	櫺	櫼	櫞	櫻	櫟	歀	歜	歎	氈	濼	瀑	瀦	瀥	瀰	瀙
20	瀏	瀅	瀠	瀧	瀷	瀾	瀤	瀹	燣	燺	燩	爁	爈	爇	爂	爄	爅	爵	犨	犪
40	獵	獱	璧	璮	璫	璸	瓗	瓛	甐	甓	曈	癅	癉	癄	皣	皞	皬	矙	矘	矚
60	瞷	矡	礃	礐	礂	礏	礔	穡	穛	竇	竉	竂	竂	竲	竳	籒	籓	籔	籇	籗
80	籐	籑	糲	糰	糷	糴	繱	繴	繵	縅	繡	繼	繁	纘	翽					

Row 54		01	02	03	04	05	06	07	08	09	10	11	12	13	14	15	16	17	18	19
00		積	聴	膸	膓	艕	艁	蕎	蔡	蔆	蕘	薐	薫	薗	蘿	蔆	蕖	蛺	蟓	蟂
20	蟎	蟵	螇	螬	蠭	蝨	蝨	蟇	蠭	襀	襬	襌	襹	褻	褒	襝	襊	襭	覲	譑
40	謟	譈	謌	譅	譔	谿	豐	貏	貗	贍	賣	蹪	蹥	蹏	躹	輴	轄	輸	轁	鏣
60	鏚	鍝	鍩	鍴	鍽	鍮	鍻	鑒	鎾	鍈	鍓	鍟	鍨	鎵	鎦	鍪	闍	闤	闍	隯
80	隭	隲	雞	霆	霧	霧	霻	霭	霫	鞞	鞛	鞟	鞮	鞝	鞣					

Row 55		01	02	03	04	05	06	07	08	09	10	11	12	13	14	15	16	17	18	19
00		鞶	顂	頯	頷	頳	頿	顈	顊	顑	颾	飋	餜	餜	餢	餗	餞	騀	騇	騀
20	騃	騊	騂	騈	骻	骼	骽	髼	髿	鬠	鬴	魍	鮟	鮇	鮣	鮢	鮙	鮝	鵞	鵖
40	鵏	鵓	鵛	鵃	鵅	鵁	鼤	鼪	麯	黖	儯	儰	燁	龎	嚛	嚟	嚛	嚞	嚜	嚧
60	嚠	壏	嬻	嬫	嬪	嬨	巁	彍	彝	懤	懆	懟	擡	擓	擌	擘	擪	擧	攅	攕
80	擻	攜	擷	斀	檫	櫈	檷	櫋	檵	櫟	櫂	檿	櫉	檬	櫁					

Row 56		01	02	03	04	05	06	07	08	09	10	11	12	13	14	15	16	17	18	19
00		櫃	櫄	歷	歷	斅	濯	濖	瀇	瀐	瀂	瀓	燽	燷	燫	璹	璼	壘	癝	癛
20	癢	盫	瞸	瞴	瞹	瞺	矅	礨	礋	礆	礇	礊	礈	礂	礍	礆	礔	禯	禮	禬
40	穙	竵	箵	簥	簪	簶	簛	簡	簸	簣	糒	糦	糧	糟	縹	繢	繝	繏	繈	繛
60	罇	羴	翷	翻	翻	翾	耮	聽	聯	臎	臒	臈	轟	蘮	薁	蘩	蘩	薆	薻	藁
80	蘧	蘒	蟒	蟨	蟢	蟰	蟴	蟒	蟚	襆	襊	襎	襍	覽	覷					

Row 57		01	02	03	04	05	06	07	08	09	10	11	12	13	14	15	16	17	18	19
00		覴	譢	譤	謬	譔	譤	譚	讀	繇	謩	貚	貙	貜	賰	趬	趩	趯	蹘	蹶
20	蹴	軁	軁	轊	辮	遷	邊	鄘	鄭	醩	鏗	鏍	鎐	鎦	鎓	鎋	鎮	鎖	鐫	鐾
40	鐾	鎜	鬪	闟	雝	霶	露	韛	韉	韡	韙	韽	額	顣	顏	顡	顛	顋	顡	顚
60	飀	飂	飀	飃	饔	饎	饋	餡	饗	饈	饈	馤	騉	騡	騈	騌	騆	騐	髶	鬐
80	鬩	鯒	鯉	鯆	鯪	鯌	鯋	鯽	鯫	鵠	鵪	鶂	鵝	鵶	鵽					

Row 58		01	02	03	04	05	06	07	08	09	10	11	12	13	14	15	16	17	18	19
00		鼂	鶩	麠	麔	麧	麵	麮	黊	黿	鼥	鼦	鼿	囃	壠	壥	嬗	嬹	嬛	嬾
20	孼	寶	寶	屩	屭	巃	攋	攈	攊	攕	攑	旟	曏	曡	疊	曟	櫎	櫔	櫣	櫼
40	櫢	櫞	藵	櫜	櫥	櫏	櫍	櫒	穮	瀅	瀞	瀨	瀉	瀋	爄	爈	爕	爕	瓊	瓚
60	瓊	璻	覴	矆	矅	礯	礚	礠	禰	穳	穤	穪	竬	籄	籆	籓	籐	籢	籙	籚
80	糲	繆	繬	纏	繮	繱	臁	臏	舋	艠	艢	艥	艶	藒	蘱					

Row 59		01	02	03	04	05	06	07	08	09	10	11	12	13	14	15	16	17	18	19
00		蘳	蘐	蘞	蘄	蘊	虩	蠖	蠵	蟎	蠍	蠏	蠡	蠁	衞	覇	覸	覶	覿	譑
20	譢	譃	譌	貚	贋	蹻	蹸	躅	躇	躄	軄	軃	鏡	鏨	鐏	鏋	鏴	鏆	鏻	鏾
40	鏓	鐾	鏥	鐀	鏤	鏑	鏫	鏠	鏁	鐅	鐨	闞	隱	雓	雟	霱	霫	霺	鞨	鞴
60	鞤	韝	鞴	韜	韞	韲	韹	韸	顡	顣	飅	飈	饒	饓	騞	騘	騟	騘	騦	騗
80	髈	鬉	鬒	鬸	鯅	鰊	鯘	鰑	鯡	鯩	鯮	鰇	鯯	鵦	鶘					

Row 60		01	02	03	04	05	06	07	08	09	10	11	12	13	14	15	16	17	18	19
00		鶺	鴿	鷥	鶂	鴺	鶡	鴹	鵂	麢	黣	黧	鼆	鼀	黿	鼅	鼖	儽	儶	儷
20	匶	嚝	嬞	孅	孽	孍	孆	孾	巆	巕	巖	廳	攩	斆	曨	朤	曫	櫒	櫤	櫴
40	櫱	櫚	欖	欘	櫰	欕	殰	瀼	瀵	瀸	灂	爏	爤	爒	爏	爗	爟	爡	雙	犨
60	獼	瓐	瓌	瓓	瓑	瓗	疉	礑	穤	籋	籄	籀	糴	纀	纚	纛	纑	羻	翾	穫
80	聹	聻	聽	虆	藻	蘈	蘮	蘐	蘗	蘟	蘢	蘵	蘩	蘱	虇					

Row 61		01	02	03	04	05	06	07	08	09	10	11	12	13	14	15	16	17	18	19
00		蘒	蘔	蘏	蠘	蠒	蠈	襛	襧	襆	覰	譩	譢	譺	譮	譚	譡	譤	譥	譍
20	豒	贘	趭	躃	軆	鍱	鐟	鏢	鐄	鐗	鐈	鏨	鐏	鐕	鐞	鐂	鐚	鐛	鐧	鏊
40	鏖	隵	雜	雙	霳	霬	霴	霱	鞞	鞚	韐	韃	顛	飃	飂	饐	饍	饊	騯	騞
60	騤	騙	髗	髒	髈	髓	鬪	鬸	魓	魏	鰊	鰂	鰔	鰻	鰋	鰇	鰲	鰢	鰂	鰈
80	鰛	鰉	鰕	鰐	鯿	鰀	鰌	鰲	鶃	鶓	鶌	鶙	鶘	鶪	鶋					

Row 62		01	02	03	04	05	06	07	08	09	10	11	12	13	14	15	16	17	18	19
00		麡	麔	麅	齚	鼁	躡	嚂	壦	孈	亹	廫	巏	巁	彏	彏	懰	攑	攓	橙
20	櫾	灥	欚	欝	灌	灒	瀿	灍	灇	瓓	癨	癧	癪	矐	矑	礰	礲	礮	穲	穮
40	竉	竈	籉	籤	籑	籡	纈	纃	纅	纉	纎	纕	羄	艪	蘫	蘯	蘨	蘿	蘖	蘳
60	蘞	蘲	蠛	襲	覿	覼	讃	讆	贍	贑	贕	轜	醻	鑀	鑅	鑆	鑈	鑉	鑊	鑓
80	韇	霷	霿	韇	韡	韢	韥	顈	顚	飈	飉	飋	饏	饑	饕					

Row 63		01	02	03	04	05	06	07	08	09	10	11	12	13	14	15	16	17	18	19
00		馩	驆	驐	驋	髎	鬖	鬘	鬕	鬞	鰮	鰪	鰟	鱂	鱃	鰩	鷈	鶽	鷃	鷇
20	鷔	鷂	鷄	鰜	壜	廳	廲	黰	鼂	鼩	鼧	齩	囇	圞	孊	巓	彎	彲	懘	懫
40	戳	攧	攤	攡	曬	曮	櫺	欆	欇	灞	灩	爣	爦	競	籓	籯	籘	纙	纏	罎
60	矓	蘳	蠦	蠹	蠹	讁	讃	讀	讟	獵	趲	轊	轋	鑣	鑍	鑔	鑖	鑯	鑃	鑡
80	鑿	甐	霿	韂	韣	韽	顯	饆	饁	驑	驜	髝	鱇	鱅	鱞					

Row 64		01	02	03	04	05	06	07	08	09	10	11	12	13	14	15	16	17	18	19
00		鱎	鱅	鰺	鱉	鱉	鷗	鷭	鷸	黱	鼸	龐	劚	囑	囒	夔	巕	攋	攦	欏
20	欑	欐	欒	灙	灡	爜	犨	癯	礸	禷	籞	籱	蘻	虀	虈	虇	蠊	蠭	蠫	讈
40	讇	讐	豅	躝	躘	酇	鑶	鑟	鑤	鑴	鑯	鑷	鑛	鑽	鑹	鑥	霴	靃	韃	韄
60	顪	顬	顰	饔	馩	驜	贏	驝	鱂	鱏	鱝	鱠	鱓	鷿	鸀	鸂	鸍	鼷	齵	儺
80	廳	囒	囍	孏	欆	礸	穲	穳	纝	禶	禴	讑	贛	轜	醿					

Row 65		01	02	03	04	05	06	07	08	09	10	11	12	13	14	15	16	17	18	19
00		鐃	鑬	鑴	鑶	雥	韇	霺	韄	韤	饝	驞	鬖	鬤	鬭	魒	鱰	鱜	鱝	鱵
20	鱥	鸓	鸔	麢	麡	麷	黿	齀	龠	孿	戇	曯	欞	灪	爧	爤	籭	糷	虉	虌
40	虌	襸	蠣	讘	貜	貛	贜	躣	躙	讎	靉	霽	韉	顳	饙	驄	鸗	鱹	鱻	鸌
60	鸇	鸎	黵	鼈	讚	龣	戀	孌	護	欔	灦	礵	籯	蠜	讟	讆	躐	醾	鑺	钃
80	钀	鑾	鱳	驨	髗	鱴	黷	龥	爞	灩	爨	犫	虊	襴	讞					

Row 66	00	01	02	03	04	05	06	07	08	09	10	11	12	13	14	15	16	17	18	19
00		豓	轥	[illegible]	[illegible]	飍	飝	[illegible]	鬱	鸛	[illegible]	[illegible]	[illegible]	[illegible]	[illegible]	[illegible]	[illegible]	[illegible]	[illegible]	齼
20	[illegible]	纞	钄	驘	鸜	[illegible]	[illegible]	韊	[illegible]	[illegible]	[illegible]	[illegible]	[illegible]	鱻	[illegible]	[illegible]	[illegible]	靐	[illegible]	
40																				
60																				
80																				

CNS 11643-1992 Plane 4

Row 1		01	02	03	04	05	06	07	08	09	10	11	12	13	14	15	16	17	18	19
00		𠂆	乀	乁	乚	𡿨	丂	丩	乃	几	刂	㔾	巜	冃	凵	勹	卂	卩	孑	孓
20	尢	屮	忄	扌	犭	刄	丯	亖	仐	兂	冃	尖	刖	刐	乍	吧	产	丛	叱	冋
40	壬	矢	允	㕣	帀	开	不	氾	灬	亣	冈	艹	辶	丗	丫	缶	仄	佀	仢	任
60	兂	再	夰	瓜	凷	玎	卮	幼	扐	医	厈	尾	岁	叏	叽	谷	另	囚	囙	囘
80	先	压	夲	尔	层	户	屵	帆	羊	佀	扣	抖	甲	米	禾					

Row 2		01	02	03	04	05	06	07	08	09	10	11	12	13	14	15	16	17	18	19
00		罒	阢	阬	西	甬	辰	汞	迺	优	佤	伶	吏	伍	伛	佃	伎	似	兆	兵
20	矣	伞	冄	㕣	沁	刻	制	别	荆	刘	判	劢	劲	劧	劯	区	市	刋	即	所
40	厽	叒	兊	妥	言	吕	否	占	吁	托	寻	尒	奂	矿	好	妐	姿	奷	亏	宜
60	赤	尪	启	并	屽	岦	肖	巩	帄	帆	帚	兹	庥	后	幵	犽	弜	彵	往	忍
80	忖	忑	戋	扭	抻	拐	扚	技	邑	助	利	呆	歹	奴	壳					

Row 3		01	02	03	04	05	06	07	08	09	10	11	12	13	14	15	16	17	18	19
00		毕	沕	沴	癶	灸	牰	犳	狂	玔	玐	田	羊	肞	艻	芃	边	邦	邗	纫
20	阡	卵	乱	亢	佅	俶	伞	戾	冲	泯	刚	刮	剑	刨	刷	利	勑	旎	砌	助
40	励	劲	叵	叵	卲	卤	卸	吏	叟	吮	吨	吒	吠	呁	吟	呼	呚	咬	昏	呈
60	呀	告	坢	坃	垩	坙	奁	奄	夯	夾	奎	妷	敌	妑	妽	姆	孥	孖	宵	宋
80	齐	冠	尖	尬	尬	岙	室	劵	岓	岿	峁	岦	峨	岸	昆					

Row 4		01	02	03	04	05	06	07	08	09	10	11	12	13	14	15	16	17	18	19
00		帉	帊	帍	帙	帣	乘	纱	庎	延	弅	弜	往	怢	怖	忬	怄	忞	忟	忕
20	扈	拌	抪	拗	技	抐	挖	批	抚	斋	攼	攺	敌	斘	於	昇	昆	枕	来	杞
40	松	杀	改	欣	殃	叙	毡	派	汕	沵	灭	灾	抆	牰	犹	狃	狙	狐	犹	犯
60	玑	玨	瓬	畇	疫	疝	疠	登	盷	旬	昆	砚	秃	穸	罗	罖	芈	耴	肝	肌
80	股	臣	百	舡	臼	芊	芤	芓	芫	芙	苫	芇	芼	芝	迒					

Row 5		01	02	03	04	05	06	07	08	09	10	11	12	13	14	15	16	17	18	19
00		迁	迈	迗	迎	邗	郊	郝	邠	邳	邽	長	陀	陧	陈	崩	乳	哲	兹	枣
20	亩	众	侙	俄	俅	偛	俶	侍	侲	侮	金	兟	津	洛	洇	净	凬	凨	剎	刮
40	刣	刜	制	刿	刹	到	刽	勑	劲	匋	匍	卑	卣	卝	卻	卸	厈	叓	咸	哇
60	吰	咙	昭	呗	咃	哙	哘	哃	呢	垺	垙	抹	坺	坬	叁	垩	尌	垷	坰	娶
80	姓	卒	查	查	奔	套	奈	臭	扶	夸	奻	姑	妫	娍	婩					

Row 6

		01	02	03	04	05	06	07	08	09	10	11	12	13	14	15	16	17	18	19
00		娚	孡	学	乳	宐	导	尳	尮	尪	层	屃	屄	屇	岋	岯	岼	岜	岙	岂
20	峀	岾	峂	帑	应	庞	庢	庣	庠	庝	庚	弆	弡	彼	希	彭	怎	怂	忬	怢
40	怦	怰	怦	悔	怞	怂	怤	怟	恶	恮	戕	或	戋	扉	扊	拜	抗	挝	攲	歧
60	敚	敁	敓	敳	敧	昖	昔	昬	朊	柴	枬	枛	茉	柹	枞	柒	欣	欿	欤	欲
80	欣	欸	歮	殃	殁	殅	殌	殈	殶	毰	毻	沠	泎	泲	泭					

Row 7

		01	02	03	04	05	06	07	08	09	10	11	12	13	14	15	16	17	18	19
00		泅	流	沶	泒	泈	泺	炳	炒	艾	炎	炛	垩	脉	股	料	牞	牫	粉	犻
20	犬	狨	狕	猌	狘	狮	狭	玞	玫	瓷	盱	畇	畇	畁	畹	疔	疟	疢	瘚	盁
40	盂	盂	盼	盽	眈	盱	彤	眍	昇	矜	矤	砓	砭	秄	杓	秔	穸	空	窔	弃
60	紈	罕	罡	耈	耄	耓	肕	肥	肷	肬	朋	胣	肚	肹	肯	肩	臤	臽	舑	舟
80	舸	舣	芜	苆	芙	苴	芮	苹	芥	芫	芴	苊	芹	芸	苁					

Row 8

		01	02	03	04	05	06	07	08	09	10	11	12	13	14	15	16	17	18	19
00		芈	匡	衎	衍	迓	运	迹	进	邱	邿	邮	邾	郇	邛	郙	阬	阾	陉	陒
20	邑	剁	仯	侪	侼	佩	侨	促	供	俩	偶	修	冶	冞	泾	浸	剥	剌	剞	剬
40	刭	勆	勍	勈	匑	匙	匽	匧	匩	卣	卸	卼	厌	原	叕	叙	呼	哦	咔	咊
60	咝	哦	垴	垐	垩	夎	奍	奃	奘	姗	姞	娱	娞	娶	妾	妛	敞	姤	孨	孛
80	孪	宨	宦	宋	尯	尵	属	屋	眉	眉	屎	峴	峷	峕	峇					

Row 9

		01	02	03	04	05	06	07	08	09	10	11	12	13	14	15	16	17	18	19
00		帨	峠	衫	帮	帡	帼	扁	宦	彦	席	咸	弫	张	弇	骈	弯	往	徊	洛
20	徐	恶	恚	怨	恁	恈	恀	使	恼	悧	恗	恾	恄	恦	悇	恳	恶	态	悲	思
40	使	恎	悔	悦	戒	扂	挍	洲	拭	挒	插	捍	捆	批	佩	挤	掐	排	挨	挣
60	拚	敷	敢	敁	故	料	昕	昛	晙	昭	昌	昪	昔	脘	湖	梡	桴	柠	柿	栟
80	歌	歔	欿	吹	欿	歁	歮	殅	殊	殦	殓	毞	涅	洲	淋					

Row 10

		01	02	03	04	05	06	07	08	09	10	11	12	13	14	15	16	17	18	19
00		浃	涑	泽	泶	海	炦	烔	烰	省	再	埏	沼	洑	牸	牱	辈	狇	狭	律
20	狻	独	玻	琊	珇	瓞	瓴	瓩	瓯	瓶	瓴	牧	眭	畹	野	畢	留	疣	疢	疼
40	疔	疲	瘁	疻	皅	臭	皱	皲	盆	盈	昉	盼	眒	眖	眹	映	眮	明	盷	曼
60	県	眠	昏	矼	殺	矜	砕	砿	砐	砶	祆	祉	神	秅	秩	秺	秫	秺	烁	耕
80	耙	窦	窆	窭	穽	吧	戏	粔	紆	缸	罡	罢	罨	宜	群					

Row 11

		01	02	03	04	05	06	07	08	09	10	11	12	13	14	15	16	17	18	19
00		翐	翍	翊	翡	耇	者	耞	耡	耗	肱	胜	脉	胝	腁	胇	胋	舤	舡	舣
20	舦	舵	芸	茉	苴	苋	茾	苐	芸	茈	虖	虔	蚩	蚨	蚉	蚩	罗	衸	衩	衽
40	覀	觔	負	赳	趴	軐	軑	迭	逃	迺	迢	迌	郊	郄	邦	郁	郞	陈	陜	陕
60	陎	陒	半	亭	倥	侪	侚	倃	倊	侯	倷	偑	倠	兕	森	涵	剅	刭	則	契
80	剚	剭	刹	剒	劾	勈	匑	匣	匵	卤	厚	厡	厧	哷	哦					

Row 12	00	01	02	03	04	05	06	07	08	09	10	11	12	13	14	15	16	17	18	19
00		唔	唻	咏	啞	哩	啊	狢	啅	哾	迺	喜	啫	咺	唾	垸	埻	坶	坒	埒
20	尩	就	奝	奎	奄	娧	娣	娮	娟	娨	娐	娷	娶	孫	宦	寔	宷	宮	孝	寯
40	宼	窄	寀	宲	党	屜	屎	屢	孱	峠	峵	峽	崖	崐	崾	峔	崼	崩	峻	崖
60	峼	崜	峆	峵	崺	逝	峕	岑	巸	蚤	幗	峄	幰	幌	帑	庡	庰	庢	庚	弄
80	弳	弢	弸	彩	彭	徜	徚	徬	徫	徉	徬	復	後	涊	峃					

Row 13	00	01	02	03	04	05	06	07	08	09	10	11	12	13	14	15	16	17	18	19
00		怠	恒	慨	惚	性	悖	悅	恚	恣	惡	慌	悑	悏	悭	戫	戕	挐	挐	掌
20	拏	挼	搣	挋	拗	挮	挮	捍	捬	捣	掞	敍	敂	敉	敊	敕	敌	敉	敏	斖
40	斠	斱	旈	杲	晗	皆	栎	桊	栐	栙	梈	桗	栕	栿	桅	栮	桭	棄	染	桊
60	梅	欵	欵	欶	欯	欹	欹	殆	殺	殺	毬	毯	毪	毳	氀	洰	活	洎	浧	浕
80	流	涅	洶	烗	涿	奂	脅	狩	牂	膠	牌	牑	牯	犎	狽					

Row 14	00	01	02	03	04	05	06	07	08	09	10	11	12	13	14	15	16	17	18	19
00		猂	猄	猈	猀	狢	猒	猊	珚	琛	璽	瓝	瓪	瓶	畈	畇	畛	留	畫	疨
20	疪	痃	痂	痗	痔	痡	痔	瘋	痐	痕	痕	痼	痓	昧	皐	皍	皷	皸	皽	盄
40	盜	盓	盈	眝	眆	眡	眝	眗	眚	眛	眹	眰	眞	眾	矠	矯	矲	砆	砩	砷
60	砆	砌	砂	砦	砢	砵	砥	祩	袖	秭	窈	窣	窪	窩	窜	窗	竕	竦	竬	竪
80	笠	笋	笺	笑	笓	笻	笑	笇	絚	絪	絨	絲	絨	絞	絠					

Row 15	00	01	02	03	04	05	06	07	08	09	10	11	12	13	14	15	16	17	18	19
00		縻	綮	紼	綏	綷	縱	絲	缺	缶	罠	罟	罣	罢	羚	羘	羑	翕	羾	翍
20	翃	翤	翕	翇	耍	耑	耺	联	聐	聕	胠	胆	胊	胗	胻	脅	胭	胵	胉	胎
40	背	茸	肺	导	舌	荳	舲	舦	般	舥	舣	絶	茦	莖	茜	茵	茨	苗	茉	苹
60	荕	茚	茳	茾	莛	茾	荄	萸	茵	莠	萱	虓	虒	蚰	蚵	蚗	蚘	蚈	蚜	衕
80	袓	袡	袚	覂	弆	覝	覍	覞	觳	觵	訐	訒	訊	訔	訬					

Row 16	00	01	02	03	04	05	06	07	08	09	10	11	12	13	14	15	16	17	18	19
00		奓	谿	谹	谻	豣	貟	赵	赺	赶	跀	趼	軔	逗	建	迣	迨	速	逞	郝
20	郈	邵	郮	郿	郤	郞	臥	臥	陽	陼	陖	陗	陞	隺	飤	鼻	亳	俾	倣	傪
40	御	傳	倸	侖	冕	凘	凚	剳	剸	剪	剅	剾	劉	劆	劖	劊	劂	劓	勡	匎
60	匔	匑	匘	匬	勘	卙	卛	厁	卨	卾	厨	厳	原	唁	咳	唼	啯	啾	咽	唄
80	啯	啫	吼	唇	商	啺	啓	唽	啾	嗟	唽	埔	堵	埊	埞					

Row 17	00	01	02	03	04	05	06	07	08	09	10	11	12	13	14	15	16	17	18	19
00		堘	堅	堂	够	奞	奝	爽	婘	婚	婢	媄	堅	宿	空	寍	寃	寁	嶠	嶦
20	嵁	扁	嶼	嵤	嵿	峨	葛	崴	嶟	嵌	嶁	嶗	峴	蔵	員	棕	崆	嶇	幘	幓
40	帕	帽	弟	屠	扇	虎	庣	廖	廧	弢	徒	循	徬	徭	徯	徣	淞	徥	恩	恁
60	惈	悚	悎	悜	悛	惚	惓	悍	惧	悀	惚	惆	惂	悱	惵	悥	悟	惙	或	戰
80	戝	掊	掄	掐	掀	掫	掏	掕	掚	掯	掽	掾	捋	掟	掹					

Row 18		01	02	03	04	05	06	07	08	09	10	11	12	13	14	15	16	17	18	19
00		揩	掭	揚	捆	揔	撑	敊	敵	敨	敵	啟	救	敝	敋	儆	豉	寇	斲	旇
20	旒	旆	眼	晫	晒	晘	㬥	倃	晅	勉	朗	梈	梳	概	棚	桴	棒	桰	樓	棄
40	歕	欶	殘	殑	殺	殶	殼	殿	毆	毜	毦	毴	毲	毲	毹	塈	洸	淁	湃	湦
60	溝	滁	洭	渝	涠	涓	溝	浰	溜	浢	桼	涺	淙	淚	涇	淹	涸	浜	浞	原
80	焞	焌	焅	羡	焜	焫	覂	犖	牻	犍	犑	犃	犉	犃	犂					

Row 19		01	02	03	04	05	06	07	08	09	10	11	12	13	14	15	16	17	18	19
00		猆	猔	猄	猅	猣	猲	猈	猪	猧	猅	猹	猕	猍	猣	珹	豊	塁	琝	琭
20	瓰	瓶	瓸	瓷	甃	瓻	瓬	瓶	甀	晀	晔	痊	痛	痀	痳	痴	痰	痢	略	瘐
40	皱	皶	盎	盔	盡	睆	睦	睊	睯	睹	睟	睺	睆	睖	睜	矟	矝	矬	矲	矪
60	矫	硃	硐	硦	硻	硃	祬	桊	梚	梂	梄	桃	梁	格	案	梁	梆	桂	窔	窩
80	窂	窨	窅	竳	竟	笺	笞	笘	笶	笋	筏	筡	箳	筯	筰					

Row 20		01	02	03	04	05	06	07	08	09	10	11	12	13	14	15	16	17	18	19
00		粧	粝	粘	粫	粜	絘	絙	絧	絤	綖	絾	絻	綹	綮	綝	絅	絣	絫	罬
20	罨	罺	羓	羴	羷	翐	翍	翑	翓	翖	翭	翸	翲	聃	聒	聍	聳	胙	胖	膩
40	脂	脡	脛	脤	脟	脜	脞	脗	脥	脴	脿	腂	腄	腍	臺	舁	舃	艇	艆	艄
60	艴	苽	莟	莾	莬	莣	莕	莍	莔	莯	莿	菇	菍	菥	菁	菫	萒	萷	萻	菟
80	菘	菥	莖	茆	莾	菌	虒	虗	虘	蚣	蚭	蛅	蚰	蛤	蛛					

Row 21		01	02	03	04	05	06	07	08	09	10	11	12	13	14	15	16	17	18	19
00		蛪	蚩	蛄	蝆	蚮	蠱	衕	袈	衺	衸	袉	袘	袚	袖	袝	袮	覂	覝	覞
20	觃	覞	覡	觥	觩	觝	觡	觤	觧	訮	訣	訵	詎	詙	許	詀	詒	証	詾	谻
40	谽	谺	豉	豙	豜	豥	豣	豣	貀	貯	購	貶	賢	趄	趆	趇	趍	跊	跙	跡
60	跏	跺	跳	跽	躰	軏	軗	軚	軥	裹	遁	逞	逡	逮	逽	郙	鄙	郥	郲	郶
80	郷	郚	鄊	鄐	酭	酞	酹	酾	酏	酬	醒	釭	閎	陳	隉					

Row 22		01	02	03	04	05	06	07	08	09	10	11	12	13	14	15	16	17	18	19
00		障	陽	隼	雅	雯	彭	鞯	韭	韮	靡	颸	飥	高	亮	寇	僨	傐	傸	傆
20	傛	傜	傊	傀	傷	傜	僆	傻	傴	僰	凗	凕	剴	剩	剬	剷	剽	劇	劉	劆
40	剁	剚	剷	勏	勤	匔	匑	匰	匲	匳	厦	厲	叡	啻	喃	嗁	嗨	喋	喵	嗙
60	嘟	噔	嗽	喑	嘝	嘐	嚶	嵒	嚳	嚳	嚆	嘘	圚	堠	塴	墄	塓	塄	墆	塅
80	墡	墛	壼	墮	壝	壡	壨	夎	奞	奧	奰	敌	婚	媪	媜					

Row 23		01	02	03	04	05	06	07	08	09	10	11	12	13	14	15	16	17	18	19
00		嬮	寠	寘	寏	尅	尌	尋	尟	尠	尡	屇	屠	犀	屧	嵖	嵢	嵦	嵱	嶞
20	嵔	嵬	幍	巸	幄	幢	幡	幣	嵍	嵇	幫	廌	廎	廇	廜	廁	彉	彋	徖	徣
40	徬	徸	徤	慈	惷	惫	愐	慘	愼	慄	愸	愷	慄	偶	慣	懰	憧	像	慸	慷
60	戜	擊	揱	揬	揆	撽	揹	揆	揳	搓	揖	搜	揆	搬	搳	搮	搲	搳	搢	搖
80	搵	摠	敫	樕	豰	敼	皷	敜	敳	敾	救	敼	斲	斱	晞					

Row 24		01	02	03	04	05	06	07	08	09	10	11	12	13	14	15	16	17	18	19
00		㫾	睔	晁	晷	昪	昼	㫷	晧	脝	柢	椄	棭	梎	梙	梚	梱	梠	棙	棗
20	棐	棸	棨	椕	椉	欪	欶	欷	欲	欿	歮	殍	殔	殗	殛	殜	殘	殙	殑	殤
40	殠	殶	殸	殹	毪	毯	毱	毹	毻	涳	淠	淕	淶	淲	淴	淸	淢	淰	淦	淣
60	淫	淜	淄	淑	焨	焣	焯	焱	焲	焴	焷	焦	焭	焫	爲	爳	犂	犃	犈	犄
80	犆	犌	犎	犇	犊	猎	猈	猇	猑	猫	猸	猹	琁	琊	瓠					

Row 25		01	02	03	04	05	06	07	08	09	10	11	12	13	14	15	16	17	18	19
00		瓪	瓶	瓵	瓻	瓼	瓽	瓾	甡	甤	甥	甦	畬	畯	疏	疌	痃	痆	痏	痁
20	痊	痎	痑	痙	痚	痛	痠	皴	皵	盝	盼	眼	眹	眽	睎	睅	睈	睋	睆	睇
40	睺	睩	睧	晢	睯	睥	睪	睫	睬	睭	矬	矱	硧	硩	硯	硩	硰	祴	祷	禼
60	秼	稑	稍	稌	稓	稇	稙	稰	稘	窔	窋	窘	窔	窒	竦	竧	笁	笛	笭	笯
80	笨	笩	笫	笮	笰	笴	笲	笳	筫	筬	粘	粩	粣	粦	粪					

Row 26		01	02	03	04	05	06	07	08	09	10	11	12	13	14	15	16	17	18	19
00		絜	絊	絁	絉	絖	絏	紲	絞	絓	罝	罤	罟	羠	羜	羦	翀	翄	翇	翈
20	翎	耞	耕	耛	耠	聍	脰	脡	脧	脹	脨	腊	脪	腂	腃	脝	腦	腩	腸	腰
40	腻	膛	豚	腽	臭	舑	舤	舥	舦	舨	舩	舭	莁	莀	莫	莻	莶	莿	菀	菁
60	菂	菨	菩	菲	菭	菮	菰	菴	菹	菸	菻	菾	萀	萂	萆	萈	萃	蛇	蛐	蛑
80	蛓	蛒	蛙	蛘	蛙	蛢	蛤	蛩	衖	衭	衯	袳	袴	袵	裥					

Row 27		01	02	03	04	05	06	07	08	09	10	11	12	13	14	15	16	17	18	19
00		覂	覘	覗	覕	覙	觛	觞	觝	訷	訹	詎	詓	詑	詷	詐	訣	詖	評	詏
20	詒	詄	詅	詇	詉	詍	詌	詗	豞	貁	貂	貯	貱	貶	貵	貹	貺	趃	趁	趄
40	趆	跀	跂	跈	跉	跊	跍	跐	跒	跓	跔	跇	軯	軶	逤	逯	逳	逷	逽	逿
60	鄐	郰	郱	郲	酖	酡	酤	酣	酧	酩	釬	鈇	鈊	閖	閕	閗	閜	隊	隄	隇
80	雂	雄	雲	雳	雴	雷	靬	靪	靭	靰	靸	頍	頎	頏	颪					

Row 28		01	02	03	04	05	06	07	08	09	10	11	12	13	14	15	16	17	18	19
00		颫	餅	餀	餃	餇	餈	凱	偳	傋	傐	傚	傛	傞	傟	傪	僧	僉	僊	僬
20	凓	剺	剶	剷	勦	勴	勸	匒	匑	匙	匯	厤	厨	厩	厭	喣	喥	喭	喯	喷
40	喺	嗂	嗃	嗄	嗅	嗆	嗈	嗋	嗏	嗐	園	塕	塡	塧	塰	塳	塴	塶	塷	塸
60	夅	奨	奪	媲	媿	媾	嫄	嫁	嫆	嫐	孯	孰	孱	孲	寗	寘	寙	寠	寝	寯
80	尞	嵯	嵰	嵳	嵰	嵩	嵭	嵲	嵴	崔	嵻	嵾	嵯	嵼	嵿					

Row 29		01	02	03	04	05	06	07	08	09	10	11	12	13	14	15	16	17	18	19
00		幌	幏	幐	幏	幍	幐	幒	幑	幓	幐	廌	廍	弑	彁	彂	彃	彄	徫	徧
20	徲	愳	愂	愋	愅	愇	愊	愓	愶	惄	愍	惷	愚	戠	戡	戦	截	毅	搓	搙
40	搷	搸	搹	損	搽	搾	摑	搞	搊	擊	摆	搃	敼	敨	敦	敹	敽	敺	敫	敯
60	敳	敱	敻	斀	斂	斚	斛	斮	旐	旎	旓	暌	暑	暊	楧	楨	楲	楩	楫	楢
80	楸	楺	楾	楶	楳	楱	榕	榜	榔	榛	榫	歀	歄	歅	歇					

Row 30		01	02	03	04	05	06	07	08	09	10	11	12	13	14	15	16	17	18	19
00		歋	欶	殜	殨	殩	臭	毨	毪	毮	毤	毰	氂	渻	滓	滙	溮	淠	湫	滝
20	渚	消	溭	潸	湝	溆	滊	溼	滮	渺	溲	溕	滽	湞	浩	清	煟	萛	畝	燉
40	焰	照	焘	煔	煠	煏	煇	煸	猫	猒	獮	猹	猶	猫	猳	臭	猛	瑚	豎	瑙
60	瓢	甆	瓿	瓶	甈	瓶	瓶	瓶	甌	戡	睬	睞	睭	睥	睅	畫	畊	腥	痞	痙
80	瘏	瘯	瘎	痵	痳	瘵	瘭	瘍	瘷	瘝	瘥	瘨	瘥	瘆	皠					

Row 31		01	02	03	04	05	06	07	08	09	10	11	12	13	14	15	16	17	18	19
00		皵	睚	睆	睕	睟	睳	睮	睙	睗	睒	睿	睯	瞖	瞔	瞓	睻	瞓	矝	矨
20	矬	碕	碑	硪	碊	碱	硻	碢	碠	碊	碏	碌	碑	碯	碖	碑	碅	禙	禂	禣
40	禒	稇	稡	稒	稑	稐	稧	稲	稖	稰	窴	窭	竫	竱	竰	竨	竩	竮	竪	筥
60	筠	箟	箽	箳	箝	篁	箶	箭	箹	箻	箽	箪	粽	紗	緦	緒	緗	緐	緊	緅
80	緂	綄	緆	緐	緢	罾	羜	羸	羻	翊	翝	翛	聕	腷	腺					

Row 32		01	02	03	04	05	06	07	08	09	10	11	12	13	14	15	16	17	18	19
00		腪	腟	腜	腤	腩	膝	腱	腷	腨	腬	膱	腭	艆	艃	艅	莿	荐	莪	莪
20	菒	菶	菦	萘	萲	葅	萸	葚	葛	葃	葍	葿	蒨	蓤	蒽	葾	萮	葎	蓸	蒗
40	蒒	蓛	蒟	萻	葉	萲	葙	虜	蛛	蛝	蛚	蛺	蜥	蜻	蜍	蜥	蜤	蜏	蜇	蜙
60	蜡	蝍	蝗	衙	裿	裓	裍	裧	裬	褅	褂	觤	誂	誎	誚	誳	誄	誆	誩	諀
80	誷	諃	諫	諀	諍	豋	豿	貘	貇	貆	貎	貑	貒	貍	賆					

Row 33		01	02	03	04	05	06	07	08	09	10	11	12	13	14	15	16	17	18	19
00		賍	賋	趂	趄	趚	趙	趦	趛	踙	軫	輇	輂	輪	辡	遰	遫	遙	遻	酨
20	鄗	鄋	鄭	鄨	鄹	鄸	醂	醆	醁	醓	醔	鍂	鍗	鍈	鍒	鍗	鍓	鍏	鍦	鍜
40	鍦	駣	駣	閜	閮	閫	閳	閸	閵	閷	閾	闀	隍	隋	雜	雃	霅	霝	霛	霣
60	靰	鞍	鞎	鞀	鞅	鞆	鞁	鞈	頫	頛	頪	頩	頲	頦	頨	頮	頳	颶	颽	颼
80	颾	颼	飀	飴	飶	飿	飵	餂	餟	餅	餗	餕	餘	餟	餱					

Row 34		01	02	03	04	05	06	07	08	09	10	11	12	13	14	15	16	17	18	19
00		骫	稾	鬶	鬿	魄	魗	魧	魫	魜	魣	鮇	黕	僚	傢	儆	僫	僁	僻	僣
20	僬	僟	奈	僨	僝	僷	僯	剸	剹	剷	劄	劅	劂	劇	劕	劓	劗	勩	勢	匔
40	匱	厥	噎	嘍	嗔	嘀	嘢	嘝	嘒	嘥	嘞	嘒	嘐	嘼	嘗	嘊	圖	墂	墳	墑
60	墁	墤	墜	墫	墹	墓	壿	奮	奭	嫌	嫓	嫞	嫭	嫂	嫭	嫱	嫪	嫳	嫛	嫚
80	嫯	嫫	嫬	嫸	寋	寍	寑	尌	尟	尠	屫	屩	屪	屬	屭					

Row 35		01	02	03	04	05	06	07	08	09	10	11	12	13	14	15	16	17	18	19
00		嶂	嶆	嶈	嶙	嵲	嶂	嶇	嶉	嵷	嶊	嶓	嶅	嶄	嶓	嶆	嶆	嶁	嶐	嶍
20	幑	幑	廘	廙	廕	廞	廱	彰	徙	徛	徧	徱	徾	徿	慁	慦	慚	慛	慸	慣
40	慓	慝	憀	慴	慺	慹	慨	憲	憁	憎	憋	憏	戚	戤	摛	摚	摳	摝	摭	撇
60	摧	撐	撻	撽	搗	撓	撥	撚	撊	擺	敹	敿	敼	敲	斢	晝	暽	暿	曌	暤
80	朄	槲	槮	槢	槶	槸	構	樫	樏	滕	槻	槃	櫻	樌	樞					

Row 36	01	02	03	04	05	06	07	08	09	10	11	12	13	14	15	16	17	18	19
00		槝	樛	榔	檜	楠	尌	槇	槁	歀	欶	欲	歎	翌	殦	殘	殟	殩	殨	魂
20	殑	殼	毀	毁	毦	毰	乾	毷	毹	毺	毻	毼	氈	滐	濔	激	漊	消	漎	瀘
40	溵	漆	潧	臬	滂	溅	漂	滄	滅	澍	滏	温	滜	熣	烊	燁	煬	燋	穀	熜
60	豩	牮	牔	牗	犨	犪	犤	犪	犙	獄	殼	獶	獮	獵	獷	獼	獵	瑑	瑱	瓟
80	瓬	瓶	甃	甄	甌	甎	甑	甒	甓	睬	睼	暘	睳	瘞	瘴					

Row 37	01	02	03	04	05	06	07	08	09	10	11	12	13	14	15	16	17	18	19
00		瘌	癘	瘬	瘖	瘚	瘃	瘦	瘺	瘸	瘏	瘱	瘻	瘤	瘰	皞	皠	皶	皺	皵
20	皷	盞	盬	眝	睧	睞	睠	睦	睺	睳	睸	瞁	瞦	瞍	睹	瞙	瞜	睃	瞗	瞩
40	矡	矲	猴	矯	碌	磹	碏	碊	碍	碵	碣	磸	碶	磣	禍	種	稽	稜	碭	積
60	穑	稧	穢	穀	粹	窶	竪	豎	箢	箈	箮	箬	簍	篊	箴	箣	箕	箵	範	箳
80	箥	箫	糍	糲	粿	綹	緌	緄	緀	絅	緒	綼	綜	緫	綅					

Row 38	01	02	03	04	05	06	07	08	09	10	11	12	13	14	15	16	17	18	19
00		綷	緫	綦	緘	緟	羫	羻	羿	翐	翑	翗	耥	耤	耧	耩	耨	耰	耫	聙
20	聜	聡	聦	聫	腽	膅	臃	膗	膉	膞	膭	膸	膹	膻	膯	膱	膬	膭	膆	觳
40	膟	膰	膞	膕	膾	舔	舓	艕	艙	艘	艗	莘	萓	萫	萻	葼	葽	蒃	蒇	蒐
60	蓍	蓪	蒫	蒸	蓍	蓄	蔦	蒎	蓁	蓏	蓇	蓋	蓑	蓖	蓛	蓣	蓯	蓰	虢	虧
80	蜫	蜮	蜯	蜺	蜡	蜰	蝃	蜳	螯	蝋	蝊	蜷	蝋	蝂	蜂					

Row 39	01	02	03	04	05	06	07	08	09	10	11	12	13	14	15	16	17	18	19
00		蝂	蝗	蛒	衙	衚	裎	裞	裱	褄	裷	裾	褀	褂	褆	褌	褎	裰	褋	褷
20	覆	覞	覡	覢	觓	觕	觖	誄	誆	語	誆	誒	誋	誏	誖	誧	誐	誃	誘	誗
40	誚	誤	誒	誰	豨	豪	豩	豬	豫	豥	貌	豢	貋	賕	賓	賔	賖	經	趄	趑
60	趙	趖	趜	趟	趡	跿	踃	踊	踒	踖	輁	輑	輦	輥	輶	農	遯	鄙	鄘	鄝
80	鄢	鄤	鄥	酮	酪	鉵	銁	銂	銤	銽	鋓	鋠	鋺	闓	闕					

Row 40	01	02	03	04	05	06	07	08	09	10	11	12	13	14	15	16	17	18	19
00		闅	閔	開	隉	隕	隔	隃	隁	隩	傷	雂	霋	霎	霙	霤	霤	霫	霵	霶
20	靁	靦	靧	靨	鞀	鞄	鞃	鞉	鞎	鞊	鞍	鞘	鞕	鞔	鞖	鞗	鞚	鞛	鞟	鞞
40	頛	頝	頠	頡	頢	頣	頦	頨	颭	颮	颯	颰	颱	颳	颲	颵	颶	餕	餂	餑
60	餅	餦	馲	馳	駆	駈	駔	駘	駗	駙	駚	駛	駜	駝	駟	駢	駣	駤	駥	駦
80	鳫	鳯	鳰	鳱	鳲	鳳	鳴	鳵	鴃	鴄	鴅	鴆	鴇	鴈	鴉					

Row 41	01	02	03	04	05	06	07	08	09	10	11	12	13	14	15	16	17	18	19
00		僇	劁	劃	劄	劉	劈	劌	劈	勦	勢	嘈	嘘	嘲	嘸	嘵	嘹	嘼	器	墱
20	墥	墭	墱	蚤	墺	嫶	嬃	嫸	嬈	嫚	嬰	嬰	嫵	孻	孺	寯	寭	寮	寰	寱
40	寷	嶦	嶭	嶰	嶲	嶰	嶴	嶳	嶵	嶶	嶷	嶺	嶼	嶽	巂	廠	廡	廣	廥	廧
60	廚	彈	彉	彋	彍	彰	徹	徼	徾	憄	憌	憍	憓	憔	憚	憛	憜	憝	憞	憠
80	憪	憮	憯	憰	憳	憶	憸	憺	憼	擃	擁	擄	擉	擋	擌					

Row 42		01	02	03	04	05	06	07	08	09	10	11	12	13	14	15	16	17	18	19
00		攄	搿	擳	摟	撜	擽	撝	擒	敹	㪍	斀	斅	斛	斢	斷	旟	旞	瞟	膔
20	膋	榱	橽	槺	檇	橄	樬	榟	櫒	槵	榯	樎	槐	榾	穎	檕	樸	橤	槃	榔
40	槲	櫨	虢	獉	歁	歆	殰	殨	殦	殨	殻	毹	氊	氋	氌	潓	澘	瀆	潡	瀰
60	瀵	瀄	瀾	潩	潫	澁	潴	潳	濳	濬	濕	澔	澘	潀	熇	爕	爴	牗	犓	犞
80	犤	犢	獂	犨	獂	獜	獥	獖	獳	獮	獋	獖	獡	獻	璥					

Row 43		01	02	03	04	05	06	07	08	09	10	11	12	13	14	15	16	17	18	19
00		璓	璭	瓎	瓟	甀	甂	甈	甋	暛	瞵	畾	疁	瘣	瘷	瘜	瘸	瘨	瘟	瘵
20	瘯	瘺	瘨	瘵	瘚	瘥	瘳	瘴	暜	皶	暗	瞸	瞘	瞩	暥	瞡	瞋	瞝	瞜	瞣
40	暚	暪	暰	瞠	瞢	瞥	畀	瞜	瞥	矠	矡	矞	粮	碚	磚	碉	碥	磒	磒	磟
60	磤	磤	礐	禣	禢	稯	穅	穛	穓	穟	穠	穢	穋	穭	穤	穮	竇	窞	窾	落
80	筷	箈	箻	箺	簄	簹	篈	篍	篃	篟	篘	篥	篈	篧	篡					

Row 44		01	02	03	04	05	06	07	08	09	10	11	12	13	14	15	16	17	18	19
00		篁	篕	篑	篰	簐	簘	簇	簍	簉	簂	簟	簆	簑	簁	篡	簆	簃	糌	糍
20	糲	粟	糷	糧	縍	縼	縺	縿	縜	縿	縭	繐	縶	繫	繂	縩	繓	繩	繫	繼
40	罿	羶	羷	翬	翻	翷	翾	翾	耼	聱	聵	膑	膪	膵	膣	膭	膘	臌	膯	膠
60	膠	膧	膬	膴	膏	膸	臲	臨	臷	艕	艘	艙	艞	藻	蕿	蒁	蔕	蒔	蒨	蒸
80	蒳	蒱	蒩	蒩	蒐	蒟	蒷	蒖	蒬	蒳	蓾	蓭	蓳	蓷	蓳					

Row 45		01	02	03	04	05	06	07	08	09	10	11	12	13	14	15	16	17	18	19
00		蔋	蔩	蔳	蔸	蕏	虡	蜐	蜊	蜨	蜜	蜡	蝹	蝿	蝍	蝶	蝨	蝼	蝍	蝹
20	蟵	蟼	蟌	蟓	褑	褑	褸	褐	褚	褆	褍	褔	褓	褳	褸	褼	褾	褸	襘	襢
40	覙	覡	覞	覟	觪	觱	觩	觴	觶	觶	觹	觬	觵	諕	諪	諷	諿	謌	謐	謉
60	謏	謑	謅	謗	謖	謚	謢	諿	諩	豄	豂	豰	豩	豯	豰	豲	賥	賩	賥	賾
80	賨	趍	趙	趠	趨	趞	踂	踋	踕	踙	踁	踍	踙	踞	踨					

Row 46		01	02	03	04	05	06	07	08	09	10	11	12	13	14	15	16	17	18	19
00		踊	踛	踺	踹	躄	躖	輐	輊	輇	暈	輨	輙	輪	辟	逮	遾	遛	遺	遬
20	達	遳	邍	鄘	鄃	鄬	鄸	鄙	鄱	鄲	醘	醨	醞	醫	鉾	鈔	鋆	鋈	鋣	鋸
40	閕	閿	閬	隸	靅	靓	靧	鞟	鞔	鞍	鞌	鞦	鞎	鞮	韄	韂	頻	頣	頣	頸
60	頟	頫	頳	颬	颭	颮	颯	養	餅	餘	餌	餛	餝	餧	餞	餟	餔	駭	駮	駯
80	駺	骲	骸	骯	骹	骴	骿	髆	髀	髍	髩	髯	髻	髲	鬇					

Row 47		01	02	03	04	05	06	07	08	09	10	11	12	13	14	15	16	17	18	19
00		髩	鬅	鬼	魋	魅	魒	魂	鮏	鮑	鮞	鮬	鮘	鮖	鮫	鮮	鮍	鮗	鮯	鮿
20	鯊	鯍	鯎	鯇	鯡	鯐	鳶	鴪	鴻	鴆	鴾	鵈	鵃	鵂	鵌	鵁	鵐	鵑	鵬	鵬
40	鶲	麌	麗	麬	麮	麵	麷	麧	麼	黀	黗	黔	黕	默	鼎	鼏	儑	儷	儳	儻
60	僢	僵	僸	儔	劆	劉	劇	劕	劒	劕	嗤	嘬	嘁	嘞	嘓	嘔	噗	嘀	嘯	噪
80	囍	噵	嚇	嚪	嚭	圝	墀	墇	墬	墻	墣	墶	奭	嫸	嫞					

Row 48		01	02	03	04	05	06	07	08	09	10	11	12	13	14	15	16	17	18	19
00		嬂	寴	巁	嶂	嶭	嶏	巇	幢	襱	彔	鬉	廣	廛	㢊	羿	彏	徲	㦖	戫
20	儃	㥏	意	憃	惷	懤	憁	懕	蕙	㥞	擂	擂	擳	擺	擒	撁	擩	擫	擉	擇
40	擤	敼	敹	斁	斀	蔪	斯	旘	曂	嘯	暩	曾	曌	曓	朁	檍	樻	櫢	櫇	櫼
60	檞	櫗	麭	橡	㮚	樬	檽	樣	檏	樽	歅	歆	歔	殗	彭	殰	殲	殨	磬	毲
80	氈	氉	氀	毰	潒	湏	瀘	漓	潛	滅	潡	澫	漌	潎	潭					

Row 49		01	02	03	04	05	06	07	08	09	10	11	12	13	14	15	16	17	18	19
00		瀉	瀀	燍	燂	燛	爵	犓	燧	熏	爏	犕	牘	犜	犢	獟	獛	獚	獮	獵
20	獽	獶	獿	瓎	璙	璏	璑	璿	璃	瓢	瓥	甇	甂	甌	甀	瞙	瞜	瞞	瞬	療
40	癠	癥	瘤	癉	癢	瘸	瘯	瘮	癕	瘺	發	發	皟	皠	皵	皽	皺	盧	盬	盭
60	瞞	瞮	瞣	瞶	瞜	瞰	瞜	瞭	瞧	瞻	督	瞟	矁	矔	矕	磘	磜	磯	磦	磼
80	礔	礚	礡	礞	禠	禣	禮	禯	穆	穮	穆	穇	穢	穄	穗					

Row 50		01	02	03	04	05	06	07	08	09	10	11	12	13	14	15	16	17	18	19
00		穊	窔	窩	窻	窋	窳	窶	竂	箬	篘	篛	篇	篝	篠	篚	篭	篘	篾	篸
20	篙	簪	簹	篼	篔	篬	篣	篜	篳	篸	節	篺	篾	簌	糗	糠	糖	緂	緪	緆
40	緌	緦	縦	纍	縘	緜	縠	罷	羅	罿	羫	羥	羲	羶	翕	翷	耩	耬	聹	聦
60	聵	膾	膷	臆	臄	膻	臂	膭	臎	臉	膝	膐	膼	臩	臺	艖	艜	艗	艞	艟
80	蒹	蔙	蔌	蔞	蕣	蔏	蔆	蔮	蔯	蔄	蔭	蔪	蔫	蔢	蓵					

Row 51		01	02	03	04	05	06	07	08	09	10	11	12	13	14	15	16	17	18	19
00		蕺	蕮	蕋	蕢	蕻	蕒	蕖	蕤	蕙	蕈	蕭	蕾	蕩	蕷	蕅	蕽	蕰	蕮	蕐
20	虢	虧	虩	虪	虡	螠	蝙	螓	螆	螃	螆	螡	螏	螅	螱	螌	螌	螬	螵	螢
40	螣	蠡	衛	衝	衡	褏	褡	褯	褰	褦	褪	褠	褫	褲	褵	覦	覥	覨	覢	覶
60	覯	覘	覡	觷	觶	觵	觸	觺	觹	謏	謕	諫	謎	謖	謚	謟	謧	謥	謦	謨
80	謪	謫	謬	謼	豰	豵	貐	貒	貓	賉	賊	賍	賏	賧	賮					

Row 52		01	02	03	04	05	06	07	08	09	10	11	12	13	14	15	16	17	18	19
00		趍	趤	趨	趥	趧	趪	趬	趮	踺	踧	踵	踁	踛	蹍	踶	蹈	軀	輸	輪
20	輯	輰	遬	遷	鄒	鄉	醅	醙	醚	醍	醋	醔	醃	醄	醫	鋟	鋸	錿	鍏	銹
40	錭	鍃	鉼	闇	闍	闌	闒	闑	閞	隤	隦	隟	隭	雜	霍	霆	霤	霹	霍	霓
60	靨	靧	鞔	鞕	鞧	鞅	鞝	鞬	鞣	鞦	鞴	鞨	鞶	韽	韺	韴	頮	頫	頻	頯
80	頤	頪	頳	颺	颸	颼	颽	飆	餮	饞	餬	餳	餴	餺	餵					

Row 53		01	02	03	04	05	06	07	08	09	10	11	12	13	14	15	16	17	18	19
00		餴	餇	餘	骳	骴	髓	駛	駐	駒	駟	猽	傌	駧	骻	骽	骹	骺	骿	髁
20	髹	髲	髮	髭	髽	髾	髫	髺	鬉	鬷	鬺	魾	魼	鮇	鮓	鮁	鮌	鮊	鮉	鮗
40	鮒	鮞	鮍	鮏	鮐	鴂	鴃	鴒	鴐	鴝	鴑	鳴	鴎	鴟	鴇	麁	麈	麨	麵	麮
60	麩	黏	黏	黓	默	黽	鼩	鼱	齎	儥	儌	儸	儰	儭	瀆	劇	劐	劗	劙	勩
80	勸	嘌	嚵	嚝	嚈	嚶	嚳	嚽	嚋	嚎	嚍	壇	壒	壘	壞					

Row 54		01	02	03	04	05	06	07	08	09	10	11	12	13	14	15	16	17	18	19
00		奞	𡤢	嬦	嫵	嬪	簝	𡾋	嶸	礊	對	幩	幨	幰	歸	𢕟	𢕪	懫	懕	懗
20	懝	懢	懱	攕	擊	擎	擨	撲	斅	斆	斢	斣	曦	曓	檈	槢	贏	權	欆	櫶
40	櫞	櫩	櫼	櫝	櫛	櫵	歆	歔	檗	礔	殬	毃	氉	氈	氍	瀐	瀎	瀕	瀵	瀼
60	辮	瀞	瀩	瀵	瀰	爊	爦	爕	爏	爾	牄	犝	犤	獬	獚	玀	獴	獻	瓂	瓕
80	瓎	甍	甑	甐	甗	甋	甒	甔	瞫	曆	皪	甜	瘽	癀	癚					

Row 55		01	02	03	04	05	06	07	08	09	10	11	12	13	14	15	16	17	18	19
00		癀	癠	癇	癁	癀	瘄	皡	皜	皷	盭	盬	盫	盨	矰	矯	瞚	瞵	瞟	瞦
20	瞶	瞸	矘	罺	穜	礵	礦	磻	礁	礒	碭	礬	磵	礛	穗	穡	穮	穳	穯	穲
40	穙	穬	穧	竁	窩	竇	竂	竄	竴	竤	竵	篔	篕	篛	篰	篞	篻	簃	簅	簈
60	簉	簀	簌	簇	簍	簐	簜	簙	簪	簫	簬	簸	簹	糲	糰	糭	糷	縮	纏	縳
80	繳	縿	繄	繒	罿	羆	羵	羶	翱	翿	耩	耪	耰	耱	耬					

Row 56		01	02	03	04	05	06	07	08	09	10	11	12	13	14	15	16	17	18	19
00		聜	聽	聻	聯	聵	膵	臁	臂	臛	臚	膹	舋	臞	膿	艱	艢	艣	艠	艡
20	艤	艷	薑	藁	蘑	鞸	藦	藮	藲	藟	薨	藤	藭	藪	藨	蘡	藯	薇	藾	蘊
40	薳	藹	蔃	蘁	虧	蠐	螊	蠨	蟈	蟔	螞	蟵	蠘	蟬	蠑	蠚	蟲	蠐	蠙	蠓
60	蠜	蠼	蠍	蠯	蠶	衞	褽	襦	襪	襹	襨	襱	覞	覯	艫	觹	觽	謑	謎	譋
80	謞	謚	譅	譩	譽	譟	蹓	豋	貙	貗	賗	賟	蹇	趚	趢					

Row 57		01	02	03	04	05	06	07	08	09	10	11	12	13	14	15	16	17	18	19
00		趦	趨	趧	趪	趫	蹗	蹁	蹎	蹓	蹸	蹥	蹠	蹑	蹳	蹻	軆	轁	轃	轄
20	轀	轌	輯	轚	遾	邅	邆	鄗	鄹	醢	醨	醯	醴	醶	醰	鋳	鎬	鏩	鍄	鄆
40	鍬	鏓	鏚	鏟	闤	闦	闧	闋	闛	闟	闞	闠	闢	隮	隸	雘	雚	雛	雝	雞
60	霂	霏	霚	霝	霠	霤	靧	靪	鞎	鞚	鞠	鞏	鞔	鞗	鞜	鞠	鞴	韍	顤	頣
80	頼	頜	頞	頓	頣	頲	頹	頫	頴	頭	颸	颹	颺	颼	飀					

Row 58		01	02	03	04	05	06	07	08	09	10	11	12	13	14	15	16	17	18	19
00		颸	飄	飃	飆	飇	餍	饕	餸	餰	餹	餿	駿	騂	騄	騇	骯	骽	髁	髆
20	髈	髊	豪	髟	鬉	鬊	鬘	鬛	鬙	魒	魑	鮃	鮇	鮧	鮔	鮳	鮵	鯛	鯎	鮊
40	鮒	鮎	鮟	鮼	鵂	鵅	鵟	鵝	鵡	鵳	鵿	鶬	鶮	鷂	鶶	鶻	鷁	鶡	鷍	鷑
60	鷹	黏	黏	黖	黟	黿	鼳	齡	鼽	齊	齎	儴	儓	億	儴	儴	儢	礨	勴	蹈
80	嚌	嚟	嚛	嚝	嚵	皰	囑	嚥	嚙	嚓	獱	奮	嫽	寡	巁					

Row 59		01	02	03	04	05	06	07	08	09	10	11	12	13	14	15	16	17	18	19
00		廫	彲	辯	懇	懇	戀	懢	懾	懇	懟	懕	懲	攄	擻	攋	攞	攥	攕	攂
20	擿	攖	擂	攕	擟	斀	斆	斅	斸	旟	曚	曖	曨	暴	櫈	櫪	櫨	櫪	欃	欅
40	樸	櫜	櫫	櫹	櫾	殲	毄	氄	氌	氍	瀀	瀨	瀙	瀾	瀶	瀷	瀸	瀻	瀺	瀦
60	瀞	灑	灂	灇	瀧	爆	爕	爚	辦	犩	犪	玃	獮	璽	璺	瓀	瓟	瓥	甖	甗
80	甄	蹊	甿	疆	疅	癔	癠	癈	癰	癕	癘	癛	曖	皇	皸					

Row 60		01	02	03	04	05	06	07	08	09	10	11	12	13	14	15	16	17	18	19
00		醰	盬	盭	瞕	矃	瞲	矆	瞸	瞮	礜	䁐	矎	礃	礡	礚	礛	磈	礏	穡
20	襗	穯	穨	櫜	櫛	竈	竂	竁	簴	籦	簻	籓	簛	籈	簃	簎	篲	籑	簽
40	簮	籛	簝	籓	䉓	籉	籊	籋	籗	籚	䉢	籀	糩	糦	糣	糔	糳	糨	糤	糯
60	繰	繓	繥	繎	繅	繀	繏	縹	繻	罾	羄	罼	羉	羶	羻	羵	羷	羱	聸	翻
80	耰	耭	聸	臛	臖	膞	臱	闛	艓	艐	艥	艚	艛	艴	蘔					

Row 61		01	02	03	04	05	06	07	08	09	10	11	12	13	14	15	16	17	18	19
00		蕟	藉	蕺	蕬	藮	蓺	䕙	稨	穓	䕯	蘅	蘼	蘢	蘛	蘙	蘱	䖘	麚	廣
20	蟐	蟞	蟜	蠘	蟮	蠂	蟍	蟳	蝨	蟓	蠤	㠋	畿	衞	𧝝	褢	襘	襭	襏	襀
40	襹	襩	襴	襸	襢	襦	覿	覸	覶	覴	觹	譊	譅	譂	譀	譃	譈	謏	讐	譍
60	譥	譺	誶	諡	譢	徾	蹕	豑	貗	貙	獽	貚	貐	賿	趬	趯	趲	趭	趱	蹳
80	躯	蹹	躤	蹩	蹵	躉	躄	躖	躞	轅	轏	轕	轓	轁	轚					

Row 62		01	02	03	04	05	06	07	08	09	10	11	12	13	14	15	16	17	18	19
00		轞	邆	醯	醶	醲	醱	鍷	鍹	鎶	鍺	鏪	鍴	鍡	鎃	鐸	鏴	鎪	鐓	闊
20	隮	霬	霤	靧	霡	醹	鞗	鞾	鞻	韣	鞺	韐	鞹	鞼	鞬	鞧	鞲	韝	韘	頣
40	頥	頳	顂	顎	顭	顩	顊	遰	颾	飀	飉	飃	飋	餧	餻	䭠	餷	餪	䭔	餸
60	饍	餵	饈	馘	馧	駏	駁	騚	騝	騍	驋	騲	騹	驆	騷	驊	騊	騼	骫	髀
80	髺	鬅	鬈	鬋	鬖	鬞	鬏	鬙	鬗	闠	灈	魌	魖	魓	魐					

Row 63		01	02	03	04	05	06	07	08	09	10	11	12	13	14	15	16	17	18	19
00		鮔	鯘	鮛	鯆	鯅	鮷	鮑	鮬	鮺	鯘	鯊	駚	鷖	鷙	舄	鵖	鴨	鶚	鴗
20	鷞	鶸	鶅	鵙	鵭	齱	麜	麳	麷	黋	黇	黕	鼃	鼉	鼔	鼕	鼘	鼪	鼭	齖
40	齞	儽	勩	匵	噭	嚩	嚭	嚫	噫	圞	嬰	嬬	孂	寴	寯	寱	廬	巏	巑	巄
60	幱	彏	彲	彇	懝	憨	懠	懮	懥	戲	擓	擹	攕	擿	攄	擧	斣	斶	櫍	櫉
80	櫑	櫖	櫋	櫼	欎	檵	櫛	歟	毊	瀇	澗	潤	瀾	澩	爔					

Row 64		01	02	03	04	05	06	07	08	09	10	11	12	13	14	15	16	17	18	19
00		爇	爑	燸	犪	獹	甓	瓆	璺	環	璣	豓	甗	齰	曘	癗	癦	癜	癯	瘨
20	癋	癠	瓕	疇	盪	矃	矙	頷	辬	矒	甥	磜	矱	礡	礉	穠	穧	穥	穛	篹
40	籃	竇	竈	竆	簺	簹	簶	簸	簲	簷	簿	篾	簜	簩	籅	籌	箐	籐	糫	糒
60	糗	粲	糓	糲	縿	繐	繴	繸	縸	緆	繏	繟	繶	繇	繅	繁	罽	罾	羄	羉
80	翷	聹	臕	臑	臏	赯	蘨	蘭	蕑	蘡	蕌	薰	藪	舊	麛					

Row 65		01	02	03	04	05	06	07	08	09	10	11	12	13	14	15	16	17	18	19
00		螠	蟠	蝸	蜁	甕	簠	黨	蠡	褶	䙡	襏	覼	覷	覶	覹	覻	艐	艥	艒
20	艞	艢	艡	艣	譑	譱	譄	譆	譋	讉	譮	譶	譿	譾	讇	讗	讛	譣	豶	獜
40	貛	貕	貜	贖	趫	趩	趮	蹱	蹥	蹻	躚	躝	躐	鬄	軄	轈	轙	轒	轜	轛
60	邅	獶	遹	邃	鄷	醽	醷	醑	醣	醼	鋺	鏉	鏾	鏊	鏓	錊	鐝	闤	闟	靃
80	雝	靇	霼	霖	霎	鞔	轉	韛	鞳	鞨	韉	鞥	韞	韈	鞟					

Row 66		01	02	03	04	05	06	07	08	09	10	11	12	13	14	15	16	17	18	19
00		韻	鶲	謍	頰	顈	顂	頪	顅	䫗	顗	顙	顣	顊	顐	顖	顚	颸	飀	飂
20	飅	飃	餦	餰	餺	餸	饎	饂	髾	馠	馞	騨	騙	騠	騴	騛	騬	騷	騣	骸
40	髃	髃	髇	鬠	鬃	鬡	鬟	鬆	鬄	魋	鰟	鮻	鯢	鰄	鯺	鯌	鯭	鯮	鯩	鯠
60	鰛	鰍	鰝	鰯	鰦	鰰	鰵	鱂	鰲	鶢	鱑	鰔	鰳	鷺	鶞	鶡	鵬	鵳	鵰	鵧
80	鴿	鼬	麩	麌	麐	麖	麰	麱	麲	麷	麴	麨	麳	黧	黐

Row 67		01	02	03	04	05	06	07	08	09	10	11	12	13	14	15	16	17	18	19
00		鼭	鼵	黵	黢	堯	鼛	鼶	齋	齙	齲	齡	獵	龔	儲	儡	劚	嚱	圝	壧
20	孁	孆	寠	巇	巘	懶	懺	懵	廙	徽	儳	懇	懮	懵	懚	懿	懇	懰	攢	攥
40	撜	撲	擮	擻	戲	斅	櫶	櫂	櫞	櫍	欄	櫄	櫺	瀝	瀎	瀓	瀾	瀷	灖	灃
60	瀸	瀨	瀯	燿	瀡	爊	爕	獼	獻	獵	獮	獿	甌	疊	癙	癃	皺	皪	矇	矓
80	矂	矙	矖	矕	礡	礑	礛	穎	穖	穲	穳	竊	竉	籀	籚

Row 68		01	02	03	04	05	06	07	08	09	10	11	12	13	14	15	16	17	18	19
00		籡	籓	糯	繾	纗	纅	罍	聺	臙	臢	臡	艭	艬	虆	蘲	蘻	蘸	蘱	蘠
20	蘞	蘛	蘴	蘢	蘜	蘋	蠨	蠦	蠸	蠹	蠰	蠿	蠼	蠱	蠡	襼	襹	襶	觼	觷
40	讈	讕	讓	讖	讘	讙	讞	贕	贒	贘	趲	趰	趮	趯	趲	趪	趬	躔	躝	躘
60	躉	躑	躚	躟	轥	轞	轠	鄺	酈	醶	鑯	鑶	鑳	鑸	鑹	鑽	鑾	钁	钂	鑷
80	闥	闢	闞	隴	霮	霳	靇	靃	靄	靅	靆	靉	韈	韊	韞

Row 69		01	02	03	04	05	06	07	08	09	10	11	12	13	14	15	16	17	18	19
00		鞨	鞻	韃	韄	韅	韉	韠	韡	韣	韤	鼇	顡	顣	顛	顪	顃	顟	顢	顳
20	贅	颼	飋	颵	飄	饕	饛	饡	饞	饜	饗	饑	驊	驎	驒	驙	驢	驥	驫	鶾
40	驄	髗	髕	鬐	鬙	鬘	鬞	鬟	鬤	鬲	鬹	鰤	鰮	鰿	鱊	鰑	鰨	鰥	鰶	鱀
60	鰷	鱝	鱢	鱓	鱋	鶫	鷥	鶺	鷄	鷊	鷐	鷍	鷝	鷞	鷡	鷥	鷧	鷩	鷯	麠
80	麷	麯	麝	麤	黻	黷	黸	黹	黺	黼	黽	黿	鼂	黯	黲

Row 70		01	02	03	04	05	06	07	08	09	10	11	12	13	14	15	16	17	18	19
00		齇	齛	齹	齋	齝	齟	齣	齤	齧	齣	齨	龜	儳	儺	儸	孿	孌	囈	囍
20	嚽	囆	壩	孆	孎	巏	巑	巕	廱	彏	戄	攣	攫	攩	攭	斅	斆	斄	欐	氍
40	灟	灡	灚	灪	灥	灩	爙	爞	爟	瓕	瓙	瓛	甗	癵	矔	癰	癯	癲	矘	矙
60	虧	矕	曯	礸	礹	礴	礶	禴	穱	穳	竷	竸	籧	籩	籫	籭	籯	籮	籰	籱
80	簒	籑	糷	纅	纏	纐	纕	纖	纗	纘	罏	罍	躐	聽	耱

Row 71		01	02	03	04	05	06	07	08	09	10	11	12	13	14	15	16	17	18	19
00		耀	臁	臎	臟	臘	臛	虉	虈	虌	虃	虆	蘧	虇	虊	蠖	蠗	蠛	蠕	蠯
20	蠵	蠚	襳	襺	譸	譳	譿	讅	讇	讕	讗	讘	讚	讛	讟	讜	豒	豷	貜	贙
40	趯	趲	趱	躚	躣	躤	躠	躡	躦	軉	轕	轗	轝	邎	酆	醽	醾	醿	釁	釂
60	鑦	鑴	鑵	鑻	鑼	鑽	钀	钃	镵	闤	闠	隵	雥	靈	靋	靌	靎	靍	靏	韇
80	韂	韀	韄	韉	韊	韛	顬	顴	顳	顲	顱	顥	顧	飍	飌

Row 72		01	02	03	04	05	06	07	08	09	10	11	12	13	14	15	16	17	18	19
00		颾	饝	饆	饋	饘	騯	騺	騷	驃	驀	騉	騋	騣	髊	髗	髎	鶾	鬞	鬏
20	鬙	鷪	鷽	魌	鰿	鰪	鰝	鰦	鮻	鰫	騰	鱄	鷲	鶪	鶺	鶬	鶡	鸁	麡	麠
40	鼜	麧	麮	黼	黿	麶	麷	鼕	黰	黱	黮	黭	黯	黴	黷	黻	鼖	鼛	鼥	鼨
60	鼭	齃	齄	齅	齆	齈	齾	龕	囑	孏	巘	巙	巚	巕	巗	巎	巏	巑	巐	巒
80	欇	欈	灃	灉	玁	瓛	甗	矔	矕	矖	矙	礸	礹	禶	穳					

Row 73		01	02	03	04	05	06	07	08	09	10	11	12	13	14	15	16	17	18	19
00		穲	竊	籑	籒	籓	籔	籗	籚	纕	纙	纚	纝	罍	羉	聶	臛	臝	艭	艷
20	蘵	蘶	蘷	蘸	蘺	蘻	蘼	蘽	蠃	蠇	蠈	蠉	襶	襹	觀	觻	觽	觾	讂	讄
40	讅	讆	讇	變	讔	趲	躞	躟	轠	轣	邎	醾	醿	闤	雥	雤	靋	靌	靎	靏
60	靃	韇	韈	韊	韏	韣	顆	顑	顲	饏	饖	饘	饙	驈	驋	驙	驖	髗	髖	髕
80	髓	鬝	鬟	鬢	鬣	鬤	魑	魒	魖	魘	鱇	鱋	鱍	鱒	鱌					

Row 74		01	02	03	04	05	06	07	08	09	10	11	12	13	14	15	16	17	18	19
00		鷙	鷭	鷯	鷺	鷩	鷲	鷷	鷼	鸀	鸆	鸉	鸃	鸊	麢	齫	齴	齳	黶	黸
20	黳	鼊	鼲	鼉	鼘	鼙	鼱	鼶	齂	齃	齇	齈	儺	儻	儸	囐	囍	廱	巘	彏
40	攜	攡	攦	攣	攭	斄	灖	灙	灚	欆	瓖	瓹	矘	瘮	癅	矐	矕	矗	玂	礵
60	籑	籲	籫	籮	籯	籱	籥	糵	糷	纖	纗	纘	纚	纞	罏	罐	罆	聵	臟	艫
80	虉	虋	虌	蠸	蠹	蠺	蠽	蠾	蠿	衋	衋	襶	讀	讜	讟					

Row 75		01	02	03	04	05	06	07	08	09	10	11	12	13	14	15	16	17	18	19
00		豅	贙	趯	躝	邁	酆	鑐	鑹	鑸	鑼	雞	韉	顝	顲	顴	飅	饡	驖	驌
20	鸐	髍	髕	髏	鬅	鬈	鬻	鰍	鰤	鰽	鰼	鱉	鰽	鱢	鱦	鷩	鷮	鷯	鷬	鷫
40	鷞	鷥	鷽	鸍	鹼	鹽	麷	麶	麼	黀	黐	黐	黧	黫	黯	鼇	鼈	鼈	鼶	齒
60	齇	齈	齎	齏	齗	齞	齘	齟	齧	齺	囂	囈	巎	巏	巕	攍	欉	灇	灋	玁
80	矡	癰	癱	矙	矖	穳	籆	籊	纅	纆	纔	羅	麗	虈	蠶					

Row 76		01	02	03	04	05	06	07	08	09	10	11	12	13	14	15	16	17	18	19
00		蠱	蠹	蠶	蠹	襵	襶	讓	趲	躍	躤	躪	邐	釂	釀	釁	鑪	霴	霵	礶
20	韤	韥	讚	顛	顯	顪	飂	飆	饟	驝	髁	髏	鬡	鬣	鬠	鬤	鬟	鬻	鬺	魑
40	魋	魒	鰄	鰈	鰒	鱠	鱷	鱵	鷚	鸆	鸇	鸉	鸌	鸐	鸊	鹹	麟	麶	黌	黷
60	黟	黸	黲	黳	黶	黷	黸	鼷	齳	齴	齵	齶	齾	齹	齺	龞	龕	巖	壤	歐
80	歐	灃	灉	曭	曮	矆	矍	穭	穮	籦	糲	纑	纓	虆	蠬					

Row 77		01	02	03	04	05	06	07	08	09	10	11	12	13	14	15	16	17	18	19
00		觀	觼	讕	躩	貗	趯	趲	躩	闟	闠	靎	霹	韉	顣	飌	饟	驪	驟	髒
20	髗	鬤	鬢	鬭	鰭	鱝	鸌	鶴	鸐	鸏	鸔	鹻	麟	麶	黐	黷	黲	黳	黵	鼉
40	鼕	鼶	鼸	齤	齸	齵	齹	齺	齻	龠	龥	匶	寱	欞	歎	氈	灄	灝	灥	籆
60	巖	欗	蘮	鼇	艫	韇	鑶	鍥	靊	韉	飀	鑴	驨	鬛	鸕	鸔	鼉	麡	黐	纂
80	齇	孈	孏	攊	灆	礶	籧	纗	纞	虈	蠤	虆	蘾	襹	讙					

Row 78	00	01	02	03	04	05	06	07	08	09	10	11	12	13	14	15	16	17	18	19
00		[illegible]	[illegible]	[illegible]	[illegible]	[illegible]	[illegible]	[illegible]	[illegible]	[illegible]	[illegible]	[illegible]	[illegible]	[illegible]	[illegible]	[illegible]	[illegible]	[illegible]	[illegible]	[illegible]
20	[illegible]	[illegible]	[illegible]	[illegible]	[illegible]	[illegible]	[illegible]	[illegible]	[illegible]	[illegible]	[illegible]	[illegible]	[illegible]	[illegible]	[illegible]	[illegible]	[illegible]	[illegible]	[illegible]	[illegible]
40	[illegible]	[illegible]	[illegible]	[illegible]	[illegible]	[illegible]	[illegible]	[illegible]	[illegible]	[illegible]	[illegible]	[illegible]	[illegible]	[illegible]	[illegible]	[illegible]	[illegible]	[illegible]	[illegible]	[illegible]
60	[illegible]																			
80																				

CNS 11643-1992 Plane 5

Row 1		01	02	03	04	05	06	07	08	09	10	11	12	13	14	15	16	17	18	19
00		ㄣ	ㄥ	乙	𠃊	㔾	𠂇	丩	𠄎	凵	马	廿	屮	丑	厺	干	屯	心	少	巨
20	卂	仐	从	仈	宂	凼	𠚣	切	叻	匃	卯	厄	殳	叉	艮	吃	玊	屹	岂	𢎘
40	朩	歹	毛	爪	王	亥	弗	乱	𠆭	早	冋	夙	由	刉	庀	刅	朸	尥	本	夅
60	庄	芦	刻	肉	叱	另	妣	孔	宂	尪	召	叫	开	幻	弘	㣆	忆	户	乳	扒
80	此	卣	毌	汴	汉	年	夹	犳	犰	而	聿	艼	邙	阠	阨					

Row 2		01	02	03	04	05	06	07	08	09	10	11	12	13	14	15	16	17	18	19
00		阪	阞	阢	自	曲	伒	伶	弁	完	冲	刯	刿	刋	刭	刟	韧	劮	励	劯
20	匃	甸	匌	匼	亞	卌	芈	厍	屏	厍	厚	厎	反	叹	叐	吠	吐	吩	吕	呇
40	囘	囪	妖	妏	示	尪	辰	带	岦	君	召	岂	岁	巛	弝	帍	帙	帉	帐	彬
60	甫	庇	安	弥	弛	代	彸	忏	忹	忕	忋	忣	怮	忟	戕	扯	判	抒	抙	抨
80	扐	扶	抓	旱	束	杍	氿	独	犽	犮	犾	犿	疙	癿	矶					

Row 3		01	02	03	04	05	06	07	08	09	10	11	12	13	14	15	16	17	18	19
00		禾	肶	肚	肷	肌	芇	言	言	豕	邗	邙	邜	邪	阣	阺	邻	丙	伐	侀
20	佡	尧	合	岔	伞	谷	肯	洞	兊	刻	刚	刕	刭	刹	刦	刜	刧	制	刎	劾
40	匊	匋	仓	匤	匦	華	卢	卤	厍	岜	呶	咢	呃	呟	咀	呼	吣	启	旱	岳
60	呓	坆	呈	坢	望	庭	夆	癸	委	姬	妮	娈	犴	孥	孪	尥	尮	尳	尯	屁
80	岎	岄	岭	岕	岻	岇	岠	岭	岫	炭	岂	岵	巩	帙	帡					

Row 4		01	02	03	04	05	06	07	08	09	10	11	12	13	14	15	16	17	18	19
00		帐	帔	帆	岭	帛	纴	幽	庞	庡	床	庄	庠	庣	弍	弜	弫	弡	灵	彖
20	彶	彷	御	忉	忹	忸	怿	戋	扭	拼	抛	攺	敀	敚	吾	盼	肩	柿	奈	饮
40	欧	歮	毗	氐	叔	毯	殷	毕	采	泫	泼	汾	炻	炘	奕	尔	爰	朏	犴	狂
60	狞	狗	狉	狑	玟	玘	瓦	甹	疝	疚	癿	矴	矽	取	卧	旱	矸	矾	秄	穸
80	究	羽	肮	肫	舡	虹	西	谷	迖	邦	邻	陕	陉	阪	阺					

Row 5		01	02	03	04	05	06	07	08	09	10	11	12	13	14	15	16	17	18	19
00		咻	亟	亰	伏	你	侰	佫	侣	佨	侷	侃	杲	冋	活	佟	剆	刹	劳	剃
20	刺	刹	剑	劷	劫	劬	励	劶	劶	劣	匡	医	卙	厓	杏	君	味	呃	咔	呀
40	咡	呼	咻	咧	听	呟	昌	号	呆	吉	咕	囪	囸	囮	垙	至	豸	奔	夯	姑
60	妭	妮	姘	姗	姄	狐	妾	娄	宦	宗	穿	妙	徂	尪	尥	尳	屌	声	峒	峡
80	岫	岷	岬	峡	峄	峋	岙	帏	帏	帔	怔	怖	怫	帕	怍					

Row 6		01	02	03	04	05	06	07	08	09	10	11	12	13	14	15	16	17	18	19
00		岣	帲	岰	纱	丝	床	庯	庋	扈	庙	庡	床	庣	卅	弞	叠	彸	征	徜
20	忢	恒	怭	忡	忕	所	扻	抯	抧	抝	拺	敀	敁	敂	龛	旄	旿	昛	昳	映
40	昫	昙	肬	柔	柹	枕	杫	校	杚	枠	柢	柨	柰	栗	欣	欥	欪	欶	炊	欿
60	歙	欲	歮	歰	殶	残	殁	殂	殅	殀	殎	段	殶	殸	毨	毜	毤	毲	沉	洰
80	泾	涆	沢	泗	炦	炎	犾	牠	牣	犹	犾	犄	牠	犳	犴					

Row 7		01	02	03	04	05	06	07	08	09	10	11	12	13	14	15	16	17	18	19
00		毕	牮	牛	犯	狚	狁	狜	狠	狆	犱	狖	猫	狉	狢	炊	珒	瓞	岷	瓪
20	甡	备	畀	疫	疗	卹	盱	帛	皃	财	盂	盍	盯	眂	眅	晃	矨	矴	秆	秀
40	秅	竞	竘	竽	笅	竻	籽	紏	纡	纨	罘	羿	耷	耸	肺	胫	肑	肸	股	胣
60	肷	胝	肦	舡	芎	芾	芠	苜	茾	乎	衩	覓	迅	迸	迭	迲	迣	述	迖	迫
80	迦	迯	邦	邪	邮	陁	陋	陊	陷	陑	夵	庖	侔	佊	侙					

Row 8		01	02	03	04	05	06	07	08	09	10	11	12	13	14	15	16	17	18	19
00		俫	侳	俿	俉	夵	龛	畬	况	浗	洦	淙	涊	剆	鬲	勠	勉	努	叵	叵
20	叵	毕	叙	叟	郗	厌	言	昏	哼	吁	呃	哸	哇	喝	咧	哧	咸	咳	吾	咛
40	唧	嗰	唪	唷	味	啙	喍	鬲	肩	唍	杏	嗮	囷	囮	囯	垅	垌	埛	埏	坬
60	壐	垩	垶	夠	奆	奙	奓	婋	婟	媮	婇	婡	婘	媓	媪	嫪	宔	宺	容	尌
80	罘	尳	尶	尯	屖	屑	岺	峕	峢	峋	嵃	峷	帡	帹	嵨					

Row 9		01	02	03	04	05	06	07	08	09	10	11	12	13	14	15	16	17	18	19
00		帗	峒	帵	峑	帘	康	庾	庑	庮	庴	弉	弴	徙	徜	徚	徑	徕	徛	徖
20	恷	惰	愧	悻	扅	扇	挐	抨	挋	拆	捞	挕	捺	捅	捼	搓	括	捵	择	揿
40	搄	敋	敃	敀	敕	旊	旐	晲	晸	晛	昫	曹	朊	栀	栻	梳	梐	梱	梋	桍
60	欿	欧	欭	欶	欸	欷	歇	歧	殊	殉	殙	殃	殈	殅	殉	殗	殩	毶	毷	毴
80	毬	毧	毰	毤	毪	毼	氉	氩	桄	泋	浃	泧	洟	涃	涭					

Row 10		01	02	03	04	05	06	07	08	09	10	11	12	13	14	15	16	17	18	19
00		浯	洶	涉	泾	炫	炬	炅	炁	颮	曼	受	犷	牉	版	犺	牸	犻	牻	牭
20	牵	犾	献	猦	狴	狗	狡	狫	狴	狎	狱	狳	猺	玺	珋	玑	珦	珔	瓬	瓬
40	瓬	瓶	歪	眏	眇	盼	畚	畘	畲	疷	疢	痱	症	痒	疾	眆	眦	盼	眘	皸
60	盅	盏	盔	盱	眣	眮	眐	睓	眮	眲	眸	眦	眼	眼	眚	眘	眢	昂	矤	砬
80	砣	硫	秵	秐	秡	秢	秨	窕	窐	窂	窣	笆	笔	竽	笅					

Row 11		01	02	03	04	05	06	07	08	09	10	11	12	13	14	15	16	17	18	19
00		笏	粑	粝	紖	紩	紓	紟	缸	罥	罘	翁	耆	耵	取	聆	肄	肮	朊	胅
20	胝	胒	朋	胥	貸	胂	臬	芫	茄	茵	茵	茇	虬	衎	衧	衱	衬	衲	衦	覂
40	舸	訆	豻	豹	貼	趵	軒	迷	迹	迴	迟	迵	迳	速	迨	逐	郅	郢	郦	郜
60	郇	郷	郕	娜	凱	閂	陆	陏	陷	陪	陚	烝	倥	倴	倰	假	倈	倢	俾	俨
80	偺	倴	偍	偬	傜	偾	匏	帖	晟	淬	淟	淫	凷	剆	剳					

Row 12		01	02	03	04	05	06	07	08	09	10	11	12	13	14	15	16	17	18	19
00		剕	則	剘	剢	删	㓘	剳	㓡	勭	励	勵	勈	㔤	匒	匌	匩	匧	奂	叜
20	厠	厙	叕	㕏	哫	咊	咯	哆	咰	咡	㖃	呦	唔	哘	㖆	哌	唔	哎	啰	唁
40	哂	哝	唉	哚	唤	哊	唕	唲	唗	唘	哃	咰	哪	唎	唜	唽	唛	啝	唯	啇
60	圁	圂	垕	垎	垛	垩	垤	垫	垾	垦	姟	娦	姰	姁	契	登	奆	奔	娮	娴
80	娫	娍	娓	娯	娖	娪	娬	娞	娄	娣	孮	孯	宮	宭	宯

Row 13		01	02	03	04	05	06	07	08	09	10	11	12	13	14	15	16	17	18	19
00		害	尓	尳	尵	屁	屃	屄	峄	峌	峬	峾	峴	峭	峵	峞	峘	峼	峀	峝
20	崖	峖	峷	帍	帩	帪	帣	庈	庉	庍	庢	庫	庐	庛	庾	弳	弰	弬	弮	徆
40	徠	徖	徟	徝	恶	恙	恩	恮	悂	悃	悈	悐	悋	悒	悀	悁	悇	悕	悯	悦
60	悭	戓	戋	毁	扂	扆	扉	挛	拳	捽	掂	捤	掓	捆	掐	挢	挲	挳	捀	敁
80	敁	敓	敳	敥	敂	料	斛	旃	旄	玺	晘	晥	晙	晒	晟

Row 14		01	02	03	04	05	06	07	08	09	10	11	12	13	14	15	16	17	18	19
00		晌	晉	暑	朐	胶	枇	枭	梯	梈	染	梵	梟	欣	欸	欧	欷	款	欨	欱
20	欲	发	殊	殅	殀	殒	殉	殑	殜	殗	毳	毁	眷	毰	毹	毷	毸	涉	汪	洲
40	淖	浣	涯	烒	炬	货	袋	衰	狐	爭	捌	脂	狮	独	铜	桃	格	坐	球	狟
60	猚	猘	猎	狸	猁	珀	瓳	瓵	瓴	瓯	瓶	瓸	眦	毒	眀	眑	眝	眒	串	痃
80	痍	痃	痩	痊	痳	痭	痊	跛	被	盅	盆	眬	眼	眯	眨

Row 15		01	02	03	04	05	06	07	08	09	10	11	12	13	14	15	16	17	18	19
00		眩	聊	貮	罝	督	罛	矜	秫	炫	祛	祓	砰	砨	砝	砮	砹	硐	硄	硃
20	硌	砒	砵	砦	硑	祠	祹	秭	秠	秧	秮	窕	窖	窔	窦	笭	竜	竝	竡	竤
40	竱	笄	笉	笎	笰	笑	笷	笨	筓	筍	筕	笼	粈	粜	粪	綈	綫	絃	綁	絣
60	罭	罘	罟	罣	羓	翃	翊	翣	聊	聃	胅	脉	胆	胫	胬	脛	脆	胖	脑	脎
80	胸	脆	夏	舑	舌舌	舻	舶	苇	莘	莒	莠	其	茚	莀	荺

Row 16		01	02	03	04	05	06	07	08	09	10	11	12	13	14	15	16	17	18	19
00		葩	莽	茺	茴	荐	菜	荮	蚈	虾	蚿	蚨	蚾	蚯	蚍	蚳	蚼	釜	氤	畏
20	胄	盂	衕	裙	袞	袈	袤	衺	衦	衸	衹	衼	袃	要	兹	訏	訙	訐	谷	豕
40	豚	財	貟	赤工	赿	趄	趆	距	趴	躬	躯	軒	軕	害	迨	迸	逆	逕	迺	迴
60	遾	郋	郘	邦	郙	郢	郕	郲	郜	郟	郯	郞	郗	兩	閂	閈	陌	陞	陒	陌
80	雩	飤	哭	鈗	魝	芀	倭	倴	倰	倾	倈	俽	俣	俜	倪

Row 17		01	02	03	04	05	06	07	08	09	10	11	12	13	14	15	16	17	18	19
00		偊	傍	倹	翅	菈	兡	冕	涪	凰	剡	剷	剬	勠	匐	匍	厞	叙	叡	叕
20	啦	啩	啽	唔	啺	啡	替	啰	啐	唳	啹	啸	啯	毁	唵	唿	啫	啷	唫	唉
40	啘	啞	喂	喿	喀	唲	喏	喀	罢	喔	喺	圉	圊	圛	圕	圙	堆	堯	埆	堅
60	奎	猝	娞	婉	婀	婚	婚	奢	爽	婷	婕	媚	婧	婿	媄	娶	婆	媐	寃	寝
80	窨	乳	尴	尵	尳	欻	屋	屃	屎	屌	屍	屣	崿	崰	崸

Row 18	01	02	03	04	05	06	07	08	09	10	11	12	13	14	15	16	17	18	19
00		𡸁	𡹷	𡹞	事	𡯘	𡯝	崮	𡵵	𡺶	豎	𡼏	𢁁	巷	帢	㟨	㠇	𢄼	幁	帽
20	𢅏	𢂻	啓	棄	㡰	𢇍	㢂	㡿	𢈸	𢈛	𢈤	𢉛	𢉉	廝	𢈺	𢉁	𢊬	𢌬	𢍸	𢏢
40	號	弹	𢐞	彫	𢓊	徬	𢔀	俺	御	㣤	㥶	𢙐	𢚩	𢝬	悴	㥘	惛	恇	㥅	㥈
60	㥪	㥮	㦅	㤷	𢧐	㦃	挎	搋	捎	揑	搆	掉	拵	掁	敁	敺	敜	𢾅	敞	㛚
80	𣀑	𢽼	斛	𣅁	𣈶	𣇉	腕	柳	椛	椓	槑	梭	椃	梀	梍					

Row 19	01	02	03	04	05	06	07	08	09	10	11	12	13	14	15	16	17	18	19
00		椴	𣉡	棄	歆	欽	歪	殍	殩	𣩿	殧	殍	殛	殻	毨	毹	毿	氁	毰	湾
20	涑	浩	沮	淼	淫	沘	洛	洇	滷	泗	浙	溹	浣	渢	淦	焐	煆	契	牃	牉
40	牗	牲	犊	犇	牸	犛	犲	猊	猴	猰	猣	猸	猉	猫	㺬	琊	堅	瓻	瓶	瓿
60	甌	甐	甁	㼜	甡	葡	畊	畔	畱	畊	疘	痏	痞	痜	疫	痥	瘵	瘌	皏	皮
80	皶	盓	盈	眩	眡	眶	睓	睉	瞅	瞳	睞	瞄	瞍	眡	甜					

Row 20	01	02	03	04	05	06	07	08	09	10	11	12	13	14	15	16	17	18	19
00		脩	矻	矬	矪	矺	砘	研	砿	硎	硶	砯	硪	硎	硝	硜	碀	硧	砸	硃
20	峇	祼	祇	稻	稅	稏	稃	稘	秕	稃	乘	稠	窅	窪	窰	窴	窿	竈	竷	竝
40	竽	管	笨	筅	笺	筸	箳	筍	筺	箊	籽	粒	粃	粍	粞	粨	粫	粰	絮	結
60	結	紙	絣	絮	綷	罹	罨	羝	羗	羚	翍	翻	耔	聳	腳	脈	腓	腩	腥	膜
80	腹	臈	脚	膐	舶	艒	艂	艇	艉	艅	艴	芻	苍	艶	艷					

Row 21	01	02	03	04	05	06	07	08	09	10	11	12	13	14	15	16	17	18	19
00		荣	菸	葶	萼	萘	菪	菴	萇	菴	菴	萁	葛	菌	葵	葧	蓍	蒩	蓿	萘
20	歔	虒	虗	蛀	蚢	蚫	蚯	蛾	蛳	蛔	蛶	蛱	蛴	蝥	蚕	衷	袊	裪	褓	袹
40	袮	袥	衹	覓	覜	覝	覸	覵	現	䚂	舦	舭	詳	詥	訦	訞	詨	詛	詾	詉
60	詚	詖	詅	豝	豩	豿	貁	貃	豣	負	赩	趑	趍	趄	趚	趐	趡	超	趑	趓
80	跀	跣	踘	跳	跨	跉	跫	踀	躲	躲	躱	軜	軽	輧	軸					

Row 22	01	02	03	04	05	06	07	08	09	10	11	12	13	14	15	16	17	18	19
00		軷	朝	軻	𨔝	𨔞	迶	逜	逩	逭	通	逦	遀	逾	郗	郜	郞	郾	鄐	郘
20	鄄	郣	酦	酡	酌	酩	酟	䣺	䣿	釨	鼓	毀	敨	閆	閔	陮	隩	夆	頇	飽
40	飹	飢	飣	馬	馬	傞	傺	衾	保	傚	偯	傁	僂	傿	倨	僙	逸	滂	濂	涵
60	勝	匒	匎	劑	劉	剡	斣	劂	剮	劕	勂	勱	勨	勴	勶	甥	養	叟	喳	嗖
80	嘅	嗑	噠	喊	噎	嗬	噀	嗬	嗟	嗷	嘩	嘁	嘆	嘧	噛					

Row 23	01	02	03	04	05	06	07	08	09	10	11	12	13	14	15	16	17	18	19
00		嘎	喤	嗵	咠	𠷒	喫	嗦	噁	嗶	啇	匙	嘗	㗖	嗋	嘐	嗚	圗	圕	圓
20	埼	墟	墒	堶	墸	墪	塏	墭	壺	姞	姹	娍	娧	媂	媜	夏	彝	嫁	嬉	媟
40	嫐	嫊	嫭	婼	嫚	媢	嫙	嫂	嫂	嫡	嫥	嬔	嫇	嫣	嬛	嬡	嬖	嬰	嬖	孰
60	孺	寫	審	寬	寳	寞	寠	堂	屠	屚	屣	嵁	崿	嶇	嶇	嶠	嶙	嶱	嶠	巘
80	崤	嶐	嵡	嵱	嵹	嶓	嶡	幟	幪	幗	幠	幜	幭	幮	幰					

Row 24		01	02	03	04	05	06	07	08	09	10	11	12	13	14	15	16	17	18	19
00		剬	罘	豻	冡	庴	庫	庯	庭	庚	庪	庹	扁	庲	弑	徥	弻	弲	弶	冪
20	徬	偕	復	偵	從	御	徆	徾	怩	怯	恧	惏	愗	怨	艎	恔	悏	偽	揆	假
40	極	悖	惐	悋	愊	惹	惛	惈	悒	惐	悄	惀	惦	惤	愢	惊	愱	㥑	揉	戜
60	戚	扅	扆	扉	扊	掊	挍	挍	掠	捸	挽	掛	捧	揮	揪	捌	捋	捐	掴	揖
80	掎	掭	掐	捭	揀	敓	敨	敧	敤	敆	敜	敁	敹	敡	敯					

Row 25		01	02	03	04	05	06	07	08	09	10	11	12	13	14	15	16	17	18	19
00		敪	敧	斯	旝	旍	晇	晉	晸	晪	晐	晻	暴	腄	桂	棧	棒	棫	棆	棸
20	椛	椃	椪	棲	桯	椅	棼	棽	椉	棗	椎	椈	棺	椑	棭	欽	欽	欿	歅	欹
40	歆	歃	歧	齒	殑	殏	殛	殍	殛	殘	殌	殟	殙	毼	毴	毷	毵	毸	毹	毣
60	毯	渍	湤	淀	湶	湉	湉	湆	湔	湚	湢	渿	湫	湇	湷	湃	湨	湖	焾	焥
80	焎	烈	焳	焥	焙	焿	焲	犂	犐	犑	犃	犉	犎	犋	猘					

Row 26		01	02	03	04	05	06	07	08	09	10	11	12	13	14	15	16	17	18	19
00		猤	猬	猼	猽	猩	猺	猛	猣	琀	琜	琒	琔	琡	瑛	瓝	瓠	瓟	瓳	瓶
20	瓴	痞	痔	痋	痓	痹	痾	痥	痏	痗	痠	痵	痰	痯	皷	盗	睆	睫	睦	睜
40	瞠	睩	睭	睓	睕	睔	睘	睮	睲	矟	矠	矡	硞	硶	硽	碌	碎	碗	碚	碇
60	碄	碕	碆	碌	碞	碖	禂	禆	稃	稊	窼	窨	窹	窶	窵	窳	窱	窴	窺	竂
80	窒	竁	竆	竇	竈	竩	竦	竨	竩	筥	筆	筩	筬	筠	筡					

Row 27		01	02	03	04	05	06	07	08	09	10	11	12	13	14	15	16	17	18	19
00		筦	筭	筹	筿	箚	粞	粡	粧	綎	綄	綂	綍	綷	綹	綵	絢	綸	緊	綼
20	罜	罣	罟	羖	羘	羙	羬	羭	翓	翙	翝	翤	翮	翜	聏	聐	聑	聣	聕	聠
40	腡	腆	腇	腉	腒	腋	腏	腳	腮	腷	臿	舂	舑	舓	舔	菈	菁	菱	菹	菿
60	萅	萆	萈	萉	萊	萋	萌	萏	萐	萑	菌	萓	萓	萗	菫	萘	菇	萙	菟	萚
80	蛇	蛐	蛕	蛗	蛜	蛤	蛦	蛪	蛱	蛾	蛴	蜩	蜋	蛔	蛽					

Row 28		01	02	03	04	05	06	07	08	09	10	11	12	13	14	15	16	17	18	19
00		蛭	蜂	蛸	蛩	蛬	蛷	蛪	衕	衙	衉	裂	裊	裏	裓	裖	裑	裘	裚	裗
20	裎	覓	覝	觓	觙	訤	訬	訯	訴	詁	詛	貀	貁	貂	貃	貄	貆	貈	貉	貊
40	豣	貶	貼	貾	賆	賁	趀	趄	趆	趉	超	趁	趋	趎	跓	跕	跗	跘	距	跛
60	跙	跚	跚	跕	跡	跠	跨	跳	跣	跪	跬	跱	軶	軷	軸	軼	軥	軲	軹	軻
80	輊	軺	逦	逿	遈	遐	遏	遒	遙	遛	遝	鄎	鄏	鄐	鄓					

Row 29		01	02	03	04	05	06	07	08	09	10	11	12	13	14	15	16	17	18	19
00		鄅	鄛	鄆	鄈	酢	酣	釵	鈜	鈕	鈒	鈯	閘	閜	閞	閟	閡	閣	閤	閦
20	陵	陏	隁	隄	隕	隟	隇	隊	隍	隋	雱	雯	雰	電	輩	靫	靬	預	頎	頏
40	頌	頊	頍	颳	飧	飢	飩	飭	馲	骯	髣	魁	魪	鳱	鼽	傲	傔	傗	傘	傖
60	傚	傞	傕	傒	傓	傔	傞	僌	僑	僰	僂	僄	僆	僇	僈	僋	僒	僓	僔	僕
80	僗	僘	僙	僛	僜	僝	僡	僣	僤	僦	僨	僩	僪	僫	僭					

Row 30		01	02	03	04	05	06	07	08	09	10	11	12	13	14	15	16	17	18	19
00		絲	啌	哹	喉	嗒	喀	㖪	嗐	嘁	嗽	嗉	喔	嗑	嘆	嗄	嗝	唄	嗌	嘐
20	嘍	嚨	嗖	嗅	嗆	嗺	嘔	啓	啚	啤	嚶	嗡	圕	圗	圞	堙	墤	堺	塌	墈
40	墋	墒	壟	墊	壑	墾	墮	墁	嫉	嫋	嫒	嬌	嬖	嬃	嫪	嫃	嫌	嫄	嫺	嫭
60	嫿	嬀	嬋	嬰	嬸	孺	孽	寮	寯	寱	屢	屣	屧	屪	嶝	嶟	嶢	嶙	嶧	嶨
80	嶠	嶫	嶧	嶬	嶰	嶸	幍	幎	幔	幣	幤	幪	幬	廑	廔					

Row 31		01	02	03	04	05	06	07	08	09	10	11	12	13	14	15	16	17	18	19
00		庳	廋	廇	廗	廜	廥	弊	彍	彉	韶	徾	徻	徿	慂	慹	憗	憂	憃	慁
20	慘	愭	惸	慞	慉	慛	慯	憪	憊	慴	慺	憏	憟	憰	慅	愪	愧	慉	憖	憂
40	戩	戫	扇	搯	摖	摻	摋	摠	摾	摼	撻	摐	摲	擠	敱	敡	敼	敹	敿	斅
60	斂	斀	斛	新	旛	暉	暍	暔	暓	暕	暥	暭	槩	榃	槅	榾	槷	槬	槉	槲
80	槁	槢	粘	槳	槧	歀	歁	歂	歃	歈	歋	歊	殠	殨	殦					

Row 32		01	02	03	04	05	06	07	08	09	10	11	12	13	14	15	16	17	18	19
00		轂	瞞	毹	氈	潒	漉	溢	滅	潛	潢	潿	澈	潡	澆	潯	爤	熇	熗	熘
20	熜	熨	牓	牔	牕	犕	犗	犘	犝	犡	犞	猷	獻	猿	獉	獏	獡	獛	獶	獽
40	玃	獚	獦	獳	獲	璽	瑛	瑀	甃	瓤	甏	甄	瞇	疃	瞖	疐	瘟	瘌	瘢	瘦
60	瘼	瘽	瘸	瘴	癈	瘻	瘴	癏	瘞	瘺	癤	皪	皫	皭	豎	皺	皻	皹	皽	盬
80	盩	睢	瞈	瞘	瞣	瞲	瞶	瞁	瞕	瞠	瞷	瞉	备	瞴	矓					

Row 33		01	02	03	04	05	06	07	08	09	10	11	12	13	14	15	16	17	18	19
00		穇	穊	穈	穉	磧	磲	磴	磶	磬	禥	禌	凱	稽	稑	穃	穊	稈	稬	稗
20	稦	稯	稞	稸	黎	窔	窬	窴	窯	窱	窻	窾	竃	竘	竦	竩	箬	篩	篼	箎
40	箂	箑	篇	篔	篝	篗	篛	篚	篟	篧	篯	篰	簁	簃	簈	粮	糈	糅	糋	糗
60	糣	糷	縋	縍	縪	縰	繄	縿	罷	罯	罹	罼	羰	羵	羶	羺	羻	翱	翾	翿
80	聒	聧	聨	聵	禽	脝	腁	腋	腈	腄	膜	腸	膘	膃	腯					

Row 34		01	02	03	04	05	06	07	08	09	10	11	12	13	14	15	16	17	18	19
00		膄	膈	膍	膌	膾	膟	贏	臀	臂	甄	艐	艒	艕	艞	誊	蔆	萊	蒮	蔑
20	蓓	蓉	蓒	蓛	蓪	蓫	蓸	蔟	蔥	蔪	蔂	蔎	蔽	蕐	蕞	蕎	蕪	蕔	蕈	蕃
40	蕛	蕘	蕣	蕦	蕫	蕿	蕻	蔓	蕵	虤	虥	虦	虩	號	蝀	蝒	蝗	蝠	蝈	蝣
60	蝍	蝤	蝨	蟓	褱	褢	褠	褨	褶	褿	襆	襇	襋	襏	襖	襪	襫	覩	覭	覯
80	覶	觬	觵	觶	諄	諼	諕	諪	諓	諫	諕	諜	諵	諭	谽					

Row 35		01	02	03	04	05	06	07	08	09	10	11	12	13	14	15	16	17	18	19
00		豞	豰	豴	豯	豷	貐	貔	貗	貘	貙	貛	賅	賆	賊	賏	賔	賑	賓	賝
20	賙	越	趦	趞	趠	趣	趡	趨	趧	趬	跰	跠	跬	跮	跲	踁	踄	踂	踃	踊
40	踌	踖	踗	踙	踥	躬	軓	軟	輢	輣	輗	輪	輡	退	遊	逮	過	遠	鄐	鄑
60	鄒	鄓	鄔	鄕	鄗	鄖	鄘	鄙	鄜	鄛	鄶	鄧	醃	醊	醎	醢	醦	鋄	鍂	鑷
80	鍚	閱	閶	閘	関	隞	隇	隕	隁	隑	隟	隱	隲	隳	雉					

Row 36		01	02	03	04	05	06	07	08	09	10	11	12	13	14	15	16	17	18	19
00		霈	雯	雷	雩	零	雵	酖	酢	鞋	靷	歁	靲	歆	殙	訢	逭	頏	頙	頪
20	頚	頏	頞	頢	頒	頓	頡	颱	颲	颭	颸	颪	颯	餂	餅	餌	餁	餇	飽	餓
40	飴	馲	馰	閦	魃	魄	瑰	傀	鬽	鴇	鴇	麰	黕	黰	傑	儲	粭	毿	淼	剷
60	剸	剽	劗	剳	剴	劉	劊	勬	勬	勲	劵	勬	塹	勞	匓	勫	匯	离	卿	厬
80	叡	啖	噫	嗛	嘻	呤	嘆	嗓	嘜	嗏	嗽	嘍	晳	巽	輯					

Row 37		01	02	03	04	05	06	07	08	09	10	11	12	13	14	15	16	17	18	19
00		噁	嵷	嗷	圜	墂	墫	墽	墠	墺	塈	墼	嫤	嫢	嫫	嫛	嬀	嬄	嫞	嫺
20	嫮	嫵	嬍	嫯	嫭	寥	寠	寣	寵	尋	尌	屨	巁	嶋	嶠	嶬	嶕	嶗	嶗	嶟
40	嶗	廉	廖	廓	廛	廚	廝	幩	幢	幡	幟	幨	幪	幯	幫	幬	幭	幮	彝	彠
60	廝	廡	廞	廠	廧	弳	彍	徵	徸	徹	徼	德	徽	徾	徿	憖	憙	憩	憾	懆
80	懁	懌	懍	懏	懞	懟	懢	懤	懨	懰	戩	戫	戭	戮	扆					

Row 38		01	02	03	04	05	06	07	08	09	10	11	12	13	14	15	16	17	18	19
00		攳	撓	撨	擁	撟	撊	撍	擷	擇	擋	擽	擼	斁	斂	斄	斅	斆	敲	敺
20	敽	斅	斀	敮	旉	旝	旛	暟	暤	曀	曎	曈	曒	曔	朁	朆	朇	朧	榟	榤
40	槓	槑	榲	槢	槧	橏	樧	橀	橑	樃	橠	橁	橧	橪	橬	檥	檡	歡	歈	歊
60	歍	歒	歜	歞	殭	毀	毰	毿	氄	氅	氆	氋	氍	氎	瀰	漩	潹	潐	潓	潳
80	潚	澗	澋	澘	澆	澌	澏	澑	澛	熑	熇	熻	爾	犉	犛					

Row 39		01	02	03	04	05	06	07	08	09	10	11	12	13	14	15	16	17	18	19
00		熦	犖	甀	甏	牖	甃	犒	犗	犝	犞	犡	犥	犦	犨	犫	犪	犧	獡	獢
20	獥	獦	獧	獨	獩	獪	獫	獬	獭	獮	獯	獰	獱	獲	瓠	瓡	瓢	甄	甂	甈
40	甍	甐	甑	瘆	瘈	瘉	瘊	瘋	瘌	瘍	瘎	瘏	瘐	瘑	瘒	瘓	瘔	瘕	瘖	皓
60	皳	瞄	瞅	瞇	瞈	瞉	瞋	瞍	瞎	瞏	瞐	瞕	瞙	瞚	瞛	瞜	瞝	矠	矡	瞀
80	磊	磈	磌	磍	磏	磑	磓	磔	磕	磖	磙	磛	磜	磝	磞					

Row 40		01	02	03	04	05	06	07	08	09	10	11	12	13	14	15	16	17	18	19
00		禃	禑	禖	禡	穀	穎	穄	穆	穈	穉	穊	穋	程	穐	穖	窴	窸	窽	窾
20	竨	竮	管	箮	箸	箺	箷	箹	箾	篅	篆	篋	篍	篎	篏	篐	篗	篘	篛	篜
40	篧	糲	糉	糋	糒	糓	糔	緗	緌	緍	緎	緓	緔	緗	緙	緛	緝	罯	罳	罶
60	羪	羻	羾	翀	翂	翃	翄	翍	翏	翐	翓	翖	翗	翙	翜	翝	翞	聢	聣	聤
80	聥	聦	聧	聨	聫	聬	聭	脺	腣	腤	腪	腲	腵	膆	膉					

Row 41		01	02	03	04	05	06	07	08	09	10	11	12	13	14	15	16	17	18	19
00		膕	膖	膗	膘	膙	臺	舋	舓	舕	舙	舚	舝	舠	舤	萋	萐	萒	萓	萕
20	萘	萛	萞	萟	萠	萡	萢	萣	萩	萪	萫	萬	萭	萮	萯	萰	萲	萳	萴	萵
40	萶	萷	萹	萺	萻	萾	虢	虡	虣	螋	蜳	蝍	蝦	蝰	蝱	蝲	蝳	蝴	蝷	蝹
60	蟵	蠶	蠸	蠽	衊	衋	衇	衈	衉	衊	褧	褩	褪	褬	褭	褯	褰	褲	覞	覟
80	覠	覡	覣	觤	觥	觧	詬	詷	誗	誘	誝	誸	豯	豰	豱					

Row 42		01	02	03	04	05	06	07	08	09	10	11	12	13	14	15	16	17	18	19
00		猣	𤞏	猏	豨	𤝔	𧵳	賊	賈	資	袷	䞤	𧺯	䞶	䞩	趕	𧻓	𧻘	䞱	𧻚
20	䞴	𨂍	踤	䟵	踻	䠢	踼	䟥	䟧	踾	䟴	䟨	䟰	䟸	跨	踱	䟽	䠃	跸	𨀐
40	𧰃	䠳	䠷	䡁	䡇	䡊	𨌈	𨍃	䡮	䤕	𨐨	𨔨	𨗏	𨗬	𨘯	𨞹	鄒	𨞪	𨟂	鄸
60	𨟊	𨟟	𨟠	鄭	𨟲	鄘	𨟼	鄉	𨠉	醾	醒	𨦠	𨧱	𨨝	𨰪	𨷝	閣	闓	闍	闔
80	闢	閰	閨	閳	閽	闃	閺	陪	陳	隩	陸	翟	雅	雂	霁

Row 43		01	02	03	04	05	06	07	08	09	10	11	12	13	14	15	16	17	18	19
00		𩂈	𩂍	霋	𩈴	𩈻	鞄	鞊	𩋐	鞞	𩋸	鞦	䩷	𩌄	𩌐	韋	𩎕	𩏌	韡	韠
20	韸	𩒞	頡	頴	頼	頤	頙	頯	顃	顋	顛	顳	顣	顚	顉	頣	顮	颸	颼	飀
40	飂	餕	餡	餑	餄	餾	𩟔	駁	駍	駑	駡	騂	骬	骰	髚	髫	髩	髮	髿	鬧
60	鬩	魃	魁	魅	魄	魋	魆	魤	魣	魛	鯊	魟	鮣	鴒	鴆	鳺	麐	麂	𪊠	麠
80	麃	𪏖	𪓑	𪖑	𪗁	𪘁	𪙋	𪚀	𪚁	𪚏	𪚜	𪛁	𪛃	鼎	濃

Row 44		01	02	03	04	05	06	07	08	09	10	11	12	13	14	15	16	17	18	19
00		㓩	𠞝	剠	劃	剩	剿	劁	勬	勱	勭	勨	歐	區	匲	犟	犀	厲	叕	叟
20	叡	噾	嚏	噜	嚞	噧	噿	嚁	嚁	嘓	嚗	嚰	嚿	囒	嚋	嚵	噷	嚕	噲	嚦
40	嚚	壥	壛	壈	壉	壓	壡	壜	夔	夠	奭	奯	嬘	嬝	嬭	嬲	嬳	嬫	孅	孌
60	嬪	孵	曾	登	寱	寵	尠	尣	屚	屭	屢	嶟	幢	嶜	嶰	嶫	嶲	嶕	巕	巒
80	嚚	巔	巑	幰	幱	幧	幨	彘	彌	彍	廣	廥	廪	廌	廦

Row 45		01	02	03	04	05	06	07	08	09	10	11	12	13	14	15	16	17	18	19
00		彃	彍	彯	徵	徲	怒	愁	愿	慹	憄	懐	憏	懫	懪	懙	憬	懾	懔	懭
20	懅	懀	戳	戮	摩	擥	攄	擻	擯	撻	擛	攃	攫	攚	戲	斀	斁	斂	斅	斃
40	斄	斔	斝	斷	斸	斵	曤	曦	曚	曨	曪	曫	朆	朁	朇	朣	朦	朧	梻	棒
60	棴	梓	櫃	檷	榕	橑	櫦	櫢	棚	椅	椅	櫋	櫜	櫱	櫽	欅	欚	欃	歁	歑
80	歊	歏	殢	殧	殨	殩	毅	毳	毸	氈	氌	溉	瀨	淯	溥

Row 46		01	02	03	04	05	06	07	08	09	10	11	12	13	14	15	16	17	18	19
00		濴	潒	漢	潛	瀲	瀞	瀑	灘	燦	燉	熉	熨	爲	煎	爏	牐	牉	牊	膢
20	牗	犕	犥	犟	犦	犨	犫	猏	獵	獭	獴	獶	獷	獼	獽	玁	玂	玃	玁	瓃
40	璛	瓕	甇	甌	甈	甗	甄	彊	瘖	瘟	瘌	瘰	瘯	瘵	瘛	瘖	瘍	皞	皦	皺
60	皽	盝	瞜	瞜	瞪	瞵	瞶	睹	瞞	瞯	瞪	瞟	瞰	瞫	瞡	矇	矉	矊	矟	矲
80	碭	礓	破	礑	礤	礬	磅	礱	礴	穛	穞	穮	穭	黎	窹

Row 47		01	02	03	04	05	06	07	08	09	10	11	12	13	14	15	16	17	18	19
00		竇	竊	竈	窸	窾	竃	竄	竅	竆	竀	竂	竇	竨	箬	箵	篣	筝	篔	篗
20	簁	篪	篤	簃	簇	簞	簟	簪	簧	簸	簹	簽	籅	籓	籍	籙	籛	籤	籦	糉
40	糅	糠	糜	糌	糥	糙	糐	糳	縦	綡	緉	緌	緹	縔	縡	緺	縎	縨	緖	綟
60	縫	緬	縛	罼	罿	羀	羅	羇	羱	羴	羵	羶	羷	翺	翽	翾	翻	耧	耩	耪
80	耬	耮	聕	聰	聵	聲	聹	聶	聾	肆	膴	膝	膢	膳	賊

Row 48		01	02	03	04	05	06	07	08	09	10	11	12	13	14	15	16	17	18	19
00		琮	薹	睡	睺	鬃	粼	粦	艅	艖	艏	艑	艋	艥	艎	艒	艓	彝	菼	菲
20	蓬	蕢	蕁	萹	蓏	蕃	蓤	蓶	蓁	蒤	蒧	蔓	葳	蓸	蒡	蓮	萄	菻	蕒	葰
40	莧	菰	萯	菓	蔀	薛	覤	蜊	蝙	螇	蝀	蝢	螥	蝰	蝟	蟡	蜂	颯	螅	蜒
60	蜳	蜚	蝐	蝅	蝨	蟗	衕	褭	褰	褫	禨	裩	裿	褋	覸	覼	覾	覬	覷	觖
80	觳	觫	觲	觵	觶	觻	諓	諕	諟	諲	謊	諍	諙	諲	謕					

Row 49		01	02	03	04	05	06	07	08	09	10	11	12	13	14	15	16	17	18	19
00		諒	諸	諄	請	諑	諔	謝	謅	嘗	隋	謔	諓	豰	豏	貂	貉	貐	貅	貑
20	貏	貄	貔	貓	貛	賑	賣	發	趑	趚	趣	趦	趪	趬	趥	趫	趪	趯	楚	踞
40	踷	踞	踧	踟	踖	踦	踒	踑	踕	踘	踣	踌	踥	踽	躲	輯	輲	輪	輯	輝
60	輷	輢	輅	輠	輣	輩	辥	遄	遂	遐	遾	遑	遒	遫	遱	遳	遺	還	鼇	鄸
80	鄻	鄹	鄺	鄱	鄧	醎	醄	醐	醓	醃	醃	鋉	鋏	鋽	鋈					

Row 50		01	02	03	04	05	06	07	08	09	10	11	12	13	14	15	16	17	18	19
00		踪	長	雎	肆	雝	閱	閹	闌	閿	闇	闍	闐	闑	闑	隮	隱	隮	隔	障
20	隴	隧	隳	隟	隢	雄	雅	霡	霞	霫	霹	霶	霴	霚	霜	霸	霺	霯	酬	酪
40	酲	鞋	鞋	鞠	鞣	鞈	鞙	鞾	韓	韞	韡	誹	韻	韶	韻	韽	響	韶	頡	頡
60	頫	頰	頫	頿	頿	颱	颼	飧	飽	餉	餔	餘	餳	餞	餕	餗	餡	駢	駚	駢
80	駓	駟	駘	駒	駌	駡	駑	骨	骳	骿	髍	髑	髕	髗	髻					

Row 51		01	02	03	04	05	06	07	08	09	10	11	12	13	14	15	16	17	18	19
00		髻	髮	髯	髲	魑	魅	魈	魋	魍	魎	鬯	魝	魟	魠	魰	魴	魶	魵	魿
20	鳩	鳪	鳫	鳬	鳭	鳶	鳸	鴃	鴂	鴄	鴆	鴇	鴉	鴒	鴝	鴦	麀	麃	麂	麇
40	麩	麰	麯	麴	麱	麿	黁	黍	點	鼎	鼐	夐	僾	儁	儃	儆	儇	儷	儉	儌
60	兟	兢	剿	劃	劊	劌	劈	勸	匿	厲	叡	嚅	嚯	嚾	嚅	嚽	嚵	嚶	嚷	囌
80	囐	嚟	嚩	嚳	嚽	嚿	嚶	嚼	囒	壔	壑	壐	夔	奱	孋					

Row 52		01	02	03	04	05	06	07	08	09	10	11	12	13	14	15	16	17	18	19
00		嬉	嫪	嬁	嬃	嬈	嬖	嬰	嬽	嬰	孭	寰	寯	寯	尀	屏	巇	巆	巉	巊
20	巋	巌	巍	巏	巔	巕	巘	巙	巚	幭	幰	幱	廞	廥	廯	廮	廦	弆	彏	彲
40	徾	徽	徸	憋	憠	憩	憨	憩	懌	懤	懭	懊	懨	懰	懼	懞	懵	擧	擷	擷
60	擽	擼	擸	攂	斀	斁	斂	斃	斆	斅	斀	斁	旛	暾	暿	曤	曥	曧	曩	檮
80	檬	檯	檺	檽	櫂	櫄	櫅	櫆	櫉	櫐	櫜	櫱	櫳	櫸	歋					

Row 53		01	02	03	04	05	06	07	08	09	10	11	12	13	14	15	16	17	18	19
00		殭	殯	殲	穀	毇	氂	氀	濢	濭	瀼	瀨	瀧	瀷	瀧	瀶	瀷	瀲	瀯	瀰
20	瀸	瀺	灕	燾	燻	爃	爄	爅	爈	爍	爕	爏	爐	爕	爜	爣	爟	牒	牓	牘
40	牔	牛曾	犑	犢	犣	犦	犧	獃	獄	獷	獼	獺	獻	猺	獴	獮	玂	璞	璢	瓘
60	璪	璭	瓋	瓊	甌	甐	甗	甓	瘵	瘸	瘺	瘻	瘽	癃	癆	癉	癒	癄	癗	癥
80	癪	癬	瞟	瞕	瞚	瞍	瞰	瞴	瞺	矗	盬	瞿	矅	矊	矏					

Row 54	01	02	03	04	05	06	07	08	09	10	11	12	13	14	15	16	17	18	19
00		瞜	瞨	瞘	瞦	瞮	瞜	瞟	瞶	瞗	瞺	磿	瞽	積	磏	磙	磠	磛	磩	磝
20	礬	磸	禠	禮	禪	禭	禯	穚	穟	穛	穮	穬	穧	穫	穯	穳	穲	穭	穱	穲
40	穮	窻	窼	竆	竉	竊	竁	竇	竂	竈	竄	竅	窽	窾	竌	篖	篺	篻	篹	篼
60	簑	簕	簚	簝	簥	簰	簬	簱	簵	簳	簶	簷	簹	籆	粹	糘	糚	糝	糨	糬
80	糞	絜	絣	縞	縹	繚	繉	繝	纍	纝	罏	罍	罾	羀	羂					

Row 55	01	02	03	04	05	06	07	08	09	10	11	12	13	14	15	16	17	18	19
00		翇	翍	翎	翶	翷	翸	翻	耆	聐	聜	聝	聤	聠	聥	聳	膍	膕	膞	膭
20	膱	臑	臇	臈	臕	臛	臗	臝	臠	臡	臢	艥	艩	艬	艭	艴	艵	艶	艾	芃
40	蓟	蔆	蔋	蔎	蔑	蔒	蔕	蔛	蔵	蔾	蕑	蕟	蕣	蕥	蕦	蕻	薪	薵	藙	蘎
60	藋	藴	蘐	蘈	蘒	蘓	蘙	蘚	蘝	蘬	蘮	虤	虦	虪	虧	虩	虪	蛲	螟	螭
80	螳	螵	螶	螷	螸	螹	螼	蟀	蟂	蟃	蠶	蟹	蠱	蠽	蠿					

Row 56	01	02	03	04	05	06	07	08	09	10	11	12	13	14	15	16	17	18	19
00		衋	衈	衊	衎	衏	衺	褬	褫	褯	褶	襐	襆	覞	覟	覛	覠	覢	覣	覥
20	覬	覰	觎	觿	觾	觽	觸	觻	謏	謑	謒	譄	譑	譽	谼	豋	豈	豵	豷	貒
40	貗	貙	貚	貛	貜	賟	賩	賮	賫	賲	贎	趥	趧	趫	趭	趯	趰	趬	趱	趲
60	趞	趨	跼	踦	踑	踀	踋	踆	踖	踗	踛	踓	踔	踏	軆	軇	軈	軉	軐	軑
80	輯	輵	輹	輼	輽	辳	遭	邅	邂	邃	邆	邇	邈	邌	鄰					

Row 57	01	02	03	04	05	06	07	08	09	10	11	12	13	14	15	16	17	18	19
00		鄿	酄	酅	酆	酇	酈	酁	酂	醰	醑	醡	醫	釐	鍄	鍆	鍋	鍬	鍭	鏃
20	鑢	鑥	鑱	鑿	钁	钂	钃	钄	闛	闟	闠	闣	闤	隨	隮	隯	隳	隸	隺	雊
40	雗	霒	霚	霟	霠	霣	霦	靐	靌	靍	靎	靏	鞃	鞄	鞋	鞬	鞭	鞮	鞾
60	韠	韡	韢	韣	韤	韥	韨	韪	韫	韬	韮	韯	韰	韱	韸	韹	韺	韻	飀	飁
80	飂	飃	飄	飅	飆	飇	飈	飉	飨	飧	餗	餕	餡	餦	餧					

Row 58	01	02	03	04	05	06	07	08	09	10	11	12	13	14	15	16	17	18	19
00		餶	餷	餺	餼	餾	馞	駆	駇	駛	駝	駞	駣	駒	駇	駄	駧	駕	駡	駭
20	駕	骴	骳	髣	髤	髧	髩	骲	骹	魅	魆	魕	魛	魟	魋	魏	魈	魓	魺	魭
40	魶	魼	鮁	鮂	鮄	鮃	鮈	鮍	鮎	鳶	鴦	鴇	鴎	鴏	鴒	鴗	鴔	鴩	鹵	齡
60	麄	麇	麋	麇	麌	麃	黆	黇	黈	黏	黐	黧	黩	野	默	黯	黓	鼳	鼵	僜
80	僇	熵	龠	凓	澖	龢	圎	剸	剳	劀	劙	勵	劉	鎊	錋					

Row 59	01	02	03	04	05	06	07	08	09	10	11	12	13	14	15	16	17	18	19
00		嚉	嚛	嚝	嚫	嚽	嚶	嚿	嚥	嚗	嚺	嚾	墍	墅	墻	壕	壥	數	獝	夓
20	嬨	嬩	嬳	孴	寱	嶟	嶥	嶠	嶯	嶐	嶻	巓	巙	巘	廦	廧	廮	廩	徲	徾
40	徿	憋	憩	懇	懟	懍	懨	懾	戁	戃	戄	戫	扅	擏	擳	擿	攐	斀	斂	斆
60	斅	斖	斕	旞	曍	曬	曯	曶	朧	構	槊	槵	櫜	櫝	櫣	櫨	櫪	櫰	櫟	欒
80	欕	歗	殩	殲	毇	毊	氇	渻	湃	溞	潶	瀕	瀖	瀾	漊					

Row 60		01	02	03	04	05	06	07	08	09	10	11	12	13	14	15	16	17	18	19
00		熢	熰	葀	豎	牅	牑	舉	獃	獦	獶	璬	璙	璩	甑	瞺	曊	罶	罻	翼
20	螀	癈	癒	癀	瘸	癞	癐	癆	瘍	瘸	瘰	癐	瘸	矰	瞪	曉	瞨	瞸	盧	瞾
40	瞱	聽	矙	矐	瞵	矄	矋	矌	禮	磃	磼	磝	磩	礐	礌	礪	礐	礡	穚	穟
60	穫	穭	積	穞	穤	穭	穮	穯	穱	窶	窼	竃	竆	竇	竈	竪	竰	簹	籋	籒
80	籓	篁	篷	篾	簅	簉	簪	簾	簲	簷	簸	簻	籊	籑	籖					

Row 61		01	02	03	04	05	06	07	08	09	10	11	12	13	14	15	16	17	18	19
00		簌	簏	簒	簙	簛	簝	簢	簥	簦	簬	簴	簵	簶	簼	簿	籀	籄	籈	籉
20	籍	籎	糒	糓	糘	糚	糝	糣	糤	糦	縪	縳	縺	繃	繈	繐	繒	繓	繘	繛
40	罏	罐	罾	羵	羷	翸	翹	耩	聧	聶	聸	聹	聽	聾	膽	臉	臑	臎	臘	臚
60	臜	艥	舋	舉	舄	舉	舋	艠	艣	艤	艦	艪	艫	艭	艷	艟	艥	蒞	薎	蔽
80	薐	薒	薖	薚	薝	薣	薧	薭	薾	藀	藂	藃	藇	藈	藋					

Row 62		01	02	03	04	05	06	07	08	09	10	11	12	13	14	15	16	17	18	19
00		藪	藊	藐	藑	藒	藔	藷	蟓	蟟	蟧	蟨	蟩	蟫	蟬	蟯	蟵	蟶	蟷	蟸
20	蟺	蟻	蟽	蠁	蠂	襀	襊	襏	襐	襑	襓	襕	襚	襜	襝	觀	覲	覷	觴	觶
40	觶	觻	觼	譁	譂	譃	譅	譆	譇	譈	譊	譋	譌	譍	譎	谿	豏	豐	豒	豓
60	豶	豷	豻	貆	貋	貍	貙	貗	貘	贅	贆	贇	贈	贉	赯	趫	趬	趭	趮	趯
80	趲	趲	趵	趷	蹥	蹦	蹪	蹫	蹮	蹯	蹱	蹲	蹳	蹸	蹔					

Row 63		01	02	03	04	05	06	07	08	09	10	11	12	13	14	15	16	17	18	19
00		躕	轆	轄	轅	轉	轊	轋	轌	轍	轎	辴	辬	辟	辥	邆	邇	邅	邈	邍
20	邊	邋	邌	邎	鄿	酆	酄	酅	酆	醘	醙	醡	醤	醉	醫	醨	醭	醲	釐	鏃
40	鏤	鏢	鏞	鏁	鏗	鏶	鏊	鏊	鏴	闠	闤	闥	闦	闧	隳	隴	雞	霳	霴	霵
60	霶	霿	靂	靃	靄	靅	靆	靉	靐	鞉	鞊	鞋	鞚	鞛	鞝	鞞	鞟	鞡	鞢	鞤
80	鞪	韡	韣	顀	顂	顃	顅	顆	顇	顉	顊	顋	颸	颹	颻					

Row 64		01	02	03	04	05	06	07	08	09	10	11	12	13	14	15	16	17	18	19
00		颾	颿	飀	飁	飂	飃	餓	餐	餮	餯	餰	餱	餲	餳	餵	餶	餷	餸	餺
20	餼	餽	餿	饀	饁	饃	騂	騃	騄	騅	騆	騇	騈	騉	騊	騋	騌	騍	騎	鬁
40	魃	魆	魈	魊	魋	魍	魎	魏	魑	魮	魰	魱	魲	魳	魴	魵	魶	魷	魸	魹
60	魺	魻	魼	魽	鴆	鴇	鴈	鴉	鴊	鴋	鴌	鴍	鴎	鴏	鴐	鴑	鴒	鴓	麌	麎
80	麏	麐	麕	麖	麮	麯	麰	麲	麳	麵	麶	麷	麸	麹	麺					

Row 65		01	02	03	04	05	06	07	08	09	10	11	12	13	14	15	16	17	18	19
00		黈	黙	黚	黽	鼙	鼰	鼲	鼴	鼳	鼵	鼶	鼷	齋	齓	儭	儮	儯	儶	兤
20	兣	瀌	瀨	瀝	劙	劚	劗	劘	劚	嚐	嚙	嚞	嚠	嚥	嚦	嚧	嚪	嚫	嚬	壂
40	壃	壈	壏	壐	嬏	嬐	嬑	嬒	嬓	嬔	嬕	嬘	嬙	嬚	嬛	嬜	嬞	嬟	嬠	嬡
60	嬢	嬣	嬤	嬥	嬦	嬧	嬨	嬩	嬪	嬫	嬬	嬭	嬮	嬯	嬰	嬱	嬲	嬳	嬴	嬵
80	嬶	嬷	嬸	嬹	嬺	嬻	嬼	嬽	嬾	嬿	孀	孁	孂	孃	孄					

Row 66		01	02	03	04	05	06	07	08	09	10	11	12	13	14	15	16	17	18	19
00		檬	樽	檖	標	橶	樹	椶	檠	檕	𣡕	欅	歡	歒	齣	殬	殩	穀	盤	氉
20	毲	毷	氈	氍	辨	瀨	潛	澪	濤	灌	漢	潭	澗	瀘	滴	澿	潓	灑	瀸	瀉
40	潢	瀈	瀐	瀕	淍	澌	熆	爟	嫛	牅	牓	𤗼	獱	獼	獹	璋	瓤	甄	甎	甗
60	瘟	瘮	瘨	癃	癘	癥	癭	癙	瘴	瘓	瞸	瞞	瞾	瞳	矓	瞟	瞶	瞺	矇	矕
80	矂	罤	礹	稸	禮	襽	礒	礫	礆	礑	礜	禦	穟	穋	穛					

Row 67		01	02	03	04	05	06	07	08	09	10	11	12	13	14	15	16	17	18	19
00		穡	穞	穈	穭	穠	贏	竅	寥	巇	竵	篴	簫	籋	籖	篁	篴	簿	簨	籌
20	籍	簣	簠	簜	簦	籓	簸	籀	簞	簟	簻	簒	簡	籄	繁	舒	繄	繇	繁	籠
40	籦	緦	繈	繯	繽	繠	繥	繏	纁	纇	繼	纍	贏	纘	繼	纏	繵	纚	纍	羅
60	羈	羆	羃	羮	翻	耩	耩	聸	聹	聵	聽	膞	臆	臑	臛	臐	臑	臈	臌	臟
80	蠡	艐	曬	艂	彈	艥	艪	艬	艫	艢	艣	艤	艨	艩	蘄					

Row 68		01	02	03	04	05	06	07	08	09	10	11	12	13	14	15	16	17	18	19
00		蒴	虆	蕢	蘢	蘂	薦	蘴	蘞	蘰	蘬	蘸	蘀	蘵	虈	蘷	蘜	虇	蘿	蘺
20	虉	虅	虓	虤	虩	虪	虧	虩	虦	虪	螟	蟋	蟢	蟨	蟰	蟧	蟦	蟫	蟬	蟟
40	蟱	蟤	蠔	蠢	蠈	蠱	蠿	蠹	蠶	衊	襞	襄	襪	襭	襫	襩	襤	襴	襹	襸
60	襶	襹	襼	襽	覝	覦	覽	觴	讄	譴	譲	譽	讅	護	豨	豯	豵	豷	賵	賻
80	贐	贒	贓	贕	贖	贘	趯	趲	趰	趱	趬	趭	趮	趠	趧					

Row 69		01	02	03	04	05	06	07	08	09	10	11	12	13	14	15	16	17	18	19
00		踩	蹉	蹥	蹢	蹤	蹁	蹾	蹸	蹬	蹯	躂	躣	蹺	躁	躐	軀	轅	轆	轊
20	轚	轍	辦	辬	遴	邆	過	邅	邇	邊	邌	鄭	鄘	鄙	鄰	鄺	鄭	醽	醰	醭
40	醜	醨	醲	釂	釅	釁	鏃	鏇	鐵	鏻	鐿	鏺	鏽	鐔	鏩	閿	闟	雋	闠	闤
60	闞	闌	闥	闍	闖	闓	隮	雝	雙	霏	霆	霳	霆	霍	霹	霻	靋	靄	靉	靏
80	靦	靧	靨	鞍	鞓	鞜	鞴	鞨	鞭	鞴	韓	韝	韞	韡	韣					

Row 70		01	02	03	04	05	06	07	08	09	10	11	12	13	14	15	16	17	18	19
00		韢	韡	韥	韨	韹	韷	韻	韽	韾	頯	頹	顆	顋	顑	顥	顡	顛	飀	飂
20	飅	飉	飃	飌	飋	颿	飆	饎	餳	饋	餴	饈	饡	饟	饞	騂	騃	騌	騍	騂
40	騕	騞	騠	騤	騵	騶	驅	騬	騽	骯	骰	骹	骻	骿	髁	髂	髖	髕	鬘	鬞
60	鬠	鬡	鬢	鬤	鬣	鬢	魑	魒	魖	魕	魘	魔	魗	魑	鮸	鮋	鮓	鮚	鮣	鮱
80	鮿	鯃	鯎	鯃	鯫	鯉	鯱	鯸	鯒	鯗	鯱	鵞	鶦	鶩	鶴					

Row 71		01	02	03	04	05	06	07	08	09	10	11	12	13	14	15	16	17	18	19
00		鷐	鷗	鷚	鷴	鷳	鷵	鷸	鷽	鸃	鸆	鸌	鸒	麡	麤	麢	麣	麢	麲	麷
20	麰	麴	黐	黖	黗	黙	黟	黣	黤	黦	黧	黭	黰	黱	黿	鼙	鼛	鼵	鼶	鼸
40	鼷	齃	儃	儏	儠	儣	儦	儨	儰	儹	儻	孏	孻	嬨	嬸	嚷	嚹	嚱	嚼	囆
60	囂	壈	壞	孏	孆	孅	孈	孇	孃	孋	孌	孍	孎	孏	廱	廲	懍	懾	懼	懿
80	戀	戇	戃	戄	戅	戁	戆	攃	攄	攋	攍	攎	攏	攐	攔					

Row 72		01	02	03	04	05	06	07	08	09	10	11	12	13	14	15	16	17	18	19
00		繳	嚛	䁿	爵	樢	檶	橽	檄	櫢	樹	櫵	檍	㰈	轃	鎮	衛	歟	歎	殲
20	氈	瀻	瀈	齕	孌	衛	犥	獮	璺	瓖	瓗	歟	瓐	歷	癴	癮	癭	矔	矇	瞤
40	睤	曆	黻	盧	瞭	矆	疇	赫	矖	縣	聰	瞑	曆	獳	獎	爾	瓕	硯	磬	禰
60	櫶	稿	擬	窸	竇	簷	籠	篴	懿	簀	篗	籍	篡	邁	豐	篾	簗	篘	籬	籊
80	篬	瀏	糠	糟	糬	綮	縕	縑	繢	繟	羸	罽	羈	翻	翽

Row 73		01	02	03	04	05	06	07	08	09	10	11	12	13	14	15	16	17	18	19
00		耫	聕	聲	齋	臏	臞	舓	閼	舋	艃	艥	艨	艂	薔	蕉	蘳	藙	蘢	蘈
20	蘻	蘩	蘷	蘛	蘭	蘮	蘟	藤	蘫	蘯	蘲	蘵	蠣	蠕	蠨	蟾	蠯	蠽	蟲	蠮
40	襍	襐	襒	覆	觶	譏	譒	譸	譩	謠	譈	讐	譢	曆	豋	豶	貗	貔	貓	貘
60	瞰	贃	贎	贉	贆	趯	趰	趲	趬	趭	趮	趫	趲	趧	蹡	蹳	蹖	躐	躇	躍
80	蹸	躐	躂	躇	躋	躄	躃	轃	轁	轄	轒	轕	轜	邊	邋

Row 74		01	02	03	04	05	06	07	08	09	10	11	12	13	14	15	16	17	18	19
00		邍	酁	酅	酄	酇	醦	醏	醭	醱	醶	醷	醹	醻	醳	醼	醾	鏗	鍽	鐍
20	鍪	鐙	鐒	鐊	鐈	鬭	闖	闞	鬳	隳	囊	雗	雝	霏	霣	霚	霫	霬	霧	霳
40	霽	霿	靧	靦	鞊	鞢	鞼	鞱	鞜	鞨	鞽	韃	韄	鞼	韇	韓	韽	韾	頮	瀨
60	賴	顉	顊	飀	飆	飄	饁	饆	饉	饅	饇	饍	饈	饐	饑	饒	饙	騌	騒	騚
80	騝	騞	騢	騮	鬐	鬑	鬒	鬗	骽	髈	髊	髍	髎	髏	鬀

Row 75		01	02	03	04	05	06	07	08	09	10	11	12	13	14	15	16	17	18	19
00		鬆	鬖	鬗	鬇	鬷	魌	魑	魒	魗	鮔	鮓	鯨	鯦	鯇	鰆	鯱	鯈	鮸	鰖
20	魤	鯥	鯩	鰵	鯀	鴐	鰶	鰷	鶩	鶩	鷲	鴘	鴾	鴟	鵀	鵗	鵜	鵨	鴯	鴰
40	鵲	鵣	鶬	鶗	鵂	鶢	麡	麢	麤	麠	麯	麴	麵	麰	麼	黀	黍	黎	黖	黝
60	黯	黫	鼙	鼛	鼞	鼟	齇	齏	鼪	鼫	齕	齗	齚	齾	龜	儹	儻	龤	㔶	嚵
80	嚸	嚶	嚼	囒	囖	罄	壏	壣	壧	嬅	嬲	嬰	孽	羸	彌

Row 76		01	02	03	04	05	06	07	08	09	10	11	12	13	14	15	16	17	18	19
00		幰	廨	廲	廞	彋	彍	徾	懃	懈	懌	懰	鹹	擧	擘	攀	攑	攚	攕	擈
20	黴	歠	歡	麞	曦	櫰	櫻	櫂	櫰	櫸	櫜	檖	櫒	櫜	蘮	斷	氈	毊	瀋	灄
40	瀠	瀵	瀸	瀼	瀱	爁	爛	爊	燮	爆	癧	癧	癢	癯	玃	瓌	癟	癮	皽	皾
60	鹽	矗	矘	矙	矌	矇	瞭	矕	礥	礮	礦	礵	禝	穋	穮	穳	穆	穲	竊	籋
80	籗	籙	籛	籚	籔	籓	籖	籧	籣	籰	籑	籒	籏	籅	籞

Row 77		01	02	03	04	05	06	07	08	09	10	11	12	13	14	15	16	17	18	19
00		纍	繶	纎	纊	罍	罻	羉	羀	舉	翿	朧	臝	臅	臜	鼻	艪	艦	艭	艬
20	輿	輿	饌	餳	艷	艷	蘁	蘍	蘙	藾	蘧	藻	蘒	蘮	蘦	蘫	蘘	蘠	蘗	蘺
40	蘹	蘾	虩	蠡	蠍	蠝	蠠	螟	蠿	蠶	蠹	蠷	蠺	蠽	蠿	齋	襝	襪	襦	襖
60	襥	襺	覼	觀	讃	讇	讅	讈	讌	讍	豊	豒	豬	貛	豪	鼕	貜	貙	貐	贐
80	贓	趩	趯	躉	躓	躞	躔	躒	躕	躙	躚	躡	躛	躧	蹩

Row 78	01	02	03	04	05	06	07	08	09	10	11	12	13	14	15	16	17	18	19
00		轐	轞	轗	轖	轙	轛	邋	邀	遷	䫲	醨	鄺	醰	醶	醹	醻	醫	鏏	鐓
20	鏱	鏦	鐦	鏻	鑋	鐶	闠	闟	闥	闤	闢	闣	闞	闡	𢿫	雦	霱	霣	䨆	𩅦
40	韗	韀	韇	韈	韣	韤	韅	韊	韎	韄	韄	韹	韺	韱	顥	顛	顧	顨	顩	顪
60	颮	颷	颾	飀	飅	飉	飍	餧	餫	餬	騂	騃	騄	騅	騆	騇	騉	騊	騋	騌
80	騊	鬺	鬻	髁	髃	髄	髆	髺	髻	鬃	鬄	鬅	鬆	鬇	鬈					

Row 79	01	02	03	04	05	06	07	08	09	10	11	12	13	14	15	16	17	18	19
00		魌	魍	鰫	鰬	鰟	鰢	鄉	鰴	鰻	鯛	鯸	鯩	鯜	鯯	鯝	鯻	鶯	鶪	鶯
20	鴿	鶟	鶠	鶦	鶨	鶩	鶪	鶫	鶬	鶭	鶮	鶯	鶰	鶱	鶲	鶳	鶴	鶵	鶶	鶷
40	麳	麶	麷	麹	麺	麼	麽	麾	麿	黀	黁	黂	黃	黅	黆	黇	黈	黉	黊	黋
60	鼰	鼱	鼲	鼳	鼴	鼵	齀	齁	齂	齃	齄	齅	齆	齇	齈	齉	嚽	嚾	嚿	囄
80	囂	疊	壘	壛	壢	孈	孎	彯	巏	巍	巑	巘	巕	巗	巆					

Row 80	01	02	03	04	05	06	07	08	09	10	11	12	13	14	15	16	17	18	19
00		戳	屨	攎	攉	巇	㩧	欆	欙	櫼	欏	欑	櫹	檈	櫜	鐒	鑼	鐃	釐	歎
20	歟	歔	歛	臮	瀤	瀸	瀶	纍	灘	瀿	灪	瀲	灖	灒	灎	灛	櫻	獿	獹	玃
40	獵	璐	瓟	甗	矙	皾	癒	癧	癠	癬	瞫	矚	矘	矗	礭	礪	穲	竇	竊	竈
60	竷	篶	籀	簾	籑	籔	籐	籓	籗	籜	籚	籠	籛	籤	籪	籬	籫	籭	籰	籲
80	粩	纏	纖	纘	罍	羵	聵	臕	臡	臢	舋	艬	艭	艫	蘿					

Row 81	01	02	03	04	05	06	07	08	09	10	11	12	13	14	15	16	17	18	19
00		韝	蘥	蘨	虇	蘪	蘭	虆	虉	虈	獼	蠘	蠦	蠨	蠬	蠮	蠯	蠵	蠹	蠧
20	襲	襵	襶	艦	讅	讄	讇	讉	讋	讌	讍	讏	讐	貛	貜	贓	贔	贕	贖	趯
40	趲	趭	躎	躒	躔	躘	躗	躙	躚	躛	躝	躞	轔	轗	躧	闊	闋	闌	闔	闐
60	闔	隔	霮	霯	霵	霻	靅	靆	靇	靉	靊	韅	韇	韈	韊	韍	韛	韜	韤	韡
80	韣	韥	韟	韠	韡	顚	顛	顜	顝	顟	顢	飂	飃	飡	饜					

Row 82	01	02	03	04	05	06	07	08	09	10	11	12	13	14	15	16	17	18	19
00		餝	饖	饡	饇	饛	饎	饠	饟	饘	饙	饚	驔	驕	驚	驊	驋	驉	驚	驁
20	驒	軀	髏	髀	髖	鬆	鬈	鬋	鬌	鬍	鬎	鬏	鬩	鬫	鬻	鬾	魋	魑	魖	魒
40	魙	鰱	鰩	鰫	鰯	鰲	鰳	鰷	鰹	鱄	鱇	鱊	鱋	鱗	鱝	韓	鱙	鷵	鷹	鷲
60	鷻	鷽	鸂	鸉	鸊	鸋	鸌	鸑	鸒	鸓	鸔	鸕	鸖	鸗	麗	麤	麮	麯	麳	麴
80	夔	黷	黰	黶	黸	黭	黺	黻	黼	黿	鼂	鼇	鼉	鼊	鼷					

Row 83	01	02	03	04	05	06	07	08	09	10	11	12	13	14	15	16	17	18	19
00		鼶	鼸	鼺	鼼	齊	齌	齎	齒	齘	齝	齡	齣	龕	龘	攙	斸	儽	灑	囈
20	壟	壧	孋	寷	寶	巎	巕	巗	巘	巙	廱	攢	彏	彨	攣	攏	攔	攖	攘	攛
40	斅	曨	欄	欃	欂	欅	欆	欒	欖	歷	殲	氌	灑	灕	爛	爜	犧	犨	甗	贏
60	癦	癥	癪	癬	舋	矏	矐	矙	矓	矚	矘	纓	礦	礨	礶	礨	穮	竷	竸	籔
80	甄	籂	籗	籮	籲	籩	籥	糴	纔	纚	纈	纗	纇	纕	聽					

Row 84		01	02	03	04	05	06	07	08	09	10	11	12	13	14	15	16	17	18	19
00		𦪙	艪	蘁	蘒	蘐	蘜	蘉	蘔	蘫	蘬	蟻	蠎	蠝	蠣	蠷	蠰	鑾	蟹	蓬
20	罶	蠹	蘏	轂	襰	覼	觼	讁	讄	讇	讅	讂	讖	讙	豴	賝	贚	贎	趯	趲
40	趮	趭	蹪	躑	躦	躩	躪	躨	躐	躡	邍	醲	醰	鑘	鑝	鑤	闟	鬮	霱	霳
60	霵	霺	霷	靁	韄	韇	韣	韤	韥	韾	韡	韢	韣	韘	顩	顪	顲	飂	饓	饛
80	饞	驨	驌	驝	驙	驫	驓	驥	驦	驨	驧	鬞	鬠	鬤	鬢

Row 85		01	02	03	04	05	06	07	08	09	10	11	12	13	14	15	16	17	18	19
00		鬡	鬟	鬣	鬤	鬛	鬚	鬻	魖	魕	魙	魗	鮺	鰖	鰫	鰶	鱃	鰸	鱉	鱉
20	鱟	鷩	鷹	鷺	鶯	鷲	鸐	鶾	鷮	鷞	鷭	鷳	鸀	鸆	鸄	鸋	鸓	鸔	鸕	麠
40	麶	麷	麳	麴	麮	麯	麰	黀	黁	黫	黭	鼀	鼁	鼂	鼅	鼆	鼉	鼊	齂	齆
60	齾	齻	龤	龢	龣	龘	㒽	䫄	䴙	齇	齃	嚵	奲	嬱	廱	斆	旟	曮	曩	朧
80	欞	欗	欘	欄	欃	欏	欑	欒	㰆	殰	殲	氌	氍	灇	灑

Row 86		01	02	03	04	05	06	07	08	09	10	11	12	13	14	15	16	17	18	19
00		灡	灢	爨	瓖	瓘	瓚	甗	甗	癭	癰	矙	矡	礹	礵	礷	穳	竊	竉	籙
20	籚	籛	籝	籣	糶	糷	纅	纆	纇	羅	羉	虀	虇	虌	虉	虊	蘼	蠼	蠽	蠾
40	蠻	蠹	蠿	襶	讁	讂	讆	趲	趱	躖	躘	躙	躚	躛	軃	轞	轟	轠	釃	釄
60	鑮	鑯	鑱	鑲	鑴	鑶	靌	靏	靐	韇	韈	韊	韉	韤	顬	顭	顮	顯	饟	饞
80	饠	驠	驡	髗	髖	髕	鬖	鬘	鬠	鬻	魑	鱁	鱛	鱝	鱢

Row 87		01	02	03	04	05	06	07	08	09	10	11	12	13	14	15	16	17	18	19
00		鱧	鱮	齋	鱨	鱭	鷔	鷺	鷹	鷲	鸕	鸂	鸃	鸛	鸑	鸓	鸞	鸈	鸐	鸖
20	鸎	鸄	鸑	鸍	鸌	鸉	麟	麢	麡	麶	麷	麴	麳	黐	黙	黸	黷	黶	黰	鼆
40	鼉	齇	齈	齉	齤	齬	齺	齾	龕	龔	龜	龝	䶵	囋	囐	囕	孏	孎	憲	爛
60	攫	攦	曤	朧	欇	欉	欗	歡	灨	灪	灠	灝	爢	犨	玃	瓥	鬱	虋	礶	禰
80	穰	竈	籗	籰	籭	籱	纙	纞	纕	羇	羈	蠹	蠸	臞	鸜

Row 88		01	02	03	04	05	06	07	08	09	10	11	12	13	14	15	16	17	18	19
00		蘻	蘠	蘳	蘴	蘭	蠗	蠛	蠓	蠖	蠶	蠽	蠹	蠺	襺	覿	觾	讜	躐	趯
20	趲	躩	躪	躝	躟	轣	轤	轥	贏	邐	醹	醽	醼	鑱	闤	闥	靂	韇	韊	韱
40	顪	飍	饕	饡	饢	驉	驫	驥	髐	鬗	鬘	鬭	鬮	魒	鱥	鱞	鱣	鱧	鱨	鱮
60	鱵	鱳	鱴	鱶	鱹	鸁	鸄	鸅	鸆	鸇	鸉	鸌	鸏	鸐	鸑	鸒	鸔	鸕	麏	麥
80	麷	麴	黂	黏	黷	黳	黵	黶	鼊	鼛	鼱	鼶	鼸	齂	齁

Row 89		01	02	03	04	05	06	07	08	09	10	11	12	13	14	15	16	17	18	19
00		齵	鬖	囉	孌	寷	巑	巕	儽	戁	攂	攊	攠	欏	欙	歡	灥	爏	犪	穫
20	癰	籩	糶	纞	纗	纚	纝	纘	贏	讚	覵	虉	虆	蘹	蘺	蘸	蠿	蠽	蠻	蠼
40	蠹	蠺	蠶	襹	觀	覽	讙	讘	鑾	軆	轞	轠	闠	灩	靉	靊	韉	韊	顳	飋
60	飌	饟	驩	驐	驏	驌	驎	驑	鬤	鬣	鬵	魗	鱢	鱶	黶	鼈	鶩	鸏	鸓	鸛
80	鸘	鸗	齹	齸	麢	麣	豔	黷	黸	鼊	黯	龜	齹	鼷	鼶

Row 90

	00	01	02	03	04	05	06	07	08	09	10	11	12	13	14	15	16	17	18	19
00		觮	齍	齏	齰	齸	䶥	覊	蘚	欒	灨	灢	瓚	礹	穰	籑	籟	籚	鞿	豅
20	鬱	囊	鷨	襶	覼	讋	讞	躒	躕	躍	轣	韡	鑭	鑽	靐	霦	靈	醶	韉	韣
40	顳	顴	飌	饟	驩	驤	髗	鬞	鬻	鱹	鱇	鱲	驛	驖	鸛	鸑	鸏	鸐	鸘	鸜
60	黶	鼉	鼊	鼈	鼶	齴	齵	龤	龕	龖	靈	靡	廬	灑	灥	爣	甗	癵	礸	臠
80	麟	艬	虆	蠋	覶	讐	讕	躔	玁	趯	轥	醽	鑣	闟	隱					

Row 91

	00	01	02	03	04	05	06	07	08	09	10	11	12	13	14	15	16	17	18	19
00		隴	韝	譣	飌	饕	鬟	鱝	鱶	鱠	鳠	鷩	鷩	鸑	鷷	鸛	鸇	鸝	鸏	黬
20	鼉	蠶	鼸	齱	齫	齹	龜	穀	虁	巕	欙	躔	欞	灪	癧	矔	籭	臢	轡	圞
40	鹽	躗	躐	鸎	羅	韃	鬛	闤	鬱	魒	鑳	鱄	鑻	鱴	鷬	鷭	鬘	貛	醴	鷩
60	黶	齟	龕	鐢	覵	檽	穖	竈	籆	纆	蘭	蠬	齜	黲	躚	轋	靈	鞻	鸞	灩
80	鱎	鱺	鱩	鱥	鸕	鶪	驤	饕	鼵	鼸	軆	爨	鑵	糯	禳					

Row 92

	00	01	02	03	04	05	06	07	08	09	10	11	12	13	14	15	16	17	18	19
00		鑯	韾	驫	鸑	鱧	鰻	鑼	鸊	鸐	齾	鑰	鑑	鸒	鱑	鸜	鑾	鸄	鱙	鼲
20	巙	顯	鰝	鰪	灪	鸝	龤	鸎	灦	虋	鬱	讔	虪	龘	靋	礹	觀	顱	鱸	驪
40	鸞	鼺	黷	襶	欆	鸁	豐	蘭	齉	龖										
60																				
80																				

CNS 11643-1992 Plane 6

Row 1		01	02	03	04	05	06	07	08	09	10	11	12	13	14	15	16	17	18	19
00		乀	⺊	乂	丩	乙	乚	二	二	二	七	巳	卜	工	丂	丌	午	丸	凡	丂
20	天	个	亼	六	刃	勹	力	可	云	飞	户	光	亡	亏	旦	丘	万	丑	川	禾
40	丱	去	区	仃	㔾	元	穴	同	内	丹	兂	出	凶	瓜	刊	叨	加	㠯	廿	卬
60	冄	冄	戏	丕	殳	及	收	乜	囚	囙	因	史	太	凧	寸	不	屮	巛	王	五
80	王	巳	乡	刃	廾	廾	弍	弓	弓	弓	弓	弓	弓	礼	忄					

Row 2		01	02	03	04	05	06	07	08	09	10	11	12	13	14	15	16	17	18	19
00		忆	斗	斤	氵	日	王	爪	皿	四	丑	亏	北	日	丐	丰	夭	亏	世	氶
20	仙	令	仈	会	冋	冊	囚	冗	冬	爪	缶	由	冂	功	叫	丑	如	巛	包	旬
40	匀	北	完	卡	冃	厇	厄	序	厄	牟	区	汉	叹	反	史	凸	各	旦	吗	叫
60	叱	色	各	西	圩	左	孕	斉	外	夙	夾	处	予	杀	无	尥	尺	半	屺	岂
80	屿	出	岔	出	巵	币	帘	红	务	弁	弓	弓	弢	弟	弘					

Row 3		01	02	03	04	05	06	07	08	09	10	11	12	13	14	15	16	17	18	19
00		弘	弗	令	彤	彡	忆	尼	毛	扐	扠	百	旿	自	玉	火	爬	厂	犸	丐
20	日	生	疋	内	艹	舟	身	公	⺁	彐	而	系	死	中	宇	冊	耒	飞	荒	孖
40	亙	虫	从	仑	佇	併	饮	尬	伧	今	充	元	元	介	夌	尖	冉	冊	冊	宊
60	冴	兖	凤	夙	凭	凹	卤	凶	区	由	刖	刿	別	刑	匈	刖	劲	医	匠	匭
80	半	去	犴	車	伞	亩	卡	支	皮	卯	旧	厌	厌	底	忝					

Row 4		01	02	03	04	05	06	07	08	09	10	11	12	13	14	15	16	17	18	19
00		肮	公	去	叚	及	尧	夆	吉	召	足	旱	号	吼	看	回	目	困	四	壮
20	仳	巫	夆	夆	麦	夋	丑	多	夸	奎	奕	夺	肉	娇	妃	妫	抒	孜	它	宁
40	亏	穴	宄	当	尚	昼	局	吊	屁	尸	岩	艸	玄	屺	屹	峡	岂	岔	屾	帀
60	忿	厄	布	忙	忙	希	庄	序	庆	庇	広	圳	弓	吊	弘	曳	彐	妆	当	丐
80	珍	伶	悖	悖	怀	任	戎	序	厄	找	盲	旦	叭	肌	呆					

Row 5		01	02	03	04	05	06	07	08	09	10	11	12	13	14	15	16	17	18	19
00		系	机	次	吹	正	岂	劲	夙	气	氛	永	床	泛	汎	汪	汶	汹	炙	灸
20	杰	叔	钉	犹	丕	生	用	定	卑	皂	后	否	礼	季	年	网	咒	罔	孝	肉
40	肛	肯	凶	凹	芒	芋	芦	芍	芷	艾	芋	衣	豕	身	底	迁	迴	边	邵	邸
60	邦	阝	所	先	丰	垂	肃	引	周	亘	亘	苴	丞	炎	信	佈	伎	休	体	傍
80	但	作	你	佢	爸	克	兑	免	兵	全	共	良	兵	谷	凶					

Row 6	01	02	03	04	05	06	07	08	09	10	11	12	13	14	15	16	17	18	19
00	同	㒳	冊	冾	兇	凬	凪	丙	刘	创	刹	刿	劶	劵	㘉	吙	旨	吴	仓
20 匨	匩	匫	匲	匧	㶴	平	尘	卤	压	厍	厌	㐰	皇	交	叓	㔔	㕣	吽	吘
40 㠯	荒	品	吐	吃	吼	吸	㕾	召	因	囚	囘	囲	囘	丐	囟	回	囲	囻	囮
60 囚	圫	至	圬	坛	坐	圪	坍	均	坐	㘰	坚	垩	壮	𡉏	宔	夆	夂	夗	夻
80 妶	妥	妄	妟	姄	妗	孖	孛	孙	写	穷	宫	宦	安	穷					

Row 7	01	02	03	04	05	06	07	08	09	10	11	12	13	14	15	16	17	18	19
00	寿	岂	尖	尜	尬	尸	层	屁	启	㞢	孡	峀	屹	岉	岎	岙	岚	岫	峋
20 凹	凹	巡	乎	帬	帑	帇	帐	帕	帔	帍	帍	余	帠	幵	应	庰	庂	庋	底
40 庞	弅	弁	弃	井	弄	弈	武	肯	弪	弦	弮	彤	徘	征	彸	从	彴	彾	彼
60 发	忐	志	忍	忽	念	忼	怑	怕	怲	怮	役	怐	物	㐴	成	或	犮	屉	扨
80 扭	抚	扣	抨	扒	拎	扮	抡	㕮	皱	孪	穷	百	盹	旦					

Row 8	01	02	03	04	05	06	07	08	09	10	11	12	13	14	15	16	17	18	19
00	旻	昌	沓	舌	各	朋	胥	朗	肌	来	耒	杲	杪	杓	屎	峨	欲	欸	歨
20 歨	夗	歼	殇	殁	殂	殊	殉	死	毐	毕	毡	毪	汁	汙	汛	沬	汐	汰	汧
40 沁	浡	没	炖	炁	爬	号	牠	朊	牧	牤	牣	牲	狒	犹	狱	狮	狐	狃	犯
60 弦	狄	狐	玩	玹	室	助	畄	甹	疔	疖	疣	疬	号	食	针	昊	启	祟	权
80 杉	卧	亢	网	咢	老	肥	胧	肱	胴	同	胃	臣	卤	阜					

Row 9	01	02	03	04	05	06	07	08	09	10	11	12	13	14	15	16	17	18	19
00	至	芀	芔	芎	苊	芩	芝	花	虫	豕	辛	辰	辻	迣	迭	邑	邸	邵	邦
20 兵	阝	丽	囱	匈	太	秀	串	乘	乌	臣	乱	事	亨	佚	保	侣	侄	佤	傀
40 假	作	倭	俩	佥	免	兖	兕	甝	光	光	兜	其	冈	冈	凫	浛	凅	刭	凯
60 咸	飢	凭	凶	甾	刺	刿	刻	制	凼	刚	删	删	刚	刹	刨	刎	劾	劲	劼
80 匐	匐	阜	匿	隶	協	卅	垂	卉	卞	库	直	卣	卣	卣					

Row 10	01	02	03	04	05	06	07	08	09	10	11	12	13	14	15	16	17	18	19
00	卤	谷	即	弜	厗	厗	盾	厦	厕	厝	美	余	弯	丝	羿	叔	系	叒	昏
20 屃	咦	哑	咏	咽	哅	吻	哼	周	邑	园	囵	囿	图	囬	回	垦	垸	埠	坼
40 垯	埠	垍	埇	坨	垂	奇	垒	垂	堅	垡	長	疋	奚	猷	费	芥	共	奔	奎
60 哭	奂	婺	姊	媸	娉	孤	孝	孪	宾	家	宴	宦	时	村	尖	庖	户	屏	屌
80 峑	伞	岊	罡	岪	岠	妾	岵	克	岀	岐	岸	岑	至	香					

Row 11	01	02	03	04	05	06	07	08	09	10	11	12	13	14	15	16	17	18	19
00	帛	帝	斋	卒	娄	庛	庘	彦	庄	底	庛	延	殄	廻	弇	弄	弃	弑	弨
20 弧	弦	彗	弱	彝	彔	彬	彦	徂	作	徇	佟	忠	㐫	患	忞	忽	忑	忠	怀
40 快	恨	怄	怍	怢	怬	怺	命	怆	我	戕	戚	戮	戚	戒	戋	戚	房	扈	拏
60 扠	汞	拼	扼	拔	拐	抹	抱	扶	拜	攴	致	鼓	枚	鼓	赦	攸	斉	祈	斫
80 旁	亘	昊	皆	佰	厄	旺	昰	昅	盵	晬	昝	㫖	旨	艮					

Row 12		01	02	03	04	05	06	07	08	09	10	11	12	13	14	15	16	17	18	19
00		畁	枂	肭	隶	宋	杬	柄	杵	柭	枝	杈	析	枲	欪	炊	欧	歫	豆	歪
20	岸	岜	肯	歨	齿	歭	炭	表	岸	歼	殂	殁	殉	毒	毐	毕	毘	毙	毤	毦
40	畏	氛	氖	氚	沝	汆	沆	汧	沷	沬	泄	沍	泝	沒	泹	涝	泂	泳	沧	沿
60	涂	斉	页	炙	災	爬	爮	丞	爻	斧	牀	牁	牂	肧	朐	朌	牝	牱	犷	犵
80	牧	犿	狂	狀	狁	弦	狔	犮	狃	狜	狲	犾	狝	狝	狝					

Row 13		01	02	03	04	05	06	07	08	09	10	11	12	13	14	15	16	17	18	19
00		玬	玩	玹	玥	玔	玖	瓩	香	牧	奎	甬	甭	甫	甪	畂	甿	亩	畐	畕
20	画	疔	疚	疛	彼	皱	盂	盍	盱	盰	眈	眃	盷	省	导	昆	直	直	矿	矽
40	祋	秇	秎	穽	空	穸	究	窀	竻	罕	糺	罜	罘	伞	美	羽	耇	耐	耍	耓
60	耒	耷	耽	勘	肏	肴	胪	胎	胍	胘	肼	肫	肥	育	脊	脊	胥	胄	胃	胐
80	直	垔	蚤	舀	舁	舥	舡	舡	芐	苷	芋	芫	芸	苙	芔					

Row 14		01	02	03	04	05	06	07	08	09	10	11	12	13	14	15	16	17	18	19
00		苹	芽	苦	若	蚕	虭	号	衍	衵	衮	衩	觅	见	角	觓	訇	豇	豕	赴
20	趴	足	辛	辰	迂	迥	迄	迣	迯	迫	迺	迵	邵	邦	邶	邬	長	自	陈	陣
40	陜	非	笋	垂	乳	佤	尥	東	函	亳	囱	龟	觔	倣	促	俣	俌	俄	俻	使
60	俶	俾	俘	俳	倯	倪	俗	倨	倉	傘	奄	苋	兕	典	典	衍	凋	役	冽	栓
80	冑	刦	刮	函	函	到	剅	刻	刲	刺	刑	制	刚	剛	剛					

Row 15		01	02	03	04	05	06	07	08	09	10	11	12	13	14	15	16	17	18	19
00		剃	剌	刽	努	勇	勅	勁	乖	匌	甸	匍	匊	畠	帚	埃	兆	盆	区	匿
20	陘	是	陘	匾	卑	南	却	卻	卿	即	厚	厎	厉	厓	庢	厡	厧	座	屐	叄
40	卺	叔	咎	季	叟	岳	咠	呞	呈	呱	吻	咚	响	哌	呰	周	凬	呇	咎	囩
60	畕	囪	图	囫	圂	垩	垫	垞	垔	坆	垸	坸	垚	垈	垦	垗	全	声	壶	妥
80	妻	故	㪅	宴	媚	娃	娩	姗	娘	姹	娞	姰	娯	娙	晏					

Row 16		01	02	03	04	05	06	07	08	09	10	11	12	13	14	15	16	17	18	19
00		孧	孖	孫	孝	孚	學	害	宅	宊	宓	宝	官	宬	帮	尉	射	尌	党	尜
20	尦	尬	尰	尯	尴	尲	屐	尾	屆	屄	屏	屍	亭	岇	岑	岕	峀	岫	岙	岀
40	峕	岳	崗	峗	峯	峷	峽	崩	峖	岺	峝	岿	峃	峇	峛	差	巹	巵	希	帍
60	帟	帬	帘	帠	帨	帛	帻	帙	帳	帱	帑	帝	弄	举	㝣	庑	庢	庬	券	㢷
80	弉	弁	弅	弆	弇	弍	弎	弑	弯	弸	弼	费	弗	習	弩					

Row 17		01	02	03	04	05	06	07	08	09	10	11	12	13	14	15	16	17	18	19
00		录	彖	彗	彔	佟	徘	征	徒	忝	忌	忎	忐	忑	息	悠	慌	恔	悖	悚
20	恛	悍	悄	悴	怕	悯	恼	我	戒	戟	戡	戚	戚	戮	屋	扉	扈	扁	扆	拳
40	挛	享	拼	指	挂	拞	拙	挥	投	挖	掬	揪	掏	抑	摒	捷	敁	改	敎	效
60	鼓	敛	钱	敦	斛	所	於	秀	旃	旼	昇	昙	昌	昔	易	昳	書	冒	旱	昷
80	昱	胎	栄	栗	柿	柘	栓	柃	款	欺	軟	契	欧	妖	弥					

Row 18		01	02	03	04	05	06	07	08	09	10	11	12	13	14	15	16	17	18	19
00		㱍	殶	殅	殈	殊	殇	殹	毀	毇	毒	毟	毡	毢	毪	毩	氐	氝	氛	隶
20	泉	泎	泥	洸	流	洖	沿	涊	溢	浤	洦	浌	滋	浾	派	炣	炦	炼	羑	费
40	炭	炱	烝	省	㳒	爭	采	𥝢	𦓴	𠄨	牊	牑	牏	牗	牕	牓	牠	特	牫	犋
60	犑	犓	犌	犐	犕	犿	狃	狅	狊	狉	狛	狝	狆	玻	珂	珄	珊	瓞	瓠	瓨
80	昏	青	畂	畋	畕	畏	畟	画	畠	畢	畠	疣	疦	疩	痃					

Row 19		01	02	03	04	05	06	07	08	09	10	11	12	13	14	15	16	17	18	19
00		疣	痒	痕	痨	登	皈	皉	皍	皐	皏	皔	盉	盘	盽	眃	眎	眡	眩	眸
20	眦	眽	眘	看	眢	眥	眞	晏	眲	睤	苗	敃	翣	炭	砚	砝	硐	砏	砨	祈
40	祓	衾	祖	祝	祗	禽	稀	秧	秫	秝	科	秞	秎	秊	采	乖	窕	窍	窚	窞
60	窮	粦	竽	笄	笲	笧	紆	紂	紦	紅	紃	紌	紕	罕	罔	罡	罟	罨	罝	罠
80	羝	幸	羢	翌	翏	翠	翍	耙	耛	舧	舦	离	肢	胴	胉					

Row 20		01	02	03	04	05	06	07	08	09	10	11	12	13	14	15	16	17	18	19
00		胠	胲	胇	胱	脈	服	脉	胳	胐	脊	胥	扁	肩	扃	脊	朗	玺	臬	臾
20	甜	舦	舠	舥	艮	莞	荨	茱	茉	茺	茀	茧	荂	茜	茶	茶	荼	苍	莈	虐
40	虒	虓	虫	蚩	蚂	蚑	虵	衍	術	衰	衮	衹	觔	豋	員	豺	豨	赳	赲	趸
60	軛	軥	軎	迒	迋	迊	迡	迹	追	途	邦	郭	邵	邺	郊	邺	郰	郶	郰	陀
80	陇	陏	陶	隙	降	陜	除	陜	阽	青	面	覓	倉	倉	倉					

Row 21		01	02	03	04	05	06	07	08	09	10	11	12	13	14	15	16	17	18	19
00		倉	飢	鼻	韭	韭	棗	非	叠	飫	昝	亂	胥	亞	危	章	亮	亮	炎	佸
20	偄	傲	俩	倒	倸	例	俺	炙	尭	畲	與	奔	眞	異	冕	侖	冕	涮	淵	凬
40	凷	剫	刮	劵	剃	剅	刨	剳	剬	剎	剼	剭	劁	勃	勇	努	勉	働	勃	匔
60	匑	匑	匒	匓	匐	匜	匯	匚	匭	卹	单	隶	皁	泉	卤	卤	卲	厚	厥	厥
80	盾	厚	厍	厔	摩	隼	单	器	叝	叟	叟	叚	叆	吉	唐					

Row 22		01	02	03	04	05	06	07	08	09	10	11	12	13	14	15	16	17	18	19
00		高	咳	唡	咽	喽	啫	香	哉	嗽	圁	圊	圁	圎	坔	型	垩	埭	埲	埸
20	垗	城	垾	埕	埇	埌	埏	堆	垩	堲	基	堲	垒	喜	寿	奎	夔	夶	嬴	奔
40	奩	奞	舆	奥	姬	娱	婹	婴	婴	婴	婺	娉	嫄	婚	婚	媦	孨	孴	寐	寄
60	宴	寔	寤	寷	寖	宷	寔	寀	家	宜	宗	将	尋	尐	尲	尳	尵	尨	尖	屖
80	屃	屄	屎	屎	屠	草	宫	嵜	峑	岂	岡	岦	岩	峄	峔					

Row 23		01	02	03	04	05	06	07	08	09	10	11	12	13	14	15	16	17	18	19
00		肯	業	峴	峹	垂	巡	凰	差	郙	帶	帛	帨	帾	幆	帿	帹	帲	帾	幏
20	帑	羿	弅	庮	廍	廙	庿	庡	廇	弆	弇	弊	弫	彅	彉	彔	彐	彖	彏
40	徒	循	徎	徎	徢	徯	俗	徲	徯	慈	恐	恭	烈	恩	惠	悤	恖	怨	急	惣
60	悴	悴	悚	惆	悁	性	愕	惦	愀	惪	惱	戜	戲	戚	扆	扉	扂	擘	掱	搋
80	拙	挽	捭	掴	揣	揆	揑	掭	掟	搖	掏	揞	採	掾	揃					

Row 24		01	02	03	04	05	06	07	08	09	10	11	12	13	14	15	16	17	18	19
00		敁	㪅	赦	敉	敦	敡	敊	敍	敒	猣	敆	柰	敇	敳	兆	斴	旂	旗	旆
20	旍	㬊	書	春	曺	昰	昵	昦	昢	冣	曑	㫚	皆	曹	會	胖	窣	亲	東	栗
40	栫	梹	枅	栖	栲	栐	柵	栶	栅	栤	舂	枲	柴	欲	欣	欶	欿	跟	埲	垚
60	凿	酋	㡴	殆	殜	殕	殎	殑	殌	殏	殈	毒	毗	毕	毘	髦	毢	毣	毞	毤
80	粟	泓	沝	流	浸	涺	浢	浅	泿	洛	洄	洮	減	淡	浡					

Row 25		01	02	03	04	05	06	07	08	09	10	11	12	13	14	15	16	17	18	19
00		涅	洲	浣	洄	浬	浸	洹	洋	沸	泫	涵	涇	浩	洎	浿	涽	洦	淹	渉
20	袂	烸	焍	家	焚	焦	焉	烝	魚	牉	牊	牏	牓	牕	舀	舌	犅	犾	狱	狟
40	狣	狢	猓	猰	猚	猻	狩	獭	玹	球	班	琲	瑙	琥	瓞	瓟	瓜	瓵	豈	甁
60	瓶	甭	瑚	眠	畈	畎	畚	畁	畏	畀	痒	痃	痂	疪	痗	痈	痹	痔	痐	疮
80	痋	症	癸	癸	皋	皛	皮	皷	皱	皰	皲	皵	盂	盈	盔					

Row 26		01	02	03	04	05	06	07	08	09	10	11	12	13	14	15	16	17	18	19
00		盈	盅	盒	留	盞	眮	眵	眹	眽	省	眘	鼎	真	眞	矜	矞	矧	知	矬
20	研	破	砠	确	砺	礉	祎	祒	祉	祫	祗	祢	祭	祩	秺	秫	秧	秳	秙	黍
40	窊	窭	窌	窕	竒	竟	竒	笎	笄	笔	粒	粚	粆	籸	粌	紌	紼	絎	紺	絰
60	紛	綳	紇	約	紟	紪	索	紧	紊	罙	缽	罨	罘	罝	罥	罣	罚	罟	羚	羫
80	羝	羠	羛	羕	牂	羝	翑	翓	翥	耽	聅	聆	聉	聘	聙					

Row 27		01	02	03	04	05	06	07	08	09	10	11	12	13	14	15	16	17	18	19
00		聳	聑	聏	肁	肕	胥	肯	胬	胼	脛	脖	胉	脯	胦	脡	胔	脒	胍	脳
20	臯	畾	皇	臱	臸	致	致	乖	舭	舦	舋	舄	舀	舙	舚	舙	舥	舨	舩
40	舷	舨	舨	芼	芃	芺	芳	荒	茯	荳	茝	茵	茾	荖	莧	莔	茜	茮	荷	荽
60	萄	莽	莾	茁	茆	茨	莽	虎	蚁	蚕	蚨	蚓	蚪	蚍	蚤	蚩	蛋	蛍	蛋	蛩
80	衄	蚩	蚨	蚴	盃	盅	衕	衙	衮	衰	衾	袁	衷	袅	衾					

Row 28		01	02	03	04	05	06	07	08	09	10	11	12	13	14	15	16	17	18	19
00		袞	袨	袝	袛	袗	袙	袧	衩	衹	覃	觓	觟	訏	訉	訐	訑	訦	託	逭
20	豆	豈	豣	豕	豤	財	貟	起	赴	赶	赳	趵	趴	趶	跜	趸	躬	軏	軒	軎
40	迕	迎	迃	迠	迒	迳	迹	迷	迺	逰	迹	逮	逛	逝	迣	迭	逡	郄	郡	郫
60	郿	郜	郪	郝	酞	量	釜	釗	釡	釿	閂	阪	陞	陏	陘	陋	陵	陒	陪	隆
80	雉	雅	惟	非	非	飛	飠	飢	飤	胥	鹵	乘	發	圈	卷					

Row 29		01	02	03	04	05	06	07	08	09	10	11	12	13	14	15	16	17	18	19
00		亟	亹	亭	侾	倌	倚	俜	俶	倷	侵	倮	侸	俦	便	保	倾	倣	倸	倏
20	傛	偕	候	佘	侖	龠	奚	冥	與	崙	冞	凘	凗	處	凬	兇	函	函	剭	剻
40	剃	剉	劑	剛	勍	勧	勩	勣	勢	勦	匐	匑	匰	匱	卓	卣	厦	卿	卿	厥
60	厥	厬	厨	叚	厴	叆	叇	叕	叡	叟	叞	叡	叔	叙	叟	叟	善	誓	启	唻
80	唍	哆	啐	哶	啊	喹	嗵	員	嗰	嘍	阜	岳	嘟	品	周					

Row 30		01	02	03	04	05	06	07	08	09	10	11	12	13	14	15	16	17	18	19
00		𠕒	函	囼	㘣	𡇂	𡇈	㙂	𡋾	埭	塔	堄	埴	臺	堺	堺	垮	埢	堥	堲
20	奎	坐	亹	夋	畓	夏	奊	夓	㚄	𡚇	乘	爽	執	奩	奞	奤	桊	奥	娶	娑
40	嫈	婁	𡞖	娄	嬰	嬰	敄	娕	婦	婟	娷	媳	姘	奕	卒	寂	寀	寇	寛	宺
60	寞	尉	尉	尊	尞	尞	尞	岀	尧	岔	㞙	屜	屁	屈	屋	屎	犀	屚	屜	屡
80	阻	毒	峇	㠀	屉	弥	崫	崣	巷	崮	峿	嵏	峎	峴	岨

Row 31		01	02	03	04	05	06	07	08	09	10	11	12	13	14	15	16	17	18	19
00		崮	崓	崢	崧	峪	嵐	峪	㠓	嵂	峴	嵘	嵫	巤	巽	巷	巻	帣	幕	帑
20	帑	幣	帽	幩	幬	幔	幓	幌	幗	幒	扁	咸	康	唐	庋	庰	庞	庳	屛	庬
40	庫	弇	弇	庸	弈	畀	畁	弑	弶	弦	弢	弴	弽	张	弨	彅	彖	彘	影	彪
60	彰	彬	彫	徜	徑	徫	徃	修	御	徇	徭	徫	徬	徳	惪	恐	恭	憂	恳	悬
80	啞	恩	忩	悘	愡	慈	惸	慄	慍	憦	愖	悁	慖	懘	悽

Row 32		01	02	03	04	05	06	07	08	09	10	11	12	13	14	15	16	17	18	19
00		愘	慀	戛	戜	戕	戺	挈	挛	捺	捞	掃	搧	揖	押	搡	拼	押	掴	搖
20	掾	攔	捨	捻	鼓	攲	敲	敥	敞	鞍	敳	散	敪	敹	斋	斣	敍	将	斛	斫
40	斯	旃	旃	晝	量	晶	晜	晬	晭	晃	晙	昌	晥	昪	旨	晁	望	胳	腁	腰
60	梔	梖	亲	榉	栽	桓	梾	椕	棍	椢	椁	桂	桤	椗	桀	欧	款	欻	欶	眘
80	歬	殕	殌	殯	殞	殚	殸	殹	殿	殽	殺	毀	毚	毘	毣

Row 33		01	02	03	04	05	06	07	08	09	10	11	12	13	14	15	16	17	18	19
00		毦	毧	毨	毤	毴	毯	毶	毷	氉	泉	源	浣	浯	消	涝	滅	涠	涷	浇
20	淀	淖	淵	淬	淜	湑	滑	淔	渶	泮	湫	湽	港	湓	溆	溛	溫	溳	滁	滌
40	烜	煜	煸	焻	烰	裁	尉	娶	熨	爱	㚇	炭	爨	煹	爬	爱	夆	爺	爸	牾
60	牉	牃	牓	牍	牖	牌	牕	牊	犸	犆	犂	犔	犗	犘	犀	献	犹	獄	狴	猕
80	猍	猑	猸	猾	獀	猻	瑯	琈	琨	瑁	琁	瑹	瑰	瓜	甃

Row 34		01	02	03	04	05	06	07	08	09	10	11	12	13	14	15	16	17	18	19
00		瓶	瓾	甂	甌	甿	畒	畫	畮	畹	畤	畾	畫	畬	畧	疐	疼	疫	痍	病
20	痈	瘦	瘊	瘁	痃	痴	登	盅	鼻	皱	皺	盜	盚	盝	睺	睸	眤	睗	睒	瞍
40	睥	略	瞆	截	畊	眘	眷	習	眉	泉	昇	晟	刪	矧	矬	矬	庾	㑴	嫉	笑
60	碰	硃	硬	碕	碗	硝	磁	禔	禹	秤	稊	秈	税	稐	粱	窖	窒	窦	窩	窪
80	竏	竧	竨	笙	笓	筤	筵	筑	筴	筌	筎	箄	箹	粊	粓

Row 35		01	02	03	04	05	06	07	08	09	10	11	12	13	14	15	16	17	18	19
00		粛	粫	絍	絽	絣	綒	綊	緩	紺	絝	縶	綮	緌	缻	緎	罣	罠	罟	罝
20	罨	罧	罛	罜	罥	羞	羞	羑	羢	羝	翊	翔	翍	翐	翋	翗	翎	翑	翓	翚
40	耆	耕	聃	聑	聏	聍	聻	聜	晝	肭	胖	胠	閣	脅	脀	腰	腒	腗	腘	腚
60	胸	腳	膝	膠	膨	膐	膂	脩	臥	臯	臬	舁	舡	舻	舀	舋	舵	艢	艒	舤
80	舵	艄	艀	艏	茨	苋	茋	菱	葸	葏	葬	蒿	蔚	華	蒟

Row 36		01	02	03	04	05	06	07	08	09	10	11	12	13	14	15	16	17	18	19
00		茿	菆	茾	荕	莗	莍	莂	莕	莆	荁	莫	草	蒪	茶	莾	莽	菱	莇	苷
20	草	莧	茵	莜	菍	莬	莽	著	菌	菜	菊	虝	虖	虒	虘	蚤	蚷	蛔	蚔	蚌
40	蛉	蛇	蛩	蛙	蛩	蚕	蚮	衏	衺	衾	袰	袞	衷	袠	疾	衦	袜	袹	衹	堊
60	跜	跜	舤	舺	舨	舸	舷	舨	舵	舶	牑	阜	脂	詔	訴	詖	詃	詽	詾	詘
80	詨	訖	訰	詉	詅	寘	詈	詹	誊	詡	婄	容	貁	豿	豪

Row 37		01	02	03	04	05	06	07	08	09	10	11	12	13	14	15	16	17	18	19
00		象	豗	貥	貅	貀	貥	貱	貯	貶	貣	貰	貸	貾	赶	赽	趁	跘	跖	跱
20	跐	跅	跃	跏	跃	跀	跰	跂	跶	跰	躰	躭	躯	躯	躶	躳	躹	軏	軓	軕
40	軠	軦	軸	軵	軨	軥	軟	豜	迯	迷	逞	逞	逍	逋	迣	逵	逦	逄	逕	逡
60	逷	逼	峇	烜	邑	肥	鄀	邧	郛	部	郿	都	郪	酛	酛	酤	酮	酘	酥	酤
80	酘	畣	媎	湎	粟	量	鈚	金	瓬	瓨	瓬	閚	閑	閈	阺

Row 38		01	02	03	04	05	06	07	08	09	10	11	12	13	14	15	16	17	18	19
00		陵	陋	隟	陾	隁	陳	陘	险	陶	隆	隊	雇	雀	雁	雅	隻	雂	雩	雯
20	蜚	頍	颰	倉	飽	飾	飪	飭	湑	麃	麻	鹵	黼	縣	殰	兜	殗	麞	覓	傪
40	偵	偣	偶	傫	傠	偾	偭	傉	偐	偿	個	偰	偓	傩	傳	傑	僉	僶	傘	無
60	典	隻	剷	呂	冢	覂	減	兗	匏	風	剩	割	剳	剶	劲	剮	剔	剸	剡	舅
80	券	勓	皃	匿	博	鼎	卤	觔	叠	厥	厝	厚	厔	厩	厞

Row 39		01	02	03	04	05	06	07	08	09	10	11	12	13	14	15	16	17	18	19
00		羑	曼	參	叅	叄	犇	叚	曼	営	善	詹	善	嵐	啛	唻	喙	喫	嗄	喳
20	最	嗪	嘄	嘄	嗖	嘮	咽	喭	嘳	嗽	嗺	嵩	團	圕	圖	嚪	圛	塀	堘	埆
40	堧	墒	執	畣	塀	塈	墅	壷	墾	塭	壴	趄	壴	猋	奢	奦	報	執	奱	奧
60	奥	奡	婆	婁	敹	嫏	婧	婼	婕	媙	婷	婽	孥	孱	孱	寀	寊	家	寪	寔
80	家	就	掌	尮	尵	淹	就	尳	尳	屆	屢	屠	屖	屁	屎

Row 40		01	02	03	04	05	06	07	08	09	10	11	12	13	14	15	16	17	18	19
00		屐	屜	屘	屐	屏	嶼	嵒	嵙	奎	崖	嵾	嵛	崀	崩	嵏	嵧	嵊	嵲	嵮
20	嶮	巺	巽	巽	帑	幄	幃	幂	帽	幒	幒	業	幐	帶	幷	幫	幍	廄	康	廛
40	廆	廇	廖	廬	廈	廐	廕	廸	弊	彝	弊	彖	彜	强	弻	弼	彍	弱	弱	彚
60	彝	彰	影	彡	彭	徥	徲	徥	徱	悉	惥	惠	惠	惦	肅	悶	惫	愛	惣	悳
80	悬	悳	愬	恩	焦	愈	愈	慌	惇	慠	愀	慽	慷	惰	愜

Row 41		01	02	03	04	05	06	07	08	09	10	11	12	13	14	15	16	17	18	19
00		慄	憏	愶	慹	戚	戥	戢	戮	裁	摮	掔	摮	搴	拳	擊	捘	捘	捥	揆
20	揥	揵	捹	撰	揊	搹	揰	搜	揲	揶	捽	揃	揨	搋	掩	掭	揔	捊	掬	掐
40	插	掛	揤	揘	揔	揶	鼓	敳	敥	敘	敍	敊	敔	敳	敕	敬	敭	散	敨	斪
60	斛	斛	新	斲	斯	斵	斵	斳	斷	斯	斸	旒	旌	旛	旍	旐	晳	晜	晋	晾
80	晏	暈	朂	喇	暏	暑	暋	暋	最	壺	暮	會	冐	脯	朎

Row 42		01	02	03	04	05	06	07	08	09	10	11	12	13	14	15	16	17	18	19
00		柬	棃	稟	柚	栟	楄	梳	楻	楠	楙	椊	椇	梋	棭	栚	梣	棽	棚	椤
20	格	棓	畓	棄	栔	棨	欵	歃	歔	歁	癸	欶	匵	崇	歨	嶹	炊	蒴	歮	殊
40	殨	殨	娎	殊	殦	殿	殻	毄	毦	毷	毹	毵	毽	毴	毸	毠	毬	毱	浚	淋
60	澄	津	潩	減	溻	涑	湩	湮	涸	港	涯	溙	滓	溘	潲	溢	洿	滔	溢	洚
80	浸	澤	浏	烤	烙	烕	焽	烘	熘	覂	賁	㚅	絜	臭	敕					

Row 43		01	02	03	04	05	06	07	08	09	10	11	12	13	14	15	16	17	18	19
00		烈	綖	𡆼	牋	牻	牒	牓	牘	牑	牗	牼	牌	牏	牕	酉	犃	犆	犋	物
20	犃	㹆	犀	厞	契	獎	猷	猴	狻	猇	猓	猲	獤	獀	猶	猴	猩	猏	猹	瑀
40	琡	瑢	斑	瑽	璧	基	琫	飍	颻	甀	甄	甌	甞	睬	異	畢	曼	臬	痕	疸
60	㾮	痳	瘊	痠	痒	瘃	瘀	瘩	瘵	痄	瘢	癸	發	登	飆	皋	皓	皻	皺	皸
80	盜	盄	盈	盞	盇	眯	睇	眩	眲	睅	睽	睔	睙	睨	睧					

Row 44		01	02	03	04	05	06	07	08	09	10	11	12	13	14	15	16	17	18	19
00		瞁	瞅	瞓	睪	省	睿	瞀	瞤	矜	矲	規	殹	斑	礎	砿	硯	磁	碯	磬
20	碧	桎	補	禬	禞	祾	禒	祲	禍	祽	新	稞	萬	秠	稷	稆	稀	稖	剿	粱
40	稾	窂	穽	窆	窠	窣	窞	窅	窡	窮	窳	穿	竤	竪	笑	笵	筫	箟	箎	箘
60	筋	篜	粞	粣	糕	粡	粱	粲	糞	粼	綈	紐	綵	絡	緬	經	綵	綄	綠	絡
80	縐	緊	絣	罃	罟	罭	罙	罶	罤	罠	罩	莛	翔	羾	翎					

Row 45		01	02	03	04	05	06	07	08	09	10	11	12	13	14	15	16	17	18	19
00		詳	執	美	翏	翍	翑	翐	翖	翤	翧	翨	習	翶	翼	習	翷	耆	聅	耕
20	耟	耿	書	胺	胳	离	胭	胹	腤	脎	脂	腰	膣	膴	腶	膕	膜	腑	膆	腖
40	脾	腩	脉	膶	腮	膌	臏	膀	腳	舺	臂	膂	脊	臀	臣	𦣞	雁	皇	臯	臺
60	舀	舀	舃	舐	詹	舔	舜	舡	舥	郍	艌	帶	營	菸	菅	萏	菾	萃	菁	菫
80	蒿	蒿	蕐	蕿	芸	菊	萬	萁	菹	莋	荐	萩	菻	葵	蓃					

Row 46		01	02	03	04	05	06	07	08	09	10	11	12	13	14	15	16	17	18	19
00		萼	蕒	蔥	蔑	萵	葺	葜	葛	蒿	蕤	蕑	葳	薑	董	萑	菰	茹	薺	莽
20	萉	葩	荷	萑	萏	莽	艹	蒿	虙	虛	蚌	蚢	蚌	蛛	蚗	蚕	蚜	蚍	蛸	蜍
40	蛘	蚷	蚩	蚤	蚃	蛤	衁	衉	衈	衔	衙	衚	裛	褒	袁	袝	裙	裰	裂	襀
60	裥	覎	覩	覢	視	覥	覘	舵	舳	舷	舶	艄	舨	艒	詼	謐	詨	譴	訴	詎
80	詛	謣	証	訴	諒	誇	望	登	譬	警	䨮	登	豻	冢	象					

Row 47		01	02	03	04	05	06	07	08	09	10	11	12	13	14	15	16	17	18	19
00		豫	豫	象	豨	貔	貊	貅	貆	眩	賊	貶	賚	貧	賀	頂	豩	趑	趄	趙
20	越	趄	趼	跂	跟	趺	跑	跳	跋	船	躹	躭	躲	躷	軖	輇	軞	輴	輳	輪
40	遨	遺	遣	適	逎	遥	遡	過	逵	遊	送	迹	遞	遜	遡	疊	粑	艉	肥	郟
60	鄙	鄘	鄧	鄮	郄	郤	鄹	卿	鄉	酥	酗	酞	酟	酩	酷	酡	畚	垂	壘	鈃
80	鈋	鈿	鈒	鈐	鈺	鉞	鉅	鑿	釜	璽	窈	閜	閔	閉	閒					

Row 48	01	02	03	04	05	06	07	08	09	10	11	12	13	14	15	16	17	18	19
00		閅	隖	院	隡	隔	隠	隑	陵	陲	雁	雔	雄	难	稚	雲	雋	霁	雯	零
20	靚	婓	啡	爽	酐	耐	靭	乾	頌	颶	颫	颮	备	夆	餂	飷	飽	飳	飰	駄
40	馮	髡	髢	勉	鳶	鳰	鼻	鬥	腸	乾	亭	偽	偼	傱	傍	偲	傐	僻	俾	備
60	傻	雩	僉	鴝	偉	傘	氽	爬	龠	冀	冨	冥	剏	剪	劃	劈	剄	剟	剮	剢
80	劊	勔	勉	匔	匎	匲	匭	麥	卑	萁	準	斡	卣	聖	厞				

Row 49	01	02	03	04	05	06	07	08	09	10	11	12	13	14	15	16	17	18	19
00		厫	厨	厰	厳	叁	雍	叡	叟	叡	賽	咰	啇	啬	暴	駆	嘗	喀	嗃	嗡
20	嗍	嗏	嘆	嗂	嗀	嚣	單	嗌	嘞	嗥	嗥	嗾	嘹	嘐	嘶	嗠	嘏	嚞	國	圙
40	圖	墉	報	墀	堅	埆	堞	墋	墚	墓	墜	墜	墊	壆	墅	壺	壼	壹	桑	慶
60	嫛	移	夢	奐	奪	奭	嫛	嬰	婹	婠	婢	媘	嫜	婥	媺	學	孴	孱	寤	寍
80	寷	寚	宣	東	寅	寧	寎	寝	尌	尃	尌	㞅	屡	屣	屎				

Row 50	01	02	03	04	05	06	07	08	09	10	11	12	13	14	15	16	17	18	19
00		扇	扉	屈	屈	屛	屦	屍	屐	履	岦	赛	峰	嵱	嶭	嵮	嶅	嵩	嵴	嵫
20	峊	幽	韋	戟	巢	巋	幃	幂	幅	幗	禽	辦	廊	廥	廮	庚	廃	廬	廖	麻
40	廄	弊	貳	粥	虢	鬻	劉	影	彰	彌	徢	徧	得	徥	從	徙	意	悳	慈	惔
60	愡	惎	愢	愠	愢	愬	愿	惩	愹	愮	慎	惄	慉	慨	憛	慅	慌	像	慨	憚
80	戚	戢	献	搴	挲	揎	揆	揆	擾	揔	搜	揀	揊	捶	搞				

Row 51	01	02	03	04	05	06	07	08	09	10	11	12	13	14	15	16	17	18	19
00		搠	掬	拚	搜	攢	鼓	鼓	敍	敕	敀	敲	敲	敳	斆	敱	毀	毀	萎	颳
20	斷	鼎	斮	斲	旃	旂	就	旣	暑	晷	暆	晷	曉	暠	暩	暬	曾	留	冀	朣
40	胼	樜	楙	稟	棨	棗	棱	棶	楄	榖	楧	椁	榼	楀	楩	楂	榧	楂	椅	梓
60	楔	椽	榴	榭	榲	橡	檗	檠	櫜	歃	歆	歇	歁	歉	歊	歈	歀	歐	歟	鶩
80	赭	殘	殂	亮	婚	殄	殜	殟	殤	殭	殛	殺	殽	毅	勞				

Row 52	01	02	03	04	05	06	07	08	09	10	11	12	13	14	15	16	17	18	19
00		毄	毃	殺	磬	毤	毨	毪	毰	毹	毺	毿	氀	氁	氆	氇	氍	毧	氳	淼
20	蕅	㳽	滴	淳	溾	漾	潑	涵	溪	浸	溥	瀰	滿	淵	潮	澀	溼	湵	溼	湿
40	滋	滋	溯	滑	漢	淨	滝	滇	漭	熗	煐	煤	熤	熄	熇	燴	燒	燭	燽	煳
60	威	燹	殳	爽	燕	點	熙	爲	煮	熏	變	羡	爬	爵	變	爿	爽	牕	牓	牓
80	牆	犒	牸	犞	犠	犩	犪	犫	犪	犫	猷	獻	猽	獁	獖				

Row 53	01	02	03	04	05	06	07	08	09	10	11	12	13	14	15	16	17	18	19
00		獈	獶	獦	獧	獬	獵	獄	獶	瑩	璧	瑇	瑻	瑯	瑫	瑽	璿	渠	甹	豎
20	甚	豎	甗	甄	瓶	甃	甍	畜	睧	瞰	睇	畛	畧	畨	畬	畲	畢	惠	棶	痏
40	瘕	瘓	瘍	瘵	瘝	瘚	瘠	普	皐	皷	皺	皸	盜	盫	盩	監	盬	睫	睯	睆
60	睞	瞘	睚	睒	瞂	瞢	瞀	矒	瞸	矍	罼	綴	矬	矲	碌	碌	碌	碻	磵	碔
80	碑	硯	碠	磫	禓	禚	禭	稑	稭	稞	稗	稷	稱	穊	穋				

Row 54		01	02	03	04	05	06	07	08	09	10	11	12	13	14	15	16	17	18	19
00		豩	窐	宼	寑	寈	寙	寘	寠	竆	竰	竤	竮	蓏	蕹	箕	箇	築	箽	箮
20	箮	篔	笐	箽	筱	篠	篺	粫	糈	粆	糠	糜	粜	粢	綷	緪	綩	綎	綻	緰
40	緫	紫	絜	綒	纍	纝	縧	經	紓	罟	罦	罜	罛	罤	罨	罽	羝	羖	羫	觲
60	善	翗	翓	翢	粿	聕	䎴	聏	聑	聎	䎰	聊	聒	聬	聠	章	徛	肃	書	脚
80	腑	胾	胳	腠	腤	腖	腢	腣	䐈	腗	腦	𦜕	腤	腤	腩					

Row 55		01	02	03	04	05	06	07	08	09	10	11	12	13	14	15	16	17	18	19
00		罯	罳	嵤	𪖐	甥	欲	舮	舎	舔	艇	舭	舲	般	艐	艳	艴	艵	䒂	覔
20	蒵	葬	萍	菡	萿	萤	萀	莞	蒳	菋	菱	萁	葦	萋	萸	蓿	葛	蓔	蔀	蓝
40	蓁	蓢	蒼	蓒	蔍	蓭	蒁	蒭	蓦	葬	蔓	蔏	蕪	蓪	著	蔓	蔄	蔺	蔸	蕧
60	蔆	蒕	蒩	䒨	蒷	蒻	葭	莧	蒥	蒞	薊	蕹	蔐	虝	虞	虓	蝛	蛛	蜆	蚣
80	蛞	蜔	蚴	蛮	蜚	蚤	蚕	蛩	蜇	蜑	蚰	蜍	盜	盟	衕					

Row 56		01	02	03	04	05	06	07	08	09	10	11	12	13	14	15	16	17	18	19
00		衙	衞	衛	袚	裁	袭	装	衷	裛	裵	衮	裞	袳	裗	衹	褔	褫	黔	貶
20	賍	覘	覔	覗	觗	誁	詘	詎	詔	誠	諄	詽	詩	諛	詸	說	訟	誂	詤	叙
40	敍	產	詈	誓	谿	豨	豝	豪	豣	獨	貉	貈	貯	賊	貹	賉	貺	賍	贁	賨
60	貣	賁	賚	賀	貴	買	債	赧	赩	赾	趚	趄	趆	趟	趵	跦	趹	跐	踂	跋
80	跨	蹕	跚	踋	踈	踅	跧	跼	趸	踖	躭	躰	躬	躲	躳					

Row 57		01	02	03	04	05	06	07	08	09	10	11	12	13	14	15	16	17	18	19
00		躲	䠷	輥	輊	輞	輚	輡	輁	輦	辦	農	辳	辱	逸	遝	遂	遯	逑	達
20	遉	逵	適	遐	逞	遽	邏	邊	遣	逌	逋	運	連	通	遴	逷	酌	酱	鈀	鄙
40	鄆	鄂	卿	鄖	醌	醑	醍	鈄	鈹	鉄	鈗	釩	鉋	鎣	䟫	既	路	跛	開	閤
60	閘	閫	閼	陪	降	陟	陘	陸	陛	隉	陵	隋	隆	隗	隑	隨	隕	畫	翟	奞
80	堆	雅	雎	琟	雄	雕	翟	雉	雁	雓	睢	雒	霏	靖	靠					

Row 58		01	02	03	04	05	06	07	08	09	10	11	12	13	14	15	16	17	18	19
00		韭	靦	靤	鞀	鞍	鞆	鞈	鞃	鞋	韝	鞫	韻	韮	頃	頂	頍	頓	頤	頎
20	颸	颹	颾	颶	飡	飿	餂	餅	餉	餈	饈	飽	飯	餃	飪	香	馭	騖	馮	屠
40	骭	骰	骫	骪	髪	髾	鬲	魁	魈	寇	魋	甖	奐	鮫	鮊	鷫	鴻	鳩	鳩	鼻
60	鼻	齔	豹	乳	帶	齒	鬣	豬	黍	傢	傷	傲	僑	僭	僉	傳	僂	僩	僊	個
80	僭	僊	像	僬	僚	倉	傘	龠	蠱	與	膁	累	蜀	滄	淼					

Row 59		01	02	03	04	05	06	07	08	09	10	11	12	13	14	15	16	17	18	19
00		剃	刳	剗	劈	剝	副	劃	劉	飭	創	剳	勵	勦	勝	匍	匱	匭	匵	厦
20	厫	廠	厤	厲	厝	原	厭	厴	參	叒	叟	吞	嗽	嘵	嘶	噚	嘔	嗡	嘸	嗻
40	啡	嗁	嚚	壘	參	嘩	嘣	嗺	嗐	暮	萬	嗇	圂	圏	圍	圓	圈	團	鳥	圖
60	墡	墻	墘	豈	墳	整	塔	塴	墍	墠	墓	墜	壹	壺	壼	喜	麥	复	勞	夐
80	奐	奮	奭	嬰	嬃	數	嬈	嬧	嫜	嫿	嬾	媳	婭	學	濡					

Row 60		01	02	03	04	05	06	07	08	09	10	11	12	13	14	15	16	17	18	19
00		寀	寧	寍	窒	寷	寪	寘	寠	寴	寐	寱	寲	賓	奮	壽	尌	對	兟	絲
20	㞜	數	屗	屢	屪	屚	嶲	嵍	嶀	嵼	嵻	崚	嶐	崋	嵾	嵱	嶁	㠥	㠑	嶨
40	巤	巢	肄	㡎	幏	幅	㡭	廞	廍	廫	弇	弆	㢳	貳	弩	彯	彄	彈	彁	趃
60	彖	㣉	彙	隸	彣	徛	復	徖	徹	微	徾	徵	復	御	徿	徲	寨	㤹	惥	惪
80	飃	惠	惪	㥑	㥎	㥫	愬	慯	㦔	悆	㥶	愼	㦁	慉	憒					

Row 61		01	02	03	04	05	06	07	08	09	10	11	12	13	14	15	16	17	18	19
00		懜	懔	懽	慺	㦙	慌	慵	戩	戟	戴	裁	擊	殬	撇	搷	摍	搥	擲	擓
20	攬	攜	撇	擮	掩	搸	㨶	擠	搭	搽	擨	搋	㝹	殺	敷	敁	𢿜	鼓	㪇	敦
40	數	斆	斁	敷	斜	斳	斲	斱	斴	斷	旛	暀	晋	暈	暅	晀	暊	學	曾	普
60	朝	朝	腠	檕	棘	榦	樜	樓	榎	橪	楦	樫	榣	棇	櫜	桼	梟	楙	歆	款
80	歃	歎	歇	歀	歐	欺	欽	歙	殛	殪	殝	殯	殗	殼	殽					

Row 62		01	02	03	04	05	06	07	08	09	10	11	12	13	14	15	16	17	18	19
00		毈	毀	毞	毤	毨	毢	氂	氅	毹	毿	氁	氆	氃	毾	氄	毬	毇	樕	渜
20	淮	溸	浡	漻	漏	濕	潯	湏	滿	溢	淹	濇	濄	澣	𤅃	滌	滳	澮	熛	煊
40	燖	煌	熿	㷥	爂	㷷	爆	煎	熬	䲝	羹	熥	爲	爰	爼	爾	牕	牖	牗	牒
60	牒	犢	犕	犞	犚	犘	犦	犑	犡	犪	犩	豰	猍	猶	獥	獱	獼	獯	獿	獹
80	獴	獨	獦	瑄	璌	璓	琶	琵	瓞	瓹	甍	甌	甈	睹	璧					

Row 63		01	02	03	04	05	06	07	08	09	10	11	12	13	14	15	16	17	18	19
00		膂	畷	暖	畤	畫	畾	甥	畱	疐	痠	瘴	瘠	瘖	瘵	瘨	瘟	瘨	瘟	癡
20	瘙	瘯	瘡	瘡	瘴	暘	甿	皝	皠	皻	皺	皽	盬	盦	瞭	瞘	瞒	瞕	瞝	瞵
40	煦	瞗	矆	矗	矟	畀	叟	矍	矠	矦	矬	矪	磦	磇	礄	礒	磕	磥	磮	磬
60	禍	禬	禮	禧	禖	祿	禪	禽	禭	禲	稼	稷	稿	稭	穡	穄	穠	穗	穆	穋
80	龠	窟	窶	窸	窴	竊	竄	竅	竈	竇	竢	篠	篺	簠	簫					

Row 64		01	02	03	04	05	06	07	08	09	10	11	12	13	14	15	16	17	18	19
00		箬	篋	篛	篇	篔	篘	篸	箾	糇	糈	糐	糋	糒	糪	糧	糌	糜	糞	粺
20	縩	縪	縂	繞	繝	綷	縎	縒	繼	紳	繪	緎	縈	縶	縅	罈	罊	罋	罌	署
40	罧	罝	罨	罩	罪	罹	罻	罷	罽	罿	羉	羬	羣	羨	羶	翔	翩	翿	翽	耦
60	耘	聠	聃	聳	肇	肈	肆	腌	腍	腐	腐	腐	腌	腑	腷	腹	腺	膳	膢	膡
80	羸	臖	臝	舀	興	舉	舁	舊	舔	舐	舙	舝	舑	舒	舔					

Row 65		01	02	03	04	05	06	07	08	09	10	11	12	13	14	15	16	17	18	19
00		舜	舽	艚	艄	艵	艓	艆	艷	艶	艴	芔	茻	芔	芔	芔	芔	芔	芔	蔻
20	蓀	蓊	蓳	薄	蒗	蓟	蔡	蓷	蔛	葵	蓤	蔀	蔓	蔻	蔻	蔚	蔔	蔽	蕆	蕈
40	蕉	葉	薛	蔆	蔾	蓍	蕣	蕐	蔏	蕫	蕃	蔐	蕁	蕻	蕺	蕠	蕍	菊	蕓	蒻
60	蕙	蕣	薧	蕗	蔙	蕤	虡	虘	虓	虒	虜	虞	蛈	蛸	蝠	蛶	蝴	蝕	蝛	蝹
80	蜱	蜍	蜕	蜖	蛩	蜇	蜤	蜠	蜯	蝨	螶	螘	螱	蟗	螚					

Row 66	01	02	03	04	05	06	07	08	09	10	11	12	13	14	15	16	17	18	19
00		䍃	𥂕	蝍	崡	監	盟	衜	衕	䙔	製	䘭	䘮	䘻	裏	襊	褍	襝	裚	䘾
20	䘺	䘽	𦋸	𦌋	𥁶	覬	䚁	睍	觛	𧣍	䚩	觨	𧣄	誓	誁	設	諚	䜸	䛎	誠
40	詍	諟	𧩯	調	䛠	誤	謥	詹	詈	善	䜰	䝡	𨀌	猍	猸	𧳇	豝	𧴊	豰	膝
60	𧲤	𧳑	𧲲	𧲸	𧳈	𧳍	𧳉	𧵳	𧶁	𧵠	賓	賨	賈	賫	責	𧴧	䝿	趍	趹	䞻
80	䞶	趞	䞣	䞯	䞘	趥	䞼	䟸	𨁵	𨂐	𨂂	𨂄	𨂃	𨁺	𨀗					

Row 67	01	02	03	04	05	06	07	08	09	10	11	12	13	14	15	16	17	18	19
00		𨑓	倐	𨉭	𨉢	躽	𨉟	𨋍	𨋙	輍	𨌆	𨍃	䡝	𨋩	𨌡	𨍈	𨋷	載	𨕬	𨗋
20	遷	逋	遚	𨘢	𨗎	𨕹	𨗈	𨘋	遒	戲	𢱢	䣀	郶	郻	鄁	鄙	鄭	鄰	御	醮
40	醍	𢧢	囍	𩿧	晉	輋	鉶	鋘	鋝	鎊	鍒	鋗	鏠	銳	跡	踩	閞	闐	闢	闟
60	閼	餓	餑	陘	隘	隱	陳	隮	隁	隰	隵	降	翟	翟	雈	翟	雝	誰	雁	錐
80	雗	礁	雔	雞	糴	雛	雖	睢	雋	霅	霝	霽	電	霝	霧					

Row 68	01	02	03	04	05	06	07	08	09	10	11	12	13	14	15	16	17	18	19
00		靤	靼	靲	鞊	鞞	靶	鞄	韋	韋	鞔	韜	韒	頊	頏	頍	顧	頰	碩	頣
20	顊	領	須	颷	颸	颶	颺	飀	餮	饕	飱	飧	餞	餌	餛	餠	餂	館	馘	馡
40	馢	馥	馦	馧	馬	駛	駝	駍	騧	騵	驫	骯	骸	骻	骳	骱	骰	髙	亭	髮
60	髶	髭	髮	髲	長	髽	鬩	鬪	鬷	魊	魅	魍	魎	魑	魆	鬼	魖	鬼	槐	鮀
80	馯	鳥	鳶	鳩	鳩	麪	罴	黝	黔	黽	鼓									

CNS 11643-1992 Plane 7

Row 1		01	02	03	04	05	06	07	08	09	10	11	12	13	14	15	16	17	18	19
00		壹	寱	奞	奭	僆	僥	僬	僫	儩	僤	傀	僿	僚	僻	傀	御	㒗	兢	㚓
20	魌	圖	凜	淜	劃	劇	鼑	剝	剸	劕	劊	劉	韓	寫	厦	厰	愿	嵫	壼	离
40	壘	嗇	喑	嚷	喹	嚓	嘙	喊	啶	嚩	喱	嘰	啍	哦	嗜	啼	嚜	嚅	毀	買
60	器	嚎	喀	嗤	嘷	啞	盃	疊	園	圏	國	壘	墖	堨	壨	墑	堤	壖	塝	賁
80	齒	埡	堮	復	墻	薹	墜	壘	壄	壽	臺	猧	奏	囊	翗					

Row 2		01	02	03	04	05	06	07	08	09	10	11	12	13	14	15	16	17	18	19
00		氀	奪	嫢	婁	娛	嫛	嬃	嬉	媥	嬬	㜸	嬌	媢	婨	頟	宿	康	宣	窨
20	窯	寧	寑	㣜	寘	對	尊	纍	就	橦	尵	屛	履	嶣	巎	嵒	畢	崵	嵋	嶺
40	嶼	嶭	嶗	嶨	嶚	嶅	嵚	嵲	嶝	嶠	巕	巠	巽	巹	巂	幭	幪	幧	幦	幽
60	幾	嶻	廔	廇	廏	廎	廥	廎	巽	猷	彌	彊	彖	彰	彲	徲	徾	徻	徼	徹
80	徫	憑	慝	憝	憝	憓	黝	慕	懬	憽	懋	憯	懎	懰	懆					

Row 3		01	02	03	04	05	06	07	08	09	10	11	12	13	14	15	16	17	18	19
00		懵	憘	戴	截	截	戚	戫	戲	戩	戴	扉	摹	摩	擎	摩	擧	摯	擦	撖
20	攘	撚	撟	撼	擇	擷	擂	擲	攝	撐	擟	擇	揃	攉	擿	擲	擡	攤	孿	鼓
40	鼕	整	歐	數	數	敳	斁	敲	敷	黴	斂	斃	斁	尉	膘	暜	暳	曹	暴	曬
60	曦	嘶	嘔	暴	最	智	曾	普	朦	櫳	橐	櫜	樁	櫓	櫃	橋	檉	樹	樆	樺
80	橼	橠	概	樅	檜	槃	歗	歘	歔	歆	歌	歇	歈	歆	歛					

Row 4		01	02	03	04	05	06	07	08	09	10	11	12	13	14	15	16	17	18	19
00		歭	整	歨	歱	歱	齒	殦	殨	殧	殩	殲	毼	殼	毇	毲	毵	毷	氅	氇
20	氍	氂	氌	氆	氂	氅	氳	氎	氊	潙	漯	滿	淋	潹	滾	潼	潸	漩	滛	涿
40	濄	潿	澱	濕	濤	濈	濹	潮	濟	潸	澗	漊	濡	澄	瀸	溹	瀉	澂	澈	瀉
60	瀟	潤	溫	潔	滄	滌	澹	滜	潄	濺	涎	漸	潽	熼	燡	燧	竇	熛	爕	燮
80	爂	爨	爨	爨	爩	燮	爣	爴	爵	爰	爵	毀	爾	牘	牆					

Row 5		01	02	03	04	05	06	07	08	09	10	11	12	13	14	15	16	17	18	19
00		牄	牘	牗	牖	牕	犔	犕	犡	獒	獻	獲	獭	獵	獝	獮	獺	獹	獨	獫
20	獼	獶	堅	豎	壂	壐	斑	璪	璶	璃	璷	瑾	環	瑭	瑟	甌	瓢	瓢	甄	甖
40	甗	甐	甎	甏	畾	畯	畷	畿	疃	疊	疐	瘀	瘵	痛	瘦	瘝	瘠	癡	癰	癄
60	癒	癃	癥	登	皜	皚	皤	皨	皫	盬	瞋	瞏	瞜	瞟	瞴	瞧	瞨	矇	瞡	瞖
80	瞽	瞻	矓	皿	矟	矡	矱	矲	矷	礜	磽	磌	礲	磁	磔					

Row 6		01	02	03	04	05	06	07	08	09	10	11	12	13	14	15	16	17	18	19
00		磱	磂	䃺	䃶	穀	祲	福	䄉	禬	禋	禺	禼	禽	稐	稱	稗	稫	稽	稷
20	穛	穋	䵓	槃	舂	窴	窾	竸	竧	䇕	竨	竭	篓	箛	箎	箁	箄	箯	箖	箢
40	篝	箴	節	篋	篺	篥	篨	篟	篕	篔	篌	篍	糇	糄	糉	糈	糍	㯺	糒	糕
60	縨	縒	縩	緺	縍	縪	縔	縐	縑	縋	縌	縴	縦	総	繈	緊	縶	縿	罊	罍
80	罉	罶	罸	罼	罿	羀	羄	羉	羈	羍	羏	羗	羛	羜	羝					

Row 7		01	02	03	04	05	06	07	08	09	10	11	12	13	14	15	16	17	18	19
00		翞	翜	翤	翪	翨	翯	翴	耑	耑	耭	聙	聜	聢	聝	聲	聤	書	肈	肅
20	膞	膱	膷	膹	臄	臆	臈	臎	臔	臕	臖	臗	臛	臞	臡	臤	臩	臫	臮	臯
40	臲	臷	舝	舠	艘	艜	艞	艡	艴	艵	艷	艸	芀	芇	芁	芃	芈	芔	芕	芘
60	蔛	蔙	蔣	蔤	蔥	蔫	蔭	蔯	蔱	蔲	蔳	蔴	蔵	蔶	蔸	蔹	蔺	蔻	蔼	蔾
80	蕀	蕂	蕃	蕅	蕇	蕉	蕊	蕋	蕍	蕎	蕏	蕐	蕑	蕓	蕕					

Row 8		01	02	03	04	05	06	07	08	09	10	11	12	13	14	15	16	17	18	19
00		蕍	蕤	蕣	蕦	蕨	虪	虤	虥	虦	蛭	蝃	蝖	蝠	蝫	蝬	蝒	蝛	蝡	蝣
20	蝹	螃	螅	螐	螑	螖	螘	螝	螡	螢	螣	螤	螥	螧	螩	螪	螮	螰	螱	螲
40	螴	螶	螷	螸	螹	螼	螾	螿	蟁	褡	褫	褵	褸	褻	褶	褹	褼	褾	襂	襃
60	覃	覗	覟	覢	覣	覥	覦	覫	觩	觫	觭	觬	觯	觰	觳	謚	謂	謅	謀	謝
80	謎	謏	謑	謒	謓	謔	謕	謖	謗	謙	謘	謣	謤	謥	謦					

Row 9		01	02	03	04	05	06	07	08	09	10	11	12	13	14	15	16	17	18	19
00		諡	謍	謽	讐	諆	豋	豊	豑	豯	豵	豰	豲	豫	豨	貗	貚	貜	賗	賝
20	賖	賫	賲	賷	賾	贁	赾	趆	趉	趐	趒	趓	趕	趖	趗	趘	趛	趜	趝	趞
40	踝	踑	踔	踕	踗	踘	踛	踞	躶	躹	輨	輖	輕	輣	輤	輦	輧	輬	輱	輯
60	轀	轄	轋	轑	轒	轔	轕	轗	辡	辥	辤	逯	遮	遴	遼	遺	遵	遶	遷	選
80	遞	遂	遧	邂	邀	邉	郮	郯	郰	郲	郳	郴	郹	鄄	鄂					

Row 10		01	02	03	04	05	06	07	08	09	10	11	12	13	14	15	16	17	18	19
00		鄹	鄭	鄮	鄱	鄹	鄽	醇	醅	醞	醘	醑	醋	醃	醟	醬	醫	醰	醲	醱
20	醳	鐾	鋙	鋓	鋔	鋤	鋠	鋪	鋸	鋺	鋿	鋞	鋾	鍛	鍪	鍫	鍬	鍯	闊	闒
40	闌	闍	闐	闑	闒	闓	闖	隮	隴	隔	際	隝	隖	障	隥	隸	隷	雁	雈	雊
60	雐	雓	雔	雖	雗	雘	雙	雚	雛	雜	雝	雟	雡	霒	霓	霞	霬	霸	霻	靁
80	靃	勳	靪	靮	鞓	鞙	鞚	鞛	鞝	鞞	鞟	鞠	鞡	鞢	鞤					

Row 11		01	02	03	04	05	06	07	08	09	10	11	12	13	14	15	16	17	18	19
00		韽	韾	頪	頫	頤	頥	頭	頮	頯	頲	頳	頵	頶	頷	頸	頹	頺	颾	颼
20	飀	飂	旟	餛	餐	餚	餜	餟	餤	餫	餬	餭	餱	餲	餳	馬	駈	駋	駍	駐
40	駭	駷	駹	駾	骬	骭	骰	骲	骳	骴	骵	骶	骷	骸	骹	髃	髈	髭	髶	髹
60	髼	鬩	鬪	鬫	鬾	魄	魏	魐	魞	魣	魤	魥	魦	魧	魪	魭	魮	魴	魳	魵
80	魶	魸	魹	魺	鴉	鴊	鴋	鴌	鴍	鴎	鴏	鴐	鴒	鴓	鴞					

Row 12		01	02	03	04	05	06	07	08	09	10	11	12	13	14	15	16	17	18	19
00		毤	亶	敳	斵	勶	麀	庳	麌	麑	欻	欯	欶	欶	数	毲	廝	廠	毸	毣
20	黓	黗	奞	龜	龜	鼦	鼀	畾	鴝	鼜	鼛	鼛	傕	棽	尉	甄	灧	灝	曓	羹
40	剿	剮	剳	劍	劉	劅	剿	勦	劅	復	厩	厪	㪍	繇	甛	鬲	曡	嗞	逿	嚍
60	嗷	嘐	嘛	嘜	嘮	嘷	嚜	戳	嘩	嘖	嘯	嘈	嘲	嘵	嘹	嘿	墼	嬴	墳	墜
80	墈	墹	墻	墽	墾	壼	夓	夔	莫	菉	燊	爊	龕	㸚	嬴					

Row 13		01	02	03	04	05	06	07	08	09	10	11	12	13	14	15	16	17	18	19
00		嬰	嬱	嬬	嫻	嬌	嬇	嫽	嫭	嫺	嫩	孌	嬴	孷	孼	孫	孹	孿	豬	寶
20	審	憲	寢	寅	尌	對	尞	尶	就	獻	猷	屩	屧	嶴	隱	崛	嶺	嵺	踏	巕
40	嶦	嵳	嵕	嶀	嶼	嶖	翯	巃	幕	幨	幪	幩	幯	幰	幦	幭	幨	廩	彝	弊
60	弸	弑	彌	彏	彍	彙	彡	彲	彯	徵	徲	徾	徺	憲	懕	懟	閤	閔	懮	閾
80	憙	憖	憶	懏	懛	懖	懜	懇	懒	憒	憪	憁	懴	憭	懍					

Row 14		01	02	03	04	05	06	07	08	09	10	11	12	13	14	15	16	17	18	19
00		懾	懏	戴	戫	戩	戲	戳	截	戧	戬	摯	摩	摰	撓	攣	摲	撫	撹	撻
20	握	撢	擛	撲	擁	撈	撤	擄	擐	擷	擋	擯	擻	敨	敺	斆	敹	整	敼	敾
40	斀	斁	敵	斅	數	斄	斳	斷	斸	斲	斵	旟	暬	曡	曹	曝	暈	曖	曷	曟
60	朁	朆	楳	槿	椅	橧	樏	檕	橋	橀	橘	濾	櫶	欐	檈	櫨	櫅	櫧	權	樣
80	橮	檞	櫳	鬆	歉	歟	歡	聶	殭	殰	殮	殯	殲	殧	殥					

Row 15		01	02	03	04	05	06	07	08	09	10	11	12	13	14	15	16	17	18	19
00		毄	殸	毀	毅	毇	毆	毈	毚	氉	氀	氃	氄	氊	演	瀉	濂	濾	瀐	滓
20	澀	濤	濉	瀏	瀆	澨	潛	溻	溜	澾	潑	澛	滅	湯	瀆	瀍	澤	溢	激	滏
40	瀡	瀀	澳	爂	熚	燸	燧	燗	熫	燎	爛	熹	熨	爨	熯	熹	爇	爟	燚	爨
60	燹	戳	燚	燵	焰	燄	煎	煞	爨	燮	爤	爔	燹	爏	爋	爐	牘	牘	犒	犛
80	犩	犣	獻	獄	獷	獠	獮	獵	獴	獸	墊	甈	瑁	瓆	瑀					

Row 16		01	02	03	04	05	06	07	08	09	10	11	12	13	14	15	16	17	18	19
00		璂	璥	璯	瓊	甭	甗	甏	甗	瓾	甓	甏	畬	疄	疑	瘍	瘠	瘟	瘼	癧
20	瘕	瘤	癥	瘦	瘻	癌	發	皙	皕	皤	皺	皶	盨	盪	盧	監	盭	盟	瞰	瞓
40	瞍	瞟	瞼	瞿	瞻	矇	矊	矞	矎	學	矙	矱	矯	磨	礪	礎	礦	礐	礜	禮
60	禢	穌	稘	稟	萬	稽	稑	穆	穗	穢	穩	穀	穆	穆	穌	穌	穧	秉	窖	窆
80	窯	寑	窶	竮	竟	篅	筌	篝	篋	篘	籀	篙	篝	篓	簩					

Row 17		01	02	03	04	05	06	07	08	09	10	11	12	13	14	15	16	17	18	19
00		簌	簟	簞	籀	簽	簠	簸	簺	簿	籈	簾	糗	糒	糅	糞	糧	縷	纖	繾
20	縞	繕	繞	繡	繯	繩	繃	繶	繂	繗	緜	縜	縵	總	縳	縩	縿	繠	纍	羃
40	羆	罿	羃	罳	罽	羈	羆	章	羔	羶	翦	翻	翱	翽	翾	耗	耆	耡	耑	耤
60	耩	耨	聰	聽	聳	聵	肅	腴	腮	膨	膩	膳	膞	膦	膮	膵	齋	臍	臂	臀
80	臙	臛	輿	艖	晉	艒	艓	會	艗	艙	艦	艇	艜	艞	艎					

Row 18	01	02	03	04	05	06	07	08	09	10	11	12	13	14	15	16	17	18	19
00		艒	艒	韓	艶	艴	器	葺	蕰	蓓	蒹	蓃	蒋	蒧	蓄	蒭	蒸	蓕	蕀	蕎
20	蒦	蔨	蔂	蔣	蔭	蔂	蓧	蓑	蔡	蔳	蔹	蓳	蔣	蔵	蔔	蔃	蔌	蔱	蔵	蔤
40	蔡	蕣	蕤	蕨	蕪	蕮	蕨	蕃	蕘	蕈	蕬	蕿	蕹	蕻	蕿	蘀	蘎	蘗	蘳	蘇
60	虘	虓	虤	虥	虦	虢	蝤	蝲	螟	螻	螺	蟖	蟥	蟮	蟆	蠅	蠖	蟀	蠂	蠏
80	蟌	蟂	蟅	蠢	蠠	蠤	蠱	蠹	蠶	蠸	蠻	蠿	蠽	蠡	衊					

Row 19	01	02	03	04	05	06	07	08	09	10	11	12	13	14	15	16	17	18	19
00		衊	衋	衞	衟	衠	衋	衺	袤	裦	褔	褘	褷	襆	褲	襢	襬	襸	覇	覞
20	覢	觙	觡	觨	觲	觼	觽	訰	誁	誰	誘	諲	諛	誡	諺	諺	詗	諍	諧	諰
40	謕	謏	謈	謎	謶	謼	譁	譎	譌	譓	譬	譬	譻	譢	譺	豆	豯	豷	豶	豩
60	豩	貐	貗	貛	貜	貟	貦	貮	貓	賩	賮	賲	賱	賟	賥	賹	賷	賸	賾	賴
80	趧	趮	趰	趪	趯	趲	趲	趰	趲	趴	路	蹄	蹊	蹎	蹕					

Row 20	01	02	03	04	05	06	07	08	09	10	11	12	13	14	15	16	17	18	19
00		蹎	蹓	蹕	蹠	躉	躛	躋	軀	輅	輎	輧	輵	輵	轀	轄	輪	輸	轞	轟
20	辇	辈	辣	辥	辟	適	逋	遴	遶	遭	遰	還	邀	邉	過	遂	道	遥	遮	遯
40	遲	遻	邈	邋	邍	郾	鄀	鄈	鄍	鄙	鄺	醛	酸	醜	醱	醞	醢	醇	醯	釀
60	醬	醫	釁	釃	醜	釆	鍊	鍐	鍍	鍾	鏉	鏑	鍛	鑒	鑿	鑾	鐻	鑹	鑔	璧
80	鐩	鐧	闊	闌	闕	闖	闐	闓	闠	闢	開	闛	隨	隧	隆					

Row 21	01	02	03	04	05	06	07	08	09	10	11	12	13	14	15	16	17	18	19
00		隸	誰	雁	雄	雅	雒	雔	雗	雘	雛	離	雖	雗	錐	雜	雞	雔	雕	雟
20	離	雟	難	雽	靈	霰	霹	霾	霿	靔	靄	靦	靶	靸	鞦	鞦	鞧	鞭	韜	韙
40	韗	韻	韽	頀	頑	頒	頗	頌	頏	頒	頓	頔	頗	頛	頠	頤	頢	頩	頫	頲
60	頵	颸	颹	颽	颾	颿	飧	餇	餘	餞	餪	餖	餠	餦	餳	餸	餹	饇	饃	饒
80	館	餔	餚	餡	餹	馲	騐	騙	騚	騡	騬	騿	驌	驌	驒					

Row 22	01	02	03	04	05	06	07	08	09	10	11	12	13	14	15	16	17	18	19
00		騽	驉	驎	驐	驕	驗	驚	驫	骿	髂	髓	髝	髞	髟	髥	髮	鬂	鬘	鬠
20	鬧	鬩	鬲	鬷	鬻	魁	魃	魅	魈	鮭	鮪	鮰	鯍	鮋	鯠	鯗	魯	鳿	鴕	鴐
40	鴑	鴘	鴩	鴬	鵇	鵗	鵰	鵲	鶊	鶏	鶡	鶚	鷁	鷀	鷂	鷀	鷌	鷓	鷫	鸕
60	麖	麠	麩	麭	麯	麵	麷	麰	黁	黄	黐	黔	黑	黕	黙	黜	黝	黿	鼐	鼎
80	鼽	齃	齅	齆	齇	齈	齉	儇	儍	凴	凴	圝	劇	劉	勩					

Row 23	01	02	03	04	05	06	07	08	09	10	11	12	13	14	15	16	17	18	19
00		勇	勳	匑	匓	匽	韋	卷	叟	嗀	嘖	嗽	嘽	噓	嚉	嚆	嚬	嚹	嚷	嚵
20	嚽	嚵	嚾	囃	對	囍	圁	圝	圞	墪	墉	墜	墶	壓	壐	壛	壟	壣	叟	夾
40	奙	婁	嬴	嬰	孌	孋	嬪	嫭	嫌	孎	孏	嫿	嬏	嬝	孿	寋	寐	寢	寫	廳
60	導	就	孱	甥	嵺	屪	嶙	嶦	巂	巀	巉	巑	巕	巘	巙	巖	廜	廥	廨	廰
80	弔	弗	彅	彈	彛	彝	彲	徹	德	恣	悫	隱	懇	憖	懋					

Row 24		01	02	03	04	05	06	07	08	09	10	11	12	13	14	15	16	17	18	19
00		𢥞	㦦	懄	憐	㦗	憶	𢥵	攣	擊	擇	擯	擿	撲	撥	攄	摎	撩	攮	擐
20	𢸦	攝	攀	擡	擺	摷	𣀔	𣪊	鼓	敲	𣪠	豰	獨	斳	斵	旞	嚮	噥	罯	噢
40	曍	曑	朦	曒	櫝	檾	櫜	櫈	檸	櫇	櫼	櫨	櫚	櫃	櫯	檝	歗	巢	槃	鑫
60	櫜	歡	歞	歜	歟	櫡	孿	殯	殜	殲	轂	毈	毲	氀	氈	氋	氌	氍	瀋	灖
80	瀵	灑	瀡	瀢	灊	瀾	瀆	瀘	瀁	瀞	瀺	瀥	瀰	爓	燨					

Row 25		01	02	03	04	05	06	07	08	09	10	11	12	13	14	15	16	17	18	19
00		燺	燎	燡	燿	爇	燹	爂	熬	熸	燚	犘	牆	牒	犞	犡	獨	獒	獻	獳
20	獜	獵	璺	瓄	瓋	璵	瓙	瓌	璯	瓏	甗	甗	甋	瞭	畽	疅	癃	癅	癄	癉
40	癥	癓	癟	癩	癄	癧	癒	療	癟	癵	皭	皺	盬	盭	盦	盬	瞥	瞦	瞸	瞟
60	矊	矇	矂	矙	矘	矆	矃	矉	矐	矠	矱	矍	礉	礌	礤	礎	礫	礧	礪	礬
80	禮	禮	禰	禨	禳	禶	禷	穖	穆	穈	穌	竄	竅	竇	竉					

Row 26		01	02	03	04	05	06	07	08	09	10	11	12	13	14	15	16	17	18	19
00		籆	竴	籦	籒	簐	簇	籘	籌	築	籑	簹	籈	籔	籚	籙	粹	糒	槃	緊
20	籉	籦	縀	纈	縮	纖	編	縲	績	繝	縺	縵	緣	繼	麋	緊	綮	纆	纗	麗
40	羅	罷	罽	羉	羃	羄	羇	羏	羗	羶	聲	聘	聵	翻	翿	聰	耨	耰	耬	聽
60	聲	聳	膜	膋	膂	膞	膝	腫	膾	臂	臆	舉	舀	艚	艜	艠	艞	薄	薀	藍
80	藍	藤	薹	藃	藎	藐	藷	藸	蘈	藙	藍	蘞	蘢	蘦	蘖					

Row 27		01	02	03	04	05	06	07	08	09	10	11	12	13	14	15	16	17	18	19
00		蕖	蓁	蕾	蕜	蘭	蕣	蕯	蕈	蕹	蔚	藛	蔜	蘘	蘞	藤	蘀	薛	藕	藾
20	蕣	蘧	舊	蘠	虧	虪	螢	螻	蠊	蟈	蟛	蟙	螬	蟯	蠍	蠏	蟕	蟋	蠦	蟟
40	螐	螯	蟊	蟴	蠚	蠣	蠶	蠸	蠻	蠽	蟲	蝨	蠡	蝕	衞	褻	褽	褧	褭	褰
60	襀	褴	襘	襖	襋	襜	襊	襍	襛	襺	覽	覵	親	覼	覶	覷	艕	艑	艥	艞
80	艛	艟	艪	艢	艤	講	謔	謐	謗	謖	謫	謣	謥	謨	謪					

Row 28		01	02	03	04	05	06	07	08	09	10	11	12	13	14	15	16	17	18	19
00		諰	謥	譂	論	謕	斱	繇	譻	譽	譆	譞	譗	豐	豵	貀	貐	貗	賕	賬
20	賚	賣	贅	贄	賷	趨	趲	蹅	蹤	蹝	蹥	蹫	蹽	蹸	蹤	躂	躉	躑	躺	軀
40	軀	輳	輹	輻	轉	轀	轄	轇	轃	轁	轂	犖	轆	遴	邁	邂	邅	邍	邋	還
60	邏	邐	邀	邇	邉	遻	選	邈	醞	鄰	鄲	鄿	鄺	鄱	鄳	鄕	醱	醲	醣	醭
80	醎	醻	醿	醫	醴	釂	釀	錽	鍍	銛	鍱	鏂	鈃	鍉	鍛					

Row 29		01	02	03	04	05	06	07	08	09	10	11	12	13	14	15	16	17	18	19
00		鐓	鐭	鑿	鑒	鑫	鏚	鏵	鏈	鏟	鏺	闆	闉	闥	闔	闓	闖	闡	隊	隆
20	鬠	隣	隙	隮	翟	雓	雞	雛	雔	雝	雚	雟	雗	雘	雙	雖	雋	雊	雔	離
40	雕	雜	靡	雪	霯	霍	霮	靝	靟	靈	鞍	鞣	韞	韁	韉	韍	韇	韈	鞬	鞵
60	鞯	韖	韛	韠	韤	夏	韰	韻	頟	頫	頲	頻	顄	顈	顊	顐	顓	顠	颸	颺
80	飋	飕	飄	飠	餐	餮	餎	餕	饌	餅	餷	餢	饑	餉	餘					

Row 30	01	02	03	04	05	06	07	08	09	10	11	12	13	14	15	16	17	18	19
00		餜	䭩	𩞔	𩞯	騅	騂	騉	騊	騌	鴐	𩣡	𩣪	骿	髃	髆	髋	髍	髈	髌
20	髊	鬃	鬇	鬆	鬈	鬋	鬏	鬕	鬦	鬷	魈	魊	魌	魋	魕	魏	鮀	鮄	鮂	鮌
40	鮙	鮆	鮉	鮋	鮏	鮣	鴬	鴦	鴩	鴳	鴴	鵁	鵃	鵑	鵒	鵓	鵔	鵘	麣	麑
60	麛	麜	麗	麳	麶	麷	黀	黁	黎	黏	黐	黦	黬	黿	鼀	鼁	鼆	鼜	鼤	鼩
80	鼫	鼷	齁	齘	龜	龝	儌	儓	儚	兢	㔆	凜	劚	劉	勞					

Row 31	01	02	03	04	05	06	07	08	09	10	11	12	13	14	15	16	17	18	19
00		𠠍	𠤒	匷	𠫓	𠫯	噩	嚚	嚣	嚽	囆	嚸	囇	嚧	嚊	嚩	壈	壂	壘	墬
20	墜	壝	壞	壡	夒	夓	夔	夑	嬰	嬾	嬻	孃	嬛	孈	寶	屪	巑	巘	巢	巔
40	巕	巗	巚	疊	廲	廥	廧	廬	廱	廰	𢇞	彏	彍	彘	彯	徸	徹	懋	懇	懸
60	懾	懼	戄	戃	戲	撽	擵	攃	攄	攎	攌	攑	攗	攖	攜	攠	敲	斁	斅	斳
80	斴	旙	旛	旝	旞	曩	曓	曜	曨	曭	曬	曯	曫	曮	曭					

Row 32	01	02	03	04	05	06	07	08	09	10	11	12	13	14	15	16	17	18	19
00		櫜	櫜	櫢	櫤	櫱	櫎	櫷	櫯	櫼	櫺	櫽	欂	欶	欷	殲	殯	毅	毊	毇
20	毽	毾	氀	氉	氋	瀟	瀡	灌	瀳	灑	灕	灛	灖	灟	灡	灢	灩	瀈	灒	瀓
40	瀹	燅	爅	爋	爊	爌	爗	爨	爧	牃	犃	犦	犨	犪	犤	獮	獶	獠	獵	獺
60	獼	玀	瑿	璈	璘	璬	璷	瓅	瓄	甗	癃	癉	癖	癀	癠	癣	癥	癘	癡	皨
80	皫	皭	皬	皺	盋	盦	盬	盭	盭	盧	瞚	瞺	矙	瞿	矚					

Row 33	01	02	03	04	05	06	07	08	09	10	11	12	13	14	15	16	17	18	19
00		矎	矑	矕	矖	礊	礶	礗	礸	礐	礬	禢	禧	禦	穮	穳	穧	竉	竄	篋
20	籍	籧	籔	籛	籌	籚	籋	籓	籎	籕	籐	籓	籙	籫	籯	糐	糣	糤	糫	糮
40	緊	繵	繨	繻	纆	繾	纀	纃	纅	纉	纑	纒	纗	纕	纚	纝	纞	纎	纃	纋
60	纈	罈	罊	罍	罏	罎	羀	羁	羉	羴	羻	羼	羸	羺	羷	翵	翸	翹	翼	翿
80	翽	翾	耤	耰	耯	聵	聸	聹	聻	聾	腐	膂	臘	臛	臡					

Row 34	01	02	03	04	05	06	07	08	09	10	11	12	13	14	15	16	17	18	19
00		臘	臁	臀	臆	臊	舉	舋	舆	舔	舘	艛	艝	艜	艞	薏	蔏	薞	薃	薑
20	薧	薺	藫	藪	藚	藧	藩	藭	藺	藹	藾	藬	蘪	蘮	蘤	蘭	蘵	蘲	蘸	蘹
40	蘇	蘷	蘺	虂	虆	虇	虈	虊	虧	虩	虪	蟏	蟓	蟺	蠛	蠑	蠙	蠣	蠟	蠨
60	蠭	蠕	蠸	蠴	蠲	蠳	蠵	蠶	蠺	蠹	蠿	蠽	蠾	蠽	蠢	蠁	衊	衋	衁	衇
80	蠵	衉	衊	衋	衛	衞	裂	褭	褱	襄	襘	襜	襛	襍	襝					

Row 35	01	02	03	04	05	06	07	08	09	10	11	12	13	14	15	16	17	18	19
00		襃	襗	襞	覂	覽	觽	觿	觶	觺	譅	譈	譇	譋	譔	譗	譟	譬	譠	譺
20	譛	譯	譿	譾	讂	讄	讅	讆	讋	讌	讎	讐	讔	讛	豃	豅	豷	貄	貙	貜
40	賾	贓	贃	贅	贇	贉	贐	贒	贔	贕	贖	贗	趯	趲	趰	趱	趮	趬	趭	趫
60	蹴	蹸	蹺	蹼	躅	躂	躍	躔	躐	躑	躒	躖	躘	躞	躠	躗	躛	轎	轒	轓
80	轘	轙	轚	辭	邃	邅	邆	邊	邍	邐	邋	邌	邏	邎	邈					

Row 36		01	02	03	04	05	06	07	08	09	10	11	12	13	14	15	16	17	18	19
00		趪	謍	譫	鄜	鄹	鄜	鄸	鄭	鄰	鄯	鄺	醛	醑	醺	醁	醮	醊	醮	醫
20	醢	䣞	醬	𩱛	鍐	鍤	鍘	鍰	鍋	鍠	鍬	鬮	鑋	鐵	鏟	鐕	闟	闠	闤	闞
40	鵮	陸	隴	隱	隧	隸	隸	雔	虢	翟	雖	雜	雖	雝	雒	霻	霏	霫	霸	霰
60	𩅦	靇	𩃬	霤	霳	靁	䨳	霣	靄	霖	艏	靤	鞍	鞢	鞎	鞕	鞚	鞔	鞨	鞔
80	鞱	韥	韗	韏	韍	韝	䪝	韠	韖	頿	顑	顐	顡	飆	颼					

Row 37		01	02	03	04	05	06	07	08	09	10	11	12	13	14	15	16	17	18	19
00		颾	颹	颼	飀	颿	飃	颺	飄	餛	餐	餐	餙	餗	餝	餚	餣	餜	餶	蒏
20	馤	馛	馞	駢	騯	騸	騺	騖	騘	骿	髆	隓	䯧	鬍	鬌	鬁	鬆	鬪	鬴	鬺
40	鬶	鬷	魒	魌	魊	魖	魓	魡	魋	蒐	䱣	鮻	鰟	鯗	鮷	鯆	鮑	鰤	鷃	鴑
60	鴻	鵝	鴿	鶒	鶝	鵺	鴝	鵜	鴿	鴨	鴉	鷗	鳩	鴦	䴎	䴓	麏	麖	麢	麵
80	麩	麪	麯	麰	黚	黴	黷	鼃	鼅	鼇	鼛	鼝	鼯	斛	斁					

Row 38		01	02	03	04	05	06	07	08	09	10	11	12	13	14	15	16	17	18	19
00		敱	齊	齋	齕	齔	竈	乾	窨	糶	貫	巽	齏	劘	剸	劃	繇	綴	變	齧
20	嚣	騇	謦	嚎	嚆	嚬	嚴	嚴	嚐	嚂	墳	壇	壇	壈	壘	壞	壆	罄	豅	壁
40	嬙	壽	夒	夔	嬃	嬰	嫈	歔	嬪	嬾	孀	寧	寭	寰	㝥	寫	寵	導	巎	巔
60	嶂	巏	桑	巇	巘	辟	萬	巒	壓	幑	嬾	幫	廡	廳	彈	彍	彌	彊	蠹	彌
80	蕭	蕾	彙	德	徹	瀝	徽	寇	德	懕	惠	慇	懾	懿	懲					

Row 39		01	02	03	04	05	06	07	08	09	10	11	12	13	14	15	16	17	18	19
00		懲	懇	辨	憣	懥	懍	懞	懶	懽	懂	懵	懵	戴	戴	攣	攘	擂	擽	攩
20	擽	擋	搔	攀	撫	斲	旛	曠	曆	曬	曒	羈	鹵	櫃	櫬	欖	檈	櫯	櫶	穠
40	櫪	欀	繫	纖	毅	毆	毪	氄	氈	毹	氋	潭	豫	選	瀆	瀋	瀬	瀣	瀛	瀑
60	瀐	濤	瀇	瀞	瀊	瀠	瀥	瀎	瀵	瀼	瀷	爈	爛	爣	燾	燹	䨻	爨	縠	翕
80	牆	犢	犪	犛	獵	獺	獄	獳	獙	璁	瓆	瓇	璯	巃	矓					

Row 40		01	02	03	04	05	06	07	08	09	10	11	12	13	14	15	16	17	18	19
00		瓏	甗	甖	艠	癘	癥	癮	癠	癚	癋	癰	皡	皫	盭	盢	瞵	矅	矉	矊
20	矑	罻	穔	矝	磴	礚	礜	礨	襤	礭	礱	礸	禮	禶	穼	竀	竈	簀	蘼	篾
40	穭	穗	簿	籛	籣	籖	籘	糧	糫	糮	糯	糲	糳	糵	糴	檜	繀	繈	縷	纆
60	繚	繂	繕	緒	繹	綢	縕	綃	縭	豹	縲	繇	罏	罽	罤	羀	羃	羅	攫	擷
80	擐	翳	獳	耪	釋	耮	聰	聱	聾	肭	䏰	䐿	膐	臀	臀					

Row 41		01	02	03	04	05	06	07	08	09	10	11	12	13	14	15	16	17	18	19
00		膢	臓	臢	臌	膧	臏	臐	臍	臓	臙	臑	臱	粵	罍	瞿	艭	艬	籌	艶
20	粸	芻	蒸	蘆	藻	蕭	薜	蕩	蔗	鄭	蘄	蘑	蕑	蔪	蘇	懟	蘳	殤	蕼	蘘
40	藷	薔	蓋	蘖	薹	藉	蘊	蔓	葬	藥	薅	藹	蒨	虨	虪	虩	蠐	蠦	蟋	蠍
60	蝤	蝟	蠛	蟈	蠅	蠆	蠚	蠶	蠹	蠱	蠶	蠡	蠢	蠡	蠭	蠱	蠭	蠶	蠢	蠿
80	衛	襄	贏	襲	褢	襞	襛	襤	襱	襴	襶	襵	襹	櫬	覰					

Row 42		01	02	03	04	05	06	07	08	09	10	11	12	13	14	15	16	17	18	19
00		觹	觵	䚫	觿	譁	譇	謀	譂	譀	譃	譈	譄	譆	譤	譾	譝	譩	戴	謵
20	曡	䀁	䝤	䝥	貖	貚	𧲿	𧳂	𧳶	䝨	䝮	𧳣	𧳧	𧳾	𧴂	𧴃	𧸣	賦	賫	賧
40	𧸘	贉	贌	艢	寳	贒	𩔰	樴	檽	趨	趲	趮	蹢	蹻	蹣	蹼	蹭	蹶	躁	躅
60	躐	躎	蹬	蹼	躤	跳	蹈	躇	踩	躕	躄	躉	躠	軂	軃	軅	軀	軉	轋	轒
80	轒	韓	䨬	辮	辯	辦	變	邇	遾	邋	邌	邂	邈	邍	還					

Row 43		01	02	03	04	05	06	07	08	09	10	11	12	13	14	15	16	17	18	19
00		邉	邊	鬙	鄳	鄿	鄷	酆	鄺	酇	酈	醾	醽	醟	醧	醶	醼	鍐	鍦	鏜
20	鐵	鐎	鏍	鐮	鐴	鏝	鐊	鐅	鏧	闟	闠	闥	闞	闛	隨	隮	隮	隴	鏞	雚
40	暫	雈	難	雛	雝	難	雞	雙	霁	霵	霫	霬	霮	霯	霱	霵	霺	鞯	鞢	鞫
60	鞸	鞹	鞼	韃	韄	韅	韉	韊	韝	韡	韢	韣	韤	韥	韛	韟	韠	額	顡	顙
80	類	顡	顧	顯	顰	顥	顫	燰	飉	飂	飃	飄	飇	韐	饕					

Row 44		01	02	03	04	05	06	07	08	09	10	11	12	13	14	15	16	17	18	19
00		饗	饙	饚	饛	饝	饞	饟	馦	馩	馥	驈	驉	驊	驕	驖	驗	驌	驗	騷
20	驒	驛	骴	骶	骻	髀	髂	髃	髈	髊	髍	豪	鬘	鬖	鬚	鬠	鬢	鬜	鬡	鬑
40	鬤	鬫	鬰	鬿	魑	魌	鮄	鮍	鮷	鯗	鰤	鯪	鯛	鯵	鯾	鰍	鰗	鰛	鯰	鶩
60	鶉	鶖	鶚	鶄	鶬	鶜	鶤	鶨	鶯	鶻	鶼	鷀	鷂	鷉	鷋	鷑	鷔	鷘	鷨	鷫
80	鹺	麏	麙	麔	麡	麥	麨	麮	麳	麶	麷	麹	麼	黂	黈					

Row 45		01	02	03	04	05	06	07	08	09	10	11	12	13	14	15	16	17	18	19
00		黰	黱	黽	鼃	鼂	鼇	鼙	鼛	鼲	鼴	鼵	鼶	鼷	鼸	齍	齗	齘	齚	齞
20	齕	齗	齡	龐	龜	龝	龞	龥	僂	顛	顛	𩔳	謳	剸	勦	匔	匱	麗	嚋	嚔
40	嚽	嚸	器	嚹	嚪	囒	墬	夒	嬃	嬖	嬧	孏	嬸	嶾	巁	巆	巑	巒	巕	廱
60	廮	廓	廞	彏	彊	彎	彞	徽	懇	懋	懜	懤	懬	懍	懫	懰	擠	擛	擨	擷
80	攆	斀	斁	斄	斅	斆	斈	數	斷	曌	曹	曬	櫔	櫟	櫺					

Row 46		01	02	03	04	05	06	07	08	09	10	11	12	13	14	15	16	17	18	19
00		櫕	歡	歟	殲	毇	毲	毾	瀛	瀑	瀠	瀚	瀏	瀝	瀞	瀧	燫	爆	爍	爕
20	爨	犨	犪	犩	犦	犧	犪	犬	獻	獾	圝	獐	獻	猛	獲	璺	瓌	甗	疇	疊
40	疉	癌	癥	癲	癜	癢	癧	瞶	瞱	瞻	盬	盧	盭	盩	矈	矎	矆	礍	礭	礴
60	礦	礵	禮	穡	穤	穲	窾	竄	竅	竇	竊	竂	竇	竃	籩	籭	籰	籯	籲	籮
80	籦	籧	籥	綜	縡	縂	繠	繫	纀	繽	纆	纏	纓	纙	纚					

Row 47		01	02	03	04	05	06	07	08	09	10	11	12	13	14	15	16	17	18	19
00		繕	縱	繝	繼	纇	纎	纘	罍	羆	羄	羅	羉	羈	羵	羼	羸	羴	羷	羺
20	翻	翾	翿	耰	聾	聹	聺	臏	臙	臚	臛	臜	臞	臡	舝	艣	艱	艷	艼	虊
40	藻	藹	藾	蘁	蘄	蘆	蘇	蘋	蘐	蘑	蘔	蘕	蘙	蘛	蘜	蘝	蘞	蘟	蘠	蘡
60	蘢	蘤	蘥	蘦	蘧	蘩	蘪	蘫	蘬	蘭	蘮	虪	虩	虪	虧	蠆	蠓	蠔	蠛	蠝
80	蠙	蠟	蠨	蠮	蠰	蠶	蠸	蠹	蠺	蠻	蠽	蠾	蠿	衊	襲					

Row 48	01	02	03	04	05	06	07	08	09	10	11	12	13	14	15	16	17	18	19
00		襄	褍	襊	襜	襛	襓	覆	覶	覺	觶	譆	譇	譈	譐	譑	謬	譎	譋	譕
20	譯	諱	謂	譤	譂	警	譋	貚	貗	貙	贂	賭	贆	趪	趫	趬	蹟	蹪	蹫	蹯
40	蹮	蹝	蹧	躚	躖	躃	躅	轒	轍	轑	轕	轗	轘	辴	農	遳	遷	邌	邇	鄃
60	鄈	鄉	鄒	鄭	鄹	鄲	醊	醋	醎	醳	醱	醹	鏶	鏑	鐵	鐠	鐉	鐍	鐌	鐏
80	鐍	鐾	鑒	闒	闔	闑	闓	闐	闠	闢	闤	隸	隵	靉	鞲					

Row 49	01	02	03	04	05	06	07	08	09	10	11	12	13	14	15	16	17	18	19
00		雘	雟	雛	雝	雗	靨	鞾	雚	雖	雞	雟	雜	雡	雥	霤	霦	霧	霩	霪
20	霢	霨	霮	霯	霏	霴	霾	鞭	鞳	鞻	鞵	韃	韉	韇	韋	韌	鞴	韄	韅	韝
40	韣	韙	韞	顢	顛	顣	顗	顠	顤	顥	顦	顧	顨	顩	顪	饉	饊	饋	饌	饍
60	饐	饑	饒	饎	饏	饓	饙	饚	馘	馦	騅	騇	騂	騃	騄	騋	騍	騑	騞	騠
80	鷺	髆	髏	髐	髖	髕	鬇	鬈	鬉	鬊	鬋	鬌	鬍	鬮	鬰					

Row 50	01	02	03	04	05	06	07	08	09	10	11	12	13	14	15	16	17	18	19
00		鬺	鬷	鬹	鬻	鬵	魌	魖	魈	魋	魏	魐	鮥	鯙	鯫	鯦	鰻	鯝	鯷	鰱
20	鬻	鯿	鯷	鷙	鷔	鷖	鷄	鷉	鷗	鵬	鶤	鶘	鶙	鶡	鶥	鶨	鶬	鶴	鷃	鷂
40	鹵	鹺	麕	麢	麖	麜	麧	麬	麮	麯	麰	麱	麳	麴	黂	黃	黅	黇	黏	黐
60	黕	黽	黿	鼂	鼇	鼈	鼉	鼊	鼢	鼫	鼯	鼱	鼳	齙	齚	齛	齜	齝	齞	龐
80	龕	龖	龗	爔	儺	儷	瀿	劚	嚫	嚬	嚭	嚳	嚴	嚶	嚹					

Row 51	01	02	03	04	05	06	07	08	09	10	11	12	13	14	15	16	17	18	19
00		圞	圝	壙	壛	壜	壝	壟	壢	奮	孃	孆	孅	孊	孍	對	孴	巉	巍	幰
20	廬	彏	彏	徿	懍	懎	懪	懫	懮	戴	擨	擽	攡	攤	攦	攫	攭	旜	曤	曥
40	欒	櫏	櫙	櫺	櫿	欂	欃	欄	欆	欇	欈	瀵	瀷	瀸	瀹	瀺	瀼	瀿	灃	灄
60	灊	灑	灒	灙	灕	爥	爧	爦	爨	爩	犪	犫	犨	犢	犤	犩	犪	獶	獿	瓅
80	瓐	甐	甗	甒	疊	疉	疅	疊	疊	癃	癭	皪	皶	矆	矇					

Row 52	01	02	03	04	05	06	07	08	09	10	11	12	13	14	15	16	17	18	19
00		矊	矌	矐	礡	禱	禴	穡	穲	穤	竈	竊	竆	竄	竷	籃	籊	籌	籓	籐
20	籑	籔	籗	籚	籛	籜	糬	糭	糰	纀	續	纁	纆	纏	纑	纕	繼	纘	纙	纛
40	飄	罍	罏	罐	耰	聯	聵	臈	臇	臊	臏	藻	藉	蘀	蘁	蘄	蘅	藍	蘗	蘜
60	蘞	蘢	蘥	蘦	蘨	蘩	蘪	蘫	蘬	蘱	蘲	蘳	蘷	蘺	蠁	蠂	蠄	蠈	蠊	蠋
80	蠙	蠚	蠹	蠺	蠻	蠱	蠸	蠾	蠢	衊	衋	衢	襋	襽	襲					

Row 53	01	02	03	04	05	06	07	08	09	10	11	12	13	14	15	16	17	18	19
00		襲	襹	襛	襳	襶	襵	覉	覶	覹	譟	譜	譅	譯	譹	譿	讀	議	讒	論
20	讌	讍	讓	豅	豬	貜	贏	贖	趲	趱	躍	躒	躖	躕	躔	躃	躘	躙	躞	躦
40	軀	軃	轔	轙	轢	轣	邐	邋	邌	邍	鄚	鄜	鄝	鄟	鄠	鄡	鄨	醴	醵	醶
60	鑓	鑛	鑜	鑝	鑞	鑟	鑡	鑢	鑣	鑥	鑪	鑰	鑿	贏	闠	闡	隮	隯	隳	雚
80	雛	雜	雝	雞	難	雡	雥	離	霴	霵	霽	霿	靃	靄	靏					

Row 54	00	01	02	03	04	05	06	07	08	09	10	11	12	13	14	15	16	17	18	19
00		醶	髂	䰛	夔	韄	韅	韇	韊	韉	鞼	韝	韡	韲	韹	顪	顢	顣	顥	顡
20	顤	顪	顟	顫	顚	飂	飃	飋	飌	飉	飆	飇	飄	飅	飇	飜	饗	饔	饞	饟
40	饚	饝	饠	驓	驔	驖	驛	驟	驞	驚	骳	髕	髖	髐	髜	鬇	鬖	鬘	鬗	鬟
60	鬠	鬡	鬤	鬭	鬵	鬶	鬻	鬺	鬸	鬹	鬺	魖	魙	魕	鰝	鰞	鰶	鰻	鱃	鱙
80	鱛	鱧	鱨	鱭	鱶	鱵	鷁	鷈	鷔	鷖	鷘	鷚	鷞	鷫	鷯					

Row 55	00	01	02	03	04	05	06	07	08	09	10	11	12	13	14	15	16	17	18	19
00		鷴	鷵	鷸	鸈	鷭	鸀	鷂	鸇	䴏	麡	麠	麗	麢	麧	麴	麯	麷	黁	黏
20	黐	黐	黐	黳	黵	黶	黷	鼇	鼈	鼉	鼱	鼲	齀	齃	齄	齅	齆	齇	齈	齉
40	龕	龜	龞	㒦	儽	儹	儾	冐	匷	夒	囒	囓	囕	囖	囔	嚴	嚴	囐	囖	𡔖
60	壥	壧	孋	孆	孇	孌	孏	孊	孅	寷	寶	屭	巕	巏	巖	巘	巙	巚	廮	廱
80	彏	彐	彲	𢩗	𢩘	懹	懺	攀	攎	攔	攕	攖	攛	斸	旟					

Row 56	00	01	02	03	04	05	06	07	08	09	10	11	12	13	14	15	16	17	18	19
00		曡	霳	櫸	欄	欆	欅	欏	歡	歡	毊	氎	灊	灖	瀆	灕	瀨	灪	灙	灚
20	爚	爣	爆	爧	爕	爢	爆	玁	瓓	瓕	瓥	瓥	矑	矒	矙	蠱	盩	盟	矚	矘
40	礸	礸	禷	禴	穥	穰	穱	穳	竊	籙	籛	籜	籡	籢	籣	繫	纜	纖	纈	纏
60	纘	纛	纕	纚	糴	罍	羇	羉	聸	臞	臡	臢	艭	艬	蘬	蘯	蘱	蘲	蘼	蘽
80	蘿	虇	虆	虌	蠆	虈	虋	蠠	蠥	蠦	蠨	蠩	蠫	蠬	蠱					

Row 57	00	01	02	03	04	05	06	07	08	09	10	11	12	13	14	15	16	17	18	19
00		蠹	蠹	蠺	蠻	蠶	蠸	蠼	蠽	蠾	蠹	蠹	襲	襹	襼	襽	襾	襷	襸	覼
20	觿	讐	讄	讅	讖	讕	讗	讘	讙	讛	讜	讞	讟	變	讝	貜	貛	貕	貗	贎
40	贍	贕	贚	趲	躦	躧	躨	躩	軉	轞	轟	轠	轣	轤	轥	輚	轞	邇	邍	邐
60	鑒	酅	醽	醾	釂	釃	醺	鑈	鑉	鐵	鑊	鑋	鑌	鑍	鑎	鑏	鑐	鑑	鑰	闤
80	隮	雥	雧	雦	雚	雝	雛	雟	靆	靈	靍	靎	靏	靐	靓					

Row 58	00	01	02	03	04	05	06	07	08	09	10	11	12	13	14	15	16	17	18	19
00		韆	韇	韈	韉	韊	鞫	韡	韢	韣	韤	韥	顫	顯	顯	顰	顭	顮	飀	飍
20	饘	饙	饚	饞	驜	驝	驕	驏	驫	驪	驥	驦	驧	驨	髒	髏	髖	髗	鬠	鬢
40	鬤	鬮	鬱	鬸	鬹	魑	魒	魓	魕	鰻	鱅	鱃	鱇	鱋	鱄	鱗	鱘	鱓	鱢	鱥
60	鱋	鱉	鱉	鱉	鱉	鱐	鱐	鱓	鱵	鷹	鷺	鸂	鸇	鸗	鸛	鸚	鸕	鸝	鸞	鸛
80	鸖	鸍	麣	麤	麯	麩	麷	麵	麶	麷	麰	麲	黀	黎	黂					

Row 59	00	01	02	03	04	05	06	07	08	09	10	11	12	13	14	15	16	17	18	19
00		黬	黰	黷	黸	黹	黻	黭	黮	黴	黶	鼉	鼊	鼈	鼂	鼇	鼅	釃	釄	鼖
20	鼞	鼟	鼷	鼸	鼿	齀	齁	齂	齃	齄	齅	齾	齹	齺	齻	齼	龎	儾	勷	囍
40	囐	囒	囔	巙	孅	孍	孏	孄	孈	戀	戁	戄	戃	戅	戆	攣	攘	變	巘	鼞
60	灘	欇	蠡	欒	欓	欗	欚	欛	殭	氍	灋	瀼	灂	灃	灅	爕	爙	爛	爣	躑
80	爨	玂	玁	玃	玀	玁	玂	玃	玀	瓛	瓝	甗	矗	矚	矙					

Row 60		01	02	03	04	05	06	07	08	09	10	11	12	13	14	15	16	17	18	19
00		虪	癯	皪	盬	瞜	矒	礔	礕	禮	穜	禫	鬤	穲	穦	竈	篹	籔	篘	劉
20	籋	籣	籃	籆	糯	縺	纗	纉	罍	羝	羺	翳	臕	臁	臍	膞	虪	贏	䨇	轡
40	䌰	鬵	瓌	黮	艫	蘢	藰	蕬	蓫	蘟	蘋	蘏	蘻	蘤	藁	蘙	蘿	蘀	蘛	蘶
60	蠳	蠛	蠓	蠘	蘖	蠡	蠪	蠶	衢	鷥	譚	讜	讚	罍	罍	㬫	貛	蠹	饕	獺
80	獵	贖	贗	贅	澀	趲	躪	躍	躓	蹢	轙	轋	轍	輪	翟

Row 61		01	02	03	04	05	06	07	08	09	10	11	12	13	14	15	16	17	18	19
00		轞	邇	遷	遺	邁	鄮	醇	醲	醿	釃	醬	鏤	鑄	鐵	鏴	鐁	壘	闠	鼜
20	虉	難	鞿	雛	雝	離	雜	霰	靅	靋	韇	韉	韀	鞻	韄	韡	韣	韅	韝	靡
40	瓙	隴	顟	瞵	顡	顬	類	顧	顗	顤	顛	颾	饔	饡	饈	馧	驍	驕	驞	驎
60	驉	騤	驛	驧	驚	髗	髏	髍	髊	髎	髆	髇	髐	髑	髌	髟	鬂	鬊	鬎	鬹
80	鬷	鬻	鬻	鬻	鬻	鱑	鰝	鰛	鰟	鱛	鯡	鰫	鰷	鰺	鱠

Row 62		01	02	03	04	05	06	07	08	09	10	11	12	13	14	15	16	17	18	19
00		鰎	鱹	鱶	鱚	鷲	鷙	鷟	鶕	鵺	鵷	鵰	鵩	鵻	鶈	鶛	鶚	鷗	鶠	鶖
20	鶬	鶪	鷉	鷫	鷸	鸐	鸉	麜	麳	麡	黈	黶	黧	黰	鼊	鼇	鼭	鼶	鼷	鼸
40	鼵	鼾	齇	齵	齸	齺	齹	齾	壓	䜌	饋	嚈	巖	嚙	囆	壢	孁	孅	孏	孇
60	孃	彛	嶸	寱	巕	巤	巆	幱	廲	懃	懬	懝	攃	攡	攭	擽	旟	曔	櫫	櫓
80	櫃	櫫	歗	鬣	瀰	瀶	瀼	灊	爦	爨	玁	皪	矑	癮	癰

Row 63		01	02	03	04	05	06	07	08	09	10	11	12	13	14	15	16	17	18	19
00		皭	盪	盬	矆	礙	礛	礞	穖	竇	籤	籮	籓	籢	籖	籍	籧	籯	籵	纈
20	纞	纓	纃	纏	纛	罌	罍	羅	羉	臙	艬	艭	蘈	蘥	蘳	蘵	蘷	蘸	蘹	蘺
40	虇	虆	蠹	蠶	蠽	蠾	蠻	襮	襴	襬	覼	覾	讅	讍	譸	譞	讂	讁	讇	讋
60	豅	虋	贙	贛	贔	躔	躕	躚	轔	轖	轣	轞	辥	邍	邏	酈	酁	醽	醾	鑄
80	鑵	鑚	鑰	鑠	鑲	鑴	闤	闥	闢	雥	靐	離	雗	霺	靇

Row 64		01	02	03	04	05	06	07	08	09	10	11	12	13	14	15	16	17	18	19
00		霿	醿	韇	顣	顥	飋	飉	饜	饞	饡	醫	騮	驎	驕	驝	驜	驖	驏	驠
20	驔	驧	鬺	韠	鬍	鬮	鬩	鬻	鬹	魑	魕	魖	魙	鱇	鰿	鱝	鰪	鱷	鰟	鱡
40	鱵	鱉	鱍	鱶	鷁	鷂	鸊	鸂	鸃	鷫	鷬	鷭	鷮	鸁	麘	麖	麷	麳	黂	黯
60	黴	黶	鼜	鼘	鼟	齆	齗	齰	齵	齸	齺	齾	龐	匷	韠	韇	癟	覿	巙	灪
80	灝	爂	欄	檑	爵	爞	爟	瀼	灂	瀿	灃	爗	爚	爛	爨

Row 65		01	02	03	04	05	06	07	08	09	10	11	12	13	14	15	16	17	18	19
00		爩	犣	犪	獵	瓓	瓖	癭	礜	穮	穳	竊	籉	籗	籚	籛	籜	籦	糴	糶
20	纅	纕	纘	纚	罽	羼	艨	艭	蘴	虂	虃	虆	蠦	蠨	蠩	蠽	蠿	蠸	襸	襽
40	襹	覶	讄	讆	讓	豅	趯	躩	躨	躪	躙	躢	躧	邐	鑢	鑪	鑛	闥	韄	霸
60	韉	韇	韈	韇	饟	飍	驐	驑	驒	髍	髂	髀	鬤	鬘	鬛	鬻	鬻	鰻	鱗	鱄
80	鱑	鱐	鱕	鱗	鸕	鸔	鸙	鸘	鸛	麢	麣	黷	黸	鼷	齻

Row 66	01	02	03	04	05	06	07	08	09	10	11	12	13	14	15	16	17	18	19
00		[illegible]	[illegible]	[illegible]	[illegible]	[illegible]	[illegible]	[illegible]	[illegible]	[illegible]	[illegible]	[illegible]	[illegible]	[illegible]	[illegible]	[illegible]	[illegible]	[illegible]	[illegible]	[illegible]
20	[illegible]	[illegible]	[illegible]	[illegible]	[illegible]	[illegible]	[illegible]	[illegible]	[illegible]	[illegible]	[illegible]	[illegible]	[illegible]	[illegible]	[illegible]	[illegible]	[illegible]	[illegible]	[illegible]	[illegible]
40	[illegible]	[illegible]	[illegible]	[illegible]	[illegible]	[illegible]	[illegible]	[illegible]	[illegible]	[illegible]	[illegible]	[illegible]	[illegible]	[illegible]	[illegible]	[illegible]	[illegible]	[illegible]	[illegible]	[illegible]
60	[illegible]	[illegible]	[illegible]	[illegible]	[illegible]	[illegible]	[illegible]	[illegible]	[illegible]	[illegible]	[illegible]	[illegible]	[illegible]	[illegible]	[illegible]	[illegible]	[illegible]	[illegible]	[illegible]	[illegible]
80	[illegible]	[illegible]	[illegible]	[illegible]	[illegible]	[illegible]	[illegible]	[illegible]	[illegible]	[illegible]	[illegible]	[illegible]	[illegible]	[illegible]	[illegible]					

Row 67	01	02	03	04	05	06	07	08	09	10	11	12	13	14	15	16	17	18	19
00		[illegible]	[illegible]	[illegible]	[illegible]	[illegible]	[illegible]	[illegible]	[illegible]	[illegible]	[illegible]	[illegible]	[illegible]	[illegible]	[illegible]	[illegible]	[illegible]	[illegible]	[illegible]	[illegible]
20	[illegible]	[illegible]	[illegible]	[illegible]	[illegible]	[illegible]	[illegible]	[illegible]	[illegible]	[illegible]	[illegible]	[illegible]	[illegible]	[illegible]	[illegible]	[illegible]	[illegible]	[illegible]	[illegible]	[illegible]
40	[illegible]	[illegible]	[illegible]	[illegible]	[illegible]	[illegible]	[illegible]	[illegible]	[illegible]	[illegible]	[illegible]	[illegible]	[illegible]	[illegible]	[illegible]	[illegible]	[illegible]	[illegible]	[illegible]	[illegible]
60	[illegible]	[illegible]	[illegible]	[illegible]	[illegible]	[illegible]	[illegible]	[illegible]	[illegible]	[illegible]	[illegible]	[illegible]	[illegible]	[illegible]	[illegible]	[illegible]	[illegible]	[illegible]	[illegible]	[illegible]
80	[illegible]	[illegible]	[illegible]	[illegible]	[illegible]	[illegible]	[illegible]	[illegible]	[illegible]	[illegible]	[illegible]	[illegible]	[illegible]	[illegible]	[illegible]					

Row 68	01	02	03	04	05	06	07	08	09	10	11	12	13	14	15	16	17	18	19
00		[illegible]	[illegible]	[illegible]	[illegible]	[illegible]	[illegible]	[illegible]	[illegible]	[illegible]	[illegible]	[illegible]	[illegible]	[illegible]	[illegible]	[illegible]	[illegible]	[illegible]	[illegible]	[illegible]
20	[illegible]	[illegible]	[illegible]	[illegible]	[illegible]	[illegible]	[illegible]	[illegible]	[illegible]	[illegible]	[illegible]	[illegible]	[illegible]	[illegible]	[illegible]	[illegible]	[illegible]	[illegible]	[illegible]	[illegible]
40	[illegible]	[illegible]	[illegible]	[illegible]	[illegible]	[illegible]	[illegible]	[illegible]	[illegible]	[illegible]	[illegible]	[illegible]	[illegible]	[illegible]	[illegible]	[illegible]	[illegible]	[illegible]	[illegible]	[illegible]
60	[illegible]	[illegible]	[illegible]	[illegible]	[illegible]	[illegible]	[illegible]	[illegible]	[illegible]	[illegible]	[illegible]	[illegible]	[illegible]	[illegible]	[illegible]	[illegible]	[illegible]	[illegible]	[illegible]	[illegible]
80	[illegible]	[illegible]	[illegible]	[illegible]	[illegible]	[illegible]	[illegible]	[illegible]	[illegible]	[illegible]	[illegible]	[illegible]	[illegible]	[illegible]	[illegible]					

Row 69	01	02	03	04	05	06	07	08	09	10	11	12	13	14	15	16	17	18	19
00		[illegible]	[illegible]	[illegible]	[illegible]	[illegible]	[illegible]	[illegible]	[illegible]	[illegible]	[illegible]	[illegible]	[illegible]	[illegible]	[illegible]	[illegible]	[illegible]	[illegible]	[illegible]	[illegible]
20	[illegible]	[illegible]	[illegible]	[illegible]	[illegible]	[illegible]	[illegible]	[illegible]	[illegible]	[illegible]	[illegible]	[illegible]	[illegible]	[illegible]	[illegible]	[illegible]	[illegible]	[illegible]	[illegible]	[illegible]
40	[illegible]	[illegible]	[illegible]	[illegible]	[illegible]	[illegible]	[illegible]	[illegible]	[illegible]	[illegible]	[illegible]	[illegible]	[illegible]	[illegible]	[illegible]	[illegible]	[illegible]	[illegible]	[illegible]	[illegible]
60	[illegible]	[illegible]	[illegible]	[illegible]	[illegible]	[illegible]	[illegible]	[illegible]	[illegible]	[illegible]	[illegible]	[illegible]	[illegible]	[illegible]	[illegible]	[illegible]	[illegible]	[illegible]	[illegible]	[illegible]
80	[illegible]	[illegible]	[illegible]	[illegible]	[illegible]	[illegible]	[illegible]	[illegible]	[illegible]	[illegible]	[illegible]	[illegible]	[illegible]	[illegible]	[illegible]					

Row 70	01	02	03	04	05	06	07	08	09	10	11	12	13	14	15	16	17	18	19
00		[illegible]	[illegible]	[illegible]	[illegible]	[illegible]	[illegible]	[illegible]	[illegible]	[illegible]	[illegible]	[illegible]	[illegible]	[illegible]	[illegible]	[illegible]	[illegible]	[illegible]	[illegible]	[illegible]
20	[illegible]	[illegible]	[illegible]	[illegible]	[illegible]	[illegible]	[illegible]	[illegible]	[illegible]	[illegible]	[illegible]	[illegible]	[illegible]	[illegible]	[illegible]	[illegible]	[illegible]	[illegible]	[illegible]	[illegible]
40	[illegible]	[illegible]	[illegible]	[illegible]	[illegible]	[illegible]	[illegible]	[illegible]	[illegible]	[illegible]	[illegible]	[illegible]	[illegible]	[illegible]						
60																				
80																				

CNS 11643-1986 Plane 15

Row 1		01	02	03	04	05	06	07	08	09	10	11	12	13	14	15	16	17	18	19
00		乙	千	乣	㕚	生	么	厄	夯	从	区	肌	允	尺	亢	刘	匁	匚	匜	厇
20	邓	亘	卟	囟	亣	不	龙	亏	开	彡	屯	中	乔	企	乇	仔	仉	风	有	冄
40	冗	安	次	充	凶	厄	叻	叽	叺	扔	圣	不	夸	尬	奶	存	孙	龙	尥	巳
60	町	屮	岙	巨	并	羊	幻	处	尨	杢	汉	水	癸	爿	辶	乔	肙	辰	卹	亦
80	朩	仪	伝	关	佰	伂	伊	址	攸	低	任	冰	罕	汾	汗					

Row 2		01	02	03	04	05	06	07	08	09	10	11	12	13	14	15	16	17	18	19
00		囯	买	务	刘	劝	劣	邑	励	饱	匈	芒	华	厖	去	吕	吋	旱	吣	呅
20	吹	囥	坎	坊	寻	奵	妵	安	妒	宇	宄	开	穴	宁	宜	尨	尼	岸	光	岁
40	时	帆	希	廷	廷	武	弐	忿	扣	扨	扐	㕛	旦	助	东	杂	杀	瓜	刨	刉
60	汙	汢	炎	奶	犾	炇	牝	犯	牞	狗	玑	盯	初	禹	私	羊	胞	肱	艾	芒
80	芑	过	込	邠	厖	卹	丞	豆	车	牽	佽	秋	佲	侞	冬					

Row 3		01	02	03	04	05	06	07	08	09	10	11	12	13	14	15	16	17	18	19
00		佤	任	佊	枣	佛	佳	佨	欣	佘	佪	作	佯	伞	宗	冠	冹	泪	枣	冾
20	兂	兇	亟	刾	劲	劭	劬	舅	匧	匼	岸	厖	肏	圣	籾	受	叐	乏	哘	咔
40	哎	旺	叻	呙	岔	告	呴	囝	困	国	坛	杢	歪	坙	坤	坍	坈	坒	坉	壳
60	奋	炎	夸	奉	柴	枣	买	癸	妐	姺	妫	妭	妀	娟	姈	姹	妏	妍	妟	妤
80	孢	孝	实	寀	屆	峑	岀	宏	岙	岩	岐	峀	岗	岎	名					

Row 4		01	02	03	04	05	06	07	08	09	10	11	12	13	14	15	16	17	18	19
00		岿	杢	帙	帵	忻	纭	廷	奔	弢	弫	孜	彾	彡	忯	恆	忛	怯	忼	志
20	忉	攸	忬	屏	厦	护	扱	拐	拼	挖	拃	抻	拥	挑	技	拘	扨	拌	尖	㞢
40	首	邑	旺	妲	昳	杲	机	杫	枲	東	枂	杦	杺	毡	毣	毛	秋	香	毯	毡
60	氨	沈	沐	剎	半	汧	汚	沪	沉	沪	汻	汔	洋	尔	抉	灬	炁	杰	奸	爻
80	只	灿	炽	斧	谷	牧	犹	狄	玑	玫	甭	甸	瓶	盃	亩					

Row 5		01	02	03	04	05	06	07	08	09	10	11	12	13	14	15	16	17	18	19
00		砌	矾	矶	衫	朴	竺	釆	罕	罗	咒	舌	芳	苐	芫	芭	芋	芨	迈	迅
20	迄	邠	邵	邹	邦	阂	陂	阡	所	阶	陈	阪	䑼	兹	学	奕	侫	佪	全	俄
40	伐	侂	俊	俞	色	侹	併	仰	侔	偹	究	壳	尭	宥	究	淡	凬	胣	荆	劼
60	剐	剬	刭	刽	刿	劻	旒	缽	甸	朐	匼	卓	幸	辈	東	怕	䒤	扉	厚	柔
80	咩	咤	省	别	若	和	哐	昆	喃	哑	春	呵	啵	咆	唧					

Row 6		01	02	03	04	05	06	07	08	09	10	11	12	13	14	15	16	17	18	19
00		呏	吻	岱	困	坛	坊	延	体	坳	坏	估	怯	叔	坤	押	坚	拍	坷	坐
20	奏	夸	冥	奃	查	臭	妃	妕	妹	妊	妮	妡	婆	妳	姑	姊	委	妪	妈	妣
40	姁	娇	籽	孖	孚	孪	學	孥	孳	宕	宠	宕	官	宾	孛	冠	帛	旭	冠	屦
60	茂	岊	岐	岂	昆	峨	峀	峬	岬	峝	峑	峞	岳	巢	崩	绖	帽	针	轩	应
80	庋	府	庙	应	庈	忱	忼	恚	忝	忑	态	怨	丕	忩	毟					

Row 7		01	02	03	04	05	06	07	08	09	10	11	12	13	14	15	16	17	18	19
00		恁	你	戕	叓	抾	抺	技	拈	搒	拊	扺	拸	拗	扳	抢	拃	鼓	攽	扮
20	料	放	斉	香	眉	吡	昨	晃	昼	昕	昙	昊	昪	肛	杈	杬	秋	枳	栟	杀
40	栈	轰	杝	相	茉	毒	枡	秉	栌	构	栯	枭	枀	栍	欥	政	肯	岔	毣	毬
60	毡	叒	玹	毪	洗	汅	汯	汞	沓	汥	沾	浅	沥	冲	泼	沫	泅	湧	炕	炷
80	炷	灬	炎	炦	炪	炰	炁	炘	奚	殷	殴	牀	牵	牪	软					

Row 8		01	02	03	04	05	06	07	08	09	10	11	12	13	14	15	16	17	18	19
00		罕	狄	玆	玩	玗	玣	玫	玚	玡	瓩	革	畀	时	疋	疨	矾	矸	矼	矶
20	矾	矶	袄	衪	衬	衽	衩	衲	衣	衿	秃	秋	秔	季	衫	穿	窆	籾	纨	系
40	约	罡	罗	瓶	罕	耒	耵	助	肖	肢	肛	肩	肹	肸	肩	芦	苧	芙	芏	苶
60	劳	苀	芢	茎	芛	芭	花	芶	芲	虔	蚋	虺	蚪	虬	蚩	衵	豸	迷	迟	迈
80	迟	远	迹	迂	廷	迸	邦	郊	邪	邰	邳	却	郊	陀	陆					

Row 9		01	02	03	04	05	06	07	08	09	10	11	12	13	14	15	16	17	18	19
00		赴	玚	秩	笏	拥	龟	奄	衮	倖	傍	佌	俗	俤	侑	佶	佉	值	侘	倡
20	佪	你	俸	侌	侽	罟	涤	枣	浦	涓	浬	浚	旁	刷	剂	勴	刿	勔	匌	匩
40	郡	啉	卧	卣	原	庭	厩	妙	帕	麦	延	旺	唛	哑	哂	咾	咗	哇	嗡	害
60	耆	呲	曳	哭	唧	哪	咆	和	唸	唓	唸	垤	室	垈	垪	垐	垭	垵	城	垩
80	埻	垫	基	垴	垚	坐	里	坒	埔	埏	垤	埒	垧	垤	剖					

Row 10		01	02	03	04	05	06	07	08	09	10	11	12	13	14	15	16	17	18	19
00		夹	衮	奋	奂	叁	奕	奔	焌	爽	娅	娓	婳	婷	娶	姝	娟	娼	始	娥
20	娜	孜	孤	阜	窑	宋	容	宰	客	尉	泰	犀	屣	屄	屐	屏	岕	学	炭	峒
40	崁	崑	崐	岜	崊	峃	峯	峉	峋	峋	带	帼	帾	帷	歪	床	庚	庚	庑	庵
60	庋	弢	徙	宓	悚	悛	恕	悖	恶	咸	恛	悈	恣	悦	悲	悒	悉	恪	佩	恍
80	怨	战	戗	扉	扈	扇	捋	挟	捤	挼	捻	拔	捩	拒	掇					

Row 11		01	02	03	04	05	06	07	08	09	10	11	12	13	14	15	16	17	18	19
00		抛	掃	抽	挹	拼	揗	挫	捡	抹	艳	拨	捬	恣	圣	炮	炫	胥	号	吴
20	咀	眨	昭	艮	泉	昆	肪	杍	栊	梾	梂	栖	松	栭	枯	梁	栩	根	梣	杪
40	树	相	枭	祭	板	棚	臬	板	殍	毠	毡	毯	毪	毬	毡	毭	毪	毡	毡	毥
60	毯	毳	毽	氰	没	洨	汲	湃	汞	溺	派	沓	浏	浸	浥	洦	沯	涣	涂	觅
80	炮	炻	炼	炶	炪	烧	烝	熙	炭	栅	烟	焦	炒	炁	焰					

Row 12		01	02	03	04	05	06	07	08	09	10	11	12	13	14	15	16	17	18	19
00		烏	炲	炂	哥	庛	凮	泧	牀	犁	狁	狦	狐	狾	玏	珋	玨	珑	玵	玸
20	玧	玿	玦	玥	珦	坒	玻	珎	釜	玞	玠	玪	蚕	瓟	瓬	杳	斟	玹	畜	瞅
40	畓	昔	畓	畔	昍	明	昒	畟	疛	疹	癸	皷	皐	盒	眈	眞	眲	矶	砜	砙
60	砘	砎	砸	砯	硫	砌	砼	硫	砣	祉	祀	祉	祢	袗	祎	秄	秇	秖	秎	秎
80	析	窓	窦	穿	竝	竝	竗	竗	竗	笔	笙	笒	笧	笯	籽					

Row 13		01	02	03	04	05	06	07	08	09	10	11	12	13	14	15	16	17	18	19
00		籾	粃	紈	羌	翆	翕	䝷	肚	肮	胙	昭	胐	胅	胋	脅	臭	致	學	茉
20	芓	苿	苩	苇	苬	茆	茹	荈	荐	虾	虾	蚯	蚁	蚕	蚓	蚐	备	衒	衷	袓
40	袱	祈	貟	赵	赳	赴	赸	赵	赳	趵	軒	軏	軓	迓	迗	迣	迦	迵	郘	陀
60	陏	陉	雯	乘	鶱	執	亟	亭	倨	倿	倨	倩	倂	倎	倇	倯	俟	卼	卽	俞
80	倂	倃	倣	倂	偿	俊	俻	偲	倫	倯	倫	倫	倫	酒	棘					

Row 14		01	02	03	04	05	06	07	08	09	10	11	12	13	14	15	16	17	18	19
00		㮾	空	剣	剦	亮	寄	冨	烜	匜	淀	淥	兜	剞	剺	刷	剢	刷	剢	留
20	務	勢	営	姸	凖	卙	厝	厦	延	猗	曼	叔	咯	咔	唠	唔	唧	呢	咊	唱
40	哓	呢	哂	啤	呰	哹	哛	哫	哻	哸	晦	啾	啗	坳	埘	垮	坴	球	堊	堂
60	埗	挫	塹	埠	垢	埝	亮	叟	麥	敫	夋	奄	奕	奮	奂	婉	婷	娧	媥	娼
80	婢	妻	娽	婣	妙	媛	娉	嫺	娒	婭	舒	孷	容	窑	宾					

Row 15		01	02	03	04	05	06	07	08	09	10	11	12	13	14	15	16	17	18	19
00		常	龚	屐	展	尉	孱	屁	昼	峌	崀	崑	崁	崀	峪	崇	崌	崍	崇	崀
20	竟	帶	帑	庳	庚	逋	逞	逢	逪	弢	徠	徹	徒	悖	悺	悦	悪	惡	恿	悤
40	偲	愉	徑	悋	挖	挠	捳	挸	挻	掷	搵	挐	捥	捬	捸	捯	捧	掙	捹	撇
60	翔	挨	捙	捵	捽	掚	捶	翌	翊	章	斩	旆	旃	旂	旅	昢	晁	眯	晌	晁
80	晹	鲊	昪	皆	泰	柠	栌	梵	树	林	极	栓	树	桀	梔					

Row 16		01	02	03	04	05	06	07	08	09	10	11	12	13	14	15	16	17	18	19
00		椤	楠	春	棕	梱	梟	梱	桑	梨	袋	榹	树	楓	梅	棑	梼	欤	毴	毬
20	毯	毹	毯	毯	毵	毯	羕	渊	淳	淋	淶	淙	浣	浣	湾	渼	湊	涌	湧	渌
40	湑	恭	浡	津	湩	游	湧	渤	油	浞	淏	淏	浣	涓	添	燚	湧	添	澉	滏
60	烘	烑	烌	烋	焞	焘	炳	焐	焘	煐	烟	烈	焚	焦	焨	焞	焜	烧	照	焖
80	焖	焙	焕	焈	爽	牅	猸	猈	猊	珱	珠	珊	瑀	琁	琊					

Row 17		01	02	03	04	05	06	07	08	09	10	11	12	13	14	15	16	17	18	19
00		琍	珠	琍	琊	琊	琔	琁	堅	威	畟	瓩	畎	畫	留	痞	発	皋	珀	皍
20	皛	晳	皌	盏	盄	睉	眤	眚	會	眕	砳	矪	矷	砝	砧	砫	砥	砯	砄	硼
40	硎	祥	祾	祭	袿	祺	秦	裕	祵	祷	祈	祚	祼	秥	秠	窑	窠	窈	窬	窗
60	庨	竡	竩	站	竫	章	竒	笅	笍	芸	筝	笧	笶	筀	笉	粒	粘	粦	粙	綒
80	紼	絃	絖	紬	紁	絹	絣	紤	欿	罡	姜	祥	羴	羜	箂					

Row 18		01	02	03	04	05	06	07	08	09	10	11	12	13	14	15	16	17	18	19
00		耷	耴	聁	聃	聆	聅	聊	朞	脷	朖	腻	胐	肏	胎	盼	胥	舡	艳	芸
20	芋	苂	苸	茌	苿	苁	荣	茂	茉	苭	莱	荶	苊	茰	莫	茆	莑	莖	前	茺
40	芬	荄	荐	茶	荃	茀	庴	蚌	衷	袂	哀	貼	訊	豻	豺	貯	敗	赸	赳	赶
60	起	赶	軛	軒	亀	郁	郝	郵	邸	酕	鈌	閂	陌	陈	陪	陑	陛	陊	隽	难
80	兖	查	奐	亶	恵	亶	郷	倭	侖	倸	郷	倓	俶	倨	俑					

Row 19		01	02	03	04	05	06	07	08	09	10	11	12	13	14	15	16	17	18	19
00		倏	倸	倓	偎	偽	偵	傌	粡	尅	晄	涼	漏	斈	鄉	湛	涼	堯	執	凳
20	剛	剢	剮	剺	勬	勰	匰	凖	郷	厤	夐	啞	唼	唊	號	唛	們	哆	喘	咢
40	咽	唽	啺	啲	勪	啉	埂	堏	埿	埝	埋	埌	埇	埜	堊	埧	堕	据	埩	堀
60	堒	埢	塝	埠	埽	塔	靠	鄉	焚	瓶	孳	婅	婞	婆	婁	惣	媪	嫩	媿	屢
80	婳	妻	娩	婗	婷	媏	婑	婧	媒	媪	媵	婗	媙	婀	嫂					

Row 20		01	02	03	04	05	06	07	08	09	10	11	12	13	14	15	16	17	18	19
00		嬌	嫪	媍	孯	孴	孻	冠	宵	宗	寀	寂	寞	窜	寁	寉	京	屛	屐	屏
20	扇	屏	属	屖	屈	屈	屃	崈	峞	崩	嵩	嵜	嵛	崥	崀	崽	嵩	嶌	峻	嵯
40	峥	幃	幘	幗	幙	庭	崩	廒	庶	廐	廋	廌	廧	碇	彌	弱	彭	影	彰	後
60	徹	愐	愣	意	忝	怔	悾	悅	恚	恣	惡	想	恙	惋	惜	慽	悒	惘	惘	悍
80	倢	悅	悋	戠	戡	戝	戚	扃	掖	掬	掠	撓	捅	捘	撓					

Row 21		01	02	03	04	05	06	07	08	09	10	11	12	13	14	15	16	17	18	19
00		掾	揖	揆	捞	揁	揣	提	挎	搠	撇	搋	捶	搋	捶	挽	掷	敎	敵	敉
20	敬	敃	卿	覌	斊	斠	昜	旗	杲	晲	晆	暎	昺	晧	晾	暠	晸	鼎	晬	晱
40	勉	晁	晶	朠	棶	林	棨	梆	棸	梳	棕	梡	槲	梲	桔	棣	棗	棘	棚	極
60	棟	椇	楢	棨	椄	栏	椛	椭	楷	相	乘	畝	窬	歃	歆	歐	歆	歀	歍	殊
80	卿	殏	殷	殸	殼	彀	殿	殷	毺	毻	毠	毹	毬	氈	氳					

Row 22		01	02	03	04	05	06	07	08	09	10	11	12	13	14	15	16	17	18	19
00		沾	湠	淀	焚	渤	溁	洛	涳	渕	淼	渏	清	泉	涵	淠	涸	涵	湄	渿
20	淽	涟	湏	涔	湜	淒	淦	湘	湧	淑	焮	焠	焞	焱	焭	焘	焚	煙	焉	熜
40	熥	烝	煮	焜	煺	焽	煇	烟	烈	觅	腖	犁	犐	犑	玟	琓	班	琑	琰	琺
60	瑳	琿	琊	琢	珽	珊	琀	璽	珍	瓞	瓶	甋	甌	甡	畚	畹	畈	痞	痱	痓
80	瘂	登	皇	皷	皴	皆	皖	皷	皺	盋	盜	盝	盠	盚	笽					

Row 23		01	02	03	04	05	06	07	08	09	10	11	12	13	14	15	16	17	18	19
00		盒	盕	盘	瞑	眛	會	矞	硃	硖	晏	硣	硭	硌	硽	硌	砺	硫	碹	硊
20	祴	裡	裑	祳	褡	秸	秎	桊	稖	稀	稦	秼	窠	窔	窓	窖	窯	竒	音	竝
40	逃	笞	筌	筠	筋	笹	筫	筍	粈	粰	糀	粨	紘	緸	絿	絅	綑	織	紑	綍
60	罰	辜	羝	羴	耋	耆	耞	眠	眛	睎	聆	皺	矞	膊	膞	朧	腊	皐	皛	鼠
80	舨	舡	舭	香	蕊	荽	芨	莘	莹	荽	荡	菩	菆	萘	莩					

Row 24		01	02	03	04	05	06	07	08	09	10	11	12	13	14	15	16	17	18	19
00		荴	莽	荕	荂	蒍	葢	萲	莢	䒮	莩	莬	菫	荼	荾	茶	袊	蓌	萿	莓
20	茉	菻	蚌	蚊	蚸	蚕	蛏	蛛	蚵	蛾	蛆	蛉	蛩	衃	衕	袮	袴	脊	酠	䝨
40	焜	覎	覍	覘	覞	觜	䚗	般	訧	訝	訨	訔	詠	訏	訒	昚	豉	資	䞞	䝱
60	貭	賁	貾	暴	明	赦	赳	赻	趏	起	趐	赿	䟓	䞣	跳	躴	躮	軌	䡊	遻
80	遊	逳	進	郖	邱	郲	郝	酕	釶	欿	閌	閈	陓	陗	陭					

Row 25		01	02	03	04	05	06	07	08	09	10	11	12	13	14	15	16	17	18	19
00		隌	陵	陬	陭	陦	陫	隆	雩	雯	雫	雺	奜	暃	靭	骬	骳	鬲	歪	稙
20	亂	兗	就	䞓	俊	倷	併	偠	飽	傚	傘	倦	挑	剴	粭	瓶	勛	稜	翢	貢
40	冩	兜	兕	剅	剷	剨	剮	募	頖	敬	眞	㪺	輊	庵	夆	婜	嫏	鷄	叟	嗊
60	嗦	嗟	嗒	嗤	啬	喪	喇	噆	嘻	嗎	嗇	喈	嗢	嘮	嗃	噗	噓	嗾	嘶	噔
80	垉	嗵	圁	圄	圖	堡	塗	墼	塱	塌	堰	壼	塥	墡	堪					

Row 26		01	02	03	04	05	06	07	08	09	10	11	12	13	14	15	16	17	18	19
00		坔	埾	垔	埌	埔	埃	姱	奢	嬨	婈	娉	媕	婡	婕	娶	嫗	嫄	媛	媿
20	婹	嫗	嬀	嫮	嫩	嫛	婉	媞	媎	媓	媤	嫇	媼	媪	嫁	婚	嫂	婒	孺	孳
40	寀	寏	害	寍	宿	寋	寞	寠	灷	就	匳	魅	魃	崢	崀	崄	崌	崊	嵋	嶔
60	飈	秫	瑕	祀	蚤	祐	幔	峸	幄	庢	庤	庽	庨	庿	廑	邏	邉	彝	黎	徦
80	衚	恀	怒	恺	恁	恣	恖	悳	惊	琵	悲	愌	恴	悊	怊					

Row 27		01	02	03	04	05	06	07	08	09	10	11	12	13	14	15	16	17	18	19
00		惌	慧	惰	悪	恩	惵	恷	惩	惟	愍	慍	愈	愫	愬	戥	摅	擎	捲	掜
20	搋	捸	搠	掤	捷	摓	撐	搯	擫	撇	掖	拸	摸	搇	搳	挝	擷	擠	擲	摠
40	搩	撿	搶	擊	菝	攽	㸚	旒	旍	晾	昻	暱	暟	暛	晬	睍	暍	暪	罩	暵
60	暆	暲	曧	厰	曆	曢	朤	朥	橐	梁	桴	榐	桎	榇	槨	桽	梸	榜	樺	槩
80	榢	棼	槐	棗	棰	棠	棫	梆	棘	椗	森	棦	楊	梯	椕					

Row 28		01	02	03	04	05	06	07	08	09	10	11	12	13	14	15	16	17	18	19
00		椛	椘	棚	椞	棤	樨	椰	架	檢	梍	喬	槍	檜	楗	穌	款	歈	殖	毅
20	毹	毿	毰	毵	毲	毳	毸	毴	毼	氂	毾	氁	毺	氉	氄	涵	潔	滾	流	滷
40	滅	濺	滌	潀	溢	濙	添	潾	濃	溅	瀦	溭	潶	涚	涌	滎	源	溵	濊	溜
60	湧	湼	熜	點	煤	焟	焊	焄	焮	焩	煊	煁	焏	熏	焌	燚	熂	燭	燒	煜
80	焦	熔	烟	烱	燬	燹	焗	焌	熙	烿	烮	爁	燦	燚	燭					

Row 29		01	02	03	04	05	06	07	08	09	10	11	12	13	14	15	16	17	18	19
00		羹	翁	翌	翦	猪	猹	犟	犨	猤	猱	猻	琮	瑳	瑥	瓞	琴	璘	瑎	琰
20	琿	珑	琪	琄	瑅	琀	琳	珊	瑃	琟	甄	瑝	琊	甌	蛾	秀	睆	瞿	晨	畐
40	畟	痳	瘵	孊	盜	盥	盼	睹	睬	睥	皰	皴	碟	硉	磞	砂	綜	祺	褸	赫
60	裾	袝	袴	裀	裬	裱	裼	裸	褕	稃	秋	碌	稞	犂	稌	窠	窒	球	韵	豹
80	谾	竿	筑	箍	筂	箬	簞	筠	箹	篙	筌	粸	粱	糉	粺					

Row 30		01	02	03	04	05	06	07	08	09	10	11	12	13	14	15	16	17	18	19
00		糆	粯	粙	絮	綏	紵	紊	絭	綴	裁	紼	絗	絳	絈	罳	罸	罩	罽	姜
20	辣	翔	翍	耽	眼	晒	䎀	聆	聦	聊	聖	聘	聯	膌	腋	膇	睦	朠	腸	腠
40	腮	肥	腈	腮	禽	脬	脡	臯	舐	餠	艶	菙	菈	萨	葬	荏	菼	菭	蒖	萝
60	蒡	蒂	蓁	蓳	蒸	蔎	蒙	荳	莕	蔎	蒂	莽	蔆	蕖	荻	葛	葸	葹	蔌	蕖
80	蕮	蔘	薊	蕀	葩	貓	蕀	蕏	蓯	貓	蕱	蕃	蕰	蒬	蕒					

Row 31		01	02	03	04	05	06	07	08	09	10	11	12	13	14	15	16	17	18	19
00		蕃	膚	處	虧	蝕	蚷	蛭	蛇	蛇	衕	術	裎	褙	袞	誘	袏	載	畱	觛
20	詎	窖	詧	話	詧	詘	話	詒	詾	豋	貁	貣	賑	賕	買	賻	貾	賀	赦	赴
40	趸	趆	趎	趕	趉	趨	趑	趌	趁	趵	跂	跋	跮	躬	軲	躳	躲	遼	迸	逹
60	遺	遏	遞	迦	逧	遱	遯	鄬	鄺	鄙	鄖	鄭	酡	酸	酥	酹	鋆	鉚	鉉	鑫
80	舒	鉼	鍪	鉀	鈐	甜	甌	閈	閿	閔	開	閙	閑	閞	閡					

Row 32		01	02	03	04	05	06	07	08	09	10	11	12	13	14	15	16	17	18	19
00		閒	隥	陰	悪	壅	霐	霄	斐	蓰	甚	帽	歆	順	嵐	飭	飦	馴	魁	鳦
20	齊	乖	壓	寐	孰	俸	倌	儎	偬	傈	僨	僘	僉	傻	僴	傭	僤	僶	劍	匏
40	箟	畓	斯	蒯	劉	募	匏	匏	舉	壓	嵾	嗾	嚎	嘵	嘮	嚷	嚮	嚷	嚼	嘩
60	喜	嘩	嘲	嘕	嚇	嘵	嘷	嗔	嘟	圊	墺	墉	墯	墅	壋	墅	墢	墋	塹	墊
80	樫	塣	墬	壍	夐	奚	奘	嬈	嬬	嬃	嫱	嫠	嬗	嬥	孌					

Row 33		01	02	03	04	05	06	07	08	09	10	11	12	13	14	15	16	17	18	19
00		媞	媯	嫈	嫌	孾	孜	寛	寲	寶	寒	寘	寰	塞	寱	堂	尟	屢	屧	嵒
20	嶲	嵗	嶧	嶸	嶋	嶹	巖	廋	廔	彜	彝	彄	彈	彰	徬	徹	得	徦	徉	循
40	愢	慥	慷	懒	懊	憋	懇	憚	蕙	慫	懃	懍	截	戴	撩	撚	撍	撓	擁	擻
60	搽	擬	擦	擠	擽	攏	攖	攤	攢	撇	攟	攝	攞	攥	攭	敹	敺	斛	斝	旗
80	暺	暵	暸	曉	曙	曬	曮	曠	曨	曖	曣	曤	曫	曭	曪					

Row 34		01	02	03	04	05	06	07	08	09	10	11	12	13	14	15	16	17	18	19
00		朗	槌	菘	楠	槆	榁	楼	榊	林	乘	乘	棬	棗	棗	棱	棨	棝	棵	楹
20	榎	楙	棸	楈	檮	樫	棄	棽	檆	栞	槼	槢	檷	櫁	櫂	櫌	檽	櫍	櫃	櫺
40	槵	樒	楮	櫟	槊	欹	歋	歘	殯	殽	殷	毶	毹	氍	氌	氎	溶	滚	滾	澄
60	漸	漭	漂	漆	漏	溝	滾	渺	漷	潽	澾	濕	潭	潝	澍	潫	澨	滌	滬	瀏
80	瀉	漊	滔	鑫	瀫	漨	熿	熇	焞	烝	燚	熒	熨	熡	鄭					

Row 35		01	02	03	04	05	06	07	08	09	10	11	12	13	14	15	16	17	18	19
00		榣	煡	熱	煻	熼	熹	熨	燉	燬	燳	熸	熲	燹	爐	煅	燛	熠	熰	燢
20	熊	熡	熻	熿	燜	燚	燛	燩	燺	燦	燪	牖	犪	犢	猣	猷	猛	獑	獵	璇
40	琈	璇	琴	璞	璐	琪	璪	琴	璧	璞	瓔	瑪	琴	瑚	瑆	瑳	瑧	瑳	瑳	瓔
60	瓏	瓓	璱	瑥	瑔	瑍	璺	瑒	瑜	瓊	瓤	甆	甈	畦	畏	痞	瘉	睒	睽	盎
80	盟	瞀	瞚	睥	碟	硾	磑	磝	碸	磖	磠	磧	碻	硝	磋					

Row 36		01	02	03	04	05	06	07	08	09	10	11	12	13	14	15	16	17	18	19
00		硯	磓	碣	碍	磣	砦	袼	褩	禧	禘	禖	禐	禛	禑	禮	禂	褪	褊	稅
20	稜	棣	稄	梨	椒	稔	稞	窣	箸	窩	窲	窒	寃	遍	淇	逷	篓	箽	箪	箸
40	箂	笓	箄	箴	箹	篋	箬	篠	箢	粞	粺	粫	粨	粭	糕	綂	綌	綘	絧	絰
60	綒	緒	綪	綜	綁	綑	綾	綤	翟	耜	睍	聘	滕	膜	膛	膆	膂	膈	膞	貼
80	腩	臌	艆	菨	蒙	萿	淬	菲	菼	葳	葵	菡	蔡	菳	萶					

Row 37		01	02	03	04	05	06	07	08	09	10	11	12	13	14	15	16	17	18	19
00		荶	萅	菷	萂	菍	萯	萛	萺	葱	葯	蓮	葿	菱	蓶	蔋	葭	蕗	蛏	蜓
20	蛋	蜉	蜉	蜙	蜓	蜂	衕	裓	裺	褖	裹	裿	覞	覞	覓	誒	詎	論	詾	貊
40	貯	賕	賊	賧	賫	賰	賖	賴	趑	趗	趧	趨	趙	趌	趏	趚	踋	跿	躾	躰
60	鶱	輆	輮	軲	軨	翔	遮	迺	遣	遲	遷	遺	遳	遏	遊	逢	遁	郶	郒	郲
80	鼁	鉢	鍳	鈸	鉼	鉥	鉦	鉆	鉏	鉽	锻	閏	閬	閫	閽					

Row 38		01	02	03	04	05	06	07	08	09	10	11	12	13	14	15	16	17	18	19
00		闒	陯	隔	隡	陰	陪	隁	陽	隨	霑	霎	霄	霧	靖	靲	鞈	鞑	靻	頔
20	頊	頍	餕	飪	餂	飧	髭	鬿	鮒	麂	麺	麮	幔	毹	黿	儆	儔	儫	僾	儚
40	儯	僫	儊	僂	傱	嵳	傞	僙	儶	儰	僤	僩	僴	僔	僟	僯	傑	粿	糊	鴔
60	寫	潺	凜	剺	剹	劀	劂	劌	劕	劖	劙	匏	匔	匭	匰	匶	厚	厞	厥	厬
80	鑊	嘡	嗟	嘻	嗽	嘍	嘹	嘶	嘹	嘽	嘾	噃	嘦	噬	噂					

Row 39		01	02	03	04	05	06	07	08	09	10	11	12	13	14	15	16	17	18	19
00		喂	嗰	噉	噹	噹	噹	嗷	嗥	嗽	嘢	嚳	嗏	唵	圞	圜	圕	墉	墈	墭
20	墖	墪	墭	墷	墼	墱	壚	壜	壚	壽	夐	夑	奦	奱	奰	奮	嬲	嫩	嬈	嫞
40	嬈	嫰	嫮	嫵	嫩	嫚	嫡	嫼	嫺	嫕	嫵	嫣	嫳	嫸	嫲	塞	寵	寰	寠	尉
60	對	屜	嶘	嵗	嵽	嶐	巃	幓	巏	幰	廓	廔	廝	曆	廘	摩	廩	慶	廗	廞
80	張	彁	徶	徹	徵	徾	憖	憼	愡	惑	憑	憙	慨	慝	慯					

Row 40		01	02	03	04	05	06	07	08	09	10	11	12	13	14	15	16	17	18	19
00		愷	憫	憸	憮	愨	憰	慨	愻	戲	戳	摘	搽	摧	擦	摽	搧	搲	撅	搓
20	摓	撻	撲	撥	撙	撽	擠	撕	撥	撶	撮	擶	撖	攄	撫	擼	摇	擁	擜	擻
40	擾	擦	翻	曒	暇	鼎	暌	暁	槦	樺	槅	槐	穼	窸	槙	槌	樫	標	薹	榛
60	椎	樊	橧	琹	樋	橐	橑	棋	樾	樹	櫛	樓	棘	榜	樋	檔	檻	櫟	櫨	櫘
80	櫛	樹	櫵	橦	樛	欒	欲	歆	歐	歲	殿	毓	毷	氈	氉					

Row 41		01	02	03	04	05	06	07	08	09	10	11	12	13	14	15	16	17	18	19
00		氌	漀	滮	漾	溶	漆	漉	潻	溧	籀	漏	潌	澜	漤	漦	潄	漬	減	滐
20	滿	潉	漼	灩	潤	潖	潆	澕	潒	澼	灒	澌	澈	澮	澯	溟	潐	燊	燚	燓
40	熴	熨	熛	熕	熰	熶	熇	燓	熨	熙	熛	熺	熨	焉	熿	燢	燧	燬	燐	燁
60	燈	燌	燾	燴	燯	燴	爃	爓	爔	爷	牖	牕	犞	犨	犝	犞	犚	獩	獥	獮
80	獻	璭	璯	璲	璷	璸	璾	瓈	瓉	瓋	瓐	瓏	瓓	瓙	瓞					

Row 42	01	02	03	04	05	06	07	08	09	10	11	12	13	14	15	16	17	18	19
00		現	璩	琛	瑞	璥	毳	瑿	瑸	璁	瓝	甡	罯	廻	痨	鴖	碎	鴽	鴞	鵅
20	皡	皶	盪	睽	瞔	瞦	瞴	瞲	睸	瞬	矲	碹	磋	磓	碜	磡	磲	磦	磸	磪
40	磆	碗	磈	磄	碨	碴	碻	磏	磂	磇	碿	禐	禀	禒	禛	禞	禝	禟	禡	稦
60	稫	稀	穕	稡	穖	稐	黎	穛	穏	穆	窩	竨	竲	竬	竪	箖	箟	箬	箴	箙
80	篞	篹	篵	篺	篼	簕	簩	簚	簦	簹	簺	籒	粳	糕	糍					

Row 43	01	02	03	04	05	06	07	08	09	10	11	12	13	14	15	16	17	18	19
00		精	糎	糂	糆	糈	糌	糀	糉	糏	糊	糁	糍	糈	絽	縕	緁	緋	緃	緊
20	緣	緵	緺	緿	縍	縡	綿	縛	罩	翔	翥	翻	翌	聉	聤	聘	聛	聟	聢	聾
40	聜	脘	腭	腥	腭	腹	腱	膊	膪	膷	膻	臂	臆	膽	臊	臞	舆	臨	臯	臺
60	舚	艇	艖	艕	艟	芺	莸	蓑	蔆	莎	萈	萕	萩	葷	葇	蕐	蒈	蒖	蓋	蓱
80	蕠	蕻	蕖	蕼	蕾	薪	薤	薰	藏	蘷	蘤	蘳	蘴	蘸	蘺					

Row 44	01	02	03	04	05	06	07	08	09	10	11	12	13	14	15	16	17	18	19
00		菣	蒮	蓍	蓏	蓑	蓒	蓕	蓋	蓣	蓧	虧	虩	蚤	蝴	蝍	蝗	蝤	蝔	蝖
20	褒	褙	褧	褩	褯	覃	覅	覘	覝	謯	諉	諄	諛	諫	諴	謊	謖	謝	諤	謇
40	貇	貌	賍	賄	賚	賁	貭	賊	賒	賚	賕	趦	趌	趑	趙	趟	趚	趣	跓	跙
60	躲	躶	躷	軗	軽	輆	輀	輈	輗	辟	辞	辱	辵	逖	逢	遄	遌	遳	遲	邋
80	邂	邀	邅	醇	醌	酥	醋	醎	醏	釜	釡	鈁	鉅	鋑	鋀					

Row 45	01	02	03	04	05	06	07	08	09	10	11	12	13	14	15	16	17	18	19
00		鋑	鉷	鈑	鉅	鈁	鉚	鉌	銓	鋻	鋗	鋼	閦	開	陲	陞	隉	隴	階	陸
20	雍	雒	雔	雫	雯	霄	霫	靑	靊	韓	頏	頍	頞	頜	薦	駑	駁	駈	斠	敼
40	鬪	魁	魄	魅	魯	鰂	鳶	鳰	鴦	鵈	麂	麩	鼓	敲	豩	亮	賔	桌	儐	儵
60	龕	歏	儒	傜	傷	僂	傯	獘	嬖	歏	澀	滄	凱	匏	匯	擋	撽	廲	埶	嚐
80	嚆	噴	嘖	嗌	嗷	嘮	嗣	嚬	嗵	嚀	嚾	圖	壇	墡	墁					

Row 46	01	02	03	04	05	06	07	08	09	10	11	12	13	14	15	16	17	18	19
00		墦	埶	壄	墩	墈	塨	壓	墟	墰	壔	增	墽	埀	墶	夐	夤	奬	奮	嫗
20	嬢	嫌	嬓	嫷	媢	嫪	嬉	嫙	嬛	嫮	嫻	嬨	嬖	嫩	嬈	嫺	嫂	嫺	辣	寨
40	寬	嶢	寏	竃	寱	寣	寰	寯	寵	尊	屣	屪	屣	屘	屧	寂	嶭	嵥	巇	寡
60	嶒	嶰	幣	幓	廜	廕	廩	廯	弻	彖	徊	徹	憯	憇	憓	憾	愼	憋	懇	憖
80	憶	懈	機	懥	愧	懲	懵	戩	戰	截	戲	戲	擸	撲	攄					

Row 47	01	02	03	04	05	06	07	08	09	10	11	12	13	14	15	16	17	18	19
00		搒	搦	擀	摁	搖	搥	搠	搯	擽	撚	擽	撖	擤	擂	撪	撹	斀	斅	斒
20	嫖	旗	戳	曙	嘗	暱	暋	舶	膀	棼	槩	樺	橄	檻	樫	橥	棘	樓	槺	檣
40	櫚	檵	樰	檑	橏	櫃	樸	鼐	欉	檪	樹	檻	歊	殐	殫	鍼	毿	滬	漠	溢
60	湄	澆	滾	滴	滴	漨	灉	漂	漪	漪	灌	滅	濃	漂	滲	漾	漦	漀	潰	滲
80	潵	漭	潊	潰	瀐	潊	潸	澤	潏	潔	澔	潡	漏	灣	潏					

Row 48		01	02	03	04	05	06	07	08	09	10	11	12	13	14	15	16	17	18	19
00		潒	熑	熱	燈	煌	爋	燋	熾	熛	熲	熝	煿	熓	熙	熏	熬	熜	焦	煨
20	熒	爃	熴	畓	熆	熱	爊	熑	燴	熜	熾	犓	犹	琡	琋	琣	琜	琦	琥	瑔
40	瑆	瑔	瑐	瑔	瑲	瓪	瓾	甈	瘃	瘀	瘭	瘵	瘦	盨	盤	盩	盤	盤	盭	瞈
60	瞅	瞝	瞨	瞋	瞝	矮	磽	礲	磚	磟	磌	磖	磤	禘	禚	禪	稨	稪	稳	稅
80	穆	穆	穐	竪	竨	竳	竵	箁	箒	箶	箷	箾	篕	篨	篩					

Row 49		01	02	03	04	05	06	07	08	09	10	11	12	13	14	15	16	17	18	19
00		篟	篋	篆	篍	篙	篦	篢	篠	篯	篦	糕	糌	糎	糆	糞	縎	縐	縮	縺
20	縛	縐	縝	縷	縹	繌	繃	繋	繩	繂	繖	繩	罅	罉	罭	罷	翶	翏	翹	耄
40	聗	聚	聝	聕	聘	聳	聬	聰	肅	膗	膜	膠	膃	膵	膐	鼻	臻	舐	艆	艴
60	艵	艷	蒸	蒦	蓈	蓏	蓥	蓳	蓛	蓜	蓳	蓻	蓭	蔂	蔮	蓓	蓍	蔧	蔺	蔄
80	蔽	蔜	蔥	蕠	蕷	蕻	蕹	蕶	蕕	蕣	蟯	蟬	蟌	蟔	蟦					

Row 50		01	02	03	04	05	06	07	08	09	10	11	12	13	14	15	16	17	18	19
00		蠢	蝳	蝹	蝭	融	螂	螖	螂	螋	螉	螒	褯	褱	褫	覆	覃	覥	諫	誇
20	謍	謚	謐	謨	謧	謪	謤	謽	豯	貘	賵	賶	趁	趠	蹐	踸	踍	踊	軅	軧
40	輱	輕	轟	轟	輂	辶	遲	邎	邍	遴	邁	鄧	鄚	鄩	鄺	醇	醮	醰	醇	鍌
60	鍷	鍛	鍊	鍤	鍾	鍯	鍽	鎛	鎝	鎞	鎬	鎶	鎿	鏧	鏊	鏔	鏺	鐲	闒	闟
80	闕	闙	隳	隴	隲	隵	隰	隯	隸	隸	雡	霅	霘	霹	霳					

Row 51		01	02	03	04	05	06	07	08	09	10	11	12	13	14	15	16	17	18	19
00		霍	霸	頵	頷	颸	颻	餚	餥	馡	馦	駢	駦	駗	骹	髙	髳	髮	髻	髺
20	魼	魁	魄	鮺	鮻	鮁	鮺	鯅	鮎	鮣	鯚	鮗	鵞	麗	黢	齇	齈	儕	儚	儱
40	龠	儨	儫	禯	禮	糗	糠	糎	騎	黴	凗	濈	劈	劉	劗	勞	斴	厭	曆	叡
60	嚒	嘶	嚱	嚔	嚾	嚍	嚛	嚧	嚕	嚘	嚙	嚧	嚪	疊	嚼	罍	囈	嚵	嚽	囇
80	嚂	氱	氳	團	壑	壚	壜	壛	壇	夔	燮	嬀	嬟	嬮	孅					

Row 52		01	02	03	04	05	06	07	08	09	10	11	12	13	14	15	16	17	18	19
00		嫼	嬁	嬮	嬳	嬪	嬨	嬫	嬲	嬶	嬸	嬺	孌	孳	孱	寋	寙	寢	賽	寧
20	寷	寡	寧	寮	尌	嶝	嶅	嶒	嶜	嶔	龐	廙	廥	廩	廦	彝	衞	徻	廉	懸
40	憔	憡	憙	憃	憹	懁	憪	憰	懓	懃	懯	懲	撓	撽	擌	攕	擮	擓	擽	攬
60	擕	擕	擟	擊	擦	斀	斁	斀	膰	曍	曃	曘	曞	曛	曝	曶	曓	朝	曑	檔
80	檕	檟	檇	檣	樣	檥	檸	檹	檵	橋	檑	檴	櫋	櫃	櫉					

Row 53		01	02	03	04	05	06	07	08	09	10	11	12	13	14	15	16	17	18	19
00		櫊	櫛	櫂	櫄	櫫	櫔	櫥	櫼	櫺	櫚	櫹	櫞	櫓	櫳	櫶	櫱	櫯	櫽	櫼
20	欂	欃	欐	欞	欆	歖	歗	歘	殪	殨	毇	毊	毄	氉	氌	氊	氎	氀	瀼	瀿
40	瀉	瀘	瀠	瀾	瀰	灁	灂	灃	灄	灅	灊	灉	灍	灑	灒	灣	灥	灔	灕	灙
60	灛	灝	爃	燷	燲	爄	爋	爌	爏	爑	爖	爗	爜	爝	爞	爛	爥	爧	爨	爩
80	熥	犃	犥	犦	犧	犨	犩	獵	玃	璡	璬	璭	璯	璷	璻					

Row 54		01	02	03	04	05	06	07	08	09	10	11	12	13	14	15	16	17	18	19
00		璱	璮	瓔	蕢	瑟	璥	璭	瓚	瑠	瓘	瑀	瑑	璚	瑝	瓈	璢	瓅	疊	鴪
20	癄	瘵	皷	盩	盡	盦	盥	盤	盬	瞔	瞟	矂	矋	磗	磶	礵	礌	礴	礭	礎
40	礵	礡	礥	礩	礶	礜	禩	禯	禪	穎	穦	穢	穫	穄	竂	竈	竉	竅	竆	竰
60	塹	篾	簅	簾	簃	籃	簺	籐	籛	籙	籢	籗	籚	籜	籠	籦	籫	籯	籩	籪
80	籫	籐	籔	紏	粸	糌	緣	總	繙	繱	繼	纏	纖	縮	緱					

Row 55		01	02	03	04	05	06	07	08	09	10	11	12	13	14	15	16	17	18	19
00		罅	罈	罾	羶	羵	翬	翺	耰	耱	聯	聴	聸	聹	職	聵	膀	膇	膞	膬
20	膟	礜	艉	莪	蘋	蘫	虢	蘙	蕤	蘷	蘀	蕺	蕿	蒸	薀	薔	蕸	蕙	蕿	蕤
40	蔭	蘍	蕖	藺	藺	蘛	蘿	蕉	藺	蕈	蕇	蕅	薛	薯	藐	藐	藉	藶	蘤	蘣
60	蘚	蘑	蘑	麒	蜷	螢	蝗	蟓	蝮	蜂	蟆	褊	褊	襆	褶	覞	覷	覼	諭	諑
80	詁	諡	諟	謳	謠	諰	譁	譖	謜	譹	貌	賸	賰	餮	賮					

Row 56		01	02	03	04	05	06	07	08	09	10	11	12	13	14	15	16	17	18	19
00		賥	賵	赮	趬	趣	趰	超	趧	趕	趖	趨	趮	趲	趡	趯	趪	踈	踋	躾
20	軄	軀	軁	轉	轋	轆	輸	辣	邅	遴	逼	霆	鄒	郶	醑	醌	鋈	鋷	錇	錟
40	錻	鍾	鏞	鎅	鍏	鍼	鍔	鍞	鏊	鏃	鏨	鏇	鏱	鐀	鐉	鍟	鐑	鎊	鎕	鎼
60	鑈	鑯	鑿	銛	鍰	鏻	鈐	鎘	鏒	鑀	闒	闛	闥	隉	隌	隡	隩	雖	霏	霤
80	霐	霮	霿	霻	霳	霫	靤	靤	鞣	韻	顈	頪	顡	類	顛					

Row 57		01	02	03	04	05	06	07	08	09	10	11	12	13	14	15	16	17	18	19
00		顆	顜	顉	頷	颶	餅	餑	饅	餾	馩	駭	駕	驕	骿	髮	鬌	鬋	鬍	鬕
20	魄	魳	鮊	鮺	鮎	鮿	鯈	鯡	鯳	鳶	鴗	鴣	鵂	鹹	麏	麠	麅	麰	黁	黵
40	儀	僚	儤	斂	龕	儁	儠	嫪	嫶	嫸	嫠	濵	嬓	嬖	劉	孅	叡	嚌	嚩	囃
60	嚋	嚐	嚁	嘔	嘸	嚪	鼉	壙	墊	壝	墀	墻	壇	墝	墍	墺	嬑	嬔	嬤	嬥
80	嫘	嫺	寫	寰	窶	勸	徹	錤	簹	窯	寵	縭	巏	歸	廩					

Row 58		01	02	03	04	05	06	07	08	09	10	11	12	13	14	15	16	17	18	19
00		廦	廮	廲	彌	懥	憝	憓	懼	懟	蕙	懷	懢	懇	戀	戲	攆	攋	攑	擬
20	攂	搖	斆	戵	斁	斄	暈	曄	曤	曖	軀	遭	檸	檝	櫍	櫵	櫼	欅	櫺	欌
40	橙	櫎	檉	櫛	櫦	檜	櫆	構	樸	欄	櫘	櫻	歛	歡	整	蹺	鏄	谿	疆	殲
60	殲	聲	瀞	瀟	瀣	瀰	澤	瀆	瀶	灃	灑	瀘	瀹	灈	灖	瀯	瀯	爨	瀱	灂
80	瀅	燗	爊	燵	爐	燢	爟	爧	爆	爁	爤	爥	爍	爨	熵					

Row 59		01	02	03	04	05	06	07	08	09	10	11	12	13	14	15	16	17	18	19
00		燹	爈	爑	爔	爵	爓	牆	牒	獡	獵	獶	獷	瓎	瓍	璲	瓛	瑠	璁	瓔
20	環	瓌	甡	疇	癛	癀	皷	監	盤	瞌	翹	矐	瞞	礒	礸	礒	礋	礀	礙	礁
40	礫	礧	礮	禧	襆	襟	禕	禣	禩	襝	襖	穡	穩	穎	穩	穆	穫	穠	竇	竊
60	潔	篆	篧	簑	簒	籌	箱	簁	籓	籥	籜	纂	簪	簞	節	糠	糯	糲	糮	糳
80	糯	糲	綮	繡	繽	繊	繳	繶	繇	繒	繞	織	繐	縷	緄					

Row 60		01	02	03	04	05	06	07	08	09	10	11	12	13	14	15	16	17	18	19
00		綉	縉	軀	鴇	翜	翸	翰	翾	耩	耭	檣	聟	聰	膝	臑	臛	臙	臏	臍
20	臢	舋	膔	膹	艦	艆	薕	蕠	薶	蕢	蓜	藎	藭	蕊	搖	蔉	藜	蕓	蕘	菓
40	蘀	蔦	蔏	蕣	蕗	蕅	蕆	蕠	蕟	虓	虞	蘧	蜯	蜨	蛾	蝨	蟄	蝂	蝭	蠦
60	蠸	衁	衛	衞	襈	襯	襭	談	誏	謝	警	彭	諄	說	讃	詟	箋	貘	賢	賒
80	賺	糡	趨	趠	趫	趲	蹌	跳	蹤	蹝	軀	軁	轀	輸	翹					

Row 61		01	02	03	04	05	06	07	08	09	10	11	12	13	14	15	16	17	18	19
00		辟	壁	辮	遁	遛	遄	遳	遂	遶	醋	醾	醶	醟	錡	錗	鍷	錞	鍘	鉉
20	鋎	鋒	鏤	鎼	鏍	鍆	鋕	鏊	鉽	鑿	鎓	鎊	錕	鎅	鎼	鑫	鏬	鎚	鏵	鎔
40	錎	鍔	錠	鍎	錄	鑢	鎰	鍔	闌	隴	隥	隲	隳	雈	雒	雛	霨	霭	霰	霱
60	鞚	韞	顏	頵	頤	穎	頭	顛	颼	颸	饈	饌	馞	駸	驁	髃	髆	髣	髻	髾
80	髋	魑	魎	魷	鯠	鯎	鮀	鰍	鯐	鯀	鳶	鵝	鷥	梟	鵟					

Row 62		01	02	03	04	05	06	07	08	09	10	11	12	13	14	15	16	17	18	19
00		肆	鷟	鵖	鴾	鵻	麐	麺	麵	黁	黔	黿	學	儇	僎	鑫	儃	儚	贔	冀
20	滾	縲	劓	匯	鍚	壓	曆	廬	嚏	嚮	嚙	嚱	嚶	嚦	嚍	嚜	嚚	嚗	嚳	境
40	墻	壿	嚢	壍	壣	壖	壝	壕	嫽	孅	嬀	嬉	嬫	嬾	寵	嵏	巍	巕	廮	廩
60	廳	彊	徽	彰	悉	恩	懋	憲	憒	憗	憝	懇	攬	撐	攄	播	撩	撤	攢	擶
80	攕	攜	擇	擯	攂	爁	曠	曹	疇	曣	矆	鶻	艢	欖	櫄					

Row 63		01	02	03	04	05	06	07	08	09	10	11	12	13	14	15	16	17	18	19
00		櫟	醬	櫼	櫹	黏	檰	轟	樹	櫾	機	櫪	櫳	櫋	攀	櫞	樽	鏦	檄	灑
20	瀵	瀌	瀷	濃	澥	瀹	濱	瀨	瀾	瀓	瀾	瀐	瀟	瀷	瀑	瀊	燧	鎣	燮	燹
40	爔	熄	燕	煎	燚	爕	獬	獵	璨	璩	璝	璸	瓓	瓖	璧	璟	璭	璿	瓏	瓊
60	璞	鑫	璁	璷	瓝	甋	盪	督	償	磼	磧	礎	磬	礐	穟	穤	穇	穆	稷	穌
80	穌	穋	穐	穨	窵	韻	簞	篁	簸	簸	籥	籛	簪	籔	簌					

Row 64		01	02	03	04	05	06	07	08	09	10	11	12	13	14	15	16	17	18	19
00		篹	纂	粺	篸	簆	簇	糧	糢	糅	緖	織	繾	繹	繰	繱	繳	繝	繩	繞
20	羶	羴	翗	翽	聯	聵	聵	聞	臚	臛	臘	臝	膾	臔	膲	舁	舉	舉	毬	舞
40	蕕	薦	藩	藭	蒻	蘼	翠	蘤	藏	舊	藝	薿	蘡	蘾	蘩	蘟	蘦	蘱	蘺	蘵
60	獄	薅	蘠	蘗	虧	蟳	蟰	蟵	蠉	蠔	蟿	蠗	蠛	蠮	蠻	衱	襁	襽	醉	覸
80	覶	覹	諍	謐	謲	譎	贗	贈	贐	賫	贄	賠	賵	趯	趲					

Row 65		01	02	03	04	05	06	07	08	09	10	11	12	13	14	15	16	17	18	19
00		躂	踐	蹚	踱	蹡	軟	軀	轟	軫	轊	遴	還	邂	醋	醺	鋋	鐔	鐃	鐩
20	鑿	鐠	鐋	銖	鏼	鎖	鑾	鏞	鏟	鏃	鏶	鏠	鑐	鍏	鏵	鎛	鐏	鏦	鍾	闉
40	闇	闐	闆	闔	闕	隙	隥	隨	隱	霆	霡	鞴	鞵	顓	鞼	穎	頭	飄	饁	餚
60	騂	鮑	驚	駹	驗	髀	髀	髦	鬖	鬆	魋	魏	鮐	鮤	鯐	鯇	鰲	鰲	鯉	鯛
80	鱇	鯚	鯏	鰂	鱥	鷂	鵾	鶻	麕	麖	麔	麰	麐	罌	黴					

Row 66		01	02	03	04	05	06	07	08	09	10	11	12	13	14	15	16	17	18	19
00		歛	豇	嘕	嚵	畵	嚳	隓	壞	豨	嬶	孅	孽	孵	蹇	豁	憲	嶺	斅	幭
20	廲	廖	癩	鬄	懩	懿	懥	憔	憪	斆	攓	擷	擽	攕	攕	擲	擇	擤	攡	攪
40	擫	摖	孌	孌	斸	曠	櫎	櫹	欞	櫨	櫚	櫼	欋	聲	櫺	欏	欉	櫥	欑	欓
60	櫟	欐	欒	欖	欘	櫳	歗	穡	瀝	瀫	瀆	瀕	瀞	瀣	瀦	瀑	瀗	瀋	瀕	瀘
80	灑	瀹	澩	燎	燴	燵	燳	燚	瓃	璠	璉	璒	璣	璿	瓀					

Row 67		01	02	03	04	05	06	07	08	09	10	11	12	13	14	15	16	17	18	19
00		瓍	瓆	瓔	瓊	甏	甐	癗	盬	盭	矇	礋	礬	礄	礂	礐	穳	竇	籀	籓
20	籚	籓	籣	籡	籢	籥	籧	籭	籫	糉	糪	糮	繡	纆	纓	纈	纖	纔	罅	聯
40	職	聺	臆	臢	臟	臊	臁	臺	艫	蘘	蘫	蘽	蘨	蕙	蘠	蘸	蘼	藺	蘛	蘷
60	虈	虆	蘐	虋	虇	虌	虃	虁	虉	虊	虅	虂	虄	虀	虃	蠊	蠛	蠟	蠨	蠘
80	蠘	蠑	蟋	蠮	蟈	蠏	襮	覵	譌	譑	豫	禮	贚	贚	贜					

Row 68		01	02	03	04	05	06	07	08	09	10	11	12	13	14	15	16	17	18	19
00		贖	贌	趲	趱	躑	躕	轓	轞	轥	邋	遺	邐	鄷	邍	鏳	鏡	鏐	鏦	鏈
20	鏚	鏌	鏔	鏮	鏓	鏺	鏿	鏃	鏢	鏠	鏷	鐋	鏹	鏄	鐍	鏞	鐞	鐛	闟	闤
40	闠	闞	闡	闥	隴	靡	靄	韡	韇	韞	韝	韻	類	顛	飂	飃	饈	饋	鴿	驊
60	驀	騷	驕	驩	髻	鬍	鬆	鬈	魏	魑	魒	魌	鮬	鯸	鮳	鯱	鰊	鰔	鰗	鰣
80	鰮	鰫	鯛	鰈	鷹	鶼	鶬	鷊	鶝	鷈	鷽	體	廳	囊	囍					

Row 69		01	02	03	04	05	06	07	08	09	10	11	12	13	14	15	16	17	18	19
00		罍	壥	壦	壨	孆	孊	孎	屭	巕	巆	巎	戳	攊	攑	攣	攛	攞	曮	櫳
20	櫼	欇	欈	欉	欌	欑	欏	欐	欗	欖	欙	欛	櫹	畾	灈	灡	灦	爦	爧	爠
40	爡	爣	爤	爥	爩	爦	爨	爫	爮	玃	瓓	瓖	瓗	瓙	鑄	矚	曦	礦	礵	礮
60	礴	礵	鸚	襸	穭	穮	穳	穲	竊	竊	龝	籏	纂	纙	纕	纘	纚	纓	纏	纏
80	繏	纔	纗	纙	聵	聯	聰	臗	臖	臡	蘗	蘗	藤	蘾	蘵					

Row 70		01	02	03	04	05	06	07	08	09	10	11	12	13	14	15	16	17	18	19
00		蘤	蘳	蘩	蘨	蘳	蘭	蘺	蘬	蘮	蘶	蘱	蘸	蠋	蠜	蠛	蠟	蠬	蠐	襵
20	襲	覾	譴	譯	譺	譽	譾	贇	贐	贌	贕	贍	趲	趲	躂	躅	躉	躑	躔	躒
40	軅	軀	轉	轐	邎	酆	醶	醻	鐯	鐐	鐢	鐵	鐺	鐻	鐹	鐿	鑀	鑁	鑂	鑃
60	鑄	鑅	鑈	鑉	鑊	鑋	鑌	鑍	鑎	鑐	鑑	鑒	鑓	鑔	鑕	鑖	鑗	鑘	鑙	鑚
80	闀	闗	隮	隱	雤	霫	霴	韀	韁	韞	顛	飀	饕	驉	驜					

Row 71		01	02	03	04	05	06	07	08	09	10	11	12	13	14	15	16	17	18	19
00		驓	驔	驕	驖	驙	鬗	鬘	鬙	魒	鱧	鱶	鯇	鱸	鱺	鱻	鰲	鱥	鱚	鱖
20	鰕	鯽	鷕	鷭	鷲	鷸	鷽	鸂	黯	鼙	黿	齸	齻	齽	龕	龔	劙	灑	囒	囊
40	巒	壛	壠	壧	孾	嬃	孍	孌	孏	屭	巃	巖	彏	戇	攥	攬	攮	攭	欎	欓
60	欔	欙	欚	欛	欜	欝	欞	欟	欒	欝	氈	灃	灜	灝	灢	灟	灣	灤	灩	灨
80	灘	爟	爥	爆	爔	爠	瓕	癁	癬	矘	盬	盭	礬	礪	纙					

Row 72		01	02	03	04	05	06	07	08	09	10	11	12	13	14	15	16	17	18	19
00		穇	䫻	簝	篟	簻	蕢	簹	鄭	鬖	糉	糎	縿	繟	繡	纋	瞶	職	膶	臋
20	覽	贇	霿	繇	蘑	蘗	藻	聽	孽	蘐	蕿	藜	蕊	穗	蕙	藏	蘅	蠡	蠘	蠽
40	蠢	蟒	襟	觀	覷	贖	矅	贜	趯	遷	躕	轘	譬	遷	遲	遭	遼	聰	鄙	醜
60	糴	鼇	鏉	壓	鐩	鏩	鐀	鏀	鐈	鑫	勳	鐣	鐵	鑪	鐐	鐫	鐓	鐶	鑕	鑣
80	闤	闠	闥	闞	闟	闢	雔	霻	霰	齍	顛	顣	纈	飄	饎					

Row 73		01	02	03	04	05	06	07	08	09	10	11	12	13	14	15	16	17	18	19
00		積	驌	髗	鬗	魌	魑	鯀	鱗	鱘	鰯	鰛	鯽	鰳	鰶	鰲	鰲	鯄	鯴	鶼
20	魏	麐	黏	龐	儚	儼	勸	嚻	嚽	壥	夔	孆	孅	孋	巓	攙	攠	孃	蹴	欏
40	櫝	欅	鬱	欄	櫼	欈	檻	欆	鬱	欞	穢	瀨	灕	燹	爛	爦	爤	瓊	瓛	礁
60	礤	襘	聰	懋	籊	籦	籧	纉	纚	纏	纖	瞗	蘸	虇	蘯	蘙	蒼	蠸	蠛	襝
80	贜	贜	讀	譓	譕	變	賿	璺	贇	趨	躉	躏	臟	醿	鏐					

Row 74		01	02	03	04	05	06	07	08	09	10	11	12	13	14	15	16	17	18	19
00		鑸	鏌	爚	鑄	鐦	鑮	鑽	鑇	鐻	鐸	鑞	闌	闞	闚	闛	闤	闡	雚	韶
20	顉	颾	餅	饐	驖	驛	驛	鬠	鬃	魄	鰊	鱅	鰕	鱴	鰾	鰲	鷁	鷯	鷗	騩
40	鷄	鷊	蟹	儹	禶	嚀	欌	廱	戇	戇	戇	櫼	攦	攬	撞	欅	欝	欐	艫	灞
60	灑	灃	獻	爛	變	瓕	瓘	環	矚	礦	確	欅	鷙	籤	糯	鬱	矚	灕	霧	鑾
80	蠙	蠟	蠬	蠷	讙	譜	謐	豔	贑	趲	醾	鑞	鐯	鑮	鑊					

Row 75		01	02	03	04	05	06	07	08	09	10	11	12	13	14	15	16	17	18	19
00		鐙	鎢	鐐	鏵	鐩	鐵	鐪	鑕	鏈	鑿	鑳	鐫	鐸	鑡	鑯	闞	闤	闥	霽
20	髻	顱	顲	饞	驖	驥	鬮	鬆	鰱	鰲	鰶	鱳	鷁	龤	龜	譱	爨	孎	蠹	戇
40	戇	攮	攩	攝	攦	矚	欞	欝	欟	欐	爵	欖	欖	獺	鑾	穰	穌	雞	籠	籯
60	臨	纖	蠥	聽	欉	蔿	蘐	蘸	贜	讗	讚	躪	鑞	鑼	鑮	鑽	鑱	鑾	闢	闤
80	靇	驤	顆	韻	鬢	鱇	鰻	鱳	鯵	飍	騣	齡	麟	黷	齆					

Row 76		01	02	03	04	05	06	07	08	09	10	11	12	13	14	15	16	17	18	19
00		鹹	礦	嚼	嬪	寒	巙	鬱	戇	戇	攡	攬	攮	攢	歐	瀲	灘	犪	瓓	鷫
20	䆳	穰	矖	戀	蘭	蘯	讕	讚	鑵	鑵	鑾	鑕	鐏	耀	鬟	鬈	覿	鱝	鑑	飄
40	鰱	鑾	孍	欞	鬱	灊	巖	騰	矙	彎	鑣	鑯	鑗	鑑	鑾	鑽	鑊	霸	鄉	鱶
60	鰿	鱠	鷩	鱴	鷽	攪	鹽	欗	爥	虀	蠱	籮	籬	纔	黨	虆	蘸	戀	讓	鑿
80	靏	鷫	鬢	鬱	鶩	鱺	鷰	鷳	鸎	龘	囑	廳	懿	懰	髏					

Row 77		01	02	03	04	05	06	07	08	09	10	11	12	13	14	15	16	17	18	19
00		鑴	鑽	鑁	黨	鸙	灡	籠	蹤	鑸	闥	鑑	鱵	鼈	灥	欏	饕	蠶	鷹	躩
20	戀	鑫	嚻	鸞	鑾	鑽														
40																				
60																				
80																				

H

Big Five Table

This appendix constitutes a table for the complete Big Five character set, printed here using the typeface 宋體 (MSung-Light), developed by Monotype. Each character is indexed by hexadecimal Big Five value, and each level is in a separate section.

Big Five Level 1

The following rows constitute Big Five Level 1. Note that 0xA140 of Level 1 is a full-width space character.

Row A1	0	1	2	3	4	5	6	7	8	9	A	B	C	D	E	F
4		，	、	。	．	•	；	：	？	！	︰	…	‥	﹐	﹑	﹒
5	·	﹔	﹕	﹖	﹗	｜	–	︱	—	︳	＿	︴	﹏	（	）	︵
6	︶	｛	｝	︷	︸	〔	〕	︹	︺	【	】	︻	︼	《	》	︽
7	︾	〈	〉	︿	﹀	「	」	﹁	﹂	『	』	﹃	﹄	﹙	﹚	
A		﹛	﹜	﹝	﹞	‘	’	“	”	〝	〞	‵	′	＃	＆	＊
B	※	§	〃	○	●	△	▲	◎	☆	★	◇	◆	□	■	▽	▼
C	㊣	%	‾	￣	＿	ˍ	﹉	﹊	﹍	﹎	﹋	﹌	﹟	﹠	﹡	＋
D	－	×	÷	±	√	＜	＞	＝	≦	≧	≠	∞	≒	≡	﹢	﹣
E	﹤	﹥	﹦	～	∩	∪	⊥	∠	∟	⊿	log	ln	∫	∮	∵	∴
F	♀	♂	⊕	⊙	↑	↓	←	→	↖	↗	↙	↘	∥	∣	／	

Row A2	0	1	2	3	4	5	6	7	8	9	A	B	C	D	E	F
4	＼	∕	﹨	＄	￥	〒	￠	￡	％	＠	℃	℉	﹩	﹪	﹫	㏕
5	㎜	㎝	㎞	㏎	㎡	㎎	㎏	㏄	°	兙	兛	兞	兝	兡	兣	嗧
6	瓩	糎	▁	▂	▃	▄	▅	▆	▇	█	▏	▎	▍	▌	▋	▊
7	▉	┼	┴	┬	┤	├	▔	─	│	▕	┌	┐	└	┘	╭	
A		╮	╰	╯	═	╞	╪	╡	◢	◣	◥	◤	╱	╲	╳	０
B	１	２	３	４	５	６	７	８	９	Ⅰ	Ⅱ	Ⅲ	Ⅳ	Ⅴ	Ⅵ	Ⅶ
C	Ⅷ	Ⅸ	Ⅹ	〡	〢	〣	〤	〥	〦	〧	〨	〩	十	卄	卅	Ａ
D	Ｂ	Ｃ	Ｄ	Ｅ	Ｆ	Ｇ	Ｈ	Ｉ	Ｊ	Ｋ	Ｌ	Ｍ	Ｎ	Ｏ	Ｐ	Ｑ
E	Ｒ	Ｓ	Ｔ	Ｕ	Ｖ	Ｗ	Ｘ	Ｙ	Ｚ	ａ	ｂ	ｃ	ｄ	ｅ	ｆ	ｇ
F	ｈ	ｉ	ｊ	ｋ	ｌ	ｍ	ｎ	ｏ	ｐ	ｑ	ｒ	ｓ	ｔ	ｕ	ｖ	

Row A3	0	1	2	3	4	5	6	7	8	9	A	B	C	D	E	F
4	ｗ	ｘ	ｙ	ｚ	Α	Β	Γ	Δ	Ε	Ζ	Η	Θ	Ι	Κ	Λ	Μ
5	Ν	Ξ	Ο	Π	Ρ	Σ	Τ	Υ	Φ	Χ	Ψ	Ω	α	β	γ	δ
6	ε	ζ	η	θ	ι	κ	λ	μ	ν	ξ	ο	π	ρ	σ	τ	υ
7	φ	χ	ψ	ω	ㄅ	ㄆ	ㄇ	ㄈ	ㄉ	ㄊ	ㄋ	ㄌ	ㄍ	ㄎ	ㄏ	
A		ㄐ	ㄑ	ㄒ	ㄓ	ㄔ	ㄕ	ㄖ	ㄗ	ㄘ	ㄙ	ㄚ	ㄛ	ㄜ	ㄝ	ㄞ
B	ㄟ	ㄠ	ㄡ	ㄢ	ㄣ	ㄤ	ㄥ	ㄦ	ㄧ	ㄨ	ㄩ	˙		ˊ	ˇ	ˋ
C	NULL	TC1 (SOH)	TC2 (STX)	TC3 (ETX)	TC4 (EOT)	TC5 (ENQ)	TC6 (ACK)	BELL	FE0 (BS)	FE1 (HT)	FE2 (LF)	FE3 (VT)	FE4 (FF)	FE5 (CR)	SO	SI
D	TC7 (DLE)	DC1	DC2	DC3	DC4	TC8 (NAK)	TC9 (SYN)	TC10 (ETB)	CAN	EM	SUB	ESC	IS4 (FS)	IS3 (GS)	IS2 (RS)	IS1 (US)
E	DEL															
F																

Row A4	0	1	2	3	4	5	6	7	8	9	A	B	C	D	E	F
4	一	乙	丁	七	乃	九	了	二	人	儿	入	八	几	刀	刁	力
5	匕	十	卜	又	三	下	丈	上	丫	丸	凡	久	么	也	乞	于
6	亡	兀	刃	勺	千	叉	口	土	士	夕	大	女	子	孑	孓	寸
7	小	尢	尸	山	川	工	己	已	巳	巾	干	廾	弋	弓	才	
A		丑	丐	不	中	丰	丹	之	尹	予	云	井	互	五	亢	仁
B	什	仃	仆	仇	仍	今	介	仄	元	允	內	六	兮	公	冗	凶
C	分	切	刈	勻	勾	勿	化	匹	午	升	卅	卞	厄	友	及	反
D	壬	天	夫	太	夭	孔	少	尤	尺	屯	巴	幻	廿	弔	引	心
E	戈	戶	手	扎	支	文	斗	斤	方	日	曰	月	木	欠	止	歹
F	毋	比	毛	氏	水	火	爪	父	爻	片	牙	牛	犬	王	丙	

Row A5	0	1	2	3	4	5	6	7	8	9	A	B	C	D	E	F
4	世	丕	且	丘	主	乍	乏	乎	以	付	仔	仕	他	仗	代	令
5	仙	仞	充	兄	冉	冊	冬	凹	出	凸	刊	加	功	包	匆	北
6	匝	仟	半	卉	卡	占	卯	卮	去	可	古	右	召	叮	叩	叨
7	叼	司	叵	叫	另	只	史	叱	台	句	叭	叻	四	囚	外	
A		央	失	奴	奶	孕	它	尼	巨	巧	左	市	布	平	幼	弁
B	弘	弗	必	戊	打	扔	扒	扑	斥	旦	朮	本	未	末	札	正
C	母	民	氐	永	汁	汀	氾	犯	玄	玉	瓜	瓦	甘	生	用	甩
D	田	由	甲	申	疋	白	皮	皿	目	矛	矢	石	示	禾	穴	立
E	丞	丟	乒	乓	乩	亙	交	亦	亥	仿	伉	伙	伊	伕	伍	伐
F	休	伏	仲	件	任	仰	仳	份	企	伋	光	兇	兆	先	全	

Row A6	0	1	2	3	4	5	6	7	8	9	A	B	C	D	E	F
4	共	再	冰	列	刑	划	刎	刖	劣	匈	匡	匠	印	危	吉	吏
5	同	吊	吐	吁	吋	各	向	名	合	吃	后	吆	吒	因	回	囝
6	圳	地	在	圭	圬	圯	圩	夙	多	夷	夸	妄	奸	妃	好	她
7	如	妁	字	存	宇	守	宅	安	寺	尖	屹	州	帆	并	年	
A		式	弛	忙	忖	戎	戌	戍	成	扣	扛	托	收	早	旨	旬
B	旭	曲	曳	有	朽	朴	朱	朵	次	此	死	氖	汝	汗	汙	江
C	池	汐	汕	污	汛	汍	汎	灰	牟	牝	百	竹	米	糸	缶	羊
D	羽	老	考	而	耒	耳	聿	肉	肋	肌	臣	自	至	臼	舌	舛
E	舟	艮	色	艾	虫	血	行	衣	西	阡	串	亨	位	住	佇	佗
F	佞	伴	佛	何	估	佐	佑	伽	伺	伸	佃	佔	似	但	佣	

Row A7	0	1	2	3	4	5	6	7	8	9	A	B	C	D	E	F
4	作	你	伯	低	伶	余	佝	佈	佚	兌	克	免	兵	冶	冷	別
5	判	利	刪	刨	劫	助	努	劬	匣	即	卵	吝	吭	吞	吾	否
6	呎	吧	呆	呃	吳	呈	呂	君	吩	告	吹	吻	吸	吮	吵	吶
7	吠	吼	呀	吱	含	吟	听	囪	困	囤	囫	坊	坑	址	坍	
A		均	坎	圾	坐	坏	圻	壯	夾	妝	妒	妨	妞	妣	妙	妖
B	妍	妤	妓	妊	妥	孝	孜	孚	孛	完	宋	宏	尬	局	屁	尿
C	尾	岐	岑	岔	岌	巫	希	序	庇	床	廷	弄	弟	彤	形	彷
D	役	忘	忌	志	忍	忱	快	忸	忪	戒	我	抄	抗	抖	技	扶
E	抉	扭	把	扼	找	批	扳	抒	扯	折	扮	投	抓	抑	抆	改
F	攻	攸	旱	更	束	李	杏	材	村	杜	杖	杞	杉	杆	杠	

Row A8	0	1	2	3	4	5	6	7	8	9	A	B	C	D	E	F
4	杓	宋	步	每	求	汞	沙	沁	沈	沉	沅	沛	汪	決	沐	汰
5	沌	汨	沖	沒	汽	沃	汲	汾	汴	沆	汶	沍	沔	沘	沂	灶
6	灼	災	灸	牢	牡	牠	狄	狂	玖	甬	甫	男	甸	皂	盯	矣
7	私	秀	禿	究	系	罕	肖	肓	肝	肘	肛	肚	育	良	芒	
A		芋	芍	見	角	言	谷	豆	豕	貝	赤	走	足	身	車	辛
B	辰	迂	迆	迅	迄	巡	邑	邢	邪	邦	那	酉	釆	里	防	阮
C	阱	阪	阬	並	乖	乳	事	些	亞	享	京	佯	依	侍	佳	使
D	佬	供	例	來	侃	佰	併	侈	佩	佻	侖	佾	侏	侑	佺	兔
E	兒	兕	兩	具	其	典	冽	函	刻	券	刷	刺	到	刮	制	剁
F	劾	劻	卒	協	卓	卑	卦	卷	卸	卹	取	叔	受	味	呵	

Row A9	0	1	2	3	4	5	6	7	8	9	A	B	C	D	E	F
4	咖	呸	咕	咀	呻	呷	咄	咒	咆	呼	咐	呱	呶	和	咚	呢
5	周	咋	命	咎	固	垃	坷	坪	坩	坡	坦	坤	坼	夜	奉	奇
6	奈	奄	奔	妾	妻	委	妹	妮	姑	姆	姐	姍	始	姓	姊	妯
7	妳	姒	姅	孟	孤	季	宗	定	官	宜	宙	宛	尚	屈	居	
A		屆	岷	岡	岸	岩	岫	岱	岳	帘	帚	帖	帕	帛	帑	幸
B	庚	店	府	底	庖	延	弦	弧	弩	往	征	彿	彼	忝	忠	忽
C	念	忿	怏	怔	怯	怵	怖	怪	怕	怡	性	怩	怫	怛	或	戕
D	房	戾	所	承	拉	拌	拄	抿	拂	抹	拒	招	披	拓	拔	拋
E	拈	抨	抽	押	拐	拙	拇	拍	抵	拚	抱	拘	拖	拗	拆	抬
F	拎	放	斧	於	旺	昔	易	昌	昆	昂	明	昀	昏	昕	昊	

Row AA	0	1	2	3	4	5	6	7	8	9	A	B	C	D	E	F
4	昇	服	朋	杭	枋	枕	東	果	杳	杷	枇	枝	林	杯	杰	板
5	枉	松	析	杵	枚	枓	杼	杪	杲	欣	武	歧	歿	氓	氛	泣
6	注	泳	沱	泌	泥	河	沽	沾	沼	波	沫	法	泓	沸	泄	油
7	況	沮	泗	泅	泱	沿	治	泡	泛	泊	沬	泯	泜	泖	泠	
A		炕	炎	炒	炊	炙	爬	爭	爸	版	牧	物	狀	狎	狙	狗
B	狐	玩	玨	玟	玫	玥	甽	疝	疙	疚	的	盂	盲	直	知	矽
C	社	祀	祁	秉	秈	空	穹	竺	糾	罔	羌	羋	者	肺	肥	肢
D	肱	股	肫	肩	肴	肪	肯	臥	臾	舍	芳	芝	芙	芭	芽	芟
E	芹	花	芬	芥	芯	芸	芣	芰	芾	芷	虎	虱	初	表	軋	迎
F	返	近	邵	邸	邱	邯	采	金	長	門	阜	陀	阿	阻	附	

Row AB	0	1	2	3	4	5	6	7	8	9	A	B	C	D	E	F
4	陔	佳	雨	青	非	亟	亭	亮	信	侵	侯	便	俠	俑	俏	保
5	促	侶	俘	俟	俊	俗	侮	俐	俄	係	俚	俎	俞	侷	兗	冒
6	冑	冠	剎	剃	削	前	剌	剋	則	勇	勉	勃	勁	匍	南	卻
7	厚	叛	咬	哀	咨	哎	哉	咸	咦	咳	哇	哂	咽	咪	品	
A		哄	哈	咯	咫	咱	咻	咩	咧	咿	囿	垂	型	垠	垣	垢
B	城	垮	垓	奕	契	奏	奎	奐	姜	姘	姿	姣	姨	娃	姥	姪
C	姚	姦	威	姻	孩	宣	宦	室	客	宥	封	屎	屏	屍	屋	峙
D	峒	巷	帝	帥	帟	幽	庠	度	建	弈	弭	彥	很	待	徊	律
E	徇	後	徉	怒	思	怠	急	怎	怨	恍	恰	恨	恢	恆	恃	恬
F	恫	恪	恤	扁	拜	挖	按	拼	拭	持	拮	拽	指	拱	拷	

Row AC	0	1	2	3	4	5	6	7	8	9	A	B	C	D	E	F
4	拯	括	拾	拴	挑	挂	政	故	斫	施	既	春	昭	映	昧	是
5	星	昨	昱	昤	曷	柿	染	柱	柔	某	柬	架	枯	柵	柩	柯
6	柄	柑	枴	柚	查	枸	柏	柞	柳	枰	柙	柢	柝	柒	歪	殃
7	殆	段	毒	毗	氟	泉	洋	洲	洪	流	津	洌	洱	洞	洗	
A		活	洽	派	洶	洛	泵	洹	洧	洸	洩	洮	洵	洎	洫	炫
B	為	炳	炬	炯	炭	炸	炮	炤	爰	牲	牯	牴	狩	狠	狡	玷
C	珊	玻	玲	珍	珀	玳	甚	甭	畏	界	畎	畋	疫	疤	疥	疢
D	疣	癸	皆	皇	皈	盈	盆	盃	盅	省	盹	相	眉	看	盾	盼
E	眇	矜	砂	研	砌	砍	祆	祉	祈	祇	禹	禺	科	秒	秋	穿
F	突	竿	竽	籽	紂	紅	紀	紉	紇	約	紆	缸	美	羿	耄	

Row AD	0	1	2	3	4	5	6	7	8	9	A	B	C	D	E	F
4	耐	耍	耑	耶	胖	胥	胚	胃	胄	背	胡	胛	胎	胞	胤	胝
5	致	舢	苧	范	茅	苣	苛	苦	茄	若	茂	茉	苒	苗	英	茁
6	苜	苔	苑	苞	苓	苟	苯	茆	虐	虹	虻	虺	衍	衫	要	觔
7	計	訂	訃	貞	負	赴	赳	趴	軍	軌	述	迦	迢	迪	迥	
A		迭	迫	迤	迨	郊	郎	郁	郃	酋	酊	重	閂	限	陋	陌
B	降	面	革	韋	韭	音	頁	風	飛	食	首	香	乘	亳	倌	倍
C	倣	俯	倦	倥	俸	倩	倖	倆	值	借	倚	倒	們	俺	倀	倔
D	倨	俱	倡	個	候	倘	俳	修	倭	倪	俾	倫	倉	兼	冤	冥
E	冢	凍	凌	准	凋	剖	剜	剔	剛	剝	匪	卿	原	厝	叟	哨
F	唐	唁	唷	哼	哥	哲	唆	哺	唔	哩	哭	員	唉	哮	哪	

Row AE	0	1	2	3	4	5	6	7	8	9	A	B	C	D	E	F
4	哦	唧	唇	哽	唏	圃	圄	埂	埔	埋	埃	堉	夏	套	奘	奚
5	娑	娘	娜	娟	娛	娓	姬	娠	娣	娩	娥	娌	娉	孫	屘	宰
6	害	家	宴	宮	宵	容	宸	射	屑	展	屐	峭	峽	峻	峪	峨
7	峰	島	崁	峴	差	席	師	庫	庭	座	弱	徒	徑	徐	恙	
A		恣	恥	恐	恕	恭	恩	息	悄	悟	悚	悍	悔	悌	悅	悖
B	扇	拳	挈	拿	捎	挾	振	捕	捂	捆	捏	捉	挺	捐	挽	挪
C	挫	挨	捍	捌	效	敉	料	旁	旅	時	晉	晏	晃	晒	晌	晅
D	晁	書	朔	朕	朗	校	核	案	框	桓	根	桂	桔	栩	梳	栗
E	桌	桑	栽	柴	桐	桀	格	桃	株	桅	栓	栘	桁	殊	殉	殷
F	氣	氧	氨	氦	氤	泰	浪	涕	消	涇	浦	浸	海	浙	涓	

Row AF	0	1	2	3	4	5	6	7	8	9	A	B	C	D	E	F
4	浬	涉	浮	浚	浴	浩	涌	涊	浹	涅	浥	涔	烊	烘	烤	烙
5	烈	烏	爹	特	狼	狹	狽	狸	狷	玆	班	琉	珮	珠	珪	珞
6	畔	畝	畜	畚	留	疾	病	症	疲	疳	疽	疼	疹	痂	疸	皋
7	皰	益	盍	盎	眩	真	眠	眨	矩	砰	砧	砸	砝	破	砷	
A		砥	砭	砠	砟	砲	祕	祐	祠	祟	祖	神	祝	祗	祚	秤
B	秣	秧	租	秦	秩	秘	窄	窈	站	笆	笑	粉	紡	紗	紋	紊
C	素	索	純	紐	紕	級	紜	納	紙	紛	缺	罟	羔	翅	翁	耆
D	耘	耕	耙	耗	耽	耿	胱	脂	胰	脅	胭	胴	脆	胸	胳	脈
E	能	脊	胼	胯	臭	臬	舀	舐	航	舫	舨	般	芻	茫	荒	荔
F	荊	茸	荐	草	茵	茴	荏	茲	茹	茶	茗	荀	茱	茨	荃	

Row B0	0	1	2	3	4	5	6	7	8	9	A	B	C	D	E	F
4	虔	蚊	蚪	蚓	蚤	蚩	蚌	蚣	蚜	衰	衷	袁	袂	衽	衹	記
5	訐	討	訌	訕	訊	託	訓	訖	訏	訑	豈	豺	豹	財	貢	起
6	躬	軒	軔	軏	辱	送	逆	迷	退	迺	迴	逃	追	逅	迸	邕
7	郡	郝	郢	酒	配	酌	釘	針	釗	釜	釙	閃	院	陣	陡	
A		陛	陝	除	陘	陞	隻	飢	馬	骨	高	鬥	鬲	鬼	乾	偺
B	偽	停	假	偃	偌	做	偉	健	偶	偎	偕	偵	側	偷	偏	倏
C	偯	偭	兜	冕	凰	剪	副	勒	務	勘	動	匐	匏	匙	匿	區
D	匾	參	曼	商	啪	啦	啄	啞	啡	啃	啊	唱	啖	問	啕	唯
E	啤	唸	售	啜	唬	啣	唳	啁	啗	圈	國	圉	域	堅	堊	堆
F	埠	埤	基	堂	堵	執	培	夠	奢	娶	婁	婉	婦	婪	婀	

Row B1	0	1	2	3	4	5	6	7	8	9	A	B	C	D	E	F
4	娼	婢	婚	婆	婊	孰	寇	寅	寄	寂	宿	密	尉	專	將	屠
5	屜	屝	崇	崆	崎	崛	崖	崢	崑	崩	崔	崙	崤	崧	崗	巢
6	常	帶	帳	帷	康	庸	庶	庵	庾	張	強	彗	彬	彩	彫	得
7	徙	從	徘	御	徠	徜	恿	患	悉	悠	您	惋	悴	惦	悽	
A		情	悻	悵	惜	悼	惘	惕	惆	惟	悸	惚	惇	戚	戛	扈
B	掠	控	捲	掖	探	接	捷	捧	掘	措	捱	掩	掉	掃	掛	捫
C	推	掄	授	掙	採	掬	排	掏	掀	捻	捩	捨	捺	敝	敖	救
D	教	敗	啟	敏	敘	敕	敔	斜	斛	斬	族	旋	旌	旎	晝	晚
E	晤	晨	晦	晞	曹	勗	望	梁	梯	梢	梓	梵	桿	桶	梱	梧
F	梗	械	梃	棄	梭	梆	梅	梔	條	梨	梟	梡	梂	欲	殺	

Row B2	0	1	2	3	4	5	6	7	8	9	A	B	C	D	E	F
4	毫	毬	氫	涎	涼	淳	淙	液	淡	淌	淤	添	淺	清	淇	淋
5	涯	淑	涮	淞	淹	涸	混	淵	淅	淒	渚	涵	淚	淫	淘	淪
6	深	淮	淨	淆	淄	涪	淬	涿	淦	烹	焉	焊	烽	烯	爽	牽
7	犁	猜	猛	猖	猓	猙	率	琅	琊	球	理	現	琍	瓠	瓶	
A		瓷	甜	產	略	畦	畢	異	疏	痔	痕	疵	痊	痍	皎	盔
B	盒	盛	眷	眾	眼	眶	眸	眺	硫	硃	硎	祥	票	祭	移	窒
C	窕	笠	笨	笛	第	符	笙	笞	笮	粒	粗	粕	絆	絃	統	紮
D	紹	紼	絀	細	紳	組	累	終	紲	紱	缽	羞	羚	翌	翎	習
E	耜	聊	聆	脯	脖	脣	脫	脩	脰	脤	舂	舵	舷	舶	船	莎
F	莞	莘	莩	莢	莖	莽	莫	莒	莊	莓	莉	莠	荷	荻	荼	

Row B3	0	1	2	3	4	5	6	7	8	9	A	B	C	D	E	F
4	莆	莧	處	彪	蛇	蛀	蚶	蛄	蚵	蛆	蛋	蚱	蚯	蛉	術	袞
5	袈	被	袒	袖	袍	袋	覓	規	訪	訝	訣	訥	許	設	訟	訛
6	訢	豉	豚	販	責	貫	貨	貪	貧	赧	赦	趾	趺	軛	軟	這
7	逍	通	逗	連	速	逝	逐	逕	逞	造	透	逢	逖	逛	途	
A		部	郭	都	酗	野	釵	釦	釣	釧	釭	釩	閉	陪	陵	陳
B	陸	陰	陴	陶	陷	陬	雀	雪	雩	章	竟	頂	頃	魚	鳥	鹵
C	鹿	麥	麻	傢	傍	傅	備	傑	傀	傖	傘	傚	最	凱	割	剴
D	創	剩	勞	勝	勛	博	厥	啻	喀	喧	啼	喊	喝	喘	喂	喜
E	喪	喔	喇	喋	喃	喳	單	喟	唾	喲	喚	喻	喬	喱	啾	喉
F	喫	喙	圍	堯	堪	場	堤	堰	報	堡	堝	堠	壹	壺	奠	

Row B4	0	1	2	3	4	5	6	7	8	9	A	B	C	D	E	F
4	婷	媚	婿	媒	媛	媧	孳	孱	寒	富	寓	寐	尊	尋	就	嵌
5	嵐	崴	嵇	巽	幅	帽	幀	幃	幾	廊	廁	廂	廄	弼	彭	復
6	循	徨	惑	惡	悲	悶	惠	愜	愣	惺	愕	惰	惻	惴	慨	惱
7	愎	惶	愉	愀	愒	戟	扉	掣	掌	描	揀	揩	揉	揆	揍	
A		插	揣	提	握	揖	揭	揮	捶	援	揪	換	摒	揚	揹	敞
B	敦	敢	散	斑	斐	斯	普	晰	晴	晶	景	暑	智	晾	晷	曾
C	替	期	朝	棺	棕	棠	棘	棗	椅	棟	棵	森	棧	棹	棒	棲
D	棣	棋	棍	植	椒	椎	棉	棚	楮	棻	款	欺	欽	殘	殖	殼
E	毯	氮	氯	氬	港	游	湔	渡	渲	湧	湊	渠	渥	渣	減	湛
F	湘	渤	湖	湮	渭	渦	湯	渴	湍	渺	測	湃	渝	渾	滋	

Row B5	0	1	2	3	4	5	6	7	8	9	A	B	C	D	E	F
4	溉	渙	湎	湣	湄	湲	湩	湟	焙	焚	焦	焰	無	然	煮	焜
5	牌	犄	犀	猶	猥	猴	猩	琺	琪	琳	琢	琥	琵	琶	琴	琯
6	琛	琦	琨	甥	甦	畫	番	痢	痛	痣	痙	痘	痞	痠	登	發
7	皖	皓	皴	盜	睏	短	硝	硬	硯	稍	稈	程	稅	稀	窘	
A		窗	窖	童	竣	等	策	筆	筐	筒	答	筍	筋	筏	筑	粟
B	粥	絞	結	絨	絕	紫	絮	絲	絡	給	絢	絰	絳	善	翔	翕
C	耋	聒	肅	腕	腔	腋	腑	腎	脹	腆	脾	腌	腓	腴	舒	舜
D	菩	萃	菸	萍	菠	菅	萋	菁	華	菱	菴	著	萊	菰	萌	菌
E	菽	菲	菊	萸	萎	萄	菜	萇	菔	菟	虛	蛟	蛙	蛭	蛔	蛛
F	蛤	蛐	蛞	街	裁	裂	袱	覃	視	註	詠	評	詞	証	詁	

Row B6	0	1	2	3	4	5	6	7	8	9	A	B	C	D	E	F
4	詔	詛	詐	詆	訴	診	訶	詖	象	貂	貯	貼	貳	貽	賁	費
5	賀	貴	買	貶	貿	貸	越	超	趁	跎	距	跋	跚	跑	跌	跛
6	跆	軻	軸	軼	辜	逮	逵	週	逸	進	逶	鄂	郵	鄉	鄒	酣
7	酥	量	鈔	鈕	鈣	鈉	鈞	鈍	鈐	鈇	鈑	閔	閏	開	閑	
A		間	閒	閎	隊	階	隋	陽	隅	隆	隍	陲	隄	雁	雅	雄
B	集	雇	雯	雲	韌	項	順	須	飧	飪	飯	飩	飲	飭	馮	馭
C	黃	黍	黑	亂	傭	債	傲	傳	僅	傾	催	傷	傻	傯	僇	剿
D	剷	剽	募	勦	勤	勢	勣	匯	嗟	嗨	嗓	嗦	嗎	嗜	嗇	嗑
E	嗣	嗤	嗯	嗚	嗡	嗅	嗆	嗥	嗉	園	圓	塞	塑	塘	塗	塚
F	塔	填	塌	塭	塊	塢	塒	塋	奧	嫁	嫉	嫌	媾	媽	媼	

Row B7	0	1	2	3	4	5	6	7	8	9	A	B	C	D	E	F
4	媳	嫂	媲	嵩	嵯	幌	幹	廉	廈	弒	彙	徬	微	愚	意	慈
5	感	想	愛	惹	愁	愈	慎	慌	慄	慍	愾	愴	愧	愍	愆	愷
6	戡	戢	搓	搾	搞	搪	搭	搽	搬	搏	搜	搔	損	搶	搖	搗
7	搆	敬	斟	新	暗	暉	暇	暈	暖	暄	暘	暍	會	榔	業	
A		楚	楷	楠	楔	極	椰	概	楊	楨	楫	楞	楓	楹	榆	楝
B	楣	楛	歇	歲	毀	殿	毓	毽	溢	溯	滓	溶	滂	源	溝	滇
C	滅	溥	溘	溼	溺	溫	滑	準	溜	滄	滔	溪	溧	溴	煎	煙
D	煩	煤	煉	照	煜	煬	煦	煌	煥	煞	煆	煨	煖	爺	牒	猷
E	獅	猿	猾	瑯	瑚	瑕	瑟	瑞	瑁	琿	瑙	瑛	瑜	當	畸	瘀
F	痰	瘁	痲	痱	痺	痿	痴	痳	盞	盟	睛	睫	睦	睞	督	

Row B8	0	1	2	3	4	5	6	7	8	9	A	B	C	D	E	F
4	睹	睪	睬	睜	睥	睨	睢	矮	碎	碰	碗	碘	碌	碉	硼	碑
5	碓	硿	祺	祿	禁	萬	禽	稜	稚	稠	稔	稟	稞	窟	窠	筷
6	節	筠	筮	筧	粱	粳	粵	經	絹	綑	綁	綏	絛	置	罩	罪
7	署	義	羨	群	聖	聘	肆	肄	腱	腰	腸	腥	腮	腳	腫	
A		腹	腺	腦	舅	艇	蒂	葷	落	萱	葵	葦	葫	葉	葬	葛
B	萼	萵	葡	董	葩	葭	葆	虞	虜	號	蛹	蜓	蜈	蜇	蜀	蛾
C	蛻	蜂	蜃	蜆	蜊	衙	裟	裔	裙	補	裘	裝	裡	裊	裕	裒
D	覜	解	詫	該	詳	試	詩	詰	誇	詼	詣	誠	話	誅	詭	詢
E	詮	詬	詹	詻	訾	詨	豢	貊	貉	賊	資	賈	賄	貲	賃	賂
F	賅	跡	跟	跨	路	跳	跺	跪	跤	跦	躲	較	載	軾	輊	

Row B9	0	1	2	3	4	5	6	7	8	9	A	B	C	D	E	F
4	辟	農	運	遊	道	遂	達	逼	違	遐	遇	遏	過	遍	遑	逾
5	遁	鄒	鄗	酬	酪	酩	釉	鈷	鉗	鈸	鈽	鉀	鈾	鉛	鉋	鉤
6	鉑	鈴	鉉	鉍	鉅	鈹	鈿	鉚	閘	隘	隔	隕	雍	雋	雉	雊
7	雷	電	雹	零	靖	靴	靶	預	頑	頓	頊	頒	頌	飼	飴	
A		飽	飾	馳	馱	馴	髡	鳩	麂	鼎	鼓	鼠	僧	僮	僥	僖
B	僭	僚	僕	像	僑	僱	僎	僩	兢	凳	劃	劂	匱	厭	嗾	嘀
C	嘛	嘗	嗽	嘔	嘆	嘉	嘍	嘎	嗷	嘖	嘟	嘈	嘐	嗶	團	圖
D	塵	塾	境	墓	墊	塹	墅	塽	壽	夥	夢	夤	奪	奩	嫡	嫦
E	嫩	嫗	嫖	嫘	嫣	孵	寞	寧	寡	寥	實	寨	寢	寤	察	對
F	屢	嶄	嶇	幛	幣	幕	幗	幔	廓	廖	弊	彆	彰	徹	慇	

Row BA	0	1	2	3	4	5	6	7	8	9	A	B	C	D	E	F
4	愿	態	慷	慢	慣	慟	慚	慘	慵	截	撇	摘	摔	撤	摸	摟
5	摺	摑	摧	搴	摭	摻	敲	斡	旗	旖	暢	暨	暝	榜	榨	榕
6	槁	榮	槓	構	榛	榷	榻	榫	榴	槐	槍	榭	槌	榦	槃	榣
7	歉	歌	氳	漳	演	滾	漓	滴	漩	漾	漠	漬	漏	漂	漢	
A		滿	滯	漆	漱	漸	漲	漣	漕	漫	漯	澈	漪	滬	漁	滲
B	滌	滷	熔	熙	煽	熊	熄	熒	爾	犒	犖	獄	獐	瑤	瑣	瑪
C	瑰	瑭	甄	疑	瘧	瘍	瘋	瘉	瘓	盡	監	瞄	睽	睿	睡	磁
D	碟	碧	碳	碩	碣	禎	福	禍	種	稱	窪	窩	竭	端	管	箕
E	箋	筵	算	箝	箔	箏	箸	箇	箄	粹	粽	精	綻	綰	綜	綽
F	綾	綠	緊	綴	網	綱	綺	綢	綿	綵	綸	維	緒	緇	綬	

Row BB	0	1	2	3	4	5	6	7	8	9	A	B	C	D	E	F
4	罰	翠	翡	翟	聞	聚	肇	腐	膀	膏	膈	膊	腿	膂	臧	臺
5	與	舔	舞	艋	蓉	蒿	蓆	蓄	蒙	蒞	蒲	蒜	蓋	蒸	蓀	蓓
6	蒐	蒼	蓑	蓊	蜿	蜜	蜻	蜢	蜥	蜴	蜘	蝕	蜷	蜩	裳	褂
7	裴	裹	裸	製	裨	褚	裯	誦	誌	語	誣	認	誡	誓	誤	
A		說	誥	誨	誘	誑	誚	誧	豪	貍	貌	賓	賑	賒	赫	趙
B	趕	跼	輔	輒	輕	輓	辣	遠	遘	遜	遣	遙	遞	遢	遝	遛
C	鄙	鄘	鄞	酵	酸	酷	酴	鉸	銀	銅	銘	銖	鉻	銓	銜	銨
D	鉼	銑	閡	閨	閩	閣	閥	閤	隙	障	際	雌	雒	需	靼	鞅
E	韶	頗	領	颯	颱	餃	餅	餌	餉	駁	骯	骰	髦	魁	魂	鳴
F	鳶	鳳	麼	鼻	齊	億	儀	僻	僵	價	儂	儈	儉	儅	凜	

Row BC	0	1	2	3	4	5	6	7	8	9	A	B	C	D	E	F
4	劇	劈	劉	劍	劊	勰	厲	嘮	嘻	嘹	嘲	嘿	嘴	嘩	噓	噎
5	噗	噴	嘶	嘯	嘰	墀	墟	增	墳	墜	墮	墩	墦	奭	嬉	嫻
6	嬋	嫵	嬌	嬈	寮	寬	審	寫	層	履	嶝	嶔	幢	幟	幡	廢
7	廚	廟	廝	廣	廠	彈	影	德	徵	慶	慧	慮	慝	慕	憂	
A		慼	慰	慫	慾	憧	憐	憫	憎	憬	憚	憤	憔	憮	戮	摩
B	摯	摹	撞	撲	撈	撐	撰	撥	撓	撕	撩	撒	撮	播	撫	撚
C	撬	撙	撢	撳	敵	敷	數	暮	暫	暴	暱	樣	樟	槨	樁	樞
D	標	槽	模	樓	樊	槳	樂	樅	槭	樑	歐	歎	殤	毅	毆	漿
E	潼	澄	潑	潦	潔	澆	潭	潛	潸	潮	澎	潺	潰	潤	澗	潘
F	滕	潯	潠	潟	熟	熬	熱	熨	牖	犛	獎	獗	瑩	璋	璃	

Row BD	0	1	2	3	4	5	6	7	8	9	A	B	C	D	E	F
4	瑾	璀	畿	瘠	瘩	瘟	瘤	瘦	瘡	瘢	皚	皺	盤	瞎	瞇	瞌
5	瞑	瞋	磋	磅	確	磊	碾	磕	碼	磐	稿	稼	穀	稽	稷	稻
6	窯	窮	箭	箱	範	箴	篆	篇	篁	箠	篌	糊	締	練	緯	緻
7	緘	緬	緝	編	緣	線	緞	緩	綞	緙	緲	緹	罵	罷	羯	
A		翩	耦	膛	膜	膝	膠	膚	膘	蔗	蔽	蔚	蓮	蔬	蔭	蔓
B	蔑	蔣	蔡	蔔	蓬	蔥	蓿	蔆	螂	蝴	蝶	蝠	蝦	蝸	蝨	蝙
C	蝗	蝌	蝓	衛	衝	褐	複	褒	褓	褕	褊	誼	諒	談	諄	誕
D	請	諸	課	諉	諂	調	誰	論	諍	誶	誹	諛	豌	豎	豬	賠
E	賞	賦	賤	賬	賭	賢	賣	賜	質	賡	赭	趟	趣	踫	踐	踝
F	踢	踏	踩	踟	踡	踞	躺	輝	輛	輟	輩	輦	輪	輜	輞	

Row BE	0	1	2	3	4	5	6	7	8	9	A	B	C	D	E	F
4	輥	適	遮	遨	遭	遷	鄰	鄭	鄧	鄱	醇	醉	醋	醃	鋅	銻
5	銷	鋪	銬	鋤	鋁	銳	銼	鋒	鋇	鋰	銲	閭	閱	霄	霆	震
6	霉	靠	鞍	鞋	鞏	頡	頫	頜	颳	養	餓	餒	餘	駝	駐	駟
7	駛	駑	駕	駒	駙	骷	髮	髯	鬧	魅	魄	魷	魯	鴆	鴉	
A		鴃	麩	麾	黎	墨	齒	儒	儘	儔	儐	儕	冀	冪	凝	劑
B	劓	勳	噙	噫	噹	噩	噤	噸	噪	器	噥	噱	噯	噬	噢	噶
C	壁	墾	壇	壅	奮	嬝	嬴	學	寰	導	彊	憲	憑	憩	憊	懍
D	憶	憾	懊	懈	戰	擅	擁	擋	撻	撼	據	擄	擇	擂	操	撿
E	擒	擔	撾	整	曆	曉	暹	曄	曇	暸	樽	樸	樺	橙	橫	橘
F	樹	橄	橢	橡	橋	橇	樵	機	橈	歙	歷	氅	濂	澱	澡	

Row BF	0	1	2	3	4	5	6	7	8	9	A	B	C	D	E	F
4	濃	澤	濁	澧	澳	激	澹	澶	澦	澠	澴	熾	燉	燐	燒	燈
5	燕	熹	燎	燙	燜	燃	燄	獨	璜	璣	璘	璟	璞	瓢	甌	甍
6	瘴	瘸	瘺	盧	盥	瞠	瞞	瞟	瞥	磨	磚	磬	磧	禦	積	穎
7	穆	穌	穋	窺	篙	簑	築	篤	篛	篡	篩	篦	糕	糖	縊	
A		縑	縈	縛	縣	縞	縝	縉	縐	罹	羲	翰	翱	翮	耨	膳
B	膩	膨	臻	興	艘	艙	蕊	蕙	蕈	蕨	蕩	蕃	蕉	蕭	蕪	蕞
C	螃	螟	螞	螢	融	衡	褪	褲	褥	褫	褡	親	覦	諦	諺	諫
D	諱	謀	諜	諧	諮	諾	謁	謂	諷	諭	諳	諶	諼	豫	豭	貓
E	賴	蹄	踱	踴	蹂	踹	踵	輻	輯	輸	輳	辨	辦	遵	遴	選
F	遲	遼	遺	鄴	醒	錠	錶	鋸	錳	錯	錢	鋼	錫	錄	錚	

Row C0	0	1	2	3	4	5	6	7	8	9	A	B	C	D	E	F
4	錐	錦	錡	錕	錮	錙	閻	隧	隨	險	雕	霎	霑	霖	霍	霓
5	霏	靛	靜	靦	鞘	頰	頸	頻	頷	頭	頹	頤	餐	館	餞	餛
6	餡	餚	駭	駢	駱	骸	骼	髻	髭	鬨	鮑	鴕	鴣	鴦	鴨	鴒
7	鴛	默	黔	龍	龜	優	償	儡	儲	勵	嚎	嚀	嚐	嚅	嚇	
A		嚏	壕	壓	壑	壎	嬰	嬪	嬤	孺	尷	屨	嶼	嶺	嶽	嶸
B	幫	彌	徽	應	懂	懇	懦	懋	戲	戴	擎	擊	擘	擠	擰	擦
C	擬	擱	擢	擤	斂	斃	曙	曖	檀	檔	檄	檢	檜	櫛	檣	橾
D	檗	檐	檠	歜	殮	毚	氈	濘	濱	濟	濠	濛	濤	濫	濯	澀
E	濬	濡	濩	濕	濮	濰	燧	營	燮	燦	燥	燭	燬	燴	燠	爵
F	牆	獰	獲	璩	環	璦	璨	癆	療	癌	盪	瞳	瞪	瞰	瞬	

Row C1	0	1	2	3	4	5	6	7	8	9	A	B	C	D	E	F
4	瞧	瞭	矯	磷	磺	磴	磯	礁	禧	禪	穗	窿	簇	簍	篾	篷
5	簌	篠	糠	糜	糞	糢	糟	糙	糝	縮	績	繆	縷	縲	繃	縫
6	總	縱	繅	繁	縴	縹	繈	縵	縿	縯	罄	翳	翼	聱	聲	聰
7	聯	聳	臆	臃	膺	臂	臀	膿	膽	臉	膾	臨	舉	艱	薪	
A		薄	蕾	薜	薑	薔	薯	薛	薇	薨	薊	虧	蟀	蟑	螳	蟒
B	蟆	螫	螻	螺	蟈	蟋	褻	褶	襄	褸	褽	覬	謎	謗	謙	講
C	謊	謠	謝	謄	謐	豁	谿	豳	賺	賽	購	賸	賻	趨	蹉	蹋
D	蹈	蹊	轄	輾	轂	轅	輿	避	遽	還	邁	邂	邀	鄹	醣	醞
E	醜	鍍	鎂	錨	鍵	鍊	鍥	鍋	錘	鍾	鍬	鍛	鍰	鍚	鍔	闊
F	闋	闌	闈	闆	隱	隸	雖	霜	霞	鞠	韓	顆	颶	餵	騁	

Row C2	0	1	2	3	4	5	6	7	8	9	A	B	C	D	E	F
4	駿	鮮	鮫	鮪	鮭	鴻	鴿	麋	黏	點	黜	黝	黛	鼾	齋	叢
5	嚕	嚮	壙	壘	嬸	彝	懣	戳	擴	擲	擾	攆	擺	擻	擷	斷
6	曜	朦	檳	檬	櫃	檻	檸	櫂	檮	檯	歟	歸	殯	瀉	瀋	濾
7	瀆	濺	瀑	瀏	燻	燼	燾	燸	獷	獵	璧	璿	甕	癖	癘	
A		癒	瞽	瞿	瞻	瞼	礎	禮	穡	穢	穠	竄	竅	簫	簧	簪
B	簞	簣	簡	糧	織	繕	繞	繚	繡	繒	繙	罈	翹	翻	職	聶
C	臍	臏	舊	藏	薩	藍	藐	藉	薰	薺	薹	薦	蟯	蟬	蟲	蟠
D	覆	覲	觴	謨	謹	謬	謫	豐	贅	蹙	蹣	蹦	蹤	蹟	蹕	軀
E	轉	轍	邇	邃	邈	醫	醬	釐	鎔	鎊	鎖	鎢	鎳	鎮	鎬	鎰
F	鎘	鎚	鎗	闔	闖	闐	闕	離	雜	雙	雛	雞	霤	鞣	鞦	

Row C3	0	1	2	3	4	5	6	7	8	9	A	B	C	D	E	F
4	鞭	韹	額	顏	題	顎	顓	颺	餾	餿	餽	餮	馥	騎	髁	鬃
5	鬆	魏	魍	魎	鯊	鯉	鯽	鯈	鯀	鵑	鵝	鵠	黠	鼕	鼬	儳
6	嚥	壞	壟	壢	寵	龐	廬	懲	懷	懶	懵	攀	攏	曠	曝	櫥
7	櫝	櫚	櫓	瀛	瀟	瀨	瀚	瀝	瀕	瀘	爆	爍	牘	犢	獸	
A		獺	璽	瓊	瓣	疇	疆	癟	癡	矇	礙	禱	穫	穩	簾	簿
B	簸	簽	簷	籀	繫	繭	繹	繩	繪	羅	繳	羶	羹	羸	臘	藩
C	藝	藪	藕	藤	藥	藷	蟻	蠅	蠍	蟹	蟾	襠	襟	襖	襞	譁
D	譜	識	證	譚	譎	譏	譆	譙	贈	贊	蹼	蹲	躇	蹶	蹬	蹺
E	蹴	轔	轎	辭	邊	邋	醱	醮	鏡	鏑	鏟	鏃	鏈	鏜	鏝	鏖
F	鏢	鏍	鏘	鏤	鏗	鏨	關	隴	難	霪	霧	靡	韜	韻	類	

Row C4	0	1	2	3	4	5	6	7	8	9	A	B	C	D	E	F
4	願	顛	颼	饅	饉	騖	騙	鬍	鯨	鯧	鯖	鯛	鶉	鵡	鵲	鵪
5	鵬	麒	麗	麓	麴	勸	嚨	嚷	嚶	嚴	嚼	壤	孀	孃	孽	寶
6	巉	懸	懺	攘	攔	攙	曦	朧	櫬	瀾	瀰	瀲	爐	獻	瓏	癢
7	癥	礦	礪	礬	礫	竇	競	籌	籃	籍	糯	糰	辮	繽	繼	
A		纂	罌	耀	臚	艦	藻	藹	蘑	藺	蘆	蘋	蘇	蘊	蠔	蠕
B	襤	覺	觸	議	譬	警	譯	譟	譫	贏	贍	躉	躁	躅	躂	醴
C	釋	鐘	鐃	鏽	闡	霰	飄	饒	饑	馨	騫	騰	騷	騵	鰓	鰍
D	鹹	麵	黨	鼯	齟	齣	齡	儷	儸	囁	囀	囂	夔	屬	巍	懼
E	懾	攝	攜	斕	曩	櫻	欄	櫺	殲	灌	爛	犧	瓖	瓔	癩	矓
F	籐	纏	續	羼	蘗	蘭	蘚	蠣	蠢	蠡	蠟	襪	襬	覽	譴	

Row C5	0	1	2	3	4	5	6	7	8	9	A	B	C	D	E	F
4	護	譽	贓	躊	躍	躋	轟	辯	醺	鐮	鐳	鐵	鐺	鐸	鐲	鐫
5	闢	霸	霹	露	響	顧	顥	饗	驅	驃	驀	騾	髏	魔	魑	鰭
6	鰥	鶯	鶴	鷂	鶸	麝	黯	鼙	齜	齦	齧	儼	儻	囈	囊	囉
7	孿	巔	巒	彎	懿	攤	權	歡	灑	灘	玀	瓤	疊	癮	癬	
A		禳	籠	籟	聾	聽	臟	襲	襯	觼	讀	贖	贗	躑	躓	轡
B	酈	鑄	鑑	鑒	霽	霾	韃	韁	顫	饕	驕	驍	髒	鬚	鱉	鰱
C	鰾	鰻	鷓	鷗	鼴	齬	齪	龔	囌	巖	戀	攣	攫	攪	曬	欐
D	瓚	竊	籤	籣	籥	纓	纖	纔	臢	蘸	蘿	蠱	變	邐	邏	鑣
E	鑠	鑤	靨	顯	饜	驚	驛	驗	髓	體	髑	鱔	鱗	鱖	鷥	麟
F	黴	囑	壩	攬	灞	癱	癲	矗	罐	羈	蠶	蠹	衢	讓	讒	

Row C6	0	1	2	3	4	5	6	7	8	9	A	B	C	D	E	F
4	讖	艷	贛	釀	鑪	靂	靈	靄	韆	顰	驟	鬢	魘	鱟	鷹	鷺
5	鹼	鹽	鼇	齷	齲	廳	欖	灣	籬	籮	蠻	觀	躡	釁	鑲	鑰
6	顱	饞	髖	鬣	黌	灤	矚	讚	鑷	韉	驢	驥	纜	讜	躪	釅
7	鑽	鑾	鑼	鱷	鱸	黷	豔	鑿	鸚	爨	驪	鬱	鸛	鸞	籲	
A																
B																
C																
D																
E																
F																

Big Five Level 2

Row C9	0	1	2	3	4	5	6	7	8	9	A	B	C	D	E	F
4	乂	乜	凵	匚	厂	万	丌	乇	亍	囗	兀	屮	彳	丏	冇	与
5	丮	亓	仂	仉	仈	冘	勼	卬	厹	圠	夃	夬	尐	巿	旡	殳
6	毌	气	爿	丱	丼	仨	仜	仩	仡	仝	冚	刌	匜	卌	圢	圣
7	夗	夯	宁	宄	尒	尻	屴	屳	帄	庀	庂	忉	戉	扐	氕	
A		氶	汃	氿	氻	犮	犰	玊	禸	肊	阞	伎	优	伬	仵	伔
B	仱	伀	价	伈	伝	伂	伅	伢	伓	伄	仴	伒	冱	刓	刉	刐
C	劦	匢	匟	卍	厊	吇	囡	囟	圮	圪	圴	夼	妀	奼	妅	奻
D	奾	奷	奿	孖	尕	尥	屼	屺	屻	屾	巟	幵	庄	异	弚	彴
E	忕	忔	忏	扜	扞	扤	扡	扦	扢	扙	扠	扚	扥	旯	旮	朾
F	朹	朸	朻	机	朿	朼	朳	氘	汆	汒	汜	汏	汊	汔	汋	

Row CA	0	1	2	3	4	5	6	7	8	9	A	B	C	D	E	F
4	汌	灱	牞	犴	犵	玎	甪	癿	穵	网	艸	艼	芀	艽	艿	虍
5	襾	邙	邗	邘	邛	邔	阢	阤	阠	阣	佖	伻	佢	佉	体	佤
6	伾	佧	佒	佟	佁	佘	伭	伳	伿	佡	冏	冹	刜	刞	刡	劭
7	劮	匉	卣	卲	厎	厏	吰	吷	吪	呔	呅	吙	吜	吥	吘	
A		吽	呏	呁	吨	吤	呇	囮	囧	囥	坁	坅	坌	坉	坋	坒
B	夆	奀	妦	妘	妠	妗	妎	妢	妐	妏	妧	妡	宎	宒	尨	尪
C	岍	岏	岈	岋	岉	岒	岊	岆	岓	岕	巠	帊	帎	庋	庉	庌
D	庈	庍	弅	弝	彸	彶	忒	忑	忐	忭	忨	忮	忳	忡	忤	忣
E	忺	忯	忷	忻	怀	忴	戺	抃	抌	抎	抏	抔	抇	扱	扻	扺
F	扰	抁	抈	扷	扽	扲	扴	攷	旰	旴	旳	旲	旵	杅	杇	

Row CB	0	1	2	3	4	5	6	7	8	9	A	B	C	D	E	F
4	杙	杕	杌	杈	杝	杍	杚	杋	毐	氙	氚	汸	汧	汫	沄	沋
5	沏	汱	汯	汩	沚	汭	沇	沕	沜	汦	汳	汥	汻	沎	灴	灺
6	牣	犿	犽	狃	狆	狁	犺	狅	玕	玗	玓	玔	玒	町	甹	疔
7	疕	皁	礽	耴	肕	肙	肐	肒	肜	芐	芏	芅	芎	芑	芓	
A		芊	芃	芄	豸	迉	辿	邟	邡	邥	邞	邧	邠	阰	阨	阯
B	阭	丳	侘	佼	侅	佽	侀	侇	佶	佴	侉	侄	佷	佌	侗	佪
C	侚	佹	侁	佸	侐	侜	侔	侞	侒	侂	侕	佫	佮	冞	冼	冾
D	刵	刲	刳	剆	刱	劼	匊	匋	匼	厒	厔	咇	呿	咁	咑	咂
E	咈	呫	呺	呾	呥	呬	呴	呦	咍	呯	呡	呠	咘	呣	呧	呤
F	囷	囹	坯	坲	坭	坫	坱	坰	坶	垀	坵	坻	坳	坴	坢	

Row CC	0	1	2	3	4	5	6	7	8	9	A	B	C	D	E	F
4	坨	坽	夌	奆	妵	妺	姏	姎	妲	姌	姁	妶	妼	姃	姖	妱
5	妽	妭	姈	婴	妿	孢	孥	宓	宕	屄	屆	岮	岓	岠	岵	岯
6	岨	岬	岟	岣	岭	岢	岪	岧	岸	岥	岶	岰	岦	帗	帔	帙
7	弨	弢	弣	弤	彔	徂	彾	彽	忞	忥	怭	怦	怙	怲	怋	
A		怴	怊	怗	怳	怚	怞	怬	怢	怍	怐	怮	怓	怑	怌	怉
B	怜	戔	戽	抭	抴	拑	抾	抪	抶	拊	抮	抳	抯	抻	抩	抰
C	抸	攽	斨	斻	昉	旼	昄	昒	昈	旻	昃	昋	昍	昅	旽	昑
D	昐	昭	朊	枅	杭	枎	枒	杶	杻	枘	枆	构	杴	枔	枌	杺
E	枟	枑	枙	枃	杽	极	杸	枇	柃	欥	殀	歾	毞	氝	沓	泬
F	泫	泮	泙	沶	泔	沭	泧	沷	泐	泂	沺	泃	泆	泭	泲	

Row CD	0	1	2	3	4	5	6	7	8	9	A	B	C	D	E	F
4	泒	泝	沴	沊	沝	汿	泞	泀	洰	泍	泇	沰	泹	泏	泩	泑
5	炔	炘	炅	炓	炆	炄	炑	炖	炂	炚	炃	牪	狖	狋	狘	狉
6	狜	狒	狔	狚	狌	狑	玤	玡	玭	玦	玢	玠	玬	玝	瓝	瓨
7	甿	畀	甾	疌	疘	皯	盳	盱	盰	盵	矸	矼	矹	矻	矺	
A		矷	祂	礿	秅	穸	穻	竻	籵	糽	耵	肏	肮	肣	肸	肵
B	肭	舠	芠	苀	芫	芚	芘	芛	芵	芧	芮	芼	芞	芺	芴	芨
C	芡	芩	苂	芤	苃	芶	芢	虰	虯	虭	虮	豖	迒	迋	迓	迍
D	迖	迕	迗	邲	邴	邯	邳	邰	阹	阽	阼	阺	陃	俍	俅	俓
E	侲	俉	俋	俁	俔	俜	俙	侻	侳	俛	俇	俖	侉	俀	侹	俬
F	剄	剉	勀	勂	匽	卼	厗	厖	厙	厘	咺	咡	咭	咥	哏	

Row CE	0	1	2	3	4	5	6	7	8	9	A	B	C	D	E	F
4	哃	茍	咷	咮	哖	咶	哅	哆	咠	呰	咼	咢	咾	呲	哞	咰
5	垵	垞	垟	垤	垌	垗	垝	垛	垔	垘	垏	垙	垥	垚	垕	壴
6	复	奓	姡	姞	姮	娀	姱	姝	姺	姽	姼	姶	姤	姲	姷	姛
7	姩	姳	姵	姠	姾	姴	姭	宨	屌	峐	峘	峌	峗	峋	峛	
A		峞	峚	峉	峇	峊	峖	峓	峔	峏	峈	峆	峎	峟	峸	巹
B	帡	帢	帣	帠	帤	庰	庤	庢	庛	庣	庥	弇	弮	彖	徆	怷
C	怹	恔	恲	恞	恅	恓	恇	恉	恛	恌	恀	恂	恟	怤	恄	恘
D	恦	恮	扂	扃	拏	挍	挋	拵	挎	挃	拫	拹	挏	挌	拸	拶
E	挀	挓	挔	拺	挕	挾	挻	敁	敂	斪	斿	衵	昡	昲	昵	易
F	昦	昢	昳	昫	昺	昝	昻	昹	昜	朏	朐	柁	柲	柈	枺	

Row CF	0	1	2	3	4	5	6	7	8	9	A	B	C	D	E	F
4	柜	枻	柸	柘	柀	枷	柅	柫	柤	柟	枵	柍	枳	柷	柶	柮
5	柣	柂	枹	柎	柧	柰	枲	柼	柆	柭	柌	枮	柦	柛	柺	柉
6	柊	柃	柪	柋	欨	殂	殄	殶	毖	毘	毠	氠	氡	洨	洴	洭
7	洟	洼	洿	洒	洊	泚	洳	洄	洙	洺	洚	洑	洀	洝	浂	
A		洁	洘	洷	洃	洏	浀	洇	浲	渢	洈	洢	洉	洐	炷	炟
B	炾	炱	炰	炡	炔	炵	炩	牁	牉	牊	牬	牰	牳	牮	狊	狤
C	狨	狫	狟	狪	狦	狣	玅	珌	珂	珈	珅	玹	玶	玵	玴	珫
D	玿	珇	玾	珃	珆	玸	珋	瓬	瓮	甮	畇	畈	疧	疪	癹	盄
E	眈	眃	眄	眅	眊	盷	盻	盺	矧	矨	砆	砑	砒	砅	砐	砏
F	砎	砉	砃	砓	祊	祌	祋	祅	祄	秕	种	秏	秖	秎	窀	

Row D0	0	1	2	3	4	5	6	7	8	9	A	B	C	D	E	F
4	穾	竑	笀	笁	籺	籸	籹	籿	粀	粁	紃	紈	紁	罘	羑	羍
5	羾	耇	耎	耏	耔	耷	胘	胇	胠	胑	胈	胂	胐	胅	胣	胙
6	胜	胊	胕	胉	胏	胗	胦	胍	臿	舡	芔	苙	苾	苹	茇	苨
7	茀	苕	茺	苫	苖	苴	苬	苡	苲	苵	茌	苻	苶	苰	苪	
A		苤	苠	苺	苳	苭	虷	虴	虼	虳	衁	衎	衧	衪	衩	觓
B	訄	訇	赲	迣	迡	迮	迠	郱	邽	邿	郕	郅	邾	郇	郋	郈
C	釔	釓	陔	陏	陑	陓	陊	陎	倞	倅	倇	倓	倢	倰	倛	俵
D	俴	倳	倷	倬	俶	俷	倗	倜	倠	倧	倵	倯	倱	倎	党	冔
E	冓	凊	凄	凅	凈	凎	剡	剚	剒	剞	剟	剕	剢	勍	匎	厞
F	唦	哢	唗	唒	哧	哳	哤	唚	哿	唄	唈	哫	唑	唅	哱	

Row D1	0	1	2	3	4	5	6	7	8	9	A	B	C	D	E	F
4	唊	哻	哷	唩	哠	唎	唍	唋	圁	圂	埌	堲	埕	埒	垺	埆
5	垽	垼	垸	垶	垿	埇	埐	垹	埁	夎	奊	娙	娖	娭	娮	娕
6	娏	娗	娊	娞	娳	孬	宧	宭	宬	尃	屖	屔	峬	峿	峮	峱
7	峷	崀	峹	帩	帨	庨	庮	庪	庬	弳	弰	彧	恝	恚	恧	
A		恁	悢	悈	悀	悒	悁	悝	悃	悕	悛	悗	悇	悜	悎	戙
B	扆	拲	挐	捖	挬	捄	捅	挶	捃	揤	挹	捋	捊	挼	挩	捁
C	挴	捘	捔	捙	挭	捇	挳	捚	捑	挸	捗	捀	捈	敊	敆	旆
D	旃	旄	旂	晊	晟	晇	晑	朒	朓	栟	栚	桉	栲	栳	栻	桋
E	桏	栖	栱	栜	栵	栫	栭	栯	桎	桄	栴	栝	栒	栔	栦	栨
F	栮	桍	栺	栥	栠	欬	欯	欭	欱	欴	歭	肂	殈	毦	毤	

Row D2	0	1	2	3	4	5	6	7	8	9	A	B	C	D	E	F
4	毨	毣	毢	毧	氤	浺	浣	浤	淬	洍	浡	涒	浘	浢	浭	浯
5	涑	涍	涓	浿	涆	浞	浧	浠	涚	浰	浼	浟	涂	涘	栔	浨
6	浹	浾	涀	湾	淏	涃	淍	涹	浵	涐	烜	烓	烑	烝	烋	焏
7	烢	烗	烒	烞	烠	烔	烍	烅	烆	烇	烚	烎	烡	牂	牸	
A		牷	牶	犻	狺	狴	狾	狶	狳	狻	猁	珓	珙	珥	珖	玼
B	珧	珣	珩	珜	珒	珛	珔	珝	珚	珗	珘	珨	瓞	瓟	瓴	瓿
C	甡	畛	畟	疰	痁	疻	痄	痀	疿	痆	疺	皊	盋	眝	眛	眐
D	眓	眒	眣	眑	眕	眙	眚	眢	眧	砣	砬	砢	砵	砯	砨	砮
E	砫	砭	砩	砳	砪	砱	祔	祛	祏	祜	祓	祒	祑	秫	秬	秠
F	秮	秭	秪	秜	秞	秝	窆	窉	窅	窒	窌	窊	窀	竘	笐	

Row D3	0	1	2	3	4	5	6	7	8	9	A	B	C	D	E	F
4	笄	笓	笅	笏	笈	笊	笎	笉	笒	粄	粑	粊	粌	粈	粍	粅
5	紞	紝	紑	紎	紘	紖	紓	紟	紒	紏	紌	罜	罡	罞	罠	罝
6	罛	羖	羒	翃	翂	翀	耖	聇	耹	胺	胲	胹	胵	脁	胻	脀
7	舁	舯	舥	茳	茭	荄	茙	荑	茥	荖	茿	荁	茦	茜	茢	
A		荂	荎	茛	茪	茈	茼	荍	茖	茤	茠	茷	茯	茩	荇	荅
B	荌	荓	茵	茬	荋	茧	莽	虓	虒	蚢	蚨	蚖	蚍	蚑	蚞	蚇
C	蚗	蚆	蚋	蚚	蚅	蚥	蚙	蚡	蚧	蚕	蚘	蚎	蚝	蚐	蚔	衃
D	衄	衭	衵	衶	衲	袀	衱	衿	衯	袃	衾	衴	衼	訒	豇	豗
E	豻	貤	貣	赶	赸	趵	趷	趶	軑	軓	迾	迵	适	迿	迻	逄
F	迼	迶	邳	郠	郙	郚	郣	郯	郥	郘	郛	郗	郜	郤	酐	

Row D4	0	1	2	3	4	5	6	7	8	9	A	B	C	D	E	F
4	酎	酏	釔	釢	釚	陜	陟	隼	飣	髟	鬯	乿	偰	偪	偡	偞
5	偠	偓	偋	偝	偲	偈	偍	偁	偛	偊	偢	倕	偅	偟	偩	偫
6	偣	偤	偆	偀	偮	偳	偗	偑	凐	剫	剭	剬	剮	勖	勓	匭
7	厜	啵	啶	唼	啍	啐	唴	唪	啑	啢	唶	唵	唰	啒	啅	
A		唌	唲	啥	啎	唹	啈	唭	唻	啀	啋	圊	圇	埻	堔	埢
B	埶	埜	埴	堀	埭	埽	堈	埸	堋	埳	埏	堇	埮	埣	埲	埥
C	埬	埡	堎	埼	堐	埧	堁	堌	埱	埩	埰	堍	堄	奜	婠	婘
D	婕	婧	婞	娸	娵	婭	婐	婟	婥	婬	婓	婤	婗	婃	婝	婒
E	婄	婛	婈	媎	娾	婍	娹	婌	婰	婩	婇	婑	婖	婂	婜	孲
F	孮	寁	寀	屙	崞	崋	崝	崚	崠	崌	崨	崍	崦	崥	崏	

Row D5	0	1	2	3	4	5	6	7	8	9	A	B	C	D	E	F
4	崰	崒	崣	崟	崮	帾	帴	庱	庴	庹	庲	庳	弶	弸	徛	徖
5	徟	悊	悐	悆	悾	悰	悺	惓	惔	惏	惤	惙	惝	惈	悱	惛
6	悷	惊	悿	惃	惍	惀	挲	捥	掊	掂	捽	掽	掞	掭	掝	掗
7	掫	掎	捯	掇	掐	据	掯	捵	掜	捭	掮	捼	掤	挻	掟	
A		捸	掅	掁	掑	掍	捰	敓	旍	晥	晡	晛	晙	晜	晢	朘
B	桹	梇	梐	梜	桭	桮	梮	梫	楖	桯	梣	梬	梩	桵	桴	梲
C	梏	桷	梒	桼	桫	桲	梪	梀	桱	桾	梛	梖	梋	梠	梉	梤
D	桸	桻	梑	梌	梊	桽	欶	欳	欷	欸	殑	殏	殍	殎	殌	氪
E	淀	涫	涴	涳	湴	涬	淩	淢	涷	淶	淔	渀	淈	淠	淟	淖
F	涾	淥	淜	淝	淛	淴	淊	涽	淭	淰	涺	淕	淂	淏	淉	

Row D6	0	1	2	3	4	5	6	7	8	9	A	B	C	D	E	F
4	淐	淲	淓	淽	淗	淍	淣	涻	烺	焍	烷	焗	烴	焌	烰	焄
5	烳	焐	烼	烿	焆	焓	焀	烸	烶	焋	焂	焎	牾	牻	牼	牿
6	猝	猗	猇	猑	猘	猊	猈	狿	猏	猞	玈	珶	珸	珵	琄	琁
7	珽	琇	琀	珺	珼	珿	琌	琋	珴	琈	畤	畣	痎	痒	痏	
A		痋	痌	痑	痐	皏	皉	盓	眹	眯	眭	眱	眲	眴	眳	眽
B	眥	眻	眵	硈	硒	硉	硍	硊	硌	砦	硅	硐	祤	祧	祩	祪
C	祣	祫	祡	离	秺	秸	秶	秷	窏	窔	窐	笵	筇	笴	笥	笰
D	笢	笤	笳	笘	笪	笝	笱	笫	笭	笯	笲	笸	笚	笣	粔	粘
E	粖	粣	紵	紽	紸	紶	紺	絅	紬	紩	絁	絇	紾	紿	絊	紻
F	紨	罣	羕	羜	羝	羛	翊	翋	翍	翐	翑	翇	翏	翉	耟	

Row D7	0	1	2	3	4	5	6	7	8	9	A	B	C	D	E	F
4	耞	耛	聇	聃	聈	脘	脥	脙	脛	脭	脟	脬	脞	脡	脕	脧
5	脝	脢	舑	舸	舳	舺	舴	舲	艴	莐	莣	莨	莍	荺	荳	莤
6	荴	莏	莁	莕	莙	荵	莔	莩	荽	莃	莌	莝	莛	莪	莋	荾
7	莥	莯	莈	莗	莰	荿	莦	莇	莮	荶	莚	虙	虖	蚿	蚷	
A		蛂	蛁	蛅	蚺	蚰	蛈	蚹	蚳	蚸	蛌	蚴	蚻	蚼	蛃	蚽
B	蚾	衒	袉	袕	袨	袢	袪	袚	袑	袡	袟	袘	袧	袙	袛	袗
C	袤	袬	袌	袓	袎	覂	觖	觙	觕	訰	訧	訬	訞	谹	谻	豜
D	豝	豽	貥	赽	赻	赹	趼	跂	趹	趿	跁	軘	軞	軝	軜	軗
E	軠	軡	逤	逋	逑	逜	逌	逡	郯	郪	郰	郴	郲	郳	郔	郫
F	郬	郩	酖	酘	酚	酓	酕	釬	釴	釱	釳	釸	釤	釹	釪	

Row D8	0	1	2	3	4	5	6	7	8	9	A	B	C	D	E	F
4	釾	釷	舒	釮	跃	閆	閈	陼	陭	陫	陶	陯	雂	靪	頄	飥
5	馗	傛	傕	傔	傞	傋	傣	傃	傌	傎	偈	偞	傜	傒	傂	傇
6	兟	凔	匒	匑	厤	厧	喑	喨	喥	喭	啷	嗚	喢	喓	喈	喏
7	喵	喁	喣	喒	喤	嘹	喌	喦	啿	喕	喡	喎	圌	堐	堷	
A		堙	堞	堧	堣	堨	埵	塈	堥	埬	堛	堳	堿	堉	堮	堹
B	堸	堭	堬	堻	奡	媯	媔	媟	婺	媢	媞	婸	媦	婼	媥	媬
C	媕	媮	娷	媄	媊	媗	媃	媋	媩	婻	婽	媌	媜	媏	媓	媝
D	寪	寍	寋	寔	寑	寊	寎	尌	尰	崷	嵃	嵫	嵁	嵋	崿	崵
E	嵑	嵎	嵕	崳	崺	嵒	崽	崱	嵙	嵂	崹	嵉	嵿	崼	崲	尌
F	嵟	嵗	幄	幁	彘	徦	徥	徫	惉	悹	惌	惢	惎	惄	愔	

Row D9	0	1	2	3	4	5	6	7	8	9	A	B	C	D	E	F
4	惲	愊	愖	愅	惵	愓	惸	惼	惾	惁	愃	愘	愝	愐	惿	愄
5	愋	扊	掔	掱	掰	揎	揥	揨	揯	揃	撝	揳	揊	揠	揶	揕
6	揲	揵	摡	揟	掾	揝	揜	揄	揘	揓	揂	揇	揌	揋	揈	揰
7	揗	揙	攲	敧	敪	敤	敜	敨	敥	斌	斝	斞	斮	旐	旒	
A		晼	晬	晻	晀	晱	晹	晪	晲	暜	椌	棓	椄	棜	椪	棬
B	棪	棱	椏	棖	棷	棫	棤	棶	椓	椐	棳	棡	椇	棌	椈	楰
C	梴	椑	棯	棆	椔	棸	棐	棽	棼	棨	椋	椊	椗	棎	棈	棝
D	棞	棦	棴	棑	椆	棔	棩	椕	椥	棇	欹	欻	欿	欼	殔	殗
E	殙	殕	殽	毰	毲	毳	氰	淼	湆	湇	渟	湉	溈	渼	渽	湅
F	湢	渫	渿	湁	湝	湳	渜	渳	湋	湀	湑	渻	渃	渮	湞	

Row DA	0	1	2	3	4	5	6	7	8	9	A	B	C	D	E	F
4	湨	湜	湡	湂	渨	湠	湱	湫	渹	渢	渰	湓	湥	渧	湸	湤
5	湷	湕	湹	湒	湦	渵	渶	湚	焠	焞	焯	烻	焮	焱	焣	焥
6	焢	焲	焟	焆	焺	焛	牋	牚	犈	犉	犆	犅	犋	猒	猋	猰
7	猢	猱	猳	猧	猲	猭	猦	猣	猵	猌	琮	琬	琰	琫	琖	
A		琚	琡	琭	琱	琤	琣	琝	琩	琠	琲	瓻	甯	畯	畬	痧
B	痚	痡	痦	痝	痟	痤	痗	皕	皒	盚	睆	睇	睄	睍	睅	睊
C	睎	睋	睌	矞	矬	硠	硤	硥	硜	硭	硱	硪	确	硰	硩	硨
D	硞	硢	祴	祳	祲	祰	稂	稊	稃	稌	稄	窙	竦	竤	筊	笻
E	筄	筈	筌	筎	筀	筘	筅	粢	粞	粨	粡	絘	絯	絣	絓	絖
F	絧	絪	絏	絭	絜	絫	絒	絔	絩	絑	絟	絎	缾	缿	罥	

Row DB	0	1	2	3	4	5	6	7	8	9	A	B	C	D	E	F
4	罜	羢	羦	羕	翋	聑	聏	聐	胾	胔	腃	腊	腒	腏	腇	脽
5	腍	脺	臦	臮	臷	臸	臹	舄	舼	舽	舿	艵	茻	菏	菹	萣
6	菀	萋	荛	菧	菤	菼	菶	萐	菆	菈	菫	菣	莿	萁	菝	菥
7	菘	菿	菡	菋	菎	菖	菵	菉	萉	萏	萂	萑	萆	菂	菳	
A		菕	菺	菇	菑	菪	萓	萿	落	菮	菄	菻	菗	菢	萛	苒
B	恭	蛘	蛢	蛦	蛓	蛣	蛚	蛪	蛝	蛫	蛜	蛬	蛩	蝗	蛨	蜂
C	衈	衖	衕	袺	裗	袹	袸	裀	袾	袶	袼	袷	袽	衮	裹	裉
D	覎	覐	覞	觝	觚	觛	詎	詍	訹	詓	詀	詷	詘	詄	詅	詒
E	詈	詑	詊	詌	詏	豟	貁	貀	貺	貾	貰	貹	貵	趄	趆	趉
F	跘	跓	跍	跇	跖	跜	跏	跕	跙	跈	跗	跅	軯	軷	軺	

Row DC	0	1	2	3	4	5	6	7	8	9	A	B	C	D	E	F
4	軹	軦	軮	軥	軵	軧	軨	軶	軫	軱	軬	軴	軩	逭	逴	逯
5	鄆	鄋	鄏	鄇	鄎	鄈	郥	鄐	鄁	郡	鄉	鄅	鄃	酡	酤	酟
6	酢	酠	鈁	鈊	鈥	鈃	鈚	鈦	鈏	鈌	鈀	鈒	釿	釽	鈆	鈄
7	鈧	鈂	鈜	鈤	鈙	鈗	鈅	鈖	鉄	閍	閌	閐	陙	陜	限	
A		隍	隃	陲	雃	雈	雅	雩	雰	靬	靰	靮	頊	颩	飫	魀
B	丵	亃	亄	亶	傽	傿	僆	傮	僄	僊	傴	僈	僂	偂	傒	傺
C	從	僨	僉	傶	俠	凗	勞	剸	剻	剼	嗃	嗛	嗌	嗐	噌	嗊
D	嗝	嗀	嗔	嗄	嗩	喿	嗒	喋	嗏	嗕	嗢	嗖	嗈	嗲	嘣	嗙
E	嗂	圔	埧	塨	塤	塏	塍	塉	塯	塕	塎	塝	塙	塥	塛	塓
F	塗	塱	壼	嫇	嫄	嫋	媺	嫅	媱	媵	媯	媿	嫈	嫛	嫆	

Row DD	0	1	2	3	4	5	6	7	8	9	A	B	C	D	E	F
4	媷	嫀	媴	婛	嫧	嫍	嫎	嬰	寖	寘	寙	尟	層	嵱	嵣	嵊
5	嵥	嵲	嵬	嵞	嶋	嵧	嵢	巰	幏	幎	幁	幍	幣	廅	廌	廆
6	廋	廇	彀	徯	徭	惷	慉	慊	愫	慅	慛	愲	愮	慆	愯	慏
7	愪	慀	戠	截	戣	戜	戥	擘	掌	撆	搐	搒	摧	搠	搤	
A		搳	摃	摲	搕	搢	搹	搷	揩	摵	搌	搦	搰	搨	揌	搵
B	搯	搊	擠	摀	搥	搧	搋	挈	搛	摽	搡	搎	殹	旐	旓	暆
C	暌	暕	暐	暋	暊	暙	暔	最	朠	楦	楟	椸	楎	楢	楱	椿
D	楅	楪	椹	楂	楗	楙	楺	楈	楉	椵	楬	椳	椽	楥	棰	楸
E	椴	楩	楀	楯	楄	窠	棨	楁	楴	椮	椻	楋	椷	楜	楏	楑
F	椲	楒	椯	楻	椼	歆	歅	歃	歂	歛	歁	殛	殼	毻	毼	

Row DE	0	1	2	3	4	5	6	7	8	9	A	B	C	D	E	F
4	毹	毷	毸	溛	滖	滈	溏	滀	溟	溓	溔	溠	溱	溹	滆	滒
5	溽	滁	溞	滉	溷	溰	滍	溦	滏	溲	溾	滃	滜	滘	溙	溒
6	溎	溍	溤	溡	溿	溳	滐	滊	溗	溮	溣	煇	煔	煒	煣	煠
7	煁	煝	煢	煲	煸	煪	煡	熚	煘	煃	煋	煰	煟	煐	煓	
A		煄	煍	煚	牏	犍	犌	犑	犐	犎	猼	獂	猻	猺	獀	獊
B	獉	瑄	瑊	瑋	瑒	瑑	瑗	瑀	瑏	瑐	瑎	瑂	瑆	瑍	瑔	瓡
C	瓿	瓾	瓽	甝	畹	畷	榃	痯	瘏	瘃	痷	痾	痼	痹	痸	瘐
D	痻	痶	痭	痵	痽	皙	皵	盝	睕	睟	睠	睒	睖	睚	睩	睧
E	睔	睙	睭	矠	碇	碚	碔	碏	碄	碕	碅	碆	碡	碃	硹	碙
F	碀	碖	硻	祼	禂	祽	祹	稑	稘	稙	稒	稗	稕	稢	稓	

Row DF	0	1	2	3	4	5	6	7	8	9	A	B	C	D	E	F
4	稛	稐	窣	窢	窞	竫	筦	筤	筭	筴	筩	筲	筥	筳	筱	筰
5	筡	筸	筶	筣	粲	粴	粯	綈	綆	綀	綍	絿	綅	絺	綎	絻
6	綃	絼	綌	綔	綄	絽	綒	罭	罫	罧	罨	罬	羦	羥	羧	翛
7	翜	耡	腤	腠	腷	腜	腩	腛	腢	腲	朡	腞	腶	腧	腯	
A		腄	腡	舝	艉	艄	艀	艂	艅	蓱	萿	葖	葶	葹	蒏	蒍
B	葥	葑	葀	蒆	葧	萰	葍	葽	葚	葙	葴	葳	葝	蔇	葞	萷
C	萺	萴	葺	葃	葸	萲	葅	萩	菙	葋	萯	葂	萭	葟	葰	萹
D	葎	葌	葒	葯	蓅	蒎	萻	葇	萶	萳	葨	葾	葄	萫	葠	葔
E	葮	葐	蜋	蜄	蛷	蜌	蛺	蛖	蛵	蝍	蛸	蜎	蜉	蜁	蛶	蜍
F	蜅	裖	裋	裍	裎	裞	裛	裚	裌	裐	覅	覛	觟	觥	觤	

Row E0	0	1	2	3	4	5	6	7	8	9	A	B	C	D	E	F
4	觡	觠	觢	觜	触	詶	誆	詿	詡	訿	詷	誂	誄	詵	誃	誁
5	詴	詺	谼	豋	豊	豥	豤	豦	貆	貄	貅	賌	赨	赩	趑	趌
6	趎	趏	趍	趓	趔	趐	趒	跰	跠	跬	跱	跮	跐	跩	跣	跢
7	跧	跲	跫	跴	輆	軿	輁	輀	輅	輇	輈	輂	輋	遒	逿	
A		遄	遉	逽	鄐	鄍	鄏	鄑	鄖	鄔	鄋	鄎	酮	酯	鉈	鉒
B	鈰	鈺	鉦	鈳	鉥	鉞	銃	鈮	鉊	鉆	鉭	鉬	鉏	鉠	鉧	鉯
C	鈶	鉡	鉰	鈱	鉔	鉣	鉐	鉲	鉎	鉓	鉌	鉖	鈲	閟	閜	閞
D	閛	隒	隓	隑	隗	雎	雺	雽	雸	雵	靳	靷	靸	靲	頏	頍
E	頎	颬	飶	飹	馯	馲	馰	馵	骭	骫	魛	鳨	鳭	鳧	麀	黽
F	僦	僔	僗	僨	僳	儌	僪	僝	僤	僓	僬	僸	僯	僭	僠	

Row E1	0	1	2	3	4	5	6	7	8	9	A	B	C	D	E	F
4	凘	劀	劁	勩	勫	匰	厬	嘧	嘕	嘌	嘒	嗼	嘏	嘐	嘁	嘓
5	嘂	嘊	嘝	嘄	嗿	嗹	墉	塼	墐	墘	墆	墁	塿	塴	墋	塺
6	墇	墑	墎	塶	墂	墈	塻	墔	墍	墿	嬭	嫜	嫮	嫥	嫕	嫪
7	嫚	嫭	嫫	嫳	嫢	嫠	嫛	嫬	嫞	嫝	嫙	嫨	嫟	孷	寠	
A		寣	屣	嶂	嶀	嵽	嶆	嵺	嶁	嵷	嶊	嶉	嶈	嵾	嵼	嶍
B	嵹	嵿	幘	幙	幓	廘	廑	廗	廎	廜	廕	廙	廒	廔	彄	彃
C	彯	徶	愬	愨	慁	慞	慱	慳	慒	慓	慲	慬	憀	慴	慔	慺
D	慛	慥	愻	慪	慡	慖	戩	戧	戫	搫	摍	摛	摝	摴	摶	摲
E	摳	摽	摵	摦	撦	摎	撂	摞	摜	摋	摓	摠	摐	摿	搿	摬
F	摫	摙	摥	摷	敳	斠	暡	暠	暟	朅	朄	朢	榱	榶	槉	

Row E2	0	1	2	3	4	5	6	7	8	9	A	B	C	D	E	F
4	榠	槎	榖	榰	榬	榼	榑	榙	榎	榧	榍	榩	榾	榯	榿	槄
5	榽	榤	槔	榹	槊	榚	槏	榳	槛	榪	榡	榞	槙	榗	榐	槂
6	榵	榥	榒	歊	歍	歋	殞	殟	殠	毃	毄	毾	滎	滵	滱	漃
7	漥	滸	漷	滻	漮	漉	潎	漙	漚	漧	漘	漻	漒	滭	漊	
A		漶	潳	滹	滮	漭	潀	漰	漼	漵	滫	漇	漎	潃	漅	滽
B	滶	漹	漜	滼	漺	漟	漍	漞	漈	漡	熇	熐	熉	熀	熅	熂
C	熏	煻	熆	熁	熗	牄	牓	犗	犕	犓	獃	獍	獑	獌	瑢	瑳
D	瑱	瑵	瑲	瑧	瑮	甀	甂	甃	畽	疐	瘖	瘈	瘌	瘕	瘑	瘊
E	瘔	皸	瞁	睼	瞅	瞂	睮	瞀	睯	睾	瞃	碲	碪	碴	碭	碨
F	硾	碫	碞	碥	碠	碬	碢	碤	禘	禊	禋	禖	禕	禔	禓	

Row E3	0	1	2	3	4	5	6	7	8	9	A	B	C	D	E	F
4	禗	禈	禒	禐	稫	穊	稰	稯	稨	稦	窨	窫	窬	竮	箈	箜
5	箊	箑	箐	箖	箍	箌	箛	箎	箅	箘	劄	箙	箤	箂	粻	粿
6	粼	粺	綧	綷	緂	綣	綪	緁	緀	緅	綝	緎	緄	緆	緋	緌
7	綯	綹	綖	綼	綟	綦	綮	綩	綡	緉	罳	翢	翣	翥	翞	
A		耤	聝	聜	膉	膆	膃	膇	膍	膌	膋	舕	蒗	蒤	蒡	蒟
B	蒺	蓎	蓂	蒬	蒮	蒫	蒹	蒴	蓁	蓍	蒪	蒚	蒱	蓐	蒝	蒧
C	蒻	蒢	蒔	蓇	蓌	蒛	蒩	蒯	蒨	蓖	蒘	蒶	蓏	蒠	蓗	蓔
D	蓒	蓛	蒰	蒑	虡	蜳	蜣	蜨	蝫	蝀	蜮	蜞	蜡	蜙	蜛	蝃
E	蜬	蝁	蜾	蝆	蜠	蜲	蜪	蜭	蜼	蜒	蜺	蜱	蜵	蝂	蜦	蜧
F	蜸	蜤	蜚	蜰	蜑	裷	裧	裱	裲	裺	裾	裮	裼	裶	裻	

Row E4	0	1	2	3	4	5	6	7	8	9	A	B	C	D	E	F
4	裰	裬	裫	覝	覡	覟	覞	觩	觫	觨	誫	誙	誋	誒	誏	誖
5	谽	豨	豩	賕	賏	賗	趖	踉	踂	跿	踍	跽	踊	踃	踇	踆
6	踅	跾	踀	踄	輐	輑	輎	輍	鄣	鄜	鄠	鄢	鄟	鄝	鄚	鄤
7	鄡	鄛	酺	酲	酹	酳	銥	銤	鉶	銛	鉺	銠	銔	銪	銍	
A		銦	銚	銫	鉹	銗	鉿	銣	鋮	銎	銂	銕	銢	鉽	銈	銡
B	銊	銆	銌	銙	銧	銋	銇	銩	銝	鋋	鉴	隞	隡	雿	靘	靽
C	靺	靾	鞃	鞀	鞂	靻	鞄	鞁	靿	韎	韍	頖	颭	颮	餂	餀
D	餇	馝	馜	駃	馹	駀	馺	駍	馽	駇	骱	髣	髧	鬾	鬿	魠
E	魡	魟	鳿	鳲	鳵	麧	僿	儃	儰	僸	儆	儇	僶	僾	儋	儌
F	僽	儊	剸	劌	勱	勯	噈	噂	噌	嘵	噁	噊	噉	噆	噘	

Row E5	0	1	2	3	4	5	6	7	8	9	A	B	C	D	E	F
4	噚	噀	噴	嘽	嘬	嘾	嘸	嘪	嘺	圚	墫	墝	墱	墠	墣	憻
5	墬	墥	墡	壿	嫿	嫴	嫽	嫞	嫶	嬃	嫸	嬂	嫹	嬁	嬇	嬅
6	嬏	屧	嶙	嶗	嶟	嶒	嶢	嶓	嶕	嶠	嶜	嶡	嶚	嶞	幘	幝
7	幠	幜	緳	廛	廞	廡	彉	徲	憋	憃	慹	憱	憰	憢	憉	
A		憛	憓	憯	憭	憟	憒	憪	憡	憍	慦	憳	戭	撆	擎	撖
B	擨	撅	撗	撜	撏	撋	撊	撌	撣	撟	撨	撱	撘	敶	敺	敹
C	敻	斲	斳	暵	暰	暩	暲	暷	暪	暯	樀	樆	樗	樥	槸	樕
D	樖	槤	樠	槿	㯳	槢	樛	樝	槾	樧	槲	槮	樔	槷	槧	橀
E	樈	槦	槻	樍	槼	槫	樉	樄	樘	樥	樏	槶	樦	樇	樞	歈
F	歒	殥	殣	殢	殦	氁	氀	毿	氂	潁	漦	潾	澇	濆	澒	

Row E6	0	1	2	3	4	5	6	7	8	9	A	B	C	D	E	F
4	澍	澉	澌	潢	潏	澅	潚	澖	潶	潬	澂	潕	潲	潒	潐	潗
5	澔	澓	滃	漀	潡	潫	潽	潧	澐	潓	澋	潩	潿	澕	潣	潷
6	潪	潻	熲	熯	熛	熰	熠	熚	熩	熵	熝	熥	熞	熤	熡	熪
7	熜	熧	熳	犘	犚	獘	獒	獞	獟	獠	獝	獛	獡	獚	獙	
A		獢	璇	璉	璊	璆	璁	瑽	璅	璈	瑼	瑧	甂	甃	畾	瘥
B	瘞	瘙	瘵	瘜	瘣	瘚	瘨	瘛	皜	皝	皞	皛	瞍	瞏	瞉	瞈
C	磍	碻	磏	磌	磑	磎	磔	磈	磃	磄	磉	禚	禡	禠	禜	禢
D	禛	嶲	稹	窲	窴	窳	箷	篋	箾	箬	篎	箯	箹	篊	箵	糅
E	糈	糌	糋	緷	緛	緪	緧	緗	緡	縃	緺	緦	緶	緱	緰	緮
F	緟	罶	羬	羰	羭	翭	翫	翪	翬	翦	翨	聤	聧	膣	膟	

Row E7	0	1	2	3	4	5	6	7	8	9	A	B	C	D	E	F
4	膞	膕	膢	腦	膗	舖	艄	艓	艒	艐	艎	艑	蔤	蔻	蔏	蔀
5	蔩	蔎	蔉	蔍	蔟	蔊	蔧	蔜	蓻	蔫	蓺	蔈	蔌	蓴	蔪	蓲
6	蔕	蓷	蓫	蓳	蓼	蕏	蓪	蓩	蓖	蓾	蔨	蔝	蔮	蔂	蕐	蔞
7	蓶	蔱	蔦	蓧	蓨	蓰	蓯	蓹	蔘	蔠	蔰	蔋	蔙	蔯	虢	
A		蝖	蝣	蝤	蝷	蟡	蝳	蝘	蝔	蝛	蝒	蝡	蝚	蝑	蝞	蝭
B	蝪	蝐	蝎	蝟	蝝	蝯	蝬	蝺	蝮	蝜	蝥	蝏	蝻	蝵	蝢	蝧
C	蝩	衚	褅	褌	褔	褋	褗	褘	褙	褆	褖	褑	褎	褉	覢	覤
D	覣	觭	觰	觬	諏	諆	誸	諓	諑	諔	諕	誻	諗	誾	諀	諅
E	諘	諃	諌	説	語	谾	豍	貏	賥	賟	賙	賨	賚	賝	賧	趠
F	趜	趡	趛	踠	踣	踥	踤	踮	踕	踛	踖	踑	踙	踦	踧	

Row E8	0	1	2	3	4	5	6	7	8	9	A	B	C	D	E	F
4	踔	踒	踘	踓	踜	踗	踚	輬	輤	輘	輚	輠	輣	輖	輗	遳
5	遰	遯	遧	遫	鄯	鄫	鄩	鄪	鄲	鄦	鄮	醅	醆	醊	醁	醂
6	醄	醀	鋐	鋃	鋄	鋀	鋙	銶	鋏	鋱	鋟	鋘	鋩	鋗	鋝	鋌
7	鋯	鋂	鋨	鋊	鋈	鋎	鋦	鋍	鋕	鋉	鋠	鋞	鋧	鋑	鋓	
A		銵	鋡	鋆	銴	镼	閬	閫	閮	閰	隤	隢	雓	霅	霈	霂
B	靚	鞊	鞎	鞈	鞐	鞏	頞	頝	頦	頩	頨	頠	頛	頧	颲	餈
C	飺	餑	餔	餖	餗	餕	駜	駍	駏	駓	駔	駎	駉	駖	駘	駋
D	駗	駌	骳	髬	髫	髳	髲	髱	魆	魃	魧	魴	魱	魦	魶	魵
E	魰	魨	魤	魬	鴋	鴃	鴅	鴗	鴑	鴙	鴘	鴓	鴝	鴈	鴖	鴫
F	麀	黓	鼏	鼐	儜	儓	儗	儚	儑	凞	匴	叡	嚀	噠	嚄	

Row E9	0	1	2	3	4	5	6	7	8	9	A	B	C	D	E	F
4	嘆	噦	噣	噭	噲	噞	噉	圜	圛	壈	墽	壉	墿	墺	壂	墼
5	壆	嬗	嬙	嬛	嬡	嬔	嬓	嬐	嬖	嬨	嬚	嬠	嬞	寯	嶬	嶱
6	嶩	嶧	嶵	嶰	嶮	嶪	嶨	嶲	嶭	嶯	嶴	幧	幨	幦	幯	廩
7	廧	廦	廨	廥	彋	徼	憝	憨	憖	懅	憴	懆	懁	懌	憺	
A		憿	憸	憌	擗	擖	擐	擏	擉	撽	擊	擃	擛	擳	擙	攳
B	敿	敼	斢	曈	暾	曀	曊	曋	曏	暽	暻	暺	曌	朣	樴	橦
C	橉	橧	樲	橨	樾	橝	橭	橶	橛	橑	樨	橚	樻	樿	橗	橪
D	檠	橐	橏	橔	橯	橩	橠	樳	橞	檏	樽	橍	橎	橆	歕	歔
E	歖	殧	殪	殫	毈	毇	氄	氃	氆	澭	濋	澣	濇	澼	濎	濈
F	潞	濄	澽	澞	濊	澨	瀄	澥	澮	澺	澬	澪	濏	澿	澸	

Row EA	0	1	2	3	4	5	6	7	8	9	A	B	C	D	E	F
4	澢	濉	澫	濨	潹	澲	澰	燅	燂	熿	熸	燖	燀	燁	燋	燔
5	燊	燇	燏	燫	燗	熼	燆	燚	燢	犝	犞	獩	獦	獧	獬	獥
6	獫	獪	瑿	璚	璠	璔	璒	璕	璡	甗	鞬	瘯	瘭	瘱	瘴	瘳
7	瘼	瘵	瘲	瘰	皻	盦	瞚	瞝	瞡	瞜	瞛	瞢	瞣	瞕	瞙	
A		瞗	礉	磩	磥	磪	磞	磣	磛	磡	磢	磆	磟	磠	褶	穄
B	穈	穇	窶	窸	窵	窱	窷	篞	篣	篧	篝	篕	篥	篚	篨	篹
C	篔	篪	簀	篜	篫	篛	篟	糒	糔	糗	糐	糑	縒	綷	縗	縌
D	縟	縠	縓	縃	縜	縕	縚	縢	縋	繄	縖	縍	緣	縥	縳	罃
E	罻	罼	罽	羱	翯	耪	耩	聬	膱	膦	膮	膹	膵	膫	膰	臕
F	膴	膲	膷	膧	艄	艕	艖	艗	蕖	蕅	蕫	蕍	蕓	蒷	蕘	

Row EB	0	1	2	3	4	5	6	7	8	9	A	B	C	D	E	F
4	蕀	蕆	蕤	蕁	蕢	蕄	蕑	蕇	蕣	蔾	蕛	蕱	蕎	蕮	蕵	蕕
5	蕧	蕠	薌	蕦	蕝	蕔	蕥	蕬	虣	虥	虤	螛	螏	螗	螓	螒
6	螈	螁	螖	螘	蝹	螇	螣	螅	螐	螑	螝	螄	螔	螜	螚	螉
7	褞	褦	褰	褭	褮	褧	褱	褢	褩	褣	褯	褬	褟	觱	諠	
A		諢	諲	諴	諵	諝	謔	諤	諟	諰	諈	諞	諡	諨	諿	諯
B	諻	貑	貒	貐	賵	賮	賱	賰	賳	赬	赮	趥	趧	踳	踾	踸
C	蹀	蹅	踶	踼	踽	蹁	踰	踿	躽	輶	輮	輵	輲	輹	輷	輴
D	遶	遹	遻	邆	郺	鄳	鄵	鄶	醓	醐	醑	醍	醏	錧	錞	錈
E	錟	錆	錏	鍺	錸	錼	錛	錣	錒	錁	鍆	錭	錎	錍	鋋	錝
F	鋺	錥	錓	鋹	鋷	錴	錂	錤	鋿	錩	錹	錵	錪	錔	錌	

Row EC	0	1	2	3	4	5	6	7	8	9	A	B	C	D	E	F
4	錋	鋾	錉	錀	鋻	鋈	閼	闍	閾	閹	閺	閶	閿	閵	閽	隩
5	雔	霋	霒	霐	鞙	鞗	鞔	韰	韸	頛	頠	頲	餤	餟	餧	餩
6	馞	駮	駬	駥	駤	駰	駣	駪	駩	駧	骹	骿	骴	骻	髶	髺
7	髹	髷	鬳	鮀	鮅	鮇	魼	魾	魻	鮂	鮓	鮒	鮐	魺	鮎	
A		魽	鮈	鴥	鴗	鴠	鴞	鴯	鴆	鴘	鴅	鴑	鴐	鴂	鴖	麈
B	麆	麇	麮	麭	黕	黖	黺	鼒	鼽	儦	儥	儢	儤	儠	儩	勴
C	嚓	嚌	嚍	嚆	嚄	嚃	噾	嚂	噿	嚁	壖	壔	壏	壒	嬭	嬥
D	嬲	嬣	嬬	嬧	嬦	嬯	嬮	孻	寱	寲	嶷	幬	幪	徾	徻	懃
E	憵	憼	懧	懠	懥	懤	懨	懞	擯	擩	擣	擫	擤	擨	斁	斀
F	斶	旚	曒	檍	檖	檁	檥	檉	檟	檛	檡	檞	檇	檓	檎	

Row ED	0	1	2	3	4	5	6	7	8	9	A	B	C	D	E	F
4	檕	檗	檨	檤	檑	橿	檦	檚	檅	檌	檒	歛	殭	氉	黏	欅
5	澯	濔	濣	濜	濭	濧	濦	濞	濲	濸	澤	濨	燡	燱	燨	燪
6	燸	燰	爂	獳	獮	獯	璗	璲	璫	璐	璪	璭	璱	璥	璯	甐
7	甑	甒	甓	疄	癃	癈	癉	癇	皤	盩	瞵	瞫	瞲	瞷	瞶	
A		瞴	瞱	瞨	矰	磳	磽	礂	磻	磼	磲	礅	磹	磾	礄	禫
B	禨	穜	穛	穖	穘	穔	穚	窾	竀	竁	簅	簏	簨	簣	簙	簟
C	簎	篴	篹	簞	簂	簉	簃	簁	篸	篽	簒	篰	篱	簌	簺	糙
D	縭	縼	繂	縳	顈	縸	縪	繉	繀	繇	縩	縬	縰	縻	縶	繄
E	縺	罅	罿	罾	罽	翴	翲	耬	膻	臄	臌	臊	臅	臇	膼	臩
F	艛	艚	艜	蕖	蕰	薏	蕘	薕	薠	薋	薣	藄	薙	薚	薞	

Row EE	0	1	2	3	4	5	6	7	8	9	A	B	C	D	E	F
4	蕷	蕼	薉	薡	蕺	蕸	蕗	薎	薖	薆	薍	蕹	薝	薁	薢	薂
5	薈	薵	薭	蕶	薘	薐	薟	虨	蠙	螪	螭	蟅	螰	螬	螹	螵
6	螼	螮	蟉	蟃	蟂	蟌	䗪	螯	蟄	蟊	蟘	蟲	蟚	螢	蠡	蟞
7	螲	褵	褳	褼	褾	襁	襒	褷	襂	覎	覯	覺	觲	觳	謞	
A		謘	謖	謑	謅	謋	謢	謏	謒	謕	謇	謍	謈	謆	謜	謓
B	謚	豏	豰	豲	豱	豯	貕	貔	賧	赯	蹎	蹍	蹓	蹐	蹌	蹇
C	轃	轀	邅	遾	鄸	醚	醘	醛	醙	醟	醡	醝	醠	鎡	鎃	鎯
D	銛	鍖	鍇	鍼	鍘	鍜	鍶	鍉	鍐	鍑	鍠	鍭	鎏	鎣	鍪	鍹
E	鍗	鍕	鍒	鍏	鍱	鍷	鍻	鍡	鍞	鍣	鍧	鎀	鍎	鍫	闇	闍
F	闉	闃	闅	䦧	隮	隰	隬	霋	霟	霘	霝	霙	鞚	鞡	鞜	

Row EF	0	1	2	3	4	5	6	7	8	9	A	B	C	D	E	F
4	鞞	鞝	鞟	韔	韱	頯	頢	頣	頦	頧	頪	飺	餫	餬	餪	餳
5	餲	餯	餭	餱	餰	馘	馣	馡	騂	駺	駴	駷	駹	駸	駶	駻
6	駽	駾	駼	騃	骾	髾	髽	鬁	鬈	魈	鮚	鮨	鮞	鮇	鮦	鮡
7	鮥	鮤	鮆	鮢	鮠	鮯	鴳	鵁	鵧	鴶	鴮	鵒	鵊	鵅	鵇	
A		鵮	鵩	鵃	鵢	鵷	鵻	鴐	鵹	鵖	麙	麍	黂	麮	黈	黚
B	黻	鼂	鼤	鼣	鼢	齔	龠	儱	儭	儮	嚘	嚜	嚗	嚚	嚝	嚙
C	嬰	嬼	屩	屫	巀	幭	幮	瀵	懟	懭	懮	懱	懪	懰	懫	懖
D	懩	擿	攄	擽	攌	攁	攃	擼	䩟	旛	曚	曛	曘	櫅	檹	檽
E	櫡	櫆	櫲	榼	檷	櫇	檴	檭	歖	毉	氋	瀇	瀌	瀍	瀁	瀅
F	瀔	瀎	濿	瀀	濻	瀦	濼	灊	瀊	爁	燿	燹	爍	燽	獶	

Row F0	0	1	2	3	4	5	6	7	8	9	A	B	C	D	E	F
4	璸	瓀	璵	瓁	璾	璶	璻	瓂	甔	甓	癜	癤	癙	癐	癓	癗
5	癚	皦	皽	盬	矂	瞺	磿	礌	礓	礔	礉	礐	礒	礑	禭	禬
6	穟	簜	簩	簙	簠	簟	簭	簝	簦	簨	簢	簥	簰	繜	繐	繖
7	繣	繘	繢	繟	繑	繠	繗	繓	羵	羳	翷	翸	聵	臑	臒	
A		臐	艟	艞	薴	藆	藀	藃	藂	薳	薵	薽	藇	藄	薿	藋
B	藎	藈	藅	薱	薶	藒	蘤	薸	薷	薾	虩	蟧	蟦	蟢	蟛	蟫
C	蟪	蟥	蟟	蟳	蟤	蟔	蟜	蟓	蟭	蟘	蟣	螤	蟗	蟙	蠁	蟴
D	蟨	蟝	襓	襋	襏	襌	襆	襐	襑	襉	謪	謧	謣	謳	謰	謵
E	譇	謯	謼	謾	謱	謥	謷	謦	謶	謮	謤	謻	謽	謺	豂	豵
F	貙	貘	貗	賾	贄	賿	賢	蹈	蹢	蹠	蹗	踣	蹞	蹥	蹧	

Row F1	0	1	2	3	4	5	6	7	8	9	A	B	C	D	E	F
4	蹛	蹚	蹡	蹝	蹩	蹔	轆	轇	轈	轋	鄨	鄺	鄻	鄾	醨	醥
5	醧	醘	醪	鎵	鎌	鎒	鎷	鎛	鎝	鎉	鎧	鎎	鎪	鎞	鎦	鎕
6	鎈	鎙	鎟	鎍	鎱	鎑	鎲	鎤	鎨	鎴	鎣	鎥	闒	闓	闑	隓
7	雗	雚	巂	雟	雘	雝	霣	霢	霥	鞬	鞮	鞨	鞫	鞤	鞪	
A		鞢	鞥	韗	韙	韖	韘	韺	顐	顑	顒	颸	饁	餼	餺	騏
B	騋	騉	騍	騄	騑	騊	騅	騇	騆	髀	髜	鬈	鬄	鬅	鬩	鬵
C	魊	魌	魋	鯇	鯆	鯃	鮿	鯁	鮵	鮸	鯓	鮶	鯄	鮹	鮽	鵜
D	鵓	鵏	鵊	鵛	鵋	鵙	鵖	鵌	鵗	鵒	鵔	鵟	鵘	鵚	麎	麌
E	黟	鼁	鼀	鼖	鼥	鼫	鼪	鼩	鼨	齌	齕	儴	儵	劖	勷	厴
F	嚫	嚭	嚦	嚧	嚪	嚬	壚	壝	壛	夒	嬽	嬾	嬿	巃	幰	

Row F2	0	1	2	3	4	5	6	7	8	9	A	B	C	D	E	F
4	徿	懻	攇	攐	攍	攉	攌	攎	斄	旞	旝	曞	櫧	櫠	櫌	櫑
5	櫙	櫋	櫟	櫜	櫐	櫫	櫏	櫍	櫞	歠	殰	氌	瀙	瀧	瀠	瀖
6	瀫	瀡	瀢	瀣	瀩	瀗	瀤	瀜	瀪	爌	爊	爇	爂	爅	犥	犦
7	犤	犣	犡	瓋	瓅	璷	瓃	甖	癠	矉	矊	矄	矱	礝	礛	
A		礡	礜	礥	礞	禰	穧	穨	簳	簼	簹	簬	簻	糬	糪	繶
B	繵	繸	繰	繷	繯	繺	繲	繴	繨	罋	罊	羃	羆	羷	翽	翾
C	聸	臗	臕	艤	艡	艣	艫	艱	藭	藙	藡	藨	藚	藗	藬	藲
D	藸	藘	藟	藣	藜	藑	藰	藦	藯	藞	藢	蠀	蟺	蠃	蟶	蟷
E	蠉	蠌	蠋	蠆	蟼	蠈	蟿	蠊	蠂	襢	襚	襛	襗	襡	襜	襘
F	襝	襙	覈	覷	覶	觶	譐	譈	譊	譀	譓	譖	譔	譋	譕	

Row F3	0	1	2	3	4	5	6	7	8	9	A	B	C	D	E	F
4	譑	譂	譒	譇	徵	豷	豶	貚	賰	贊	贉	趬	趪	趭	趫	蹭
5	蹸	蹳	蹪	蹯	蹻	軂	轒	轑	轏	轐	轓	辴	酀	鄿	醰	醭
6	鏞	鏇	鏏	鏂	鏚	鏐	鏹	鏬	鏌	鏙	錣	鏦	鏊	鑌	鏮	鏣
7	鏕	鏄	鏎	鏑	鏒	鏧	蹽	闚	闛	雗	霩	霫	霬	霨	霦	
A		鞳	鞷	鞶	韝	韞	韟	顜	顙	顝	顗	颿	飃	颻	飂	饎
B	饇	饃	馦	馧	騚	騕	騥	騝	騤	騛	騢	騠	騧	騣	騞	騜
C	騔	髂	鬋	鬊	鬎	鬌	鬷	鯪	鯫	鯠	鯞	鯤	鯦	鯢	鯰	鯔
D	鯗	鯬	鯜	鯙	鯥	鯕	鯡	鯚	鵷	鵼	鵩	鵲	鵺	鵹	鶀	鶅
E	鵸	鶌	鶗	鵽	鶉	鶊	鶒	鶓	鶕	鶹	鶬	鵰	鶠	鶤	鶩	鶪
F	鵯	鶮	麔	麑	麌	黼	鼭	鼏	鼩	齌	齖	齗	齘	匷	嚲	

Row F4	0	1	2	3	4	5	6	7	8	9	A	B	C	D	E	F
4	嚵	嚳	囃	孅	巆	巇	廮	廯	忀	徾	懹	攗	攖	攕	攓	旟
5	曨	曣	曤	櫳	櫰	櫪	櫨	櫹	櫱	櫮	櫯	瀼	瀵	瀯	瀷	瀴
6	瀱	灂	瀸	瀿	瀺	瀹	灀	瀻	瀳	灁	爓	爔	犨	獽	獼	璺
7	皫	皪	皾	盭	矌	矎	矏	矍	矲	礥	礣	礧	礨	礤	礩	
A		禲	穮	穬	穭	竷	籉	籈	籊	籇	籅	糮	繻	繾	纁	纀
B	羺	翷	耰	臐	臑	臒	艨	艩	蘢	藿	蘁	藾	蘛	蘀	藶	蘄
C	蘎	蘅	蘌	蘔	蠙	蠐	蠑	蠗	蠓	蠖	襓	襦	聰	覺	譠	譪
D	譝	譨	譣	譥	譧	譭	趮	躆	躈	躄	轙	轖	轗	轕	轘	轚
E	邍	酄	酅	醷	醹	醲	醳	鐋	鐓	鏻	鐠	鐏	鐔	鐌	鐕	鐐
F	鑟	鐙	鐍	鏎	鐼	鐷	鐇	鐎	鐖	鐒	鏺	鐉	鏸	鐊	鐆	

Row F5	0	1	2	3	4	5	6	7	8	9	A	B	C	D	E	F
4	鏿	鐌	鏶	鏴	鐩	闞	闠	闤	霵	霯	鞹	鞻	韽	韾	顠	顢
5	顣	顟	飁	飂	饐	饎	饙	饌	饋	饓	騲	騴	騱	騬	騪	騶
6	騩	騮	騸	騭	髇	髊	髆	鬐	鬒	鬑	鰋	鰈	鯷	鰅	鰒	鯸
7	鱀	鰇	鰎	鰆	鰗	鰔	鰉	鶟	鶙	鶤	鶝	鶒	鶘	鶐	鶛	
A		鶠	鶔	鶜	鶪	鶗	鶡	鶚	鶢	鶨	鶞	鶣	鶿	鶩	鶖	鶦
B	鶧	麙	麛	麚	黥	黤	黧	黦	鼰	鼮	齛	齠	齞	齝	齙	龑
C	儺	儹	劘	劗	囃	嚽	嚾	孈	孇	巋	巏	廱	懽	攛	欂	櫼
D	欃	櫸	欀	灃	灄	灊	灈	灉	灅	灆	爝	爚	爙	獾	甗	癪
E	矐	礭	礱	礯	籔	籓	糲	纊	纇	纈	纋	纆	纍	罍	羻	耰
F	臝	蘘	蘪	蘦	蘟	蘣	蘜	蘙	蘧	蘮	蘡	蘠	蘩	蘞	蘥	

Row F6	0	1	2	3	4	5	6	7	8	9	A	B	C	D	E	F
4	蠩	蠝	蠛	蠠	蠤	蠜	蠫	巇	襭	襩	襮	襫	觺	譹	譸	譅
5	譺	譻	贐	贔	趯	躎	躌	轞	轛	轝	酆	酄	酅	醹	鐿	鐻
6	鐶	鐩	鐽	鐼	鐰	鐹	鐪	鐷	鐬	鑀	鐱	闤	闠	闟	霩	霺
7	鞿	韡	顤	飉	飂	飀	饘	饖	騹	騽	驆	驄	驂	驁	驇	
A		騿	髍	鬕	鬗	鬘	鬖	鬺	魒	鰫	鰝	鰜	鰬	鰣	鰨	鰩
B	鰤	鰡	鶓	鶂	鶋	鶌	鷇	鶅	鶍	鶾	鶗	鶘	鶙	鶒	鶠	鶡
C	鶬	鶣	鷈	鶱	鶯	騢	鷉	鶹	鶺	鹺	麢	黫	黮	黭	鼛	鼘
D	饕	鼶	齎	齥	蠭	龔	亹	囆	囅	囋	奱	孋	孌	巕	巑	廲
E	攤	攠	攦	攢	欋	欌	欑	氍	灘	灖	灗	灒	爞	爟	犪	玃
F	瓘	瓕	瓖	瓗	癭	矔	礵	禴	穰	穱	籗	籜	籙	籛	籚	

Row F7	0	1	2	3	4	5	6	7	8	9	A	B	C	D	E	F
4	羅	蘗	纑	罏	羇	臞	艫	蘴	蘵	蘳	蘬	蘺	蘶	蠬	蠨	蠦
5	襲	豅	襱	覼	覿	觻	讂	讄	讅	讆	譒	讃	贕	躕	躔	躚
6	躒	躐	躖	躛	轠	轢	酇	鑌	鑐	鑊	鑋	鑏	鑇	鑠	鑈	鑉
7	鑆	霿	韣	顪	顩	飋	饔	饛	驎	驓	驔	驌	驏	騷	驊	
A		驉	驒	驐	髐	鬙	鬫	鬻	魖	魕	鱆	鱈	鰿	鱄	鰹	鱂
B	鱁	鰼	鰷	徽	鰲	鰽	鰶	鷉	鶾	鷃	鷊	鷏	鷓	鷒	鷂	鷙
C	鷩	鷙	鷔	鷖	鷗	鷕	鷤	麷	黰	鼨	鼰	鼳	鼞	齹	龕	龢
D	儽	劙	壨	壧	奲	孍	巘	廮	彏	戁	儻	戄	攩	攥	曡	曫
E	欑	欒	欐	馨	灡	灚	爢	獑	獵	玃	癰	矔	籧	籦	纕	艬
F	蘺	蘷	櫰	蘼	蘛	蘻	褱	蠰	蠲	蠽	蠳	襶	襴	襳	觾	

Row F8	0	1	2	3	4	5	6	7	8	9	A	B	C	D	E	F
4	讌	讎	讋	讈	襱	贊	躘	轤	轣	醼	鑢	鑕	鑝	鑗	鑞	韄
5	韅	頀	驖	驙	鬞	鬢	鬠	鱒	鱘	鱐	鱊	鱍	鱋	鱕	鱙	鱌
6	鱎	鷟	鷷	鶾	鸏	鷫	鷸	鷤	鷶	鷡	鷮	鷦	鷲	鷰	鷢	鷬
7	鷳	鷴	鷨	鷱	麡	麶	黲	黳	鼀	鼜	鼶	鼷	鼸	鼳	齋	
A		齱	齰	齮	齯	囓	嚞	孎	屭	攭	曭	曮	欓	灟	灡	灝
B	灚	爣	瓛	蠡	變	礸	禷	襸	籪	纗	纞	艭	蘵	蠸	蠷	蠵
C	蠹	譾	讕	躞	躟	躠	躝	醾	醽	釂	鑫	鑨	鑸	雥	靆	靃
D	靇	韇	韥	驞	髕	鬤	鱣	鱧	鱦	鱢	鱞	鱠	鸂	鸃	鸇	鱶
E	鸆	鸏	鸐	羸	鸉	鸑	鸒	鸞	鼊	鼙	龖	齴	齵	齶	囔	攮
F	斸	欘	欙	欗	欚	灢	爦	犪	矘	矙	礹	籩	籫	糶	纚	

Row F9	0	1	2	3	4	5	6	7	8	9	A	B	C	D	E	F
4	纘	纛	纚	臠	臡	虆	虇	虈	襹	襺	襼	襻	觿	讘	讙	躥
5	躤	躣	鑮	鑭	鑯	鑱	鑳	靉	顲	饟	鱨	鱮	鱭	鸋	鸍	鸐
6	鸏	鸒	鸑	麡	黵	鼉	齇	齸	齻	齺	齹	圞	灝	籯	蠼	趲
7	躦	釃	鑴	鑸	鑶	鑵	驠	鱴	鱳	鱱	鱵	鸔	鸓	黶	鼊	
A		龤	灨	灥	糷	虪	蠾	蠿	鑾	讞	玃	躩	軉	靂	顳	顴
B	飌	饡	馫	驤	驦	驧	鬤	鸕	鸗	齈	戇	欞	爧	虌	躨	钂
C	钀	钁	驩	驨	鬮	鸙	爩	虋	讟	钃	鱹	麷	癵	驫	鱺	鸝
D	灩	灪	麤	齾	齉	龘										
E																
F																

I

Hong Kong GCCS Table

This appendix constitutes a complete code table for the 3,049 hanzi defined in Hong Hong GCCS, as described in Chapter 3, *Character Set Standards*. The characters are printed using Monotype's 宋體 (MSung-Light) typeface design. Also included is an additional set of 145 hanzi specified by Hong Kong's Department of Judiciary. Unlike the other code tables in this book, this code table is indexed by hexadecimal Big Five values. This is because the Big Five character set and its encoding does not, unfortunately, fit the usual 94×94 model.

Row 8E	0	1	2	3	4	5	6	7	8	9	A	B	C	D	E	F
4	湪	埕	程	焾	稭		椽	鐟	舂	穉	穪	頮	𥟂	穽	窞	寭
5	窨	竂	竈	燑	翻	竑	竚	竝	竪	笡	咲	箍	笲	筕	笩	䁸
6	筠	箢	筋	筱	筗	莜	篭	菹	籌	箸	纂		筱	篩	𥲤	篹
7	簬	籚	簣	粃	㹻	莽		粧	糉	糇	糦	籴	繫	糵	糎	
A		繧	䓞	綤	絝	蓫		綉	綫	焵	綳	緒	𤄓	緞	緤	𣸣
B	𦃙	嫩	綵	轉	縝	緆	繇	繮	纏	纜	鑬	縧	銚	鋼	鐏	礶
C	罩	罵	羌	羗	羣	羨	𤕭	萃	檡		輸	翺	熠	者	耇	耝
D	耨	耬	䳯	耶	耻	聃	聡	恕	嗢	肇	泂	膀	朥	肧	錆	脇
E	脚	墰	恧	汓	翻		擧	壆	舘	𡢃	橓	㻐	𤩱	䑺	舩	
F	𦨣	𣶭	俹	壎	萠	荢	芑	𤥶	𣐤	𡛟	𣳟	芪	椛	劳	笁	

Row 8F	0	1	2	3	4	5	6	7	8	9	A	B	C	D	E	F
4	蒁	茀	茚	咚	媄	姘	昆	棧	芳	苜	荔	湇	烮	苫	菌	楏
5	焞	茝	啇	菈	萩	蒳	菟	菁	菓		萲	楄	蕚	儰	䅗	
6	菑	篫	葱	熜	蔥	檧	莽		祘	蒨	芺	蓓	蓓	莒	莒	葎
7	芊	蒓	蔆	蔓	蕉	蔚	蔭	蔴	嫲	萃	蔾	蔄	蔆	栟	蘖	
A		遺	還	藁	藻	蘂	夒	夔	夔	濹	蘇	埦	嫭	号	蝦	虾
B	蝨	鴹	蟮	搒	蠠	蠫	蟹	噜	虬	楓	郵	蚌	衆	衍	洐	衎
C	衞	袜	褍	袴	袏		装		褻	覇	覊	覞	覩	覽	觀	鍒
D	觧	觿	譖	詨	詶	訝	誐	誳	諠	諦		譔	譛	爝	詗	謟
E	砈	磭	譋	譌	譍	諳	璣	讐	讔	詚	娍	衏	衎	貜	貝	貢
F	貫	嬛	昭	賖	賚	賜	贊	聰	嬻	賛	瀛	贑		琝	起	

Row 90	0	1	2	3	4	5	6	7	8	9	A	B	C	D	E	F
4	趧	趸	喀	瑢	楷	蹰	躉	竧	躭	躲	軃	鋺	輙	輭	輹	辞
5	辪	鋈	軞	辰	蔯	錸	鍶	迦	迣	迪	䟾	迹			逌	逞
6	逢	蓮	逿	遊	遜	遡	遻	遨	邨	郎	郄	郌	郮	都	酧	
7	醩	醾	粬	蘲	崖	鈎	沟	鈐	鉢	鉶	銹	鋋	釆	錕	鐢	
A		嘓	鍊	鍪	鍵	鎛		媜	鏑	鏨	鐮	鉃	鐶	鑾	鑑	鍳
B	鑛	鋹	閅	閔	鐗	閨	潤	紆		郢	坣	淦	陷	氰	陻	隝
C	穃	隣	蔭	憶	隶	碉	錐	隽	双	闇	萠	俌	叟	霂	霝	瓌
D	嬃	曔	霮	蕗	霶	霙	澫	蘦	瓀	灵	霻	霚	靜	彭	靟	嬚
E	孶	毪	鞳	偆	靳	靳	鞦	鞟	鞱	鞾	韉	韒	韓	硎	韮	琜
F	頡	響	韵	韸	詾	頟	頴	頼	顒	顛	縣	韡	濵	凶	瀷	

Row 91	0	1	2	3	4	5	6	7	8	9	A	B	C	D	E	F
4	颹	飆	颾	飈	飃	颳	䬙	姘	喰	滄	飦	餋	餬	餹	瑳	錡
5	馛	駶	騑	騌	騋	騐	贏	䄻	㛹	雺	鬆	髡	髢	髯	鬋	鬒
6	鬔	鬭	遉	侎	鬴		鬻	魁	魆	魐	魑	婅	婳	鮎		鯽
7	鯿	鰌	鰕	鷔	鳷	鴴	鵦	鵵	鴻	鷩	鶡	鶂	鷩	鸓		
A		鷄		鶵	鸇	孅	驪	羯	鶒	麌	麐	麛	麞	麤	黏	麪
B	麯	燁	麿	桄	挄	黎	伲	岻	钄	黿	鼈	騆	鏰	蔬	鼗	鼖
C	鼹	嚓	嗅	齅	斲	霂	齏	萺	齡	齩	竜	龎	爖	驡	琜	琓
D	熿	瑴	燈	瓛	玞	鐃	嬈	禟	鈃	阡	鍩	鐿	鍉	鋈	鎁	鏀
E	鋻	爗	燁	琕	瞠	榕	焫	爈	熐	熜	媤	炣	嫖	榚	琟	嫤
F	砿	嫆	嫂	妺	嫦	婉	娡	嬪	簽	嬨	妭	坛	璃	埼	垓	

Row 92	0	1	2	3	4	5	6	7	8	9	A	B	C	D	E	F
4	垪	墷	蔃	檰	蘠	荇	琷	蘷	滖	碽	滧	樼	萸	榼	驢	葳
5	栫	嬢	檥	熐	塬	孋	朸	暟	樸	瀨	藻	灕	菲	吡	矗	胒
6	噟	啓	叻	咩	鑚	鏾	鏧	仸	傢	噱	爆	亼	儔	價	佋	侊
7	祧	婨	伆	偲	愢	粑	僯	仟	伩	僗	隚	促	䠟	欻	亘	
A		働	儍	倆	伃	琢	涿	佂	倮	傯	傁	俌	俥	偪	僼	赴
B	趌	趑	趆	淚	栟	浻	滏	浲	嫺	淋	冨	涂	溘	葢	尯	尳
C	尫	趍	鍶	刬	掰	劤	劥	勬	鑰	焜	燜	熥	吷	琀	嚫	槑
D	啶	瑧	瑂	璙	琔	瑕	玘	騱	璉	漣	叐	喌	爏	瀝	喊	倰
E	响	𠯫	圞	鉝	雲		埝	垍	坿	垺	壋	𡠢	鍼	妥	娽	娍
F	娬	妸		媮	嫏	娒	穸	𡧳	嫘	焥	㛚	涌	瑃	姑	粭	

Row 93	0	1	2	3	4	5	6	7	8	9	A	B	C	D	E	F
4	媁	鐙	僜	鏠	瑼	垰	焅	钀	鐈	鎡	鋒	屡	奆	岞	幞	幈
5	𤢖	預	毐	廊	孏	嫺	孄	嫅	嫮	𡛜	姍	㛢	脪	鋪	𢅗	楓
6	𨫓	弌	弍	嬪	㚷	妮	妹	孄		衏	衕	恾	𢢣	恶	忛	垡
7	𢖾	忼	悪	蕙	懀	夽	亶	㤁	憙	憘	恵	𢫬	𢷬	摱	憂	
A		搜	㹁	抗	挺	掃	棉	騂	擛	挷		撶	抄	捏	𤩂	撊
B	护	撙	弇	敫	槭	榕	濢	冒	𡌵	𥊣	唍	𣋑	𡟱	𧭈	曎	𣋲
C	哽	畔		礒	鎂	礩	娗	碁	矶	磻	旗	𡞵	喵	𠈓	唶	昙
D	煜	暎	莢	晫	騲	昰	覞	烖	晣	暌	曚	昞	䅵	彭	機	𣛮
E	樗	櫵	栈	瓐	樺		枬	梶	栞	楚	燊		橾	燥	樳	橒
F	樹	櫸	𡤋	擧	梘	橌	𣙮	橺	歔	瀑	汇	鋥	鋲	鎓	鎖	

Row 94	0	1	2	3	4	5	6	7	8	9	A	B	C	D	E	F
4	銉	踕	鉡	鏡	涥	漨		浧	𣸠	濦	渄	𣿷	娽	渊	塇	洤
5	硂	焻	煏	㷈	烱	牐	犇	𤛓	𤝔	𤜣	兹	璨	涣	瑺	𣽏	𣚭
6	𤩽	𤤒	䋿	璒	垡	瓑	鏫	𣶂	悧	琍	瓌	琼	鎇	珖	苒	蔆
7	𦼻	曈	嘁	曉	嚋	𣅙	畕	癋	𢋈	嘕	瑨	鐕	琌	𤦧	𣇵	
A		𤈶	琱	㺘	𤩝	玕	釺	圲	銓	𨩲	𡣢	僟	𣉺	𣋎	睸	𣇉
B	昹	映	暄	㸷	榤	搩	𤤃	琸	璛	𤥎	璠	𤩙	𥔲	璬	繳	錇
C	𥖁	砞	碍	碈	磒	珐	祙	襧	襨	裿	禛	蒖	䙳	椹	湛	𥟵
D	秴	𥡝	𡛊	𥝝	鈵	秱	喧	瑄	𠈃	渲	婠	哆	啫	吒	奼	仛
E	哇	族	婙	㥤	𥫝	𥪃	媙	㑴	𥕾	娪	䈡	笹	䇹	籯	籭	篙
F	䈂	𥺆	粘	糍	𤥊	嬨	粎	籼	粮	檲	緜	縇	綊	鑸	鏝	

Row 95	0	1	2	3	4	5	6	7	8	9	A	B	C	D	E	F
4	縡	譐	綗	粡	䈡	芉	靟	柖	䙡	桻	埄	羿	牠		翃	箣
5	劉	笉	簦	笋	䲢	鴦	藤	驣	樜	㭉		琚	聈	騟	聅	菡
6	蘊	葉	葛	脷	腺	胆	脉	腂	腌	飃	舵	艢	艥	艕	蒎	袞
7	蘐	鱵	嫖	䅨	婿	嫈	嫜	嫤	嫁	岔	蜓	涍	蠭	蝗	娸	
A		衮	佅	袝	袿	裦	襆	褋	裡	褠	褳	襘	鐭	鑊	鑿	鍸
B	玗	蒤	諼	詎	嵊	詢	訜	讟	彍	釹	棋	楗	堋	烄	媿	鵭
C	負	賩	賶	妳	疇	姰		烽	踨	躧	屛	暢	轉	綵	汘	潒
D	迥	迵	潹	溋	媼	鰞	柊	珎	邻	邦	啱	醆	醻	鑛	鋗	瞛
E	鐵	錭	鏽	鑮	鎣	訫	鬧	閧	閗	閑	閱	堤	琎	玾	璊	爀
F	瓅	喻	随	溜	堡	陫	琮	琹	璨	瀿	琒	瑫	璌	靁	霝	

Row 96	0	1	2	3	4	5	6	7	8	9	A	B	C	D	E	F
4	架	霄	零	䋤	蘸	鍨	鋉	鑕	鐴	攊	鋈	嬉	譩	鍄	珹	烑
5	韐	靭	餸	嚘	巁	鑛	瓓	頟	頨	鋶	颸	釙	苦	鐔	璭	鏻
6	麣	錤	璉	鉅	鑤	菇	餻	饍	譱	熔	菝	甜	蘋	蹼	鏷	樸
7	檏	騄	嬚	騯	駐	駉	騾	駁	驝	騂	鍽	塲	埣	堺	琛	
A		韃	硄	惘	溓	楝	灆	鐳	恬	悳	愑	覬	愇	鱒	鱓	鱻
B	鰲	鰐	鯪	鯏	鯇	鮟	鸝	鴿	鴟	鴻	鵴	鶵	鴣	鷮	鵝	鶲
C	鷰	鷧	鵑	蒠	蕕	蔚	萺	蕙	菸	蒬	蓈	葧	蒴	蓶	萁	櫸
D	総	柃	楣	橄		璞	澐	鏛	鍒	鏌	偅	碹	鉷	礨	俤	伕
E	邁	磃	硼	碁	磢	硋	婼	晿	珞	夈	佫	澲	潑	瀞	瀞	吔
F	炬	埧	壳	坻	鴎	埗	熖	燁	炁	熑	脊	煌	嫙	奐	鐭	

Row 97	0	1	2	3	4	5	6	7	8	9	A	B	C	D	E	F
4	愌	嫎	娋	紸	爔	嬸	馚	鎊	鎻	鐫	嬛	嚟	菒	葤	墉	熉
5	揰	濦	炕	焱	腆	綨	縳	緋	瑱	瑓	鎌	鍉	珢	璊	璏	鏈
6	嬧	瑻	璒	欂	珳	珻	球	琨	璔	媞	瓈	儤	壈	瑝	瑈	琲
7	炥	琊	鉤	珦	鍟	鑫	鑫	鑫	琴	鏑	鐎	礁	鋍	鎵	燝	
A		玵	喸	嚀	濘	吱	呣	啽	秄	嫚	纏	姸	瑡	嘶	蕲	鐁
B	媛	鋨	琦	妰	嬞	嫺	蟵	婡	嫍	涍	娅	鉟	嫕	鏤	婕	鍴
C	沛	歷	韝	憚	僴	瀵	潘	墉	煝	緗	躭	渏	霌	蒟	浗	贜
D	灩	砻	浓	瀁	溼	澋	漌	灦	礹	烟	媌	沰	艉	瑚	轀	妮
E	鉀	鋶	韬	鐍	莝	堒	埈	婏	墩	埊	墬	壂	鼕	堌	弢	梹
F	椟	堧	澯	轄	樸	鐋	蘑	杋	晴	樚	楠	菈	蓋	蔄	药	

Row 98	0	1	2	3	4	5	6	7	8	9	A	B	C	D	E	F
4	蒈	葯	药	蕿	漗	蔥	荋	婼	萿	萡	蘵	孱	妔	媂	娭	娕
5	媝	孏	烪	嫬	姚	媚	姙	媱	鎐	暚	烵	娓	娫	烷	樫	瀅
6	襂	爋	孱	婚	焄	鋸	倨	蓶	峂	爦	纘	熌	櫝	煇	堚	炦
7	烇	勛	烆	浈	勇			姬			彝					
A				曦												穀
B							謹			禧				調	遨	
C			痵		県		沢	国								
D																
E				塩				条						属		
F	壳		点										枥			

Row 99	0	1	2	3	4	5	6	7	8	9	A	B	C	D	E	F
4				辻		込										両
5																
6											笹				焺	
7						猪			畠							
A			堺												芦	
B							榊				惣					
C																
D																
E			仮													
F					駄											

Row 9A	0	1	2	3	4	5	6	7	8	9	A	B	C	D	E	F
4											磨		匁			
5										枠						
6		惨							汭							
7				窃											鯵	
A																
B			竈					椚		姤		塀				
C								呪								
D	惧		嘶							椿	鰯	蝓				
E			勘		帋				耔							
F			蒻				讁					蛑				

Row 9B	0	1	2	3	4	5	6	7	8	9	A	B	C	D	E	F
4							拃				柏		槼			
5					苽				覥		皐		韠		頳	骰
6																
7	僄	晈	暿	詑			爁	琦	蟲			類	俌		肣	
A		埜		祐	紘			衡	亭	郟	頣		鏵			濼
B			瑢	涇	溰	漽	晏	嵔	楰	浮					愳	
C	逵	驤	寓	絲	譞	鐥	馻				爑		咺			
D	刑	軑	剻			煱			溶	琫	唸			芷	釔	傷
E		祉		譈				珀		偦	剅	杞	惞		睛	鈀
F				咖			澶		蟈	適		鰉	譢			

Row 9C	0	1	2	3	4	5	6	7	8	9	A	B	C	D	E	F
4	嵛	莎	輶		鼕	諄	頊		濛		驫			愍	鏴	稯
5	憕	娧	晋	倪		爲		迺	珏	陵	涏	莰		襷		
6	翊		營		笵	霆	卬		郪		穅	鷰		聰		堋
7	獮	旡	禃			柬	楸	菏		詈		画	补		墶	
A		嬾	衞			歩			鉤	譁		鈦		瑍	飞	
B		嗣	蠹	裹	懂	廷	嫪	溱	琛	媓	懿		㣺	秣	蕁	璇
C	魃	駈	褒				礅	奋	爍	檯	屨	塱	蔧	苹		霹
D	婧	梟	蘊	鈳					澰	箇	祾		漸	髆	棚	輘
E	厢	蘅	鎿	栶	飆	蹕		繇	梟	暠		嶅	鑟		圖	頤
F	鈤	嶫	玢	旆	槔	叒	㻯	淇	櫟	朶				瞖		

Row 9D	0	1	2	3	4	5	6	7	8	9	A	B	C	D	E	F
4							品			醑	揦		砈	鉅		睇
5		胣				妍		峯			筑					
6			嚋		鏂											
7										逓					唬	
A						菻	繿	浥	槙		刮		覼	嬪	蹟	
B	跦			誗		熒		涸					鎛	嚿		跖
C	孭			揞	拐			劶	嘭		吚			魧	鯰	嘢
D	嘞	鏷		奵	浧	蝰					腔	鶩	贖	瘻	鱅	癇
E	曖	鉣	吲	腈	苷	嗺	脲	萘	肽	嗪	祢	噃	吖	喀	喋	嘅
F	啍	甲	𨋢	坳	甴	嘓	喙	咗	啲	㗎	咴	廘		𠿪	搽	

Row 9E	0	1	2	3	4	5	6	7	8	9	A	B	C	D	E	F
4	喙	麪	絙	嗞	嚟	抝	靭	咔	賍	燶	酶	揼	搣	揾	啩	搲
5	鱲	攞	冚	剫	啫	冧	呍	呌	啤	癦	踭	膶	疱	朏	蠄	螆
6	䘏	膶	萜		草	猄			芪		噻					
7		酰		鈈				㖭	牦		猯		踇		礳	
A		鱝	攠		酮	猬	鮁			恢	蠻		罐	椌		熣
B	纖	鴉			咱		淹	卧		揯			牨			舭
C	呋				髒	㩜		獴	䰾	鶡	鯭		鰦	鰔		
D	鴇	葜		蛙			捒	紮			㨪	逈	勬	㹔	㙫	蝛
E	皃	癀	嫩	㖠	硺	䞼	墧	碏	噼	鮋	嵴	癔	黈	魔	鴾	㿝
F	暫	窸		熁	踕	𡃶				䱌	剢		嗦	汶	䳌	

Row 9F	0	1	2	3	4	5	6	7	8	9	A	B	C	D	E	F
4	篾	鬹	埞		屓	擁	頯	罹		蚭	唍			㕭	纆	凾
5	㵎	蔚	霃	泶	麂	還	笟	髩	峑	箣	扨	拼	鬖	篏	鬪	籾
6	鬮	篩	粆	鰕	筧	髮	鼗	鰮		齚	啳	寃	俽	麘	㑪	剠
7		勑	坧	偖	妷	佾	韆	鵼	轜	呩	鞴	餡	韹	匬	㤹	
A		楦	叚	鰊	鴩	魰	陁	榀	傦	畆	娟	駃	劄	嗯	酙	隁
B	酜	䣙	酐	陡	捿		欄	嘑	醎	畺	抅		獏	篡	簸	
C	薜		盖	鵞	个	咂	莽	峁	丞	届	亶	僭	坺	卲	卮	从
D	氯	佅	伹	咜	㖑	劚	趆	嘁	弌	嗒	贋	歒	䤃	顉	鮗	頪
E	廮	骺	麩	簏		笔	滮	碖	蠘	罰	罸	嘎	鷜	壢	亂	鋤
F	跔	蹏	鸛	踁	抂	轃	蹤	蹩	㐂		亶	磘	泪	詧	瘇	

Row A0	0	1	2	3	4	5	6	7	8	9	A	B	C	D	E	F
4		韶	泎	蟖	痃	麐	硓		䐗	狢	獱	謭	猂	瓩	賚	璿
5	藫	僥	袠	苦	衩		蔻	熵	詾	倖	毟	惛	癧	髗	鴗	鍮
6	鮭	蠣	癰	蠏	賣	猬	霦	鮰	啗	犲	髻	養	鐵		慙	憲
7	廩	慽	奼	坟	愓	抦	戹	拎	擥	懢	厘		捤	栂	㖨	
A		嵗		迚	阫	嗽	僙		礆	匳	阸	嗏	暱	磬	矾	糏
B	糂	糕	糚	稭	聰	睨	紝	硱	砘	覔	譫	肦	聢	蟳	聛	础
C	脃	眤	覊	脤	畓		螩	蟎	臈	盤	諔	貭	謔	畔	頙	蓚
D		楹	趦	亂	靚	瑨	涹	鬸	濟	砒	倸	煶	悤	憜	洫	梵
E	㤝	憔	罱		牔	徰	駄									
F																

Row FA	0	1	2	3	4	5	6	7	8	9	A	B	C	D	E	F
4	有	鉟	浼	漌	葍	紈	珯	况	埧	琊	錞	鍄	府	茽	汕	砼
5	杆	拟	玖	鉚	倣	茬	僆	侫	㣍	俫	蓓	諦	槮	璆	倴	倩
6	偃	健	傑	傑	滔	僚	偽	儁	儁	儀	灝	挽	莬	現	兒	挑
7	不	兪	吹	帽	㑵	徾	叕	兔	斈	宂	蝽	沕	冰	冲	洋	
A		鴴	凉	减	凑	淋	凓	凝	决	凢	凡	凭	苶	楠	橅	彻
B	刋	刦	刧	券	劃	劔	効	勅	勪	勝	勠	勷	艽	包	鏕	啉
C	滙	滙	匯	滙	匧	卄	卌	洴	妾	栛	珕	恊	玐	彭	姤	爆
D	茚	卭	却	卻	鄂	卿	卿	矦	矦	厓	鏍	厠	厥	厮	玧	秔
E	晥	玜	叁	叅	汉	义	埾	叙	叡	叡	叠	澄	撜	叶	咯	吓
F	炨	唫	晗	浛	呭	苣	唅	唎	咏	咤	趦	姰	參	炵	晢	

Row FB	0	1	2	3	4	5	6	7	8	9	A	B	C	D	E	F
4	鋯	恄	商	鵬	启	琗	喆	喩	嘅	嬉	譆	嚞	熺	嘻	嚏	嗥
5	嗥	曍	嘷	暤	噍	噏	磅	囱	鞫	召	囫	国	园	鐗	圁	圯
6	坆	灼	汮	炋	坂	垢	荓	垸	壂	堃	螌	熚	堦	塋	塜	墪
7	叙	壠	壜	壬	堉	寿	坑	鷀	焻	鏓	啾	够	梦	㓞	湙	
A		奘	娄	啟	奮	蔨	姊	呫	菀	蓰	媄	姙	嫱	娉	娜	泒
B	娣	妚	姹	蓹	娖	媚	婇	珽	婷	婆	媖	瑥	媲	嬴	徫	
C	嬙	嬴	妐	広	勐	孳	孛	孽	誽	滵	輐	佢	寧		寕	寐
D	寵	寶	宝	鸐	尅	尉	尔	珎	尓	尳	芦	屜	鄜	岅	峩	峯
E	嶋	崑	娸	崐	崘	嵇	嵐	岑	巘	茥	珏	玬	巽	㠠	帀	帆
F	帯	帮	榦	幵	幺	巘	庛	厦	廉	廐	厨	嫎	岎	廴	延	

Row FC	0	1	2	3	4	5	6	7	8	9	A	B	C	D	E	F
4	廹	廻	迴	廼	弈	鏍	弍	弔	弢	畯		埪	强	彌	弦	彛
5	彝	彣		彭	彫	鍀	御	徧	徽	瀓	暌	徽	黴	恠	釖	偲
6	鍃	忽	恒		憃	猋	些	垐	愢	涚	特	悞	悤	悳	璗	璁
7	謥	璁	傯	婧	慤		湎	慈	墓	憁	凴	凴	甜	宪	潏	
A		懋	懮	鑿	驄	懷	愗	戇	慣	忝	憨	擺	搌	承	担	媣
B	拕	攘	揦	瑢	掟	搸	揸	塤	㩟	撐	澊	攝		灝	褶	擡
C	擎	鑻	擕	携	攜	敍	潡	墩	整	斅	斆	敷	斗	斱	珍	餚
D	旖	礳	嫼	无	既	忟	杈	昘	昉	春	晀	沓	炟	晋	㬊	晧
E	晣	晳	晴		暢	暹	晓	曙	曜	懼	藹	朂	燗	瑚		槺
F	櫰	杞	朾	李	朮	霳	枱	莜	栢	湘	鈼	柳	枈	蓘	栟	

Row FD	0	1	2	3	4	5	6	7	8	9	A	B	C	D	E	F
4	尨	槡	樋	鏁	楳	棃	棋	楟	椀		楂	槩	椷	枏	楡	鐠
5	縕	椶	榘	渠	榦	荣	槗	槹	橄	嵺	橅	樻	樴	檄	枱	欖
6	霊	龔	鬱	皀	忻	欵	歴	歷	溵	毅	傢	斈	毜	吡	毱	毡
7	滝	毟	氷	衫	玘	芀	汚	舦	汹	涝	渐	沄	炕	玩	玝	
A		沓	婚	沓	嗒	鮃	涽	彩	彬	样	萄	菩	海	涖	浜	湼
B	漼	玹	澍	滬	菁	蒨	淞	洸	渝	荊	錁	港	游	琜	湝	烋
C	湏	媑	敚	潳	嫞	濘	漽	淴	塑	漪	蔓	鏰	漱	潛	潤	潴
D	霘	澍	澟	灘	濂	濃	濤	濬	濬	濮	濼	瀆	瀕	瀛	瀛	縈
E	瀘	灾	炖	炁	焚	烕	烖	烟	裀	烽	焜	焰	焱	炳	煅	媈
F	煊	煮		煦	煏	鍢	燙	煬	燈	瑮	瑛	熺	鐔	炽	燎	

Row FE	0	1	2	3	4	5	6	7	8	9	A	B	C	D	E	F
4	鑂	燹	燮	鑃	爤	鍁	爪	爮	牀	珐	柹	憁	牅	覃	牵	牲
5	漽	犂	猪	猫	猴	猷	酞	酖	猨	献	珏	玲	吠	舦	珉	瑫
6	炰	妗	珍	眕	珥	珩	珮	璇	珷	琕	椃	琦	琹		琲	瑜
7	瑜	瑠	隅	璹	琉	瑶	莹	塗		瑴	鐔	樬	堪	鍖	璩	
A		潞	璧	鏮	孆	鑍	嬰	璆	衾	甎	瓩	甞	隗	甯	寗	阱
B	鈃	盼	畊	畧	晦	畹	璣	疋	疎	瑝	疞	疴	痖	痮	癑	癏
C	癯	癶	犾	皐	皋	嵲	皐	臯	暤	皞	皷	盌	蓋	葢	盦	會
D	嵿	眞	眦	着	掿	睿	睘	瞬	瞷	矷	矸	矽	矴	砉		
E	碁	硇	磈	磓	磴	礉	礪	磚	礴	碱	礽	辺	祆			恫
F	禆	祺	椂	禀	禡	禝	禮	礼	禩	湡	蕿	玜	秆	霖	秔	

The following two code tables provide an additional set of 145 hanzi specified by Hong Kong's Department of Judiciary, encoded in rows 0x8A and 0x8B:

Row 8A	0	1	2	3	4	5	6	7	8	9	A	B	C	D	E	F
4	呼	呤	唪	㕭	呦	眨	嘟	撽	挐	傲	踶	㾓	頢	瞍	蹢	睺
5	撾	擨	跂	蹲	䠥	猛	搵	唖	唪	吵	啃	搢	蹾	噉	吠	嘰
6	掇	闛	燿	銼	咀	骬	蹋	踬	瘤	揮	骲	㩧	飇	𦙶	罰	瞠
7	鐐	悼	搢	鴿	頕	窗	肮	嘹	撴	啞	揨	揃	嗍	掾	凹	
A		脜	脛	詎	擪	盆	呬	蹨	胼	𨭆	剌	扑	踔	仉	皺	墶
B	搔	糝	腠	俺	絜	嘍	軭	啹	橙	聊	胗	煩	乳	嘖	膳	飵
C	喇	挤	揔	毳	跀	嚾	摼	辈	鵒	齡	喀	拡	絮	摧	嚡	殀
D	悺	掭	軅	啦	粫	𢃇	咽	㩟	揶	𩚵	莔	氽	癴	趵	叻	蠪
E	擊	启	鹽	閂	哩	呃										
F																

Row 8B	0	1	2	3	4	5	6	7	8	9	A	B	C	D	E	F
4		祆	掮			㨦		𢭏		𡁻		齻		閇	闒	閲
5	闁				𠵴				穖		𤈦					
6																
7																
A																
B																
C																
D																
E																
F																

J

JIS X 0208:1997 Table

This appendix constitutes a table for the complete JIS X 0208:1997 character set, printed here using the typeface 平成明朝W3 (HeiseiMin-W3), developed by FDPC. Each character is indexed by Row-Cell value.

Note that Row-Cell 01-01 is a full-width space character.

Row 1		01	02	03	04	05	06	07	08	09	10	11	12	13	14	15	16	17	18	19
00			、	。	，	．	・	：	；	？	！	゛	゜	´	｀	¨	＾	￣	＿	ヽ
20	ヾ	ゝ	ゞ	〃	仝	々	〆	〇	ー	―	‐	／	＼	～	∥	｜	…	‥	‘	’
40	“	”	（	）	〔	〕	［	］	｛	｝	〈	〉	《	》	「	」	『	』	【	】
60	＋	－	±	×	÷	＝	≠	＜	＞	≦	≧	∞	∴	♂	♀	°	′	″	℃	￥
80	＄	¢	£	％	＃	＆	＊	＠	§	☆	★	○	●	◎	◇					

Row 2		01	02	03	04	05	06	07	08	09	10	11	12	13	14	15	16	17	18	19
00		◆	□	■	△	▲	▽	▼	※	〒	→	←	↑	↓	〓					
20							∈	∋	⊆	⊇	⊂	⊃	∪	∩						
40			∧	∨	¬	⇒	⇔	∀	∃											
60	∠	⊥	⌒	∂	∇	≡	≒	≪	≫	√	∽	∝	∵	∫	∬					
80			Å	‰	♯	♭	♪	†	‡	¶					◯					

Row 3		01	02	03	04	05	06	07	08	09	10	11	12	13	14	15	16	17	18	19
00																	０	１	２	３
20	４	５	６	７	８	９								Ａ	Ｂ	Ｃ	Ｄ	Ｅ	Ｆ	Ｇ
40	Ｈ	Ｉ	Ｊ	Ｋ	Ｌ	Ｍ	Ｎ	Ｏ	Ｐ	Ｑ	Ｒ	Ｓ	Ｔ	Ｕ	Ｖ	Ｗ	Ｘ	Ｙ	Ｚ	
60						ａ	ｂ	ｃ	ｄ	ｅ	ｆ	ｇ	ｈ	ｉ	ｊ	ｋ	ｌ	ｍ	ｎ	ｏ
80	ｐ	ｑ	ｒ	ｓ	ｔ	ｕ	ｖ	ｗ	ｘ	ｙ	ｚ									

Row 4

		01	02	03	04	05	06	07	08	09	10	11	12	13	14	15	16	17	18	19
00		ぁ	あ	ぃ	い	ぅ	う	ぇ	え	ぉ	お	か	が	き	ぎ	く	ぐ	け	げ	こ
20	ご	さ	ざ	し	じ	す	ず	せ	ぜ	そ	ぞ	た	だ	ち	ぢ	っ	つ	づ	て	で
40	と	ど	な	に	ぬ	ね	の	は	ば	ぱ	ひ	び	ぴ	ふ	ぶ	ぷ	へ	べ	ぺ	ほ
60	ぼ	ぽ	ま	み	む	め	も	ゃ	や	ゅ	ゆ	ょ	よ	ら	り	る	れ	ろ	ゎ	わ
80	ゐ	ゑ	を	ん																

Row 5

		01	02	03	04	05	06	07	08	09	10	11	12	13	14	15	16	17	18	19
00		ァ	ア	ィ	イ	ゥ	ウ	ェ	エ	ォ	オ	カ	ガ	キ	ギ	ク	グ	ケ	ゲ	コ
20	ゴ	サ	ザ	シ	ジ	ス	ズ	セ	ゼ	ソ	ゾ	タ	ダ	チ	ヂ	ッ	ツ	ヅ	テ	デ
40	ト	ド	ナ	ニ	ヌ	ネ	ノ	ハ	バ	パ	ヒ	ビ	ピ	フ	ブ	プ	ヘ	ベ	ペ	ホ
60	ボ	ポ	マ	ミ	ム	メ	モ	ャ	ヤ	ュ	ユ	ョ	ヨ	ラ	リ	ル	レ	ロ	ヮ	ワ
80	ヰ	ヱ	ヲ	ン	ヴ	ヵ	ヶ													

Row 6

		01	02	03	04	05	06	07	08	09	10	11	12	13	14	15	16	17	18	19
00		Α	Β	Γ	Δ	Ε	Ζ	Η	Θ	Ι	Κ	Λ	Μ	Ν	Ξ	Ο	Π	Ρ	Σ	Τ
20	Υ	Φ	Χ	Ψ	Ω									α	β	γ	δ	ε	ζ	η
40	θ	ι	κ	λ	μ	ν	ξ	ο	π	ρ	σ	τ	υ	φ	χ	ψ	ω			
60																				
80																				

Row 7

		01	02	03	04	05	06	07	08	09	10	11	12	13	14	15	16	17	18	19
00		А	Б	В	Г	Д	Е	Ё	Ж	З	И	Й	К	Л	М	Н	О	П	Р	С
20	Т	У	Ф	Х	Ц	Ч	Ш	Щ	Ъ	Ы	Ь	Э	Ю	Я						
40										а	б	в	г	д	е	ё	ж	з	и	й
60	к	л	м	н	о	п	р	с	т	у	ф	х	ц	ч	ш	щ	ъ	ы	ь	э
80	ю	я																		

Row 8

		01	02	03	04	05	06	07	08	09	10	11	12	13	14	15	16	17	18	19
00		─	│	┌	┐	┘	└	├	┬	┤	┴	┼	━	┃	┏	┓	┛	┗	┣	┳
20	┫	┻	╋	┠	┯	┨	┷	┿	┝	┰	┥	┸	╂							
40																				
60																				
80																				

Row 16

		01	02	03	04	05	06	07	08	09	10	11	12	13	14	15	16	17	18	19
00		亜	唖	娃	阿	哀	愛	挨	姶	逢	葵	茜	穐	悪	握	渥	旭	葦	芦	鯵
20	梓	圧	斡	扱	宛	姐	虻	飴	絢	綾	鮎	或	粟	袷	安	庵	按	暗	案	闇
40	鞍	杏	以	伊	位	依	偉	囲	夷	委	威	尉	惟	意	慰	易	椅	為	畏	異
60	移	維	緯	胃	萎	衣	謂	違	遺	医	井	亥	域	育	郁	磯	一	壱	溢	逸
80	稲	茨	芋	鰯	允	印	咽	員	因	姻	引	飲	淫	胤	蔭					

Row 17		01	02	03	04	05	06	07	08	09	10	11	12	13	14	15	16	17	18	19
00		院	陰	隠	韻	吋	右	宇	烏	羽	迂	雨	卯	鵜	窺	丑	碓	臼	渦	嘘
20	唄	欝	蔚	鰻	姥	厩	浦	瓜	閏	噂	云	運	雲	荏	餌	叡	営	嬰	影	映
40	曳	栄	永	泳	洩	瑛	盈	穎	頴	英	衛	詠	鋭	液	疫	益	駅	悦	謁	越
60	閲	榎	厭	円	園	堰	奄	宴	延	怨	掩	援	沿	演	炎	焔	煙	燕	猿	縁
80	艶	苑	薗	遠	鉛	鴛	塩	於	汚	甥	凹	央	奥	往	応					

Row 18		01	02	03	04	05	06	07	08	09	10	11	12	13	14	15	16	17	18	19
00		押	旺	横	欧	殴	王	翁	襖	鴬	鴎	黄	岡	沖	荻	億	屋	憶	臆	桶
20	牡	乙	俺	卸	恩	温	穏	音	下	化	仮	何	伽	価	佳	加	可	嘉	夏	嫁
40	家	寡	科	暇	果	架	歌	河	火	珂	禍	禾	稼	箇	花	苛	茄	荷	華	菓
60	蝦	課	嘩	貨	迦	過	霞	蚊	俄	峨	我	牙	画	臥	芽	蛾	賀	雅	餓	駕
80	介	会	解	回	塊	壊	廻	快	怪	悔	恢	懐	戒	拐	改					

Row 19		01	02	03	04	05	06	07	08	09	10	11	12	13	14	15	16	17	18	19
00		魁	晦	械	海	灰	界	皆	絵	芥	蟹	開	階	貝	凱	劾	外	咳	害	崖
20	慨	概	涯	碍	蓋	街	該	鎧	骸	浬	馨	蛙	垣	柿	蛎	鈎	劃	嚇	各	廓
40	拡	撹	格	核	殻	獲	確	穫	覚	角	赫	較	郭	閣	隔	革	学	岳	楽	額
60	顎	掛	笠	樫	橿	梶	鰍	潟	割	喝	恰	括	活	渇	滑	葛	褐	轄	且	鰹
80	叶	椛	樺	鞄	株	兜	竃	蒲	釜	鎌	噛	鴨	栢	茅	萱					

Row 20		01	02	03	04	05	06	07	08	09	10	11	12	13	14	15	16	17	18	19
00		粥	刈	苅	瓦	乾	侃	冠	寒	刊	勘	勧	巻	喚	堪	姦	完	官	寛	干
20	幹	患	感	慣	憾	換	敢	柑	桓	棺	款	歓	汗	漢	澗	潅	環	甘	監	看
40	竿	管	簡	緩	缶	翰	肝	艦	莞	観	諌	貫	還	鑑	間	閑	関	陥	韓	館
60	舘	丸	含	岸	巌	玩	癌	眼	岩	翫	贋	雁	頑	顔	願	企	伎	危	喜	器
80	基	奇	嬉	寄	岐	希	幾	忌	揮	机	旗	既	期	棋	棄					

Row 21		01	02	03	04	05	06	07	08	09	10	11	12	13	14	15	16	17	18	19
00		機	帰	毅	気	汽	畿	祈	季	稀	紀	徽	規	記	貴	起	軌	輝	飢	騎
20	鬼	亀	偽	儀	妓	宜	戯	技	擬	欺	犠	疑	祇	義	蟻	誼	議	掬	菊	鞠
40	吉	吃	喫	桔	橘	詰	砧	杵	黍	却	客	脚	虐	逆	丘	久	仇	休	及	吸
60	宮	弓	急	救	朽	求	汲	泣	灸	球	究	窮	笈	級	糾	給	旧	牛	去	居
80	巨	拒	拠	挙	渠	虚	許	距	鋸	漁	禦	魚	亨	享	京					

Row 22		01	02	03	04	05	06	07	08	09	10	11	12	13	14	15	16	17	18	19
00		供	侠	僑	兇	競	共	凶	協	匡	卿	叫	喬	境	峡	強	彊	怯	恐	恭
20	挟	教	橋	況	狂	狭	矯	胸	脅	興	蕎	郷	鏡	響	饗	驚	仰	凝	尭	暁
40	業	局	曲	極	玉	桐	粁	僅	勤	均	巾	錦	斤	欣	欽	琴	禁	禽	筋	緊
60	芹	菌	衿	襟	謹	近	金	吟	銀	九	倶	句	区	狗	玖	矩	苦	躯	駆	駈
80	駒	具	愚	虞	喰	空	偶	寓	遇	隅	串	櫛	釧	屑	屈					

Row 23		01	02	03	04	05	06	07	08	09	10	11	12	13	14	15	16	17	18	19
00		掘	窟	沓	靴	轡	窪	熊	隈	粂	栗	繰	桑	鍬	勲	君	薫	訓	群	軍
20	郡	卦	袈	祁	係	傾	刑	兄	啓	圭	珪	型	契	形	径	恵	慶	慧	憩	掲
40	携	敬	景	桂	渓	畦	稽	系	経	継	繋	罫	茎	荊	蛍	計	詣	警	軽	頚
60	鶏	芸	迎	鯨	劇	戟	撃	激	隙	桁	傑	欠	決	潔	穴	結	血	訣	月	件
80	倹	倦	健	兼	券	剣	喧	圏	堅	嫌	建	憲	懸	拳	捲					

Row 24		01	02	03	04	05	06	07	08	09	10	11	12	13	14	15	16	17	18	19
00		検	権	牽	犬	献	研	硯	絹	県	肩	見	謙	賢	軒	遣	鍵	険	顕	験
20	鹸	元	原	厳	幻	弦	減	源	玄	現	絃	舷	言	諺	限	乎	個	古	呼	固
40	姑	孤	己	庫	弧	戸	故	枯	湖	狐	糊	袴	股	胡	菰	虎	誇	跨	鈷	雇
60	顧	鼓	五	互	伍	午	呉	吾	娯	後	御	悟	梧	檎	瑚	碁	語	誤	護	醐
80	乞	鯉	交	佼	侯	候	倖	光	公	功	効	勾	厚	口	向					

Row 25		01	02	03	04	05	06	07	08	09	10	11	12	13	14	15	16	17	18	19
00		后	喉	坑	垢	好	孔	孝	宏	工	巧	巷	幸	広	庚	康	弘	恒	慌	抗
20	拘	控	攻	昂	晃	更	杭	校	梗	構	江	洪	浩	港	溝	甲	皇	硬	稿	糠
40	紅	紘	絞	綱	耕	考	肯	肱	腔	膏	航	荒	行	衡	講	貢	購	郊	酵	鉱
60	砿	鋼	閤	降	項	香	高	鴻	剛	劫	号	合	壕	拷	濠	豪	轟	麹	克	刻
80	告	国	穀	酷	鵠	黒	獄	漉	腰	甑	忽	惚	骨	狛	込					

Row 26		01	02	03	04	05	06	07	08	09	10	11	12	13	14	15	16	17	18	19
00		此	頃	今	困	坤	墾	婚	恨	懇	昏	昆	根	梱	混	痕	紺	艮	魂	些
20	佐	叉	唆	嵯	左	差	査	沙	瑳	砂	詐	鎖	裟	坐	座	挫	債	催	再	最
40	哉	塞	妻	宰	彩	才	採	栽	歳	済	災	采	犀	砕	砦	祭	斎	細	菜	裁
60	載	際	剤	在	材	罪	財	冴	坂	阪	堺	榊	肴	咲	崎	埼	碕	鷺	作	削
80	咋	搾	昨	朔	柵	窄	策	索	錯	桜	鮭	笹	匙	冊	刷					

Row 27		01	02	03	04	05	06	07	08	09	10	11	12	13	14	15	16	17	18	19
00		察	拶	撮	擦	札	殺	薩	雑	皐	鯖	捌	錆	鮫	皿	晒	三	傘	参	山
20	惨	撒	散	桟	燦	珊	産	算	纂	蚕	讃	賛	酸	餐	斬	暫	残	仕	仔	伺
40	使	刺	司	史	嗣	四	士	始	姉	姿	子	屍	市	師	志	思	指	支	孜	斯
60	施	旨	枝	止	死	氏	獅	祉	私	糸	紙	紫	肢	脂	至	視	詞	詩	試	誌
80	諮	資	賜	雌	飼	歯	事	似	侍	児	字	寺	慈	持	時					

Row 28		01	02	03	04	05	06	07	08	09	10	11	12	13	14	15	16	17	18	19
00		次	滋	治	爾	璽	痔	磁	示	而	耳	自	蒔	辞	汐	鹿	式	識	鴫	竺
20	軸	宍	雫	七	叱	執	失	嫉	室	悉	湿	漆	疾	質	実	蔀	篠	偲	柴	芝
40	屡	蕊	縞	舎	写	射	捨	赦	斜	煮	社	紗	者	謝	車	遮	蛇	邪	借	勺
60	尺	杓	灼	爵	酌	釈	錫	若	寂	弱	惹	主	取	守	手	朱	殊	狩	珠	種
80	腫	趣	酒	首	儒	受	呪	寿	授	樹	綬	需	囚	収	周					

Row 29		01	02	03	04	05	06	07	08	09	10	11	12	13	14	15	16	17	18	19
00		宗	就	州	修	愁	拾	洲	秀	秋	終	繍	習	臭	舟	蒐	衆	襲	讐	蹴
20	輯	週	酋	酬	集	醜	什	住	充	十	従	戎	柔	汁	渋	獣	縦	重	銃	叔
40	夙	宿	淑	祝	縮	粛	塾	熟	出	術	述	俊	峻	春	瞬	竣	舜	駿	准	循
60	旬	楯	殉	淳	準	潤	盾	純	巡	遵	醇	順	処	初	所	暑	曙	渚	庶	緒
80	署	書	薯	藷	諸	助	叙	女	序	徐	恕	鋤	除	傷	償					

Row 30		01	02	03	04	05	06	07	08	09	10	11	12	13	14	15	16	17	18	19
00		勝	匠	升	召	哨	商	唱	嘗	奨	妾	娼	宵	将	小	少	尚	庄	床	廠
20	彰	承	抄	招	掌	捷	昇	昌	昭	晶	松	梢	樟	樵	沼	消	渉	湘	焼	焦
40	照	症	省	硝	礁	祥	称	章	笑	粧	紹	肖	菖	蒋	蕉	衝	裳	訟	証	詔
60	詳	象	賞	醤	鉦	鍾	鐘	障	鞘	上	丈	丞	乗	冗	剰	城	場	壌	嬢	常
80	情	擾	条	杖	浄	状	畳	穣	蒸	譲	醸	錠	嘱	埴	飾					

Row 31		01	02	03	04	05	06	07	08	09	10	11	12	13	14	15	16	17	18	19
00		拭	植	殖	燭	織	職	色	触	食	蝕	辱	尻	伸	信	侵	唇	娠	寝	審
20	心	慎	振	新	晋	森	榛	浸	深	申	疹	真	神	秦	紳	臣	芯	薪	親	診
40	身	辛	進	針	震	人	仁	刃	塵	壬	尋	甚	尽	腎	訊	迅	陣	靭	笥	諏
60	須	酢	図	厨	逗	吹	垂	帥	推	水	炊	睡	粋	翠	衰	遂	酔	錐	錘	随
80	瑞	髄	崇	嵩	数	枢	趨	雛	据	杉	椙	菅	頗	雀	裾					

Row 32		01	02	03	04	05	06	07	08	09	10	11	12	13	14	15	16	17	18	19
00		澄	摺	寸	世	瀬	畝	是	凄	制	勢	姓	征	性	成	政	整	星	晴	棲
20	栖	正	清	牲	生	盛	精	聖	声	製	西	誠	誓	請	逝	醒	青	静	斉	税
40	脆	隻	席	惜	戚	斥	昔	析	石	積	籍	績	脊	責	赤	跡	蹟	碩	切	拙
60	接	摂	折	設	窃	節	説	雪	絶	舌	蝉	仙	先	千	占	宣	専	尖	川	戦
80	扇	撰	栓	栴	泉	浅	洗	染	潜	煎	煽	旋	穿	箭	線					

Row 33		01	02	03	04	05	06	07	08	09	10	11	12	13	14	15	16	17	18	19
00		繊	羨	腺	舛	船	薦	詮	賎	践	選	遷	銭	銑	閃	鮮	前	善	漸	然
20	全	禅	繕	膳	糎	噌	塑	岨	措	曾	曽	楚	狙	疏	疎	礎	祖	租	粗	素
40	組	蘇	訴	阻	遡	鼠	僧	創	双	叢	倉	喪	壮	奏	爽	宋	層	匝	惣	想
60	捜	掃	挿	掻	操	早	曹	巣	槍	槽	漕	燥	争	痩	相	窓	糟	総	綜	聡
80	草	荘	葬	蒼	藻	装	走	送	遭	鎗	霜	騒	像	増	憎					

Row 34		01	02	03	04	05	06	07	08	09	10	11	12	13	14	15	16	17	18	19
00		臓	蔵	贈	造	促	側	則	即	息	捉	束	測	足	速	俗	属	賊	族	続
20	卒	袖	其	揃	存	孫	尊	損	村	遜	他	多	太	汰	詑	唾	堕	妥	惰	打
40	柁	舵	楕	陀	駄	騨	体	堆	対	耐	岱	帯	待	怠	態	戴	替	泰	滞	胎
60	腿	苔	袋	貸	退	逮	隊	黛	鯛	代	台	大	第	醍	題	鷹	滝	瀧	卓	啄
80	宅	托	択	拓	沢	濯	琢	託	鐸	濁	諾	茸	凧	蛸	只					

Row 35

	00	01	02	03	04	05	06	07	08	09	10	11	12	13	14	15	16	17	18	19
00		叩	但	達	辰	奪	脱	巽	竪	辿	棚	谷	狸	鱈	樽	誰	丹	単	嘆	坦
20	担	探	旦	歎	淡	湛	炭	短	端	箪	綻	耽	胆	蛋	誕	鍛	団	壇	弾	断
40	暖	檀	段	男	談	値	知	地	弛	恥	智	池	痴	稚	置	致	蜘	遅	馳	築
60	畜	竹	筑	蓄	逐	秩	窒	茶	嫡	着	中	仲	宙	忠	抽	昼	柱	注	虫	衷
80	註	酎	鋳	駐	樗	瀦	猪	苧	著	貯	丁	兆	凋	喋	寵					

Row 36

	00	01	02	03	04	05	06	07	08	09	10	11	12	13	14	15	16	17	18	19
00		帖	帳	庁	弔	張	彫	徴	懲	挑	暢	朝	潮	牒	町	眺	聴	脹	腸	蝶
20	調	諜	超	跳	銚	長	頂	鳥	勅	捗	直	朕	沈	珍	賃	鎮	陳	津	墜	椎
40	槌	追	鎚	痛	通	塚	栂	掴	槻	佃	漬	柘	辻	蔦	綴	鍔	椿	潰	坪	壷
60	嬬	紬	爪	吊	釣	鶴	亭	低	停	偵	剃	貞	呈	堤	定	帝	底	庭	廷	弟
80	悌	抵	挺	提	梯	汀	碇	禎	程	締	艇	訂	諦	蹄	逓					

Row 37

	00	01	02	03	04	05	06	07	08	09	10	11	12	13	14	15	16	17	18	19
00		邸	鄭	釘	鼎	泥	摘	擢	敵	滴	的	笛	適	鏑	溺	哲	徹	撤	轍	迭
20	鉄	典	填	天	展	店	添	纏	甜	貼	転	顛	点	伝	殿	澱	田	電	兎	吐
40	堵	塗	妬	屠	徒	斗	杜	渡	登	菟	賭	途	都	鍍	砥	砺	努	度	土	奴
60	怒	倒	党	冬	凍	刀	唐	塔	塘	套	宕	島	嶋	悼	投	搭	東	桃	梼	棟
80	盗	淘	湯	涛	灯	燈	当	痘	祷	等	答	筒	糖	統	到					

Row 38

	00	01	02	03	04	05	06	07	08	09	10	11	12	13	14	15	16	17	18	19
00		董	蕩	藤	討	謄	豆	踏	逃	透	鐙	陶	頭	騰	闘	働	動	同	堂	導
20	憧	撞	洞	瞳	童	胴	萄	道	銅	峠	鴇	匿	得	徳	涜	特	督	禿	篤	毒
40	独	読	栃	橡	凸	突	椴	届	鳶	苫	寅	酉	瀞	噸	屯	惇	敦	沌	豚	遁
60	頓	呑	曇	鈍	奈	那	内	乍	凪	薙	謎	灘	捺	鍋	楢	馴	縄	畷	南	楠
80	軟	難	汝	二	尼	弐	迩	匂	賑	肉	虹	廿	日	乳	入					

Row 39

	00	01	02	03	04	05	06	07	08	09	10	11	12	13	14	15	16	17	18	19
00		如	尿	韮	任	妊	忍	認	濡	禰	祢	寧	葱	猫	熱	年	念	捻	撚	燃
20	粘	乃	廼	之	埜	嚢	悩	濃	納	能	脳	膿	農	覗	蚤	巴	把	播	覇	杷
40	波	派	琶	破	婆	罵	芭	馬	俳	廃	拝	排	敗	杯	盃	牌	背	肺	輩	配
60	倍	培	媒	梅	楳	煤	狽	買	売	賠	陪	這	蝿	秤	矧	萩	伯	剥	博	拍
80	柏	泊	白	箔	粕	舶	薄	迫	曝	漠	爆	縛	莫	駁	麦					

Row 40

	00	01	02	03	04	05	06	07	08	09	10	11	12	13	14	15	16	17	18	19
00		函	箱	硲	箸	肇	筈	櫨	幡	肌	畑	畠	八	鉢	溌	発	醗	髪	伐	罰
20	抜	筏	閥	鳩	噺	塙	蛤	隼	伴	判	半	反	叛	帆	搬	斑	板	氾	汎	版
40	犯	班	畔	繁	般	藩	販	範	釆	煩	頒	飯	挽	晩	番	盤	磐	蕃	蛮	匪
60	卑	否	妃	庇	彼	悲	扉	批	披	斐	比	泌	疲	皮	碑	秘	緋	罷	肥	被
80	誹	費	避	非	飛	樋	簸	備	尾	微	枇	毘	琵	眉	美					

Row 41		01	02	03	04	05	06	07	08	09	10	11	12	13	14	15	16	17	18	19
00		鼻	柊	稗	匹	疋	髭	彦	膝	菱	肘	弼	必	畢	筆	逼	桧	姫	媛	紐
20	百	謬	俵	彪	標	氷	漂	瓢	票	表	評	豹	廟	描	病	秒	苗	錨	鋲	蒜
40	蛭	鰭	品	彬	斌	浜	瀕	貧	賓	頻	敏	瓶	不	付	埠	夫	婦	富	冨	布
60	府	怖	扶	敷	斧	普	浮	父	符	腐	膚	芙	譜	負	賦	赴	阜	附	侮	撫
80	武	舞	葡	蕪	部	封	楓	風	葺	蕗	伏	副	復	幅	服					

Row 42		01	02	03	04	05	06	07	08	09	10	11	12	13	14	15	16	17	18	19
00		福	腹	複	覆	淵	弗	払	沸	仏	物	鮒	分	吻	噴	墳	憤	扮	焚	奮
20	粉	糞	紛	雰	文	聞	丙	併	兵	塀	幣	平	弊	柄	並	蔽	閉	陛	米	頁
40	僻	壁	癖	碧	別	瞥	蔑	箆	偏	変	片	篇	編	辺	返	遍	便	勉	娩	弁
60	鞭	保	舗	鋪	圃	捕	歩	甫	補	輔	穂	募	墓	慕	戊	暮	母	簿	菩	倣
80	俸	包	呆	報	奉	宝	峰	峯	崩	庖	抱	捧	放	方	朋					

Row 43		01	02	03	04	05	06	07	08	09	10	11	12	13	14	15	16	17	18	19
00		法	泡	烹	砲	縫	胞	芳	萌	蓬	蜂	褒	訪	豊	邦	鋒	飽	鳳	鵬	乏
20	亡	傍	剖	坊	妨	帽	忘	忙	房	暴	望	某	棒	冒	紡	肪	膨	謀	貌	貿
40	鉾	防	吠	頬	北	僕	卜	墨	撲	朴	牧	睦	穆	釦	勃	没	殆	堀	幌	奔
60	本	翻	凡	盆	摩	磨	魔	麻	埋	妹	昧	枚	毎	哩	槙	幕	膜	枕	鮪	柾
80	鱒	桝	亦	俣	又	抹	末	沫	迄	侭	繭	麿	万	慢	満					

Row 44		01	02	03	04	05	06	07	08	09	10	11	12	13	14	15	16	17	18	19
00		漫	蔓	味	未	魅	巳	箕	岬	密	蜜	湊	蓑	稔	脈	妙	粍	民	眠	務
20	夢	無	牟	矛	霧	鵡	椋	婿	娘	冥	名	命	明	盟	迷	銘	鳴	姪	牝	滅
40	免	棉	綿	緬	面	麺	摸	模	茂	妄	孟	毛	猛	盲	網	耗	蒙	儲	木	黙
60	目	杢	勿	餅	尤	戻	籾	貰	問	悶	紋	門	匁	也	冶	夜	爺	耶	野	弥
80	矢	厄	役	約	薬	訳	躍	靖	柳	薮	鑓	愉	愈	油	癒					

Row 45		01	02	03	04	05	06	07	08	09	10	11	12	13	14	15	16	17	18	19
00		諭	輸	唯	佑	優	勇	友	宥	幽	悠	憂	揖	有	柚	湧	涌	猶	猷	由
20	祐	裕	誘	遊	邑	郵	雄	融	夕	予	余	与	誉	輿	預	傭	幼	妖	容	庸
40	揚	揺	擁	曜	楊	様	洋	溶	熔	用	窯	羊	耀	葉	蓉	要	謡	踊	遥	陽
60	養	慾	抑	欲	沃	浴	翌	翼	淀	羅	螺	裸	来	莱	頼	雷	洛	絡	落	酪
80	乱	卵	嵐	欄	濫	藍	蘭	覧	利	吏	履	李	梨	理	璃					

Row 46		01	02	03	04	05	06	07	08	09	10	11	12	13	14	15	16	17	18	19
00		痢	裏	裡	里	離	陸	律	率	立	葎	掠	略	劉	流	溜	琉	留	硫	粒
20	隆	竜	龍	侶	慮	旅	虜	了	亮	僚	両	凌	寮	料	梁	涼	猟	療	瞭	稜
40	糧	良	諒	遼	量	陵	領	力	緑	倫	厘	林	淋	燐	琳	臨	輪	隣	鱗	麟
60	瑠	塁	涙	累	類	令	伶	例	冷	励	嶺	怜	玲	礼	苓	鈴	隷	零	霊	麗
80	齢	暦	歴	列	劣	烈	裂	廉	恋	憐	漣	煉	簾	練	聯					

Row 47		01	02	03	04	05	06	07	08	09	10	11	12	13	14	15	16	17	18	19
00		蓮	連	錬	呂	魯	櫓	炉	賂	路	露	労	婁	廊	弄	朗	楼	榔	浪	漏
20	牢	狼	篭	老	聾	蝋	郎	六	麓	禄	肋	録	論	倭	和	話	歪	賄	脇	惑
40	枠	鷲	亙	亘	鰐	詫	藁	蕨	椀	湾	碗	腕								
60																				
80																				

Row 48		01	02	03	04	05	06	07	08	09	10	11	12	13	14	15	16	17	18	19
00		弌	丐	丕	个	丱	丶	丼	丿	乂	乖	乘	亂	亅	豫	亊	舒	弍	于	亞
20	亟	亠	亢	亰	亳	亶	从	仍	仄	仆	仂	仗	仞	仭	仟	价	伉	佚	估	佛
40	佝	佗	佇	佶	侈	侏	侘	佻	佩	佰	侑	佯	來	侖	儘	俔	俟	俎	俘	俛
60	俑	俚	俐	俤	俥	倚	倨	倔	倪	倥	倅	伜	俶	倡	倩	倬	俾	俯	們	倆
80	偃	假	會	偕	偐	偈	做	偖	偬	偸	傀	傚	傅	傴	傲					

Row 49		01	02	03	04	05	06	07	08	09	10	11	12	13	14	15	16	17	18	19
00		僉	僊	傳	僂	僖	僞	僥	僭	僣	僮	價	僵	儉	儁	儂	儖	儕	儔	儚
20	儡	儺	儷	儼	儻	儿	兀	兒	兌	兔	兢	竸	兩	兪	兮	冀	冂	囘	册	冉
40	冏	冑	冓	冕	冖	冤	冦	冢	冩	冪	冫	决	冱	冲	冰	况	冽	凅	凉	凛
60	几	處	凩	凭	凰	凵	凾	刄	刋	刔	刎	刧	刪	刮	刳	刹	剏	剄	剋	剌
80	剞	剔	剪	剴	剩	剳	剿	剽	劍	劔	劒	剱	劈	劑	辨					

Row 50		01	02	03	04	05	06	07	08	09	10	11	12	13	14	15	16	17	18	19
00		辧	劬	劭	劼	劵	勁	勍	勗	勞	勣	勦	飭	勠	勳	勵	勸	勹	匆	匈
20	甸	匍	匐	匏	匕	匚	匣	匯	匱	匳	匸	區	卆	卅	丗	卉	卍	凖	卞	卩
40	卮	夘	卻	卷	厂	厖	厠	厦	厥	厮	厰	厶	參	簒	雙	叟	曼	燮	叮	叨
60	叭	叺	吁	吽	呀	听	吭	吼	吮	吶	吩	吝	呎	咏	呵	咎	呟	呱	呷	呰
80	咒	呻	咀	呶	咄	咐	咆	哇	咢	咸	咥	咬	哄	哈	咨					

Row 51		01	02	03	04	05	06	07	08	09	10	11	12	13	14	15	16	17	18	19
00		咫	哂	咤	咾	咼	哘	哥	哦	唏	唔	哽	哮	哭	哺	哢	唹	啀	啣	啌
20	售	啜	啅	啖	啗	唸	唳	啝	喙	喀	咯	喊	喟	啻	啾	喘	喞	單	啼	喃
40	喩	喇	喨	嗚	嗅	嗟	嗄	嗜	嗤	嗔	嘔	嗷	嘖	嗾	嗽	嘛	嗹	噎	噐	營
60	嘴	嘶	嘲	嘸	噫	噤	嘯	噬	噪	嚆	嚀	嚊	嚠	嚔	嚏	嚥	嚮	嚶	嚴	囂
80	嚼	囁	囃	囀	囈	囎	囑	囓	囗	囮	囹	圀	囿	圄	圉					

Row 52		01	02	03	04	05	06	07	08	09	10	11	12	13	14	15	16	17	18	19
00		圈	國	圍	圓	團	圖	嗇	圜	圦	圷	圸	坎	圻	址	坏	坩	埀	垈	坡
20	坿	垉	垓	垠	垳	垤	垪	垰	埃	埆	埔	埒	埓	堊	埖	埣	堋	堙	堝	塲
40	堡	塢	塋	塰	毀	塒	堽	塹	墅	墹	墟	墫	墺	壞	墻	墸	墮	壅	壓	壑
60	壗	壙	壘	壥	壜	壤	壟	壯	壺	壹	壻	壼	壽	夂	夊	夐	夛	梦	夥	夬
80	夭	夲	夸	夾	竒	奕	奐	奎	奚	奘	奢	奠	奥	奬	奩					

Row 53		01	02	03	04	05	06	07	08	09	10	11	12	13	14	15	16	17	18	19
00		奸	妁	妝	佞	侫	妣	妲	姆	姨	姜	妍	姙	姚	娥	娟	娑	娜	娉	娚
20	婀	婬	婉	娵	娶	婢	婪	媚	媼	媾	嫋	嫂	媽	嫣	嫗	嫦	嫩	嫖	嫺	嫻
40	嬌	嬋	嬖	嬲	嫐	嬪	嬶	嬾	孃	孅	孀	孑	孕	孚	孛	孥	孩	孰	孳	孵
60	學	斈	孺	宀	它	宦	宸	寃	寇	寉	寔	寐	寤	實	寢	寞	寥	寫	寰	寶
80	寳	尅	將	專	對	尓	尠	尢	尨	尸	尹	屁	屆	屎	屓					

Row 54		01	02	03	04	05	06	07	08	09	10	11	12	13	14	15	16	17	18	19
00		屐	屏	孱	屬	屮	乢	屶	屹	岌	岑	岔	妛	岫	岻	岶	岼	岷	峅	岾
20	峇	峙	峩	峽	峺	峭	嶌	峪	崋	崕	崗	嵜	崟	崛	崑	崔	崢	崚	崙	崘
40	嵌	嵒	嵎	嵋	嵬	嵳	嵶	嶇	嶄	嶂	嶢	嶝	嶬	嶮	嶽	嶐	嶷	嶼	巉	巍
60	巓	巒	巖	巛	巫	已	巵	帋	帚	帙	帑	帛	帶	帷	幄	幃	幀	幎	幗	幔
80	幟	幢	幤	幇	幵	并	幺	麼	广	庠	廁	廂	廈	廐	廏					

Row 55		01	02	03	04	05	06	07	08	09	10	11	12	13	14	15	16	17	18	19
00		廖	廣	廝	廚	廛	廢	廡	廨	廩	廬	廱	廳	廰	廴	廸	廾	弃	弉	彝
20	彜	弋	弑	弖	弩	弭	弸	彁	彈	彌	彎	弯	彑	彖	彗	彙	彡	彭	彳	彷
40	徃	徂	彿	徊	很	徑	徇	從	徙	徘	徠	徨	徭	徼	忖	忻	忤	忸	忱	忝
60	悳	忿	怡	恠	怙	怐	怩	怎	怱	怛	怕	怫	怦	怏	怺	恚	恁	恪	恷	恟
80	恊	恆	恍	恣	恃	恤	恂	恬	恫	恙	悁	悍	惧	悃	悚					

Row 56		01	02	03	04	05	06	07	08	09	10	11	12	13	14	15	16	17	18	19
00		悄	悛	悖	悗	悒	悧	悋	惡	悸	惠	惓	悴	忰	悽	惆	悵	惘	慍	愕
20	愆	惶	惷	愀	惴	惺	愃	愡	惻	惱	愍	愎	慇	愾	愨	愧	慊	愿	愼	愬
40	愴	愽	慂	慄	慳	慷	慘	慙	慚	慫	慴	慯	慥	慱	慟	慝	慓	慵	憙	憖
60	憇	憬	憔	憚	憊	憑	憫	憮	懌	懊	應	懷	懈	懃	懆	憺	懋	罹	懍	懦
80	懣	懶	懺	懴	懿	懽	懼	懾	戀	戈	戉	戍	戌	戔	戛					

Row 57		01	02	03	04	05	06	07	08	09	10	11	12	13	14	15	16	17	18	19
00		戞	戡	截	戮	戰	戲	戳	扁	扎	扞	扣	扛	扠	扨	扼	抂	抉	找	抒
20	抓	抖	拔	抃	抔	拗	拑	抻	拏	拿	拆	擔	拈	拜	拌	拊	拂	拇	抛	拉
40	挌	拮	拱	挧	挂	挈	拯	拵	捐	挾	捍	搜	捏	掖	掎	掀	掫	捶	掣	掏
60	掉	掟	掵	捫	捩	掾	揩	揀	揆	揣	揉	插	揶	揄	搖	搴	搆	搓	搦	搶
80	攝	搗	搨	搏	摧	摯	摶	摎	攪	撕	撓	撥	撩	撈	撼					

Row 58		01	02	03	04	05	06	07	08	09	10	11	12	13	14	15	16	17	18	19
00		據	擒	擅	擇	撻	擘	擂	擱	擧	舉	擠	擡	抬	擣	擯	攬	擶	擴	擲
20	擺	攀	擽	攘	攜	攅	攤	攣	攫	攴	攵	攷	收	攸	畋	效	敖	敕	敍	敘
40	敞	敝	敲	數	斂	斃	變	斛	斟	斫	斷	旃	旆	旁	旄	旌	旒	旛	旙	无
60	旡	旱	杲	昊	昃	旻	杳	昵	昶	昴	昜	晏	晄	晉	晁	晞	晝	晤	晧	晨
80	晟	晢	晰	暃	暈	暎	暉	暄	暘	暝	曁	暹	曉	暾	暼					

Row 59		01	02	03	04	05	06	07	08	09	10	11	12	13	14	15	16	17	18	19
00		曄	暸	曖	曚	曠	昿	曦	曩	曰	曵	曷	朏	朖	朞	朦	朧	霸	朮	朿
20	朶	杁	朸	朷	杆	杞	杠	杙	杣	杤	枉	杰	枩	杼	杪	枌	枋	枦	枡	枅
40	枷	柯	枴	柬	枳	柩	枸	柤	柞	柝	柢	柮	枹	柎	柆	柧	檜	栞	框	栩
60	桀	桍	栲	桎	梳	栫	桙	档	桷	桿	梟	梏	梭	梔	條	梛	梃	檮	梹	桴
80	梵	梠	梺	椏	梍	桾	椁	棊	椈	棘	椢	椦	棡	椌	棍					

Row 60		01	02	03	04	05	06	07	08	09	10	11	12	13	14	15	16	17	18	19
00		棔	棧	棕	椶	椒	椄	棗	棣	椥	棹	棠	棯	椨	椪	椚	椣	椡	棆	楹
20	楷	楜	楸	楫	楔	楾	楮	椹	楴	椽	楙	椰	楡	楞	楝	榁	楪	榲	榮	槐
40	榿	槁	槓	榾	槎	寨	槊	槝	榻	槃	榧	樮	榑	榠	榜	榕	榴	槞	槨	樂
60	樛	槿	權	槹	槲	槧	樅	榱	樞	槭	樔	槫	樊	樒	櫁	樣	樓	橄	樌	橲
80	樶	橸	橇	橢	橙	橦	橈	樸	樢	檐	檍	檠	檄	檢	檣					

Row 61		01	02	03	04	05	06	07	08	09	10	11	12	13	14	15	16	17	18	19
00		檗	蘗	檻	櫃	櫂	檸	檳	檬	櫞	櫑	櫟	檪	櫚	櫪	櫻	欅	蘖	櫺	欒
20	欖	鬱	欟	欸	欷	盜	欹	飮	歇	歃	歉	歐	歙	歔	歛	歟	歡	歸	歹	歿
40	殀	殄	殃	殍	殘	殕	殞	殤	殪	殫	殯	殲	殱	殳	殷	殼	毆	毋	毓	毟
60	毬	毫	毳	毯	麾	氈	氓	气	氛	氤	氣	汞	汕	汢	汪	沂	沍	沚	沁	沛
80	汾	汨	汳	沒	沐	泄	泱	泓	沽	泗	泅	泝	沮	沱	沾					

Row 62		01	02	03	04	05	06	07	08	09	10	11	12	13	14	15	16	17	18	19
00		沺	泛	泯	泙	泪	洟	衍	洶	洫	洽	洸	洙	洵	洳	洒	洌	浣	涓	浤
20	浚	浹	浙	涎	涕	濤	涅	淹	渕	渊	涵	淇	淦	涸	淆	淬	淞	淌	淨	淒
40	淅	淺	淙	淤	淕	淪	淮	渭	湮	渮	渙	湲	湟	渾	渣	湫	渫	湶	湍	渟
60	湃	渺	湎	渤	滿	渝	游	溂	溪	溘	滉	溷	滓	溽	溯	滄	溲	滔	滕	溏
80	溥	滂	溟	潁	漑	灌	滬	滸	滾	漿	滲	漱	滯	漲	滌					

Row 63		01	02	03	04	05	06	07	08	09	10	11	12	13	14	15	16	17	18	19
00		漾	漓	滷	澆	潺	潸	澁	澀	潯	潛	濳	潭	澂	潼	潘	澎	澑	濂	潦
20	澳	澣	澡	澤	澹	濆	澪	濟	濕	濬	濔	濘	濱	濮	濛	瀉	瀋	濺	瀑	瀁
40	瀏	濾	瀛	瀚	潴	瀝	瀘	瀟	瀰	瀾	瀲	灑	灣	炙	炒	炯	烱	炬	炸	炳
60	炮	烟	烋	烝	烙	焉	烽	焜	焙	煥	煕	熈	煦	煢	煌	煖	煬	熏	燻	熄
80	熕	熨	熬	燗	熹	熾	燒	燉	燔	燎	燠	燬	燧	燵	燼					

Row 64		01	02	03	04	05	06	07	08	09	10	11	12	13	14	15	16	17	18	19
00		燹	燿	爍	爐	爛	爨	爭	爬	爰	爲	爻	爼	爿	牀	牆	牋	牘	牴	牾
20	犂	犁	犇	犒	犖	犢	犧	犹	犲	狃	狆	狄	狎	狒	狢	狠	狡	狹	狷	倏
40	猗	猊	猜	猖	猝	猴	猯	猩	猥	猾	獎	獏	默	獗	獪	獨	獰	獸	獵	獻
60	獺	珈	玳	珎	玻	珀	珥	珮	珞	璢	琅	瑯	琥	珸	琲	琺	瑕	琿	瑟	瑙
80	瑁	瑜	瑩	瑰	瑣	瑪	瑶	瑾	璋	璞	璧	瓊	瓏	瓔	珱					

Row 65		01	02	03	04	05	06	07	08	09	10	11	12	13	14	15	16	17	18	19
00		瓠	瓣	瓧	瓩	瓮	瓲	瓰	瓱	瓸	瓷	甄	甃	甅	甌	甎	甍	甕	甓	甞
20	甦	甬	甼	畄	畍	畊	畉	畛	畆	畚	畩	畤	畧	畫	畭	畸	當	疆	疇	畴
40	疊	疉	疂	疔	疚	疝	疥	疣	痂	疳	痃	疵	疽	疸	疼	疱	痍	痊	痒	痙
60	痣	痞	痾	痿	痼	瘁	痰	痺	痲	痳	瘋	瘍	瘉	瘟	瘧	瘠	瘡	瘢	瘤	瘴
80	瘰	瘻	癇	癈	癆	癜	癘	癡	癢	癨	癩	癪	癧	癬	癰					

Row 66		01	02	03	04	05	06	07	08	09	10	11	12	13	14	15	16	17	18	19
00		癲	癶	癸	發	皀	皃	皈	皋	皎	皖	皓	皙	皚	皰	皴	皸	皹	皺	盂
20	盍	盖	盒	盞	盡	盥	盧	盪	蘯	盻	眈	眇	眄	眩	眤	眞	眥	眦	眛	眷
40	眸	睇	睚	睨	睫	睛	睥	睿	睾	睹	瞎	瞋	瞑	瞠	瞞	瞰	瞶	瞹	瞿	瞼
60	瞽	瞻	矇	矍	矗	矚	矜	矣	矮	矼	砌	砒	礦	砠	礪	硅	碎	硴	碆	硼
80	碚	碌	碣	碵	碪	碯	磑	磆	磋	磔	碾	碼	磅	磊	磬					

Row 67		01	02	03	04	05	06	07	08	09	10	11	12	13	14	15	16	17	18	19
00		磧	磚	磽	磴	礇	礒	礑	礙	礬	礫	祀	祠	祗	祟	祚	祕	祓	祺	祿
20	禊	禝	禧	齋	禪	禮	禳	禹	禺	秉	秕	秧	秬	秡	秣	稈	稍	稘	稙	稠
40	稟	禀	稱	稻	稾	稷	穃	穗	穉	穡	穢	穩	龝	穰	穹	穽	窈	窗	窕	窘
60	窖	窩	竈	窰	窶	竅	竄	窿	邃	竇	竊	竍	竏	竕	竓	站	竚	竝	竡	竢
80	竦	竭	竰	笂	笏	笊	笆	笳	笘	笙	笞	笵	笨	笶	筐					

Row 68		01	02	03	04	05	06	07	08	09	10	11	12	13	14	15	16	17	18	19
00		筺	笄	筍	笋	筌	筅	筵	筥	筴	筧	筰	筱	筬	筮	箝	箘	箟	箍	箜
20	箚	箋	箒	箏	筝	箙	篋	篁	篌	篏	箴	篆	篝	篩	簑	簔	篦	篥	籠	簀
40	簇	簓	篳	篷	簗	簍	篶	簣	簧	簪	簟	簷	簫	簽	籌	籃	籔	籏	籀	籐
60	籘	籟	籤	籖	籥	籬	籵	粃	粐	粤	粭	粢	粫	粡	粨	粳	粲	粱	粮	粹
80	粽	糀	糅	糂	糘	糒	糜	糢	鬻	糯	糲	糴	糶	糺	紆					

Row 69		01	02	03	04	05	06	07	08	09	10	11	12	13	14	15	16	17	18	19
00		紂	紜	紕	紊	絅	絋	紮	紲	紿	紵	絆	絳	絖	絎	絲	絨	絮	絏	絣
20	經	綉	絛	綏	絽	綛	綺	綮	綣	綵	緇	綽	綫	總	綢	綯	緜	綸	綟	綰
40	緘	緝	緤	緞	緻	緲	緡	縅	縊	縣	縡	縒	縱	縟	縉	縋	縢	繆	繦	縻
60	縵	縹	繃	縷	縲	縺	繧	繝	繖	繞	繙	繚	繹	繪	繩	繼	繻	纃	緕	繽
80	辮	繿	纈	纉	續	纒	纐	纓	纔	纖	纎	纛	纜	缸	缺					

Row 70		01	02	03	04	05	06	07	08	09	10	11	12	13	14	15	16	17	18	19
00		罅	罌	罍	罎	罐	网	罕	罔	罘	罟	罠	罨	罩	罧	罸	羂	羆	羃	羈
20	羇	羌	羔	羞	羝	羚	羣	羯	羲	羹	羮	羶	羸	譱	翅	翆	翊	翕	翔	翡
40	翦	翩	翳	翹	飜	耆	耄	耋	耒	耘	耙	耜	耡	耨	耿	耻	聊	聆	聒	聘
60	聚	聟	聢	聨	聳	聲	聰	聶	聹	聽	聿	肄	肆	肅	肛	肓	肚	肭	冐	肬
80	胛	胥	胙	胝	胄	胚	胖	脉	胯	胱	脛	脩	脣	脯	腋					

Row 71		01	02	03	04	05	06	07	08	09	10	11	12	13	14	15	16	17	18	19
00		隋	腆	脾	腓	腑	胼	腱	腮	腥	腦	腴	膃	膈	膊	膀	膂	膠	膕	膤
20	膣	腟	膓	膩	膰	膵	膾	膸	膽	臀	臂	膺	臉	臍	臑	臙	臘	臈	臚	臟
40	臠	臧	臺	臻	臾	舁	舂	舅	與	舊	舍	舐	舖	舩	舫	舸	舳	艀	艙	艘
60	艝	艚	艟	艤	艢	艨	艪	艫	舮	艱	艷	艸	艾	芍	芒	芫	芟	芻	芬	苡
80	苣	苟	苒	苴	苳	苺	莓	范	苻	苹	苞	茆	苜	茉	苙					

Row 72		01	02	03	04	05	06	07	08	09	10	11	12	13	14	15	16	17	18	19
00		茵	茴	茖	茲	茱	荀	茹	荐	荅	茯	茫	茗	茘	莅	莚	莪	莟	莢	莖
20	茣	莎	莇	莊	荼	莵	荳	荵	莠	莉	莨	菴	萓	菫	菎	菽	萃	菘	萋	菁
40	菷	萇	菠	菲	萍	萢	萠	莽	萸	蔆	菻	葭	萪	萼	蕚	蒄	葷	葫	蒭	葮
60	蒂	葩	葆	萬	葯	葹	萵	蓊	葢	蒹	蒿	蒟	蓙	蓍	蒻	蓚	蓐	蓁	蓆	蓖
80	蒡	蔡	蓿	蓴	蔗	蔘	蔬	蔟	蔕	蔔	蓼	蕀	蕣	蕘	蕈					

Row 73		01	02	03	04	05	06	07	08	09	10	11	12	13	14	15	16	17	18	19
00		蕁	蘂	蕋	蕕	薀	薤	薈	薑	薊	薨	蕭	薔	薛	藪	薇	薜	蕷	蕾	薐
20	藉	薺	藏	薹	藐	藕	藝	藥	藜	藹	蘊	蘓	蘋	藾	藺	蘆	蘢	蘚	蘰	蘿
40	虍	乕	虔	號	虧	虱	蚓	蚣	蚩	蚪	蚋	蚌	蚶	蚯	蛄	蛆	蚰	蛉	蠣	蚫
60	蛔	蛞	蛩	蛬	蛟	蛛	蛯	蜒	蜆	蜈	蜀	蜃	蛻	蜑	蜉	蜍	蛹	蜊	蜴	蜿
80	蜷	蜻	蜥	蜩	蜚	蝠	蝟	蝸	蝌	蝎	蝴	蝗	蝨	蝮	蝙					

Row 74		01	02	03	04	05	06	07	08	09	10	11	12	13	14	15	16	17	18	19
00		蝓	蝣	蝪	蠅	螢	螟	螂	螯	蟋	螽	蟀	蟐	雖	螫	蟄	螳	蟇	蟆	螻
20	蟯	蟲	蟠	蠏	蠍	蟾	蟶	蟷	蠎	蟒	蠑	蠖	蠕	蠢	蠡	蠱	蠶	蠹	蠧	蠻
40	衄	衂	衒	衙	衞	衢	衫	袁	衾	袞	衵	衽	袵	衲	袂	袗	袒	袮	袙	袢
60	袍	袤	袰	袿	袱	裃	裄	裔	裘	裙	裝	裹	褂	裼	裴	裨	裲	褄	褌	褊
80	褓	襃	褞	褥	褪	褫	襁	襄	褻	褶	褸	襌	褝	襠	襞					

Row 75		01	02	03	04	05	06	07	08	09	10	11	12	13	14	15	16	17	18	19
00		襦	襤	襭	襪	襯	襴	襷	襾	覃	覈	覊	覓	覘	覡	覩	覦	覬	覯	覲
20	覺	覽	覿	觀	觚	觜	觝	觧	觴	觸	訃	訖	訐	訌	訛	訝	訥	訶	詁	詛
40	詒	詆	詈	詼	詭	詬	詢	誅	誂	誄	誨	誡	誑	誥	誦	誚	誣	諄	諍	諂
60	諚	諫	諳	諧	諤	諱	謔	諠	諢	諷	諞	諛	謌	謇	謚	諡	謖	謐	謗	謠
80	謳	鞫	謦	謫	謾	謨	譁	譌	譏	譎	證	譖	譛	譚	譫					

Row 76		01	02	03	04	05	06	07	08	09	10	11	12	13	14	15	16	17	18	19
00		譟	譬	譯	譴	譽	讀	讌	讎	讒	讓	讖	讙	讚	谺	豁	谿	豈	豌	豎
20	豐	豕	豢	豬	豸	豺	貂	貉	貅	貊	貍	貎	貔	豼	貘	戝	貭	貪	貽	貲
40	貳	貮	貶	賈	賁	賤	賣	賚	賽	賺	賻	贄	贅	贊	贇	贏	贍	贐	齎	贓
60	賍	贔	贖	赧	赭	赱	赳	趁	趙	跂	趾	趺	跏	跚	跖	跌	跛	跋	跪	跫
80	跟	跣	跼	踈	踉	跿	踝	踞	踐	踟	蹂	踵	踰	踴	蹊					

Row 77		01	02	03	04	05	06	07	08	09	10	11	12	13	14	15	16	17	18	19
00		蹇	蹉	蹌	蹐	蹈	蹙	蹤	蹠	踪	蹣	蹕	蹶	蹲	蹼	躁	躇	躅	躄	躋
20	躊	躓	躑	躔	躙	躪	躡	躬	躰	軆	躱	躾	軅	軈	軋	軛	軣	軼	軻	軫
40	軾	輊	輅	輕	輒	輙	輓	輜	輟	輛	輌	輦	輳	輻	輹	轅	轂	輾	轌	轉
60	轆	轎	轗	轜	轢	轣	轤	辜	辟	辣	辭	辯	辷	迚	迥	迢	迪	迯	邇	迴
80	逅	迹	迺	逑	逕	逡	逍	逞	逖	逋	逧	逶	逵	逹	迸					

Row 78		01	02	03	04	05	06	07	08	09	10	11	12	13	14	15	16	17	18	19
00		遏	遐	遑	遒	逎	遉	逾	遖	遘	遞	遨	遯	遶	隨	遲	邂	遽	邁	邀
20	邊	邉	邏	邨	邯	邱	邵	郢	郤	扈	郛	鄂	鄒	鄙	鄲	鄰	酊	酖	酘	酣
40	酥	酩	酳	酲	醋	醉	醂	醢	醫	醯	醪	醵	醴	醺	釀	釁	釉	釋	釐	釖
60	釟	釡	釛	釼	釵	釶	鈞	釿	鈔	鈬	鈕	鈑	鉞	鉗	鉅	鉉	鉤	鉈	銕	鈿
80	鉋	鉐	銜	銖	銓	銛	鉚	鋏	銹	銷	鋩	錏	鋺	鍄	錮					

Row 79		01	02	03	04	05	06	07	08	09	10	11	12	13	14	15	16	17	18	19
00		錙	錢	錚	錣	錺	錵	錻	鍜	鍠	鍼	鍮	鍖	鎰	鎬	鎭	鎔	鎹	鏖	鏗
20	鏨	鏥	鏘	鏃	鏝	鏐	鏈	鏤	鐚	鐔	鐓	鐃	鐇	鐐	鐶	鐫	鐵	鐡	鐺	鑁
40	鑒	鑄	鑛	鑠	鑢	鑞	鑪	鈩	鑰	鑵	鑷	鑽	鑚	鑼	鑾	钁	鑿	閂	閇	閊
60	閔	閖	閘	閙	閠	閨	閧	閭	閼	閻	閹	閾	闊	濶	闃	闍	闌	闕	闔	闖
80	關	闡	闥	闢	阡	阨	阮	阯	陂	陌	陏	陋	陷	陜	陞					

Row 80		01	02	03	04	05	06	07	08	09	10	11	12	13	14	15	16	17	18	19
00		陝	陟	陦	陲	陬	隍	隘	隕	隗	險	隧	隱	隲	隰	隴	隶	隸	隹	雎
20	雋	雉	雍	襍	雜	霍	雕	雹	霄	霆	霈	霓	霎	霑	霏	霖	霙	霤	霪	霰
40	霹	霽	霾	靄	靆	靈	靂	靉	靜	靠	靤	靦	靨	勒	靫	靱	靹	鞅	靼	鞁
60	靺	鞆	鞋	鞏	鞐	鞜	鞨	鞦	鞣	鞳	鞴	韃	韆	韈	韋	韜	韭	齏	韲	竟
80	韶	韵	頏	頌	頸	頤	頡	頷	頽	顆	顏	顋	顫	顯	顰					

Row 81		01	02	03	04	05	06	07	08	09	10	11	12	13	14	15	16	17	18	19
00		顱	顴	顳	颪	颯	颱	颶	飄	飃	飆	飩	飫	餃	餉	餒	餔	餘	餡	餝
20	餞	餤	餠	餬	餮	餽	餾	饂	饉	饅	饐	饋	饑	饒	饌	饕	馗	馘	馥	馭
40	馮	馼	駟	駛	駝	駘	駑	駭	駮	駱	駲	駻	駸	騁	騏	騅	駢	騙	騫	騷
60	驅	驂	驀	驃	騾	驕	驍	驛	驗	驟	驢	驥	驤	驩	驫	驪	骭	骰	骼	髀
80	髏	髑	髓	體	髞	髟	髢	髣	髦	髯	髫	髮	髴	髱	髷					

Row 82		01	02	03	04	05	06	07	08	09	10	11	12	13	14	15	16	17	18	19
00		髻	鬆	鬘	鬚	鬟	鬢	鬣	鬥	鬧	鬨	鬩	鬪	鬮	鬯	鬲	魄	魃	魏	魍
20	魎	魑	魘	魴	鮓	鮃	鮑	鮖	鮗	鮟	鮠	鮨	鮴	鯀	鯊	鮹	鯆	鯏	鯑	鯒
40	鯣	鯢	鯤	鯔	鯡	鰺	鯲	鯱	鯰	鰕	鰔	鰉	鰓	鰌	鰆	鰈	鰒	鰊	鰄	鰮
60	鰛	鰥	鰤	鰡	鰰	鱇	鰲	鱆	鰾	鱚	鱠	鱧	鱶	鱸	鳧	鳬	鳰	鴉	鴈	鳫
80	鴃	鴆	鴪	鴦	鶯	鴣	鴟	鵄	鴕	鴒	鵁	鴿	鴾	鵆	鵈					

Row 83		01	02	03	04	05	06	07	08	09	10	11	12	13	14	15	16	17	18	19
00		鵝	鵞	鵤	鵑	鵐	鵙	鵲	鶉	鶇	鶫	鵯	鵺	鶚	鶤	鶩	鶲	鷄	鷁	鶻
20	鶸	鶺	鷆	鷏	鷂	鷙	鷓	鷸	鷦	鷭	鷯	鷽	鸚	鸛	鸞	鹵	鹹	鹽	麁	麈
40	麋	麌	麒	麕	麑	麝	麥	麩	麸	麪	麭	靡	黌	黎	黏	黐	黔	黜	點	黝
60	黠	黥	黨	黯	黴	黶	黷	黹	黻	黼	黽	鼇	鼈	皷	鼕	鼡	鼬	鼾	齊	齒
80	齔	齣	齟	齠	齡	齦	齧	齬	齪	齷	齲	齶	龕	龜	龠					

Row 84		01	02	03	04	05	06	07	08	09	10	11	12	13	14	15	16	17	18	19
00		堯	槇	遙	瑤	凜	熙													
20																				
40																				
60																				
80																				

K

JIS X 0212-1990 Table

This appendix constitutes a table for the complete JIS X 0212-1990 character set, printed here using the typeface 平成明朝W3 (HeiseiMin-W3H), developed by FDPC. Each character is indexed by Row-Cell value.

Row 2		01	02	03	04	05	06	07	08	09	10	11	12	13	14	15	16	17	18	19
00																˘	ˇ	¸	˙	˝
20	¯	˛	˚	~	΄	΅									¡	¦	¿			
40																				
60																º	ª	©	®	™
80	¤	№																		

Row 5		01	02	03	04	05	06	07	08	09	10	11	12	13	14	15	16	17	18	19
00																				
20																				
40																				
60																				
80								ヷ	ヸ	ヹ	ヺ									

Row 6		01	02	03	04	05	06	07	08	09	10	11	12	13	14	15	16	17	18	19
00																				
20																				
40																				
60						Ά	Έ	Ή	Ί	Ϊ		Ό		Ύ	Ϋ		Ώ			
80		ά	έ	ή	ί	ϊ	ΐ	ό	ς	ύ	ϋ	ΰ	ώ							

Row 7		01	02	03	04	05	06	07	08	09	10	11	12	13	14	15	16	17	18	19
00																				
20															Ђ	Ѓ	Є	Ѕ	І	Ї
40	Ј	Љ	Њ	Ћ	Ќ	Ў	Џ													
60																				
80			ђ	ѓ	є	ѕ	і	ї	ј	љ	њ	ћ	ќ	ў	џ					

Row 9		01	02	03	04	05	06	07	08	09	10	11	12	13	14	15	16	17	18	19
00		Æ	Đ		Ħ		Ĳ		Ł	Ŀ		Ŋ	Ø	Œ		Ŧ	Þ			
20														æ	đ	ð	ħ	ı	ĳ	ĸ
40	ł	ŀ	ŉ	ŋ	ø	œ	ß	ŧ	þ											
60																				
80																				

Row 10		01	02	03	04	05	06	07	08	09	10	11	12	13	14	15	16	17	18	19
00		Á	À	Ä	Â	Ă	Ǎ	Ā	Ą	Å	Ã	Ć	Ĉ	Č	Ç	Ċ	Ď	É	È	Ë
20	Ê	Ě	Ė	Ē	Ę		Ĝ	Ğ	Ģ	Ġ	Ĥ	Í	Ì	Ï	Î	Ǐ	İ	Ī	Į	Ĩ
40	Ĵ	Ķ	Ĺ	Ľ	Ļ	Ń	Ň	Ņ	Ñ	Ó	Ò	Ö	Ô	Ǒ	Ő	Ō	Õ	Ŕ	Ř	Ŗ
60	Ś	Ŝ	Š	Ş	Ť	Ţ	Ú	Ù	Ü	Û	Ŭ	Ǔ	Ű	Ū	Ų	Ů	Ũ	Ǘ	Ǜ	Ǚ
80	Ǖ	Ŵ	Ý	Ÿ	Ŷ	Ź	Ž	Ż												

Row 11		01	02	03	04	05	06	07	08	09	10	11	12	13	14	15	16	17	18	19
00		á	à	ä	â	ă	ǎ	ā	ą	å	ã	ć	ĉ	č	ç	ċ	ď	é	è	ë
20	ê	ě	ė	ē	ę	ǵ	ĝ	ğ		ġ	ĥ	í	ì	ï	î	ǐ		ī	į	ĩ
40	ĵ	ķ	ĺ	ľ	ļ	ń	ň	ņ	ñ	ó	ò	ö	ô	ǒ	ő	ō	õ	ŕ	ř	ŗ
60	ś	ŝ	š	ş	ť	ţ	ú	ù	ü	û	ŭ	ǔ	ű	ū	ų	ů	ũ	ǘ	ǜ	ǚ
80	ǖ	ŵ	ý	ÿ	ŷ	ź	ž	ż												

Row 16		01	02	03	04	05	06	07	08	09	10	11	12	13	14	15	16	17	18	19
00		丂	丄	丅	丌	丒	丟	丣	两	丨	丫	丮	丯	丰	丵	乀	乁	乄	乇	乑
20	乚	乜	乣	乨	乩	乴	乵	乹	乿	亍	亖	亗	亝	亯	亹	仃	仐	仚	仛	仠
40	仡	仢	仨	仯	仱	仳	仵	份	仾	仿	伀	伂	伃	伈	伋	伌	伒	伕	伖	众
60	伙	伮	伱	你	伳	伵	伷	伹	伻	伾	佀	佂	佈	佉	佋	佌	佒	佔	佖	佘
80	佟	佣	佪	佬	佮	佱	佷	佸	佹	佺	佽	佾	侁	侂	侄					

Row 17		01	02	03	04	05	06	07	08	09	10	11	12	13	14	15	16	17	18	19
00		侅	侉	侊	侌	侎	侐	侒	侓	侔	侗	侙	侚	侞	侟	侲	侷	侹	侻	侼
20	侽	侾	俀	俁	俅	俆	俈	俉	俋	俌	俍	俏	俒	俜	俠	俢	俰	俲	俼	俽
40	俿	倀	倁	倄	倇	倊	倌	倎	倐	倓	倗	倘	倛	倜	倝	倞	倢	倧	倮	倰
60	倲	倳	倵	偀	偁	偂	偅	偆	偊	偌	偎	偑	偒	偓	偗	偙	偟	偠	偢	偣
80	偦	偧	偪	偭	偰	偱	倻	傁	傃	傄	傆	傊	傎	傏	傐					

Row 18		01	02	03	04	05	06	07	08	09	10	11	12	13	14	15	16	17	18	19
00		傒	傓	傔	傖	傛	傜	傞	傟	傠	傡	傢	傪	傯	傰	傹	傺	傽	僀	僃
20	僄	僇	僌	僎	僐	僓	僔	僘	僜	僝	僟	僢	僤	僦	僨	僩	僯	僱	僶	僺
40	僾	儃	儆	儇	儈	儋	儌	儍	儎	僲	儐	儗	儙	儛	儜	儞	儣	儧	儨	儬
60	儭	儯	儱	儳	儴	儵	儸	儹	兂	兊	兏	兓	兕	兗	兘	兟	兤	兦	兾	冃
80	冄	冋	冎	冘	冝	冡	冣	冭	冸	冺	冼	冾	冿	凂						

Row 19		01	02	03	04	05	06	07	08	09	10	11	12	13	14	15	16	17	18	19
00		凈	减	凑	凒	凓	凕	凘	凞	凢	凥	凮	凲	凳	凴	凷	刁	刂	刅	划
20	刓	刕	刖	刘	刢	刨	刱	刲	刵	刼	剅	剉	剕	剗	剘	剚	剜	剟	剠	剡
40	剦	剮	剷	剸	剹	劀	劂	劅	劊	劌	劓	劕	劖	劗	劘	劚	劜	劤	劥	劦
60	劧	劯	劰	劶	劵	劸	劺	劻	劽	勀	勄	勆	勈	勌	勏	勑	勔	勖	勛	勜
80	勠	勥	勨	勩	勪	勬	勰	勱	勴	勶	勷	匀	匃	匊	匋					

Row 20		01	02	03	04	05	06	07	08	09	10	11	12	13	14	15	16	17	18	19
00		匌	匑	匒	匘	匛	匜	匞	匟	匢	匧	匨	匩	匫	匬	匭	匰	匲	匵	匼
20	匽	區	卂	卌	卋	卙	卛	卡	卣	卥	卬	卭	卲	卹	卾	厃	厇	厈	厎	厓
40	厔	厙	厝	厡	厤	厪	厫	厯	厲	厴	厵	厷	厸	厺	厽	叀	叅	叏	叒	叓
60	叕	叚	叝	叞	叠	叧	另	叵	吉	吒	吚	吡	吧	吨	吪	启	吱	吴	吵	呃
80	呄	呇	呍	呏	呞	呢	呤	呦	呧	呩	呫	呭	呮	呴	呿					

Row 21		01	02	03	04	05	06	07	08	09	10	11	12	13	14	15	16	17	18	19
00		咁	咃	咅	咈	咉	咍	咑	咕	咖	咜	咟	咡	咦	咧	咩	咪	咭	咮	咱
20	咷	咹	咺	咻	咿	哆	哊	响	哎	哠	哪	哬	哯	哶	哼	哾	哿	唀	唁	唅
40	唈	唉	唌	唍	唎	唕	唪	唫	唲	唵	唶	唻	唼	唽	啁	啇	啉	啊	啍	啐
60	啑	啘	啚	啛	啞	啠	啡	啤	啦	啿	喁	喂	喆	喈	喎	喏	喑	喒	喓	喔
80	喗	喣	喤	喭	喲	喿	嗁	嗃	嗆	嗉	嗋	嗌	嗎	嗑	嗒					

Row 22		01	02	03	04	05	06	07	08	09	10	11	12	13	14	15	16	17	18	19
00		嗓	嗗	嗘	嗛	嗞	嗢	嗩	嗶	嗿	嘅	嘈	嘊	嘍	嘎	嘏	嘐	嘑	嘒	嘙
20	嘬	嘰	嘳	嘵	嘷	嘹	嘻	嘼	嘽	嘿	噀	噁	噃	噄	噆	噉	噋	噍	噏	噔
40	噞	噠	噡	噢	噣	噦	噩	噭	噯	噱	噲	噵	嚄	嚅	嚈	嚋	嚌	嚕	嚙	嚚
60	嚝	嚞	嚟	嚦	嚧	嚨	嚩	嚫	嚬	嚭	嚱	嚳	嚷	嚾	囅	囉	囊	囋	囏	囐
80	囌	囍	囙	囜	囝	囟	囡	囤	囥	囦	囧	囨	囪	囫	园					

Row 23		01	02	03	04	05	06	07	08	09	10	11	12	13	14	15	16	17	18	19
00		囶	囷	圁	圂	圇	圊	圌	圑	圕	圚	圛	圝	圠	圢	圣	圤	圥	圩	圪
20	圬	圮	圯	圳	圴	圽	圾	圿	坅	坆	坌	坍	坒	坢	坥	坧	坨	坫	坭	坮
40	坯	坰	坱	坳	坴	坵	坷	坹	坺	坻	坼	坾	垁	垃	垌	垔	垗	垙	垚	垜
60	垝	垞	垟	垡	垕	垧	垨	垩	垬	垸	垽	埇	埈	埌	埏	埕	埝	埞	埤	埦
80	埧	埩	埭	埰	埵	埶	埸	埽	埾	埿	堃	堄	堈	堉	埡					

Row 24		01	02	03	04	05	06	07	08	09	10	11	12	13	14	15	16	17	18	19
00		堌	堍	堝	堞	堟	堠	堦	堧	堭	堲	堹	堿	塉	塌	塍	塏	塐	塕	塟
20	塡	塤	塧	塨	塸	塼	塿	墀	墁	墇	墈	墉	墊	墌	墍	墏	墐	墔	墖	墝
40	墠	墡	墢	墦	墩	墱	墲	壄	墼	壂	壈	壍	壎	壐	壒	壔	壖	壚	壝	壡
60	壢	壩	壳	夅	夆	夋	夌	夒	夓	夔	虁	夝	夡	夣	夤	夨	夯	夰	夳	夵
80	夶	夿	奃	奆	奒	奓	奙	奛	奝	奞	奟	奡	奣	奫	奭					

Row 25		01	02	03	04	05	06	07	08	09	10	11	12	13	14	15	16	17	18	19
00		奯	奲	奵	奶	她	奻	奼	妋	妌	妎	妒	妕	妗	妟	妤	妧	妭	妮	妯
20	妰	妳	妷	妺	妼	姁	姃	姄	姈	姊	姍	姒	姝	姞	姟	姣	姤	姧	姮	姯
40	姱	姲	姴	姷	娀	娄	娌	娍	娎	娒	娓	娞	娣	娤	娧	娨	娪	娭	娰	婄
60	婅	婇	婈	婌	婐	婕	婞	婣	婥	婧	婭	婷	婺	婻	婾	媋	媐	媓	媖	媙
80	媜	媞	媟	媠	媢	媧	媬	媱	媲	媳	媵	媸	媺	媻	媿					

Row 26		01	02	03	04	05	06	07	08	09	10	11	12	13	14	15	16	17	18	19
00		嫄	嫆	嫈	嫏	嫚	嫜	嫠	嫥	嫪	嫮	嫵	嫶	嫽	嬀	嬁	嬈	嬗	嬴	嬙
20	嬛	嬝	嬡	嬥	嬭	嬸	孁	孋	孌	孒	孖	孞	孨	孮	孯	孼	孽	孾	孿	宂
40	宄	宆	宊	宎	宐	宑	宓	宔	宖	宨	宩	宬	宭	宯	宱	宲	宷	宺	宼	寀
60	寁	寍	寏	寖	寗	寘	寙	寚	寠	寯	寱	寴	寽	尌	尗	尞	尟	尣	尦	尩
80	尫	尬	尮	尰	尲	尵	尶	屙	屚	屜	屢	屣	屧	屨	屩					

Row 27		01	02	03	04	05	06	07	08	09	10	11	12	13	14	15	16	17	18	19
00		屭	屰	屴	屵	屺	屻	屼	屽	岇	岈	岊	岏	岒	岝	岞	岠	岢	岣	岦
20	岪	岲	岴	岵	岺	峉	峋	峒	峝	峗	峮	峱	峲	峴	崁	崆	崍	崒	崫	崣
40	崤	崦	崧	崱	崴	崹	崽	崿	嵂	嵃	嵆	嵈	嵕	嵑	嵙	嵊	嵟	嵠	嵡	嵢
60	嵤	嵪	嵭	嵰	嵹	嵺	嵾	嵿	嶁	嶃	嶈	嶊	嶒	嶓	嶔	嶕	嶙	嶛	嶟	嶠
80	嶧	嶫	嶰	嶴	嶸	嶹	巃	巇	巋	巐	巎	巘	巙	巠	巤					

Row 28		01	02	03	04	05	06	07	08	09	10	11	12	13	14	15	16	17	18	19
00		巩	巸	巹	帀	帇	帍	帒	帔	帕	帘	帟	帠	帮	帨	帲	帵	帾	幋	幐
20	幉	幑	幖	幘	幛	幜	幞	幨	幪	幫	幬	幭	幮	幰	庂	庋	庎	庢	庤	庥
40	庨	庪	庬	庱	庳	庽	庾	庿	廆	廌	廋	廎	廑	廒	廔	廕	廜	廞	廥	廫
60	异	弆	弇	弈	弎	弙	弜	弝	弡	弢	弣	弤	弨	弫	弬	弮	弰	弴	弶	弻
80	弽	弿	彀	彄	彅	彇	彍	彐	彔	彘	彛	彠	彣	彤	彧					

Row 29		01	02	03	04	05	06	07	08	09	10	11	12	13	14	15	16	17	18	19
00		彯	彲	彴	彵	彸	彺	彽	彾	徉	徍	徏	徖	徜	徝	徢	徧	徫	徤	徬
20	徯	徰	徱	徸	忄	忇	忈	忉	忋	忐	忑	忒	忓	忔	忞	忡	忢	忨	忩	忪
40	忬	忭	忮	忯	忲	忳	忶	忺	忼	怇	怊	怍	怓	怔	怗	怘	怚	怟	怤	怭
60	怳	怵	恀	恇	恈	恉	恌	恑	恔	恖	恗	恝	恡	恧	恱	恾	恿	悂	悆	悈
80	悊	悎	悑	悓	悕	悘	悝	悞	悢	悤	悥	您	悰	悱	悷					

Row 30		01	02	03	04	05	06	07	08	09	10	11	12	13	14	15	16	17	18	19
00		悻	悾	惂	惄	惈	惉	惊	惋	惎	惏	惔	惕	惙	惛	惝	惞	惢	惥	惲
20	惵	惸	惼	惽	愂	愇	愊	愌	愐	愑	愒	愓	愔	愖	愗	愙	愜	愞	愢	愪
40	愫	愰	愱	愵	愶	愷	愹	慁	慅	慆	慉	慞	慠	慬	慲	慸	慻	慼	慿	憀
60	憁	憃	憄	憋	憍	憒	憓	憗	憘	憜	憝	憟	憠	憥	憨	憪	憭	憸	憹	憼
80	懀	懁	懂	懎	懏	懕	懜	懝	懞	懟	懡	懢	懧	懩	懥					

Row 31		01	02	03	04	05	06	07	08	09	10	11	12	13	14	15	16	17	18	19
00		懬	懫	懯	戁	戃	戄	戇	戓	戕	戜	戠	戢	戣	戧	戩	戫	戹	戺	扂
20	扃	扄	扆	扌	扐	扑	扒	扔	扖	扚	扜	扤	扭	扯	扳	扺	扽	抍	抎	抏
40	抐	抦	抨	抳	抶	抷	抸	抾	抿	拄	拎	拕	拖	拚	拪	拲	拴	拼	拽	挃
60	挄	挊	挋	挍	挐	挓	挖	挘	挩	挪	挭	挵	挶	挹	挼	捁	捂	捃	捄	捆
80	捊	捋	捎	捒	捓	捔	捘	捛	捥	捦	捬	捭	捱	捴	捵					

Row 32		01	02	03	04	05	06	07	08	09	10	11	12	13	14	15	16	17	18	19
00		捸	捼	捽	捿	掂	掄	掇	掊	掐	掔	掕	掙	掚	掞	掤	掦	掭	掮	掯
20	掽	揁	揅	揈	揎	揑	揓	揔	揕	揜	揠	揥	揪	揬	揲	揳	揵	揸	揹	搉
40	搊	搐	搒	搔	搘	搞	搠	搢	搤	搥	搩	搪	搯	搰	搵	搽	搿	摋	摏	摑
60	摒	摓	摔	摚	摛	摜	摝	摟	摠	摡	摣	摭	摳	摴	摻	摽	撅	撇	撏	撐
80	撑	撘	撙	撛	撝	撟	撡	撣	撦	撨	撬	撳	撽	撾	撿					

Row 33		01	02	03	04	05	06	07	08	09	10	11	12	13	14	15	16	17	18	19
00		擄	擉	擊	擋	擌	擎	擐	擑	擕	擗	擤	擥	擩	擪	擭	擰	擵	擷	擻
20	擿	攁	攄	攈	攉	攊	攏	攓	攔	攖	攙	攛	攞	攟	攢	攦	攩	攮	攱	攺
40	攼	攽	敃	敇	敉	敐	敒	敔	敟	敠	敧	敫	敺	敿	斁	斅	斊	斒	斕	斘
60	斝	斠	斣	斦	斮	斲	斳	斴	斿	旂	旈	旉	旎	旐	旔	旖	旘	旟	旰	旲
80	旴	旵	旹	旾	旿	昀	昄	昈	昉	昍	昑	昒	昕	昖	昝					

Row 34		01	02	03	04	05	06	07	08	09	10	11	12	13	14	15	16	17	18	19
00		昞	昡	昢	昣	昤	昦	昩	昪	昫	昬	昮	昰	昱	昳	昹	昷	晀	晅	晆
20	晊	晌	晑	晎	晗	晘	晙	晛	晜	晠	晡	[illegible]	晪	晫	晬	晾	晢	晵	晿	暏
40	最	暘	晻	暀	晼	暋	暌	暍	暐	暒	暙	暚	暛	暜	暟	暠	暤	暭	暱	暲
60	暵	暻	暿	曀	曂	曃	曈	曌	曎	曏	曔	曛	曟	曨	曫	曬	曮	曺	朅	朇
80	朎	朓	朙	朜	朠	朢	朳	朾	杅	杇	杈	杌	杔	杕	杝					

Row 35		01	02	03	04	05	06	07	08	09	10	11	12	13	14	15	16	17	18	19
00		杦	杬	杮	杴	杶	杻	极	构	枎	枏	枑	枓	枖	枘	枙	枛	枰	枱	枲
20	枵	枻	枼	枽	枾	柀	柂	柃	柅	柈	柉	柒	柗	柙	柜	柡	柦	柰	柲	柶
40	柷	桒	栔	栙	栝	栟	栨	栧	栬	栭	栯	栰	栱	栳	栻	栿	桄	桅	桊	桌
60	桕	桗	桘	桛	桫	栝	桯	桰	桱	桲	桵	桹	桺	桻	桼	梂	梄	梆	楟	梋
80	梘	梚	梜	梡	梣	梥	梩	梪	梮	梲	梻	棅	棈	棌	棏					

Row 36		01	02	03	04	05	06	07	08	09	10	11	12	13	14	15	16	17	18	19
00		棐	棑	棓	棖	棙	棜	棝	棥	棨	棪	棫	棬	棭	棰	棱	棵	棶	棻	棼
20	棽	椆	椉	椊	椐	椑	椓	椖	椗	椱	椳	椵	椸	椻	楂	楅	楉	楎	楗	楛
40	楣	楤	楥	楦	楨	楩	楬	楰	楱	楲	楺	楻	楿	榀	榍	榒	榖	榘	榡	榥
60	榦	榨	榫	榭	榯	榷	榸	榺	榼	槅	槈	槑	槖	槗	槢	槥	槮	槯	槱	槳
80	槵	槾	樀	樁	樃	樏	樑	樕	樚	樝	樠	樤	樨	樰	樲					

Row 37		01	02	03	04	05	06	07	08	09	10	11	12	13	14	15	16	17	18	19
00		樴	樷	樻	樾	樿	橅	橆	橉	橊	橎	橐	橑	橒	橕	橖	橛	橤	橧	橪
20	橱	橳	橾	檁	檃	檆	檇	檉	檋	檑	檛	檝	檞	檟	檥	檫	檯	檰	檱	檴
40	檽	檾	檿	櫆	櫉	櫈	櫌	櫐	櫔	櫕	櫖	櫜	櫝	櫤	櫧	櫬	櫰	櫱	櫲	櫼
60	櫽	欂	欃	欆	欇	欉	欏	欐	欑	欗	欛	欞	欤	欨	欫	欬	欯	欵	欶	欻
80	欿	歂	歊	歍	歒	歖	歘	歡	歠	歧	歫	歭	歰	歵	歽					

Row 38		01	02	03	04	05	06	07	08	09	10	11	12	13	14	15	16	17	18	19
00		歾	殂	殅	殗	殛	殟	殠	殢	殣	殨	殩	殬	殭	殮	殰	殸	殹	殽	殾
20	毃	毄	毉	毌	毖	毚	毡	毣	毦	毧	毮	毱	毷	毹	毿	氂	氄	氅	氉	氍
40	氎	氐	氒	氙	氟	氦	氧	氨	氬	氮	氳	氵	氶	氺	氻	氿	汊	汋	汍	汏
60	汒	汔	汙	汛	汜	汫	汭	汯	汴	汶	汸	汹	汻	沅	沆	沇	沉	沔	沕	沗
80	沘	沜	沟	沰	沲	沴	泂	泆	泍	泏	泐	泑	泒	泔	泖					

Row 39		01	02	03	04	05	06	07	08	09	10	11	12	13	14	15	16	17	18	19
00		泚	泜	泠	泧	泩	泫	泬	泮	泲	泴	洄	洇	洊	洎	洏	洑	洓	洚	洦
20	洧	洨	汧	洮	洯	洱	洹	洼	洿	浗	浞	浟	浡	浥	浧	浯	浰	浼	涂	涇
40	涑	涒	涔	涖	涗	涘	涪	涬	涴	涷	涹	涽	涿	淄	淈	淊	淎	淏	淖	淛
60	淝	淟	淠	淢	淥	淩	淯	淰	淴	淶	淼	渀	渄	渞	渢	渧	渲	渶	渹	渻
80	渼	湄	湅	湈	湉	湋	湏	湑	湒	湓	湔	湗	湜	湝	湞					

Row 40		01	02	03	04	05	06	07	08	09	10	11	12	13	14	15	16	17	18	19
00		湢	湣	湨	湳	湻	湽	溍	溓	溙	溠	溧	溭	溮	溱	溳	溻	溿	滀	滁
20	滃	滇	滈	滊	滍	滎	滏	滫	滭	滮	滹	滻	滽	漄	漈	漊	漍	漖	漘	漚
40	漛	漦	漩	漪	漯	漰	漳	漶	漻	漼	漭	潏	潑	潒	潓	潗	潙	潚	潝	潞
60	潡	潢	潨	潬	潽	潾	澃	澇	澉	澋	澌	澍	澐	澒	澓	澔	澖	澚	澟	澠
80	澥	澦	澧	澨	澮	澯	澰	澵	澶	澼	濅	濇	濈	濊						

Row 41		01	02	03	04	05	06	07	08	09	10	11	12	13	14	15	16	17	18	19
00		濚	濞	濨	濩	濰	濵	濹	濼	濽	瀀	瀅	瀆	瀇	瀍	瀗	瀠	瀣	瀯	瀴
20	瀷	瀹	瀼	灃	灄	灈	灉	灊	灋	灔	灕	灝	灞	灎	灤	灥	灬	灮	灵	灶
40	灾	炁	炅	炆	炔	炕	炖	炗	炘	炛	炤	炫	炰	炱	炴	炷	烊	烑	烓	烔
60	烕	烖	烘	烜	烤	烺	焃	焄	焅	焆	焇	焋	焌	焏	焞	焠	焫	焭	焯	焰
80	焱	焸	煁	煅	煆	煇	煊	煋	煐	煒	煗	煚	煜	煞	煠					

Row 42		01	02	03	04	05	06	07	08	09	10	11	12	13	14	15	16	17	18	19
00		煨	煹	熀	熅	熇	熌	熒	熚	熛	熠	熢	熯	熰	熲	熳	熺	熿	燀	燁
20	燄	燋	燌	燓	燖	燙	燚	燜	燸	燾	爀	爇	爈	爉	爓	爗	爚	爝	爟	爤
40	爫	爯	爴	爸	爹	牁	牂	牃	牅	牎	牏	牐	牓	牕	牖	牚	牜	牞	牠	牣
60	牨	牫	牮	牯	牱	牷	牸	牻	牼	牿	犄	犉	犍	犎	犓	犛	犨	犭	犮	犱
80	犴	犾	狁	狇	狉	狌	狕	狖	狘	狟	狥	狳	狴	狺	狻					

Row 43		01	02	03	04	05	06	07	08	09	10	11	12	13	14	15	16	17	18	19
00		狾	猂	猄	猅	猇	猋	猍	猒	猓	猘	猙	猞	猢	猤	猧	猨	猬	猱	猲
20	猵	猺	猻	猽	獃	獍	獐	獒	獖	獘	獝	獞	獟	獠	獦	獧	獩	獫	獬	獮
40	獯	獱	獷	獹	獼	玀	玁	玃	玅	玆	玎	玐	玓	玕	玗	玘	玜	玞	玟	玠
60	玢	玥	玦	玪	玫	玭	玵	玷	玹	玼	玽	玿	珅	珆	珢	珋	珌	珏	珒	珓
80	珖	珙	珝	珡	珣	珦	珧	珩	珴	珵	珷	珹	珺	珻	珽					

Row 44		01	02	03	04	05	06	07	08	09	10	11	12	13	14	15	16	17	18	19
00		珿	琀	琁	琄	琇	瑘	琑	琚	琛	琤	琦	琨	琩	琪	琫	琬	琭	琮	琯
20	琰	琱	琹	瑀	瑃	瑄	瑆	瑇	瑋	瑍	瑑	瑒	瑗	瑝	瑢	瑦	瑧	瑨	瑫	瑭
40	瑮	瑱	瑲	璀	璁	璅	璆	璇	璉	璏	璐	璑	璒	璘	璙	璚	璜	璟	璠	璡
60	璣	璦	璨	璩	璪	璫	璮	璯	璱	璲	璵	璹	璻	璿	瓈	瓉	瓌	瓐	瓓	瓘
80	瓚	瓛	瓞	瓟	瓤	瓨	瓪	瓫	瓯	瓴	瓺	瓻	甅	瓿	甍					

Row 45		01	02	03	04	05	06	07	08	09	10	11	12	13	14	15	16	17	18	19
00		甒	甖	甗	甠	甡	甤	甧	甩	甪	甯	甶	甹	甽	甾	甿	畀	畃	畇	畈
20	畎	畐	畒	畗	畞	畟	畡	畯	畱	畹	畺	畻	畼	畽	畾	疁	疅	疐	疒	疓
40	疕	疙	疜	疢	疤	疴	疺	疿	痀	痁	痄	痆	痌	痎	痏	痗	痚	痟	痠	痡
60	痤	痧	痬	痮	痯	痱	痹	瘀	瘂	瘃	瘄	瘇	瘈	瘊	瘌	瘏	瘒	瘓	瘕	瘖
80	瘙	瘛	瘜	瘝	瘞	瘣	瘥	瘦	瘩	瘭	瘲	瘳	瘵	瘸	瘹					

Row 46		01	02	03	04	05	06	07	08	09	10	11	12	13	14	15	16	17	18	19
00		瘺	瘼	癊	癀	癁	癃	癄	癅	癉	癋	癕	癙	癟	癤	癥	癭	癮	癯	癱
20	癵	皁	皅	皌	皍	皕	皛	皜	皝	皟	皠	皢	皣	皤	皥	皦	皧	皨	皪	皭
40	皽	盁	盅	盉	盋	盌	盇	盙	盝	盠	盦	盨	盬	盰	盱	盶	盹	盼	眀	眆
60	眊	眎	眒	眔	眕	眗	眙	眚	眛	眢	眨	眭	眮	眯	眴	眵	眶	眹	眽	眾
80	睂	睅	睆	睊	睍	睎	睏	睒	睖	睗	睜	睞	睟	睠	睢					

Row 47		01	02	03	04	05	06	07	08	09	10	11	12	13	14	15	16	17	18	19
00		睤	睧	睪	睬	睰	睲	睳	睴	睺	睽	瞀	瞄	瞌	瞍	瞔	瞕	瞖	瞚	瞟
20	瞢	瞧	瞪	瞮	瞯	瞱	瞵	瞾	矃	矉	矑	矒	矕	矙	矞	矟	矠	矤	矦	矪
40	矬	矰	矱	矴	矸	矻	砅	砆	砉	砍	砎	砑	砝	砡	砢	砤	砭	砮	砰	砵
60	砷	硃	硄	硇	硈	硌	硎	硒	硜	硞	硠	硡	硣	硤	硨	硪	确	硺	硾	碊
80	碏	碔	碘	碡	碝	碞	碟	碤	碨	碬	碭	碰	碱	碲	碳					

Row 48		01	02	03	04	05	06	07	08	09	10	11	12	13	14	15	16	17	18	19
00		碻	碽	磀	磇	磈	磉	磌	磎	磒	磓	磕	磖	磤	磛	磟	磠	磡	磦	磪
20	磲	磳	磵	磶	磷	磺	磻	磿	礆	礌	礐	礚	礜	礞	礟	礠	礥	礧	礩	礭
40	礱	礴	礵	礻	礽	礿	祄	祅	祆	祊	祋	祏	祑	祔	祘	祛	祜	祧	祩	祫
60	祲	祹	祻	祼	祾	禋	禌	禑	禓	禔	禕	禖	禘	禛	禜	禡	禨	禩	禫	禯
80	禱	禴	禸	离	秂	秄	秇	秈	秊	秏	秔	秖	秚	秝	秞					

Row 49		01	02	03	04	05	06	07	08	09	10	11	12	13	14	15	16	17	18	19
00		秠	秢	秥	秪	秫	秭	秱	秸	秼	稂	稃	稇	稉	稊	稌	稑	稕	稛	稞
20	稡	稧	稫	稭	稯	稰	稴	稵	稸	稹	稺	穄	穅	穇	穈	穌	穕	穖	穙	穜
40	穝	穟	穠	穥	穧	穪	穭	穵	穸	穾	窀	窂	窅	窆	窊	窋	窐	窑	窔	窞
60	窠	窣	窬	窳	窵	窹	窻	窼	竆	竉	竌	竎	竑	竛	竨	竩	竫	竬	竱	竴
80	竻	竽	竾	笇	笔	笟	笣	笧	笩	笪	笫	笭	笮	笯	笰					

Row 50		01	02	03	04	05	06	07	08	09	10	11	12	13	14	15	16	17	18	19
00		笱	笴	笽	笿	筀	筁	筇	筎	筕	筠	筤	筦	筩	筪	筭	筯	筲	筳	筷
20	箄	箉	箎	箐	箑	箖	箛	箞	箠	箥	箬	箯	箰	箲	箵	箶	箺	箻	箼	箽
40	篂	篅	篈	篊	篔	篖	篗	篙	篚	篛	篨	篪	篲	篴	篵	篸	篹	篺	篼	篾
60	簁	簂	簃	簄	簆	簉	簋	簌	簎	簏	簙	簛	簠	簥	簦	簨	簬	簱	簳	簴
80	簶	簹	簺	籆	籊	籀	籑	籒	籓	籙	籚	籛	籜	籝	籞					

Row 51		01	02	03	04	05	06	07	08	09	10	11	12	13	14	15	16	17	18	19
00		籡	籣	籧	籩	籭	籮	籰	籲	籹	籼	籽	粆	粇	粏	粔	粞	粠	粦	粰
20	粶	粷	粺	粻	粼	粿	糄	糇	糈	糉	糍	糏	糓	糔	糕	糗	糙	糚	糝	糦
40	糩	糫	糵	紃	紇	紈	紉	紏	紑	紒	紓	紖	紝	紞	紣	紦	紪	紭	紱	紼
60	紽	紾	絀	絁	絇	絈	絍	絑	絓	絗	絙	絚	絜	絝	絥	絧	絪	絰	絸	絺
80	絻	絿	綁	綂	綃	綅	綆	綈	綋	綌	綍	綑	綖	綗	綝					

Row 52		01	02	03	04	05	06	07	08	09	10	11	12	13	14	15	16	17	18	19
00		綞	綦	綧	綪	綳	綶	綷	綹	緂	緃	緄	緅	緆	緌	緍	緎	緗	緙	縀
20	緢	緥	緦	緪	緫	緭	緱	緵	緶	緹	緺	縈	縐	縑	縕	縗	縜	縝	縠	縧
40	縨	縬	縭	縯	縳	縶	縿	繄	繅	繇	繎	繐	繒	繘	繟	繡	繢	繥	繫	繮
60	繯	繳	繸	繾	纁	纆	纇	纊	纍	纑	纕	纘	纚	纝	纞	缼	缻	缽	缾	缿
80	罃	罄	罇	罏	罒	罓	罛	罜	罝	罡	罣	罤	罥	罦	罭					

Row 53		01	02	03	04	05	06	07	08	09	10	11	12	13	14	15	16	17	18	19
00		罱	罽	罾	罿	羀	羋	羍	羏	羐	羑	羖	羗	羜	羡	羢	羦	羪	羭	羴
20	羼	羿	翀	翃	翈	翎	翏	翛	翟	翣	翥	翨	翬	翮	翯	翲	翺	翽	翾	翿
40	耇	耈	耊	耍	耎	耏	耑	耓	耔	耖	耝	耞	耟	耠	耤	耦	耬	耮	耰	耴
60	耵	耷	耹	耺	耼	耾	聀	聄	聠	聤	聦	聭	聱	聵	肁	肈	肎	肜	肞	肦
80	肧	肫	肸	肹	胈	胍	胏	胒	胔	胕	胗	胘	胠	胭	胮					

Row 54		01	02	03	04	05	06	07	08	09	10	11	12	13	14	15	16	17	18	19
00		胰	胲	胳	胶	胹	胺	胾	脃	脋	脖	脗	脘	脜	脞	脠	脤	脧	脬	脰
20	脵	脺	脼	腅	腇	腊	腌	腒	腗	腠	腡	腧	腨	腩	腭	腯	腷	膁	膐	膄
40	膅	膆	膋	膎	膖	膘	膛	膞	膢	膮	膲	膴	膻	臋	臃	臅	臊	臎	臏	臕
60	臗	臛	臝	臞	臡	臤	臫	臬	臰	臱	臲	臵	臶	臸	臹	臽	臿	舀	舃	舑
80	舓	舔	舙	舚	舝	舡	舢	舨	舲	舴	舺	艃	艄	艅	艆					

Row 55		01	02	03	04	05	06	07	08	09	10	11	12	13	14	15	16	17	18	19
00		艋	艎	艏	艑	艖	艜	艠	艣	艧	艭	艴	艻	艽	艿	芀	芁	芃	芄	芇
20	芉	芊	芎	芑	芔	芖	芘	芚	芛	芠	芡	芣	芤	芧	芨	芩	芪	芮	芰	芲
40	芴	芷	芺	芼	芾	芿	苆	苐	苕	苚	苠	苢	苤	苨	苪	苭	苯	苶	苷	苽
60	苾	茀	茁	茇	茈	茊	茋	荔	茛	茝	茞	茟	茡	茢	茬	茭	茮	茰	茳	茷
80	茺	茼	茽	荂	荃	荄	荇	荍	荎	荑	荕	荖	荗	荰	荸					

Row 56		01	02	03	04	05	06	07	08	09	10	11	12	13	14	15	16	17	18	19
00		荽	荿	莀	莂	莄	莆	莍	莒	莔	莕	莘	莙	莛	莜	莝	莦	莧	莩	莬
20	莾	莿	菀	菇	菉	菏	菐	菑	菔	菝	荓	菨	菪	菶	菸	菹	菼	萁	萆	萊
40	萏	萑	萕	萙	莭	萯	萹	葅	葇	葈	葊	葍	葏	葑	葒	葖	葘	葙	葚	葜
60	葠	葤	葥	葧	葪	葰	葳	葴	葶	葸	葼	葽	蒁	蒅	蒒	蒓	蒕	蒞	蒦	蒨
80	蒩	蒪	蒯	蒱	蒴	蒺	蒽	蒾	蓀	蓂	蓇	蓈	蓌	蓏	蓓					

Row 57		01	02	03	04	05	06	07	08	09	10	11	12	13	14	15	16	17	18	19
00		蓜	蓧	蓪	蓯	蓰	蓱	蓲	蓷	蔲	蓺	蓻	蓽	蔂	蔃	蔇	蔌	蔎	蔐	蔜
20	蔞	蔢	蔣	蔤	蔥	蔧	蔪	蔫	蔯	蔳	蔴	蔶	蔿	蕆	蕏	蕐	蕑	蕒	蕓	蕖
40	蕙	蕜	蕝	蕞	蕟	蕠	蕡	蕢	蕤	蕫	蕯	蕹	蕺	蕻	蕽	蕿	薁	薅	薆	薉
60	薋	薌	薏	薓	薘	薝	薟	薠	薢	薥	薧	薴	薶	薷	薸	薼	薽	薾	薿	藂
80	藇	藊	藋	藎	薭	藘	藚	藟	藠	藦	藨	藭	藳	藶	藼					

Row 58		01	02	03	04	05	06	07	08	09	10	11	12	13	14	15	16	17	18	19
00		藿	蘀	蘄	蘅	蘍	蘎	蘐	蘑	蘒	蘘	蘙	蘛	蘞	蘡	蘧	蘩	蘶	蘸	蘺
20	蘼	蘽	虀	虂	虆	虒	虓	虖	虗	虘	虙	虝	虠	虡	虢	虣	虤	虩	虬	虯
40	虵	虶	虷	虺	蚍	蚑	蚖	蚘	蚚	蚜	蚡	蚦	蚧	蚨	蚭	蚱	蚳	蚴	蚵	蚷
60	蚸	蚹	蚿	蛀	蛁	蛃	蛅	蛑	蛒	蛕	蛗	蛚	蛜	蛡	蛣	蛥	蛧	蛨	蛪	蛫
80	蛽	蜄	蜅	蜇	蜋	蜎	蜏	蜐	蜓	蜔	蜙	蜞	蜟	蜡	蜣					

Row 59		01	02	03	04	05	06	07	08	09	10	11	12	13	14	15	16	17	18	19
00		蜨	蜮	蜯	蜱	蜲	蜹	蜺	蜼	蜽	蜾	蝀	蝃	蝅	蝍	蝘	蝝	蝡	蝤	蝥
20	蝯	蝱	蝲	蝻	螃	螄	螅	螆	螇	螈	螉	螋	螌	螐	螓	螕	螗	螘	螙	螞
40	螠	螣	螧	螬	螭	螮	螱	螵	螾	螿	蟁	蟈	蟉	蟊	蟎	蟕	蟖	蟙	蟚	蟜
60	蟟	蟢	蟣	蟤	蟪	蟫	蟭	蟱	蟳	蟸	蟺	蟿	蠁	蠃	蠆	蠉	蠊	蠋	蠐	蠙
80	蠒	蠓	蠔	蠘	蠚	蠛	蠜	蠞	蠟	蠨	蠭	蠮	蠰	蠲	蠵					

Row 60		01	02	03	04	05	06	07	08	09	10	11	12	13	14	15	16	17	18	19
00		蠺	蠼	衁	衃	衅	衈	衉	衊	衋	衎	衐	衕	衖	衘	衚	衜	衟	衠	衤
20	衩	衱	衹	衻	袀	袘	袚	袛	袜	袟	袠	袨	袪	袺	袽	袾	裀	裊	裋	裌
40	裍	裎	裑	裒	裓	裛	裞	裧	裯	裰	裱	裵	裷	褁	褆	褍	褎	褏	褕	褖
60	褘	褙	褚	褜	褠	褦	褧	褨	褰	褱	褲	褵	褹	褺	褾	襀	襂	襅	襆	襉
80	襏	襒	襗	襚	襛	襜	襡	襢	襣	襫	襮	襰	襳	襵	襺					

Row 61		01	02	03	04	05	06	07	08	09	10	11	12	13	14	15	16	17	18	19
00		襻	襼	襽	覉	覍	覐	覔	覕	覛	覜	覟	覠	覥	覤	覬	覵	覶	覷	覼
20	觔	觕	觖	觗	觘	觥	觩	觫	觭	觱	觳	觶	觹	觽	觿	訄	訅	訇	訏	訑
40	訒	訔	訕	訞	訠	訢	訤	訦	訫	訬	訯	訵	訷	訽	訾	詀	詃	詅	詇	詉
60	詍	詎	詓	詖	詗	詘	詜	詝	詡	詥	詧	詵	詶	詷	詹	詺	詻	詾	詿	誀
80	誃	誆	誋	誏	誐	誒	誖	誗	誙	誟	誧	誩	誮	誯	誳					

Row 62		01	02	03	04	05	06	07	08	09	10	11	12	13	14	15	16	17	18	19
00		誶	誷	誻	誾	諃	諆	諈	諉	諊	諑	諓	諔	諕	諗	諝	諟	諬	諰	諴
20	諵	諶	諼	諿	謅	謆	謋	謑	謜	謞	謟	謊	謭	謰	謷	謼	譂	譃	譄	譅
40	譆	譈	譒	譓	譔	譙	譍	譞	譣	譭	譶	譸	譹	譼	譾	讁	讄	讅	讋	讍
60	讐	讔	讕	讜	讞	讟	谸	谹	谽	谾	豅	豇	豉	豋	豍	豏	豓	豔	豗	豘
80	豛	豝	豙	豣	豤	豦	豨	豩	豭	豳	豵	豶	豻	豾	貆					

Row 63		01	02	03	04	05	06	07	08	09	10	11	12	13	14	15	16	17	18	19
00		貇	貋	貐	貒	貓	貙	貛	貜	貤	貹	貺	賅	賆	賉	賋	賏	賖	賕	賙
20	賝	賡	賨	賬	賯	賰	賲	賵	賷	賸	賾	賿	贁	贃	贉	贒	贗	贛	赥	赩
40	赬	赮	赿	趀	趄	趈	趍	趐	趑	趧	趞	趏	趠	趦	趫	趬	趯	趲	趵	趷
60	趹	趻	跀	跅	跆	跇	跈	跊	跎	跑	跔	跕	跗	跙	跤	跥	跧	跬	跰	趼
80	跱	跲	跴	跽	踁	踄	踅	踆	踋	踑	踔	踖	踠	踡	踢					

Row 64		01	02	03	04	05	06	07	08	09	10	11	12	13	14	15	16	17	18	19
00		踣	踦	踧	踱	踳	踶	踷	踸	踹	踽	蹀	蹁	蹋	蹍	蹎	蹏	蹔	蹛	蹜
20	蹝	蹞	蹡	蹢	蹩	蹬	蹭	蹯	蹰	蹱	蹹	蹺	蹻	躂	躃	躉	躐	躒	躕	躚
40	躛	躝	躞	躢	躧	躩	躭	躮	躳	躵	躺	躻	軀	軁	軃	軄	軇	軏	軑	軔
60	軜	軨	軮	軰	軱	軷	軹	軺	軭	輀	輂	輇	輈	輏	輐	輖	輗	輘	輞	輠
80	輡	輣	輥	輧	輨	輬	輭	輮	輴	輵	輶	輷	輺	轀	轁					

Row 65		01	02	03	04	05	06	07	08	09	10	11	12	13	14	15	16	17	18	19
00		轃	轇	轏	轑	轒	轓	轔	轕	轘	轝	轞	轥	辝	辠	辡	辤	辥	辦	辵
20	辶	辸	达	迀	迁	迆	迊	迋	迍	运	迒	迓	迕	迠	迣	迤	迨	迮	迱	迵
40	迶	迻	迾	适	逄	逈	逌	逘	逛	逨	逩	逯	逪	逬	逭	逳	逴	逷	逿	遃
60	遄	遌	遛	遝	遢	遦	遧	遬	遰	遴	遹	邅	邈	邋	邌	邎	邐	邕	邗	邘
80	邙	邛	邠	邡	邢	邩	邰	邲	邳	邴	邶	邽	郌	邾	郃					

Row 66	01	02	03	04	05	06	07	08	09	10	11	12	13	14	15	16	17	18	19
00		郄	郅	郇	郈	郕	郗	郘	郙	郜	郝	郟	郥	郒	郶	郫	郯	郰	郴	郾
20	郿	鄀	鄄	鄅	鄆	鄈	鄍	鄐	鄔	鄖	鄗	鄘	鄚	鄜	鄞	鄠	鄥	鄢	鄣	鄧
40	鄩	鄪	鄫	鄱	鄰	鄶	鄷	鄹	鄺	鄻	鄽	酃	酇	酈	酏	酓	酗	酙	酚	酛
60	酡	酤	酧	酭	酴	酹	酺	醇	醁	醃	醅	醆	醊	醎	醑	醘	醔	醕	醢	醞
80	醡	醦	醨	醬	醭	醮	醰	醱	醲	醳	醶	醻	醼	醽	醿				

Row 67	01	02	03	04	05	06	07	08	09	10	11	12	13	14	15	16	17	18	19
00		釂	釃	釅	釓	釔	釗	釙	釚	釞	釤	釥	釩	釪	釬	釭	釮	釯	釰	釱
20	釷	釹	釻	釽	鈀	鈁	鈄	鈅	鈆	鈇	鈉	鈊	鈌	鈐	鈒	鈓	鈖	鈘	鈜	鈝
40	鈣	鈤	鈥	鈦	鈨	鈮	鈯	鈰	鈳	鈵	鈶	鈸	鈹	鈺	鈼	鈾	鉀	鉂	鉃	鉆
60	鉇	鉊	鉍	鉎	鉏	鉑	鉘	鉙	鉜	鉝	鉠	鉡	鉥	鉧	鉨	鉩	鉮	鉯	鉰	鉵
80	鉶	鉷	鉸	鉹	鉻	鉼	鉽	鉿	銈	銉	銊	銍	銎	銒	銗				

Row 68	01	02	03	04	05	06	07	08	09	10	11	12	13	14	15	16	17	18	19
00		銙	銟	銠	銤	銥	銧	銨	銫	銯	銲	銶	銸	銺	銻	銼	銽	銿	鋀	鋁
20	鋂	鋃	鋅	鋆	鋇	鋈	鋋	鋌	鋍	鋎	鋐	鋓	鋕	鋗	鋘	鋙	鋜	鋝	鋟	鋠
40	鋡	鋣	鋥	鋧	鋨	鋬	鋮	鋰	鋹	鋻	鋿	錀	錂	錈	錍	錑	錔	錕	錜	錝
60	錞	錟	錡	錤	錥	錧	錩	錪	錳	錴	錶	錷	鍇	鍈	鍉	鍐	鍑	鍒	鍕	鍗
80	鍘	鍚	鍞	鍤	鍥	鍧	鍩	鍪	鍭	鍯	鍰	鍱	鍳	鍴	鍶				

Row 69	01	02	03	04	05	06	07	08	09	10	11	12	13	14	15	16	17	18	19
00		鍺	鍽	鍿	鎀	鎁	鎂	鎈	鎊	鎋	鎍	鎏	鎒	鎕	鎘	鎛	鎞	鎡	鎣	鎤
20	鎦	鎨	鎪	鎴	鎵	鎶	鎺	鎩	鏁	鏄	鏅	鏆	鏇	鏉	鏊	鏋	鏌	鏍	鏓	鏙
40	鏜	鏞	鏠	鏢	鏦	鏧	鏹	鏷	鏸	鏺	鏻	鏽	鐁	鐂	鐄	鐈	鐉	鐍	鐎	鐏
60	鐕	鐖	鐗	鐟	鐮	鐯	鐱	鐲	鐳	鐴	鐻	鐿	鐽	鑃	鑅	鑈	鑊	鑌	鑕	鑙
80	鑚	鑛	鑡	鑣	鑨	鑫	鑭	鑮	鑯	鑱	鑲	鑻	钃	镸	镹				

Row 70	01	02	03	04	05	06	07	08	09	10	11	12	13	14	15	16	17	18	19
00		镾	閁	閈	閌	閍	閎	閝	閞	閟	閡	閦	閩	閫	閬	閴	閶	閺	閽	閿
20	闆	闈	闉	闋	闐	闑	闒	闓	闙	闚	闝	闞	闟	闠	闤	闦	阝	阞	阢	阤
40	阥	阦	阬	阱	阳	阷	阸	阹	阺	阼	阽	陁	陒	陔	陖	陗	陘	陡	陮	陴
60	陻	陼	陾	陿	隁	隂	隃	隄	隉	隑	隖	隚	隝	隟	隤	隥	隦	隩	隮	隯
80	隳	隺	雊	雒	嶲	雘	雚	雝	雞	巂	雩	雯	雱	雺	霂				

Row 71	01	02	03	04	05	06	07	08	09	10	11	12	13	14	15	16	17	18	19
00		霃	霅	霉	霚	霛	霝	霡	霢	霣	霨	霱	霳	靁	靃	靊	靎	靏	靕	靗
20	靘	靚	靛	靣	靧	靪	靮	靳	靶	靹	靸	靻	靽	靿	鞀	鞉	鞕	鞖	鞗	鞙
40	鞚	鞞	鞟	鞢	鞬	鞮	鞱	鞲	鞵	鞶	鞸	鞹	鞺	鞼	鞾	鞿	韁	韄	韅	韇
60	韉	韊	韌	韍	韎	韐	韑	韔	韗	韘	韙	韝	韞	韠	韛	韡	韤	韯	韱	韴
80	韷	韸	韺	頇	頊	頙	頍	頎	頔	頖	頜	頞	頠	頣	頦				

Row 72		01	02	03	04	05	06	07	08	09	10	11	12	13	14	15	16	17	18	19
00		頪	頮	頠	頬	頲	頳	頵	頥	頿	顄	顇	顊	顑	顒	顗	顖	顜	顡	顛
20	顤	顣	顥	顦	顪	顬	颫	颭	颮	颰	颴	颷	颸	颺	颻	颿	飂	飅	飈	飌
40	飡	飣	飥	飦	飧	飪	飳	飶	餂	餇	餈	餑	餕	餖	餗	餚	餛	餜	餟	餢
60	餦	餧	餫	餱	餲	餳	餴	餵	餹	餺	餻	餼	饀	饁	饆	饇	饈	饍	饎	饔
80	饘	饋	饛	饜	饞	饟	饠	馛	馝	馟	馦	馰	馱	馲	馵					

Row 73		01	02	03	04	05	06	07	08	09	10	11	12	13	14	15	16	17	18	19
00		駎	馺	馽	馿	駃	駉	駓	駔	駙	駚	駜	駞	駧	駪	駫	駬	駰	駴	駵
20	駹	駽	駾	騂	騃	騄	騋	騌	騐	騑	騖	騞	騠	騢	騣	騤	騧	騭	騮	騳
40	騵	騶	騸	驇	驁	驄	驊	驋	驌	驎	驑	驔	驖	驤	骪	骭	骮	骯	骲	骴
60	骵	骶	骹	骻	骾	骿	髁	髃	髆	髈	髎	髐	髒	髕	髖	髗	髛	髜	髠	髤
80	髥	髧	髩	髬	髲	髳	髵	髹	髺	髽	髿	鬀	鬁	鬂	鬃					

Row 74		01	02	03	04	05	06	07	08	09	10	11	12	13	14	15	16	17	18	19
00		鬄	鬅	鬈	鬉	鬋	鬌	鬍	鬎	鬐	鬒	鬖	鬙	鬛	鬜	鬠	鬦	鬫	鬭	鬳
20	鬴	鬵	鬷	鬹	鬺	鬽	魈	魋	魌	魕	魖	魗	魛	魞	魡	魣	魥	魦	魨	魪
40	魫	魬	魭	魮	魳	魵	魷	魸	魹	魿	鮀	鮄	鮅	鮆	鮇	鮉	鮊	鮋	鮍	鮏
60	鮐	鮔	鮚	鮝	鮞	鮦	鮧	鮩	鮬	鮰	鮱	鮲	鮷	鮸	鮻	鮼	鮾	鮿	鯁	鯇
80	鯈	鯎	鯐	鯗	鯘	鯝	鯟	鯥	鯧	鯪	鯫	鯯	鯳	鯷	鯸					

Row 75		01	02	03	04	05	06	07	08	09	10	11	12	13	14	15	16	17	18	19
00		鯹	鯺	鯽	鯿	鰀	鰂	鰋	鰏	鰑	鰖	鰘	鰙	鰚	鰜	鰞	鰢	鰣	鰦	鰧
20	鰨	鰩	鰪	鰱	鰵	鰶	鰷	鰽	鱁	鱃	鱄	鱅	鱉	鱊	鱎	鱏	鱐	鱓	鱔	鱖
40	鱘	鱛	鱝	鱞	鱟	鱣	鱬	鱪	鱜	鱫	鱭	鱮	鱰	鱲	鱵	鱷	鱻	鳦	鳲	鳷
60	鳹	鴋	鴂	鴑	鴗	鴘	鴜	鴝	鴞	鴯	鴰	鴲	鴳	鴴	鴺	鴼	鵅	鴽	鵂	鵃
80	鵇	鵊	鵓	鵔	鵟	鵣	鵢	鵥	鵩	鵪	鵫	鵰	鵶	鵷	鵻					

Row 76		01	02	03	04	05	06	07	08	09	10	11	12	13	14	15	16	17	18	19
00		鵼	鵾	鶃	鶄	鶆	鶊	鶍	鶎	鶒	鶓	鶕	鶖	鶗	鶘	鶡	鶪	鶬	鶮	鶱
20	鶵	鶹	鶼	鶿	鷃	鷇	鷉	鷊	鷔	鷕	鷖	鷗	鷚	鷞	鷟	鷠	鷥	鷧	鷩	鷫
40	鷮	鷰	鷳	鷴	鷾	鸊	鸂	鸇	鸎	鸐	鸑	鸒	鸕	鸖	鸙	鸜	鸝	鹺	鹻	鹼
60	麀	麅	麃	麄	麇	麉	麊	麌	麍	麎	麏	麐	麕	麤	麨	麬	麮	麯	麳	麴
80	麵	黆	黈	黋	黕	黟	黤	黧	黬	黭	黮	黰	黱	黲	黵					

Row 77		01	02	03	04	05	06	07	08	09	10	11	12	13	14	15	16	17	18	19
00		黸	黿	鼂	鼃	鼉	鼏	鼐	鼑	鼒	鼔	鼖	鼗	鼙	鼚	鼛	鼟	鼢	鼦	鼪
20	鼫	鼯	鼱	鼲	鼴	鼷	鼹	鼺	鼼	鼽	鼿	齁	齃	齄	齅	齆	齇	齓	齕	齖
40	齗	齘	齚	齝	齞	齨	齩	齭	齮	齯	齰	齱	齳	齵	齺	齽	龏	龐	龑	龒
60	龔	龖	龗	龞	龡	龢	龣	龥												
80																				

L

KS X 1001:1992 Table

This appendix constitutes a table for the complete KS X 1001:1992 character set, printed here using the typeface HY신명조 (HYSMyeongJo-Medium), developed by Hanyang Systems. Each character is indexed by Row-Cell value.

Note that Row-Cell 01-01 is a full-width space character.

Row 1		01	02	03	04	05	06	07	08	09	10	11	12	13	14	15	16	17	18	19
00			、	。	·	‥	…	¨	〃	-	―	∥	＼	∼	‘	’	“	”	〔	〕
20	〈	〉	《	》	「	」	『	』	【	】	±	×	÷	≠	≤	≥	∞	∴	°	′
40	″	℃	Å	￠	￡	￥	♂	♀	∠	⊥	⌒	∂	∇	≡	≒	§	※	☆	★	○
60	●	◎	◇	◆	□	■	△	▲	▽	▼	→	←	↑	↓	↔	〓	≪	≫	√	∽
80	∝	∵	∫	∬	∈	∋	⊆	⊇	⊂	⊃	∪	∩	∧	∨	￢					

Row 2		01	02	03	04	05	06	07	08	09	10	11	12	13	14	15	16	17	18	19
00		⇒	⇔	∀	∃	´	～	ˇ	˘	˝	˚	˙	¸	˛	¡	¿	ː	∮	∑	∏
20	¤	℉	‰	◁	◀	▷	▶	♤	♠	♡	♥	♧	♣	⊙	◈	▣	◐	◑	▒	▤
40	▥	▨	▧	▦	▩	♨	☏	☎	☜	☞	¶	†	‡	↕	↗	↙	↖	↘	♭	♩
60	♪	♬	㉿	㈜	№	㏇	™	㏂	㏘	℡										
80																				

Row 3		01	02	03	04	05	06	07	08	09	10	11	12	13	14	15	16	17	18	19
00		！	＂	＃	＄	％	＆	＇	（	）	＊	＋	，	－	．	／	０	１	２	３
20	４	５	６	７	８	９	：	；	＜	＝	＞	？	＠	Ａ	Ｂ	Ｃ	Ｄ	Ｅ	Ｆ	Ｇ
40	Ｈ	Ｉ	Ｊ	Ｋ	Ｌ	Ｍ	Ｎ	Ｏ	Ｐ	Ｑ	Ｒ	Ｓ	Ｔ	Ｕ	Ｖ	Ｗ	Ｘ	Ｙ	Ｚ	［
60	￦	］	＾	＿	｀	ａ	ｂ	ｃ	ｄ	ｅ	ｆ	ｇ	ｈ	ｉ	ｊ	ｋ	ｌ	ｍ	ｎ	ｏ
80	ｐ	ｑ	ｒ	ｓ	ｔ	ｕ	ｖ	ｗ	ｘ	ｙ	ｚ	｛	｜	｝	￣					

Row 4		01	02	03	04	05	06	07	08	09	10	11	12	13	14	15	16	17	18	19
00		ㄱ	ㄲ	ㄳ	ㄴ	ㄵ	ㄶ	ㄷ	ㄸ	ㄹ	ㄺ	ㄻ	ㄼ	ㄽ	ㄾ	ㄿ	ㅀ	ㅁ	ㅂ	ㅃ
20	ㅄ	ㅅ	ㅆ	ㅇ	ㅈ	ㅉ	ㅊ	ㅋ	ㅌ	ㅍ	ㅎ	ㅏ	ㅐ	ㅑ	ㅒ	ㅓ	ㅔ	ㅕ	ㅖ	ㅗ
40	ㅘ	ㅙ	ㅚ	ㅛ	ㅜ	ㅝ	ㅞ	ㅟ	ㅠ	ㅡ	ㅢ	ㅣ		ㅥ	ㅦ	ㅧ	ㅨ	ㅩ	ㅪ	ㅫ
60	ㅬ	ㅭ	ㅮ	ㅯ	ㅰ	ㅱ	ㅲ	ㅳ	ㅴ	ㅵ	ㅶ	ㅷ	ㅸ	ㅹ	ㅺ	ㅻ	ㅼ	ㅽ	ㅾ	ㅿ
80	ㆀ	ㆁ	ㆂ	ㆃ	ㆄ	ㆅ	ㆆ	ㆇ	ㆈ	ㆉ	ㆊ	ㆋ	ㆌ	ㆍ	ㆎ					

Row 5		01	02	03	04	05	06	07	08	09	10	11	12	13	14	15	16	17	18	19
00		ⅰ	ⅱ	ⅲ	ⅳ	ⅴ	ⅵ	ⅶ	ⅷ	ⅸ	ⅹ						Ⅰ	Ⅱ	Ⅲ	Ⅳ
20	Ⅴ	Ⅵ	Ⅶ	Ⅷ	Ⅸ	Ⅹ								Α	Β	Γ	Δ	Ε	Ζ	Η
40	Θ	Ι	Κ	Λ	Μ	Ν	Ξ	Ο	Π	Ρ	Σ	Τ	Υ	Φ	Χ	Ψ	Ω			
60						α	β	γ	δ	ε	ζ	η	θ	ι	κ	λ	μ	ν	ξ	ο
80	π	ρ	σ	τ	υ	φ	χ	ψ	ω											

Row 6		01	02	03	04	05	06	07	08	09	10	11	12	13	14	15	16	17	18	19
00		─	│	┌	┐	┘	└	├	┬	┤	┴	┼	━	┃	┏	┓	┛	┗	┣	┳
20	┫	┻	╋	┠	┯	┨	┷	┿	┝	┰	┥	┸	╂	┒	┑	┚	┙	┖	┕	┎
40	┍	┞	┟	┡	┢	┦	┧	┩	┪	┭	┮	┱	┲	┵	┶	┹	┺	┽	┾	╀
60	╁	╃	╄	╅	╆	╇	╈	╉	╊											
80																				

Row 7		01	02	03	04	05	06	07	08	09	10	11	12	13	14	15	16	17	18	19
00		㎕	㎖	㎗	ℓ	㎘	㏄	㎣	㎤	㎥	㎦	㎙	㎚	㎛	㎜	㎝	㎞	㎟	㎠	㎡
20	㎢	㏊	㎍	㎎	㎏	㏏	㎈	㎉	㏈	㎧	㎨	㎰	㎱	㎲	㎳	㎴	㎵	㎶	㎷	㎸
40	㎹	㎀	㎁	㎂	㎃	㎄	㎺	㎻	㎼	㎽	㎾	㎿	㎐	㎑	㎒	㎓	㎔	Ω	㏀	㏁
60	㎊	㎋	㎌	㏖	㏅	㎭	㎮	㎯	㏛	㎩	㎪	㎫	㎬	㏝	㏐	㏓	㏃	㏉	㏜	㏆
80																				

Row 8		01	02	03	04	05	06	07	08	09	10	11	12	13	14	15	16	17	18	19
00		Æ	Đ	ª	Ħ		Ĳ		Ŀ	Ł	Ø	Œ	º	Þ	Ŧ	Ŋ		㉠	㉡	㉢
20	㉣	㉤	㉥	㉦	㉧	㉨	㉩	㉪	㉫	㉬	㉭	㉮	㉯	㉰	㉱	㉲	㉳	㉴	㉵	㉶
40	㉷	㉸	㉹	㉺	㉻	ⓐ	ⓑ	ⓒ	ⓓ	ⓔ	ⓕ	ⓖ	ⓗ	ⓘ	ⓙ	ⓚ	ⓛ	ⓜ	ⓝ	ⓞ
60	ⓟ	ⓠ	ⓡ	ⓢ	ⓣ	ⓤ	ⓥ	ⓦ	ⓧ	ⓨ	ⓩ	①	②	③	④	⑤	⑥	⑦	⑧	⑨
80	⑩	⑪	⑫	⑬	⑭	⑮	½	⅓	⅔	¼	¾	⅛	⅜	⅝	⅞					

Row 9		01	02	03	04	05	06	07	08	09	10	11	12	13	14	15	16	17	18	19
00		æ	đ	ð	ħ	ı	ĳ	ĸ	ŀ	ł	ø	œ	ß	þ	ŧ	ŋ	ŉ	㈀	㈁	㈂
20	㈃	㈄	㈅	㈆	㈇	㈈	㈉	㈊	㈋	㈌	㈍	㈎	㈏	㈐	㈑	㈒	㈓	㈔	㈕	㈖
40	㈗	㈘	㈙	㈚	㈛	⒜	⒝	⒞	⒟	⒠	⒡	⒢	⒣	⒤	⒥	⒦	⒧	⒨	⒩	⒪
60	⒫	⒬	⒭	⒮	⒯	⒰	⒱	⒲	⒳	⒴	⒵	⑴	⑵	⑶	⑷	⑸	⑹	⑺	⑻	⑼
80	⑽	⑾	⑿	⒀	⒁	⒂	^{1}	^{2}	^{3}	^{4}	^{n}	$_{1}$	$_{2}$	$_{3}$	$_{4}$					

Row 10		01	02	03	04	05	06	07	08	09	10	11	12	13	14	15	16	17	18	19
00		ぁ	あ	ぃ	い	ぅ	う	ぇ	え	ぉ	お	か	が	き	ぎ	く	ぐ	け	げ	こ
20	ご	さ	ざ	し	じ	す	ず	せ	ぜ	そ	ぞ	た	だ	ち	ぢ	っ	つ	づ	て	で
40	と	ど	な	に	ぬ	ね	の	は	ば	ぱ	ひ	び	ぴ	ふ	ぶ	ぷ	へ	べ	ぺ	ほ
60	ぼ	ぽ	ま	み	む	め	も	ゃ	や	ゅ	ゆ	ょ	よ	ら	り	る	れ	ろ	ゎ	わ
80	ゐ	ゑ	を	ん																

Row 11		01	02	03	04	05	06	07	08	09	10	11	12	13	14	15	16	17	18	19
00		ァ	ア	ィ	イ	ゥ	ウ	ェ	エ	ォ	オ	カ	ガ	キ	ギ	ク	グ	ケ	ゲ	コ
20	ゴ	サ	ザ	シ	ジ	ス	ズ	セ	ゼ	ソ	ゾ	タ	ダ	チ	ヂ	ッ	ツ	ヅ	テ	デ
40	ト	ド	ナ	ニ	ヌ	ネ	ノ	ハ	バ	パ	ヒ	ビ	ピ	フ	ブ	プ	ヘ	ベ	ペ	ホ
60	ボ	ポ	マ	ミ	ム	メ	モ	ャ	ヤ	ュ	ユ	ョ	ヨ	ラ	リ	ル	レ	ロ	ヮ	ワ
80	ヰ	ヱ	ヲ	ン	ヴ	ヵ	ヶ													

Row 12		01	02	03	04	05	06	07	08	09	10	11	12	13	14	15	16	17	18	19
00		А	Б	В	Г	Д	Е	Ё	Ж	З	И	Й	К	Л	М	Н	О	П	Р	С
20	Т	У	Ф	Х	Ц	Ч	Ш	Щ	Ъ	Ы	Ь	Э	Ю	Я						
40										а	б	в	г	д	е	ё	ж	з	и	й
60	к	л	м	н	о	п	р	с	т	у	ф	х	ц	ч	ш	щ	ъ	ы	ь	э
80	ю	я																		

Row 16		01	02	03	04	05	06	07	08	09	10	11	12	13	14	15	16	17	18	19
00		가	각	간	갇	갈	갉	갊	감	갑	값	갓	갔	강	갖	갗	같	갚	갛	개
20	객	갠	갤	갬	갭	갯	갰	갱	갸	갹	갼	걀	걋	걍	걔	걘	걜	거	걱	건
40	걷	걸	걺	검	겁	것	겄	겅	겆	겉	겊	겋	게	겐	겔	겜	겝	겟	겠	겡
60	겨	격	겪	견	겯	결	겸	겹	겻	겼	경	곁	계	곈	곌	곕	곗	고	곡	곤
80	곧	골	곪	곬	곯	곰	곱	곳	공	곶	과	곽	관	괄	괆					

Row 17		01	02	03	04	05	06	07	08	09	10	11	12	13	14	15	16	17	18	19
00		괌	괍	괏	광	괘	괜	괠	괩	괬	괭	괴	괵	괸	괼	굄	굅	굇	굉	교
20	굔	굘	굡	굣	구	국	군	굳	굴	굵	굶	굻	굼	굽	굿	궁	궂	궈	궉	권
40	궐	궜	궝	궤	궷	귀	귁	귄	귈	귐	귑	귓	규	균	귤	그	극	근	귿	글
60	긁	금	급	긋	긍	긔	기	긱	긴	긷	길	긺	김	깁	깃	깅	깆	깊	까	깍
80	깎	깐	깔	깖	깜	깝	깟	깠	깡	깥	깨	깩	깬	깰	깸					

Row 18		01	02	03	04	05	06	07	08	09	10	11	12	13	14	15	16	17	18	19
00		깹	깻	깼	깽	꺄	꺅	꺌	꺼	꺽	꺾	껀	껄	껌	껍	껏	껐	껑	께	껙
20	껜	껨	껫	껭	껴	껸	껼	꼇	꼈	꼍	꼐	꼬	꼭	꼰	꼲	꼴	꼼	꼽	꼿	꽁
40	꽂	꽃	꽈	꽉	꽐	꽜	꽝	꽤	꽥	꽹	꾀	꾄	꾈	꾐	꾑	꾕	꾜	꾸	꾹	꾼
60	꿀	꿇	꿈	꿉	꿋	꿍	꿎	꿔	꿜	꿨	꿩	꿰	꿱	꿴	꿸	뀀	뀁	뀄	뀌	뀐
80	뀔	뀜	뀝	뀨	끄	끅	끈	끊	끌	끎	끓	끔	끕	끗	끙					

Row 19		01	02	03	04	05	06	07	08	09	10	11	12	13	14	15	16	17	18	19
00		끝	끼	끽	낀	낄	낌	낍	낏	낑	나	낙	낚	난	낟	날	낡	낢	남	납
20	낫	났	낭	낮	낯	낱	낳	내	낵	낸	낼	냄	냅	냇	냈	냉	냐	냑	냔	냘
40	냠	냥	너	넉	넋	넌	널	넒	넓	넘	넙	넛	넜	넝	넣	네	넥	넨	넬	넴
60	넵	넷	넸	넹	녀	녁	년	녈	념	녑	녔	녕	녘	녜	녠	노	녹	논	놀	놂
80	놈	놉	놋	농	높	놓	놔	놘	놜	놨	뇌	뇐	뇔	뇜	뇝					

Row 20		01	02	03	04	05	06	07	08	09	10	11	12	13	14	15	16	17	18	19
00		뇟	뇨	뇩	뇬	뇰	뇹	뇻	뇽	누	눅	눈	눋	눌	눔	눕	눗	눙	눠	눴
20	눼	뉘	뉜	뉠	뉨	뉩	뉴	뉵	뉼	늄	늅	늉	느	늑	는	늘	늙	늚	늠	늡
40	늣	능	늦	늪	늬	늰	늴	니	닉	닌	닐	닒	님	닙	닛	닝	닢	다	닥	닦
60	단	닫	달	닭	닮	닯	닳	담	답	닷	닸	당	닺	닻	닿	대	댁	댄	댈	댐
80	댑	댓	댔	댕	댜	더	덕	덖	던	덛	덜	덞	덟	덤	덥					

Row 21		01	02	03	04	05	06	07	08	09	10	11	12	13	14	15	16	17	18	19
00		덧	덩	덫	덮	데	덱	덴	델	뎀	뎁	뎃	뎄	뎅	뎌	뎐	뎔	뎠	뎡	뎨
20	뎬	도	독	돈	돋	돌	돎	돐	돔	돕	돗	동	돛	돝	돠	돤	돨	돼	됐	되
40	된	될	됨	됩	됫	됴	두	둑	둔	둘	둠	둡	둣	둥	둬	뒀	뒈	뒝	뒤	뒨
60	뒬	뒵	뒷	뒹	듀	듄	듈	듐	듕	드	득	든	듣	들	듦	듬	듭	듯	등	듸
80	디	딕	딘	딛	딜	딤	딥	딧	딨	딩	딪	따	딱	딴	딸					

Row 22		01	02	03	04	05	06	07	08	09	10	11	12	13	14	15	16	17	18	19
00		땀	땁	땃	땄	땅	땋	때	땍	땐	땔	땜	땝	땟	땠	땡	떠	떡	떤	떨
20	떪	떫	떰	떱	떳	떴	떵	떻	떼	떽	뗀	뗄	뗌	뗍	뗏	뗐	뗑	뗘	뗬	또
40	똑	똔	똘	똥	똬	똴	뙈	뙤	뙨	뚜	뚝	뚠	뚤	뚫	뚬	뚱	뛔	뛰	뛴	뛸
60	뜀	뜁	뜅	뜨	뜩	뜬	뜯	뜰	뜸	뜹	뜻	띄	띈	띌	띔	띕	띠	띤	띨	띰
80	띱	띳	띵	라	락	란	랄	람	랍	랏	랐	랑	랒	랖	랗					

Row 23		01	02	03	04	05	06	07	08	09	10	11	12	13	14	15	16	17	18	19
00		래	랙	랜	랠	램	랩	랫	랬	랭	랴	략	랸	럇	량	러	럭	런	럴	럼
20	럽	럿	렀	렁	렇	레	렉	렌	렐	렘	렙	렛	렝	려	력	련	렬	렴	렵	렷
40	렸	령	례	롄	롑	롓	로	록	론	롤	롬	롭	롯	롱	롸	롼	뢍	뢨	뢰	뢴
60	뢸	룀	룁	룃	룅	료	룐	룔	룝	룟	룡	루	룩	룬	룰	룸	룹	룻	룽	뤄
80	뤘	뤠	뤼	뤽	륀	륄	륌	륏	륑	류	륙	륜	률	륨	륩					

Row 24		01	02	03	04	05	06	07	08	09	10	11	12	13	14	15	16	17	18	19
00		륫	륭	르	륵	른	를	름	릅	릇	릉	릊	릍	릎	리	릭	린	릴	림	립
20	릿	링	마	막	만	많	맏	말	맑	맒	맘	맙	맛	망	맞	맡	맣	매	맥	맨
40	맬	맴	맵	맷	맸	맹	맺	먀	먁	먈	먕	머	먹	먼	멀	멂	멈	멉	멋	멍
60	멎	멓	메	멕	멘	멜	멤	멥	멧	멨	멩	며	멱	면	멸	몃	몄	명	몇	몌
80	모	목	몫	몬	몰	몲	몸	몹	못	몽	뫄	뫈	뫘	뫙	뫼					

Row 25		01	02	03	04	05	06	07	08	09	10	11	12	13	14	15	16	17	18	19
00		묀	묄	묍	묏	묑	묘	묜	묠	묩	묫	무	묵	묶	문	묻	물	묽	묾	뭄
20	뭅	뭇	뭉	뭍	뭏	뭐	뭔	뭘	뭡	뭣	뭬	뮈	뮌	뮐	뮤	뮨	뮬	뮴	뮷	므
40	믄	믈	믐	믓	미	믹	민	믿	밀	밂	밈	밉	밋	밌	밍	및	밑	바	박	밖
60	밗	반	받	발	밝	밞	밟	밤	밥	밧	방	밭	배	백	밴	밸	뱀	뱁	뱃	뱄
80	뱅	뱉	뱌	뱍	뱐	뱝	버	벅	번	벋	벌	벎	범	법	벗					

Row 26		01	02	03	04	05	06	07	08	09	10	11	12	13	14	15	16	17	18	19
00		벙	벚	베	벡	벤	벧	벨	벰	벱	벳	벴	벵	벼	벽	변	별	볍	볏	볐
20	병	볕	볘	볜	보	복	볶	본	볼	봄	봅	봇	봉	봐	봔	봤	봬	뵀	뵈	뵉
40	뵌	뵐	뵘	뵙	뵤	뵨	부	북	분	붇	불	붉	붊	붐	붑	붓	붕	붙	붚	붜
60	붤	붰	붸	뷔	뷕	뷘	뷜	뷩	뷰	뷴	뷸	븀	븃	븅	브	븍	븐	블	븜	븝
80	븟	비	빅	빈	빌	빎	빔	빕	빗	빙	빚	빛	빠	빡	빤					

Row 27		01	02	03	04	05	06	07	08	09	10	11	12	13	14	15	16	17	18	19
00		빨	빪	빰	빱	빳	빴	빵	빻	빼	빽	뺀	뺄	뺌	뺍	뺏	뺐	뺑	뺘	뺙
20	뺨	뻐	뻑	뻔	뻗	뻘	뻠	뻣	뻤	뻥	뻬	뼁	뼈	뼉	뼘	뼙	뼛	뼜	뼝	뽀
40	뽁	뽄	뽈	뽐	뽑	뽕	뾔	뾰	뿅	뿌	뿍	뿐	뿔	뿜	뿟	뿡	쀼	쁑	쁘	쁜
60	쁠	쁨	쁩	삐	삑	삔	삘	삠	삡	삣	삥	사	삭	삯	산	삳	살	삵	삶	삼
80	삽	삿	샀	상	샅	새	색	샌	샐	샘	샙	샛	샜	생	샤					

Row 28		01	02	03	04	05	06	07	08	09	10	11	12	13	14	15	16	17	18	19
00		샥	샨	샬	샴	샵	샷	샹	섀	섄	섈	섐	섕	서	석	섞	섟	선	섣	설
20	섦	섧	섬	섭	섯	섰	성	섶	세	섹	센	셀	셈	셉	셋	셌	셍	셔	셕	션
40	셜	셤	셥	셧	셨	셩	셰	셴	셸	솅	소	속	솎	손	솔	솖	솜	솝	솟	송
60	솥	솨	솩	솬	솰	솽	쇄	쇈	쇌	쇔	쇗	쇘	쇠	쇤	쇨	쇰	쇱	쇳	쇼	쇽
80	숀	숄	숌	숍	숏	숑	수	숙	순	숟	술	숨	숩	숫	숭					

Row 29		01	02	03	04	05	06	07	08	09	10	11	12	13	14	15	16	17	18	19
00		숯	숱	숲	숴	쉈	쉐	쉑	쉔	쉘	쉠	쉥	쉬	쉭	쉰	쉴	쉼	쉽	쉿	슁
20	슈	슉	슐	슘	슛	슝	스	슥	슨	슬	슭	슴	습	슷	승	시	식	신	싣	실
40	싫	심	십	싯	싱	싶	싸	싹	싻	싼	쌀	쌈	쌉	쌌	쌍	쌓	쌔	쌕	쌘	쌜
60	쌤	쌥	쌨	쌩	썅	써	썩	썬	썰	썲	썸	썹	썼	썽	쎄	쎈	쎌	쏀	쏘	쏙
80	쏜	쏟	쏠	쏢	쏨	쏩	쏭	쏴	쏵	쏸	쐈	쐐	쐤	쐬	쐰					

Row 30		01	02	03	04	05	06	07	08	09	10	11	12	13	14	15	16	17	18	19
00		쐴	쐼	쐽	쑈	쑤	쑥	쑨	쑬	쑴	쑵	쑹	쒀	쒔	쒜	쒸	쒼	쓩	쓰	쓱
20	쓴	쓸	쓺	쓿	씀	씁	씌	씐	씔	씜	씨	씩	씬	씰	씸	씹	씻	씽	아	악
40	안	앉	않	알	앍	앎	앓	암	압	앗	았	앙	앝	앞	애	액	앤	앨	앰	앱
60	앳	앴	앵	야	약	얀	얄	얇	얌	얍	얏	양	얕	얗	얘	얜	얠	얩	어	억
80	언	얹	얻	얼	얽	얾	엄	업	없	엇	었	엉	엊	엌	엎					

Row 31		01	02	03	04	05	06	07	08	09	10	11	12	13	14	15	16	17	18	19
00		에	엑	엔	엘	엠	엡	엣	엥	여	역	엮	연	열	엶	엷	염	엽	엾	엿
20	였	영	옅	옆	옇	예	옌	옐	옘	옙	옛	옜	오	옥	온	올	옭	옮	옰	옳
40	옴	옵	옷	옹	옻	와	왁	완	왈	왐	왑	왓	왔	왕	왜	왝	왠	왬	왯	왱
60	외	왹	왼	욀	욈	욉	욋	욍	요	욕	욘	욜	욤	욥	욧	용	우	욱	운	울
80	욹	욺	움	웁	웃	웅	워	웍	원	월	웜	웝	웠	웡	웨					

Row 32		01	02	03	04	05	06	07	08	09	10	11	12	13	14	15	16	17	18	19
00		웩	웬	웰	웸	웹	웽	위	윅	윈	윌	윔	윕	윗	윙	유	육	윤	율	윰
20	윱	윳	융	윷	으	윽	은	을	읊	음	읍	읏	응	읒	읓	읔	읕	읖	읗	의
40	읜	읠	읨	읫	이	익	인	일	읽	읾	잃	임	입	잇	있	잉	잊	잎	자	작
60	잔	잖	잗	잘	잚	잠	잡	잣	잤	장	잦	재	잭	잰	잴	잼	잽	잿	쟀	쟁
80	쟈	쟉	쟌	쟎	쟐	쟘	쟝	쟤	쟨	쟬	저	적	전	절	젊					

Row 33		01	02	03	04	05	06	07	08	09	10	11	12	13	14	15	16	17	18	19
00		점	접	젓	정	젖	제	젝	젠	젤	젬	젭	젯	젱	져	젼	졀	졈	졉	졌
20	졍	졔	조	족	존	졸	졺	좀	좁	좃	종	좆	좇	좋	좌	좍	좔	좝	좟	좡
40	좨	좼	좽	죄	죈	죌	죔	죕	죗	죙	죠	죡	죤	죵	주	죽	준	줄	줅	줆
60	줌	줍	줏	중	줘	줬	줴	쥐	쥑	쥔	쥘	쥠	쥡	쥣	쥬	쥰	쥴	쥼	즈	즉
80	즌	즐	즘	즙	즛	증	지	직	진	짇	질	짊	짐	집	짓					

Row 34		01	02	03	04	05	06	07	08	09	10	11	12	13	14	15	16	17	18	19
00		징	짖	짙	짚	짜	짝	짠	짢	짤	짧	짬	짭	짯	짰	짱	째	짹	짼	쨀
20	쨈	쨉	쨋	쨌	쨍	쨔	쨘	쨩	쩌	쩍	쩐	쩔	쩜	쩝	쩟	쩠	쩡	쩨	쩽	쪄
40	쪘	쪼	쪽	쫀	쫄	쫌	쫍	쫏	쫑	쫓	쫘	쫙	쫠	쫬	쫴	쬈	쬐	쬔	쬘	쬠
60	쬡	쭁	쭈	쭉	쭌	쭐	쭘	쭙	쭝	쭤	쭸	쭹	쮜	쮸	쯔	쯤	쯧	쯩	찌	찍
80	찐	찔	찜	찝	찡	찢	찧	차	착	찬	찮	찰	참	찹	찻					

Row 35		01	02	03	04	05	06	07	08	09	10	11	12	13	14	15	16	17	18	19
00		찼	창	찾	채	책	챈	챌	챔	챕	챗	챘	챙	챠	챤	챦	챨	챰	챵	처
20	척	천	철	첨	첩	첫	첬	청	체	첵	첸	첼	쳄	쳅	쳇	쳉	쳐	쳔	쳤	쳬
40	쳰	촁	초	촉	촌	촐	촘	촙	촛	총	촤	촨	촬	촹	최	쵠	쵤	쵬	쵭	쵯
60	쵱	쵸	춈	추	축	춘	출	춤	춥	춧	충	춰	췄	췌	췐	취	췬	췰	췸	췹
80	췻	췽	츄	츈	츌	츔	츙	츠	측	츤	츨	츰	츱	츳	층					

Row 36		01	02	03	04	05	06	07	08	09	10	11	12	13	14	15	16	17	18	19
00		치	칙	친	칟	칠	칡	침	칩	칫	칭	카	칵	칸	칼	캄	캅	캇	캉	캐
20	캑	캔	캘	캠	캡	캣	캤	캥	캬	캭	컁	커	컥	컨	컫	컬	컴	컵	컷	컸
40	컹	케	켁	켄	켈	켐	켑	켓	켕	켜	켠	켤	켬	켭	켯	켰	켱	켸	코	콕
60	콘	콜	콤	콥	콧	콩	콰	콱	콴	콸	쾀	쾅	쾌	쾡	쾨	쾰	쿄	쿠	쿡	쿤
80	쿨	쿰	쿱	쿳	쿵	쿼	퀀	퀄	퀑	퀘	퀭	퀴	퀵	퀸	퀼					

Row 37		01	02	03	04	05	06	07	08	09	10	11	12	13	14	15	16	17	18	19
00		큄	큅	큇	큉	큐	큔	큘	큠	크	큭	큰	클	큼	큽	킁	키	킥	킨	킬
20	킴	킵	킷	킹	타	탁	탄	탈	탉	탐	탑	탓	탔	탕	태	택	탠	탤	탬	탭
40	탯	탰	탱	탸	턍	터	턱	턴	털	턺	텀	텁	텃	텄	텅	테	텍	텐	텔	템
60	텝	텟	텡	텨	텬	텼	톄	톈	토	톡	톤	톨	톰	톱	톳	통	톺	톼	퇀	퇘
80	퇴	퇸	툇	툉	툐	투	툭	툰	툴	툼	툽	툿	퉁	퉈	퉜					

Row 38		01	02	03	04	05	06	07	08	09	10	11	12	13	14	15	16	17	18	19
00		퉤	튀	튁	튄	튈	튐	튑	튕	튜	튠	튤	튬	튱	트	특	튼	튿	틀	틂
20	틈	틉	틋	틔	틘	틜	틤	틥	티	틱	틴	틸	팀	팁	팃	팅	파	팍	팎	판
40	팔	팖	팜	팝	팟	팠	팡	팥	패	팩	팬	팰	팸	팹	팻	팼	팽	퍄	퍅	퍼
60	퍽	펀	펄	펌	펍	펏	펐	펑	페	펙	펜	펠	펨	펩	펫	펭	펴	편	펼	폄
80	폅	폈	평	폐	폘	폡	폣	포	폭	폰	폴	폼	폽	폿	퐁					

Row 39		01	02	03	04	05	06	07	08	09	10	11	12	13	14	15	16	17	18	19
00		퐈	퐝	푀	푄	표	푠	푤	푭	푯	푸	푹	푼	푿	풀	풂	품	풉	풋	풍
20	풔	풩	퓌	퓐	퓔	퓜	퓟	퓨	퓬	퓰	퓸	퓻	퓽	프	픈	플	픔	픕	픗	피
40	픽	핀	필	핌	핍	핏	핑	하	학	한	할	핥	함	합	핫	항	해	핵	핸	핼
60	햄	햅	햇	했	행	햐	향	허	헉	헌	헐	헒	험	헙	헛	헝	헤	헥	헨	헬
80	헴	헵	헷	헹	혀	혁	현	혈	혐	협	혓	혔	형	혜	혠					

Row 40		01	02	03	04	05	06	07	08	09	10	11	12	13	14	15	16	17	18	19
00		혤	혭	호	혹	혼	홀	홅	홈	홉	홋	홍	홑	화	확	환	활	홧	황	홰
20	홱	홴	횃	횅	회	획	횐	횔	횝	횟	횡	효	횬	횰	횹	횻	후	훅	훈	훌
40	훑	훔	훗	훙	훠	훤	훨	훰	훵	훼	훽	휀	휄	휑	휘	휙	휜	휠	휨	휩
60	휫	휭	휴	휵	휸	휼	흄	흇	흉	흐	흑	흔	흖	흗	흘	흙	흠	흡	흣	흥
80	흩	희	흰	흴	흼	흽	힁	히	힉	힌	힐	힘	힙	힛	힝					

Row 42		01	02	03	04	05	06	07	08	09	10	11	12	13	14	15	16	17	18	19
00		伽	佳	假	價	加	可	呵	哥	嘉	嫁	家	暇	架	枷	柯	歌	珂	痂	稼
20	苛	茄	街	袈	訶	賈	跏	軻	迦	駕	刻	却	各	恪	慤	殼	珏	脚	覺	角
40	閣	侃	刊	墾	奸	姦	干	幹	懇	揀	杆	柬	桿	澗	癎	看	磵	稈	竿	簡
60	肝	艮	艱	諫	間	乫	喝	曷	渴	碣	竭	葛	褐	蝎	鞨	勘	坎	堪	嵌	感
80	憾	戡	敢	柑	橄	減	甘	疳	監	瞰	紺	邯	鑑	鑒	龕					

Row 43		01	02	03	04	05	06	07	08	09	10	11	12	13	14	15	16	17	18	19
00		匣	岬	甲	胛	鉀	閘	剛	堈	姜	岡	崗	康	强	彊	慷	江	畺	疆	糠
20	絳	綱	羌	腔	舡	薑	襁	講	鋼	降	鱇	介	价	個	凱	塏	愷	愾	慨	改
40	槪	漑	疥	皆	盖	箇	芥	蓋	豈	鎧	開	喀	客	坑	更	粳	羹	醵	倨	去
60	居	巨	拒	据	據	擧	渠	炬	祛	距	踞	車	遽	鉅	鋸	乾	件	健	巾	建
80	愆	楗	腱	虔	蹇	鍵	騫	乞	傑	杰	桀	儉	劍	劒	檢					

Row 44		01	02	03	04	05	06	07	08	09	10	11	12	13	14	15	16	17	18	19
00		瞼	鈐	黔	劫	怯	迲	偈	憩	揭	擊	格	檄	激	膈	覡	隔	堅	牽	犬
20	甄	絹	繭	肩	見	譴	遣	鵑	抉	決	潔	結	缺	訣	兼	慊	箝	謙	鉗	鎌
40	京	俓	倞	傾	儆	勁	勍	卿	坰	境	庚	徑	慶	憬	擎	敬	景	暻	更	梗
60	涇	炅	烱	璟	璥	瓊	痙	硬	磬	竟	競	絅	經	耕	耿	脛	莖	警	輕	逕
80	鏡	頃	頸	驚	鯨	係	啓	堺	契	季	屆	悸	戒	桂	械					

Row 45		01	02	03	04	05	06	07	08	09	10	11	12	13	14	15	16	17	18	19
00		棨	溪	界	癸	磎	稽	系	繫	繼	計	誡	谿	階	鷄	古	叩	告	呱	固
20	姑	孤	尻	庫	拷	攷	故	敲	暠	枯	槁	沽	痼	皐	睾	稿	羔	考	股	膏
40	苦	苽	菰	藁	蠱	袴	誥	賈	辜	錮	雇	顧	高	鼓	哭	斛	曲	梏	穀	谷
60	鵠	困	坤	崑	昆	梱	棍	滾	琨	袞	鯤	汨	滑	骨	供	公	共	功	孔	工
80	恐	恭	拱	控	攻	珙	空	蚣	貢	鞏	串	寡	戈	果	瓜					

Row 46		01	02	03	04	05	06	07	08	09	10	11	12	13	14	15	16	17	18	19
00		科	菓	誇	課	跨	過	鍋	顆	廓	槨	藿	郭	串	冠	官	寬	慣	棺	款
20	灌	琯	瓘	管	罐	菅	觀	貫	關	館	刮	恝	括	适	侊	光	匡	壙	廣	曠
40	洸	炚	狂	珖	筐	胱	鑛	卦	掛	罫	乖	傀	塊	壞	怪	愧	拐	槐	魁	宏
60	紘	肱	轟	交	僑	咬	喬	嬌	嶠	巧	攪	敎	校	橋	狡	皎	矯	絞	翹	膠
80	蕎	蛟	較	轎	郊	餃	驕	鮫	丘	久	九	仇	俱	具	勾					

Row 47		01	02	03	04	05	06	07	08	09	10	11	12	13	14	15	16	17	18	19
00		區	口	句	咎	嘔	坵	垢	寇	嶇	廐	懼	拘	救	枸	柩	構	歐	毆	毬
20	求	溝	灸	狗	玖	球	瞿	矩	究	絿	耉	臼	舅	舊	苟	衢	謳	購	軀	逑
40	邱	鉤	銶	駒	驅	鳩	鷗	龜	國	局	菊	鞠	鞫	麴	君	窘	群	裙	軍	郡
60	堀	屈	掘	窟	宮	弓	穹	窮	芎	躬	倦	券	勸	卷	圈	拳	捲	權	淃	眷
80	厥	獗	蕨	蹶	闕	机	櫃	潰	詭	軌	饋	句	晷	歸	貴					

Row 48		01	02	03	04	05	06	07	08	09	10	11	12	13	14	15	16	17	18	19
00		鬼	龜	叫	圭	奎	揆	槻	珪	硅	窺	竅	糾	葵	規	赳	逵	閨	勻	均
20	畇	筠	菌	鈞	龜	橘	克	剋	劇	戟	棘	極	隙	僅	劤	勤	懃	斤	根	槿
40	瑾	筋	芹	菫	覲	謹	近	饉	契	今	妗	擒	昑	檎	琴	禁	禽	芩	衾	衿
60	襟	金	錦	伋	及	急	扱	汲	級	給	亘	兢	矜	肯	企	伎	其	冀	嗜	器
80	圻	基	埼	夔	奇	妓	寄	岐	崎	己	幾	忌	技	旗	旣					

Row 49		01	02	03	04	05	06	07	08	09	10	11	12	13	14	15	16	17	18	19
00		朞	期	杞	棋	棄	機	欺	氣	汽	沂	淇	玘	琦	琪	璂	璣	畸	畿	碁
20	磯	祁	祇	祈	祺	箕	紀	綺	羈	耆	耭	肌	記	譏	豈	起	錡	錤	飢	饑
40	騎	騏	驥	麒	緊	佶	吉	拮	桔	金	喫	儺	喇	奈	娜	懦	懶	拏	拿	癩
60	羅	蘿	螺	裸	邏	那	樂	洛	烙	珞	落	諾	酪	駱	亂	卵	暖	欄	煖	爛
80	蘭	難	鸞	捏	捺	南	嵐	枏	楠	湳	濫	男	藍	襤	拉					

Row 50		01	02	03	04	05	06	07	08	09	10	11	12	13	14	15	16	17	18	19
00		納	臘	蠟	衲	囊	娘	廊	朗	浪	狼	郎	乃	來	內	奈	柰	耐	冷	女
20	年	撚	秊	念	恬	拈	捻	寧	寗	努	勞	奴	弩	怒	擄	櫓	爐	瑙	盧	老
40	蘆	虜	路	露	駑	魯	鷺	碌	祿	綠	菉	錄	鹿	論	壟	弄	濃	籠	聾	膿
60	農	惱	牢	磊	腦	賂	雷	尿	壘	屢	樓	淚	漏	累	縷	陋	嫩	訥	杻	紐
80	勒	肋	凜	凌	稜	綾	能	菱	陵	尼	泥	匿	溺	多	茶					

Row 51		01	02	03	04	05	06	07	08	09	10	11	12	13	14	15	16	17	18	19
00		丹	亶	但	單	團	壇	彖	斷	旦	檀	段	湍	短	端	簞	緞	蛋	袒	鄲
20	鍛	撻	澾	獺	疸	達	啖	坍	憺	擔	曇	淡	湛	潭	澹	痰	聃	膽	蕁	覃
40	談	譚	錟	沓	畓	答	踏	遝	唐	堂	塘	幢	戇	撞	棠	當	糖	螳	黨	代
60	垈	坮	大	對	岱	帶	待	戴	擡	玳	臺	袋	貸	隊	黛	宅	德	悳	倒	刀
80	到	圖	堵	塗	導	屠	島	嶋	度	徒	悼	挑	掉	搗	桃					

Row 52		01	02	03	04	05	06	07	08	09	10	11	12	13	14	15	16	17	18	19
00		棹	櫂	淘	渡	滔	濤	燾	盜	睹	禱	稻	萄	覩	賭	跳	蹈	逃	途	道
20	都	鍍	陶	韜	毒	瀆	牘	犢	獨	督	禿	篤	纛	讀	墩	惇	敦	旽	暾	沌
40	焞	燉	豚	頓	乭	突	仝	冬	凍	動	同	憧	東	桐	棟	洞	潼	疼	瞳	童
60	胴	董	銅	兜	斗	杜	枓	痘	竇	荳	讀	豆	逗	頭	屯	臀	芚	遁	遯	鈍
80	得	嶝	橙	燈	登	等	藤	謄	鄧	騰	喇	懶	拏	癩	羅					

Row 53		01	02	03	04	05	06	07	08	09	10	11	12	13	14	15	16	17	18	19
00		蘿	螺	裸	邏	樂	洛	烙	珞	絡	落	諾	酪	駱	丹	亂	卵	欄	欒	瀾
20	爛	蘭	鸞	剌	辣	嵐	擥	攬	欖	濫	籃	纜	藍	襤	覽	拉	臘	蠟	廊	朗
40	浪	狼	琅	瑯	螂	郞	來	崍	徠	萊	冷	掠	略	亮	倆	兩	凉	梁	樑	粮
60	粱	糧	良	諒	輛	量	侶	儷	勵	呂	廬	慮	戾	旅	櫚	濾	礪	藜	蠣	閭
80	驢	驪	麗	黎	力	曆	歷	瀝	礫	轢	靂	憐	戀	攣	漣					

Row 54		01	02	03	04	05	06	07	08	09	10	11	12	13	14	15	16	17	18	19
00		煉	璉	練	聯	蓮	輦	連	鍊	冽	列	劣	洌	烈	裂	廉	斂	殮	濂	簾
20	獵	令	伶	囹	寧	岺	嶺	怜	玲	笭	羚	翎	聆	逞	鈴	零	靈	領	齡	例
40	澧	禮	醴	隸	勞	怒	撈	擄	櫓	潞	瀘	爐	盧	老	蘆	虜	路	輅	露	魯
60	鷺	鹵	碌	祿	綠	菉	錄	鹿	麓	論	壟	弄	朧	瀧	瓏	籠	聾	儡	瀨	牢
80	磊	賂	賚	賴	雷	了	僚	寮	廖	料	燎	療	瞭	聊	蓼					

Row 55		01	02	03	04	05	06	07	08	09	10	11	12	13	14	15	16	17	18	19
00		遼	鬧	龍	壘	婁	屢	樓	淚	漏	瘻	累	縷	蔞	褸	鏤	陋	劉	旒	柳
20	榴	流	溜	瀏	琉	瑠	留	瘤	硫	謬	類	六	戮	陸	侖	倫	崙	淪	綸	輪
40	律	慄	栗	率	隆	勒	肋	凜	凌	楞	稜	綾	菱	陵	俚	利	厘	吏	唎	履
60	悧	李	梨	浬	犁	狸	理	璃	異	痢	籬	罹	羸	莉	裏	裡	里	釐	離	鯉
80	吝	潾	燐	璘	藺	躪	隣	鱗	麟	林	淋	琳	臨	霖	砬					

Row 56		01	02	03	04	05	06	07	08	09	10	11	12	13	14	15	16	17	18	19
00		立	笠	粒	摩	瑪	痲	碼	磨	馬	魔	麻	寞	幕	漠	膜	莫	邈	万	卍
20	娩	巒	彎	慢	挽	晩	曼	滿	漫	灣	瞞	萬	蔓	蠻	輓	饅	鰻	唜	抹	末
40	沫	茉	襪	靺	亡	妄	忘	忙	望	網	罔	芒	茫	莽	輞	邙	埋	妹	媒	寐
60	昧	枚	梅	每	煤	罵	買	賣	邁	魅	脈	貊	陌	驀	麥	孟	氓	猛	盲	盟
80	萌	冪	覓	免	冕	勉	棉	沔	眄	眠	綿	緬	面	麵	滅					

Row 57		01	02	03	04	05	06	07	08	09	10	11	12	13	14	15	16	17	18	19
00		蔑	冥	名	命	明	暝	椧	溟	皿	瞑	茗	蓂	螟	酩	銘	鳴	袂	侮	冒
20	募	姆	帽	慕	摸	摹	暮	某	模	母	毛	牟	牡	瑁	眸	矛	耗	芼	茅	謀
40	謨	貌	木	沐	牧	目	睦	穆	鶩	歿	沒	夢	朦	蒙	卯	墓	妙	廟	描	昴
60	杳	渺	猫	竗	苗	錨	務	巫	憮	懋	戊	拇	撫	无	楙	武	毋	無	珷	畝
80	繆	舞	茂	蕪	誣	貿	霧	鵡	墨	默	們	刎	吻	問	文					

Row 58		01	02	03	04	05	06	07	08	09	10	11	12	13	14	15	16	17	18	19
00		汶	紊	紋	聞	蚊	門	雯	勿	沕	物	味	媚	尾	嵋	彌	微	未	梶	楣
20	渼	湄	眉	米	美	薇	謎	迷	靡	黴	岷	悶	愍	憫	敏	旻	旼	民	泯	玟
40	珉	緡	閔	密	蜜	謐	剝	博	拍	搏	撲	朴	樸	泊	珀	璞	箔	粕	縛	膊
60	舶	薄	迫	雹	駁	伴	半	反	叛	拌	搬	攀	斑	槃	泮	潘	班	畔	瘢	盤
80	盼	磐	磻	礬	絆	般	蟠	返	頒	飯	勃	拔	撥	渤	潑					

Row 59		01	02	03	04	05	06	07	08	09	10	11	12	13	14	15	16	17	18	19
00		發	跋	醱	鉢	髮	魃	倣	傍	坊	妨	尨	幇	彷	房	放	方	旁	昉	枋
20	榜	滂	磅	紡	肪	膀	舫	芳	蒡	蚌	訪	謗	邦	防	龐	倍	俳	北	培	徘
40	拜	排	杯	湃	焙	盃	背	胚	裴	裵	褙	賠	輩	配	陪	伯	佰	帛	柏	栢
60	白	百	魄	幡	樊	煩	燔	番	磻	繁	蕃	藩	飜	伐	筏	罰	閥	凡	帆	梵
80	氾	汎	泛	犯	範	范	法	琺	僻	劈	壁	擘	檗	璧	癖					

Row 60		01	02	03	04	05	06	07	08	09	10	11	12	13	14	15	16	17	18	19
00		碧	蘗	闢	霹	便	卞	弁	變	辨	辯	邊	別	瞥	鱉	鼈	丙	倂	兵	屛
20	幷	昞	昺	柄	棅	炳	甁	病	秉	竝	輧	餠	騈	保	堡	報	寶	普	步	洑
40	湺	潽	珤	甫	菩	補	褓	譜	輔	伏	僕	匐	卜	宓	復	服	福	腹	茯	蔔
60	複	覆	輹	輻	馥	鰒	本	乶	俸	奉	封	峯	峰	捧	棒	烽	熢	琫	縫	蓬
80	蜂	逢	鋒	鳳	不	付	俯	傅	剖	副	否	咐	埠	夫	婦					

Row 61		01	02	03	04	05	06	07	08	09	10	11	12	13	14	15	16	17	18	19
00		孚	孵	富	府	復	扶	敷	斧	浮	溥	父	符	簿	缶	腐	腑	膚	艀	芙
20	莩	訃	負	賦	賻	赴	趺	部	釜	阜	附	駙	鳧	北	分	吩	噴	墳	奔	奮
40	忿	憤	扮	昐	汾	焚	盆	粉	糞	紛	芬	賁	雰	不	佛	弗	彿	拂	崩	朋
60	棚	硼	繃	鵬	丕	備	匕	匪	卑	妃	婢	庇	悲	憊	扉	批	斐	枇	榧	比
80	毖	毗	毘	沸	泌	琵	痺	砒	碑	秕	秘	粃	緋	翡	肥					

Row 62		01	02	03	04	05	06	07	08	09	10	11	12	13	14	15	16	17	18	19
00		脾	臂	菲	蜚	裨	誹	譬	費	鄙	非	飛	鼻	嚬	嬪	彬	斌	檳	殯	浜
20	濱	瀕	牝	玭	貧	賓	頻	憑	氷	聘	騁	乍	事	些	仕	伺	似	使	俟	僿
40	史	司	唆	嗣	四	士	奢	娑	寫	寺	射	巳	師	徙	思	捨	斜	斯	柶	査
60	梭	死	沙	泗	渣	瀉	獅	砂	社	祀	祠	私	篩	紗	絲	肆	舍	莎	蓑	蛇
80	裟	詐	詞	謝	賜	赦	辭	邪	飼	駟	麝	削	數	朔	索					

Row 63		01	02	03	04	05	06	07	08	09	10	11	12	13	14	15	16	17	18	19
00		傘	刪	山	散	汕	珊	産	疝	算	蒜	酸	霰	乷	撒	殺	煞	薩	三	參
20	杉	森	滲	芟	蔘	衫	揷	澁	鈒	颯	上	傷	像	償	商	喪	嘗	孀	尙	峠
40	常	床	庠	廂	想	桑	橡	湘	爽	牀	狀	相	祥	箱	翔	裳	觴	詳	象	賞
60	霜	塞	璽	賽	嗇	塞	穡	索	色	牲	生	甥	省	笙	墅	壻	嶼	序	庶	徐
80	恕	抒	捿	敍	暑	曙	書	栖	棲	犀	瑞	筮	絮	緖	署					

Row 64		01	02	03	04	05	06	07	08	09	10	11	12	13	14	15	16	17	18	19
00		胥	舒	薯	西	誓	逝	鋤	黍	鼠	夕	奭	席	惜	昔	晳	析	汐	淅	潟
20	石	碩	蓆	釋	錫	仙	僊	先	善	嬋	宣	扇	敾	旋	渲	煽	琁	瑄	璇	璿
40	癬	禪	線	繕	羨	腺	膳	船	蘚	蟬	詵	跣	選	銑	鐥	饍	鮮	卨	屑	楔
60	泄	洩	渫	舌	薛	褻	設	說	雪	齧	剡	暹	殲	纖	蟾	贍	閃	陝	攝	涉
80	燮	葉	城	姓	宬	性	惺	成	星	晟	猩	珹	盛	省	筬					

Row 65		01	02	03	04	05	06	07	08	09	10	11	12	13	14	15	16	17	18	19
00		聖	聲	腥	誠	醒	世	勢	歲	洗	稅	笹	細	說	貰	召	嘯	塑	宵	小
20	少	巢	所	掃	搔	昭	梳	沼	消	溯	瀟	炤	燒	甦	疏	疎	瘙	笑	篠	簫
40	素	紹	蔬	蕭	蘇	訴	逍	遡	邵	銷	韶	騷	俗	屬	束	涑	粟	續	謖	贖
60	速	孫	巽	損	蓀	遜	飡	率	宋	悚	松	淞	訟	誦	送	頌	刷	殺	灑	碎
80	鎖	衰	釗	修	受	嗽	囚	垂	壽	嫂	守	岫	峀	帥	愁					

Row 66		01	02	03	04	05	06	07	08	09	10	11	12	13	14	15	16	17	18	19
00		戍	手	授	搜	收	數	樹	殊	水	洙	漱	燧	狩	獸	琇	璲	瘦	睡	秀
20	穗	竪	粹	綏	綬	繡	羞	脩	茱	蒐	蓚	藪	袖	誰	讐	輸	遂	邃	酬	銖
40	銹	隋	隧	隨	雖	需	須	首	髓	鬚	叔	塾	夙	孰	宿	淑	潚	熟	琡	璹
60	肅	菽	巡	徇	循	恂	旬	栒	楯	橓	殉	洵	淳	珣	盾	瞬	筍	純	脣	舜
80	荀	蓴	蕣	詢	諄	醇	錞	順	馴	戌	術	述	鉥	崇	崧					

Row 67		01	02	03	04	05	06	07	08	09	10	11	12	13	14	15	16	17	18	19
00		嵩	瑟	膝	蝨	濕	拾	習	褶	襲	丞	乘	僧	勝	升	承	昇	繩	蠅	陞
20	侍	匙	嘶	始	媤	尸	屎	屍	市	弑	恃	施	是	時	枾	柴	猜	矢	示	翅
40	蒔	蓍	視	試	詩	諡	豕	豺	埴	寔	式	息	拭	植	殖	湜	熄	篒	蝕	識
60	軾	食	飾	伸	侁	信	呻	娠	宸	愼	新	晨	燼	申	神	紳	腎	臣	莘	薪
80	藎	蜃	訊	身	辛	辰	迅	失	室	實	悉	審	尋	心	沁					

Row 68		01	02	03	04	05	06	07	08	09	10	11	12	13	14	15	16	17	18	19
00		沈	深	瀋	甚	芯	諶	什	十	拾	雙	氏	亞	俄	兒	啞	娥	峨	我	牙
20	芽	莪	蛾	衙	訝	阿	雅	餓	鴉	鵝	堊	岳	嶽	幄	惡	愕	握	樂	渥	鄂
40	鍔	顎	鰐	齷	安	岸	按	晏	案	眼	雁	鞍	顔	鮟	斡	謁	軋	閼	唵	岩
60	巖	庵	暗	癌	菴	闇	壓	押	狎	鴨	仰	央	怏	昻	殃	秧	鴦	厓	哀	埃
80	崖	愛	曖	涯	碍	艾	隘	靄	厄	扼	掖	液	縊	腋	額					

Row 69		01	02	03	04	05	06	07	08	09	10	11	12	13	14	15	16	17	18	19
00		櫻	罌	鶯	鸚	也	倻	冶	夜	惹	揶	椰	爺	耶	若	野	弱	掠	略	約
20	若	葯	蒻	藥	躍	亮	佯	兩	凉	壤	孃	恙	揚	攘	敭	暘	梁	楊	樣	洋
40	瀁	煬	痒	瘍	禳	穰	糧	羊	良	襄	諒	讓	釀	陽	量	養	圄	御	於	漁
60	瘀	禦	語	馭	魚	齬	億	憶	抑	檍	臆	偃	堰	彦	焉	言	諺	孼	蘖	俺
80	儼	嚴	奄	掩	淹	嶪	業	円	予	余	勵	呂	女	如	廬					

Row 70		01	02	03	04	05	06	07	08	09	10	11	12	13	14	15	16	17	18	19
00		旅	歟	汝	濾	璵	礖	礪	與	艅	茹	輿	轝	閭	餘	驪	麗	黎	亦	力
20	域	役	易	曆	歷	疫	繹	譯	轢	逆	驛	嚥	堧	姸	娟	宴	年	延	憐	戀
40	捐	挻	撚	椽	沇	沿	涎	涓	淵	演	漣	烟	然	煙	煉	燃	燕	璉	硏	硯
60	秊	筵	緣	練	縯	聯	衍	軟	輦	蓮	連	鉛	鍊	鳶	列	劣	咽	悅	涅	烈
80	熱	裂	說	閱	厭	廉	念	捻	染	殮	炎	焰	琰	艶	苒					

Row 71		01	02	03	04	05	06	07	08	09	10	11	12	13	14	15	16	17	18	19
00		簾	閻	髥	鹽	曄	獵	燁	葉	令	囹	塋	寧	嶺	嶸	影	怜	映	暎	楹
20	榮	永	泳	渶	潁	濚	瀛	瀯	煐	營	獰	玲	瑛	瑩	瓔	盈	穎	纓	羚	聆
40	英	詠	迎	鈴	鍈	零	霙	靈	領	乂	倪	例	刈	叡	曳	汭	濊	猊	睿	穢
60	芮	藝	蘂	禮	裔	詣	譽	豫	醴	銳	隸	霓	預	五	伍	俉	傲	午	吾	吳
80	嗚	塢	墺	奧	娛	寤	悟	惡	懊	敖	旿	晤	梧	汚	澳					

Row 72		01	02	03	04	05	06	07	08	09	10	11	12	13	14	15	16	17	18	19
00		烏	熬	獒	筽	蜈	誤	鰲	鼇	屋	沃	獄	玉	鈺	溫	瑥	瘟	穩	縕	蘊
20	兀	壅	擁	瓮	甕	癰	翁	邕	雍	饔	渦	瓦	窩	窪	臥	蛙	蝸	訛	婉	完
40	宛	梡	椀	浣	玩	琓	琬	碗	緩	翫	脘	腕	莞	豌	阮	頑	曰	往	旺	枉
60	汪	王	倭	娃	歪	矮	外	嵬	巍	猥	畏	了	僚	僥	凹	堯	夭	妖	姚	寥
80	寮	尿	嶢	拗	搖	撓	擾	料	曜	樂	橈	燎	燿	瑤	療					

Row 73		01	02	03	04	05	06	07	08	09	10	11	12	13	14	15	16	17	18	19
00		窈	窯	繇	繞	耀	腰	蓼	蟯	要	謠	遙	遼	邀	饒	慾	欲	浴	縟	褥
20	辱	俑	傭	冗	勇	埇	墉	容	庸	慂	榕	涌	湧	溶	熔	瑢	用	甬	聳	茸
40	蓉	踊	鎔	鏞	龍	于	佑	偶	優	又	友	右	宇	寓	尤	愚	憂	旴	牛	玗
60	瑀	盂	祐	禑	禹	紆	羽	芋	藕	虞	迂	遇	郵	釪	隅	雨	雩	勖	彧	旭
80	昱	栯	煜	稶	郁	頊	云	暈	橒	殞	澐	熉	耘	芸	蕓					

Row 74		01	02	03	04	05	06	07	08	09	10	11	12	13	14	15	16	17	18	19
00		運	隕	雲	韻	蔚	鬱	亐	熊	雄	元	原	員	圓	園	垣	媛	嫄	寃	怨
20	愿	援	沅	洹	湲	源	爰	猿	瑗	苑	袁	轅	遠	阮	院	願	鴛	月	越	鉞
40	位	偉	僞	危	圍	委	威	尉	慰	暐	渭	爲	瑋	緯	胃	萎	葦	蔿	蝟	衛
60	褘	謂	違	韋	魏	乳	侑	儒	兪	劉	唯	喩	孺	宥	幼	幽	庾	悠	惟	愈
80	愉	揄	攸	有	杻	柔	柚	柳	楡	楢	油	洧	流	游	溜					

Row 75		01	02	03	04	05	06	07	08	09	10	11	12	13	14	15	16	17	18	19
00		濡	猶	猷	琉	瑜	由	留	癒	硫	紐	維	臾	萸	裕	誘	諛	諭	踰	蹂
20	遊	逾	遺	酉	釉	鍮	類	六	堉	戮	毓	肉	育	陸	倫	允	奫	尹	崙	淪
40	潤	玧	胤	贇	輪	鈗	閏	律	慄	栗	率	聿	戎	瀜	絨	融	隆	垠	恩	慇
60	殷	誾	銀	隱	乙	吟	淫	蔭	陰	音	飮	揖	泣	邑	凝	應	膺	鷹	依	倚
80	儀	宜	意	懿	擬	椅	毅	疑	矣	義	艤	薏	蟻	衣	誼					

Row 76		01	02	03	04	05	06	07	08	09	10	11	12	13	14	15	16	17	18	19
00		議	醫	二	以	伊	利	吏	夷	姨	履	已	弛	彛	怡	易	李	梨	泥	爾
20	珥	理	異	痍	痢	移	罹	而	耳	肄	苡	荑	裏	裡	貽	貳	邇	里	離	飴
40	餌	匿	溺	瀷	益	翊	翌	翼	謚	人	仁	刃	印	吝	咽	因	姻	寅	引	忍
60	湮	燐	璘	絪	茵	藺	蚓	認	隣	靭	靷	鱗	麟	一	佚	佾	壹	日	溢	逸
80	鎰	馹	任	壬	妊	姙	恁	林	淋	稔	臨	荏	賃	入	卄					

Row 77		01	02	03	04	05	06	07	08	09	10	11	12	13	14	15	16	17	18	19
00		立	笠	粒	仍	剩	孕	芿	仔	刺	咨	姉	姿	子	字	孜	恣	慈	滋	炙
20	煮	玆	瓷	疵	磁	紫	者	自	茨	蔗	藉	諮	資	雌	作	勺	嚼	斫	昨	灼
40	炸	爵	綽	芍	酌	雀	鵲	孱	棧	殘	潺	盞	岑	暫	潛	箴	簪	蠶	雜	丈
60	仗	匠	場	墻	壯	奬	將	帳	庄	張	掌	暲	杖	樟	檣	欌	漿	牆	狀	獐
80	璋	章	粧	腸	臟	臧	莊	葬	蔣	薔	藏	裝	贓	醬	長					

Row 78		01	02	03	04	05	06	07	08	09	10	11	12	13	14	15	16	17	18	19
00		障	再	哉	在	宰	才	材	栽	梓	渽	滓	災	縡	裁	財	載	齋	齎	爭
20	箏	諍	錚	佇	低	儲	咀	姐	底	抵	杵	楮	樗	沮	渚	狙	猪	疽	箸	紵
40	苧	菹	著	藷	詛	貯	躇	這	邸	雎	齟	勣	吊	嫡	寂	摘	敵	滴	狄	炙
60	的	積	笛	籍	績	翟	荻	謫	賊	赤	跡	蹟	迪	迹	適	鏑	佃	佺	傳	全
80	典	前	剪	塡	塼	奠	專	展	廛	悛	戰	栓	殿	氈	澱					

Row 79		01	02	03	04	05	06	07	08	09	10	11	12	13	14	15	16	17	18	19
00		煎	琠	田	甸	畑	癲	筌	箋	箭	篆	纏	詮	輾	轉	鈿	銓	錢	鐫	電
20	顚	顫	餞	切	截	折	浙	癤	竊	節	絶	占	岾	店	漸	点	粘	霑	鮎	點
40	接	摺	蝶	丁	井	亭	停	偵	呈	姃	定	幀	庭	廷	征	情	挺	政	整	旌
60	晶	晸	柾	楨	檉	正	汀	淀	淨	渟	湞	瀞	炡	玎	珽	町	睛	碇	禎	程
80	穽	精	綎	艇	訂	諪	貞	鄭	酊	釘	鉦	鋌	錠	霆	靖					

Row 80		01	02	03	04	05	06	07	08	09	10	11	12	13	14	15	16	17	18	19
00		靜	頂	鼎	制	劑	啼	堤	帝	弟	悌	提	梯	濟	祭	第	臍	薺	製	諸
20	蹄	醍	除	際	霽	題	齊	俎	兆	凋	助	嘲	弔	彫	措	操	早	晁	曺	曹
40	朝	條	棗	槽	漕	潮	照	燥	爪	璪	眺	祖	祚	租	稠	窕	粗	糟	組	繰
60	肇	藻	蚤	詔	調	趙	躁	造	遭	釣	阻	雕	鳥	族	簇	足	鏃	存	尊	卒
80	拙	猝	倧	宗	從	悰	慫	棕	淙	琮	種	終	綜	縱	腫					

Row 81		01	02	03	04	05	06	07	08	09	10	11	12	13	14	15	16	17	18	19
00		踪	踵	鍾	鐘	佐	坐	左	座	挫	罪	主	住	侏	做	姝	胄	呪	周	嗾
20	奏	宙	州	廚	晝	朱	柱	株	注	洲	湊	澍	炷	珠	疇	籌	紂	紬	綢	舟
40	蛛	註	誅	走	躊	輳	週	酎	酒	鑄	駐	竹	粥	俊	儁	准	埈	寯	峻	晙
60	樽	浚	準	濬	焌	畯	竣	蠢	逡	遵	雋	駿	茁	中	仲	衆	重	卽	櫛	楫
80	汁	葺	增	憎	曾	拯	烝	甑	症	繒	蒸	證	贈	之	只					

Row 82		01	02	03	04	05	06	07	08	09	10	11	12	13	14	15	16	17	18	19
00		咫	地	址	志	持	指	摯	支	旨	智	枝	枳	止	池	沚	漬	知	砥	祉
20	祗	紙	肢	脂	至	芝	芷	蜘	誌	識	贄	趾	遲	直	稙	稷	織	職	唇	嗔
40	塵	振	搢	晉	晋	桭	榛	殄	津	溱	珍	瑨	璡	畛	疹	盡	眞	瞋	秦	縉
60	縝	臻	蔯	袗	診	賑	軫	辰	進	鎭	陣	陳	震	侄	叱	姪	嫉	帙	桎	瓆
80	疾	秩	窒	膣	蛭	質	跌	迭	斟	朕	什	執	潗	緝	輯					

Row 83		01	02	03	04	05	06	07	08	09	10	11	12	13	14	15	16	17	18	19
00		鏶	集	徵	懲	澄	且	侘	借	叉	嗟	嵯	差	次	此	磋	箚	茶	蹉	車
20	遮	捉	搾	着	窄	錯	鑿	齪	撰	澯	燦	璨	瓚	竄	簒	纂	粲	纘	讚	贊
40	鑽	餐	饌	刹	察	擦	札	紮	僭	參	塹	慘	慙	懺	斬	站	讒	讖	倉	倡
60	創	唱	娼	廠	彰	愴	敞	昌	昶	暢	槍	滄	漲	猖	瘡	窓	脹	艙	菖	蒼
80	債	埰	寀	寨	彩	採	砦	綵	菜	蔡	采	釵	冊	柵	策					

Row 84		01	02	03	04	05	06	07	08	09	10	11	12	13	14	15	16	17	18	19
00		責	凄	妻	悽	處	倜	刺	剔	尺	慽	戚	拓	擲	斥	滌	瘠	脊	蹠	陟
20	隻	仟	千	喘	天	川	擅	泉	淺	玔	穿	舛	薦	賤	踐	遷	釧	闡	阡	韆
40	凸	哲	喆	徹	撤	澈	綴	輟	轍	鐵	僉	尖	沾	添	甛	瞻	簽	籤	詹	諂
60	堞	妾	帖	捷	牒	疊	睫	諜	貼	輒	廳	晴	淸	聽	菁	請	靑	鯖	切	剃
80	替	涕	滯	締	諦	逮	遞	體	初	剿	哨	憔	抄	招	梢					

Row 85		01	02	03	04	05	06	07	08	09	10	11	12	13	14	15	16	17	18	19
00		椒	楚	樵	炒	焦	硝	礁	礎	秒	稍	肖	艸	苕	草	蕉	貂	超	酢	醋
20	醮	促	囑	燭	矗	蜀	觸	寸	忖	村	邨	叢	塚	寵	悤	憁	摠	總	聰	蔥
40	銃	撮	催	崔	最	墜	抽	推	椎	楸	樞	湫	皺	秋	芻	萩	諏	趨	追	鄒
60	酋	醜	錐	錘	鎚	雛	騶	鰍	丑	畜	祝	竺	筑	築	縮	蓄	蹙	蹴	軸	逐
80	春	椿	瑃	出	朮	黜	充	忠	沖	蟲	衝	衷	悴	膵	萃					

Row 86		01	02	03	04	05	06	07	08	09	10	11	12	13	14	15	16	17	18	19
00		贅	取	吹	嘴	娶	就	炊	翠	聚	脆	臭	趣	醉	驟	鷲	側	仄	厠	惻
20	測	層	侈	値	嗤	峙	幟	恥	梔	治	淄	熾	痔	痴	癡	稚	穉	緇	緻	置
40	致	蚩	輜	雉	馳	齒	則	勅	飭	親	七	柒	漆	侵	寢	枕	沈	浸	琛	砧
60	針	鍼	蟄	秤	稱	快	他	咤	唾	墮	妥	惰	打	拖	朶	楕	舵	陀	馱	駝
80	倬	卓	啄	坼	度	托	拓	擢	晫	柝	濁	濯	琢	琸	託					

Row 87		01	02	03	04	05	06	07	08	09	10	11	12	13	14	15	16	17	18	19
00		鐸	呑	嘆	坦	彈	憚	歎	灘	炭	綻	誕	奪	脫	探	眈	耽	貪	塔	搭
20	榻	宕	帑	湯	糖	蕩	兌	台	太	怠	態	殆	汰	泰	笞	胎	苔	跆	邰	颱
40	宅	擇	澤	撑	攄	兎	吐	土	討	慟	桶	洞	痛	筒	統	通	堆	槌	腿	褪
60	退	頹	偸	套	妬	投	透	鬪	慝	特	闖	坡	婆	巴	把	播	擺	杷	波	派
80	爬	琶	破	罷	芭	跛	頗	判	坂	板	版	瓣	販	辦	鈑					

Row 88		01	02	03	04	05	06	07	08	09	10	11	12	13	14	15	16	17	18	19
00		阪	八	叭	捌	佩	唄	悖	敗	沛	浿	牌	狽	稗	覇	貝	彭	澎	烹	膨
20	愎	便	偏	扁	片	篇	編	翩	遍	鞭	騙	貶	坪	平	枰	萍	評	吠	嬖	幣
40	廢	弊	斃	肺	蔽	閉	陛	佈	包	匍	匏	咆	哺	圃	布	怖	抛	抱	捕	暴
60	泡	浦	疱	砲	胞	脯	苞	葡	蒲	袍	褒	逋	鋪	飽	鮑	幅	暴	曝	瀑	爆
80	輻	俵	剽	彪	慓	杓	標	漂	瓢	票	表	豹	飇	飄	驃					

Row 89		01	02	03	04	05	06	07	08	09	10	11	12	13	14	15	16	17	18	19
00		品	稟	楓	諷	豊	風	馮	彼	披	疲	皮	被	避	陂	匹	弼	必	泌	珌
20	畢	疋	筆	苾	馝	乏	逼	下	何	厦	夏	廈	昰	河	瑕	荷	蝦	賀	遐	霞
40	鰕	壑	學	虐	謔	鶴	寒	恨	悍	旱	汗	漢	澣	瀚	罕	翰	閑	閒	限	韓
60	割	轄	函	含	咸	啣	喊	檻	涵	緘	艦	銜	陷	鹹	合	哈	盒	蛤	閤	闔
80	陜	亢	伉	姮	嫦	巷	恒	抗	杭	桁	沆	港	缸	肛	航					

Row 90		01	02	03	04	05	06	07	08	09	10	11	12	13	14	15	16	17	18	19
00		行	降	項	亥	偕	咳	垓	奚	孩	害	懈	楷	海	瀣	蟹	解	該	諧	邂
20	駭	骸	劾	核	倖	幸	杏	荇	行	享	向	嚮	珦	鄕	響	餉	饗	香	噓	墟
40	虛	許	憲	櫶	獻	軒	歇	險	驗	奕	爀	赫	革	俔	峴	弦	懸	晛	泫	炫
60	玄	玹	現	眩	睍	絃	絢	縣	舷	衒	見	賢	鉉	顯	孑	穴	血	頁	嫌	俠
80	協	夾	峽	挾	浹	狹	脅	脇	莢	鋏	頰	亨	兄	刑	型					

Row 91		01	02	03	04	05	06	07	08	09	10	11	12	13	14	15	16	17	18	19
00		形	泂	滎	瀅	灐	炯	熒	珩	瑩	荊	螢	衡	逈	邢	鎣	馨	兮	彗	惠
20	慧	暳	蕙	蹊	醯	鞋	乎	互	呼	壕	壺	好	岵	弧	戶	扈	昊	晧	毫	浩
40	淏	湖	滸	澔	濠	濩	灝	狐	琥	瑚	瓠	皓	祜	糊	縞	胡	芦	葫	蒿	虎
60	號	蝴	護	豪	鎬	頀	顥	惑	或	酷	婚	昏	混	渾	琿	魂	忽	惚	笏	哄
80	弘	汞	泓	洪	烘	紅	虹	訌	鴻	化	和	嬅	樺	火	畵					

Row 92		01	02	03	04	05	06	07	08	09	10	11	12	13	14	15	16	17	18	19
00		禍	禾	花	華	話	譁	貨	靴	廓	擴	攫	確	碻	穫	丸	喚	奐	宦	幻
20	患	換	歡	晥	桓	渙	煥	環	紈	還	驩	鰥	活	滑	猾	豁	闊	凰	幌	徨
40	恍	惶	愰	慌	晃	晄	榥	況	湟	滉	潢	煌	璜	皇	篁	簧	荒	蝗	遑	隍
60	黃	匯	回	廻	徊	恢	悔	懷	晦	會	檜	淮	澮	灰	獪	繪	膾	茴	蛔	誨
80	賄	劃	獲	宖	橫	鐄	哮	嚆	孝	效	斅	曉	梟	涍	淆					

Row 93		01	02	03	04	05	06	07	08	09	10	11	12	13	14	15	16	17	18	19
00		爻	肴	酵	驍	侯	候	厚	后	吼	喉	嗅	帿	後	朽	煦	珝	逅	勛	勳
20	塤	壎	焄	熏	燻	薰	訓	暈	薨	喧	暄	煊	萱	卉	喙	毁	彙	徽	揮	暉
40	煇	諱	輝	麾	休	携	烋	畦	虧	恤	譎	鷸	兇	凶	匈	洶	胸	黑	昕	欣
60	炘	痕	吃	屹	紇	訖	欠	欽	歆	吸	恰	洽	翕	興	僖	凞	喜	噫	囍	姬
80	嬉	希	憙	憘	戱	晞	曦	熙	熹	熺	犧	禧	稀	羲	詰					

M

KS X 1002:1991 Hanja Table

This appendix constitutes a table for only the 2,856 hanja in the KS X 1002:1991 character set standard, printed here using the typeface HY신명조 (HYSMyeongJo-Medium), developed by Hanyang Systems. Each character is indexed by Row-Cell value.

Row 55		01	02	03	04	05	06	07	08	09	10	11	12	13	14	15	16	17	18	19
00		仮	傢	咖	哿	坷	宊	斝	榎	檟	珈	笳	耞	舸	葭	譌	卻	咯	埆	搉
20	擱	桷	偘	慳	栞	榦	玕	秆	茛	衎	赶	迀	齦	噶	楬	秸	羯	蠍	鶡	坩
40	埳	嵁	弇	憨	撼	欿	歛	泔	淦	澉	矙	轗	酣	鹻	韐	傋	僵	壃	忼	扛
60	杠	橿	殭	矼	穅	繈	罡	羌	羫	茳	豇	韁	剴	匃	揩	槩	玠	磕	闓	硜
80	賡	鏗	呿	昛	秬	筥	籧	胠	腒	苣	莒	蕖	蘧	袪	裾					

Row 56		01	02	03	04	05	06	07	08	09	10	11	12	13	14	15	16	17	18	19
00		駏	揵	犍	睷	褰	謇	鞬	乬	朅	榤	撿	芡	刦	刼	挌	毄	闃	骼	鬲
20	鴃	樫	狷	畎	筧	縳	繾	羂	蠲	鰹	抉	觖	闋	傔	嗛	岒	拑	歉	縑	蒹
40	黚	鼸	冏	剄	哽	惸	憼	扃	檠	熒	煢	熲	畊	竸	綆	顈	罄	褧	謦	駉
60	鯁	黥	堦	烓	瘈	禊	笄	綮	縘	罽	葪	薊	雞	髻	估	凅	刳	塙	杲	栲
80	槀	槹	櫜	牯	皐	盬	瞽	稾	箍	篙	糕	罟	羖	翶	胯					

Row 57		01	02	03	04	05	06	07	08	09	10	11	12	13	14	15	16	17	18	19
00		觚	詁	郜	酤	鈷	靠	鴣	鷱	嚳	斛	縠	觳	轂	堃	崐	悃	捆	緄	袞
20	裍	褌	錕	閫	髡	鵾	鶤	齫	搰	榾	矻	鶻	倥	崆	悾	栱	槓	箜	蛩	蛬
40	贛	跫	釭	龔	侉	堝	夥	夸	撾	猓	稞	窠	蝌	裹	踝	銙	騍	椁	癨	躩
60	霍	鞹	丱	涫	爟	盥	祼	窾	筦	綰	輨	錧	鑵	雚	顴	髖	鸛	佸	栝	筈
80	聒	髺	鴰	恇	桄	框	爌	獷	磺	絖	纊	茪	誆	誑	咼					

Row 58		01	02	03	04	05	06	07	08	09	10	11	12	13	14	15	16	17	18	19
00		挂	罣	詿	媿	廥	恠	瑰	璝	蒯	襘	馘	浤	觥	訇	閎	佼	嘄	嘐	噭
20	嚙	姣	憍	撟	晈	暞	榷	磽	窖	趫	蹻	鉸	骹	鵁	齩	佉	佝	俅	傴	冓
40	劬	匶	厹	叴	坸	姤	媾	嫗	屨	岣	彀	戵	扣	捄	搆	摳	昫	榘	漚	璆
60	甌	疚	痀	癯	窛	窶	篝	糗	胊	蒟	蚯	裘	覯	詬	遘	釦	韝	韭	韮	颶
80	駈	鬮	鷇	鸜	匊	掬	跼	麴	捃	桾	皸	倔	崛	淈	詘					

Row 59		01	02	03	04	05	06	07	08	09	10	11	12	13	14	15	16	17	18	19
00		躳	勌	惓	棬	睠	綣	蜷	佹	几	劂	匱	憒	撅	樻	氿	簣	繢	跪	闠
20	餽	麂	刲	嫢	嬀	巋	暌	楏	樛	潙	睽	糺	虬	虯	跬	邽	闚	頍	馗	囷
40	麕	亟	尅	屐	郄	卺	厪	墐	巹	廑	漌	觔	跟	釿	靳	唫	噤	嶔	笒	黔
60	圾	岌	皀	礏	笈	芨	亙	殑	儆	剞	墍	屺	庋	弃	忮	愭	掎	攲	旂	暣
80	暨	朞	歧	炁	猉	禨	綥	綦	羇	肵	芪	芰	蘄	蘷	蜝					

Row 60		01	02	03	04	05	06	07	08	09	10	11	12	13	14	15	16	17	18	19
00		蟣	覊	覬	跂	隑	頎	鬐	鰭	黖	姞	蛣	挐	挪	梛	穤	糯	偄	煗	赧
20	餪	喃	柟	曩	匂	奶	嬭	迺	鼐	怒	碾	佞	儜	嚀	濘	呶	孥	獶	猱	笯
40	臑	儂	噥	穠	醲	餒	嫋	嬲	淖	碯	裊	鐃	吼	耨	吶	肭	忸	靵	衄	呢
60	怩	柅	祢	禰	膩	昵	暱	爹	慱	担	椴	漙	癉	耑	胆	腶	蜑	妲	怛	闥
80	靼	韃	儋	啗	噉	墰	壜	毯	禫	罈	薝	郯	黮	黵	倘					

Row 61		01	02	03	04	05	06	07	08	09	10	11	12	13	14	15	16	17	18	19
00		儻	党	搪	檔	溏	瑭	璫	瞠	礑	蟷	襠	讜	鏜	鐺	餳	餹	儓	懟	旲
20	汏	碓	鐓	叨	壔	弢	忉	慆	掏	搯	擣	檮	洮	涂	稌	菟	酴	闍	鞀	鞱
40	饕	鼗	櫝	黷	弴	潡	蕫	咄	堗	侗	僮	哃	垌	峒	彤	朣	橦	涷	艟	苳
60	茼	董	蝀	鍊	鮗	抖	斁	肚	脰	蚪	蠹	陡	窀	迍	乭	凳	墱	滕	磴	籐
80	縢	螣	鐙	倮	囉	曪	瘰	砢	蠃	鑼	騾	羸	駱	犖	嬾					

Row 62		01	02	03	04	05	06	07	08	09	10	11	12	13	14	15	16	17	18	19
00		幱	攔	欒	襴	鑾	闌	埒	䔩	婪	惏	鑞	榔	硠	稂	莨	蜋	閬	淶	騋
20	畧	哴	悢	椋	涼	踉	魎	儢	厲	唳	梠	癘	糲	膂	臚	蠡	邌	鑢	攊	櫟
40	櫪	癧	轣	酈	孌	楝	湅	臠	鏈	鰊	鰱	挒	捩	颲	奩	瀲	磏	躐	鬣	另
60	呤	姈	岭	昤	櫺	泠	秢	苓	蛉	軨	鴒	齡	隸	鱧	壚	滷	玈	癆	窂	艪
80	艫	轤	鐪	鑪	顱	髗	鱸	鸕	先	彔	淥	漉	簏	轆	騄					

Row 63		01	02	03	04	05	06	07	08	09	10	11	12	13	14	15	16	17	18	19
00		儱	攏	曨	礱	蘢	隴	龐	攂	礌	礧	籟	纇	罍	耒	蕾	誄	酹	頪	嘹
20	嫽	撩	暸	潦	獠	繚	膋	醪	鐐	飂	飉	龔	僂	嘍	嶁	慺	摟	螻	髏	橊
40	縲	纍	遛	鶹	劉	掄	崙	溧	瘻	窿	泐	凜	廩	澟	倰	蔆	俐	剺	哩	嫠
60	漓	灕	离	莅	蜊	螭	貍	邐	魑	黐	嶙	悋	獜	磷	粦	粼	繗	躪	轔	鄰
80	鏻	驎	痳	岦	劘	媽	螞	蟇	麽	麿	瞙	鏌	墁	嫚	幔					

Row 64		01	02	03	04	05	06	07	08	09	10	11	12	13	14	15	16	17	18	19
00		縵	謾	蹣	鏋	鏝	鬘	帕	秣	惘	汒	漭	莽	蟒	魍	呆	楳	沬	玫	眛
20	苺	莓	酶	霉	脉	貊	貘	儚	甍	甿	虻	幎	糸	俛	湎	糆	緜	麫	篾	蠛
40	洺	侔	姥	媢	嫫	恈	旄	皃	眊	粍	糢	耄	蝥	蟊	鉾	髦	凨	苜	幪	懞
60	曚	溕	濛	瞢	矇	艨	雺	鸏	淼	眇	藐	貓	儛	嘸	廡	膴	騖	嘿	匁	悗
80	懣	抆	捫	炆	璊	亹	娓	媄	媺	弥	弭	敉	瀰	獼	麋					

Row 65		01	02	03	04	05	06	07	08	09	10	11	12	13	14	15	16	17	18	19
00		糜	茉	蘼	虋	忞	忟	暋	湣	緡	罠	苠	閩	鰵	黽	榓	滵	亳	欂	膊
20	鎛	駁	髆	媻	扳	攀	攽	肦	胖	盤	頖	哱	浡	脖	鈸	鵓	仿	厖	幫	徬
40	搒	旊	梆	牓	艕	螃	鎊	髣	魴	坏	坯	扒	琲	蓓	粨	繙	翻	膰	蘩	袢
60	橃	罸	笵	訉	颿	擗	甓	疈	襞	鷿	鼊	忭	抃	籩	辮	胼	賆	駢	骿	鴘
80	瞥	鷩	並	塀	絣	缾	迸	鈵	鋲	鉼	俌	盙	簠	葆	寶					

Row 66		01	02	03	04	05	06	07	08	09	10	11	12	13	14	15	16	17	18	19
00		鴇	黼	墣	幞	扑	濮	箙	菔	蝠	蝮	鵩	丰	夆	篷	綘	菶	鴌	仆	俘
20	婄	抔	拊	掊	桴	榑	涪	玞	祔	筟	罘	罦	胕	芣	苻	蔀	蚨	蜉	袝	裒
40	跗	鈇	頫	鮒	麩	体	坌	帉	枌	棻	棼	氛	湓	濆	犇	畚	砏	笨	肦	膹
60	蕡	轒	黺	鼖	岪	祓	紱	艴	茀	韍	髴	黻	堋	淜	鬅	仳	俾	剕	圮	埤
80	妣	屁	庳	悱	棐	椑	沘	淝	渒	濞	狉	狒	痞	痺	睥					

Row 67		01	02	03	04	05	06	07	08	09	10	11	12	13	14	15	16	17	18	19
00		祕	篦	紕	羆	腓	芘	芾	萆	蓖	蚍	貔	贔	轡	邳	郫	閟	陴	霏	鞴
20	騑	騛	髀	鼙	儐	擯	矉	繽	臏	蘋	豳	邠	鑌	霦	顰	鬂	鬢	冰	凭	凴
40	娉	傞	剚	卸	咋	姒	楂	榭	汜	痧	皶	竢	笥	缷	蜡	覗	駛	魦	鯊	鰤
60	槊	爍	蒴	鑠	剷	姍	攣	橵	潸	澘	狻	繖	訕	鏟	閂	毿	糝	釤	鬖	卅
80	唼	歃	翣	鍤	霅	霎	塽	徜	晌	殤	甞	緗	鎟	顙	鬺					

Row 68		01	02	03	04	05	06	07	08	09	10	11	12	13	14	15	16	17	18	19
00		鰓	槭	濇	瀒	眚	鉎	噬	婿	揟	撕	湑	澨	紓	耡	芧	鉏	晰	矽	腊
20	舄	蜥	鉐	䬊	墡	嫙	尟	尠	仚	愃	歚	熯	筅	綫	譔	譱	鏇	騸	鱓	鱻
40	偰	媟	揲	暬	爇	碟	稧	紲	孅	憸	摻	睒	譫	銛	韱	囁	懾	灄	聶	躡
60	鑷	顳	珵	騂	帨	洒	繐	蛻	佋	俏	卲	嗉	埽	塐	愬	捎	樔	泝	筱	箾
80	繅	翛	膆	艘	蛸	踈	酥	霄	魈	鮹	鰺	溯	遬	飧	飱					

Row 69		01	02	03	04	05	06	07	08	09	10	11	12	13	14	15	16	17	18	19
00		窣	蟀	柗	竦	鬆	忩	曬	瑣	叟	售	廋	晬	殳	泗	溲	濉	睟	睢	瞍
20	祟	籔	脺	膄	膸	讎	豎	陲	颼	饈	俶	倏	儵	婌	橚	驌	鷫	侚	狥	盹
40	眴	紃	肫	駨	鬊	鶉	絨	菘	倅	淬	焠	虱	慴	熠	隰	塍	鬙	偲	兕	厮
60	啻	塒	廝	枲	柹	澌	緦	翤	諟	諰	豉	釃	鍉	題	喰	媳	栻	哂	噺	囟
80	姺	汛	矧	脤	贐	頣	駪	蟋	颸	梣	潯	燖	葚	鐔	鱏					

Row 70	00	01	02	03	04	05	06	07	08	09	10	11	12	13	14	15	16	17	18	19
00		辻	丫	哦	娿	婀	峩	疴	砑	笌	迓	錏	鵞	偓	鄂	咢	喔	噩	腭	萼
20	覨	諤	鶚	齶	桉	犴	贋	鴈	嘎	戛	搵	穵	訐	遏	頞	鵪	唵	婩	嵓	晻
40	腤	葊	菴	諳	頷	醃	黯	卬	坱	泱	盎	鞅	僾	唉	啀	噯	娭	崕	挨	捱
60	欸	漄	獃	皚	睚	瞹	磑	礙	薆	藹	靉	騃	呃	戹	搤	阨	嚶	嫈	罃	鸎
80	埜	爚	禴	篛	籥	鑰	鰯	鶸	龠	徉	漾	瀁	烊	癢	眻					

Row 71	00	01	02	03	04	05	06	07	08	09	10	11	12	13	14	15	16	17	18	19
00		蘘	暘	鑲	颺	驤	圉	敔	淤	飫	繶	傿	匽	嫣	讞	鄢	鶠	鼴	臬	崦
20	广	曮	罨	醃	閹	嶫	鄴	恚	噎	舁	嶧	懌	淢	閾	兗	囦	埏	嬿	悁	掾
40	曣	櫞	涴	臙	莚	蜵	蠕	讌	鷰	曀	冉	塩	懕	厭	檿	檐	灎	灔	釅	黶
60	魘	黶	曅	熀	爗	饜	咏	嬴	嬰	浧	濴	癭	碤	縈	蠑	贏	郢	韺	囈	嫛
80	拽	掜	枘	獩	睨	瞖	緊	翳	苅	蕊	蕋	薉	蚋	蜺	鯢					

Row 72	00	01	02	03	04	05	06	07	08	09	10	11	12	13	14	15	16	17	18	19
00		鷔	𧢌	仵	俁	唔	嗷	噁	圬	媪	嫯	忤	慠	捂	汙	窹	聱	莫	襖	謷
20	迃	迕	遨	鏊	鏖	隩	驁	鼯	媼	慍	昷	氳	熅	蘊	轀	醞	韞	饂	鰮	嗢
40	膃	喁	廱	滃	癰	禺	罋	蓊	雝	顒	哇	囮	婐	梔	洼	猧	窊	萵	譌	刓
60	垸	妧	岏	忨	惋	涴	盌	朊	瀇	迋	媧	偎	崴	嵔	渨	煨	碨	磈	聵	隗
80	偠	喓	坳	墝	嬈	幺	徭	徼	殀	澆	祆	窔	窅	蕘	邀					

Row 73	00	01	02	03	04	05	06	07	08	09	10	11	12	13	14	15	16	17	18	19
00		鷂	溽	蓐	傛	宂	嵱	慵	惷	槦	硧	舂	蛹	踴	亐	亮	俁	偊	吁	堣
20	嵎	庽	杅	疣	盱	竽	耦	耰	謣	踽	隅	麀	夒	齵	燠	惲	沄	篔	紜	霣
40	韵	冤	圜	杬	楥	猨	綄	芫	薗	蚖	謜	鋺	騵	鵷	黿	刖	粵	喟	幃	煒
60	熨	痿	葳	衞	諉	逶	闈	韙	韡	餧	骫	冘	呦	囿	壝	帷	揉	斿	泑	牖
80	瘉	瘐	窬	窳	籲	粈	緌	腴	莠	蕕	蕤	蚰	蚴	蝤	褕					

Row 74	00	01	02	03	04	05	06	07	08	09	10	11	12	13	14	15	16	17	18	19
00		讉	迶	鞣	鮪	黝	鼬	龥	儥	昀	壡	潏	矞	狨	听	嚚	圁	垽	慭	檼
20	溵	狺	珢	癮	訔	鄞	齗	齕	喑	崟	瘖	愔	霠	悒	挹	浥	儗	嵦	劓	嶷
40	欹	漪	猗	礒	螘	饐	咿	圯	尔	彝	栮	洟	珆	訑	詑	迤	隶	弋	熤	鷁
60	仞	堙	夤	婣	扨	氤	洇	禋	籾	芢	裀	泆	軼	紝	衽	銋	飪	廿	媵	呰
80	嬨	孜	孶	柘	泚	牸	眥	眦	粢	耔	薋	茈	茲	莿	虸					

Row 75	00	01	02	03	04	05	06	07	08	09	10	11	12	13	14	15	16	17	18	19
00		觜	訾	貲	赭	鎡	頿	髭	鮓	鷟	鷓	岝	怍	斮	柞	汋	焯	犳	碏	剗
20	戔	驏	涔	潛	灊	卡	囃	眨	磼	襍	傽	奘	妝	嬙	嶂	廧	戕	漳	牂	瘴
40	糚	胖	萇	裝	賬	鄣	鏘	餦	鼜	条	崽	扗	梓	灾	纔	崢	猙	琤	鎗	宁
60	岨	杼	柢	氐	潴	瀦	牴	罝	羝	苴	蛆	衹	褚	觝	詆	豬	陼	樀	磧	糴
80	菂	覿	逖	馰	吮	囀	嫥	屆	巔	戩	揃	旃	栴	槙	湔					

Row 76		01	02	03	04	05	06	07	08	09	10	11	12	13	14	15	16	17	18	19
00		澶	牋	瑱	甎	畋	畠	痓	癜	磚	籛	擅	翦	腆	膞	荃	躔	輇	邅	鄽
20	鋑	錪	靛	靦	顓	飦	餰	鬋	鱣	鸇	岊	晢	窃	佔	墊	玷	笘	簟	苫	蔪
40	蛅	覘	颭	黏	椄	楪	蜨	跕	蹀	鰈	征	叮	婧	婷	怔	掟	桯	梃	棖	灯
60	珵	疔	筳	莛	証	遉	酲	鋥	靚	儕	娣	擠	猘	瑅	睇	禔	稊	緹	踶	蹏
80	躋	鍗	隄	韲	鮧	鯷	佻	傮	刁	厝	嘈	噪	嬥	徂	懆					

Row 77		01	02	03	04	05	06	07	08	09	10	11	12	13	14	15	16	17	18	19
00		找	殂	澡	琱	皁	祧	竈	笊	糙	糶	絩	絛	胙	臊	艚	蔦	蜩	誂	譟
20	鈟	銚	鋽	鯛	鵰	鼂	瘯	拵	伀	悰	柊	椶	樅	琮	瘇	粽	螽	踨	剉	痤
40	莝	髽	丟	侜	儔	尌	幬	拄	硃	籒	肘	腠	蔟	蛀	裯	詋	賙	趎	輈	遒
60	銋	霌	霔	鼄	噂	埻	墫	惷	撙	皴	繜	罇	踆	蹲	鐏	隼	餕	鱒	駿	茁
80	眾	即	喞	騭	櫛	蕺	嶒	矰	罾	坻	墀	抵	榰	泜	痣					

Row 78		01	02	03	04	05	06	07	08	09	10	11	12	13	14	15	16	17	18	19
00		秪	篪	舐	踟	躓	軹	阯	鮨	鷙	禝	侲	儘	瑨	稹	蓁	塦	趁	鉁	鬒
20	垤	絰	蒺	郅	鑕	鴆	咠	戢	濈	潗	癥	瞪	佽	偖	奓	岔	徣	槎	瑳	硨
40	戳	擉	蹔	儧	儹	劗	巑	攢	欑	爨	趲	扎	拶	儳	叅	嶄	巉	慚	憯	攙
60	槧	欃	毚	譖	塹	鑱	饞	驂	黲	倀	傖	滄	刱	悵	惝	戧	搶	椙	氅	瑲
80	窗	窻	蹌	鋹	錆	閶	鬯	鶬	棌	茝	嘖	幘	磔	笧	簀					

Row 79		01	02	03	04	05	06	07	08	09	10	11	12	13	14	15	16	17	18	19
00		蚱	淒	萋	褄	覷	郪	呎	坧	塉	惕	捗	摭	蜴	跖	躑	俴	倩	僢	儃
20	洊	濺	阡	祆	粁	踐	芊	茜	荐	蒨	蕆	蚕	辿	韉	剟	啜	埑	惙	掇	歠
40	銕	錣	餟	饕	幨	忝	沾	檐	櫼	瀸	簷	襜	倢	呫	喋	怗	褺	凊	圊	蜻
60	鶄	嚏	彘	棣	殢	砌	蒂	蔕	蕞	軆	隸	髢	偢	僬	劭	勦	噍	嫶	岧	峭
80	嶕	怊	悄	愀	杪	燋	綃	耖	誚	譙	趠	軺	迢	鈔	鍫					

Row 80		01	02	03	04	05	06	07	08	09	10	11	12	13	14	15	16	17	18	19
00		鍬	鞘	顦	髫	鷦	齠	曯	爥	矚	薥	躅	髑	吋	葱	蓯	鏦	騘	驄	嘬
20	摧	榱	漼	璀	磪	縗	脧	僦	啾	娵	帚	惆	捶	揫	搥	甃	瘳	穐	箒	箠
40	篴	縋	縐	蒭	陬	隹	鞦	騅	魋	鰌	雛	鶖	鶵	麄	麤	妯	舳	豖	蹜	鼀
60	秫	冲	忡	珫	惴	揣	疩	瘁	顇	冣	橇	毳	厠	昃	卮	哆	寘	巵	畤	痓
80	絺	菑	薙	褫	豸	跱	錙	阤	鯔	鳷	鴟	鵄	敕	櫬	藽					

Row 81		01	02	03	04	05	06	07	08	09	10	11	12	13	14	15	16	17	18	19
00		襯	齔	寖	忱	椹	沉	郴	鋟	駸	噲	夬	佗	坨	拕	柁	橢	沱	詑	跎
20	躱	駞	鮀	鴕	鼉	拆	橐	沰	涿	矺	籜	蘀	踔	逴	憚	攤	殫	癱	驒	侻
40	嗿	忐	酖	傝	塌	搨	燙	盪	碭	蘯	埭	娧	孡	抬	迨	駄	駘	撐	牚	噋
60	噸	迵	恫	樋	筩	隤	妒	渝	骰	侈	忒	叵	妑	岥	怕	灞	爸	玻	皤	笆
80	簸	耙	菠	葩	鄱	汴	朳	汃	孛	旆	珮	霈	霸	砰	祊					

Row 82		01	02	03	04	05	06	07	08	09	10	11	12	13	14	15	16	17	18	19
00		鬔	蟚	匾	徧	惼	緶	艑	萹	蝙	褊	諞	砭	窆	怦	抨	泙	苹	蓱	鮃
20	敝	狴	獘	癈	傈	庖	哺	㬥	炮	炰	舖	誧	鉋	鞄	餔	鯆	僄	勡	嘌	嫖
40	摽	殍	熛	縹	裱	鏢	鑣	髟	鰾	禀	瘋	葑	詖	辟	鞁	髲	愊	佖	咇	滭
60	篳	罼	蓽	鷩	蹕	鞸	韠	駜	鵯	偪	呀	嚇	岈	[illegible]	煆	瘕	罅	鍜	狢	瘧
80	矐	确	郝	鸖	僩	嫺	嫻	捍	暵	閈	駻	鷴	鼾	瞎	荅					

Row 83		01	02	03	04	05	06	07	08	09	10	11	12	13	14	15	16	17	18	19
00		菡	諴	轞	闞	匌	嗑	柙	榼	溘	盍	郃	夯	恆	炕	缿	頏	哈	嶰	廨
20	欬	獬	瑎	痎	薤	醢	頦	鮭	翮	覈	悻	薌	歔	巘	[illegible]	攇	嶮	獫	玁	弈
40	洫	焱	闃	儇	嬛	昡	琄	痃	県	繯	翾	蜆	誢	鋗	駽	絜	趐	匧	叶	埉
60	恊	悏	愜	篋	夐	娙	詗	迥	陘	傒	嘒	惠	徯	槥	盻	謑	譿	儫	冱	嘷
80	嫭	嫮	怙	沍	滈	滬	犒	猢	皜	皞	箎	聕	醐	餬	鬍					

Row 84		01	02	03	04	05	06	07	08	09	10	11	12	13	14	15	16	17	18	19
00		圂	惛	溷	焜	閽	囫	哄	澒	篊	鉷	閧	俰	嘩	婲	擭	畫	驊	龢	矍
20	玃	礭	鑊	寰	懽	擐	瓛	皖	睆	絙	豢	轘	鍰	鐶	鬟	蛞	喤	媓	恍	瑝
40	肓	貺	鍠	佪	栃	洄	滙	盔	詼	迴	頮	鱠	嚄	澋	鈜	黌	傚	囂	崤	殽
60	熇	皛	虓	餚	吽	煦	垕	堠	涸	猴	篌	詡	譃	酗	餱	曛	爋	獯	纁	葷
80	鑂	欻	烜	諠	諼	燬	芔	虫	虺	撝	翬	咻	擕	隳	髹					

Row 85		01	02	03	04	05	06	07	08	09	10	11	12	13	14	15	16	17	18	19
00		鵂	卹	恟	胷	很	忻	掀	焮	訢	釁	仡	汔	疙	迄	齕	廞	噏	歙	潝
20	翖	咥	唏	嘻	悕	戲	暿	欷	燹	爔	豨	餼	犵	纈	襭	頡	黠			
40																				
60																				
80																				

N

Hangul Reading Table

The first table in this appendix is a jamo-based index into the second table that provides page numbers for quicker access. The second table provides a complete reading index for all 2,350 hangul that are enumerated in the KS X 1001:1992 character set standard. The ISO/TR 11941:1996 transliteration method, specifically Method 2, is used along with KS X 1001:1992 Row-Cell codes.

Reading		Page
ㄱ	G	863
ㄲ	GG	863
ㄴ	N	864
ㄷ	D	865
ㄸ	DD	865
ㄹ	R	866
ㅁ	M	867
ㅂ	B	867
ㅃ	BB	868
ㅅ	S	868
ㅆ	SS	869
아 (ㅏ)	A	870
애 (ㅐ)	AE	870
야 (ㅑ)	YA	870
얘 (ㅒ)	YAE	870
어 (ㅓ)	EO	870
에 (ㅔ)	E	870
여 (ㅕ)	YEO	870
예 (ㅖ)	YE	870
오 (ㅗ)	O	870
와 (ㅘ)	WA	870
왜 (ㅙ)	WAE	870
외 (ㅚ)	OE	870
요 (ㅛ)	YO	870
우 (ㅜ)	U	870
워 (ㅝ)	WEO	870
웨 (ㅞ)	WE	870
위 (ㅟ)	WI	871
유 (ㅠ)	YU	871
으 (ㅡ)	EU	871
의 (ㅢ)	YI	871
이 (ㅣ)	I	871
ㅈ	J	871
ㅉ	JJ	872
ㅊ	C	872
ㅋ	K	873
ㅌ	T	873
ㅍ	P	874
ㅎ	H	874

	Code	Reading
가	16-01	ga
각	16-02	gag
간	16-03	gan
갇	16-04	gad
갈	16-05	gal
갉	16-06	galg
갊	16-07	galm
감	16-08	gam
갑	16-09	gab
값	16-10	gabs
갓	16-11	gas
갔	16-12	gass
강	16-13	gang
갖	16-14	gaj
갗	16-15	gac
같	16-16	gat
갚	16-17	gap
갛	16-18	gah
개	16-19	gae
객	16-20	gaeg
갠	16-21	gaen
갤	16-22	gael
갬	16-23	gaem
갭	16-24	gaeb
갯	16-25	gaes
갰	16-26	gaess
갱	16-27	gaeng
갸	16-28	gya
갹	16-29	gyag
갼	16-30	gyan
걀	16-31	gyal
걋	16-32	gyas
걍	16-33	gyang
걔	16-34	gyae
걘	16-35	gyaen
걜	16-36	gyael
거	16-37	geo
걱	16-38	geog
건	16-39	geon
걷	16-40	geod
걸	16-41	geol
걺	16-42	geolm
검	16-43	geom
겁	16-44	geob
것	16-45	geos
겄	16-46	geoss
겅	16-47	geong
겆	16-48	geoj
겉	16-49	geot
겊	16-50	geop
겋	16-51	geoh
게	16-52	ge
겐	16-53	gen
겔	16-54	gel
겜	16-55	gem
겝	16-56	geb
겟	16-57	ges
겠	16-58	gess
겡	16-59	geng
겨	16-60	gyeo
격	16-61	gyeog
겪	16-62	gyeogg
견	16-63	gyeon
겯	16-64	gyeod
결	16-65	gyeol
겸	16-66	gyeom
겹	16-67	gyeob
겻	16-68	gyeos
겼	16-69	gyeoss
경	16-70	gyeong
곁	16-71	gyeot
계	16-72	gye
곈	16-73	gyen
곌	16-74	gyel
곕	16-75	gyeb
곗	16-76	gyes
고	16-77	go
곡	16-78	gog
곤	16-79	gon
곧	16-80	god
골	16-81	gol
곪	16-82	golm
곬	16-83	gols
곯	16-84	golh
곰	16-85	gom
곱	16-86	gob
곳	16-87	gos
공	16-88	gong
곶	16-89	goj
과	16-90	gwa
곽	16-91	gwag
관	16-92	gwan
괄	16-93	gwal
괆	16-94	gwalm
괌	17-01	gwam
괍	17-02	gwab
괏	17-03	gwas
광	17-04	gwang
괘	17-05	gwae
괜	17-06	gwaen
괠	17-07	gwael
괩	17-08	gwaeb
괬	17-09	gwaess
괭	17-10	gwaeng
괴	17-11	goe
괵	17-12	goeg
괸	17-13	goen
괼	17-14	goel
굄	17-15	goem
굅	17-16	goeb
굇	17-17	goes
굉	17-18	goeng
교	17-19	gyo
굔	17-20	gyon
굘	17-21	gyol
굡	17-22	gyob
굣	17-23	gyos
구	17-24	gu
국	17-25	gug
군	17-26	gun
굳	17-27	gud
굴	17-28	gul
굵	17-29	gulg
굶	17-30	gulm
굻	17-31	gulh
굼	17-32	gum
굽	17-33	gub
굿	17-34	gus
궁	17-35	gung
궂	17-36	guj
궈	17-37	gweo
궉	17-38	gweog
권	17-39	gweon
궐	17-40	gweol
궜	17-41	gweoss
궝	17-42	gweong
궤	17-43	gwe
궷	17-44	gwes
귀	17-45	gwi
귁	17-46	gwig
귄	17-47	gwin
귈	17-48	gwil
귐	17-49	gwim
귑	17-50	gwib
귓	17-51	gwis
규	17-52	gyu
균	17-53	gyun
귤	17-54	gyul
그	17-55	geu
극	17-56	geug
근	17-57	geun
귿	17-58	geud
글	17-59	geul
긁	17-60	geulg
금	17-61	geum
급	17-62	geub
긋	17-63	geus
긍	17-64	geung
긔	17-65	gyi
기	17-66	gi
긱	17-67	gig
긴	17-68	gin
긷	17-69	gid
길	17-70	gil
긺	17-71	gilm
김	17-72	gim
깁	17-73	gib
깃	17-74	gis
깅	17-75	ging
깆	17-76	gij
깊	17-77	gip
까	17-78	gga
깍	17-79	ggag
깎	17-80	ggagg
깐	17-81	ggan
깔	17-82	ggal
깖	17-83	ggalm
깜	17-84	ggam
깝	17-85	ggab
깟	17-86	ggas
깠	17-87	ggass
깡	17-88	ggang
깥	17-89	ggat
깨	17-90	ggae
깩	17-91	ggaeg
깬	17-92	ggaen
깰	17-93	ggael
깸	17-94	ggaem

	Code	Reading
깹	18-01	ggaeb
깻	18-02	ggaes
깼	18-03	ggaess
깽	18-04	ggaeng
꺄	18-05	ggya
꺅	18-06	ggyag
꺌	18-07	ggyal
꺼	18-08	ggeo
꺽	18-09	ggeog
꺾	18-10	ggeogg
껀	18-11	ggeon
껄	18-12	ggeol
껌	18-13	ggeom
껍	18-14	ggeob
껏	18-15	ggeos
껐	18-16	ggeoss
껑	18-17	ggeong
께	18-18	gge
껙	18-19	ggeg
껜	18-20	ggen
껨	18-21	ggem
껫	18-22	gges
껭	18-23	ggeng
껴	18-24	ggyeo
껸	18-25	ggyeon
껼	18-26	ggyeol
꼇	18-27	ggyeos
꼈	18-28	ggyeoss
꼍	18-29	ggyeot
꼐	18-30	ggye
꼬	18-31	ggo
꼭	18-32	ggog
꼰	18-33	ggon
꼲	18-34	ggonh
꼴	18-35	ggol
꼼	18-36	ggom
꼽	18-37	ggob
꼿	18-38	ggos
꽁	18-39	ggong
꽂	18-40	ggoj
꽃	18-41	ggoc
꽈	18-42	ggwa
꽉	18-43	ggwag
꽐	18-44	ggwal
꽜	18-45	ggwass
꽝	18-46	ggwang
꽤	18-47	ggwae
꽥	18-48	ggwaeg
꽹	18-49	ggwaeng
꾀	18-50	ggoe
꾄	18-51	ggoen
꾈	18-52	ggoel
꾐	18-53	ggoem
꾑	18-54	ggoeb
꾕	18-55	ggoeng
꾜	18-56	ggyo
꾸	18-57	ggu
꾹	18-58	ggug
꾼	18-59	ggun
꿀	18-60	ggul
꿇	18-61	ggulh
꿈	18-62	ggum
꿉	18-63	ggub
꿋	18-64	ggus
꿍	18-65	ggung
꿎	18-66	gguj
꿔	18-67	ggweo
꿜	18-68	ggweol
꿨	18-69	ggweoss
꿩	18-70	ggweong
꿰	18-71	ggwe
꿱	18-72	ggweg
꿴	18-73	ggwen
꿸	18-74	ggwel
뀀	18-75	ggwem
뀁	18-76	ggweb
뀄	18-77	ggwess
뀌	18-78	ggwi
뀐	18-79	ggwin
뀔	18-80	ggwil
뀜	18-81	ggwim
뀝	18-82	ggwib
뀨	18-83	ggyu
끄	18-84	ggeu
끅	18-85	ggeug
끈	18-86	ggeun
끊	18-87	ggeunh
끌	18-88	ggeul
끎	18-89	ggeulm
끓	18-90	ggeulh
끔	18-91	ggeum
끕	18-92	ggeub
끗	18-93	ggeus
끙	18-94	ggeung
끝	19-01	ggeut
끼	19-02	ggi
끽	19-03	ggig
낀	19-04	ggin
낄	19-05	ggil
낌	19-06	ggim
낍	19-07	ggib
낏	19-08	ggis
낑	19-09	gging
나	19-10	na
낙	19-11	nag
낚	19-12	nagg
난	19-13	nan
낟	19-14	nad
날	19-15	nal
낡	19-16	nalg
낢	19-17	nalm
남	19-18	nam
납	19-19	nab
낫	19-20	nas
났	19-21	nass
낭	19-22	nang
낮	19-23	naj
낯	19-24	nac
낱	19-25	nat
낳	19-26	nah
내	19-27	nae
낵	19-28	naeg
낸	19-29	naen
낼	19-30	nael
냄	19-31	naem
냅	19-32	naeb
냇	19-33	naes
냈	19-34	naess
냉	19-35	naeng
냐	19-36	nya
냑	19-37	nyag
냔	19-38	nyan
냘	19-39	nyal
냠	19-40	nyam
냥	19-41	nyang
너	19-42	neo
넉	19-43	neog
넋	19-44	neogs
넌	19-45	neon
널	19-46	neol
넒	19-47	neolm
넓	19-48	neolb
넘	19-49	neom
넙	19-50	neob
넛	19-51	neos
넜	19-52	neoss
넝	19-53	neong
넣	19-54	neoh
네	19-55	ne
넥	19-56	neg
넨	19-57	nen
넬	19-58	nel
넴	19-59	nem
넵	19-60	neb
넷	19-61	nes
넸	19-62	ness
넹	19-63	neng
녀	19-64	nyeo
녁	19-65	nyeog
년	19-66	nyeon
녈	19-67	nyeol
념	19-68	nyeom
녑	19-69	nyeob
녔	19-70	nyeoss
녕	19-71	nyeong
녘	19-72	nyeok
녜	19-73	nye
녠	19-74	nyen
노	19-75	no
녹	19-76	nog
논	19-77	non
놀	19-78	nol
놂	19-79	nolm
놈	19-80	nom
놉	19-81	nob
놋	19-82	nos
농	19-83	nong
높	19-84	nop
놓	19-85	noh
놔	19-86	nwa
놘	19-87	nwan
놜	19-88	nwal
놨	19-89	nwass
뇌	19-90	noe
뇐	19-91	noen
뇔	19-92	noel
뇜	19-93	noem
뇝	19-94	noeb

	Code	Reading
뇟	20-01	noes
뇨	20-02	nyo
뇩	20-03	nyog
뇬	20-04	nyon
뇰	20-05	nyol
뇹	20-06	nyob
뇻	20-07	nyos
뇽	20-08	nyong
누	20-09	nu
눅	20-10	nug
눈	20-11	nun
눋	20-12	nud
눌	20-13	nul
눔	20-14	num
눕	20-15	nub
눗	20-16	nus
눙	20-17	nung
눠	20-18	nweo
눴	20-19	nweoss
눼	20-20	nwe
뉘	20-21	nwi
뉜	20-22	nwin
뉠	20-23	nwil
뉨	20-24	nwim
뉩	20-25	nwib
뉴	20-26	nyu
뉵	20-27	nyug
뉼	20-28	nyul
늄	20-29	nyum
늅	20-30	nyub
늉	20-31	nyung
느	20-32	neu
늑	20-33	neug
는	20-34	neun
늘	20-35	neul
늙	20-36	neulg
늚	20-37	neulm
늠	20-38	neum
늡	20-39	neub
늣	20-40	neus
능	20-41	neung
늦	20-42	neuj
늪	20-43	neup
늬	20-44	nyi
늰	20-45	nyin
늴	20-46	nyil
니	20-47	ni
닉	20-48	nig
닌	20-49	nin
닐	20-50	nil
닒	20-51	nilm
님	20-52	nim
닙	20-53	nib
닛	20-54	nis
닝	20-55	ning
닢	20-56	nip
다	20-57	da
닥	20-58	dag
닦	20-59	dagg
단	20-60	dan
닫	20-61	dad
달	20-62	dal
닭	20-63	dalg
닮	20-64	dalm
닯	20-65	dalb
닳	20-66	dalh
담	20-67	dam
답	20-68	dab
닷	20-69	das
닸	20-70	dass
당	20-71	dang
닺	20-72	daj
닻	20-73	dac
닿	20-74	dah
대	20-75	dae
댁	20-76	daeg
댄	20-77	daen
댈	20-78	dael
댐	20-79	daem
댑	20-80	daeb
댓	20-81	daes
댔	20-82	daess
댕	20-83	daeng
댜	20-84	dya
더	20-85	deo
덕	20-86	deog
덖	20-87	deogg
던	20-88	deon
덛	20-89	deod
덜	20-90	deol
덞	20-91	deolm
덟	20-92	deolb
덤	20-93	deom
덥	20-94	deob
덧	21-01	deos
덩	21-02	deong
덫	21-03	deoc
덮	21-04	deop
데	21-05	de
덱	21-06	deg
덴	21-07	den
델	21-08	del
뎀	21-09	dem
뎁	21-10	deb
뎃	21-11	des
뎄	21-12	dess
뎅	21-13	deng
뎌	21-14	dyeo
뎐	21-15	dyeon
뎔	21-16	dyeol
뎠	21-17	dyeoss
뎡	21-18	dyeong
뎨	21-19	dye
뎬	21-20	dyen
도	21-21	do
독	21-22	dog
돈	21-23	don
돋	21-24	dod
돌	21-25	dol
돎	21-26	dolm
돐	21-27	dols
돔	21-28	dom
돕	21-29	dob
돗	21-30	dos
동	21-31	dong
돛	21-32	doc
돝	21-33	dot
돠	21-34	dwa
돤	21-35	dwan
돨	21-36	dwal
돼	21-37	dwae
됐	21-38	dwaess
되	21-39	doe
된	21-40	doen
될	21-41	doel
됨	21-42	doem
됩	21-43	doeb
됫	21-44	does
됴	21-45	dyo
두	21-46	du
둑	21-47	dug
둔	21-48	dun
둘	21-49	dul
둠	21-50	dum
둡	21-51	dub
둣	21-52	dus
둥	21-53	dung
둬	21-54	dweo
뒀	21-55	dweoss
뒈	21-56	dwe
뒝	21-57	dweng
뒤	21-58	dwi
뒨	21-59	dwin
뒬	21-60	dwil
뒵	21-61	dwib
뒷	21-62	dwis
뒹	21-63	dwing
듀	21-64	dyu
듄	21-65	dyun
듈	21-66	dyul
듐	21-67	dyum
듕	21-68	dyung
드	21-69	deu
득	21-70	deug
든	21-71	deun
듣	21-72	deud
들	21-73	deul
듦	21-74	deulm
듬	21-75	deum
듭	21-76	deub
듯	21-77	deus
등	21-78	deung
듸	21-79	dyi
디	21-80	di
딕	21-81	dig
딘	21-82	din
딛	21-83	did
딜	21-84	dil
딤	21-85	dim
딥	21-86	dib
딧	21-87	dis
딨	21-88	diss
딩	21-89	ding
딪	21-90	dij
따	21-91	dda
딱	21-92	ddag
딴	21-93	ddan
딸	21-94	ddal

	Code	Reading
땀	22-01	ddam
땁	22-02	ddab
땃	22-03	ddas
땄	22-04	ddass
땅	22-05	ddang
땋	22-06	ddah
때	22-07	ddae
땍	22-08	ddaeg
땐	22-09	ddaen
땔	22-10	ddael
땜	22-11	ddaem
땝	22-12	ddaeb
땟	22-13	ddaes
땠	22-14	ddaess
땡	22-15	ddaeng
떠	22-16	ddeo
떡	22-17	ddeog
떤	22-18	ddeon
떨	22-19	ddeol
떪	22-20	ddeolm
떫	22-21	ddeolb
떰	22-22	ddeom
떱	22-23	ddeob
떳	22-24	ddeos
떴	22-25	ddeoss
떵	22-26	ddeong
떻	22-27	ddeoh
떼	22-28	dde
떽	22-29	ddeg
뗀	22-30	dden
뗄	22-31	ddel
뗌	22-32	ddem
뗍	22-33	ddeb
뗏	22-34	ddes
뗐	22-35	ddess
뗑	22-36	ddeng
뗘	22-37	ddyeo
뗬	22-38	ddyeoss
또	22-39	ddo
똑	22-40	ddog
똔	22-41	ddon
똘	22-42	ddol
똥	22-43	ddong
똬	22-44	ddwa
똴	22-45	ddwal
뙈	22-46	ddwae
뙤	22-47	ddoe
뙨	22-48	ddoen
뚜	22-49	ddu
뚝	22-50	ddug
뚠	22-51	ddun
뚤	22-52	ddul
뚫	22-53	ddulh
뚬	22-54	ddum
뚱	22-55	ddung
뛔	22-56	ddwe
뛰	22-57	ddwi
뛴	22-58	ddwin
뛸	22-59	ddwil
뜀	22-60	ddwim
뜁	22-61	ddwib
뜅	22-62	ddwing
뜨	22-63	ddeu
뜩	22-64	ddeug
뜬	22-65	ddeun
뜯	22-66	ddeud
뜰	22-67	ddeul
뜸	22-68	ddeum
뜹	22-69	ddeub
뜻	22-70	ddeus
띄	22-71	ddyi
띈	22-72	ddyin
띌	22-73	ddyil
띔	22-74	ddyim
띕	22-75	ddyib
띠	22-76	ddi
띤	22-77	ddin
띨	22-78	ddil
띰	22-79	ddim
띱	22-80	ddib
띳	22-81	ddis
띵	22-82	dding
라	22-83	ra
락	22-84	rag
란	22-85	ran
랄	22-86	ral
람	22-87	ram
랍	22-88	rab
랏	22-89	ras
랐	22-90	rass
랑	22-91	rang
랒	22-92	raj
랖	22-93	rap
랗	22-94	rah
래	23-01	rae
랙	23-02	raeg
랜	23-03	raen
랠	23-04	rael
램	23-05	raem
랩	23-06	raeb
랫	23-07	raes
랬	23-08	raess
랭	23-09	raeng
랴	23-10	rya
략	23-11	ryag
랸	23-12	ryan
럇	23-13	ryas
량	23-14	ryang
러	23-15	reo
럭	23-16	reog
런	23-17	reon
럴	23-18	reol
럼	23-19	reom
럽	23-20	reob
럿	23-21	reos
렀	23-22	reoss
렁	23-23	reong
렇	23-24	reoh
레	23-25	re
렉	23-26	reg
렌	23-27	ren
렐	23-28	rel
렘	23-29	rem
렙	23-30	reb
렛	23-31	res
렝	23-32	reng
려	23-33	ryeo
력	23-34	ryeog
련	23-35	ryeon
렬	23-36	ryeol
렴	23-37	ryeom
렵	23-38	ryeob
렷	23-39	ryeos
렸	23-40	ryeoss
령	23-41	ryeong
례	23-42	rye
롄	23-43	ryen
롑	23-44	ryeb
롓	23-45	ryes
로	23-46	ro
록	23-47	rog
론	23-48	ron
롤	23-49	rol
롬	23-50	rom
롭	23-51	rob
롯	23-52	ros
롱	23-53	rong
롸	23-54	rwa
롼	23-55	rwan
뢍	23-56	rwang
뢨	23-57	rwaess
뢰	23-58	roe
뢴	23-59	roen
뢸	23-60	roel
룀	23-61	roem
룁	23-62	roeb
룃	23-63	roes
룅	23-64	roeng
료	23-65	ryo
룐	23-66	ryon
룔	23-67	ryol
룝	23-68	ryob
룟	23-69	ryos
룡	23-70	ryong
루	23-71	ru
룩	23-72	rug
룬	23-73	run
룰	23-74	rul
룸	23-75	rum
룹	23-76	rub
룻	23-77	rus
룽	23-78	rung
뤄	23-79	rweo
뤘	23-80	rweoss
뤠	23-81	rwe
뤼	23-82	rwi
뤽	23-83	rwig
륀	23-84	rwin
륄	23-85	rwil
륌	23-86	rwim
륏	23-87	rwis
륑	23-88	rwing
류	23-89	ryu
륙	23-90	ryug
륜	23-91	ryun
률	23-92	ryul
륨	23-93	ryum
륩	23-94	ryub

	Code	Reading
륫	24-01	ryus
륭	24-02	ryung
르	24-03	reu
륵	24-04	reug
른	24-05	reun
를	24-06	reul
름	24-07	reum
릅	24-08	reub
릇	24-09	reus
릉	24-10	reung
릊	24-11	reuj
릍	24-12	reut
릎	24-13	reup
리	24-14	ri
릭	24-15	rig
린	24-16	rin
릴	24-17	ril
림	24-18	rim
립	24-19	rib
릿	24-20	ris
링	24-21	ring
마	24-22	ma
막	24-23	mag
만	24-24	man
많	24-25	manh
맏	24-26	mad
말	24-27	mal
맑	24-28	malg
맒	24-29	malm
맘	24-30	mam
맙	24-31	mab
맛	24-32	mas
망	24-33	mang
맞	24-34	maj
맡	24-35	mat
맣	24-36	mah
매	24-37	mae
맥	24-38	maeg
맨	24-39	maen
맬	24-40	mael
맴	24-41	maem
맵	24-42	maeb
맷	24-43	maes
맸	24-44	maess
맹	24-45	maeng
맺	24-46	maej
먀	24-47	mya
먁	24-48	myag
먈	24-49	myal
먕	24-50	myang
머	24-51	meo
먹	24-52	meog
먼	24-53	meon
멀	24-54	meol
멂	24-55	meolm
멈	24-56	meom
멉	24-57	meob
멋	24-58	meos
멍	24-59	meong
멎	24-60	meoj
멓	24-61	meoh
메	24-62	me
멕	24-63	meg
멘	24-64	men
멜	24-65	mel
멤	24-66	mem
멥	24-67	meb
멧	24-68	mes
멨	24-69	mess
멩	24-70	meng
며	24-71	myeo
멱	24-72	myeog
면	24-73	myeon
멸	24-74	myeol
몃	24-75	myeos
몄	24-76	myeoss
명	24-77	myeong
몇	24-78	myeoc
몌	24-79	mye
모	24-80	mo
목	24-81	mog
몫	24-82	mogs
몬	24-83	mon
몰	24-84	mol
몲	24-85	molm
몸	24-86	mom
몹	24-87	mob
못	24-88	mos
몽	24-89	mong
뫄	24-90	mwa
뫈	24-91	mwan
뫘	24-92	mwass
뫙	24-93	mwang
뫼	24-94	moe
묀	25-01	moen
묄	25-02	moel
묍	25-03	moeb
묏	25-04	moes
묑	25-05	moeng
묘	25-06	myo
묜	25-07	myon
묠	25-08	myol
묩	25-09	myob
묫	25-10	myos
무	25-11	mu
묵	25-12	mug
묶	25-13	mugg
문	25-14	mun
묻	25-15	mud
물	25-16	mul
묽	25-17	mulg
묾	25-18	mulm
뭄	25-19	mum
뭅	25-20	mub
뭇	25-21	mus
뭉	25-22	mung
뭍	25-23	mut
뭏	25-24	muh
뭐	25-25	mweo
뭔	25-26	mweon
뭘	25-27	mweol
뭡	25-28	mweob
뭣	25-29	mweos
뭬	25-30	mwe
뮈	25-31	mwi
뮌	25-32	mwin
뮐	25-33	mwil
뮤	25-34	myu
뮨	25-35	myun
뮬	25-36	myul
뮴	25-37	myum
뮷	25-38	myus
므	25-39	meu
믄	25-40	meun
믈	25-41	meul
믐	25-42	meum
믓	25-43	meus
미	25-44	mi
믹	25-45	mig
민	25-46	min
믿	25-47	mid
밀	25-48	mil
밂	25-49	milm
밈	25-50	mim
밉	25-51	mib
밋	25-52	mis
밌	25-53	miss
밍	25-54	ming
및	25-55	mic
밑	25-56	mit
바	25-57	ba
박	25-58	bag
밖	25-59	bagg
밗	25-60	bags
반	25-61	ban
받	25-62	bad
발	25-63	bal
밝	25-64	balg
밞	25-65	balm
밟	25-66	balb
밤	25-67	bam
밥	25-68	bab
밧	25-69	bas
방	25-70	bang
밭	25-71	bat
배	25-72	bae
백	25-73	baeg
밴	25-74	baen
밸	25-75	bael
뱀	25-76	baem
뱁	25-77	baeb
뱃	25-78	baes
뱄	25-79	baess
뱅	25-80	baeng
뱉	25-81	baet
뱌	25-82	bya
뱍	25-83	byag
뱐	25-84	byan
뱝	25-85	byab
버	25-86	beo
벅	25-87	beog
번	25-88	beon
벋	25-89	beod
벌	25-90	beol
벎	25-91	beolm
범	25-92	beom
법	25-93	beob
벗	25-94	beos

	Code	Reading
벙	26-01	beong
벚	26-02	beoj
베	26-03	be
벡	26-04	beg
벤	26-05	ben
벧	26-06	bed
벨	26-07	bel
벰	26-08	bem
벱	26-09	beb
벳	26-10	bes
벴	26-11	bess
벵	26-12	beng
벼	26-13	byeo
벽	26-14	byeog
변	26-15	byeon
별	26-16	byeol
볍	26-17	byeob
볏	26-18	byeos
볐	26-19	byeoss
병	26-20	byeong
볕	26-21	byeot
볘	26-22	bye
볜	26-23	byen
보	26-24	bo
복	26-25	bog
볶	26-26	bogg
본	26-27	bon
볼	26-28	bol
봄	26-29	bom
봅	26-30	bob
봇	26-31	bos
봉	26-32	bong
봐	26-33	bwa
봔	26-34	bwan
봤	26-35	bwass
봬	26-36	bwae
뵀	26-37	bwaess
뵈	26-38	boe
뵉	26-39	boeg
뵌	26-40	boen
뵐	26-41	boel
뵘	26-42	boem
뵙	26-43	boeb
뵤	26-44	byo
뵨	26-45	byon
부	26-46	bu
북	26-47	bug
분	26-48	bun
붇	26-49	bud
불	26-50	bul
붉	26-51	bulg
붊	26-52	bulm
붐	26-53	bum
붑	26-54	bub
붓	26-55	bus
붕	26-56	bung
붙	26-57	but
붚	26-58	bup
붜	26-59	bweo
붤	26-60	bweol
붰	26-61	bweoss
붸	26-62	bwe
뷔	26-63	bwi
뷕	26-64	bwig
뷘	26-65	bwin
뷜	26-66	bwil
뷩	26-67	bwing
뷰	26-68	byu
뷴	26-69	byun
뷸	26-70	byul
븀	26-71	byum
븃	26-72	byus
븅	26-73	byung
브	26-74	beu
븍	26-75	beug
븐	26-76	beun
블	26-77	beul
븜	26-78	beum
븝	26-79	beub
븟	26-80	beus
비	26-81	bi
빅	26-82	big
빈	26-83	bin
빌	26-84	bil
빎	26-85	bilm
빔	26-86	bim
빕	26-87	bib
빗	26-88	bis
빙	26-89	bing
빚	26-90	bij
빛	26-91	bic
빠	26-92	bba
빡	26-93	bbag
빤	26-94	bban
빨	27-01	bbal
빪	27-02	bbalm
빰	27-03	bbam
빱	27-04	bbab
빳	27-05	bbas
빴	27-06	bbass
빵	27-07	bbang
빻	27-08	bbah
빼	27-09	bbae
빽	27-10	bbaeg
뺀	27-11	bbaen
뺄	27-12	bbael
뺌	27-13	bbaem
뺍	27-14	bbaeb
뺏	27-15	bbaes
뺐	27-16	bbaess
뺑	27-17	bbaeng
뺘	27-18	bbya
뺙	27-19	bbyag
뺨	27-20	bbyam
뻐	27-21	bbeo
뻑	27-22	bbeog
뻔	27-23	bbeon
뻗	27-24	bbeod
뻘	27-25	bbeol
뻠	27-26	bbeom
뻣	27-27	bbeos
뻤	27-28	bbeoss
뻥	27-29	bbeong
뻬	27-30	bbe
뼁	27-31	bbeng
뼈	27-32	bbyeo
뼉	27-33	bbyeog
뼘	27-34	bbyeom
뼙	27-35	bbyeob
뼛	27-36	bbyeos
뼜	27-37	bbyeoss
뼝	27-38	bbyeong
뽀	27-39	bbo
뽁	27-40	bbog
뽄	27-41	bbon
뽈	27-42	bbol
뽐	27-43	bbom
뽑	27-44	bbob
뽕	27-45	bbong
뾔	27-46	bboe
뾰	27-47	bbyo
뿅	27-48	bbyong
뿌	27-49	bbu
뿍	27-50	bbug
뿐	27-51	bbun
뿔	27-52	bbul
뿜	27-53	bbum
뿟	27-54	bbus
뿡	27-55	bbung
쀼	27-56	bbyu
쁑	27-57	bbyung
쁘	27-58	bbeu
쁜	27-59	bbeun
쁠	27-60	bbeul
쁨	27-61	bbeum
쁩	27-62	bbeub
삐	27-63	bbi
삑	27-64	bbig
삔	27-65	bbin
삘	27-66	bbil
삠	27-67	bbim
삡	27-68	bbib
삣	27-69	bbis
삥	27-70	bbing
사	27-71	sa
삭	27-72	sag
삯	27-73	sags
산	27-74	san
삳	27-75	sad
살	27-76	sal
삵	27-77	salg
삶	27-78	salm
삼	27-79	sam
삽	27-80	sab
삿	27-81	sas
샀	27-82	sass
상	27-83	sang
샅	27-84	sat
새	27-85	sae
색	27-86	saeg
샌	27-87	saen
샐	27-88	sael
샘	27-89	saem
샙	27-90	saeb
샛	27-91	saes
샜	27-92	saess
생	27-93	saeng
샤	27-94	sya

	Code	Reading
샥	28-01	syag
샨	28-02	syan
샬	28-03	syal
샴	28-04	syam
샵	28-05	syab
샷	28-06	syas
샹	28-07	syang
섀	28-08	syae
섄	28-09	syaen
섈	28-10	syael
섐	28-11	syaem
섕	28-12	syaeng
서	28-13	seo
석	28-14	seog
섞	28-15	seogg
섟	28-16	seogs
선	28-17	seon
섣	28-18	seod
설	28-19	seol
섦	28-20	seolm
섧	28-21	seolb
섬	28-22	seom
섭	28-23	seob
섯	28-24	seos
섰	28-25	seoss
성	28-26	seong
섶	28-27	seop
세	28-28	se
섹	28-29	seg
센	28-30	sen
셀	28-31	sel
셈	28-32	sem
셉	28-33	seb
셋	28-34	ses
셌	28-35	sess
셍	28-36	seng
셔	28-37	syeo
셕	28-38	syeog
션	28-39	syeon
셜	28-40	syeol
셤	28-41	syeom
셥	28-42	syeob
셧	28-43	syeos
셨	28-44	syeoss
셩	28-45	syeong
셰	28-46	sye
셴	28-47	syen
셸	28-48	syel
솅	28-49	syeng
소	28-50	so
속	28-51	sog
솎	28-52	sogg
손	28-53	son
솔	28-54	sol
솖	28-55	solm
솜	28-56	som
솝	28-57	sob
솟	28-58	sos
송	28-59	song
솥	28-60	sot
솨	28-61	swa
솩	28-62	swag
솬	28-63	swan
솰	28-64	swal
솽	28-65	swang
쇄	28-66	swae
쇈	28-67	swaen
쇌	28-68	swael
쇔	28-69	swaem
쇗	28-70	swaes
쇘	28-71	swaess
쇠	28-72	soe
쇤	28-73	soen
쇨	28-74	soel
쇰	28-75	soem
쇱	28-76	soeb
쇳	28-77	soes
쇼	28-78	syo
쇽	28-79	syog
숀	28-80	syon
숄	28-81	syol
숌	28-82	syom
숍	28-83	syob
숏	28-84	syos
숑	28-85	syong
수	28-86	su
숙	28-87	sug
순	28-88	sun
숟	28-89	sud
술	28-90	sul
숨	28-91	sum
숩	28-92	sub
숫	28-93	sus
숭	28-94	sung
숯	29-01	suc
숱	29-02	sut
숲	29-03	sup
숴	29-04	sweo
쉈	29-05	sweoss
쉐	29-06	swe
쉑	29-07	sweg
쉔	29-08	swen
쉘	29-09	swel
쉠	29-10	swem
쉥	29-11	sweng
쉬	29-12	swi
쉭	29-13	swig
쉰	29-14	swin
쉴	29-15	swil
쉼	29-16	swim
쉽	29-17	swib
쉿	29-18	swis
슁	29-19	swing
슈	29-20	syu
슉	29-21	syug
슐	29-22	syul
슘	29-23	syum
슛	29-24	syus
슝	29-25	syung
스	29-26	seu
슥	29-27	seug
슨	29-28	seun
슬	29-29	seul
슭	29-30	seulg
슴	29-31	seum
습	29-32	seub
슷	29-33	seus
승	29-34	seung
시	29-35	si
식	29-36	sig
신	29-37	sin
싣	29-38	sid
실	29-39	sil
싫	29-40	silh
심	29-41	sim
십	29-42	sib
싯	29-43	sis
싱	29-44	sing
싶	29-45	sip
싸	29-46	ssa
싹	29-47	ssag
싻	29-48	ssags
싼	29-49	ssan
쌀	29-50	ssal
쌈	29-51	ssam
쌉	29-52	ssab
쌌	29-53	ssass
쌍	29-54	ssang
쌓	29-55	ssah
쌔	29-56	ssae
쌕	29-57	ssaeg
쌘	29-58	ssaen
쌜	29-59	ssael
쌤	29-60	ssaem
쌥	29-61	ssaeb
쌨	29-62	ssaess
쌩	29-63	ssaeng
썅	29-64	ssyang
써	29-65	sseo
썩	29-66	sseog
썬	29-67	sseon
썰	29-68	sseol
썲	29-69	sseolm
썸	29-70	sseom
썹	29-71	sseob
썼	29-72	sseoss
썽	29-73	sseong
쎄	29-74	sse
쎈	29-75	ssen
쎌	29-76	ssel
쏀	29-77	ssyen
쏘	29-78	sso
쏙	29-79	ssog
쏜	29-80	sson
쏟	29-81	ssod
쏠	29-82	ssol
쏢	29-83	ssolm
쏨	29-84	ssom
쏩	29-85	ssob
쏭	29-86	ssong
쏴	29-87	sswa
쏵	29-88	sswag
쏸	29-89	sswan
쐈	29-90	sswass
쐐	29-91	sswae
쐤	29-92	sswaess
쐬	29-93	ssoe
쐰	29-94	ssoen

	Code	Reading
쐴	30-01	ssoel
쐼	30-02	ssoem
쐽	30-03	ssoeb
쑈	30-04	ssyo
쑤	30-05	ssu
쑥	30-06	ssug
쑨	30-07	ssun
쑬	30-08	ssul
쑴	30-09	ssum
쑵	30-10	ssub
쑹	30-11	ssung
쒀	30-12	ssweo
쒔	30-13	ssweoss
쒜	30-14	sswe
쒸	30-15	sswi
쒼	30-16	sswin
쓩	30-17	ssyung
쓰	30-18	sseu
쓱	30-19	sseug
쓴	30-20	sseun
쓸	30-21	sseul
쓺	30-22	sseulm
쓿	30-23	sseulh
씀	30-24	sseum
씁	30-25	sseub
씌	30-26	ssyi
씐	30-27	ssyin
씔	30-28	ssyil
씜	30-29	ssyim
씨	30-30	ssi
씩	30-31	ssig
씬	30-32	ssin
씰	30-33	ssil
씸	30-34	ssim
씹	30-35	ssib
씻	30-36	ssis
씽	30-37	ssing
아	30-38	a
악	30-39	ag
안	30-40	an
앉	30-41	anj
않	30-42	anh
알	30-43	al
앍	30-44	alg
앎	30-45	alm
앓	30-46	alh
암	30-47	am
압	30-48	ab
앗	30-49	as
았	30-50	ass
앙	30-51	ang
앝	30-52	at
앞	30-53	ap
애	30-54	ae
액	30-55	aeg
앤	30-56	aen
앨	30-57	ael
앰	30-58	aem
앱	30-59	aeb
앳	30-60	aes
앴	30-61	aess
앵	30-62	aeng
야	30-63	ya
약	30-64	yag
얀	30-65	yan
얄	30-66	yal
얇	30-67	yalb
얌	30-68	yam
얍	30-69	yab
얏	30-70	yas
양	30-71	yang
얕	30-72	yat
얗	30-73	yah
얘	30-74	yae
얜	30-75	yaen
얠	30-76	yael
얩	30-77	yaeb
어	30-78	eo
억	30-79	eog
언	30-80	eon
얹	30-81	eonj
얻	30-82	eod
얼	30-83	eol
얽	30-84	eolg
얾	30-85	eolm
엄	30-86	eom
업	30-87	eob
없	30-88	eobs
엇	30-89	eos
었	30-90	eoss
엉	30-91	eong
엊	30-92	eoj
엌	30-93	eok
엎	30-94	eop
에	31-01	e
엑	31-02	eg
엔	31-03	en
엘	31-04	el
엠	31-05	em
엡	31-06	eb
엣	31-07	es
엥	31-08	eng
여	31-09	yeo
역	31-10	yeog
엮	31-11	yeogg
연	31-12	yeon
열	31-13	yeol
엶	31-14	yeolm
엷	31-15	yeolb
염	31-16	yeom
엽	31-17	yeob
엾	31-18	yeobs
엿	31-19	yeos
였	31-20	yeoss
영	31-21	yeong
옅	31-22	yeot
옆	31-23	yeop
옇	31-24	yeoh
예	31-25	ye
옌	31-26	yen
옐	31-27	yel
옘	31-28	yem
옙	31-29	yeb
옛	31-30	yes
옜	31-31	yess
오	31-32	o
옥	31-33	og
온	31-34	on
올	31-35	ol
옭	31-36	olg
옮	31-37	olm
옰	31-38	ols
옳	31-39	olh
옴	31-40	om
옵	31-41	ob
옷	31-42	os
옹	31-43	ong
옻	31-44	oc
와	31-45	wa
왁	31-46	wag
완	31-47	wan
왈	31-48	wal
왐	31-49	wam
왑	31-50	wab
왓	31-51	was
왔	31-52	wass
왕	31-53	wang
왜	31-54	wae
왝	31-55	waeg
왠	31-56	waen
왬	31-57	waem
왯	31-58	waes
왱	31-59	waeng
외	31-60	oe
왹	31-61	oeg
왼	31-62	oen
욀	31-63	oel
욈	31-64	oem
욉	31-65	oeb
욋	31-66	oes
욍	31-67	oeng
요	31-68	yo
욕	31-69	yog
욘	31-70	yon
욜	31-71	yol
욤	31-72	yom
욥	31-73	yob
욧	31-74	yos
용	31-75	yong
우	31-76	u
욱	31-77	ug
운	31-78	un
울	31-79	ul
욹	31-80	ulg
욺	31-81	ulm
움	31-82	um
웁	31-83	ub
웃	31-84	us
웅	31-85	ung
워	31-86	weo
웍	31-87	weog
원	31-88	weon
월	31-89	weol
웜	31-90	weom
웝	31-91	weob
웠	31-92	weoss
웡	31-93	weong
웨	31-94	we

	Code	Reading		Code	Reading		Code	Reading		Code	Reading
웩	32-01	weg	읽	32-48	ilg	점	33-01	jeom	죗	33-48	joes
웬	32-02	wen	읾	32-49	ilm	접	33-02	jeob	죙	33-49	joeng
웰	32-03	wel	잃	32-50	ilh	젓	33-03	jeos	죠	33-50	jyo
웸	32-04	wem	임	32-51	im	정	33-04	jeong	죡	33-51	jyog
웹	32-05	web	입	32-52	ib	젖	33-05	jeoj	죤	33-52	jyon
웽	32-06	weng	잇	32-53	is	제	33-06	je	죵	33-53	jyong
위	32-07	wi	있	32-54	iss	젝	33-07	jeg	주	33-54	ju
윅	32-08	wig	잉	32-55	ing	젠	33-08	jen	죽	33-55	jug
윈	32-09	win	잊	32-56	ij	젤	33-09	jel	준	33-56	jun
윌	32-10	wil	잎	32-57	ip	젬	33-10	jem	줄	33-57	jul
윔	32-11	wim	자	32-58	ja	젭	33-11	jeb	줅	33-58	julg
윕	32-12	wib	작	32-59	jag	젯	33-12	jes	줆	33-59	julm
윗	32-13	wis	잔	32-60	jan	젱	33-13	jeng	줌	33-60	jum
윙	32-14	wing	잖	32-61	janh	져	33-14	jyeo	줍	33-61	jub
유	32-15	yu	잗	32-62	jad	젼	33-15	jyeon	줏	33-62	jus
육	32-16	yug	잘	32-63	jal	졀	33-16	jyeol	중	33-63	jung
윤	32-17	yun	잚	32-64	jalm	졈	33-17	jyeom	줘	33-64	jweo
율	32-18	yul	잠	32-65	jam	졉	33-18	jyeob	줬	33-65	jweoss
윰	32-19	yum	잡	32-66	jab	졌	33-19	jyeoss	줴	33-66	jwe
윱	32-20	yub	잣	32-67	jas	졍	33-20	jyeong	쥐	33-67	jwi
윳	32-21	yus	잤	32-68	jass	졔	33-21	jye	쥑	33-68	jwig
융	32-22	yung	장	32-69	jang	조	33-22	jo	쥔	33-69	jwin
윷	32-23	yuc	잦	32-70	jaj	족	33-23	jog	쥘	33-70	jwil
으	32-24	eu	재	32-71	jae	존	33-24	jon	쥠	33-71	jwim
윽	32-25	eug	잭	32-72	jaeg	졸	33-25	jol	쥡	33-72	jwib
은	32-26	eun	잰	32-73	jaen	졺	33-26	jolm	쥣	33-73	jwis
을	32-27	eul	잴	32-74	jael	좀	33-27	jom	쥬	33-74	jyu
읊	32-28	eulp	잼	32-75	jaem	좁	33-28	job	쥰	33-75	jyun
음	32-29	eum	잽	32-76	jaeb	좃	33-29	jos	쥴	33-76	jyul
읍	32-30	eub	잿	32-77	jaes	종	33-30	jong	쥼	33-77	jyum
읏	32-31	eus	쟀	32-78	jaess	좆	33-31	joj	즈	33-78	jeu
응	32-32	eung	쟁	32-79	jaeng	좇	33-32	joc	즉	33-79	jeug
읒	32-33	euj	쟈	32-80	jya	좋	33-33	joh	즌	33-80	jeun
읓	32-34	euc	쟉	32-81	jyag	좌	33-34	jwa	즐	33-81	jeul
읔	32-35	euk	쟌	32-82	jyan	좍	33-35	jwag	즘	33-82	jeum
읕	32-36	eut	쟎	32-83	jyanh	좔	33-36	jwal	즙	33-83	jeub
읖	32-37	eup	쟐	32-84	jyal	좝	33-37	jwab	즛	33-84	jeus
읗	32-38	euh	쟘	32-85	jyam	좟	33-38	jwas	증	33-85	jeung
의	32-39	yi	쟝	32-86	jyang	좡	33-39	jwang	지	33-86	ji
읜	32-40	yin	쟤	32-87	jyae	좨	33-40	jwae	직	33-87	jig
읠	32-41	yil	쟨	32-88	jyaen	좼	33-41	jwaess	진	33-88	jin
읨	32-42	yim	쟬	32-89	jyael	좽	33-42	jwaeng	짇	33-89	jid
읫	32-43	yis	저	32-90	jeo	죄	33-43	joe	질	33-90	jil
이	32-44	i	적	32-91	jeog	죈	33-44	joen	짊	33-91	jilm
익	32-45	ig	전	32-92	jeon	죌	33-45	joel	짐	33-92	jim
인	32-46	in	절	32-93	jeol	죔	33-46	joem	집	33-93	jib
일	32-47	il	젊	32-94	jeolm	죕	33-47	joeb	짓	33-94	jis

	Code	Reading
징	34-01	jing
짖	34-02	jij
짙	34-03	jit
짚	34-04	jip
짜	34-05	jja
짝	34-06	jjag
짠	34-07	jjan
짢	34-08	jjanh
짤	34-09	jjal
짧	34-10	jjalb
짬	34-11	jjam
짭	34-12	jjab
짯	34-13	jjas
짰	34-14	jjass
짱	34-15	jjang
째	34-16	jjae
짹	34-17	jjaeg
짼	34-18	jjaen
쨀	34-19	jjael
쨈	34-20	jjaem
쨉	34-21	jjaeb
쨋	34-22	jjaes
쨌	34-23	jjaess
쨍	34-24	jjaeng
쨔	34-25	jjya
쨘	34-26	jjyan
쨩	34-27	jjyang
쩌	34-28	jjeo
쩍	34-29	jjeog
쩐	34-30	jjeon
쩔	34-31	jjeol
쩜	34-32	jjeom
쩝	34-33	jjeob
쩟	34-34	jjeos
쩠	34-35	jjeoss
쩡	34-36	jjeong
쩨	34-37	jje
쩽	34-38	jjeng
쪄	34-39	jjyeo
쪘	34-40	jjyeoss
쪼	34-41	jjo
쪽	34-42	jjog
쫀	34-43	jjon
쫄	34-44	jjol
쫌	34-45	jjom
쫍	34-46	jjob
쫏	34-47	jjos
쫑	34-48	jjong
쫓	34-49	jjoc
쫘	34-50	jjwa
쫙	34-51	jjwag
쫠	34-52	jjwal
쫬	34-53	jjwass
쫴	34-54	jjwae
쬈	34-55	jjwaess
쬐	34-56	jjoe
쬔	34-57	jjoen
쬘	34-58	jjoel
쬠	34-59	jjoem
쬡	34-60	jjoeb
쭁	34-61	jjyong
쭈	34-62	jju
쭉	34-63	jjug
쭌	34-64	jjun
쭐	34-65	jjul
쭘	34-66	jjum
쭙	34-67	jjub
쭝	34-68	jjung
쭤	34-69	jjweo
쭸	34-70	jjweoss
쭹	34-71	jjweong
쮜	34-72	jjwi
쮸	34-73	jjyu
쯔	34-74	jjeu
쯤	34-75	jjeum
쯧	34-76	jjeus
쯩	34-77	jjeung
찌	34-78	jji
찍	34-79	jjig
찐	34-80	jjin
찔	34-81	jjil
찜	34-82	jjim
찝	34-83	jjib
찡	34-84	jjing
찢	34-85	jjij
찧	34-86	jjih
차	34-87	ca
착	34-88	cag
찬	34-89	can
찮	34-90	canh
찰	34-91	cal
참	34-92	cam
찹	34-93	cab
찻	34-94	cas
찼	35-01	cass
창	35-02	cang
찾	35-03	caj
채	35-04	cae
책	35-05	caeg
챈	35-06	caen
챌	35-07	cael
챔	35-08	caem
챕	35-09	caeb
챗	35-10	caes
챘	35-11	caess
챙	35-12	caeng
챠	35-13	cya
챤	35-14	cyan
챦	35-15	cyanh
챨	35-16	cyal
챰	35-17	cyam
챵	35-18	cyang
처	35-19	ceo
척	35-20	ceog
천	35-21	ceon
철	35-22	ceol
첨	35-23	ceom
첩	35-24	ceob
첫	35-25	ceos
첬	35-26	ceoss
청	35-27	ceong
체	35-28	ce
첵	35-29	ceg
첸	35-30	cen
첼	35-31	cel
쳄	35-32	cem
쳅	35-33	ceb
쳇	35-34	ces
쳉	35-35	ceng
쳐	35-36	cyeo
쳔	35-37	cyeon
쳤	35-38	cyeoss
쳬	35-39	cye
쳰	35-40	cyen
촁	35-41	cyeng
초	35-42	co
촉	35-43	cog
촌	35-44	con
촐	35-45	col
촘	35-46	com
촙	35-47	cob
촛	35-48	cos
총	35-49	cong
촤	35-50	cwa
촨	35-51	cwan
촬	35-52	cwal
촹	35-53	cwang
최	35-54	coe
쵠	35-55	coen
쵤	35-56	coel
쵬	35-57	coem
쵭	35-58	coeb
쵯	35-59	coes
쵱	35-60	coeng
쵸	35-61	cyo
춈	35-62	cyom
추	35-63	cu
축	35-64	cug
춘	35-65	cun
출	35-66	cul
춤	35-67	cum
춥	35-68	cub
춧	35-69	cus
충	35-70	cung
춰	35-71	cweo
췄	35-72	cweoss
췌	35-73	cwe
췐	35-74	cwen
취	35-75	cwi
췬	35-76	cwin
췰	35-77	cwil
췸	35-78	cwim
췹	35-79	cwib
췻	35-80	cwis
췽	35-81	cwing
츄	35-82	cyu
츈	35-83	cyun
츌	35-84	cyul
츔	35-85	cyum
츙	35-86	cyung
츠	35-87	ceu
측	35-88	ceug
츤	35-89	ceun
츨	35-90	ceul
츰	35-91	ceum
츱	35-92	ceub
츳	35-93	ceus
층	35-94	ceung

	Code	Reading
치	36-01	ci
칙	36-02	cig
친	36-03	cin
칟	36-04	cid
칠	36-05	cil
칡	36-06	cilg
침	36-07	cim
칩	36-08	cib
칫	36-09	cis
칭	36-10	cing
카	36-11	ka
칵	36-12	kag
칸	36-13	kan
칼	36-14	kal
캄	36-15	kam
캅	36-16	kab
캇	36-17	kas
캉	36-18	kang
캐	36-19	kae
캑	36-20	kaeg
캔	36-21	kaen
캘	36-22	kael
캠	36-23	kaem
캡	36-24	kaeb
캣	36-25	kaes
캤	36-26	kaess
캥	36-27	kaeng
캬	36-28	kya
캭	36-29	kyag
컁	36-30	kyang
커	36-31	keo
컥	36-32	keog
컨	36-33	keon
컫	36-34	keod
컬	36-35	keol
컴	36-36	keom
컵	36-37	keob
컷	36-38	keos
컸	36-39	keoss
컹	36-40	keong
케	36-41	ke
켁	36-42	keg
켄	36-43	ken
켈	36-44	kel
켐	36-45	kem
켑	36-46	keb
켓	36-47	kes
켕	36-48	keng
켜	36-49	kyeo
켠	36-50	kyeon
켤	36-51	kyeol
켬	36-52	kyeom
켭	36-53	kyeob
켯	36-54	kyeos
켰	36-55	kyeoss
켱	36-56	kyeong
켸	36-57	kye
코	36-58	ko
콕	36-59	kog
콘	36-60	kon
콜	36-61	kol
콤	36-62	kom
콥	36-63	kob
콧	36-64	kos
콩	36-65	kong
콰	36-66	kwa
콱	36-67	kwag
콴	36-68	kwan
콸	36-69	kwal
쾀	36-70	kwam
쾅	36-71	kwang
쾌	36-72	kwae
쾡	36-73	kwaeng
쾨	36-74	koe
쾰	36-75	koel
쿄	36-76	kyo
쿠	36-77	ku
쿡	36-78	kug
쿤	36-79	kun
쿨	36-80	kul
쿰	36-81	kum
쿱	36-82	kub
쿳	36-83	kus
쿵	36-84	kung
쿼	36-85	kweo
퀀	36-86	kweon
퀄	36-87	kweol
퀑	36-88	kweong
퀘	36-89	kwe
퀭	36-90	kweng
퀴	36-91	kwi
퀵	36-92	kwig
퀸	36-93	kwin
퀼	36-94	kwil
큄	37-01	kwim
큅	37-02	kwib
큇	37-03	kwis
큉	37-04	kwing
큐	37-05	kyu
큔	37-06	kyun
큘	37-07	kyul
큠	37-08	kyum
크	37-09	keu
큭	37-10	keug
큰	37-11	keun
클	37-12	keul
큼	37-13	keum
큽	37-14	keub
킁	37-15	keung
키	37-16	ki
킥	37-17	kig
킨	37-18	kin
킬	37-19	kil
킴	37-20	kim
킵	37-21	kib
킷	37-22	kis
킹	37-23	king
타	37-24	ta
탁	37-25	tag
탄	37-26	tan
탈	37-27	tal
탉	37-28	talg
탐	37-29	tam
탑	37-30	tab
탓	37-31	tas
탔	37-32	tass
탕	37-33	tang
태	37-34	tae
택	37-35	taeg
탠	37-36	taen
탤	37-37	tael
탬	37-38	taem
탭	37-39	taeb
탯	37-40	taes
탰	37-41	taess
탱	37-42	taeng
탸	37-43	tya
턍	37-44	tyang
터	37-45	teo
턱	37-46	teog
턴	37-47	teon
털	37-48	teol
턺	37-49	teolm
텀	37-50	teom
텁	37-51	teob
텃	37-52	teos
텄	37-53	teoss
텅	37-54	teong
테	37-55	te
텍	37-56	teg
텐	37-57	ten
텔	37-58	tel
템	37-59	tem
텝	37-60	teb
텟	37-61	tes
텡	37-62	teng
텨	37-63	tyeo
텬	37-64	tyeon
텼	37-65	tyeoss
톄	37-66	tye
톈	37-67	tyen
토	37-68	to
톡	37-69	tog
톤	37-70	ton
톨	37-71	tol
톰	37-72	tom
톱	37-73	tob
톳	37-74	tos
통	37-75	tong
톺	37-76	top
톼	37-77	twa
퇀	37-78	twan
퇘	37-79	twae
퇴	37-80	toe
퇸	37-81	toen
툇	37-82	toes
툉	37-83	toeng
툐	37-84	tyo
투	37-85	tu
툭	37-86	tug
툰	37-87	tun
툴	37-88	tul
툼	37-89	tum
툽	37-90	tub
툿	37-91	tus
퉁	37-92	tung
퉈	37-93	tweo
퉜	37-94	tweoss

	Code	Reading		Code	Reading		Code	Reading		Code	Reading
퉤	38-01	twe	패	38-48	pae	퐈	39-01	pwa	학	39-48	hag
튀	38-02	twi	팩	38-49	paeg	퐝	39-02	pwang	한	39-49	han
튁	38-03	twig	팬	38-50	paen	푀	39-03	poe	할	39-50	hal
튄	38-04	twin	팰	38-51	pael	푄	39-04	poen	핥	39-51	halt
튈	38-05	twil	팸	38-52	paem	표	39-05	pyo	함	39-52	ham
튐	38-06	twim	팹	38-53	paeb	푠	39-06	pyon	합	39-53	hab
튑	38-07	twib	팻	38-54	paes	푤	39-07	pyol	핫	39-54	has
튕	38-08	twing	팼	38-55	paess	푭	39-08	pyob	항	39-55	hang
튜	38-09	tyu	팽	38-56	paeng	푯	39-09	pyos	해	39-56	hae
튠	38-10	tyun	퍄	38-57	pya	푸	39-10	pu	핵	39-57	haeg
튤	38-11	tyul	퍅	38-58	pyag	푹	39-11	pug	핸	39-58	haen
튬	38-12	tyum	퍼	38-59	peo	푼	39-12	pun	핼	39-59	hael
튱	38-13	tyung	퍽	38-60	peog	푿	39-13	pud	햄	39-60	haem
트	38-14	teu	펀	38-61	peon	풀	39-14	pul	햅	39-61	haeb
특	38-15	teug	펄	38-62	peol	풂	39-15	pulm	햇	39-62	haes
튼	38-16	teun	펌	38-63	peom	품	39-16	pum	했	39-63	haess
튿	38-17	teud	펍	38-64	peob	풉	39-17	pub	행	39-64	haeng
틀	38-18	teul	펏	38-65	peos	풋	39-18	pus	햐	39-65	hya
틂	38-19	teulm	펐	38-66	peoss	풍	39-19	pung	향	39-66	hyang
틈	38-20	teum	펑	38-67	peong	풔	39-20	pweo	허	39-67	heo
틉	38-21	teub	페	38-68	pe	풩	39-21	pweong	헉	39-68	heog
틋	38-22	teus	펙	38-69	peg	퓌	39-22	pwi	헌	39-69	heon
틔	38-23	tyi	펜	38-70	pen	퓐	39-23	pwin	헐	39-70	heol
틘	38-24	tyin	펠	38-71	pel	퓔	39-24	pwil	헒	39-71	heolm
틜	38-25	tyil	펨	38-72	pem	퓜	39-25	pwim	험	39-72	heom
틤	38-26	tyim	펩	38-73	peb	퓟	39-26	pwis	헙	39-73	heob
틥	38-27	tyib	펫	38-74	pes	퓨	39-27	pyu	헛	39-74	heos
티	38-28	ti	펭	38-75	peng	퓬	39-28	pyun	헝	39-75	heong
틱	38-29	tig	펴	38-76	pyeo	퓰	39-29	pyul	헤	39-76	he
틴	38-30	tin	편	38-77	pyeon	퓸	39-30	pyum	헥	39-77	heg
틸	38-31	til	펼	38-78	pyeol	퓻	39-31	pyus	헨	39-78	hen
팀	38-32	tim	폄	38-79	pyeom	퓽	39-32	pyung	헬	39-79	hel
팁	38-33	tib	폅	38-80	pyeob	프	39-33	peu	헴	39-80	hem
팃	38-34	tis	폈	38-81	pyeoss	픈	39-34	peun	헵	39-81	heb
팅	38-35	ting	평	38-82	pyeong	플	39-35	peul	헷	39-82	hes
파	38-36	pa	폐	38-83	pye	픔	39-36	peum	헹	39-83	heng
팍	38-37	pag	폘	38-84	pyel	픕	39-37	peub	혀	39-84	hyeo
팎	38-38	pagg	폡	38-85	pyeb	픗	39-38	peus	혁	39-85	hyeog
판	38-39	pan	폣	38-86	pyes	피	39-39	pi	현	39-86	hyeon
팔	38-40	pal	포	38-87	po	픽	39-40	pig	혈	39-87	hyeol
팖	38-41	palm	폭	38-88	pog	핀	39-41	pin	혐	39-88	hyeom
팜	38-42	pam	폰	38-89	pon	필	39-42	pil	협	39-89	hyeob
팝	38-43	pab	폴	38-90	pol	핌	39-43	pim	혓	39-90	hyeos
팟	38-44	pas	폼	38-91	pom	핍	39-44	pib	혔	39-91	hyeoss
팠	38-45	pass	폽	38-92	pob	핏	39-45	pis	형	39-92	hyeong
팡	38-46	pang	폿	38-93	pos	핑	39-46	ping	혜	39-93	hye
팥	38-47	pat	퐁	38-94	pong	하	39-47	ha	혠	39-94	hyen

	Code	Reading
혤	40-01	hyel
혭	40-02	hyeb
호	40-03	ho
혹	40-04	hog
혼	40-05	hon
홀	40-06	hol
홅	40-07	holt
홈	40-08	hom
홉	40-09	hob
홋	40-10	hos
홍	40-11	hong
홑	40-12	hot
화	40-13	hwa
확	40-14	hwag
환	40-15	hwan
활	40-16	hwal
홧	40-17	hwas
황	40-18	hwang
홰	40-19	hwae
홱	40-20	hwaeg
홴	40-21	hwaen
홷	40-22	hwaes
홹	40-23	hwaeng
회	40-24	hoe
획	40-25	hoeg
횐	40-26	hoen
횔	40-27	hoel
횝	40-28	hoeb
횟	40-29	hoes
횡	40-30	hoeng
효	40-31	hyo
횬	40-32	hyon
횰	40-33	hyol
횹	40-34	hyob
횻	40-35	hyos
후	40-36	hu
훅	40-37	hug
훈	40-38	hun
훌	40-39	hul
훑	40-40	hult
훔	40-41	hum
훗	40-42	hus
훙	40-43	hung
훠	40-44	hweo
훤	40-45	hweon
훨	40-46	hweol
훰	40-47	hweom
훵	40-48	hweong
훼	40-49	hwe
훽	40-50	hweg
휀	40-51	hwen
휄	40-52	hwel
휑	40-53	hweng
휘	40-54	hwi
휙	40-55	hwig
휜	40-56	hwin
휠	40-57	hwil
휨	40-58	hwim
휩	40-59	hwib
휫	40-60	hwis
휭	40-61	hwing
휴	40-62	hyu
휵	40-63	hyug
휸	40-64	hyun
휼	40-65	hyul
흄	40-66	hyum
흇	40-67	hyus
흉	40-68	hyung
흐	40-69	heu
흑	40-70	heug
흔	40-71	heun
흖	40-72	heunh
흗	40-73	heud
흘	40-74	heul
흙	40-75	heulg
흠	40-76	heum
흡	40-77	heub
흣	40-78	heus
흥	40-79	heung
흩	40-80	heut
희	40-81	hyi
흰	40-82	hyin
흴	40-83	hyil
흼	40-84	hyim
흽	40-85	hyib
힁	40-86	hying
히	40-87	hi
힉	40-88	hig
힌	40-89	hin
힐	40-90	hil
힘	40-91	him
힙	40-92	hib
힛	40-93	his
힝	40-94	hing

O

TCVN 6056:1995 Table

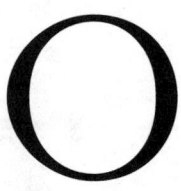

This appendix constitutes a table for the complete TCVN 6056:1995 character set, printed here using the typeface 文鼎中明CNS11643 (MingTiEG-Medium), developed by Arphic Technology. Each character is indexed by Row-Cell value.

Row 42		01	02	03	04	05	06	07	08	09	10	11	12	13	14	15	16	17	18	19
00		一	丁	七	万	丈	三	上	下	不	与	丐	丑	且	丕	世	丘	丙	丞	丟
20	丫	中	丰	串	丸	丹	主	丿	乂	乃	久	之	乍	乎	乏	乖	乘	乙	九	乞
40	也	乱	乳	乾	亂	了	予	事	二	亍	于	云	互	五	井	亙	些	亟	亡	亢
60	交	亥	亨	享	京	亭	人	什	仁	仃	仄	仆	仇	今	介	仍	仔	仕	他	仗
80	付	仙	仝	代	令	仰	件	价	任	份	仿	企	伊	伍	伎					

Row 43		01	02	03	04	05	06	07	08	09	10	11	12	13	14	15	16	17	18	19
00		伏	伐	休	会	伮	伯	伴	似	伽	佃	位	低	住	佐	体	余	佚	佛	作
20	佞	你	佳	併	佻	使	來	侈	例	侔	侖	侘	供	依	侯	侱	侵	侶	侼	便
40	係	促	俊	俐	俑	俗	保	俠	信	修	俱	俸	俺	俵	倂	倈	個	倍	們	倒
60	倖	倘	候	倚	借	倡	倣	値	倦	倩	倪	倫	倬	倭	偃	偈	偉	偏	停	健
80	偪	側	偵	偶	偽	傅	傌	傍	傑	傘	備	催	從	傲	傳					

Row 44		01	02	03	04	05	06	07	08	09	10	11	12	13	14	15	16	17	18	19
00		債	傷	傾	僂	僄	像	僑	僕	僚	僥	僧	僭	僮	價	儂	億	儈	儉	儒
20	儳	儼	兀	元	兄	充	兆	兇	先	光	克	免	兑	兔	兜	兢	入	全	兩	八
40	公	六	兮	共	兵	其	具	典	兼	内	冉	冊	再	冒	冕	冗	冘	冠	冢	冤
60	冥	冬	冰	况	冶	冷	冽	准	凌	凍	凜	凝	几	凡	凭	凱	凶	出	函	刀
80	刁	刃	分	切	刊	刌	刎	刑	列	初	刪	判	別	刦	刨					

Row 45		01	02	03	04	05	06	07	08	09	10	11	12	13	14	15	16	17	18	19
00		利	到	制	刷	刺	刻	則	削	前	剥	剧	剪	副	割	創	剷	剿	劂	劃
20	劄	劇	劍	劑	劕	力	功	加	助	劬	効	劾	勁	勃	勇	勉	勅	勒	動	勖
40	勘	務	勛	勝	勞	勢	勤	勦	勵	勸	勹	勿	包	匈	匍	匏	匐	化	匝	匡
60	匣	匪	匱	匹	匼	匿	區	十	千	卅	升	午	半	卌	卒	卓	協	南	博	卜
80	卞	占	卦	卬	卯	印	危	卲	即	卷	却	卿	厄	厓	厔					

Row 46		01	02	03	04	05	06	07	08	09	10	11	12	13	14	15	16	17	18	19
00		厘	厮	厝	原	厭	厲	去	參	又	及	友	双	反	叔	取	受	叛	叠	口
20	古	句	另	叩	只	叫	召	叮	可	台	叱	史	右	号	司	叻	吁	各	合	吉
40	同	名	后	吏	吐	向	吒	吓	吔	君	吝	吟	吣	否	吩	含	听	吳	吵	吹
60	吻	吼	吾	告	呂	呃	呆	呈	呌	呎	呞	呠	呡	呢	周	呫	呱	味	呵	呶
80	呸	呼	命	咀	咂	咄	咆	咈	咋	和	咏	咐	咒	咚	咢					

Row 47		01	02	03	04	05	06	07	08	09	10	11	12	13	14	15	16	17	18	19
00		咧	咬	咮	咯	咷	咻	咼	咽	哀	品	哃	哄	哆	哇	哈	哉	响	員	哢
20	哥	哦	哪	哭	哮	哲	哽	哿	唇	唈	唎	唐	唑	唩	唯	唱	唼	唾	啄	商
40	啌	啐	啒	啛	啜	啣	啨	啩	啷	啺	啿	喁	喃	善	喇	喉	喋	喍	喎	喔
60	喘	喚	喜	喝	喟	喡	喦	喧	喪	單	喻	嗦	嗎	嗔	嗙	嗚	嗛	嗢	嗣	嘆
80	嘈	嘍	嘫	嘬	嘮	嘲	嘶	嘺	嘻	噎	噔	噙	噞	噤	噦					

Row 48		01	02	03	04	05	06	07	08	09	10	11	12	13	14	15	16	17	18	19
00		器	噪	噬	噯	噴	噶	嚂	嚄	嚅	嚋	嚎	嚓	嚛	嚜	嚦	嚧	嚨	嚯	嚴
20	嚶	囂	囉	囑	囒	囕	囚	四	回	因	园	困	囱	囷	固	囻	圃	圈	國	圍
40	園	圓	圖	團	土	圣	在	圩	圭	圯	地	址	坂	均	坊	坎	坏	坑	坡	坤
60	坦	坧	垂	垉	垌	垓	垢	垵	垹	垮	埃	埇	埈	埋	城	域	埣	埩	埮	埶
80	執	培	基	堂	堅	堆	堤	堪	堯	報	場	堷	塊	塗	塞					

Row 49		01	02	03	04	05	06	07	08	09	10	11	12	13	14	15	16	17	18	19
00		塡	塵	塾	境	墅	墆	墓	墜	增	墮	墳	墻	墾	壁	壇	壑	壓	壕	壘
20	壙	壞	壟	壢	壤	士	壬	壯	壴	壻	壼	壽	复	夕	外	夙	多	夜	大	天
40	太	夫	夭	央	失	夷	夸	夾	奄	奇	奈	奉	奏	契	奢	奧	奪	奬	奮	女
60	奴	奶	奸	好	如	妃	妍	妒	妓	妖	妙	妝	妥	妮	妯	妲	妹	妻	妾	姈
80	姊	始	姐	姑	姓	委	姚	姤	姥	姦	姪	姻	姿	威	娓					

Row 50		01	02	03	04	05	06	07	08	09	10	11	12	13	14	15	16	17	18	19
00		娘	娜	娥	娶	婁	婆	婉	婍	婢	婦	婭	媒	媧	媽	嫁	嫂	嫌	嫖	嫗
20	嫡	嫦	嫩	嬌	嬖	嬰	嬸	子	孔	孕	字	存	孛	孝	孟	季	孤	孥	孩	孫
40	學	孺	孽	宁	宇	守	安	宋	完	宗	官	宙	定	宛	宜	宝	客	宣	室	宮
60	宰	害	宴	家	容	宿	寂	寄	寅	密	寇	富	寐	寒	寓	寔	寞	察	寠	寡
80	實	寨	審	寫	寬	寵	寶	寸	对	寿	封	射	將	專	尊					

Row 51		01	02	03	04	05	06	07	08	09	10	11	12	13	14	15	16	17	18	19
00		尋	對	導	小	少	尔	尖	尙	尚	尸	尹	尺	尼	尽	尾	局	居	屈	屋
20	屍	屏	展	屠	屢	層	屬	屯	山	屹	岌	岑	岧	岩	岱	岵	岸	島	峽	崇
40	崍	崑	崒	崔	崖	崙	嵁	嵋	嵎	嵩	嵬	嶄	嶢	巍	巖	川	州	巡	巢	工
60	左	巧	差	己	已	巳	巴	巽	巾	帀	市	布	希	帑	帖	帝	帥	師	帳	帶
80	常	帽	幀	幔	幃	幟	幡	幢	幣	干	平	年	幻	幼	庄					

Row 52		01	02	03	04	05	06	07	08	09	10	11	12	13	14	15	16	17	18	19
00		床	序	底	店	庙	庚	府	度	座	庫	庭	庵	庶	康	廁	廂	廈	廉	廊
20	廓	廕	廚	廛	廟	廠	廡	廢	廣	廩	延	廷	建	廾	弄	弊	弋	弎	式	弑
40	弓	弔	引	弗	弟	弩	弱	張	強	弼	彈	彊	彐	形	彩	彫	彬	彭	影	彷
60	役	彼	彾	彿	往	征	徂	待	徊	律	後	徐	徒	得	徘	從	徠	御	徬	微
80	徵	德	徹	心	必	忉	忌	忍	忑	忒	忖	志	忘	忙	忝					

Row 53		01	02	03	04	05	06	07	08	09	10	11	12	13	14	15	16	17	18	19
00		忠	忤	快	忱	念	忽	忿	怍	怎	怒	怖	怜	思	急	性	怨	怫	怯	怳
20	怵	恋	恍	恐	恕	恜	恟	恨	恩	恪	恬	恭	息	悁	悅	悉	悌	悍	悔	悗
40	悛	患	悲	悴	悶	悼	悽	情	惇	惊	惑	惕	惚	惛	惜	惠	惡	惦	惱	想
60	惴	惶	惷	愀	愁	愆	愈	愍	意	愕	愚	感	愿	慄	慇	慈	態	慌	慎	慕
80	慘	慚	慛	慟	慢	慣	慤	慨	慫	慮	慰	慵	慷	慼	慾					

Row 54		01	02	03	04	05	06	07	08	09	10	11	12	13	14	15	16	17	18	19
00		憂	憑	憔	憚	憤	憨	憫	憲	憶	憾	懃	懇	應	懊	懷	戀	戈	戊	戌
20	戍	戎	成	我	戒	或	戚	戛	戟	截	戰	戲	户	戾	房	所	扁	扇	手	才
40	扎	扑	打	扗	扛	扠	扣	扳	扶	批	扼	技	抄	抆	把	抑	抒	抓	投	抗
60	折	抛	抨	披	担	抳	抷	抹	押	抽	拂	拍	拒	拔	拖	拗	拘	拙	招	拜
80	拥	拪	括	拭	拯	拱	拳	拽	拾	拿	持	挂	指	按	挍					

Row 55		01	02	03	04	05	06	07	08	09	10	11	12	13	14	15	16	17	18	19
00		挏	挪	挫	振	挰	挹	挾	捁	捅	捉	捍	捕	捧	捨	据	捲	捷	捺	掂
20	掃	掇	授	掉	掏	排	掘	掙	掛	掠	採	探	掣	接	控	推	措	掬	掮	揀
40	揂	揆	描	提	插	揖	揚	揭	揮	揳	援	損	搏	搔	搖	搗	搜	搬	搭	摘
60	摸	摹	撐	撒	撓	撞	撢	撤	撩	撫	播	撮	撰	擅	擇	據	擦	擬	擲	擾
80	攔	攘	攙	攜	攝	攬	支	收	攷	攻	放	政	故	效	敏					

Row 56		01	02	03	04	05	06	07	08	09	10	11	12	13	14	15	16	17	18	19
00		救	敕	敖	敗	敘	教	敝	敢	散	敦	敬	敲	整	敵	數	文	斎	斐	斗
20	料	斜	斟	斤	斥	斧	斬	断	新	方	於	施	旁	旅	旋	旌	族	旗	旛	日
40	旦	旨	早	旭	旱	旺	昂	昆	昇	明	昏	易	昔	星	映	昧	是	時	晃	晚
60	晤	晦	晨	普	景	晴	晶	智	暄	暇	暈	暗	暢	暫	暮	暴	暹	曀	曆	曉
80	曖	曠	曩	曰	曲	曳	更	曷	書	曹	曼	曾	替	最	會					

Row 57		01	02	03	04	05	06	07	08	09	10	11	12	13	14	15	16	17	18	19
00		月	有	朋	服	朏	朔	朕	朗	望	朝	期	木	未	末	本	札	朱	朴	朵
20	机	朽	杄	杍	杆	杇	李	杏	村	杕	杖	杜	束	杠	杣	杯	杰	東	松	板
40	枉	料	枕	林	枚	果	枝	枮	枯	架	枷	枸	柁	柃	柄	柆	柊	柏	某	柑
60	染	柔	柚	查	柩	柪	柱	柳	柴	柿	栍	栐	栓	栖	栗	栘	校	栢	核	根
80	格	桀	桁	桂	桃	桄	案	桑	桶	梁	梅	梆	梏	桧	條					

Row 58		01	02	03	04	05	06	07	08	09	10	11	12	13	14	15	16	17	18	19
00		梨	梭	械	梳	梶	梹	棣	棆	棍	棒	棖	棗	棘	棟	棧	森	棯	棱	棵
20	棹	棺	棿	植	椎	椒	椳	楊	楓	楚	楛	楢	楨	業	楱	楴	極	榔	榖	榜
40	榛	榩	榮	榱	榴	槃	槊	槌	槍	槐	槓	槔	槞	椅	槯	槶	槽	椿	樂	樊
60	樋	樑	樓	標	樞	模	樣	横	樳	樶	樸	樹	樾	橉	橊	橋	橘	橙	橛	機
80	檾	橽	檀	檁	檄	檜	檢	檬	檺	櫂	櫃	欖	櫊	櫟	櫳					

Row 59		01	02	03	04	05	06	07	08	09	10	11	12	13	14	15	16	17	18	19
00		欄	權	欗	欠	次	欣	欲	欺	欽	款	歆	歇	歌	歎	歛	歟	歡	止	正
20	此	步	武	歪	歲	歷	歹	死	殀	殃	殉	殊	殘	殪	殮	殯	段	殷	殺	殼
40	殿	毀	毅	毋	母	每	毒	比	毛	毫	毬	毯	氂	氈	氏	民	氓	氣	水	永
60	汁	求	汉	汐	汕	汛	汜	汝	江	池	污	汩	汰	汲	決	沁	沃	沉	沌	沐
80	沒	沓	沔	沖	沙	沚	沛	沱	河	沸	油	治	沼	沾	沿					

Row 60		01	02	03	04	05	06	07	08	09	10	11	12	13	14	15	16	17	18	19
00		泄	泅	泆	泉	泊	法	泗	泛	泜	泡	波	泣	泥	注	泪	泮	泰	洁	洄
20	洋	洌	洒	洗	洙	洛	洞	洩	洪	洮	洲	泇	洷	活	派	流	浗	浠	浥	浮
40	浰	海	浸	涂	涅	涇	消	涉	涓	涖	涗	涯	液	涸	涼	淁	淋	淒	淘	淚
60	淟	淡	淢	淥	淩	淪	淫	淬	淮	淯	深	淳	淵	淶	混	淹	淺	清	減	渠
80	渡	渤	渥	温	測	渭	港	渴	湄	湅	湆	渫	溢	湖	湘					

Row 61		01	02	03	04	05	06	07	08	09	10	11	12	13	14	15	16	17	18	19
00		湧	湨	湯	湲	源	準	溧	溪	溳	溶	滂	滅	滈	滌	滑	滔	滝	滯	滲
20	滴	滾	滿	漁	漂	漉	漏	漓	演	漠	漢	漣	漨	漫	漲	漸	漼	潐	潔	潗
40	潛	潠	潤	潦	潭	潮	潯	潰	潺	澄	澆	澎	澤	澮	激	濁	濃	濈	濔	濕
60	濛	濞	濡	濤	濫	濼	瀉	瀋	瀐	瀘	瀝	瀾	灑	灟	火	灯	灰	灵	灶	灸
80	灼	災	灾	炊	炎	炐	炒	炖	炤	炩	炭	炮	炳	点	烈					

Row 62		01	02	03	04	05	06	07	08	09	10	11	12	13	14	15	16	17	18	19
00		烊	烏	烘	烛	烝	烤	烹	焉	焙	焞	無	然	煉	煤	照	煩	煽	熄	熅
20	熊	熑	熙	熟	熱	熶	熾	燃	燈	燎	燐	燒	燕	燥	燦	燭	燻	燼	爉	爌
40	爐	爛	爪	爬	争	爰	爲	爵	爽	爾	牀	牆	片	版	牋	牌	牒	牙	牛	牟
60	牢	牣	物	牲	特	犀	犯	狀	狂	狃	狄	狐	狗	狡	狹	狼	猊	猢	献	猴
80	猿	獄	獅	獒	獨	獬	獲	獵	獸	獻	玄	玉	王	玩	玲					

Row 63		01	02	03	04	05	06	07	08	09	10	11	12	13	14	15	16	17	18	19
00		玳	玷	珀	珊	珍	珠	珥	班	現	球	理	琉	琢	琴	琵	琶	瑁	瑙	瑚
20	瑟	瑤	瑪	璃	璧	璽	瓊	瓜	瓢	瓦	瓶	瓷	甌	甍	甓	甕	甘	甚	生	產
40	用	甫	田	由	甲	男	界	畏	留	畜	畢	略	番	畫	畱	當	畺	疊	疋	疏
60	疔	疚	疵	疫	疲	疹	疽	疾	病	症	痊	痔	痕	痘	痛	痢	痰	痺	痹	瘀
80	瘁	瘋	瘟	瘢	瘦	瘴	療	癆	癐	癡	癰	癲	癸	登	發					

Row 64		01	02	03	04	05	06	07	08	09	10	11	12	13	14	15	16	17	18	19
00		白	百	的	皆	皇	皋	皐	皮	皿	盃	盆	盈	益	盎	盒	盔	盜	盛	盞
20	盡	監	盤	盧	目	盲	相	盾	省	眇	眉	看	眛	真	眠	眩	眪	眭	眷	眼
40	眾	睒	督	睦	睍	睹	瞋	瞑	瞞	瞭	瞳	瞻	瞼	矇	矗	矛	矜	矢	矣	知
60	矧	矩	短	矯	石	研	砧	砭	砲	破	硫	硬	硯	碁	碎	碞	碧	碩	確	磊
80	磋	磨	磬	磷	磺	礌	礎	礙	礦	礬	示	礼	社	祚	祝					

Row 65		01	02	03	04	05	06	07	08	09	10	11	12	13	14	15	16	17	18	19
00		神	祠	祭	祿	稟	禁	禍	福	禦	禫	禮	禱	禹	离	禽	禿	秀	私	秉
20	秋	科	租	秤	秧	秩	称	移	稀	程	税	稔	種	稱	稽	穊	積	穎	穢	穩
40	穫	穴	究	穹	空	穿	突	窈	窒	窕	窗	窘	窞	窮	竅	立	站	竟	章	童
60	竭	端	竹	竿	笀	笈	笙	笛	笠	笣	笤	符	笪	第	笱	笵	筆	等	筋	筏
80	筑	筒	笄	答	策	筤	筩	筭	筮	筥	箇	箏	箕	算	管					

Row 66		01	02	03	04	05	06	07	08	09	10	11	12	13	14	15	16	17	18	19
00		箤	箭	箱	箸	節	篆	築	篘	篙	篝	簒	篤	簗	篩	篷	簡	簩	簪	簫
20	簬	簾	籃	籤	籠	籺	粉	粒	粗	粹	精	糊	糖	糝	糞	糧	系	紀	約	紅
40	紆	紇	紋	納	紐	純	紗	紙	級	紛	素	紡	索	紫	紬	累	細	紳	紹	終
60	組	絆	絏	結	絞	絡	給	絨	絬	統	絲	絶	絸	絺	綉	經	綠	綣	綱	網
80	綸	綽	綾	綿	緊	緘	緞	締	緡	緣	編	緯	練	縈	縊					

Row 67		01	02	03	04	05	06	07	08	09	10	11	12	13	14	15	16	17	18	19
00		縟	縣	縱	縷	總	績	繁	織	繚	繞	繩	繭	繰	繲	繳	繶	繸	繹	繼
20	繾	續	纏	缶	缸	缺	缽	缾	罄	罔	罪	置	罰	署	罵	罷	羅	羊	美	羝
40	羨	群	義	羹	羽	翁	習	翕	翠	翡	翥	翩	翼	老	考	耒	耕	耗	耞	耨
60	耳	耽	聖	聘	聚	聯	聰	聲	職	聽	肝	股	肢	肣	肥	肭	肯	肱	育	胄
80	胆	背	胎	胖	胗	胜	胝	胞	胤	胭	胱	胸	胼	能	脅					

Row 68		01	02	03	04	05	06	07	08	09	10	11	12	13	14	15	16	17	18	19
00		脫	脹	脾	腋	腎	腐	腑	腔	腕	腥	腦	腫	腰	腹	腿	膁	膏	膠	膨
20	膽	臘	臟	臣	臧	自	臭	至	致	臼	舂	舅	與	興	舉	舌	舍	舒	舖	舘
40	舜	舞	航	般	船	艋	艟	艮	良	艱	色	艷	艸	艾	艽	芍	芎	芒	芙	芝
60	芟	芮	花	芷	芹	芻	芼	芾	芿	苑	苓	苔	苗	茎	若	苦	苫	英	苳	苾
80	茀	茁	茌	茙	茫	茶	茹	茺	茼	荄	荇	草	莜	荎	荒					

Row 69		01	02	03	04	05	06	07	08	09	10	11	12	13	14	15	16	17	18	19
00		荔	荸	茶	莆	莊	莓	莖	茜	莪	莫	莯	菊	菟	菩	菫	華	菱	菴	菶
20	萊	萌	萍	萏	萬	萻	落	葉	著	董	葩	葫	葬	葯	葵	葸	蒂	蒙	蒜	蒲
40	蒸	蓉	蓋	蓬	蓮	蓺	蔑	蔓	蔗	蔘	蕁	蔄	蕉	蕊	蔬	蕙	蕞	蕩	蕷	薆
60	薈	薑	薷	藉	藍	藕	藝	藞	藤	藥	藶	蘇	蘋	蘞	蘺	虎	虐	虔	處	虛
80	號	虧	虫	虬	虯	虷	蚕	蚜	蚤	蚨	蚩	蚵	蛀	蛇	蛒					

Row 70		01	02	03	04	05	06	07	08	09	10	11	12	13	14	15	16	17	18	19
00		蛛	蛟	蛮	蜀	蜂	蜅	蜇	蜍	蜚	蜜	蜦	蝎	蝩	蝳	蝴	蝶	螉	螢	螬
20	螻	蟄	蟒	蟯	蟲	蟳	蠅	蠐	蠟	蠡	蠢	蠶	蠻	血	行	術	衛	衣	表	衫
40	衰	衲	衾	袄	袈	袋	袍	袖	袙	袞	裁	裊	裒	裕	裘	裙	補	裝	裱	裴
60	裸	製	褓	褲	褶	襆	襌	襲	襵	西	要	見	規	視	親	覺	覽	觀	角	解
80	觸	言	訂	訃	計	討	訓	託	記	訛	訟	訥	訪	設	許					

Row 71		01	02	03	04	05	06	07	08	09	10	11	12	13	14	15	16	17	18	19
00		訴	診	註	証	詐	詔	評	詛	詞	詠	試	詩	詰	話	詳	誅	誇	誌	認
20	誓	誘	語	誠	誣	誦	誨	説	課	調	諂	談	請	諒	論	諛	諜	諧	諫	諭
40	諱	諳	諶	諷	諸	諺	諾	謀	謁	謎	謔	謗	謙	講	謝	謠	謨	謫	謹	證
60	譎	譜	警	譬	譯	議	譴	護	譽	讀	變	讎	讒	讓	讚	谷	谿	豆	豉	豐
80	豕	象	豪	豬	豸	豹	豺	貅	貓	貝	貞	負	財	貢	貧					

Row 72		01	02	03	04	05	06	07	08	09	10	11	12	13	14	15	16	17	18	19
00		貨	貪	貫	責	貯	貰	貳	貴	貶	買	費	賀	賂	賊	賓	賞	賢	賣	賤
20	賥	賦	質	賭	賵	贈	贍	贓	贖	赤	赦	赧	赫	走	赴	起	趁	超	越	趣
40	趨	足	趾	跌	距	跟	跡	跪	跬	路	跳	踏	踔	踖	踘	踪	蹄	[illegible]	蹇	蹈
60	蹉	蹜	蹟	躁	躇	躊	躍	躐	躘	身	躬	躹	軀	車	軌	軍	軏	軒	軟	軸
80	軿	載	輕	輝	輞	輩	輪	輸	轄	轉	轎	轟	辛	辭	辟					

Row 73		01	02	03	04	05	06	07	08	09	10	11	12	13	14	15	16	17	18	19
00		辣	辨	辱	農	迂	迄	过	迎	近	返	远	迡	迢	迫	迭	述	迴	迷	迹
20	追	迾	退	送	逃	逆	逋	逎	透	逐	途	通	逞	速	造	逢	連	逭	週	進
40	逴	逸	逼	逾	遁	遂	遇	遊	運	過	遏	道	達	違	遙	遞	遠	遣	遨	適
60	遭	遯	遲	遴	遵	遶	遷	選	遺	避	邁	還	邅	邊	邏	邑	卬	那	邦	邪
80	郟	郎	郡	部	郭	都	鄉	鄙	鄧	鄭	鄰	酉	酌	配	酖					

Row 74		01	02	03	04	05	06	07	08	09	10	11	12	13	14	15	16	17	18	19
00		酪	酬	酲	酷	醒	醜	醫	醬	釋	里	重	野	金	釪	釘	針	釧	釭	釵
20	鈇	鈍	鈐	鈸	鉊	鉋	鉑	鉗	鉛	鉞	鉤	鉦	鉻	銀	銃	銅	銑	銷	鋟	鍋
40	鋪	鋭	鋯	鋸	鋼	錁	錆	錐	錚	錠	錢	錦	錫	錯	鍊	鍮	鍺	鍼	鍾	鎖
60	鎗	鎮	鎰	鏌	鏡	鏢	鐘	鐙	鐮	鐲	鐵	鐸	鑊	鑠	鑨	鑿	長	門	閉	開
80	閍	閏	閑	間	閣	閧	閨	閱	閾	闌	闖	關	闡	阮	防					

Row 75		01	02	03	04	05	06	07	08	09	10	11	12	13	14	15	16	17	18	19
00		阻	陂	附	陋	降	限	陛	陞	院	陣	除	陰	陲	陳	陵	陷	陸	陽	隄
20	隆	隊	階	隔	隘	隙	障	隨	險	隰	隱	隴	隻	雀	雄	雅	集	雉	雋	雍
40	雖	雙	雜	離	難	雲	雩	零	雷	霆	需	霍	霏	霑	霓	霖	霜	霧	露	霸
60	靀	靂	靈	青	非	靡	鞅	鞋	鞍	鞏	鞠	韁	音	韵	韶	韻	響	頂	頃	項
80	順	須	頌	預	頑	頓	頗	領	頡	頭	頴	頹	額	顏	願					

Row 76		01	02	03	04	05	06	07	08	09	10	11	12	13	14	15	16	17	18	19
00		顛	類	顧	顯	風	颯	飄	飛	飢	飭	飲	餅	養	餒	餘	館	餲	饌	饑
20	饒	饞	首	香	馥	馨	馬	馭	馴	駁	駐	駒	駕	駙	駝	駢	駭	駸	駿	騅
40	騎	騷	驅	驕	驗	驚	驛	驟	驢	骨	骸	骾	髓	體	高	髦	髯	鬢	鬚	鬠
60	門	閗	閙	閲	鬪	鬭	鬼	魁	魂	魄	魔	魚	魯	鮮	鮹	鯢	鯨	鳥	鳩	鳳
80	鳶	鴛	鴦	鴻	鵝	鵡	鵬	鵲	鶯	鶴	鶵	鷄	鷺	鷗	鷹					

Row 77		01	02	03	04	05	06	07	08	09	10	11	12	13	14	15	16	17	18	19
00		鸞	鹿	麂	麑	麒	麗	麝	麟	麥	麵	麻	麼	黃	黎	黑	默	點	鼎	齊
20	齒	龍																		
40																				
60																				
80																				

P

Code Table Indexes

This appendix includes reading, radical, and stroke-count indexes that may help you to locate Chinese characters in various appendixes throughout this book, specifically Appendixes E through H, and J through M. The information provided in this appendix is similar to what you could infer from the manuals for the various national character set standards, but perhaps in a somewhat more convenient (or available) format.

GB 2312-80 Level 1 Reading Index

The following table is a reading index for the 3,755 hanzi in GB 2312-80 Level 1 hanzi (also applies to GB/T 12345-90 Level 1 hanzi). The "Reading" column corresponds to the first character in a Pinyin reading. A Row-Cell range is provided, which can be subsequently used to locate hanzi in Appendixes E, *GB 2312-80 Table*, and F, *GB/T 12345-90 Table*.

Reading	Range	Reading	Range	Reading	Range
A	1601–1636	J	2787–3105	R	4027–4085
B	1637–1832	K	3106–3211	S	4086–4389
C	1833–2077	L	3212–3471	T	4390–4557
D	2078–2273	M	3472–3534	W	4558–4683
E	2274–2301	N	3635–3721	X	4684–4924
F	2302–2432	O	3722–3729	Y	4925–5248
G	2433–2593	P	3730–3857	Z	5249–5589
H	2594–2786	Q	3858–4026		

GB 2312-80 Level 2 Radical Index

The following is a radical index for the 3,008 GB 2312-80 Level 2 hanzi, arranged according to a reduced set of 186 radicals (this index also applies to GB/T 12345-90 Level 2 hanzi). The GB 2312-80 Row-Cell codes for the radicals themselves are also provided under the "Radical" column. Note that some radicals do not have a corresponding range—hanzi categorized under such radicals are in GB 2312-80 Level 1 hanzi.

Number	Radical		GB 2312-80
1	50-27	一	5601–5612
2	56-13	丨	5613–5614
3	56-15	丿	5615–5627
4	56-28	丶	5628
5	50-50	乙	5629–5632
6	22-94	二	5633
7	42-14	十	5634–5637
8	19-07	厂	5638–5645
9	56-46	匚	5646–5651
10	18-23	卜	5652–5653
11	56-54	刂	5654–5670
12	56-71	冂	5671–5672
13	56-73	亻	5673–5757
14	40-43	人	5758–5765
15	16-43	八	5766–5771
16	57-72	勹	5772–5775
17	28-24	几	5776–5777
18	22-89	儿	5778
19	57-79	亠	5779–5790
20	57-91	冫	5791–5801
21	58-02	冖	5802–5804
22	58-05	讠	5805–5863
23	58-64	卩	5864–5865
24	58-66	阝	5866–5926
25	21-22	刀	5927–5928
26	33-06	力	5929–5936
27	51-54	又	5937–5939
28	59-40	廴	5940
29	59-41	凵	5941–5943
30	59-44	厶	5944–5946
31	25-04	工	5947
32	45-33	土	5948–6015
33	42-31	士	6016–6018
34	60-19	艹	6019–6234
35	62-35	廾	6235–6236
36	20-83	大	6237–6243
37	62-44	尢	6244–6247
38	62-48	扌	6248–6313
39	20-71	寸	
40	63-14	弋	6314–6317
41	31-58	口	6318–6476
42	64-77	囗	6477–6487
43	29-77	巾	6488–6506
44	41-29	山	6507–6559
45	65-60	彳	6560–6573
46	65-74	彡	6574
47	65-75	犭	6575–6621
48	47-06	夕	6622–6625
49	66-26	夂	6626
50	66-27	饣	6627–6646
51	25-67	广	6647–6663
52	66-64	忄	6664–6736
53	35-37	门	6737–6759
54	67-60	丬	6760–6762
55	67-63	氵	6763–6917
56	69-18	宀	6918–6932
57	69-33	辶	6933–6969
58	69-70	彐	6970–6973

Number	Radical		GB 2312-80
59	42-12	尸	6974–6981
60	25-13	弓	6982–6987
61	28-26	己	
62	69-88	屮	6988
63	37-14	女	6989–7055
64	48-01	小	7056–7057
65	55-51	子	7058–7063
66	34-77	马	7064–7088
67	70-89	纟	7089–7158
68	71-59	幺	7159–7160
69	71-61	巛	7161–7163
70	45-85	王	7164–7223
71	46-04	韦	7224–7226
72	36-30	木	7227–7363
73	40-14	犬	7364–7365
74	20-85	歹	7366–7376
75	19-21	车	7377–7406
76	24-74	戈	7407–7416
77	17-40	比	
78	45-63	瓦	7417–7422
79	54-25	止	
80	74-23	攴	7423
81	40-53	日	7424–7457
82	17-20	贝	7458–7471
83	28-91	见	7472–7479
84	37-03	牛	7480–7491
85	42-54	手	7492–7502
86	35-11	毛	7503–7512
87	38-88	气	7513–7521
88	75-22	攵	7522–7524
89	38-12	片	7525–7527
90	29-79	斤	
91	55-06	爪	7528–7529
92	52-34	月	7530–7602
93	39-23	欠	7603–7608
94	23-71	风	7609–7614
95	76-15	殳	7615–7618
96	46-36	文	7619–7621
97	23-29	方	7622–7629
98	22-23	斗	
99	27-80	火	7630–7664
100	24-24	父	
101	76-65	灬	7665–7668
102	27-07	户	7669–7673
103	76-74	礻	7674–7692
104	48-36	心	7693–7716
105	77-17	聿	7717–7718
106	43-14	水	7719–7721
107	46-67	毋	
108	42-30	示	
109	42-15	石	7722–7771
110	33-90	龙	7772
111	50-21	业	7773–7775
112	36-31	目	7776–7813
113	44-79	田	7814–7822
114	43-36	四	7823–7832
115	35-83	皿	7833–7835
116	78-36	钅	7836–7981
117	42-24	矢	7982–7984
118	26-44	禾	7985–8006
119	16-55	白	8007–8011
120	25-47	瓜	8012–8013
121	51-35	用	8014
122	36-81	鸟	8015–8057
123	80-58	疒	8058–8119
124	33-02	立	8120–8121
125	49-08	穴	8122–8133
126	81-34	衤	8134–8165
127	81-66	疋	8166–8167
128	38-04	皮	8168–8169
129	35-12	矛	8170
130	81-71	耒	8171–8182
131	32-47	老	8183
132	22-90	耳	8184–8190

Number	Radical	GB 2312-80
133	19-28 臣	
134	46-87 西	8191
135	50-19 页	8192–8213
136	82-14 虍	8214–8215
137	19-70 虫	8216–8329
138	83-30 缶	8330–8333
139	41-64 舌	8334
140	54-81 竹	8335–8406
141	30-42 臼	8407–8410
142	55-52 自	8411
143	49-10 血	8412
144	54-59 舟	8413–8431
145	50-34 衣	8432–8437
146	49-82 羊	8438–8443
147	35-55 米	8444–8461
148	84-62 艮	8462–8463
149	51-80 羽	8464–8472
150	84-73 糸	8473–8478
151	34-83 麦	8479–8480
152	55-63 走	8481–8485
153	19-64 赤	8486–8487
154	22-25 豆	8488–8489
155	51-47 酉	8490–8524
156	19-29 辰	
157	85-25 豕	8525
158	34-17 卤	8526
159	32-79 里	
160	55-67 足	8527–8583
161	41-77 身	
162	18-41 采	
163	85-84 豸	8584–8589
164	29-39 角	8590–8603
165	49-52 言	8604–8605
166	48-33 辛	
167	25-40 谷	
168	39-64 青	8606
169	38-68 其	
170	51-74 雨	8607–8618
171	19-61 齿	8619–8627
172	86-28 黾	8628–8630
173	86-31 隹	8631–8637
174	29-80 金	8638–8646
175	51-67 鱼	8647–8715
176	24-79 革	8716–8725
177	25-39 骨	8726–8739
178	25-77 鬼	8740–8746
179	42-19 食	8747–8751
180	50-84 音	
181	87-52 髟	8752–8764
182	34-73 麻	8765–8767
183	34-25 鹿	8768–8775
184	26-58 黑	8776–8786
185	42-83 鼠	8787–8791
186	17-39 鼻	8792–8794

Big Five and CNS 11643-1992 Stroke Index

The following table is a stroke count index for the hanzi in the two levels of Big Five and the seven planes of CNS 11643-1992. A Row-Cell range is provided for each stroke count (hexadecimal for Big Five), which can be subsequently used to locate hanzi in Appendix G, *CNS 11643-1992 Table*, and Appendix H, *Big Five Table*.

Strokes	B5 L1	B5 L2	CNS P1	CNS P2	CNS P3	CNS P4	CNS P5	CNS P6	CNS P7
1	A440–A441		3601–3602		0101–0104	0101–0105	0101–0104	0101	
2	A442–A453	C940–C944	3603–3620	0101–0105	0105–0111	0106–0112	0105–0110	0102–0112	

Strokes	B5 L1	B5 L2	CNS P1	CNS P2	CNS P3	CNS P4	CNS P5	CNS P6	CNS P7
3	A454–A47E	C945–C94C	3621–3663	0106–0112	0112–0135	0113–0124	0111–0118	0113–0132	
4	A4A1–A4FD	C94D–C962	3664–3762	0113–0134	0136–0174	0125–0152	0119–0144	0133–0209	
5	A4FE–A5DF	C963–C9AA	3763–3901	0135–0173	0175–0264	0153–0203	0145–0203	0210–0329	
6	A5E0–A6E9	C9AB–CA59	3902–4074	0174–0289	0265–0430	0204–0320	0204–0314	0330–0561	
7	A6EA–A8C2	CA5A–CBB0	4075–4367	0290–0516	0431–0731	0321–0514	0315–0494	0562–0921	
8	A8C3–AB44	CBB1–CDDC	4368–4770	0517–0892	0732–1101	0515–0820	0501–0789	0922–1441	
9	AB45–ADBB	CDDD–D0C7	4771–5192	0893–1372	1102–1534	0821–1161	0790–1170	1442–2103	
10	ADBC–B0AD	D0C8–D44A	5193–5680	1373–1945	1535–2026	1162–1635	1171–1681	2104–2890	
11	B0AE–B3C2	D44B–D850	5681–6208	1946–2620	2027–2576	1636–2213	1682–2244	2891–3830	
12	B3C3–B6C2	D851–DCB0	6209–6709	2621–3353	2577–3218	2214–2807	2245–2952	3831–4847	
13	B6C3–B9AB	DCB1–E0EF	6710–7181	3354–4085	3219–3774	2808–3412	2953–3652	4848–5865	
14	B9AC–BBF4	E0F0–E4E5	7182–7593	4086–4745	3775–4303	3413–4088	3653–4380	5866–6890	
15	BBF5–BEA6	E4E6–E8F3	7594–8015	4746–5430	4304–4815	4089–4755	4381–5149		0101–1226
16	BEA7–C074	E8F4–ECB8	8016–8331	5431–6036	4816–5230	4756–5368	5150–5878		1227–2282
17	C075–C24E	ECB9–EFB6	8332–8626	6037–6534	5231–5549	5369–5870	5879–6514		2283–3084
18	C24F–C35E	EFB7–F1EA	8627–8810	6535–6922	5550–5812	5871–6340	6515–7141		3085–3806
19	C35F–C454	F1EB–F3FC	8811–8964	6923–7273	5813–6016	6341–6713	7142–7574		3807–4525
20	C455–C4D6	F3FD–F5BF	8965–9065	7274–7545	6017–6204	6714–7012	7575–7971		4526–5083
21	C4D7–C56A	F5C0–F6D5	9066–9154	7546–7735	6205–6331	7013–7267	7972–8316		5084–5543
22	C56B–C5C7	F6D6–F7CF	9155–9219	7736–7892	6332–6411	7268–7431	8317–8565		5544–5936
23	C5C8–C5F0	F7D0–F8A4	9220–9260	7893–8018	6412–6478	7432–7568	8566–8750		5937–6247
24	C5F1–C654	F8A5–F8ED	9261–9301	8019–8091	6479–6527	7569–7674	8751–8902		6248–6472
25	C655–C664	F8EE–F96A	9302–9317	8092–8157	6528–6565	7675–7749	8903–9006		6473–6611
26	C665–C66B	F96B–F9A1	9318–9324	8158–8179	6566–6587	7750–7780	9007–9068		6612–6742
27	C66C–C675	F9A2–F9B9	9325–9334	8180–8209	6588–6612	7781–7819	9069–9127		6743–6834
28	C676–C678	F9BA–F9C5	9335–9337	8210–8220	6613–6619	7820–7839	9128–9162		6835–6918
29	C679–C67C	F9C7–F9CB	9338–9341	8221–8225	6620–6624	7840–7844	9163–9190		6919–6957
30	C67D	F9CC–F9CF	9342	8226–8229	6625–6627	7845–7851	9191–9210		6958–6983
31		F9D0		8230	6628–6631		9211–9219		6984–7005
32	C67E	F9D1	9343	8231	6632	7852–7853	9220–9227		7006–7018
33		F9C6–F9D2		8232–8233	6633–6634	7854	9228–9234		7019–7026
34						7855–7857	9235–9237		7027–7029
35		F9D3		8234	6635	7858	9238		7030–7033
36		F9D4		8235	6636		9239–9240		7034–7040
37							9241–9242		7041–7044
38							9243–9244		7045–7046
39					6637				7047–7048

Strokes	B5 L1	B5 L2	CNS P1	CNS P2	CNS P3	CNS P4	CNS P5	CNS P6	CNS P7
40							9245–9246		7049
41									7050
43							9247		7051
44						7859			7052–7053
48		F9D5		8236		7860	9248		
52					6638				
64							9249		

JIS X 0208:1997 Level 1 Reading Index

The following table is a reading index for the 2,965 JIS X 0208:1997 Level 1 kanji. A Row-Cell range is provided for each basic sound of the 50 Sounds Table, which can be subsequently used to locate kanji in Appendix J, *JIS X 0208:1997 Table*. Each reading is represented in hiragana and transliterated.

Reading		Range	Reading		Range	Reading		Range
あ	A	1601–1641	た	TA	3430–3544	ま	MA	4364–4402
い	I	1642–1705	ち	CHI	3545–3636	み	MI	4403–4418
う	U	1706–1732	つ	TSU	3637–3665	む	MU	4419–4428
え	E	1733–1786	て	TE	3666–3737	め	ME	4429–4445
お	O	1787–1827	と	TO	3738–3863	も	MO	4446–4472
か	KA	1828–2074	な	NA	3864–3882	や	YA	4473–4490
き	KI	2075–2268	に	NI	3883–3907	ゆ	YU	4491–4528
く	KU	2269–2320	ぬ	NU	3908	よ	YO	4529–4568
け	KE	2321–2434	ね	NE	3909–3920	ら	RA	4569–4587
こ	KO	2435–2618	の	NO	3921–3934	り	RI	4588–4659
さ	SA	2619–2736	は	HA	3935–4058	る	RU	4660–4664
し	SHI	2737–3157	ひ	HI	4059–4151	れ	RE	4665–4703
す	SU	3158–3203	ふ	FU	4152–4225	ろ	RO	4704–4732
せ	SE	3204–3324	へ	HE	4226–4260	わ	WA	4733–4751
そ	SO	3325–3429	ほ	HO	4261–4363			

JIS Radical Index

The following table is a radical index for the 3,384 JIS X 0208:1997 Level 2 kanji and the 5,801 JIS X 0212-1990 kanji. For each of the 214 radicals, their number, form (with JIS X 0208:1997 or JIS X 0212-1990 Row-Cell code—JIS X 0212-1990 Row-Cell codes are shaded for easy identification), name (in Japanese and transliterated—the Japanese names are derived from Jack Halpern's *New Japanese-English*

Character Dictionary, pp 1772–1780), and Row-Cell ranges are provided. Note that some of these radicals do not have a corresponding Row-Cell range in a particular character set standard—JIS X 0208:1997 Level 1 typically includes such kanji.

Number	Radical		Name	JIS X 0208:1997	JIS X 0212-1990
			1 Stroke		
1	16-76	一	一 *ichi*	4801–4803	1601–1608
2	16-09	丨	棒 *bō*	4804–4805	1609–1614
3	48-06	丶	点 *ten*	4806–4807	
4	48-08	丿	ノ *no*	4808–4811	1615–1619
5	18-21	乙	乙 *otsu*	4812	1620–1628
6	48-13	亅	撥棒 *hanebō*	4813–4816	
			2 Strokes		
7	38-83	二	二 *ni*	4817–4820	1629–1632
8	48-21	亠	鍋蓋 *nabebuta*	4821–4825	1633–1634
9	31-45	人	人 *hito*	4826–4924	1635–1868
10	49-25	儿	人繞 *ninnyō*, 人足 *hitoashi*	4925–4931	1869–1877
11	38-94	入	入 *iru*	4932–4933	1878
12	40-12	八	八 *hachi*, 八頭 *hachigashira*	4934–4935	1879
13	49-36	冂	冂構 *keigamae*	4936–4943	1880–1883
14	49-44	冖	ワ冠 *wakanmuri*	4944–4949	1884–1887
15	49-50	冫	二水 *nisui*	4950–4959	1888–1908
16	49-60	几	机, 几 *tsukue*	4960–4964	1909–1914
17	49-65	凵	凵繞 *kannyō*, 受け箱 *ukebako*	4965–4966	1915
18	37-65	刀	刀 *katana*	4967–5001	1916–1955
19	46-47	力	力 *chikara*	5002–5016	1956–1990
20	50-17	勹	包構 *tsutsumigamae*	5017–5023	1991–2003
21	50-24	匕	匕のヒ *sajinohi*	5024	2004
22	50-25	匚	匚構 *hakogamae*	5025–5029	2005–2018
23	50-30	匸	隠構, 匸構 *kakushigamae*	5030–5031	2019–2021
24	29-29	十	十 *jū*	5032–5037	2022–2026
25	43-46	卜	トのト *bokunoto*	5038	2027–2029
26	50-39	卩	節旁 *fushizukuri*	5039–5043	2030–2034
27	50-44	厂	雁垂 *gandare*	5044–5050	2035–2050
28	50-51	厶	ム *mu*	5051–5053	2051–2056
29	43-84	又	又 *mata*	5054–5057	2057–2064
			3 Strokes		
30	24-93	口	口 *kuchi*	5058–5187	2065–2281
31	51-88	囗	国構 *kunigamae*	5188–5208	2282–2312

Number	Radical		Name	JIS X 0208:1997	JIS X 0212-1990
32	37-58	土	土 *tsuchi*	5209–5266	2313–2461
33	27-46	士	士 *samurai*	5267–5272	2462
34	52-73	夂	冬頭 *fuyugashira*	5273	2463–2464
35	52-74	夊	夊繞 *suinyō*	5274–5275	2465–2470
36	45-28	夕	夕 *yūbe*	5276–5278	2471–2474
37	34-71	大	大 *ōkii, dai*	5279–5294	2475–2502
38	29-87	女	女 *onna*	5301–5350	2503–2628
39	27-50	子	子 *ko*	5351–5362	2629–2638
40	53-63	宀	ウ冠 *ukanmuri*	5363–5380	2639–2671
41	32-03	寸	寸 *sun*	5381–5384	2672–2673
42	30-14	小	小 *chiisai*	5385–5386	2674–2676
43	53-87	尢	曲足 *mageashi*	5387–5388	2677–2686
44	53-89	尸	尸 *shikabane*	5389–5404	2687–2701
45	54-05	屮	屮 *tetsu*	5405	2702
46	27-19	山	山 *yama*	5406–5462	2703–2792
47	54-63	巛	曲がり川 *magarigawa*	5463	2793–2794
48	25-09	工	工 *takumi*	5464	2801
49	24-42	己	己 *onore*	5465–5466	2802–2803
50	22-50	巾	巾 *haba*	5467–5483	2804–2833
51	20-19	干	干 *hosu*	5484–5485	
52	54-86	幺	糸頭 *itogashira*	5486–5487	
53	54-88	广	麻垂 *madare*	5488–5513	2834–2859
54	55-14	廴	延繞 *ennyō*	5514–5515	
55	55-16	廾	廿脚 *nijūashi*	5516–5520	2860–2863
56	55-21	弋	式構 *shikigamae*	5521–5522	2864
57	21-61	弓	弓 *yumi*	5523–5531	2865–2886
58	28-87	彐	彐頭 *keigashira*	5532–5535	2887–2891
59	55-36	彡	彡旁 *sanzukuri*	5536–5537	2892–2902
60	55-38	彳	行人偏 *gyōninben*	5538–5553	2903–2923
4 Strokes					
61	31-20	心	心 *kokoro*	5554–5688	2924–3107
62	56-89	戈	戈 *kanohoko*	5689–5707	3108–3116
63	24-45	戸	扉の戸 *tobiranoto*	5708	3117–3122
64	28-74	手	手 *te*	5709–5828	3123–3337
65	27-57	支	支繞 *shinyō*, 十又 *jūmata*		3338
66	58-29	攴	攴旁 *bokuzukuri*, 攴 *tomata*	5829–5846	3339–3355
67	42-24	文	文 *bun*, 文繞 *bunnyō*		3356–3358

Number	Radical		Name	JIS X 0208:1997	JIS X 0212-1990
68	37-45	斗	斗 *tomasu*	5847–5848	3359–3362
69	22-52	斤	斧 *ono*	5849–5850	3363–3367
70	42-93	方	方 *kata*	5851–5858	3368–3377
71	58-59	无	无繞 *munyō*	5859–5860	
72	38-92	日	日 *nichi*	5861–5908	3378–3476
73	59-09	曰	平日 *hirabi*	5909–5911	3477–3479
74	23-78	月	月 *tsuki*	5912–5917	3480–3485
75	44-58	木	木 *ki*	5918–6122	3486–3771
76	23-71	欠	欠伸 *akubi*	6123–6136	3772–3788
77	27-63	止	止 *tomeru*	6137	3789–3793
78	61-38	歹	歹偏 *gatsuhen*	6138–6152	3794–3815
79	61-53	殳	ル又 *rumata*, 殳旁 *hokozukiri*	6153–6156	3816–3822
80	61-57	毋	母 *haha, nakare*	6157–6158	3823
81	40-70	比	比 *kuraberu, hi*		3824–3825
82	44-51	毛	毛 *ke*	6159–6165	3826–3840
83	27-65	氏	氏 *uji*	6166	3841–3842
84	61-67	气	気構 *kigamae*	6167–6170	3843–3850
85	31-69	水	水 *mizu*	6171–6352	3851–4135
86	18-48	火	火 *hi*	6353–6406	4136–4239
87	36-62	爪	爪 *tsume*	6407–6410	4240–4242
88	41-67	父	父 *chichi*		4243–4244
89	64-11	爻	メメ *meme*	6411–6412	
90	64-13	爿	爿偏 *shōhen*	6413–6415	4245–4248
91	42-50	片	片 *kata*	6416–6417	4249–4254
92	18-71	牙	牙 *kiba*		4255
93	21-77	牛	牛 *ushi*	6418–6426	4256–4276
94	24-04	犬	犬 *inu*	6427–6460	4277–4347
			5 Strokes		
95	24-28	玄	玄 *gen*		4348–4349
96	22-44	玉	玉 *tama*	6461–6494	4350–4481
97	17-27	瓜	瓜 *uri*	6501–6502	4482–4484
98	20-04	瓦	瓦 *kawara*	6503–6518	4485–4503
99	20-37	甘	甘 *amai*	6519	
100	32-24	生	生 *umareru*	6520	4504–4507
101	45-49	用	用 *mochiiru*	6521	4508–4510
102	37-36	田	田 *ta*	6522–6542	4511–4536
103	41-05	疋	疋 *hiki*		4537

Number	Radical		Name	JIS X 0208:1997	JIS X 0212-1990
104	45-38	疒	病垂 *yamaidare*	6543–6601	4538–4620
105	66-02	癶	発頭 *hatsugashira*	6602–6604	
106	39-82	白	白 *shiro*	6605–6613	4621–4639
107	40-73	皮	毛皮 *kegawa*	6614–6618	4640
108	27-14	皿	皿 *sara*	6619–6628	4641–4652
109	44-60	目	目 *me*	6629–6665	4653–4733
110	44-23	矛	矛 *hoko*	6666	4734–4736
111	44-80	矢	矢 *ya*	6667–6668	4737–4742
112	32-48	石	石 *ishi*	6669–6710	4743–4842
113	28-08	示	示 *shimesu*	6711–6726	4843–4881
114	48-82	禸	禺脚 *gūnoashi*	6727–6728	4882–4883
115	18-51	禾	ノ木 *nogi*	6729–6753	4884–4946
116	23-74	穴	穴 *ana*	6754–6770	4947–4969
117	46-09	立	立 *tatsu*	6771–6782	4970–4979
			6 Strokes		
118	35-61	竹	竹 *take*	6783–6865	4980–5108
119	42-38	米	米 *kome*	6866–6892	5109–5142
120	27-69	糸	糸 *ito*	6893–6992	5143–5274
121	20-44	缶	缶 *hotogi*	6993–7005	5275–5283
122	70-06	网	網頭 *amigashira*	7006–7020	5284–5305
123	45-51	羊	羊 *hitsuji*	7021–7033	5306–5320
124	17-09	羽	羽 *hane*	7034–7044	5321–5339
125	47-23	老	老 *oi*	7045–7047	5340–5342
126	28-09	而	而して *shikashite*		5343–5346
127	70-48	耒	耒 *raisuki*	7048–7053	5347–5358
128	28-10	耳	耳 *mimi*	7054–7069	5359–5373
129	70-70	聿	筆旁 *fudezukuri*	7070–7073	5374–5375
130	38-89	肉	肉 *niku*	7074–7140	5376–5464
131	31-35	臣	臣 *shin*	7141	5465
132	28-11	自	自 *mizukara*		5466–5470
133	27-74	至	至 *itaru*	7142–7143	5471–5474
134	17-17	臼	臼 *usu*	7144–7149	5475–5478
135	32-69	舌	舌 *shita*	7150–7152	5479–5483
136	33-04	舛	升 *masu*		5484
137	29-14	舟	舟 *fune*	7153–7168	5485–5510
138	26-17	艮	艮 *kon, ushitora*	7169	
139	31-07	色	色 *iro*	7170	5511

Number	Radical		Name	JIS X 0208:1997	JIS X 0212-1990
140	71-71	艸	草 *kusa*	7171–7339	5512–5824
141	73-40	虍	虎冠 *torakanmuri*	7340–7344	5825–5837
142	35-78	虫	虫 *mushi*	7345–7439	5838–6002
143	23-76	血	血 *chi*	7440–7441	6003–6009
144	25-52	行	行 *gyō*	7442–7445	6010–6018
145	16-65	衣	衣 *koromo*	7446–7507	6019–6103
146	75-08	襾	西 *nishi*	7508–7511	6104
			7 Strokes		
147	24-11	見	見 *miru*	7512–7523	6105–6119
148	19-49	角	角 *tsuno*	7524–7529	6120–6134
149	24-32	言	言葉 *kotoba*	7530–7613	6135–6265
150	35-11	谷	谷 *tani*	7614–7616	6266–6270
151	38-06	豆	豆 *mame*	7617–7620	6271–6277
152	76-21	豕	豕 *inoko*	7621–7623	6278–6291
153	76-24	豸	貉 *mujina*	7624–7634	6292–6308
154	19-13	貝	貝 *kai*	7635–7662	6309–6337
155	32-54	赤	赤 *aka*	7663–7664	6338–6341
156	33-86	走	走 *hashiru*	7665–7668	6342–6357
157	34-13	足	足 *ashi*	7669–7726	6358–6445
158	31-40	身	身 *mi*	7727–7733	6446–6456
159	28-54	車	車 *kuruma*	7734–7766	6457–6512
160	31-41	辛	辛 *karai*	7767–7771	6513–6518
161	35-04	辰	辰の辰 *shinnotatsu*		
162	65-19	辵	之繞 *shinnyō, shinnyū*	7772–7822	6519–6576
163	45-24	邑	邑 *mura*	7823–7835	6577–6653
164	38-51	酉	日読みの酉 *sakenotori*	7836–7855	6654–6703
165	40-48	釆	ノ米 *nogome*	7856–7857	
166	46-04	里	里 *sato*	7858	
			8 Strokes		
167	22-66	金	金 *kane*	7859–7956	6704–6992
168	36-25	長	長 *nagai*		6993–7001
169	44-71	門	門 *mon*	7957–7983	7002–7035
170	41-76	阜	岐阜の阜 *gifunofu*	7984–8015	7036–7080
171	80-16	隶	隷旁 *reizukuri*	8016–8017	
172	80-18	隹	隹 *furutori*	8018–8026	7081–7089
173	17-11	雨	雨 *ame*	8027–8047	7090–7117
174	32-36	青	青 *ao*	8048	7118–7122
175	40-83	非	非 *arazu*	8049	

Number	Radical		Name	JIS X 0208:1997	JIS X 0212-1990
9 Strokes					
176	44-44	面	面 *men*	8050–8052	7123–7124
177	19-55	革	革 *kawa*	8053–8073	7125–7161
178	80-74	韋	鞣革 *nameshigawa*	8074–8075	7162–7176
179	80-76	韭	韭 *nira*	8076–8078	7177–7178
180	18-27	音	音 *oto*	8079–8081	7179–7182
181	42-39	頁	大貝 *ōgai*	8082–8103	7183–7225
182	41-87	風	風 *kaze*	8104–8110	7226–7239
183	40-84	飛	飛 *tobu*		
184	31-09	食	食 *shoku*	8111–8135	7240–7286
185	28-83	首	首 *kubi*	8136–8137	
186	25-65	香	匂い香 *nioikō*	8138	7287–7290
10 Strokes					
187	39-47	馬	馬 *uma*	8139–8175	7291–7353
188	25-92	骨	骨 *hone*	8176–8183	7354–7375
189	25-66	高	高 *takai*	8184	7376–7377
190	81-85	髟	髪冠 *kamikanmuri*	8185–8207	7378–7415
191	82-08	鬥	鬪構 *tōgamae*	8208–8213	7416–7418
192	82-14	鬯	鬯 *chō*	8214	
193	82-15	鬲	鬲 *kaku*	8215	7419–7424
194	21-20	鬼	鬼 *oni*	8216–8222	7425–7431
11 Strokes					
195	21-91	魚	魚 *uo*	8223–8273	7432–7556
196	36-27	鳥	鳥 *tori*	8274–8334	7557–7656
197	83-35	鹵	鹵 *ro*	8335–8337	7657–7659
198	28-15	鹿	鹿 *shika*	8338–8345	7660–7672
199	83-46	麥	麦 *baku*	8346–8350	7673–7680
200	43-67	麻	麻 *asa*	8351	
12 Strokes					
201	18-11	黄	黄色 *kiiro*	8352	7681–7683
202	21-48	黍	黍 *kibi*	8353–8355	
203	25-85	黒	黒 *kuro*	8356–8366	7684–7701
204	83-67	黹	黹 *futsu*	8367–8369	
13 Strokes					
205	83-70	黽	黽 *ben*	8370–8372	7702–7705
206	37-04	鼎	鼎 *kanae*		7706–7709
207	24-61	鼓	鼓 *tsuzumu*	8373–8374	7710–7716
208	33-45	鼠	鼠 *nezumi*	8375–8376	7717–7727

Number	Radical	Name	JIS X 0208:1997	JIS X 0212-1990
		14 Strokes		
209	41-01 鼻	鼻 *hana*	8377	7728–7736
210	83-78 齊	斉 *sei*	8378	
		15 Strokes		
211	83-79 齒	歯 *ha*	8379–8391	7737–7755
		16 Strokes		
212	46-22 龍	竜 *ryū*	8392	7756–7762
213	83-93 龜	亀 *kame*	8393	7763
		17 Strokes		
214	83-94 龠	龠 *yaku*	8394	7764–7767

KS Hanja Reading Index

The following table represents a reading index for the 4,888 hanja in KS X 1001:1992 (see Appendix L, *KS X 1001:1992 Table*), and the 2,856 hanja in KS X 1002:1991 (see Appendix M, *KS X 1002:1991 Hanja Table*), indexed by jamo (and transliterated according to ISO/TR 11941:1996 Method 2), and using Row-Cell codes. Note that some jamo do not have any corresponding hanja in one or both standards.

Reading		KS X 1001	KS X 1002
ㄱ	G	4201–4949	5501–6011
ㄲ	GG	4950	
ㄴ	N	4951–5092	6012–6066
ㄷ	D	5093–5289	6067–6182
ㄸ	DD		
ㄹ	R	5290–5603	6183–6383
ㅁ	M	5604–5845	6384–6516
ㅂ	B	5846–6230	6517–6740
ㅃ	BB		
ㅅ	S	6231–6809	6741–7001
ㅆ	SS	6810–6811	
아 (ㅏ)	A	6812–6876	7002–7051
애 (ㅐ)	AE	6877–6904	7052–7079
야 (ㅑ)	YA	6905–6955	7080–7105
얘 (ㅒ)	YAE		
어 (ㅓ)	EO	6956–6986	7106–7126
에 (ㅔ)	E	6987	7127–7128
여 (ㅕ)	YEO	6988–7148	7129–7177
예 (ㅖ)	YE	7149–7172	7178–7202
오 (ㅗ)	O	7173–7229	7203–7249
와 (ㅘ)	WA	7230–7261	7250–7269
왜 (ㅙ)	WAE	7262–7265	7270
외 (ㅚ)	OE	7266–7270	7271–7279
요 (ㅛ)	YO	7271–7344	7280–7313
우 (ㅜ)	U	7345–7409	7314–7340
워 (ㅝ)	WEO	7410–7439	7341–7356
웨 (ㅞ)	WE		
위 (ㅟ)	WI	7440–7464	7357–7370
유 (ㅠ)	YU	7465–7556	7371–7413
으 (ㅡ)	EU	7557–7577	7414–7435
의 (ㅢ)	YI	7578–7602	7436–7445
이 (ㅣ)	I	7603–7707	7446–7478
ㅈ	J	7708–8305	7479–7831
ㅉ	JJ		
ㅊ	C	8306–8664	7832–8109
ㅋ	K	8665	8110–8111

Reading		KS X 1001	KS X 1002
ㅌ	T	8666–8770	8112–8170
ㅍ	P	8771–8926	8171–8269

Reading		KS X 1001	KS X 1002
ㅎ	H	8927–9394	8270–8536

Q

Character Lists and Mapping Tables

This appendix provides various character lists and mapping tables that are useful to anyone who needs to know more details about some CJKV character sets, besides simply their descriptions in Chapter 3, *Character Set Standards*, and their code tables as provided in various appendixes throughout this book.

GB 2312-80 Versus GB/T 12345-90

As discussed in Chapter 3, GB/T 12345-90 is considered the traditional analog of GB 2312-80. This section provides the *exact* differences between these two standards.

The following are four simplified/traditional hanzi pairs whose code points were swapped between Levels 1 and 2 (GB 2312-80 forms shown below):

Level 1		Level 2	
后	26-83	後	65-65
征	53-87	徵	65-71
余	51-64	馀	66-37
么	35-20	麽	87-65

Note that one of the GB 2312-80 hanzi in Level 2 (馀 66-37), after being swapped with a hanzi in Level 1 (余 51-64), had its left-side radical unsimplified. This new hanzi 餘, now at position 51-64, is also included in the following long list.

The hanzi—2,118 in all—in the "GB/T" (GB/T 12345-90) column of the following table are traditional replacements for simplified hanzi in the "GB" (GB 2312-80) column, which span rows 16 through 87. Note how the code points are identical.

GB	GB/T	
皑	皚	16-08
蔼	藹	16-10
碍	礙	16-13
爱	愛	16-14
肮	骯	16-25
袄	襖	16-32
坝	壩	16-51
罢	罷	16-53
摆	擺	16-58
败	敗	16-60
颁	頒	16-68
办	辦	16-76
绊	絆	16-77
帮	幫	16-79
绑	綁	16-83
镑	鎊	16-87
谤	謗	16-89
饱	飽	17-05
宝	寶	17-06
报	報	17-08
鲍	鮑	17-11
辈	輩	17-18
贝	貝	17-20
钡	鋇	17-21
狈	狽	17-23
备	備	17-24
惫	憊	17-25
绷	綳	17-33
笔	筆	17-42
毕	畢	17-47
毙	斃	17-48
币	幣	17-50
闭	閉	17-53
边	邊	17-63
编	編	17-64
贬	貶	17-65
变	變	17-68
辩	辯	17-71
辫	辮	17-72
标	標	17-74
鳖	鱉	17-78

GB	GB/T	
瘪	癟	17-81
濒	瀕	17-84
滨	濱	17-85
宾	賓	17-86
摈	擯	17-87
饼	餅	17-93
拨	撥	18-06
钵	鉢	18-07
铂	鉑	18-12
驳	駁	18-21
补	補	18-25
财	財	18-38
参	參	18-46
蚕	蠶	18-47
残	殘	18-48
惭	慚	18-49
惨	慘	18-50
灿	燦	18-51
苍	蒼	18-52
舱	艙	18-53
仓	倉	18-54
沧	滄	18-55
厕	厠	18-62
侧	側	18-64
测	測	18-66
层	層	18-67
诧	詫	18-79
搀	攙	18-83
掺	摻	18-84
蝉	蟬	18-85
馋	饞	18-86
谗	讒	18-87
缠	纏	18-88
铲	鏟	18-89
产	産	18-90
阐	闡	18-91
颤	顫	18-92
场	場	19-01
尝	嘗	19-02
长	長	19-04
偿	償	19-05

GB	GB/T	
肠	腸	19-06
厂	廠	19-07
畅	暢	19-09
钞	鈔	19-14
车	車	19-21
彻	徹	19-25
尘	塵	19-30
陈	陳	19-34
衬	襯	19-36
称	稱	19-38
惩	懲	19-45
诚	誠	19-47
骋	騁	19-50
迟	遲	19-57
驰	馳	19-59
齿	齒	19-61
炽	熾	19-67
冲	衝	19-69
虫	蟲	19-70
宠	寵	19-72
畴	疇	19-75
踌	躊	19-76
筹	籌	19-79
绸	綢	19-81
丑	醜	19-83
锄	鋤	19-90
雏	雛	19-91
础	礎	20-01
储	儲	20-02
触	觸	20-05
处	處	20-06
传	傳	20-11
疮	瘡	20-15
闯	闖	20-19
创	創	20-20
锤	錘	20-24
纯	純	20-31
绰	綽	20-34
辞	辭	20-39
词	詞	20-42
赐	賜	20-45

GB	GB/T	
聪	聰	20-47
从	從	20-51
丛	叢	20-52
蹿	躥	20-58
窜	竄	20-60
错	錯	20-77
达	達	20-79
带	帶	20-88
贷	貸	20-91
担	擔	21-03
单	單	21-05
郸	鄲	21-06
掸	撣	21-07
胆	膽	21-08
惮	憚	21-12
诞	誕	21-14
弹	彈	21-15
当	當	21-17
挡	擋	21-18
党	黨	21-19
荡	蕩	21-20
档	檔	21-21
捣	搗	21-23
岛	島	21-26
祷	禱	21-27
导	導	21-28
灯	燈	21-38
邓	鄧	21-43
敌	敵	21-48
涤	滌	21-51
递	遞	21-61
缔	締	21-62
颠	顛	21-63
点	點	21-67
垫	墊	21-70
电	電	21-71
淀	澱	21-77
钓	釣	21-86
调	調	21-87
谍	諜	21-93
钉	釘	22-04
顶	頂	22-05
锭	錠	22-07
订	訂	22-09
东	東	22-11
动	動	22-15
栋	棟	22-16
冻	凍	22-19
斗	鬥	22-23
犊	犢	22-31
独	獨	22-32
读	讀	22-33
赌	賭	22-36
镀	鍍	22-38
锻	鍛	22-45
断	斷	22-47
缎	緞	22-48
队	隊	22-51
对	對	22-52
吨	噸	22-54
顿	頓	22-57
钝	鈍	22-59
夺	奪	22-65
堕	墮	22-73
鹅	鵝	22-76
额	額	22-78
讹	訛	22-79
恶	惡	22-81
饿	餓	22-86
儿	兒	22-89
尔	爾	22-91
饵	餌	22-92
贰	貳	23-01
发	發	23-02
罚	罰	23-03
阀	閥	23-07
矾	礬	23-15
钒	釩	23-16
烦	煩	23-19
范	範	23-22
贩	販	23-23
饭	飯	23-25
访	訪	23-35
纺	紡	23-36
飞	飛	23-41
诽	誹	23-44
废	廢	23-47
费	費	23-49
纷	紛	23-55
坟	墳	23-56
奋	奮	23-60
愤	憤	23-63
粪	糞	23-64
丰	豐	23-65
枫	楓	23-67
锋	鋒	23-70
风	風	23-71
疯	瘋	23-72
冯	馮	23-75
缝	縫	23-76
讽	諷	23-77
凤	鳳	23-79
肤	膚	23-84
辐	輻	23-88
抚	撫	24-07
辅	輔	24-08
赋	賦	24-19
复	復	24-20
负	負	24-26
讣	訃	24-28
妇	婦	24-30
缚	縛	24-31
该	該	24-35
钙	鈣	24-38
盖	蓋	24-39
干	幹	24-41
赶	趕	24-47
赣	贛	24-51
冈	岡	24-52
刚	剛	24-53
钢	鋼	24-54
纲	綱	24-57
岗	崗	24-58

GB	GB/T	
镐	鎬	24-68
搁	擱	24-73
鸽	鴿	24-75
阁	閣	24-83
铬	鉻	24-85
个	個	24-86
给	給	24-88
龚	龔	25-08
巩	鞏	25-14
贡	貢	25-17
钩	鈎	25-19
沟	溝	25-21
构	構	25-25
购	購	25-26
蛊	蠱	25-38
顾	顧	25-43
剐	剮	25-48
关	關	25-56
观	觀	25-59
馆	館	25-61
惯	慣	25-63
贯	貫	25-65
广	廣	25-67
规	規	25-70
归	歸	25-73
龟	龜	25-74
闺	閨	25-75
轨	軌	25-76
诡	詭	25-78
柜	櫃	25-81
贵	貴	25-83
刽	劊	25-84
辊	輥	25-85
锅	鍋	25-88
国	國	25-90
过	過	25-93
骇	駭	26-07
韩	韓	26-11
汉	漢	26-26
号	號	26-37
阂	閡	26-50

GB	GB/T	
鹤	鶴	26-55
贺	賀	26-56
轰	轟	26-68
鸿	鴻	26-72
红	紅	26-76
壶	壺	26-88
护	護	27-04
沪	滬	27-06
哗	嘩	27-09
华	華	27-10
画	畫	27-13
划	劃	27-14
话	話	27-16
怀	懷	27-19
坏	壞	27-21
欢	歡	27-22
环	環	27-23
还	還	27-25
缓	緩	27-26
谎	謊	27-49
挥	揮	27-51
辉	輝	27-52
贿	賄	27-63
秽	穢	27-64
会	會	27-65
烩	燴	27-66
汇	匯	27-67
讳	諱	27-68
诲	誨	27-69
绘	繪	27-70
荤	葷	27-71
浑	渾	27-75
获	獲	27-81
货	貨	27-85
祸	禍	27-86
击	擊	27-87
机	機	27-90
积	積	27-93
饥	饑	28-02
讥	譏	28-05
鸡	鷄	28-06

GB	GB/T	
绩	績	28-08
缉	緝	28-09
极	極	28-11
辑	輯	28-13
级	級	28-22
挤	擠	28-23
几	幾	28-24
蓟	薊	28-27
剂	劑	28-33
济	濟	28-35
计	計	28-38
记	記	28-39
际	際	28-42
继	繼	28-44
纪	紀	28-45
夹	夾	28-48
荚	莢	28-52
颊	頰	28-53
贾	賈	28-54
钾	鉀	28-56
价	價	28-59
驾	駕	28-61
歼	殲	28-63
监	監	28-64
坚	堅	28-65
笺	箋	28-67
间	間	28-68
艰	艱	28-72
缄	緘	28-74
茧	繭	28-75
检	檢	28-76
硷	鹼	28-79
拣	揀	28-80
捡	撿	28-81
简	簡	28-82
俭	儉	28-83
荐	薦	28-86
槛	檻	28-87
鉴	鑒	28-88
践	踐	28-89
贱	賤	28-90

GB	GB/T	
见	見	28-91
键	鍵	28-92
舰	艦	29-02
剑	劍	29-03
饯	餞	29-04
渐	漸	29-05
溅	濺	29-06
涧	澗	29-07
将	將	29-11
浆	漿	29-12
蒋	蔣	29-15
桨	槳	29-16
奖	獎	29-17
讲	講	29-18
酱	醬	29-20
胶	膠	29-26
浇	澆	29-29
骄	驕	29-30
娇	嬌	29-31
搅	攪	29-33
铰	鉸	29-34
矫	矯	29-35
侥	僥	29-36
饺	餃	29-40
缴	繳	29-41
绞	絞	29-42
轿	轎	29-46
较	較	29-47
阶	階	29-55
节	節	29-58
洁	潔	29-64
结	結	29-65
诫	誡	29-75
紧	緊	29-84
锦	錦	29-85
仅	僅	29-86
谨	謹	29-87
进	進	29-88
烬	燼	29-93
尽	盡	30-01
劲	勁	30-02
茎	莖	30-05
鲸	鯨	30-08
惊	驚	30-10
经	經	30-13
颈	頸	30-17
镜	鏡	30-21
径	徑	30-22
痉	痙	30-23
竞	競	30-26
纠	糾	30-32
旧	舊	30-41
驹	駒	30-52
举	舉	30-57
据	據	30-61
锯	鋸	30-66
惧	懼	30-69
剧	劇	30-71
鹃	鵑	30-73
绢	絹	30-78
觉	覺	30-85
诀	訣	30-87
绝	絶	30-88
钧	鈞	30-91
军	軍	30-92
骏	駿	31-05
开	開	31-10
凯	凱	31-13
颗	顆	31-37
壳	殼	31-39
课	課	31-46
垦	墾	31-49
恳	懇	31-50
抠	摳	31-57
库	庫	31-66
裤	褲	31-67
夸	誇	31-68
块	塊	31-73
侩	儈	31-75
宽	寬	31-77
矿	礦	31-83
旷	曠	31-85
亏	虧	31-87
岿	巋	31-89
窥	窺	31-90
馈	饋	32-01
溃	潰	32-03
扩	擴	32-09
阔	闊	32-11
蜡	蠟	32-15
腊	臘	32-16
莱	萊	32-19
来	來	32-20
赖	賴	32-21
蓝	藍	32-22
栏	欄	32-24
拦	攔	32-25
篮	籃	32-26
阑	闌	32-27
兰	蘭	32-28
澜	瀾	32-29
谰	讕	32-30
揽	攬	32-31
览	覽	32-32
懒	懶	32-33
缆	纜	32-34
烂	爛	32-35
滥	濫	32-36
捞	撈	32-44
劳	勞	32-45
涝	澇	32-52
乐	樂	32-54
镭	鐳	32-56
垒	壘	32-61
类	類	32-64
篱	籬	32-73
离	離	32-75
漓	灕	32-76
里	裏	32-79
鲤	鯉	32-80
礼	禮	32-81
丽	麗	32-86
厉	厲	32-87

GB	GB/T	
励	勵	32-88
砾	礫	32-89
历	歷	32-90
沥	瀝	33-04
隶	隸	33-05
俩	倆	33-09
联	聯	33-10
莲	蓮	33-11
连	連	33-12
镰	鐮	33-13
怜	憐	33-15
涟	漣	33-16
帘	簾	33-17
敛	斂	33-18
脸	臉	33-19
链	鏈	33-20
恋	戀	33-21
炼	煉	33-22
练	練	33-23
粮	糧	33-24
两	兩	33-29
辆	輛	33-30
谅	諒	33-34
疗	療	33-38
辽	遼	33-41
镣	鐐	33-45
猎	獵	33-52
临	臨	33-57
邻	鄰	33-58
鳞	鱗	33-59
赁	賃	33-62
龄	齡	33-68
铃	鈴	33-69
灵	靈	33-73
岭	嶺	33-75
领	領	33-76
馏	餾	33-83
刘	劉	33-85
龙	龍	33-90
聋	聾	33-91
咙	嚨	33-92

GB	GB/T	
笼	籠	33-93
垄	壟	34-02
拢	攏	34-03
陇	隴	34-04
楼	樓	34-05
娄	婁	34-06
搂	摟	34-07
篓	簍	34-08
芦	蘆	34-11
卢	盧	34-12
颅	顱	34-13
庐	廬	34-14
炉	爐	34-15
掳	擄	34-16
卤	滷	34-17
虏	虜	34-18
鲁	魯	34-19
赂	賂	34-24
录	錄	34-28
陆	陸	34-29
驴	驢	34-31
铝	鋁	34-33
屡	屢	34-37
缕	縷	34-38
虑	慮	34-39
滤	濾	34-43
绿	綠	34-44
峦	巒	34-45
挛	攣	34-46
孪	孿	34-47
滦	灤	34-48
乱	亂	34-50
抡	掄	34-53
轮	輪	34-54
伦	倫	34-55
仑	侖	34-56
沦	淪	34-57
纶	綸	34-58
论	論	34-59
萝	蘿	34-60
罗	羅	34-62

GB	GB/T	
逻	邏	34-63
锣	鑼	34-64
箩	籮	34-65
骡	騾	34-66
骆	駱	34-70
络	絡	34-71
妈	媽	34-72
玛	瑪	34-74
码	碼	34-75
蚂	螞	34-76
马	馬	34-77
骂	罵	34-78
吗	嗎	34-80
买	買	34-82
麦	麥	34-83
卖	賣	34-84
迈	邁	34-85
瞒	瞞	34-87
馒	饅	34-88
蛮	蠻	34-89
满	滿	34-90
谩	謾	35-01
锚	錨	35-10
铆	鉚	35-13
贸	貿	35-19
镁	鎂	35-30
门	門	35-37
闷	悶	35-38
们	們	35-39
锰	錳	35-44
梦	夢	35-46
谜	謎	35-53
弥	彌	35-54
觅	覓	35-57
绵	綿	35-64
缅	緬	35-69
庙	廟	35-77
灭	滅	35-80
悯	憫	35-85
闽	閩	35-86
鸣	鳴	35-89

GB	GB/T	
铭	銘	35-90
谬	謬	35-93
谋	謀	36-17
亩	畝	36-22
钠	鈉	36-38
纳	納	36-41
难	難	36-49
挠	撓	36-51
脑	腦	36-52
恼	惱	36-53
闹	鬧	36-54
馁	餒	36-57
拟	擬	36-66
腻	膩	36-69
撵	攆	36-76
酿	釀	36-80
鸟	鳥	36-81
聂	聶	36-84
啮	嚙	36-86
镊	鑷	36-87
镍	鎳	36-88
柠	檸	36-91
狞	獰	36-92
宁	寧	36-94
拧	擰	37-01
泞	濘	37-02
钮	鈕	37-05
纽	紐	37-06
脓	膿	37-07
浓	濃	37-08
农	農	37-09
疟	瘧	37-17
诺	諾	37-21
欧	歐	37-23
鸥	鷗	37-24
殴	毆	37-25
呕	嘔	37-27
沤	漚	37-29
盘	盤	37-44
庞	龐	37-51
赔	賠	37-66
喷	噴	37-71
鹏	鵬	37-84
骗	騙	38-13
飘	飄	38-14
频	頻	38-21
贫	貧	38-22
苹	蘋	38-27
凭	憑	38-30
评	評	38-32
泼	潑	38-35
颇	頗	38-36
扑	撲	38-43
铺	鋪	38-44
仆	僕	38-45
朴	樸	38-51
谱	譜	38-55
脐	臍	38-74
齐	齊	38-75
骑	騎	38-79
岂	豈	38-81
启	啓	38-84
气	氣	38-88
讫	訖	38-93
牵	牽	39-03
钎	釺	39-05
铅	鉛	39-06
迁	遷	39-08
签	簽	39-09
谦	謙	39-11
钱	錢	39-14
钳	鉗	39-15
浅	淺	39-19
谴	譴	39-20
堑	塹	39-21
枪	槍	39-25
呛	嗆	39-26
墙	墻	39-29
蔷	薔	39-30
抢	搶	39-32
锹	鍬	39-34
桥	橋	39-37
乔	喬	39-39
侨	僑	39-40
翘	翹	39-44
窍	竅	39-47
窃	竊	39-52
钦	欽	39-53
亲	親	39-55
寝	寢	39-62
轻	輕	39-65
氢	氫	39-66
倾	傾	39-67
顷	頃	39-74
请	請	39-75
庆	慶	39-76
琼	瓊	39-77
穷	窮	39-78
趋	趨	39-87
区	區	39-88
躯	軀	39-91
驱	驅	39-93
龋	齲	40-03
颧	顴	40-07
权	權	40-08
劝	勸	40-16
鹊	鵲	40-21
确	確	40-23
让	讓	40-35
饶	饒	40-36
扰	擾	40-37
绕	繞	40-38
热	熱	40-40
韧	韌	40-45
认	認	40-47
纫	紉	40-50
荣	榮	40-57
绒	絨	40-62
软	軟	40-77
锐	鋭	40-81
闰	閏	40-82
润	潤	40-83
洒	灑	40-87

GB	GB/T		GB	GB/T		GB	GB/T	
萨	薩	40-88	识	識	42-22	岁	歲	43-74
鳃	鰓	40-90	驶	駛	42-27	孙	孫	43-79
赛	賽	40-92	势	勢	42-38	损	損	43-80
伞	傘	41-01	适	適	42-42	缩	縮	43-85
丧	喪	41-05	释	釋	42-45	琐	瑣	43-86
骚	騷	41-07	饰	飾	42-46	锁	鎖	43-88
扫	掃	41-08	视	視	42-51	獭	獺	44-01
涩	澀	41-12	试	試	42-52	挞	撻	44-02
杀	殺	41-17	寿	壽	42-57	台	臺	44-08
纱	紗	41-20	兽	獸	42-62	态	態	44-12
筛	篩	41-24	枢	樞	42-64	摊	攤	44-15
晒	曬	41-25	输	輸	42-68	贪	貪	44-16
闪	閃	41-33	书	書	42-73	瘫	癱	44-17
陕	陝	41-34	赎	贖	42-74	滩	灘	44-18
赡	贍	41-36	属	屬	42-84	坛	壇	44-19
缮	繕	41-41	术	術	42-85	谭	譚	44-23
伤	傷	41-43	树	樹	42-87	谈	談	44-24
赏	賞	41-45	竖	豎	42-90	叹	嘆	44-30
烧	燒	41-53	数	數	42-93	汤	湯	44-32
绍	紹	41-60	帅	帥	43-07	烫	燙	44-44
赊	賒	41-62	双	雙	43-11	涛	濤	44-46
舍	捨	41-65	谁	誰	43-13	绦	縧	44-48
摄	攝	41-67	顺	順	43-19	讨	討	44-54
慑	懾	41-69	说	說	43-21	腾	騰	44-58
设	設	41-72	硕	碩	43-22	誊	謄	44-60
绅	紳	41-80	烁	爍	43-24	锑	銻	44-64
审	審	41-83	丝	絲	43-31	题	題	44-66
婶	嬸	41-84	饲	飼	43-39	体	體	44-69
肾	腎	41-86	松	鬆	43-41	条	條	44-85
渗	滲	41-88	耸	聳	43-42	贴	貼	44-89
声	聲	41-89	怂	慫	43-43	铁	鐵	44-90
绳	繩	41-94	颂	頌	43-44	厅	廳	44-92
胜	勝	42-04	讼	訟	43-47	听	聽	44-93
圣	聖	42-05	诵	誦	43-48	烃	烴	44-94
师	師	42-06	擞	擻	43-51	铜	銅	45-13
狮	獅	42-08	苏	蘇	43-53	统	統	45-19
湿	濕	42-10	诉	訴	43-63	头	頭	45-23
诗	詩	42-11	肃	肅	43-64	图	圖	45-28
时	時	42-17	虽	雖	43-68	涂	塗	45-31
蚀	蝕	42-20	随	隨	43-70	团	團	45-37
实	實	42-21	绥	綏	43-71	颓	頹	45-39

GB	GB/T	
鸵	鴕	45-50
驮	馱	45-52
驼	駝	45-53
椭	橢	45-54
洼	窪	45-61
袜	襪	45-64
弯	彎	45-68
湾	灣	45-69
顽	頑	45-71
万	萬	45-82
网	網	45-88
韦	韋	46-04
违	違	46-05
围	圍	46-07
为	爲	46-10
潍	濰	46-11
维	維	46-12
苇	葦	46-13
伟	偉	46-16
伪	僞	46-17
纬	緯	46-19
谓	謂	46-29
卫	衛	46-32
闻	聞	46-37
纹	紋	46-38
稳	穩	46-40
问	問	46-42
挝	撾	46-46
蜗	蝸	46-47
涡	渦	46-48
窝	窩	46-49
呜	嗚	46-56
钨	鎢	46-57
乌	烏	46-58
诬	誣	46-60
无	無	46-62
芜	蕪	46-63
坞	塢	46-75
雾	霧	46-77
务	務	46-81
误	誤	46-83
锡	錫	46-93
牺	犧	46-94
袭	襲	47-14
习	習	47-16
铣	銑	47-19
戏	戲	47-23
细	細	47-24
虾	蝦	47-26
辖	轄	47-29
峡	峽	47-31
侠	俠	47-32
狭	狹	47-33
吓	嚇	47-37
锨	鍁	47-39
鲜	鮮	47-42
纤	纖	47-43
贤	賢	47-45
衔	銜	47-46
闲	閑	47-48
显	顯	47-52
险	險	47-53
现	現	47-54
献	獻	47-55
县	縣	47-56
馅	餡	47-58
宪	憲	47-60
线	綫	47-63
镶	鑲	47-66
乡	鄉	47-71
详	詳	47-74
响	響	47-76
项	項	47-78
萧	蕭	47-84
嚣	囂	47-89
销	銷	47-90
晓	曉	47-94
啸	嘯	48-05
协	協	48-13
挟	挾	48-14
胁	脅	48-18
谐	諧	48-19
写	寫	48-20
泻	瀉	48-26
谢	謝	48-27
锌	鋅	48-31
衅	釁	48-38
兴	興	48-43
锈	銹	48-66
绣	綉	48-69
须	須	48-75
许	許	48-77
绪	緒	48-87
续	續	48-88
轩	軒	48-89
悬	懸	48-92
选	選	49-01
癣	癬	49-02
绚	絢	49-04
学	學	49-07
勋	勛	49-11
询	詢	49-15
寻	尋	49-16
驯	馴	49-17
训	訓	49-21
讯	訊	49-22
逊	遜	49-23
压	壓	49-25
鸦	鴉	49-27
鸭	鴨	49-28
哑	啞	49-38
亚	亞	49-39
讶	訝	49-40
阉	閹	49-43
盐	鹽	49-46
严	嚴	49-47
颜	顔	49-53
阎	閻	49-54
艳	艷	49-62
厌	厭	49-65
砚	硯	49-66
谚	諺	49-72
验	驗	49-73

GB	GB/T		GB	GB/T		GB	GB/T	
鸯	鴦	49-76	萤	螢	51-09	阅	閱	52-36
杨	楊	49-78	营	營	51-10	云	雲	52-38
扬	揚	49-79	荧	熒	51-11	郧	鄖	52-39
疡	瘍	49-81	蝇	蠅	51-12	陨	隕	52-41
阳	陽	49-84	赢	贏	51-14	运	運	52-43
痒	癢	49-87	颖	穎	51-17	蕴	蘊	52-44
养	養	49-88	哟	喲	51-20	酝	醞	52-45
样	樣	49-89	拥	擁	51-21	晕	暈	52-46
尧	堯	50-02	佣	傭	51-22	杂	雜	52-51
谣	謠	50-05	痈	癰	51-24	载	載	52-56
药	藥	50-09	踊	踴	51-27	攒	攢	52-60
爷	爺	50-15	优	優	51-37	暂	暫	52-61
页	頁	50-19	忧	憂	51-39	赞	贊	52-62
业	業	50-21	邮	郵	51-42	赃	贜	52-63
叶	葉	50-22	铀	鈾	51-43	脏	臟	52-64
医	醫	50-29	犹	猶	51-44	凿	鑿	52-68
铱	銥	50-31	诱	誘	51-53	枣	棗	52-70
颐	頤	50-35	舆	輿	51-63	灶	竈	52-78
遗	遺	50-37	余	餘	51-64	责	責	52-80
仪	儀	50-39	鱼	魚	51-67	择	擇	52-81
蚁	蟻	50-47	渔	漁	51-70	则	則	52-82
艺	藝	50-53	与	與	51-75	泽	澤	52-83
亿	億	50-58	屿	嶼	51-76	贼	賊	52-84
忆	憶	50-68	语	語	51-79	赠	贈	52-89
义	義	50-69	郁	鬱	51-84	轧	軋	52-94
诣	詣	50-72	狱	獄	51-92	铡	鍘	53-01
议	議	50-73	誉	譽	51-94	闸	閘	53-02
谊	誼	50-74	预	預	52-04	诈	詐	53-09
译	譯	50-75	驭	馭	52-06	斋	齋	53-11
绎	繹	50-79	鸳	鴛	52-07	债	債	53-14
荫	蔭	50-81	渊	淵	52-08	毡	氈	53-17
阴	陰	50-85	辕	轅	52-15	盏	盞	53-21
银	銀	50-88	园	園	52-16	斩	斬	53-22
饮	飲	50-91	员	員	52-17	辗	輾	53-23
隐	隱	50-94	圆	圓	52-18	崭	嶄	53-24
樱	櫻	51-03	缘	緣	52-21	栈	棧	53-27
婴	嬰	51-04	远	遠	52-22	战	戰	53-29
鹰	鷹	51-05	愿	願	52-24	绽	綻	53-32
应	應	51-06	约	約	52-28	张	張	53-37
缨	纓	51-07	跃	躍	52-30	涨	漲	53-39
莹	瑩	51-08	钥	鑰	52-31	帐	帳	53-42

GB	GB/T		GB	GB/T		GB	GB/T	
账	賬	53-43	嘱	囑	54-86	剀	剴	56-60
胀	脹	53-45	贮	貯	54-92	伛	傴	56-81
赵	趙	53-52	铸	鑄	54-93	伥	倀	56-86
蛰	蟄	53-61	筑	築	54-94	伧	傖	56-87
辙	轍	53-62	驻	駐	55-04	侪	儕	57-13
锗	鍺	53-64	专	專	55-08	侬	儂	57-15
这	這	53-66	砖	磚	55-09	俦	儔	57-17
贞	貞	53-74	转	轉	55-10	俨	儼	57-18
针	針	53-75	赚	賺	55-12	俪	儷	57-19
侦	偵	53-76	桩	樁	55-14	偾	僨	57-39
诊	診	53-79	庄	莊	55-15	偻	僂	57-45
镇	鎮	53-82	装	裝	55-16	傥	儻	57-46
阵	陣	53-83	妆	妝	55-17	傧	儐	57-47
帧	幀	54-01	壮	壯	55-19	傩	儺	57-48
症	癥	54-02	状	狀	55-20	佥	僉	57-61
郑	鄭	54-03	锥	錐	55-22	籴	糴	57-65
证	證	54-04	赘	贅	55-24	黉	黌	57-68
织	織	54-15	坠	墜	55-25	冁	囅	57-70
职	職	54-16	缀	綴	55-26	凫	鳧	57-76
执	執	54-20	谆	諄	55-27	亵	褻	57-84
只	祇	54-27	准	準	55-28	脔	臠	57-85
纸	紙	54-29	浊	濁	55-39	讠	言	58-05
挚	摯	54-31	资	資	55-42	讦	訐	58-06
掷	擲	54-32	渍	漬	55-53	讧	訌	58-07
帜	幟	54-36	综	綜	55-59	讪	訕	58-08
质	質	54-42	总	總	55-60	讴	謳	58-09
滞	滯	54-45	纵	縱	55-61	讵	詎	58-10
钟	鐘	54-51	邹	鄒	55-62	讷	訥	58-11
终	終	54-53	诅	詛	55-71	诂	詁	58-12
种	種	54-54	组	組	55-73	诃	訶	58-13
肿	腫	54-55	钻	鑽	55-74	诋	詆	58-14
众	衆	54-58	啬	嗇	56-36	诏	詔	58-15
诌	謅	54-63	厍	厙	56-39	诎	詘	58-16
轴	軸	54-65	厣	厴	56-41	诒	詒	58-17
皱	皺	54-69	靥	靨	56-44	诓	誆	58-18
昼	晝	54-71	赝	贋	56-45	诔	誄	58-19
骤	驟	54-72	匦	匭	56-48	诖	詿	58-20
诸	諸	54-78	匮	匱	56-49	诘	詰	58-21
诛	誅	54-79	赜	賾	56-51	诙	詼	58-22
烛	燭	54-82	刭	剄	56-57	诜	詵	58-23
瞩	矚	54-85	刿	劌	56-59	诟	詬	58-24

GB	GB/T		GB	GB/T		GB	GB/T	
诠	詮	58-25	邬	鄔	58-89	荪	蓀	61-05
诤	諍	58-26	邺	鄴	58-94	荭	葒	61-06
诨	諢	58-27	郏	郟	59-03	荮	葤	61-07
诩	詡	58-28	郐	鄶	59-06	莳	蒔	61-10
诮	誚	58-29	郓	鄆	59-09	莴	萵	61-11
诰	誥	58-30	郦	酈	59-10	莶	薟	61-18
诳	誑	58-31	刍	芻	59-27	莸	蕕	61-21
诶	誒	58-32	劢	勱	59-29	莺	鶯	61-26
诹	諏	58-33	巯	巰	59-47	莼	蓴	61-27
诼	諑	58-34	垩	堊	59-49	萦	縈	61-51
诿	諉	58-35	圹	壙	59-59	蒇	蕆	61-59
谀	諛	58-36	坜	壢	59-62	蒉	蕢	61-62
谂	諗	58-37	垅	壟	59-66	蒌	蔞	61-68
谄	諂	58-38	垆	壚	59-68	蓦	驀	61-75
谇	誶	58-39	垭	埡	59-75	蓠	蘺	61-81
谌	諶	58-40	垲	塏	59-78	蓥	鎣	61-86
谏	諫	58-41	垴	堖	59-81	蓣	蕷	61-87
谑	謔	58-42	埘	塒	59-85	蔹	蘞	61-92
谒	謁	58-43	埚	堝	59-86	蔺	藺	61-94
谔	諤	58-44	埙	塤	59-87	蕲	蘄	62-13
谕	諭	58-45	芗	薌	60-28	薮	藪	62-20
谖	諼	58-46	芸	蕓	60-31	藓	蘚	62-26
谙	諳	58-47	苈	藶	60-34	奁	奩	62-38
谛	諦	58-48	苋	莧	60-40	尴	尷	62-47
谘	諮	58-49	苌	萇	60-41	扪	捫	62-49
谝	諞	58-50	苁	蓯	60-42	抟	摶	62-50
谟	謨	58-51	苎	苧	60-49	挢	撟	62-56
谠	讜	58-52	茏	蘢	60-55	掴	摑	62-66
谡	謖	58-53	茑	蔦	60-64	掼	摜	62-72
谥	謚	58-54	茔	塋	60-67	揿	撳	62-76
谧	謐	58-55	茕	煢	60-68	摅	攄	62-83
谪	謫	58-56	荛	蕘	60-73	撄	攖	62-92
谫	謭	58-57	荜	蓽	60-74	撷	擷	63-02
谮	譖	58-58	荞	蕎	60-81	撸	擼	63-03
谯	譙	58-59	荟	薈	60-86	撺	攛	63-05
谲	譎	58-60	荠	薺	60-89	叽	嘰	63-20
谳	讞	58-61	荦	犖	60-93	呒	嘸	63-28
谵	譫	58-62	荥	滎	60-94	呓	囈	63-29
谶	讖	58-63	荨	蕁	61-01	呖	嚦	63-31
陉	陘	58-74	荩	藎	61-03	呗	唄	63-34
邝	鄺	58-87	荬	蕒	61-04	呙	咼	63-35

GB	GB/T		GB	GB/T		GB	GB/T	
咛	嚀	63-44	狲	猻	65-88	闫	閆	67-38
咝	噝	63-48	猃	獫	65-93	闱	闈	67-39
哒	噠	63-53	猡	玀	66-04	闳	閎	67-40
哓	嘵	63-56	猕	獼	66-08	闵	閔	67-41
哔	嗶	63-57	饣	飠	66-27	闶	閌	67-42
哕	噦	63-60	饧	餳	66-28	闼	闥	67-43
哙	噲	63-64	饨	飩	66-29	闾	閭	67-44
哜	嚌	63-66	饩	餼	66-30	阃	閫	67-45
哝	噥	63-70	饪	飪	66-31	阄	鬮	67-46
唛	嘜	63-73	饫	飫	66-32	阆	閬	67-47
唠	嘮	63-75	饬	飭	66-33	阈	閾	67-48
唢	嗩	63-79	饴	飴	66-34	阊	閶	67-49
啧	嘖	63-85	饷	餉	66-35	阋	鬩	67-50
啭	囀	63-89	饽	餑	66-36	阌	閿	67-51
喽	嘍	64-22	馄	餛	66-38	阍	閽	67-52
喾	嚳	64-23	馇	餷	66-39	阏	閼	67-53
嗫	囁	64-31	馊	餿	66-40	阒	闃	67-54
嗳	噯	64-40	馍	饃	66-41	阕	闋	67-55
辔	轡	64-46	馐	饈	66-42	阖	闔	67-56
嘤	嚶	64-51	馑	饉	66-43	阗	闐	67-57
噜	嚕	64-64	馓	饊	66-44	阙	闕	67-58
囵	圇	64-80	馔	饌	66-45	阚	闞	67-59
帏	幃	64-88	馕	饢	66-46	沣	灃	67-67
帱	幬	64-92	庑	廡	66-48	沩	溈	67-77
帻	幘	64-93	赓	賡	66-57	泷	瀧	67-81
帼	幗	64-94	忏	懺	66-67	泸	瀘	67-82
岖	嶇	65-11	怃	憮	66-68	泺	濼	67-88
岘	峴	65-13	怄	慪	66-70	泾	涇	67-94
岚	嵐	65-16	忾	愾	66-73	浃	浹	68-04
岽	崬	65-20	怅	悵	66-74	浈	湞	68-05
峄	嶧	65-27	怆	愴	66-75	浍	澮	68-11
峤	嶠	65-29	怿	懌	66-88	浏	瀏	68-15
崂	嶗	65-32	恸	慟	66-90	浒	滸	68-16
崃	崍	65-33	恹	懨	66-91	浔	潯	68-17
嵘	嶸	65-41	恻	惻	66-92	涞	淶	68-21
嵝	嶁	65-48	恺	愷	66-93	涠	潿	68-22
巅	巔	65-59	恽	惲	67-02	渎	瀆	68-34
徕	徠	65-66	悭	慳	67-05	渑	澠	68-37
犷	獷	65-78	惬	愜	67-11	渖	瀋	68-41
犸	獁	65-79	愦	憒	67-20	滟	灩	68-57
狯	獪	65-86	闩	閂	67-37	滠	灄	68-60

GB	GB/T	
滢	瀅	68-62
浐	滻	68-68
潆	瀠	68-75
潇	瀟	68-76
潋	瀲	68-82
濑	瀨	68-94
灏	灝	69-16
骞	騫	69-25
迩	邇	69-39
迳	逕	69-41
逦	邐	69-46
屦	屨	69-80
弪	弳	69-82
妩	嫵	69-92
妪	嫗	69-93
妫	媯	70-03
娅	婭	70-11
娆	嬈	70-12
娈	孌	70-14
娲	媧	70-20
娴	嫻	70-21
婵	嬋	70-31
嫒	嬡	70-40
嫔	嬪	70-41
嫱	嬙	70-45
驵	駔	70-64
驷	駟	70-65
驸	駙	70-66
驺	騶	70-67
驿	驛	70-68
驽	駑	70-69
骀	駘	70-70
骁	驍	70-71
骅	驊	70-72
骈	駢	70-73
骊	驪	70-74
骐	騏	70-75
骒	騍	70-76
骓	騅	70-77
骖	驂	70-78
骘	騭	70-79
骛	騖	70-80
骜	驁	70-81
骝	騮	70-82
骟	騸	70-83
骠	驃	70-84
骢	驄	70-85
骣	驏	70-86
骥	驥	70-87
骧	驤	70-88
纟	糹	70-89
纡	紆	70-90
纣	紂	70-91
纥	紇	70-92
纨	紈	70-93
纩	纊	70-94
纭	紜	71-01
纰	紕	71-02
纾	紓	71-03
绀	紺	71-04
绁	紲	71-05
绂	紱	71-06
绉	縐	71-07
绋	紼	71-08
绌	絀	71-09
绐	紿	71-10
绔	絝	71-11
绗	絎	71-12
绛	絳	71-13
绠	綆	71-14
绡	綃	71-15
绨	綈	71-16
绫	綾	71-17
绮	綺	71-18
绯	緋	71-19
绱	緔	71-20
绲	緄	71-21
缍	綞	71-22
绶	綬	71-23
绺	綹	71-24
绻	綣	71-25
绾	綰	71-26
缁	緇	71-27
缂	緙	71-28
缃	緗	71-29
缇	緹	71-30
缈	緲	71-31
缋	繢	71-32
缌	緦	71-33
缏	緶	71-34
缑	緱	71-35
缒	縋	71-36
缗	緡	71-37
缙	縉	71-38
缜	縝	71-39
缛	縟	71-40
缟	縞	71-41
缡	縭	71-42
缢	縊	71-43
缣	縑	71-44
缤	繽	71-45
缥	縹	71-46
缦	縵	71-47
缧	縲	71-48
缪	繆	71-49
缫	繅	71-50
缬	纈	71-51
缭	繚	71-52
缯	繒	71-53
缰	繮	71-54
缱	繾	71-55
缲	繰	71-56
缳	繯	71-57
缵	纘	71-58
玑	璣	71-65
玮	瑋	71-66
珑	瓏	71-71
顼	頊	71-79
玺	璽	71-84
珲	琿	71-85
琏	璉	71-86
瑷	璦	72-08
璎	瓔	72-12

GB	GB/T	
瓒	瓚	72-22
趱	趲	72-24
韫	韞	72-25
韬	韜	72-26
杩	榪	72-31
枥	櫪	72-32
枧	梘	72-37
枨	棖	72-39
枞	樅	72-40
枭	梟	72-41
栉	櫛	72-46
栊	櫳	72-48
栌	櫨	72-51
栎	櫟	72-61
柽	檉	72-63
桠	椏	72-66
桡	橈	72-67
桢	楨	72-69
桤	榿	72-71
桦	樺	72-75
桧	檜	72-77
栾	欒	72-79
棂	櫺	72-89
椟	櫝	72-92
椠	槧	72-93
椤	欏	73-01
榄	欖	73-13
榇	櫬	73-20
榈	櫚	73-21
榉	櫸	73-23
槟	檳	73-36
槠	櫧	73-38
樯	檣	73-41
橹	櫓	73-54
橼	櫞	73-58
殇	殤	73-68
殒	殞	73-70
殓	殮	73-71
殚	殫	73-73
殡	殯	73-75
轫	軔	73-77

GB	GB/T	
轭	軛	73-78
轱	軲	73-79
轲	軻	73-80
轳	轤	73-81
轵	軹	73-82
轶	軼	73-83
轸	軫	73-84
轷	軤	73-85
轹	轢	73-86
轺	軺	73-87
轼	軾	73-88
轾	輊	73-89
辁	輇	73-90
辂	輅	73-91
辄	輒	73-92
辇	輦	73-93
辋	輞	73-94
辍	輟	74-01
辎	輜	74-02
辏	輳	74-03
辘	轆	74-04
辚	轔	74-05
戋	戔	74-07
戗	戧	74-08
瓯	甌	74-17
昙	曇	74-28
晔	曄	74-42
晖	暉	74-45
暧	曖	74-51
贲	賁	74-58
贳	貰	74-59
贶	貺	74-60
贻	貽	74-61
贽	贄	74-62
赀	貲	74-63
赅	賅	74-64
赆	贐	74-65
赈	賑	74-66
赉	賚	74-67
赇	賕	74-68
赍	賫	74-69

GB	GB/T	
赕	賧	74-70
赙	賻	74-71
觇	覘	74-72
觊	覬	74-73
觋	覡	74-74
觌	覿	74-75
觎	覦	74-76
觏	覯	74-77
觐	覲	74-78
觑	覷	74-79
毵	毿	75-07
氇	氌	75-10
氲	氳	75-18
牍	牘	75-25
胧	朧	75-42
胨	腖	75-43
胪	臚	75-45
胫	脛	75-54
脍	膾	75-58
脶	腡	75-65
膑	臏	75-87
欤	歟	76-03
飑	颮	76-09
飒	颯	76-10
飓	颶	76-11
飕	颼	76-12
飙	飆	76-13
飚	飈	76-14
毂	轂	76-17
齑	齏	76-20
斓	斕	76-21
炀	煬	76-30
炜	煒	76-31
炝	熗	76-33
烨	燁	76-39
焖	燜	76-43
焘	燾	76-66
祢	禰	76-82
祯	禎	76-85
禅	禪	76-88
怼	懟	77-01

GB	GB/T	
悫	愨	77-08
懑	懣	77-15
戆	戇	77-16
泶	澩	77-20
矶	磯	77-22
砀	碭	77-24
砗	硨	77-26
砜	碸	77-31
砺	礪	77-34
砻	礱	77-35
硖	硤	77-44
硗	磽	77-45
碛	磧	77-51
碜	磣	77-55
龛	龕	77-72
眍	瞘	77-78
睐	睞	77-89
睑	瞼	77-90
罴	羆	78-28
羁	羈	78-31
钅	釒	78-36
钆	釓	78-37
钇	釔	78-38
钋	釙	78-39
钊	釗	78-40
钌	釕	78-41
钍	釷	78-42
钏	釧	78-43
钐	釤	78-44
钔	鍆	78-45
钗	釵	78-46
钕	釹	78-47
钚	鈈	78-48
钛	鈦	78-49
钜	鉅	78-50
钣	鈑	78-51
钤	鈐	78-52
钫	鈁	78-53
钪	鈧	78-54
钭	鈄	78-55
钬	鈥	78-56
钯	鈀	78-57
钰	鈺	78-58
钲	鉦	78-59
钴	鈷	78-60
钶	鈳	78-61
钷	鉕	78-62
钸	鈽	78-63
钹	鈸	78-64
钺	鉞	78-65
钼	鉬	78-66
钽	鉭	78-67
钿	鈿	78-68
铄	鑠	78-69
铈	鈰	78-70
铉	鉉	78-71
铊	鉈	78-72
铋	鉍	78-73
铌	鈮	78-74
铍	鈹	78-75
铎	鐸	78-76
铐	銬	78-77
铑	銠	78-78
铒	鉺	78-79
铕	銪	78-80
铖	鋮	78-81
铗	鋏	78-82
铙	鐃	78-83
铘	鋣	78-84
铛	鐺	78-85
铞	銱	78-86
铟	銦	78-87
铠	鎧	78-88
铢	銖	78-89
铤	鋌	78-90
铦	銛	78-91
铧	鏵	78-92
铨	銓	78-93
铪	鉿	78-94
铩	鎩	79-01
铫	銚	79-02
铮	錚	79-03
铯	銫	79-04
铳	銃	79-05
铴	鍚	79-06
铵	銨	79-07
铷	銣	79-08
铹	鐒	79-09
铼	錸	79-10
铽	鋱	79-11
铿	鏗	79-12
锃	鋥	79-13
锂	鋰	79-14
锆	鋯	79-15
锇	鋨	79-16
锉	銼	79-17
锊	鋝	79-18
锍	鋶	79-19
锎	鐦	79-20
锏	鐧	79-21
锒	鋃	79-22
锓	鋟	79-23
锔	鋦	79-24
锕	錒	79-25
锖	錆	79-26
锘	鍩	79-27
锛	錛	79-28
锝	鍀	79-29
锞	錁	79-30
锟	錕	79-31
锢	錮	79-32
锪	鍃	79-33
锫	錇	79-34
锩	錈	79-35
锬	錟	79-36
锱	錙	79-37
锲	鍥	79-38
锴	鍇	79-39
锶	鍶	79-40
锷	鍔	79-41
锸	鍤	79-42
锼	鎪	79-43
锾	鍰	79-44

GB	GB/T	
锿	鑀	79-45
镂	鏤	79-46
锵	鏘	79-47
镄	鐨	79-48
镅	鎇	79-49
镆	鏌	79-50
镉	鎘	79-51
镌	鐫	79-52
镎	鎿	79-53
镏	鎦	79-54
镒	鎰	79-55
镓	鎵	79-56
镔	鑌	79-57
镖	鏢	79-58
镗	鏜	79-59
镘	鏝	79-60
镙	鏍	79-61
镛	鏞	79-62
镞	鏃	79-63
镟	鏇	79-64
镝	鏑	79-65
镡	鐔	79-66
镢	鐝	79-67
镤	鏷	79-68
镥	鑥	79-69
镦	鐓	79-70
镧	鑭	79-71
镨	鐠	79-72
镩	鑹	79-73
镪	鏹	79-74
镫	鐙	79-75
镬	鑊	79-76
镯	鐲	79-77
镱	鐿	79-78
镲	鑔	79-79
镳	鑣	79-80
锺	鍾	79-81
穑	穡	80-03
鸠	鳩	80-15
鸢	鳶	80-16
鸨	鴇	80-17
鸩	鴆	80-18
鸪	鴣	80-19
鸫	鶇	80-20
鸬	鸕	80-21
鸲	鴝	80-22
鸱	鴟	80-23
鸶	鷥	80-24
鸸	鴯	80-25
鸷	鷙	80-26
鸹	鴰	80-27
鸺	鵂	80-28
鸾	鸞	80-29
鹁	鵓	80-30
鹂	鸝	80-31
鹄	鵠	80-32
鹆	鵒	80-33
鹇	鷳	80-34
鹈	鵜	80-35
鹉	鵡	80-36
鹋	鶓	80-37
鹌	鵪	80-38
鹎	鵯	80-39
鹑	鶉	80-40
鹕	鶘	80-41
鹗	鶚	80-42
鹚	鷀	80-43
鹛	鶥	80-44
鹜	鶩	80-45
鹞	鷂	80-46
鹣	鶼	80-47
鹦	鸚	80-48
鹧	鷓	80-49
鹨	鷚	80-50
鹩	鷯	80-51
鹪	鷦	80-52
鹫	鷲	80-53
鹬	鷸	80-54
鹱	鸌	80-55
鹭	鷺	80-56
鹳	鸛	80-57
疖	癤	80-60
疠	癘	80-61
疬	癧	80-63
痖	瘂	80-73
痨	癆	80-76
痫	癇	80-79
瘅	癉	80-87
瘗	瘞	80-89
瘘	瘻	80-92
瘿	癭	81-08
瘾	癮	81-11
癞	癩	81-14
癫	癲	81-18
窦	竇	81-28
窭	窶	81-32
裆	襠	81-41
裢	褳	81-45
裣	襝	81-47
裥	襉	81-48
褛	褸	81-58
褴	襤	81-60
皲	皸	81-68
耢	耮	81-76
耧	耬	81-79
聍	聹	81-87
聩	聵	81-89
顸	頇	81-92
颀	頎	81-93
颃	頏	81-94
颉	頡	82-01
颌	頜	82-02
颍	潁	82-03
颏	頦	82-04
颔	頷	82-05
颚	顎	82-06
颛	顓	82-07
颞	顳	82-08
颟	顢	82-09
颡	顙	82-10
颢	顥	82-11
颥	顬	82-12
颦	顰	82-13

GB	GB/T	
虮	蟣	82-17
虿	蠆	82-18
蚬	蜆	82-25
蛎	蠣	82-35
蛏	蟶	82-41
蛱	蛺	82-44
蛲	蟯	82-45
蛳	螄	82-47
蛴	蠐	82-51
蝈	蟈	82-69
蝾	蠑	82-78
蝼	螻	82-87
螨	蟎	82-93
罂	罌	83-31
笃	篤	83-38
笕	筧	83-40
笾	籩	83-54
筚	篳	83-57
箦	簀	83-69
箧	篋	83-70
箨	籜	83-74
箪	簞	83-76
箫	簫	83-79
篑	簣	83-81
簖	籪	83-93
籁	籟	84-05
舣	艤	84-15
舻	艫	84-21
袅	裊	84-33
羟	羥	84-39
粝	糲	84-47
粜	糶	84-48
糁	糝	84-54
絷	縶	84-74
麸	麩	84-79
趱	趲	84-85
酽	釅	85-06
酾	釃	85-07
鹾	鹺	85-26
趸	躉	85-27
跄	蹌	85-36

GB	GB/T	
跞	躒	85-40
跷	蹺	85-46
跸	蹕	85-47
跹	躚	85-49
跻	躋	85-50
踬	躓	85-57
踯	躑	85-60
蹑	躡	85-70
蹒	蹣	85-71
躏	躪	85-79
躜	躦	85-82
觞	觴	85-92
觯	觶	86-03
靓	靚	86-06
雳	靂	86-08
霁	霽	86-11
霭	靄	86-16
龀	齔	86-19
龃	齟	86-20
龅	齙	86-21
龆	齠	86-22
龇	齜	86-23
龈	齦	86-24
龉	齬	86-25
龊	齪	86-26
龌	齷	86-27
黾	黽	86-28
鼋	黿	86-29
鼍	鼉	86-30
雠	讎	86-37
銮	鑾	86-39
錾	鏨	86-41
鱿	魷	86-47
鲂	魴	86-48
鲅	鮁	86-49
鲆	鮃	86-50
鲇	鮎	86-51
鲈	鱸	86-52
稣	穌	86-53
鲋	鮒	86-54
鲎	鱟	86-55

GB	GB/T	
鲐	鮐	86-56
鲑	鮭	86-57
鲒	鮚	86-58
鲔	鮪	86-59
鲕	鮞	86-60
鲚	鱭	86-61
鲛	鮫	86-62
鲞	鯗	86-63
鲟	鱘	86-64
鲠	鯁	86-65
鲡	鱺	86-66
鲢	鰱	86-67
鲣	鰹	86-68
鲥	鰣	86-69
鲦	鰷	86-70
鲧	鯀	86-71
鲨	鯊	86-72
鲩	鯇	86-73
鲫	鯽	86-74
鲭	鯖	86-75
鲮	鯪	86-76
鲰	鯫	86-77
鲱	鯡	86-78
鲲	鯤	86-79
鲳	鯧	86-80
鲴	鯝	86-81
鲵	鯢	86-82
鲶	鯰	86-83
鲷	鯛	86-84
鲺	鯴	86-85
鲻	鯔	86-86
鲼	鱝	86-87
鲽	鰈	86-88
鳄	鰐	86-89
鳅	鰍	86-90
鳆	鰒	86-91
鳇	鰉	86-92
鳊	鯿	86-93
鳋	鰠	86-94
鳌	鰲	87-01
鳍	鰭	87-02

GB	GB/T		GB	GB/T		GB	GB/T	
鳎	鰨	87-03	鳜	鱖	87-12	髋	髖	87-37
鳏	鰥	87-04	鳝	鱔	87-13	髌	髕	87-38
鳐	鰩	87-05	鳟	鱒	87-14	魇	魘	87-42
鳓	鰳	87-06	鳢	鱧	87-15	魉	魎	87-43
鳔	鰾	87-07	鞑	韃	87-18	飨	饗	87-47
鳕	鱈	87-08	鞒	鞽	87-19	餍	饜	87-48
鳗	鰻	87-09	鞯	韉	87-21	鬓	鬢	87-62
鳘	鰵	87-10	鹘	鶻	87-29	黩	黷	87-82
鳙	鱅	87-11	髅	髏	87-35	黪	黲	87-85

The 103 hanzi included in GB/T 12345-90 rows 88 (94 hanzi) and 89 (nine hanzi) are in some way or another related to the hanzi in rows 16 through 87. Those that are shaded are actually hanzi that were moved from GB 2312-80 rows 16 through 87 (the "GB" column code point) to make way for a traditional form. Those that are unshaded simply indicate that the hanzi is related—usually an alternate traditional form—to the hanzi indicated by the code point in the "GB" column.

	GB/T	GB		GB/T	GB		GB/T	GB
襬	88-01	16-58	广	**88-24**	**25-67**	曆	88-47	32-90
闆	88-02	16-69	閤	88-25	26-47	帘	**88-48**	**33-17**
錶	88-03	17-77	鬍	88-26	26-90	瞭	88-49	33-43
彆	88-04	17-80	划	**88-27**	**27-14**	鹵	88-50	34-17
蔔	88-05	18-23	迴	88-28	27-56	囉	88-51	34-62
纔	88-06	18-37	彙	88-29	27-67	黴	88-52	35-25
厂	**88-07**	**19-07**	穫	88-30	27-81	濛	88-53	35-41
冲	**88-08**	**19-69**	飢	88-31	28-02	懞	88-54	35-41
丑	**88-09**	**19-83**	几	**88-32**	**28-24**	矇	88-55	35-41
齣	88-10	19-86	傢	88-33	28-50	瀰	88-56	35-54
噹	88-11	21-17	价	**88-34**	**28-59**	麵	88-57	35-70
党	**88-12**	**21-19**	荐	**88-35**	**28-86**	衊	88-58	35-79
淀	**88-13**	**21-77**	薑	88-36	29-10	闢	88-59	17-57
鼕	88-14	22-12	儘	88-37	30-01	苹	**88-60**	**38-27**
斗	**88-15**	**22-23**	据	**88-38**	**30-61**	凭	**88-61**	**38-30**
噁	88-16	22-81	捲	88-39	30-77	扑	**88-62**	**38-43**
髮	88-17	23-02	尅	88-40	31-43	仆	**88-63**	**38-45**
范	**88-18**	**23-22**	夸	**88-41**	**31-68**	朴	**88-64**	**38-51**
丰	**88-19**	**23-65**	睏	88-42	32-07	韆	88-65	39-07
複	88-20	24-20	蜡	**88-43**	**32-15**	籤	88-66	39-09
干	**88-21**	**24-41**	腊	**88-44**	**32-16**	縴	88-67	47-43
穀	88-22	25-40	纍	88-45	32-59	鞦	88-68	39-79
颳	88-23	25-46	里	**88-46**	**32-79**	麯	88-69	39-90

	GB/T	GB
确	88-70	40-23
舍	88-71	41-65
术	88-72	42-85
松	88-73	43-41
囌	88-74	43-53
台	88-75	44-08
颱	88-76	44-08
檯	88-77	44-08
鑪	88-78	44-19
涂	88-79	45-31
糰	88-80	45-37
万	88-81	45-82
係	88-82	47-21
繫	88-83	47-21
鹹	88-84	47-44
嚮	88-85	47-82
鬚	88-86	48-75
葯	88-87	50-09
叶	88-88	50-22
郁	88-89	51-84
禦	88-90	51-89
籲	88-91	51-85
愿	88-92	52-24
云	88-93	52-38
髒	88-94	52-64
症	89-01	54-02
隻	89-02	54-27
只	89-03	54-27
緻	89-04	54-34
製	89-05	54-38
种	89-06	54-54
硃	89-07	54-76
筑	89-08	54-94
准	89-09	55-28

CNS 11643-1986 Versus CNS 11643-1992

The 171 hanzi at the end of CNS 11643-1986 Plane 14, Row-Cell 66-39 through 68-21, became part of CNS 11643-1992 Plane 4, and were scattered throughout according to their number of strokes and indexing radical.

	1986	1992
汔	66-39	01-47
㐰	66-40	01-57
压	66-41	01-81
尔	66-42	01-83
矣	66-43	02-20
勼	66-44	02-32
幵	66-45	02-37
奷	66-46	02-54
妍	66-47	02-57
宂	66-48	02-65
忘	66-49	02-81
扫	66-50	02-83
邢	66-51	03-18
冠	66-52	03-81
岂	66-53	03-91
忞	66-54	04-17
来	66-55	04-38
杞	66-56	04-39
侍	66-57	05-27
列	66-58	05-48
𡛰	66-59	06-01
学	66-60	06-03
丕	66-61	06-18
旹	66-62	06-66
柴	66-63	06-69
泦	66-64	06-91
济	66-65	06-93
㑗	66-66	08-28
侽	66-67	08-30
徍	66-68	09-17
珁	66-69	09-21
怘	66-70	09-22
恈	66-71	09-31
栟	66-72	09-79
欿	66-73	09-82
炦	66-74	10-06
珇	66-75	10-24
昉	66-76	10-50
秎	66-77	10-73
烌	66-78	10-78
咒	66-79	11-73
娐	66-80	12-30
峼	66-81	12-60
洒	66-82	12-65
捬	66-83	13-28
杲	66-84	13-43
略	66-85	13-44
皆	66-86	13-45
梤	66-87	13-50
恭	66-88	13-59
奂	66-89	13-85
猩	66-90	14-02
留	66-91	14-17
盄	66-92	14-42
砋	66-93	14-66
袖	66-94	14-68
覂	67-01	15-83
轫	67-02	16-12
敃	67-03	16-26
陖	67-04	16-30

	1986	1992
寉	67-05	16-33
湳	67-06	16-45
㤳	67-07	17-76
坙	67-08	18-55
洴	67-09	18-58
覂	67-10	18-86
豊	67-11	19-16
硓	67-12	19-65
笩	67-13	19-90
腖	67-14	20-48
莭	67-15	20-83
訮	67-16	21-29
廊	67-17	21-83
酞	67-18	21-85
脭	67-19	21-90
高	67-20	22-13
堿	67-21	22-75
堫	67-22	22-79
塅	67-23	22-81
臵	67-24	23-18
搖	67-25	23-79
搕	67-26	23-80
喩	67-27	24-02
梚	67-28	24-15
淑	67-29	24-63
煠	67-30	24-65
焯	67-31	24-66
葱	67-32	26-65
菍	67-33	26-76
跓	67-34	27-49
塧	67-35	28-51
㙞	67-36	28-56
寝	67-37	28-78
敲	67-38	29-61
蜂	67-39	30-43
晭	67-40	30-72
碑	67-41	31-29

	1986	1992
貇	67-42	32-88
時	67-43	33-01
偖	67-44	34-13
僟	67-45	34-21
僨	67-46	34-23
嫞	67-47	34-70
廱	67-48	35-26
踻	67-49	35-48
膡	67-50	35-89
榥	67-51	35-90
殜	67-52	36-17
滅	67-53	36-45
睛	67-54	38-19
萎	67-55	38-68
逨	67-56	39-76
鄧	67-57	39-77
郒	67-58	39-81
鉶	67-59	39-86
雷	67-60	40-20
䑙	67-61	40-61
藝	67-62	41-10
集	67-63	41-47
寗	67-64	41-51
韮	67-65	41-53
廥	67-66	41-60
漙	67-67	42-55
濢	67-68	42-72
䁠	67-69	43-31
篃	67-70	43-88
篁	67-71	44-01
蔌	67-72	45-01
蓓	67-73	45-04
䛹	67-74	45-56
䛢	67-75	45-59
䛥	67-76	46-27
䝗	67-77	46-44
頣	67-78	46-58

	1986	1992
嬂	67-79	48-01
䁐	67-80	48-50
𣟳	67-81	48-68
歖	67-82	48-71
謦	67-83	48-78
燍	67-84	49-03
璙	67-85	49-24
蕌	67-86	51-12
闇	67-87	52-44
鳸	67-88	53-52
澍	67-89	54-62
䭲	67-90	57-28
頼	67-91	57-80
癛	67-92	59-91
䐿	67-93	60-84
隮	67-94	57-53
璣	68-01	64-10
𦌾	68-02	64-79
霖	68-03	65-83
霎	68-04	65-84
櫇	68-05	67-49
燿	68-06	67-63
疊	68-07	67-73
贎	68-08	68-47
鍇	68-09	68-76
額	68-10	69-12
嚦	68-11	70-59
篇	68-12	70-74
譳	68-13	71-27
鑿	68-14	71-67
臟	68-15	72-30
霓	68-16	73-58
鑘	68-17	75-09
曬	68-18	75-84
鬮	68-19	77-23
蘦	68-20	78-23
鱻	68-21	78-59

JIS C 6226-1978 Versus JIS X 0208-1983

The differences between JIS C 6226-1978 and JIS X 0208-1983 can be classified into four categories, each of which is described here with complete examples. These differences vary depending on the source of the information. The first three categories are consistently treated the same by all sources I have referenced, but the fourth category gets different treatment depending on the source of the information. While the transition from JIS C 6226-1978 to JIS X 0208-1983 is generally viewed as involving only kanji simplification, there are a handful of cases where a simplified kanji in JIS C 6226-1978 was restored to its traditional form in JIS X 0208-1983. In some case, these changes can be considered corrections.

Category 1

Several non-kanji were added to the character set. The first set consists of 39 miscellaneous characters added to row 2, and the second set consists of 32 line-drawing elements added to row 8.

JIS X 0208-1983		JIS X 0208-1983		JIS X 0208-1983	
∈	02-26	√	02-69	┴	08-10
∋	02-27	∽	02-70	┼	08-11
⊆	02-28	∝	02-71	━	08-12
⊇	02-29	∵	02-72	┃	08-13
⊂	02-30	∫	02-73	┏	08-14
⊃	02-31	∬	02-74	┓	08-15
∪	02-32	Å	02-82	┛	08-16
∩	02-33	‰	02-83	┗	08-17
∧	02-42	♯	02-84	┣	08-18
∨	02-43	♭	02-85	┳	08-19
¬	02-44	♪	02-86	┫	08-20
⇒	02-45	†	02-87	┻	08-21
⇔	02-46	‡	02-88	╋	08-22
∀	02-47	¶	02-89	┠	08-23
∃	02-48	◯	02-94	┯	08-24
∠	02-60	─	08-01	┨	08-25
⊥	02-61	│	08-02	┷	08-26
⌒	02-62	┌	08-03	┿	08-27
∂	02-63	┐	08-04	┝	08-28
∇	02-64	┘	08-05	┰	08-29
≡	02-65	└	08-06	┥	08-30
≒	02-66	├	08-07	┸	08-31
≪	02-67	┬	08-08	╂	08-32
≫	02-68	┤	08-09		

Category 2

The kanji shape in the original code position had simplified, and the unsimplified kanji was given a new code position after JIS Level 2 kanji. The final result was an addition of four kanji to row 84.

Original Character		Added Character	
尭	22-38	堯	84-01
槙	43-74	槇	84-02
遥	45-58	遙	84-03
瑶	64-86	瑤	84-04

Category 3

22 simplified and traditional kanji pairs exchanged code positions between JIS Level 1 kanji and JIS Level 2 kanji (44 affected code points). The table below shows the characters as found in JIS X 0208-1983, so the simplified form is in the JIS Level 1 column, and the traditional form is in the JIS Level 2 column.

JIS Level 1		JIS Level 2	
鯵	16-19	鰺	82-45
鴬	18-09	鶯	82-84
蛎	19-34	蠣	73-58
撹	19-41	攪	57-88
竃	19-86	竈	67-62
潅	20-35	灌	62-85
諌	20-50	諫	75-61
頚	23-59	頸	80-84
砿	25-60	礦	66-72
蕊	28-41	蘂	73-02
靭	31-57	靱	80-55

JIS Level 1		JIS Level 2	
賎	33-08	賤	76-45
壷	36-59	壺	52-68
砺	37-55	礪	66-74
梼	37-78	檮	59-77
涛	37-83	濤	62-25
迩	38-86	邇	77-78
蝿	39-72	蠅	74-04
桧	41-16	檜	59-56
侭	43-89	儘	48-54
薮	44-89	藪	73-14
篭	47-22	籠	68-38

Category 4

The shapes of several kanji were altered. This category of change is quite subjective (that is the nature of glyph changes), and what appears below are 250 such characters. The actual number of affected kanji depends on your source. The source used here is the Adobe-Japan1-3 character collection. 18 kanji restored to their traditional (or correct, as the case may be) forms in JIS X 0208-1983 are indicated with shading.

1978	1983	
啞	唖	16-02
逢	逢	16-09
芦	芦	16-18
飴	飴	16-27
溢	溢	16-78
鰯	鰯	16-83
淫	淫	16-92
迂	迂	17-10
欝	欝	17-21
厩	厩	17-25
噂	噂	17-29
餌	餌	17-34
焰	焔	17-75
襖	襖	18-08
鷗	鴎	18-10
迦	迦	18-64
恢	恢	18-90
拐	拐	18-93
晦	晦	19-02
喝	喝	19-69
葛	葛	19-75
鞄	鞄	19-83
嚙	噛	19-90
澗	澗	20-34
翰	翰	20-45
翫	翫	20-69
徽	徽	21-11
祇	祇	21-32
俠	侠	22-02
卿	卿	22-10
僅	僅	22-47
軀	躯	22-77
屛	喰	22-84
櫛	櫛	22-91
屑	屑	22-93
靴	靴	23-04
祁	祁	23-23
慧	慧	23-37
稽	稽	23-46
繫	繋	23-50
荆	荊	23-53

1978	1983	
隙	隙	23-68
倦	倦	23-81
嫌	嫌	23-89
捲	捲	23-94
鹼	鹸	24-20
諺	諺	24-33
巷	巷	25-11
昂	昂	25-23
溝	溝	25-34
麴	麹	25-77
鵠	鵠	25-84
甑	甑	25-89
采	采	26-51
榊	榊	26-71
栅	柵	26-84
薩	薩	27-07
鯖	鯖	27-10
錆	錆	27-12
珊	珊	27-25
屢	屢	28-40
遮	遮	28-55
杓	杓	28-61
灼	灼	28-62
繡	繍	29-11
酋	酋	29-22
曙	曙	29-76
渚	渚	29-77
薯	薯	29-82
藷	藷	29-83
哨	哨	30-05
廠	廠	30-19
梢	梢	30-31
蔣	蒋	30-53
醬	醤	30-63
鞘	鞘	30-68
蝕	蝕	31-10
靭	靭	31-57
逗	逗	31-64
翠	翠	31-73
摺	摺	32-02
逝	逝	32-34

1978	1983	
蟬	蝉	32-70
撰	撰	32-81
栓	栓	32-82
煎	煎	32-89
煽	煽	32-90
詮	詮	33-07
噌	噌	33-25
遡	遡	33-44
創	創	33-47
搔	掻	33-63
痩	痩	33-73
遜	遜	34-29
驒	騨	34-45
腿	腿	34-60
黛	黛	34-67
啄	啄	34-79
濯	濯	34-85
琢	琢	34-86
蛸	蛸	34-93
巽	巽	35-07
辿	辿	35-09
棚	棚	35-10
鱈	鱈	35-13
樽	樽	35-14
簞	箪	35-29
註	註	35-80
瀦	瀦	35-85
凋	凋	35-92
捗	捗	36-29
槌	槌	36-40
鎚	鎚	36-42
塚	塚	36-45
摑	掴	36-47
辻	辻	36-52
鄭	鄭	37-02
擢	擢	37-07
溺	溺	37-14
塡	填	37-22
顚	顛	37-31
堵	堵	37-40
屠	屠	37-43

1978	1983		1978	1983		1978	1983	
菟	菟	37-49	鱒	鱒	43-80	爨	爨	64-06
賭	賭	37-50	迄	迄	43-88	珎	珎	64-63
塘	塘	37-68	麵	麺	44-45	甄	甄	65-11
禱	祷	37-88	儲	儲	44-57	甍	甍	65-16
鴇	鴇	38-30	餠	餅	44-63	甕	甕	65-17
瀆	涜	38-34	籾	籾	44-66	皓	皓	66-11
瀞	瀞	38-52	鑓	鑓	44-90	硼	硼	66-79
噸	噸	38-53	愈	愈	44-92	稱	稱	67-42
遁	遁	38-59	癒	癒	44-94	穐	穐	67-52
頓	頓	38-60	猷	猷	45-18	篦	篦	68-25
那	那	38-65	熔	熔	45-48	粐	粐	68-68
謎	謎	38-70	耀	耀	45-52	粮	粮	68-78
灘	灘	38-71	萊	莱	45-73	絽	絽	69-25
楢	楢	38-74	遼	遼	46-43	綮	綮	69-27
禰	禰	39-09	漣	漣	46-90	綟	綟	69-38
囊	嚢	39-25	煉	煉	46-91	翔	翔	70-38
牌	牌	39-55	蓮	蓮	47-01	舮	舮	71-68
這	這	39-71	榔	榔	47-17	芎	芎	71-73
秤	秤	39-73	蠟	蝋	47-25	苒	苒	71-82
剝	剥	39-77	兔	兎	49-29	萁	萁	72-20
箸	箸	40-04	冉	冉	49-39	葱	葱	72-27
潑	溌	40-14	冕	冕	49-43	蔗	蔗	72-84
醱	醗	40-16	冤	冤	49-45	螂	螂	74-07
挽	挽	40-52	吩	吩	51-16	蟒	蟒	74-29
扉	扉	40-66	唳	唳	51-26	褊	褊	74-79
樋	樋	40-85	嘲	嘲	51-62	覯	覯	75-18
柊	柊	41-02	嚥	嚥	51-75	諞	諞	75-70
稗	稗	41-03	堋	堋	52-36	譁	譁	75-86
逼	逼	41-15	媾	媾	53-29	跚	跚	76-73
媛	媛	41-18	寃	寃	53-67	踉	踉	76-84
謬	謬	41-21	屏	屏	54-02	輓	輓	77-46
廟	廟	41-32	悗	悗	56-04	迪	迪	77-76
瀕	瀕	41-46	捩	捩	57-64	迩	邇	77-78
頻	頻	41-49	搆	搆	57-76	邁	邁	78-09
蔽	蔽	42-35	攅	攅	58-25	扈	扈	78-29
瞥	瞥	42-45	斃	斃	58-45	釁	釁	78-55
娩	娩	42-58	枦	枦	59-37	霤	霤	80-37
庖	庖	42-89	枴	枴	59-42	靠	靠	80-49
泡	泡	43-02	梛	梛	59-75	靭	靱	80-55
蓬	蓬	43-09	梍	梍	59-84	頤	頤	80-85
頰	頬	43-43	湮	湮	62-48	鬮	鬮	82-13

1978	1983	
鮗	鮗	82-28
鰺	鰺	82-46

1978	1983	
麪	麪	83-49
龜	龜	83-93

Other definitions of JIS C 6226-1978 and JIS X 0208-1983 differences *may* include the following characters:

1978	1983	
閏	閏	17-28
慨	慨	19-20
概	概	19-21
冴	冴	26-67
捌	捌	27-11

1978	1983	
叱	叱	28-24
噛	噛	51-48
幤	幤	54-82
燗	燗	63-83
藜	藜	73-28

1978	1983	
蛛	蛛	73-65
邉	邉	78-21
閻	閻	79-69
雎	雎	80-19

JIS X 0208-1983 Versus JIS X 0208-1990

This section also supplements Chapter 3. Changes made to JIS X 0208-1983 to create JIS X 0208-1990 were very minor, and basically consist of two categories. The first category consists of characters added to the character set standard. In the case of JIS X 0208-1990, the following two kanji characters were appended after JIS Level 2 kanji:

JIS X 0208-1990	
凜	84-05
熙	84-06

However, there were some very subtle glyph changes introduced with JIS X 0208-1990. These glyph changes can be categorized into approximately six different types. See the following table for several examples of such glyph changes. Furthermore, some of these changes involve simplified kanji being restored to their traditional (or, in some cases, correct) forms.

JIS X 0208-1983	JIS X 0208-1990
帰	帰
公	公
邪	邪
埴	埴
緋	緋
匕	匕

What? You cannot see the differences? This then goes to show how subtle (and subjective) glyph changes can be. The following is a complete list of the 145 affected kanji. Seven kanji restored to their traditional (or correct, as the case may be) forms in JIS X 0208-1990 are indicated with shading.

1983	1990		1983	1990		1983	1990	
偉	偉	16-46	訟	訟	30-57	吏	吏	45-89
緯	緯	16-62	丈	丈	30-70	隣	隣	46-57
違	違	16-67	埴	埴	30-93	麗	麗	46-79
厩	厩	17-25	職	職	31-06	聯	聯	46-94
衛	衛	17-50	船	船	33-05	匕	匕	**50-24**
延	延	17-68	総	総	33-77	雙	雙	50-54
沿	沿	17-72	聡	聡	33-79	喩	喩	51-40
鉛	鉛	17-84	像	像	33-92	圍	圍	52-03
翁	翁	18-07	誕	誕	35-34	姚	姚	53-13
慨	慨	19-20	恥	恥	35-49	娶	娶	53-24
概	概	19-21	兆	兆	35-91	巉	巉	54-58
殻	殻	19-44	眺	眺	36-15	巓	巓	54-60
敢	敢	20-26	聴	聴	36-16	弭	弭	55-25
頑	頑	20-72	跳	跳	36-23	徘	徘	55-49
帰	帰	21-02	庭	庭	36-77	惘	惘	56-17
窮	窮	21-71	廷	廷	36-78	扨	扨	57-14
均	均	22-49	艇	艇	36-90	擲	擲	58-19
傑	傑	23-70	桃	桃	37-77	敝	敝	58-41
穴	穴	23-74	逃	逃	38-08	晟	晟	58-80
健	健	23-82	排	排	39-51	杳	杳	59-32
建	建	23-90	輩	輩	39-58	柧	柧	59-55
交	交	24-82	班	班	40-41	椰	椰	60-31
公	公	24-88	頒	頒	40-50	榧	榧	60-50
更	更	25-25	悲	悲	40-65	橄	橄	60-77
校	校	25-27	扉	扉	40-66	檐	檐	**60-89**
硬	硬	25-37	斐	斐	40-69	氈	氈	**61-65**
絞	絞	25-42	緋	緋	40-76	渣	渣	**62-54**
考	考	25-45	誹	誹	40-80	漑	漑	62-84
降	降	25-63	貧	貧	41-47	滾	滾	62-88
拷	拷	25-73	父	父	41-67	漾	漾	63-01
罫	罫	26-65	分	分	42-12	燿	燿	64-02
使	使	27-40	粉	粉	42-20	珥	珥	64-66
史	史	27-43	紛	紛	42-22	琲	琲	64-74
邪	邪	28-57	雰	雰	42-23	瓠	瓠	65-01
収	収	28-93	便	便	42-56	癲	癲	66-01
瞬	瞬	29-54	盆	盆	43-63	磔	磔	66-89
舜	舜	29-56	桝	桝	43-81	窕	窕	67-58
松	松	30-30	耶	耶	44-77	緝	緝	69-41

1983	1990	
縵	縵	69-60
翡	翡	70-39
聚	聚	70-60
聰	聰	70-66
聶	聶	70-67
腓	腓	71-04
膵	膵	71-25
菲	菲	72-43
蜚	蜚	73-84
蠶	蠶	74-36
衮	衮	74-49

1983	1990	
裴	裴	74-74
褫	褫	74-85
褻	褻	74-88
襪	襪	75-04
襯	襯	75-05
訝	訝	75-35
贅	贅	76-52
贏	贏	76-55
躑	躑	77-22
躡	躡	77-26
鑷	鑷	79-50

1983	1990	
隘	隘	80-07
靠	靠	80-49
靱	靱	80-55
頌	頌	80-83
顳	顳	81-03
魍	魍	82-19
鯡	鯡	82-44
鯱	鯱	82-47
鵈	鵈	82-94

JIS X 0212-1990 Versus JIS C 6226-1978

The following table supplements material about JIS X 0212-1990 in Chapter 3 by illustrating the 28 kanji that were removed from the JIS X 0208 series in 1983, but were subsequently included in JIS X 0212-1990.

JIS C 6226-1978		JIS X 0208:1997		JIS X 0212-1990	
俠	22-02	侠	22-02	俠	17-34
啞	16-02	唖	16-02	啞	21-64
嚙	19-90	噛	19-90	嚙	22-58
囊	39-25	嚢	39-25	囊	22-76
塡	37-22	填	37-22	塡	24-20
屢	28-40	屡	28-40	屢	26-90
搔	33-63	掻	33-63	搔	32-43
摑	36-47	掴	36-47	摑	32-59
攢	58-25	攅	58-25	攢	33-34
潑	40-14	溌	40-14	潑	40-53
瀆	38-34	涜	38-34	瀆	41-12
焰	17-75	焔	17-75	焰	41-79
瘦	33-73	痩	33-73	瘦	45-87
禱	37-88	祷	37-88	禱	48-80
繡	29-11	繍	29-11	繡	52-55
繫	23-50	繋	23-50	繫	52-58
萊	45-73	莱	45-73	萊	56-39
蔣	30-53	蒋	30-53	蔣	57-22
蠟	47-25	蝋	47-25	蠟	59-88
軀	22-77	躯	22-77	軀	64-52
醬	30-63	醤	30-63	醬	66-83
醱	40-16	醗	40-16	醱	66-87

JIS C 6226-1978		JIS X 0208:1997		JIS X 0212-1990	
頰	43-43	頬	43-43	頰	72-04
顚	37-31	顛	37-31	顚	72-19
鷗	18-10	鴎	18-10	鷗	76-31
鹼	24-20	鹸	24-20	鹼	76-59
麴	25-77	麹	25-77	麴	76-79
麵	44-45	麺	44-45	麵	76-80

Jōyō Kanji

The following table lists the 95 kanji that were added to Tōyō Kanji in 1981 to form Jōyō Kanji. This brought the total number of kanji from 1,850 to 1,945. JIS X 0208:1997 Row-Cell codes are provided.

	JIS X 0208:1997		JIS X 0208:1997		JIS X 0208:1997
渦	17-18	桟	27-23	塚	36-45
猿	17-78	肢	27-72	漬	36-50
凹	17-90	遮	28-55	釣	36-64
稼	18-52	蛇	28-56	亭	36-66
拐	18-93	酌	28-64	偵	36-69
涯	19-22	汁	29-33	泥	37-05
垣	19-32	塾	29-46	搭	37-75
殻	19-44	宵	30-12	棟	37-79
潟	19-67	尚	30-16	洞	38-22
喝	19-69	壌	30-77	凸	38-44
褐	19-76	唇	31-16	屯	38-54
缶	20-44	甚	31-51	縄	38-76
頑	20-72	据	31-88	猫	39-13
挟	22-20	杉	31-89	把	39-36
矯	22-26	逝	32-34	覇	39-38
襟	22-63	斉	32-38	漠	39-89
隅	22-89	仙	32-71	肌	40-09
靴	23-04	栓	32-82	鉢	40-13
渓	23-44	挿	33-62	扉	40-66
蛍	23-54	曹	33-66	披	40-68
嫌	23-89	槽	33-69	頻	41-49
洪	25-31	藻	33-84	瓶	41-51
溝	25-34	駄	34-44	雰	42-23
昆	26-11	濯	34-85	塀	42-29
崎	26-74	棚	35-10	俸	42-80
皿	27-14	挑	36-09	泡	43-02
傘	27-17	眺	36-15	褒	43-11

	JIS X 0208:1997
僕	43-45
朴	43-49
堀	43-57
磨	43-65
抹	43-85

	JIS X 0208:1997
岬	44-08
妄	44-49
戻	44-65
厄	44-81
癒	44-94

	JIS X 0208:1997
悠	45-10
羅	45-69
竜	46-21
枠	47-40

The Jōyō Kanji document lists official traditional forms for 355 of the 1,945 Jōyō Kanji, as shown in the following table. JIS X 0208:1997 Row-Cell codes are provided. Those traditional forms that map to IBM Selected Kanji or Unicode include hexadecimal codes prefixed with "I+" and "U+," respectively. Those traditional forms that are considered JIS78 variants are marked as "JIS78" (same code point as standard form, but different vintage of JIS X 0208). The one instance that maps to JIS X 0212-1990 has been shaded. Note how Row-Cell 42-59 has three traditional forms.

Standard		Traditional	
亜	16-01	亞	48-19
悪	16-13	惡	56-08
圧	16-21	壓	52-58
囲	16-47	圍	52-03
為	16-57	爲	64-10
医	16-69	醫	78-48
壱	16-77	壹	52-69
逸	16-79	逸	`I+FBB4`
稲	16-80	稻	67-43
隠	17-03	隱	80-12
営	17-36	營	51-59
栄	17-41	榮	60-38
衛	17-50	衞	74-44
駅	17-56	驛	81-67
謁	17-58	謁	
円	17-63	圓	52-04
縁	17-79	緣	`U+7DE3`
塩	17-86	鹽	83-37
奥	17-92	奧	52-92
応	17-94	應	56-70
横	18-03	橫	`I+FAEE`
欧	18-04	歐	61-31
殴	18-05	毆	61-56
黄	18-11	黃	`U+9EC3`
温	18-25	溫	`U+6EAB`

Standard		Traditional	
穏	18-26	穩	67-51
仮	18-30	假	48-81
価	18-33	價	49-11
禍	18-50	禍	
画	18-72	畫	65-33
会	18-81	會	48-82
壊	18-85	壞	52-53
悔	18-89	悔	
懐	18-91	懷	56-71
海	19-04	海	
絵	19-08	繪	69-73
慨	19-20	慨	
概	19-21	槪	
拡	19-40	擴	58-18
殻	19-44	殼	61-55
覚	19-48	覺	75-20
学	19-56	學	53-60
岳	19-57	嶽	54-54
楽	19-58	樂	60-59
喝	19-69	喝	*JIS78*
渇	19-73	渴	`U+6E34`
褐	19-76	褐	
勧	20-11	勸	50-16
巻	20-12	卷	50-43
寛	20-18	寬	`I+FAAA`

Standard		Traditional	
歓	20-31	歡	61-36
漢	20-33	漢	
缶	20-44	罐	70-05
観	20-49	觀	75-23
関	20-56	關	79-80
陥	20-57	陷	79-92
器	20-79	器	
既	20-91	既	
帰	21-02	歸	61-37
気	21-04	氣	61-70
祈	21-07	祈	
偽	21-22	僞	49-06
戯	21-26	戲	57-06
犠	21-30	犧	64-26
旧	21-76	舊	71-49
拠	21-82	據	58-01
挙	21-83	擧	58-09
虚	21-85	虛	`U+865B`
峡	22-14	峽	54-23
挟	22-20	挾	57-49
狭	22-25	狹	64-37
郷	22-31	鄕	`I+FBB8`
響	22-33	響	
暁	22-39	曉	58-92
勤	22-48	勤	

Standard		Traditional	
謹	22-64	謹	
区	22-72	區	50-31
駆	22-78	驅	81-60
勲	23-14	勳	50-14
薫	23-16	薰	I+FB9E
径	23-34	徑	55-45
恵	23-35	惠	56-10
掲	23-39	揭	U+63ED
渓	23-44	溪	62-68
経	23-48	經	69-20
継	23-49	繼	69-75
茎	23-52	莖	72-19
蛍	23-54	螢	74-05
軽	23-58	輕	77-43
鶏	23-60	鷄	83-17
芸	23-61	藝	73-26
撃	23-66	擊	33-03
欠	23-71	缺	69-94
倹	23-80	儉	49-13
剣	23-85	劍	49-88
圏	23-87	圈	52-01
検	24-01	檢	60-93
権	24-02	權	60-62
献	24-05	獻	64-59
研	24-06	硏	U+784F
県	24-09	縣	69-49
険	24-17	險	80-10
顕	24-18	顯	80-93
験	24-19	驗	81-68
厳	24-23	嚴	51-78
効	24-90	效	58-35
広	25-13	廣	55-02
恒	25-17	恆	55-81
鉱	25-59	鑛	79-42
号	25-70	號	73-43
国	25-81	國	52-02
穀	25-82	穀	
黒	25-85	黑	I+FC4B
済	26-49	濟	63-27
砕	26-53	碎	66-76
斎	26-56	齋	67-23
剤	26-62	劑	49-93
桜	26-89	櫻	61-15
殺	27-06	殺	
雑	27-08	雜	80-24
参	27-18	參	50-52
惨	27-20	慘	56-46
桟	27-23	棧	60-02
蚕	27-29	蠶	74-36
賛	27-31	贊	76-53
残	27-36	殘	61-44
祉	27-67	祉	
糸	27-69	絲	69-15
視	27-75	視	
歯	27-85	齒	83-79
児	27-89	兒	49-27
辞	28-13	辭	77-70
湿	28-30	濕	63-28
実	28-34	實	53-73
写	28-44	寫	53-77
煮	28-49	煮	
社	28-50	社	
者	28-52	者	
釈	28-65	釋	78-57
寿	28-87	壽	52-72
収	28-93	收	58-32
臭	29-13	臭	
従	29-30	從	55-47
渋	29-34	澁	63-07
獣	29-35	獸	64-57
縦	29-36	縱	69-52
祝	29-43	祝	
粛	29-45	肅	70-73
処	29-72	處	49-61
暑	29-75	暑	
緒	29-79	緖	I+FB8E
署	29-80	署	
諸	29-84	諸	I+FBA9
叙	29-86	敍	58-38
奨	30-09	奬	52-93
将	30-13	將	53-82
渉	30-36	涉	U+6D89
焼	30-38	燒	63-86
祥	30-45	祥	I+FB80
称	30-46	稱	67-42
証	30-58	證	75-90
乗	30-72	乘	48-11
剰	30-74	剩	49-84
壌	30-77	壤	52-65
嬢	30-78	孃	53-48
条	30-82	條	59-74
浄	30-84	淨	62-38
状	30-85	狀	U+72C0
畳	30-86	疊	65-40
譲	30-89	讓	76-10
醸	30-90	釀	78-54
嘱	30-92	囑	51-86
触	31-08	觸	75-29
寝	31-18	寢	53-74
慎	31-21	愼	56-38
真	31-31	眞	66-35
神	31-32	神	I+FB7E
尽	31-52	盡	66-24
図	31-62	圖	52-06
粋	31-72	粹	68-79
酔	31-76	醉	78-45
随	31-79	隨	78-14
髄	31-81	髓	81-82
数	31-84	數	58-43
枢	31-85	樞	60-68
瀬	32-05	瀨	I+FB50
声	32-28	聲	70-65
静	32-37	靜	80-48
斉	32-38	齊	83-78
摂	32-61	攝	57-80
窃	32-64	竊	67-70
節	32-65	節	
専	32-76	專	53-83
戦	32-79	戰	57-05
浅	32-85	淺	62-41
潜	32-88	潛	63-10
繊	33-01	纖	69-89
践	33-09	踐	76-88

Standard		Traditional	
銭	33-12	錢	79-02
禅	33-21	禪	67-24
祖	33-36	祖	
僧	33-46	僧	
双	33-48	雙	50-54
壮	33-52	壯	52-67
層	33-56	層	
捜	33-60	搜	57-51
挿	33-62	插	57-71
巣	33-67	巢	U+5DE2
争	33-72	爭	64-07
総	33-77	總	69-33
荘	33-81	莊	72-23
装	33-85	裝	74-70
騒	33-91	騷	81-59
増	33-93	增	I+FA9D
憎	33-94	憎	
臓	34-01	臟	71-39
蔵	34-02	藏	73-22
贈	34-03	贈	
即	34-08	卽	U+537D
属	34-16	屬	54-04
続	34-19	續	69-84
堕	34-36	墮	52-56
体	34-46	體	81-83
対	34-48	對	53-84
帯	34-51	帶	54-72
滞	34-58	滯	62-92
台	34-70	臺	71-42
滝	34-76	瀧	34-77
択	34-82	擇	58-04
沢	34-84	澤	63-23
単	35-17	單	51-37
嘆	35-18	嘆	
担	35-20	擔	57-31
胆	35-32	膽	71-28
団	35-36	團	52-05
弾	35-38	彈	55-28
断	35-39	斷	58-50
痴	35-52	癡	65-87
遅	35-57	遲	78-15
昼	35-75	晝	58-76
虫	35-78	蟲	74-21
鋳	35-82	鑄	79-41
著	35-88	著	
庁	36-03	廳	55-12
徴	36-07	徵	U+5FB5
懲	36-08	懲	
聴	36-16	聽	70-69
勅	36-28	敕	58-37
鎮	36-35	鎭	79-15
塚	36-45	塚	*JIS78*
逓	36-94	遞	78-10
鉄	37-20	鐵	79-36
転	37-30	轉	77-59
点	37-32	點	83-58
伝	37-33	傳	49-03
都	37-52	都	I+FBB7
党	37-62	黨	83-62
盗	37-80	盜	61-25
灯	37-84	燈	37-85
当	37-86	當	65-36
闘	38-14	鬪	82-12
徳	38-33	德	I+FABA
独	38-40	獨	64-55
読	38-41	讀	76-06
突	38-45	突	
届	38-47	屆	53-92
縄	38-76	繩	69-74
難	38-81	難	
弐	38-85	貳	76-40
悩	39-26	惱	56-29
脳	39-30	腦	71-10
覇	39-38	霸	59-17
廃	39-49	廢	55-06
拝	39-50	拜	57-33
梅	39-63	梅	
売	39-68	賣	76-46
麦	39-94	麥	83-46
発	40-15	發	66-04
髪	40-17	髮	81-91
抜	40-20	拔	57-22
繁	40-43	繁	
晩	40-53	晚	
蛮	40-58	蠻	74-39
卑	40-60	卑	
碑	40-74	碑	
秘	40-75	祕	67-16
浜	41-45	濱	63-32
賓	41-48	賓	
頻	41-49	頻	*JIS78*
敏	41-50	敏	
瓶	41-51	甁	I+FB6E
侮	41-78	侮	
福	42-01	福	I+FB82
払	42-07	拂	57-36
仏	42-09	佛	48-39
併	42-27	倂	U+5002
塀	42-29	塀	
並	42-34	竝	67-77
変	42-49	變	58-46
辺	42-53	邊	78-20
勉	42-57	勉	
弁	42-59	辨	49-94
弁	42-59	瓣	65-02
弁	42-59	辯	77-71
歩	42-66	步	U+6B65
穂	42-70	穗	67-47
宝	42-85	寶	53-79
褒	43-11	襃	74-81
豊	43-13	豐	76-20
墨	43-47	墨	
翻	43-61	飜	70-44
毎	43-72	每	
万	43-92	萬	72-63
満	43-94	滿	62-64
免	44-40	免	
黙	44-59	默	64-52
戻	44-65	戾	U+623E
薬	44-84	藥	73-27
訳	44-85	譯	76-03
予	45-29	豫	48-14
余	45-30	餘	81-17

Standard		Traditional		Standard		Traditional		Standard		Traditional	
与	45-31	與	71-48	虜	46-26	虜		歴	46-82	歷	U+6B77
誉	45-32	譽	76-05	両	46-30	兩	49-32	恋	46-88	戀	56-88
揺	45-41	搖	57-74	猟	46-36	獵	64-58	練	46-93	練	
様	45-45	樣	60-75	緑	46-48	綠	I+FB8D	錬	47-03	鍊	U+934A
謡	45-56	謠	75-79	塁	46-61	壘	52-62	炉	47-07	爐	64-04
来	45-72	來	48-52	涙	46-62	淚	U+6DDA	労	47-11	勞	50-09
頼	45-74	賴	I+FBAE	類	46-64	類		廊	47-13	廊	
乱	45-80	亂	48-12	励	46-69	勵	50-15	朗	47-15	朗	I+FAE0
欄	45-83	欄		礼	46-73	禮	67-25	楼	47-16	樓	60-76
覧	45-87	覽	75-21	霊	46-78	靈	80-45	郎	47-26	郎	I+FBB6
隆	46-20	隆	I+FBE9	齢	46-80	齡	83-84	録	47-31	錄	U+9304
竜	46-21	龍	46-22	暦	46-81	曆	U+66C6	湾	47-49	灣	63-52

The following table lists the 10 kanji in the Jinmei-yō Kanji list that have official traditional forms:

Standard		Traditional		Standard		Traditional		Standard		Traditional	
巌	20-64	巖	54-62	猪	35-86	猪	I+FB5E	禄	47-29	祿	67-19
渚	29-77	渚	*JIS78*	禎	36-87	禎		亘	47-43	亙	47-42
穣	30-87	穰	67-53	弥	44-79	彌	55-29				
琢	34-86	琢	*JIS78*	祐	45-20	祐					

IBM Selected Kanji and Non-Kanji

The tables in this section supplement material found in Appendix C, *Vendor Character Set Standards*. Specifically, they illustrate how the 388 IBM Selected Kanji and Selected Non-kanji are mapped from DBCS-PC (Shift-JIS) to DBCS-EUC (EUC-JP) encoding.

The following table illustrates how two IBM Selected Non-kanji and one Selected Kanji are mapped to JIS X 0208:1997 code points in DBCS-EUC encoding:

	IBM DBCS-PC	JIS X 0208:1997
¬	FA54	02-44
∵	FA5B	02-72
昂	FAD0	25-23

The following table illustrates how one IBM Selected Non-kanji and 279 Selected Kanji are mapped to JIS X 0212-1990 code points in DBCS-EUC encoding:

	IBM	JIS X 0212
￤	FA55	02-35
纊	FA5C	52-67
褜	FA5D	60-63
鍈	FA5E	68-73
銈	FA5F	67-88
蓜	FA60	57-01
俉	FA61	17-27
昱	FA63	34-13
棈	FA64	35-92
鋹	FA65	68-48
曻	FA66	34-31
彅	FA67	28-84
丨	FA68	16-09
仡	FA69	16-40
伀	FA6B	16-50
伃	FA6C	16-52
伹	FA6D	16-67
佖	FA6E	16-78
侒	FA6F	17-07
侊	FA70	17-03
侚	FA71	17-12
侔	FA72	17-09
俍	FA73	17-30
偀	FA74	17-63
倢	FA75	17-56
俿	FA76	17-40
倞	FA77	17-55
偆	FA78	17-67
偰	FA79	17-84
偂	FA7A	17-65
傔	FA7B	18-03
僘	FA7D	18-27
兊	FA7E	18-70
兤	FA80	18-77
冝	FA81	18-85
冾	FA82	18-92
刕	FA84	19-21
劜	FA85	19-56
劦	FA86	19-59
勀	FA87	19-69
勛	FA88	19-78

	IBM	JIS X 0212
匀	FA89	19-91
卲	FA8C	20-32
厓	FA8D	20-39
厲	FA8E	20-48
叝	FA8F	20-62
咜	FA91	21-10
咩	FA93	21-15
哿	FA94	21-36
喆	FA95	21-72
坥	FA97	23-34
垬	FA98	23-68
埈	FA99	23-72
埇	FA9A	23-71
墲	FA9E	24-46
夋	FA9F	24-65
奓	FAA0	24-85
奛	FAA1	24-87
奝	FAA2	24-88
奣	FAA3	24-92
妤	FAA4	25-15
妺	FAA5	25-23
孖	FAA6	26-30
寀	FAA7	26-59
甯	FAA8	45-10
寘	FAA9	26-65
尞	FAAB	26-75
岦	FAAC	27-19
岺	FAAD	27-24
崧	FAAF	27-42
嵂	FAB2	27-48
嵭	FAB3	27-62
嶸	FAB4	27-84
嶹	FAB5	27-85
巐	FAB6	27-89
弡	FAB7	28-68
弴	FAB8	28-77
彧	FAB9	28-94
忞	FABB	29-34
恝	FABC	29-71
悊	FABE	29-80
惞	FABF	30-16

	IBM	JIS X 0212
惕	FAC0	30-12
惲	FAC2	30-19
愑	FAC3	30-29
愷	FAC4	30-45
愰	FAC5	30-41
憘	FAC6	30-68
戓	FAC7	31-08
抦	FAC8	31-41
揵	FAC9	32-36
摠	FACA	32-68
撝	FACB	32-84
擎	FACC	33-06
昀	FACE	33-85
昕	FACF	33-92
昉	FAD1	33-88
昮	FAD2	34-11
昞	FAD3	34-01
昤	FAD4	34-05
晗	FAD6	34-24
晙	FAD7	34-26
晳	FAD9	34-36
暙	FADA	34-50
暠	FADB	34-55
暲	FADC	34-59
暿	FADD	34-62
曺	FADE	34-77
朎	FADF	34-80
杦	FAE1	35-01
枻	FAE2	35-21
桒	FAE3	35-41
柀	FAE4	35-25
桄	FAE6	35-56
棏	FAE7	35-94
楨	FAE9	36-44
榘	FAEB	36-57
槢	FAEC	36-74
樰	FAED	36-93
橆	FAEF	37-07
橳	FAF0	37-21
橾	FAF1	37-22
櫤	FAF3	37-53

	IBM	JIS X 0212		IBM	JIS X 0212		IBM	JIS X 0212
毖	FAF4	38-24	琇	FB65	44-05	訷	FBA4	61-52
氿	FAF5	38-55	珵	FB66	43-89	詹	FBA5	61-74
汜	FAF6	38-64	琦	FB67	44-11	誧	FBA6	61-90
沆	FAF7	38-74	琪	FB68	44-14	誾	FBA7	62-04
汯	FAF8	38-67	琩	FB69	44-13	諟	FBA8	62-16
泚	FAF9	39-01	琮	FB6A	44-18	諶	FBAA	62-21
洄	FAFA	39-11	瑢	FB6B	44-34	譓	FBAB	62-43
涇	FAFB	39-39	璉	FB6C	44-48	賰	FBAD	63-25
浯	FAFC	39-35	璟	FB6D	44-57	贒	FBAF	63-35
涖	FB40	39-43	畯	FB6F	45-27	軏	FBB2	64-57
涬	FB41	39-47	皜	FB71	46-27	遧	FBB5	65-66
淏	FB42	39-57	皛	FB73	46-26	鄧	FBB9	66-39
淼	FB45	39-70	皦	FB74	46-35	釚	FBBA	67-08
渹	FB46	39-78	睆	FB76	46-82	釗	FBBB	67-06
湜	FB47	39-92	劯	FB77	19-61	釞	FBBC	67-09
渧	FB48	39-75	砡	FB78	47-53	釭	FBBD	67-15
渼	FB49	39-80	硎	FB79	47-66	釮	FBBE	67-16
溿	FB4A	40-17	硤	FB7A	47-73	釤	FBBF	67-10
澈	FB4B	40-69	硺	FB7B	47-77	釥	FBC0	67-11
澵	FB4C	40-88	禔	FB81	48-69	鈆	FBC1	67-28
濵	FB4D	41-06	禛	FB83	48-73	鈐	FBC2	67-33
瀅	FB4E	41-11	竑	FB84	49-72	鈊	FBC3	67-31
瀇	FB4F	41-13	竫	FB87	49-76	鈺	FBC4	67-53
炅	FB51	41-42	箞	FB88	50-27	鉀	FBC5	67-56
炫	FB52	41-51	絈	FB8A	51-65	鈼	FBC6	67-54
焏	FB53	41-73	絜	FB8B	51-72	鉎	FBC7	67-63
焄	FB54	41-67	綷	FB8C	52-07	鉙	FBC8	67-67
煜	FB55	41-92	繒	FB8F	52-52	鉑	FBC9	67-65
煆	FB56	41-84	罇	FB90	52-82	鈹	FBCA	67-52
煇	FB57	41-85	羡	FB91	53-14	鉧	FBCB	67-73
燁	FB59	42-19	茁	FB93	55-62	銧	FBCC	68-06
燾	FB5A	42-29	荿	FB95	56-02	鉷	FBCD	67-81
犱	FB5B	42-79	菇	FB96	56-23	鉸	FBCE	67-82
犾	FB5C	42-81	菶	FB97	56-33	鋧	FBCF	68-43
猤	FB5D	43-14	葈	FB98	56-49	鋗	FBD0	68-33
獷	FB5F	43-42	蒴	FB99	56-84	鋙	FBD1	68-35
玽	FB60	43-70	蕓	FB9A	57-38	鋐	FBD2	68-30
珉	FB61	43-74	蕙	FB9B	57-40	鋕	FBD4	68-32
珖	FB62	43-80	蕫	FB9C	57-49	鋠	FBD5	68-39
珣	FB63	43-84	裵	FBA2	60-51	鋓	FBD6	68-31
珒	FB64	43-78	訒	FBA3	61-40	錥	FBD7	68-64

	IBM	JIS X 0212
錡	FBD8	68-62
鋻	FBD9	68-49
錞	FBDB	68-60
鋿	FBDC	68-50
錝	FBDD	68-59
錂	FBDE	68-52
鍰	FBDF	68-90
鍗	FBE0	68-79
鎤	FBE1	69-19
鏆	FBE2	69-31
鏞	FBE3	69-41
鏸	FBE4	69-48

	IBM	JIS X 0212
鐱	FBE5	69-66
鑅	FBE6	69-74
鑈	FBE7	69-75
隝	FBEB	70-72
隯	FBEC	70-79
霳	FBED	71-12
靃	FBEF	71-14
靏	FBF1	71-17
靕	FBF3	71-18
顗	FBF4	72-17
顥	FBF5	72-22
餧	FBF8	72-61

	IBM	JIS X 0212
驎	FBFB	73-49
髜	FC40	73-77
魵	FC41	74-45
鮏	FC43	74-59
鮱	FC44	74-70
鮻	FC45	74-74
鰀	FC46	75-05
鵰	FC47	75-91
鵫	FC48	75-90
鸙	FC4A	76-54

The following table illustrates how the remaining 25 IBM Select Non-kanji and 81 Selected Kanji are mapped to JIS X 0212-1990 user-defined code points, according to IBM and OSF (only 80 IBM Selected Kanji are covered in the "IBM" column):

	PC	IBM	OSF
ⅰ	FA40	83-01	83-83
ⅱ	FA41	83-02	83-84
ⅲ	FA42	83-03	83-85
ⅳ	FA43	83-04	83-86
ⅴ	FA44	83-05	83-87
ⅵ	FA45	83-06	83-88
ⅶ	FA46	83-07	83-89
ⅷ	FA47	83-08	83-90
ⅸ	FA48	83-09	83-91
ⅹ	FA49	83-10	83-92
Ⅰ	FA4A	83-11	83-93
Ⅱ	FA4B	83-12	83-94
Ⅲ	FA4C	83-13	84-01
Ⅳ	FA4D	83-14	84-02
Ⅴ	FA4E	83-15	84-03
Ⅵ	FA4F	83-16	84-04
Ⅶ	FA50	83-17	84-05
Ⅷ	FA51	83-18	84-06
Ⅸ	FA52	83-19	84-07
Ⅹ	FA53	83-20	84-08
'	FA56	83-21	84-09
"	FA57	83-22	84-10
㈱	FA58	83-23	84-11

	PC	IBM	OSF
№	FA59	83-24	84-12
℡	FA5A	83-25	84-13
炻	FA62	84-01	84-14
仼	FA6A	84-02	84-15
僴	FA7C	84-03	84-16
凬	FA83	84-04	84-17
匇	FA8A	84-05	84-18
匤	FA8B	84-06	84-19
﨎	FA90	84-07	84-20
咊	FA92	84-08	84-21
坙	FA96	84-09	84-22
﨏	FA9B	84-10	84-23
塚	FA9C	84-11	84-24
增	FA9D	84-12	84-25
寬	FAAA	84-14	84-26
峵	FAAE	84-15	84-27
嵓	FAB0	84-16	84-28
﨑	FAB1	84-17	84-29
德	FABA	84-18	84-30
悅	FABD	84-19	84-31
愠	FAC1	84-20	84-32
敎	FACD	84-21	84-33
昻	FAD0		84-34

	PC	IBM	OSF
晥	FAD5	84-23	84-35
晴	FAD8	84-24	84-36
朗	FAE0	84-25	84-37
栁	FAE5	84-26	84-38
﨓	FAE8	84-27	84-39
﨔	FAEA	84-28	84-40
橫	FAEE	84-29	84-41
櫢	FAF2	84-30	84-42
淸	FB43	84-31	84-43
淲	FB44	84-32	84-44
瀨	FB50	84-34	84-45
凞	FB58	84-36	84-46
猪	FB5E	84-37	84-47
甁	FB6E	84-38	84-48
皂	FB70	84-39	84-49
皞	FB72	84-40	84-50
益	FB75	84-41	84-51
礰	FB7C	84-43	84-52
礼	FB7D	84-44	84-53
神	FB7E	84-45	84-54
祥	FB80	84-46	84-55
福	FB82	84-47	84-56
竫	FB85	84-48	84-57

	PC	IBM	OSF
靖	FB86	84-49	84-58
精	FB89	84-51	84-59
綠	FB8D	84-52	84-60
緖	FB8E	84-53	84-61
羽	FB92	84-54	84-62
荢	FB94	84-55	84-63
蕅	FB9D	84-56	84-64
薰	FB9E	84-57	84-65
穐	FB9F	84-58	84-66
蚟	FBA0	84-59	84-67
蠇	FBA1	84-60	84-68
諸	FBA9	84-62	84-69
譿	FBAC	84-63	84-70
賴	FBAE	84-64	84-71

	PC	IBM	OSF
赶	FBB0	84-65	84-72
𧺆	FBB1	84-66	84-73
𨑨	FBB3	84-67	84-74
逸	FBB4	84-68	84-75
郞	FBB6	84-69	84-76
都	FBB7	84-70	84-77
鄕	FBB8	84-71	84-78
鋳	FBD3	84-72	84-79
鋅	FBDA	84-73	84-80
閒	FBE8	84-74	84-81
隆	FBE9	84-75	84-82
隝	FBEA	84-76	84-83
靊	FBEE	84-77	84-84
靏	FBF0	84-78	84-85

	PC	IBM	OSF
靑	FBF2	84-79	84-86
飯	FBF6	84-81	84-87
飼	FBF7	84-82	84-88
館	FBF9	84-83	84-89
馞	FBFA	84-84	84-90
髙	FBFC	84-85	84-91
𩵽	FC42	84-86	84-92
鶴	FC49	84-87	84-93
黑	FC4B	84-88	84-94

The following table illustrates a single special-case mapping, according to IBM:

	IBM	JIS X 0212
昻	8D56	84-22

Duplicate Hanja in KS X 1001:1992

The KS X 1001:1992 character set standard, because of its design, includes 268 duplicate hanja. This is because the designers of this character set standard decided to order the hanja according to reading (which is fine), but decided to duplicately encode those hanja that have multiple readings. The following table illustrates these 268 duplicate hanja arranged by unique hanja. KS X 1001:1992 Row-Cell codes, the corresponding Unicode values, and readings (using hangul and transliterated) are also provided.

Hanja	KS X 1001:1992	Unicode	Hangul	Readings
賈	42-25,45-47	8CC8,F903	가,고	*ga,go*
降	43-29,90-02	964D,FA09	강,항	*gang,hang*
豈	43-48,49-34	F900,8C48	개,기	*gae,gi*
更	43-54,44-58	F901,66F4	갱,경	*gaeng,gyeong*
車	43-71,83-19	F902,8ECA	거,차	*geo,ca*
見	44-24,90-70	898B,FA0A	견,현	*gyeon,hyeon*
契	44-88,48-48	5951,F909	계,글	*gye,geul*
滑	45-72,92-33	F904,6ED1	골,활	*gol,hwal*
串	45-90,46-13	4E32,F905	곶,관	*goj,gwan*
廓	46-09,92-09	5ED3,FA0B	곽,확	*gwag,hwag*

Hanja	KS X 1001:1992	Unicode	Hangul	Readings
句	47-03,47-91	53E5,F906	구,귀	*gu,gwi*
龜	47-47,48-02,48-24	9F9C,F907,F908	구,귀,균	*gu,gwi,gyun*
金	48-61,49-49	F90A,91D1	금,김	*geum,gim*
喇	49-52,52-90	F90B,5587	나,라	*na,ra*
奈	49-53,50-15	F90C,5948	나,내	*na,nae*
懶	49-56,52-91	F90D,61F6	나,라	*na,ra*
拏	49-57,52-92	62CF,F95B	나,라	*na,ra*
癩	49-59,52-93	F90E,7669	나,라	*na,ra*
羅	49-60,52-94	F90F,7F85	나,라	*na,ra*
蘿	49-61,53-01	F910,863F	나,라	*na,ra*
螺	49-62,53-02	F911,87BA	나,라	*na,ra*
裸	49-63,53-03	F912,88F8	나,라	*na,ra*
邏	49-64,53-04	F913,908F	나,라	*na,ra*
樂	49-66,53-05,68-37,72-89	F914,F95C,6A02,F9BF	낙,락,악,요	*nag,rag,ag,yo*
洛	49-67,53-06	F915,6D1B	낙,락	*nag,rag*
烙	49-68,53-07	F916,70D9	낙,락	*nag,rag*
珞	49-69,53-08	F917,73DE	낙,락	*nag,rag*
落	49-70,53-10	F918,843D	낙,락	*nag,rag*
諾	49-71,53-11	8AFE,F95D	낙,락	*nag,rag*
酪	49-72,53-12	F919,916A	낙,락	*nag,rag*
駱	49-73,53-13	F91A,99F1	낙,락	*nag,rag*
亂	49-74,53-15	F91B,4E82	난,란	*nan,ran*
卵	49-75,53-16	F91C,5375	난,란	*nan,ran*
欄	49-77,53-17	F91D,6B04	난,란	*nan,ran*
爛	49-79,53-20	F91E,721B	난,란	*nan,ran*
蘭	49-80,53-21	F91F,862D	난,란	*nan,ran*
鸞	49-82,53-22	F920,9E1E	난,란	*nan,ran*
嵐	49-86,53-25	F921,5D50	남,람	*nam,ram*
濫	49-90,53-29	F922,6FEB	남,람	*nam,ram*
藍	49-92,53-32	F923,85CD	남,람	*nam,ram*
襤	49-93,53-33	F924,8964	남,람	*nam,ram*
拉	49-94,53-35	F925,62C9	납,랍	*nab,rab*
臘	50-02,53-36	F926,81D8	납,랍	*nab,rab*
蠟	50-03,53-37	F927,881F	납,랍	*nab,rab*
廊	50-07,53-38	F928,5ECA	낭,랑	*nang,rang*
朗	50-08,53-39	F929,6717	낭,랑	*nang,rang*
浪	50-09,53-40	F92A,6D6A	낭,랑	*nang,rang*
狼	50-10,53-41	F92B,72FC	낭,랑	*nang,rang*
郎	50-11,53-45	F92C,90DE	낭,랑	*nang,rang*
來	50-13,53-46	F92D,4F86	내,래	*nae,rae*
冷	50-18,53-50	F92E,51B7	냉,랭	*naeng,raeng*

Hanja	KS X 1001:1992	Unicode	Hangul	Readings
女	50-19,69-92	5973,F981	녀,여	*nyeo,yeo*
年	50-20,70-36	5E74,F98E	년,연	*nyeon,yeon*
撚	50-21,70-42	649A,F991	년,연	*nyeon,yeon*
秊	50-22,70-60	79CA,F995	년,연	*nyeon,yeon*
念	50-23,70-86	5FF5,F9A3	념,염	*nyeom,yeom*
捻	50-26,70-87	637B,F9A4	념,염	*nyeom,yeom*
寧	50-27,54-24,71-12	5BE7,F95F,F9AA	녕,령,영	*nyeong,ryeong,yeong*
勞	50-30,54-44	F92F,52DE	노,로	*no,ro*
怒	50-33,54-45	6012,F960	노,로	*no,ro*
擄	50-34,54-47	F930,64C4	노,로	*no,ro*
櫓	50-35,54-48	F931,6AD3	노,로	*no,ro*
爐	50-36,54-51	F932,7210	노,로	*no,ro*
盧	50-38,54-52	F933,76E7	노,로	*no,ro*
老	50-39,54-53	F934,8001	노,로	*no,ro*
蘆	50-40,54-54	F935,8606	노,로	*no,ro*
虜	50-41,54-55	F936,865C	노,로	*no,ro*
路	50-42,54-56	F937,8DEF	노,로	*no,ro*
露	50-43,54-58	F938,9732	노,로	*no,ro*
魯	50-45,54-59	F939,9B6F	노,로	*no,ro*
鷺	50-46,54-60	F93A,9DFA	노,로	*no,ro*
碌	50-47,54-62	F93B,788C	녹,록	*nog,rog*
祿	50-48,54-63	F93C,797F	녹,록	*nog,rog*
綠	50-49,54-64	F93D,7DA0	녹,록	*nog,rog*
菉	50-50,54-65	F93E,83C9	녹,록	*nog,rog*
錄	50-51,54-66	F93F,9304	녹,록	*nog,rog*
鹿	50-52,54-67	F940,9E7F	녹,록	*nog,rog*
論	50-53,54-69	F941,8AD6	논,론	*non,ron*
壟	50-54,54-70	F942,58DF	농,롱	*nong,rong*
弄	50-55,54-71	F943,5F04	농,롱	*nong,rong*
籠	50-57,54-75	F944,7C60	농,롱	*nong,rong*
聾	50-58,54-76	F945,807E	농,롱	*nong,rong*
牢	50-62,54-79	F946,7262	뇌,뢰	*noe,roe*
磊	50-63,54-80	F947,78CA	뇌,뢰	*noe,roe*
賂	50-65,54-81	F948,8CC2	뇌,뢰	*noe,roe*
雷	50-66,54-84	F949,96F7	뇌,뢰	*noe,roe*
尿	50-67,72-81	5C3F,F9BD	뇨,요	*nyo,yo*
壘	50-68,55-04	F94A,58D8	누,루	*nu,ru*
屢	50-69,55-06	F94B,5C62	누,루	*nu,ru*
樓	50-70,55-07	F94C,6A13	누,루	*nu,ru*
淚	50-71,55-08	F94D,6DDA	누,루	*nu,ru*
漏	50-72,55-09	F94E,6F0F	누,루	*nu,ru*

Hanja	KS X 1001:1992	Unicode	Hangul	Readings
累	50-73,55-11	F94F;7D2F	누,루	*nu,ru*
縷	50-74,55-12	F950,7E37	누,루	*nu,ru*
陋	50-75,55-16	F951,964B	누,루	*nu,ru*
杻	50-78,74-84	677B,F9C8	뉴,유	*nyu,yu*
紐	50-79,75-10	7D10,F9CF	뉴,유	*nyu,yu*
勒	50-80,55-45	F952,52D2	늑,륵	*neug,reug*
肋	50-81,55-46	F953,808B	늑,륵	*neug,reug*
凜	50-82,55-47	F954,51DC	늠,름	*neum,reum*
凌	50-83,55-48	F955,51CC	능,릉	*neung,reung*
稜	50-84,55-50	F956,7A1C	능,릉	*neung,reung*
綾	50-85,55-51	F957,7DBE	능,릉	*neung,reung*
菱	50-87,55-52	F958,83F1	능,릉	*neung,reung*
陵	50-88,55-53	F959,9675	능,릉	*neung,reung*
泥	50-90,76-18	6CE5,F9E3	니,이	*ni,i*
匿	50-91,76-41	533F,F9EB	닉,익	*nig,ig*
溺	50-92,76-42	6EBA,F9EC	닉,익	*nig,ig*
茶	50-94,83-17	8336,F9FE	다,차	*da,ca*
丹	51-01,53-14	4E39,F95E	단,란	*dan,ran*
糖	51-56,87-24	7CD6,FA03	당,탕	*dang,tang*
宅	51-75,87-40	5B85,FA04	댁,택	*daeg,taeg*
度	51-88,86-84	5EA6,FA01	도,탁	*do,tag*
讀	52-33,52-70	8B80,F95A	독,두	*dog,du*
洞	52-55,87-51	6D1E,FA05	동,통	*dong,tong*
掠	53-51,69-17	63A0,F975	략,약	*ryag,yag*
略	53-52,69-18	7565,F976	략,약	*ryag,yag*
亮	53-53,69-25	4EAE,F977	량,양	*ryang,yang*
兩	53-55,69-27	5169,F978	량,양	*ryang,yang*
凉	53-56,69-28	51C9,F979	량,양	*ryang,yang*
梁	53-57,69-36	6881,F97A	량,양	*ryang,yang*
糧	53-61,69-46	7CE7,F97B	량,양	*ryang,yang*
良	53-62,69-48	826F,F97C	량,양	*ryang,yang*
諒	53-63,69-50	8AD2,F97D	량,양	*ryang,yang*
量	53-65,69-54	91CF,F97E	량,양	*ryang,yang*
勵	53-68,69-90	52F5,F97F	려,여	*ryeo,yeo*
呂	53-69,69-91	5442,F980	려,여	*ryeo,yeo*
廬	53-70,69-94	5EEC,F982	려,여	*ryeo,yeo*
旅	53-73,70-01	65C5,F983	려,여	*ryeo,yeo*
濾	53-75,70-04	6FFE,F984	려,여	*ryeo,yeo*
礪	53-76,70-07	792A,F985	려,여	*ryeo,yeo*
閭	53-79,70-13	95AD,F986	려,여	*ryeo,yeo*
驪	53-81,70-15	9A6A,F987	려,여	*ryeo,yeo*

Hanja	KS X 1001:1992	Unicode	Hangul	Readings
麗	53-82,70-16	9E97,F988	려,여	*ryeo,yeo*
黎	53-83,70-17	9ECE,F989	려,여	*ryeo,yeo*
力	53-84,70-19	529B,F98A	력,역	*ryeog,yeog*
曆	53-85,70-23	66C6,F98B	력,역	*ryeog,yeog*
歷	53-86,70-24	6B77,F98C	력,역	*ryeog,yeog*
轢	53-89,70-28	8F62,F98D	력,역	*ryeog,yeog*
憐	53-91,70-38	6190,F98F	련,연	*ryeon,yeon*
戀	53-92,70-39	6200,F990	련,연	*ryeon,yeon*
漣	53-94,70-50	6F23,F992	련,연	*ryeon,yeon*
煉	54-01,70-54	7149,F993	련,연	*ryeon,yeon*
璉	54-02,70-57	7489,F994	련,연	*ryeon,yeon*
練	54-03,70-63	7DF4,F996	련,연	*ryeon,yeon*
聯	54-04,70-65	806F,F997	련,연	*ryeon,yeon*
蓮	54-05,70-69	84EE,F999	련,연	*ryeon,yeon*
輦	54-06,70-68	8F26,F998	련,연	*ryeon,yeon*
連	54-07,70-70	9023,F99A	련,연	*ryeon,yeon*
鍊	54-08,70-72	934A,F99B	련,연	*ryeon,yeon*
列	54-10,70-74	5217,F99C	렬,열	*ryeol,yeol*
劣	54-11,70-75	52A3,F99D	렬,열	*ryeol,yeol*
烈	54-13,70-79	70C8,F99F	렬,열	*ryeol,yeol*
裂	54-14,70-81	88C2,F9A0	렬,열	*ryeol,yeol*
廉	54-15,70-85	5EC9,F9A2	렴,염	*ryeom,yeom*
殮	54-17,70-89	6BAE,F9A5	렴,염	*ryeom,yeom*
簾	54-19,71-01	7C3E,F9A6	렴,염	*ryeom,yeom*
獵	54-20,71-06	7375,F9A7	렵,엽	*ryeob,yeob*
令	54-21,71-09	4EE4,F9A8	령,영	*ryeong,yeong*
囹	54-23,71-10	56F9,F9A9	령,영	*ryeong,yeong*
嶺	54-26,71-13	5DBA,F9AB	령,영	*ryeong,yeong*
怜	54-27,71-16	601C,F9AC	령,영	*ryeong,yeong*
玲	54-28,71-31	73B2,F9AD	령,영	*ryeong,yeong*
羚	54-30,71-38	7F9A,F9AF	령,영	*ryeong,yeong*
聆	54-32,71-39	8046,F9B0	령,영	*ryeong,yeong*
鈴	54-34,71-43	9234,F9B1	령,영	*ryeong,yeong*
零	54-35,71-45	96F6,F9B2	령,영	*ryeong,yeong*
靈	54-36,71-47	9748,F9B3	령,영	*ryeong,yeong*
領	54-37,71-48	9818,F9B4	령,영	*ryeong,yeong*
例	54-39,71-51	4F8B,F9B5	례,예	*rye,ye*
禮	54-41,71-63	79AE,F9B6	례,예	*rye,ye*
醴	54-42,71-68	91B4,F9B7	례,예	*rye,ye*
隸	54-43,71-70	96B7,F9B8	례,예	*rye,ye*
了	54-85,72-71	4E86,F9BA	료,요	*ryo,yo*

Hanja	KS X 1001:1992	Unicode	Hangul	Readings
僚	54-86,72-72	50DA,F9BB	료,요	*ryo,yo*
寮	54-87,72-80	5BEE,F9BC	료,요	*ryo,yo*
料	54-89,72-87	6599,F9BE	료,요	*ryo,yo*
燎	54-90,72-91	71CE,F9C0	료,요	*ryo,yo*
療	54-91,72-94	7642,F9C1	료,요	*ryo,yo*
蓼	54-94,73-07	84FC,F9C2	료,요	*ryo,yo*
遼	55-01,73-12	907C,F9C3	료,요	*ryo,yo*
龍	55-03,73-44	9F8D,F9C4	룡,용	*ryong,yong*
劉	55-17,74-69	5289,F9C7	류,유	*ryu,yu*
柳	55-19,74-87	67F3,F9C9	류,유	*ryu,yu*
流	55-21,74-92	6D41,F9CA	류,유	*ryu,yu*
溜	55-22,74-94	6E9C,F9CB	류,유	*ryu,yu*
琉	55-24,75-04	7409,F9CC	류,유	*ryu,yu*
留	55-26,75-07	7559,F9CD	류,유	*ryu,yu*
硫	55-28,75-09	786B,F9CE	류,유	*ryu,yu*
類	55-30,75-26	985E,F9D0	류,유	*ryu,yu*
六	55-31,75-27	516D,F9D1	륙,육	*ryug,yug*
戮	55-32,75-29	622E,F9D2	륙,육	*ryug,yug*
陸	55-33,75-33	9678,F9D3	륙,육	*ryug,yug*
倫	55-35,75-34	502B,F9D4	륜,윤	*ryun,yun*
崙	55-36,75-38	5D19,F9D5	륜,윤	*ryun,yun*
淪	55-37,75-39	6DEA,F9D6	륜,윤	*ryun,yun*
輪	55-39,75-44	8F2A,F9D7	륜,윤	*ryun,yun*
律	55-40,75-47	5F8B,F9D8	률,율	*ryul,yul*
慄	55-41,75-48	6144,F9D9	률,율	*ryul,yul*
栗	55-42,75-49	6817,F9DA	률,율	*ryul,yul*
率	55-43,65-67,75-50	F961,7387,F9DB	률,솔,율	*ryul,sol,yul*
隆	55-44,75-56	9686,F9DC	륭,융	*ryung,yung*
利	55-55,76-06	5229,F9DD	리,이	*ri,i*
吏	55-57,76-07	540F,F9DE	리,이	*ri,i*
履	55-59,76-10	5C65,F9DF	리,이	*ri,i*
李	55-61,76-16	674E,F9E1	리,이	*ri,i*
梨	55-62,76-17	68A8,F9E2	리,이	*ri,i*
理	55-66,76-21	7406,F9E4	리,이	*ri,i*
異	55-68,76-22	F962,7570	리,이	*ri,i*
痢	55-69,76-24	75E2,F9E5	리,이	*ri,i*
罹	55-71,76-26	7F79,F9E6	리,이	*ri,i*
裏	55-74,76-32	88CF,F9E7	리,이	*ri,i*
裡	55-75,76-33	88E1,F9E8	리,이	*ri,i*
里	55-76,76-37	91CC,F9E9	리,이	*ri,i*
離	55-78,76-38	96E2,F9EA	리,이	*ri,i*

Hanja	KS X 1001:1992	Unicode	Hangul	Readings
吝	55-80,76-53	541D,F9ED	린,인	*rin,in*
燐	55-82,76-61	71D0,F9EE	린,인	*rin,in*
璘	55-83,76-62	7498,F9EF	린,인	*rin,in*
藺	55-84,76-65	85FA,F9F0	린,인	*rin,in*
隣	55-86,76-68	96A3,F9F1	린,인	*rin,in*
鱗	55-87,76-71	9C57,F9F2	린,인	*rin,in*
麟	55-88,76-72	9E9F,F9F3	린,인	*rin,in*
林	55-89,76-87	6797,F9F4	림,임	*rim,im*
淋	55-90,76-88	6DCB,F9F5	림,임	*rim,im*
臨	55-92,76-90	81E8,F9F6	림,임	*rim,im*
立	56-01,77-01	7ACB,F9F7	립,입	*rib,ib*
笠	56-02,77-02	7B20,F9F8	립,입	*rib,ib*
粒	56-03,77-03	7C92,F9F9	립,입	*rib,ib*
磻	58-82,59-68	78FB,F964	반,번	*ban,beon*
北	59-37,61-33	F963,5317	배,북	*bae,bug*
便	60-05,88-21	F965,4FBF	변,편	*byeon,pyeon*
復	60-54,61-05	5FA9,F966	복,부	*bog,bu*
輻	60-63,88-80	8F3B,FA07	복,폭	*bog,pog*
不	60-84,61-53	4E0D,F967	부,불	*bu,bul*
泌	61-84,89-18	F968,6CCC	비,필	*bi,pil*
數	62-92,66-06	F969,6578	삭,수	*sag,su*
索	62-94,63-67	F96A,7D22	삭,색	*sag,saeg*
殺	63-15,65-77	6BBA,F970	살,쇄	*sal,swae*
參	63-19,83-49	F96B,53C3	삼,참	*sam,cam*
狀	63-50,77-78	72C0,F9FA	상,장	*sang,jang*
塞	63-61,63-65	585E,F96C	새,색	*sae,saeg*
省	63-72,64-93	F96D,7701	생,성	*saeng,seong*
說	64-67,65-13,70-82	8AAA,F96F,F9A1	설,세,열	*seol,se,yeol*
葉	64-81,71-08	F96E,8449	섭,엽	*seob,yeob*
拾	67-06,68-09	62FE,F973	습,십	*seub,sib*
識	67-59,82-29	8B58,F9FC	식,지	*sig,ji*
辰	67-85,82-67	F971,8FB0	신,진	*sin,jin*
沈	68-01,86-56	F972,6C88	심,침	*sim,cim*
什	68-07,82-90	4EC0,F9FD	십,집	*sib,jib*
惡	68-34,71-87	60E1,F9B9	악,오	*ag,o*
若	69-14,69-20	F974,82E5	야,약	*ya,yag*
易	70-22,76-15	6613,F9E0	역,이	*yeog,i*
咽	70-76,76-54	F99E,54BD	열,인	*yeol,in*
瑩	71-33,91-09	F9AE,7469	영,형	*yeong,hyeong*
阮	72-54,74-33	962E,F9C6	완,원	*wan,weon*
暈	73-87,93-27	F9C5,6688	운,훈	*un,hun*

Hanja	KS X 1001:1992	Unicode	Hangul	Readings
刺	77-09,84-07	523A,F9FF	자,척	*ja,ceog*
炙	77-19,78-59	7099,F9FB	자,적	*ja,jeog*
切	79-23,84-78	5207,FA00	절,체	*jeol,ce*
拓	84-12,86-86	62D3,FA02	척,탁	*ceog,tag*
暴	88-59,88-76	FA06,66B4	포,폭	*po,pog*
行	90-01,90-28	FA08,884C	항,행	*hang,haeng*

R

Chinese Character Lists

This appendix provides various Chinese character lists based on non-coded character set standards in printed form, as described in Chapter 3, *Character Set Standards*. All of these Chinese character lists can be generated using the *CJKV Character Set Server*.*

Hanzi Lists From China

This section includes two hanzi lists from China that total 3,500 characters: Chángyòng Hànzì and Cìchángyòng Hànzì. While most of the hanzi in these lists are included in the GB 2312-80 character set standard, there are a handful that are not.

China's Chángyòng Hànzì

The following is a complete listing of China's hanzi list entitled 现代汉语常用字表 (*xiàndài hànyǔ chángyòngzì biǎo*), also called Chángyòng Hànzì. All 2,500 of these hanzi are included in the GB 2312-80 character set standard. 2,495 of them are in Level 1 hanzi, and the remaining five are in Level 2 hanzi.

GB 2312-80 Level 1—2,495 hanzi

啊阿挨唉哀矮碍爱安按暗岸案昂袄傲奥扒吧八疤巴拔把坝霸罢爸白柏
百摆败拜斑班搬般板版扮拌伴瓣半办帮榜膀绑棒傍胞包剥薄雹保堡饱
宝抱报暴爆杯碑悲北辈背贝倍备被奔本笨蹦逼鼻比鄙笔彼碧蔽毕毙币
闭弊必辟壁臂避鞭边编扁便变辨辩辫遍标表别滨宾兵冰柄丙饼病并玻

* *http://www.oreilly.com/~lunde/cjkv-char.html*

菠播拨波博搏伯脖膊泊驳捕卜补不布步部怖擦猜裁材才财睬踩采彩菜
餐参蚕残惭惨灿苍舱仓藏操槽草厕策侧册测层插叉茶查察岔差拆柴馋
缠铲产颤昌场尝常长偿肠厂敞畅唱倡超抄钞朝潮吵炒车扯撤彻臣辰尘
晨沉陈趁衬撑称城成呈乘程惩诚承秤吃持匙池迟驰耻齿尺赤翅斥充冲
虫崇抽酬稠愁筹仇绸丑臭初出厨锄除楚础储触处川穿传船喘串疮窗床
闯创吹炊锤垂春唇纯蠢磁辞慈词此刺次聪葱匆从丛凑粗醋促窜摧催脆
翠村存寸错搭达答打大呆戴带代贷袋待逮怠耽担丹单胆旦但淡诞弹蛋
当挡党荡档刀蹈倒岛导到稻悼道盗德得的灯登等凳堤低滴敌笛抵底地
第帝弟递颠点典垫电店殿叼雕掉吊钓调跌爹蝶叠丁盯叮钉顶定订丢东
冬董懂动栋冻洞抖斗陡豆逗都督毒独读堵赌杜肚度渡端短锻段断缎堆
队对吨蹲顿盾多夺躲朵惰蛾鹅额恶饿恩而儿耳二发罚伐乏阀法帆番翻
繁凡烦反返范贩犯饭泛坊芳方房防妨仿访纺放非飞肥匪肺废沸费芬吩
分纷坟粉奋份愤粪丰封蜂峰锋风疯逢缝讽奉凤佛否夫肤扶幅符伏俘服
浮福抚辅俯斧府腐赴副覆复傅付父腹负富附妇咐该改概盖溉干甘杆竿
肝赶感秆敢冈刚钢缸纲岗港杠高膏糕搞稿告哥歌搁鸽胳割革葛格阁隔
个各给根跟耕更工攻功恭供躬公宫弓巩贡共钩勾沟狗构购够辜估孤姑
鼓古骨谷股故顾固刮瓜挂乖拐怪关官冠观管馆罐惯灌贯光广规归龟轨
鬼桂柜跪贵滚棍锅国果裹过哈孩海害含寒喊旱汗汉航豪毫好耗号浩喝
荷核禾和何合盒河贺黑痕很狠恨横衡恒轰哄烘虹洪宏红喉猴吼厚候后
呼乎忽壶胡蝴狐糊湖虎护互户花哗华猾滑画划化话槐怀坏欢环还缓换
患唤幻荒慌黄皇煌晃谎灰挥辉恢回毁悔慧惠贿会汇绘昏婚魂浑混活伙
火获或惑货祸击圾基机积肌饥迹激鸡绩吉极籍集及急疾即级挤几脊已
技季剂济寄计记既忌际继纪嘉夹佳家加甲假稼价架驾嫁歼监坚尖间煎
兼肩艰奸茧检拣捡简俭剪减荐鉴践贱见键箭件健舰剑渐建僵姜将浆江
疆桨奖讲匠酱降蕉椒焦胶交郊浇骄娇嚼搅脚狡角饺缴绞教轿较叫揭接
皆街阶截劫节杰捷竭洁结解姐戒界借介届巾筋斤金今津紧锦仅谨进晋
禁近浸尽劲茎睛晶京惊精经井警景颈静境敬镜径竟竞净揪究纠久九酒
救旧舅就鞠拘居菊局矩举聚拒据巨具距锯俱句惧剧捐倦卷绢掘觉决绝
均菌军君俊卡开凯慨刊堪砍看康糠扛抗炕考烤靠棵颗科壳咳可渴克刻
客课肯垦恳坑空恐孔控口扣寇枯哭苦酷库裤夸垮挎跨块快宽款筐狂框
矿旷况亏葵愧昆捆困括扩阔垃拉喇蜡腊辣啦来赖蓝栏拦篮兰览懒烂滥
狼廊郎朗浪捞劳牢老姥涝勒乐雷累垒类泪冷厘梨犁黎狸离理李里礼栗
丽厉励历利例立粒隶力璃俩联莲连镰廉怜帘脸链恋炼练粮凉梁粱良两
辆量亮谅僚疗辽了料列裂烈劣猎林临邻淋零龄铃伶灵陵岭领另令溜榴
留刘流柳六龙聋笼隆垄拢楼搂漏芦炉虏鲁碌露路鹿录陆驴旅屡虑律率
滤绿卵乱掠略轮论萝螺罗锣箩骡落骆络妈麻码蚂马骂吗埋买麦卖迈脉

瞒馒蛮满慢漫芒茫盲忙猫茅毛矛茂冒帽貌贸么梅霉煤没眉每美妹门闷
们萌蒙盟猛梦孟眯迷谜米秘蜜密棉眠绵免勉面苗描秒庙妙蔑灭民敏明
鸣名命摸模膜磨摩魔抹末莫墨默沫漠谋某亩母墓暮幕慕木目牧拿哪那
纳乃奶耐南男难囊挠脑恼闹呢内嫩能泥尼你逆年念娘酿鸟尿捏您凝宁
牛扭纽浓农弄奴努怒女暖挪欧偶趴爬怕拍排牌派攀盘盼判叛乓旁胖抛
炮袍跑泡培赔陪配佩喷盆蓬棚膨朋捧碰批披劈脾疲皮匹僻篇偏片骗飘
漂票撇拼贫品乒苹萍平凭瓶评坡泼婆破魄迫剖扑铺仆葡朴普谱期欺戚
妻七漆其棋奇齐旗骑起岂乞企启砌器气弃汽恰洽牵铅千迁签谦钱钳前
潜遣浅欠歉枪腔墙强抢锹敲悄桥瞧乔侨巧切茄且窃侵亲琴勤芹禽青轻
倾清晴情顷请庆穷秋丘球求趋区曲屈驱渠取趣去圈权泉全拳犬券劝缺
却鹊确雀裙群然燃染壤嚷让饶扰绕惹热仁人忍任认刃扔仍日荣融熔容
绒揉柔肉如辱乳入软瑞锐润若弱撒洒塞赛三伞散桑嗓丧扫嫂色森杀沙
纱傻筛晒山删衫闪陕善扇伤商赏晌上尚裳梢捎稍烧勺少哨绍蛇舌舍摄
射涉社设申伸身深神沈审婶甚肾慎渗声生牲升绳省盛剩胜圣师失狮施
湿诗尸十石拾时什食蚀实识史使驶始式示士世柿事誓逝势是适侍释饰
氏市室视试收手首守寿授售受瘦兽蔬梳殊输叔舒疏书熟薯暑鼠属术述
树束竖数刷耍摔衰甩帅拴霜双爽谁水睡税顺说斯撕思私司丝死肆寺四
似饲松颂送宋诵搜艘嗽苏俗素速塑宿诉肃酸蒜算虽随碎岁穗孙损笋缩
索锁所塌他它她塔踏抬台泰太态摊贪滩坛痰谈坦毯探叹炭汤塘堂膛唐
糖倘躺趟烫掏涛滔萄桃逃淘陶讨套特腾疼梯踢提题蹄体替惕剃天添填
田甜挑条跳贴铁帖厅听停亭庭挺艇通桐同铜童桶筒统痛偷投头透秃突
图徒途涂屠土吐兔团推腿退吞屯拖托脱驼妥挖蛙娃瓦袜歪外弯湾玩顽
丸完碗挽晚万汪王亡网往旺望忘妄威微危违围唯为维委伟伪尾未味畏
胃喂位慰卫温蚊文闻纹稳问翁窝我卧握沃呜乌污屋无吴武五午舞伍侮
雾物勿务悟误析西吸锡牺稀息希悉膝夕惜熄溪袭席习喜洗系隙戏细瞎
虾霞峡狭下厦夏吓掀先仙鲜纤咸贤衔闲弦嫌显险现献县馅羡宪陷限线
相香箱乡祥详想响享项巷橡像向象削销消宵晓小孝校笑效些歇鞋协携
邪斜胁写械卸泄泻谢屑薪欣辛新心信星腥兴刑型形行醒幸杏性姓兄凶
胸雄熊休修羞朽锈秀袖绣需虚须徐许蓄叙序畜絮绪续宣悬旋选学穴雪
血循旬询寻巡训讯迅压押鸦鸭呀芽牙崖雅哑亚咽烟淹盐严研岩延言颜
炎沿掩眼演艳燕厌雁焰宴验殃央秧杨扬羊洋阳氧仰痒养样邀腰妖摇遥
窑谣咬药要耀爷野冶也页业叶夜液一医依衣遗移仪疑宜姨椅蚁倚已乙
以艺易亿役疫亦意毅忆义益议谊译异翼因音阴姻银饮引隐印英樱鹰应
营蝇迎赢盈影硬映拥佣庸咏泳涌永勇用优悠忧尤由邮犹油游有友右诱
又幼于榆愚余鱼愉渔予娱雨与屿宇语羽玉域遇御愈欲狱育誉浴裕预冤
元原援园员圆源缘远愿怨院约越跃钥月悦阅云匀允运晕韵孕杂栽灾宰

载再在咱暂赞脏葬遭糟枣早澡躁造皂灶燥责择则泽贼怎增曾赠扎渣轧
闸眨榨炸摘宅窄债寨粘沾盏斩崭展占战站章张掌涨丈帐仗胀障招找赵
照罩兆召遮折哲者这浙珍真贞针侦枕诊震振镇阵蒸挣睁征争整正政症
郑证芝枝支蜘知肢脂汁之织职直植殖执值侄址指止只旨纸志至致置帜
制智秩质治中忠钟终种肿重众舟周州洲粥皱宙昼骤珠株蛛朱猪诸逐竹
烛煮嘱主著柱助铸筑住注祝驻抓爪专砖转赚庄装撞壮状追准捉桌啄着
浊资姿滋紫仔子自字棕踪宗总纵走奏租足族祖阻组钻嘴醉最罪尊遵昨
左做作坐座

GB 2312-80 Level 2—5 hanzi

叨橘蜓蜻筝

China's Cìchángyòng Hànzì

The following is a complete listing of China's other hanzi list entitled 现代汉语次常用字表 (*xiàndài hànyǔ cìchángyòngzì biǎo*), also called Cìchángyòng Hànzì. This hanzi list is broken into three parts. The 880 hanzi that are included in GB 2312-80 Level 1 hanzi, the 118 that are included in GB 2312-80 Level 2 hanzi, and the remaining two hanzi that are included in GB 7589-87 (these two hanzi are also included in GB 8565.2-88 and thus ISO-IR-165:1992).

GB 2312-80 Level 1—880 hanzi

埃哎癌蔼艾隘鞍氨俺肮凹熬懊澳芭捌叭笆跋靶耙扳颁绊邦梆磅蚌谤苞
褒豹卑狈惫焙崩绷泵蓖庇痹贬彪膘鳖憋瘪彬濒秉勃舶渤哺埠簿沧糙曹
蹭茬碴豺搀掺蝉阐猖嘲巢澈忱橙澄逞痴弛侈宠畴橱雏矗揣幢捶椿醇淳
戳绰雌瓷赐囱簇篡崔粹撮搓措挫瘩歹掸氮捣祷蹬瞪邓涤嫡蒂缔掂碘佃
甸惦奠淀碉刁碟谍鼎锭兜痘睹镀妒兑墩敦囤钝哆垛跺舵堕俄讹扼遏尔
饵贰筏樊矾肪菲啡诽吠氛焚忿枫冯敷孵拂辐袱甫脯赋缚钙柑肛篙羔镐
戈疙蛤羹埂耿梗汞拱苟垢菇咕箍沽雇寡褂棺逛瑰硅闺诡刽郭亥骇酣憨
韩涵函罕翰撼捍憾悍焊夯杭壕嚎呵赫褐鹤嘿哼鸿侯葫弧唬沪徊淮痪焕
涣宦磺蝗凰惶幌恍徽蛔晦秽讳诲荤豁霍畸稽箕讥棘辑嫉冀祭寂妓枷荚
颊贾钾柬碱溅涧蒋礁矫侥剿酵窖秸芥诫襟荆兢鲸靖窘玖韭灸臼疚驹沮
炬鹃眷倔爵诀钧峻竣骏咖揩楷勘坎慷拷坷苛磕啃吭抠窟胯筷眶盔窥魁
傀溃坤廓莱澜揽缆琅榔酪烙蕾儡擂肋棱楞篱漓鲤莉荔吏砾俐痢沥哩敛
晾撩聊燎寥潦镣琳磷鳞凛赁吝玲菱凌琉硫馏瘤咙窿娄篓陋卢颅庐卤赂
吕铝侣履缕氯峦抡伦仑沦逻裸洛玛蔓曼氓莽锚铆玫枚媒昧媚檬锰靡糜
弥觅泌冕娩缅瞄藐渺皿悯闽螟铭谬摹蘑寞陌拇牡姆募睦穆呐钠娜奈馁

拟匿腻溺蔫碾撵捻聂孽镊柠狞拧泞钮脓虐疟懦糯诺鸥殴藕呕帕徘湃潘
畔庞咆刨胚沛砰烹澎彭硼篷鹏坯霹啤屁譬瓢频聘坪屏颇菩蒲圃浦瀑栖
凄柒歧畦崎脐祈契迄泣掐乾黔谴嵌呛撬翘峭俏窍怯钦秦擒寝氢卿擎琼
囚蛆躯娶痊瘸瓤攘韧纫茸蓉溶冗蠕儒褥蕊闰萨腮叁搔骚瑟涩僧砂刹啥
煞珊苫杉擅赡膳芍奢赊赦呻绅甥虱矢屎拭嗜恃枢抒淑赎曙署蜀黍墅庶
漱恕栓吮瞬硕烁嘶伺耸讼酥粟溯髓遂隧祟梭唆琐蹋胎苔汰瘫檀潭谭袒
碳搪棠淌藤誊剔啼涕屉恬舔廷瞳彤捅凸颓蜕褪臀鸵驮椭拓唾洼豌惋宛
婉腕枉巍桅苇萎纬蔚魏谓尉瘟吻紊嗡瓮蜗涡巫诬芜梧捂坞晤昔熙晰犀
媳铣匣辖暇侠锨舷涎腺厢镶湘翔萧硝哮嚣淆肖啸楔蝎挟谐蟹懈芯锌衅
猩邢匈汹嗅酗旭恤婿轩喧玄癣靴薛勋熏驯殉汛逊蚜衙涯讶蜒阎奄衍堰
砚唁谚鸯漾姚舀椰掖腋壹揖伊夷胰抑邑屹逸肄溢绎茵殷吟淫婴缨莹萤
荧颖哟踊蛹幽佑迂淤舆逾隅芋郁吁喻寓豫鸳渊袁辕猿岳粤耘陨蕴酝砸
攒赃凿藻蚤噪憎喳铡栅乍诈斋瞻毡蘸栈绽樟彰杖账昭沼辙蔗斟疹狰怔
拯吱趾挚掷稚滞窒盅衷仲轴肘帚咒拄蛀贮撰桩妆椎锥赘坠缀谆拙卓琢
茁酌灼咨籽滓综揍卒诅

GB 2312-80 Level 2—118 hanzi

丐噩匕夭匾卦偎凫禀谒阱芙茉苘荞荠莩莺蒿薇奕拗捺叽吆咧咪唠唧嗦
嗤喊嘀嘹幔岖徙猬馍庵悴愕憔沐涮漩姊嬉缤缭缰玷璧杈桦榄楣榛榕橄
檐檩昙昵掰牍肴胧腌朦臊飒炫祠盹铸铛锉秕秫鸠鹉鹦瘾癞衩裆蚣蚪蚓
蚯蛉蜈蝠蝌蝙螟螃蟋蟀笙笤箫篾翎翩麸跛跷踱蹂蹦雳霎鲫鳄鳍鬓

GB 7589-87—2 hanzi

啰瞭

Hanzi Lists From Taiwan

This section includes two hanzi lists from Taiwan: Chángyòng Hànzì and Cìchángyòng Hànzì. All of the hanzi in these lists are included in the CNS 11643-1992 character set standard, spread across Planes 1 and 2.

Taiwan's Chángyòng Hànzì

The following are the 4,808 hanzi as defined in Taiwan's list entitled 常用國字標準字體表 (*chángyòng guózì biāozhǔn zìtǐ biǎo*), sometimes known as their Chángyòng Hànzì set. All of these hanzi are included in CNS 11643-1992 Plane 1.

一乙丁七乃九了二人入八几刀刁力匕十卜又三下丈上丫丸凡久么也乞
于亡兀刃千叉口土士夕大女子孑孓寸小尸山川工己已巳巾干弓才丑丐
不中丹之尹予云井互五仁什仃仆仇仍今介仄元允內六兮公冗凶分切刈
勻勾勿化匹午升卅卞厄友及反壬天夫太夭孔少尤尺屯巴幻廿弔引心戈
戶手扎支文斗斤方日曰月木欠止歹毋比毛氏水火爪父爻片牙牛犬王丙
世丕且丘主乍乏乎以付仔仕他仗代令仙仞充兄冉冊冬凹出凸刊加功包
匆北匝仟半卉卡占卯卮去可古右召叮叩叨叼司叵叫另只史叱台句叭四
囚外央失奴奶孕它尼巨巧左市布平幼弁弘弗必戊打扔扒斥旦朮本未末
札正母民氐永汁汀氾犯玄玉瓜瓦甘生用甩田由甲申疋白皮皿目矛矢石
示禾穴立丞丟乒乓乩亙交亦亥仿伉伙伊伕伍伐休伏仲件任仰仳份企光
兇兆先全共再冰列刑划刎劣匈匡匠印危吉吏同吊吐吁吋各向名合吃后
吆吒因回圳地在圭圬圯夙多夷夸妄奸妃好她如妁字存宇守宅安寺尖屹
州帆并年式弛忙忖戎戌戍成扣扛托收早旨旬旭曲曳有朽朴朱朵次此死
氖汝汗汙江池汐汕灰牟牝百竹米糸缶羊羽老考而耒耳聿肉肋肌臣自至
臼舌舛舟艮色艾虫血行衣西阡串亨位住佇佗佞伴佛何估佐佑伽伺伸佃
佔似但佣作你伯低伶余佝兌克免兵冶冷別判利刪刨劫助努劬匣即卵吝
吭吞吾否呎吧呆呃吳呈呂君吩告吹吻吸吮吵吶吠吼呀吱含吟囪困囤坊
坑址坍均坎圾坐坏壯夾妝妒妨妞妣妙妖妍妤妓妊妥孝孜孚完宋宏尬局
屁尿尾岐岑岔岌巫希序庇床廷弄弟彤形彷役忘忌志忍忱快戒我抄抗抖
技扶抉扭把扼找批扳抒扯折扮投抓抑改攻旱更束李杏材村杜杖杞杉步
每求汞沙沁沈沉沅沛汪決沐汰沌汨沖沒汽沃汲汾灶灼災灸牢牡牠狄狂
玖甬甫男甸皂盯矣私秀禿究系罕肖肓肝肘肛肚育良芒芋芍見角言谷豆
豕貝赤走足身車辛辰迂迆迅迄巡邑邢邪邦那酉里防阮阱阪並乖乳事些
亞享京佯依侍佳使佬供例來侃佰併侈佩佻侖佾侏兔兒兕兩具其典冽函
刻券刷刺到刮制剁劾卒協卓卑卦卷卸卹取叔受味呵咖呸咕咀呻呷咄咒
咆呼咐呱呶和咚呢周咋命咎固垃坷坪坩坡坦坤坼夜奉奇奈奄奔妾妻委
妹妮姑姆姐姍始姓姊妯妳姒孟孤季宗定官宜宙宛尚屈居屆岷岡岸岩岫
岱岳帘帚帖帕帛帑幸庚店府底庖延弦弧弩往征彿彼忝忠忽念忿怏怔怯
怵怖怪怕怡性或戕房戾所承拉拌拄抿拂抹拒招披拓拔拋拈抨抽押拐拙
拇拍抵拚抱拘拖拗拆抬拎放斧於旺昔易昌昆昂明昀昏服朋杭枋枕東果
杳杷枇枝林杯杰板枉松析杵枚欣武歧歿氓氛泣注泳沱泌泥河沽沾沼波
沫法泓沸泄油況沮泗泅泱沿治泡泛泊炕炎炒炊炙爬爭爸版牧物狀狎狙
狗狐玩玨玟玫甽疝疙疚的盂盲直知矽社祀祁秉空穹竺糾罔羌羋者肺肥
肢肱股肫肩肴肪肯臥臾舍芳芝芙芭芽芟芹花芬芥虎虱初表軋迎返近邵
邸邱采金長門阜陀阿阻附雨青非亟亭亮信侵侯便俠俑俏保促侶俘俟俊
俗侮俐俄係俚俎俞兗冒冑冠剎剃削前剌剋則勇勉勃勁匍南卻厚叛咬哀

咨哎哉咸咦咳哇哂咽咪品哄哈咯咫咱咻垂型垠垣垢城垮奕契奏奎奐姜
姘姿姣姨娃姥姪姚姦威姻孩宣宦室客宥封屎屏屍屋峙巷帝帥幽庠度建
弈弭彥很待徊律徇後怒思怠急怎怨恍恰恨恢恆恃恬恫恪恤扁拜挖按拼
拭持拮拽指拱拷拯括拾拴挑政故斫施既春昭映昧是星昨曷柿染柱柔某
柬架枯柵柩柯柄柑枴柚查枸柏柞柳歪殃殆段毒毗氟泉洋洲洪流津洌洱
洞洗活洽派洶洛炫為炳炬炯炭炸炮爰牲牯牴狩狠狡玷珊玻玲珍珀玳甚
甭畏界疫疤疥癸皆皇皈盈盆盃省盹相眉看盾盼矜砂研砌砍祆祉祈祇禹
科秒秋穿突竿竽紂紅紀紉紇約缸美羿耐耍耶胖胥胚胃胄背胡胛胎胞胤
致舢苧范茅苣苛苦茄若茂茉苒苗英茁苜苔苑苞苓苟虐虹衍衫要計訂訃
貞負赴赳趴軍軌述迦迢迪迥迭迫郊郎郁酋酊重閂限陋陌降面革韋韭音
頁風飛食首香乘倌倍倣俯倦倥俸倩倖倆值借倚倒們俺倀倔倨俱倡個候
倘俳修倭倪俾倫倉兼冤冥冢凍凌准凋剖剜剔剛剝匪卿原厝叟哨唐唁唷
哼哥哲唆哺唔哩哭員唉哮哪哦唧圃埂埔埋埃夏套奘奚娑娘娜娟娛娓姬
娠娣娩娥娌孫宰害家宴宮宵容宸射屑展屐峭峽峻峪峨峰島崁差席師庫
庭座弱徒徑徐恙恣恥恐恕恭恩息悄悟悚悍悔悌悅悖扇拳挈拿捎挾振捕
捂捆捏捉挺捐挽挪挫挨效料旁旅時晉晏晃晒晌書朔朕朗校核案框桓根
桂桔栩梳栗桌桑栽柴桐桀格桃株桅栓殊殉殷氣氧氨氦氤泰浪涕消涇浦
浸海浙涓浬涉浮浚浴浩烊烘烤烙烈烏爹特狼狹狽狸狷班琉珮珠畔畝畜
畚留疾病症疲疳疽疼疹痂益盍盎眩真眠眨矩砰砧砸砝破砷砥砭祕祐祠
祟祖神祝祗祚秤秣秧租秦秩窄窈站笆笑粉紡紗紋紊素索純紐紕級紜納
紙紛缺罟羔翅翁耆耘耕耙耗耽耿胱脂胰脅胭胴脆胸胳脈能脊臭臬舀舐
航舫舨般芻茫荒荔荊茸荐草茵茴荏茲茹茶茗荀茱虔蚊蚪蚓蚤蚩蚌蚣衰
衷袁袂記訐討訌訕訊託訓訖豈豺豹財貢起躬軒軔辱送逆迷退迺迴逃追
逅邕郡酒配酌釘針釗釜閃院陣陡陛陝除隻飢馬骨高鬥鬲鬼乾偕偽停假
偃偌做偉健偶偎偕偵側偷偏倏兜冕凰剪副勒務勘動匐匏匙匿區匾參曼
商啪啦啄啞啡啃啊唱啖問啕唯啤唸售啜唬啣唳圈國域堅堊堆埠埤基堂
堵執培夠奢娶婁婉婦婪婀娼婢婚婆婊孰寇寅寄寂宿密尉專將屠屜崇崆
崎崛崖崢崑崩崔崙巢常帶帳帷康庸庶庵庚張強彗彬彩彫得徙從徘御悤
患悉悠您惋悴惦悽情悻悵惜悼惘惕惆惟悸惚戚戛扈掠控捲掖探接捷捧
掘措捱掩掉掃掛捫推掄授掙採掬排掏掀捻捩捨敝敖救教敗啟敏敘斜斬
族旋旌旎晝晚晤晨晦曹勗望梁梯梢梓梵桿桶梱梧梗械梃棄梭梆梅梔條
梨梟欲殺毫氫涎涼淳淙液淡淌淤添淺清淇淋涯淑涮淞淹涸混淵淅淒渚
涵淚淫淘淪深淮淨淆淄烹焉焊烽爽牽犁猜猛猖猓猙率琅琊球理現琍瓠
瓶瓷甜產略畦畢異疏痔痕疵痊皎盔盒盛眷眾眼眶眸眺硫硃祥票祭移窒
窕笠笨笛第符笙笞粒粗絆絃統紮紹紼絀細紳組累終缽羞羚翌翎習耜聊
聆脯脖脣脫脩春舵舷舶船莎莞莘莩莢莖莽莫莒莊莓莉莠荷荻荼處彪蛇

蛀蚶蛄蚵蛆蛋蚱蚯術袞袈被袒袖袍袋覓規訪訝訣訥許設訟訛豉豚販責
貫貨貪貧赧赦趾軛軟這逍通逗連速逝逐逕逞造透逢逖逛途部郭都酗野
釵釦釣釧閉陪陵陳陸陰陴陶陷雀雪章竟頂頃魚鳥鹿麥麻傢傍傅備傑傀
傖傘最凱割剴創剩勞勝勛博厥啻喀喧啼喊喝喘喂喜喪喔喇喋喃喳單喟
唾喲喚喻喬喱啾喉圍堯堪場堤堰報堡壹壺奠婷媚婿媒媛孳孱寒富寓寐
尊尋就嵌嵐巽幅帽幀幾廊廁廂弼彭復循徨惑惡悲悶惠愜愣惺愕惰惻惴
慨惱愎惶愉愀戟扉掣掌描揀揩揉揆揍插揣提握揖揭揮捶援揪換摒揚敞
敦敢散斑斐斯普晰晴晶景暑智曾替期朝棺棕棠棘棗椅棟棵森棧棹棒棲
棣棋棍植椒椎棉棚款欺欽殘殖殼毯氮氯港游湔渡渲湧湊渠渥渣減湛湘
渤湖湮渭渦湯渴湍渺測湃渝渾滋溉渙焙焚焦焰無然煮牌犄犀猶猥猴猩
琺琪琳琢琥琵琶琴甥甦畫番痢痛痣痙痘痞登發皖皓皴盜睏短硝硬硯稍
稈程稅稀窘窗窖童竣等策筆筐筒答筍筋筏粟粥絞結絨絕紫絮絲絡給絢
善翔翕肅腕腔腋腑腎脹腆脾舒舜菩萃菸萍菠菅萋菁華菱菴著萊菰萌菌
菽菲菊萸萎萄菜虛蛟蛙蛭蛔蛛蛤街裁裂袱覃視註詠評詞証詁詔詛詐詆
訴診象貂貯貼貳貽賁費賀貴買貶貿貸越超趁跎距跋跚跑跌跛跆軻軸軼
辜逮逵週逸進鄂郵鄉酣酥量鈔鈕鈣鈉鈞鈍鈐閔閏開閑間閒隊階隋陽隅
隆隍陲雁雅雄集雇雯雲韌項順須飧飪飯飩飲飭馮馭黃黍黑亂傭債傲傳
僅傾催傷傻傯剿剷剽募勦勤勢匯嗟嗨嗓嗦嗎嗜嗇嗑嗣嗤嗯嗚嗡嗅嗆嗥
園圓塞塑塘塗塚塔填塌塭塊塢奧嫁嫉嫌媾媽媼媳嫂媲嵩幌幹廉廈弒彙
徬微愚意慈感想愛惹愁愈慎慌慄慍愾愴愧戡戢搓搾搞搪搭搽搬搏搜搔
損搶搖搗敬斟新暗暉暇暈暖會椰業楚楷楠楔極椰概楊楨楫楞楓楹榆歇
歲毀殿毓毽溢溯滓溶滂源溝滇滅溥溘溼溺溫滑準溜滄滔溪煎煙煩煤煉
照煜煬煦煌煥煞爺牒猷獅猿猾瑯瑚瑕瑟瑞瑁琿瑙瑛瑜當畸瘀痰瘁痲痱
痺痿痴盞盟睛睫睦睞督睹睪睬睜睥睨矮碎碰碗碘碌碉硼碑祺祿禁萬禽
稜稚稠稔稟窟窠筷節筠粱粳粵經絹綑綁綏置罩罪署義羨群聖聘肆肄腱
腰腸腥腮腳腫腹腺腦舅艇蒂葷落萱葵葦葫葉葬葛萼萵葡董葩虞虜號蛹
蜓蜈蜇蜀蛾蛻蜂蜃衙裟裔裙補裘裝裡裊裕解詫該詳試詩詰誇詼詣誠話
誅詭詢詮詬詹豢貊貉賊資賈賄貲賃賂賅跡跟跨路跳跺跪躲較載軾輊辟
農運遊道遂達逼違遐遇遏過遍遑逾遁鄒酬酪酩釉鈷鉗鈸鈽鉀鈾鉛鉋鉤
鉑鈴閘隘隔隕雍雋雉雷電雹零靖靴靶預頑頓頊頒頌飼飴飽飾馳馱馴鳩
麂鼎鼓鼠僧僮僥僖僭僚僕像僑僱兢凳劃匱厭嗾嘀嘛嘗嗽嘔嘆嘉嘍嘎嗷
嘖嘟嘈團圖塵塾境墓墊塹墅壽夥夢夤奪奩嫡嫦嫩嫗嫖嫘嫣孵寞寧寡寥
實寨寢寤察對屢嶄嶇幛幣幕幗幔廓廖弊彆彰徹慇愿態慷慢慣慟慚慘截
撇摘摔撤摸摟摺摑摧敲斡旗旖暢暨榜榨榕槁榮槓構榛榷榻榫榴槐槍榭
槌歉歌氳漳演滾漓滴漩漾漠漬漏漂漢滿滯漆漱漸漲漣漕漫漯漱漪滬漁
滲滌熔熙煽熊熄爾犒犖獄獐瑤瑣瑪瑰甄疑瘧瘍瘋瘉瘓盡監瞄睽睿睡磁

碟碧碳碩禎福禍種稱窪窩竭端管箕箋筵算箝箔箏粹粽精綻綰綜綽綾綠
緊綴網綱綺綢綿綵綸維緒緇罰翠翡翟聞聚肇腐膀膏膈膊腿臧臺與舔舞
蓉蒿蓆蓄蒙蒞蒲蒜蓋蒸蓀蓓蒐蒼蜿蜜蜻蜢蜥蜴蜘蝕裳褂裴裹裸製裨褚
誦誌語誣認誡誓誤說誥誨誘誑豪貍貌賓賑賒赫趙趕踊輔輒輕輓辣遠遘
遜遣遙遞鄙酵酸酷鉸銬銀銅銘銖鉻銓銜閡閨閩閣閥閤隙障際雌需靼鞅
韶頗領颯颱餃餅餌餉駁骯骰髦魁魂鳴鳶鳳麼鼻齊億儀僻僵價儂儈儉凜
劇劈劉劍厲嘮嘻嘹嘲嘿嘴嘩噓噎噗噴嘶嘯嘰墀墟增墳墜墮嬉嫻嬋嫵嬌
寮寬審寫層履嶝幢幟廢廚廟廝廣廠彈影德徵慶慧慮慝慕憂慼慰慫慾憧
憐憫憎憬憚憤憔戮摩摯摹撞撲撈撐撰撥撓撕撩撒撮播撫撚撬敵敷數暮
暫暴樣樟槨椿樞標槽模樓樊槳樂樅歐殤毅毆漿潼澄潑潦潔澆潭潛潸潮
澎潺潰潤澗潘熟熬熱熨牖犛獎獗瑩璋璃瘠瘩瘟瘤瘦瘡皚皺盤瞎瞇瞌瞑
磋磅確磊碾磕碼磐稿稼穀稽稷稻窯窮箭箱範箴篆篇篁糊締練緯緻緘緬
緝編緣線緞緩綞罵罷羯翩膛膜膝膠膚蔗蔽蔚蓮蔬蔭蔓蔑蔣蔡蔔蓬蔥蓿
螂蝴蝶蝠蝦蝸蝨蝙蝗蝌衛衝褐複褒褓誼諒談諄誕請諸課諉諂調誰論諍
豌豎豬賠賞賦賤賬賭賢賣賜質赭趟趣踫踐踝踢踏踩踟躺輝輛輟輩輦輪
輜適遮遨遭遷鄰鄭鄧鄱醇醉醋醃鋅銻銷鋪鋤鋁銳銼鋒閭閱霄霆震霉靠
鞍鞋鞏頡颳養餓餒餘駝駐駟駛駑駕駒駙骷髮髯鬧魅魄魷魯鴆鴉麩麾黎
墨齒儒儘儔儐冀凝劑噙噫噹噩噤噸噪器噥噱噯噬噢壁墾壇壅奮嬝嬴學
導憲憑憩憊懍憶憾懊懈戰擅擁擋撻撼據擄擇擂操撿擒擔整曆曉暹樽樸
樺橙橫橘樹橄橢橡橋橇樵機歙歷濂澱澡濃澤濁澧澳激澹熾燉燐燒燈燕
熹燎燙燜燃燄獨璜璣瓢甌瘴瘸盧盥瞠瞞瞟瞥磨磚磬禦積穎穆穌窺篙簑
築篤篛篡篩糕糖縊縑縈縛縣罹羲翰翱膳膩膨臻興艘艙蕊蕙蕈蕨蕩蕃蕉
蕭蕪螃螟螞螢融衡褪褲褥褫親覦諦諺諫諱謀諜諧諮諾謁謂諷諭豫貓賴
蹄踱踴蹂踹踵輻輯輸辨辦遵遴選遲遼遺醒錠錶鋸錳錯錢鋼錫錄錚錐錦
閻隧隨險雕霎霑霖霍霓霏靛靜靦鞘頰頸頻頷頭頹頤餐館餞餛餡駭駢駱
骸骼髻髭鬨鮑鴕鴣鴦鴨鴒鴛默黔龍龜優償儡儲勵嚎嚀嚐嚅嚇嚏壕壓壑
嬰嬪嬤孺尷嶼嶺嶽幫彌徽應懂懇懦戲戴擎擊擘擠擰擦擬擱斂斃曙曖檀
檔檄檢檜櫛殮濘濱濟濠濛濤濫濯澀濬濡燧營燮燦燥燭燬燴爵牆獰獲璩
環璦癆療癌盪瞳瞪瞰瞬瞧瞭矯磷磺磴磯礁禧禪穗簇簍篾篷糠糜糞糢糟
糙縮績繆縷縲繃縫總縱繅繁罄翳翼聱聲聰聯聳臆臃膺臂臀膿膽臉膾臨
舉艱薪薄蕾薜薑薔薯薛薇虧蟀蟑螳蟒蟆螫螻螺蟈蟋褻褶襄褸覬謎謗謙
講謊謠謝謄豁谿賺賽購趨蹉蹋蹈蹊轄輾轂轅輿避遽還邁邂邀鄒醣醞醜
鍍鎂錨鍵鍊鍥鍋錘鍾鍬鍛鍰闊闋闌闈闆隱隸雖霜霞鞠韓顆颶餵騁駿鮮
鮫鮪鴻鴿麋黏點黜黝黛鼾齋叢嚕嚮壙壘嬸彝懣戳擴擲擾攆擺擻斷朦檳
檬櫃檻檸櫂歟歸殯瀉瀋濾瀆濺瀑瀏燻獷獵璧甕癖癘癒瞽瞿瞻礎禮穡穢
竄竅簫簧簪簞簣簡糧織繕繞繚繡罈翹翻職聶臍臏舊藏薩藍藐藉薰蟯蟬

蟲覆覲觴謨謹謬豐贅蹙蹣蹦蹤軀轉轍邇醫醬釐鎔鎊鎖鎢鎳鎮闔闖闐離
雜雙雛雞鞣鞦鞭額顏題顎顓颺餾餿魄馥騎鬃鬆魏鯊鯉鯽鵑鵝鵠黠鼕鼬
嚥嚨壞壟壢寵龐廬懲懷懶懵攀攏曠曝櫥櫝櫚櫓瀛瀟瀨瀚瀝瀕爆爍牘犢
獸獺璽瓊瓣疇疆矇礙禱穫穩簾簿簸簽簷繫繭繹繩繪羅羶羹羸臘藩藝藪
藕藤藥蟻蠅蠍蟹襠襟襖譁譜識證譚譎譏贈贊蹼蹲躇蹶蹬蹺轔轎辭邊鏡
鏑鏟鏃鏈鏜鏝鏖鏢鏍鏘鏤鏗關隴難霪霧靡韜韻類願顛颼饅鶩騙鬍鯨鯧
鶉鵡鵲鵪鵬麒麗麓麴勸嚷嚶嚴嚼壤孀孽寶懸懺攘攔攙曦朧瀾瀰爐獻瓏
癢癥礦礪礬礫竇競籌籃籍糯辮繽繼纂耀臚艦藻藹蘑藺蘆蘋蘇蘊蠔蠕襤
覺觸議譬警譯贏贍躉躁躅躂釋鐘鐃鏽闡飄饒饑馨騫騰騷鰓鰍鹹麵黨齟
齣齡儷囁囀囂夔屬巍懼懾攝攜櫻欄殲灌爛犧癩矓籐纏續蘖蘭蘚蠣蠢蠡
蠟襪覽譴護譽贓躊躍轟辯醺鐮鐳鐵鐺鐸鐲闢霸霹露響顧驅驃驀騾髏魔
鰭鰥鶯鶴鷂麝黯鼙齜齦儼囈囊囉孿巔巒彎懿攤權歡灑灘玀疊癮癬籠籟
聾聽臟襲襯讀贖贗躑轡鑄鑑鑒霽霾韃韁顫驕髒鬚鱉鰱鰾鰻鷓鷗鼴齬齪
龔囌巖戀攣攫攪竊籤纓纖蘸蘿蠱變邐邏鑣鑠靨顯饜驚驛驗髓體鱔鱗鱖
鷥麟黴囑壩攬灞癲矗罐羈蠶蠹衢讓讒讖贛釀靂靈靄韆顰驟鬢魘鷹鷺鹼
鹽鼇齷齲廳欖灣籬籮蠻觀躡釁鑲鑰顱饞灤矚讚驢驥纜躪鑽鑾鑼鱷鱸黷
豔鑿鸚爨驪鬱鸞籲

Taiwan's Cìchángyòng Hànzì

The following are the 6,341 hanzi as defined in Taiwan's list entitled 次常用國字標準字體表 (*cìchángyòng guózì biāozhǔn zìtǐ biǎo*), sometimes known as their Cìchángyòng Hànzì set. This list is separated into those hanzi that are in CNS 11643-1992 Plane 1 (577 hanzi) and those that are in Plane 2 (5,764 hanzi).

CNS 11643-1992 Plane 1—577 hanzi

尣尫𡯆𡯋𡯏尰龠瓩糎兀勺廾弋丰亢叻扑伋刖囝圩污汛汍汎佈佚听囫圻
孛忸忪扠攸杆杠杓宋汴沆汶沍沔沘沂釆阮侑佺怩怫怛昕昊昇料杼杪杲
沬泯泜泖泠秈芯芸芣芰芾芷邶陂隹侷咩咧咿囿垓峒帘徉挂昱枰柙柢柝
柰泵洹洧洸洩洮洵洎洫炤畎畋疢疣盅眇禺籽紆耑胝苯茆虻虺觔迤迨郜
亳唇哽唏圄娉屘峴捍捌敉晅晁栘桁涌浞浹涅浥涔茲珪珞痂疽皋砠砟砲
秘耄胼胯茨荃蚜衽衹訏訑軏迸郝郢釙陘陞倞偭啁啗圉屝崤崧崗徠徜惇
捺敕敔斛晞梡梂毬涪淬涿淦烯痍硎笮粕紲紱脰脤莆莧蛉訢趺釭釩陬雩
鹵傚喫喙堝堠媧崴嵇幃廄愒揹晾晷楮棻氬湎湣湄湲湩湟焜琯琛琦琨痠
筑絰絳耋聒腌腓腴萇萉菟蚰蛞訶詖逶鄢鈇鈑閎隄僇勣嗦塒塋嵯愍愆愷
搆暄暘暍楝楣楛溧溴煆煨煖痳睢碓稞筮筧絛葭葆蜆蜊裒覜詻訾跤跦鄗
鉉鉍鉅鈹鈿鉚雊髡僎僩劂嘐嗶慵搴摭摻暝榦槃滷滎碣箸箇箄綏膂艋蓑

蓊蜷蜩裯誚遏逫遛鄜鄞酴銨鉼銑雒劊勰墩墦奭嬈嶔幡憮撙撢撳暱槭歎
滕潯潠潟瑾璀畿瘢瞋箠篌緈緲緹耦膘蔆蝓褕褊誶誹諛賡踡踞輞輥鋇鋰
銲頫頜駃儕冪劓噶寰彊撾曄曇橈氅澶澦澠澴璘璟璞甍瘺磧穇篦縞縝縉
縐翮耨蕞褡諳諶諼貑輳鄴錡錕錮錙餚壎屨嶸懋擢擭檣橾檗檐檠歜毚氈
濩濕濮濰燠璨礲簌篠糝縴縹繈縵縿薨薊褻謠豳賸賻錫鍔鮭擷曜檮檯燼
燾璿瞼穠繒繙薺薹蟠謫蹟蹕邃邈鎬鎰鎘鎚鎗闕霤韹餮髁魎魍鯈鯀儳瀘
癟籀繳藷蟾襞譆譙蹴邋醱醮鏨饉鯖鯛孃巉櫬瀲糰瞿譟醴霰騵鶤儸爛囊
櫺瓖瓔蘼襬躋鐫顥饗魑齧儻甗襶艨躓酈饕驍櫳瓚籣籥纔臢髑灞鑪鬻髕
鬣贙鑷鑣讜釃鸛

CNS 11643-1992 Plane 2—5,764 hanzi

乂乜凵厂万丌亍囗屮彳丏冇与丮亓仂仉冘卬厹圠夃夬尐巿殳毌气爿仨
仜仩仡仝刌刉匜卌夗夯宁宄尒尻屴庀庂忉戉扐氕氶汃氿犮犰玊禸肊阞
伎优伬仵伔仱伀价冱刓劦匢卍囡囟圮攺妀屼屺巟幵异弚彴忕忔扜扞扤
扡扦扢攷旯旮朾朹朸朻机朿朼氘汆汒汜汏汊汔汋犴犵玎甪网艸艼芀艽
襾邙邗邘邛邔阢阤阠佖伻佢佉体佤伾佧佒佟佁佘冏刜刞劭卣厎吰吷吪
呔囮囧坁坅坌夆妦妘妠妗妎妢妐宎尨尪岍岏岈岋岉岒岜帊庋庉庌庈弅
弝彸忒忑忐忭忨忮忳忡忤忣忺忯忷忻戺抃抌抎抏抔抇扱扻扺旰旴旳杅
杇杙杕杌杈杝毐氙氚汸汧汫沄沋沏汱汯汩沚汭沇沕汼汦汳牣犿犽狃狆
犺玕玗玓玔町甹疔疕皁礽耴肕肙肐肒肜芐芏芅芎芑芓芊芃芄豸迉邟邡
邥邞邧邠阰阨阯侘佼侅佽侀侇佶佴侉侄佷佌侗佪侚佹侁佸侐侜侔侞冞
冼刵刲刳剆刱劼匊匼厒咇呿咁咑咂咈呫呺呾呥呬呴呦咍囷囹坯坲坭坫
坱坰坶垀坵坻坳坴夌奅妵妺姏姎妲姌姁孢孥宓宕屄岮岤岠岵岯岨岬岟
岣岭岢岪岧岝帗帔帙弨弢弣弤彔徂彾忞忥怭怦怙怲怋怴怊怗怳怚怞怬
怢怍怐怮怓戔戽抭抴拑抾抪抶拊抮攽斨斻昉旼昄昒昈旻昃曶枅杬枎枒
杶杻枘枆构杴枍枌欥殀歾毞沓泬泫泮泙沶泔沭泧沷泑泂沺泃泆泭泲泒
泝沴炔炘炅狖狋狘狉狜狒狔狚狌狑玤玡玭玦玢玠瓝瓨甿畀甾疌皯盳盱
矸矼矹矻矺祂礿秅穸耵肏肮肣肸肵舠芠苀芫芚芘芛芵芧芮芼芞芺芴芨
芡芩虰虯虭虮迒迋迓迍迖迕邲邴邯邳郃阹阽阼阺俍俅俓侲俉俋俁俔俜
俙侻侳俛俇剄剉匽卼厗厖咺咡咭咥哏哃茍咷咮哖咶哅哆咠呰咼咢垵垞
垟垤垌垗垝垛垔垘壴复奓姡姞姮娀姱姝姺姽姼姶姤宨屌峐峘峌峗峋峛
峞峚峉峇峊叠帡帢帣帠帤庰庤庢庛庣庥弇弮彖怷怹恔恲恞恅恓恇恉恛
恌㤖恂恟扂扃拏挍挋拵挎挃拫拹挏挌拸拶振战斪斿袒昡昲昵昜昪昢昳
昫昺昝昴朏朐柁柲柈枺柜枻柸柘柀枷柅柫柤柟枵柍枳柷柶柮柣桅枹柎
柧柰臬欨殂殄殶毖毘氡洨洴洭洟洼洿洒洊泚洳洄洙洺洚洑洀烓炟炾皃
炰牁牉牬牰狊狤狨狫狟狪狦狣玅珌珂珈珅瓬瓮甮畇疧癹盄眈眃眄眅眊

昀昑矝矵砄砒砅砐砏砎砉竓神祋祅秕种秏秖秎窀突竑粌粎籹紃紈罘羑
羍羾耇耎耏耔耷肱胇胠肵胈胂胐胅胣胙胜朐胕胉胏胗臿舡舁苙苾苹茇
苨苐苕苦苦苗苴茵苡苲苵荏苻茶虷虴衁衎衦衪衩觓訄訇迣迡迮邾邽郘
郕郅郖郇郎郈釔陔陏陑陓陊倞倅倇倓倢倰倛俵俴傳倷倬俶倕倗倜倠党
尋冓凊凄凅剆剸剳剞劉剕勍匪吵哢哇哂哧哳哤哻哿唄唈唲唑唫囯圂埌
垔埕埒垺埆垐垡娄埧娙娖娭孬宧専屖屔峬峿峮猑峷峭帨庨庮庪庬弳彧
恝恚恧恁悢悈悀悒悁悝悃悕悛悗悇扆拲挈捖挬挗捅挴捃挶挹捋捊挼挩
捁挴捘捔敁敓旆旃旄旂晊晟晇朒朓栟栚桉栲栳栻桋桏栖栱栜栵栫栭栯
桎桄栴栝栒栔欸欯欧欱欮峙殉殈毦毪毨毮冲浣浤浫浰浮涒浘浢浭浯涑
浡涘淏淐泥涅浠浞浰浼浟涂涘烜烓烑烝烋焦牂牸牷狻猙狴狾狶狳狻玹
琪珥珖玼珧珣珩颱颮瓞瓟甡畛畟疰痁疻痄痀盻盂貯眛眐眓眒眏眑眕眙
眚眢砣砬砢砵砯砨砮祔祛祏祜祓祒祑秫秬秠秮秭秪窆窉窅窋窌窊竘笊
笄笓笅笏笈笊笎笉紫紞紝紁紇紘紖紓紟紒罜罡罦罠罣罛羖羒翃翋耖耾
聆胺胲胹胵胇朌脊舁舯茳茭荄荗荑荎荖荊荁茦茜茢荂荃荅荋茝茼茷荍
荄莯茯茯茩荇荅虓虒蚢蚨蚚蚳蚑蚹蚸蚗蚆蚋蚔蚅蚽蚰蚡蚧蚕蚸蚰衭衵
衶衲衸衱衹衿袈衾訒豇豗豻貤貣赶趂趵趵軏軓迵迥适迿迻逄郘郙郬郜
郣郷郥郘郛郗部郤酐酎酏釘釢陜陟隼飣髟鬯偰偪偡偞偠偓偋偗偲偈偍
偁偛偊偢倕偅偟偩偫劇劚剬勔匭匽唦啶唼啍啐唴唪啑啢唶唵啒啀啅啐
唲啥锫圊圇埻埰埢埶埜埴堀埭埽堈場堋埳埏堇婠婘婕婧婞娸婌婭婐婟
婥婬婓婣婗娾婞寁寀屚崞崋崝崚崠崌崨崍崦崥崏崰崒崣崟崧帾帴庱庴庹庲
庳弶弸徛悊惄悆悾悰悺惓惔惏惤惙惝惈悱惛悷掔捥掊掂捽掽掞掭掝掗
掫掎掜掇掐据掯掑掜捭掮掕捆挺敒旍晥晡晛晙晜晢腧根梻桯梜棟桮梮
梫梛梣梺梈梩梾梯棁梏梒梎桼欶歒欹欽殑毬殍氪淀涫涴涳湴涬淩淢涷
淶渞淽淈淠淟淖淚淥淜淝淛淴淊淓淭淰焌焋焏焫焥焩焇焍煮牿犁牼牿猝
猗猇猑猘猊猈猺猗琁琈琣琟琤琁琁琇琀晴畬痃痒痏痋痌痑畊盐眳眯眭
睐眲眴眳眽眥硈硒硉硍硊硌砦祤祧祩裍祫祰紫离秸秸䅟穿窔窒笵笷笱
筍第筤笤笳笘笪笸笥筇等筊笲粔粘紵紽紸紶紼絅紬絑紾絇紾給罣羕羜
羝羦翊翍翑翐翗翣翏耟耞聎聃聄脘脥脙脛脭脬脬脞脡腕腖䏰舸舳舺舴
舲艴莰莣莨莱莍荳茜莢莌菳茸莙葱莤莩荽莃莌莝莛莪莋莇菝虙虖蛌蚷
蚑蛁蛅蚺蚰蚨蚥蚳蚸蚸蚴蛆蚼衖衼衩衸袢袪袚袑袖袟袘袧袙袛袗袠袁
袞覂觖觙觕訰訦訬訞訽訩訮豜豝豽趿跂跌趼躰軘軞軝迯逋逑逜逌逡郯郪郰
郴郲郳郵郫酘酖酚盒釬釴鈃釳釸釶鈌鈋閂閈陼陭陫隿靪頄頏馗脩傕傔傞
傋傣傿傌傎傝傑傜傒傊傖厤喑喨喥喭喞鳴喢喓喈喏喵喁喣喒喤喫喎邑
圖堋堷堙堞堧堨堨埵堅堲冪媯媔媟婺媢媞媋媦婼媥媇媜媮媣爲寍寋寔
寑尌廬崳嵃嵫嵁嵋崿崵嵑嵎崺崳嵇嵐崽嵚嵛崕嵍假徥惉悳惌惢惎惄
愔惲愊愖愅惵惕愂惼慃扊掔掱掰揎揥揨揯揃撝揳揑揠揶揕揲揵摡揟掾

揝揜揄揘敧敧敪黓敘斌斝斞斮旐旒晥晬晻晠暜椌棓椄棜椪棬棪棱椏棖
椒棫棤棶椓椐棳椆椇棌椈楔梴椑棯棆椔棸棐棽棼棨欹欻欿殔殗殙殽毼
毲毳氰淼湆渧渟湉溈渼湤湅湢渫渿湁湝湳渜渳湋湀湑湇渃渮湞湨湜湡
湴渨湠渚湫淘渢湃湓焠焞焯烻焮焱焣牋牚犈犉犆犅猒猋猰猢猱猳猧猲
猭猦猤猵琮琬琰琫琖琚琡琭琱琤甯畯畬痧痚痡痦痝痟痤痗皕睆睇睄睍
睅睊睎睋睌矞矬硍硤硥硜硭硱硪确硰硩祴祳祲稂稊稃稌窙竦筊筇筅筈
筌粢絘絯絣絓絖絧絪絏絭絜絫缾缿罥罦羢羠羡聑聏胾胔腃腊腒腏腇脽
腍弫臮臷舙舄舼艂艴艵菏菹萣菀萋莬菧菤菼菶萐菆菈菫菣莿萁菝菥菘
菿菡菋菎菖菵菉萉萏莉萑萆菂菳萮菺菇菑蛘蛢蛦蛓蛣蛚蛪蛝蛫蛜蛬蛩
蛗衈衕衏袺裗袹袸裀袾袶袼袷袽袲裒覗覘觗觚詎詍訹詙詀詗詘詄詅詒
詈貎貁貀貺貾貰趄趀跘跓跕跇跖跜跏跍跙跈跗跅軯軷軺軹軦軮軥軵軧
軨軶軫軱軬逭逴逯鄆鄬鄄郿鄗郯郹鄏鄁郪郲郾鄃酡酤酟酢鈁鈊鈥鈃鈋
鈦鈏鈌鈀鈒釿鈲鈆鉄閍閌隇陜隈隉隃雃雈雱雺靬靰靮頇飫馺黹亶傽傿
僆傮僄僊傴僈僂僃僁傺從僨僉勥剸剻剹嗃嗛嗌嗐嗋嗊嗝嗀嗀嗔嗄嗩喿
嗒喋嗏嗕嗢嗖嗈嗲塓塨塤塏塍塉塯塕壼嫇嫄嫋嫐嫅媱媵嫏媿嫈嫛寖寘
寙尟尳嵱嵣嵊嵥嵲嵬嵞巰幏幎廅廌廆廋廇彀徯徭惷慉慊愫慅愶愲愮慆
㥮戠戤戣戥掔搴搫搐搒搉搠搤搳損摲搕搘搞搷搢搣搌搦搰搨摠搵搯搊
搚搗搥搧搋敱斒旖暆暌暕暐暋楦楟椸楎楢楱椿楅楪椹楂楗楙楺楈楉椵
楬椳椽楥棰楸椴楩楀楯楄楶楘歆歅歃歀歈殛毹毷毻溛滾滈溏滄溟溓溔
溠溱溹滆滒溽滁溞滉溷溰滍溦滏溲溾滃滜煇煔煒煣煠煁煝煢煲牏犍犌
犑犐犎猼獂猻猺獀獊瑄瑊瑋瑒瑑瑗瑀瓡瓿甄甞甝畹畷痯瘏瘃痷痾痼痹
瘌瘐痻皙皵盝睕睟睠睒睖睚睩睧睔矠碇碚碔碏碄碕碅碆祼禂稑稘稙稛
稗窣窢窞竫筦筤筭筴筩筲筥筳筱筰筡粲綈綆綀綍綠綅絺綎絻綃絼綌絲
罭罫罧罨罬羦羥羧翛翜耡腤腠腷腜腩腛腢腲腰腞腶腧腯腄舝艉艄艀艂
艅蓱萿葵葶葹葿蔿葥葑葀葽葧萰葍萋葚葙葴葳葝蔇葞葪萺萴葺葄葸萲
葅萩葐葋蒷葂萬葟葰萹葎葌葒葯蜋蜄蛷蜌蛺蛖蛵蝍蛸蜎蜉蜓蛶蜍裖裋
裍裎裞裛裚觔覛觟觥觤觡觠觢觜詶誆詿詡詘詷誂誄詵誃詴豋豥貇虡貆
貄貅賌赨赩趑趌趎趏趍趓跰跠跬跱跮跐跩跣跢跧跲跫輆軿輁輀輅輇輈
輂輋遒逿遄鄐鄍鄏鄑鄓鄔鄕鄎酮酯鉈鉒鈰鈺鉦鈳鉥鉞銃鈮鉊鉆鉭鉬鉏
鉠鉧鉯鈶閟閜閞隒陸隑隗雎雽雸靳靷靸靲頏頍頎颭飿馯馲馰畀骭骫鳭
鳩鳧麀黽僦僔僗僨僳僛僪僝僤僓僬僰凘劀劁勩匰厬嘧嘕嘌嘒嗼嘏嘍嘁
嘓嘂嗺嘝嚊嗩墉塼墐墘墆墁塿塴墋墬墊奫嫜嫮嫥嫕嫪嫚嫭嫫嫳嫢嫠嫛
孷寠屣嶂嶀嵽嶆嵺嶁嵷嶊嶉嶈嵾幘幙幓廘廑廗廎廜廕廙彄彃彰愬愨慁
慞慱慳慒慓慲慬憀慴慔慺慛慥戩戧摮摍摛摝摴摶摲摳摽摵摦摣摎摺摞
摜摋摓摠摐摿敳斠暡暠暍楝槷榬榶槉榠槎榖榰榱榼榑榙榎榧榍榩榾榯
榿槄榽榤槔榹槊歊歍歋殞殟殠毃毄毾滎滵滱漃漥滸漷漨漮漉漵漙漚漧

潳漻漒滭漊漶漍滹滮漭澴漰漼潡滫漇潀瀄漅熇熐熉熀熅熂熏牄牓犗犕
獦獃獍獑獀瑢瑳瑱瑤瑲甄甂甃畽疐瘖瘓瘌瘕瘑瘊皸瞑睼瞅瞂睮瞀瞖睪
碲碪碴碭碨硾碫碞禘禊禋禖禕禔禓禗稫穊稰稯窨窫窬箈箜箊箑箐箖箷
箌箛箎箄箘箚箙粻粿粼粺綧綷緂綣綪緁緀緅綝緎緄緆緋緌綯綹綖綼綟
綦綮罳翢翣翥耤聝腦膝膃膇䐓膌膋談蒗蒤蒡蒟蒺蓎蓂蒬蓶蒫蒹蒴蓁蓍
蒪蒚蒱蓐蒝蒧蒻蒢蒔蓇蓌蒛蒩蒯蒨蓖蓻蒶蓅蒠虡蜳蛲蜨蝫蝀蜮蜞蜡蜙
蜛蝃蜬蜑蜾蜯蜠蜲蜪蜭蜼蜒蜺蜱蜵蝂蜦蜧蜸蜇蜚蜰蜑裷裧裱裲裺裾裮
裼裶裻覞覛觩觫誂誙誋誒谽豨賕跟跜跿踍跽踊踃踇踆踅跾輐輑鄣鄜鄠
鄡鄟鄝鄭鄤鄥鄲酺醒酹酳銥銖銂銛鉺銠銒銪銍銦銚銫鉹銗鉿銣鋮鋈隞
霂靬靺靶鞃鞀鞂靻鞄韎韍頖颭颮餂餀馝駃駔駞馺駂鬳髫髲魃魆魠魡鳿
鳲鳵麧僿儃僞僸儆儇僶僾儋儌僁劋劇勱噈噂噌嘵噁嘺噉噆噘噚噀噴嘽
嘬嘾嘸墫墝墱墠墣墯墬壿嫿嫴嫽嫷嫶嬃屧嶙嶗嶟嶒嶢嶓嶕嶠嶜嶡嶚隓
幩幝幠廔廛廞廡彉徲憋憃慹憱憍憢憉憛憓憯憭憟憒憪憮憰戭撆撉撖撠
撅撗撜撏撊撋撌撣撟敶敺敹敻斳暵暰暩樀樆樗槥槸樕樔槤樠槿槬橊樛
槇槾樧槲槮樸槷槧橀殥殣殢殦毸氀毿氂潁漦潾澇潰澒澍澈澌潢潏澅潚
澗潶潬潵潕潲潒潐潗澔澓潝熲熯熛熰熠熚摩熨獎獒獐獟獠獝獛獦璇璉
璊璆璁瑽璅甈瘥瘞瘙瘭瘜瘣皜皝皞皛瞍罼瞉磍碻磏磌磑磎磔磈磃禚禡
禠禜禛積穉窴窳篪篋篍篙篎箯篘糅糈糌緷緛緪緧緗緍緭緺緦緶緱緰罶
羬羰羭羦翫翪翬翦翨膣膟膞膕膢舖艄艓艒艐艎艑蔤蔻蔏蔀蔩蔎蓑蔍蔟
蔊蔧蔜蓻蔫蓺蔈蔌蓴蔪蓲蔕蓷蓫蓳蓼蔗蓪蓩蓭蓾蔨蓛蔮蔂蓽蔞蓶蔱蔦
蓧蓨蓰蓯蓹蔘蔠蔖虢蝖蝣蝤蝏蝺蝳蝘蝔蝛蝒蝡蝚蝑蝞蝭蝪蝐蝎蝟蝝蝯
蝬蝺蝮蝜螌衚褅褌褔褋褗褘褙褆褖褑褎覠覤覣觭觰觬諏諆誸諓諑諔諕
諎諗誾諀諅谾豍貏賥賟賙賨賚趠趜趡踠踣踥踤踮踕踛踖踑踙踦踧踔踒
踘踓輬輤輘輚輠輣輖輗遳遰遯鄑鄫鄩鄚鄲鄦鄮醅醆醊醁鋐鋃鋟鋀鋙錄
鋏鋱鋟鋘鋩鋗鋅鋋鋯鋂鋨鋊鋈踞閬閣隤雓雱霈霂靚鞊鞎鞈韐鞏頞頝頨
頩頪頯颲餈餥餑餔餖餗餕駜駍駏駓駔駎駉駖駘髺髻髳髮魋魊魧魴魱魦
魶魵鴃鳺鴅鳿鴀鴂鴇鴋鴆鴈鴒麀黓鼏鼒儜儓儗儚儑匴叡噰噠噮噳噦噣
噭噲噞圜壞墽嬗嬙嬛嬡嬔嬓嬐嬖嶬嶱嶩嶧嶵嶰嶮嶪嶨嶲嶭嶫嶦幦廩廧
廦廨廥彋徼憝憨憖懅憴懆懁懌憺憿憸擗擖擐擏擉撽撾斀曈暾曀曊曋歸
朣樴橦橉橧樲橨樾橝榛機橛橑樨橚樻樿橁橪檠橐歖歔殧殪殫毈毇氄澭
濋澣濇澼濎濈潞濄澽澞濊澨瀄澥澮燚燂熿熸燖燀燁燋燔燊犝犞獗獦獧
獬獥獫獪瑿璚璠瓻甋瘯瘰瘱瘽瘳瘼瘵瘲皻盦瞚瞝瞡瞜瞛瞢磝磩磥磪磞
磣磛穄穈窶窸窵篠篞篣篧篝篕篥篚篨篹篔篪糒糔糗縒縡縗縌縟縠縓縎
縜縕縚縢縋縏縈罻罼罺羱翯耪膱膦膮膹膵膫膰膬膴膲膷艗艕蕖蕅蕫蕍
蕓蕢蕘蕀蕆蕤蕁蕡蕄蕑蕇蕣蔾蕛蕱蕎蕮蕵蕕蕧蕠薌蕦蕝虩螛螏螗螓螒
螈螁螖螘蝹螇螣螅螐螑螝螄螔螌螚褞褦褰褭褮褧褢褱褩覮諠諢諲諴諵

諝諕諤諟諰諈諞諡貑貒賵賫赬赮趥趧踳踾踸蹀踖踶踼踽蹁踰軀輶輮輵
輲輹輷輴遶遹遻遳邆鄈鄍鄐醓醐醑醍錧錞錈錟錆錏鍺錸錝錛錣錒錁鍆
錭錎錍鋋閼閽閾閹閿閶閺閳闇隩雔霎黔霃鞙僌鞔鬁頲頯頣餤餟餧駮駬
駥駤駰駣駪駩骹骿骳髶髺髹鬳鮀鮅鮇鮚鮃鮋鮓鮒鮐鴃鴂鴠鴉鴆鴇
鴋鴌鴐麈麏麇麧黕黓黺鼒鼽儦儥儢儤儠勵嚓嚌嚂嚆嚄嚃壖嬭嬥嬲寱嶷
嶹嶿徾懃懁懋懧懠懝懤懨懞擯擩擣擫擤擨斁斀斣旚曒檍檖檁檥檉櫃櫆
檡檞檇檓檎檕檃歛殭黏斷澩濴濔濣濭濧濸濦濞燡獳獮獯璗璲璫璐璪甑甑
甋癃癈癉癇瞚瞝瞵瞫瞲瞯瞶瞴矰磳磽磹磻磼磿禫穖穜穛穟窾竀竁篷簁
簂簀簉篻簎篴篕篳篽簉簃篵篸篽縭縼繂縳縨縸縪繉縰縩繇縼縷縰縻縶縶
罅罿罾罽翴翷耬臆臄臌臊臅臇舉艛薀藍蕙薨薕蕡薋薣蕻薞薚薖薟薛薉
薡蕺薝薜薇薖薆薍薙薝薁薢薂薈薅螾螭螭螷螺螬螹螵螼螮螵螬螇螂螂
螯蟄蟊螴蟲螿螫蟇蟞褵褳褸褾襁襒褷襂覬覬覭覯觲觳謅謑謖謘謋謍謢謏
謞謕謇謍謈謰謷貘貙貕貗貔賵賧蹗蹡蹎蹍蹌蹇轃轀遭遰鄚醚醝醛醙醟鎡鎃
鎯鍤鍖鍇鍼鍘鍜鍶鍉鍐鍑鍠鍭鎏鎏鍪闇闉闌闋闃闍隮隱雿鞚鞡鞈鞞鞟
韔韱顀顄顇顉顅饈餬餱餳餲餘餭餿餶饌餯騂騇騑騋騅騂騌騄騅騃騁騬騌
騐骾鬁鬄鬈鬊鬾鮚鮨鮪鮛鮦鮡鮥鮤鮭鴰鴳鴶鴷鴸鴹鴻鴺鴼鴾鵀鵁鵂鴛
鵅鴐麋麀麏麆黚黻黿鼢鼤鼩鼬龠儱嚘嚜嚗嚚嚙屩巀幭瀎懟懫懮懱懪懰
懥擿擥擽攇攋攌旛曚曛櫅櫥櫺櫂櫆竪濱濾瀍瀁瀅瀔瀐瀉瀀瀆瀦濼爁燿
燹獶璸瓀璵瓁甗甓癜癙癟癚癠皦皧盬瞾礌礓礔礅礜禭禬禮簜簩簙簠簞
簦簝簪簣簡簥繜繐繖繏繘繢繟繑繁繛繙聵臑臒臕艟薴薾藂蘔藂藼薵甊
藇藆藐藋藎藔藅藙藦蘇藒虩蟧蟦蟢蟛蟫蟪蟥蟟蟳蟤蟝蟜蟓蟭蟣蟻蟲蟙
蠁蟗蟨襓襋襏襌襆襐謫謪謣謳謰謵謯謱謼謾謱謥謷謽謸謺謷謹謻謾蹢
蹢蹠蹝蹡蹞蹥蹧蹯蹚蹣蹤蹩蹔轆轇轐鄨鄸鄹鄿醨醩醧醙醪鎵鎌鎒鎢鎛
鎝鎉鎧鎎鎪鎞鎦闑闓闒隳雗雚巂雟雘雝霣霢鞭鞮鞨鞫鞪鞶鞥鞿顗顜顒
颸颺餽騏騋騉騍騤騑騊騅騋鬆鬈鬅鬩鬵魈魌魋鯇鯆鯃鯁鯅鯈鯊鯓鵊
鵎鵏鵐鵑鵒鵓鵔鵕鵖鵗鵘鵙鵝鵚黟黿鼀鼁鼂鼃鼄鼆齋齕儴儵劖嚫嚭
嚦嚧嚪嚬壚壝壛夒嬽嬾嬿巃巄巇懬懭攄攘攈攉攌櫜旞旝櫙櫋櫌櫗櫓櫟
櫜櫝櫫歠殰瀙瀧瀠瀯瀫瀡瀢瀣瀨爄爊爇爂犢犣犥犡瓀瓆瓅疇矌礦矱礛
礞礡礨禰穬穰穧穩籆簵簻糬糪繶繵繷繰繳繯繲繵繺罋罌羃羆羶翶翷臏
臕臖艤藫藬藭藯藹蘅蘀蘁藨藰藸藷藶藾藿蘈蠈蟺蠃蠉蠊蠋蠌蠍蠓蟷
蠑蠒襗襘襚襛襜襞襝襡覈覷覶觶譊譓譔譈譏譖譒譙譍譎譌譐譑譕譓譗蹺
趬趫趭蹭蹸蹬蹪蹯蹻轒轑轓轔轕轖鄺醰醱鏞鏇鏈鏂鏚鏐鏕鏑鏌鏕鏓鏦
鏊鏉闚闛霪霫霬鞳鞷鞸鞺鞹顜顝顚顛颼颽颾颿餾餼餽饃騚騙騜騝騟騕
騛騢騠騗騣騤騥騦鬊鬌鬋鬌鬐鬍鯆鯉鯎鯏鯑鯒鯓鯔鯕鯖鯗鯘鵛鵞鵟鵠鵢
鵣鵤鵥鵦鵧鵨鵩鵪鵫鵬鵭鵮鵯鵰鵱鵲鵳鵴麛麜麞黼鼭齗齘齙齚齛齜
曩嚳嬫嶒巁廮廯徿徾攐攖攕攓攏旟曨曣櫳櫰櫪櫨櫬櫱瀼瀵瀯瀷瀴瀱瀺瀸

瀿瀺瀹爓犨獶獼瓙皫皾盭矌矆矏矍礥礤礯礨穮穡穭竷籉籈籀繻繾纁
纀羺翷聹臛臙艨蘢藿蘁藾蘛蘀藶蘄蘐蘅蘗蠙蠐蠑蠗蠓蠖襣襦觷譠譪譝
譨譣謦趮躆躈躄轙轖轗轕轘鏧邍鄙鄚醷醵醲醳鐊鐓鏻鐕鏄鐔鏾鐕鐐鐼
鐙鐍鏵鐀鏷鐇鐎鐖闟闠闤霘鞹鞻韽顠顂顣顟飄飂饐饎饋饌饙驔驐騱騬
騪騶騩騮騸騭髚髊髆髻鬒鰸鰈鯷鰅鰒鯸鷖鷄鶬鶤鶅鶘鶠鶪鷗鶵鶲鶹
鶺鶼鶾鷀鷂鷃鷄鷙鷙鷥麑麛麙黖黗黛鼮鼵齙齝齞齡儺儹劘劗囃嚽嚾孅
巋巏廱懽攛欂櫼欃櫸灃灄灉灈灊爚爚獾甗癪矐礭礱籔糲纊纇纈纋纆纍
罍穮羸蘘蘖蘦隱蘟蘜蘺蘧藯蘡蘠蘩蘞蘥蠩蠝蠛蠠蠤蠜襫襭襮襮觼譹
譸譾譺譻贐贔趯艦轛轝酆酇酈醹鐿鐻鐶闔闥霹鞿韡顤飋飆饘騹騽驆驄
驂驁鶖驌鬖鬗鬘鬕鬺鰫鰝鰜鰚鰣鰨鰩鷁鷋鷚鷀鷇鷅鷌鷑鶾鷉鷍鷒鷗
鷏鷐鷈鷋鷔鷔鹺麝黮黭黰齎齣鼶齧齩嚿囆囈囄囋囍囏巑巕廲巇攤攦攞攢欋
欔氍灘灖灗爞爟犩玀瓘癭皭礵禴穰穱籗籜籙籛籠籟纑纐羇臞艫艬蘸蘼
虈蠬蠨蠦蠪蠥覿覵襤讂讄讅讆贖躕躔躚躒躐躖躝轠轢酅鑌鑐鑊鑋鑏霾鐲顪
顩飀饔饛驎驓驔驌驏驕驊驉驒驍鬡鬫鬻魖鱆鱈鱋鱄鰹鱂鱁鱃鱎鱉鰲鷻
鷼鷽鷾鸀鷵鷺鷸鷹鷲鷘鷫鷩鸂黐黕齴鼸鼹鼀齬龕龢儽劙鑺巎巃孋斖
戁攩攥疊櫕欒虋灆灖灙灦玁癰矔籧籦纕蘳虆虇虋蘻蘱蘲韠蠯蠰讇蠮蠷襳襴
襶觻讌讎讐讚轤醾鐻鑕韤韅韄驖鬤鬠鬹鱒鱘鱐鱊鱍鱋鱕驐鷭鷮鷯鷳鷴鸔
鷿鷥鷦鷦鷩鷯鷲鷹麡麧黂鼊鼕鼶鼷鼺齅齰齮齯齵囓囍囑攎曭曮灟灡
灝爣瓛蠡讋襹纚纝虇蠸蠼蠵蠹讔讕躞躟躠醿醽醻鑫鑯靃韥韣驞髕鱣鱧
鱦鱳鱞鱠灉鸁鸉鸃鸆鸊鸓鸁鸞鸒鸑鸕鸕鸖鸛鸙鸜囔攮欘欆矘矙籑糶纗纘
蠹欒鬭虉虈蘸襶襽觽讘讙躥躤躣鑚鑭鑯鑱鑳鑴韇饟饠鱨鸐鸍鸛鸎鸑鸑鸒
黸鼉鱸鹼顓齾黷麠麢麷蠼趲躦醲鑷驤闤鑹鑵鑽鑾鼊齹灨糷钃蠾蠿讜讞
貜躩趯覾覿饞饡驦驧鬞鸕鸔戇鼺躨钁钂钀驩驨鱺鑼讝钃鑸戵癵鸁鱱鸓灎
灩麤爩驪

Kanji Lists From Japan

There are three basic kanji lists used in Japan: Jōyō Kanji, Gakushū Kanji, and Jinmei-yō Kanji. The following sections provides each list in printed form.

Jōyō Kanji

The following are the 1,945 Jōyō Kanji (常用漢字 *jōyō kanji*), listed in the order they appear in the JIS X 0208:1997 character set standard. They are all included in JIS X 0208:1997 Level 1 kanji.

亜哀愛悪握圧扱安暗案以位依偉囲委威尉意慰易為異移維緯胃衣違遺
医井域育一壱逸稲芋印員因姻引飲院陰隠韻右宇羽雨渦浦運雲営影映

栄永泳英衛詠鋭液疫益駅悦謁越閲円園宴延援沿演炎煙猿縁遠鉛塩汚
凹央奥往応押横欧殴王翁黄沖億屋憶乙卸恩温穏音下化仮何価佳加可
夏嫁家寡科暇果架歌河火禍稼箇花荷華菓課貨過蚊我画芽賀雅餓介会
解回塊壊快怪悔懐戒拐改械海灰界皆絵開階貝劾外害慨概涯街該垣嚇
各拡格核殻獲確穫覚角較郭閣隔革学岳楽額掛潟割喝括活渇滑褐轄且
株刈乾冠寒刊勘勧巻喚堪完官寛干幹患感慣憾換敢棺款歓汗漢環甘監
看管簡緩缶肝艦観貫還鑑間閑関陥館丸含岸眼岩頑顔願企危喜器基奇
寄岐希幾忌揮机旗既期棋棄機帰気汽祈季紀規記貴起軌輝飢騎鬼偽儀
宜戯技擬欺犠疑義議菊吉喫詰却客脚虐逆丘久休及吸宮弓急救朽求泣
球究窮級糾給旧牛去居巨拒拠挙虚許距漁魚享京供競共凶協叫境峡強
恐恭挟教橋況狂狭矯胸脅興郷鏡響驚仰凝暁業局曲極玉勤均斤琴禁筋
緊菌襟謹近金吟銀九句区苦駆具愚虞空偶遇隅屈掘靴繰桑勲君薫訓群
軍郡係傾刑兄啓型契形径恵慶憩掲携敬景渓系経継茎蛍計警軽鶏芸迎
鯨劇撃激傑欠決潔穴結血月件倹健兼券剣圏堅嫌建憲懸検権犬献研絹
県肩見謙賢軒遣険顕験元原厳幻弦減源玄現言限個古呼固孤己庫弧戸
故枯湖誇雇顧鼓五互午呉娯後御悟碁語誤護交侯候光公功効厚口向后
坑好孔孝工巧幸広康恒慌抗拘控攻更校構江洪港溝甲皇硬稿紅絞綱耕
考肯航荒行衡講貢購郊酵鉱鋼降項香高剛号合拷豪克刻告国穀酷黒獄
腰骨込今困墾婚恨懇昆根混紺魂佐唆左差査砂詐鎖座債催再最妻宰彩
才採栽歳済災砕祭斎細菜裁載際剤在材罪財坂咲崎作削搾昨策索錯桜
冊刷察撮擦札殺雑皿三傘参山惨散桟産算蚕賛酸暫残仕伺使刺司史嗣
四士始姉姿子市師志思指支施旨枝止死氏祉私糸紙紫肢脂至視詞詩試
誌諮資賜雌飼歯事似侍児字寺慈持時次滋治璽磁示耳自辞式識軸七執
失室湿漆疾質実芝舎写射捨赦斜煮社者謝車遮蛇邪借勺尺爵酌釈若寂
弱主取守手朱殊狩珠種趣酒首儒受寿授樹需囚収周宗就州修愁拾秀秋
終習臭舟衆襲週酬集醜住充十従柔汁渋獣縦重銃叔宿淑祝縮粛塾熟出
術述俊春瞬准循旬殉準潤盾純巡遵順処初所暑庶緒署書諸助叙女序徐
除傷償勝匠升召商唱奨宵将小少尚床彰承抄招掌昇昭晶松沼消渉焼焦
照症省硝礁祥称章笑粧紹肖衝訟証詔詳象賞鐘障上丈乗冗剰城場壌嬢
常情条浄状畳蒸譲醸錠嘱飾植殖織職色触食辱伸信侵唇娠寝審心慎振
新森浸深申真神紳臣薪親診身辛進針震人仁刃尋甚尽迅陣酢図吹垂帥
推水炊睡粋衰遂酔錘随髄崇数枢据杉澄寸世瀬畝是制勢姓征性成政整
星晴正清牲生盛精聖声製西誠誓請逝青静斉税隻席惜斥昔析石積籍績
責赤跡切拙接摂折設窃節説雪絶舌仙先千占宣専川戦扇栓泉浅洗染潜
旋線繊船薦践選遷銭銑鮮前善漸然全禅繕塑措疎礎祖租粗素組訴阻僧
創双倉喪壮奏層想捜掃挿操早曹巣槽燥争相窓総草荘葬藻装走送遭霜

騒像増憎臓蔵贈造促側則即息束測足速俗属賊族続卒存孫尊損村他多
太堕妥惰打駄体対耐帯待怠態替泰滞胎袋貸退逮隊代台大第題滝卓宅
択拓沢濯託濁諾但達奪脱棚谷丹単嘆担探淡炭短端胆誕鍛団壇弾断暖
段男談値知地恥池痴稚置致遅築畜竹蓄逐秩窒茶嫡着中仲宙忠抽昼柱
注虫衷鋳駐著貯丁兆帳庁弔張彫徴懲挑朝潮町眺聴脹腸調超跳長頂鳥
勅直朕沈珍賃鎮陳津墜追痛通塚漬坪釣亭低停偵貞呈堤定帝底庭廷弟
抵提程締艇訂逓邸泥摘敵滴的笛適哲徹撤迭鉄典天展店添転点伝殿田
電吐塗徒斗渡登途都努度土奴怒倒党冬凍刀唐塔島悼投搭東桃棟盗湯
灯当痘等答筒糖統到討謄豆踏逃透陶頭騰闘働動同堂導洞童胴道銅峠
匿得徳特督篤毒独読凸突届屯豚曇鈍内縄南軟難二尼弐肉日乳入如尿
任妊忍認寧猫熱年念燃粘悩濃納能脳農把覇波派破婆馬俳廃拝排敗杯
背肺輩配倍培媒梅買売賠陪伯博拍泊白舶薄迫漠爆縛麦箱肌畑八鉢発
髪伐罰抜閥伴判半反帆搬板版犯班畔繁般藩販範煩頒飯晩番盤蛮卑否
妃彼悲扉批披比泌疲皮碑秘罷肥被費避非飛備尾微美鼻匹必筆姫百俵
標氷漂票表評描病秒苗品浜貧賓頻敏瓶不付夫婦富布府怖扶敷普浮父
符腐膚譜負賦赴附侮武舞部封風伏副復幅服福腹複覆払沸仏物分噴墳
憤奮粉紛雰文聞丙併兵塀幣平弊柄並閉陛米壁癖別偏変片編辺返遍便
勉弁保舗捕歩補穂募墓慕暮母簿倣俸包報奉宝峰崩抱放方法泡砲縫胞
芳褒訪豊邦飽乏亡傍剖坊妨帽忘忙房暴望某棒冒紡肪膨謀貿防北僕墨
撲朴牧没堀奔本翻凡盆摩磨魔麻埋妹枚毎幕膜又抹末繭万慢満漫味未
魅岬密脈妙民眠務夢無矛霧婿娘名命明盟迷銘鳴滅免綿面模茂妄毛猛
盲網耗木黙目戻問紋門匁夜野矢厄役約薬訳躍柳愉油癒諭輸唯優勇友
幽悠憂有猶由裕誘遊郵雄融夕予余与誉預幼容庸揚揺擁曜様洋溶用窯
羊葉要謡踊陽養抑欲浴翌翼羅裸来頼雷絡落酪乱卵欄濫覧利吏履理痢
裏里離陸律率立略流留硫粒隆竜慮旅虜了僚両寮料涼猟療糧良量陵領
力緑倫厘林臨輪隣塁涙累類令例冷励礼鈴隷零霊麗齢暦歴列劣烈裂廉
恋練連錬炉路露労廊朗楼浪漏老郎六録論和話賄惑枠湾腕

Gakushū Kanji

The following are the 1,006 Gakushū Kanji (学習漢字 *gakushū kanji*), arranged by grade level, and in the order they appear in the JIS X 0208:1997 character set standard. They are all in JIS X 0208:1997 Level 1. They also form a subset of Jōyō Kanji, listed in the previous section.

Grade 1—80 kanji

一右雨円王音下火花貝学気休玉金九空月犬見五口校左三山四子糸字
耳七車手十出女小上森人水正生青石赤先千川早草足村大男竹中虫町
天田土二日入年白八百文本名木目夕立力林六

Grade 2—160 kanji

引羽雲園遠黄何夏家科歌画会回海絵外角楽活間丸岩顔帰汽記弓牛魚
京強教近兄形計元原言古戸午後語交光公工広考行高合国黒今才細作
算姉市思止紙寺時自室社弱首秋週春書少場色食心新親図数星晴声西
切雪線船前組走多太体台谷知地池茶昼朝長鳥直通弟店点電冬刀東当
答頭同道読内南肉馬買売麦半番父風分聞米歩母方北妹毎万明鳴毛門
夜野矢友曜用来理里話

Grade 3—200 kanji

悪安暗委意医育員飲院運泳駅横屋温化荷界開階寒感漢館岸期起客宮
急球究級去橋業局曲銀区苦具君係軽決血研県庫湖向幸港号根祭坂皿
仕使始指死詩歯事持次式実写者主取守酒受州拾終習集住重宿所暑助
勝商昭消章乗植深申真神身進世整昔全想相送息速族他打対待代第題
炭短談着柱注丁帳調追定庭笛鉄転登都度島投湯等豆動童農波配倍箱
畑発反板悲皮美鼻筆氷表病秒品夫負部服福物平返勉放味命面問役薬
油有由遊予様洋羊葉陽落流旅両緑礼列練路和

Grade 4—200 kanji

愛案以位囲胃衣印栄英塩央億加果課貨芽改械害街各覚完官管観関願
喜器希旗機季紀議救求泣給挙漁競共協鏡極訓軍郡型径景芸欠結健建
験固候功好康航告差最菜材昨刷察札殺参散産残司史士氏試児治辞失
借種周祝順初唱松焼照省笑象賞信臣成清静席積折節説戦浅選然倉巣
争側束続卒孫帯隊達単置仲貯兆腸低停底的典伝徒努灯働堂得特毒熱
念敗梅博飯費飛必標票不付府副粉兵別変辺便包法望牧末満未脈民無
約勇要養浴利陸料良量輪類令例冷歴連労老録

Grade 5—185 kanji

圧易移因営永衛液益演往応恩仮価可河過賀解快格確額刊幹慣眼基寄
規技義逆久旧居許境興均禁句群経潔件券検険減現限個故護効厚構耕
講鉱混査再妻採災際在罪財桜雑賛酸師志支枝資飼似示識質舎謝授修
術述準序承招証常情条状織職制勢性政精製税績責接設絶舌銭祖素総

像増造則測属損態貸退団断築張提程敵適統導銅徳独任燃能破判版犯比肥非備俵評貧婦富布武復複仏編弁保墓報豊暴貿防務夢迷綿輸余預容率略留領

Grade 6—181 kanji

異遺域宇映延沿我灰拡閣革割株巻干看簡危揮机貴疑吸供胸郷勤筋敬系警劇激穴憲権絹厳源呼己誤后孝皇紅鋼降刻穀骨困砂座済裁策冊蚕姿私至視詞誌磁射捨尺若樹収宗就衆従縦縮熟純処署諸除傷将障城蒸針仁垂推寸盛聖誠宣専泉洗染善創奏層操窓装臓蔵存尊宅担探誕暖段値宙忠著庁潮頂賃痛展党糖討届難乳認納脳派俳拝背肺班晩否批秘腹奮並閉陛片補暮宝訪亡忘棒枚幕密盟模訳優郵幼欲翌乱卵覧裏律臨朗論

Jinmei-Yō Kanji

The following are the 285 Jinmei-yō Kanji (人名用漢字 *jinmei-yō kanji*), listed in the order they appear in the JIS X 0208:1997 character set standard. They are separated into two parts: those that are in JIS Level 1 kanji (245 kanji), and those that are in JIS Level 2 kanji (40 kanji).

JIS X 0208:1997 Level 1—245 kanji

阿葵茜渥旭梓絢綾鮎杏伊惟亥郁磯允胤卯丑唄叡瑛艶苑於旺伽嘉茄霞魁凱馨叶樺鎌茅侃莞巌伎嬉毅稀亀誼鞠橘亨匡喬尭桐錦欣欽芹衿玖矩駒熊栗袈圭慧桂拳絃胡虎伍吾梧瑚鯉倖宏弘昂晃浩紘鴻嵯沙瑳裟哉采冴朔笹皐燦爾蒔汐鹿偲紗洲峻竣舜駿淳醇曙渚恕庄捷昌梢菖蕉丞穣晋榛秦須翠瑞嵩雛碩爽惣綜聡蒼汰黛鯛鷹啄琢只辰巽旦檀智猪暢蝶椎槻蔦椿紬鶴悌汀禎杜藤憧瞳寅酉惇敦奈那凪捺楠虹乃之巴萩肇鳩隼斐緋眉柊彦媛彪彬芙楓蕗碧甫輔朋萌鳳鵬睦槙柾亦麿巳稔椋孟也冶耶弥靖佑宥柚湧祐邑楊耀蓉遥嵐藍蘭李梨璃琉亮凌瞭稜諒遼琳麟瑠伶嶺怜玲蓮呂禄倭亘

JIS X 0208:1997 Level 2—40 kanji

侑勁奎崚彗昴晏晨晟暉栞椰毬洸洵滉漱澪燎燿瑶皓眸笙綺綸翔脩茉莉菫詢諄赳迪頌颯黎凜熙

Hanja Lists From Korea

There are two basic hanja lists used in Korean: Sangyong Hanja and its middle school subset. The following sections provides each list in printed form. Both lists have been expanded to accomodate multiple-encoding as found in KS X 1001:1992, so don't be surprised if you encounter multiple instances of some hanja.

Sangyong Hanja

The following is a complete listing of Korea's hanja set entitled Sangyong Hanja (상용 한자/常用漢字 *sangyong hanja*), in which there are 1,800 hanja. Because there are multiple instances of some hanja in KS X 1001-1992, these 1,800 hanja become 1,953 in the list below.

佳假價加可家暇架歌街刻却各脚覺角閣刊姦干幹懇看簡肝間渴感敢減
甘監鑑甲剛康强江綱講鋼降介個慨改概皆蓋豈開客更去居巨拒據擧距
車乾件健建傑儉劍檢憩擊格激堅犬絹肩見遣決潔結缺兼謙京傾卿境庚
徑慶敬景更硬竟競經耕警輕鏡頃驚係啓契季戒桂械溪界癸系繼計階鷄
古告固姑孤庫故枯稿考苦顧高鼓哭曲穀谷困坤骨供公共功孔工恐恭攻
空貢寡戈果瓜科誇課過郭冠官寬慣管觀貫關館光廣鑛掛塊壞怪愧交巧
敎校橋矯較郊丘久九俱具區口句懼拘救構求狗球究舊苟驅鷗龜國局菊
君群軍郡屈宮弓窮券勸卷拳權厥句歸貴鬼龜叫規閨均菌龜克劇極僅勤
斤根謹近契今琴禁禽金錦及急級給肯企其器基奇寄己幾忌技旗旣期棄
機欺氣畿祈紀記豈起飢騎緊吉金奈羅那樂洛落諾亂卵暖欄爛蘭難南濫
男藍納娘廊朗浪郎乃來內奈耐冷女年念寧努勞奴怒爐老路露祿綠錄鹿
論弄濃農惱腦雷屢樓淚漏累能陵泥多茶丹但單團壇斷旦檀段短端達擔
淡潭談畓答踏唐堂當糖黨代大對帶待臺貸隊宅德倒刀到圖導島度徒挑
桃渡盜稻跳逃途道都陶毒獨督篤讀敦豚突冬凍動同東桐洞童銅斗讀豆
頭鈍得燈登等羅樂洛絡落諾丹亂卵欄爛蘭濫藍覽廊朗浪郎來冷掠略兩
涼梁糧良諒量勵慮旅麗力曆歷憐戀練聯蓮連鍊列劣烈裂廉令寧嶺零靈
領例禮勞怒爐老路露祿綠錄鹿論弄賴雷了料龍屢樓淚漏累柳流留類六
陸倫輪律栗率隆陵利吏履李梨理異裏里離隣林臨立磨馬痲幕漠莫慢晩
滿漫萬蠻末亡妄忘忙望罔茫埋妹媒梅每買賣脈麥孟猛盲盟免勉眠綿面
滅冥名命明銘鳴募慕暮某模母毛矛謀貌木沐牧目睦沒夢蒙卯墓妙廟苗
務戊武無舞茂貿霧墨默問文聞門勿物味尾微未眉米美迷憫敏民密蜜博
拍朴泊薄迫半反叛班盤般返飯拔發髮倣傍妨房放方芳訪邦防倍北培拜
排杯背輩配伯栢白百煩番繁飜伐罰凡汎犯範法壁碧便變辨辯邊別丙兵
屛病竝保報寶普步補譜伏卜復服福腹複本奉封峯蜂逢鳳不付副否夫婦

富府復扶浮父符簿腐膚負賦赴部附北分墳奔奮憤粉紛不佛弗拂崩朋備
卑妃婢悲批比碑秘肥費非飛鼻貧賓頻氷聘事仕似使史司四士寫寺射巳
師思捨斜斯査死沙社祀私絲舍蛇詐詞謝賜辭邪削數朔索山散産算酸殺
三參森上傷像償商喪嘗尚常床想桑狀相祥裳詳象賞霜塞塞索色生省序
庶徐恕敍暑書緒署西夕席惜昔析石釋仙先善宣旋禪線船選鮮舌設說雪
涉葉城姓性成星盛省聖聲誠世勢歲洗稅細說召小少所掃昭消燒疏笑素
蔬蘇訴騷俗屬束粟續速孫損率松訟誦送頌刷殺鎖衰修受囚壽守帥愁手
授收數樹殊水獸睡秀誰輸遂隨雖需須首叔孰宿淑熟肅巡循旬殉盾瞬純
脣順戌術述崇濕拾習襲乘僧勝升承昇侍始市施是時矢示視試詩式息植
識食飾伸信愼新晨申神臣身辛辰失室實審尋心沈深甚十拾雙氏亞兒我
牙芽阿雅餓岳惡樂安岸案眼雁顔謁巖暗壓仰央殃哀愛涯厄額也夜耶若
野弱掠略約若藥兩凉壤揚梁楊樣洋糧羊良諒讓陽量養御於漁語魚億憶
抑焉言嚴業予余勵女如旅汝與輿餘麗亦力域役易曆歷疫譯逆驛宴年延
憐戀沿演然煙燃燕研硯緣練聯軟蓮連鉛鍊列劣悅烈熱裂說廉念染炎鹽
葉令寧嶺影映榮永泳營英詠迎零靈領例藝禮譽豫銳五傲午吾嗚娛悟惡
梧汚烏誤屋獄玉溫翁瓦臥完緩曰往王外畏了搖料樂腰要謠遙慾欲浴辱
勇容庸用龍于偶優又友右宇尤愚憂牛羽遇郵雨云運雲韻雄元原員圓園
怨援源遠院願月越位偉僞危圍委威慰爲緯胃衛謂違乳儒唯幼幽悠惟愈
有柔柳油流猶由留維裕誘遊遺酉類六肉育陸倫潤輪閏律栗率隆恩銀隱
乙吟淫陰音飮泣邑應依儀宜意疑矣義衣議醫二以利吏夷履已易李梨泥
理異移而耳裏貳里離益翼人仁刃印因姻寅引忍認隣一壹日逸任壬林臨
賃入立刺姉姿子字恣慈玆紫者自資雌作昨爵酌殘暫潛蠶雜丈場壯獎將
帳張掌牆狀章粧腸臟莊葬藏裝長障再哉在才材栽災裁財載爭低底抵著
貯寂摘敵滴的積笛籍績賊赤跡蹟適傳全典前專展戰田轉錢電切折節絶
占店漸點接蝶丁井亭停定庭廷征情政整正淨程精訂貞靜頂制堤帝弟提
濟祭第製諸除際題齊兆助弔操早朝條潮照燥祖租組調造鳥族足存尊卒
拙宗從種終縱鐘佐坐左座罪主住周宙州晝朱柱株注洲舟走酒竹俊準遵
中仲衆重卽增憎曾症蒸證贈之只地志持指支智枝止池知紙至誌識遲直
織職振珍盡眞辰進鎭陣陳姪疾秩質執集徵懲且借差次此茶車捉着錯讚
贊察參慘塹倉創唱昌暢滄窓蒼債彩採菜冊策責妻悽處刺尺戚拓斥千天
川泉淺薦賤踐遷哲徹鐵尖添妾廳晴淸聽請靑切替體初抄招礎肖草超促
燭觸寸村總聰銃催最抽推秋追醜丑畜祝築縮蓄逐春出充忠蟲衝取吹就
臭趣醉側測層値恥治稚置致齒則親七漆侵寢枕沈浸針稱快他墮妥打度
托拓濁濯琢彈歎炭奪脫探貪塔湯糖太怠態殆泰宅擇澤兎吐土討洞痛統
通退投透鬪特播波派破罷頗判板版販八敗貝便片篇編遍平評幣廢弊肺
蔽閉包布抱捕暴浦胞飽幅暴爆標漂票表品楓豊風彼疲皮被避匹必畢筆

下何夏河荷賀學鶴寒恨旱汗漢閑限韓割含咸陷合巷恒抗港航行降項亥
奚害海解該核幸行享向鄕響香虛許憲獻軒險驗革弦懸玄現絃縣見賢顯
穴血協脅亨兄刑形螢兮惠慧乎互呼好戶毫浩湖胡虎號護豪惑或婚昏混
魂忽弘洪紅鴻化和火畵禍禾花華話貨擴確穫丸患換歡環還活況皇荒黃
回悔懷會灰劃獲橫孝效曉侯候厚喉後訓毁揮輝休携凶胸黑吸興喜噫希
戱熙稀

Sangyong Hanja Middle School Subset

The following is a complete listing of the 900 hanja that constitute the middle school subset of Sangyong Hanja. Because there are multiple instances of some hanja in KS X 1001:1992, these 900 hanja become 978 in the listing below.

佳假價加可家歌街各脚角干看間渴感敢減甘甲強江講降個改皆開客更
去居巨擧車乾建堅犬見決潔結京庚慶敬景更競經耕輕驚季溪界癸計鷄
古告固故考苦高曲穀谷困坤骨公共功工空果科課過官觀關光廣交敎校
橋久九口句救求究舊國君軍郡弓勸卷權句歸貴均極勤根近今禁金及急
給其基己幾技旣期氣記起吉金樂落卵暖難南男浪郎乃來內冷女年念勞
怒老路露綠論農能多丹但單短端達談答堂當代大對待宅德刀到圖島度
徒道都獨讀冬動同東洞童斗讀豆頭得燈登等樂落丹卵浪郞來冷兩凉良
量旅力歷練連列烈令領例禮勞怒老路露綠論料柳流留六陸倫律利理異
里林立馬莫晩滿萬末亡忘忙望妹每買賣麥免勉眠面名命明鳴暮母毛木
目卯妙務戊武無舞茂墨問文聞門勿物味尾未米美民密半反飯發房放方
訪防北拜杯白百番伐凡法便變別丙兵病保報步伏復服福本奉逢不否夫
婦富復扶浮父部北分不佛朋備悲比非飛鼻貧氷事仕使史四士寺射巳師
思死私絲舍謝數山散産算殺三參上傷商喪尙常想相賞霜色生省序暑書
西夕席惜昔石仙先善線船選鮮設說雪葉城姓性成星盛省聖聲誠世勢歲
洗稅細說小少所消笑素俗續速孫松送殺修受壽守愁手授收數樹水秀誰
雖須首叔宿淑純順戌崇拾習乘勝承始市施是時示視試詩式植識食信新
申神臣身辛辰失室實心深甚十拾氏兒我惡樂安案眼顔巖暗仰哀愛也夜
若野弱約若藥兩凉揚洋羊良讓陽量養於漁語魚億憶言嚴業余女如旅汝
與餘亦力易歷逆年然煙硏硯練連列悅烈熱說念炎葉令榮永英迎領例藝
禮五午吾悟惡烏誤屋玉溫瓦臥完曰往王外料樂要欲浴勇容用于又友右
宇尤憂牛遇雨云運雲雄元原圓園怨遠願月位偉危威爲唯幼有柔柳油流
猶由留遊遺酉六肉育陸倫律恩銀乙吟陰音飮泣邑應依意矣義衣議醫二
以利已易理異移而耳貳里益人仁印因寅引忍認一壹日壬林入立姉子字
慈者自作昨場壯將章長再哉在才材栽財爭低著貯敵的赤適傳全典前展
戰田錢電節絶店接丁井停定庭情政正淨精貞靜頂帝弟祭第製諸除題兆

助早朝祖調造鳥族足存尊卒宗從種終鐘坐左罪主住宙晝朱注走酒竹中
衆重卽增曾證之只地志持指支枝止知紙至識直盡眞辰進質執集且借次
此車着察參唱昌窓採菜冊責妻處尺千天川泉淺鐵晴淸聽請靑體初招草
寸村最推秋追丑祝春出充忠蟲取吹就治致齒則親七針快他打度脫探太
泰宅土洞統通退投特波破判八敗貝便片篇平閉布抱暴暴表品楓豊風彼
皮匹必筆下何夏河賀學寒恨漢閑限韓合恒行降亥害海解幸行向鄕香虛
許現見賢血協兄刑形惠乎呼好戶湖虎號或婚混紅化和火畫花華話貨患
歡活皇黃回會孝效厚後訓休凶胸黑興喜希

S

Single-Byte Code Tables

This appendix provides code tables that illustrate the characters in a variety of single-byte character sets, indexed by hexadecimal values. Control characters, when defined, appear as visual tags.

Non-CJKV Code Tables

This section provides code tables for non-CJKV character sets, such as ASCII, EBCDIC, and ISO 8859-1:1998. All of these character sets, as described in the beginning sections of Chapter 3, *Character Set Standards*, form the foundation for locale-specific instances.

ASCII Code Table

The following is an ASCII code table, including the C0 control code region (0x00 through 0x1F and 0x7F) expressed as visual tags:

	0	1	2	3	4	5	6	7	8	9	A	B	C	D	E	F
0	<NUL>	<SOH>	<STX>	<ETX>	<EOT>	<ENQ>	<ACK>	<BEL>	<BS>	<HT>	<LF>	<VT>	<FF>	<CR>	<SO>	<SI>
1	<DLE>	<DC1>	<DC2>	<DC3>	<DC4>	<NAK>	<SYN>	<ETB>	<CAN>	<EM>	<SUB>	<ESC>	<FS>	<GS>	<RS>	<US>
2	<SP>	!	"	#	$	%	&	'	(	)	*	+	,	-	.	/
3	0	1	2	3	4	5	6	7	8	9	:	;	<	=	>	?
4	@	A	B	C	D	E	F	G	H	I	J	K	L	M	N	O
5	P	Q	R	S	T	U	V	W	X	Y	Z	[	\	]	^	_
6	`	a	b	c	d	e	f	g	h	i	j	k	l	m	n	o
7	p	q	r	s	t	u	v	w	x	y	z	{	|	}	~	<DEL>

EBCDIC Code Table

The following is an EBCDIC code table, including control characters expressed as visual tags:

	0	1	2	3	4	5	6	7	8	9	A	B	C	D	E	F
0	<NUL>	<SOH>	<STX>	<ETX>	<SEL>	<HT>	<RNL>	<DEL>	<GE>	<SPS>	<RPT>	<VT>	<FF>	<CR>	<SO>	<SI>
1	<DLE>	<DC1>	<DC2>	<DC3>	<RES>	<NL>	<BS>	<POC>	<CAN>	<EM>	<UBS>	<CU1>	<IFS>	<IGS>	<IRS>	<IUS>
2	<DS>	<SOS>	<FS>	<WUS>	<BYP>	<LF>	<ETB>	<ESC>	<SA>	<SFE>	<SM>	<CSP>	<MFA>	<ENQ>	<ACK>	<BEL>
3			<SYN>	<IR>	<PP>	<TRN>	<NBS>	<EOT>	<SBS>	<IT>	<RFF>	<CU3>	<DC4>	<NAK>		<SUB>
4	<SP>										[	.	<	(	+	!
5	&										]	$	*	)	;	^
6	-	/									|	,	%	_	>	?
7										`	:	#	@	'	=	"
8		a	b	c	d	e	f	g	h	i						
9		j	k	l	m	n	o	p	q	r						
A		~	s	t	u	v	w	x	y	z						
B																
C	{	A	B	C	D	E	F	G	H	I						
D	}	J	K	L	M	N	O	P	Q	R						
E	\		S	T	U	V	W	X	Y	Z						
F	0	1	2	3	4	5	6	7	8	9						

ISO 8859-1:1998 Code Table

The table at the top of the following page illustrates the complete ISO 8859-1:1998 character set and its encoding. Note how the region up until 0x7F is identical to ASCII, which is a common property for the remaining parts of ISO 8859. The control codes <NBSP> and <SHY> stand for "non-breaking space" and "soft hyphen," respectively.

Chinese Code Tables

This section provides Chinese single-byte code tables, specifically for GB-Roman and CNS-Roman.

	0	1	2	3	4	5	6	7	8	9	A	B	C	D	E	F
0	<NUL>	<SOH>	<STX>	<ETX>	<EOT>	<ENQ>	<ACK>	<BEL>	<BS>	<HT>	<LF>	<VT>	<FF>	<CR>	<SO>	<SI>
1	<DLE>	<DC1>	<DC2>	<DC3>	<DC4>	<NAK>	<SYN>	<ETB>	<CAN>	<EM>	<SUB>	<ESC>	<FS>	<GS>	<RS>	<US>
2	<SP>	!	"	#	$	%	&	'	(	)	*	+	,	-	.	/
3	0	1	2	3	4	5	6	7	8	9	:	;	<	=	>	?
4	@	A	B	C	D	E	F	G	H	I	J	K	L	M	N	O
5	P	Q	R	S	T	U	V	W	X	Y	Z	[	\	]	^	_
6	`	a	b	c	d	e	f	g	h	i	j	k	l	m	n	o
7	p	q	r	s	t	u	v	w	x	y	z	{	|	}	~	<DEL>
8																
9																
A	<NBSP>	¡	¢	£	¤	¥	¦	§	¨	©	ª	«	¬	<SHY>	®	¯
B	°	±	²	³	´	µ	¶	·	¸	¹	º	»	¼	½	¾	¿
C	À	Á	Â	Ã	Ä	Å	Æ	Ç	È	É	Ê	Ë	Ì	Í	Î	Ï
D	Ð	Ñ	Ò	Ó	Ô	Õ	Ö	×	Ø	Ù	Ú	Û	Ü	Ý	Þ	ß
E	à	á	â	ã	ä	å	æ	ç	è	é	ê	ë	ì	í	î	ï
F	ð	ñ	ò	ó	ô	õ	ö	÷	ø	ù	ú	û	ü	ý	þ	ÿ

GB-Roman Code Table

The following is a GB-Roman (GB 1988-89) code table, including control characters. Note how the characters at 0x24 and 0x7E are different from ASCII.

	0	1	2	3	4	5	6	7	8	9	A	B	C	D	E	F
0	<NUL>	<SOH>	<STX>	<ETX>	<EOT>	<ENQ>	<ACK>	<BEL>	<BS>	<HT>	<LF>	<VT>	<FF>	<CR>	<SO>	<SI>
1	<DLE>	<DC1>	<DC2>	<DC3>	<DC4>	<NAK>	<SYN>	<ETB>	<CAN>	<EM>	<SUB>	<ESC>	<FS>	<GS>	<RS>	<US>
2	<SP>	!	"	#	¥	%	&	'	(	)	*	+	,	-	.	/
3	0	1	2	3	4	5	6	7	8	9	:	;	<	=	>	?
4	@	A	B	C	D	E	F	G	H	I	J	K	L	M	N	O
5	P	Q	R	S	T	U	V	W	X	Y	Z	[	\	]	^	_
6	`	a	b	c	d	e	f	g	h	i	j	k	l	m	n	o
7	p	q	r	s	t	u	v	w	x	y	z	{	|	}	‾	<DEL>

CNS-Roman Code Table

There is no need to actually include a CNS-Roman (CNS 5205-1989) code table here because it is identical to the ASCII code table on page 965 of this appendix.

Japanese Code Tables

The following sections provide Japanese single-byte code tables, specifically JIS-Roman, half-width katakana (seven- and eight-bit forms), and EBCDIK.

JIS-Roman and Half-Width Katakana Code Table

The following is a single code table that includes both JIS-Roman and half-width katakana (eight-bit form)—JIS X 0201-1997. Note how the characters at 0x5C and 0x7E are different from ASCII.

	0	1	2	3	4	5	6	7	8	9	A	B	C	D	E	F
0	<NUL>	<SOH>	<STX>	<ETX>	<EOT>	<ENQ>	<ACK>	<BEL>	<BS>	<HT>	<LF>	<VT>	<FF>	<CR>	<SO>	<SI>
1	<DLE>	<DC1>	<DC2>	<DC3>	<DC4>	<NAK>	<SYN>	<ETB>	<CAN>	<EM>	<SUB>	<ESC>	<FS>	<GS>	<RS>	<US>
2	<SP>	!	"	#	$	%	&	'	(	)	*	+	,	-	.	/
3	0	1	2	3	4	5	6	7	8	9	:	;	<	=	>	?
4	@	A	B	C	D	E	F	G	H	I	J	K	L	M	N	O
5	P	Q	R	S	T	U	V	W	X	Y	Z	[	¥	]	^	_
6	`	a	b	c	d	e	f	g	h	i	j	k	l	m	n	o
7	p	q	r	s	t	u	v	w	x	y	z	{	|	}	‾	<DEL>
8																
9																
A		｡	｢	｣	､	･	ｦ	ｧ	ｨ	ｩ	ｪ	ｫ	ｬ	ｭ	ｮ	ｯ
B	ｰ	ｱ	ｲ	ｳ	ｴ	ｵ	ｶ	ｷ	ｸ	ｹ	ｺ	ｻ	ｼ	ｽ	ｾ	ｿ
C	ﾀ	ﾁ	ﾂ	ﾃ	ﾄ	ﾅ	ﾆ	ﾇ	ﾈ	ﾉ	ﾊ	ﾋ	ﾌ	ﾍ	ﾎ	ﾏ
D	ﾐ	ﾑ	ﾒ	ﾓ	ﾔ	ﾕ	ﾖ	ﾗ	ﾘ	ﾙ	ﾚ	ﾛ	ﾜ	ﾝ	ﾞ	ﾟ
E																
F																

Half-Width Katakana Code Table

The following is the seven-bit form of the half-width katakana code table, which includes a "space" character at 0x20:

	0	1	2	3	4	5	6	7	8	9	A	B	C	D	E	F
0	<NUL>	<SOH>	<STX>	<ETX>	<EOT>	<ENQ>	<ACK>	<BEL>	<BS>	<HT>	<LF>	<VT>	<FF>	<CR>	<SO>	<SI>
1	<DLE>	<DC1>	<DC2>	<DC3>	<DC4>	<NAK>	<SYN>	<ETB>	<CAN>	<EM>	<SUB>	<ESC>	<FS>	<GS>	<RS>	<US>
2	<SP>	｡	｢	｣	､	･	ｦ	ｧ	ｨ	ｩ	ｪ	ｫ	ｬ	ｭ	ｮ	ｯ
3	ｰ	ｱ	ｲ	ｳ	ｴ	ｵ	ｶ	ｷ	ｸ	ｹ	ｺ	ｻ	ｼ	ｽ	ｾ	ｿ
4	ﾀ	ﾁ	ﾂ	ﾃ	ﾄ	ﾅ	ﾆ	ﾇ	ﾈ	ﾉ	ﾊ	ﾋ	ﾌ	ﾍ	ﾎ	ﾏ
5	ﾐ	ﾑ	ﾒ	ﾓ	ﾔ	ﾕ	ﾖ	ﾗ	ﾘ	ﾙ	ﾚ	ﾛ	ﾜ	ﾝ	ﾞ	ﾟ
6																
7																

EBCDIK Code Table

The following is an EBCDIK code table, similar to EBCDIC on page 966 of this chapter, but with lowercase Latin replaced by half-width katakana:

	0	1	2	3	4	5	6	7	8	9	A	B	C	D	E	F
0	<NUL>	<SOH>	<STX>	<ETX>	<SEL>	<HT>	<RNL>	<DEL>	<GE>	<SPS>	<RPT>	<VT>	<FF>	<CR>	<SO>	<SI>
1	<DLE>	<DC1>	<DC2>	<DC3>	<RES>	<NL>	<BS>	<POC>	<CAN>	<EM>	<UBS>	<CU1>	<IFS>	<IGS>	<IRS>	<IUS>
2	<DS>	<SOS>	<FS>	<WUS>	<BYP>	<LF>	<ETB>	<ESC>	<SA>	<SFE>	<SM>	<CSP>	<MFA>	<ENQ>	<ACK>	<BEL>
3			<SYN>	<IR>	<PP>	<TRN>	<NBS>	<EOT>	<SBS>	<IT>	<RFF>	<CU3>	<DC4>	<NAK>		<SUB>
4	<SP>	｡	｢	｣	､	･	ｦ	ｧ	ｨ	ｩ	£	.	<	(	+	|
5	&	ｪ	ｫ	ｬ	ｭ	ｮ	ｯ		ｰ		!	¥	*	)	;	¬
6	-	/									|	,	%	_	>	?
7										`	:	#	@	'	=	"
8		ｱ	ｲ	ｳ	ｴ	ｵ	ｶ	ｷ	ｸ	ｹ	ｺ		ｻ	ｼ	ｽ	ｾ
9	ｿ	ﾀ	ﾁ	ﾂ	ﾃ	ﾄ	ﾅ	ﾆ	ﾇ	ﾈ	ﾉ			ﾊ	ﾋ	ﾌ
A		ｰ	ﾍ	ﾎ	ﾏ	ﾐ	ﾑ	ﾒ	ﾓ	ﾔ	ﾕ		ﾖ	ﾗ	ﾘ	ﾙ
B											ﾚ	ﾛ	ﾜ	ﾝ	ﾞ	ﾟ
C	{	A	B	C	D	E	F	G	H	I						
D	}	J	K	L	M	N	O	P	Q	R						
E	$		S	T	U	V	W	X	Y	Z						
F	0	1	2	3	4	5	6	7	8	9						

Korean Code Tables

The following sections include Korean single-byte code tables, specifically those for KS-Roman and single-byte jamo.

KS-Roman Code Table

The following code table is for KS-Roman (KS X 1003:1993). Note how 0x5C and 0x7E are different from ASCII.

	0	1	2	3	4	5	6	7	8	9	A	B	C	D	E	F
0	<NUL>	<SOH>	<STX>	<ETX>	<EOT>	<ENQ>	<ACK>	<BEL>	<BS>	<HT>	<LF>	<VT>	<FF>	<CR>	<SO>	<SI>
1	<DLE>	<DC1>	<DC2>	<DC3>	<DC4>	<NAK>	<SYN>	<ETB>	<CAN>	<EM>	<SUB>	<ESC>	<FS>	<GS>	<RS>	<US>
2	<SP>	!	"	#	$	%	&	'	(	)	*	+	,	-	.	/
3	0	1	2	3	4	5	6	7	8	9	:	;	<	=	>	?
4	@	A	B	C	D	E	F	G	H	I	J	K	L	M	N	O
5	P	Q	R	S	T	U	V	W	X	Y	Z	[	₩	]	^	_
6	`	a	b	c	d	e	f	g	h	i	j	k	l	m	n	o
7	p	q	r	s	t	u	v	w	x	y	z	{	|	}	‾	<DEL>

Jamo Code Table

The following is a single-byte jamo code table. It includes the 51 modern jamo. Consonants are encoded in the range 0x41–0x5E, and vowels are in the range 0x62–0x7C. 0x40 is a "fill" character that serves to indicate a syllable boundary.

	0	1	2	3	4	5	6	7	8	9	A	B	C	D	E	F
0	<NUL>	<SOH>	<STX>	<ETX>	<EOT>	<ENQ>	<ACK>	<BEL>	<BS>	<HT>	<LF>	<VT>	<FF>	<CR>	<SO>	<SI>
1	<DLE>	<DC1>	<DC2>	<DC3>	<DC4>	<NAK>	<SYN>	<ETB>	<CAN>	<EM>	<SUB>	<ESC>	<FS>	<GS>	<RS>	<US>
2	<SP>															
3																
4	<FILL>	ㄱ	ㄲ	ㄳ	ㄴ	ㄵ	ㄶ	ㄷ	ㄸ	ㄹ	ㄺ	ㄻ	ㄼ	ㄽ	ㄾ	ㄿ
5	ㅀ	ㅁ	ㅂ	ㅃ	ㅄ	ㅅ	ㅆ	ㅇ	ㅈ	ㅉ	ㅊ	ㅋ	ㅌ	ㅍ	ㅎ	
6			ㅏ	ㅐ	ㅑ	ㅒ	ㅓ	ㅔ			ㅕ	ㅖ	ㅗ	ㅘ	ㅙ	ㅚ
7			ㅛ	ㅜ	ㅝ	ㅞ	ㅟ	ㅠ			ㅡ	ㅢ	ㅣ			

Vietnamese Code Tables

This section includes a variety of Vietnamese code tables, such as those defined in TCVN 5712:1993, registered with ISO, and those defined by Microsoft, IBM, and other organizations.

The following is the TCVN 5712:1993 VN1 encoding table, which includes all characters necessary for expressing the complete Quốc ngữ character set. Note that a handful of characters are encoded within what is normally reserved for control characters, specifically within the range 0x00 through 0x20.

	0	1	2	3	4	5	6	7	8	9	A	B	C	D	E	F
0	<NUL>	Ú	Ụ	<ETX>	Ừ	Ử	Ữ	<BEL>	<BS>	<HT>	<LF>	<VT>	<FF>	<CR>	<SO>	<SI>
1	<DLE>	Ứ	Ự	Ỳ	Ỷ	Ỹ	Ý	Ỵ	<CAN>	<EM>	<SUB>	<ESC>	<FS>	<GS>	<RS>	<US>
2	<SP>	!	"	#	$	%	&	'	(	)	*	+	,	-	.	/
3	0	1	2	3	4	5	6	7	8	9	:	;	<	=	>	?
4	@	A	B	C	D	E	F	G	H	I	J	K	L	M	N	O
5	P	Q	R	S	T	U	V	W	X	Y	Z	[	\	]	^	_
6	`	a	b	c	d	e	f	g	h	i	j	k	l	m	n	o
7	p	q	r	s	t	u	v	w	x	y	z	{	|	}	~	<DEL>
8	À	Ả	Ã	Á	Ạ	Ặ	Ậ	È	Ẻ	Ẽ	É	Ẹ	Ệ	Ì	Ỉ	Ĩ
9	Í	Ị	Ò	Ỏ	Õ	Ó	Ọ	Ộ	Ờ	Ở	Ỡ	Ớ	Ợ	Ù	Ủ	Ũ
A	<NBSP>	Ă	Â	Ê	Ô	Ơ	Ư	Đ	ă	â	ê	ô	ơ	ư	đ	Ằ
B	◌̀	◌̉	◌̃	◌́	◌̣	à	ả	ã	á	ạ	Ẳ	ằ	ẳ	ẵ	ắ	Ẵ
C	Ắ	Ầ	Ẩ	Ẫ	Ấ	Ề	ặ	ầ	ẩ	ẫ	ấ	ậ	è	Ể	ẻ	ẽ
D	é	ẹ	ề	ể	ễ	ế	ệ	ì	ỉ	Ễ	Ế	Ồ	ĩ	í	ị	ò
E	Ổ	ỏ	õ	ó	ọ	ồ	ổ	ỗ	ố	ộ	ờ	ở	ỡ	ớ	ợ	ù
F	Ỗ	ủ	ũ	ú	ụ	ừ	ử	ữ	ứ	ự	ỳ	ỷ	ỹ	ý	ỵ	Ố

The following is the TCVN 5712:1993 VN2 encoding table, which is identical to VN1 except that the uppercase characters with diacritic marks that occupy the C0 (0x00–0x1F) and C1 (0x80–0x9F) control code regions are not included. This is because some environments use control characters for special purposes, and encoding of graphic characters would be futile.

Note that TCVN 5712:1993 VN2 is identical to VSCII (specifically, VSCII-2), which is ISO International Registration 180 (ISO IR 180), established on November 1, 1993.

	0	1	2	3	4	5	6	7	8	9	A	B	C	D	E	F
0	<NUL>	<SOH>	<STX>	<ETX>	<EOT>	<ENQ>	<ACK>	<BEL>	<BS>	<HT>	<LF>	<VT>	<FF>	<CR>	<SO>	<SI>
1	<DLE>	<DC1>	<DC2>	<DC3>	<DC4>	<NAK>	<SYN>	<ETB>	<CAN>	<EM>	<SUB>	<ESC>	<FS>	<GS>	<RS>	<US>
2	<SP>	!	"	#	$	%	&	'	(	)	*	+	,	-	.	/
3	0	1	2	3	4	5	6	7	8	9	:	;	<	=	>	?
4	@	A	B	C	D	E	F	G	H	I	J	K	L	M	N	O
5	P	Q	R	S	T	U	V	W	X	Y	Z	[	\	]	^	_
6	`	a	b	c	d	e	f	g	h	i	j	k	l	m	n	o
7	p	q	r	s	t	u	v	w	x	y	z	{	|	}	~	<DEL>
8																
9																
A	<NBSP>	Ă	Â	Ê	Ô	Ơ	Ư	Đ	ă	â	ê	ô	ơ	ư	đ	Ằ
B	◌̀	◌̉	◌̃	◌́	◌̣	à	ả	ã	á	ạ	Ẳ	ằ	ẳ	ẵ	ắ	Ẵ
C	Ắ	Ầ	Ẩ	Ẫ	Ấ	Ề	ặ	ầ	ẩ	ẫ	ấ	ậ	è	Ể	ẻ	ẽ
D	é	ẹ	ề	ể	ễ	ế	ệ	ì	ỉ	Ễ	Ế	Ồ	ĩ	í	ị	ò
E	Ổ	ỏ	õ	ó	ọ	ồ	ổ	ỗ	ố	ộ	ờ	ở	ỡ	ớ	ợ	ù
F	Ỗ	ủ	ũ	ú	ụ	ừ	ử	ữ	ứ	ự	ỳ	ỷ	ỹ	ý	ỵ	Ố

The following is the TCVN 5712:1993 VN3 encoding table, which is identical to VN2 except that the uppercase characters with diacritic tone marks and the five tone marks themselves have been removed:

	0	1	2	3	4	5	6	7	8	9	A	B	C	D	E	F
0	<NUL>	<SOH>	<STX>	<ETX>	<EOT>	<ENQ>	<ACK>	<BEL>	<BS>	<HT>	<LF>	<VT>	<FF>	<CR>	<SO>	<SI>
1	<DLE>	<DC1>	<DC2>	<DC3>	<DC4>	<NAK>	<SYN>	<ETB>	<CAN>	<EM>	<SUB>	<ESC>	<FS>	<GS>	<RS>	<US>
2	<SP>	!	"	#	$	%	&	'	(	)	*	+	,	-	.	/
3	0	1	2	3	4	5	6	7	8	9	:	;	<	=	>	?
4	@	A	B	C	D	E	F	G	H	I	J	K	L	M	N	O
5	P	Q	R	S	T	U	V	W	X	Y	Z	[	\	]	^	_
6	`	a	b	c	d	e	f	g	h	i	j	k	l	m	n	o
7	p	q	r	s	t	u	v	w	x	y	z	{	|	}	~	<DEL>
8																
9																
A	<NBSP>	Ă	Â	Ê	Ô	Ơ	Ư	Đ	ă	â	ê	ô	ơ	ư	đ	
B						à	ả	ã	á	ạ		ằ	ẳ	ẵ	ắ	
C							ặ	ầ	ẩ	ẫ	ấ	ậ	è		ẻ	ẽ
D	é	ẹ	ề	ể	ễ	ế	ệ	ì	ỉ				ĩ	í	ị	ò
E		ỏ	õ	ó	ọ	ồ	ổ	ỗ	ố	ộ	ờ	ở	ỡ	ớ	ợ	ù
F		ủ	ũ	ú	ụ	ừ	ử	ữ	ứ	ự	ỳ	ỷ	ỹ	ý	ỵ	

The following is a code table for Microsoft Code Page 1258:

	0	1	2	3	4	5	6	7	8	9	A	B	C	D	E	F
0	<NUL>	<SOH>	<STX>	<ETX>	<EOT>	<ENQ>	<ACK>	<BEL>	<BS>	<HT>	<LF>	<VT>	<FF>	<CR>	<SO>	<SI>
1	<DLE>	<DC1>	<DC2>	<DC3>	<DC4>	<NAK>	<SYN>	<ETB>	<CAN>	<EM>	<SUB>	<ESC>	<FS>	<GS>	<RS>	<US>
2	<SP>	!	"	#	$	%	&	'	(	)	*	+	,	-	.	/
3	0	1	2	3	4	5	6	7	8	9	:	;	<	=	>	?
4	@	A	B	C	D	E	F	G	H	I	J	K	L	M	N	O
5	P	Q	R	S	T	U	V	W	X	Y	Z	[	\	]	^	_
6	`	a	b	c	d	e	f	g	h	i	j	k	l	m	n	o
7	p	q	r	s	t	u	v	w	x	y	z	{	|	}	~	<DEL>
8			‚	ƒ	„	…	†	‡	ˆ	‰		‹	Œ			
9		‘	’	“	”	•	–	—	˜	™		›	œ			Ÿ
A	<NBSP>	¡	¢	£	¤	¥	¦	§	¨	©	ª	«	¬	<SHY>	®	¯
B	°	±	²	³	´	µ	¶	·	¸	¹	º	»	¼	½	¾	¿
C	À	Á	Â	Ă	Ä	Å	Æ	Ç	È	É	Ê	Ë	◌̀	Í	Î	Ï
D	Đ	Ñ	◌̉	Ó	Ô	Ơ	Ö	×	Ø	Ù	Ú	Û	Ü	Ư	◌̃	ß
E	à	á	â	ă	ä	å	æ	ç	è	é	ê	ë	◌́	í	î	ï
F	đ	ñ	◌̣	ó	ô	ơ	ö	÷	ø	ù	ú	û	ü	ư	₫	ÿ

The following is a code table for IBM Code Page 01129:

	0	1	2	3	4	5	6	7	8	9	A	B	C	D	E	F
0	<NUL>	<SOH>	<STX>	<ETX>	<EOT>	<ENQ>	<ACK>	<BEL>	<BS>	<HT>	<LF>	<VT>	<FF>	<CR>	<SO>	<SI>
1	<DLE>	<DC1>	<DC2>	<DC3>	<DC4>	<NAK>	<SYN>	<ETB>	<CAN>	<EM>	<SUB>	<ESC>	<FS>	<GS>	<RS>	<US>
2	<SP>	!	"	#	$	%	&	'	(	)	*	+	,	-	.	/
3	0	1	2	3	4	5	6	7	8	9	:	;	<	=	>	?
4	@	A	B	C	D	E	F	G	H	I	J	K	L	M	N	O
5	P	Q	R	S	T	U	V	W	X	Y	Z	[	\	]	^	_
6	`	a	b	c	d	e	f	g	h	i	j	k	l	m	n	o
7	p	q	r	s	t	u	v	w	x	y	z	{	|	}	~	<DEL>
8																
9																
A	<NBSP>	¡	¢	£	¤	¥	¦	§	œ	©	ª	«	¬	<SHY>	®	¯
B	°	±	²	³	Ÿ	µ	¶	·	Œ	¹	º	»	¼	½	¾	¿
C	À	Á	Â	Ă	Ä	Å	Æ	Ç	È	É	Ê	Ë	◌̀	Í	Î	Ï
D	Đ	Ñ	◌̉	Ó	Ô	Ơ	Ö	×	Ø	Ù	Ú	Û	Ü	Ư	◌̃	ß
E	à	á	â	ă	ä	å	æ	ç	è	é	ê	ë	◌́	í	î	ï
F	đ	ñ	◌̣	ó	ô	ơ	ö	÷	ø	ù	ú	û	ü	ư	₫	ÿ

Note the similarities in Microsoft Code Page 1258 and IBM Code Page 01129, particularly in the range 0xA0 through 0xFF.

Finally, the following is a complete VISCII code table:

	0	1	2	3	4	5	6	7	8	9	A	B	C	D	E	F
0	<NUL>	<SOH>	Ẳ	<ETX>	<EOT>	Ẵ	Ẫ	<BEL>	<BS>	<HT>	<LF>	<VT>	<FF>	<CR>	<SO>	<SI>
1	<DLE>	<DC1>	<DC2>	<DC3>	Ỷ	<NAK>	<SYN>	<ETB>	<CAN>	Ỹ	<SUB>	<ESC>	<FS>	<GS>	Ỵ	<US>
2	<SP>	!	"	#	$	%	&	'	(	)	*	+	,	-	.	/
3	0	1	2	3	4	5	6	7	8	9	:	;	<	=	>	?
4	@	A	B	C	D	E	F	G	H	I	J	K	L	M	N	O
5	P	Q	R	S	T	U	V	W	X	Y	Z	[	\	]	^	_
6	`	a	b	c	d	e	f	g	h	i	j	k	l	m	n	o
7	p	q	r	s	t	u	v	w	x	y	z	{	|	}	~	<DEL>
8	Ạ	Ắ	Ằ	Ặ	Ấ	Ầ	Ẩ	Ậ	Ẽ	Ẹ	Ế	Ề	Ể	Ễ	Ệ	Ố
9	Ồ	Ổ	Ỗ	Ộ	Ợ	Ớ	Ờ	Ở	Ị	Ỏ	Ọ	Ỉ	Ủ	Ũ	Ụ	Ỳ
A	Õ	ắ	ằ	ặ	ấ	ầ	ẩ	ậ	ẽ	ẹ	ế	ề	ể	ễ	ệ	ố
B	ồ	ổ	ỗ	Ỡ	Ơ	ộ	ờ	ở	ị	Ự	Ứ	Ừ	Ử	ơ	ớ	Ư
C	À	Á	Â	Ã	Ả	Ă	ẳ	ẵ	È	É	Ê	Ẻ	Ì	Í	Ĩ	ỳ
D	Đ	ứ	Ò	Ó	Ô	ạ	ỷ	ừ	ử	Ù	Ú	ỹ	ỵ	Ý	ỡ	ư
E	à	á	â	ã	ả	ă	ữ	ẫ	è	é	ê	ẻ	ì	í	ĩ	ỉ
F	đ	ự	ò	ó	ô	õ	ỏ	ọ	ụ	ù	ú	ũ	ủ	ý	ợ	Ữ

T

Software and Document Sources

Here you will find addresses and other contact information for the authors and vendors of the software and documents described in this book. This information will be divided into two sections: those available free online and those available through commercial distribution. ISBNs and part numbers for documents can be found in this book's bibliography.

Anonymous FTP

FTP stands for file transfer protocol, and is a very convenient way to obtain files and programs from Internet sites worldwide. Using FTP is usually a simple matter of typing the command *ftp* followed by the site name or IP number.* Below is an example:

```
% ftp ftp.oreilly.com
```

Once you initialize an FTP session, you will be greeted with a prompt from the FTP server. This prompt will ask you for a login name. The login string to use is *anonymous* (after all, this is "anonymous" FTP). You will then be prompted for a password in the form of your real login ID or full email address (preferred). This allows the site administrators keep track of anonymous FTP access to their site.

If you use a web browser, you can alternatively feed it a complete URL, as follows:

ftp://ftp.oreilly.com/

Using a complete URL has the added advantage of being able to specify the path and optionally the target filename. Consider the following:

ftp://ftp.oreilly.com/pub/examples/nutshell/cjkv/doc/cjk.inf

* While specifying an IP number is the most accurate way to identify an Internet host, it is problematic because IP numbers have a tendency to change over time.

Sometimes you will find a file called *ls-lR.Z* or *ls-lR* (or some other incarnation thereof) at the root level of an FTP server. This file typically contains a complete directory and file listing for the entire FTP site. If you are not sure where a file is located on an FTP server, you can often use the *get* command to obtain this file, then use *grep* or some other searching mechanism to find exactly where on the FTP server a particular file is located. You can also use an Internet search engine or guide, described in the next section, to locate files.

Searching for Files

Before the proliferation of the Web in the mid-1990s, a common method for searching for files on FTP servers was to use Archie. While you can still use Archie for this purpose, a better method is to use an Internet search engine or an Internet guide.

The most common Internet search engine is AltaVista.* It is used by a variety of other services called Internet guides. Popular Internet guides include Excite,† Infoseek,‡ Lycos,** and Yahoo!†† I encourage you to use these Internet guides as a convenient way to search for files on the Internet, whether they are web pages or programs.

Useful URLs

There is much more software available than I could possibly describe in this book. I encourage you to browse several key URLs for other new and interesting software packages. I plan to consolidate some of these software packages and information sources at the following URL:

ftp://ftp.oreilly.com/pub/examples/nutshell/cjkv/

This same URL will also contain code fragments, mapping tables, and character lists from this book in machine-readable form.

The various RFCs (Request for Comments) mentioned throughout this book can all be found at a common URL.‡‡

Note that some software packages, such as Apple Computer's ResEdit and most operating system software, cannot be transported to other URLs due to licensing and other restrictions.

---

* *http://www.altavista.com/*
† *http://www.excite.com/*
‡ *http://www.infoseek.com/*
** *http://www.lycos.com/*
†† *http://www.yahoo.com/*
‡‡ *http://www.rfc-editor.org/*

Commercial Sources

Below you will find contact information that should help you to find software, hardware, and documents mentioned in this book. I encourage you to contact these companies for more information, and how to order their products. While no address, phone number, facsimile number, email address, or URL is permanent, the contact information provided below should help you to make contact with each company.

Adobe Systems Incorporated — Software developer, type foundry
345 Park Avenue, San Jose, CA 95110-2704 USA
+1-408-536-6000 (phone), +1-408-537-6000 (facsimile)
http://www.adobe.com/

The Aegis Society — ISP
1-6 Minami Hirao, Imazato, Nagaokakyo-shi, Kyoto-fu 617 JAPAN
+81-75-951-1168 (phone), +81-75-957-1087 (facsimile)
aegis@aegis.org
http://www.aegis.org/aegis/

AI-Net Corporation — 今昔文字鏡 CD-ROM
1-17-3 Okano, Nishi-ku, Yokohama-shi 222 JAPAN
+81-45-311-0124 (phone), +81-45-314-3002 (facsimile)

Aladdin Enterprises — Ghostscript (PostScript clone)
203 Santa Margarita Avenue, Menlo Park, CA 94025 USA
+1-650-322-0103 (phone), +1-650-322-1734 (facsimile)
ghost@aladdin.com
http://www.cs.wisc.edu/~ghost/

Alis Technologies Incorporated — Batam, Tango
100 Alexis Nihon Boulevard, Suite 600, Montreal, Quebec H4M 2P2 CANADA
+1-514-747-2547 (phone), +1-514-747-2561 (facsimile)
info@alis.com
http://www.alis.com/

AltaVista Technology, Incorporated — Internet search engine
1671 Dell Avenue, Suite 209, Campbell, CA 95008 USA
+1-408-364-8777 (phone), +1-408-364-8778 (facsimile)
http://www.altavista.com/

America Online, Incorporated — ISP
8619 Roswell Road, Suite 535, Atlanta, GA 30328 USA
800-827-6364 (phone), +1-404-250-0054 (phone), +1-404-250-1848 (facsimile)
http://www.aol.com/

American National Standards Institute (ANSI) — ANSI standards, ISO standards
11 West 42nd Street, New York, NY 10036 USA
+1-212-642-4900 (phone), +1-212-398-0023 (facsimile)
http://www.ansi.org/

Apple Computer Incorporated — AppleWorks, Macintosh, MacOS, MacWriteII
1 Infinite Loop, Cupertino, CA 95014 USA
800-544-8554 (phone), +1-408-996-1010 (phone), +1-408-974-6726 (facsimile)
http://www.apple.com/

Apropos Customer Service — Smart Characters
8 Belknap Street, Arlington, MA 02174 USA
800-676-4021 (phone), +1-617-648-2041 (phone), +1-617-641-0342 (facsimile/bbs)
custsvc@aproposinc.com
http://www.aproposinc.com/

Arphic Technology Company, Limited — Chinese type foundry
11F, 168, Yung Chi Road, Taipei 110 TAIWAN
+886-2-7607976 (phone), +886-2-7673474 (facsimile)
http://www.arphic.com.tw/

ASCII Corporation — Publisher
Toshin Building, 4-33-10 Yoyogi, Shibuya-ku, Tokyo 151-8024 JAPAN
+81-3-5351-8111 (phone)
http://www.ascii.co.jp/

ASCII SOMETHING GOOD Corporation — Katana
IK Building, 2-24-9 Kamiosaki, Shinagawa-ku, Tokyo 141-8670 JAPAN
http://www.asg.co.jp/

Asian Technology Information Program (ATIP) — Information about Asia
Harks Roppongi Building 1F, 6-15-21 Roppongi, Minato-ku, Tokyo, 106-0032 JAPAN
+81-3-5411-6670 (phone), +81-3-5411-6671 (facsimile)
www-admin@atip.org
http://www.atip.org/

AsiaSoft, Incorporated — Software distributor
1766 20th Avenue, Vero Beach, FL 32960 USA
800-882-8856 (phone), +1-561-794-9888 (phone), +1-561-794-9039 (facsimile)
asiasoft@asiasoft.com
http://www.asiasoft.com/

Basis Technology Corporation — RJ, Rosette: C++ Library for Unicode, Uniconv
One Kendall Square, Building 200, Cambridge, MA 02139 USA
800-973-3775 (phone), +1-617-252-5636 (phone), +1-617-252-9150 (facsimile)
info@basistech.com
http://www.basistech.com/

Be, Incorporated — BeOS, NetPositive
800 El Camino Real, Suite 300, Menlo Park, CA 94025 USA
+1-650-462-4100 (phone), +1-650-462-4129 (facsimile)
info@be.com
http://www.be.com/

Bitstream Incorporated — Type foundry
215 First Street, Cambridge, MA 02142 USA
800-522-3668 (phone), +1-617-497-6222 (phone), +1-617-868-0784 (facsimile)
sales@bitstream.com
http://www.bitstream.com/

Bridge Incorporated — Japanese fonts
13F NSS Building, 7-1-2, Kita-ku, Sapporo 060 JAPAN
+81-11-717-1171 (phone), +81-11-716-2190 (facsimile)
http://www.bridge.co.jp/

Canon, Incorporated — Canon WordTank, PostScript printers
3-30-2 Shimomaruko, Ohta-ku, Tokyo 146-8501 JAPAN
+81-3-3758-2111 (phone)
http://www.canon.co.jp/

Catena Corporation これ和英, コリャ英和
2-10-24 Shiomi, Koto-ku, Tokyo 135-8565 JAPAN
+81-3-3615-3211 (phone)
http://www.catena.co.jp/

CCiC System Pacifica Software distributor
605 Addison Street, Suite A, Berkeley, CA 94710-1919 USA
+1-510-548-2242 (phone), +1-510-843-5173 (facsimile)
sales@ccic.janet.com
http://www.janet.com/ccic/

Chanzhou SinoType Technology Company, Limited Chinese type foundry
Lujia Xiang Town, Changzhou, Jiangsu 213169 CHINA
+86-519-635-1076 (phone)
sinotype@sinotype.com

Cheng & Tsui Company Software and book distributor
25 West Street, Boston, MA 02111-1268 USA
800-554-1963 (phone), +1-617-988-2401 (phone), +1-617-426-3669 (facsimile)
http://www.cheng-tsui.com/

Chinese Information Processing *Chinese Information Processing*
Chengdu University of Science & Technology, P.O. Box 263, Chengdu, Sichuan 610065 CHINA
+86-581554-21221 (phone)

Chinese and Oriental Languages Information Processing Society (COLIPS) *CommCOLIPS*
c/o DISCS, National University of Singapore, Kent Ridge 0511 SINGAPORE
luakt@iscs.nus.sg
http://www.iscs.nus.sg/~colips/

CJK Dictionary Publishing Society (CDPS) CJK consulting and dictionary services
1-3-502 3-Chome Niiza, Niiza-shi, Saitama-ken 352-0006 JAPAN
+81-48-481-3103 (phone), +81-48-479-1323 (facsimile)
jhalpern@cjk.org
http://www.cjk.org/

Communication Intelligence Corporation (CIC) Handwriter, MacHandwriter
275 Shoreline Drive, Suite 500, Redwood Shores, CA 94065-1413 USA
+1-650-802-7888 (phone), +1-650-802-7777 (facsimile)
http://www.cic.com/

CompuServe Incorporated ISP
5000 Arlington Center Boulevard, Columbus, OH 43220 USA
800-848-8199 (phone), +1-614-457-8600 (phone), +1-614-457-0348 (facsimile)
postmaster@compuserve.com
http://www.compuserve.com/

CTM Development PowerMail
P.O. Box 629000, El Dorado Hills, CA 95762 USA
800-424-9933 (phone), +1-415-840-0276 (facsimile)
info@ctmdev.com
http://www.ctmdev.com/

Dainippon Screen Corporation Japanese type foundry
Teranouchi-agaru 4-Chome, Horikawa-dori, Kamigyo-ku, Kyoto 602-8585 JAPAN
+81-75-417-2568 (phone)
http://www.screen.co.jp/

Dialect Group LLC Language learning and productivity tools
Dialect Plaza, 2211 North Wilson Way, Stockton, CA 95205-3127 USA
800-527-2607 (phone), +1-209-462-6300 (phone), +1-209-462-9717 (facsimile)
catalog@dialect.com
http://www.dialect.com/

Digital Equipment Corporation PostScript printers
146 Main Street, Maynard, MA 01754-2571 USA
800-344-4825 (phone)
http://www.digital.com/

Directorate for Standards & Quality (STAMEQ) TCVN standards
Nghia Do, Cau Giay, Hanoi VIETNAM
+84-4-834-4268 (phone), +84-4-836-1556 (facsimile)
http://home.vnn.vn/tcvn/

DTP center Biblos Biblos "Gaiji" fonts
6-28-8 Itaya, Tsuchiura-shi, Ibaraki 300-0007 JAPAN
+81-298-26-0220 (phone), +81-298-26-0550 (facsimile)
info@biblosfont.co.jp
http://www.biblosfont.co.jp/

DynaLab Incorporated Chinese and Japanese type foundry
4F, 115 Ming Sheng East Road Section 3, Taipei TAIWAN
+886 2-717-1518 (phone), +886 2-713-8041 (facsimile)
info@dynalab.com.tw
http://www.dynalab.com/

Dynaware Corporation MacVJE, MacWORD
CASA Buidling 3F, 3-3-11 Senba-Higashi, Minoo-shi, Osaka 562 JAPAN
+81-727-27-2051 (phone), +81-727-27-3011 (facsimile)
http://www.dynaware.co.jp/

EAST Company, Limited PS Print
2-22-8 Yoyogi, Shibuya-ku, Tokyo 151-0053 JAPAN
+81-3-3374-0544 (phone), +81-3-3374-2998 (facsimile)
http://www.est.co.jp/

Eastwind Books & Arts, Incorporated Chinese books and software
1435A Stockton Street, San Francisco, CA 94133 USA
+1-415-772-5888 (phone), +1-415-772-5885 (facsimile)
info@eastwindsf.com
http://www.eastwindsf.com/

EJ Bilingual Incorporated EZ JapaneseOCR, EZ JapaneseReader, EZ JapaneseWriter
2463 Torrance Boulevard, Suite 1, Torrance, CA 90501 USA
+1-310-320-8139 (phone), +1-310-320-3228 (facsimile)
http://www.ejbilingual.com/

Electronics for Imaging (EFI), Incorporated PostScript printers
2855 Campus Drive, San Mateo, CA 94403 USA
+1-650-286-8600 (phone), +1-650-286-8686 (facsimile)
http://www.efi.com/

Enfour Media Laboratory Pty. Limited Enfour "Gaiji" fonts
4-19-12 Sendagaya, Shibuya-ku, Tokyo 151-0051 JAPAN
+81-3-5411-7736 (phone), +81-3-5474-8934 (facsimile)
enfour@enfour.com
http://www.enfour.com/

Ergosoft Corporation EGBook, EGBridge, EGTalk, EGWord, EGWord Pure
3-9-1 Akasaka, Kiyo Building 3F, Minato-ku, Tokyo 107 JAPAN
+81-45-565-3330 (phone), +81-45-565-3331 (facsimile)
http://www.ergo.co.jp/

Excite, Incorporated Internet guide
555 Broadway, Redwood City, CA 94063 USA
+1-650-568-6000 (phone), +1-650-568-6030 (facsimile)
http://www.excite.com/

5D Solutions Limited Jaws (PostScript clone)
Guardian House Suite 1, Borough Road, Godalming, Surrey GU7 2AE UNITED KINGDOM
+44-1483-426421 (phone), +44-1483-419541 (facsimile)
ian@5-d.com
http://www.5-d.com/

FlashWare International Chinese Character Tutor
6440 Weidner Road, Franklin, OH 45005 USA
+1-513-748-8182 (phone/facsimile)
71045.3475@compuserve.com
http://ourworld.compuserve.com/homepages/fergab/

Fontworks Limited Japanese type foundry
19/F Podium Plaza, 5 Hanoi Road, Tsim Sha Tsui HONG KONG
+852-2851-2739 (phone), +852-2544-3543 (facsimile)
general@fontworks.com
http://www.fontworks.co.jp/

Foreign Ink Limited Service bureau
5735 Washburn Avenue South, Minneapolis, MN 55410-2636 USA
+1-612-920-4884 (phone), +1-612-924-9075 (facsimile)
fi-sales@fornink.com
http://www.fornink.com/

Founder Incorporated Founder FIT
SpaceArea Iijima 7F, 2-23-1 Nishi-Gotanda, Shinagawa-ku, Tokyo 141-0031 JAPAN
+81-3-3779-2551 (phone), +81-3-3779-2566 (facsimile)
http://www.founder.co.jp/

Free Software Foundation, Incorporated GNU General Public License, GNU software
59 Temple Place, Suite 330, Boston, MA 02111-1307 USA
+1-617-542-5942 (phone), +1-617-542-2652 (facsimile)
gnu@gnu.org
http://www.gnu.org/

Fujitsu Business Systems Fujitsu technical manuals
Shiraishi Dai2 Building, 6F, 1-14 Kanda, Chiyoda-ku, Tokyo 101 JAPAN
+81-3-3253-4151 (phone)
http://www.fujitsu.co.jp/

Fujitsu Software Corporation ATLAS
3055 Orchard Drive, San Jose, CA 95134 USA
800-603-8105 (phone), +1-408-456-7771 (phone), +1-408-456-7050 (facsimile)
http://www.fsc.fujitsu.com/language/

Gamma Productions, Incorporated Gamma UniType, Gamma UniVerse
12625 High Bluff Drive, Suite 218, San Diego, CA 92130 USA
+1-619-794-6399 (phone), +1-619-794-7294 (facsimile)
info@gammapro.com
http://www.gammapro.com/

Hangul & Computer HWP
Shindae Building, Dongjak-gu, Seoul 360-185 KOREA
+82-2-639-8700 (phone), +82-2-822-0136 (facsimile)
http://www.hnc.co.kr/

Hanyang Systems Incorporated Korean type foundry
Jinyeong Building 3F, 935-25 Bangbae1-dong, Seocho-gu, Seoul 137-061 KOREA
+82-2-598-0050 (phone), +82-2-591-9745 (facsimile)
http://www.hanyang.co.kr/

Harlequin Incorporated ScriptWorks RIP (PostScript clone)
One Cambridge Center, Cambridge, MA 02142 USA
+1-617-374-2400 (phone)
+1-617-252-6505 (facsimile)
web@harlequin.com
http://www.harlequin.com/

Heidelberger Druckmaschinen Aktiengesellschaft PostScript printers
Kurfürsten-Anlage 52-60, D-69115 Heidelberg GERMANY
+49-6221-92-0 (phone), +49-6221-92-6999 (facsimile)
http://www.hdpp.de/

Hewlett-Packard Hewlett-Packard technical manuals
Department C2MO HP-UX, Box 1145, Roseville, CA 95678 USA
800-227-8164 (phone)
http://www.hp.com/

Hitachi Corporation Hitachi technical manuals
Omori Bell Port B, 6-26-2 Minamiooi, Shinagawa-ku, Tokyo 140 JAPAN
+81-3-5471-2183 (phone), +81-3-5471-2947 (facsimile)
http://www.hitachi.co.jp/

InfoLogic, Incorporated IW PS Font Installer
Hyojin Building 2F, 53-4, Nonhyun-dong, Kangnam-gu, Seoul 135-011 KOREA
+82-2-516-6030 (phone), +82-2-518-5285 (facsimile)
info@infologic.net
http://www.infologic.net/

Information Processing Society of Japan (IPSJ) 『情報処理』(*jōhō shori*) journal
Shibaura-Maekawa Buidling 7F, 3-16-20 Shibaura, Minato-ku, Tokyo 108-0023 JAPAN
+81-3-5484-3535 (phone), +81-3-5484-3534 (facsimile)
somu@ipsj.or.jp
http://www.ipsj.or.jp/

Infoseek Corporation Internet guide
1399 Moffett Park Drive, Sunnyvale, CA 94089 USA
800-781-4636 (phone), +1-408-543-6000 (phone), +1-408-734-9350 (facsimile)
info@infoseek.com
http://www.infoseek.com/

International Business Machines (IBM) Corporation AIX, IBM publications
IBM Standards Program, Old Orchard Road, Armonk, NY 10504 USA
+1-303-924-4807 (phone)
1-800-879-2755 (phone), +1-919-713-4072 (phone)—*for ordering IBM publications*
http://www.ibm.com/
http://www.elink.ibmlink.ibm.com/pbl/pbl—for ordering IBM publications

International Macintosh Users Group IMUG
3891 Corina Way, Palo Alto, CA 94303 USA
http://www.imug.org/

International Organization for Standardization (ISO) ISO standards
1, rue de Varembe, Case Postale 56, CH-1211, Geneva 20 SWITZERLAND
+41-22-749-0111 (phone), +41-22-733-3430 (facsimile)
central@iso.ch
http://www.iso.ch/

International Typeface Corporation Type foundry, *U&lc*
866 Second Avenue, New York, NY 10017 USA
800-634-9325 (phone), +1-212-371-0699 (phone), +1-212-752-4752 (facsimile)

Internet Initiative Japan (IIJ), Incorporated ISP
Sanbancho Annex Building 1-4, Sanban-cho, Chiyoda-ku, Tokyo 102 JAPAN
+81-3-5276-6240 (phone), +81-3-5276-6239 (facsimile)
info@iij.ad.jp
http://www.iij.ad.jp/

Japan Association of Graphic Arts Technology (JAGAT) FAGAT
1-29-11 Wada, Suginami-ku, Tokyo 166-8539 JAPAN
+81-3-3384-3111 (phone), +81-3-3384-3481 (facsimile)
asiaforum@jagat.or.jp
http://www.jagat.or.jp/

Japan Network Information Center (JPNIC) Japanese network information
Fuundo Building 3F, 1-2 Kanda-Ogawamachi, Chiyoda-ku, Tokyo 101-0052 JAPAN
+81-3-5297-2311 (phone)
+81-3-5297-2312 (facsimile)
query@nic.ad.jp
http://www.nic.ad.jp/

Japan Organization InterNetwork (JOIN) Bitnet
Science University of Tokyo, 1-3 Kagurazaka, Shinjuku-ku, Tokyo 162-8601 JAPAN
+81-3-5228-8114 (phone), +81-3-3260-2280 (facsimile)
official@join.ad.jp
http://www.join.ad.jp/

Japan Pacific Publications, Incorporated Japanese service bureau
419 Occidental Avenue South #509, Seattle, WA 98104 USA
+1-206-622-7443 (phone), +1-206-621-1786 (facsimile)
japanpac@halcyon.com

Japanese Language Services, Incorporated *Japan Insider*
One Kendall Square, Building 200, Cambridge, MA 02139 USA
800-872-5272 (phone), +1-617-577-8000 (phone), +1-617-577-8011 (facsimile)
info@japanese.com
http://www.japanese.com/

Japanese Standards Association Heisei typefaces, JIS standards
1-24 Akasaka 4-Chome, Minato-ku, Tokyo 107-8440 JAPAN
+81-3-3583-8071 (phone), +81-3-3582-3372 (facsimile)
http://www.jsa.or.jp/

John Benjamins Publishing Company *Language International*
Amsteldijk 44, P.O. Box 75577, 1070 AN Amsterdam THE NETHERLANDS
+31-20-676-2325 (phone), +31-20-673-9773 (facsimile)
language.international@benjamins.nl
http://www.language-international.com/

JUSTSYSTEM Corporation ATOK, Ichitaro
Brains Park, Tokushima-shi 771-0189 JAPAN
+81-886-66-1000 (phone), +81-886-66-1010 (facsimile)
www@justsystem.co.jp
http://www.justsystem.co.jp/

Juxian Guan Limited Publisher
Flat A, 17/F, Kam Man Fung Fty. Buidling, 6 Hong Man Street, Chai-wan HONG KONG
+852-2889-8012 (phone), +852-2515-9239 (facsimile)
juxian@juxian.com.hk
http://www.juxian.com.hk/

K Denshi Kogyo Incorporated Japanese software distributor
Japan Center, 1581 Webster Street, San Francisco, CA 94115 USA
+1-415-346-5964 (phone), +1-415-346-0764 (facsimile)
info@kdenshi.com
http://www.kdenshi.com/

Kanji Dictionary Publishing Society (KDPS) Japanese consulting and dictionary services
1-3-502 3-Chome Niiza, Niiza-shi, Saitama-ken 352-0006 JAPAN
+81-48-481-3103 (phone), +81-48-479-1323 (facsimile)
jhalpern@kanji.org
http://www.kanji.org/

Kanji-Flash Softworks Kanji-Flash/BTJ
2121 Redrock Court, Los Angeles, CA 90039-3549 USA
+1-213-661-3694 (phone)
kanjiflash@compuserve.com
http://ourworld.compuserve.com/homepages/KanjiFlash/

KiCompWare MOKE, WinJDIC
P.O. Box 240418, Apple Valley, MN 55044 USA
http://www1.minn.net/~medwards/kicomp.html

Kinokuniya Bookstores of America Japanese books, EBs, magazines, and software
Japan Center, 1581 Webster Street, San Francisco, CA 94115-9948 USA
+1-415-567-7625 (phone), +1-415-567-4109 (facsimile)
psale@kinokuniya.co.jp
http://bookweb.kinokuniya.co.jp/

Korean Technical Communications Korean service bureau, translation services
556 Weddell Drive, Suite 8, Sunnyvale, CA 94089 USA
+1-408-745-1112 (phone), +1-408-745-1113 (facsimile)
info@ktcus.com
http://www.ktcus.com/

Kuni Research International Corporation Eudora Pro-J
Edobori Center Building 11F, 2-1-1 Edobori, Nishi-ku, Osaka 550-0002 JAPAN
+81-6-441-0234 (phone), +81-6-441-0235 (facsimile)
eudora-sales@kuni.co.jp
http://www.kuni.co.jp/

Kureo Technology Limited InTransNet translation service, KCOM2, Kmail, Kview
314-3602 Gilmore Way, Suite 303, Burnaby, BC V5G 4W9 CANADA
+1-604-433-7715 (phone), +1-604-433-3393 (facsimile)
http://www.kureo.com/

Language Engineering Corporation LogoVista, online translation service
385 Concord Avenue, Belmont, MA 02178-3037 USA
800-458-7267 (phone), +1-617-489-4000 (phone), +1-617-489-3850 (facsimile)
info@lec.com
http://www.lec.com/

LaserMaster Corporation PostScript-compatible printers
6900 Shady Oak Road, Eden Prairie, MN 55344 USA
800-300-5479 (phone), +1-612-944-6069 (phone), +1-612-944-0522 (facsimile)
http://www.lmt.com/

Lava Software Pty. Limited Japanese WordMage
GPO Box 215, Adelaide 5001 AUSTRALIA
+61-8-8235-0003 (phone), +61-8-8235-0668 (facsimile)
service@lavasoft.com
http://www.lavasoft.com/

Lernout & Hauspie Speech Products N.V. KanjiScan OCR, Tsunami MT, Typhoon MT
Sint-Krispijnstraat 7, 8900 Ieper, BELGIUM
+32-57-22-8888 (phone), +32-57-20-8489 (facsimile)
http://www.lhs.com/

LINC Media, Incorporated *Computing Japan*
Odakyu Minami-Aoyama Building 10F, 7-8-1 Minami Aoyama, Minato-ku, Tokyo 107-0062 JAPAN
800-330-5822 (phone), +81-3-3499-2099 (phone), +81-3-3499-2199 (facsimile)
subs@cjmag.co.jp
http://www.cjmag.co.jp/

LineLabo Company, Limited Service bureau
2-18-1102, Shimomiyabi-cho, Shinjuku-ku, Tokyo 162-0822 JAPAN
+81-3-5229-8041 (phone), +81-3-5229-8047 (facsimile)
linelabo@po.jah.or.jp
http://www.linelabo.com/

Linguist's Software Incorporated Foreign language fonts
P.O. Box 580, Edmonds, WA 98020-0580 USA
+1-425-775-1130 (phone), +1-425-771-5911 (facsimile)
fonts@linguistsoftware.com
http://www.linguistsoftware.com/

The Localisation Industry Standards Association (LISA) LISA
7 Route du Monastère, 1173 Féchy SWITZERLAND
+41-21-821-3210 (phone), +41-21-821-3219 (facsimile)
lisa@lisa.org
http://www.lisa.org/

Lycos, Incorporated Internet guide
500 Old Connecticut Path, Framingham, MA 01701-4576 USA
+1-508-424-0400 (phone)
http://www.lycos.com/

Macromedia, Incorporated Fontographer, Dreamweaver, Macromedia FreeHand
600 Townsend Street, San Francisco, CA 94103 USA
+1-415-252-2000 (phone), +1-415-626-0554 (facsimile)
http://www.macromedia.com/

MacSTATION Incorporated Japanese software distributor
Grande Maison Rokubancho #206, 6-2 Rokubancho, Chiyoda-ku, Tokyo 102 JAPAN
+81-3-5276-7981 (phone), +81-3-5276-7985 (facsimile)
http://www.macstation.co.jp/

MCI Mail ISP
1111 19th Street NW #500, Washington, DC 20036 USA
800-444-6245 (phone), +1-202-833-8484 (phone), +1-202-416-5858 (facsimile)
http://www.mcimail.com/

Media Drive Corporation Japanese OCR software
2-3-14 Kajicho Felis Building, Chiyoda-ku, Tokyo 101 JAPAN
+81-3-3710-4133 (phone), +81-3-3716-8104 (facsimile)
http://www.mediadrive.co.jp/

Mediator Technologies Shodouka
111 Ripley Street, San Francisco, CA 94110 USA
+1-415-282-2184 (phone and facsimile)
info@shodouka.com
http://www.shodouka.com/

MEGASOFT Incorporated MIFES
Nishitani-Tokyu Building, 1-38 Enoki-cho, Suita-shi, Osaka 564-0053 JAPAN
+81-6-386-2058 (phone), +81-6-386-2123 (facsimile)
http://www.megasoft.co.jp/

Mercury Software Japan, Incorporated Solo PowerLite, Solo Publisher, Solo Writer
Rengezo-cho 20 Shogoin, Hassei Building 2F, Sakyo-ku, Kyoto 606 JAPAN
+81-75-751-0205 (phone), +81-75-751-0206 (facsimile)

Microsoft Corporation Internet Explorer, Microsoft Office, Microsoft Windows
One Microsoft Way, Redmond, WA 98052-6399 USA
800-426-9400 (phone), +1-425-936-6697 (phone), +1-425-936-7329 (facsimile)
http://www.microsoft.com/

MIQ Japan, Incorporated ANS
SIT Nishi Shinjuku Building, 4-7-1 Nishi Shinjuku, Shinjuku-ku, Tokyo 160 JAPAN
+81-3-3299-7377 (phone), +81-3-3299-7371 (facsimile)

Monotype Typography Incorporated Type foundry
985 Busse Road, Elk Grove Village, IL 60007-2400 USA
+1-847-718-0400 (phone), +1-847-718-0500 (facsimile)
http://www.monotype.com/

Morisawa & Company, Limited Dr. Kerning, Fuzzy Kerning, Japanese type foundry
2-6-25 Shikitsu-Higashi, Naniwa-ku, Osaka 556 JAPAN
+81-6-649-2151 (phone), +81-6-647-0918 (facsimile)
http://www.morisawa.co.jp/

MultiLingual Computing, Incorporated *MultiLingual Communications & Technology*
319 North First Avenue, Sandpoint, ID 83864 USA
+1-208-263-8178 (phone), +1-208-263-6310 (facsimile)
info@multilingual.com
http://www.multilingual.com/

MultiMedia PrePress Technologies Service bureau, translation services
3310 West Big Beaver, Sheffield Office Park, Suite 137, Troy, MI 48084 USA
+1-248-649-4490 (phone), +1-248-649-6031 (facsimile)
info@mmpt.com
http://www.mmpt.com/

Nakanishi Printing Company, Limited — Service bureau
Shimodachuri-ogawa Kamigyo-ku, Kyoto 602-8048 JAPAN
+81-75-441-3155 (phone), +81-75-417-2050 (facsimile)
info@nacos.com
http://www.nacos.com/nakanishi/

NEC Corporation — NEC technical manuals
1-4-2 Mita, Minato-ku, Tokyo 108 JAPAN
+81-3-3455-0333 (phone)
http://www.nec.co.jp/

NeocorTech LLC — KanjiScan OCR, Tsunami MT, Typhoon MT
9909 Huennekens Street, Suite 205, San Diego, CA 92103 USA
800-693-9283 (phone), +1-619-784-3579 (phone), +1-619-784-3664 (facsimile)
info@neocor.com
http://www.neocor.com/

NETCOM On-Line Communication Services, Incorporated — ISP
3031 Tisch Way, San Jose, CA 95128 USA
800-353-6600 (phone), +1-408-983-5950 (phone), +1-408-241-9145 (facsimile)
info@netcom.com
http://www.netcom.com/

NetObjects, Incorporated — NetObjects Fusion
602 Galveston Drive, Redwood City, CA 94063 USA
+1-650-482-3200 (phone), +1-650-562-0288 (facsimile)
info@netobjects.com
http://www.netobjects.com/

Netscape Communications Corporation — JavaScript, Netscape Communicator
501 East Middlefield Road, Mountain View, CA 94043 USA
+1-650-937-3777 (phone), +1-650-528-4124 (facsimile)
sales@netscape.com
http://www.netscape.com/

Nichigai Associates, Incorporated — Publisher
1-23-8 Ohmori-kita, Ohta-ku, Tokyo 143-8550 JAPAN
+81-3-3763-7581 (phone), +81-3-3764-1350 (facsimile)
info@nichigai.co.jp
http://www.nichigai.co.jp/

NIFTY Corporation — ISP
Omori Bellport A, 6-26-1 Minami-oi, Shinagawa-ku, Tokyo 140-8544 JAPAN
+81-3-5471-5800 (phone), +81-3-5471-5890 (facsimile)
http://www.nifty.ne.jp/

Nippon Information Science (NIS) Corporation — Japanese type foundry
Sumire Building 3F, 5-4-4 Koishigawa, Bunkyo-ku, Tokyo 112-0002 JAPAN
+81-3-3818-6184 (phone), +81-3-3814-3206 (facsimile)
nischan@magical.egg.or.jp
http://www.nisfont.co.jp/

Nisus Software Incorporated — MacQWERTY, Nisus Compact, Nisus Writer
107 South Cedros Avenue, Solana Beach, CA 92075 USA
+1-619-481-1477 (phone), +1-619-481-6154 (facsimile)
info@nisus.com
http://www.nisus.com/

NJStar Software Company — NJStar, NJWin
P.O. Box 40, Epping NSW 2121 AUSTRALIA
+61-2-9869-0821 (phone), +61-2-9869-0823 (facsimile)
info@njstar.com
http://www.njstar.com/

Oki Electric Industry Company, Limited — PostScript printers
1-7-12 Toranomon, Minato-ku, Tokyo 105 JAPAN
+81-3-3501-3111 (phone), +81-3-3581-5522 (facsimile)
http://www.oki.co.jp/

O'Reilly & Associates, Incorporated — Publisher
101 Morris Street, Sebastopol, CA 95472 USA
800-998-9938 (phone), +1-707-829-0515 (phone), +1-707-829-0104 (facsimile),
info@oreilly.com
http://www.oreilly.com/

Pacific HiTech, Incorporated — CD-ROM–based software
3855 South 500 West, Suite M, Salt Lake City, UT 84115 USA
+1-801-261-1024 (phone), +1-801-261-0310 (facsimile)
http://www.pht.com/

Pacific Rim Connections, Incorporated — Consulting services, software distributor
1838 El Camino Real, Suite 219, Burlingame, CA 94010-3126 USA
+1-650-697-0911 (phone), +1-650-697-9439 (facsimile)
pacrim@sirius.com
http://www.sirius.com/~pacrim/

Pacific Software Publishing, Incorporated — KanjiKit, KanjiWORD
600 108th Avenue NE, Suite 104, Bellevue, WA 98004 USA
800-232-3989 (phone), +1-206-688-8080 (phone), +1-206-990-3388 (facsimile)
http://www.pspinc.com/

PC-VAN — ISP
NEC Corporation, 5-7-1 Shiba, Minato-ku, Tokyo 108 JAPAN
+81-3-3454-6909 (phone)
http://www.pcvan.com/

Peking University Founder Group Corporation — FIT, Chinese type foundry
204, Cheng Fu Road, Hai Dian, Beijing 100871 CHINA
+86-10-6257-9955 (phone), +86-10-6256-3881 (facsimile)
helin@founderpku.com
http://www.founderpku.com/

The Perl Journal — *The Perl Journal*
P.O. Box 54, Boston, MA 02101 USA
+1-617-623-8718 (facsimile)
subscriptions@tpj.com
http://www.tpj.com/

Personal Media Corporation — BTRON, *TRONWARE*
MY Building, 1-7-7 Hiratsuka, Shinagawa-ku, Tokyo 142-0051 JAPAN
+81-3-5702-7858 (phone), +81-3-5702-7857 (facsimile)
spd@personal-media.co.jp
http://www.personal-media.co.jp/

The Portal Information Network — ISP
20863 Stevens Creek Boulevard, Suite 200, Cupertino, CA 95014 USA
+1-408-343-4400 (phone), +1-408-343-4401 (facsimile)
http://www.portal.com/

Pyrus North America, Limited — FontLab, FontLab Composer, ScanFont, TypeTool
Box 465, 474 Old Orchard Circle, Millersville, MD 21108 USA
+1-410-987-5616 (phone), +1-410-987-4980 (facsimile)
info@pyrus.com
http://www.pyrus.com/ or *http://www.fontlab.com/*

QUALCOMM Incorporated — Eudora Pro
6455 Lusk Boulevard, San Diego, CA 92121-2779 USA
+1-619-587-1121 (phone), +1-619-658-2100 (facsimile)
http://www.qualcomm.com/

Qualitas Trading Company — Japanese software distributor
2029 Durant Avenue, Berkeley, CA 94704 USA
+1-510-848-8080 (phone), +1-510-848-8009 (facsimile)
inquire@qtc.com
http://www.qtc.com/

Quark, Incorporated — QuarkXPress
1800 Grant Street, Denver, CO 80203 USA
800-676-4575 (phone), +1-303-894-8888 (phone), +1-303-894-3395 (facsimile)
http://www.quark.com/

Rasmussen Software, Incorporated — Anzio
10240 SW Nimbus Avenue, Suite L9, Portland, Oregon 97223 USA
+1-503-624-0360 (phone), +1-503-624-0760 (facsimile)
rsi@anzio.com
http://www.anzio.com/

Ryobi Imagix Corporation — Japanese type foundry
Ryobi Imagix Building 6F, 2-10-11 Kaji-cho, Chiyoda-ku, Tokyo 101-0044 JAPAN
+81-3-3257-1283 (phone)

Sandoll Communication — Korean type foundry
110-524, Kwangweon New Building, 188-21 Myongryun-dong, Chongro-gu, Seoul KOREA
+82-2-741-3685 (phone), +82-2-742-0310 (facsimile)
taurus@soback.kornet.nm.kr

Sasuga Japanese Bookstore — Japanese books, EBs, magazines, and software
7 Upland Road, Cambridge, MA 02140 USA
+1-617-497-5460 (phone), +1-617-497-5362 (facsimile)
sasuga@world.std.com
http://world.std.com/~sasuga/

Scriptics Corporation — Tcl
2275 East Bayshore Road, Suite 101, Palo Alto, CA 94303 USA
+1-650-843-6900 (phone), +1-650-843-6909 (facsimile)
http://www.scriptics.com/

Seiko Instruments Incorporated — Electronic dictionaries
1-8 Nakase, Mihama-ku, Chiba 261-8507 JAPAN
+81-43-211-1111 (phone), +81-43-211-8050 (facsimile)
http://www.sii.co.jp/

Sentius Corporation — Mikan, Sentius Electronic Book Player, Sentius Read!
580 College Avenue, Palo Alto, CA 94306 USA
800-434-0474 (phone), +1-650-856-1296 (phone), +1-650-856-1297 (facsimile)
info@sentius.com
http://www.sentius.com/

Seoul Systems Company, Limited — Korean type foundry
150-1, Pyungchang Building, Pyungchang-dong, Jongro-gu, Seoul 110-011 KOREA
+82-2-396-3630 (phone), +82-2-391-2341 (facsimile)
http://www.ssc.co.kr/

Sesame Computer Projects — *SESAME Bulletin*
8 Avenue Road, Harrogate, North Yorkshire HG2 7PG UNITED KINGDOM
+44-0423-888-432 (phone), +44-0423-883-918 (facsimile)
european@sesame.demon.co.uk

Seybold Publications — Seybold Reports
P.O. Box 644, 428 East Baltimore Avenue, Media, PA 19063 USA
800-325-3820 (phone), +1-610-565-2480 (phone), +1-610-565-4659 (facsimile)
pubsvcs@seyboldreport.com
http://www.seyboldreport.com/

Shaken Corporation — Japanese type foundry
2-26-13 Higashi Otsuka, Toshima-ku, Tokyo 170 JAPAN
+81-3-3942-2211 (phone)

Silicon Graphics, Incorporated — IRIX
2011 North Shoreline Boulevard, Mountain View, CA 94039-7311 USA
+1-650-960-1980 (phone), +1-650-961-0595 (facsimile)
ird@esd.sgi.com
http://www.sgi.com/

SimulTrans — Localization and internationalization services
2606 Bayshore Parkway, Mountain View, CA 94043 USA
+1-650-969-3500 (phone), +1-650-969-9959 (facsimile)
http://www.simultrans.com/

SOFTBANK Corporation — Publisher
24-1 Nihonbashi-Hakozakicho, Chuo-ku, Tokyo 103-8501 JAPAN
+81-3-5642-8101 (phone), +81-3-5641-3424 (facsimile)
http://www.softbank.co.jp/

SoftMagic Incorporated — Korean type foundry
Han Chungang Building 9F, 646-7 Yoksam-dong, Kangnam-gu, Seoul 135-080 KOREA
+82-2-558-0222 (phone), +82-2-558-5850 (facsimile)
info@softmagic.co.kr
http://www.softmagic.co.kr/

SOFTWARE Too Corporation — Japanese software distributor and developer
3-6-2 Rinkai-cho, Edogawa-ku, Tokyo JAPAN
+81-3-5676-2177 (phone), +81-3-5676-2171 (facsimile)
http://www.swtoo.com/

Sony Corporation — DD-DR1 (Data Discman drive), PalmTop computer
6-7-35 Kitashinagawa, Shinagawa-ku, Tokyo 141 JAPAN
+81-3-3448-3311 (phone)
http://www.sony.co.jp/

Star+Globe Technologies Pte. Limited — WinMASS, xMASS
1 International Business Park, #09-02 The Synergy, SINGAPORE 609917
+65-665-6969 (phone), +65-665-7912 (facsimile)
info@starglobe.com.sg
http://www.starglobe.com.sg/

Stone Bridge Press MacSunrise Script
P.O. Box 8208, Berkeley, CA 94707 USA
800-947-7271 (phone), +1-510-524-8732 (phone), +1-510-524-8711 (facsimile)
sbp@stonebridge.com
http://www.stonebridge.com/

Stone RichSight (SRS) Information Technology Company, Limited RichWin
#A1 Wanquanzhuang, Beijing 100080 CHINA
+86-10-6263-0930 (phone), +86-10-6257-7954 (facsimile)
http://www.richwin.com/

Sumitomo Metal Systems Development Company, Limited SMI EDICOLOR, SpellViser
Mita-Nittodai Building 1F, Mita 3-11-36, Minato-ku, Tokyo 108-0073 JAPAN
+81-3-5476-9805 (phone), +81-3-5476-9801 (facsimile)
info_edicol@ssd.co.jp
http://www.smisoft.ssd.co.jp/

Sun Microsystems, Incorporated Java, Solaris, SPARC workstations
2550 Garcia Avenue, Mountain View, CA 94043 USA
+1-650-691-4343 (phone)
users@sun.com
http://www.sun.com/

Sybase, Incorporated Unilib
1650 65th Street, Emeryville, CA 94608 USA
+1-510-922-5248 (phone), +1-510-922-4228 (facsimile)
http://www.sybase.com/

SystemSoft Corporation Japanese software distributor
3-10-30 Tenjin, Chuo-ku, Fukuoka 810-8665 JAPAN
+81-92-722-4857 (phone)
http://www.systemsoft.co.jp/

Taishukan Shoten Publishing Company, Limited Publisher
3-24 Kanda Nishiki-cho, Chiyoda-ku, Tokyo 101-8466 JAPAN
+81-3-5476-8334 (phone), +81-3-5999-5435 (facsimile)
http://www.taishukan.co.jp/

TEX Users Group *TUGboat*
1466 NW Front Avenue, Portland, OR 97209 USA
+1-503-223-9994 (phone), +1-503-223-3960 (facsimile)
tug@tug.org
http://www.tug.org/

Technical Japanese Program Technical Japanese courses
University of Wisconsin-Madison, Department of Engineering Professional Development,
1510 Engineering Drive, Madison, WI 53706-1573 USA
+1-608-262-4810 (phone), +1-608-265-4734 (facsimile)
jdavis@engr.wisc.edu
http://epdwww.engr.wisc.edu/japan/ or *http://www.engr.wisc.edu/epd/tjc/*

TransPac Software, Incorporated TurboWriter
467 Saratoga Avenue, Suite 550, San Jose, CA 95129 USA
+1-408-261-7550 (phone), +1-408-984-6303 (facsimile)
http://www.transpac.com/

TRON Association TRON
Katsuta Building 5F, 1-3-39 Mita, Minato-ku, Tokyo 108-0073 JAPAN
+81-3-3454-3191 (phone), +81-3-3454-3224 (facsimile)
http://www.tokyoweb.or.jp/tron/

Tulip, Incorporated — Service bureau
1725 Montgomery Street, San Francisco, CA 94111 USA
+1-415-544-0900 (phone), +1-415-544-0244 (facsimile)
sf@tulipgraphics.com
http://www.tulipgraphics.com/

TWICS Company, Limited — ISP
NichiBei Kaiwa Gakuin, 1-21 Yotsuya, Shinjuku-ku, Tokyo 160 JAPAN
+81-3-3351-5977 (phone), +81-3-3353-6096 (facsimile)
info@twics.com
http://www.twics.com/

TwinBridge Software Corporation — AsianViewer, Chinese Partner, Japanese Partner
1055 Corporate Center Drive, Suite 400, Monterey Park, CA 91754 USA
800-894-6114 (phone), +1-213-263-3926 (phone), +1-213-263-8126 (facsimile)
tbsales@twinbridge.com
http://www.twinbridge.com/

TypeBank Company, Limited — Japanese type foundry
1-33-5 Sendagaya, Shibuya-ku, Tokyo 151-0051 JAPAN
+81-3-3359-6013 (phone), +81-3-3359-6016 (facsimile)
http://www.typebank.co.jp/

The Unicode Consortium — The Unicode Standard
P.O. Box 700519, San Jose, CA 95170-0519 USA
+1-408-777-3721 (phone), +1-408-777-3784 (facsimile)
unicode-inc@unicode.org
http://www.unicode.org/

UnionWay International Corporation — UnionWay AsianSuite
820 South Garfield Avenue #202, Alhambra, CA 91801 USA
+1-626-576-8866 (phone), +1-626-282-7152 (facsimile)
sales@unionway.com
http://www.unionway.com/

UniScape, Incorporated — Global C, Global Checker, Global Xchange
303 Twin Dolphin Drive, Suite 510, Redwood Shores, CA 94065 USA
+1-650-596-1430 (phone), +1-650-596-1436 (facsimile)
http://www.uni-scape.com/

Unitrendix Corporation — Software distributor
23900 Hawthorne Boulevard, Torrance, CA 90505 USA
+1-310-791-2300 (phone), +1-310-378-2079 (facsimile)
info@unitrendix.com
http://www.unitrendix.com/

URW++ Design & Development GmbH — Type foundry
Poppenbütteler Bogen 29A, D-22399 Hamburg GERMANY
+49-4060-60-50 (phone), +49-4060-60-5111 (facsimile)
juergen@urwpp.de
http://www.urwpp.de/

UUNET Technologies, Incorporated — ISP
3060 Williams Drive, Fairfax, VA 22031 USA
800-488-6383 (phone), +1-703-206-5600 (phone), +1-703-206-5601 (facsimile)
info@uu.net
http://www.uu.net/

VACS Corporation VJE
Daiichi-Yazawa Building, 1-34-10 Morino, Machida-shi, Tokyo 194-0022 JAPAN
+81-427-24-9200 (phone), +81-427-28-6864 (facsimile)
http://www.vacs.co.jp/

Village Center, Incorporated WZ
Sunlight Building, 3-2 Jinbocho, Kanda, Chiyoda-ku, Tokyo 101 JAPAN
+81-3-3221-3520 (phone), +81-3-3221-3528 (facsimile)
http://www.villagecenter.co.jp/

Walnut Creek CDROM CD-ROM–based software
4041 Pike Lane, Suite E, Concord, CA 94520 USA
800-786-9907 (phone), +1-510-674-0783 (phone), +1-510-674-0821 (facsimile)
info@cdrom.com
http://www.cdrom.com/

Windows NT Extended Kanji Processing Council XKP
Sasazuka NA Building, 1-50-1 Sasazuka, Shibuya-ku, 151-8533 JAPAN
http://www.xkp.or.jp/

Wnn Consortium Wnn
c/o ASTEM Research Institute, Kyoto Research Park, 17 Chudoji Minami-machi, Shimogyo-ku, Kyoto 600 JAPAN
+81-75-315-2897 (facsimile)
wnn@astem.or.jp

World Language Resources Software distributor
2130 Sawtelle Boulevard, Suite 304, Los Angeles, CA 90025 USA
310-996-2300 (phone), +1-310-996-2300 (facsimile)
moreinfo@worldlanguage.com
http://www.worldlanguage.com/

X/Open Company Limited X/Open standards
Apex Plaza, Foxbury Road, Reading, Berkshire RG1 1AX UNITED KINGDOM
+44-1734-508311 (phone), +44-1734-500110 (facsimile)
xospecs@xopen.co.uk
http://www.xopen.co.uk/

Xerox Systems Institute XCCS, Xerox technical manuals
3400 Hillview Avenue, Box 10034, Palo Alto, CA 94303 USA
+1-650-813-7839 (phone), +1-650-813-7811 (facsimile)
http://www.xerox.com/

Yahoo! Corporation Internet guide
3400 Central Expressway, Suite 201, Santa Clara, CA 95051 USA
+1-408-731-3300 (telephone), +1-408-731-3301 (facsimile)
info@yahoo.com
http://www.yahoo.com/

Yinu System, Incorporated Bitmapped fonts for the X Window System, Wnn for MacOS
Owariya Building 2F, Yamabuki-cho 130, Shinjuku-ku, Tokyo 162-0801 JAPAN
+81-3-5261-8587 (phone), +81-3-5261-8584 (facsimile)
service@yinu.co.jp
http://www.yinu.co.jp/

Yoon Design Institute & Yoon Media Korean type foundry
29-22 Zamwon-dong Seocho-gu, Seoul 137-030 KOREA
+82-2-516-6030 (phone), +82-2-518-5285 (facsimile)
http://www.yoonfont.co.kr/

Zhong Yi Electronics Corporation Chinese type foundry
1 Bei Sun Huan Zhong Road, Beijing 100029 CHINA
+86-10-6237-9375 (phone), +86-10-6202-7031 (facsimile)
zhongmz@public.bta.net.cn

U

Mailing Lists

There are many mailing lists which you can, without charge, join to get more information, or better yet, to participate in a discussion on a topic of interest. So, fire up your email client, and start sending those subscription requests!

Joining a mailing list, such as those that I describe below, usually entails sending an email message to a subscription address. The user name that you use is generally *majordomo*, *listserv*, or the name of the mailing list plus *-request*. Do *not* send subscription requests to an actual discussion list as this bothers its participants. This is basic mailing list etiquette.

For more detailed information about mailing lists and mailing list management, I suggest that you read Alan Schwartz's *Managing Mailing Lists* (O'Reilly & Associates, 1998).

General Mailing Lists

The mailing lists that are provided in this section are not specific to any one language, so are potentially useful to a broad audience.

AsianDOC Electronic Newsletter

The AsianDOC (Asian Database Online Community) Electronic Newsletter supports scholars, librarians, and researchers world-wide who are developing text and image databases in the various fields of Asian Studies, or who are incorporating materials in Asian languages into larger databases, and to promote better communication among them. Table U-1 provides the information necessary to subscribe to the AsianDOC Electronic Newsletter.

Table U-1: AsianDOC Electronic Newsletter Information

Subscribing address	*listproc@lists.acs.ohio-state.edu*
Subscribing command	subscribe asiandoc *your_name*
Submission address	*asiandoc@lists.acs.ohio-state.edu*
URL	*http://asiandoc.lib.ohio-state.edu/*
FAQ	*http://asiandoc.lib.ohio-state.edu/info.html*

Maureen Donovan is the maintainer and editor of the AsianDOC Electronic Newsletter.*

BeOS Mailing Lists

A number of interesting BeOS-related mailing lists are available from the maker of BeOS itself, far too many to list here in this book.†

Framers Mailing List

The Framers Mailing List, also available in a daily digest form, is a forum for sharing experiences and information about Adobe FrameMaker. Information about this mailing list is in Table U-2.

Table U-2: Framers Mailing List Information

Subscribing address	*majordomo@frameusers.com*
Subscribing command	subscribe framers[a]
Submission address	*framers@frameusers.com*
URL	*http://www.frameusers.com/*
FAQ	*http://www.frameusers.com/framefaq.shtml*

[a] Or use "subscribe framers-digest" to receive the daily digest instead of individual messages based on each posting.

FreeHand-L Mailing List

Users of Macromedia FreeHand can subscribe to a mailing list that serves as a forum to discuss FreeHand-related issues. Table U-3 provides information about the FreeHand-L Mailing List.

Table U-3: FreeHand-L Mailing List Information

Subscribing address	*listserv@galileo.uafadm.alaska.edu*
Subscribing command	subscribe freehand-l *your_name*

* *donovan.1@osu.edu*

† *http://www.be.com/aboutbe/mailinglists.html*

Table U-3: FreeHand-L Mailing List Information (continued)

Submission address	*freehand-l@galileo.uafadm.alaska.edu*
Usenet News	*comp.graphics.apps.freehand, alt.aldus.freehand*

IETF Charsets Mailing List

When charset names get registered, there is generally a discussion then ensues. Becoming a member of the IETF Charsets Mailing List allows you to monitor or participate in these discussions. They also have archives of postings, going back several years.* Table U-4 lists the information necessary to join this mailing list.

Table U-4: IETF Charsets Mailing List Information

Subscribing address	*ietf-charsets-request@iana.org*
Subscribing command	subscribe *your_name*
Submission address	*ietf-charsets@iana.org*

ISO 10646 Mailing List

Similar to Unicode, there is also a mailing list for ISO 10646-1:1993 issues. Table U-5 lists the relevant information for the ISO 10646 Mailing List.

Table U-5: ISO 10646 Mailing List Information

Subscribing address	*listserv@listproc.hcf.jhu.edu*
Subscribing command	subscribe iso10646 *your_name*
Submission address	*iso10646@listproc.hcf.jhu.edu*

Language Tech News Mailing List

The magazine entitled *MultiLingual Communications & Technology* offers the Language Tech News Mailing List as a way to provide interesting and timely information about developments in multilingual computing. Table U-6 lists the information needed to join this mailing list.

Table U-6: Language Tech News Mailing List Information

Subscribing address	*listserv@multilingual.com*
Subscribing command	subscribe news-l *your_name*

Unlike the other mailing lists in this appendix, this one is read-only. This means that submissions are not sent. Consider it a news service.

* *http://lists.w3.org/Archives/Public/ietf-charsets/*

Mule Mailing Lists

There are two mailing lists that offer discussions about Mule, whose multilingual functionality has since been merged back into GNU Emacs. They differ only in the language used for discussions. Table U-7 lists the information necessary to subscribe to the Mule Mailing Lists.

Table U-7: Mule Mailing List Information

Subscribing address	*mule-request@etl.go.jp*
Subscribing command	subscribe mule *your_name*
Subscribing command (mule-jp)[a]	subscribe mule-jp *your_name*
Submission address	*mule@etl.go.jp*
Submission address (mule-jp)	*mule-jp@etl.go.jp*

[a] The "mule-jp" mailing list includes all postings from the "mule" mailing list, so there is no need to subscribe to both.

Mozilla Language Enabling Project

Although not really a mailing list *per se*, the Mozilla Language Enabling Project is a group that is working to enhance the multilingual support in Netscape Communication's web-browsing software and related products. There are a number of mailing lists, too many to list here in this book.*

Nisus Mailing List

Nisus Writer is a MacOS-based word processor that has been adapted to handle Japanese and other non-Western scripts. Table U-8 provides the information necessary to join this mailing list.

Table U-8: Nisus Mailing List Information

Subscribing address	*listserv@listserv.dartmouth.edu*
Subscribing command	subscribe nisus *your_name*
Submission address	*nisus@listserv.dartmouth.edu*
URL	*http://tile.net/lists/nisus.html*

PAGEMAKR Mailing List

The PAGEMAKR Mailing List can serve as a forum for discussing Adobe PageMaker issues with potentially more experienced users. Table U-9 provides the information necessary to join this mailing list.

* *http://www.mozilla.org/community.html*

Table U-9: PAGEMAKR Mailing List Information

Subscribing address	*listserv@listserv.iupui.edu*
Subscribing command	subscribe pagemakr *your_name*
Submission address	*pagemakr@listserv.iupui.edu*
URL	*http://www.hypercorp.com/gain/pm/*
FAQ	*http://www.hypercorp.com/gain/pm/faq.html*

QUARKXPR Mailing List

Users of QuarkXPress can subscribe to the QUARKXPR Mailing List to participate in or start discussions that relate to using QuarkXPress. Table U-10 provides the details about this mailing list.

Table U-10: QUARKXPR Mailing List Information

Subscribing address	*listserv@listserv.indiana.edu*
Subscribing command	subscribe quarkxpr *your_name*
Submission address	*quarkxpr@listserv.indiana.edu*
URL	*http://www.tile.net/lists/quarkxpr.html*

Unicode Mailing List

Although the Unicode books have been published, Unicode itself is constantly evolving in order to become better. Joining this mailing list will keep you better informed of changes made to the Unicode standard. Table U-11 provides the information for joining this mailing list.

Table U-11: Unicode Mailing List Information

Subscribing address	*unicode-request@unicode.org*
Subscribing command	subscribe *your_name*
Submission address	*unicode@unicode.org*
URL	*http://www.unicode.org/*

WWW International Mailing List

The World Wide Web Consortium (W3C) sponsors a mailing list for discussing internationalization issues as they affect the Web. Table U-12 lists the information necessary for joining this mailing list.

Table U-12: WWW International Mailing List Information

Subscribing address	*www-international-request@w3.org*
Subscribing command	subscribe *your_name*

Table U-12: WWW International Mailing List Information (continued)

Submission address	*www-international@w3.org*
URL	*http://www.w3.org/International/*

Chinese Mailing Lists

Unfortunately, I am aware of only one Chinese-only mailing list, specifically the CCNET-L Mailing List.

CCNET-L Mailing List

The CCNET-L (Chinese Computing Network) Mailing List is a forum for those interested in using Chinese on computer systems. Table U-13 provides the information for joining this mailing list.

Table U-13: CCNET-L Mailing List Information

Subscribing address	*listserv@uga.uga.edu*
Subscribing command	subscribe ccnet-l *your_name*
Submission address	*ccnet-l@uga.uga.edu*

Japanese Mailing Lists

The following mailing lists either provide a Japanese-language forum or are about Japanese computing—or both.

Canna Mailing List

For those who use Canna, a Japanese input method available for Windows and Unix, there is a discussion forum available in the form of a mailing list. Table U-14 provides the information for joining this mailing list.

Table U-14: Canna Mailing List Information

Subscribing address	*canna-request@nec.co.jp*
Subscribing command	subscribe *your_name*
Submission address	*canna@nec.co.jp*
Usenet News	*tnn.forum.canna*
URL	*http://www.nec.co.jp/canna/*

EDICOLOR Mailing List

The EDICOLOR Mailing List offers a forum for discussing issues about SMI EDICOLOR, a Japanese page-layout system developed by Sumitomo Metal Industries. Table U-15 provides the information necessary to join this mailing list.

Table U-15: EDICOLOR Mailing List Information

Subscribing address	*edicolor-ctl@cup.com*
Subscribing command	join (in "`Subject:`" line)
Submission address	*edicolor@cup.com*
URL	*http://www.tkp.co.jp/edi_ml/*

Font Mailing Lists

There are two font-related mailing lists managed by Akila Inouye (井上明 *inoue akira*).* They are the Font-D and Font-G Mailing Lists.† Topics of discussion can be technical in nature, but are often announcements for font- or typography-related seminars or other similar events. The language used for nearly all postings in these mailing lists is Japanese.

Font-D Mailing List

The Font-D (Font Design) Mailing List provides a forum for discussing issues about font design. Table U-16 provides the information for joining this mailing list.

Table U-16: Font-D Mailing List Information

Subscribing address	*majordomo@ml.l-h.co.jp*
Subscribing command	subscribe font-d
Submission address	*font-d@ml.l-h.co.jp*

Font-G Mailing List

The Font-G (Font General) Mailing List provides a forum for discussing issues about font in general. Table U-17 provides the information for joining this mailing list.

Table U-17: Font-G Mailing List Information

Subscribing address	*majordomo@ml.l-h.co.jp*
Subscribing command	subscribe font-g
Submission address	*font-g@ml.l-h.co.jp*

* *akilax@l-h.co.jp*
† *http://www.l-h.co.jp/lhcontents/mailinglist.html*

Honyaku Mailing List

Established by Dan Kanagy* in 1994, the Honyaku Mailing List is a forum for Japanese translators to discuss translation issues. Table U-18 provides the information for joining this mailing list.

Table U-18: Honyaku Mailing List Information

Subscribing address	*listserv@peach.ease.lsoft.com*
Subscribing command	subscribe honyaku *your_name*
Submission address	*honyaku@peach.ease.lsoft.com*
URL	*http://www.crossroads.net/h1/*
FAQ	*http://www.crossroads.net/h1/faq.html*

NIHONGO Mailing List

The NIHONGO Mailing List, maintained by Jon LaCure,† is devoted to discussions about the Japanese language, its use on computers, and Japanese culture in the context of language. Table U-19 provides the details for joining this mailing list.

Table U-19: NIHONGO Mailing List Information

Subscribing address	*listserv@utkvm1.utk.edu*
Subscribing command	subscribe nihongo *your_name*
Submission address	*nihongo@utkvm1.utk.edu*
Usenet News	*sci.lang.japan*
URL	*http://funnelweb.utcc.utk.edu/~lacure/*
FAQ	*ftp://rtfm.mit.edu/pub/usenet/news.answers/japan/language/*

The NIHONGO Mailing List FAQ was until recently maintained by Olaf Meeuwissen, and is now maintained by Ben Bullock.

Nihongo Computing Mailing List

The Nihongo Computing Mailing List, managed by Hiroshi Hasabe (長谷部宏 *hasabe hiroshi*),‡ is dedicated as a forum for discussing issues that involve Japanese computing, and differs from the NIHONGO Mailing List (also known as Usenet News *sci.lang.japan*) as follows:

- It is devoted solely to computing issues—*sci.lang.japan* also deals with the language and cultural issues
- It accommodates people who feel that *sci.lang.japan* is simply too academic

* *dkanagy@gol.com*

† *lacure@utkux.utcc.utk.edu*

‡ *hhasebe@msdi.co.jp*

- Many subscribers are professional translators who need to deal with Japanese computing issues on a daily basis
- Software developers and distributors can post information about their Japanese-capable products (such as press releases) that may be of interest to subscribers

Table U-20 provides the necessary information for subscribing to the Nihongo Computing Mailing List.

Table U-20: Nihongo Computing Mailing List Information

Subscribing address	*majordomo@msdi.co.jp*
Subscribing command	subscribe nihongo-computing
Submission address	*nihongo-computing@msdi.co.jp*
URL	*http://www.msdi.co.jp/public/info/nihongo-computing/*

RES-JAPAN-GROUP Mailing List

Rick Schlichting* at the University of Arizona has established the Japan CS Project, which collects and disseminates Japanese scientific and technical information related to computing and computer science. One of its activities is a mailing list version of the Usenet News newsgroup *comp.research.japan*. Like the NIHONGO Mailing List, it is intended for people who do not have access to Usenet News, and all posts to the mailing list are cross-posted to the Usenet News newsgroup version.

According to the mailing list's charter, the following is appropriate discussion material for this group:

- Information about CS research papers published in Japan, including titles, authors, and (where feasible) abstracts—this includes papers in both English and Japanese
- Descriptions of current Japanese computing and CS activities, trip reports to Japanese universities and companies, and so on
- Announcements related to computing and CS in Japan, including those related to conferences held in Japan, research opportunities in Japan, funding for research visits to Japan, and so on
- Queries related to computing and CS research underway in Japan
- General discussions on computing and CS in Japan, both academic and industrial

* *rick@cs.arizona.edu*

This mailing list is also used to distribute certain types of information that appear on a regular basis, including:

- Table of contents information from Japanese computing journals
- The public portions of reports from the Asian Technology Information Program (ATIP) headed by David Kahaner
- The text of program announcements from the National Science Foundation (NSF) related to Japan
- The Tokyo Report Memoranda issued by the Tokyo office of NSF

Table U-21 provides the information necessary to join the RES-GROUP-JAPAN Mailing List.

Table U-21: RES-GROUP-JAPAN Mailing List Information

Subscribing address	*res-japan-group-request@cs.arizona.edu*
Subscribing command	subscribe *your_name*
Submission address	*res-japan-group@cs.arizona.edu*
Usenet News	*comp.research.japan*
URL	*http://www.cs.arizona.edu/japan/www/japan.html*

SKK Mailing List

The Japanese input method called SKK has an associated mailing list, and allows SKK users to discuss their problems, offer suggestions for improvements, and answer others' questions. Most of the discussions are in Japanese. Table U-22 provides the information for joining this mailing list.

Table U-22: SKK Mailing List Information

Subscribing address	*skk-join@kuis.kyoto-u.ac.jp*
Submission address	*skk@kuis.kyoto-u.ac.jp*
URL	*http://skk.kuis.kyoto-u.ac.jp/skk/*

T-Code Mailing List

There is a mailing list for those who use or are interested in the two-stroke Japanese input method called T-Code. Table U-23 provides the information for joining this mailing list.

Table U-23: T-Code Mailing List Information

Subscribing address	*tcode-admin@is.s.u-tokyo.ac.jp*
Submission address	*tcode-ml@is.s.u-tokyo.ac.jp*

Korean Mailing Lists

Unfortunately, I am aware of only one Korean-only mailing list that is of potential interest to readers of this book, specifically the Hangul Mailing List.

Hangul Mailing List

The Hangul Mailing List deals with Korean computing issues, and the typical posting is in Korean. Table U-24 provides the information for joining this mailing list.

Table U-24: Hangul Mailing List Information

Subscribing address	*majordomo@cair.kaist.ac.kr*
Subscribing command	subscribe hangul
Submission address	*hangul@cair.kaist.ac.kr*
Usenet News	*han.comp.hangul*
URL	*http://standard.nca.or.kr/hangul/*
FAQ	*http://pantheon.yale.edu/~jshin/faq/*

This mailing list's FAQ, which is of tremendous value, is maintained by Jungshik Shin (신정식 *sin jeongsig*).

V

Professional Organizations

There are organizations dedicated to the advancement of processing CJKV or multilingual text on computer systems. If you find one that sparks your interest, I encourage you to join. Appendix T, *Software and Document Sources,* provides detailed contact information for these organizations (page number cross-references are provided when appropriate). Most of these professional organizations sponsor frequent conferences, and some publish journals.

Chinese and Oriental Languages Information Processing Society

The Chinese and Oriental Languages Information Processing Society (COLIPS), based in Singapore, is an organization that is dedicated to advancing the science and technology of CJKV information processing. The society publishes two issues of its journal, *Communications of COLIPS* (*CommCOLIPS*), per year at a rate of $50 (Singapore) per volume, or $30 (Singapore) for those who reside in Singapore or Malaysia. The first year of membership is free, and $25 (Singapore) per year thereafter.

For more information on COLIPS, or to join, please refer to their online information.* See page 979 in Appendix T for COLIPS' contact information.

International Macintosh Users Group

If you live in the San Francisco Bay Area, and work with computers in the context of languages other than English, then the International Macintosh Users Group

* *http://www.iscs.nus.sg/~colips/*

(IMUG) may be of interest to you. IMUG hosts talks in the San Francisco Bay Area on a variety of subjects once a month. Membership dues for individuals are $20 (US) per year but $15 (US) for renewals, and include a newsletter. Attending IMUG talks is free to members, but non-members are charged $2 (US).

Information about IMUG and its events is available online.* See page 982 in Appendix T for IMUG's complete contact information.

The Localisation Industry Standards Association

The Localisation Industry Standards Association (LISA) is an organization that promotes the development of internationalization and localization in software development.† LISA publishes *The LISA Forum*, their quarterly newsletter (ISSN 1420-3693). See page 985 in Appendix T for LISA's complete contact information.

Oriental Language Computer Society

The Oriental Language Computer Society (OLCS) is an excellent organization for any reader of this book to join if they are really serious about technical issues as they pertain to CJKV computing. Membership dues for individuals are currently $50 (US) per year, and include four issues of *Computer Processing of Oriental Languages* (CPOL), its quarterly journal. For more information, or to join OLCS, please refer to their online information.‡

The Unicode Consortium

The Unicode Consortium, which is responsible for the development and promotion of the Unicode standard, offers several levels of membership ranging from corporate to individual.** The Unicode Consortium sponsors Unicode conferences twice a year. See page 992 in Appendix T for The Unicode Consortium's complete contact information.

* *http://www.imug.org/*
† *http://www.lisa.org/*
‡ *http://cpol.csie.nctu.edu.tw/*
** *http://www.unicode.org/*

W

Perl Code Examples

This appendix provides Perl equivalents of some algorithms presented in Chapter 9, *Information Processing Techniques*, as C or Java code. While the C and Java code examples in Chapter 9 are useful for developing your own commercial-grade software, these Perl equivalents are useful for internal-use tools.

If you do not use Perl, feel free to skip this appendix. But, in the same vein, I encourage you to explore the Perl programming language to see whether it can offer you something—I use nothing but Perl for virtually all of my programming needs.

A few of these Perl code examples began their life as code courtesy of regex wizard Jeffrey Friedl, author of a most excellent book entitled *Mastering Regular Expressions* (O'Reilly & Associates, 1997). Tom Christiansen and Nathan Torkington's *Perl Cookbook* (O'Reilly & Associates, 1998) includes a short section on multiple-byte handling in regexes (specifically, on pp 202–206).

Japanese Code Conversion

The programs presented in the following sections perform Japanese code conversion. Note that all of them support ASCII (JIS-Roman), JIS X 0208:1997, and half-width katakana (even for ISO-2022-JP encoding, which, technically, does not support half-width katakana).

ISO-2022-JP to EUC-JP Conversion

The following Perl program performs ISO-2022-JP to EUC-JP conversion, and fully supports half-width katakana:

```
#!/usr/local/bin/perl -w

while (defined($line = <STDIN>)) {
  $line =~ s{ # JIS X 0208:1997
    \e\$[\@B]                       # ESC $ plus @ or B
    ((?:[\x21-\x7E][\x21-\x7E])+) # Two-byte characters
    \e\([BHJ]                       # ESC ( plus B, H, or J
  }{($x = $1) =~ tr/\x21-\x7E/\xA1-\xFE/, # From 7- to 8-bit
    $x
  }egx;
  $line =~ s{ # JIS X 0201-1997 half-width katakana
    \e\(I          # ESC ( I
    ([\x21-\x7E]+) # Half-width katakana
    \e\([BHJ]      # ESC ( plus B, H, or J
  }{($x = $1) =~ tr/\x21-\x7E/\xA1-\xFE/,  # From 7- to 8-bit
    ($y = $x) =~ s/([\xA1-\xFE])/\x8E$1/g, # Prefix with SS2
    $y
  }egx;
  print STDOUT $line;
}
```

EUC-JP to ISO-2022-JP Conversion

The following Perl program performs EUC-JP to ISO-2022-JP conversion, and fully supports half-width katakana:

```
#!/usr/local/bin/perl -w

while (defined($line = <STDIN>)) {
  $line =~ s{ # JIS X 0208:1997
    ((?:[\xA1-\xFE][\xA1-\xFE])+)
  }{\e\$B$1\e\(J}gx;
  $line =~ s{ # JIS X 0201-1997 half-width katakana
    ((?:\x8E[\xA0-\xDF])+)
  }{\e\(I$1\e\(J}gx;
  $line =~ s/\x8E//g;                 # Remove SS2s
  $line =~ tr/\xA1-\xFE/\x21-\x7E/; # From 8- to 7-bit
  print STDOUT $line;
}
```

ISO-2022-JP or EUC-JP to Shift-JIS Conversion

The following Perl program performs ISO-2022-JP or EUC-JP to Shift-JIS conversion, and fully supports half-width katakana. A single program allows this because EUC-JP can be regularized to ISO-2022-JP using simple eight- to seven-bit operations:

```
#!/usr/local/bin/perl -w

sub convert2sjis { # For EUC-JP and ISO-2022-JP to Shift-JIS
  my @euc = unpack("C*", $_[0]);
  my @out = ();
```

```
  while (($hi, $lo) = splice(@euc, 0, 2)) {
    $hi &= 127; $lo &= 127;
    push(@out, (($hi + 1) >> 1) + ($hi < 95 ? 112 : 176),
      $lo + (($hi & 1) ? ($lo > 95 ? 32 : 31) : 126));
  }
  return pack("C*", @out);
}

while (defined($line = <STDIN>)) {
  $line =~ s{( # EUC-JP
    (?:[\xA1-\xFE][\xA1-\xFE])+| # JIS X 0208:1997
    (?:\x8E[\xA0-\xDF])+         # Half-width katakana
  )}{substr($1,0,1) eq "\x8E" ? (($x = $1) =~ s/\x8E//g, $x) :
    &convert2sjis($1)}egx;
  $line =~ s{ # Handle ISO-2022-JP
    \e\$[\@B]
    ((?:[\x21-\x7E][\x21-\x7E])+)
    \e\([BHJ]
  }{&convert2sjis($1)}egx;
  $line =~ s{ # Handle ISO-2022-JP half-width katakana
    \e\(I
    ([\x20-\x5F]+)
    \e\([BHJ]
  }{($x = $1) =~ tr/\x20-\x5F/\xA0-\xDF/, $x}egx;
  print STDOUT $line;
}
```

Shift-JIS to ISO-2022-JP Conversion

The following Perl program performs Shift-JIS to ISO-2022-JP conversion, and fully supports half-width katakana:

```
#!/usr/local/bin/perl -w

sub sjis2jis { # For Shift-JIS to ISO-2022-JP and EUC-JP
  my @ord = unpack("C*", $_[0]);
  for ($i = 0; $i < @ord; $i += 2) {
    $ord[$i] = (($ord[$i]-($ord[$i]<160?112:176))<<1)-
      ($ord[$i+1]<159?1:0);
    $ord[$i+1] -= ($ord[$i+1]<159?($ord[$i+1]>127?32:31):126);
  }
  return pack("C*", @ord);
}

while (defined($line = <STDIN>)) {
  $line =~ s{( # JIS X 0208:1997 and half-width katakana
    (?:[\x81-\x9F\xE0-\xEF][\x40-\x7E\x80-\xFC])+|
    [\xA0-\xDF]+
  )}{
    ($x=$1) !~ /^[\xA0-\xDF]/ ?
    "\e\$B" . &sjis2jis($1) . "\e\(J" :
    "\e\(I" . (($y=$x) =~ tr/\xA0-\xDF/\x20-\x5F/, $y) . "\e\(J"
  }egx;
  print STDOUT $line;
}
```

Shift-JIS to EUC-JP Conversion

The following Perl program performs Shift-JIS to EUC-JP conversion, and fully supports half-width katakana:

```
#!/usr/local/bin/perl -w

sub sjis2jis { # For Shift-JIS to ISO-2022-JP and EUC-JP
  my @ord = unpack("C*", $_[0]);
  for ($i = 0; $i < @ord; $i += 2) {
    $ord[$i] = (($ord[$i]-($ord[$i]<160?112:176))<<1)-
      ($ord[$i+1]<159?1:0);
    $ord[$i+1] -= ($ord[$i+1]<159?($ord[$i+1]>127?32:31):126);
  }
  return pack("C*", @ord);
}

while (defined($line = <STDIN>)) {
  $line =~ s{( # JIS X 0208:1997 and half-width katakana
    (?:[\x81-\x9F\xE0-\xEF][\x40-\x7E\x80-\xFC])+|
    [\xA0-\xDF]+
  )}{
    ($x = $1) !~ /^[\xA0-\xDF]/ ?
    (($y = &sjis2jis($x)) =~ tr/\21-\x7E/\xA1-\xFE/, $y) :
    (($y = $x) =~ s/([\xA0-\xDF])/\x8E$1/g, $y)
  }egx;
  print STDOUT $line;
}
```

Half- to Full-Width Katakana Conversion

The following Perl program converts half-width katakana to their full-width equivalents. The default behavior assumes Shift-JIS encoding—invoking the program with the `-e` option assumes EUC-JP encoding.

```
#!/usr/local/bin/perl -w

# unkana.pl
#
# (Version with multi-encoding support without using JPerl)
# Written by Ken Lunde (lunde@oreilly.com or lunde@adobe.com)
# January 3, 1997

require 5.002;

$euc = "";

if (defined $ARGV[0] && $ARGV[0] eq "-e") {
  $euc = chr(142);
}

if ($euc) { # If EUC encoding
  $encoding = '[\xA1-\xFE][\xA1-\xFE]';
```

```
  $symbol_one = chr(161);
  $kana_one = chr(165);

  # Second-byte values (decimal) in EUC
  @two = (161, 163, 214, 215, 162, 166, 242, 161, 163, 165, 167, 169,
    227, 229, 231, 195, 188, 162, 164, 166, 168, 170, 171, 173, 175,
    177, 179, 181, 183, 185, 187, 189, 191, 193, 196, 198, 200,
    202 .. 207, 210, 213, 216, 219, 222 .. 226, 228, 230, 232 .. 237,
    239, 243, 171, 172);
} else { # If Shift-JIS encoding
  $encoding = '[\x81-\x9F\xE0-\xFC][\x40-\x7E\x80-\xFC]';
  $symbol_one = chr(129);
  $kana_one = chr(131);

  # Second-byte values (decimal) in Shift-JIS
  @two = (64, 66, 117, 118, 65, 69, 146, 64, 66, 68, 70, 72, 131, 133,
    135, 98, 91, 65, 67, 69, 71, 73, 74, 76, 78, 80, 82, 84, 86, 88,
    90, 92, 94, 96, 99, 101, 103, 105 .. 110, 113, 116, 119, 122, 125,
    126, 128 .. 130, 132, 134, 136 .. 141, 143, 147, 74, 75);
}

# Initialize lookup for kana substitution (stored in %char_hash)
foreach $value (160 .. 223) {
  $char_hash{chr($value)} = chr($two[$value - 160]);
}

# main loop
while ($line = <STDIN>) {
  $line =~ s/([\x00-\x80]+ |          # ASCII or JIS-Roman
             (?:$encoding)+ |         # JIS X 0208:1997
             (?:${euc}[\xA0-\xDF])+ # Half-width katakana
            )/&dostuff($1)/egox;
  print STDOUT $line;
}

sub dostuff {
  my ($str) = @_;

  if ($str =~ /^${euc}[\xA0-\xDF]/o) {           # If half-width kana
    $str =~ s/((?:$euc\xB3$euc\xDE)+ |            # u + dakuten
              (?:${euc}[\xCA-\xCE]$euc\xDF)+ | # KSTH-row + dakuten
              (?:${euc}[\xB6-\xC4\xCA-\xCE]$euc\xDE)+ | # H-row
              (?:${euc}[\xA0-\xDF])             # All other cases
             )/&han2zen($1)/egox;
  }
  return $str; # Returns ASCII/JIS-Roman and JIS X 0208:1997 as-is
}

sub han2zen {
  my ($hkana) = @_;

  if ($hkana =~ /^$euc\xB3$euc\xDE/o) { # Special "u + dakuten" case
    if ($euc) {
      $hkana =~ s/$euc\xB3$euc\xDE/\xA5\xF4/go;
```

```
      } else {
        $hkana =~ s/\xB3\xDE/\x83\x94/g;
      }
    } elsif ($hkana =~ /^${euc}[\xB6-\xC4\xCA-\xCE]${euc}[\xDE\xDF]/o) {
      $prefix = $kana_one;         # First byte for katakana
      if ($hkana =~ /^${euc}[\xCA-\xCE]$euc\xDF/o) {
        $suffix = 2;               # Increment value for handakuten
      } else {
        $suffix = 1;               # Increment value for dakuten
      }
      $hkana =~ s/$euc([\xB6-\xC4\xCA-\xCE])${euc}[\xDE\xDF]/
                  pack("n",unpack("n","$prefix$char_hash{$1}") +
                  $suffix)/egox;
    } else {
      if ($hkana =~ /^${euc}[\xA0-\xA5\xB0\xDE\xDF]/o) {
        $prefix = $symbol_one;   # First byte for symbol
      } else {
        $prefix = $kana_one;     # First byte for katakana
      }
      $hkana =~ s/$euc([\xA0-\xDF])/$prefix$char_hash{$1}/go;
    }
    return $hkana;
  }
```

Korean Code Conversion

Although this section does not include any complete Perl programs, the most difficult algorithms for handling Korean encodings are included as workable subroutines that can be used in Perl programs. The main focus of this section is Johab encoding, which requires an algorithm similar to that necessary for handling conversion to and from Johab encoding, which is strikingly similar to that used for handling conversion to and from Shift-JIS encoding. Because handling Johab encoding also requires mapping tables (for handling the 2,350 hangul in KS X 1001:1992) or bit-array manipulation (as an alternative for turning these 2,350 hangul into their Johab equivalents), I do not include complete programs.

ISO-2022-KR or EUC-KR to Johab Conversion

The following Perl subroutine converts strings of two-byte data encoded according to ISO-2022-KR or EUC-KR into Johab encoding:

```
sub convert2johab ($) { # Convert ISO-2022-KR or EUC-KR to Johab
  my @euc = unpack("C*", $_[0]);
  my ($fe_off,$hi_off,$lo_off) = (0,0,1);
  my @out = ();

  while (($hi, $lo) = splice(@euc, 0, 2)) {
    $hi &= 127; $lo &= 127;
    $fe_off = 21 if $hi == 73;
    $fe_off = 34 if $hi == 126;
```

```
    ($hi_off,$lo_off) = ($lo_off,$hi_off) if ($hi < 74 or $hi > 125);
    push(@out, ((($hi + $hi_off) >> 1) + ($hi < 74 ? 200 : 187) - $fe_off),
      $lo + ((($hi + $lo_off) & 1) ? ($lo > 110 ? 34 : 16) : 128));
  }
  return pack("C*", @out);
}
```

Note that any program that includes the above subroutine must *not* apply it to the code ranges provided in Table W-1, which represent modern jamo and hangul. These characters require completely different handling, as explained in Chapter 4, *Encoding Methods*.

Table W-1: Code Ranges Unaffected by Johab Code Conversion Algorithm

	ISO-2022-KR	EUC-KR
Modern jamo	2421–2454	A4A1–A4D4
Hangul	3021–487E	B0A1–C8FE

Johab to ISO-2022-KR or EUC-KR Conversion

The following Perl subroutine can be used to convert Johab-encoded symbols and hanja into ISO-2022-KR or EUC-KR encoding. This subroutine actually returns ISO-2022-KR–encoded characters, but the further transformation to EUC-KR encoding is a trivial operation.

```
sub johab2ks ($) { # Convert Johab to ISO-2022-KR
  my @johab = unpack("C*", $_[0]);
  my ($offset,$d8_off) = (0,0);
  my @out = ();

  while (($hi, $lo) = splice(@johab, 0, 2)) {
    $offset = 1 if ($hi > 223 and $hi < 250);
    $d8_off = ($hi == 216 and ($lo > 160 ? 94 : 42));
    push(@out, (((($hi - ($hi < 223 ? 200 : 187)) << 1) -
      ($lo < 161 ? 1 : 0) + $offset) + $d8_off),
      $lo - ($lo < 161 ? ($lo > 126 ? 34 : 16) : 128));
  }
  return pack("C*", @out);
}
```

Like with conversion to Johab encoding, conversion from Johab encoding using the above subroutine affects only a limited encoding region, specifically those for encoding symbols (including ancient jamo) and hanja. Two-byte codes whose first byte is within the range 0x84 through 0xD3 are hangul, and are converted through other means. Those two-byte codes whose first byte is within the range 0xD8 through 0xDE and 0xE0 through 0xF9 *are* handled by this subroutine.

TRON Code Conversion

The standard TRON character set (as described in Appendix C, *Vendor Character Set Standards*, starting on page 595) consists of the JIS X 0208:1997, JIS X 0212-1990, GB 2312-80, and KS X 1001:1992 character sets. Conversion between TRON encoding and those encodings for JIS X 0208:1997 and JIS X 0212-1990 is trivial, and requires minor adjustments to Perl code provided earlier in this chapter. However, converting between TRON encoding and those encodings for GB 2312-80 and KS X 1001:1992 is less trivial, and brings to bear a different code conversion technique, specifically zero-base code conversion.

Zero-base code conversion is a useful technique for dealing with encodings that have different dimensions, but whose character ordering is identical. Put simply, zero-base code conversion transforms one encoding into a single contiguous list of values starting at 0 (zero). For a 94×94 encoding whose encoding range is 0x2121–0x7E7E (ISO-2022 encoding with 8,836 code points), the result is the range 0–8,835 (remember that this list begins at 0, not 1). Reversing this effect, but with different parameters, can effectively fit a 94×94 encoding block into a block of different dimensions.

Consider the following line of code:

```
$char = (($hi - 33) * 94) + ($lo - 33);
```

First we assume that we are dealing with an encoding that fits within a 94×94 matrix, and whose byte values are in the range 0x21–0x7E (decimal 33–127). The first byte's value is stored in the variable `$hi`, and the second byte's is in `$lo`. Note how the lowest byte value is subtracted from each byte ("`$hi - 33`" and "`$lo - 33`"). Then, the first byte's value is multiplied by the number of code points in the second byte's range (in this case, 94).

TRON and GB 2312-80 Code Conversion

The 8,836 two-byte code points supported by the encodings for GB 2312-80, such as ISO-2022-CN (0x2121–0x7E7E) and EUC-CN (0xA1A1–0xFEFE), fall into the TRON encodings range 0x2180–0x678F. While ISO-2022-CN and EUC-CN encodings are based on encodings rows with 94 code points each (that is, 0x21–0x7E or 0xA1–0xFE), TRON encoding, for GB 2312-80, is based on encodings rows with 126 code points each (0x80–0xFD).

The following function, `gb2tron()`, converts ISO-2022-CN– or EUC-CN–encoded GB 2312-80 two-byte characters into TRON encoding:

```
sub gb2tron ($) { # EUC-CN or ISO-2022-CN to TRON
  my @euc = unpack("C*", $_[0]);
  my $char;
  my @out = ();
```

```
  while (($hi, $lo) = splice(@euc, 0, 2)) {
    $hi &= 127; $lo &= 127;                    # Normalize to ISO-2022-CN
    $char = (($hi - 33) * 94) + ($lo - 33); # Normalize to zero-base
    push(@out, (($char / 126) + 33), (($char % 126) + 128));
  }
  return pack("C*", @out);
}
```

The following function, `tron2euc_cn()`, converts TRON-encoded GB 2312-80 characters back into EUC-CN encoding:

```
sub tron2euc_cn ($) {
  my @euc = unpack("C*", $_[0]);
  my $char;
  my @out = ();

  while (($hi, $lo) = splice(@euc, 0, 2)) {
    $char = (($hi - 33) * 126) + ($lo - 128); # Normalize to zero-base
    push(@out, (($char / 94) + 161), (($char % 94) + 161));
  }
  return pack("C*", @out);
}
```

TRON and KS X 1001:1992 Code Conversion

The 8,836 two-byte code points supported by the encodings for KS X 1001:1992, such as ISO-2022-KR (0x2121–0x7E7E) and EUC-KR (0xA1A1–0xFEFE), fall into the TRON encodings range 0xB780–0xFD8F. While ISO-2022-KR and EUC-KR encodings are based on encodings rows with 94 code points each (that is, 0x21–0x7E or 0xA1–0xFE), TRON encoding, for KS X 1001:1992, is based on encodings rows with 126 code points each (0x80–0xFD), as you learned in the previous section.

The following function, `ks2tron()`, converts ISO-2022-KR– or EUC-KR–encoded KS X 1001:1992 two-byte characters into TRON encoding:

```
sub ks2tron ($) { # EUC-KR or ISO-2022-KR to TRON
  my @euc = unpack("C*", $_[0]);
  my $char;
  my @out = ();

  while (($hi, $lo) = splice(@euc, 0, 2)) {
    $hi &= 127; $lo &= 127;                    # Normalize to ISO-2022-KR
    $char = (($hi - 33) * 94) + ($lo - 33); # Normalize to zero-base
    push(@out, (($char / 126) + 183), (($char % 126) + 128));
  }
  return pack("C*", @out);
}
```

The following function, `tron2euc_kr()`, converts TRON-encoded KS X 1001:1992 characters back into EUC-KR encoding:

```
sub tron2euc_kr ($) { # TRON KS X 1001:1992 to EUC-KR
  my @euc = unpack("C*", $_[0]);
  my $char;
  my @out = ();
```

```
  while (($hi, $lo) = splice(@euc, 0, 2)) {
    $char = (($hi - 183) * 126) + ($lo - 128); # Normalize to zero-base
    push(@out, (($char / 94) + 161), (($char % 94) + 161));
  }
  return pack("C*", @out);
}
```

Unicode Code Conversion

Although conversion between Unicode and legacy encodings is table-driven, conversion between the various flavors of Unicode encoding is algorithmic. This section covers conversion between UCS-2 and UTF-8 encodings. The two subroutines that are provided in this section were adapted from code written by Gisle Aas.

UCS-2 to UTF-8 Conversion

The following subroutine converts UCS-2 data into UTF-8 encoding—this simple version does not recognize UTF-16 surrogates nor UCS-4 encoding:

```
sub UCS2toUTF8 ($$) {
  my ($one,$two) = @_;

  my $ch = ($one * 256) + $two;
  if ($ch <= 127) {
    chr($ch);
  } elsif ($ch <= 2047) {
    pack("C*", 192 | ($ch >> 6), 128 | ($ch & 63));
  } elsif ($ch <= 65535) {
    pack("C*", 224 | ($ch >> 12), 128 | (($ch >> 6) & 63), 128 | ($ch & 63));
  } else {
    die "Whoah! Bad UTF-16 data!\n";
  }
}
```

UTF-8 to UCS-2 Conversion

The following subroutine converts UTF-8 encoding (up to its three-byte representation) to UCS-2 encoding:

```
sub UTF8toUCS2 ($) {
  my ($bytes) = @_;

  if ($bytes =~ /^([\x00-\x7F])$/) {
    pack("n*",unpack("C*",$1));
  } elsif ($bytes =~ /^([\xC0-\xDF])([\x80-\xBF])$/) {
    pack("n",((ord($1) & 31) << 6) | (ord($2) & 63));
  } elsif ($bytes =~ /^([\xE0-\xEF])([\x80-\xBF])([\x80-\xBF])/) {
    pack("n",((ord($1) & 15) << 12) | ((ord($2) & 63) <<  6) | (ord($3) & 63));
  } else {
    die "Whoah! Bad UTF-8 data!\n";
  }
}
```

Encoding Detection

The following Perl program illustrates an effective way to automatically detect CJKV encodings, using Japanese encodings as an example. The two lines that have been emboldened are those that perform the actual detection.

This program applies encoding detection on every line of the file, and outputs the line prefixed with information about what encoding was detected.

```
#!/usr/local/bin/perl -w

# The function in this program, DetectJPEncoding(), checks the data
# that it is given, and returns various values depending on what
# encoding it detected. The return values are listed in the definition
# of the %codes hash below. You can feed this function as much data as
# you wish (such as single characters, lines, or the entire buffer),
# but the more you give it, the better the chance it will correctly
# return a single encoding (that is, not "Ambiguous"). It currently
# deals with Japanese encodings through the use of encoding templates.

%codes = (
  0 => "ERROR",
  1 => "Shift-JIS",
  2 => "EUC-JP",
  3 => "Ambiguous",    # Means ASCII, Shift-JIS, or EUC-JP
  4 => "ISO-2022-JP"
);

open(SJS,"<jis.sjs") or die "Cannot open Shift-JIS file!\n";
open(EUC,"<jis.euc") or die "Cannot open EUC-JP file!\n";
open(JIS,"<jis.jis") or die "Cannot open ISO-2022-JP file!\n";
open(OUT,">out") or die "Cannot open output file!\n";

while (defined($line = <SJS>)){
  print OUT $codes{&DetectJPEncoding($line)} . ": " . $line;
}
close(SJS);

while (defined($line = <EUC>)){
  print OUT $codes{&DetectJPEncoding($line)} . ": " . $line;
}
close(EUC);

while (defined($line = <JIS>)){
  print OUT $codes{&DetectJPEncoding($line)} . ": " . $line;
}
close(JIS);

sub DetectJPEncoding ($) {
  my $data = shift;
  return 4 if $data =~ m{ # Return from subroutine if ISO-2022-JP
    \e             # Escape character
    (?:
```

```
        \$[\@B]    # JIS X 0208 series
      | \([BHIJ]   # ASCII or JIS X 0201-1997
    )
  }x;
  my ($sjs_out,$euc_out) = (0,0);
  my $euc_jp = q{ # EUC-JP encoding
    [\x00-\x7F]                       # Code set 0
    | \x8E[\xA0-\xDF]                 # Code set 2
    | \x8F[\xA1-\xFE][\xA1-\xFE] # Code set 3
    | [\xA1-\xFE][\xA1-\xFE]      # Code set 1
  };
  my $sjs = q{ # Shift-JIS encoding
    [\x00-\x7F\xA0-\xDF]              # ASCII and half-width katakana
    | [\x81-\x9F\xE0-\xFC][\x40-\x7E\x80-\xFC] # Two-byte range
  };
  $sjs_out = 1 if $data =~ /\A (?:$sjs)+ \Z/ox;
  $euc_out = 2 if $data =~ /\A (?:$euc_jp)+ \Z/ox;

  return ($sjs_out + $euc_out);
}
```

Through the careful use of the encoding templates that start on page 1021, the above code can be adapted so that it can automatically detect virtually any encoding, within reason. This same code can also be used to check the integrity of a file's encoding.

Repairing ISO-2022-JP Encoding

As discussed in Chapter 4, ISO-2022-JP encoding (and other ISO-2022–based encodings) can be damaged in a number of ways. The "escape" character can be damaged as follows:

- Converted into a single space (0x20)
- URL transformation
- Converted into Quoted-Printable encoding
- Simply removed from the file

The following Perl program effectively repairs damaged ISO-2022-JP–encoded files, even if they were damaged in multiple ways (which is usually not the case).

```
#!/usr/local/bin/perl -w

# o Converted into a single space (0x20)
# o Converted into URL transformation -- "%1B"
# o Converted into quoted-printable -- "=1B"
#
# Or they are simply deleted.

while (defined($line = <STDIN>)) {
  $line =~ s{
```

```
      (?:\x20|[=%]1[Bb])?                # Optional space or escape
      (
        (?:
          \$ [\@B]                       # $ plus @ or B
          (?:[\x21-\x7E][\x21-\x7E])+    # One or more two-byte characters
        )
        |                                # Or...
        (?:
          \( I                           # ( plus I
          [\x20-\x5F]+?                  # One or more half-width katakana
        )
      )
      (?:\x20|[=%]1[Bb])?                # Optional space or escape
      (
        \( [BHJ]                         # ( plus B, H, or J
      )
    }{\e$1\e$2}gx;
    print STDOUT $line;
  }
```

Other Useful Transformations

There are other useful programs written in Perl, including libraries designed for CJKV information processing. Page 412 provides some pointers to some useful Perl modules and libraries for CJKV data manipulation.

The following sections provide some simple Perl programs for performing a number of common text-processing tasks.

URL Transformation

The following Perl program, a single line of code, is used to encode a string according to URL transformation:

```
$string =~ s/([^0-9A-Za-z])/sprintf("%%%02X",ord($1))/ge;
```

Likewise, the following Perl program effectively reverses the effect of the above:

```
$string =~ s/%([0-9A-Fa-f][0-9A-Fa-f])/chr hex $1/ge;
```

Quoted-Printable Transformation

To encode quoted-printable:

```
$string =~ s/([=\x00-\x1F\x80-\xFF])/sprintf("=%02X",ord($1))/ge;
```

To decode quoted-printable:

```
$string =~ s/=([0-9A-Fa-f][0-9A-Fa-f])/chr hex $1/ge;
$string =~ s/=[\n\r]+$//;
```

CJKV Encoding Templates

The following are some encoding specifications that can be used for handling various CJKV encodings. In particular, they are useful in conjunction with automatically detecting CJKV encodings.

EUC-CN and EUC-KR Encodings

```
$euc = q{
    [\x00-\x7F]              # Code set 0 (ASCII or equivalent)
  | [\xA1-\xFE][\xA1-\xFE] # Code set 1 (GB 2312-80 or KS X 1001:1992)
};
```

Big Five Encoding

```
$big5 = q{
    [\x00-\x7F]                        # ASCII/CNS-Roman
  | [\xA1-\xFE][\x40-\x7E\xA1-\xFE] # Big Five
};
```

GBK and Big Five Plus Encodings

```
$gbk = q{
    [\x00-\x7F]                        # ASCII or equivalent
  | [\x81-\xFE][\x40-\x7E\x80-\xFE] # Two-byte (GBK or Big Five Plus)
};
```

EUC-TW Encoding

```
$euc_tw = q{
    [\x00-\x7F]                               # Code set 0 (CNS-Roman)
  | [\xA1-\xFE][\xA1-\xFE]                   # Code set 1 (Plane 1)
  | \x8E[\xA1-\xB0][\xA1-\xFE][\xA1-\xFE] # Code set 2 (Planes 1-16)
};
```

Shift-JIS Encoding

```
$sjs = q{
    [\x00-\x7F]                                     # ASCII/JIS-Roman
  | [\x81-\x9F\xE0-\xFC][\x40-\x7E\x80-\xFC] # JIS X 0208:1997
  | [\xA0-\xDF]                                     # Half-width katakana
};
```

EUC-JP Encoding

```
$euc_jp = q{
    [\x00-\x7F]                    # Code set 0 (ASCII/JIS-Roman)
  | [\xA1-\xFE][\xA1-\xFE]        # Code set 1 (JIS X 0208:1997)
  | \x8E[\xA0-\xDF]                # Code set 2 (Half-width katakana)
  | \x8F[\xA1-\xFE][\xA1-\xFE] # Code set 3 (JIS X 0212-1990)
};
```

Johab Encoding

```
$johab = q{
    [\x00-\x7F]                                    # ASCII/KS-Roman
  | [\x84-\xD3][\x41-\x7E\x81-\xFE]                # Modern hangul
  | [\xD8-\xDE\xE0-\xF9][\x31-\x7E\x91-\xFE]       # Symbols and hanja
};
```

UHC Encoding

```
$uhc = q{
    [\x00-\x7F]                                    # One-byte
  | [\x81-\xFE][\x41-\x5A\x61-\x7A\x81-\xFE]       # Two-byte
};
```

UCS-2 and UTF-16 Encodings

The following encoding template works for UCS-2 encoding in any byte order:

```
$ucs2 = q{
  [\x00-\xFF][\x00-\xFF]
};
```

The following encoding template is for UTF-16 encoding in little-endian byte order without the surrogates area:

```
$utf16l = q{
    [\x00-\xFF][\x00-\xD7\xE0-\xFF]                        # UCS-2
  | [\x00-\xFF][\xD8-\xDB][\x00-\xFF][\xDC-\xDF]           # UTF-16 surrogates
};
```

The following encoding template is for UTF-16 encoding in big-endian byte order without the surrogates area:

```
$utf16b = q{
    [\x00-\xD7\xE0-\xFF][\x00-\xFF]                        # UCS-2
  | [\xD8-\xDB][\x00-\xFF][\xDC-\xDF][\x00-\xFF]           # UTF-16 surrogates
};
```

UTF-8 Encoding

The following UTF-8 encoding template supports the full one- to six-byte representation:

```
$utf8 = q{
    [\x00-\x7F]                                                          # One-byte
  | [\xC2-\xDF][\x80-\xBF]                                               # Two-byte
  | \xE0[\xA0-\xBF][\x80-\xBF]                                           # Three-byte
  | [\xE1-\xEF][\x80-\xBF][\x80-\xBF]                                    # Three-byte
  | \xF0[\x90-\xBF][\x80-\xBF][\x80-\xBF]                                # Four-byte
  | [\xF1-\xF7][\x80-\xBF][\x80-\xBF][\x80-\xBF]                         # Four-byte
  | \xF8[\x88-\xBF][\x80-\xBF][\x80-\xBF][\x80-\xBF]                     # Five-byte
  | [\xF9-\xFB][\x80-\xBF][\x80-\xBF][\x80-\xBF][\x80-\xBF]              # Five-byte
  | \xFC[\x84-\xBF][\x80-\xBF][\x80-\xBF][\x80-\xBF][\x80-\xBF]          # Six-byte
  | \xFD[\x80-\xBF][\x80-\xBF][\x80-\xBF][\x80-\xBF][\x80-\xBF]          # Six-byte
};
```

Multiple-Byte Anchoring

The following Perl program illustrates how to apply and test multiple-byte anchoring. This technique is critical in order to ensure that regex matches are applied according to *character* not *byte* boundaries.

```
#!/usr/local/bin/perl -w

$search = "\x8C\x95";                                   # "剣"
$text1  = "Text 1 \x90\x56\x8C\x95\x93\xB9"; # "Text 1 新剣道"
$text2  = "Text 2 \x94\x92\x8C\x8C\x95\x61"; # "Text 2 白血病"
$encoding = q{ # Shift-JIS encoding
  [\x00-\x7F]                               # ASCII
  | [\x81-\x9F\xE0-\xFC][\x40-\x7E\x80-\xFC] # Two-byte range
  | [\xA0-\xDF]                             # Half-width katakana
};

print "First attempt -- no anchoring\n";
print " Matched Text1\n" if $text1 =~ /$search/o;
print " Matched Text2\n" if $text2 =~ /$search/o;

print "Second attempt -- anchoring\n";
print " Matched Text1\n" if $text1 =~ /^(?:$encoding)*?$search/ox;
print " Matched Text2\n" if $text2 =~ /^(?:$encoding)*?$search/ox;
```

The following is the result of running the above program (assuming we name it *mb-anchor.pl*):

```
% perl mb-anchor.pl
First attempt -- no anchoring
 Matched Text1
 Matched Text2
Second attempt -- anchoring
 Matched Text1
```

Note how anchoring causes correct matching to take place. The text in the variable `$text2` does not contain the search character (0x8C95), but its byte sequence does occur between two characters (0x8C8C and 0x9561).

But, unlike the conventional regex anchors used in Perl (such as ^ and $) and other regular expression implementations, these anchors *consume* characters.

Multiple-Byte Processing

The following program illustrates how to break up data consisting of multiple-byte characters into separate list elements, where each list element contains one character. This particular program doesn't do anything terribly useful, but does check whether each character consists of one or two bytes, then prints out two-byte characters, along with their hexadecimal codes.

```
#!/usr/local/bin/perl -w

$encoding = q{ # Shift-JIS encoding
  [\x00-\x80\xFD-\xFF]            # ASCII and other one-byte
  | [\xA0-\xDF]                   # Half-width katakana
  | [\x81-\x9F\xE0-\xFC][\x40-\x7E\x80-\xFC] # Two-byte range
};

while (defined($line = <STDIN>)) {
  @enc = $line =~ /$encoding/gox; # One character per element
  foreach $element (@enc) {
    if (length($element) == 2) { # If two-byte character
      print STDOUT "0x" . ($x = uc unpack("H*",$element), $x);
    } else { # All others are one-byte characters
      print STDOUT "$element\n";
    }
  }
}
```

I find the above code useful in developing code converters that make use of table-driven conversion, such as conversion between Unicode and legacy encodings.

X

Glossary

The following glossary entries provide definitions and explanations for all terms found in this book, so I suggest that you consult it on an as-needed basis. It also makes for good reading if you have nothing else better to do on a cloudy, rainy, or otherwise nasty day.

50 Sounds array

50音配列 (*gojūon hairetsu*). The Japanese keyboard array whose keys follow the sequence of the 50 Sounds Table. *See 50 Sounds Table.*

50 Sounds order

50音順 (*gojūon jun*). A Japanese collation sequence that follows the ordering from the 50 Sounds Table. *See 50 Sounds Table.*

50 Sounds Table

50音表 (*gojūon hyō*). A table made up of a 5×10 matrix whose total number of possible sounds is 50. Kana characters are set into this table.

AAT

Apple Advanced Typography. The new name for Apple Computer's QuickDraw GX technology, which is used in conjunction with ATSUI. *See ATSUI.*

Aegis

All English General Information System. The name of an ISP based in Japan.

AFM

Adobe Font Metrics. The file format, for PostScript fonts, that encapsulates per-character width and bounding box information.

AI

Artificial Intelligence (人工知能 *jinkō chinō* in Japanese) or Adobe Illustrator.

AIX

Advanced Interactive Executive. IBM's version of the Unix operating system.

Algorithmic conversion

A type of conversion that makes use of mathematical operations to change the values of the converted objects. *See also table-driven conversion.*

America Online

An Internet service provider.

ANK

Alphabet, Numerals, and Katakana. One way to refer to the characters defined in JIS X 0201-1997, specifically JIS-Roman and half-width katakana.

ANS

Amiga Nihongo System. The Japanese operating system for Amiga computers.

ANSI

American National Standards Institute.

ANSI X3.4-1986

Coded Character Set—7-Bit American National Standard Code for Information Interchange.

The document that defines the ASCII character set standard.

ANSI Z39.64-1989

See EACC.

AOL

See America Online.

ASCII

American Standard Code for Information Interchange.

AT&T JIS

Another name for the Japanese instance of the EUC encoding method. *See EUC-JP.*

ATC

Adobe Type Composer. Refers to a front-end tool for creating rearranged fonts, and to the underlying technology for supporting rearranged fonts.

ATM

Asychronous Transfer Mode, Automated Teller Machine, or Adobe Type Manager. Go figure out which applies to this book!

ATSUI

Apple Type Services for Unicode Imaging. When considered a Japanese transliteration, it means "hot" (熱い *atsui*) or "thick" (厚い *atsui*).

Base64

A method used for safely transforming non-ASCII characters in email messages or email message headers.

Basic Multilingual Plane

See BMP.

BBS

電子掲示板 (*denshi keijiban*) in Japanese. Bulletin Board System.

BDF

Bitmap Distribution Format. A popular bitmapped font format developed by Adobe Systems.

Bézier curve

The type of curve used for representing character shape contours in the PostScript page-description language and its supported font formats.

Big endian

The byte order on machines such as Macintosh and most Unix workstations (or other systems powered by Motorola processors). Pertains only to data represented by more than 8 bits, such as Unicode encoding (16 bits), short (16 bits in Java), integer (32 bits in Java), float (32 bits in Java), long (64 bits in Java), and double (64 bits in Java) types. True multiple-byte encodings, such as Big Five, Shift-JIS, EUC, and ISO-2022, are not affected by byte order. *See also little endian.*

Big Five

大五 (*dàwŭ*). The name of the Chinese character set and encoding used extensively in Taiwan. Big Five is not a national standard, but is equivalent to the first two planes of CNS 11643-1992. *See CNS 11643-1992.*

Big Five Plus

An extension to Big Five that includes the remaining Chinese characters in ISO 10646-1:1993 that are not in Big Five.

Binary

二进制/二進制 (*èrjìnzhì*) in Chinese, 二進法 (*nishinhō*) in Japanese, and 이진법/二進法 (*ijinbeob*) in Korean. Base two. A numeric notation that uses two possible values, 0 or 1.

Bit

位 (*wèi*) or 位元 (*wèiyuán*) in Chinese, ビット (*bitto*) in Japanese, 비트 (*biteu*) in Korean. Binary digit. The basic units of memory that computers process.

Bitmapped font

A font whose character shapes are defined by arrays of bits. *See also parametric and outline font.*

Bitnet

Because It's Time Network. Also called CREN.

BMP

Basic Multilingual Plane. The plane within ISO 10646-1:1993 that contains the Unicode character set.

BOM

Byte Order Mark. A Unicode character that indicates the byte order (or endianness) of the Unicode text that follows. 0xFEFF in big endian, or 0xFFFE in little endian.

Bopomofo

ㄅㄆㄇㄈ. *See zhuyin.*

Boten

傍点 (*bōten*). A Japanese term that refers to character annotations that serve to emphasize characters, similar to the use of underlining in Western text. These annotations usually appear above the character (horizontal writing) or to its right (vertical writing).

BTRON

Business TRON. *See TRON.*

Byte

字节/字節 (*zìjié*) or 位元组 (*wèiyuánzǔ*) in Chinese, バイト (*baito*) in Japanese, and 바이트 (*baiteu*) in Korean. An eight-bit unit.

Byte order

The order of the bytes in multiple-byte storage units, which often differs depending on the platform. Also referred to as byte order. *See big endian and little endian.*

CAE

Common Applications Environment.

Calligraphic

See cursive.

Candidate

候補 (*kōho*) in Japanese. During typical CJKV input that involves Chinese characters, candidate refers to the names that are associated with keys in a conversion dictionary. Candidates are usually presented as a list from which you must select. *See also key and name.*

Cangjie

倉頡 (*cāngjié*), short for 倉頡輸入法 (*cāngjié shūrùfǎ*). A popular structure-based Chinese input method.

CCAG

國字整理小組 (*guózì zhěnglǐ xiǎozǔ*). Chinese Character Analysis Group.

CCCII

中文資訊交換碼 (*zhōngwén zīxùn jiāohuànmǎ*). Chinese Character Code for Information Interchange.

CCITT

International Telegraphy and Telephony Consultative Committee (*Comité Consultatif International Télégraphique et Téléphonique* in French).

CCS

See Coded Character Set.

CCSID

Coded Character Set Identifier. IBM terminology that uniquely identifies a coded character set.

CD

Compact Disk.

CDRA

Character Data Representation Architecture. IBM's solution for conversion among different character sets and encodings.

CD-ROM

Compact Disk Read Only Memory.

Cell

位 (*wèi*) in Chinese, 点 (*ten*) in Japanese, and 렬/列 (*ryeol*) or 열/列 (*yeol*) in Korean. In a two-byte encoding, cell refers to the second byte. In a two-dimensional matrix, cell *usually* represents the values along the horizontal axis. *See row and Row-Cell.*

CERNET

China Education & Research Network.

CES

See Character Encoding Scheme.

CGI

Common Gateway Interface. The name given to World Wide Web programs that are executed on the server side (as opposed to the client side). CGI programs are typically written in Perl.

Character

文字 (*wénzì*) in Chinese, 文字 (*moji*) in Japanese, and 문자/文字 (*munja*) in Korean. An abstract notion denoting a class of shapes declared to have the same meaning or form.

Character Encoding Scheme

A mapping from a character set (Coded Character Set) to a set of octets (or bits or bytes). All the encodings described in Chapter 4, *Encoding Methods*, are valid CESs. *See also Coded Character Set.*

Character set

文字集合 (*moji shūgo*) in Japanese. A collection of characters.

Character spanning

均登割付 (*kintō waritsuke*). A special case of justification that is done on a much smaller scale than in the West. Character spanning, sometimes known as Japanese justification, is typically used for lists of names whereby varying numbers of characters per name are made flush to the left and right, but not to the margin of the printed page.

Chinese

国语/國語 (*guóyǔ*), 汉语/漢語 (*hànyǔ*), or 中文 (*zhōngwén*). The languages spoken in the Chinese locales, such as China, Hong Kong, Singapore, and Taiwan.

Chinese character

汉字/漢字 (*hànzì*) in Chinese, 漢字 (*kanji*) in Japanese, 한자/漢字 (*hanja*) in Korean, and chữ Hán (𡨸漢) in Vietnamese. The characters that originated in China and are used in other East Asian locales, such as Hong Kong, Japan, Korea, Singapore, Taiwan, and Vietnam.

Chữ Hán

𡨸漢. Chinese characters as used in Vietnam.

Chữ Nôm

𡨸喃. Chinese characters developed by the Vietnamese.

CIC

Communication Intelligence Corporation.

CID

Character IDentifier. The key used to access outline (glyph) data in CID-keyed fonts.

CITS

China Information Technology Standardization Committee.

CJK

Chinese, Japanese, and Korean. *See CJKV.*

CJK.INF

The online document that appeared after *Understanding Japanese Information Processing*, but before this book.*

CJKV-Roman

A term that collectively refers to the instances of the ASCII character set as defined by the CJKV locales, including GB-Roman, CNS-Roman, JIS-Roman, KS-Roman, and TCVN-Roman. *See GB-Roman, CNS-Roman, JIS-Roman, KS-Roman, and TCVN-Roman.*

CJKV

中日韩越/中日韓越 (*zhōng rì hán yuè*) in Chinese, 中日韓越 (*chū nichi kan etsu*) in Japanese, and 중일한월/中日韓越 (*jung il han weol*) in Korean. Chinese, Japanese, Korean, and Vietnamese. Refers to the languages that use Chinese characters as a large part of their writing system.

CJKV6N

Abbreviation for CJKVization (in keeping with the tradition used for L10N, I18N, and J10N). *See CJKVization.*

* *http://www.oreilly.com/~lunde/cjk_inf.html*

CJKVese

A collective term that refers to the languages spoken in CJKV locales.

CJKVization

CJKV6N. The process of adapting software for CJKV markets. *See also CJKV, internationalization, Japanization, localization.*

CN

The two-letter country code for China.

CNNIC

China Network Information Center.

CNS

中國國家標準 (*zhōngguó guójiā biāozhǔn*). Chinese National Standard.

CNS 5205-1989

The document that defines CNS-Roman, which is the Taiwanese equivalent of ASCII. *See CNS-Roman.*

CNS 7654-1989

The Taiwanese version of ISO 2022:1994. *See ISO 2022:1994.*

CNS 11643-1986

The original national character set for Taiwan that contained only two planes, roughly equivalent to Big Five. The latest version if CNS 11643-1992, which contains five additional planes of hanzi. *See CNS 11643-1992. See also Big Five.*

CNS 11643-1992

The national character set for Taiwan that contains 48,027 hanzi in seven planes. Planes 1 and 2 are identical to Big Five, but this character set is used much less frequently. *See also Big Five.*

CNS-Roman

The Taiwanese equivalent of ASCII.

Code Page

IBM and Microsoft terminology for a character set and encoding combination. CJKV Code Pages, because of the sheer number of characters, rarely take up a single page.

Code position

The numeric code within an encoding method that is used to refer to a specific character. For two-byte characters, this refers to the row and the cell.

Code space

コード領域 (*kōdo ryōiki*) in Japanese. The space in which characters can be encoded according to the specifications of a given encoding method. Code positions outside the code space are considered invalid.

Coded Character Set

A mapping from a set of abstract characters to a set of integers. A character set that is intended to be encoded. All the character sets described in Chapter 3, *Character Set Standards*, are valid CCSs.

Compound

熟語 (*jukugo*) in Japanese. A word consisting of two or more characters.

Compound ideograph

会意文字/會意文字 (*huìyì wénzì*) in Chinese, 会意文字 (*kaii moji*) in Japanese, and 회의문자/會意文字 (*hoeyi munja*) in Korean. A Chinese character that is built from two or more primitive elements, which may be pictographs or simple ideographs. The Chinese character 明 is an example, which is composed of 日 and 月. *See pictograph and simple ideograph.*

CompuServe

An Internet service provider.

Computer

计算机/計算機 (*jìsuànjī*) or 电脑/電腦 (*diànnǎo*) in Chinese, コンピュータ (*konpyūta*) or 計算機 (*keisanki*) in Japanese, and 컴퓨터 (*keompyuteo*) or 계산기/計算器 (*gyesangi*) in Korean.

Control character

制御文字 (*seigyo moji*) in Japanese. A character whose purpose is to control printing devices or communication devices as opposed to actually producing visible marks on a screen or printer. Carriage return, for example, is a control character, whereas the letter A is a printing character.

Conversion dictionary

変換辞書 (*henkan jisho*) in Japanese. The dictionary that is used by input method software (front-end processor) to convert input into Chinese characters. Each entry in this dictionary is a key, along with one or more names associated with it. The size of such dictionaries is typically in the range of several tens of thousands of entries. *See also FEP, kana-to-kanji conversion, key, and name.*

CP

Code Page. *See Code Page.*

CPAN

Comprehensive Perl Archive Network.* A huge repository of Perl documentation and software.

CPGID

Code Page Global Identifier. IBM terminology for Code Page. *See Code Page.*

CPSI

Configurable PostScript Interpreter.

CPU

中央処理装置 (*chūō shori sōchi*) in Japanese. Central Processing Unit. Usually refers to the computer itself.

CREN

See Bitnet.

CS

Computer Science or Chinese Simplified.

CT

Chinese Traditional.

CTRON

Communication and Central TRON. *See TRON.*

CTS

Computerized Typesetting System.

Cubic spline curve

See Bézier curve.

Cursive

A smoother, hand-written style of a character. Hiragana is an example of a cursive writing system. Also called calligraphic writing.

Dakuten

濁点 (*dakuten*). Refers to the diacritic mark that serves to transform many kana characters into their voiced counterparts. For example, the katakana character *ta* (タ) is transformed into *da* (ダ). Also called "nigori" (濁り *nigori*) and the voiced mark. *See also handakuten.*

Dangling line breaking

See hanging line breaking.

Data

An android member of the Enterprise-D and Enterprise-E crew who constantly endeavors to become more human—created by cyberneticist Dr. Noonien Soong in the Omicron Theta colony. Also, information.

* *http://www.perl.com/CPAN/CPAN.html*

DBCS

Double-Byte Character Set. A character set whose characters are represented by two bytes.

DBCS-EUC

A double-byte character set encoded according to the specification of EUC.

DBCS-Host

A double-byte character set with an encoding method designed for running on IBM host computers.

DBCS-PC

A double-byte character set with an encoding method designed for running on PCs.

DEC

Digital Equipment Corporation.

DEC Kanji

The Japanese character set and encoding defined by DEC. There are two implementations: DEC Kanji and Super DEC Kanji.

Decimal

十进制/十進制 (*shíjìnzhì*) in Chinese, 十進法 (*jisshinhō*) in Japanese, and 십진법/十進法 (*sibjinbeob*) in Korean. Base 10. A numeric notation that uses 10 possible values, ranging from 0 to 9.

Designator sequence

A sequence used by some ISO-2022–based encodings for indicating the characters sets to use when shifting characters are used. Unlike an escape sequence, a designator sequence does not actually change character sets. *See escape sequence.*

Diachronic

A linguistic term that refers to linguistic changes that occur between different periods.

Diacritic mark

A mark that serves to annotate characters with additional information, usually a variant reading. Diacritic marks, typically found above or below characters. In the West it is common to see accented characters such as á, à, â, ä, ã, å, and ç. Japanese examples include the hiragana characters ば (*ba*) and ぱ (*pa*), which are derived from the basic hiragana character は (*ha*).

Dialect

A linguistic term that refers to different flavors of a language that are usually spoken in different regions.

Display PostScript

A special version of PostScript designed for computer monitor output. It was used as standard software on the NeXT platform.

DOS

Disk Operating System.

DPI

Dots-per-inch. A measurement for device resolution.

DPRK

조선 민주주의 인민 공화국/朝鮮民主主義人民共和國 (*coseon mincucuyi inmin konghwakuk*). Democratic People's Republic of Korea. The official name for North Korea.

DPS

See Display PostScript.

DTD

Document Type Definition. SGML and XML terminology that refers to a document's type so that it can be interpreted correctly.

DTP

Desk Top Publishing.

Dvorak array

A Western keyboard array developed by August Dvorak and William Dealey in the 1930s as an improvement over the QWERTY keyboard array. *See QWERTY array.*

EACC

East Asian Character Code. The common reference to ANSI Z39.64-1989, *East Asian Character Code For Bibliographic Use*. Based on CCCII. *See CCCII.*

EB

電子ブック (*denshi bukku*) in Japanese. Electronic book.

EBCDIC

Extended Binary-Coded-Decimal Interchange Code. An encoding for the ASCII character set standard developed by IBM for use on IBM-based computers. Used in conjunction with several double-byte character sets and encodings, such as DBCS-Host (IBM), JEF (Fujitsu), and KEIS (Hitachi). Requires eight bits for representation.

EBCDIK

Extended Binary-Coded-Decimal Interchange Kana Code. A Japanese version of EBCDIC that includes uppercase Latin characters, numerals, symbols, half-width katakana, and control characters. *See EBCDIC.*

ECMA

European Computer Manufacturers Association.

Electronic Character Set

See Coded Character Set.

Elvis

The King of Rock 'n Roll. Also, a *vi* clone written by Steve Kirkendall for which Japanese (*jelvis*) and Korean (Hangul Elvis) versions exist.

Em-square

A square space whose height and width roughly corresponds to the width of the letter "M." Also called a mutton. "Design space" is a better term because some typeface designs have a non-square design space.

Emacs

A very powerful text editor that has been ported to a variety of platforms.

en

The two-letter language code for English.

Encoding

符号化 (*fugōka*) in Japanese. The method of defining the correspondence between numerical character codes and the final printable glyphs. For instance, 0x41 is the ASCII (JIS-Roman) code for the letter A. 0xC1 is the EBCDIC (EBCDIK) code for the letter A.

Escape character

エスケープ文字 (*esukēpu moji*) in Japanese. The control character (0x1B) that is used as part of an escape sequence. Escape sequences are used in ISO-2022-JP encodings to switch between one- and two-byte modes. *See also escape sequence, ISO-2022-JP, ISO-2022-JP-1, and ISO-2022-JP-2.*

Escape sequence

エスケープシーケンス (*esukēpu shīkensu*) in Japanese. A string of characters that contains one or more escape characters, and is used to signify a shift in mode of some sort. In the case of the Japanese character set, they are used to shift between one- and two-byte modes, and to shift between different character sets or different versions of the same character set. *See also shifting sequence.*

EUC

Extended Unix Code. There are locale-specific instances of EUC encoding, each of which can specify up to four code sets.

EUC-CN

The instance of EUC encoding for China, which uses two of the four code sets, and supports the GB 1988-89 and GB 2312-80 character sets.

EUC-JP

The instance of EUC encoding for Japan, which uses all four code sets, and supports the JIS X 0201-1997, JIS X 0208:1997, and JIS X 0212-1990 character sets.

EUC-KR

The instance of EUC encoding for Korea, which uses two of the four code sets, and supports the KS X 1003:1993 and KS X 1001:1992 character sets. Sometimes called Wansung.

EUC-TW

The instance of EUC encoding for Taiwan, which uses three of the four code sets, and supports the CNS 5205-1989 and CNS 11643-1992 character set standards.

External character

See system-defined character, system-specific character, and user-defined character.

FAGAT

Forum of Asian Graphic Arts Technology. A technology forum sponsored by JAGAT. *See JAGAT.*

Fangsong

仿宋 (*fǎngsòng*) or 仿宋体 (*fǎngsòngtǐ*). The Chinese semi-script typeface style.

FAQ

Frequently Asked Questions. A document that contains answers to frequently-asked question. Most Usenet newsgroups have accompanying FAQs whose purpose is to reduce the number of "common" questions posted.

FDPC

文字フォント開発・普及センター (*moji fonto kaihatsu fukyū sentā*). Font Development and Promotion Center. The consortium, which is part of JSA, that has developed the "Heisei" series of Japanese typefaces. It is now disbanded.

FEP

Front-End Processor. A common name for Japanese input software, which is so named from the way it captures keyboard strokes before they are sent to the text buffer of the current application. These keyboard strokes are then processed, converted into a mixture of kana and kanji text, and finally sent to the current application's text buffer.

FH

FreeHand.

Fidonet

An electronic bulletin board (BBS) service that offers a gateway to the outside world. *See BBS.*

FIT

Focus on Integrated Typesetting (飞腾 *fēiténg*; meaning "to soar"). The name of a page-layout system developed by Peking University Founder Group.

Fixed-length encoding

An encoding method whereby every character in the character set is represented by the same number of bytes. Examples include Unicode, UCS-2, UCS-4, and EUC complete two-byte format. Actually, ASCII encoding, if used by itself, is fixed-length encoded. *See also modal encoding and non-modal encoding.*

fj

From Japan. The initial two letters found in the names of Usenet Newsgroups distributed within Japan. These newsgroups are also available outside of Japan.

FM

Frequency Modulation or FrameMaker.

FM-R

The name of the PC series of computers produced by Fujitsu.

FMapType

A PostScript language key (integer) that indicates which mapping algorithm to use when interpreting the sequence of bytes in a string. All PostScript Type 0 (composite) fonts must specify an FMapType.

FSF

Free Software Foundation.

FSS-UTF

File System Safe UTF. *See UTF-8.*

FTP

File Transfer Protocol. A common way to move files between host computers, and sometimes between a host computer and a personal computer.

Full-width

全形 (*quánxíng*) in Chinese, 全角 (*zenkaku*) in Japanese, and 전각/全角 (*jeongag*) in Korean. A character whose shape occupies a space roughly that of a square. Most CJKV characters are considered to be full-width. *See also half-width.*

Furigana

振り仮名 (*furigana*). *See ruby.*

G

ゴジラ (*gojira*). Godzilla. The King. The King of the Monsters. A life form first encountered in 1954 in Japan, and subsequently went through nuclear meltdown in late 1995. Survived by Junior Godzilla. A lean and mean version of Godzilla appeared sometime around Memorial Day 1998. G sometimes refers to Gamera (ガメラ *gamera*), a giant turtle-like creature. Also, an old unit of typographic measurement used strictly for type size, written 号数/號數 (*hàoshù*) in Chinese, 号数 (*gōsū*) in Japanese, and 호수/號數 (*hosu*) in Korean. Unlike other typographic units of measurement, the scale is not absolute but relative, and the larger the value of G, the smaller the relative size. For example, 0G (the largest size) is equivalent to 42 points, and 8G is equivalent to 5.25 points.

Gaiji

外字 (*gaiji*). *See system-defined character, system-specific character, and user-defined character.*

Gaiji solution

A solution that makes it possible to interchange documents that contain non-standard characters to systems that do not have such characters installed, and allows such characters to be properly displayed and printed.

Gairaigo

外来語 (*gairaigo*). Means "loan word," but usually refers to loan words written using katakana.

Gakushū Kanji

学習漢字 (*gakushū kanji*). The 1,006 kanji that are formally taught in the Japanese educational system during the first six grades. Originally enumerated 996 kanji in 1977.

GB

Short for "Guo Biao" (国标 *guóbiāo*), which is, in turn, short for "Guojia Biaozhun" (国家标准 *guójiā biāozhǔn*), and means "National Standard" in Chinese.

GB 1988-89

The document that defines GB-Roman, which is the Chinese equivalent of ASCII. Originally designated GB 1988-80. *See GB-Roman.*

GB 2311-80

The Chinese version of ISO 2022:1994. *See ISO 2022:1994.*

GB 2312-80

The document that describes the basic Chinese character set as used in China (PRC). Also known as GB0. It enumerates 7,445 characters.

GB 6345.1-86

The document that details additions (132 characters) and corrections for GB 2312-80. *See GB 2312-80.*

GB 7589-87

The document that enumerates 7,237 additional hanzi. Also known as GB2.

GB 7590-87

The document that enumerates 7,039 additional hanzi. Also known as GB4.

GB 8565.2-88

The document on which ISO-IR-165:1992 is based. It is based on GB 2312-80, but provides additional characters. *See GB 2312-80 and ISO-IR-165:1992.*

GB 13000.1-93

The Chinese version of ISO 10646-1:1993. Based on Unicode Version 1.1. *See ISO 10646-1:1993.*

GBK

The character set used in Microsoft Windows PRC version. The "K" in GBK represents the first sound in the Chinese word meaning "extension" (扩展 *kuòzhǎn*).

GB/T

The "T" is short for "Tuijian" (推荐 *tuījiàn*), which means "recommended" (as opposed to "forced" or "mandatory") in Chinese. *See GB for its meaning.*

GB/T 12345-90

The traditional analog of GB 2312-80—contains 2,180 hanzi not found in GB 2312-80. Most of these are hanzi replacements, but some are placed into additional rows, specifically rows 88 and 89. Also known as GB1. *See GB 2312-80.*

GB/T 13131-9X

The traditional analog of GB 7589-87. Also known as GB3. Not yet published. *See GB 7589-87.*

GB/T 13132-9X

The traditional analog of GB 7590-87. Also known as GB5. Not yet published. *See GB 7590-87.*

GB-Roman

The Chinese equivalent of the ASCII character set and encoding. The name of the document that defines this character set is called GB 1988-89.

GID

Glyph IDentifier. The key used to access outline (glyph) data within "sfnt" resources.

GIF

Graphics Interchange Format.

GL

Graphic Left. Usually refers to an encoding whose bytes have the eighth bit turned off, such as ISO-2022.

Gloss

See ruby.

Glyph

A specific instance of a character. A classic example is that "f" and "i" are two separate glyphs, but you can fuse these two characters into a single glyph called a ligature: fi. *See ligature.*

GNU

Short for "GNU is Not Unix." A series of Unix-based software that is provided free of charge. GNU software (and other software that seeks protection) falls under the terms of the GNU General Public License, which protects software from being exploited for commercial uses. It ensures that there will always be a large body of software freely available.

Gothic

ゴシック (*goshikku*) or ゴシック体 (*goshikku-tai*) in Japanese and 고딕 (*godig*) or 고딕체/고딕體 (*godigce*) in Korean. The name commonly given to the Japanese typeface style in which horizontal and vertical strokes are of the same relative weight. This is roughly equivalent to the sans serif typeface style in Western typography. *See sans serif.*

GR

Graphic Right. Usually refers to an encoding whose bytes have the eighth bit turned on, such as EUC.

Grep

Global regular expression print. The standard regex-based pattern-matching utility standard on most Unix systems.

Gugja

국자/國字 (*gugja*). Korean-made hanja.

GUI

Graphical User Interface.

H

歯数 (*hasū*) in Japanese. Unit of typographic measurement equivalent to 0.25mm, and its correct usage is strictly for measurements other than type size.

Half-width

半形 (*bànxíng*) in Chinese, 半角 (*hankaku*) in Japanese, and 반각/半角 (*bangag*) in Korean. A character whose shape occupies a space half that of a square. ASCII characters as used in the West are typically considered half-width. *See also full-width*.

Han Unification

The effort on the part of the Unicode Consortium to collapse the Chinese, Japanese, and Korean versions of Chinese characters down to a common code set by eliminating duplication.

Handakuten

半濁点 (*handakuten*). Refers to the circle-like diacritic mark that serves to transform *h*-row kana characters into their p-row counterparts. For example, katakana *ha* (ハ) is transformed into katakana *pa* (パ). Also called "maru" (丸 *maru*; literally means "circle.") and the semi-voiced mark. *See also dakuten*.

Hanging line breaking

ぶら下がり禁則処理 (*burasagari kinsoku shori*) in Japanese. A method of moving characters up to the previous line in order to prevent prohibited characters for ending or beginning a line. The character or characters that are moved appear to dangle outside of the right margin. Also known as hanging line wrapping. *See also line breaking, wrap-down line breaking, and wrap-up line breaking*.

Hangul

한글 (*hangeul*). The name of the native Korean writing system. Each hangul is composed of two or three hangul elements (called jamo). *See also jamo*.

Hankaku

半角 (*hankaku*). Analogous to half-width. *See half-width*.

Hanja

한자/漢字 (*hanja*). The Korean word for Chinese character. *See Chinese character*.

Hanzi

汉字/漢字 (*hànzì*). The Chinese word for Chinese character. *See Chinese character*.

Hei

黑 (*hēi*) or 黑体 (*hēitǐ*). The Chinese sans serif typeface style. 黑 means "black" in Chinese. *See sans serif*.

Heisei

平成 (*heisei*). The name of the current Japanese era, which began in 1989. Also the name of the typefaces that have been produced by developing members of FDPC. *See also FDPC*.

Hexadecimal

十六进制/十六進制 (*shíliùjìnzhì*) in Chinese, 十六進法 (*jūrokushinhō*) in Japanese, and 십육진법/十六進法 (*sibyugjinbeob*) in Korean. Base 16. A numeric notation that uses 16 possible values, 0–9 and A–F. The most common notation used in the computer world.

Hiragana

平仮名 (*hiragana*). The cursive Japanese syllabic writing system. Together with katakana is collectively called kana. *See also kana and katakana*.

HK

The two-letter country code for Hong Kong.

Hojo Kanji

補助漢字 (*hojo kanji*). Supplemental kanji. The name given to the kanji contained in JIS X 0212-1990. These kanji are ordered by radical, then by total number of strokes.

Hong Kong

香港 (*xiānggǎng*). The name of a Chinese locale, which became part of China (PRC) in 1997. Still considered a separate locale from China.

HP

Hewlett-Packard.

HP-UX

Hewlett-Packard's version of the Unix operating system.

HTML

HyperText Markup Language. An application of SGML, and the standard language used to write content-specifying documents for the Web.

I18N

Abbreviation for internationalization. *See internationalization*.

IANA

Internet Assigned Numbers Authority.

IBM

アイ・ビー・エム (*ai bī emu*) in Japanese. International Business Machines Corporation.

IBM-eucJP

A specific instance of DBCS-EUC to include ASCII/JIS-Roman and half-width katakana.

IBM-932

A specific instance of DBCS-PC to include ASCII/JIS-Roman and half-width katakana.

IBM Japanese

The name of the Japanese character set as defined by IBM. Some implementations include IBM-eucJP and IBM-932.

ID

Identification. Usually refers to the user's name as used to access an electronic service or host computer.

IE

Internet Explorer.

IEEE

Institute of Electrical and Electronics Engineers.

IETF

Internet Engineering Task Force. A volunteer organization that deals with networking issues on the Internet. Also refers to the documents produced by this organization. These are also called Internet Drafts. They are then called RFCs when they are no longer in draft status. *See RFC.*

IIJ

Internet Initiative Japan.

IKIS

Interactive Kanji Information System. The Japanese character set and encoding developed by Nippon Data General.

IM

See input method.

IME

Input Method Editor.

Inline conversion

インライン変換 (*inrain henkan*) in Japanese. The ability to handle Japanese input at the cursor position rather than in a dedicated window.

Indexing

The process of locating the encoded position of a character, thus providing access to it.

Information interchange

信息交换 (*xìnxī jiāohuàn*) or 資訊交換 (*zīxùn jiāohuàn*) in Chinese, 情報交換 (*jōhō kōkan*) in Japanese, and 정보교환/情報交換 (*jeongbo gyohwan*) in Korean. The process of moving information from one hardware or software configuration to another with no loss of data.

Information processing

信息处理 (*xìnxī chǔlǐ*) or 資訊處理 (*zīxùn chǔlǐ*) in Chinese, 情報処理 (*jōhō shori*) in Japanese, and 정보처리/情報處理 (*jeongbo ceori*) in Korean. The process of manipulating electronically encoded information at different levels. Japanese code and text processing are forms of information processing.

Input method

The software that allows users to input characters from a large character set using a limited number of keys.

Internationalization

The process of designing software (or hardware) in a flexible manner such that it becomes an easy task to adapt or localize to another country with different languages. Internationalization also makes it possible to use more than one writing system on computers. There are two main implementations of internationalization: the locale model and the multilingual model. *See locale model, localization, and multilingual model.*

Internet

The name given to the world-wide network of computers.

IP

Internet Protocol.

IRG

Ideographic Rapporteur Group. Formerly the CJK Joint Research Group (CJK-JRG).

Iroha

いろは or 伊呂波 (*iroha*). A Japanese collation sequence based on the same sounds from the 50 Sounds order. *See 50 Sounds order.*

IRV

International Reference Version.

ISO

国際標準化機構 (*kokusai hyōjunka kikō*) in Japanese. International Organization for Standardization.

ISO 639:1988

A standard that establishes two-letter lowercase language codes, used as the first part of a locale designation.

ISO 646:1991

Identical to CJKV-Roman except for some minor locale-specific differences, such as currency symbols. Equivalent to ASCII. *See ASCII and CJKV-Roman.*

ISO 2022:1994

The document that details the escape sequences used for encoding character sets beyond ISO 646:1991 or ASCII. This standard forms the foundation for ISO-2022 and EUC encodings.

ISO-2022-CN

An encoding method, based on techniques described in ISO 2022:1994, for handling a mixture of ASCII, GB 2312-80, and CNS 11643-1992 (Planes 1 and 2). Described in RFC 1922.

ISO-2022-CN-EXT

An encoding method, based on techniques described in ISO 2022:1994, for handling a mixture of ASCII, GB 2312-80, GB/T 12345-90, GB 7589-87, GB/T 13131-9X, GB 7590-87, GB/T 13132-9X, and CNS 11643-1992 (all planes). Described in RFC 1922.

ISO-2022-JP

An encoding method, based on techniques described in ISO 2022:1994, for handling a mixture of ASCII and JIS X 0208:1997. Described in RFC 1468.

ISO-2022-JP-1

An encoding method, based on techniques described in ISO 2022:1994, for handling JIS X 0212-1990. Described in RFC 2237.

ISO-2022-JP-2

An encoding method, based on techniques described in ISO 2022:1994, for handling JIS X 0212-1990 and other character sets, such as GB 2312-80, KS X 1001:1992, and two parts of ISO 8859. Described in RFC 1554.

ISO-2022-KR

An encoding method, based on techniques described in ISO 2022:1994, for handling a mixture of ASCII and KS X 1001:1992. Described in RFC 1557.

ISO 3166-1:1997

A standard that establishes two-letter uppercase country codes, used as the second part of a locale designation.

ISO 6429:1992

A standard that describes the control character range as used in ASCII.

ISO 8859

A standard divided in ten parts that describes extensions to the ASCII character set to handle other European languages.

ISO 8879:1986

The document that describes SGML. *See SGML.*

ISO 9541:1991

A set of three documents that describe the standard digital font format. Based on the Type 1 font format by Adobe Systems.

ISO 10646-1:1993

The document that describes the ISO version of the Unicode character set. ISO 10646-1:1993 specifies fixed-length 16- and 32-bit representations. National analogs of this standard include JIS X 0221-1995 (Japan), GB 13000.1-93 (China), and KS X 1005-1:1995 (Korea).

ISO-IR-165:1992

An extension to the GB 2312-80 character set that combines all other known extensions (specifically, GB 6345.1-86 and GB 8565.2-88). *See GB 2312-80, GB 6345.1-86, and GB 8565.2-88.*

ISO/TR 11941:1996

The first international standard that documents methods for transliterating Korean text using Latin characters.

ISP

Internet Service Provider.

ITC

International Typeface Corporation.

ITRON

Industrial TRON. *See TRON.*

J10N

Abbreviation for Japanization. *See Japanization.*

ja

The two-letter language code for Japanese. Also, "yes" in German.

JAGAT

日本印刷技術協会 (*nihon insatsu gijutsu kyōkai*). Japan Association of Graphic Arts Technology. The association that sponsors FAGAT. *See FAGAT.*

Jaggies

The uneven effect when fixed-size bitmapped fonts are scaled to large sizes and subsequently displayed or printed.

JAIN

Japanese Academic InterNetwork.

Jamo

자모/字母 (*jamo*). Hangul elements. Each jamo is equivalent to a character in an alphabet, either a consonant or vowel.

Japan

日本 (*nihon* or *nippon*). The country in which the Japanese language is spoken.

JAPAN.INF

The name of the (now extremely obsolete) online document on which *Understanding Japanese Information Processing* was based. *See CJK.INF.*

Japanese

日本語 (*nihongo*) in Japanese. The language spoken in Japan.

Japanese justification

See character spanning.

Japanese line wrapping

See line breaking.

Japanese punctuation logic

See line breaking.

Japanization

日本語化 (*nihongoka*). The localization of software to the Japanese market. *See localization.*

Jaso

자소/字素 (*jaso*). *See jamo.*

Java

The most populous island of Indonesia (where my wife is from), and a popular name for coffee. Incidentally, a programming language designed to be truly cross-platform. Salient features include object-oriented–only programming, cross-platform execution, associative arrays, Unicode support, and C-like syntax. Also rumored to be 100 percent secure (but, as all security specialists know, 100 percent security is but a myth). Developed by Sun Microsystems.

JEF

Japanese processing Extended Feature. A character set and encoding developed by Fujitsu. JIS C 6226-1978 is a subset.

Jinmei-yō Kanji

人名用漢字 (*jinmei-yō kanji*). The 285 kanji, above and beyond Jōyō Kanji, specified by the Japanese government as appropriate for use in writing personal names. *See Jōyō Kanji.*

JIS

日本工業規格 (*nihon kōgyō kikaku*). Its symbol is ⓙ. ジス (*jisu*). Japanese Industrial Standard. The name of the standards established by JISC. Also the name of the encoding method used for the JIS X 0208:1997 and JIS X 0212-1990 character set standards. *See JISC.*

JIS78

Short for JIS C 6226-1978. *See JIS C 6226-1978.*

JIS83

Short for JIS X 0208-1983. *See JIS X 0208-1983.*

JIS90

Short for JIS X 0208-1990. Can sometimes be confused with JIS X 0212-1990 in some contexts. *See JIS X 0208-1990.*

JIS97

Short for JIS X 0208:1997. *See JIS X 0208:1997.*

JIS array

JIS配列 (*JIS hairetsu*). The most widely-used Japanese keyboard array. Specified in the document JIS X 6002-1985. Like the QWERTY keyboard array in the West, it is also the most inefficient. Also called Old-JIS array.

JISC

日本工業標準調査会 (*nihon kōgyō hyōjun chōsakai*). Japanese Industrial Standards Committee. The name of the organization that establishes JIS standards.

JISCII

Japanese Industrial Standard Code for Information Interchange. An improper reference to the Japanese character set standards established by JIS. More correctly known as simply JIS. *See JIS.*

JIS C 6220-1976

The original designation of what is now known as JIS X 0201-1997. The name changed on March 1, 1987. *See JIS X 0201-1997.*

JIS C 6225-1979

The original designation of what is now known as JIS X 0207-1979. The name changed on March 1, 1987. *See JIS X 0207-1979.*

JIS C 6226-1978

The first double-byte character set. Developed in 1978 by Japanese Industrial Standards.

Three revisions followed, first in 1983, second in 1990, and the latest in 1997. *See JIS X 0208-1983, JIS X 0208-1990, and JIS X 0208:1997.*

JIS C 6226-1983

The original designation of what is now known as JIS X 0208-1983. The name changed on March 1, 1987. *See JIS X 0208-1983.*

JIS C 6228-1984

The original designation for what is now known as JIS X 0202:1998. The name changed on March 1, 1987. *See JIS X 0202:1998.*

JIS C 6232-1984

The original designation for what is now known as JIS X 9051-1984. The name changed on March 1, 1987. *See JIS X 9051-1984.*

JIS C 6233-1980

The original designation for what is now known as JIS X 6002-1985. The name changed on March 1, 1987. *See JIS X 6002-1985.*

JIS C 6234-1983

The original designation for what is now known as JIS X 9052-1983. The name changed on March 1, 1987. *See JIS X 9052-1983.*

JIS C 6235-1984

The original designation for what is now known as JIS X 6003-1989. The name changed on March 1, 1987. *See JIS X 6003-1989.*

JIS C 6236-1986

The original designation for what is now known as JIS X 6004-1986. The name changed on March 1, 1987. *See JIS X 6004-1986.*

JIS encoding

Usually equivalent to ISO-2022-JP encoding. The most basic Japanese encoding method that uses escape sequences to shift between one- and two-byte modes. A modal encoding method. *See ISO-2022-JP and modal encoding.*

JIS Level 1 kanji

JIS第1水準漢字 (*JIS daiichi suijun kanji*). The name given to the 2,965 characters that constitute the first set of kanji in JIS X 0208:1997. Ordered by reading (usually ON reading). *See JIS X 0208:1997.*

JIS Level 2 kanji

JIS第2水準漢字 (*JIS daini suijun kanji*). The name given to the 3,390 characters that constitute the second set of kanji in JIS X 0208:1997. The 1978 version (JIS C 6226-1978) had 3,384 such kanji, and the 1983 version (JIS X 0208-1983) had 3,388 such kanji. Ordered by radical, then by total number of strokes. *See JIS X 0208:1997.*

JIS Level 3 kanji

JIS第3水準漢字 (*JIS daisan suijun kanji*). The first set of characters enumerated by JIS X 0213:199X. Also, a name sometimes given to the kanji in JIS X 0212-1990—the correct reference to JIS X 0212-1990 is Hojo Kanji. *See Hojo Kanji, JIS X 0212-1990, and JIS X 0213:199X.*

JIS Level 4 kanji

JIS第4水準漢字 (*JIS daisan suijun kanji*). The second set of characters enumerated by JIS X 0213:199X. *See JIS X 0213:199X.*

JIS order

The order in which characters appear in the Japanese character set standards published by JSA.

JIS sorting

A sort done in JIS order. *See JIS order.*

JIS X 0201-1997

The document that describes the JIS-Roman and half-width katakana character sets, along with their encodings.

JIS X 0202:1998

The Japanese version of ISO 2022:1994. *See ISO 2022:1994.*

JIS X 0207-1979

The Japanese version of ISO 6429:1992. *See ISO 6429:1992.*

JIS X 0208-1983

The 1983 edition of the document that describes the Japanese character set standard, and was originally named JIS C 6226-1983. 6,877 characters are enumerated. *See JIS X 0208:1997.*

JIS X 0208-1990

The 1990 version of the document that describes the Japanese character set standard. 6,879 characters are enumerated. *See JIS X 0208:1997.*

JIS X 0208:1997

The 1997 revision to JIS X 0208-1990, with no changes to the number or allocation of characters. *See JIS X 0208-1990.*

JIS X 0212-1990

The document that describes the supplement to the Japanese character set standard. 6,067 characters are enumerated.

JIS X 0213:199X

The document that defines JIS Levels 3 and 4. Not yet published.

JIS X 0221-1995

The Japanese version of ISO 10646-1:1993. Based on Unicode Version 1.1. *See ISO 10646-1:1993.*

JIS X 4051-1995

The document that describes Japanese line layout rules. Originally published in 1993 as JIS X 4051-1993.

JIS X 4061-1996

The standard that sets forth the rules for sorting Japanese text.

JIS X 4062:1998

The standard that establishes an exchange format for Japanese input method conversion dictionaries.

JIS X 4161-1993

The document (part 1 of 4) that describes the standard digital font format. Based on the Type 1 font format by Adobe Systems.

JIS X 4162-1993

The document (part 2 of 4) that describes the standard digital font format. Based on the Type 1 font format by Adobe Systems.

JIS X 4163-1993

The document (part 3 of 4) that describes the standard digital font format. Based on the Type 1 font format by Adobe Systems.

JIS X 4164-1993

The document (part 4 of 4) that describes the standard digital font format. Based on the Type 1 font format by Adobe Systems.

JIS X 6002-1985

The document that spells out the specifications for the JIS keyboard array. *See JIS array.*

JIS X 6003-1989

The document that describes the layout of a kanji tablet, a large input device used to input kanji directly. *See kanji tablet.*

JIS X 6004-1986

The document that describes the New-JIS keyboard array. *See New-JIS array.*

JIS X 9051-1984

The document that illustrates the 16-by-16 dot-matrix patterns for the characters specified in JIS X 0208-1983. *See JIS X 0208-1983.*

JIS X 9052-1983

The document that illustrates the 24-by-24 dot-matrix patterns for the characters specified in JIS X 0208-1983. *See JIS X 0208-1983.*

JIS-Roman

The Japanese equivalent of ASCII.

JIS7

A variation of ISO-2022-JP encoding that encodes half-width katakana using seven bits. *See ISO-2022-JP encoding.*

JIS8

A variation of ISO-2022-JP encoding that encodes half-width katakana using eight bits. *See ISO-2022-JP encoding.*

JLE

Japanese Language Environment. The name of Sun's extension that provides a Japanese environment.

JLS

Japanese Language System. The Japanese extensions for SGI's Irix operating system.

Johab

조합/組合 (*johab*). Means "combining" in Korean. The name of a Korean encoding method that represents each hangul as a group of three five-bit–encoded jamo. Sometimes considered the opposite of Wansung. *See Wansung.*

Jōyō Kanji

常用漢字 (*jōyō kanji*). The 1,945 kanji designated by the Japanese government as the ones to be used in public documents such as newspapers. Superseded Tōyō Kanji in 1981. *See Tōyō Kanji.*

JP

The two-letter country code for Japan.

JPNIC

Japan Network Information Center.

JSA

日本規格協会 (*nihon kikaku kyōkai*). Japanese Standards Association. The publisher of the JIS standards.

JTRON

Java on Industrial TRON. *See TRON.*

JUNET

Japan Unix Network. The original designation for the Internet in Japan. *See JP.*

K

Kilobyte. 1,024 bytes.

Kai

楷 (*kǎi*) or 楷体 (*kǎitǐ*). The Chinese script typeface style.

Kana

仮名 (*kana*). The term that collectively refers to hiragana and katakana. *See hiragana and katakana.*

Kana-to-kanji conversion

仮名漢字変換 (*kana kanji henkan*). The process of converting kana input into a mixture of kana and kanji characters. The most common method of inputting Japanese text.

Kanji

漢字 (*kanji*). The Chinese characters that the Japanese borrowed from the Chinese. These number in the thousands. *See Chinese character.*

Kanji compound

漢語 (*kango*). A Japanese word consisting of two or more kanji.

Kanji ligature

漢字合字 (*kanji gōji*). A character composed of two or more kanji. Typical examples include ㍻ (平成 *heisei*; the name of a Japanese era) and ㍿ (株式会社 *kabushikigaisha*; meaning "incorporated").

Kanji tablet

A large tablet containing thousands of individual keys, one for each character. This allows for direct kanji input.

Kanji-in

漢字イン (*kanji in*). The name usually given to two-byte character escape sequences as used in ISO-2022-JP encoding. A kanji-in switches the current *n*-byte-per-character mode into two-byte mode.

Kanji-out

漢字アウト (*kanji auto*). The name usually given to one-byte character escape sequences as used in JIS encoding. A kanji-out switches the current *n*-byte-per-character mode into one-byte mode.

KanjiTalk

漢字Talk (*kanji tōku*). The name of the localized Japanese operating system for the Apple Macintosh computer. Now called MacOS-J.

KanjiTalk6 character set

Apple Computer's Japanese character set standard, used on KanjiTalk6 (now called MacOS-J) and earlier. Based largely on JIS X 0208-1983 plus NEC Row 13.

KanjiTalk7 character set

Apple Computer's latest Japanese character set standard. Based largely on JIS X 0208-1990. The KanjiTalk7 character set was introduced with KanjiTalk Version 7.1, and continues to be used today.

Katakana

片仮名 (*katakana*). The square-shaped Japanese syllabary. Usually used for writing recent words of foreign origin. Together with hiragana is collectively called kana. *See also kana and hiragana.*

Katakana ligature

片仮名合字 (*katakana gōji*). A glyph composed of two or more katakana characters. Typical examples include ㍉ (ミリ *miri*, meaning "millimeter"), ㌢ (センチ *senchi*, meaning "centimeter"), ㍍ (メートル *mētoru*, meaning "meter"), ㌕ (キログラム *kiroguramu*, meaning "kilogram"), and ㌖ (キロメートル *kiromētoru*, meaning "kilometer").

KB

Kilobyte. 1,024 bytes. Usually written as K.

KEIS

Kanji processing Extended Information System. The Japanese character set and encoding developed by Hitachi.

KEIS78

The version of KEIS which corresponds to JIS C 6226-1978. *See KEIS.*

KEIS83

The version of KEIS which corresponds to JIS X 0208-1983. *See KEIS.*

Kermit

The green frog on the popular children's television program called *Sesame Street*. A popular file transfer protocol.

Key

The basic text unit that is used to index into a conversion dictionary in order to obtain the names associated with the key. *See also candidate, conversion dictionary, and name.*

KIPS

Korean Information Processing System. One of the original Korean character sets, which enumerated 2,058 hangul and 2,392 hanja.

ko

The two-letter language code for Korean.

Kokuji

国字 (*kokuji*). Japanese-made kanji.

Korea

한국/韓國 (*hangug*). The locale or country where the Korean language is spoken. *See DPRK and ROK.*

Korean

한국어/韓國語 (*hangugeo*). The language spoken in Korea.

KP

The two-letter country code for North Korea (Democratic People's Republic of Korea).

KPS

KP Standard (remember that the two-letter country code for North Korean is KP). *See KP.*

KPS 9566-97

The first North Korean character set standard that includes hangul and hanja.

KR

The two-letter country code for South Korea (Republic of Korea).

KRNIC

Korea Network Information Center.

KS

한국 공업 규격/韓國工業規格 (*hangug gongeob gyugyeog*). Its symbol is ㉿. Korean Standard.

KS C 5601-1992

The original designation of what is now known as KS X 1001:1992. The name changed on August 20, 1997. *See KS X 1001:1992.*

KS C 5619-1982

One of the original Korean character set standards, which enumerated only 51 modern jamo, 1,316 hangul, and 1,672 hanja. Obsoleted by KS X 1001:1992.

KS C 5620-1995

The original designation of what is now known as KS X 1004:1995. The name changed on August 20, 1997. *See KS X 1004:1995.*

KS C 5636-1993

The original designation of what is now known as KS X 1003:1993. The name changed on August 20, 1997. *See KS X 1003:1993.*

KS C 5657-1991

The original designation of what is now known as KS X 1002:1991. The name changed on August 20, 1997. *See KS X 1002:1991.*

KS C 5700-1995

The original designation of what is now known as KS X 1005-1:1995. The name changed on August 20, 1997. *See KS X 1005-1:1995.*

KS C 5715-1992

The original designation of what is now known as KS X 5002:1992. The name changed on August 20, 1997. *See KS X 5002:1992.*

KS C 5861-1992

The original designation of what is now known as KS X 2901:1992. The name changed on August 20, 1997. *See KS X 2901:1992.*

KS-Roman

The Korean equivalent of the ASCII character set and encoding. The name of the document that defines this character set is called KS X 1003:1993.

KS X 1001:1992

The document that describes the basic Korean character set. It enumerates 8,224 characters. Formerly KS C 5601-1992. Previous versions were dated 1987 and 1989.

KS X 1002:1991

The document that describes the extended Korean character set, which enumerates additional symbols, hangul (in two blocks), and hanja. Formerly KS C 5657-1991.

KS X 1003:1993

The document that defines KS-Roman, which is the Korean equivalent of ASCII. Formerly KS C 5636-1993. The original version was dated 1989. *See KS-Roman.*

KS X 1004:1995

The Korean version of ISO 2022:1994. Formerly KS C 5620-1995. *See ISO 2022:1994.*

KS X 1005-1:1995

The Korean version of ISO 10646-1:1993. It differs from ISO 10646-1:1993 in that it is based on Unicode Version 2.0, which includes all 11,172 pre-combined hangul. Formerly KS C 5700-1995.

KS X 2901:1992

The document that describes the EUC encoding for Korean text. Formerly KS C 5861-1992.

KS X 5002:1992

The document that illustrates the basic Korean keyboard array, which is based on hangul elements (jamo). Formerly KS C 5715-1992. Previous versions were dated 1982 and 1985.

Kun reading

訓読み (*kun yomi*). The name given to the native Japanese reading for a kanji.

KUTEN

区点 (*kuten*). Literally means "ward [and] point" (or "row [and] cell"). *See Row-Cell.*

Kyōiku Kanji

教育漢字 (*kyōiku kanji*). The 881 kanji that were once formally taught during the first six years of school in Japan. Replaced by Gakushū Kanji in 1977. *See Gakushū Kanji.*

Kyokasho

教科書 (*kyōkasho*) or 教科書体 (*kyōkashotai*). The Japanese semi-script typeface style.

L10N

Abbreviation for localization. *See localization.*

Latin character

拉丁字母 (*lādīng zìmǔ*) in Chinese, ラテン文字 (*raten moji*) or ローマ字 (*rōmaji*) in Japanese, and 로마자 (*romaja*) in Korean. The 52 upper- and lowercase characters of the Latin alphabet.

LaTeX

A variation of TeX. *See TeX.*

Ligature

A character whose glyph consists of two or more characters fused together. An example is ﬁ, which is the ligature for the letters f and i. *See also kanji ligature and katakana ligature.*

Line breaking

禁則処理 (*kinsoku shori*) in Japanese. The proper handling of CJKV characters at the beginning and at the ends of lines. Punctuation, such as 「, should not terminate a line. Likewise, punctuation, such as 」, should not begin a new line. Also known as line breaking or punctuation logic.

Linux

りぬくす (*rinukusu*) in Japanese. A popular freely-available Unix-compatible operating system that runs on PCs for which a complete set of Japanese extensions exist.

Little endian

The byte order on machines powered by Intel or Vax processors. Pertains only to data represented by more than 8 bits, such as Unicode encoding (16 bits), short (usually 16 bits), integer (usually 32 bits), float (usually 32 bits), long (usually 64 bits), and double (usually 64 bits) types. Multiple-byte encodings, such as Shift-JIS, EUC, and ISO-2022, are not affected by byte order. *See also big endian.*

Locale model

A model of internationalization that predefines many attributes that are language- or country-specific, such as the maximum number of bytes per character, date formats, time formats, currency formats, and so on. The actual attributes are located in a library or locale object file that is loaded when required. *See also internationalization and multilingual model.*

Localization

地域化 (*chiikika*). The process of adapting software (or hardware) such that it conforms to the expectations of a specific country. This often includes rewriting menus and dialogs into the target language, but sometimes involves more complex changes, such as handling special character encoding methods. Other issues to be addressed are time zones, ways of writing dates and times, currency, culture, customs, and others. *See internationalization and Japanization.*

M

Megabyte. Exactly 1,048,576 bytes.

Machine(-aided) translation

機械(支援)翻訳 (*kikai [shien] honyaku*) in Japanese. The process of converting text in one language into another language. Most software to date cannot fully perform this task, and pre- or post-editing by a human is usually required in order to obtain acceptable results.

MacOS

Macintosh Operating System.

Maru

See handakuten.

MB

Megabyte. 1,048,576 bytes.

MBCS

Multiple-Byte Character Set. A character set that contains characters of mixed encoding lengths.

McCune-Reischauer

A Latin-based transliteration system for Korean text that was subsequently adapted by the Korean Ministry of Education in 1984.

MCI Mail

The name of the Internet service offered by MCI, a telecommunications company.

MIME

Multipurpose Internet Mail Extensions.

Mincho

明朝 (*minchō*) or 明朝体 (*minchōtai*). The name commonly given to the Japanese typeface style in which vertical strokes are heavy, and horizontal strokes are thin. This is roughly equivalent to the serif typeface style in Western typography. *See serif.*

Ming

See Mincho.

MITI

通商産業省 (*tsūshō sangyō shō*). Japan's Ministry of International Trade and Industry.

MM

Multiple master or Mincho Medium.

Modal encoding

An encoding method that uses special sequences of one or more characters to signal a change in mode. Mode changes can include shifting between one- and two-byte modes, between different character sets, and between different versions of the same character set. Examples include IBM DBCS-Host, ISO-2022, JEF, KEIS, and UTF-7 encodings. *See also fixed-length and non-modal encoding.*

MOE

Ministry of Education. Written 教育部 (*jiàoyùbù*) in Chinese, 文部省 (*monbushō*) in Japanese, and 교육부/教育部 (*gyoyugbu*) in Korean.

MOR-CODE II

Morisawa's proprietary character set and encoding.

Morisawa

モリサワ (*morisawa*). A major Japanese type foundry. *See also Ryobi and Shaken.*

M-style array

M式配列 (*emu shiki hairetsu*). A keyboard array designed by Masasuke Morita for NEC. It not only specifies an ergonomic keyboard design, but an input methods that allows users to select what part converts to kanji, and what part does not.

MS

Microsoft Corporation.

MS-DOS

Microsoft Disk Operating System.

MS Kanji

Another name for Shift-JIS. *See MS and Shift-JIS.*

MSB

Most Significant Bit. The bit with the most "weight" in an eight-bit sequence (byte). This bit is what distinguishes seven- and eight-bit bytes.

Multilingual model

A model of internationalization that uses a character set whose repertoire contains enough characters to represent most of the world's writing systems. No flipping between character sets is required. See also internationalization and locale model.

Multiple-byte character

A character that is represented by more than one byte.

Myeongjo

명조/明朝 (*myeongjo*) or 명조체/明朝體 (*myeongjoce*). The Korean serif typeface style. Sometimes called myungjo. *See serif.*

Naiji

内字 (*naiji*). The opposite of gaiji, specifically characters that are considered to be standard (on your operating system or environment). *See gaiji, system-defined character, system-specific character, and user-defined character.*

Name

One or more text strings that are associated with a key in a conversion dictionary. These are presented to the user as a list of candidates from which to choose. *See also candidate, conversion dictionary, and key.*

NCS

Non-coded Character Set (such as Japan's Jōyō Kanji; opposite of Coded Character Set). *See Non-coded Character Set.*

NEC

日本電気株式会社 (*nippon denki kabushikigaisha*). Nippon Electronics Corporation.

NEC Kanji

The Japanese character set standard and encoding developed by NEC.

NEC-JIS

See NEC Kanji.

New-JIS

新JIS (*shin JIS*). A common name given to the JIS X 0208-1983 character set standard. Usually refers to the two-byte escape sequence used to designate the JIS X 0208-1990 character set in JIS encoding.

New-JIS array

新JIS配列 (*shin JIS hairetsu*). The Japanese keyboard array that was designed to replace the JIS keyboard array. It departs from the JIS array in that there are two kana characters per key. It failed, and the JIS array is still the most commonly used among the Japanese keyboard arrays.

NIC

Network Information Center.

NIFTY-Serve

A Japanese ISP based in Japan.

Nigori

See dakuten.

NLIO

Native Language Input/Output.

NNTP

Network News Transfer Protocol.

Non-coded Character Set

A character set that was designed *without* the computer in mind. *See Coded Character Set.*

Non-electronic Character Set

See Non-coded Character Set.

Non-kanji

非漢字 (*hikanji*). Characters other than kanji, such as Latin characters, hiragana, katakana, and other symbols.

Non-modal encoding

An encoding method that does not use special sequences of characters to switch between one- and two-byte modes. *See also fixed-length and modal encoding.*

Non-printing character

A character that makes no printable marks on an output device. These include control characters and white space characters, such as a space or tab character.

North Korea

See DPRK.

Notation

A method of representing units. In the world of computers, the most commonly used notations are binary (base two), octal (base eight), decimal (base 10), and hexadecimal (base 16). *See also binary, decimal, hexadecimal, and octal.*

NTT

日本電信電話 (*nippon denshin denwa*). Nippon Telegraph and Telephone.

NTT Kanji

The name of the Japanese character set and encoding as developed by NTT. *See NTT.*

Numeral

数字 (*sūji*). The printed numbers ranging from zero through nine.

OASYS

Office Automation SYStem. The personal word processor series developed by Fujitsu.

OCR

光学的文字認識 (*kōgakuteki moji ninshiki*) in Japanese. Optical Character Recognition. A device that can scan, recognize, and convert printed shapes into meaningful units, such as characters.

Octal

八进制/八進制 (*bājìnzhì*) in Chinese, 八進法 (*hasshinhō*) in Japanese, and 팔진법/八進法 (*paljinbeob*) in Korean. Base eight. A numeric notation that uses eight possible values, ranging from 0 to 7.

Octet

An array of eight bits represented as a single unit (a byte). *See byte.*

Old-JIS

旧JIS (*kyū JIS*). A common name given to the JIS C 6226-1978 character set standard. *See JIS C 6226-1978.*

Old-JIS array

See JIS array.

On reading

音読み (*on yomi*). The Japanese name given to the approximated Chinese reading for a kanji.

OpenType

An outline font format jointly developed by Adobe Systems and Microsoft that equally supports PostScript and TrueType outlines.

Orthography

正書法 (*seishohō*) in Japanese. A linguistic term that refers to the writing system of a language.

OS

Operating System. The software that drives the hardware associated with a computer system.

OSF

Open Software Foundation.

OTF

OpenType Font. The filename extension used for OpenType fonts.

Outline font

A font whose characters are described mathematically in terms of lines and curves. Outline fonts are often referred to as scalable fonts, because they can be scan converted on demand to bitmaps of any desired size and orientation.

Parametric font

A font whose shape is described as a series of vectors. This type of font format has scalable properties, but is not as high of quality as outline fonts. *See also bitmapped and outline font.*

Particle

助詞 (*joshi*) in Japanese. Grammatical markers used in the Japanese language. They are equivalent to prepositions in English, but unlike English, they come after the noun or phrase they modify. Particles are sometimes called postpositions.

PC

パソコン (*pasokon*) in Japanese. Personal Computer. Usually refers to machines that run MS-DOS. Also, Purity Control.

PC-VAN

Personal Computer Value Added Network. A Japanese ISP based in Japan.

PCF

Portable Compiled Format. A binary representation of BDF files for use under the X Window System. *See BDF.*

PDF

Portable Document Format. The document format that is generated by Adobe Acrobat technology.

Pen input

ペン入力 (*pen nyūryoku*) in Japanese. An input method that allows the user to enter text and commands with a pen (or stylus) onto a tablet. OCR technology is often used in the process of interpreting hand-written text.

Perl

Pathologically Eclectic Rubbish Lister or Practical Extraction and Report Language (depending on your mood). An ideal programming language for performing complex text processing tasks. Salient features include no built-in limits, regular expressions, associative arrays, and C-like syntax. Developed by Larry Wall.

Phonetic ideograph

形声文字/形聲文字 (*xíngshēng wénzì*) in Chinese, 形声文字 (*keisei moji*) in Japanese, and 형성문자/形聲文字 (*hyeongseong munja*) in Korean. A Chinese character constructed from at least two radical-like elements. One element is used for its reading, and the other used for its meaning. Together they form a unique character.

Pictograph

象形文字 (*xiàngxíng wénzì*) in Chinese, 象形文字 (*shōkei moji*) in Japanese, and 상형문자/象形文字 (*sanghyeong munja*) in Korean. A character whose shape reflects the shape of the object which it represents. An example of such a Chinese character is 山, which means "mountain."

Pinyin

拼音 (*pīnyīn*). The most common Latin-based transliteration method for Chinese text.

Plan 9

The name of a classic science fiction film. Also, the multilingual Unix operating system under development at AT&T Bell Laboratories.

PM

Post Meridian or PageMaker.

Point

磅 (*bàng*) in Chinese, ポイント (*pointo*) in Japanese, and 포인트 (*pointeu*) in Korean. A unit of measure used in typography. An American point is exactly $1/_{72.28915663}$ of an inch. PostScript, on the other hand, rounds this figure to $1/_{72}$ of an inch.

POSIX

Portable Operating System Interface.

Postposition

See particle.

PostScript

ポストスクリプト (*posutosukuriputo*) in Japanese. The page description language developed by Adobe Systems.

PPP

Point-to-Point Protocol.

PRC

中华人民共和国 (*zhōnghuá rénmín gònghé guó*). People's Republic of China. The official name for China.

Printable character

A character that makes some sort of mark on an output devices. Also called a graphic character.

Pseudo ruby

擬似ルビ (*giji rubi*) in Japanese. Small characters, usually kanji or Latin characters, that appear above normal-size characters, and serve to annotate them with a reading or meaning. Similar to ruby characters. *See also ruby.*

PUA

Private Use Area. Another way to refer to the encoding regions for user-defined characters. *See user-defined character.*

Push-in line breaking

See wrap-up line breaking.

Push-out line breaking

See wrap-down line breaking.

Q

级数/級數 *jíshù* in Chinese, 級数 (*kyūsū*) in Japanese, and 급수/級數 (*geubsu*) in Korean. Unit of typographic measurement equivalent to 0.25mm. Its correct usage is strictly for type size. Also, the name of an omnipotent being from the contemporary *Star Trek* series

Quadratic spline curve

The type of curve used for representing character shape contours in the TrueType font format.

Quốc ngữ

國語. The Latin-based writing system used in contemporary Vietnam.

Quoted-Printable

A method of preserving non-ASCII characters to ensure reliable transmission.

QWERTY array

The most common keyboard in use today. Its name comes from the first six keys that have 26 letters of the Latin alphabet imprinted on them.

Radical

部首 (*bùshǒu*) in Chinese, 部首 (*bushu*) in Japanese, and 부수/部首 (*busu*) in Korean. The building blocks of Chinese characters of which the most common set contains 214 radicals. Many CJKV character set standards arrange Chinese characters by radical. For example, the hanzi of GB 2312-80 Level 2 are arranged by radical. Radicals are subcomposed of strokes. *See strokes.*

RAM

Random Access Memory.

Regex

Short for regular expression. *See regular expression.*

Regexp

Short for regular expression. *See regular expression.*

Regular expression

"Have a nice day" is one example. Also, a powerful mechanism for searching, ripping apart, shredding, or otherwise manipulating text (or sometimes, binary) data. Software tools such as *awk*, Emacs, Perl, *sed*, and *vi* include regular expression engines. JPerl, Mule, and lookup provide Japanese-capable regular expression engines.

RFC

Request For Comments. The name given to the now more than 2,000 documents that describe the inner workings of the Internet.

RKSJ

Roman, (half-width) Katakana, and Shift-JIS. An encoding used by PostScript Japanese fonts.

ROC

中華民國 (*zhōnghuá mínguó*). Republic of China. The official name for Taiwan.

ROK

대한민국/大韓民國 (*daehan mingug*). Republic of Korea. The official name for South Korea.

ROM

Read Only Memory.

Roman character

See Latin character.

Row

区 (*qū*) in Chinese, 区 (*ku*) in Japanese, and 행/行 (*haeng*) in Korean. In a two-byte encoding, row refers to the first byte. In a two-dimensional matrix, row represents the values along the vertical axis. *See cell and Row-Cell.*

Row-Cell

区位 (*qūwèi*) in Chinese, 区点 (*kuten*) in Japanese, and 행렬/行列 (*haengryeol*) in Korean. A machine-independent way of indexing characters in most CJKV character set standards (and the vendor character sets derived from them).

Ruby

ルビ (*rubi*). Small characters, usually kana, that appear above normal size characters, and serve annotate them with a reading or meaning. Some folks prefer to spell it "rubi," but that conflicts with its true history.

Ryobi

リョービ (*ryōbi*). A major Japanese type foundry. *See also Morisawa and Shaken.*

Sangyong Hanja

The set of 1,800 hanja that all students in Korea are expected to learn.

Sans serif

French for without serifs. Sans serif characters do not have little feet on them. Helvetica (this is Helvetica) is a widely used sans serif typeface. *See also serif.*

SBCS

Single-Byte Character Set.

SBCS-Host

A single-byte character set that is encoded according to EBCDIC. *See EBCDIC.*

SBCS-PC

A single-byte character set that is encoded according to ASCII. *See ASCII.*

SDC

See system-defined character.

SDK

Software Developer's Kit. A collection of software and documents that are designed to aid other developers to write software that works well with a particular technology.

Serif

Characters that have little feet to act as guide marks. Derives all the way from days when letters were carved in stone—the serifs were added to provide even height, and the overall style improves legibility. Garamond, which is used as the standard textface in this book, is an example of a serif typeface. *See also sans serif.*

SG

The two-letter country code for Singapore.

SGI

Silicon Graphics Incorporated.

SGML

Standard Generalized Markup Language. Defined in ISO 8879:1986.

Shaken

写研 (*shaken*). A major Japanese type foundry. *See also Morisawa and Ryobi.*

Shift-JIS

The most common encoding method used on Japanese PCs. So named from how the first byte range of two-byte characters shifts around the encoding range of single-byte half-width katakana. Also called MS Kanji.

Shifting characters

A sequence of one or more characters that are often used to shift between one- and two-byte modes. *See also escape sequence.*

SI

Shift-In. A control character that often serves as a shifting character in ISO-2022 encoding

Simple ideograph

指事文字 (*zhǐshì wénzì*) in Chinese, 指事文字 (*shiji moji*) in Japanese, and 지사문자/指事文字 (*jisa munja*) in Korean. A Chinese character that represents an abstract shape. Examples include characters such as 上 ("up") and 下 ("down").

Simplified Chinese character

An alternate version of a traditional Chinese character, modified to be written with fewer strokes. *See traditional Chinese character.*

Singapore

新加坡 (*xīnjiāpō*). A Chinese locale, located in Southeast Asia, where simplified hanzi are used.

SJIS

An abbreviation for Shift-JIS. *See Shift-JIS.*

SJS

Another abbreviation for Shift-JIS. *See Shift-JIS.*

SK72

The older of Shaken's proprietary character sets.

SK78

The newer of Shaken's proprietary character sets.

SKIP

System of Kanji Indexing by Patterns. A method for indexing kanji that divides it geometrically thus allowing you to find any kanji in less than 30 seconds. It is found in a kanji dictionary written by Jack Halpern, and implemented in Jim Breen's KANJIDIC and KANJD212.

SMI

エスエムアイ (*esu emu ai*). Sumitomo Metal Industries (住友金属工業 *sumitomo kinzoku kōgyō*). The developer of SMI EDICOLOR.

SMTP

Simple Mail Transfer Protocol.

SNF

Server Natural Format. A binary representation of BDF files for use under the X Window System. *See BDF.*

SO

Shift-Out. A control character that often serves as a shifting character in ISO-2022 encoding.

Solaris

The name of Sun Microsystems' operating system.

Song

宋 (*sòng*) or 宋体 (*sòngtǐ*). The Chinese serif typeface style. Also, a musical score. *See serif.*

Sony

Standard Oil of New York. Er, uh, hmm, I mean a famous Japanese electronics company.

South Korea

See ROK.

SS2

Single Shift 2. A special character or character sequence (0x8E in EUC, and 0x1B4E in ISO-2022) used as a prefix to characters beyond the standard character set (invokes code set 2 in EUC, and extended character sets in ISO-2022).

SS3

Single Shift 3. A special character or character sequence (0x8F in EUC, and 0x1B4F in ISO-2022) used as a prefix to characters beyond the standard character set (invokes code set 3 in EUC, and extended character sets in ISO-2022).

SSC

See system-specific character.

STAMEQ

Standards, Metrology and Quality Control. An English translation of TCVN. *See TCVN.*

Stroke

画/畫 (*huà*) in Chinese, 画 (*kaku*) in Japanese, and 획/畫 (*hoeg*) in Korean. The basic building blocks of radicals and kanji. A single stroke is defined as an element drawn while a writing utensil is still on the paper. These usually are straight lines, curves, and some angles.

Supplemental kanji

See hojo kanji.

Syllabary

A writing system whose characters are composed of syllables. Hiragana and katakana are examples of syllabaries. *See syllable.*

Syllable

A sound sequence consisting of a consonant plus vowel.

Synchronic

A linguistic term that is used to refer to linguistic changes that exist during the same period.

System-defined character

A character that is considered standard across operating systems.

System-specific character

A character that, while considered standard on a given operating system, is specific to that operating system. That is, it may not be generally available across all operating systems.

T1C

Adobe Type 1 Coprocessor. A computer chip designed by Adobe Systems that significantly reduces the time necessary to render characters to the screen or printer.

Table-driven conversion

A type of conversion that uses mapping tables for converting objects. *See also algorithmic conversion.*

Taiwan

臺灣 (*táiwān*). One of the Chinese locales in which traditional forms of hanzi are still used. *See ROC.*

TBCS

Triple-Byte Character Set. A character set whose characters are encoded with three bytes.

TBCS-EUC

A Triple-Byte Character Set encoded according to the specification of EUC.

TCVN

Tiêu Chuẩn Việt Nam.

TCVN 5712:1993

A vietnamese standard that defines various encodings for the Latin-based Quốc ngữ writing system.

TCVN 5773:1993

A Vietnamese character set standard that enumerates 2,357 chữ Nôm characters.

TCVN 6056:1995

A Vietnamese character set standard that enumerates 3,311 chữ Hán characters.

TES

See Transfer Encoding Syntax.

TEX

A popular typesetting language developed by Donald Knuth for which CJKV-capable versions exist.

Thumb-shift array

親指シフト配列 (*oyayubi shifuto hairetsu*). The Japanese keyboard array developed by Fujitsu.

TIMTOWTDI

There Is More Than One Way To Do It. The Perl slogan.

TISN

Todai (東大 *tōdai*; University of Tokyo) International Science Network.

Tōyō Kanji

当用漢字 (*tōyō kanji*). The 1,850 kanji designated by the Japanese government as the ones to be used in public documents such as newspapers. Superseded by Jōyō Kanji in 1981. *See Jōyō Kanji.*

Traditional Chinese character

Refers to the original, sometimes complex, shapes of Chinese characters. The opposite of simplified Chinese character. 國 is an example of a traditional Chinese character. Its simplified counterpart, as used in Japan and China, is 国. Korea and Taiwan use traditional Chinese characters. Japan and China, in general, use simplified forms. *See simplified Chinese character.*

Transfer Encoding Syntax

A transformation applied to an encoding to allow it to be safely transmitted. Examples include Base64, BinHex, Quoted-Printable, and uuencoding.

TRON

トロン (*toron*). The Real-time Operating system Nucleus. An operating system, conceived by Ken Sakamura (坂村健 *sakamura ken*), to address the interface between humans and computers. Variations include BTRON (Business TRON), CTRON (Communication and Central TRON), ITRON (Industrial TRON), and JTRON (Java on ITRON).

TrueType

An outline font format developed by Apple Computer and Microsoft.

TTF

TrueType Font. The filename extension used for TrueType fonts.

TTC

TrueType Collection. The filename extension used for TrueType Collections.

TW

The two-letter country code for Taiwan.

TWICS

Two-way Information Communication System. The name of an ISP based in Japan.

TWNIC

Taiwan Network Information Center.

Two-stroke input method

2ストローク入力方式 (*ni sutorōku nyūryoku hōshiki*). A Japanese input method that associates two key-strokes per kanji. In the case of input by association, the two keys have some sort of relationship to the kanji, usually by reading or meaning. There is also input by unassociation, which arbitrarily associates two key-strokes per kanji.

Type 0 font

Adobe Systems' composite font format. A Type 0 font contains other fonts in a hierarchical fashion, providing access to huge character sets, such as those used in Japan. A CIDFont is a Type 0 that has FMapType 9.

Type 1 font

Adobe Systems' format for describing outlines or scalable fonts. Type 1 fonts use a very special and limited subset of PostScript, optimized for compactness and speed. *See also ISO 9541:1991.*

Type 3 font

A user-defined PostScript font. Type 3 fonts can use all of the PostScript language to obtain effects (gray scale, for instance) not available to Type 1 fonts.

Type 4 font

Adobe Systems' proprietary font format. Provides no benefits over Type 1 in PostScript Level 2 and beyond.

Type 5 font

Adobe Systems' ROM-based font format.

Type 9 font

A CIDFont that uses Type 1 glyph procedures. Equivalent to CIDFontType 0.

Type 10 font

A CIDFont that uses PostScript "BuildGlyph" procedures. Equivalent to CIDFontType 1.

Type 11 font

A CIDFont that uses TrueType glyph procedures. Equivalent to CIDFontType 2.

Type 42 font

Adobe Systems' font format that provides a wrapper for a TrueType font. This allows a TrueType font to be used in much the same way as a Type 1 font. *See Type 1 font.*

Typeface

A distinctive design for a set of visually related symbols. Examples include Helvetica, Garamond, Ryumin-Light, and Heisei Mincho W3.

UCS

Universal Character Set (ISO 10646-1:1993).

UCS-2

The fixed-length two-byte (16-bit) encoding method for ISO 10646-1:1993.

UCS-4

The fixed-length four-byte (31-bit) encoding method for ISO 10646-1:1993.

UDC

See user-defined character.

UHC

See Unified Hangul Code.

UI

Unix International or User Interface.

UJIS

Short for Unixized JIS, and is identical to EUC-JP. See EUC-JP.

Unicode

The name of the international 16-bit character set and encoding developed by the members of the Unicode Consortium.

Unified Hangul Code

UHC. A character set equivalent to that of Johab, but whose encoding is backward-compatible with EUC-KR. *See EUC-KR and Johab.*

Unix

The name of the operating system that runs on most workstations.

URL

Uniform Resource Locator. The standard by which the locations of files on the Internet are described.

US

The two-letter country code for The United States of America.

User-defined character

A character that is added to a character set by an end user. Sometimes confused with a character that is not considered standard on most operating systems or environments. *See system-specific character.*

USLP

Unix System Laboratories Pacific.

UTF

UCS (Universal Character Set) Transformation Format. Obsolete. A method of encoding 16- or 32-bit encodings such that they passed as a stream of ASCII bytes. Once called UTF-1. It is now a generic way to refer to the three current UTFs: UTF-7, UTF-8, and UTF-16. *See UTF-7, UTF-8, and UTF-16.*

UTF-2

Obsolete. A version of UTF defined by AT&T Bell Labs (Plan 9) and X/Open for encoding Unicode text as a stream of ASCII bytes. Also called FSS-UTF (File System Safe UTF), and now referred to as UTF-8. *See UTF-8. See also Plan 9.*

UTF-7

A variation of Base64 encoding that transforms Unicode encodings—UCS-2, UCS-4, and UTF-16—into a form that can be safely transmitted through 7-bit pathways. Most ASCII characters represent themselves under this encoding.

UTF-8

A variable-length one- through six-byte encoding that is the result of algorithmically transforming UCS-2, UCS-4, or UTF-16 encoding into a form that is more suitable for some environments. It is considered an eight-bit encoding. Once called UTF-2 and FFS-UTF (File System Safe UTF).

UTF-16

The encoding method for Unicode Version 2.0. Its "surrogates" area makes this encoding different from UCS-2 encoding—this area encodes an additional 16 planes of UCS-4 by using combinations of two 16-bit code points. *See UCS-2.*

UUCP

Unix-to-Unix Copy.

Uudecode

A Unix utility for decoding a file encoded by uuencode. *See uuencode.*

Uuencode

A Unix utility for encoding a file (usually a binary file) such that it can pass through networks with only seven-bit paths. Decoding is performed by uudecode. *See uudecode.*

Vector font

See parametric font.

Vendor-defined character

See gaiji.

vi

The two-letter language code for Vietnamese. Also, the name of a popular Unix-based text editor.

Vietnam

Việt Nam. Also written as two words: Viet Nam. The locale where the Quốc ngữ (Latin characters), chữ Hán (Chinese characters), and chữ Nôm (Vietnamese-made Chinese characters) writing systems are used.

VIQR

VIetnamese Quoted-Readable specification.

VISCII

Vietnamese Standard Code for Information Interchange.

VN

The two-letter country code for Vietnam.

VSCII

Vietnamese Standard Code for Information Interchange.

Voice input

音声入力 (*onsei nyūryoku*) in Japanese. An input method that is driven by the human voice. Such devices must usually be trained to understand the user's voice.

Wade-Giles

韋氏 (*wéishì*). Another Latin-based transliteration system for Chinese text.

Wansung

완성/完成 (*wanseong*). Means "precomposing" in Korean. Another name for EUC-KR encoding in which each hangul is encoded as a single entity. Considered to be the opposite of Johab. *See Johab.*

Ward

See row.

Whitespace

Characters that produce empty space, such as the space character or the tab character.

Wide character

A character that consists of a larger than normal byte. A byte typically consists of seven or eight bits. A character represented by 16 bits is considered a wide character.

Word processor

ワードプロセッサ (*wādopurosessa*) or ワープロ (*wāpuro*) in Japanese. A text processing tool that manipulates text in such a way that it is possible to include multiple fonts in a single document. Sufficient formatting capabilities are also quite common.

Wrap-down line breaking

追い出し禁則処理 (*oidashi kinsoku shori*) in Japanese. A method of moving characters down to the next line in order to prevent prohibited characters for ending or beginning a line. Also known as push-out line wrapping. *See also line breaking and wrap-up line breaking.*

Wrap-up line breaking

追い込み禁則処理 (*oikomi kinsoku shori*) in Japanese. A method of moving characters up to the previous line in order to prevent prohibited characters for ending or beginning a line. Also known as push-in line wrapping. *See also line breaking and wrap-down line breaking.*

Wubi

五笔 (*wǔbǐ*), short for 五笔输入法 (*wǔbǐ shūrùfǎ*). A popular stroke-based Chinese input method.

WWW

World Wide Web or simply "web." Those with slow modems or slow Internet connections sometimes call it World Wide Wait.

WYBIWYG
: What You Buy Is What You Get.

WYSIWYG
: What You See Is What You Get.

X-Modem
: A popular file transfer protocol.

X Window System
: The name of a very popular Unix windowing system developed at MIT (Massachusetts Institute of Technology). The latest release is called X11R6.

XCCS
: Xerox Character Code Standard.

XKP
: Extended Kanji Processing. An initiative for handling external characters in the context of Windows NT.

XML
: Extensible Markup Language. An implementation of SGML for the Web, and is likely to eventually replace HTML. *See HTML and SGML.*

XPG4
: X/Open Portability Guide issue 4.

Y-Modem
: A popular file transfer protocol.

YMMV
: Your Mileage May Vary.

Z-Modem
: A popular file transfer protocol.

Zenkaku
: 全角 (*zenkaku*). Analogous to full-width. *See full-width.*

zh
: The two-letter language code for Chinese.

Zhuyin
: 注音 (*zhùyīn*), short for 注音符号 (*zhùyīn fúhào*). The name of the symbols used to represent standard readings in Chinese. Also known as *bopomofo* (named from its first four sounds: *b*, *p*, *m*, and *f*).

Bibliography

This bibliography provides a listing of some potentially useful reference works. They are separated into the following categories: books (subcategorized into languages), character dictionaries, standards, periodicals, papers and articles, and RFCs. While all of these references are all useful to some extent, it is by no means necessary to obtain them all (in fact, some may be out of print). I have included ISBNs, ISSNs, and part numbers so that ordering these references becomes an easier (or, at least, somewhat possible) task.

Books

The following listings have been broken down into sections for different languages. This will give you a better idea of whether such references would be of value to you (and whether you'll be able to read them!).

Books in English

Adobe Systems Incorporated. *Adobe Type 1 Font Format.* Version 1.1. Addison-Wesley. 1990. ISBN 0-201-57044-0.

———. *PostScript Language Tutorial and Cookbook.* Addison-Wesley. 1985. ISBN 0-201-10179-3.

———. *PostScript Language Program Design.* Addison-Wesley. 1988. ISBN 0-201-14396-8.

———. *PostScript Language Reference Manual.* Second Edition. Addison-Wesley. 1990. ISBN 0-201-18127-4.

American Electronics Association. *Software Partners: The Directory of Japanese Software Distributors.* 1992.

Ames, Patrick. *Beyond Paper: the official guide to Adobe Acrobat.* Adobe Press. 1993. ISBN 1-56830-050-6.

Apple Computer. *Guide to Macintosh Software Localization*. Addison-Wesley. 1992. ISBN 0-201-60856-1.

———. *Inside Macintosh: QuickDraw GX Typography*. Addison-Wesley. 1994. ISBN 0-201-40679-9.

Be Development Team, The. *Be Advanced Topics*. O'Reilly & Associates, Incorporated. 1998. ISBN 1-56592-396-0.

———. *Be Developer's Guide*. O'Reilly & Associates, Incorporated. 1997. ISBN 1-56592-287-5.

Bienz, Tim & Richard Cohen. *Portable Document Format Reference Manual*. Addison-Wesley. 1993. ISBN 0-201-62628-4.

Branagan, Linda & Michael Sierra. *The Frame Handbook*. O'Reilly & Associates, Incorporated. 1994. ISBN 1-56592-009-0.

Bringhurst, Robert. *The Elements of Typographic Style*. Second Edition. Hartley & Marks. 1996. ISBN 0-88179-132-6 (paper) or ISBN 0-88179-133-4 (cloth).

Cameron, Debra & Bill Rosenblatt. *Learning GNU Emacs*. Second Edition. O'Reilly & Associates, Incorporated. 1996. ISBN 1-56592-152-6.

Christiansen, Tom & Nathan Torkington. *Perl Cookbook*. O'Reilly & Associates, Incorporated. 1998. ISBN 1-56592-243-3.

Clews, John. *Language Automation Worldwide: The Development of Character Set Standards*. Sesame Computer Projects. 1988. ISBN 1-870095-01-4.

Conner, Kiersten & Ed Krol. *The Whole Internet: The Next Generation*. O'Reilly & Associates, Incorporated. 1999. ISBN 1-56592-428-2.

Connolly, Dan, editor. *XML: Principles, Tools, and Techniques. World Wide Web Journal*, Volume 2, Number 4, Winter 1997. O'Reilly & Associates, Incorporated. 1997. ISBN 1-56592-349-9.

Daniels, Peter T. & William Bright, editors. *The World's Writing Systems*. Oxford Univerisyt Press. 1996. ISBN 0-19-507993-0.

Daub, Edward E. et al. *Basic Technical Japanese*. The University of Wisconsin Press. 1990. ISBN 0-299-12730-3.

———. *Comprehending Technical Japanese*. The University of Wisconsin Press. 1975. ISBN 0-299-06680-0.

Flanagan, David. *Java in a Nutshell*. Second Edition. O'Reilly & Associates, Incorporated. 1997. ISBN 1-56592-262-X.

Frey, Donnalyn & Rick Adams. *!%@:: A Directory of Electronic Mail Addressing & Networks*. Fourth Edition. O'Reilly & Associates, Incorporated. 1994. ISBN 1-56592-046-5.

Friedl, Jeffrey E.F. *Mastering Regular Expressions*. O'Reilly & Associates, Incorporated. 1997. ISBN 1-56592-257-3.

Gottlieb, Nanette. *Kanji Politics: Language Policy and Japanese Script*. Kegan Paul International. 1995. ISBN 0-7103-0512-5.

Gundavaram, Shishir. *CGI Programming on the World Wide Web*. O'Reilly & Associates, Incorporated. 1996. ISBN 1-56592-168-2.

Heisig, James. *Remembering the Kanji I: A Complete Course on How Not to Forget the Meaning and Writing of Japanese Characters.* Third Edition. Japan Publications Trading Company. 1985. ISBN 0-87040-739-2.

———. *Remembering the Kanji II: A Systematic Guide to Reading Japanese Characters.* Japan Publications Trading Company. 1987. ISBN 0-87040-748-1.

Heisig, James with Tanya Sienko. *Remembering the Kanji III: Writing and Reading Japanese Characters for Upper-Level Proficiency.* Japan Publications Trading Company. 1994. ISBN 0-87040-931-X.

Hekman, Jessica P. et al. *Linux in a Nutshell.* O'Reilly & Associates, Incorporated. 1997. ISBN 1-56592-167-4.

Henshall, Kenneth. *A Guide to Remembering Japanese Characters.* Charles E. Tuttle Company. 1995. ISBN 0-8048-2038-4.

Hewlett-Packard. *Japanese Input Method Guide for NLIO 8.0.* 1991. Hewlett-Packard part number B2200-90003.

———. *Native Language I/O Access User's Guide.* 1991. Hewlett-Packard part number B2200-90001 (Japanese) and B2200-90005 (English).

———. *Native Language I/O System Administrator's Guide.* 1991. Hewlett-Packard part number B2200-90002 (Japanese) and B2200-90006 (Japanese).

———. *Kanji Code Book.* 1989. Hewlett-Packard part number 98861-90003.

Huang, Jack & Timothy Huang. *An Introduction to Chinese, Japanese and Korean Computing.* World Scientific Publishing. 1989. ISBN 9971-50-664-5.

IBM Corporation. *Character Data Representation Architecture Reference and Registry.* 1995. IBM part number SC09-2190-00.

———. *AIX Version 3.2 for RISC System/6000: Internationalization of AIX Software—A Programmer's Guide.* Second Edition. 1992. IBM part number SC23-2431.

———. *DBCS Design Guide for DOS/V and MS Windows Programming.* IBM DBCS Technical Coordination Office. 1992. IBM part number DTC 0-0012-0.

Jelliffe, Rick. *The XML & SGML Cookbook: Recipes for Structured Information.* Prentice-Hall. 1998. ISBN 0-13-614223-0.

Kano, Nadine. *Developing International Software for Windows 95 and Windows NT.* Microsoft Press. 1995. ISBN 1-55615-840-8.

Kaplan, Jerry. *Startup: A Silicon Valley Adventure.* Penguin Books. 1994. ISBN 0-14-025731-4.

Karow, Peter. *Typeface Statistics.* URW. 1993. ISBN 3-926515-08-2.

Kissell, Joe. *The Nisus Way.* MIS:Press. 1996. ISBN 1-55828-455-9.

Lamb, Linda & Arnold Robbins. *Learning the vi Editor.* Sixth Edition. O'Reilly & Associates, Incorporated. 1998. ISBN 1-56592-426-6.

Lunde, Ken. *Prescriptive Kanji Simplification.* PhD Dissertation. University of Wisconsin-Madison. 1994. University Microfilms International order number 9419580.

———. *Understanding Japanese Information Processing.* O'Reilly & Associates, Incorporated. 1993. ISBN 1-56592-043-0. *Made obsolete by this book.*

Luong, Tuoc V. et al. *Internationalization: Developing Software for Global Markets.* John Wiley & Sons, Incorporated. 1995. ISBN 0-471-07661-9.

Lutz, Mark. *Programming Python.* O'Reilly & Associates, Incorporated. 1996. ISBN 1-56592-197-6.

Madell, Tom et al. *Developing and Localizing International Software.* Prentice-Hall. 1994. ISBN 0-13-300674-3.

McFarland, Thomas. *X Windows on the World: Developing Internationalized Software with X, Motif, and CDE.* Prentice-Hall. 1996. ISBN 0-13-359787-3.

McGilton, Henry & Mary Campione. *PostScript by Example.* Addison-Wesley. 1992. ISBN 0-201-63228-4.

Moye, Stephen. *Fontographer: Type by Design.* MIS:Press. 1995. ISBN 1-55828-447-8.

Musciano, Chuck & Bill Kennedy. *HTML: The Definitive Guide.* Third Edition. O'Reilly & Associates, Incorporated. 1998. ISBN 1-56592-492-4.

O'Donnell, Sandra Martin. *Programming for the World: A Guide to Internationalization.* Prentice-Hall. 1994. ISBN 0-13-722190-8.

O'Quinn, Donnie. *QuarkXPress in a Nutshell.* O'Reilly & Associates, Incorporated. 1998. ISBN 1-56592-399-5.

O'Quinn, Donnie & Matt LeClair. *Photoshop in a Nutshell.* O'Reilly & Associates, Incorporated. 1997. ISBN 1-56592-313-8.

O'Reilly, Tim & Troy Mott. *Windows 95 in a Nutshell.* O'Reilly & Associates, Incorporated. 1998. ISBN 1-56592-316-2.

———. *Windows 98 in a Nutshell.* O'Reilly & Associates, Incorporated. 1999. ISBN 1-56592-486-X.

O'Reilly & Associates, Incorporated. *The UNIX CD Bookshelf.* O'Reilly & Associates, Incorporated. 1998. ISBN 1-56592-406-1.

Pearce, Eric. *Windows NT in a Nutshell.* O'Reilly & Associates, Incorporated. 1997. ISBN 1-56592-251-4.

Peek, Jerry et al. *UNIX Power Tools.* Second Edition. O'Reilly & Associates, Incorporated. 1997. ISBN 1-56592-260-3.

Pollack, David, editor. *Soft Landing in Japan: A Market Entry Handbook for U.S. Software Companies.* Version 2.0J. American Electronics Association. 1992.

Quercia, Valerie. *Internet in a Nutshell.* O'Reilly & Associates, Incorporated. 1997. ISBN 1-56592-323-5.

Reid, Glenn. *Thinking in PostScript.* Addison-Wesley. 1990. ISBN 0-201-52372-8.

Sakamura, Ken. *MicroITRON 3.0: An Open and Portable Real-Time Operating System for Embedded Systems—Concept and Specification.* IEEE Computer Society. ISBN 0-8186-7795-3.

Schwartz, Alan. *Managing Mailing Lists.* O'Reilly & Associates, Incorporated. 1998. ISBN 1-56592-259-X.

Schwartz, Randal L. & Tom Christiansen. *Learning Perl*. Second Edition. O'Reilly & Associates, Incorporated. 1997. ISBN 1-56592-284-0.

Searfoss, Glenn. *JIS-Kanji Character Recognition: Featuring the Gaiji Method*. Van Nostrand Reinhold. 1994. ISBN 0-442-01813-4.

Spainhour, Stephen et al. *Perl in a Nutshell*. O'Reilly & Associates, Incorporated. 1998. ISBN 1-56592-286-7.

Spiekermann, Erik & E.M. Ginger. *Stop Stealing Sheep & find out how type works*. Adobe Press. 1993. ISBN 0-672-48543-5.

Stallman, Richard M. *GNU Emacs Manual*. Thirteenth Edition. Free Software Foundation. 1997. ISBN 1-882114-06-X.

Stein, Lincoln. *Official Guide to Programming with CGI.pm: The Standard for Building Web Scripts*. John Wiley & Sons, Incorporated. 1998. ISBN 0-471-24744-8.

Tuthill, Bill & David Smallberg. *Creating Worldwide Software: Solaris International Developer's Guide*. Second Edition. Prentice-Hall. 1997. ISBN 0-13-494493-3.

Unger, J. Marshall. *Literacy and Script Reform in Occupation Japan: Reading Between the Lines*. Oxford University Press. 1996. ISBN 0-19-510166-9.

———. *The Fifth Generation Fallacy: Why Japan Is Betting Its Future on Artificial Intelligence*. Oxford University Press. 1987. ISBN 0-19-504939-X.

Unicode Consortium, The. *The Unicode Standard, Version 2.0*. Addison-Wesley. 1996. ISBN 0-201-48345-9.

Uren, Emmanuel et al. *Software Internationalization and Localization: An Introduction*. Van Nostrand Reinhold. 1993. ISBN 0-442-01498-8.

Vromans, Johan. *Perl 5 Pocket Reference*. Second Edition. O'Reilly & Associates, Incorporated. 1998. ISBN 1-56592-495-9.

Wall, Larry et al. *Programming Perl*. Second Edition. O'Reilly & Associates, Incorporated. 1996. ISBN 1-56592-149-6.

Walsh, Norman. *Making TEX Work*. O'Reilly & Associates, Incorporated. 1994. ISBN 1-56592-051-1.

Welsh, Matt & Lar Kaufman. *Running Linux*. Second Edition. O'Reilly & Associates, Incorporated. 1996. ISBN 1-56592-151-8.

Wong, Clinton. *Web Client Programming in Perl*. O'Reilly & Associates, Incorporated. 1997. ISBN 1-56592-214-X.

Books in Chinese

陈建平.『常用汉字输入法操作速成』. 福建科学技术出版社. 1996. ISBN 7-5335-1043-7.

国家语言文字工作委员会.『简化字总表』. Second Edition. 语文出版社. 1986. ISBN 7-80006-282-1.

国家语言文字工作委员会汉字处.『现代汉语常用字表』. 语文出版社. 1988. ISBN 7-80006-107-8.

———.『现代汉语通用字表』. 语文出版社. 1988. ISBN 7-80006-167-1.

何根泽 & 何新, editors.『汉字输入快易通』. 电子工业出版社. 1996. ISBN 7-5053-3450-6.

黃大一.『中文字碼—萬碼奔騰, 一碼當先』. Second Edition. 永麒科技股份有限公司. 1992. ISBN 957-9064-00-8.

刘之强, editor.『简化字 繁体字 选用字 异体字对照表』. 上海辞书出版社. 1983.

苏培成 et al., editors.『现代汉字规范化问题』. 语文出版社. 1995. ISBN 7-80006-889-7.

谢世涯.『新中日简体字研究』. 语文出版社. 1989. ISBN 7-80006-222-8.

行政院研究發展考核委員會, editor.『兩岸常用中文資訊名詞對照表及兩岸常用中文資訊內碼對照轉碼表之編擬』. 行政院研究發展考核委員會. 1994. ISBN 957-00-3422-X.

张乐之 et al., editors.『计算机汉字输入与编辑实用手册』. 上海交通大学出版社. 1994. ISBN 7-313-01405-8.

Books in Japanese

アスキー出版技術部責任編集.『日本語TEXテクニカルブックI』. ASCII Corporation. 1990. ISBN 4-7561-0405-3.

Apple Computer Japan.『Macintosh漢字Talkテクニカル・リファレンス』. 技術評論社. 1990. ISBN 4-87408-369-2.

泉均.『ワープロ用語図説辞典』. 山海堂. 1988. ISBN 4-381-08071-8.

遠藤紹徳.『早わかり中国簡体字』. 国書刊行会. 1986.

大木敦雄.『入門NEmacs』. ASCII Corporation. 1994. ISBN 4-7561-0287-5.

———.『入門Mule』. ASCII Corporation. 1994. ISBN 4-7561-0300-6.

岡本保.『タイプ・デザインのルール [ゴシック体漢字編]』. 富士通アプリコ株式会社. 1993.

———.『タイプ・デザインのルール [明朝体漢字編]』. 富士通アプリコ株式会社. 1993.

エツコ・オバタ・ライマン.『日本人の作った漢字』. 南雲堂. 1990. ISBN 4-523-26156-3.

樺島忠夫 et al., editors.『事典日本の文字』. 大修館書店. 1985. ISBN 4-469-01209-2.

『誤字俗字・正字一覧表』. テイハン. 1995. ISBN 4-924485-29-2.

共同通信社.『記者ハンドブック』. Eighth Edition. 共同通信社. 1997. ISBN 4-7641-0381-8.

共同通信社情報システム局通信部.『字形と入力』. Second Edition. 共同通信社. 1995.

清兼義弘 & 末廣陽一, editors.『国際化プログラミング—I18N ハンドブック』. 共立出版. 1998. ISBN 4-320-02904-6.

Lunde, Ken.『日本語情報処理』. SOFTBANK Corporation. 1995. ISBN 4-89052-708-7.

斎藤靖 et al.『新Perlの国へようこそ』. サイエンス社. 1996. ISBN 4-7819-0795-4.

坂村健.『新版トロンヒューマンインタフェース標準ハンドブック』. Personal Media corporation. 1996. ISBN 4-89362-141-6.

———.『BTRON1プログラミング標準ハンドブック』. Personal Media Corporation. 1992. ISBN 4-89362-093-2.

佐渡秀治 & 吉田智子.『Linux/FreeBSD 日本語環境の構築と活用』. ソフトバンク. 1997. ISBN 4-7973-0480-4.

佐藤喜代治 et al.『漢字講座』. 10 Volumes. 大修館書店. 1987–1989.

J-PRESS.『縦組みDTP制作の現場』. AI出版. 1997. ISBN 4-87193-524-8.

常用漢字表.『大蔵省印刷局』. 1987. ISBN 4-17-214500-0.

真堂彬 & プロビット.『JIS補助漢字』. エーアイ出版. 1991. ISBN 4-87193-158-7.

菅野岑.『中国入力方法の話』. 朝日出版社. 1991. ISBN 4-255-91006-5.

長尾真 et al., editors.『情報科学辞典』. 岩波書店. 1990. ISBN 4-00-080074-4.

中西秀彦.『活字が消えた日—コンピュータと印刷』. 晶文社. 1994. ISBN 4-7949-6172-3.

錦見美貴子 et al.『マルチリンガル環境の実現: X Window/Wnn/Mule/WWWブラウザでの多国語環境』. Prentice-Hall. 1996. ISBN 4-88735-020-1.

日本エディタースクール.『標準校正必携〈電算植字対応版〉』. Seventh Edition. 日本エディタースクール出版部. 1995. ISBN 4-88888-235-5.

野村保惠.『〈電算植字〉本づくり入門』. 日本エディタースクール出版部. 1995. ISBN 4-88888-231-2.

原田種成.『漢字小百科辞典』. 三省堂. 1990. ISBN 4-385-13590-8.

Hitachi.『HITAC文字コード表(KEIS83)』. 1989. Hitachi part number 8080-2-100-10.

府川充男.『組版原論—タイポグラフィと活字・写植・DTP』. 太田出版. 1996. ISBN 4-87233-272-5.

古瀬幸広.『ワープロここが不思議—ちょっと知的なワープロ学』. 講談社. 1994. ISBN 4-06-257018-1.

———.『最新ワープロ用語辞典』. 実業之日本社. 1991. ISBN 4-408-10095-1.

———.『ネットワーク通信活用ブック』. 実業之日本社. 1991. ISBN 4-408-10096-X.

三上吉彦 et al.『マルチリンガルWEBガイド』. O'Reilly Japan. 1997. ISBN 4-900900-23-0.

文字フォント開発・普及センター.『新フォント関連用語集—フォントと組版に関する用語解説』. 日本規格協会. 1993.

森浩孝.『パソコン通信ガイドブック』. HBJ Publishing. 1986. ISBN 4-8337-8512-9.

森田正典.『これが日本語に最適なキーボードだ』. 日本経済新聞社. 1992. ISBN 4-532-40014-7.

森田正典 & 丸山和光.『日本語だから速く入力できる』. 日刊工業新聞社. 1988. ISBN 4-526-02310-8.

吉田智子.『UNIXの日本語処理がわかる本—最新Wnn活用ガイド』. 日刊工業新聞社. 1993. ISBN 4-526-03321-9.

吉目木晴彦 et al.『電脳文化と漢字のゆくえ: 岐路に立つ日本語』. 平凡社. 1998. ISBN 4-582-40322-0.

Books in Korean

Dong-A's Prime Korean-English Dictionary. Second Edition. Doosan Dong-A Company, Limited. 1996. ISBN 89-00-04440-0.

김 경석.『컴퓨터 속의 한글 이야기』. 영진 출판사. 1995. ISBN 89-314-0578-2.

김 진평.『한글의 글자표현』. Second Edition. 미진사. 1997. ISBN 89-408-0109-1.

김 학성 (金學成).『레터링 디자인』. 조형사. 1997. ISBN 89-8307-011-0.

Character Dictionaries

赤塚忠 et al.『旺文社 漢和辞典』. Fifth Edition. 旺文社. 1993. ISBN 4-01-077703-6.

费锦昌 et al., editors.『汉字写法规范字典』. 上海辞书出版社. 1992. ISBN 7-5326-0119-6.

傅永和, editor.『汉字属性字典』. 语文出版社. 1989. ISBN 7-80006-242-2.

Fujitsu Limited.『FACOM JEF文字コード索引辞書』. 1987. Fujitsu part number 99FR-0012-3.*

Halpern, Jack, editor. *The Kodansha Kanji Learner's Dictionary*. Kodansha International Limited. 1998. ISBN 4-7700-2335-9.

———. *NTC's New Japanese-English Character Dictionary*. NTC. 1993. ISBN 0-8442-8434-3.

———. *New Japanese-English Character Dictionary*. Kenkyusha. 1990. ISBN 4-7674-9040-5.

飛田良文.『国字の字典』. 東京堂出版. 1990. ISBN 4-490-10279-8.

Hitachi.『HITAC文字パターン辞書/コードブック(KEIS83拡張文字セット3)』. 1987. Hitachi part number 8080-2-109.

———.『HITAC文字パターン辞書/コードブック(拡張文字セット3)』. 1984. Hitachi part number 8080-2-074-10.

胡双宝.『简化字 繁体字 异体字辨析手册』. 北京大学出版社. 1996. ISBN 7-301-03198-X.

石川忠久 et al.『福武 漢和辞典 新装版』. Benesse. 1997. ISBN 4-8288-0435-8.

覚田正 & 米山寅太郎.『新版 漢語林』. 大修館書店. 1994. ISBN 4-469-03107-0.

———.『大漢語林』. 大修館書店. 1992. ISBN 4-469-03154-2.

冷玉龙, editor.『中华字海』. 中华出版社. 1994. ISBN: 7-5057-0630-6.

民志書林編輯, editors.『活用玉篇』. 民志書林. 1983. ISBN 89-387-0110-7.

諸橋轍次.『大漢和辭典』. Revised Second Edition. 13 Volumes. 大修館書店. 1994.

NEC.『日本電気標準文字セット辞書 基本編』. 1983. NEC part number ZBB10-2.

———.『日本電気標準文字セット辞書 拡張編』. 1983. NEC part number ZBB11-1.

Nelson, Andrew & John H. Haig. *The New Nelson Japanese-English Character Dictionary* (『新版ネルソン漢英辞典』). New Nelson Edition. Charles E. Tuttle Company. 1997. ISBN 0-8048-2036-8.

日外アソシエーツ編集部.『漢字異体字典』. 日外アソシエーツ. 1994. ISBN 4-8169-1249-5.

小川環樹 et al.『角川 必携漢和辞典』. 角川書店. 1996. ISBN 4-04-013300-5.

———.『角川 新字源 改訂版』. 角川書店. 1994. ISBN 4-04-010804-3.

商務印書館編輯部.『辭源』. 商務印書館. 1995. ISBN 7-100-00540-X.

芝野耕司, editor.『JIS漢字字典』. 財団法人日本規格協会. 1997. ISBN 4-542-20127-9.

* FACOM is usually pronounced in a way that is close to a two-word obscenity.

新村出, editor.『広辞苑』. Fourth Edition. 岩波書店. 1991. ISBN 4-00-080101-5.

Spahn, Mark & Wolfgang Hadamitzky. *The Kanji Dictionary*. Charles E. Tuttle Company. 1996. ISBN 0-8048-2058-9.

蘇培成, editor.『漢字簡繁體字對照字典』. Second Edition. 海峰出版社 & 中信出版社 (co-publishers). 1996. ISBN 962-238-213-4.

田嶋一夫.『最新JIS漢字辞典』. 講談社. 1990. ISBN 4-06-123264-9.

竹田晃 & 坂梨隆三.『五十音引き講談社漢和辞典』. 講談社. 1997. ISBN 4-06-123269-X.

上柿力.『パソコンワープロ漢字辞典』. ナツメ社. 1987. ISBN 4-8163-0696-X.

Viện Ngôn Ngữ Học. *Bảng Tra Chữ Nôm*. Nhà Xuất Bản Khoa Học Xã Hội. 1976. Permission number 5/KHXH 76.

Vũ Văn Kính. *Tự Điển Chữ Nôm*. Nhà Xuất Bản Đà Nẵng. 1996. Permission number 10/226.

『ワープロ・パソコン最新漢字辞典』. 小学館. 1994. ISBN 4-09-505121-3.

吴伟和 et al., editors.『汉字输入速查手册』. 中国工人出版社. 1996. ISBN 7-5008-1846-7.

許慎.『說文解字』. 中華書局. 100. ISBN 962-231-208-X.

楊子來.『標準中文輸入碼大字典』. 聚賢館文化有限公司. 1996. ISBN 962-436-287-4.

張三植.『大字源』. 集文堂. 1972.

張玉書 et al.『康熙字典』. 中華書局. 1716. ISBN 962-231-006-0.

中文社会科学院语言研究所词典编辑室, editors.『现代汉语词典』. 商务印书馆. 1995. ISBN 7-100-00044-0.

周冰洋 et al., editors.『常用汉字编码字典』. 宇航出版社. 1990. ISBN 7-80034-102-X.

朱文章, editor.『字詞・成語・辨正辭典』. 文翔圖書股份有限公司. 1986.

邹华清, editor.『汉语大字典』. 13 volumes. 四川辞书出版社 & 湖北辞书出版社. 1986.

Standards

American National Standards Institute. *ANSI X3.4-1986 Coded Character Set—7-Bit American National Standard Code for Information Interchange*. 1986.

———. *ANSI Z39.64-1989 East Asian Character Code for Bibliographic Use*. 1989. ISSN 1041-5653.

Chinese National Standard. *CNS 5205-1989 Information Processing—7-Bit Coded Character Set for Information Interchange* (『資訊處理及交換用七數元碼字元集』). 1989.

———. *CNS 11643-1986 Standard Interchange Code for Generally-Used Chinese Characters* (『通用漢字標準交換碼』). 1986.

———. *CNS 11643-1992 Chinese Standard Interchange Code* (『中文標準交換碼』). 1992. *Obsoletes CNS 11643-1986.*

Fujitsu Limited.『富士通文字コード解説書』. 1989. Fujitsu part number 99FR-8010-1.

Hitachi.『KEIS概説』. 1990. Hitachi part number 6180-3-003.

IBM Corporation. *Coded Character Sets: Implementation*. IBM Standards Program. 1991. IBM part number C-S 3-3220-019 1991-10.

———. *Double-Byte Character Set (DBCS): Terminology and Code Scheme*. IBM Standards Program. 1992. IBM part number C-S 3-3220-102 1992-11.

———. *Extended BCD Interchange Code: EBCDIC*. IBM Standards Program. 1990. IBM part number C-S 3-3220-002 1990-05.

———. *IBM Japanese Graphic Character Set, Kanji, for Open Environment, DBCS-PC (New JIS Sequence)*. IBM Standards Program. 1996. IBM part number C-H 3-3220-133 1996-08.

———. *IBM Japanese Graphic Character Set for Extended UNIX Code (EUC): DBCS-EUC*. IBM Standards Program. 1993. IBM part number C-H 3-3220-127 1993-03.

———. *IBM Japanese Graphic Character Set, Kanji: DBCS-Host and DBCS-PC*. IBM Standards Program. 1992. IBM part number C-H 3-3220-024 1992-11.

———. *IBM Korean Graphic Character Set, DBCS-Host and DBCS-PC (For Windows Environment)*. IBM Standards Program. 1997. IBM part number C-H 3-3220-030 1997-09.

———. *IBM Korean Graphic Character Set for Extended UNIX Code (EUC), DBCS-EUC*. IBM Standards Program. 1993. IBM part number C-H 3-3220-128 1993-11.

———. *IBM Korean Graphic Character Set, DBCS-Host and DBCS-PC*. IBM Standards Program. 1992. IBM part number C-H 3-3220-125 1992-09.

———. *IBM Simplified Chinese Graphic Character Set, GBK Code, DBCS-Host and DBCS-PC*. IBM Standards Program. 1997. IBM part number C-H 3-3220-020 1997-02.

———. *IBM Simplified Chinese Graphic Character Set for Extended UNIX Code (EUC), DBCS-EUC*. IBM Standards Program. 1994. IBM part number C-H 3-3220-132 1994-06.

———. *IBM Simplified Chinese Graphic Character Set, DBCS-Host and DBCS-PC*. IBM Standards Program. 1993. IBM part number C-H 3-3220-130 1993-11.

———. *IBM Traditional Chinese Graphic Character Set for IBM BIG-5 Code, DBCS-PC*. IBM Standards Program. 1994. IBM part number C-H 3-3220-131 1994-01.

———. *IBM Traditional Chinese Graphic Character Set for Extended UNIX Code (EUC), DBCS-EUC and TBCS-EUC*. IBM Standards Program. 1993. IBM part number C-H 3-3220-129 1993-11.

———. *IBM Traditional Chinese Graphic Character Set, DBCS-Host and DBCS-PC*. IBM Standards Program. 1992. IBM part number C-H 3-3220-126 1992-01.

International Organization for Standardization. *International Register of Coded Character Sets to Be Used with Escape Sequences*. 1996.

———. *ISO 639:1988 Code for the Representation of Names of Languages*. 1988.

———. *ISO 639-2 Codes for the Representation of Names of Languages—Part 2: Alpha-3 Code*. Draft.

———. *ISO 646:1991 Information Technology—ISO 7-Bit Coded Character Set for Information Interchange*. 1991.

———. *ISO 2022:1994 Information Technology—Character Code Structure and Extension Techniques*. 1994.

———. *ISO 3166-1:1997 Codes for the Representation of Names of Countries and Their Subdivisions—Part 1: Country Codes*. 1997.

———. *ISO 6429:1992 Information Technology—Control Functions for Coded Character Sets*. 1992.

———. *ISO 8859 Information Processing—8-Bit Single-Byte Coded Graphic Character Sets*. Ten parts. 1987–1998.

———. *ISO 8879:1986 Information Processing—Text and Office Systems—Standard Generalized Markup Language (SGML)*. 1986.

———. *ISO 9541:1991 Information Technology—Font Information Interchange*. Three parts. 1991.

———. *ISO 10179:1996 Information Technology—Processing Languages—Document Style Semantics and Specification Language (DSSSL)*. 1996.

———. *ISO 10646-1:1993 Information Technology—Universal Multiple-Octet Coded Character Set (UCS)*. 1993.

———. *ISO/TR 11941:1996 Information Documentation—Transliteration of Korean Script into Latin Characters*. 1996.

———. *ISO 14755:1997 Information Technology—Input Methods to Enter Characters from the Repertoire of ISO/IEC 10646 With a Keyboard or Other Input Device*. 1997.

———. *ISO 15924 Codes for the Representation of Names of Scripts*. Draft.

Japanese Industrial Standards Committee. *JIS C 6226-1978 Code of the Japanese Graphic Character Set for Information Interchange* (『情報交換用漢字符号』). Japanese Standards Association. 1978.

———. *JIS X 0201-1997 7-Bit and 8-Bit Coded Character Sets for Information Interchange* (『7ビット及び8ビットの情報交換用符号化文字集合』). Japanese Standards Association. 1997. *Originally designated JIS C 6220-1976, and obsoletes JIS X 0201-1976.*

———. *JIS X 0202:1998 Information Processing—ISO 7-Bit and 8-Bit Coded Character Sets—Code Extension Techniques* (『情報技術—文字符号の構造及び拡張法』). Japanese Standards Association. 1998. *Originally designated JIS C 6228-1984, and obsoletes JIS X 0202-1984 and JIS X 0202-1991.*

———. *JIS X 0207-1979 Code of the Control Character Set for Japanese Graphic Characters for Information Interchange* (『情報交換用漢字符号のための制御文字符号』). Japanese Standards Association. 1979. *Obsoletes JIS C 6225-1979.*

———. *JIS X 0208-1983 Code of the Japanese Graphic Character Set for Information Interchange* (『情報交換用漢字符号』). Japanese Standards Association. 1983. *Originally designated JIS C 6226-1983, and obsoletes JIS C 6226-1978.*

———. *JIS X 0208-1990 Code of the Japanese Graphic Character Set for Information Interchange* (『情報交換用漢字符号』). Japanese Standards Association. 1990. *Obsoletes JIS X 0208-1983.*

———. *JIS X 0208:1997 7-Bit and 8-Bit Double Byte Coded Kanji Sets for Information Interchange* (『7ビット及び8ビットの2バイト情報交換用符号化漢字集合』). Japanese Standards Association. 1997. *Obsoletes JIS X 0208-1990.*

———. *JIS X 0212-1990 Code of the Supplementary Japanese Graphic Character Set for Information Interchange* (『情報交換用漢字符号—補助漢字』). Japanese Standards Association. 1990.

———. *JIS X 0213:199X 7-Bit and 8-Bit Double Byte Coded Extended Kanji Sets for Information Interchange* (『7ビット及び8ビットの2バイト情報交換用符号化拡張漢字集合』). Japanese Standards Association. Draft.

———. *JIS X 0221-1995 Information technology—Universal Multiple-Octet Coded Character Set (UCS)—Part 1: Architecture and Basic Multilingual Plane* (『国際符号化文字集合 (UCS)—第1部 体系及び基本多言語面』). Japanese Standards Association. 1995.

———. *JIS X 4051-1995 Line Composition Rules for Japanese Documents* (『日本語文書の行組版方法』). Japanese Standards Association. 1995. *Obsoletes JIS X 4051-1993.*

———. *JIS X 4061-1996 Collation of Japanese Character String* (『日本語文字列照合順番』). Japanese Standards Association. 1996.

———. *JIS X 4062:1998 Format for Information Interchange for Dictionaries of Japanese Input Method* (『仮名漢字変換辞書交換形式』). Japanese Standards Association. 1998.

———. *JIS X 4161-1993 Font Information Interchange—Architecture* (『フォント情報交換—体系』). Japanese Standards Association. 1993.

———. *JIS X 4162-1993 Font Information Interchange—Interchange Format* (『フォント情報交換—交換用式』). Japanese Standards Association. 1993.

———. *JIS X 4163-1993 Font Information Interchange—Glyph Shape Representation* (『フォント情報交換—グリフ形状表現』). Japanese Standards Association. 1993.

———. *JIS X 4164-1993 Font Information Interchange—Application-Specific Extensions* (『フォント情報交換—応用別拡張』). Japanese Standards Association. 1993.

———. *JIS X 6002-1985 Keyboard Layout for Information Processing Using the JIS 7-Bit Coded Character Set* (『情報処理系けん盤配列』). Japanese Standards Association. 1985. *Originally designated JIS C 6233-1980.*

———. *JIS X 6003-1989 Keyboard Layout for Japanese Text Processing* (『日本語文書処理用文字盤配列』). Japanese Standards Association. 1989. *Originally designated JIS C 6235-1984.*

———. *JIS X 6004-1986 Basic Keyboard Layout for Japanese Text Processing Using Kana-Kanji Translation Method* (『仮名漢字変換形日本文入力装置用けん盤配列』). Japanese Standards Association. 1986. *Originally designated JIS C 6236-1986.*

———. *JIS X 9052-1983 24-Dots Matrix Character Patterns for Dot Printers* (『ドットプリンタ用24ドット字形』). Japanese Standards Association. 1983. *Originally designated JIS C 6234-1983.*

———. *JIS X 9051-1984 16-Dots Matrix Character Patterns for Display Devices* (『表示装置用16ドット字形』). Japanese Standards Association. 1984. *Originally designated JIS C 6232-1984.*

Korean Industrial Standards Association. *KS X 1001:1992 Code for Information Interchange (Hangul and Hanja)* (『정보 교환용 부호 (한글 및 한자)』). Korean Industrial Standard. 1992. *Originally designated KS C 5601-1992.*

———. *KS X 1002:1991 Code for Information Interchange Supplementary Set* (『정보 교환용 부호 확장 세트』). Korean Industrial Standard. 1991. *Originally designated KS C 5657-1991.*

———. *KS X 1003:1993 Code for Information Interchange (Roman Characters)* (『정보 교환용 부호 (로마 문자)』). Korean Industrial Standard. 1993. *Originally designated KS C 5636-1993.*

———. *KS X 1004:1995 Code Extension Techniques for Use with the Code for Information Interchange* (『정보 교환용 부호의 확장법』). Korean Industrial Standard. 1995. *Originally designated KS C 5620-1995.*

———. *KS X 1005-1:1995 Information technology—Universal Multiple-Octet Coded Character Set (UCS)—Part 1: Architecture and Basic Multilingual Plane* (『국제 문자 부호계 (UCS) 제 1 부 : 구조 및 기본 다국어 평면』). Korean Industrial Standard. 1995. *Originally designated KS C 5700-1995.*

———. *KS X 2901:1992 UNIX-Hangul Environment* (『유닉스 한글 환경』). Korean Industrial Standard. 1992. *Originally designated KS C 5861-1992.*

———. *KS X 5002:1992 Keyboard Layout for Information Processing* (『정보 처리용 건반 배열』). Korean Industrial Standard. 1992. *Originally designated KS C 5715-1992.*

People's Republic of China, The. *GB 1988-89 Information Processing—7-Bit Coded Character Set for Information Interchange* (『信息处理—信息交换用七位编码字符集』). Technical Standards Press. 1990. *Obsoletes GB 1988-80.*

———. *GB 2311-80 Information Processing—7-Bit and 8-Bit Coded Character Set—Code Extension Techniques* (『信息处理—七位及八位编码字符集—代码扩充技术』). Technical Standards Press. 1980.

———. *GB 2312-80 Code of Chinese Graphic Character Set for Information Interchange Primary Set* (『信息交换用汉字编码字符集—基本集』). Technical Standards Press. 1981.

———. *GB 5007.1-85 24×24 Dot Matrix Font Set of Chinese Ideograms for Information Interchange* (『信息交换用汉字24×24点阵字模集』). Technical Standards Press. 1985.

———. *GB 5007.2-85 24×24 Dot Matrix Font Data Set of Chinese Ideograms for Information Interchange* (『信息交换用汉字24×24点阵字模数据集』). Technical Standards Press. 1985.

———. *GB 6345.1-86 32×32 Dot Matrix Font Set of Chinese Ideograms for Information Interchange* (『信息交换用汉字32×32点阵字模集』). Technical Standards Press. 1986.

———. *GB 6345.2-86 32×32 Dot Matrix Font Data Set of Chinese Ideograms for Information Interchange* (『信息交换用汉字32×32点阵字模数据集』). Technical Standards Press. 1986.

———. *GB 8565.1-88 Information Processing—Coded Character Sets for Text Communication—Part 1: General Introduction* (『信息处理—文本通信用编码字符集—第一部分—总则』). Technical Standards Press. 1988.

———. *GB 8565.2-88 Information Processing—Coded Character Sets for Text Communication—Part 2: Graphic Characters* (『信息处理—文本通信用编码字符集—第二部分—图形字符集』). Technical Standards Press. 1988.

———. *GB 8565.3-88 Information Processing—Coded Character Sets for Text Communication—Part 3: Control Functions for Page-Image Format* (『信息处理—文本通信用编码字符集—第三部分—按页成象格式用控制功能』). Technical Standards Press. 1989.

———. *GB 7589-87 Code of Chinese Ideograms Set for Information Interchange—the Second Supplementary Set* (『信息交换用汉字编码字符集—第二辅助集』). Technical Standards Press. 1987.

———. *GB 7590-87 Code of Chinese Ideograms Set for Information Interchange—the Fourth Supplementary Set* (『信息交换用汉字编码字符集—第四辅助集』). Technical Standards Press. 1987.

———. *GB 12034-89 32×32 Dot Matrix Fangsongti Font Set and Data Set of Chinese Ideograms for Information Interchange* (『信息交换用汉字32×32点阵仿宋体字模集及数据集』). Technical Standards Press. 1990.

———. *GB 12035-89 32×32 Dot Matrix Kaiti Font Set and Data Set of Chinese Ideograms for Information Interchange* (『信息交换用汉字32×32点阵楷体字模集及数据集』). Technical Standards Press. 1990.

———. *GB 12036-89 32×32 Dot Matrix Heiti Font Set and Data Set of Chinese Ideograms for Information Interchange* (『信息交换用汉字32×32点阵黑体字模集及数据集』). Technical Standards Press. 1990.

———. *GB 12052-89 Korean Character Coded Character Set for Information Interchange* (『信息交换用朝鲜文字编码字符集』). Technical Standards Press. 1990

———. *GB/T 12345-90 Code of Chinese Ideogram Set for Information Interchange Supplementary Set* (『信息交换用汉字编码字符集—辅助集』). Technical Standards Press. 1990.

———. *GB 13000.1-93 Information Technology—Universal Multiple-Octet Coded Character Set (UCS)—Part 1: Architecture and Basic Multilingual Plane* (『信息技术—通用多八位编码字符集 (UCS)—第一部分：体系结构与基本多文种平面』). Technical Standards Press. 1994.

———. *GB/T 15834-1995 Use of Punctuation Marks* (『标点符号用法』). Technical Standards Press. 1996.

———. *GB/T 15835-1995 General Rules for Writing Numerals in Publications* (『出版物上数字用法的规定』). Technical Standards Press. 1996.

———. *GB 16794.1-1997* (『信息技术—通用多八位编码字符集48点阵字形』). Technical Standards Press. 1998.

Vietnam Standards Institute. *TCVN 5712:1993 Công Nghệ Thông Tin—Bộ Mã Chuẩn 8-Bit Kí Tự Việt Dùng Trong Trao Đổi Thông Tin (Information Technology—Vietnamese 8-Bit Standard Coded Character Set for Information Interchange)*. 1993.

———. *TCVN 5773:1993 Công Nghệ Thông Tin—Bộ Mã Chuẩn 16-Bit Kí Tự Việt Dùng Trong Trao Đổi Thông Tin (Information Technology—Nom 16-Bit Standard Code Set for Information Interchange)*. 1993.

———. *TCVN 6056:1995 Công Nghệ Thông Tin—Bộ Mã Chuẩn 16-Bit Chữ Nôm Dùng Trong Trao Đổi Thông Tin—Chữ Nôm Hán (Information Technology—Nom 16-Bit Standard Code for Information Interchange—Han Nom Character)*. 1995.

X/Open Consortium. *X/Open CAE Specification: Commands and Utilities, Issue 4, Version 2.* X/Open Company Limited. 1994. ISBN 1-85912-034-2. X/Open Document Number C436.

———. *X/Open CAE Specification: File System Safe UCS Transformation Format (UTF-8).* X/Open Company Limited. 1995. ISBN 1-85912-082-2. X/Open Document Number C501.

———. *X/Open CAE Specification: System Interfaces and Headers.* Issue 4, Version 2. X/Open Company Limited. 1994. ISBN 1-85912-037-7. X/Open Document Number C435.

———. *X/Open CAE Specification: System Interface Definitions.* Issue 4, Version 2. X/Open Company Limited. 1994. ISBN 1-85912-036-9. X/Open Document Number C434.

———. *X/Open Guide: Internationalisation Guide.* Version 2. X/Open Company Limited. 1993. ISBN 1-85912-002-4. X/Open Document Number G304.

Xerox Corporation. *Xerox Character Code Standard 2.0.* Xerox Systems Institute. 1990. Xerox part number XNSS 059003.

Periodicals

Chinese and Oriental Languages Information Processing Society (COLIPS). *Communications of COLIPS (CommCOLIPS).* Published twice per year. ISSN 0218-7019.

Computing Japan. LINC Media, Incorporated. Published 10 times per year. ISSN 1340-7228.

『情報処理』. Information Processing Society of Japan. Published monthly.

『정글』(*Jungle*). Yoon Design Institute. Published quarterly. Bar-2557.

Language International. John Benjamins Publishing Company. Published bi-monthly. ISSN 0923-182X.

The LISA Forum. The Localisation Industry Standards Association. Published quarterly. ISSN 1420-3693.

MultiLingual Communications & Technology. MultiLingual Computing, Incorporated. Published bi-monthly. ISSN 1065-7657.

Oriental Language Computer Society (OLCS). *Computer Processing of Oriental Languages* (CPOL). World Scientific Publishing. Published quarterly. ISSN 0715-9048.

The Perl Journal. Published quarterly. ISSN 1087-903X.

『最新ワープロ大百科』. 実業之日本社. Published from 1986 to 1993.

SESAME Bulletin. Sesame Computer Projects. ISSN 0950-2025.

Seybold Report on Internet Publishing. Seybold Publications. Published monthly. ISSN 1090-4808.

Seybold Report on Publishing Systems. Seybold Publications. Published 22 times per year. ISSN 0889-9762.

TRONWARE. Personal Media Corporation. Pubished bi-monthly.

TUGboat. TEX Users Group. Published quarterly. ISSN 0896-3207.

U&lc. International Typeface Corporation. Published quarterly. ISSN 0362-6245.

World Wide Web Journal. O'Reilly & Associates, Incorporated. Published quarterly. ISSN 1085-2301.

『中文信息』(*Chinese Information Processing*). Chinese Information Processing Society. Published bi-monthly. ISSN 1003-9082.

Papers & Articles

Adobe Systems Incorporated. *Glyph Bitmap Distribution Format (BDF) Specification*. Adobe Developer Support. Adobe Systems Technical Note #5005.

———. *Adobe CMap and CIDFont Files Specification*. Adobe Developer Support. Adobe Systems Technical Note #5014.

———. *The Type 1 Font Format Supplement*. Adobe Developer Support. Adobe Systems Technical Note #5015.

———. *Adobe-Japan1-3 Character Collection for CID-Keyed Fonts*. Adobe Developer Support. Adobe Systems Technical Note #5078.

———. *Adobe-GB1-3 Character Collection for CID-Keyed Fonts*. Adobe Developer Support. Adobe Systems Technical Note #5079.

———. *Adobe-CNS1-2 Character Collection for CID-Keyed Fonts*. Adobe Developer Support. Adobe Systems Technical Note #5080.

———. *CID-Keyed Font Technology Overview*. Adobe Developer Support. Adobe Systems Technical Note #5092.

———. *Adobe-Korea1-2 Character Collection for CID-Keyed Fonts*. Adobe Developer Support. Adobe Systems Technical Note #5093.

———. *Adobe CJKV Character Collections and CMaps for CID-Keyed Fonts*. Adobe Developer Support. Adobe Systems Technical Note #5094.

———. *Adobe-Japan2-0 Character Collection for CID-Keyed Fonts*. Adobe Developer Support. Adobe Systems Technical Note #5097.

———. *Building CMap Files for CID-Keyed Fonts*. Adobe Developer Support. Adobe Systems Technical Note #5099.

———. *CID-Keyed Font Installation for PostScript File Systems*. Adobe Developer Support. Adobe Systems Technical Note #5174.

———. *CID-Keyed Font Installation for ATM Software*. Adobe Developer Support. Adobe Systems Technical Note #5175.

———. *The Compact Font Format Specification*. Adobe Developer Support. Adobe Systems Technical Note #5176.

———. *The Type 2 Charstring Format*. Adobe Developer Support. Adobe Systems Technical Note #5177.

———. *Building PFM Files for PostScript-Language CJK Fonts*. Adobe Developer Support. Adobe Systems Technical Note #5178.

———. *CID-Keyed sfnt Font File Format for the Macintosh*. Adobe Developer Support. Adobe Systems Technical Note #5180.

———. *PostScript Language Extensions for CID-Keyed Fonts*. Adobe Developer Support. Adobe Systems Technical Note #5213.

———. *Application Support for PostScript CJK Fonts*. Adobe Developer Support. Adobe Systems Technical Note #5640.

———. *Enabling PDF Font Embedding for CID-Keyed Fonts*. Adobe Developer Support. Adobe Systems Technical Note #5641.

———. *CID Font Tutorial*. Adobe Developer Support. Adobe Systems Technical Note #5643.

Breen, Jim. *A Japanese Electronic Dictionary Project (Part 1: The Dictionary Files), Technical Report 93/13*, Department of Robotics & Digital Technology, Monash University, November 1993.

Dillard, Troy & Ken Lunde. "Japanese Text Processing and Electronic Mail on the IBM PC and Macintosh." Sesame Computer Projects. *SESAME Bulletin*, Summer 1992, Volume 5, Part 2, pp 40–48.

Huang, Jack Kai-tung. *Status and Font Samples of Digitized Chinese (Hanzi) Font Manufacturers in Taiwan, 1993*. October, 1993.

Liu, Yucheng. *Chinese Information Processing*. MS Thesis. University of Nevada, Las Vegas. 1995.

Lunde, Ken. *CJK.INF*. Distributed and maintained electronically since 1995.

———. "Cross-Locale CJKV Code Conversion." Thirteenth International Unicode Conference, San Jose, California, September 8–11, 1998.

———. "Accessibility of Unencoded Glyphs." Thirteenth International Unicode Conference, San Jose, California, September 8–11, 1998.

———. "The Design of an Extended Japanese Character Set." Ninth International Unicode Conference, San Jose, California, September 4–6, 1996.

———. "Unicode/CJK Font Support in PostScript." Seventh International Unicode Conference, San Jose, California, September 14–15, 1995.

———. "The History of the Japanese Character Set and its Encoding." *CPCOL*, June 1993, Volume 7, Number 1, pp 85–94.

———. "Electronic Transfer of Japanese." *ATArashii*, September/October 1990, Volume 4, Number 5, pp 19–27.

———. "Using Electronic Mail as a Medium for Foreign Language Study and Instruction." *CALICO Journal*, March 1990, Volume 7, Number 3, pp 68–78.

———. *JAPAN.INF: Electronic Handling of Japanese Text*. Distributed and maintained electronically from 1989 until 1992.

Morita, Masasuke. "Japanese Text Input System." *IEEE Computer*, May 1985, Volume 18, Number 5, pp 29–35.

———. "Development of New Keyboard Optimized from Standpoint of Ergonomics. Work with Computers: Organizational, Management, Stress and Health Aspects." Proceedings of the Third International Conference on Human-Computer Interaction, September 18–22, 1989, Volume 1, pp 595–603.

Miyazawa, Akira. "Character Code for Japanese Text Processing." *Journal of Information Processing*. 1990, Volume 13, Number 1, pp 2–9.

西村恕彦.「漢字のJIS」.『標準化ジャーナル』. 1978.5, pp 3–8.

野村雅昭.「JIS C 6226情報交換用漢字符号系の改正」.『標準化ジャーナル』. 1984.3, pp 4–9.

Open Software Foundation, UNIX International, and UNIX System Laboratories Pacific. *OSF, UI, and USL Standardize on Japanese Language Support*. UI-OSF-USLP Joint Announcement. Press release dated December 12, 1991.

Schilke, Steffen. *Japanization—An Introduction to Software Japanization*. Thesis. Summer, 1992.

田嶋一夫. 「JIS 漢字表の利用上の問題—漢字処理システムにおける漢字のデザインと管理」.『情報管理』. 1979. Volume 21, Number 10, pp 753–761.

内田富雄.「JIS X 0212の制定」.『標準化ジャーナル』. 1990.11.

RFCs

Berners-Lee, Tim & Daniel Connolly. *Hypertext Markup Language—2.0*. RFC 1866. November 1995.

Choi, Uhhyung et al. *Korean Character Encoding for Internet Messages*. RFC 1557. December 1993.

Freed, Ned at al. *Multipurpose Internet Mail Extensions (MIME) Part Four: Registration Procedures*. RFC 2048. November 1996.

Freed, Ned & Nathaniel Borenstein. *Multipurpose Internet Mail Extensions (MIME) Part One: Format of Internet Message Bodies*. RFC 2045. November 1996.

———. *Multipurpose Internet Mail Extensions (MIME) Part Two: Media Types*. RFC 2046. November 1996.

———. *Multipurpose Internet Mail Extensions (MIME) Part Five: Conformance Criteria and Examples*. RFC 2049. November 1996.

Freed, Ned & Jon Postel. *IANA Charset Registration Procedures*. RFC 2278. January 1998.

Goldsmith, David & Mark Davis. *UTF-7: A Mail-Safe Transformation Format of Unicode*. RFC 2152. May 1997.

Alvestrand, Harald. *Tags for the Identification of Languages*. RFC 1766. March 1995.

Lee, Fung Fung. *HZ—A Data Format for Exchanging Files of Arbitrarily Mixed Chinese and ASCII Characters*. RFC 1843. August 1995.

Levinson, Ed. *SGML Media Types*. RFC 1874. December 1995.

Moore, Keith. *Multipurpose Internet Mail Extensions (MIME) Part Three: Message Header Extensions for Non-ASCII Text*. RFC 2047. November 1996.

Murai, Jun et al. *Japanese Character Encoding for Internet Messages*. RFC 1468. June 1993.

Ohta, Masataka. *Character Sets ISO-10646 and ISO-10646-J-1*. RFC 1815. July 1995.

Ohta, Masataka & Ken'ichi Handa. *ISO-2022-JP-2: Multilingual Extension of ISO-2022-JP*. RFC 1554. December 1993.

Tamaru, Kenzaburo. *Japanese Character Encoding for Internet Messages*. RFC 2237. November 1997.

Vietnamese Standardization Working Group. *Conventions for Encoding the Vietnamese Language—VISCII: VIetnamese Standard Code for Information Interchange—VIQR: Vietnamese Quoted-Readable Specification*. Revision 1.1. RFC 1456. May 1993.

Wei, Ya-Gui et al. *ASCII Printable Characters-Based Chinese Character Encoding for Internet Messages*. RFC 1842. August 1995.

Whitehead, E. James Jr. & Makoto Murata. *XML Media Types*. RFC 2376. July 1998.

Yergeau, François. *UTF-8, a transformation format of ISO 10646*. RFC 2279. January 1998.

Yergeau, François et al. *Internationalization of the Hypertext Markup Language*. RFC 2070. January 1997.

Zhu, Haifeng at al. *Chinese Character Encoding for Internet Messages*. RFC 1922. March 1996.

Index

Symbols

Numbers

A

D

E

I

J

L

M

N

O

U

V

W

Z

About the Author

Ken Lunde was born in Madison, Wisconsin, sometime in mid-August of the year 1965, and was subsequently raised by his caring parents in nearby greater-metropolitan Mount Horeb. His first post–high school educational stint was studying the Russian language for the United States Army Reserves at the Defense Language Institute—Foreign Language Center (DLI-FLC) in Monterey, California, for all but a couple of weeks of 1984. He was a member of the now disbanded 247th Military Intelligence Detachment for all nine years of his military career. Ken entered The University of Wisconsin-Madison (UW-Madison) in 1985 as a freshman, graduated with a Bachelor of Arts degree (linguistics) in 1987, received his Master of Arts degree (linguistics) in 1988, then finally earned his Doctor of Philosophy degree (yep, linguistics again, but this time with a minor in Japanese) in 1994. His PhD dissertation was entitled *Prescriptive Kanji Simplification.* Ken joined Adobe Systems in 1991—before even contemplating his PhD dissertation—and is currently Manager of CJKV Type Development among other things.

Ken's Japanese pen-name is 小林剣 (*kobayashi ken*). The Norwegian surname *Lunde* means "small woods" or "grove." Perhaps by sheer coincidence, the Japanese surname 小林 (*kobayashi*) conveys these same meanings. The Japanese given name 剣 (*ken*) was chosen phonemically, and from his fondness for edged and other weaponry. (In retrospect, Ken is *very* pleased that he chose the kanji 剣 for his name because it is an excellent example of a kanji that has many variants in Japan's JIS X 0208:1997 character set standard, specifically 劍, 劔, 劒, 剱, and 釼.) When Ken is in a nostalgic or otherwise old-timer mood, he sometimes prefers to use 劍 instead of 剣. When visiting China he would use the simplified form 剑.

Ken resides in Union City, California, with his family and commutes to San Jose, California. His interests include reading, writing (uh, really?), eating a good tenderloin or ribeye steak (and occasional Jumbo Jack), enjoying an action movie, listening to tunes, and spending quality time with friends and family.

Although Ken is deeply intrigued by Japanese (and now CJKV) computing, seafood is, quite astonishingly, not among his favorite foods. Needless to say, he has never eaten blowfish, and doesn't plan to start anytime soon.

Colophon

Our look is the result of reader comments, our own experimentation, and feedback from distribution channels. Distinctive covers complement our distinctive approach to technical topics, breathing personality and life into potentially dry subjects.

The animal on the cover of *CJKV Information Processing* is a blowfish, also known as a globefish, swellfish, puffer, and porcupine fish. It exists in tropical waters throughout the world. In Japan it is known as *fugu* (河豚 *fugu*), and is a treasured delicacy, usually eaten raw in thin slices. While parts of the blowfish are deliciously narcotic, other parts contain a deadly toxin. Because of this, only specially certified and licensed chefs are allowed to prepare the fish for people to eat. The skin of the blowfish is often used for making lanterns and other decorations.

Edie Freedman designed this cover of this book, using a nineteenth-century engraving from the Dover Pictorial Archive. The cover design was developed with QuarkXPress Version 3.32 using the ITC Garamond and 平成角ゴシックW5 (HeiseiKakuGo-W5) fonts.

The inside layout was designed by Nancy Priest, and implemented in Adobe FrameMaker Version 5.5 by Mike Sierra. The illustrations were created in Macromedia FreeHand Version 8.0 by Chris Reilley. Additional production work was provided by Jane Ellin. Seth Maislin reviewed the index. Text entry and page layout was done by the author on Apple Macintosh PowerBook 1400cs and PowerBook G3 Series computers running Adobe FrameMaker Version 5.5.

Illustrations and some text blocks began their life in Adobe Dimensions Version 3.0, Adobe Illustrator Version 8.0, Adobe Photoshop Version 5.0, Macromedia FreeHand Version 8.0J, QuarkXPress Version 4.0J, and SMI EDICOLOR Version 2.2. Custom typefaces were created using Adobe Systems' proprietary font production tools.

The English textface is 10-point ITC Garamond Light. Chapter and section titles are set in ITC Garamond Book Italic. Unless otherwise noted, Simplified and some Traditional Chinese text (GB standards) are set in Changzhou SinoType Technology's 华文宋体 (STSong-Light) typeface design; most Traditional Chinese text (CNS standards and Big Five) and Vietnamese text (TCVN 5773:1993 and TCVN 6056:1995) are set in Arphic Technology's 文鼎中明CNS11643 (MingTiEG-Medium) typeface design; Japanese text (JIS standards) is set in FDPC's 平成明朝W3 (HeiseiMin-W3) typeface design; and Korean text (KS standards) is set in Hanyang Systems' HY신명조 (HYSMyeongJo-Medium) typeface design. Most of these typefaces are available in from Adobe Systems or their respective type foundries.

Whenever possible, our books use RepKover™, a durable and flexible lay-flat binding. If the page count exceeds RepKover's limit, perfect binding is used.

O'REILLY™
O'Reilly & Associates, Inc.
101 Morris Street
Sebastopol, CA 95472-9902
1-800-998-9938

Visit us online at:
http://www.ora.com/

O'REILLY WOULD LIKE TO HEAR FROM YOU

Which book did this card come from?

____

Where did you buy this book?

- ❑ Bookstore
- ❑ Computer Store
- ❑ Direct from O'Reilly
- ❑ Class/seminar
- ❑ Bundled with hardware/software
- ❑ Other ____________________

What operating system do you use?

- ❑ UNIX
- ❑ Macintosh
- ❑ Windows NT
- ❑ PC(Windows/DOS)
- ❑ Other ____________________

What is your job description?

- ❑ System Administrator
- ❑ Programmer
- ❑ Network Administrator
- ❑ Educator/Teacher
- ❑ Web Developer
- ❑ Other ____________________

❑ Please send me O'Reilly's catalog, containing a complete listing of O'Reilly books and software.

Name ________________ Company/Organization ________________

Address ________________

City ________ State ________ Zip/Postal Code ________ Country ________

Telephone ________________ Internet or other email address (specify network) ________________

Nineteenth century wood engraving of a bear from the O'Reilly & Associates Nutshell Handbook® *Using & Managing UUCP.*

POST CARD

PLACE STAMP HERE

NO POSTAGE NECESSARY IF MAILED IN THE UNITED STATES

BUSINESS REPLY MAIL

FIRST CLASS MAIL PERMIT NO. 80 SEBASTOPOL, CA

Postage will be paid by addressee

O'Reilly & Associates, Inc.
101 Morris Street
Sebastopol, CA 95472-9902